© 1989

THE
NEW YORK
PUBLIC LIBRARY
DESK REFERENCE

A STONESONG PRESS BOOK

Webster's New World

New York

Designer Mark Safran
Artist Bill Russell
Copy Editor Felice Levy
Production Editor Lisa Wolff
Indexer Maro Riofrancos

 Webster's New World

Simon & Schuster, Inc.
Gulf + Western Building
1 Gulf + Western Plaza
New York, New York 10023

DISTRIBUTED BY PRENTICE HALL TRADE SALES

Library of Congress Cataloging-in-Publication Data

The New York Public Library desk reference.
  "A Stonesong Press book."
  1. Encyclopedias and dictionaries. I. New York Public Library.
AG6.N49 1989   031   89-16692
ISBN 0-13-620444-9 (alk. paper)

10 9 8 7 6 5 4 3 2 1

Printed in the United States of America on acid-free paper.

First Edition

ISBN: 0-13-620444-9

A Note from the Editors

Every attempt has been made to ensure that this publication is as accurate as possible and as comprehensive as space would allow. We are grateful to the many researchers, librarians, teachers, reference editors, and friends who contributed facts, figures, time, energy, ideas, and opinions. Our choice of what to include was aided by their advice and their voices of experience. The contents, however, remain subjective to some extent, because we could not possibly cover everything that one might look for in basic information. If errors or omissions are discovered, we would appreciate hearing from you, the user, as we prepare future editions.

We hope you find our work useful.

Contents

v

Preface

"Always the beautiful answer
who asks a more beautiful question"
e. e. cummings

I am pleased to present this *Desk Reference* to the worldwide library and reading community, which includes both reference staff and users. I hope it will be a useful and welcome addition to those who seek answers in the library and at home.

Why do we need another reference book at this time? More than 50,000 books are published each year in the United States. When I first walked into The New York Public Library as a newcomer from overseas, I was overwhelmed by and speechless at the phenomenal abundance and variety of the library's holdings. All that knowledge in one place was staggering to me. It still is. And our store of knowledge and information is doubling every five years.

Yet we face the paradox that while our information is increasing, its use is diminishing. As our mountain of facts grows, we have more to sift through to find what we want. We need quick help.

Why a book? Why not another database? The answer for most of us is in cost, convenience, and aesthetics. Information technology, including computerized databases and laser disk storage and retrieval, has given us extremely valuable supplements to the book, but a book fills a unique need for portability, individuality, and beauty. As Ralph Waldo Emerson wrote more than 100 years ago, "In the highest civilization, the book is still the highest delight." If anything, the new technologies are whetting our appetite for more and better books.

Librarians in particular may ask, "How is this book preferable to similar books already available?" The 82 branch libraries of The New York Public Library answer more than 5 million reference questions each year. The *Desk Reference* assembles into one volume the kind of basic information on popular subjects that will help staff and patrons find quick, efficient answers to the most commonly asked questions.

In planning this book, the editors informally surveyed professional researchers, librarians, and reference editors, asking them what they thought to be most essential in this sort of desk book. In deciding what to include, we have tried to remain faithful to their recommendations. One book should not try to answer every conceivable question, and we have deliberately omitted topics and details that are too specialized or obscure for the average reader. While one can find all of the information in this book in other encyclopedias and almanacs, we think readers are better served by having all of this elemental and frequently sought material assembled and condensed into one concise volume. The Table of Contents includes 26 subject categories with entries ranging from standard dimensions and common abbreviations to etiquette and the phases of the moon. What these diverse entries have in common is that they provide basic answers to commonly asked questions.

Also, unlike annuals and almanacs that need revising and updating each year, the *Desk Reference* holds a considerable amount of true *reference* information, unchanging basic facts and background. Some material, of course, changes with time and new discoveries. It is hoped that this book will become a standard work. It will be revised and brought up to date as needed. Its purpose is not so much to educate as to remind you of what you may have forgotten or to introduce you to a new area. The subjects and treatments are designed for generalists who need an answer from an unfamiliar field or a refresher for what they already know.

We also hope that our book will be easy to read and fun to browse through. Sidebars, boxed charts, graphs, tables, and lists should make it accessible and attractive. We have anticipated the reader's desire to know more by ending each topic section with lists of resources for further information, including not only books but, in some sections, special collections, associations, and agencies reachable by telephone or mail. Thus the *Desk Reference* can serve as the entry point for further study.

We at The New York Public Library are pleased that this book will help to continue our tradition of serving not only individuals but society in general. The New York Public Library has rightly been called "the poor man's university," the place where the unaffiliated scholar and the curious person of any age or background can learn and feel at home.

"Books are the true levellers," wrote William Ellery Channing. "They give to all, who will faithfully use them, the society, the spiritual presence, of the best and greatest of our race." May the *Desk Reference* help everyone in pursuit of that goal.

Finally, thanks are due to the director and staff of the Publications Department of The New York Public Library and to The Stonesong Press, who worked together to fulfill this project.

VARTAN GREGORIAN, Ph.D.
Former President and Chief
Executive Officer
The New York Public Library

Time and Dates

Reckoning Days and Hours

The Day

The mean solar day is the average length of a day as determined by noting one passage of the sun across the meridian of an observer and calculating the time that it takes for the sun to cross the same point in the sky a second time. Because the sun's time in making such a circuit varies seasonally, the uniform length of our day is based on a fictional average rather than on what is actually seen on any given day (called the apparent solar day). The mean solar day is the basis of our 24-hour calendar day. It is actually 24 hours, 3 minutes, 56.55 seconds long in sidereal time.

The mean sidereal day is determined by a procedure similar to that of fixing the solar day; however, this procedure uses a star's passage across a reference point on the celestial sphere (that point now being the vernal equinox) instead of the sun's passage. The mean sidereal day is 23 hours, 56 minutes, 4.10 seconds long in solar time. That means that the solar day appears to be about 4 minutes longer than the sidereal day because Earth in its solar orbit has to move a little farther to get back to the point at which the sun crosses the same meridian.

Names of the Days

The names of the days in English derive from either ancient Latin or Saxon systems of naming days after gods or astrological planets.

English	Latin	Saxon
Sunday	Dies Solis (Sun)	Sun's Day
Monday	Dies Lunae (Moon)	Moon's Day
Tuesday	Dies Martis (Mars)	Tiw's Day
Wednesday	Dies Mercurii (Mercury)	Woden's Day
Thursday	Dies Jovis (Jupiter)	Thor's Day
Friday	Dies Veneris (Venus)	Frigg's Day
Saturday	Dies Saturni (Saturn)	Saterne's Day

The Hours

1 mean solar day	= 24 mean solar hours
1 mean solar hour	= 60 mean solar minutes
1 mean solar minute	= 60 mean solar seconds
1 mean solar day	= 86,400 mean solar seconds

When Does a Day Begin?

The standard measurement of the day is from midnight to midnight. This is accepted for civil purposes throughout most of the world, but it has not always been so. Some ancient peoples counted the day from dawn to dawn; others, for instance certain Germanic tribes, counted nights and then grouped them into units of 14—our fortnight; still others, such as Jews, count their days from sunset to sunset.

The 12-Hour System of Counting Hours

Midnight = 12 A.M. or 12 M
Noon   = 12 P.M. or 12N
A.M. (*ante meridiem*) = before noon
P.M. (*post meridiem*) = after noon

The 24-Hour System of Counting Hours

Because the 24-hour system does not repeat numbers and clearly distinguishes between midnight and noon, it is less confusing than the 12-hour system. It is the official system of the U.S. military and it is also used generally throughout Europe. In the 24-hour system, midnight can be designated by 2400 of one day or 0000 of the day following.

How Is the Day Subdivided?

The length of the day is determined by the rotation of Earth. But the division of the day into hours is an arbitrary standard, as is the uniform length of the hour. Before the invention of mechanical clocks, hours were usually of unequal length. Different cultures divided their days in different ways. The Greeks, the Egyptians, and the Romans had a 24-hour day. But they divided it into 12 hours of light and 12 of dark, which meant that the length of the hours depended on the seasons. Only after the invention of mechanical clocks in the late Middle Ages did there develop a need for an hour of uniform length.

Standard Time Around the World

Standard time was fixed in 1883 to prevent the myriad of short time differences that would result if every locality determined the mean solar time by different meridians, depending on the longitude of the particular place. Lines at every 15° longitude were drawn down a map of Earth to create 24 international time zones differing from each preceding and following zone by one hour. Because of political boundaries, such lines often depart from the strict 15° rule and sometimes zigzag or demarcate areas that differ by half an hour only.

The continental United States has four meridians designated to determine standard times: 75°, 90°, 105°, and 120° west of Greenwich, England. Canada has two other time zones, one in the east, Atlantic Standard Time, based on 60° west of Greenwich, and the other in the far west, Yukon Standard Time, with a meridian at 135° west of Greenwich. Alaska–Hawaii Standard Time is determined by the meridian that runs through Anchorage at 150° and Nome Standard Time is set at the 165° meridian.

Greenwich Mean Time and the Prime Meridian

The mean solar time determined by the meridian that runs through Greenwich, England (Greenwich Mean Time) is called Universal Time. It is used all over the world in navigation, both air and sea, and for scientific purposes, as in astronomy. From Greenwich, too, longitudes are measured around the world, Greenwich being 0°, called the prime meridian.

CLOCKS—MEASURING TIME

The sundial may be the oldest device for measuring time, going back to the Fertile Crescent of about 2000 B.C. Its operation is based on the fact that the shadow of a fixed object will move around it from one side to the other as the sun moves from east to west. Naturally, the duration of the hours marked off by a sundial changes according to the seasons of the year. Along with sundials, ancient peoples used water clocks that measured time by a constant rate of flow of water through a bowl-like device with an outlet. Sand flowing from one compartment into another also was used in late medieval Europe to measure time. These last two methods could be used at night; they also counted more uniform units of time.

With the invention of mechanical clocks, the hours became uniform. The first mechanical clocks appeared in Europe in the thirteenth century (mechanical timepieces existed in China at least two centuries earlier, though the Chinese never developed them highly). The earliest ones were driven by weights strung around a drum. As the weight fell, the mechanism was activated. Next came spring-driven clocks, though they had the disadvantage of running differently when the spring was just wound and at its most tense position and after it had unwound somewhat. The workings of all clocks depend on a motion or vibration that is constant and regular.

In 1583 the great Italian physicist Galileo (1564–1642) observed that the time it took for a pendulum to complete one total swing (called the period of oscillation) was almost independent of its magnitude, that is, how far it swung from side to side. He understood that this could be used as a frequency mechanism for regulating a clock. In 1656 a Dutch inventor, Christian Huygens (1629–95), working independently, constructed the first pendulum clock. Pendulum clocks remained the most precise means of measuring time into the twentieth century. Pendulums could be constructed to oscillate at specified frequencies once such factors as latitude, the pull of gravity, and weather and its effect on the materials out of which the clock was made had been compensated for.

Quartz clocks, introduced in the 1930s, improved on the pendulum, though only after years of development. By controlling the frequency of an electric circuit through the regular mechanical vibration of the quartz crystal, high degrees of constancy in vibration can be achieved, making a quartz clock even more accurate than a pendulum.

In the 1940s atomic clocks were introduced. Their frequencies are based on the vibrations of certain atoms and molecules that vibrate the same number of times per second. Atomic clocks are constant to within a few seconds every 100,000 years.

A sundial showing 2:45 P.M.

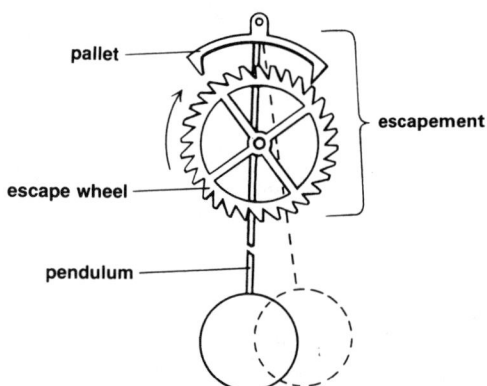

With each swing of the pendulum, the escape wheel moves one notch as the pallet moves back and forth. Notch by notch, the escapement moves the clock's mechanism to a regular rhythm.

Time Zones: International

The following list gives the time in cities around the world when it is 12 noon Eastern Standard Time. An asterisk (*) indicates the morning of the following day.

Addis Ababa	8 P.M.	Liverpool	6 P.M.
Alexandria	7 P.M.	London	5 P.M.
Amsterdam	6 P.M.	Madrid	7 P.M.
Athens	7 P.M.	Managua	11 A.M.
Baghdad	8 P.M.	Manila	1 A.M.*
Bangkok	12 M	Marseilles	6 P.M.
Barcelona	7 P.M.	Mecca	8 P.M.
Belfast	5 P.M.	Melbourne	3 A.M.*
Belgrade	6 P.M.	Mexico City	11 A.M.
Berlin	6 P.M.	Monaco	6 P.M.
Bogotá	12 N	Montreal	12 N
Bombay	10:30 P.M.	Moscow	8 P.M.
Brasilia	2 P.M.	Munich	6 P.M.
Brussels	6 P.M.	Naples	6 P.M.
Bucharest	7 P.M.	Oslo	6 P.M.
Budapest	6 P.M.	Ottawa	12 N
Buenos Aires	2 P.M.	Panama	12 N
Cairo	7 P.M.	Paris	6 P.M.
Calcutta	10:30 P.M.	Peking	1 A.M.*
Calgary	10 A.M.	Prague	6 P.M.
Cape Town	7 P.M.	Quebec	12 N
Caracas	1 P.M.	Rangoon	11:30 P.M.
Casablanca	5 P.M.	Rio de Janeiro	2 P.M.
Copenhagen	6 P.M.	Riyadh	8 P.M.
Delhi	10:30 P.M.	Rome	6 P.M.
Dublin	5 P.M.	San Juan	12 N
Edinburgh	5 P.M.	Santiago	1 P.M.
Florence	6 P.M.	Seoul	2 A.M.*
Frankfurt	6 P.M.	Shanghai	1 A.M.*
Geneva	6 P.M.	Stockholm	6 P.M.
Glasgow	5 P.M.	Sydney	3 A.M.*
Halifax	1 P.M.	Tangiers	5 P.M.
Hanoi	1 A.M.*	Teheran	8:30 P.M.
Havana	12 N	Tel Aviv	7 P.M.
Helsinki	7 P.M.	Tokyo	2 A.M.*
Ho Chi Minh City	1 A.M.*	Toronto	12 N
Hong Kong	1 A.M.*	Tripoli	7 P.M.
Istanbul	7 P.M.	Vancouver	9 A.M.
Jakarta	12 M	Venice	6 P.M.
Jerusalem	7 P.M.	Vienna	6 P.M.
Johannesburg	7 P.M.	Vladivostock	3 A.M.*
Karachi	10 P.M.	Warsaw	6 P.M.
Kuala Lumpur	1 A.M.*	Winnepeg	11 A.M.
Leningrad	8 P.M.	Yokohama	2 A.M.*
Lima	12 N	Zurich	6 P.M.
Lisbon	6 P.M.		

Standard Time Zones in Continental United States

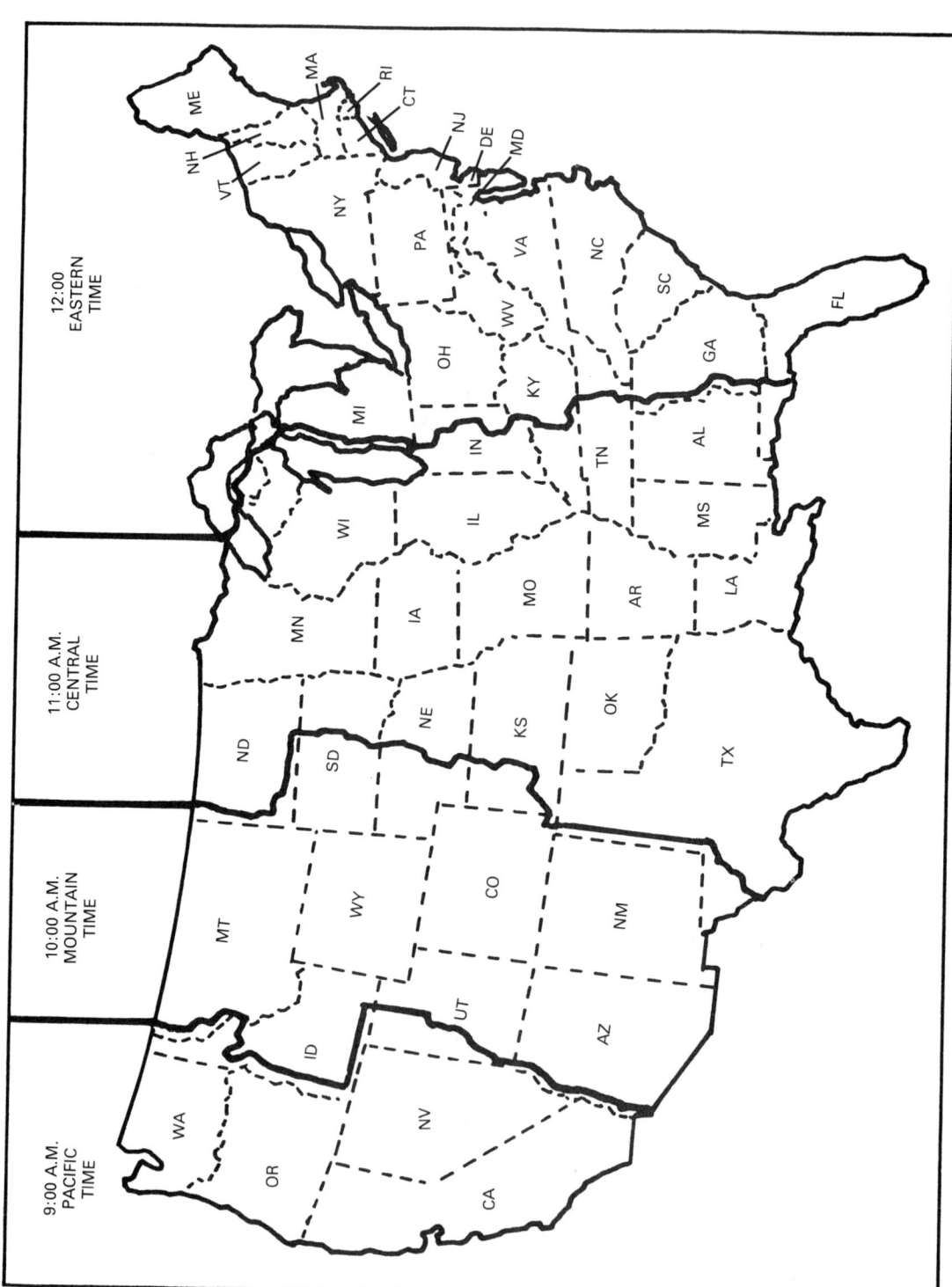

Time Zones: United States

The "lower 48" U.S. states and Washington, D.C. are divided into four time zones: Eastern, Central, Mountain, and Pacific. The time in each zone is one hour earlier than in the zone to its east and one hour later than in the zone to its west. The basic pattern of time zones in states is given below.

Eastern (12N)	*Central* (11 A.M.)	*Mountain* (10 A.M.)	*Pacific* (9 A.M.)
Connecticut	Alabama	Arizona	California
Delaware	Arkansas	Colorado	Idaho*
District of	Florida*	Idaho*	Nevada
Columbia	Illinois	Kansas*	Oregon*
Florida*	Indiana*	Montana	Washington
Georgia	Iowa	Nebraska*	
Indiana*	Kansas*	New Mexico	
Kentucky*	Kentucky*	North	
Maine	Louisiana	Dakota*	
Maryland	Minnesota	Oregon*	
Massachusetts	Mississippi	South	
Michigan	Missouri	Dakota*	
New Hampshire	Nebraska*	Texas*	
New Jersey	North	Utah	
New York	Dakota*	Wyoming	
North Carolina	Oklahoma		
Ohio	South		
Pennsylvania	Dakota*		
Rhode Island	Tennessee*		
South Carolina	Texas*		
Tennessee*	Wisconsin		
Vermont			
Virginia			
West Virginia			

* The asterisk indicates states that fall into two time zones.

Daylight Saving Time in the United States

Daylight Saving Time is attained by forwarding the clock one hour. In 1967 the Uniform Time Act went into effect in the United States. It proclaimed that all states, the District of Columbia, and U.S. possessions were to observe Daylight Saving Time starting at 2 A.M. on the last Sunday in April and ending at 2 A.M. on the last Sunday in October. Any state could exempt itself by law and a 1972 amendment to the act authorized the states split by time zones to consider that split in exempting themselves. Arizona, Hawaii, part of Indiana, Puerto Rico, the Virgin Islands, and American Samoa are now exempt. The Department of Transportation, which oversees the act, has modified some local zone boundaries in Alaska, Florida, Kansas, Michigan, and Texas over the last several years. Daylight Saving Time was extended by Congress during 1974 and 1975 to conserve energy, but the country then returned to the previous end-of-April to end-of-October system until 1987, when new legislation went into effect. The new bill, signed by President Reagan on July 8, 1986, moved the start of Daylight Saving time up to the first Sunday in April, but it did not change the end from the last Sunday in October.

International Time Adjustments

It is common throughout the world for clock time to be adjusted to use added daylight during summer.

Generally, Western Europe goes on daylight time on the last Sunday in March and changes back on the last Sunday in September. The Soviet Union stays on "advanced time" year round. China, by government order, operates as one time zone even though it should, geographically, be in 11 different zones. For religious reasons, Israel is approximately two hours behind the rest of their time zone. This means that the sun may be setting there as early as 3:30 P.M.

Paraguay, Ireland, and the Dominican Republic adjust their clock time in winter instead of summer. Thus, their time is aptly known as winter time.

International Date Line

An imaginary line set at 180° longitude runs down the Earth. When someone crosses the line traveling to the west, one day is added—that is, Sunday on the east side of the line becomes Monday as one crosses westward. The line, of course, was fixed at the longitude exactly opposite Greenwich, England, on the other side of the Earth, but it zigzags for political reasons so that parts of countries do not find themselves on the wrong side—for instance, all of Siberia is in the Asian system and all of Alaska in the American.

Divisions of Time

Unit	Duration	Abbreviation
second		sec., s., "
minute	60 seconds	min., m., '
hour	60 minutes	hr., h., hrs.
day	24 hours	da., d.
week	7 days	wk., w., wks.
fortnight	2 weeks	
month	30 days (generally)	mo., m., mos.
year	12 months	yr., yrs.
olympiad	4 years	
decade	10 years	
century	100 years	cen., c.
millenium	1,000 years	

Year: 365 days; 52 weeks; 12 months.

Calendar year: The civil or legal year from January 1 through December 31.

Fiscal year: A financial year; an accounting period of 12 months. The U.S. government's fiscal year ends September 30, but a fiscal year may end on the last day of any month.

Leap year: A span of 366 days occurring in years divisible by four, such as 1976 and 1984. Even century years, such as 1600, must be divisible by 400. Dates in ordinary years move forward a single day each year, but during leap year, they "leap" forward two days following the last day of February, the 29th.

Equinox: The day the sun crosses the equator; day and night are equal in length everywhere.

Vernal Equinox: In the Northern Hemisphere, about March 21, the first day of spring.

Autumnal Equinox: In the Northern Hemisphere, about September 22, the first day of autumn.

Solstice: The day the sun is farthest from the equator.

Summer solstice: In the Northern Hemisphere, June 21, the first day of summer; the longest day of the year.

Winter solstice: In the Northern Hemisphere, December 21, the first day of winter; the shortest day of the year.

Words Describing Periods of Time

annual	yearly
biannual	twice a year (at unequally spaced intervals)
bicentennial	relating to a period of 200 years
biennial	relating to a period of two years
bimonthly	every two months; twice a month
biweekly	every two weeks; twice a week
centennial	relating to a period of 100 years
decennial	relating to a period of 10 years
diurnal	daily; of a day
duodecennial	relating to a period of 12 years
millennial	relating to a period of 1,000 years
novennial	relating to a period of nine years
octennial	relating to a period of eight years
perennial	occurring year after year
quadrennial	relating to a period of four years
quadricentennial	relating to a period of 400 years
quincentennial	relating to a period of 500 years
quindecennial	relating to a period of 15 years
quinquennial	relating to a period of five years
semiannual	every six months (at equally spaced intervals)
semicentennial	relating to a period of 50 years
semidiurnal	twice a day
semiweekly	twice a week
septennial	relating to a period of seven years
sesquicentennial	relating to a period of 150 years
sexennial	relating to a period of six years
thrice weekly	three times a week
tricennial	relating to a period of 30 years
triennial	relating to a period of three years
trimonthly	every three months
triweekly	every three weeks; three times a week
undecennial	relating to a period of 11 years
vicennial	relating to a period of 20 years

Perpetual Calendar, 1775–2076

Look for the year you want in the following list. The number opposite each year is the number of the calendar on pages 12–13 to use for that year.

Index

1955 7	1986 4	2017 1	2048 11
1956 8	1987 5	2018 2	2049 6
1957 3	1988 13	2019 3	2050 7
1958 4	1989 1	2020 11	2051 1
1959 5	1990 2	2021 6	2052 9
1960 13	1991 3	2022 7	2053 4
1961 1	1992 11	2023 1	2054 5
1962 2	1993 6	2024 9	2055 6
1963 3	1994 7	2025 4	2056 14
1964 11	1995 1	2026 5	2057 2
1965 6	1996 9	2027 6	2058 3
1966 7	1997 4	2028 14	2059 4
1967 1	1998 5	2029 2	2060 12
1968 9	1999 6	2030 3	2061 7
1969 4	2000 14	2031 4	2062 1
1970 5	2001 2	2032 12	2063 2
1971 6	2002 3	2033 7	2064 10
1972 14	2003 4	2034 1	2065 5
1973 2	2004 12	2035 2	2066 6
1974 3	2005 7	2036 10	2067 7
1975 4	2006 1	2037 5	2068 8
1976 12	2007 2	2038 6	2069 3
1977 7	2008 10	2039 7	2070 4
1978 1	2009 5	2040 8	2071 5
1979 2	2010 6	2041 3	2072 13
1980 10	2011 7	2042 4	2073 1
1981 5	2012 8	2043 5	2074 2
1982 6	2013 3	2044 13	2075 3
1983 7	2014 4	2045 1	2076 11
1984 8	2015 5	2046 2	
1985 3	2016 13	2047 3	

1

S	M	T	W	T	F	S	S	M	T	W	T	F	S	S	M	T	W	T	F	S
JANUARY							MAY							SEPTEMBER						
1	2	3	4	5	6	7		1	2	3	4	5	6						1	2
8	9	10	11	12	13	14	7	8	9	10	11	12	13	3	4	5	6	7	8	9
15	16	17	18	19	20	21	14	15	16	17	18	19	20	10	11	12	13	14	15	16
22	23	24	25	26	27	28	21	22	23	24	25	26	27	17	18	19	20	21	22	23
29	30	31					28	29	30	31				24	25	26	27	28	29	30
FEBRUARY							JUNE							OCTOBER						
			1	2	3	4					1	2	3	1	2	3	4	5	6	7
5	6	7	8	9	10	11	4	5	6	7	8	9	10	8	9	10	11	12	13	14
12	13	14	15	16	17	18	11	12	13	14	15	16	17	15	16	17	18	19	20	21
19	20	21	22	23	24	25	18	19	20	21	22	23	24	22	23	24	25	26	27	28
26	27	28					25	26	27	28	29	30		29	30	31				
MARCH							JULY							NOVEMBER						
			1	2	3	4							1				1	2	3	4
5	6	7	8	9	10	11	2	3	4	5	6	7	8	5	6	7	8	9	10	11
12	13	14	15	16	17	18	9	10	11	12	13	14	15	12	13	14	15	16	17	18
19	20	21	22	23	24	25	16	17	18	19	20	21	22	19	20	21	22	23	24	25
26	27	28	29	30	31		23	24	25	26	27	28	29	26	27	28	29	30		
							30	31												
APRIL							AUGUST							DECEMBER						
						1			1	2	3	4	5						1	2
2	3	4	5	6	7	8	6	7	8	9	10	11	12	3	4	5	6	7	8	9
9	10	11	12	13	14	15	13	14	15	16	17	18	19	10	11	12	13	14	15	16
16	17	18	19	20	21	22	20	21	22	23	24	25	26	17	18	19	20	21	22	23
23	24	25	26	27	28	29	27	28	29	30	31			24	25	26	27	28	29	30
30														31						

2

S	M	T	W	T	F	S	S	M	T	W	T	F	S	S	M	T	W	T	F	S
JANUARY							MAY							SEPTEMBER						
	1	2	3	4	5	6			1	2	3	4	5							1
7	8	9	10	11	12	13	6	7	8	9	10	11	12	2	3	4	5	6	7	8
14	15	16	17	18	19	20	13	14	15	16	17	18	19	9	10	11	12	13	14	15
21	22	23	24	25	26	27	20	21	22	23	24	25	26	16	17	18	19	20	21	22
28	29	30	31				27	28	29	30	31			23	24	25	26	27	28	29
														30						
FEBRUARY							JUNE							OCTOBER						
				1	2	3						1	2		1	2	3	4	5	6
4	5	6	7	8	9	10	3	4	5	6	7	8	9	7	8	9	10	11	12	13
11	12	13	14	15	16	17	10	11	12	13	14	15	16	14	15	16	17	18	19	20
18	19	20	21	22	23	24	17	18	19	20	21	22	23	21	22	23	24	25	26	27
25	26	27	28				24	25	26	27	28	29	30	28	29	30	31			
MARCH							JULY							NOVEMBER						
				1	2	3	1	2	3	4	5	6	7					1	2	3
4	5	6	7	8	9	10	8	9	10	11	12	13	14	4	5	6	7	8	9	10
11	12	13	14	15	16	17	15	16	17	18	19	20	21	11	12	13	14	15	16	17
18	19	20	21	22	23	24	22	23	24	25	26	27	28	18	19	20	21	22	23	24
25	26	27	28	29	30	31	29	30	31					25	26	27	28	29	30	
APRIL							AUGUST							DECEMBER						
1	2	3	4	5	6	7				1	2	3	4							1
8	9	10	11	12	13	14	5	6	7	8	9	10	11	2	3	4	5	6	7	8
15	16	17	18	19	20	21	12	13	14	15	16	17	18	9	10	11	12	13	14	15
22	23	24	25	26	27	28	19	20	21	22	23	24	25	16	17	18	19	20	21	22
29	30						26	27	28	29	30	31		23	24	25	26	27	28	29
														30	31					

3

S	M	T	W	T	F	S	S	M	T	W	T	F	S	S	M	T	W	T	F	S
JANUARY							MAY							SEPTEMBER						
		1	2	3	4	5				1	2	3	4	1	2	3	4	5	6	7
6	7	8	9	10	11	12	5	6	7	8	9	10	11	8	9	10	11	12	13	14
13	14	15	16	17	18	19	12	13	14	15	16	17	18	15	16	17	18	19	20	21
20	21	22	23	24	25	26	19	20	21	22	23	24	25	22	23	24	25	26	27	28
27	28	29	30	31			26	27	28	29	30	31		29	30					
FEBRUARY							JUNE							OCTOBER						
					1	2							1			1	2	3	4	5
3	4	5	6	7	8	9	2	3	4	5	6	7	8	6	7	8	9	10	11	12
10	11	12	13	14	15	16	9	10	11	12	13	14	15	13	14	15	16	17	18	19
17	18	19	20	21	22	23	16	17	18	19	20	21	22	20	21	22	23	24	25	26
24	25	26	27	28			23	24	25	26	27	28	29	27	28	29	30	31		
							30													
MARCH							JULY							NOVEMBER						
					1	2		1	2	3	4	5	6						1	2
3	4	5	6	7	8	9	7	8	9	10	11	12	13	3	4	5	6	7	8	9
10	11	12	13	14	15	16	14	15	16	17	18	19	20	10	11	12	13	14	15	16
17	18	19	20	21	22	23	21	22	23	24	25	26	27	17	18	19	20	21	22	23
24	25	26	27	28	29	30	28	29	30	31				24	25	26	27	28	29	30
31																				
APRIL							AUGUST							DECEMBER						
	1	2	3	4	5	6					1	2	3	1	2	3	4	5	6	7
7	8	9	10	11	12	13	4	5	6	7	8	9	10	8	9	10	11	12	13	14
14	15	16	17	18	19	20	11	12	13	14	15	16	17	15	16	17	18	19	20	21
21	22	23	24	25	26	27	18	19	20	21	22	23	24	22	23	24	25	26	27	28
28	29	30					25	26	27	28	29	30	31	29	30	31				

4

S	M	T	W	T	F	S	S	M	T	W	T	F	S	S	M	T	W	T	F	S
JANUARY							MAY							SEPTEMBER						
			1	2	3	4					1	2	3		1	2	3	4	5	6
5	6	7	8	9	10	11	4	5	6	7	8	9	10	7	8	9	10	11	12	13
12	13	14	15	16	17	18	11	12	13	14	15	16	17	14	15	16	17	18	19	20
19	20	21	22	23	24	25	18	19	20	21	22	23	24	21	22	23	24	25	26	27
26	27	28	29	30	31		25	26	27	28	29	30	31	28	29	30				
FEBRUARY							JUNE							OCTOBER						
						1	1	2	3	4	5	6	7				1	2	3	4
2	3	4	5	6	7	8	8	9	10	11	12	13	14	5	6	7	8	9	10	11
9	10	11	12	13	14	15	15	16	17	18	19	20	21	12	13	14	15	16	17	18
16	17	18	19	20	21	22	22	23	24	25	26	27	28	19	20	21	22	23	24	25
23	24	25	26	27	28		29	30						26	27	28	29	30	31	
MARCH							JULY							NOVEMBER						
						1			1	2	3	4	5							1
2	3	4	5	6	7	8	6	7	8	9	10	11	12	2	3	4	5	6	7	8
9	10	11	12	13	14	15	13	14	15	16	17	18	19	9	10	11	12	13	14	15
16	17	18	19	20	21	22	20	21	22	23	24	25	26	16	17	18	19	20	21	22
23	24	25	26	27	28	29	27	28	29	30	31			23	24	25	26	27	28	29
30	31													30						
APRIL							AUGUST							DECEMBER						
		1	2	3	4	5						1	2		1	2	3	4	5	6
6	7	8	9	10	11	12	3	4	5	6	7	8	9	7	8	9	10	11	12	13
13	14	15	16	17	18	19	10	11	12	13	14	15	16	14	15	16	17	18	19	20
20	21	22	23	24	25	26	17	18	19	20	21	22	23	21	22	23	24	25	26	27
27	28	29	30				24	25	26	27	28	29	30	28	29	30	31			
							31													

5

S	M	T	W	T	F	S	S	M	T	W	T	F	S	S	M	T	W	T	F	S
JANUARY							MAY							SEPTEMBER						
				1	2	3						1	2			1	2	3	4	5
4	5	6	7	8	9	10	3	4	5	6	7	8	9	6	7	8	9	10	11	12
11	12	13	14	15	16	17	10	11	12	13	14	15	16	13	14	15	16	17	18	19
18	19	20	21	22	23	24	17	18	19	20	21	22	23	20	21	22	23	24	25	26
25	26	27	28	29	30	31	24	25	26	27	28	29	30	27	28	29	30			
							31													
FEBRUARY							JUNE							OCTOBER						
1	2	3	4	5	6	7		1	2	3	4	5	6					1	2	3
8	9	10	11	12	13	14	7	8	9	10	11	12	13	4	5	6	7	8	9	10
15	16	17	18	19	20	21	14	15	16	17	18	19	20	11	12	13	14	15	16	17
22	23	24	25	26	27	28	21	22	23	24	25	26	27	18	19	20	21	22	23	24
							28	29	30					25	26	27	28	29	30	31
MARCH							JULY							NOVEMBER						
1	2	3	4	5	6	7				1	2	3	4	1	2	3	4	5	6	7
8	9	10	11	12	13	14	5	6	7	8	9	10	11	8	9	10	11	12	13	14
15	16	17	18	19	20	21	12	13	14	15	16	17	18	15	16	17	18	19	20	21
22	23	24	25	26	27	28	19	20	21	22	23	24	25	22	23	24	25	26	27	28
29	30	31					26	27	28	29	30	31		29	30					
APRIL							AUGUST							DECEMBER						
			1	2	3	4							1			1	2	3	4	5
5	6	7	8	9	10	11	2	3	4	5	6	7	8	6	7	8	9	10	11	12
12	13	14	15	16	17	18	9	10	11	12	13	14	15	13	14	15	16	17	18	19
19	20	21	22	23	24	25	16	17	18	19	20	21	22	20	21	22	23	24	25	26
26	27	28	29	30			23	24	25	26	27	28	29	27	28	29	30	31		
							30	31												

6

S	M	T	W	T	F	S	S	M	T	W	T	F	S	S	M	T	W	T	F	S
JANUARY							MAY							SEPTEMBER						
					1	2							1				1	2	3	4
3	4	5	6	7	8	9	2	3	4	5	6	7	8	5	6	7	8	9	10	11
10	11	12	13	14	15	16	9	10	11	12	13	14	15	12	13	14	15	16	17	18
17	18	19	20	21	22	23	16	17	18	19	20	21	22	19	20	21	22	23	24	25
24	25	26	27	28	29	30	23	24	25	26	27	28	29	26	27	28	29	30		
31							30	31												
FEBRUARY							JUNE							OCTOBER						
	1	2	3	4	5	6			1	2	3	4	5						1	2
7	8	9	10	11	12	13	6	7	8	9	10	11	12	3	4	5	6	7	8	9
14	15	16	17	18	19	20	13	14	15	16	17	18	19	10	11	12	13	14	15	16
21	22	23	24	25	26	27	20	21	22	23	24	25	26	17	18	19	20	21	22	23
28							27	28	29	30				24	25	26	27	28	29	30
														31						
MARCH							JULY							NOVEMBER						
	1	2	3	4	5	6					1	2	3		1	2	3	4	5	6
7	8	9	10	11	12	13	4	5	6	7	8	9	10	7	8	9	10	11	12	13
14	15	16	17	18	19	20	11	12	13	14	15	16	17	14	15	16	17	18	19	20
21	22	23	24	25	26	27	18	19	20	21	22	23	24	21	22	23	24	25	26	27
28	29	30	31				25	26	27	28	29	30	31	28	29	30				
APRIL							AUGUST							DECEMBER						
				1	2	3	1	2	3	4	5	6	7				1	2	3	4
4	5	6	7	8	9	10	8	9	10	11	12	13	14	5	6	7	8	9	10	11
11	12	13	14	15	16	17	15	16	17	18	19	20	21	12	13	14	15	16	17	18
18	19	20	21	22	23	24	22	23	24	25	26	27	28	19	20	21	22	23	24	25
25	26	27	28	29	30		29	30	31					26	27	28	29	30	31	

7

S	M	T	W	T	F	S	S	M	T	W	T	F	S	S	M	T	W	T	F	S
JANUARY							MAY							SEPTEMBER						
						1	1	2	3	4	5	6	7					1	2	3
2	3	4	5	6	7	8	8	9	10	11	12	13	14	4	5	6	7	8	9	10
9	10	11	12	13	14	15	15	16	17	18	19	20	21	11	12	13	14	15	16	17
16	17	18	19	20	21	22	22	23	24	25	26	27	28	18	19	20	21	22	23	24
23	24	25	26	27	28	29	29	30	31					25	26	27	28	29	30	
30	31																			
FEBRUARY							JUNE							OCTOBER						
		1	2	3	4	5				1	2	3	4							1
6	7	8	9	10	11	12	5	6	7	8	9	10	11	2	3	4	5	6	7	8
13	14	15	16	17	18	19	12	13	14	15	16	17	18	9	10	11	12	13	14	15
20	21	22	23	24	25	26	19	20	21	22	23	24	25	16	17	18	19	20	21	22
27	28						26	27	28	29	30			23	24	25	26	27	28	29
														30	31					
MARCH							JULY							NOVEMBER						
		1	2	3	4	5						1	2			1	2	3	4	5
6	7	8	9	10	11	12	3	4	5	6	7	8	9	6	7	8	9	10	11	12
13	14	15	16	17	18	19	10	11	12	13	14	15	16	13	14	15	16	17	18	19
20	21	22	23	24	25	26	17	18	19	20	21	22	23	20	21	22	23	24	25	26
27	28	29	30	31			24	25	26	27	28	29	30	27	28	29	30			
							31													
APRIL							AUGUST							DECEMBER						
					1	2		1	2	3	4	5	6					1	2	3
3	4	5	6	7	8	9	7	8	9	10	11	12	13	4	5	6	7	8	9	10
10	11	12	13	14	15	16	14	15	16	17	18	19	20	11	12	13	14	15	16	17
17	18	19	20	21	22	23	21	22	23	24	25	26	27	18	19	20	21	22	23	24
24	25	26	27	28	29	30	28	29	30	31				25	26	27	28	29	30	31

8

S	M	T	W	T	F	S	S	M	T	W	T	F	S	S	M	T	W	T	F	S
JANUARY							MAY							SEPTEMBER						
1	2	3	4	5	6	7			1	2	3	4	5							1
8	9	10	11	12	13	14	6	7	8	9	10	11	12	2	3	4	5	6	7	8
15	16	17	18	19	20	21	13	14	15	16	17	18	19	9	10	11	12	13	14	15
22	23	24	25	26	27	28	20	21	22	23	24	25	26	16	17	18	19	20	21	22
29	30	31					27	28	29	30	31			23	24	25	26	27	28	29
														30						
FEBRUARY							JUNE							OCTOBER						
			1	2	3	4						1	2		1	2	3	4	5	6
5	6	7	8	9	10	11	3	4	5	6	7	8	9	7	8	9	10	11	12	13
12	13	14	15	16	17	18	10	11	12	13	14	15	16	14	15	16	17	18	19	20
19	20	21	22	23	24	25	17	18	19	20	21	22	23	21	22	23	24	25	26	27
26	27	28	29				24	25	26	27	28	29	30	28	29	30	31			
MARCH							JULY							NOVEMBER						
				1	2	3	1	2	3	4	5	6	7					1	2	3
4	5	6	7	8	9	10	8	9	10	11	12	13	14	4	5	6	7	8	9	10
11	12	13	14	15	16	17	15	16	17	18	19	20	21	11	12	13	14	15	16	17
18	19	20	21	22	23	24	22	23	24	25	26	27	28	18	19	20	21	22	23	24
25	26	27	28	29	30	31	29	30	31					25	26	27	28	29	30	
APRIL							AUGUST							DECEMBER						
1	2	3	4	5	6	7				1	2	3	4							1
8	9	10	11	12	13	14	5	6	7	8	9	10	11	2	3	4	5	6	7	8
15	16	17	18	19	20	21	12	13	14	15	16	17	18	9	10	11	12	13	14	15
22	23	24	25	26	27	28	19	20	21	22	23	24	25	16	17	18	19	20	21	22
29	30						26	27	28	29	30	31		23	24	25	26	27	28	29
														30	31					

9

S	M	T	W	T	F	S	S	M	T	W	T	F	S	S	M	T	W	T	F	S
JANUARY							MAY							SEPTEMBER						
	1	2	3	4	5	6				1	2	3	4	1	2	3	4	5	6	7
7	8	9	10	11	12	13	5	6	7	8	9	10	11	8	9	10	11	12	13	14
14	15	16	17	18	19	20	12	13	14	15	16	17	18	15	16	17	18	19	20	21
21	22	23	24	25	26	27	19	20	21	22	23	24	25	22	23	24	25	26	27	28
28	29	30	31				26	27	28	29	30	31		29	30					
FEBRUARY							JUNE							OCTOBER						
				1	2	3							1			1	2	3	4	5
4	5	6	7	8	9	10	2	3	4	5	6	7	8	6	7	8	9	10	11	12
11	12	13	14	15	16	17	9	10	11	12	13	14	15	13	14	15	16	17	18	19
18	19	20	21	22	23	24	16	17	18	19	20	21	22	20	21	22	23	24	25	26
25	26	27	28	29			23	24	25	26	27	28	29	27	28	29	30	31		
							30													
MARCH							JULY							NOVEMBER						
					1	2		1	2	3	4	5	6						1	2
3	4	5	6	7	8	9	7	8	9	10	11	12	13	3	4	5	6	7	8	9
10	11	12	13	14	15	16	14	15	16	17	18	19	20	10	11	12	13	14	15	16
17	18	19	20	21	22	23	21	22	23	24	25	26	27	17	18	19	20	21	22	23
24	25	26	27	28	29	30	28	29	30	31				24	25	26	27	28	29	30
31																				
APRIL							AUGUST							DECEMBER						
	1	2	3	4	5	6					1	2	3	1	2	3	4	5	6	7
7	8	9	10	11	12	13	4	5	6	7	8	9	10	8	9	10	11	12	13	14
14	15	16	17	18	19	20	11	12	13	14	15	16	17	15	16	17	18	19	20	21
21	22	23	24	25	26	27	18	19	20	21	22	23	24	22	23	24	25	26	27	28
28	29	30					25	26	27	28	29	30	31	29	30	31				

10

Month	S	M	T	W	T	F	S
JANUARY			1	2	3	4	5
	6	7	8	9	10	11	12
	13	14	15	16	17	18	19
	20	21	22	23	24	25	26
	27	28	29	30	31		
FEBRUARY						1	2
	3	4	5	6	7	8	9
	10	11	12	13	14	15	16
	17	18	19	20	21	22	23
	24	25	26	27	28	29	
MARCH							1
	2	3	4	5	6	7	8
	9	10	11	12	13	14	15
	16	17	18	19	20	21	22
	23	24	25	26	27	28	29
	30	31					
APRIL			1	2	3	4	5
	6	7	8	9	10	11	12
	13	14	15	16	17	18	19
	20	21	22	23	24	25	26
	27	28	29	30			
MAY					1	2	3
	4	5	6	7	8	9	10
	11	12	13	14	15	16	17
	18	19	20	21	22	23	24
	25	26	27	28	29	30	31
JUNE	1	2	3	4	5	6	7
	8	9	10	11	12	13	14
	15	16	17	18	19	20	21
	22	23	24	25	26	27	28
	29	30					
JULY			1	2	3	4	5
	6	7	8	9	10	11	12
	13	14	15	16	17	18	19
	20	21	22	23	24	25	26
	27	28	29	30	31		
AUGUST						1	2
	3	4	5	6	7	8	9
	10	11	12	13	14	15	16
	17	18	19	20	21	22	23
	24	25	26	27	28	29	30
	31						
SEPTEMBER		1	2	3	4	5	6
	7	8	9	10	11	12	13
	14	15	16	17	18	19	20
	21	22	23	24	25	26	27
	28	29	30				
OCTOBER				1	2	3	4
	5	6	7	8	9	10	11
	12	13	14	15	16	17	18
	19	20	21	22	23	24	25
	26	27	28	29	30	31	
NOVEMBER							1
	2	3	4	5	6	7	8
	9	10	11	12	13	14	15
	16	17	18	19	20	21	22
	23	24	25	26	27	28	29
	30						
DECEMBER		1	2	3	4	5	6
	7	8	9	10	11	12	13
	14	15	16	17	18	19	20
	21	22	23	24	25	26	27
	28	29	30	31			

11

Month	S	M	T	W	T	F	S
JANUARY				1	2	3	4
	5	6	7	8	9	10	11
	12	13	14	15	16	17	18
	19	20	21	22	23	24	25
	26	27	28	29	30	31	
FEBRUARY							1
	2	3	4	5	6	7	8
	9	10	11	12	13	14	15
	16	17	18	19	20	21	22
	23	24	25	26	27	28	29
MARCH	1	2	3	4	5	6	7
	8	9	10	11	12	13	14
	15	16	17	18	19	20	21
	22	23	24	25	26	27	28
	29	30	31				
APRIL				1	2	3	4
	5	6	7	8	9	10	11
	12	13	14	15	16	17	18
	19	20	21	22	23	24	25
	26	27	28	29	30		
MAY						1	2
	3	4	5	6	7	8	9
	10	11	12	13	14	15	16
	17	18	19	20	21	22	23
	24	25	26	27	28	29	30
	31						
JUNE		1	2	3	4	5	6
	7	8	9	10	11	12	13
	14	15	16	17	18	19	20
	21	22	23	24	25	26	27
	28	29	30				
JULY				1	2	3	4
	5	6	7	8	9	10	11
	12	13	14	15	16	17	18
	19	20	21	22	23	24	25
	26	27	28	29	30	31	
AUGUST							1
	2	3	4	5	6	7	8
	9	10	11	12	13	14	15
	16	17	18	19	20	21	22
	23	24	25	26	27	28	29
	30	31					
SEPTEMBER			1	2	3	4	5
	6	7	8	9	10	11	12
	13	14	15	16	17	18	19
	20	21	22	23	24	25	26
	27	28	29	30			
OCTOBER					1	2	3
	4	5	6	7	8	9	10
	11	12	13	14	15	16	17
	18	19	20	21	22	23	24
	25	26	27	28	29	30	31
NOVEMBER	1	2	3	4	5	6	7
	8	9	10	11	12	13	14
	15	16	17	18	19	20	21
	22	23	24	25	26	27	28
	29	30					
DECEMBER			1	2	3	4	5
	6	7	8	9	10	11	12
	13	14	15	16	17	18	19
	20	21	22	23	24	25	26
	27	28	29	30	31		

12

Month	S	M	T	W	T	F	S
JANUARY					1	2	3
	4	5	6	7	8	9	10
	11	12	13	14	15	16	17
	18	19	20	21	22	23	24
	25	26	27	28	29	30	31
FEBRUARY	1	2	3	4	5	6	7
	8	9	10	11	12	13	14
	15	16	17	18	19	20	21
	22	23	24	25	26	27	28
	29						
MARCH		1	2	3	4	5	6
	7	8	9	10	11	12	13
	14	15	16	17	18	19	20
	21	22	23	24	25	26	27
	28	29	30	31			
APRIL					1	2	3
	4	5	6	7	8	9	10
	11	12	13	14	15	16	17
	18	19	20	21	22	23	24
	25	26	27	28	29	30	
MAY							1
	2	3	4	5	6	7	8
	9	10	11	12	13	14	15
	16	17	18	19	20	21	22
	23	24	25	26	27	28	29
	30	31					
JUNE			1	2	3	4	5
	6	7	8	9	10	11	12
	13	14	15	16	17	18	19
	20	21	22	23	24	25	26
	27	28	29	30			
JULY					1	2	3
	4	5	6	7	8	9	10
	11	12	13	14	15	16	17
	18	19	20	21	22	23	24
	25	26	27	28	29	30	31
AUGUST	1	2	3	4	5	6	7
	8	9	10	11	12	13	14
	15	16	17	18	19	20	21
	22	23	24	25	26	27	28
	29	30	31				
SEPTEMBER				1	2	3	4
	5	6	7	8	9	10	11
	12	13	14	15	16	17	18
	19	20	21	22	23	24	25
	26	27	28	29	30		
OCTOBER						1	2
	3	4	5	6	7	8	9
	10	11	12	13	14	15	16
	17	18	19	20	21	22	23
	24	25	26	27	28	29	30
	31						
NOVEMBER		1	2	3	4	5	6
	7	8	9	10	11	12	13
	14	15	16	17	18	19	20
	21	22	23	24	25	26	27
	28	29	30				
DECEMBER				1	2	3	4
	5	6	7	8	9	10	11
	12	13	14	15	16	17	18
	19	20	21	22	23	24	25
	26	27	28	29	30	31	

13

Month	S	M	T	W	T	F	S
JANUARY						1	2
	3	4	5	6	7	8	9
	10	11	12	13	14	15	16
	17	18	19	20	21	22	23
	24	25	26	27	28	29	30
	31						
FEBRUARY		1	2	3	4	5	6
	7	8	9	10	11	12	13
	14	15	16	17	18	19	20
	21	22	23	24	25	26	27
	28	29					
MARCH			1	2	3	4	5
	6	7	8	9	10	11	12
	13	14	15	16	17	18	19
	20	21	22	23	24	25	26
	27	28	29	30	31		
APRIL						1	2
	3	4	5	6	7	8	9
	10	11	12	13	14	15	16
	17	18	19	20	21	22	23
	24	25	26	27	28	29	30
MAY	1	2	3	4	5	6	7
	8	9	10	11	12	13	14
	15	16	17	18	19	20	21
	22	23	24	25	26	27	28
	29	30	31				
JUNE				1	2	3	4
	5	6	7	8	9	10	11
	12	13	14	15	16	17	18
	19	20	21	22	23	24	25
	26	27	28	29	30		
JULY						1	2
	3	4	5	6	7	8	9
	10	11	12	13	14	15	16
	17	18	19	20	21	22	23
	24	25	26	27	28	29	30
	31						
AUGUST		1	2	3	4	5	6
	7	8	9	10	11	12	13
	14	15	16	17	18	19	20
	21	22	23	24	25	26	27
	28	29	30	31			
SEPTEMBER					1	2	3
	4	5	6	7	8	9	10
	11	12	13	14	15	16	17
	18	19	20	21	22	23	24
	25	26	27	28	29	30	
OCTOBER							1
	2	3	4	5	6	7	8
	9	10	11	12	13	14	15
	16	17	18	19	20	21	22
	23	24	25	26	27	28	29
	30	31					
NOVEMBER			1	2	3	4	5
	6	7	8	9	10	11	12
	13	14	15	16	17	18	19
	20	21	22	23	24	25	26
	27	28	29	30			
DECEMBER					1	2	3
	4	5	6	7	8	9	10
	11	12	13	14	15	16	17
	18	19	20	21	22	23	24
	25	26	27	28	29	30	31

14

Month	S	M	T	W	T	F	S
JANUARY							1
	2	3	4	5	6	7	8
	9	10	11	12	13	14	15
	16	17	18	19	20	21	22
	23	24	25	26	27	28	29
	30	31					
FEBRUARY			1	2	3	4	5
	6	7	8	9	10	11	12
	13	14	15	16	17	18	19
	20	21	22	23	24	25	26
	27	28	29				
MARCH				1	2	3	4
	5	6	7	8	9	10	11
	12	13	14	15	16	17	18
	19	20	21	22	23	24	25
	26	27	28	29	30	31	
APRIL							1
	2	3	4	5	6	7	8
	9	10	11	12	13	14	15
	16	17	18	19	20	21	22
	23	24	25	26	27	28	29
	30						
MAY		1	2	3	4	5	6
	7	8	9	10	11	12	13
	14	15	16	17	18	19	20
	21	22	23	24	25	26	27
	28	29	30	31			
JUNE					1	2	3
	4	5	6	7	8	9	10
	11	12	13	14	15	16	17
	18	19	20	21	22	23	24
	25	26	27	28	29	30	
JULY							1
	2	3	4	5	6	7	8
	9	10	11	12	13	14	15
	16	17	18	19	20	21	22
	23	24	25	26	27	28	29
	30	31					
AUGUST			1	2	3	4	5
	6	7	8	9	10	11	12
	13	14	15	16	17	18	19
	20	21	22	23	24	25	26
	27	28	29	30	31		
SEPTEMBER						1	2
	3	4	5	6	7	8	9
	10	11	12	13	14	15	16
	17	18	19	20	21	22	23
	24	25	26	27	28	29	30
OCTOBER	1	2	3	4	5	6	7
	8	9	10	11	12	13	14
	15	16	17	18	19	20	21
	22	23	24	25	26	27	28
	29	30	31				
NOVEMBER				1	2	3	4
	5	6	7	8	9	10	11
	12	13	14	15	16	17	18
	19	20	21	22	23	24	25
	26	27	28	29	30		
DECEMBER						1	2
	3	4	5	6	7	8	9
	10	11	12	13	14	15	16
	17	18	19	20	21	22	23
	24	25	26	27	28	29	30
	31						

Major U.S. Holidays

*January 1	New Year's Day	Third Sunday in June	Father's Day
*January 15	Martin Luther King, Jr.'s Birthday	*July 4	Independence Day
January 19	Robert E. Lee's Birthday (Southern states)	*First Monday in September	Labor Day
January 20	Inauguration Day	September 17	Citizenship Day
February 2	Groundhog Day	Fourth Friday in September	American Indian Day
February 12	Lincoln's Birthday	*October 12	Columbus Day
February 14	Valentine's Day	October 24	United Nations Day
*February 22	Washington's Birthday	October 31	Halloween
March 17	St. Patrick's Day	First Tuesday after the first Monday in November	Election Day
March or April	Easter Sunday		
April 1	April Fools' Day	*November 11	Veterans' Day
April 14	Pan American Day	*Fourth Thursday in November	Thanksgiving Day
May 1	May Day		
Second Sunday in May	Mother's Day	*December 25	Christmas Day
Third Saturday in May	Armed Forces Day		
*May 30	Memorial Day		
June 3	Jefferson Davis' Birthday (Southern states)		
June 14	Flag Day		

* These are the officially designated national holidays, but with three modifications: the days honoring **Martin Luther King**, Jr., George Washington, and Christopher Columbus are observed not on the indicated dates, but **on the Mondays** closest to those dates on the calendar.

Major Canadian Holidays

January 1	New Year's Day
March or April	Good Friday
	Easter Monday
First Monday before May 25	Victoria Day
July 1	Canada Day
First Monday in September	Labor Day
Second Monday in October	Thanksgiving Day
November 11	Remembrance Day
December 25	Christmas Day
December 26	Boxing Day

Major Foreign Holidays

January 1	New Year's Day throughout the Western world and in India, Indonesia, Japan, Korea, the Philippines, Singapore, Taiwan, and Thailand; founding of Republic of China (Taiwan)
January 2	Berchtoldstag in Switzerland
January 3	Genshi-Sai (First Beginning) in Japan
January 5	Twelfth Night (Wassail Eve or Eve of Epiphany) in England
January 6	Epiphany, observed by Catholics throughout Europe and Latin America
mid-January	Martin Luther King, Jr.'s birthday on the third Monday in the Virgin Islands
January 15	Adults' Day in Japan
January 20	St. Agnes Eve in Great Britain
January 26	Republic Day in India
January 29	Australia Day in Australia
January–February	Chinese New Year and Vietnamese New Year (Tet)
February	Hamstrom on the first Sunday in Switzerland
February 3	Setsubun (Bean-throwing Festival) in Japan
February 5	Promulgation of the Constitution Day in Mexico
February 11	National Foundation Day in Japan
February 27	Independence Day in the Dominican Republic
March 1	Independence Movement Day in Korea; Constitution Day in Panama
March 8	Women's Day in many socialist countries
March 17	St. Patrick's Day in Ireland and Northern Ireland
March 19	St. Joseph's Day in Colombia, Costa Rica, Italy, and Spain
March 21	Benito Juarez's Birthday in Mexico
March 22	Arab League Day in Arab League countries
March 23	Pakistan Day in Pakistan
March 25	Independence Day in Greece; Lady Day (Quarter Day) in Great Britain
March 26	Fiesta del Arbol (Arbor Day) in Spain
March 29	Youth and Martyrs' Day in Taiwan
March 30	Muslim New Year in Indonesia
March–April	Carnival/Lent/Easter: The pre-Lenten celebration of Carnival (Mardi Gras) and the post-Lenten celebration of Easter are movable feasts widely observed in Christian countries.
April 1	Victory Day in Spain; April Fools' Day (All Fools' Day) in Great Britain
April 5	Arbor Day in Korea
April 6	Van Riebeeck Day in South Africa
April 7	World Health Day in UN member nations
April 8	Buddha's Birthday in Korea and Japan; Hana Matsuri (Flower Festival) in Japan
April 14	Pan American Day in the Americas
April 19	Declaration of Independence Day in Venezuela
April 22	Queen Isabella Day in Spain
April 23	St. George's Day in England
April 25	Liberation Day in Italy; ANZAC Day in Australia and New Zealand
April 29	Emperor's Birthday in Japan
April 30	Queen's Birthday in The Netherlands; Walpurgis Night in Germany and Scandinavia
May	Constitution Day on first Monday in Japan
May 1	May Day–Labor Day in the U.S.S.R. and most of Europe and Latin America
May 5	Children's Day in Japan and Korea; Victory of General Zaragosa Day in Mexico; Liberation Day in The Netherlands

May 8	V-E Day in Europe
May 9	Victory over Fascism Day in the U.S.S.R.
May 31	Republic Day in South Africa
June 2	Founding of the Republic Day in Italy
June 5	Constitution Day in Denmark
June 6	Memorial Day in Korea; Flag Day in Sweden
June 8	Muhammad's Birthday in Indonesia
June 10	Portugal Day in Portugal
June 12	Independence Day in the Philippines
mid-June	Queen's Official Birthday on second Saturday in Great Britain
June 16	Soweto Day in UN member nations
June 17	German Unity Day in Germany
June 20	Flag Day in Argentina
June 22	Midsummer's Day in Finland
June 24	Midsummer's Day in Great Britain
June 29	Feast of Saints Peter and Paul in Chile, Colombia, Italy, Peru, Spain, and Venezuela
July 1	Half-year Holiday in Hong Kong; Bank Holiday in Taiwan
July 5	Independence Day in Venezuela
July 9	Independence Day in Argentina
July 10	Bon (Feast of Fortune) in Japan
July 12	Orangemen's Day in Northern Ireland
July 14	Bastille Day in France
mid-July	Feria de San Fermin during second week in Spain
July 17	Constitution Day in Korea
July 18	National Day in Spain
July 20	Independence Day in Colombia
July 21–22	National Holiday in Belgium
July 22	National Liberation Day in Poland
July 24	Simon Bolivar's Birthday in Ecuador and Venezuela
July 25	St. James Day in Spain
July 28–29	Independence Day in Peru
August	Bank Holiday on first Monday in Fiji, Grenada, Guyana, Hong Kong, Ireland, and Malawi; Independence Day on first Tuesday in Jamaica
August 1	Lammas Day in England; National Day in Switzerland
August 5	Discovery Day in Trinidad and Tobago
August 9	National Day in Singapore
August 10	Independence Day in Ecuador
August 12	Queen's Birthday in Thailand
August 14	Independence Day in Pakistan
August 15	Independence Day in India and Korea; Assumption Day in Catholic countries
August 16	National Restoration Day in the Dominican Republic
August 17	Independence Day in Indonesia
August 31	Independence Day in Trinidad and Tobago
September	Rose of Tralee Festival in Ireland
September 7	Independence Day in Brazil
September 9	Choxo-no-Sekku (Chrysanthemum Day) in Japan
September 14	Battle of San Jacinto Day in Nicaragua
mid-September	Sherry Wine Harvest in Spain
September 15	Independence Day in Costa Rica, Guatemala, and Nicaragua; Respect for the Aged Day in Japan
September 16	Independence Day in Mexico and Papua New Guinea
September 18–19	Independence Day in Chile
September 28	Confucius' Birthday in Taiwan

October 1	National Day in People's Republic of China; Armed Forces Day in Korea; National Holiday in Nigeria
October 2	National Day in People's Republic of China; Mahatma Gandhi's Birthday in India
October 3	National Foundation Day in Korea
October 5	Proclamation of the Portuguese Republic Day in Portugal
October 7	Foundation Day in the German Democratic Republic
October 9	Korean Alphabet Day in Korea
October 10	Kruger Day in South Africa; Founding of Republic of China in Taiwan
October 12	Columbus Day in Spain and widely throughout Latin America
October 19	Ascension of Muhammad Day in Indonesia
October 20	Revolution Day in Guatemala; Kenyatta Day in Kenya
October 24	United Nations Day in UN member nations
October 26	National Holiday in Austria
October 28	Greek National Day in Greece
November 1	All Saints' Day, observed by Catholics in most countries
November 2	All Souls' Day in Ecuador, El Salvador, Luxembourg, Macao, Mexico, San Marino, Uruguay, and Vatican City
November 4	National Unity Day in Italy
November 5	Guy Fawkes Day in Great Britain
November 7–8	October Revolution Day in the U.S.S.R.
November 11	Armistice Day in Belgium, France, French Guiana, and Tahiti
November 12	Sun Yat-sen's Birthday in Taiwan
November 15	Proclamation of the Republic Day in Brazil
November 17	Day of Penance in Federal Republic of Germany
November 19	National Holiday in Monaco
November 20	Anniversary of the Revolution in Mexico
November 23	Kinro-Kansha-No-Hi (Labor Thanksgiving Day) in Japan
November 30	National Heroes' Day in the Philippines
December 5	Discovery by Columbus Day in Haiti; Constitution Day in the U.S.S.R.
December 6	Independence Day in Finland
December 8	Feast of the Immaculate Conception, widely observed in Catholic countries
December 10	Constitution Day in Thailand; Human Rights Day in UN member nations
mid-December	Nine Days of Posada during third week in Mexico
December 25	Christmas Day, widely observed in all Christian countries
December 26	St. Stephen's Day in Austria, Ireland, Italy, Lichtenstein, San Marino, Switzerland, and Barcelona (Spain); Boxing Day in Great Britain and Northern Ireland
December 28	National Day in Nepal
December 31	New Year's Eve throughout the world; Omisoka (Grand Last Day) in Japan; Hogmanay Day in Scotland

Religious Holidays

Holy Days of Obligation

Members of the Roman Catholic faith are required to attend Mass on Sundays and also on Holy Days of Obligation. Saturday evening masses also fulfill the Sunday obligation in the United States. Rome recognizes 10 days of devotion (technically called ''solemnities''), but canon law permits some local selectivity regarding their observance. In this chart the starred entries are days of obligation for Catholics in the United States.

Holy Day	Date	First Observed
**Solemnity of Mary	January 1	1970*
Epiphany of Our Lord	January 6	third century
St. Joseph	March 19	fifteenth century
*Ascension of the Lord	forty days after Easter	first (?) century
Corpus Christi	Thursday after Trinity Sunday	1246
Saints Peter and Paul	June 29	third century
*Assumption of Mary	August 15	seventh century
*All Saints Day	November 1	835
*Immaculate Conception	December 8	1854
*Christmas	December 25	fourth (?) century

** The Solemnity of Mary replaces the Feast of the Maternity of Mary, which had been observed on October 11. In falling on January 1, it also replaces the feast of the Circumcision of Christ, which was celebrated on that day until 1970.

Major Jewish Holidays

Name	Approximate Date	Hebrew Date
Purim (Lots)	March	14 Adar
Pesach (Passover)	March/April	14–21 Nisan
Shavuos (Pentecost)	May/June	6 Sivan
Tisha b'Av (Ninth of Av)	mid-July	9 Av
Rosh Hashana (New Year)	September	1, 2 Tishri
Yom Kippur (Day of Atonement)	September/October	10 Tishri
Succos (Tabernacles)	September/October	15 Tishri
Hanukkah (Feast of Dedication)	winter solstice	25 Kislev

Additional Sources of Information

Chase, William D. and Helen M. *Chase's Annual Events, 1987.* Contemporary Books, 1986.

Gregory, Ruth W. *Anniversaries & Holidays,* 4th ed. American Library Association, 1983.

Harland, W. B., et al. *A Geologic Time Scale.* Cambridge University Press, 1983.

Holy Days in the United States, History, Theology, Celebration. U.S. Catholic Conference, 1984.

Kolatch, Alfred J. *The Jewish Book of Why.* David Publications, 1981.

Landes, Davis S. *Revolution in Time: Clocks and the Making of the Modern World.* Harvard University Press, 1983.

Parise, Frank, ed. *Book of Calendars.* Facts on File, 1982.

Powers, Mala. *Follow the Year: A Family Celebration of Christian Holidays.* Harper & Row, 1985.

Urdang, Laurence, and Donohue, Christina N., eds. *Holidays & Anniversaries of the World.* Gale Research, 1985.

Van Straalen, Alice. *The Book of Holidays Around the World.* Dutton, 1986.

Zerubavel, Eviator. *The Seven Day Cycle: The History and Meaning of the Week.* The Free Press, 1985.

2

Weights and Measures

U.S. System for Dry and Liquid Weights and Measures

Circular Measures

60 seconds	= 1 minute	90 degrees	= 1 quadrant
60 minutes	= 1 degree	4 quadrants	
30 degrees	= 1 sign	or	
60 degrees	= 1 sextant	360 degrees	= 1 circle

Cloth Measures

2½ inches = 1 nail   4 nails = 1 quarter   4 quarters = 1 yard

Cubic Measures

1,728 cu. inches	= 1 cu. foot	40 cu. feet	= 1 ton (shipping)
5.8 cu. feet	= 1 bulk barrel	2,150.42 cu. inches	= 1 standard bushel
27 cu. feet	= 1 cu. yard	231 cu. inches	= 1 standard gallon
128 cu. feet	= 1 cord (wood)		

Liquid Measure

1 fluid dram	= 60 minims or ⅛ fluid ounce
1 teaspoon	= ⅓ tablespoon or ⅛ fluid ounce
1 tablespoon	= 3 teaspoons or ½ fluid ounce
1 fluid ounce (fl. oz.)	= 2 tablespoons or 6 teaspoons
1 gill (gi.)	= ½ cup or 4 fluid ounces
1 cup	= 16 tablespoons or 8 fluid ounces
1 pint (pt.)	= 2 cups or 4 gills or 16 fluid ounces
1 quart (qt.)	= 2 pints or 4 cups or 32 fluid ounces
1 British imperial quart	= 1.20095 U.S. quarts
1 gallon (gal.)	= 4 quarts or 8 pints or 16 cups
1 British imperial gallon	= 1.20095 U.S. gallons
1 barrel	= 31.5 U.S. gallons (a petroleum barrel = 42 U.S. gallons)

Avoirdupois Weights

27¹¹⁄₃₂ grains	= 1 dram	100 pounds	= 1 hundredweight
16 drams	= 1 ounce	20 hundredweights	= 1 ton = 2,000 pounds
16 ounces	= 1 pound		

Square Measures

144 sq. inches	= 1 sq. foot	40 sq. rods	= 1 road	4,840 sq. yards	= 1 acre
9 sq. feet	= 1 sq. yard	4 roads	= 1 acre	640 acres	= 1 sq. mile

Miscellaneous

3 inches	= 1 palm	6 inches	= 1 span	21.8 inches	= 1 Bible cubit
4 inches	= 1 hand	18 inches	= 1 cubit	2½ feet	= 1 military pace

Customary and Metric Systems of Measurement

On December 23, 1975, the U.S. Metric Conversion Act was signed, declaring a national policy of encouraging the voluntary use of the metric system. Today, the metric system, or SI system (for Systéme International d'Unités), exists side by side with the U.S. customary system, which dates back to colonial days but is different from the British Imperial System. The debate on whether the United States should adopt the metric system has been going on for nearly 200 years. Today the United States is the only country in the world not totally committed to adopting the system.

The metric system is often considered a simpler form of measurement in that it includes only seven base units for different types of measurement:

The unit of length is the *meter.*

The unit of mass is the *kilogram.*

The unit of temperature is the *kelvin.*

The unit of time is the *second.*

The unit of electric current is the *ampere.*

The unit of light intensity is the *candela.*

The unit of substance amount is the *mole.*

All other metric units are derived from these units. For example, a newton, the unit of force, involves meters, kilograms, and seconds. A pascal, the unit of pressure, is one newton per square meter. Although the metric system was designed to fill all the needs of scientists and engineers, laymen need only know and use a few simple parts of it.

The metric system is based on the decimal system and follows a consistent name scheme using prefixes. Multiples and submultiples are always related to powers of 10. For example, *deka* means ten times, *hecto* means a hundred times, *kilo* means a thousand times, *mega* means a million times, and so on; *deci* means a tenth of, *centi* means a hundredth of, *milli* means a thousandth of, *micro* means a millionth of, and so on.

Tables of Metric Weights and Measures

Linear Measure

10 millimeters (mm) = 1 centimeter (cm)
10 centimeters = 1 decimeter (dm)
10 decimeters = 1 meter (m)
10 meters = 1 dekameter (dam)
10 dekameters = 1 hectometer (hm)
10 hectometers = 1 kilometer (km)
10 kilometers = 1 myriameter (mym)

Area Measure

100 sq. millimeters (mm^2) = 1 sq. centimeter (cm^2)
10,000 sq. centimeters = 1 sq. meter (m^2)
100 sq. meters = 1 are (a)
100 ares = 1 hectare (ha)
100 hectares = 1 sq. kilometer (km^2)

Fluid Volume Measure

10 milliliters (ml) = 1 centiliter (cl)
10 centiliters = 1 deciliter (dl)
10 deciliters = 1 liter (l)
10 liters = 1 dekaliter (dal)
10 dekaliters = 1 hectoliter (hl)
10 hectoliters = 1 kiloliter (kl)

Weight

10 milligrams (mg) = 1 centigram (cg)
10 centigrams = 1 decigram (dg)
10 decigrams = 1 gram (g)
10 grams = 1 dekagram (dag)
10 dekagrams = 1 hectogram (hg)
10 hectograms = 1 kilogram (kg)
1,000 kilograms = 1 metric ton (t)

Cubic Measure

1,000 cu. millimeters (mm³) = 1 cu. centimeter (cm³)
1,000 cu. centimeters = 1 cu. decimeter (dm³)
1,000 cu. decimeters = 1 cu. meter (m³) = 1 stere

		Comparing the commonest measurement units	
		Approximate conversions from customary to metric units and vice versa.	
	When you know:	**You can find:**	**If you multiply by:**
LENGTH	inches	millimeters	25
	feet	centimeters	30
	yards	meters	0.9
	miles	kilometers	1.6
	millimeters	inches	0.04
	centimeters	inches	0.4
	meters	yards	1.1
	kilometers	miles	0.6
AREA	square inches	square centimeters	6.5
	square feet	square meters	0.09
	square yards	square meters	0.8
	square miles	square kilometers	2.6
	acres	square hectometers (hectares)	0.4
	square centimeters	square inches	0.16
	square meters	square yards	1.2
	square kilometers	square miles	0.4
	square hectometers (hectares)	acres	2.5
MASS	ounces	grams	28
	pounds	kilograms	0.45
	short tons	megagrams (metric tons)	0.9
	grams	ounces	0.035
	kilograms	pounds	2.2
	megagrams (metric tons)	short tons	1.1
LIQUID VOLUME	ounces	milliliters	30
	pints	liters	0.47
	quarts	liters	0.95
	gallons	liters	3.8
	milliliters	ounces	0.034
	liters	pints	2.1
	liters	quarts	1.06
	liters	gallons	0.26

ELEVEN QUICK WAYS TO MEASURE WHEN YOU DON'T HAVE A RULER

1. Most credit cards are 3⅜ inches by 2⅛ inches.
2. Standard business cards are printed 3½ inches wide by 2 inches long.
3. Floor tiles are usually manufactured in 12-inch by 12-inch squares.
4. U.S. paper currency is 6⅛ inches wide by 2⅝ inches long.
5. The diameter of a quarter is approximately 1 inch, and the diameter of a penny is approximately three-quarters of an inch.
6. A standard sheet of paper is 8½ inches wide and 11 inches long.

Each of the following five items can be used as a measuring device by multiplying its length by the number of times it is used to measure an area in question.

7. A shoelace   8. A tie   9. A belt

10. Your feet—placing one in front of the other to measure floor area

11. Your outstretched arms from fingertip to fingertip

Special Weights and Measures

acre 43,560 square feet. It originally referred to the area a yoke of oxen could plow daily.

ampere A unit of electric current. A potential difference of one volt across a resistance of one ohm produces a current of one ampere.

astronomical unit (A.U.) The unit of length used in astronomy equal to the mean distance of Earth from the sun, or about 93 million miles.

bale A large bundle of goods. In the United States the approximate weight of a bale of cotton is 500 pounds.

board foot (fbm) A measurement used in lumber: 144 cubic inches (12 inches by 12 inches by 1 inch).

bolt Used in measuring cloth: 40 yards.

British thermal unit (Btu) The amount of heat needed to increase the temperature of one pound of water by 1° F.

bundle Two reams of paper.

caliber The diameter of a bore of a gun, usually expressed in modern U.S. and British usage in hundredths or thousandths of an inch and typically written as a decimal fraction.

carat or karat 200 milligrams or 3,086 grains troy. The measure was originally the weight of a seed of the carob tree in the Mediterranean region. Today it is a measure of the amount of alloy per 24 parts in gold. Thus, 24-carat gold is pure and 18-carat gold is one-quarter alloy.

case Four bundles of paper.

chain (ch) A unit of length equal to 66 feet and usually divided into 100 links. Used in surveying.

decibel A unit of relative loudness. The smallest amount of change that can be detected by the human ear is one decibel. A 20-decibel sound is 10 times as loud as a 10-decibel sound; a 30-decibel sound is 100 times as loud.

10 decibels—a light whisper
20 decibels—quiet conversation
30 decibels—normal conversation
40 decibels—light traffic
50 decibels—a typewriter; loud conversation
60 decibels—a noisy office
70 decibels—normal traffic; a quiet train
80 decibels—raucous music; the subway
90 decibels—heavy traffic; thunder
100 decibels—a plane at takeoff

The speed of sound is usually placed at 1,088 feet per second at 32° F at sea level.

ell (English) 1¼ yards or ¹⁄₃₂ bolt. Used for measuring cloth.

em A printer's measure designating the square width of any given type size. The em of 10-point type is 10 points. An en is one half of an em.

freight ton (measurement ton) 40 cubic feet of merchandise. Used for cargo freight.

gauge A measure of shotgun bore diameter. Gauge numbers originally referred to the number of lead balls of the gun barrel diameter in a pound. Today an international agreement assigns millimeter measures to each gauge.

Gauge	*Bore Diameter in mm*
6	23.34
10	19.67
12	18.52
14	17.60
16	16.81
20	15.90

great gross 12 gross, or 1,728.

gross 12 dozen, or 144.

hand A unit of measure equal to 4 inches. Used especially to measure the height of horses.

hertz A unit of electromagnetic wave frequency equal to one cycle per second.

hogshead (hhd) Two liquid barrels.

horsepower The power needed to lift 33,000 pounds a distance of 1 foot in 1 minute (about 1½ times the power an average horse can exert) or to lift 550 pounds 1 foot in 1 second. Used to measure the power of steam engines, etc.

knot The rate of speed of 1 nautical mile per hour. Used for measuring the speed of ships.

league Any of various units of distance from about 2.4 to 4.6 statute miles.

light-year A unit of length in interstellar astronomy equal to the distance that light travels in one year in a vacuum, or about 5,878,000,000,000 miles.

magnum A large bottle of wine holding about ⅖ gallon.

ohm The unit of electrical resistance in which a potential difference of one volt produces a current of one ampere.

parsec The unit of measure for interstellar space equal to a distance having a heliocentric parallax of one second, or to 206,265 times the radius of Earth's orbit, or to 3.26 light-years, or to 19.2 trillion miles.

pi The ratio of the circumference of a circle to its diameter. A transcendental number having a value to eight places of 3.14159265. For practical purposes, the value is 3.1416.

pica One-sixth, or 12 points. Used to measure typographical material.

pipe Two hogsheads. Used to measure wine and other liquids.

point .013836 (approximately ¹⁄₇₂) inch or ¹⁄₁₂ pica. Used in printing to measure type size.

quintal 100,000 grams, or 220.46 pounds avoirdupois.

quire 25 sheets of paper.

ream 500 sheets of paper, or 20 quires.

Temperature

Prefixes are not as commonly used with temperature measurements as they are with those for weight, length, and volume. The following can be used as general guidelines to tell the weather in both Celsius and Fahrenheit.

0° C	Freezing point of water (32° F)
10° C	A warm winter day (50° F)
20° C	A mild spring day (68° F)
30° C	Quite warm—almost hot (86° F)
37° C	Normal body temperature (98.6° F)
40° C	Heat wave conditions (104° F)
100° C	Boiling point of water (212° F)

To convert degrees Fahrenheit to degrees Celsius, multiply by five-ninths after subtracting 32; to convert Celsius to Fahrenheit, multiply by nine-fifths and then add 32.

(Absolute zero = −273° C = −459.4° F)

Deg. C	°F or °C	Deg. F	Deg. C	°F or °C	Deg. F	Deg. C	°F or °C	Deg. F
−17.8	0	32.0	−11.7	11	51.8	−6.1	21	69.8
−17.2	1	33.8	−11.1	12	53.6	−5.6	22	71.6
−16.7	2	35.6	−10.6	13	55.4	−5.0	23	73.4
−16.1	3	37.4	−10.0	14	57.2	−4.4	24	75.2
−15.6	4	39.2	−9.4	15	59.0	−3.9	25	77.0
−15.0	5	41.0						
−14.4	6	42.8	−8.9	16	60.8	−3.3	26	78.8
−13.9	7	44.6	−8.3	17	62.6	−2.8	27	80.6
−13.3	8	46.4	−7.8	18	64.4	−2.2	28	82.4
−12.8	9	48.2	−7.2	19	66.2	−1.7	29	84.2
−12.2	10	50.0	−6.7	20	68.0	−1.1	30	86.8

Deg. C	°F or °C	Deg. F	Deg. C	°F or °C	Deg. F	Deg. C	°F or °C	Deg. F
−0.6	31	87.8	24.4	76	168.8	49.4	121	249.8
0.0	32	89.6	25.0	77	170.6	50.0	122	251.6
0.6	33	91.4	25.6	78	172.4	50.6	123	253.4
1.1	34	93.2	26.1	79	174.2	51.1	124	255.2
1.7	35	95.0	26.7	80	176.0	51.7	125	257.0
2.2	36	96.8	27.2	81	177.8	52.2	126	258.8
2.8	37	98.6	27.8	82	179.6	52.8	127	260.6
3.3	38	100.4	28.3	83	181.4	53.3	128	262.4
3.9	39	102.2	28.9	84	183.2	53.9	129	264.2
4.4	40	104.0	29.4	85	185.0	54.4	130	266.0
5.0	41	105.8	30.0	86	186.8	55.0	131	267.8
5.6	42	107.6	30.6	87	188.6	55.6	132	269.6
6.1	43	109.4	31.1	88	190.4	56.1	133	271.4
6.7	44	111.2	31.7	89	192.2	56.7	134	273.2
7.2	45	113.9	32.2	90	194.0	57.2	135	275.0
7.8	46	114.8	32.8	91	195.8	57.8	136	276.8
8.3	47	116.6	33.3	92	197.6	58.3	137	278.6
8.9	48	118.4	33.9	93	199.4	58.9	138	280.4
9.4	49	120.2	34.4	94	201.2	59.4	139	282.2
10.0	50	122.0	35.0	95	203.0	60.0	140	284.0
10.6	51	123.8	35.6	96	204.8	60.6	141	285.8
11.1	52	125.6	36.1	97	206.6	61.1	142	287.6
11.7	53	127.4	36.7	98	208.4	61.7	143	289.4
12.2	54	129.2	37.2	99	210.2	62.2	144	291.2
12.8	55	131.0	37.8	100	212.0	62.8	145	293.0
13.3	56	132.8	38.3	101	213.8	63.3	146	294.8
13.9	57	134.6	38.9	102	215.6	63.9	147	296.6
14.4	58	136.4	39.4	103	217.4	64.4	148	298.4
15.0	59	138.2	40.0	104	219.2	65.0	149	300.2
15.6	60	140.0	40.6	105	221.6	65.4	150	392.0
16.1	61	141.8	41.1	106	222.8	66.1	151	303.8
16.7	62	143.6	41.7	107	224.6	66.7	152	305.6
17.2	63	145.4	42.2	108	226.4	67.2	153	307.4
17.8	64	147.2	42.8	109	228.2	67.8	154	309.2
18.3	65	149.0	43.3	110	230.0	68.3	155	311.0
18.9	66	150.8	43.9	111	231.8	68.9	156	312.8
19.4	67	152.6	44.4	112	233.6	69.4	157	314.6
20.0	68	154.4	45.0	113	235.4	70.0	158	316.4
20.6	69	156.2	45.6	114	237.2	70.6	159	318.2
21.1	70	158.0	46.1	115	239.0	71.1	160	320.0
21.7	71	159.8	46.7	116	240.8	71.7	161	321.8
22.2	72	161.6	47.2	117	242.6	72.2	162	323.6
22.8	73	163.4	47.8	118	244.4	72.8	163	325.4
23.3	74	165.2	48.3	119	246.2	73.3	164	327.2
23.9	75	167.0	48.9	120	248.0	73.9	165	320.0

Deg. C	°F or °C	Deg. F	Deg. C	°F or °C	Deg. F	Deg. C	°F or °C	Deg. F
74.4	166	330.8	83.3	182	359.6	92.2	198	388.4
75.0	167	332.6	83.9	183	361.4	92.8	199	390.2
75.6	168	334.4	84.4	184	363.2	93.3	200	392.0
76.1	169	336.2	85.0	185	365.0	93.9	201	393.8
76.7	170	338.0	85.6	186	366.8	94.4	202	395.6
77.2	171	339.8	86.1	187	368.6	95.0	203	397.4
77.8	172	341.6	86.7	188	370.4	95.6	204	399.2
78.3	173	343.4	87.2	189	372.2	96.1	205	401.0
78.9	174	345.2	87.8	190	374.0	96.7	206	402.8
79.4	175	347.0	88.3	191	375.8	97.2	207	404.6
80.0	176	348.8	88.9	192	377.6	97.8	208	406.4
80.5	177	350.6	89.4	193	379.4	98.3	209	408.2
81.1	178	352.4	90.0	194	381.2	98.9	210	410.0
81.7	179	354.2	90.6	195	383.0	99.4	211	411.8
82.2	180	356.0	91.1	196	384.8	100.0	212	413.6
82.8	181	357.8	91.7	197	386.6			

CONVERTING HOUSEHOLD MEASURES

From	To	Multiply by
units	dozens	12
baker's dozens	units	13
teaspoons	milliliters	4.93
teaspoons	tablespoons	0.33
tablespoons	milliliters	14.79
tablespoons	teaspoons	3
cups	liters	0.24
cups	pints	0.50
cups	quarts	0.25
pints	cups	2
pints	liters	0.47
pints	quarts	0.50
quarts	cups	4
quarts	gallons	0.25
quarts	liters	0.95
quarts	pints	2
gallons	liters	3.79
gallons	quarts	4

HISTORIC WEIGHTS AND MEASURES

Units of Volume	Location	Customary	Metric
amphora	Greece	10.3 gal.	38.8
amphora	Rome	6.84 gal.	26 l
bath	Israel	2,250 cu. in.	37 l
ephah	Israel	1.1 bu.	40 l
gallon, beer	England	282 cu. in.	4.62 l
hekat	Israel	291 cu. in.	4.77 l
tun	England	252 gal.	954 l

Units of Weight	Location	Customary	Metric
carat	England, U.S.	3⅙ grains	206 mg
denarius	Rome	0.17 oz.	4.6 g
dinar	Arabia	0.15 oz.	4.2 g
drachma	Greece	0.154 oz.	4.36 g
livre	France	1.08 lb.	490 g
livre (demikilo)	France	1.10 lb.	500 g
mite	England	0.05 grain	3.24 mg
obol	Greece	11.2 grains	0.73 g
pfund	Germany	1.1 lb.	500 g
pound, tower:	England		
12 oz.		5,400 grains	350 g
15 oz.		6,750 grains	437 g
16 oz.		7,200 grains	465 g
shekel	Israel	0.5 oz.	14.1 g
shekel, trade	Babylonia	0.3 oz.	8.37 g

Units of Length	Location	Customary	Metric
cubit	Greece	18.3 in.	46.5 cm
	Rome	17.5 in.	44.4 cm
hand	England, U.S.	4 in.	10.2 cm
stadion	Greece	622 ft.	190 m
stadium	Rome	606 ft.	185 m

COMMON FRACTIONS AND THEIR DECIMAL EQUIVALENTS

½	.5000	¹⁄₁₀	.1000	²⁄₇	.2857	³⁄₁₁	.2727	⁵⁄₉	.5556	⁷⁄₁₁	.6364
⅓	.3333	¹⁄₁₁	.0909	²⁄₉	.2222	⅘	.8000	⁵⁄₁₁	.4545	⁷⁄₁₂	.5833
¼	.2500	¹⁄₁₂	.0833	²⁄₁₁	.1818	⁴⁄₇	.5714	⁵⁄₁₂	.4167	⁸⁄₉	.8889
⅕	.2000	¹⁄₁₆	.0625	¾	.7500	⁴⁄₉	.4444	⁶⁄₇	.8571	⁸⁄₁₁	.7273
⅙	.1667	¹⁄₃₂	.0313	⅗	.6000	⁴⁄₁₁	.3636	⁶⁄₁₁	.5455	⁹⁄₁₀	.9000
⅐	.1429	¹⁄₆₄	.0156	³⁄₇	.4286	⅚	.8333	⅞	.8750	⁹⁄₁₁	.8182
⅛	.1250	⅔	.6667	⅜	.3750	⁵⁄₇	.7143	⁷⁄₉	.7778	¹⁰⁄₁₁	.9091
⅑	.1111	⅖	.4000	³⁄₁₀	.3000	⅝	.6250	⁷⁄₁₀	.7000	¹¹⁄₁₂	.9167

Metric Prefixes

The prefixes below, in combination with the basic metric units such as meter, gram, and liter, provide the multiples and submultiples in the International System. For example, centi + meter = centimeter, meaning one one-hundredth of a meter.

Prefix	Symbol	Multiples	Equivalent
exa	E	10^{18}	quintillionfold
peta	P	10^{15}	quadrillionfold
tera	T	10^{12}	trillionfold
giga	G	10^{9}	billionfold
mega	M	10^{6}	millionfold
kilo	k	10^{3}	thousandfold
hecto	h	10^{2}	hundredfold
deka	da	10	tenfold

Prefix	Symbol	Submultiples	Equivalent
deci	d	10^{-1}	tenth part
centi	c	10^{-2}	hundredth part
milli	m	10^{-3}	thousandth part
micro	u	10^{-6}	millionth part
nano	n	10^{-9}	billionth part
pico	p	10^{-12}	trillionth part
femto	f	10^{-15}	quadrillionth part
atto	a	10^{-18}	quintillionth part

Mile-to-kilometer and Kilometer-to-mile Conversions

Miles to Kilometers		Kilometers to Miles	
Miles	Kilometers	Kilometers	Miles
1	1.6	1	0.6
2	3.2	2	1.2
3	4.8	3	1.8
4	6.4	4	2.4
5	8.0	5	3.1
6	9.6	6	3.7
7	11.2	7	4.3
8	12.8	8	4.9
9	14.4	9	5.5
10	16.0	10	6.2
20	32.1	20	12.4
30	48.2	30	18.6
40	64.3	40	24.8
50	80.4	50	31.0
60	96.5	60	37.2
70	112.6	70	43.4
80	128.7	80	49.7
90	144.8	90	55.9
100	160.9	100	62.1
1,000	1,609	1,000	621

Roman Numerals

I =	1	XXX =	30
II =	2	XL =	40
III =	3	L =	50
IV =	4	LX =	60
V =	5	LXX =	70
VI =	6	LXXX =	80
VII =	7	XC =	90
VIII =	8	C =	100
IX =	9	D =	500
X =	10	M =	1,000
XX =	20		

A dash on top of a symbol multiplies its value by 1,000. For example, $\overline{V}$ signifies 5,000 and $\overline{M}$ indicates 1,000,000.

Additional Sources of Information

Dresner, Stephen. *Units of Measurement: An Encyclopaedic Dictionary of Units, Both Scientific and Popular, and the Quantities They Measure.* Books on Demand UMI.

Gerolde, Steven. *Universal Conversion Factors.* Penwell Books, 1971.

Johnstone, William D. *For a Good Measure.* Avon, 1977.

Kula, Witolde. *Measures and Men.* Princeton University Press, 1985.

Lowe, D. Armstrong. *Guide to International Recommendations on Names and Symbols for Quantities and on Units of Measurement* (WHO supplement, vol. 52), World Health, 1975.

Miller, David M. *Understanding the Metric System* (paperbound programmed learning book). Allyn & Bacon, 1965.

3

Symbols and Signs

Symbols Used in Astronomy

⊖ ☾	center	☾, ☽, ☾, ☾	last quarter
☄	comet	♆ *or* ♃	Neptune
⊕, ⊖, *or* ♁	Earth	♇	Pluto
♃	Jupiter	♄	Saturn
☉ ☾	lower limb	☆	star
♂	Mars	☆-P	star–planet altitude correction
☿	Mercury	☉	sun
●, ☾, *or* ☽	the moon	☉ ☾	upper limb
●	new moon	♁ *or* ⛢	Uranus
☽, ●, ☽, ☽,	first quarter	♀	Venus
○ *or* ☺	full moon		

Aspects and Nodes

☌	conjunction	☍	opposition
□	quadrature	☊	ascending node
△	trine	☋	descending node

Symbols Used in Biology

♃	perennial herb	∞	indefinite number
♂, ♂	male organism or cell; staminate plant or flower	×	crossed with; hybrid
♀	female organism or cell; pistillate plant or flower	+	wild type
		P	parental generation
☿	perfect, or hermaphroditic, plant or flower	F	filial generation; offspring
○	individual, especially female, organism	F_1, F_2, F_3, etc.	offspring of the first, second, third, etc., filial generation
□	individual, especially male, organism		

Symbols Used in Chemistry

+   "and," "plus," "together with," used between the symbols of reacting substances in chemical equations; when placed above a symbol or to its right as a superscript, the plus sign indicates a unit charge of positive electricity; the sign also indicates dextrorotation

—   single bond, used between the symbols of elements or groups that form a compound; when placed above a symbol or to its right as a superscript, the dash indicates a unit charge of negative electricity; it also signifies levorotation or the removal of a part from a compound

●   single bond; a unit of positive charge of electricity; separates parts of a compound considered loosely joined

⬡   Benzene ring

=   "forms" or "results in," used between the symbols of reacting substances in chemical equations;

$\equiv$	a double bond; two unit charges of negative electricity when placed above a symbol or to its right as a superscript
$\equiv$	triple bond or triple negative charge
:	unshared pair of electrons; sometimes, a double bond
⋮	triple bond
( )	groups or radicals within a compound
[ ]	with parentheses, shows certain radicals; in coordination formulas, it shows relationship to the central atom
$\frown$ *or* $\smile$	unites attached atoms or groups in

	structural formulas for cyclic compounds
$\rightarrow$	gives, passes over to, or leads to
$\rightleftarrows$	is in equilibrium with; forms and is formed from
$\downarrow$	precipitation of a substance
$\uparrow$	a substance as a gas
$\equiv$, $\backsimeq$	is equivalent to; used in equations to show how much of one substance will react with a given amount of another so that no excess of either remains
$<$	bivalent element
$>$	bivalent radical

Chemical Elements

Element	Symbol	Element	Symbol
actinium	Ac	gallium	Ga
aluminum	Al	germanium	Ge
americum	Am	gold	Au (aurum)
antimony	Sb (stibium)	hafnium	Hf
argon	Ar	helium	He
arsenic	As	holmium	Ho
astatine	At	hydrogen	H
barium	Ba	indium	In
berkelium	Bk	iodine	I
beryllium	Be	iridium	Ir
bismuth	Bi	iron	Fe (ferrum)
boron	B	krypton	Kr
bromine	Br	lanthanum	La
cadmium	Cd	lawrencium	Lr
calcium	Ca	lead	Pb (plumbum)
californium	Cf	lithium	Li
carbon	C	lutetium	Lu
cerium	Ce	magnesium	Mg
cesium	Cs	manganese	Mn
chlorine	Cl	mendelevium	Md
chromium	Cr	mercury	Hg (hydrargyrum)
cobalt	Co	molybdenum	Mo
columbium	Cb (*see* niobium)	neodymium	Nd
copper	Cu	neon	Ne
curium	Cm	neptunium	Np
dysprosium	Dy	nickel	Ni
einsteinium	Es	niobium	Nb (*formerly* columbium)
erbium	Er	nitrogen	N
europium	Eu	nobelium	No
fermium	Fm	osmium	Os
fluorine	F	oxygen	O
francium	Fr	palladium	Pd
gadolinium	Gd	phosphorus	P

Element	Symbol	Element	Symbol
platinum	Pt	strontium	Sr
plutonium	Pu	sulfur	S
polonium	Po	tantalum	Ta
potassium	K (kalium)	technetium	Tc
praseodymium	Pr	tellurium	Te
promethium	Pm	terbium	Tb
protactinium	Pa	thallium	Tl
radium	Ra	thorium	Th
radon	Rn	thulium	Tm
rhenium	Re	tin	Sn (stannum)
rhodium	Rh	titanium	Ti
rubidium	Rb	tungsten	W (wolfram)
ruthenium	Ru	uranium	U
samarium	Sm	vanadium	V
scandium	Sc	xenon	Xe
selenium	Se	ytterbium	Yb
silicon	Si	yttrium	Y
silver	Ag (argentum)	zinc	Zn
sodium	Na (natrium)	zirconium	Zr

Symbols Used in Physics

α	alpha particle	e	electronic charge of electron
Å	angstrom unit	E	electric field
β	beta ray	G	conductance; weight
γ	gamma radiation	h	Planck's constant
ϵ	electromotive force	H	enthalpy
η	efficiency	L	inductance
Λ	equivalent conductivity; permeance	n	index of refraction
λ	wavelength	P	momentum of a particle
μ	magnetic moment	R	universal gas constant
ν	frequency	S	entropy
ρ	density; specific resistance	T	absolute temperature; period
σ	conductivity; cross section; surface tension	V	electrical potential; frequency
ϕ	luminous flux; magnetic flux	W	energy
φ	fluidity	X	magnification; reactance
Ω	ohm	Y	admittance
B	magnetic induction; magnetic field	Z	impedance
c	speed of light		

Symbols Used in Medicine and Pharmacology

Å	angstrom unit	ad	up to; so as to make
$\overline{A}$, $\overline{A}\,\overline{A}$, $\overline{a}\overline{a}$, $\overline{a}a$	of each	add.	let there be added; add
a.c.	before meals	ad lib.	at pleasure; as needed or desired

agit.   shake
aq.   water
b. (i.) d.   twice daily
c̄   with
cap.   take; capsule
coch.   a spoonful
d.   give
dil.   dilute *or* dissolve
Dx   diagnosis
fldxt.   fluid extract
ft.   make
ft. mist.   let a mixture be made
ft. pulv.   let a powder be made
gr.   a grain
gtt.   drops
H.   hour
haust.   a draft
Hx   history
in d.   daily
lot.   a lotion
ⓜ heart murmur
m͡, m͡   minim
μ   micron
μμ   micromicron
mod. praesc.   in the manner prescribed
O., o.   a pint
ol.   oil
oz.   ounce
p.c.   after meals

pil.   pill(s)
p.r.n.   as circumstances may require
pulv.   powder
Px   past history
q. (i.) d.   four times daily
q.l.   as much as you please
q.s.   as much as will suffice
q.v.   as much as you like
℞   take: used at the beginning of a prescription
rep.   let it be repeated
Rh+   positive blood factor
Rh−   negative blood factor
◌   ¹⁄₁₀₀₀ of a second
s̄   without
S, Sig.   write: used in prescriptions to indicate the directions to be placed on the label of the medicine
sol.   solution
s.o.s.   if necessary
s̄s̄   one half
tab.   tablet
t. (i.) d.   three times daily
ut dict.   as directed
w/v   weight in volume
℥   ounce
f ℥   fluidounce
℈   dram
f ℈   fluidram
℈   scruple

Symbols Used in Mathematics

+   plus; positive
−   minus; negative
×   multiplied by
÷   divided by
=   equal to
±   plus or minus
∓   minus or plus
≐   plus or equal to
≠ *or* ≠   not equal to
≡   identical with
≈   nearly equal to
~   difference
≅   congruent to
>   greater than
≫   much greater than
<   less than
≪   much less than
≧ *or* ≥   greater than or equal to
≦ *or* ≤   less than or equal to

≯   not greater than
≮   not less than
∝   varies directly as; is proportional to
:   is to; the ratio of
∴   therefore
∵   because
::   proportion
∺   geometrical proportion
∞   infinity
∠   angle
∟   right angle
⊥   perpendicular
∥   parallel
⊙ *or* ○   circle
⌒   arc of a circle
○   ellipse
∅   diameter
△   triangle
□   square

▢ rectangle
⊞ cube
▱ rhomboid
√ square root
∛ cube root
∜ fourth root
ⁿ√ nth root
( ) parentheses ⎤
[ ] brackets ⎥ indicate that the quan-
{ } braces ⎥ tities enclosed by
⎦ them are to be taken
together
Σ summation of
Π product
π pi (3.1416)
∪ union

∩ intersection
! factorial
Λ *or* 0 empty set; null set
∈ is an element of
∉ is not an element of
ℓ base (2.718) of natural logarithms
⊢ assertion sign
∂ partial differential
∫ integral
∮ contour integral
﹀ horizontal integral
′ minute
″ second
° degree
% percent

Electrical Symbols

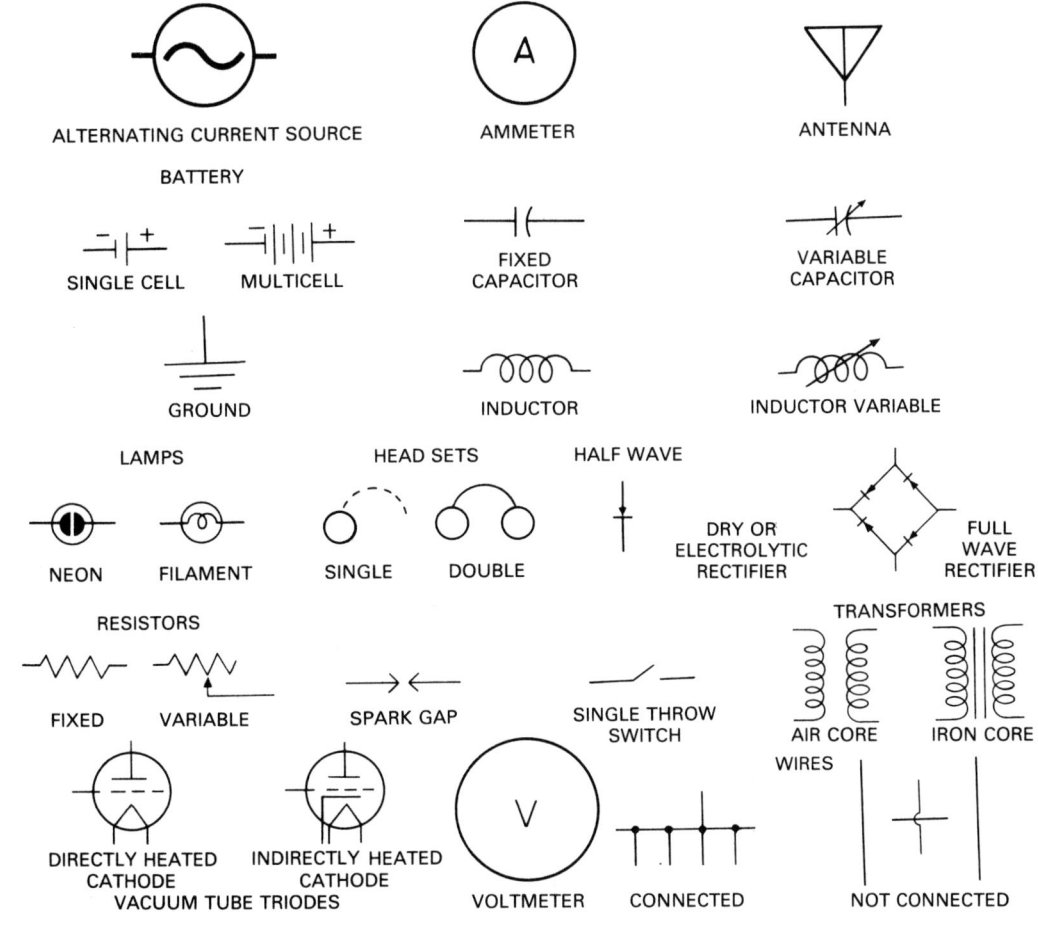

ALTERNATING CURRENT SOURCE

AMMETER

ANTENNA

BATTERY

SINGLE CELL   MULTICELL

FIXED
CAPACITOR

VARIABLE
CAPACITOR

GROUND

INDUCTOR

INDUCTOR VARIABLE

LAMPS

HEAD SETS

HALF WAVE

NEON   FILAMENT

SINGLE   DOUBLE

DRY OR
ELECTROLYTIC
RECTIFIER

FULL
WAVE
RECTIFIER

RESISTORS

TRANSFORMERS

FIXED   VARIABLE

SPARK GAP

SINGLE THROW
SWITCH

AIR CORE   IRON CORE

WIRES

DIRECTLY HEATED
CATHODE

INDIRECTLY HEATED
CATHODE

VACUUM TUBE TRIODES

VOLTMETER   CONNECTED

NOT CONNECTED

Map and Chart Symbols

Boundaries

| INTERNATIONAL | PROVINCIAL OR STATE | COUNTY | TOWNSHIP | INCORPORATED VILLAGE |

Cities and Towns

| CAPITAL CITY | URBAN AREA | TOWN OR VILLAGE |

Roads and Railroads

| SUPERHIGHWAY | SUPERHIGHWAY UNDER CONSTRUCTION | DUAL HIGHWAY | MAIN ROAD | SECONDARY ROAD |

| BRIDGE AND ROAD | DRAWBRIDGE AND ROAD | TUNNEL AND ROAD | RAILROAD TRACK, SINGLE | RAILROAD TRACKS, TWO OR MORE | RAILROAD STATION |

Hydrographic Features

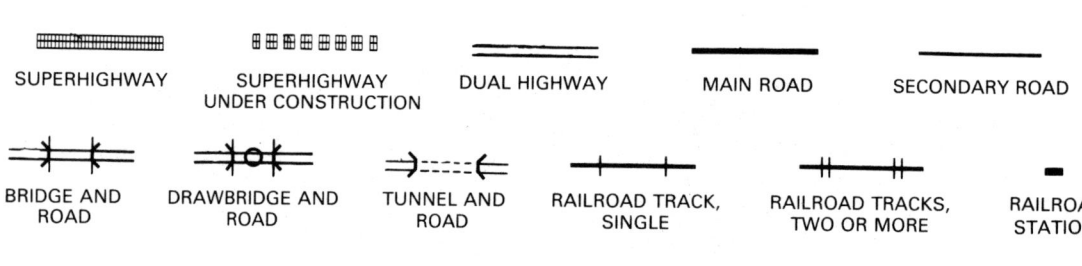

RIVER

INTERMITTENT LAKE

INTERMITTENT RIVER

FRESHWATER LAKE: RESERVOIR

DAMS

FALLS

Natural Features

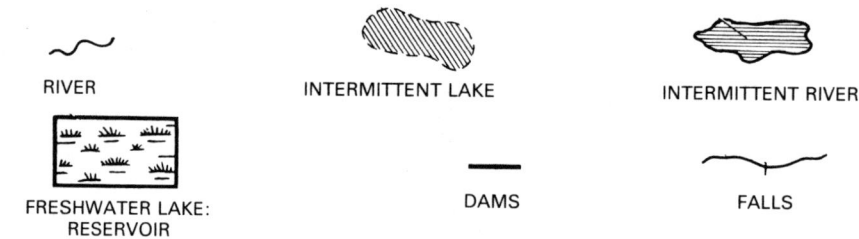

GLACIERS AND ICE SHELVES

ELEVATION ABOVE SEA LEVEL

 PASSES

Cultural, Historical, and Recreational Symbols

 POINTS OF INTEREST

 CAMPSITES

 WINTER SPORTS AREAS

STATE MONUMENTS, MEMORIALS, AND HISTORIC SITES

RUINS

NATIONAL WILDLIFE REFUGE

 RANGER STATION

Weather Symbols

Weather Conditions

CLEAR SKY

CLOUDY (PARTLY)

CLOUDY (COMPLETELY OVERCAST)

DRIZZLE

FOG (LIGHT)

FOG (HEAVY)

HAZE

HURRICANE

LIGHTNING

RAIN SHOWERS

SANDSTORM OR DUST STORM

HAIL SHOWERS

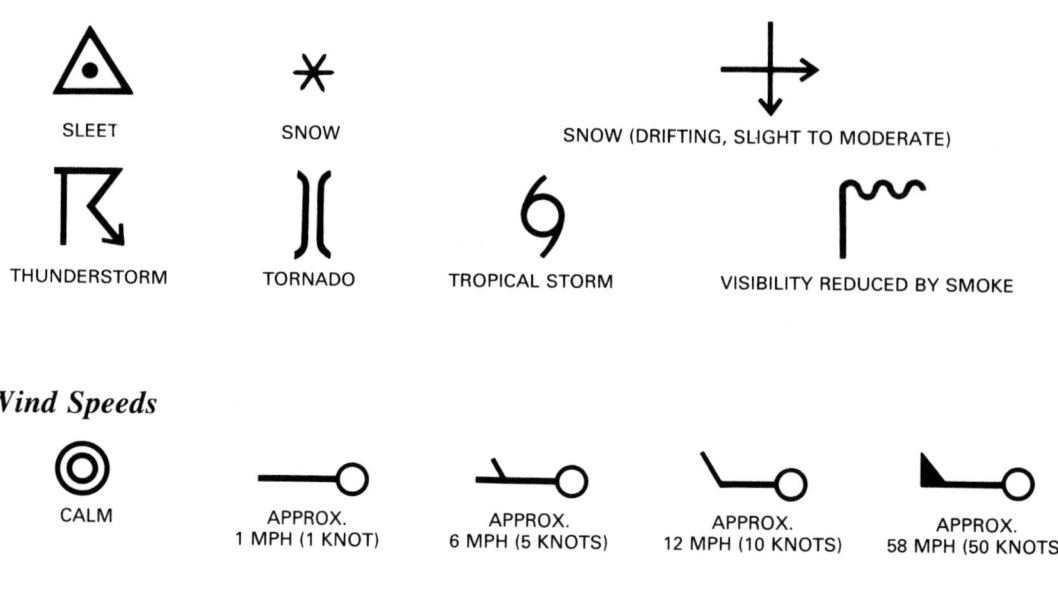

SLEET

SNOW

SNOW (DRIFTING, SLIGHT TO MODERATE)

THUNDERSTORM

TORNADO

TROPICAL STORM

VISIBILITY REDUCED BY SMOKE

Wind Speeds

CALM

APPROX.
1 MPH (1 KNOT)

APPROX.
6 MPH (5 KNOTS)

APPROX.
12 MPH (10 KNOTS)

APPROX.
58 MPH (50 KNOTS)

Weather Fronts

WARM

COLD

OCCLUDED

STATIONARY

Business and Monetary Symbols

A/C, a/c	account; account current		O/S	out of stock
A/O, a/o	account of		P/A	power of attorney
B/D	bank draft		P/C, p/c	prices current; petty cash
B/E	bill of exchange		P/N	promissory note
B/L	bill of lading		w/	with
B/P	bills payable		W/B	waybill
B/R	bills receivable		w/o	without
B/V	book value		@	at/per/priced at
C/D	carried down; certificate of deposit		#	number
			%	percent/per hundred
C/N	circular note; credit note		¢	cent
C/O	care of; carried over; cash order		$	dollar
d/d	delivered		DM	deutsche mark
D/O	delivery order		F	franc
G/A	general average		L	lira
L/C, l/c	letter of credit		£	pound
M/D, m/d	month's date		R	ruble
N/S, n/s	not sufficient funds		R	rupee
o/c	overcharge		Y	yen

Musical Symbols

𝄞	treble, or G, clef	𝅝	whole note
𝄢	bass, or F, clef	𝅗𝅥	half note
𝄡	alto, or C, clef	𝅘𝅥	quarter note
	measure	𝅘𝅥𝅮	eighth note
	final bar	𝅘𝅥𝅯	sixteenth note
𝟑𝟒	¾ time	𝅘𝅥.	dotted half note
𝄴	⁴⁄₄ time		whole rest
𝄵	²⁄₂ time		half rest
𝟔𝟖	⁶⁄₈ time	𝄽	quarter rest
♯	sharp	𝄾	eighth rest
♯♯	double sharp	𝄿	sixteenth rest
♭	flat		repeat
♭♭	double flat		repeat measure
♮	natural	*D.C.*	repeat from the beginning

p   piano (soft) $<$ crescendo

pp pianissimo (very soft) $>$ decrescendo

f   forte (loud)   tie

ff fortissimo (very loud)   ⌢   trill

Proofreaders' Marks

∧	Insert material as indicated in margin
ℒ	Delete
stet	Restore deleted material; let it stand (in text, use dots to indicate what is to be restored)
⌢	Close up; print as one word
ℒ̂	Delete and close up
tr	Transpose (in text, indicate by ∩ or ∪ to change of order)
sp	Spell out
#	Insert space
eq #	Space evenly
hr #	Insert hair space
⧠	Insert or indent one em space
⊓	Move up
⊔	Move down
⊐	Move to the right
⊏	Move to the left
⊐⊏	Center
≑	Align vertically
‖	Align horizontally; straighten type
ℓ	Turn over inverted letter
wf	Wrong font
×	Broken type; reset
¶	Begin a new paragraph

no ¶	Do not begin a new paragraph; run paragraphs together
(/)	Insert parentheses
[/]	Insert brackets
⌃	Insert comma
;/	Insert semicolon
:/	Insert colon
⊙	Insert period
?	Insert question mark
|·|·|·|	Insert ellipses
⌄	Insert apostrophe (or single quotation mark)
⌄⌄	Insert quotation marks
|=|	Insert hyphen
⊥M	Insert em dash
⊥N	Insert en dash
∨	Insert superscript or superior
∧	Insert subscript or inferior
cap	capitalize lowercase letter
lc	Lowercase capital letter
s.c.	Set in small capitals
rom	Set in roman type
bf	Set in **boldface** type
ital	Set in *italic* type

Diacritical Marks

´	acute accent (as in *café*)
˘	breve (pronunciation symbol that indicates a short vowel)
¸	cedilla (as in *François*)
^	circumflex (as in *château*)

¨	diaeresis or umlaut (as in *Köln*)
`	grave accent (as in *à la carte*)
¯	macron (pronunciation symbol that indicates a long vowel)
~	tilde (as in *São Tomé*)

Religious Symbols

Buddhism

BUDDHA

LOTUS

THE WHEEL

Christianity

CELTIC CROSS

LATIN CROSS

ORTHODOX CROSS

AGNUS DEI

CHI RHO

DESCENDING DOVE; HOLY SPIRIT

Hinduism

MANDALA

OM

SHIVA

Islam

STAR AND CRESCENT

Judaism

MENORAH

STAR OF DAVID

TEN COMMANDMENTS

Shinto

TORII

Taoism

WATER: LIFE-GIVING SOURCE   YIN-YANG

Zodiac Signs

		Planet	*Element*	*Personality Traits*
Aries The Ram Mar. 21–Apr. 19	or ♈	Mars	fire	bold, impulsive, confident, independent
Taurus The Bull Apr. 20–May 20	or ♉	Venus	earth	patient, determined, stubborn, devoted
Gemini The Twins May 21–June 21	or ♊	Mercury	air	ambitious, alert, intelligent, temperamental
Cancer The Crab June 22–July 22	or ♋	Moon	water	moody, sensitive, impressionable, sympathetic

		Planet	*Element*	*Personality Traits*
Leo The Lion July 23–Aug. 22	*or* ♌	Sun	fire	noble, generous, enthusiastic, temperamental
Virgo The Virgin Aug. 23–Sept. 22	*or* ♍	Mercury	earth	intellectual, methodical, placid, tactless
Libra The Scales Sept. 23–Oct. 23	*or* ♎	Venus	air	just, sympathetic, orderly, persuasive, sociable
Scorpio The Scorpion Oct. 24–Nov. 21	*or* ♏	Mars	water	loyal, philosophical, willful, domineering
Sagittarius The Archer Nov. 22–Dec. 21	*or* ♐	Jupiter	fire	practical, imaginative, mature, just

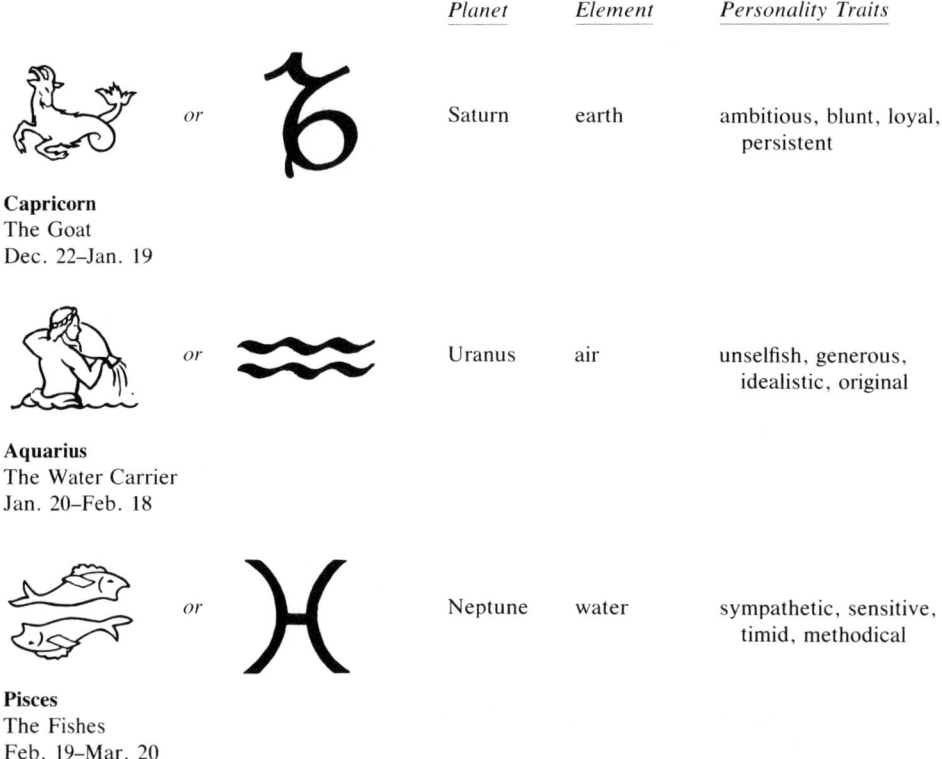

	Planet	Element	Personality Traits
Capricorn The Goat Dec. 22–Jan. 19	Saturn	earth	ambitious, blunt, loyal, persistent
Aquarius The Water Carrier Jan. 20–Feb. 18	Uranus	air	unselfish, generous, idealistic, original
Pisces The Fishes Feb. 19–Mar. 20	Neptune	water	sympathetic, sensitive, timid, methodical

International Road Signs and Travel Symbols

Danger Signs

 CURVE

 INTERSECTION

 OPENING BRIDGE

 ROAD WORKS

 TUNNEL

 PEDESTRIAN CROSSING

 WATCH OUT FOR CHILDREN

 ANIMALS CROSSING

 ROAD NARROWS

 SLIPPERY ROAD

 DANGER

 MAIN ROAD AHEAD

STOP AT INTERSECTION

Prohibition Signs

NO ENTRY

ROAD CLOSED

CLOSED TO
MOTOR VEHICLES

CLOSED TO
MOTORCYCLES

CLOSED TO
PEDESTRIANS

NO LEFT (OR RIGHT)
TURNS

NO U TURNS

OVERTAKING
PROHIBITED

SPEED LIMIT

END OF
SPEED LIMIT

Mandatory Signs

DIRECTION
TO FOLLOW

TRAFFIC
CIRCLE

PARKING

HOSPITAL

MECHANICAL
HELP

TELEPHONE

FILLING
STATION

CAMPING SITE

CARAVAN SITE

YOUTH HOSTEL

Semaphore Code

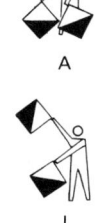
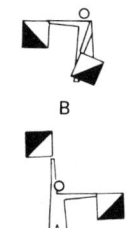
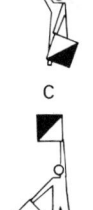

A B C D E

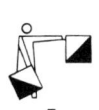

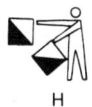

F G H I J K L M

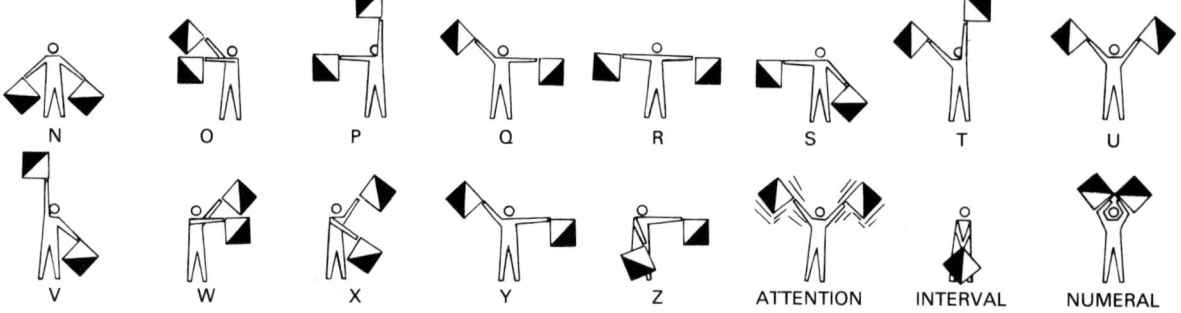

International Radio Alphabet and Morse Code

A: Alpha · —	P: Papa · — — ·	4: · · · · —
B: Bravo — · · ·	Q: Quebec (kaybec) — — · —	5: · · · · ·
C: Charlie — · — ·	R: Romeo · — ·	6: — · · · ·
D: Delta — · ·	S: Sierra · · ·	7: — — · · ·
E: Echo ·	T: Tango —	8: — — — · ·
F: Foxtrot · · — ·	U: Uniform · · —	9: — — — — ·
G: Golf — — ·	V: Victor · · · —	10: — — — — —
H: Hotel · · · ·	W: Whiskey · — —	period: · — · — · —
I: India · ·	X: X-ray — · · —	comma — — · · — —
J: Juliet · — — —	Y: Yankee — · — —	question mark: · · — — · ·
K: Kilo — · —	Z: Zulu — — · ·	semicolon: — · — · — ·
L: Lima (leema) · — · ·	1: · — — — —	colon: — — — · · ·
M: Mike — —	2: · · — — —	hyphen — · · · · —
N: November — ·	3: · · · — —	apostrophe · — — — — ·
O: Oscar — — —		

Manual Alphabet (Sign Language)

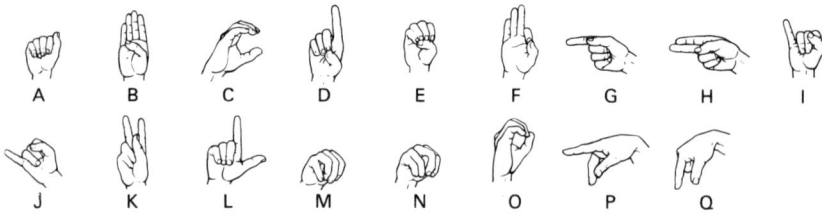

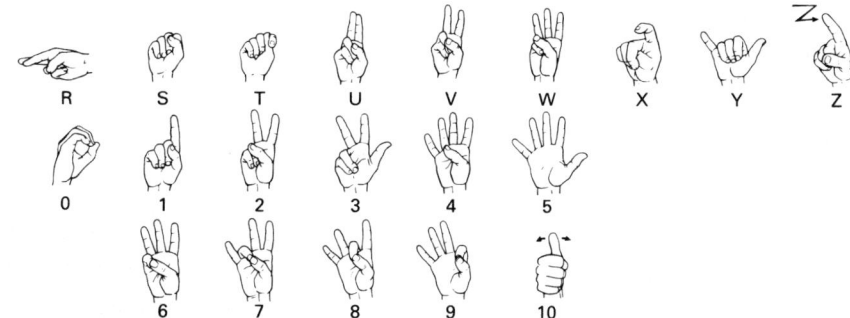

Braille Alphabet

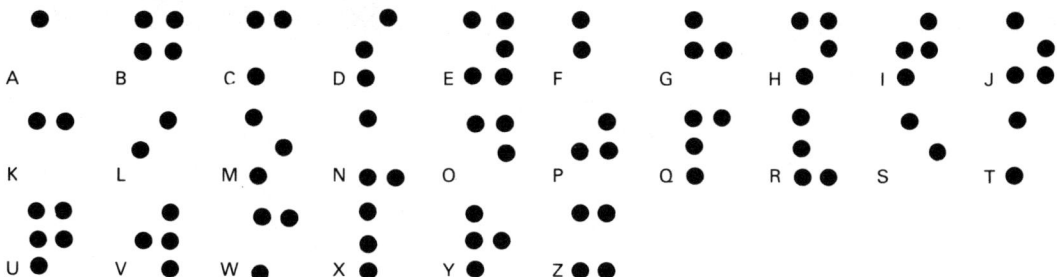

Braille Numbers

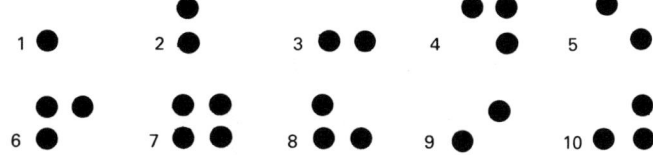

Foreign Alphabets

Arabic

Letters				Names	English Sounds	Letters				Names	English Sounds
ا	ا			alif	a	ض	ض	ضـ	ضـ	dad	d
ب	ـب	ـبـ	بـ	ba	b	ط	ـط	ـطـ	طـ	ta	t
ت	ـت	ـتـ	تـ	ta	t	ظ	ـظ	ـظـ	ظـ	za	z
ث	ـث	ـثـ	ثـ	tha	th	ع	ـع	ـعـ	عـ	'ayn	n.a.
ج	ـج	ـجـ	جـ	jim	j	غ	ـغ	ـغـ	غـ	ghayn	gh
ح	ـح	ـحـ	حـ	ha	h	ف	ـف	ـفـ	فـ	fa	f
خ	ـخ	ـخـ	خـ	kha	kh	ق	ـق	ـقـ	قـ	qaf	q
د	ـد			dal	d	ك	ـك	ـكـ	كـ	kaf	k
ذ	ـذ			dhal	dh	ل	ـل	ـلـ	لـ	lam	l
ر	ـر			rā	r	م	ـم	ـمـ	مـ	mim	m
ز	ـز			zay	z	ن	ـن	ـنـ	نـ	nun	n
س	ـس	ـسـ	سـ	sin	s	ة	ـة	ـهـ	هـ	ha	h
ش	ـش	ـشـ	شـ	shin	sh	و	ـو			waw	w
ص	ـص	ـصـ	صـ	sad	s	ى	ـى	ـيـ	يـ	ya	y

The Arabic alphabet is comprised primarily of consonants. The use of each of the four consonant forms shown above depends on whether the letter stands alone (first form), is joined to the preceding letter (second form), is joined to both the preceding and following letters (third form), or is joined only to the following letter (fourth form). In Arabic, long vowels are indicated by the consonants *alif* (for *a*), *waw* (for *u*), and *ya* (for *i*). Although short vowels are not usually written, they can be indicated by ´ *fatha* (for *a*), ‚ *kesra* (for *i*), and ˢ *damma* (for *u*). When *ha* (third letter form from bottom) has two dots over it, a new letter is made and is pronounced *t*. 'Ayn (eleventh from bottom) cannot be represented in English transliteration.

Greek

Letters		Names	English Sounds	Letters		Names	English Sounds
A	α	alpha	a	N	ν	nu	n
B	β	beta	b	Ξ	ξ	xi	x
Γ	γ	gamma	g	O	o	omicron	o
Δ	δ	delta	d	Π	π	pi	p
E	ε	epsilon	e	P	ρ	rho	r, rh
Z	ζ	zeta	z	Σ	σ ς	sigma	s
H	η	eta	ē	T	τ	tau	t
Θ	θ	theta	th	Y	υ	upsilon	y, u
I	ι	iota	i	Φ	φ	phi	ph
K	κ	kappa	k	X	χ	chi	ch
Λ	λ	lambda	l	Ψ	ψ	psi	ps
M	μ	mu	m	Ω	ω	omega	ō

Hebrew

Letters	Names	English Sounds	Letters	Names	English Sounds
א	aleph	n.a.	ל	lamed	l
ב	beth	b (bh)	מ ם	mem	m
ג	gimel	g (gh)	נ ן	nun	n
ד	daleth	d (dh)	ס	samekh	s
ה	he	h	ע	ayin	n.a.
ו	vav	w	פ ף	pe	p (ph)
ז	zayin	z	צ ץ	sadhe	s
ח	het	h	ק	koph	q
ט	teth	t	ר	resh	r
י	yod	y	שׂ	sin	s
כ ך	kaf	k (kh)	שׁ	shin	sh
			ת	tav	t (th)

Like the Arabic alphabet, the Hebrew alphabet is made up mainly of consonants. Vowels usually do not appear in Hebrew writing, but for educational purposes they are indicated by vowel points—dots or strokes—that are used with a consonant, such as יַ, which would read *day*. Five of the consonants—*kaf, mem, nun, pe,* and *sadhe*—become different (the second consonant form in the first column) when they appear at the end of a word. In terms of consonant sound, the ones shown in parentheses in the third column are used when the consonants they refer to fall at the end of a word. By themselves, the consonants *aleph* and *ayin* are silent.

Russian

Letters	English Sounds	Letters	English Sounds
А а	a	С с	s
Б б	b	Т т	t
В в	v	У у	u
Г г	g	Ф ф	f
Д д	d	Х х	kh
Е е	e	Ц ц	ts
Ж ж	zh	Ч ч	ch
З з	z	Ш ш	sh
И и Й й	i, y	Щ щ	shch
К к	k	Ъ ъ	n.a.
Л л	l	Ы ы	y
М м	m	Ь ь	n.a.
Н н	n	Э э	e
О о	o	Ю ю	yu
П п	p	Я я	ya
Р р	r		

The Russian, or Cyrillic, alphabet is based largely on the Greek alphabet. In modern Russian, the ъ is rare. It signifies that the preceding consonant remains hard even when followed by a palatal vowel. The ь signifies that the preceding consonant is palatalized even if it is not immediately followed by a palatal vowel.

Roman Numerals

1	I	70	LXX	1,910	MCMX
2	II	80	LXXX	1,920	MCMXX
3	III	90	XC	1,930	MCMXXX
4	IV	100	C	1,940	MCMXL
5	V	150	CL	1,950	MCML
6	VI	200	CC	1,960	MCMLX
7	VII	300	CCC	1,970	MCMLXX
8	VIII	400	CD	1,980	MCMLXXX
9	IX	500	D	1,990	MCMXC
10	X	600	DC	2,000	MM
15	XV	700	DCC	3,000	MMM
20	XX	800	DCCC	4,000	MMMM or M$\overline{\text{V}}$
25	XXV	900	CM	5,000	$\overline{\text{V}}$
30	XXX	1,000	M	10,000	$\overline{\text{X}}$
40	XL	1,500	MD	100,000	$\overline{\text{C}}$
50	L	1,900	MCM or	1,000,000	$\overline{\text{M}}$
60	LX		MDCCCC		

Distress Signals

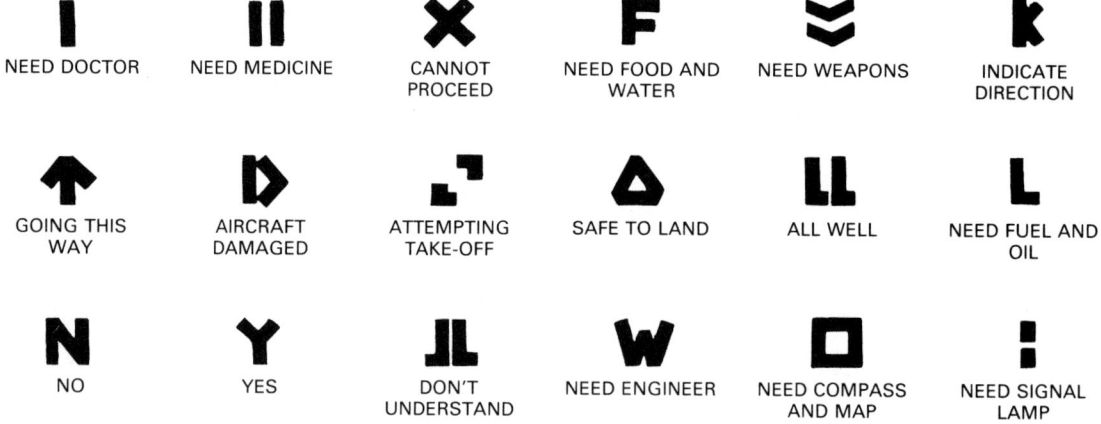

Ship's Bell Time Signals

On most ships, a day consists of six 4-hour watches. The watches change at 8 A.M., noon, 4 P.M., 8 P.M., midnight, and 4 A.M. A chime indicates each half-hour. During a 4-hour watch, one bell chimes at the first half-hour, two bells at the second, and so on up to eight, when the next watch begins and the sequence starts over again.

1 bell	12:30 or	4:30 or	8:30 A.M. or P.M.
2 bells	1:00	5:00	9:00
3 bells	1:30	5:30	9:30
4 bells	2:00	6:00	10:00
5 bells	2:30	6:30	10:30
6 bells	3:00	7:00	11:00
7 bells	3:30	7:30	11:30
8 bells	4:00	8:00	12:00

On many vessels the ship's whistle is blown at noon. On some ships a lightly struck 1 bell announces 15 minutes before the change of watch.

Birthstones and Flowers

Month	*Birthstone*	*Flower*
January	garnet	snowdrop
February	amethyst	primrose
March	aquamarine or bloodstone	violet
April	diamond	daisy
May	emerald	hawthorn
June	pearl, alexandrite, or moonstone	rose
July	ruby	water lily
August	sardonyx or peridot	poppy
September	sapphire	morning glory
October	opal or tourmaline	hops
November	topaz	chrysanthemum
December	turquoise or lapis lazuli	holly

Additional Sources of Information

Adkins, Jan. *Symbols: A Silent Language.* Walker and Company, 1984.

Campbell, Joseph, and Abadie, M.J. *The Mythic Image.* Princeton University Press, 1981.

Cirlot, J.E. *A Dictionary of Symbols.* Philosophy Library, 1972.

Cooper, J.C. *An Illustrated Encyclopedia of Traditional Symbols.* Thames and Hudson, 1987.

Dreyfuss, Henry, ed. *Symbol Sourcebook: An Authoritative Guide to International Graphic Symbols.* Van Nostrand Reinhold, 1984.

Modley, Rudolf, and Meyers, William R. *Handbook of Pictorial Symbols.* Dover, 1976.

4

The Animal World

The Orders of Mammals

Scientists have divided the natural world into three kingdoms: the animal kingdom, the mineral kingdom, and the plant kingdom. Natural objects, as opposed to man-made objects, all fall into one of those kingdoms.

The animal kingdom is classified by zoologists into groups of related animals. Each of the largest groups is called a *phylum*. Each phylum includes several *classes*. Each of these classes is divided into *orders*, which themselves are further divided into *families, genera, and species*. There are more than 1 million different species of animals in the world, including about 4,000 species of mammals.

Mammals are vertebrates, which means they have backbones. They are warm-blooded and have hairy skin. They are called mammals because they nourish their young by giving milk from their mammary glands.

There are 19 orders of mammals in the world. Ten of these live in North America. Some orders include a wide range of animals; for example, shrews, lemurs, marmosets, monkeys, apes, and humans are all primates. Other orders are made up of only one sort of creature; Order Chiroptera, for example, consists of several families of bats.

The proper names of the orders of animals are given in Latin, a convention that allows scientists who speak different languages to discuss them. The Latin names of the orders given here are followed by their common names and the families that make up each order. Examples of the various types of animals included in each family also are given.

Order Artiodactyla (even-toed hoofed animals)

Hoofed animals with an even number of toes include those that ruminate, or digest their food in four-chamber stomachs and chew cuds, and those that do not ruminate. Those that ruminate are the families *Girrafidae* (giraffes), *Cervidae* (deer, moose, reindeer, elk), *Antilocapridae* (pronghorn antelope), and *Bovidae* (cattle, bison, yaks, waterbucks, wildebeest, gazelles, springboks, sheep, musk oxen, goats). Nonruminators include the families *Suidae* (pigs), *Tayassuidae* (peccaries), *Hippopotamidae* (hippopotamuses), and *Camelidae* (camels, llamas).

Order Carnivora (meat-eaters)

There are two suborders of these toe-footed creatures. They include the *Canidae* (wolves, dogs, jackals, foxes), *Ursidae* (bears, giant pandas), *Procyonidae* (coatis, raccoons, lesser pandas), and *Mustelidae* (martens, weasels, skunks, otters), all part of one superfamily that is characterized by long snouts and unretractable claws; and *Felidae* (cats, lions, cheetahs, leopards), *Hyaenidae* (hyenas), and *Viverridae* (mongooses, civets), all of which have retractable claws.

Order Cetacea (whales and porpoises)

Two suborders of Order *Cetacea* are the toothed whales, which have regular conical teeth, and the baleen, or whalebone, whales, which have irregular whalebone surfaces instead of teeth. Toothed whales include the families *Physeteridae* (sperm whales), *Monodontidae* (narwhals, belugas), *Phocoenidae* (porpoises), and *Delphinidae* (dolphins, killer whales).

Baleens are in the Family *Eschrichtiidae* (gray whales), *Balaenidae* (right whales), or *Balaenoptridae* (fin-backed whales, hump-backed whales).

Order Chiroptera (bats)

These winged mammals fall into three families: *Phyllostomidae* (leaf-nosed bat, hog-nosed bat), *Vespertilionidae* (plain-nosed bats such as long-eared myotises, big brown bats, big-eared bats), and Molossidae (free-tailed bats, mastiff bats).

Order Dermoptera (colugos or flying lemurs)

These gliding tree mammals from Asia do not fly and are not lemurs, but they are known as flying lemurs, or Family *Cynocephalidae*.

Order Edentata (toothless mammals)

Three families of mammals get by without teeth: *Dasypodidae* (armadillos), *Bradypodidae* (sloths), and *Myrmecophagidae* (hairy anteaters).

Order Hyracoidae (hyraxes, dassies)

Family *Procaviidae* consists of a group of small hoofed mammals.

Order Insectivora (insect-eaters)

The three members are the families *Talpidae* (moles), *Soricidae* (shrews), and *Erinaceidae* (hedgehogs).

Order Lagomorpha (pikas, hares, and rabbits)

Two families make up this order: *Ochotonidae* (pikas) and *Leporidae* (hares and rabbits of all sorts).

Order Marsupialia (pouched mammals)

Included among these are the families *Caenolestidae* (rat opossums), *Diddeelphidae* (true opossums), *Dasyuridae* (native cats, native mice), *Notoryctidae* (marsupial moles), *Myrmecobiidae* (numbats), *Peramelidae* (bandicoots), *Phalangeridae* (koalas), *Vombatidae* (wombats), and *Macropodidae* (kangaroos and wallabies).

Order Monotremata (egg-laying mammals)

These more primitive mammals make up the families *Tachyglossidae* (echidnas, also called spiny anteaters) and *Ornithorhynchidae* (platypuses).

Order Perissodactyla (odd-toed hoofed animals)

The two suborders, Hippomorpha and Ceratomorpha, include creatures that have an odd number of toes. Families in this order are the *Equidae* (horses, donkeys, zebras), the *Tapiridae* (tapirs), and the *Rhinocerotidae* (rhinoceroses).

Order Pholidata

Family *Manidae* (pangolins) is the sole family in this order.

Order Pinnipedia (seals and walruses)

In the fin-footed order there are *Otariidae* (eared seals, sea lions), *Odobenidae* (walruses), and *Phocidae* (earless seals).

Order Primates (primates)

The order to which people belong is divided into two suborders: the *Prosimii*, who have longer snouts than their relatives, and the *Anthropoidea*. The first group includes the families *Tupalidae* (tree shrew), *Lemuridae* (lemurs), *Daubentonlidae* (aye-ayes), *Lorisidae* (lorises, pottos), and *Tarsiidae* (tarsiers). The anthropoids include the families *Callitrichidae* (marmosets), *Cebidae* (New World monkeys), *Cercopithecidae* (baboons, Old World monkeys), *Hylobatidae* (gibbons), *Pongidae* (gorillas, chimpanzees, orangutans), and *Hominidae* (human beings).

Order Proboscidea (elephants)

Large enough to have an order all to itself is Family *Elephantidae*.

Order Rodentia (gnawing mammals)

The most prolific mammals, Order *Rodentia* includes three suborders. It takes in the families *Aplodontidae* (mountain beavers), *Sciuridae* (chipmunks, squirrels, marmots), *Cricetidae* (field mice, lemmings, muskrats, hamsters, gerbils), *Muridae* (Old World mice, rats), *Heteromyidae* (New World mice), *Geomyidae* (gophers), and *Dipodidae* (jerboas).

Order Sirenia (dugongs and manatees)

The families *Trichechidae* (manatees) and *Dugongidae* (dugongs and other sea cows) make up the Order *Sirenia*.

Order Tubulidentata (aardvarks)

Another mammal in an order by itself is Family *Orycteropodidae*.

Invertebrates

Any animal that is made up of more than one cell but has no backbone is an invertebrate. This group includes all animals that are not amphibians, fish, mammals, birds, or reptiles. Like these chordates, invertebrates are divided into several major groups:

Annelid worms

Also called segmented worms, this group includes earthworms, leeches, and marine worms. Annelid worms have soft bodies, are symmetrical, and can be anywhere from $1/32$ of an inch (half a millimeter) to 10 feet (3 meters) in length.

Arthropods

This is the largest group of invertebrates, as well as the one comprising the most creatures; 80 percent of all animal species are arthropods. Arthropods have segmented bodies covered by external skeletons, called *exoskeletons,* which are molted from time to time to allow for growth. Their appendages ("arms" and "legs") are paired. Among the animals in this group are spiders, horseshoe crabs, crustaceans, insects, and centipedes.

Coelenterates

Mostly marine invertebrates, coelenterates have three-layered body walls, tentacles, primitive nervous systems, and special stinger cells to protect themselves. Animals in this group include jellyfish, sea anemones, and corals.

Echinoderms

Another marine invertebrate, the echinoderm, lives on the floor of the sea. Echinoderms have no heads, tube feet, and external skeletons just below the surface of the skin. They can regenerate virtually any part of their bodies. Starfish, sea urchins, sand dollars, and sea cucumbers are some of the members of this phylum.

Flatworms

As their name implies, these organisms are basically flat, soft-bodied, and symmetrical. These very primitive creatures come in two varieties: an aquatic group that includes planarians and a parasitic one that counts flukes and tapeworms among its members.

Mollusks

Most mollusks live inside shells and reside in the water. They have soft, unsegmented bodies and a powerful foot that enables them to move around. Clams, oysters, scallops, bivalves, octopuses, and squid are mollusks.

Roundworms

These wormlike animals have an outer coat made of noncellular material and a fluid-filled chamber that separates their body walls from their insides. They live both in water and on land. Among their number are rotifers, nematodes, and horsehair worms.

Sponges

Classified as plants in the eighteenth century, sponges live mostly in colonies in the water, attached to rocks. They are basically sacs taking in water through small holes; their skeletons are formed from hard substances that become stuck in their body walls.

Animal First Aid

Animals, like people, suffer medical problems. Emergency and nonemergency ailments and traumas require quick attention to prevent serious situations from turning into life-threatening ones.

Some problems—bleeding that cannot be stopped or convulsions, for instance—require the immediate attention of an expert in veterinary medicine. Many other problems, however, can be treated by the animal's owner.

The following are some common animal ailments and injuries. The symptoms and treatments for each are described. As with any medical condition, if the symptoms persist or the animal's owner is unsure about the nature of the problem, professional assistance should be sought.

Broken Bones

Symptoms. Some bone breaks show obvious symptoms: twisted or distorted limbs, or in the case of a compound fracture, bone fragments sticking through the skin. Less apparent breaks cause great pain and discomfort. The animal will cry or bite when the affected area is touched; will lie around, often on the affected area; and will usually not walk, although in some cases it will despite the break, notably when the pelvis is broken. The fracture will not bear weight. Swelling of the affected area within 24 hours can be expected from any sort of fracture.

Treatment. Treatment of compound fractures by a veterinarian should be sought as soon as possible. Other breaks should be treated by a veterinarian within 24 hours. Apply an ice pack or cold wet compress to the affected area; change regularly. Protect the animal from further injury by confining it to a small room. Apply a temporary splint to broken limbs to avoid further dislocation.

Burns

Symptoms. All burns are painful to the touch. *Electrical burns* are the most serious and can cause heart attacks and death. The burned area will show seared flesh, reddened skin, lesions, and blisters. The animal may suffer respiratory distress; paleness or blueness, especially in lips, gums, and eyelid linings; rigidity in limbs; glassy stare; collapse; and shock. *Thermal burns* cause a singed or charred area; the exposed skin is reddened or inflamed; the wound is warm or hot to the touch. *Friction burns* are similar in appearance to thermal burns, but the skin is chafed or scraped and has bare spots; bare skin is rubbed raw, is reddish in color, and is irritated or inflamed; the trauma causing the burn may leave cuts, lacerations, or embedded foreign matter.

Treatment. Depending on the type and extent of the burn, it can often be treated at home. Electrical burns can stop an animal's heart and must be treated immediately by a veterinarian; if shock occurs, keep the animal warm with heating pads or hot water bottles and a blanket or heavy coat and seek veterinary treatment immediately. Thermal burns can be treated topically by applying the jellylike substance from an aloe plant, a solution made from Domeboro (available at most pharmacies), or Vitamin E oil. Friction burns can be treated in the same way as thermal burns; however, if foreign matter is embedded, or the burn does not respond to treatment, the animal should be taken to a veterinarian.

Cat Diseases

Symptoms. Four major diseases affect the well-being of cats. *Cat distemper* induces high fever, lethargy, vomiting, and diarrhea; young kittens can develop distemper very quickly and will often die of it without exhibiting symptoms. *Rhinotracheitis* causes fever, sneezing, loss of appetite, and dehydration; additional symptoms can include discharge from eyes and nose, congestion, and swelling of membranes in the respiratory tract. *Calici virus* is characterized by sneezing and discharge from the eyes and nose; it may cause fever, lethargy, loss of appetite, dehydration, and ulcers on the tongue. *Pneumonitis* usually causes labored breathing, sneezing, coughing, snorting, wheezing, and listlessness; it may induce a loss of body fluids and very high temperatures.

Treatment. Three of these diseases—cat distemper, rhinotracheitis, and calici virus—can be prevented by annual vaccinations. All four must be treated as quickly as possible by a veterinarian if symptoms are present; professional treatment will, in most cases, effect a cure.

Constipation

Symptoms. The animal struggles or strains during a bowel movement without passing a stool; avoids food; becomes nervous or irritated.

Treatment. Feed the animal brans, cereal foods, vegetables (peas, carrots, corn), kibble; use infant-syze glycerine suppositories or soap suppositories; give an enema if the animal will allow it; add a small amount of stool softener, such as Metamucil, to food; give mineral oil or milk of magnesia, but dosages should depend on size and type of animal (consult a veterinarian).

Dental Disorders

Symptoms. Tartar, a brown crust, appears on teeth, starting at the gum line; tooth enamel erodes, especially on cats; bone fragments, foreign matter, food particles, or hair accumulate on teeth; bad breath is present. *Throat* or *mouth infections* cause coughing and discharges from mouth or nose. *Gingivitis* develops when tartar or dirty teeth are untreated. *Uremia* can cause blackish tartar, bad breath, and extraordinary thirst.

Treatment. Clean the animal's teeth monthly with a mixture of one teaspoon salt or hydrogen peroxide to half a cup of water; apply to teeth with a cotton swab or soft toothbrush. Include hard food, such as kibble, in the animal's diet; provide hard things for the animal to chew on. Infections, gingivitis, or uremia should be treated by a veterinarian.

Diarrhea

Symptoms. The animal passes liquid stool during bowel movement; there may be abnormal coloration of stool.

Treatment. Remove grease, oils, and milk from the animal's diet; avoid high-fiber foods, kibble, and dry catmeal; feed the animal a mix of one part cooked hamburger, drained of grease, and one part rice. If diarrhea results from ingestion of foreign matter (from teething or eating plants, soap, or other household materials), treat it with small doses of Pepto-Bismol or Kaopectate. If symptoms persist for more than 24 hours, or if blood is present in stool, consult a veterinarian.

Dog Diseases

Symptoms. A number of conditions affect only dogs. *Canine distemper* causes severe diarrhea and may cause high fever, discharge from eyes and nose, thickening of foot pads, coughing, muscle contractions, convulsions, and pneumonia. *Infectious canine hepatitis* usually results in fever, lethargy, and congestion of the mucous membranes; it also can cause loss of appetite and insatiable thirst. *Leptospirosis* is characterized by high fever, lethargy, loss of appetite, congestion in the whites of the eyes, and possibly pain in walking, jaundice, vomiting, and diarrhea. *Infectious canine tracheobronchitis (kennel cough)* causes high fever and severe dry coughing spasms.

Treatment. All four of these diseases can be prevented by annual vaccinations. If a dog is not vaccinated, early diagnosis of the symptoms of each disease is imperative. None of these diseases can be treated at home; bring the dog to a veterinarian as soon as possible.

External Parasites

Symptoms. Fleas, ticks, lice, maggots, and mites are common external parasites that prey on animals. All cause animals to scratch excessively, which can lead to hair loss. *Fleas* are tiny brown insects that move through the animal's coat. *Ticks* are small, round, dark-colored insects with hard shells that attach themselves to an animal's skin. *Lice* are small, dark-gray insects that remain in one place on an animal's body.

Maggots look like small worms. *Mites,* which are invisible to the unaided eye, characteristically cause skin and ear irritation.

Treatment. External parasites can be readily eliminated and controlled with commercially available powders, baths, sprays, and dips. Check the labels of such treatments carefully to be sure they are appropriate for use on your animal and that they will control the parasite in question. Fleas can be controlled with flea collars, sprays, powders, baths, or dips; treat animal and surrounding furniture and carpets to eliminate infestations. Ticks can be pulled off by hand; the animal should then be treated with spray, powder, or bath to eliminate unseen ticks; treat surrounding furniture and carpets to eliminate infestations. Lice can be treated with the same potions that work on fleas and ticks. Maggots are an increasingly rare parasite that, if present, should be treated by a veterinarian. Mites can cause recurring mange in dogs, or other recurring skin conditions in other animals; any recurring condition should be treated by a veterinarian.

Internal Parasites

Symptoms. All internal parasites drain an animal's natural defenses, leaving it susceptible to infections and diseases. All are likely to cause loss of appetite and lethargy. *Tapeworms* leave visible, light-colored segments that look like rice kernels in stools, around sleeping areas, under the animal's tail, or near its anus. *Roundworms* look like spaghetti; they are light yellow, 2 to four inches long, have slightly pointed ends, and can be seen in stools or vomit. *Hookworms* are almost invisible to the naked eye, but can cause diarrhea (often with blood present), cramps, pale gums and lips, a dry coat, a slight cough, and noticeable weight loss. *Whipworms* cause symptoms similar to those caused by hookworms, as well as possible inflammation of the colon. *Heartworms* block an animal's arteries, causing tiredness, listlessness, a poor coat, weight loss, and constant panting and coughing. *Coccidia,* one-celled protozoa, cause diarrhea, emaciation, and discharges from the animal's eyes and nose. *Toxoplasmosis* is a parasite that afflicts mostly cats; it frequently presents no symptoms at all.

Treatment. An infestation of internal parasites is a debilitating condition that should be dealt with by a veterinarian.

Rabies

Symptoms. Fever, loss of appetite, inability to swallow that results in drooling; can cause encephalitis, convulsions, or paralysis. One type of rabies causes animals to attack anything that moves (cars, animals, people); another type causes only the other symptoms.

Treatment. Prevention of rabies is possible through regular vaccinations. Once contracted, however, there is no effective treatment for rabies and the animal will have to be destroyed.

Respiratory Infections

Symptoms. Sneezing, coughing, runny eyes, swollen glands, difficulty swallowing, labored breathing, fever.

Treatment. If symptoms such as sneezing, coughing, and runny eyes are present but the animal remains active and eats normally, the condition is probably not serious and no treatment is needed. A veterinarian should examine the animal if symptoms continue for a while; if the animal becomes lethargic and loses appetite; if there are discharges of pus from its nose; if congestion becomes heavy or labored breathing is continued; or if fever of more than 102 degrees is present.

Shock

Symptoms. Weakness, collapse, pale or muddy-colored gums, fast heartbeat, difficulty breathing, no breathing, dilated pupils, low body temperature.

Treatment. Keep the animal warm by applying heating pads or hot water bottles and wrapping the animal in heavy blankets or coats. Bring the animal to a veterinarian at once.

Skin Problems

Symptoms. Localized skin conditions cause inflammation or irritation and may cause bald spots of red, raw, or discolored skin. More serious disorders such as moist eczema, wet dermatitis, or acute pruritis cause raw, oozing bald spots that may be damp to the touch or oozing pus. A lump on the animal's skin that does not go away within a few days may be a tumor. Other skin problems can cause dry, flaky skin, an oily coat, and constant biting, licking, or scratching. Symmetrical skin disorders affect both sides of an animal's body equally; a generalized condition affects the animal's whole body.

Treatment. Bald patches of red or raw skin and damp, oozing hot areas should be treated by a veterinarian. Localized inflammation can be treated with soothing topical sprays and lotions. Dry skin or coat can be soaked several times a day with water or a solution made from Domeboro tablets (available at most pharmacies); small quantities of oil added to the animal's food also will help. Itchiness can be corrected with a solution of one part Alpha-Keri (available from most pharmacies) to 20 or 30 parts water applied with a spray bottle; repeat as needed. A well-balanced diet, with appropriate levels of vitamins, can maintain healthy skin. Any skin condition that does not go away, or which reappears after treatment, should be treated by a veterinarian.

Sprains

Symptoms. Sprains usually occur in the joints of an animal's limbs, causing rapid swelling. The affected area will be hot to the touch. The animal will not walk normally, if it walks at all.

Treatment. Apply cold compresses or ice packs gently to the swollen area; keep the area cool for a day or two, changing the compress or ice when necessary. Wrap the affected area snugly with cloth, gauze, or athletic bandages; secure the wrapping to be sure the animal does not scratch or bite it off. Keep the animal quiet; discourage activity; avoid stairs. For sprains that heal and reoccur, apply hot towels or compresses; keep the injured area moist and warm for several days. If a sprain does not heal, or pain and swelling continue or are severe, see a veterinarian.

Wounds

Symptoms. *Cuts* can be recognized by the presence of smoothly separated tissue and possible bleeding. *Lacerations* result in jaggedly torn skin, bleeding, swelling, irritation, and black or blue discoloration of the skin. *Abrasions* rub or scrape away the outer layers of skin, causing pain, swelling, redness, and heat. *Bruises* or *contusions* leave black-and-blue tissue and swelling.

Treatment. Any serious wound should be treated by a veterinarian if the bleeding will not stop, if blood is gushing out, or if shock is present. Cuts that are bleeding can be dealt with by applying a pressure bandage (clean gauze or cloth wrapped around some padding) pressed firmly but gently against the wound; an ice bag, pressed firmly but gently on the area; or a tourniquet. After the bleeding has been controlled, clean the wound with hydrogen peroxide or Bactine, then dry it; keep skin from wrinkling or bunching, then apply an antiseptic or antibiotic to a gauze square and wrap snugly in place; change the dressing daily and keep the animal from removing it. Lacerations can be treated in the same way as cuts, but an ice bag must be used to reduce swelling and prevent further inflammation. Abrasions require the application of a soothing cream, ointment, or lotion (Solarcaine, Nupercainal, Unguentine ointment, or calamine lotion); a bandage is not needed, but the animal must be kept from licking the treated area. Bruises and contusions are best treated with cold compresses or ice packs.

Extinct Animals

Extinction has happened to species and subspecies throughout the time creatures have lived on this planet. The most well-known cases involved the "great dying" of the dinosaurs some 50 to 75 millions years ago.

If creatures great and small have in fact been dying off throughout the ages, why is there suddenly concern about animals becoming extinct? Isn't extinction part of the natural order of things?

The answer is no, at least not on the scale it has occurred in recent times. In the last 300 years, at least 300 vertebrate animals have become extinct. More than 150 of those extinctions have been of full species. By comparison, it is estimated that dinosaur species died off at the rate of about one per 1,000 years.

The cause of this rapid acceleration in the rate of extinctions is human activity. With some species, like the dodo, the extinction was unintentional: people introduced predators to the dodo's island home where previously there had been none. Other creatures, such as the Eastern buffalo, were purposefully killed off by human beings who wanted to "make room" for themselves.

In the late twentieth century, extinctions are more likely to be an indirect result of human activity. Rural landfills take in urban garbage, open land is blacktopped, factories produce toxins as byproducts, and engineers alter waterways. These activities all have a direct impact on the ecosystems that support animal life.

Increased awareness of the fragile links of interdependence among all of Earth's creatures, and of the impact human activities can have on those creatures, have led some to hope that the latest era of "great dying" may soon stop. It remains to be seen, however, if the forces already in motion can be stopped in time to save the hundreds of species that teeter on the brink of extinction.

The following lists comprise the number of different animals thought to be extinct as of the early 1980s and the popular names of those animals. Exact figures are difficult to determine, since endangered species often make the transition to extinction quickly and without notice. Occasionally populations of animals thought to be extinct are discovered to be extant.

Birds

Akioloa (4)	Mamo (2)
Alauwahio (2)	Merganser
Amazon (3)	Moas
Brown night heron	New Caledonian lorikeet
Caracara	Norfolk Island kaka
Chatham Island bellbird	Nukupuu (3)
Chatham Island fernbird	O-O (3)
Conure (2)	Oahu akepa
Courser	Omao (3)
Delalande's coucal	Ostrich, Arabian
Dodo (2)	Owl (10)
Duck (2)	Painted vulture
Elephant bird	Parakeet (8)
Emu (2)	Parrot (3)
Eskimo curlew	Petrel
Finch (5)	Pigeon (7)
Flycatcher (2)	Quail (2)
Gadwall	Rail (17)
Great amakihi	Reunion fody
Great auk	Ryukyu kingfisher
Guadalupe flicker	Sandpiper (2)
Heath hen	São Tomé grosbeak
Huia	Serpent eagle
Ivory-billed woodpecker	Shelduck
Jamaican pauraque	Solitaire (2)
Kioea	Spectacled cormorant
Laysan apapane	Starling (6)
Laysan millerbird	Thrush (2)
Lord Howe Island blackbird	Towhee
Lord Howe Island fantail	Ula-ai-hawane
Macaw (4)	White eye (2)
	Wren (6)

Fish

Ash Meadows killfish
Cisco (2 varieties)
Lake Titicaca orestias
Minnow (2)
New Zealand grayling
Pupfish (2)

Speckled dace
Spinedace (2)
Sucker (4)
Thicktail chub
Utah Lake sculpin

Mammals

Agouti (2)
Arizona jaguar
Aurochs
Badlands bighorn sheep
Bali tiger
Bandicoot (4)
Bat (6)
Bear (3)
Blue buck
Buffalo (2)
Burchell's zebra
Caribbean monk seal
Caucasian wisent
Christmas Island musk shrew
Dawson's caribou
Elk (2)
Greenland tundra reindeer
Hartebeest (2)
Hispaniolan hexolobodon
Hutia (5)

Ibex (2)
Isolobodon (2)
Lion (2)
Nesophont (6)
Potoroo (3)
Puerto Rican caviomorph
Quagga
Quemi (2)
Rat (12)
Rufous gazelle
Schomburgk's deer
Sea mink
Shamanu
Steller's sea cow
Syrian onager
Tarpan
Wallaby (2)
Warrah
Wolf (10)

Reptiles

Ameiva (2)
Boa
Galliwasp
Gecko (2)
Iguana (2)

Lizard (4)
Racer snake (2)
Skink (3)
Tortoise (11)
Tree snake (2)

Amphibians

Palestine painted frog

Vegas Valley leopard frog

Major U.S. and Canadian Zoos

Zoos, or zoological gardens, are private or public parks where animals of all sorts are exhibited and studied. Zoos have existed in one form or another for thousands of years, dating back to ancient China, Egypt, and Rome.

Most major cities throughout the world have zoos. The scale and type of zoo varies widely, from petting zoos that allow contact between children and animals to primate research centers to amusement parks that put on shows with trained porpoises.

The following list of major zoos is arranged by state. The name and address of each zoo is given, as well as the number of species and specimens and, where available, the zoo's specialty. Zoos of special note are marked with an asterisk (*).

United States

Alabama

Birmingham Zoo
2630 Cahaba Road
Birmingham, AL 35223
263 species, 893 specimens

Arizona

Phoenix Zoo
60th Street & East Van Buren
P.O. Box 5155
Phoenix, AZ 85010
353 species, 1,277 specimens
Specialty: Arabian oryx

Arizona-Sonora Desert Museum
Tucson Mountain Park
P.O. Box 5607
Tucson, AZ 85703
194 species, 722 specimens
Specialty: Sonoran desert fauna and flora and earth
  sciences

Arkansas

Little Rock Zoological Gardens
1 Jonesboro
Little Rock, AR 72205
76 species, 286 specimens

California

Roeding Park Zoo
894 West Belmont Avenue
Fresno, CA 93728
243 species, 728 specimens

T. Wayland Vaughan Aquarium-Museum
Scripps Institute of Oceanography
University of California
La Jolla, CA 92037
203 species, 1,402 specimens
Specialty: marine fish of Southern California

*The Los Angeles Zoo
5333 Zoo Drive
Los Angeles, CA 90027
763 species, 2,387 specimens

Oakland Baby Zoo
9777 Golf Links Road
Oakland, CA 94605
32 species, 116 specimens
Specialty: baby animals

Marine World/Africa USA
Marine World Parkway
Redwood City, CA 94065
115 species, 7,570 specimens

*San Diego Zoological Garden
Zoological Society of San Diego
Balboa Park
P.O. Box 551
San Diego, CA 92112
1,112 species, 3,988 specimens
Specialties: lemurs, tortoises, marsupials

*Sea World
1720 South Shores Road
Mission Bay
San Diego, CA 92109
594 species, 9,150 specimens
Specialties: trained marine mammals, waterfowl

San Francisco Zoological Gardens
Zoo Road and Skyline Boulevard
San Francisco, CA 94132
314 species, 1,050 specimens
Specialties: primates, bears, cats, waterfowl

Prentice Park Zoo
1700 East First Street
Santa Ana, CA 82703
98 species, 326 specimens
Specialty: children's petting zoo

Canal Zone

Summit Gardens and Zoo
P.O. Box 973
Balboa Heights
Panama Canal Zone
128 species, 232 specimens
Specialty: Panamanian animals

Colorado

Cheyenne Mountain Zoological Park
P.O. Box 158
Colorado Springs, CO 80901
220 species, 854 specimens
Specialties: giraffes, primates, felids

Denver Zoological Gardens
City Park
Denver, CO 80205
369 species, 1,482 specimens
Specialty: waterfowl

Connecticut

Beardsley Zoological Gardens
Bridgeport, CT 06610
56 species, 235 specimens
Specialty: fauna of North and South America

District of Columbia

*The National Aquarium
Commerce Building
Washington, DC 20230
380 species, 2,000+ specimens

*National Zoological Park
Smithsonian Institution
Washington, DC 20009
627 species, 2,618 specimens

Florida

Jacksonville Zoological Park
8605 Zoo Road
Jacksonville, FL 32218
268 species, 932 specimens

Crandon Park Zoo
4000 Crandon Boulevard
Key Biscayne
Miami, FL 33140
280 species, 988 specimens
Specialty: aardvarks

Marineland of Florida
RFD 1, Box 122
St. Augustine, FL 32084
106 species, 613 specimens
Specialty: performing dolphins

*Busch Gardens Zoological Park
P.O. Box 9158
Tampa, FL 33674
410 species, 2,736 specimens
Specialties: African hoofed mammals, parrots

Dreher Park Zoological Gardens
P.O. Box 6597
1301 Summit Boulevard
West Palm Beach, FL 33405
49 species, 105 specimens

Georgia

Atlanta Zoological Park
800 Cherokee Avenue, SE
Atlanta, GA 30315
401 species, 1,037 specimens
Specialties: amphibians and reptiles

Yerkes Regional Primate Research Center
Emory University
Atlanta, GA 30322
26 species, 1,310 specimens
Not open to the public

Hawaii

Honolulu Zoo
Waikiki Beach
Kapiolani Park
Honolulu, HI 96815
341 species, 1,568 specimens
Specialty: Galapagos tortoise

Idaho

Boise City Zoo
Julia Davis Park
Boise, ID 83706
81 species, 245 specimens

Illinois

*Chicago Zoological Park (Brookfield Zoo)
Brookfield, IL 60513
531 species, 2,100+ specimens
Specialty: dolphins

John G. Shedd Aquarium
1200 South Lake Shore Drive
Chicago, IL 60605

477 species, 4,786 specimens

*Lincoln Park Zoological Gardens
100 West Webster Avenue
Chicago, IL 60614

593 species, 2,036 specimens
Specialties: great apes, felids, toothless mammals

Indiana

Mesker Park Zoo
Bement Avenue
Evansville, IN 47712

192 species, 589 specimens
Specialty: large geographic exhibits

Fort Wayne Children's Zoological Gardens
3411 North Sherman Street
Fort Wayne, IN 46808

Indianapolis Zoological Park
3120 East 30th Street
Indianapolis, IN 46218

156 species, 404 specimens

Iowa

Upper Mississippi River Fishery Management Station
Iowa Conservation Commission
P.O. Box 250
Guttenberg, IA 52052

68 species, 260 specimens
Specialty: fish and reptiles of the Mississippi River

Kansas

Topeka Zoological Park
635 Gage Boulevard
Topeka, KS 66606

217 species, 520 specimens

Kentucky

Louisville Zoological Garden
1100 Trevilian Way
Louisville, KY 40213

158 species, 498 specimens

Louisiana

Greater Baton Rouge Zoo
P.O. Box 458
Baton Rouge, LA 70821

136 species, 471 specimens

Audubon Park Zoo and Odenheimer Aquarium
P.O. Box 4327
New Orleans, LA 70118

216 species, 800+ specimens

Maryland

Baltimore Zoo
Druid Hill Park
Baltimore, MD 21217

336 species, 1,061 specimens

Massachusetts

Franklin Park Zoo and Children's Zoo
Dorchester, MA 02110

New England Aquarium
Central Wharf
Boston, MA 02110

464 species, 7,416 specimens
Specialty: fish of the Atlantic Ocean

Aquarium of the National Marine Fisheries Service
Albatross Street
Woods Hole
Falmouth, MA 02543

43 species, 228 specimens
Specialty: local fauna

Michigan

*Detroit Zoological Park and Belle Isle Aquarium
8450 West 10 Mile Road
P.O. Box 39
Royal Oak, MI 48068

543 species, 4,656 specimens

Potter Park Zoo
1301 South Pennsylvania Avenue
Lansing, MI 48933

103 species, 415 specimens

Saginaw Children's Zoo
1461 South Washington
Saginaw, MI 48605

85 species, 326 specimens

Minnesota

Duluth Zoo
7210 Fremont Street
Duluth, MN 55807

89 species, 285 specimens

St. Paul's Como Zoo
Midway Parkway and Kaufman Drive
St. Paul, MN 55103

134 species, 454 specimens
Specialties: felids, great apes

Mississippi

Jackson Zoological Park
2918 West Capitol Street
Jackson, MS 39209

181 species, 752 specimens

Missouri

Kansas City Zoological Gardens
Swope Park
Kansas City, MO 64132

174 species, 586 specimens

*St. Louis Zoological Park
Forest Park
St. Louis, MO 63139

731 species, 2,216 specimens

Montana

Red Lodge Zoo
Box 820
Red Lodge, MT 59068

77 species, 210 specimens

Nebraska

Lincoln Municipal Zoo
1300 South 27th Street
Lincoln, NE 68502

146 species, 464 specimens

Henry Doorly Zoological Gardens
Riverview Park
Omaha, NE 68107

136 species, 486 specimens
Specialties: rare hoofed mammals, great apes, large
   cats

New Jersey

Turtle Back Zoo
560 Northfield Avenue
South Mountain Reservation, NJ 07052

256 species, 817 specimens
Specialty: turtles

New Mexico

Rio Grande Zoological Park
903 10th Street, SW
Albuquerque, NM 87102

184 species, 691 specimens
Specialty: hoofed mammals

New York

Bear Mountain Trailside Museum
Bear Mountain State Park
Bear Mountain, NY 10911

72 species, 148 specimens
Specialty: local natural history

*New York Zoological Park (Bronx Zoo)
185th Street and Southern Boulevard
Bronx, NY 10460

675 species, 3,200 + specimens

Buffalo Zoological Gardens
Delaware Park
Buffalo, NY 14214

340 species, 877 specimens

Staten Island Zoo
614 Broadway
Staten Island, NY 10310

430 species, 960 specimens
Specialty: reptiles

North Dakota

Dakota Zoo
Dakota Zoological Society
P.O. Box 711
Bismarck, ND 58501

109 species, 430 specimens
Specialty: North American fauna

Ohio

*Zoological Society of Cincinnati
3400 Vine Street
Cincinnati, OH 45220

564 species, 1,627 specimens

Cleveland Aquarium
Gordon Park
601 East 72nd Street
Cleveland, OH 44109

Cleveland Zoological Park
Brookside Park
P.O. Box 09040
Cleveland, OH 44109

299 species, 1,010 specimens

Columbus Zoological Gardens and Arthur C. Johnson Aquarium
9990 Riverside Drive
Powell, OH 43065

671 species, 3,399 specimens
Specialties: gorillas, reptiles, cichlids

Toledo Zoological Gardens
2700 Broadway
Toledo, OH 43609

477 species, 2,085 specimens

Oklahoma

Oklahoma City Zoo
Oklahoma City, OK 73112

510 species, 1,801 specimens

Tulsa Zoological Park
5701 East 36th Street North
Tulsa, OK 74115

238 species, 660 specimens

Oregon

Aquarium-Museum
Oregon State University Marine Science Center
Marine Science Drive
Newport, OR 97221

165 species, 2,500 specimens
Specialty: marine animals of Oregon

Portland Zoological Gardens
4001 SW Canyon Road
Portland, OR 97221

123 species, 368 specimens
Specialty: elephants

Pennsylvania

*Philadelphia Zoological Gardens
34th Street and Girard Avenue
Philadelphia, PA 19104

536 species, 2,079 specimens
Specialties: waterfowl, great apes, reptiles

Pittsburgh Zoological Gardens
P.O. Box 5072
Pittsburgh, PA 15206

633 species, 2,817 specimens

Rhode Island

Roger Williams Park Zoo
Roger Williams Park
Providence, RI 02905

102 species, 237 specimens

South Carolina

Columbia Zoological Park
Riverbanks Park
P.O. Box 1143
Columbia, SC 29202

234 species, 922 specimens

Brookgreen Gardens
Murrells Inlet, SC 29576

23 species, 162 specimens
Specialty: fauna of southeastern United States

South Dakota

Great Plains Zoo
15th and Kiwanis
Sioux Falls, SD 57102

83 species, 230 specimens
Specialty: animals of the North American Great Plains

Tennessee

Knoxville Zoological Park
915 Beaman Street at Chilhowee Park
Knoxville, TN 37914

128 species, 519 specimens

Overton Park Zoo and Aquarium
Memphis, TN 38112

425 species, 1,964 specimens
Specialties: aquatic animals, rare ruminants

Texas

Abilene Zoological Gardens
Box 60
Abilene, TX 79604

130 species, 438 specimens

Dallas Aquarium
Fair Park
First and Forest Avenue
Dallas, TX 75226

464 species, 5,859 specimens

*Dallas Zoo in Marsalis Park
621 East Clarendon Drive
Dallas, TX 75203

714 species, 2,168 specimens

Fort Worth Zoological Park and James R. Record Aquarium
2727 Zoological Park Drive
Forest Park
Fort Worth, TX 76110

791 species, 3,894 specimens

Houston Zoological Gardens
Hermann Park
P.O. Box 1562
Houston, TX 77001

507 species, 1,605 specimens

*San Antonio Zoological Garden and Aquarium
3903 North St. Mary's
San Antonio, TX 78212

775 species, 7,457 specimens

Caldwell Children's Zoo
P.O. Box 428
Tyler, TX 75701

102 species, 361 specimens

Central Texas Zoological Park
Zoo Park Drive
Waco, TX 76708

115 species, 505 specimens

Utah

Hogle Zoological Gardens
2600 Sunnyside Avenue
P.O. Box 2337
Salt Lake City, UT 84110

333 species, 1,062 specimens

Virginia

Lafayette Zoological Park
3500 Granby Street
Norfolk, VA 23501

71 species, 195 specimens

Washington

Woodland Park Zoological Gardens
5500 Phinney Avenue, N
Seattle, WA 98103

278 species, 912 specimens

Wisconsin

Henry Vilas Park Zoo
500 South Randall
Madison, WI 53715

207 species, 834 specimens

*Milwaukee County Zoological Park
10001 West Bluemound Road
Milwaukee, WI 53226

636 species, 5,130 specimens

Racine Zoological Park
2131 North Main Street
Racine, WI 53402

143 species, 543 specimens

Canada

Alberta

Calgary Zoo and National History Park
St. George's Island
Calgary 21
Alberta T2G 3H4

356 species, 1,191 specimens

Alberta Game Farm
RR 4
Sherwood Park
Edmonton
Alberta T5E 5S7

180 species, 3,400 specimens

British Columbia

Stanley Park Zoo
Stanley Park
Vancouver 5
British Columbia V6E 1V3

117 species, 515 specimens
Specialties: North American mammals and birds

Vancouver Public Aquarium
Stanley Park
P.O. Box 3232
Vancouver 3
British Columbia V6B 3X8

492 species, 11,115 specimens
Specialty: marine life of the northeast Pacific

Manitoba

Assiniboine Park Zoo
2355 Corydon Avenue
Winnipeg
Manitoba R3P 0R5

296 species, 1,156 specimens
Specialty: Nearctic animals

Ontario

Metro Toronto Zoo
P.O. Box 280
West Hill
Toronto
Ontario M1E 4R5

444 species, 3,666 specimens

<u>*Quebec*</u>

Société Zoologique de Granby
303 rue Bourget O
Casse Postale 514
Granby, PQ
Quebec J2G E8

140 species, 940 specimens

Montreal Aquarium
St. Helen's Island
Montreal, PQ H3C 1A0
Quebec

313 species, 2,244 specimens

Aquarium de Quebec
1675 Avenue du Parc
Quebec, PQ G1W 453

325 species, 2,324 specimens

Jardin Zoologique de Quebec
8191 avenue du Zoo
Orsainville, PQ G1G 4G4
Quebec

286 species, 1,081 specimens
Specialty: North American fauna

Additional Sources of Information

Allen, Thomas B. *Vanishing Wildlife of North America*. National Geographic Society, 1974.

American Kennel Club Staff. *The Complete Dog Book*, 17th ed. Howell, 1985.

Animal Medical Center Staff and Kay, William J. *Complete Book of Cat Health*. Macmillan, 1985.

Carrington, Richard. *Mermaids and Mastodons*. Rinehart, 1957.

Grzimek, Bernhard, ed. *Grzimek's Animal Life Encyclopedia*. 13 vols. Van Nostrand Reinhold, 1972–75.

Hahn, Emily. *Animal Gardens*. Doubleday, 1967.

Kirchshofer, Rosl. *The World of Zoos*. Viking Press, 1968.

Macdonald, David, ed. *The Encyclopedia of Mammals*. Facts on File, 1984.

McClung, Robert M. *Lost Wild Worlds*. William Morrow, 1976.

The New International Wildlife Encyclopedia. vols. 1–21. Purnell Reference Books, 1980.

Perrins, Christopher M., and Middleton, Alex L.A., eds. *The Encyclopedia of Birds*. Facts on File, 1985.

Scott, Peter, ed. *The Amazing World of Animals*. Praeger, 1976.

Spaulding, C. E. *A Veterinary Guide for Animal Owners*. Rodale Press, 1976.

West, Geoffrey, ed. *Encyclopedia of Animal Care*, 12th ed. Williams & Wilkins, 1977.

Whitfield, Philip. *Macmillan Illustrated Animal Encyclopedia*. Macmillan, 1984.

5

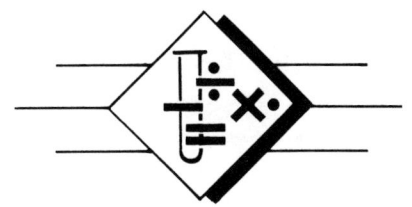

Math and Science Basics

Decimal and Percent Equivalents of Common Fractions

Fraction	Decimal	Percent (%)	Fraction	Decimal	Percent (%)
1/32	0.03125	3.125	17/32	0.53125	53.125
1/16	0.0625	6.25	9/16	0.5625	56.25
3/32	0.09375	9.375	19/32	0.59375	59.375
1/10	0.1	10	3/5	0.6	60
1/8	0.125	12.5	5/8	0.625	62.5
5/32	0.15625	15.625	21/32	0.65625	65.625
3/16	0.1875	18.75	2/3	0.6666+	66.666+
1/5	0.2	20	11/16	0.6875	68.75
7/32	0.21875	21.875	7/10	0.7	70
1/4	0.25	25	23/32	0.71875	71.87
9/32	0.28125	28.125	3/4	0.75	75
3/10	0.3	30	25/32	0.78125	78.125
5/16	0.3125	31.25	4/5	0.8	80
1/3	0.3333+	33.333+	13/16	0.8125	81.25
11/32	0.34375	34.375	27/32	0.84375	84.375
3/8	0.375	37.5	7/8	0.875	87.5
2/5	0.4	40	9/10	0.9	90
13/32	0.40625	40.625	29/32	0.90625	90.625
7/16	0.4375	43.75	15/16	0.9375	93.75
15/32	0.46875	46.875	31/32	0.96875	96.875
1/2	0.5	50			

Basic Rules of Mathematics and Mathematical Formulas

Addition and subtraction of fractions:
(Start with a common denominator)

$$\frac{2}{3} + \frac{4}{5} = \frac{10}{15} + \frac{12}{15} = \frac{22}{15} = 1\frac{7}{15}$$

$$\frac{4}{5} - \frac{2}{3} = \frac{12}{15} - \frac{10}{15} = \frac{2}{15}$$

Multiplication of fractions:

$$\frac{2}{5} \times \frac{7}{4} = \frac{14}{20} = \frac{7}{10}$$

Division of fractions:

$$\frac{1}{2} \div 2 = \frac{1}{2} \times \frac{1}{2} = \frac{1}{4}$$

Fractions to decimals:

$$\frac{3}{10} = 0.3; \frac{3}{100} = 0.03; \frac{3}{1,000} = 0.003$$

Unknown multiplied by a number:

$$5x = 10; \frac{5x}{5} = \frac{10}{5}; x = 2$$

Number added to an unknown:

$$y + 7 = 10; y + 7 - 7 = 10 - 7; y = 3$$

An unknown in a fraction:

$$\frac{a}{5} = \frac{3}{8}; a \times 8 = 5 \times 3; 8a = 15; a = 1\frac{7}{8}$$

Numbers with exponents:

$$\frac{2^3}{3^2} = 2 \times 2 \times \frac{2}{3} \times 3 = \frac{8}{9}$$

$$10^2 \times 10^3 = 10^{2+3} = 10^5$$

$$10^6 - 10^4 = 10^{6-4} = 10^2$$

$$10^{-3} = \frac{1}{10^3} = \frac{1}{1,000}$$

Area and Volume Problems

Area of a square:
Area = length × width, or length of one side (x) squared (x^2)

Area of a rectangle:
Area = length × width

Area of a triangle:
Area = $\frac{1}{2}$ × base × perpendicular height

Area of a pentagon (5 sides):
Area = square of the length of one side × 1.720

Area of a hexagon (6 sides):
Area = square of the length of one side × 2.598

Area of an octagon (8 sides):
Area = square of the length of one side × 4.828

Area of a cube:
Area = square of the length of one side × 6

Area of a sphere:
Area = square of the diameter × pi (3.1416)

Area of a circle:
Area = square of the radius × pi (3.1416)

Area of an ellipse:
Area = long diameter × short diameter × 0.7854

Circumference of a circle:
Circumference = diameter × pi (3.1416)

Volume of a cube:
Volume = cube (x^3) of the length (x) of one side

Volume of a pyramid:
Volume = area of the base × height × $\frac{1}{3}$

Volume of a cylinder:
Volume = square of the radius (r^2) of the base × pi (3.1416) × height

Volume of a sphere:
Volume = cube of the radius (r^3) × pi (3.1416) × $\frac{4}{3}$

Volume of a cone:
Volume = square of the radius (r^2) of the base × pi (3.1416) × height × $\frac{1}{3}$

Volume of a rectangular solid:
Volume = length × width × height

Basic Solutions to Triangles

Pythagorean theorem:

The square of the hypotenuse of a right-angled triangle is equal to the sum of the squares of the other two sides.

A table of trigonometric functions is required for the following formulas.

Law of Sines:

In any triangle, $a/\sin A = b/\sin B = c/\sin C$.

Right triangles:

$a = c \sin A = b \tan A$
$b = c \cos A = a \cot A$
$c = a \operatorname{cosec} A = b \sec A$

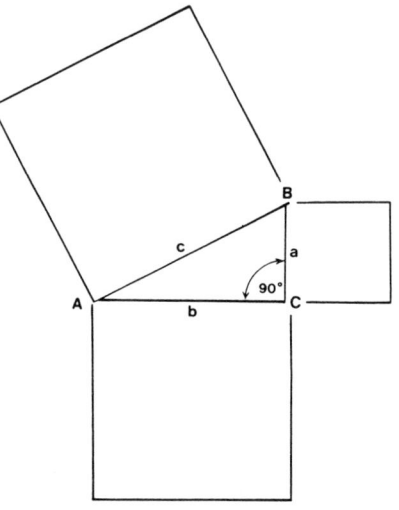

For all triangles:

The sum of the angles of a triangle $= 180$ degrees.
Given two sides (b and c) and one angle (A),
$a = \sqrt{(b^2 + c^2 - 2bc \cos A)}$
$\sin B = b/a \sin A$.
Given two angles (A and B) and one side (b),
$a = b \times \sin A/\sin B$
$c = b \times \sin C/\sin B$.
Given three sides (a, b, and c),
$\cos A = (b^2 + c^2 - a^2)/2bc$
$\sin B = b/a \times \sin A$.

Basic Formulas of Physics

acceleration: $a = v_f - v_0/t$, where v_f represents the final velocity and v_0 represents the initial velocity.

acceleration of gravity: $W = mg$, where W represents the force of weight, m represents the mass of the object, and g represents gravity.

centrifugal force: $F = mv^2/gr$, where F represents force, m represents the mass of a moving object, v represents its velocity, g represents the acceleration due to gravity (32.2 ft/sec^2), and r represents the radius of the orbit of the mass.

Coulomb's law: $F = k \times Q_aQ_b/d^2$, where F represents the electrostatic force, k represents a constant of proportionality, Q_a and Q_b represent quantities of electrostatic charge, and d represents the distance between the charges.

electrical power: $P = IV$, where P represents power, I represents electrical current, and V represents electrical potential.

energy–matter relationship: $E = mc^2$, where E represents energy, m represents mass, and c represents the velocity of light.

gravity inverse square law: $F = g \times Mm/r^2$, where F represents force, g represents the pull of gravity, M and m represent the masses of two objects, and r represents the distance between the masses.

kinetic energy: $KE = \frac{1}{2}mv^2$, where KE represents kinetic energy, m represents the mass of a moving object, and v represents the velocity.

light inverse square law: $I_1/I_2 = (d_2/d_1)^2$, where I_1 represents the light intensity at distance d_1 from the source and I_2 represents the intensity of light at distanced d_2 from the source.

mass and weight relationship: $m_1/m_2 = W_1/W_2$, where m_1 and m_2 represent two masses and W_1 and W_2 represent the size of their respective weights.

momentum: $p = mv$, where p represents momentum, m represents the mass of the object, and v represents velocity.

Newton's second law: $F = ma$, where F represents force, m represents mass of the object, and a represents the accelerated movement.

Ohm's law: $R = V/I$, where R represents electrical resistance, V represents electrical potential, and I represents electrical current.

potential energy: $PE = mgh$, where PE represents potential energy, m represents the mass of an object, g represents the pull of gravity, and h represents the distance to be traveled by m.

power: $P = $ work$/t$, where P represents power and t represents the time required to perform the indicated work.

velocity: $v = d/t$, where d represents the distance traveled in time t.

wave equation: $V = fw$, where V represents the velocity of the wave, f represents its frequency, and w represents the wavelength.

weight: $Wt = mg$, where Wt represents the weight of an object, m represents its mass, and g represents the pull of gravity.

work: $W = fd$, where W represents work, f represents the applied force, and d represents the distance over which it is applied.

Heating and Electrical Terms

ampere (amp or A) A unit of electrical current, or flow of electrons, that is equal to a charge of 1 coulomb moving through or across a conductor in 1 second. It is named for André M. Ampère, French physicist (1775–1836).

British thermal unit (Btu) A unit of heat energy measured as the amount of heat required to raise the temperature of 1 pound of water from 60° to 61° F at a constant pressure of 1 standard atmosphere (the weight of the atmosphere at mean sea level). One Btu is equal to 1054.5 joules in the meter-kilogram-second system of measurements.

coulomb (coul or C) The amount of electric charge that crosses a surface in 1 second when a steady current of 1 ampere is flowing across the surface. It is also equivalent to 6.3×10^{18} electron charges. Named for Charles A. Coulomb, French physicist (1736–1806).

joule (J) A unit of energy or work equal to the force of 1 newton magnitude when the point at which the force is applied is displaced 1 meter in the direction of the force. Named for James P. Joule, English physicist (1818–1889).

newton (N) A unit of force equal to the force that will cause an acceleration of 1 meter per second squared to a mass of 1 kilogram. Named for Sir Isaac Newton, English mathematician (1642–1727).

ohm (Ω) A unit of electrical resistance through which a current of 1 ampere will flow when there is a potential difference of 1 volt across it. Named for George S. Ohm, German physicist (1787–1854).

volt (V) A unit of electromotive force equal to the potential difference between two points for which 1 coulomb of electricity will do 1 joule of work in going from one point to the other. Named for Count Alesandro Volta (1745–1827).

watt (W) A unit of electrical power equal to 1 joule per second. It is also measured as the product of the amperes multiplied by the volts. Named for James Watt, Scottish inventor (1736–1819).

Periodic Table of the Elements

Element*	Symbol	Valence	Atomic number	Atomic weight†
Actinium	Ac	3	89	(227.0278)
Aluminum	Al	3	13	26.98154
Americium	Am	3, 4, 5, 6	95	(243.0614)
Antimony	Sb	3, 5	51	121.75
Argon	Ar	0	18	39.948
Arsenic	As	3, 5	33	74.9216
Astatine	At	1, 3, 5, 7	85	(209.987)
Barium	Ba	2	56	137.34
Berkelium	Bk	3, 4	97	(247.0703)
Beryllium	Be	2	4	9.01218
Bismuth	Bi	3, 5	83	208.9804
Boron	B	3	5	10.81
Bromine	Br	1, 3, 5, 7	35	79.904
Cadmium	Cd	2	48	112.40
Calcium	Ca	2	20	40.08
Californium	Cf	3	98	(251.0796)
Carbon	C	2, 4	6	12.011
Cerium	Ce	3, 4	58	140.12
Cesium	Cs	1	55	132.9054
Chlorine	Cl	1, 3, 5, 7	17	35.453
Chromium	Cr	2, 3, 6	24	51.996
Cobalt	Co	2, 3	27	58.9332
Columbium	(see Niobium)			
Copper	Cu	1, 2	29	63.546
Curium	Cm	3	96	(247.0704)
Dysprosium	Dy	3	66	162.50
Einsteinium	Es		99	(254.0881)
Erbium	Er	3	68	167.26
Europium	Eu	2, 3	63	151.96
Fermium	Fm		100	(257.0951)
Fluorine	F	1	9	18.9984
Francium	Fr	1	87	(223.0198)
Gadolinium	Gd	3	64	157.25
Gallium	Ga	2, 3	31	69.72
Germanium	Ge	4	32	72.59
Glucinum	(see Beryllium)			
Gold	Au	1, 3	79	196.9665
Hafnium	Hf	4	72	178.49
Helium	He	0	2	4.0026
Holmium	Ho	3	67	164.9304
Hydrogen	H	1	1	1.0079
Indium	In	3	49	114.82
Iodine	I	1, 3, 5, 7	53	126.9045
Iridium	Ir	3, 4	77	192.22
Iron	Fe	2, 3	26	55.847
Krypton	Kr	0	36	83.30
Lanthanum	La	3	57	138.9055
Lawrencium	Lw		103	(256.0986)
Lead	Pb	2, 4	82	207.2
Lithium	Li	1	3	6.941
Lutetium	Lu	3	71	174.97
Magnesium	Mg	2	12	24.305
Manganese	Mn	2, 3, 4, 6, 7	25	54.938

Element*	Symbol	Valence	Atomic number	Atomic weight†
Mendelevium	Md		101	(257.0956)
Mercury	Hg	1, 2	80	200.59
Molybdenum	Mo	3, 4, 6	42	95.94
Neodymium	Nd	3	60	144.24
Neon	Ne	0	10	20.179
Neptunium	Np	4, 5, 6	93	237.0482
Nickel	Ni	2, 3	28	58.70
Niobium	Nb	3, 5	41	92.9064
Nitrogen	N	3, 5	7	14.0067
Nobelium	No		102	(255.0933)
Osmium	Os	2, 3, 4, 8	76	190.2
Oxygen	O	2	8	15.9994
Palladium	Pd	2, 4, 6	46	106.4
Phosphorus	P	3, 5	15	30.98376
Platinum	Pt	2, 4	78	195.09
Plutonium	Pu	3, 4, 5, 6	94	(244.0642)
Polonium	Po	2, 4	84	(208.9824)
Potassium	K	1	19	39.098
Praseodymium	Pr	3	59	140.9077
Promethium	Pm	3	61	(144.9128)
Protactinium	Pa		91	(231.0359)
Radium	Ra	2	88	(226.0254)
Radon	Rn	0	86	(222.0176)
Rhenium	Re		75	186.207
Rhodium	Rh	3	45	102.9055
Rubidium	Rb	1	37	85.4678
Ruthenium	Ru	3, 4, 6, 8	44	101.07
Samarium	Sm	2, 3	62	150.4
Scandium	Sc	3	21	44.9559
Selenium	Se	2, 4, 6	34	78.96
Silicon	Si	4	14	28.086
Silver	Ag	1	47	107.868
Sodium	Na	1	11	22.98977
Strontium	Sr	2	38	87.62
Sulfur	S	2, 4, 6	16	32.06
Tantalum	Ta	5	73	180.9479
Technetium	Tc	6, 7	43	96.9062
Tellurium	Te	2, 4, 6	52	127.60
Terbium	Tb	3	65	158.9254
Thallium	Tl	1, 3	81	204.37
Thorium	Th	4	90	232.0381
Thulium	Tm	3	69	168.9342
Tin	Sn	2, 4	50	118.69
Titanium	Ti	3, 4	22	47.90
Tungsten	W	6	74	183.85
Uranium	U	4, 6	92	238.029
Vanadium	V	3, 5	23	50.9414
Xenon	Xe	0	54	131.30
Ytterbium	Yb	2, 3	70	173.04
Yttrium	Y	3	39	88.9059
Zinc	Zn	2	30	65.38
Zirconium	Zr	4	40	91.22

* The 103 chemical elements known at present are included in this table. Some of those recently discovered have been obtained only as unstable isotopes.

† Based on Carbon-12. Figures enclosed in parentheses represent the mass number of the most stable isotope.

Geological Time Chart

Age in Years	Era	Period or Epoch		Important Physical Events	Animal Life
		Period or			
			Epoch		
	CENOZOIC		Pleistocene	Repeated extensions of ice caps in arctic and north temperate areas Continents generally elevated, mountains high, deserts widespread	human beings
1.0 ±.5 ▶	CENOZOIC		Pliocene	Mountain building in northwestern North America Deformation of Tethys geosyncline; Alps and Himalayas rise	gorillas
13 ±1 ▶	CENOZOIC		Miocene	Extensive erosion surfaces cut on Appalachians and Rockies Cool, dry climates over much of world	whales, sabertooths
25 ±1 ▶	CENOZOIC		Oligocene	Initiation of mountain building in Tethys geosyncline River and floodplain deposits begin on Great Plains	apes, bats
36 ±2 ▶	CENOZOIC		Eocene	Climates warm and uniform; widespread jungles and forests	alligators
58 ±2 ▶	CENOZOIC		Paleocene	Basins develop between ranges along Pacific Coast and Rockies	kangaroos, birds, horses, camels, monkeys, elephants
65 ±2 ▶	MESOZOIC	Cretaceous		Mountain building in Rockies; seas invade much of western North America and cover Atlantic and Gulf coastal plains	ancient birds, snakes, modern fish
135 ±5 ▶	MESOZOIC	Jurassic		Widespread mild, uniform climates Mountain building along Pacific Coast of North America Extensive marine invasions of southern and central Europe	flying reptiles
180 ±5 ▶	MESOZOIC	Triassic		Fault basins in eastern North America Extensive deserts and dead seas develop in North America and Eurasia	ichthyosaurs, tyrannosaurs
230 ±10 ▶	PALEOZOIC	Permian		Continents generally elevated; Appalachian and Ural mountains complete their development Tethys geosyncline from Spain to India	ammonites, finbacked reptiles
280 ±10 ▶	PALEOZOIC	Pennsylvanian		Mountain building in southern Appalachians and southwestern United States Ice age in southern continents Coal swamps in many parts of world	dragonflies
310 ±10 ▶					

MILLIONS OF YEARS BEFORE THE PRESENT (ESTIMATES REVISED IN 1961)

Age in Years	Era	Period or		Important Physical Events	Animal Life
			Epoch		
345 ±10 ▶	PALEOZOIC	Mississippian		Mountain building in southern North America and central Europe Extensive seas over much of interior North America	amphibians, clams, lungfish
405 ±10 ▶		Devonian		Catskill delta built from New England mountains into New York and Pennsylvania Mountain building in northeastern North America Extensive submergence of geosynclines and interior of North America	starfish
425 ±10 ▶		Silurian		Formation of Caledonian mountains in northwestern Europe Dead seas in Michigan, New York, Ohio, southeastern Canada Deltas and gravel beaches along eastern edge of Appalachian geosyncline	sea scorpions, corals, sharks
500 ±10 ▶		Ordovician		Mountain building in northeastern North America Over 60 percent of North American continent covered by seas	snails, jawless fish, echinoids
		Cambrian		Climates generally mild and uniform Seas invade North American continent Geosynclines develop around edge of North America	protozoans, trilobites
?600 ▶ 1,000 ▶ 2,000 ▶ 3,000 ▶ 4,500 ▶	Precambrian			Fault basins in Lake Superior region Deformation and mountain building through central North America Geosynclines develop throughout central North America Extensive mountain building in Lake Superior region Oldest dated rocks Probable origin of Earth from solar dust cloud	jellyfish, flagellates, amoebas, worms, sponges

Phases of the Moon

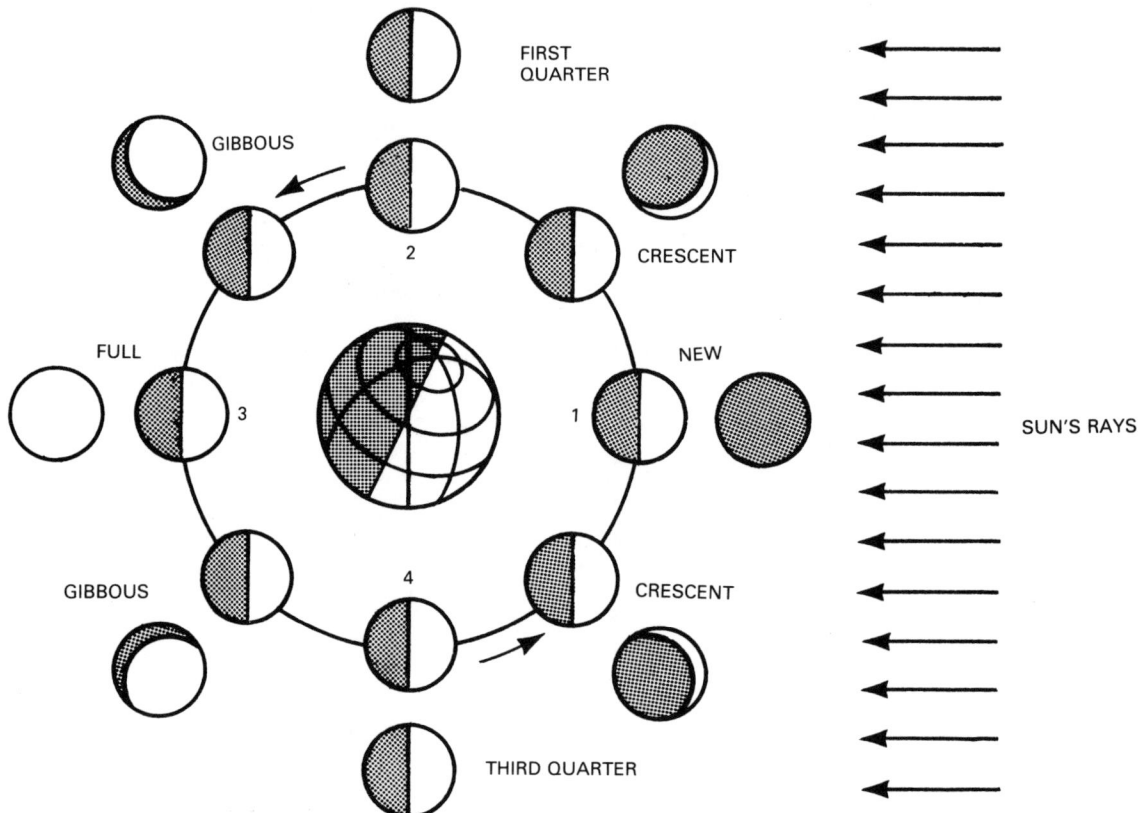

Diagram of the Solar System, with Facts About the Planets

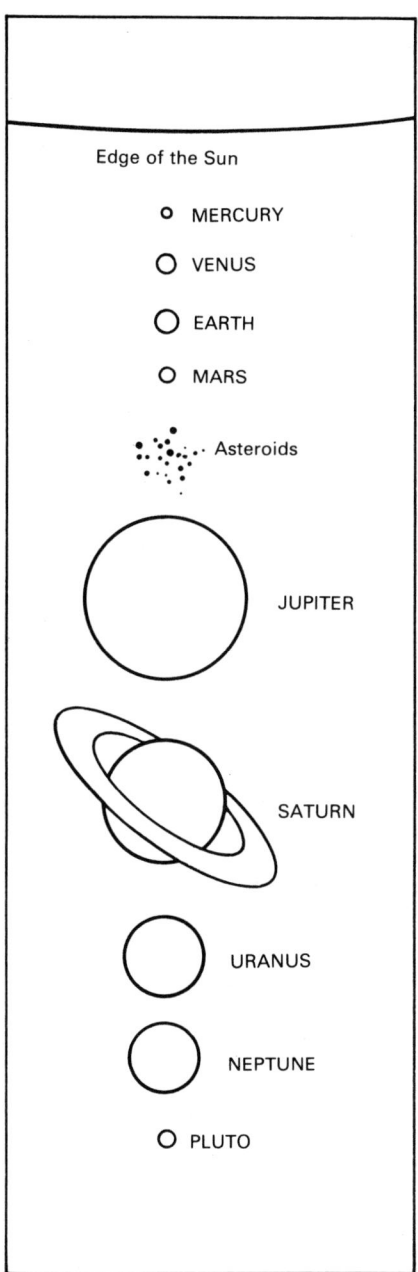

Edge of the Sun

o MERCURY

O VENUS

O EARTH

O MARS

Asteroids

JUPITER

SATURN

URANUS

NEPTUNE

O PLUTO

Relative size of the planets

The Planets

Mercury Diameter, 3,100 miles; distance from the sun, 36 million miles; orbits the sun every 88 days; rotates on its axis in 59 days.

Venus Diameter, 7,700 miles; distance from the sun, 67 million miles; orbits the sun every 225 days; rotates on its axis in 244 days.

Earth Diameter, 7,920 miles; distance from the sun, 93 million miles; orbits the sun every 365 days; rotates on its axis in 24 hours.

Mars Diameter, 4,200 miles; distance from the sun, 141 million miles; orbits the sun every 687 days; rotates on its axis in 24 hours 24 minutes.

Jupiter Diameter, 88,640 miles; distance from the sun, 483 million miles; orbits the sun every 11.9 years; rotates on its axis in 9 hours 50 minutes.

Saturn Diameter, 74,500 miles (diameter of rings, 165,000 miles); distance from the sun, 886 million miles; orbits the sun every 29.5 years; rotates on its axis in 10 hours 39 minutes.

Uranus Diameter, 32,000 miles; distance from the sun, 1,782 million miles; orbits the sun every 84 years; rotates on its axis in 23 hours.

Neptune Diameter, 31,000 miles; distance from the sun, 2,793 million miles; orbits the sun every 165 days; rotates on its axis in 15 hours 48 minutes.

Pluto Diameter, 1,500 miles; distance from the sun, 3,670 million miles; orbits the sun every 248 years; rotates on its axis in 6 days 7 hours.

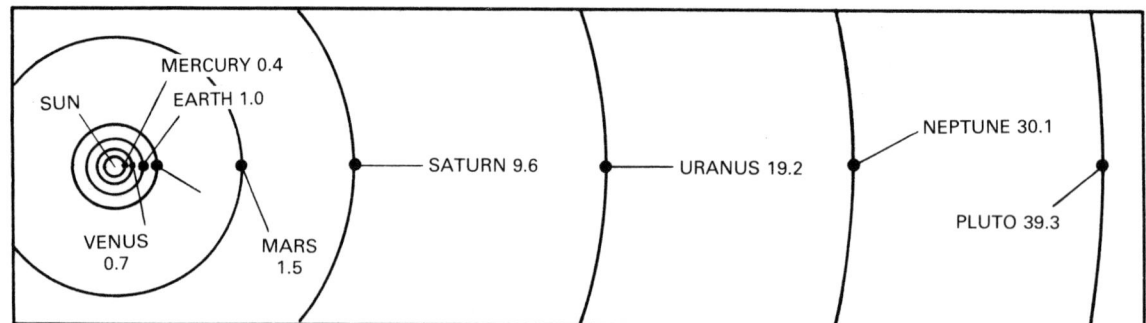

The average distances of the planets from the sun. The numbers in the diagram give the distances in terms of the astronomical unit (A.U.), or average distance between Earth and the sun. One A.U. is 9.30×10^7 miles, or 1.50×10^8 kilometers.

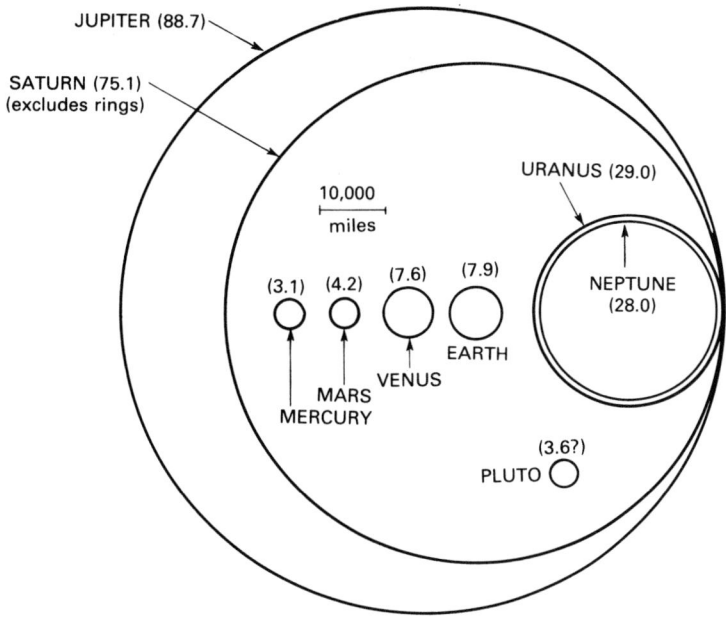

The diameters of the planets. The numbers in the diagram give the diameters in thousands of miles.

Brightest Stars

Name	Magnitude	Distance (light-years)	Location (constellation)
Sirius	−1.60	9	Canis Major
Canopus	−0.73	650	Carina
Rigil	−0.20	540	Centaurus
Arcturus	−0.06	36	Bootes
Vega	0.04	27	Lyra
Capella	0.08	45	Auriga
Rigel	0.11	900	Orion
Procyon	0.50	11	Canis Minor
Achernar	0.48	118	Eridanus
Altair	0.77	16	Aquila
Betelgeuse	0.80	520	Orion
Aldebaran	0.85	68	Taurus
Spica	0.96	220	Virgo
Antares	1.00	520	Scorpio
Pollux	1.15	35	Gemini
Fomalhaut	1.16	23	Piscis Austrinis
Deneb	1.25	1,600	Cygnus

(The brighter the star, the lower the magnitude. Compared to Sirius, the sun's magnitude would be −26.7.)

Common Terms in Science and Engineering

Astronomy

aberration The apparent displacement of a star owing to the orbital motion of Earth and the bending of light rays from the star. As Earth travels around the sun, the aberration causes the star to appear to trace an ellipse about its true position.

albedo The proportion of light reflected from a celestial body. The moon reflects only about 7 percent of the sunlight falling on it, while the albedo of Venus is more than 70 percent owing to its heavy cloud cover, which reflects a greater proportion of light.

big bang model A theory that describes the beginning of our universe as a titanic explosion. This explosion did not occur at a particular point in space, according to the theory, but rather was a transition from enormous density and temperature throughout all space to conditions of even lower density and lower temperature as space itself expanded. After the hypothetical explosion, the universe was swamped with energy in the form of radiant energy and various atomic particles. This phase was followed by a cooling and thinning out of the universe. It is believed that the universe is still expanding at this time.

black hole An ultimate state of gravitational collapse. Stars with a mass greater than two solar masses can expect to evolve into this condition, a concentration of matter so dense that even photons (light particles) cannot escape when the pressure of thermonuclear reactions are unable to counteract the force of self-gravitation. Black holes are believed to be associated with certain X-ray-emitting binary star systems, such as Cygnus X-1.

corona The outer envelope, or "atmosphere," of gas surrounding the sun, possibly extending to the orbit of Earth. During an eclipse of the sun, the corona may be visible around the edges of the moon. It has a density that is about one-millionth that of the atmosphere of Earth.

cosmology The study of the universe at large, of the distribution and behavior of the matter and energy in it, of the laws governing these factors, and of its origin and evolution.

critical density The mass density above which it is believed the expansion of the universe will slow down and reverse. Density in this case refers to all of the matter and radiant energy distributed throughout the universe.

curved space A concept of Einstein's theory of general relativity that space-time is "warped" by the presence of massive bodies. A ray of light passing near the sun will be deflected, or bent, from a perfectly straight path. As applied to cosmology, the current expansion of the universe will proceed differently according to the type of curvature. If the mass density of the universe is above critical density, it is assumed that the curvature of space is spherical; below critical density, the curvature is considered to be hyperbolic.

galaxy A large system of stars, usually containing between 1 million and 1 trillion stars, along with clouds of gas and dust. Galaxies are sometimes classified according to their shapes as spiral, elliptical, or irregular.

gravitational collapse The contraction of a star when the pressure of thermonuclear reactions can no longer sustain the force of self-gravitation. Collapse occurs at the end of a star's life when its fuel of hydrogen and other elements is depleted. Depending on its original mass, the star may evolve into a white dwarf, a neutron star, or a black hole, or it may explode as a supernova.

Hubble flow The mutual recession of celestial objects from each other by virtue of the expansion of the universe.

light-year The distance light travels in one year, approximately 9.5×10^{15} meters, or 6 trillion miles.

matter era A period in the evolution of the universe beginning about 100,000 years after the big bang and continuing to the present time. During this period, the temperature of the universe had cooled to about 3,000°, making it possible for electrons and protons to form neutral hydrogen atoms in a process of recombination. The atoms, in turn, accumulated in the clouds, stars, and galaxies that we observe today.

Milky Way The spiral galaxy in which our solar system is located. It contains about 150 billion stars, has a diameter of 500,000 light-years, and is about 12 billion years old.

neutron star A tiny star, usually a shrunken remnant of a once larger star, whose thermonuclear reactions could no longer uphold the bulk of the star's mass against the force of self-gravitation. A neutron star is only a few kilometers in diameter, midway between a white dwarf and a black hole.

perturbation The influence of one celestial body on another.

pulsar An object that emits radio waves in preferred directions and in periodic bursts. First discovered in 1967, pulsars are thought to be rapidly spinning neutron stars.

quark An elementary electrical particle that is believed to be the "building block" from which subatomic particles such as protons and neutrons are constructed. It is believed that quarks formed early in the creation of the universe, when the temperature was around a thousand billion degrees and physical forces were roughly equivalent.

quasar A contraction of the word *quasistellar,* used to describe celestial objects with a starlike appearance. Quasars are the most distant objects known. They have large red shifts indicating great recessional velocities and emit energy that is more than a thousand times that of an average galaxy.

radiation era A period early in the age of the universe when the temperature fell from about 10 billion degrees to 3,000 degrees, allowing the formation of simple nuclei, such as deuterium and helium. The radiation era was followed by the matter era.

red shift The shift of a spectrum of light toward long, red wavelengths owing to the Doppler effect of recession of a star. The faster an object recedes from Earth, the greater the shift of its light toward the red end of the spectrum. A quasar with a large red shift is moving away from Earth at a velocity of 91 percent the speed of light.

sidereal time Time that is measured by the rotation of Earth with respect to the stars, as distinguished from solar time, which is based on the rotation of Earth with respect to the sun.

supernova A gigantic explosion in which a star undergoing gravitational collapse ejects into space a large portion of its mass. This is accompanied by an immense outburst of light and charged particles.

white star A tiny star, about the size of Earth, which is the shrunken remnant of a once larger star whose thermonuclear reactions could no longer uphold the bulk of the star's mass against the force of self-gravitation. Further gravitational collapse is prevented by a condition in which the atoms are crushed very close together.

Biology

abaxial Facing away from the stem or central axis of a plant or animal.

abiogenesis A theory that living things can develop from nonliving material, as in spontaneous generation.

adaptation The modification of an organism or part of an organism to adjust to new conditions or a new environment, as in adjustment of the eyes to bright light.

adenosine triphosphate (ATP) A chemical compound present in all living cells that provides energy derived from food or sunlight for processes that require activity, such as contraction of a muscle or conduction of a nerve impulse.

appendage A structure attached to a larger structure or part of an organism, such as an arm or leg or other projection of a body area.

ATP *See* adenosine triphosphate.

bacteria Tiny, one-celled plant organisms that are generally parasitic and lacking in chlorophyll. They are commonly involved in processes of fermentation and decay, and many species are the cause of diseases in humans and animals.

bladder A saclike organ with a membranous wall that serves to collect or hold a fluid or gas, such as the urinary bladder or the air bladder of marine animals.

blastula A stage in the development of an embryo after the early phase of cell division when the cells form a hollow ball. The wall of the sphere is a single layer of cells, the blastoderm. The various organs, such as the gut, nervous system, and appendages, eventually evolve from cells of the blastula.

bud An undeveloped appendage of an organism. A plant bud may develop into flowers or leaves while the bud of an animal embryo may become an arm, leg, or wing. Some bacteria and yeast cells reproduce by issuing buds, each of which becomes a new organism.

bug Any of a large number of creeping or flying insects, mainly of the order Hemiptera. Examples of "true bugs" include bed bugs, cinch bugs, squash bugs, and giant water bugs.

calyx A cuplike portion of a plant or animal organ. Examples include the sepals, or outermost parts of a flower, and the funnel-shaped part of a kidney that collects urine as it drains toward the bladder.

carnivore Any meat-eating animal, particularly a member of the order Carnivora, which includes wolves, coyotes, bears, dogs, and cats.

cell The basic structural unit of living things. It usually consists of a membranous wall containing protoplasm, a souplike mixture of proteins, enzymes, and other organic chemicals needed for survival and reproduction. Most cells also contain a nucleus that in turn holds the DNA molecules, or genetic material, that control the various cell functions.

chlorophyll Any of nearly a dozen kinds of green pigments present in most plant cells. Chlorophylls are able to convert the energy from sunlight into carbohydrates, which plants form from carbon dioxide and water present in the environment. The carbohydrates in turn become a source of energy for animals and humans after the plant material is eaten.

chromosome A rod-shaped unit of DNA present in the nucleus of a cell that is capable of reproducing itself. It contains a portion of the genetic or hereditary traits of the species it represents. The number of chromosomes and their shapes and sizes vary among different species and sexes within a species. Human males, for example, possess a Y-shaped chromosome that is not normally present in female cells and that governs masculine physical traits.

deoxyribonucleic acid (DNA) A large molecule of nucleic acid found in the nuclei, usually in the chromosomes, of living cells. It controls such functions as the production of protein molecules in the cell and carries the template for reproduction of all the inherited characteristics of its particular species.

DNA *See* deoxyribonucleic acid.

embryo The young of a species at a very early stage of development, as the rudimentary plant that bursts forth from a seed when it germinates or the bird that has not yet hatched from its egg. In mammals, the embryo stage occurs after the cells of the blastula begin to specialize for the development of the fetus.

endogenous Pertaining to factors influencing an organism that originate within that organism, as distinguished from exogenous factors, such as environmental influences, that originate on the outside.

evolution The process by which a species of plants or animals gradually develops over a period of many generations from a simpler to a more complex form of organism. The traits of the simpler organism are often continued into the more complex form of the same organism, as can be observed in the brain and other structures of the human body.

exogenous *See* endogenous.

fauna The animal life of a region or period of history.

fermentation A process whereby complex carbohydrates or other organic substances are converted to other chemicals by the action of enzymes produced by molds, yeasts, or bacteria. An example is the conversion of sugars to alcohol.

fertilization The union of a male and a female reproductive cell resulting in the formation of a new organism. The term is also used to describe the process or enrichment of the soil for growing crops.

flora The plant life of a region or period of history.

genitalia The reproductive sex organs of a male or female of the species, particularly structures on the outside of the body.

genotype *See* phenotype.

genus A subdivision of a biological family. It is composed of a group of related species, such as the genus *Canis*, which includes various species of dogs.

gonads The male and female reproductive organs.

haploid Half the number of chromosomes ordinarily present in the nucleus of a cell. During reproduction, the offspring receives a haploid number of chromosomes from each parent, making a full, or diploid, set.

herbaceous Herblike, usually used to describe a plant in which persistent woody tissue does not develop.

herbivore An animal that feeds entirely or mainly on plant materials.

hormone A chemical secretion of a gland or other tissue that triggers an action in another gland or tissue in a different part of the body.

immunity A quality of being able to resist an infectious disease.

inbreeding The mating of closely related individuals, as in self-pollinating plants or animals that are brothers and sisters.

joint An area between two parts or segments of an organism, such as the junction of two separate bones of an animal or the node of a plant.

karyotype The general appearance of a set of chromosomes of an individual. Karyotype may be used to determine sex, genetic defects, and other chromosome-related factors.

kernel The entire grain or seed of a cereal plant.

larva The young, immature form of an organism that undergoes a change in structure to become an adult, as a caterpillar or maggot.

leaf An outgrowth of a stem of a plant, usually green, in which many living functions, such as photosynthesis, respiration, and food and water storage, take place.

lipid Any of a group of fatty substances, including oils and waxes, produced by plant or animal tissues. Lipids generally are insoluble in water but they can be dissolved in alcohol, benzene, or similar organic solvents.

male The sex of an animal that produces spermatozoa or of a plant that produces pollen.

mammal A warm-blooded, air-breathing vertebrate of the class Mammalia, possessing hair and mammary glands.

Mendel's laws A series of natural principles of heredity discovered by Gregor Mendel (1822–1884). They govern such factors as dominant and recessive traits resulting from the interaction of genes that are inherited in pairs.

metabolism The chemical and energy changes associated with the consumption of food and oxygen, the production of heat, and the calories used in physical activity.

natural selection A principle proposed by Charles Darwin (1809–1882) to explain the ability of various species to adapt to changes in the environment. Called "survival of the fittest," the theory offered an explanation for the survival of some species and extinction of others.

neuron The structural and functional unit of a nerve, including the cell body and its axon and dendrite fibers.

nucleus A structure present in most plant and animal cells. It contains the chromosomes and ribonucleic acid (RNA) molecules that direct the cell's life functions.

osmosis The diffusion of water through a semipermeable membrane from the side with a greater concentration of a solution to the side with a lesser concentration.

osseous Pertaining to bones, as something composed of bone or resembling bone.

phenotype The physical features or appearance of an individual, as distinguished from the genotype, or genetic composition of his or her cells. Two or more persons with the same physical appearance may belong to the same phenotype.

pistil The female sex structure of a plant, usually containing the ovary.

Protozoa A phylum, or large group, of one-celled animals.

receptor Any cell or group of cells that is the target of a stimulus, such as the retina of the eye.

regeneration The ability of some plants and animals to restore or replace lost tissues or structures, such as a claw or feather.

stamen The pollen-producing structure of a plant. It usually consists of an anther, the actual pollen producer, on the tip of a flower filament.

stimulus An environmental influence, such as a chemical or physical irritant, that induces or brings about a response in a cell or organism.

symbiosis A relationship in which two organisms live together for the mutual benefit of each.

terrestrial Pertaining to plant or animal life on land rather than in water.

tissue A group of cells with similar structures and functions.

tropism The involuntary response of an organism to a stimulus, such as the response of a plant to gravity or sunlight.

vacuole Any of the spaces scattered about the protoplasm of a cell, usually containing fluid.

zygote The fertilized egg cell of a plant or animal.

Chemistry

acid A substance that, in liquid form, will turn blue litmus paper red, react with alkalis (bases) to form salts, and dissolve metals to form salts. On the pH scale of 0 to 14, acids register in numbers less than 7.

alcohol Any of a group of organic compounds that contains a hydroxyl (OH) group. A common example is ethyl alcohol (C_2H_5OH).

alkali Any compound that has chemical qualities of a base, such as reacting with acids to form salts. On the pH scale, alkalis register in numbers larger than 7.

anion An ion with a negative electrical charge.

base An alkaline substance, either in molecular or ionic form, that will accept or receive a proton from another chemical unit. An example is a hydroxyl ion.

benzene ring A common organic molecule structure consisting of a ring of six carbon atoms with an equal number of attached hydrogen atoms (C_6H_6). Many organic chemicals occur in a benzene ring format with various atoms or radicals substituted for one or more hydrogen atoms, as in toluene and xylene as variations of benzene.

bond A strong electrical force that holds atoms together in molecules, crystals, and other combinations. A molecular bond may depend on the attractive force of an electron whose orbit spans the outer shells of two or more component atoms. In double bonds, two pairs of electrons may be shared equally by adjacent atoms.

catalyst A substance that accelerates a chemical reaction without becoming a part of the end product of the reaction. A catalyst can generally be recovered in its original form following the reaction.

cation An ion, atom, or group of atoms with a positive electrical charge.

compound A substance formed by the combination of two or more chemical elements that cannot be separated from the combination by physical means. The constituent atoms, however, can usually be separated by means of chemical reactions.

electrolyte Any chemical, such as a mineral, that when melted or dissolved in water will show an electrical attraction or conduct an electric current.

electron A negatively charged particle that moves in an orbit about the nucleus of an atom.

element A substance composed of atoms with the same atomic number or the same number of protons in their nuclei. Examples include oxygen, hydrogen, carbon, and gold.

hydrocarbon Any of a large group of chemical compounds consisting primarily of carbon and hydrogen atoms, usually associated with current or past life processes.

hydroxyl Pertaining to the negatively charged OH (oxygen + hydrogen) radical in an organic compound.

inorganic chemistry A branch of chemical science that deals primarily with elements and compounds that do not include hydrocarbons.

isotope One of two or more atoms having the same atomic number but a different mass number. An example is zinc, which has isotopes with five different mass numbers ranging from 64 to 70. However, all of the isotopes have equal nuclear charges, orbital electrons, and chemical properties.

mass number The atomic weight of an isotope, calculated from the numbers of protons and neutrons in the nucleus.

matter Anything that has weight or fills space, such as a solid, liquid, or gas.

organic chemistry A branch of chemistry that specializes in the composition, properties, and reactions of hydrocarbon compounds.

oxidation Any chemical reaction that increases the number of oxygen atoms in a compound, or in which the positive valence is increased by a loss of electrons.

pH A symbol for hydrogen ion activity of a substance as an expression of the negative logarithm of the concentration of hydrogen ions in moles per liter. Values of pH range from 0 to 14, with a pH of 7 representing acid-base neutrality. The degree of acidity increases as the number progresses toward zero, while alkalinity increases as the pH number approaches 14.

polymer A huge molecule composed of repeating units of the same molecule. An example is polyethylene, formed by linking ethylene molecules into a giant chain.

reduction A chemical reaction in which a substance gains electrons or loses part of its positive valence. Reduction generally occurs in a reaction that also involves oxidation.

solute A substance that is dissolved in a solution.

solvent The substance that represents the greatest proportion of parts of a solution when two or more substances, such as a solid and liquid, are mixed.

valence A number that represents the combining power of an element, ion, or radical. The valence of hydrogen is $+1$, while the valence of oxygen is -2.

Physics

acceleration The rate of change of velocity with respect to time. It is calculated by subtracting the initial or starting velocity from the final velocity and dividing the difference by the time required to reach that velocity. It may be expressed by the formula $a = v_f - v_0/t$.

achromatic An optical system that will transmit light without breaking it down into its component colors.

acoustics The science of the production, transmission, and effect of sound waves.

adiabatic Pertaining to any activity that is not accompanied by a gain or loss of heat.

anode The positive terminal of an electrical current flow. In a vacuum tube, electrons flow from a cathode toward the anode.

Bohr theory A commonly accepted concept of the atom introduced by Niels Bohr in 1913. It holds that each atom consists of a small, dense, positively charged nucleus surrounded by negatively charged electrons that move in fixed, defined orbits about the nucleus, the total number of electrons normally balancing the total positive charge of particles in the nucleus.

Boyle's law The principle that the volume of a gas times its pressure is constant at a fixed temperature.

cathode The negative terminal of an electric current system. In a vacuum tube, the filament serves as the cathode or source of electrons that are emitted.

conduction The transfer of heat by molecular motion from a source of high temperature to a region of lower temperature, tending toward a result of equalized temperatures.

convection The mechanical transfer of heated molecules of a gas or liquid from a source to another area, as when a room is warmed by the movement of air molecules heated by a radiator.

Coulomb's law The principle that an electrostatic force of attraction or repulsion between electrical charges is directly proportional to the product of the electrical charges and inversely proportional to the square of the distance between them.

electromotive force The force that causes the movement of electrons through an electrical circuit.

energy The ability to perform work. Energy may be changed from one form to another, as from heat into light, but it normally cannot be created or destroyed.

force The influence on a body that causes it to accelerate, as expressed by the formula $F = ma$.

heat A form of energy that results from the disordered motion of molecules. As the motion becomes more rapid and disordered, the amount of heat is increased.

kinetic energy Energy that is associated with the motion of an object as expressed by the formula $KE = \frac{1}{2}mv^2$.

mechanics A branch of physics that deals with the motion of objects.

momentum The mathematical product of the mass of a moving object and its velocity, as expressed by the formula $p = mv$.

potential energy Energy that is stored because of position or configuration, such as the gravitational energy of a weight that is positioned on the roof of a building.

power The rate at which work is performed, as expressed by the formula $P = W/t$.

velocity The speed with which an object travels over a specified distance during a measured amount of time. It may be expressed by the formula $v = d/t$.

weight The force on a body produced by the downward pull of gravity on it. It may be expressed by the formula $Wt = mg$, where m represents the mass of the object and g represents the effect of gravity.

work The force applied to an object times the distance over which it is applied, as expressed by the formula $W = Fd$. Work may be independent of the energy expended.

Engineering

absorbing dynamometer A device that absorbs and dissipates the power it measures. An example is the common rope brake.

abutment Any point or surface designed to withstand thrust, as the end supports of an arch or bridge.

aggregate The sand, broken stone, and similar materials that are added to cement and water to form concrete.

apomecometer A surveying instrument used to calculate the height of structures by coincident light reflected from the top and bottom of the structure when the location of the instrument is the same distance from the base of the structure as its height.

balance crane A crane with two arms, one arranged to balance the load on the other.

bearing pile In civil engineering, a column that is sunk into the ground to support a vertical load. It transmits the load to a firmer foundation at a lower depth, or it may consolidate the soil to increase its ability to bear the load.

block gauge A block of hardened steel with opposite faces ground flat and parallel and separated by a specific distance. It is used to check the accuracy of other gauges.

cable way A system of suspending cables between two towers so that a skip suspended from the cables can be raised, lowered, or otherwise maneuvered to any position along the cables.

caisson A watertight compartment built to surround a structure, such as a bridge foundation, that would otherwise be beneath the surface of the water.

camber An upwardly convex curvature applied to a structure or part of a structure for a specific purpose. Examples include the camber added to girders to allow for deflection caused by loading or to the surface of a road to facilitate drainage.

cantilever A beam or girder that is firmly attached at one end but free at the other. A bridge may be started as two cantilevered, or self-supporting, projecting arms, built inward from piers and eventually connected at the center of the span.

differential motion A mechanical movement in which the speed of a driven part is equal to the difference in the speeds of the parts connected to it.

dog Any of a variety of gripping devices, such as a steel securing piece used to fasten a pair of timbers used for shoring.

electromechanical brake A braking device in which the force is obtained partly by the attraction of two magnetized surfaces and partly by mechanical means. It is controlled by a solenoid.

engine Any machine in which power is applied to perform work. Examples include devices that convert thermal, or heat, energy into mechanical work, such as a locomotive.

engineer's chain A surveying device consisting of a chain that is 100 feet in length with each link 1 foot long.

expansion joint A joint designed between two parts of a structure so the two parts can expand when the temperature increases, as on a hot summer day, without causing distortion or damage to the structure. Examples include joints between lengths of rail in a railroad line and sliding socket joints in pipelines.

gasket A flat sheet of asbestos, cotton rope impregnated with graphite, or similar material, used to form a gas-tight joint between parts of engines, pumps, or other devices.

girder A beam, usually made of steel, used to bridge an open space.

grid In electrical engineering, a network of electrical power lines connecting various generating stations.

helical gears Gear wheels in which the teeth are set at an angle to the axis rather than parallel to the wheel axis.

impeller The rotating part of a centrifugal pump. It imparts kinetic energy to the fluid being moved.

mechanical advantage The ratio of the resistance or load to the applied force or effort of a machine.

skip A bucket, box, or similar device used to transport building materials, spoils, or mining products to or from a work site. It usually is suspended from a crane or cable way.

theodolite A surveying instrument used for measuring horizontal and vertical angles.

Geology/Geography

abyssal zone A region of greatest ocean depth, generally greater than 1,000 meters, including the deep-sea trenches. Biological activity is rare in the abyssal zone; light does not penetrate the water, as the depth and pressure are tremendous. The region represents about 250 million square kilometers of Earth's surface.

age An interval of geological time that indicates when a body of rock was formed in the surface of Earth. A group of ages forms an epoch.

alluvium The sediment carried by rivers, including deposits from estuaries, lakes, and other freshwater bodies draining into a river. The particles of sediment are generally smaller than 0.02 millimeter, depending on such factors as valleyside slopes in the watershed, the distance carried downstream, and progressive wear on the particles as they move downstream.

anthropomorphic soil Soil that is distinctive in composition and contour from the surrounding environment as a result of human activity. An example is soil that has been used for farming.

barrier beach An accumulation of sand, rock, and other material lying parallel to the coast but separated from it by a channel; it measures from a few meters to a few kilometers in width. Large barrier beaches may be identified as barrier islands. They are formed by the action of waves but are usually vulnerable to overwashing or breaching during severe storms.

bathyal zone A zone of ocean water ranging from about 200 meters to 1,000 meters in depth, generally located along continental slopes. Unlike the abyssal zone, light reaches the upper layer of the bathyal zone and there is abundant biological activity in the water. The bathyal zone of the world covers a total of about 40 million square kilometers.

bed The smallest division of stratified sedimentary rock, usually occurring as a relatively thin sheet of sedimentary material separating distinctively different layers above and below it. A bed often marks a particular event in geologic history, such as a volcanic eruption, and it may contain fossils that help identify its age.

Cambrian The earliest period of the Paleozoic Era, about 600 million years ago. Rocks formed at this period contain the earliest fossil remains of invertebrate animals.

chronostratigraphy A system of classifying the major divisions of geologic time. According to the system, the smallest segment is a chron; groups of chrons form an age; a group of ages forms an epoch; epochs form periods; periods form eras; and eras form eons. There is no uniform time scale applied to the divisions. For example, the Miocene Epoch spans 17 million years but the following Pliocene Epoch lasted only 3.7 million years.

continental drift The shifting of continental land masses from one location to another on the face of Earth owing to sea-floor spreading. Evidence supporting the concept is based on comparison of flora, fauna, rock types, and geologic formations. It indicates that until about 250 million years ago, there were just two continents—Pangaea and Gondwanaland—from which the present continents were formed.

Coriolis effect A force produced on objects moving on a north–south line on the surface of Earth because of the angular velocity of Earth as it rotates from west to east. Thus, a projectile fired directly southward from the North Pole would be deviated to the west. The Coriolis force affects mainly the flow of air in the atmosphere.

creep The slow movement of rocks and soil down slopes of hills owing to the pull of gravity. It is believed the movement involves a sliding of the entire Earth mantle over the underlying bedrock rather than changes within the mantle itself. The effect can be observed in the tendency of telephone poles and other objects to alter positions on gentle slopes over a period of years.

diagenesis The process whereby sedimentary rock is formed from sediment because of compaction, reduced pore space between particles, and chemical reactions between molecules of the compressed particles and dissolved substances in moisture between the particles.

doldrums A region between the equator and the trade wind zones where winds are light and variable, storms are frequent and severe, and navigation is difficult.

equinox A date that occurs twice each year when the sun is overhead at local solar time at the equator and day and night are both 12 hours long. It occurs on or about March 21 and September 21.

era An interval of geological time composed of a group of periods. An example is the Paleozoic Era, which spans a series of six periods of geological time.

estuary The portion of a river that is affected by ocean tides above the mouth, with a resulting mixture of salt water and fresh water. Most estuaries are former valleys that were flooded by rising ocean levels after the last glacial event. The Hudson River is an example of an estuary.

fjord A narrow sea inlet between mountain slopes. Most fjords were once glaciated valleys that became flooded by rising sea water after the last ice age. In some cases, the bottom of the fjord may be lower than the bottom of the sea at its opening into the fjord.

floodplain A relatively level area alongside a river that is subject to flooding periodically. It usually is composed of sediment that has been deposited over the surface of an original rock-cut valley.

frost hollow An area where cold air, which has a greater density than warm air, tends to collect because there is no free air outlet from the low-lying hollow. As a result, the area is more likely than the surrounding landscape to experience frost on cold days.

geology The science of the structure and composition of Earth.

glacier An accumulation of ice formed in turn by compaction of accumulated snow moving downslope from a source area because of the force of gravity. A glacier is usually confined within the limited space of a valley or basin. It may be gaining ice at the source while losing ice at a point where it melts while moving into warmer temperatures or a body of water.

induration The hardening of porous rocks or soils owing to weather conditions and the chemical actions of dissolved minerals, which form a cement. The concretelike rock formed by induration usually consists of combinations of calcium, silicon, or iron with carbon and oxygen.

leaching The action of water draining through soil layers carrying dissolved minerals or organic matter from the upper layers. Because leaching tends to remove alkaline substances, the soils eventually become acid.

Mercator projection A map in which the spherical Earth is projected as a cylinder onto a flat surface. It results in straight-line bearings that are correct and is most commonly used for navigation charts, although the projection distorts the areas toward the North and South poles.

Common Computer Terms

address A location in the computer memory where a particular unit of data is stored. The address may be in the form of an identifying label, name, or number.

ALGOL An algorithmic computer programming language, used mainly by mathematicians and scientists.

algorithm A defined set of instructions or procedural steps that will lead to a logical conclusion for a specific problem.

analog computer A computer that measures a function or behavior involving continuously variable signals, such as signals representing current, voltage, or other factors. An analog computer is also able to respond immediately to changes in input. The output may be presented in the form of a tracing on a graph or a design on a TV picture tube.

analog-to-digital computer A device that is able to convert continuous analog signals into digital data, or discrete numbers.

architecture The design of a computer so that hardware and software interface effectively.

arithmetic/logic unit The part of a computer that performs calculations and comparisons.

array An arrangement of data in which each item may be identified by a key or subscript so that a computer program can be designed to examine and extract specific data. An example is a calendar array in which a particular day of the year can be identified.

ASCII Acronym for *A*merican *S*tandard *C*ode for *I*nformation *I*nterchange, a uniform character code used by many computer systems so that data can be exchanged directly between various types of central and remote units and peripheral devices. Each alphabetic and numeric character requires a full byte.

assembler A computer program designed to assemble machine code from symbolic code or source language.

assembly language A machine-oriented computer programming language that can be translated directly into machine instructions.

BASIC Acronym for *B*eginner's *A*ll-purpose *S*ymbolic *I*nstruction *C*ode, a program that is a standard language for most personal computers. It is designed for developing programs in a "conversational mode" for on-line use.

batch A group of records or collection of transactions that may be processed together.

baud rate The rate at which information is transmitted serially from a computer. It is expressed in terms of bits per second.

BCD *See* binary coded decimal.

binary A numbering system based on twos (2's) rather than decimals (10's). Each element has a digit value of either zero (0) or one (1) and is known as a bit.

binary coded decimal (BCD) A method of encoding four bits of binary computer code to represent the 10 decimal digits. For example, 0 = 0000; 1 = 0001; 2 = 0100; and so on through 9 = 1001.

bit An acronym constructed from the words *bi*nary digi*t*. It refers to a single digit of a binary number.

bootstrap (boot) The process of initializing or loading the basic operating instructions into a computer.

buffer A temporary storage area for data that helps compensate for differences in the speed of operations of two or more parts of a computer system, such as the central processing unit and a printer.

bug Any error or malfunction in a computer operation or program.

byte A set or unit of binary digits, usually eight bits, such as a division of a word.

cathode ray tube (CRT) An electronic tube, similar to a television picture tube, on which a computer output is displayed (also called a visual display terminal).

central processing unit (CPU) The part of the computer circuitry that actually handles the data processing and controls the storage, movement, and other basic computer functions.

channel A path through which computer data flow.

character Any digit, letter, punctuation, or symbol, usually represented by a single byte of eight bits.

clock An electronic device that monitors, measures, or synchronizes various functions of a computer system.

COBOL An acronym formed from the words *CO*mmon *B*usiness *O*riented *L*anguage.

command A part of a computer code that gives input/output instructions to the computer.

compiler A set of programs that compiles or converts a program into the machine language instructions used by a particular computer.

console The part of the central processing unit from which the computer operator manually directs activities of the system, as through a keyboard.

control data Computer information that helps organize data in key categories, such as sorting sequences.

control unit The part of the central processing unit that manipulates the sequences of operations according to the program instructions.

CPU *See* central processing unit.

CRT *See* cathode ray tube.

cursor A character, such as a movable line or block of light, used to indicate a position on a cathode ray tube screen.

data acquisition system A system in which data from computers in remote locations can be transmitted to a central computer unit. The flow of data is usually governed by a program control that buffers signal inputs from the various peripheral units.

database A large file of organized information that may be updated and manipulated as needed.

data management system A set of commands used to search and retrieve content, update, and reference information from a database.

diagnostic routine A program designed to trace the source of program errors or the cause of a computer malfunction.

digital computer A computer in which discrete numbers are used to express data and instructions.

digitalization rate The speed with which digitalization occurs in an analog-to-digital converter.

direct access *See* random access.

disk (diskette) A circular plate coated with magnetic material that can be used to store computer data.

disk drive A device that is able to "read" data stored in magnetic material on a disk or to "write" data onto such a disk.

down time A period of time during which a computer system is out of operation.

dynamic range The range of voltage or input signals that results in a digital output in an analog-to-digital converter.

error message A message output by the computer, triggered by a program, indicating failure to follow a correct input/output routine, a hardware malfunction, or another problem that may cause the operation to discontinue.

execute Performance of an operation specified by a program routine or instruction.

file A collection of related data or information that is stored as a unit.

floppy disc *See* disc.

FORTRAN An acronym formed from the words *FOR*mula *TRAN*slation. It is a programming language used for mathematical and scientific operations.

garbage A popular term for meaningless data, usually the result of erroneous input/output operations or the result of data left in the computer memory from a previous unrelated project.

generation Pertaining to a group of computers developed within the same time period based on the model of an earlier product.

generator A routine designed to produce a program that will perform a specific version of a general operation, usually by filling in certain details within a predetermined framework.

hard copy A copy of the output of a computer that has been produced on paper, as distinguished from the electronic copy of the same data on disk or tape.

hardware The physical equipment or devices, such as the central processing unit, of a computer system. *See also* software.

hexadecimal A system of whole numbers with a base of 16 used in certain computer operations. Hexadecimal coding uses numerals 0 to 16 with the first 10 digits represented by 0 through 9 and the next six digits represented by the letters A through F.

high-level language Any computer language in which each instruction corresponds to a group of machine code instructions. Examples include BASIC and COBOL.

housekeeping Standard computer routines, such as deleting garbage or preliminary input/output functions, that are not directly related to a particular job.

hybrid computer A computer that is able to perform both analog and digital computing functions.

input The information a computer receives from a keyboard, tape, or disk.

input/out (I/O) terminal A computer device that is capable of both receiving and retrieving data.

instruction A part of a program that directs a computer to perform a single specific function as part of a sequence of functions.

interface A device that serves as a link or common surface boundary between two different parts of a computer system.

interrupt A temporary suspension of processing by a computer, caused by input or other activity by another part of the system.

I/O *See* input/output.

joystick A lever that is connected to a computer for use in moving the cursor from one point to another on a video display terminal.

K An abbreviation for kilo and a symbol for 1,000 (actually 2^{10}, or 1,024); it is commonly used to indicate the storage capacity of a computer memory. For example, a 64K memory has a theoretical capacity of $64 \times 1,024$, or 65,536, bytes or data storage locations.

keyboard A device that encodes characters for a computer function by depressing keys. Pressing the keys may punch holes in punched cards or provide a direct input of data to the computer.

label A group of computer characters used to identify a file, record, or memory storage area.

language A set of characters that can be used to form a meaningful set of words and symbols in writing instructions for a computer. Examples include ALGOL, BASIC, COBOL, and FORTRAN.

light pen A photoelectric device connected to the cathode ray tube of a display unit. It can be used by the operator to activate the computer to change or modify an image displayed by touching the pen to the screen.

machine language A language composed of a set of numbers and symbols that can direct computer operations without the need for translation.

magnetic memory A memory device that uses magnetic fields for storing data.

mainframe computer A large professional computer system used by a major industry or government agency, as distinguished from a smaller minicomputer or microcomputer.

memory The ability of a computer to store and retrieve data.

message A combination of characters or symbols used to communicate information between points of a computer system. *See also* error message.

microcomputer A small personal computer or word processor.

microprocessor A single large-scale integrated circuit on a fingernail-sized silicon chip. It contains thousands of individual circuit elements and is the heart of the central processing unit.

minicomputer A computer that is larger in capacity, flexibility, and cost than a microcomputer. It may commonly be used to control industrial processes.

MODEM An acronym formed from the words *MO*dulator *DEM*odulator. It is an electronic device that allows computer data to be carried over telephone lines.

mouse A movable device attached to a computer that permits the operator to reposition the cursor on the video display terminal. Manipulating the device moves the cursor vertically or horizontally on the screen.

multiprogramming The performance of two or more different computer functions at the same time.

off-line Pertaining to computer functions that are not under the direct control of a central processing unit or computer operator. The term is sometimes applied to hard copy or stored data.

on-line Computer operations that are under the direct control of the central processing unit or operator.

operating system (OS) A program that enables one to use a computer and its peripheral devices.

optical scanner An electronic device that scans direct or reflected light from a surface, such as a printed page, and converts the signals to machine-readable inputs.

OS *See* operating system.

output   The results of a computer operation, which may appear in the form of a printout or visual display.

peripheral   Any device that is separate from but connected to the computer for the purpose of supplying input or output functions, such as a modem or printer.

primary memory   The part of the computer used as the main storage area for data or programs.

RAM   *See* random access memory.

random access   The direct retrieval of data from a location in the computer memory without the need for sorting through sequential information.

random access memory (RAM)   A computer storage device that permits direct access to data independent of its location in the computer memory.

read only memory (ROM)   A type of computer memory that can be used to retrieve data for output only; new data cannot be written into it.

real time   Computer operations that permit rapid analyses of data so that decisions can be made immediately.

register   A part of the computer's central processing unit that stores information for future use. It may have specific uses, such as arithmetic functions or word processing. A computer may contain several different registers.

response time   The amount of time between the input of information into a computer and its output, or response to the input.

ROM   *See* read only memory.

serial processing   A type of computer function in which two or more programs are run in sequence rather than simultaneously.

software   The programs or instructions used to operate a computer system, as distinguished from the hardware.

storage capacity   The amount of data that can be stored in a computer memory. *See also* K.

streaming mode   A removable magnetic-tape backup system for hard disk drives. It permits copying data from the hard disk so that it can be preserved in the event of a hard drive failure.

terminal   An input/output device that allows an operator to control a computer. It may consist of a keyboard and video display screen.

time sharing   A computer function of handling two or more tasks simultaneously, as when a mainframe computer is used to process operations of several remote terminals at the same time. Such a system depends on buffering and switching inputs and outputs for each terminal. This is done at such a high rate of speed that operators of individual terminals are unaware that others are sharing the same central processing unit.

track   A segment of a disk or other magnetic storage device that stores a fixed amount of data in a designated address for rapid retrieval.

Winchester disk drive   A type of hard disk drive capable of transferring data, detecting errors, and making corrections at a high rate of speed.

word   A fixed number of bits processed by a computer as a single basic unit.

write   The process of recording data in a computer memory.

write-protected disk   A computer disk designed to prevent altering the data stored on it.

X-Y digitizer   An electronic device that allows a cursor or light pen to produce the X and Y coordinates of a graph on a video display terminal.

Additional Sources of Information

Organizations and Services

Academy of Natural Sciences
19th and the Parkway
Philadelphia, PA 19103

American Association for the Advancement of Science
1333 H Street, NW
Washington, DC 20005

American Astronomical Society
211 FitzRandolph Road
Princeton, NH 08540

American Geological Institute
5205 Leesburg Pike
Falls Church, VA 22041

American Institute of Physics
335 East 45th Street
New York, NY 10017

American Museum of Natural History
Central Park West and 79th Street
New York, NY 10024

Hale Observatories
813 Santa Barbara Street
Pasadena, CA 91101

Institute for Scientific Information
325 Chestnut Street
Philadelpha, PA 19106

National Academy of Sciences
2101 Constitution Avenue, NW
Washington, DC 20418

National Bureau of Standards
Gaithersburg, MD 20899

National Oceanic and Atmospheric Administration
Department of Commerce
Washington, DC 20230

National Science Foundation
1800 G Street, NW
Washington, DC 20550

National Technical Information Service
Department of Commerce
5285 Port Royal Road
Springfield, VA 22161

New York Academy of Sciences
2 East 63rd Street
New York, NY 10021

Scientists Institute for Public Information
355 Lexington Avenue
New York, NY 10017

Smithsonian Institution
1000 Jefferson Drive, SW
Washington, DC 20560

Books

Asimov, Isaac. *Asimov's New Guide to Science.* Basic Books, 1984.

Brown, Stanley. *The Realm of Science.* 21 vols. Touchstone, 1972.

Bunch, Bryan, and Hellemans, Alexander. *Timetables of Science: A Chronology of the Most Important People and Events in the History of Science.* Simon & Schuster, 1988.

Considine, Douglas. *Van Nostrand's Scientific Encyclopedia,* 6th ed. Van Nostrand Reinhold, 1982.

Dean, John A. *Lange's Handbook of Chemistry,* 13th ed. McGraw-Hill, 1985.

McGraw-Hill Encyclopedia of Engineering. McGraw-Hill, 1983.

McGraw-Hill Encyclopedia of Science and Technology, 5th ed. 5 vols. McGraw-Hill, 1982.

Runcorn, S. K. *Earth Science.* 3 vols. Elsevier Science, 1971.

Weast, Robert. *Handbook of Chemistry and Physics,* 69th ed. CRC Press, 1988.

6

Inventions and Scientific Discoveries

Significant Inventions and Technological Advances

Year	Invention or Achievement	Inventor/Origin
B.C. c. 6500	Potter's wheel	Asia Minor
c. 5000	Woven cloth	Mesopotamia
c. 4500	Copper working	Rudna Glava, Yugoslavia
c. 3500	Wheeled vehicles	Sumer and Syria
	Gold mining	Mesopotamia
c. 3150	Irrigation	Nile River, Upper Egypt
c. 2640	Silk production	Si-ling Chi
c. 2500	Ox-drawn plow	Egypt
	Cotton production	India
c. 1300	Musical notation	Ugarit, Syria
c. 570	Geographical and star charts	Anaximander of Miletus
c. 221	Gunpowder	Chin dynasty (China)
c. 200	Archimedean screw (lifting device)	Archimedes
c. 100	Stone bridge	Roman engineers (Tiber River, Rome)
	Wheel bearings	On a wagon found at Dejbjerg, Jutland
c. 85	Seed-planting machine	China
c. 40	Rotary winnowing machine	China
A.D. c. 100	Paper making	Ts'ai Lun
c. 180	Rotary fan	China
c. 230	Wheelbarrow	China
c. 550	Watermill	Belisarius
580	Iron-chain suspension bridge	China
640	Windmill	Persia
c. 700	Porcelain	T'ang dynasty (China)
c. 900	Moldboard plow	China
980	Canal locks	Ciao Wei-yo
1100	Rocket	China
1150	Paper mill	Xativa, Spain
1250	Magnifying glass	Roger Bacon
1260	Gun/cannon	Konstantin Anklitzen
1269	360° compass	Petrus Peregrinus de Maricourt
1280	Belt-driven spinning wheel	Hans Speyer
1285	Eyeglasses	Alessandro de Spina
1326	Metal cannon	Rinaldo di Villamagna
1335	Automatic striking clock	Palace Chapel of the Visconti, Milan, Italy
1360	Mechanical clock	Henri de Vick of Wurttemburg for King Charles V of France
1410	Wire	Rodolph of Nuremberg
1437	Perspective views (pinholes)	Leon Battista Alberti
1451	Printing press	Johannes Gutenberg
1455	Cast-iron pipe	Castle of Dillenburgh, Germany
1510	Pocket watch	Peter Henlein
1520	Spirally grooved rifle barrel	August Kotter
1525	Portable shotgun (harquebus)	Marquis of Pescara
1540	Artificial limbs	Ambroise Paré
	Pistol	Camillo Vettelli

Year	*Invention or Achievement*	*Inventor/Origin*
1550	Screwdriver	Gunsmiths and armorers (location unknown)
	Wrench	Unknown
1557	Enamel	Bernard Palissy
1561	Dredger	Pieter Breughel
1565	Graphite pencil	Konrad Gesner
1569	Screw-cutting machine and ornamental turning lathe	Jacques Besson
1585	Time bomb	Dutch siege of Antwerp
1589	Hosiery-knitting machine	Rev. William Lee
	Flush toilet	Sir John Harington
1590	Compound microscope	Zacharias Jansen
1592	Wind-powered sawmill	Cornelius Corneliszoon
1599	Silk-knitting machine	Rev. William Lee
1600	Wind-driven land vehicle	Simon Stevin
1603	Pantograph	Christopher Scheiner
1606	Surveying chain	Edmund Gunter
1609	Astronomical telescope	Galileo Galilei
1611	Double convex microscope	Johannes Kepler
1615	Solar-powered motor	Salomon de Caux
1616	Medical thermometer	Santorio Santorio
1620	Submarine	Cornelis Jocobzoon Drebbel
1621	Rectilinear slide rule	William Oughtred
1623	Calculating machine	Wilhelm Schickard
1630	Circular slide rule	Richard Delamain
1638	Micrometer	William Gascoigne
1643	Barometer (Torricellian tube)	Evangelista Torricelli and Vincenzo Viviani
1648	Hydraulic press	Blaise Pascal
1654	Air vacuum pump	Otto von Guericke
1657	Pendulum clock	Christiaan Huygens
1658	Clock balance spring	Robert Hooke
1664	Hygrometer	Francesco Folli
1667	Wind gauge	Christian Forner
1668	Reflecting telescope	Isaac Newton
1671	Silk spinning machine	Edmund Blood
1674	Tourniquet	Morel, France
1675	Calibrated foot ruler	Unknown
1676	Artificial water filtration	William Woolcott
1680	Pressure cooker	Denis Papin
1690	Steam engine	Denis Papin
1695	Epsom salts	Nehemiah Grew
1699	Portable fire pump	Daumier Duperrier
1701	Machine seed drill	Jethro Tull
1702	Tidal pump	George Sorocold
1709	Anemometer	Wolfius
1711	Tuning fork	John Shore
1712	Steam piston engine	Thomas Newcomen and John Calley
1716	True porcelain (Meissen)	Johann Friedrich Bottger
1719	Full-color printing process	Jakob Christof Le Blon
1718	Machine gun	James Puckle
1731	Octant (Hadley's quadrant)	John Hadley

Year	*Invention or Achievement*	*Inventor/Origin*
1732	Copper-zinc alloy	Christopher Pinchbeck
	Threshing machine	Michael Menzies
1733	Arsenic	George Brandt
	Flint-glass lens	Chester Moor Hall
	Flying shuttle	John Kay
1742	Crucible steel production	Benjamin Huntsman
1743	Wool carding machine	David Bourne
	Compound lever	John Wyatt
1746	Leyden jar (prototype of electrical condenser)	Pieter van Musschenbroeck and Dean E. G. von Kleist
1748	Sea quadrant	B. Cole
1750	Dynamometer	Gaspard de Prony
1752	Lightning conductor	Benjamin Franklin
1755	Iron-girder bridge	M. Garvin
1757	Sextant	John Campbell
1758	Achromatic lens (for eyeglasses)	John Dolland
	Refracting telescope	John Dolland
1760	Screw manufacturing machine	Job and William Wyatt
	Cast-iron cog wheel	Carron Iron Works, Scotland
1761	Mass production of steel scissors	Robert Hinchliffe
1762	Fire extinguisher	Dr. Godfrey
	Sandwich	Fourth Earl of Sandwich
1764	Spinning jenny	James Hargreaves
1765	Steam engine condenser	James Watt
1768	Areometer	Antoine Baumé
1770	Electric battery	John Cuthbertson
1775	Chain-driven machine	Crane (England)
1776	Submersible	David Bushnell
1777	Circular saw	Samuel Miller
	Iron boat	Yorkshire, England
1778	Mortise tumbler lock	Robert Barron
	Copying machine	James Watt
1783	Hot-air balloon	Joseph-Michel and Jacques-Etienne Montgolfier
	Hydrogen balloon	Jacques Alexandre Charles
	Tungsten	Don Fausto and Juan José d'Elhuyar
1784	Bifocal lenses	Benjamin Franklin
	Model helicopter	Launoy (France)
	Rope-spinning machine	Robert March
1785	Automatic grist mill	Oliver Evans
1787	Roller bearings	John Garnett
	Power loom	Edmund Cartwright
1790	Cotton spinning and weaving machine (first U.S. patent)	William Pollard
	Sewing machine	Thomas Saint
1794	Ball bearings	Philip Vaughan
	Cotton gin	Eli Whitney
1796	Lithography	Alois Sennefelder
1797	Parachute	André Jacques Garnerin
1798	Mass production	Eli Whitney
1800	Submarine (metal clad)	Robert Fulton
1802	Commercial steamboat	William Symington
1803	Spray gun (aerosol medication)	Alan de Vilbiss

Year	Invention or Achievement	Inventor/Origin
1804	Fishnet-making machine	Joseph Marie Charles Jacquard
	Steam locomotive	Richard Trevithick
1805	Mechanical silk loom	Joseph Marie Jacquard
	Amphibious vehicle	Oliver Evans
1806	Beaufort wind scale	Francis Beaufort
	Carbon paper	Ralph Wedgwood
1807	Patent for gas-driven automobile	Isaac de Rivez
	Long-distance steamboat	Robert Fulton
1810	Metronome	Dietrich Nikolaus Winkel
	Mowing machine	Peter Gaillard
1812	Canned food	Bryan Doukin
1813	Gun cartridge	Samuel Pauly
	Gas meter	Samuel Clegg
	Mine safety lamp	Humphrey Davy and George Stephenson
1816	Electric telegraph	Home Riggs Popham
	Stethoscope	René Théophile Hyacinthe Laënnec
1817	Dental plate	Anthony A. Plankston
1819	Dental amalgam	Charles Bell
	Dioptric system (for lighthouses)	Augustin Jean Fresnel
1821	Heliotrope	Carl Friedrich Gauss
1822	Thermocouple	Thomas Johann Seebeck
1824	Galvanometer	André-Marie Ampère
1825	Binocular telescope	J. P. Lemiere
1826	Gas stove	James Sharp
	Friction match	John Walken
1827	Astigmatic lens	George Biddell Airy
	Microphone	Charles Wheatstone
	Trifocal lens	John Isaac Hawkins
	Water turbine	Benoit Fourneyron
1828	Differential gear	Onesiphore Pecqueur
	Stethoscope with earpiece	Pierre Adolphe Poirry
1830	Thermostat	André Ure
	Phosphorous matches	Charles Sauria
	Lawn mower	Edwin Beard Budding
	Paraffin	Karl, Baron von Reichenbach
1831	Electric bell	Joseph Henry
	Reaping machine	Cyrus McCormick
1832	Hydraulic-powered factory	E. Egbers and Timothy Bail
1833	Differential calculating machine	Charles Babbage
1835	Automatic revolver	Samuel Colt
1836	Steam shovel	William Smith Otis
	Color printing	George Baxter
	Stroboscope	Joseph Antoine Ferdinand Plateau
	Combine harvester	H. Hoare and J. Hascall
1837	Braille reading system	Louis Braille
	Daguerreotype	Louis Jacques Mandé Daguerre
	Electric telegraph	William Fothergill Cooke and Charles Wheatstone
	Electric motor	Thomas Davenport
1838	Morse code	Samuel F. B. Morse
	Stereoscope	Charles Wheatstone
1840	Chronoscope	Charles Wheatstone

Year	Invention or Achievement	Inventor/Origin
1840	Electroplating	John Wright
	Vulcanization	Charles Goodyear
1842	Carbon electrode battery	Robert Wilhelm Bunsen
	Underwater telegraph cable	Samuel F. B. Morse
1845	Rotary printing press	Richard M. Hoe
	Giant telescope	William Parsons
1846	Sewing machine	Elias Howe
1849	Schrapnel shell	Edward Boxer
1850	Refrigerator	James Harrison and Alexander Catlin Twining
1851	Odometer	William Grayson
	Ophthalmoscope	Herman von Helmholtz
	Flash photography	Henry F. Talbot
1852	Steam-powered airship	Henri Giffard
	Piloted glider	George Cayley
	Microfilm	John Benjamin Dancer
1853	Gas engine	Eugenio Barsanti and Felice Matteucci
	Hypodermic syringe	Charles Gabriel Pravaz
1855	Bunsen burner	Robert Wilhelm Eberhard von Bunsen
	Stopwatch	Edward Daniel Johnson
	Safety match	Johan Edvard Lundstrom
1857	Passenger elevator	Elisha G. Otis
1860	Linoleum	Frederick Walton
	Snap button	John Newnham
1861	Pneumatic drill	Germain Sommelier
1862	Machine gun	Richard Jordan Gatling
	Ironclad ship	Jon Ericsson
1863	Phonograph (machine that wrote down what was played on a piano)	Fenby, U.S.
	Subway train (steam railway)	George Pearson
	TNT	J. Wilbrand
1865	Electric arc welding	Henry Wilde
	Reinforced concrete	W. B. Wilkinson
	Yale cylinder lock	Linus Yale, Jr.
	Offset printing (web press)	William Bullock
	Nitroglycerine	Alfred Nobel
1866	Transatlantic cable	Cyrus West Field, Samuel Canning, and Daniel Gooch
	Lip reading	Alexander Melville Bell
1867	Dynamite	Alfred Nobel
	Barbed wire	Lucien Smith
1868	Margarine	Hippolyte Mege-Mouries
	Stapler	Charles Henry Gould
	Plywood	John K. Mayo
	Pocket calculator	Charles Henry Webb
1869	Color photography	Charles Cros and Louise Ducos du Hauron
	Celluloid	John Wesley Hyatt and Isaiah Smith Hyatt
	Rayon	Paul Schutzenberger
	Vacuum cleaner	Ives W. McGaffey
1872	Hydroplane	Rev. Charles Meade Ramus
	Solar water distillation	Charles Wilson

Year	Invention or Achievement	Inventor/Origin
1873	Direct current electric motor	Zenobe Théophile Gramme
	Typewriter	Christopher Latham Sholes
1875	Mimeograph	Thomas Alva Edison
1876	Articulating telephone	Alexander Graham Bell
	Dewey decimal system	Melvil Dewey
	Carburetor (surface type)	Gottlieb Daimler
1877	Differential gear	James Starley
	Switchboard	Edwin T. Holmes
1878	Cathode ray tube	William Crookes
	Phonograph	Thomas Alva Edison
	Milking machine	L. O. Colvin
	Electric alternator	Zenobe Théophile Gramme and Hippolyte Fontaine
1879	Arc lighting system	Edwin James Houston and Elihu Thomson
	Carbon filament light bulb	Joseph Wilson Swan and Thomas Alva Edison
	Cash register	James J. Ritty
	Saccharin	Constantine Fahlberg and Ira Remsen
1880	Hearing aid	R. G. Rhodes
1881	Interferometer	Albert A. Michelson
	Rechargeable battery	Camille Faure
	Telephotography	Shelford Bidwell
1882	Induction coil	Lucien Gaulard and John Gibbs
	Commercial electric fan	Schuyler Skaats Wheeler
	Skyscraper	William Le Baron Jenny
1883	Long-span suspension bridge (Brooklyn Bridge)	John Augustus Roebling
1884	Fountain pen	Lewis Edson Waterman
	Carburetor (float-feed spray)	Edward Butler
1885	Gas-engine automobile	Gottlieb Daimler, Wilhelm Maybach, and Karl Friedrich Benz
	Gas-engine motorcycle	Gottlieb Daimler and Wilhelm Maybach
1886	Coca-Cola	John Pemberton
	Railway car brake (air brake)	George Westinghouse
	Comptometer	Dorr Eugene Felt
	Linotype machine	Ottmar Mergenthaler
1887	Mach supersonic scale	Ernst Mach
	Contact lens	Eugen A. Frick
	Electrocardiogram	Augustus Desire Waller
1888	Alternating current (AC) motor	Nikola Tesla and Galileo Ferraris
	Cellulose camera film	John Carbutt
	Monorail	Charles Lartigue
	Monotype	Tolbert Lanston
1889	Gas engine farm tractor	Charter Engine Co., Chicago
	Cotton picker	Angus Campbell
1890	Motion pictures	William Friese-Greene
	Electric subway train	London, England
1891	Electric motor car	William Morrison
	Silicon carbide	Edward Goodrich Acheson
	Flashlight	Bristol Electric Lamp Co., England
	Aluminum boat	Escher Wyss & Co., Switzerland
	Zipper	Whitcombe L. Judson

Year	Invention or Achievement	Inventor/Origin
1892	Diesel engine	Rudolf Diesel
	Vacuum flash (early thermos)	Sir James Dewar
1893	Electric toaster	Crompton & Co., England
1894	Escalator	Jesse W. Reno
	Wireless telegraphy	Guglielmo Marconi
1895	Electric hand drill	Wilhelm Fein
	Photographic typesetting	William Friese-Greene
1896	Modern manual typewriter	Herman L. Wagner
1897	Plasticine	William Harbutt
	Worm gear	Frederick W. Lanchester
1898	Loudspeaker	Horace Short
1900	Paper clip	Johann Vaaler
	Alkaline battery	Thomas Alva Edison
1901	Electric typewriter	Thaddeus Cahill
1902	Air conditioning	Willis H. Carrier
	Disc brakes	Frederick W. Lanchester
1903	Airplane	Orville and Wilbur Wright
1904	Electronic vacuum tube	John Ambrose Fleming
1905	Chemical foam fire extinguisher	Alexander Laurent
	Hydraulic centrifugal clutch	Hermann Fottinger
1906	Crystal radio apparatus	H. H. C. Dunwoody and G. W. Pickard
	Animated cartoon film	James S. Blackton and Walter Booth
	Motion picture sound	Eugen Augustin Lauset
1907	Detergents (household)	Henkel et Cie, Germany
	Gas engine helicopter	Paul Cornu and Louis Breguet
	Monoplane	Louis Bleriot
	Upright vacuum cleaner (attached dust bag)	J. Murray Spangler
1908	Bakelite	Leo Henrik Baekeland
	Cellophane	Jacques E. Brandenberger
1909	IUD (intrauterine device)	R. Richter
1910	Neon lighting	Georges Claude
1911	Binet intelligence test	Alfred Binet
	Calculating machine (full automatic multiplication and division)	Jay R. Munroe
1912	Diesel locomotive	North British Locomotive Co., England
	Cabin biplane (jetliner forerunner)	Igor Sikorsky
	Stainless steel	Harry Brearley, Elwood Hanes, Edward Maurer, and Benno Strauss
1913	Isotope labeling	Georg von Hevesy and Friedrich A. Paneth
1914	Brassiere	Mary Phelps Jacob
	Leica 35mm camera	Oskar Barnack
	Tear gas	Dr. von Tappen
1915	Amplitude modulation (AM) radio	Hendrick Johannes van der Bijl and Raymond A. Heising
1917	VHF electromagnetic waves	Guglielmo Marconi
1918	Electric food mixer	Universal Co., U.S.
	Domestic refrigerator	Nathaniel Wales and E. J. Copeland
1920	Commercial radio broadcasts	Station KDKA, Pittsburgh, PA

Year	Invention or Achievement	Inventor/Origin
1921	Hydraulic four-wheel brakes	Duesenberg Motor Co., U.S.
	Lie detector	John Larsen
	Wirephoto	Western Union Cables, U.S.
1922	Three-dimensional movies	Perfect Pictures, U.S.
1923	Frozen food	Clarence Birdseye
1924	Wash/spin dry machine	Savage Arms Corp., U.S.
1925	Hi-fi radio loudspeaker	C. W. Rice and E. W. Kellogg
1926	Aerosol can	Erik Rotheim
	Synthetic rubber	I. G. Farben, Germany
	Liquid-fueled rocket	Robert H. Goddard
	Television	John Logie Baird, C. F. Jenkins, and D. Mihaly
1927	Iron lung	Philip Drinker and Louis Shaw
	Pop-up toaster	Charles Strite
1928	Color television	John Logie Baird
	Geiger counter	Hans Geiger
	Teletype	Edward Ernst Kleinschmidt
	PVC (polyvinylchloride)	Carbide Corp., Carbon Chemical Corp., and Du Pont, U.S.
1929	Electron microscope	Max Knoll and Ernst Ruska
	Coaxial cable	Bell Telephone Laboratories, U.S.
1930	Cyclotron	Ernest O. Lawrence and N. E. Edlesfsen
	Polystyrene	I. G. Farben, Germany
1931	Photographic exposure meter	J. Thomas Rhamstine
	Fiberglass	Owens Illinois Glass Co., U.S.
	Radio astronomy	Karl Guthe Jansky
	Blood bank	Sergei Sergeivitch
	TWX (teletypewriter exchange)	Bell Telephone & Telegraph, U.S.
	Electric razor	Jacob Schick
1932	Defibrillator	William Bennett Kouwenhoven
	Wind tunnel	Ford Motor Co., U.S.
1933	Frequency modulation (FM)	Edwin H. Armstrong
	Polyethylene	Reginald Gibson and E. W. Fawcett
1935	Electronic hearing aid	Edwin A. Steven
	Richter earthquake scale	Charles Francis Richter
1936	Jet engine	Frank Whittle and Hans von Ohain
	Helicopter (contra-rotating rotors)	Henrich Focke
	Plexiglas	I. G. Farben, Germany
1937	Radio telescope	Grote Reber
	Nylon	Du Pont, U.S.
1938	Pressurized airplane cabin	Transcontinental Airways, Boeing 307 Stratoliner
	Ballpoint pen	Ladislao J. and Georg Biro
	Fluorescent lighting	Arthur H. Compton and George Inman
	Photocopy machine	Chester Carlson
1939	Jet aircraft	Hans von Ohain
	Binary calculator	John Atanasoff and George R. Stibitz
	DDT	Paul Hermann Müller
	Microfilm camera	Elgin G. Fassel
1940	Radar	Robert M. Page (word coined by S. M. Tucker)
	Automatic transmission	General Motors, U.S.

Year	*Invention or Achievement*	*Inventor/Origin*
1941	Microwave radar	U.S. Radiation Laboratory
	Dacron	John R. Whinfield
1942	Manmade atomic reaction (Manhattan Project)	Enrico Fermi and team
1943	Teflon	Du Pont, U.S.
1944	Pyrex telescope lens	Corning Glass Works and George E. Hale for the Mount Palomar Observatory
1945	Artificial kidney	Willem J. Kolff
	Atomic bomb	J. R. Oppenheimer, Arthur H. Compton, Enrico Fermi, and Leo Szilard
	Tupperware	Earl W. Tupper
	Vinyl floor covering	Du Pont, U.S.
1946	Electronic vacuum tube computer (ENIAC)	John W. Mauchly and J. Presper Eckert
1947	Holography	Dennis Gabor
	Supersonic aircraft	Bell XS-I, U.S.
1948	Transistor	William Shockley, John Bardeen, and Walter H. Brattain
	Atomic clock	William F. Libby
	Cybernetics	Norbert Wiener
	Long-playing phonograph record (microgroove record)	Peter Goldmark
	Solid electric guitar	Leo (Clarence) Fender, "Doc" Kauffman, and George Fullerton
	Velcro	Georges de Mestral
1949	Jet airliner	R. E. Bishop and team
1950	Xerographic copying machine (for office)	Haloid Co., U.S.
1952	Artificial heart valve	Charles A. Hufnagel
	Hydrogen bomb	Edward Teller and Igor Kurchatov
	Experimental videotape	John Mullin and Wayne Johnson
1953	Heart-lung machine	John H. Gibbon
1954	Regular broadcast of color television	National Television System Committee, U.S.
	Transistor radio	Regency Electronics, U.S.
1955	Felt-tip pen	Esterbrook, England
	Stereo tape recording	EMI Stereosonic Tapes
	Hovercraft	Christopher S. Cockerell
1956	Plastic contact lens	Norman Bier
1957	Sputnik (artificial satellite)	U.S.S.R.
	FORTRAN computer language	John Backus and team for IBM, U.S.
	Intercontinental ballistic missile	U.S.S.R.
1958	Laser	Charles A. Townes
	Communications satellite	SCORE, U.S.
	ALGOL computer language	Switzerland
	Hula hoop	Richard P. Knerr and Arthur K. "Spud" Melvin
1959	COBOL computer language	U.S. Conference on Data Systems Languages
	Ion engine	Alvin T. Forrester

Year	Invention or Achievement	Inventor/Origin
	Tunnel diode	Sony, Japan, based on work by Leo Esaki
	Integrated circuit	Jack S. Kilby, Texas Instruments, U.S.
	Microwave radio system	Pacific Great Eastern Railway between Vancouver and Dawson Creek-Fort St. John, British Columbia, Canada
1960	Nuclear-powered ships	USS *Enterprise*
	Argon ion laser	D. R. Herriott, A. Javan, and W. R. Bennett, Bell Laboratories, U.S.
	Vertical takeoff and lift aircraft	Frank Taylor and team at Short Brothers & Harland, Northern Ireland
	Weather satellite	NASA, U.S.
1961	Manned spaceflight	*Vostok I*, U.S.S.R.
	Stereophonic radio broadcast	Zenith and General Electric Companies, U.S.
1962	Minicomputer	Digital Corp., U.S.
	Robotics	Rand Corp. and IBM, U.S.
	X-ray sources in the constellations	Riccardo Giacconi
1963	Cassette tapes	Philips Co., The Netherlands
1964	BASIC computer language	Thomas E. Kurtz and John G. Kemeny
	Acrylic paint	Reeves Ltd., England
	Carbon fiber	RAF Farnborough, England
	Home-use transistor videotape recorder	Sony, Japan
1965	Word processor	IBM, U.S.
1966	Integrated radio circuit	Sony, Japan
	Noise reduction system	Ray M. Dolby
1967	Bubble memory prototype	A. H. Bobeck and team at Bell Telephone Laboratories, U.S.
1968	Pulsars	Jocelyn Bell
	Holographic storage technique	Bell Telephone Laboratories, U.S.
1969	Moon landing	U.S.
	PASCAL computer language	Niklaus Wirth
	Videotape cassette	Sony, Japan
	Jumbo jet airliner	Joe Sutherland and team at Boeing, U.S.
1970	Bar code system	Monarch Marking, U.S., and Plessey Telecommunications, England
	Computer floppy disk	IBM, U.S.
	Remote-controlled lunar vehicle	U.S.S.R.
1971	Earth-orbiting space station	U.S.S.R.
	Liquid crystal display (LCD)	Hoffmann-LaRoche, Switzerland
	Quartz digital watch	George Theiss and Willy Crabtree
1972	Video disk	Philips Co., The Netherlands
	Video game	Noland Bushnel
1973	Computerized tomography (CAT scan)	Allan Macleod Cormack and Godfrey N. Hounsfield
	Earth-orbiting space station	U.S.
	Microcomputer	Trong Truong
1974	Nonimpact printing	Honeywell, U.S.

Year	Invention or Achievement	Inventor/Origin
1975	Monoclonal antibodies	Cesar Milstein
	Betamax videotaping system	Sony, Japan
	Video home system (VHS)	Matsushita/JVC, Japan
1976	Mars space probes	NASA's *Viking I* and *Viking II*
1977	Neutron bomb	U.S. military
	Space shuttle	NASA, U.S.
	Alkyd paint	Winsor & Newton Ltd., England
1978	Test-tube baby	Patrick C. Steptoe and Robert G. Edwards
1979	Rubik's cube	Erno Rubik
1980	Solar-powered aircraft	Paul Macready
1981	Silicon 32-bit chip	Hewlett-Packard, U.S.
	Nuclear magnetic resonance (NMR) scanner	Thorn-EMI Research Laboratories and Nottingham University, England
1982	Artificial heart	Robert Jarvik
	Airborne observatory	NASA, U.S.
1983	Biopol (biodegradable plastic)	ICI Agricultural Division, England
	Biosensors	Cambridge Life Sciences, England
	Carbon-fiber aircraft wing	Great Britain
	512K dynamic access memory chip	IBM, U.S.
1984	Compact disk player	Sony and Fujitsu Companies, Japan, and Philips Co., The Netherlands
	Megabit computer chip	IBM, U.S.
1985	CD-ROM (compact-disk read-only memory)	Hitachi, Japan
	Image digitizer	Optronics, England
	Polymer electric conducter	Terje Skotheim and team, Brookhaven National Laboratory, U.S.
	Soft bifocal contact lens	Sofsite Contact Lens Laboratory, U.S.
1986	Uranus moons photographs	National Aeronautics and Space Administration, U.S.
	Synthetic skin	G. Gregory Gallico, III
1988	Patented animal life	Philip Leder, Timothy Stewart

Significant Scientific Discoveries

Year		Discovery	Discoverer/Origin
B.C.	c. 12,000	Fire	Unknown
	c. 10,000	Zero	Hindu priests
	c. 1300	32-letter alphabet	Ugarit, Syria
	c. 1100	Phoenician alphabet (22 letters)	
A.D.	c. 80	Magnetism	China
	200	Blood circulation	Galen
	220	Ellipse and hyperbola	Appollonius
	520	Decimal number system	Aryabhata and Varamihara
	1287	Nitric acid	Raymond Lully
	1538	Optic nerve	Constanzo Vardio

Year	*Discovery*	*Discoverer/Origin*
1550	Ligature	Ambrose Paré
1581	Pendulum motion	Galileo Galilei
1611	Coke	Simon Sturtevant
	Rainbow theory	Johannes Kepler
1614	Logarithms	John Napier
1615	Surveying by triangulation	Willebrord Snell van Roigen
1622	Lacteals	Gaspare Asellio
1631	Vernier scale	Pierre Vernier
1647	Map of moon and star catalog	Hevelius (Johannes Hewelcke)
1648	Hydrochloric acid	Johann Rudolph Glauber
1650	Lymph glands	Olvas Rudbek and Thomas Bartholin
1658	Red blood cells	Jan Swammerdam
1661	Wood (methyl) alcohol	Robert Boyle
1662	Boyle's law/gas pressure laws	Robert Boyle
1666	Principles of integral calculus	Isaac Newton
1667	Blood transfusion (lamb to boy)	Jean-Baptiste Denys, France
1669	Phosphorus	Hennig Brand
1682	Halley's comet	Edmund Halley
1684	Theory of gravity	Isaac Newton
1687	Statistical mathematics	Sir William Petty
1690	Speed of light	Ole Romer
1694	Plant pollen	Rudolph Jakob Cammerarius
1695	Epsom salts	Nehemiah Grew
1702	Boron/borax	Guillaume Homberg
1703	Binary number system	Gottfried Wilhelm Leibnitz
1709	Coke smelting (iron)	Abraham Derby
1715	Fahrenheit temperature scale	Gabriel Daniel Fahrenheit
1729	Aberration of light	Rev. James Bradley
1735	Platinum	Don Antonio de Ulloa de la Torre
1737	Plant classification system	Carl Linne
1740	Curare (drug)	Charles Marie de Lacondamine
1742	Celsius temperature scale	Anders Celsius
1747	Scurvy cure	James Lind
1751	Nickel	Axel Frederik Cronstedt
1756	Carbon dioxide	Joseph Black
1761	Medical percussion method (diagnostic technique)	Joseph Leopold Avenbrugger
1766	Hydrogen	Henry Cavendish
1770	Sulfur dioxide	Joseph Priestley
1771	Fluorine	Karl Wilhelm Scheele
1772	Nitrogen	Daniel Rutherford
	Oxygen	Karl Wilhelm Scheele and Joseph Priestley
1774	Ammonia	Joseph Priestley
	Barium	Karl Wilhelm Scheele
	Chlorine	Karl Wilhelm Scheele
	Manganese	Karl Wilhelm Scheele
1775	Digitalis (as drug)	William Withering
1778	Molybdenum	Karl Wilhelm Scheele
1779	Glycerine	Karl Wilhelm Scheele
1780	Artificial insemination	Lazzaro Spallanzani
1781	Uranus	Frederick William Herschel
1782	Tellurium	Franz Joseph Müller

Year	*Discovery*	*Discoverer/Origin*
1785	Methane and ethylene	Claude Louis Berthollet
1789	Uranium	Martin Heinrich Klaproth
	Zirconium	Martin Heinrich Klaproth
1793	Astigmatism	Thomas Young
	Strontium	Thomas Charles Hope
	Daltonism (colorblindness)	John Dalton
1796	Smallpox vaccine	Edward Jenner
1797	Chromium	Louis Nicolas Vaquelin
1799	Metric system	French Academy of Sciences
1800	Infrared light	William Herschel
1801	Asteroids	Giuseppe Piazzi
	Niobium	Charles Hatchett
	Wave theory of light	Thomas Young
	Ultraviolet light	Johann Wilhelm Ritter and William Hyde Wollaston (England)
1803	Atomic theory	John Dalton
	Iridium	Smithson Tennant
1805	Morphine	Friedrich Wilhelm Adam Serturner
1807	Potassium	Humphrey Davy
	Sodium	Humphrey Davy
	Sensory-motor nerve system	Charles Bell
1810	Homeopathy	Samuel Hahnemann
	Ammonia-soda reaction	Augustin Jean Fresnel
1811	Avogadro's law	Amedeo de Quaregna e di Ceretto
	Iodine	Bernard Courteois
1817	Parkinson's disease	James Parkinson
	Lithium	John August Arfwedson
1818	Cadmium	Friedrich Strohmeyer
	Blood transfusion (early attempt)	Thomas Blundell
	Selenium	Johan Jakob Berzelius
	Hydrogen peroxide	Baron Louis-Jacques Thénard
	Strychnine	Pierre-Joseph Pelletier and Joseph Biènaimé Caventou
	Geothermal energy experiment	F. de Larderel
1819	Magnetic field	Hans Cristian Oersted
1820	Diphtheria	Pierre Fidèle Bretonneau
	Quinine	Pierre Joseph Pelletier
1821	Caffeine	Pierre Joseph Pelletier
1824	Electromagnetism	William Sturgeon
	Magnetic pull	François Dominique Arago
1827	Aluminum	Friedrich Wohler
	Electrical resistance	George Simon Ohm
1828	Cocoa	Conrad van Houten
	Beryllium	Friedrich Wohler
	Thorium	Johan Jakob Berzelius
1830	Vanadium	Nils Gabriel Sefstrom
1831	Electromagnetic induction	Michael Faraday
	Electromagnetic balance	Antoine César Becquerel
	Magnetic north pole	James Clark Ross
1833	Creosote	Karl, Baron von Reichenbach
	Nervous reflex	Marshall Hall
1834	Galvanic cells (continuous electric light)	James Bowman Lindsay

Year	Discovery	Discoverer/Origin
1836	Acetylene	Edmund Davy
1838	Plant cells	Matthias Jakob Schleiden
1839	Animal cells	Theodore Schwann
	Protoplasm	Jan Evangelista Purkinje
1840	Ozone	Christian Friedrich Schonbein
1842	Ether anesthesia	Crawford Williamson
1844	Nitrous oxide anesthesia	Horace Wells and Gardner Q. Colton
1846	Neptune	Johann Gottfield Galle and Heinrich Ludwig d'Arrest
1847	Nitroglycerine	Ascanio Sobrero
	Chloroform anesthesia	Jacob Bell and James Young Simpson
1850	Foucault's pendulum (proving Earth's rotation)	Jean Bernard Léon Foucault
1851	Doppler principle	Christian Doppler
1852	Fluorescence	George Gabriel Stokes
1854	Paleozoic fossils	Adam Sedgwick
1855	Spinal anesthesia	J. L. Corning, U.S.
1858	Cell replication theory	Rudolf Virchow
	Mobius band	August Mobius
	Atomic and molecular weights	Stanislao Cannizzaro
1859	Cathode rays	Julius Plucker
	Evolution theory	Charles Darwin
1860	Cesium	Robert Wilhelm Bunsen and Gustav Robert Kirchhoff
1861	Speech center of brain	Pierre Paul Broca
	Sodium carbonate process	Ernest Solvay
1864	Electromagnetic wave transmission	Mahlon Loomis
	Pasteurization	Louis Pasteur
1865	Genetics	Gregor Johann Mendel
1867	Formaldehyde	August Wilhelm von Hofmann
1868	Helium (in sun's chromosphere)	Edward Frankland and Joseph Norman Lockyer
1869	Periodic law	Dmitri Ivanovitch Mendeleyev
1873	Electromagnetic radiation	James Clerk Maxwell
1877	Liquid oxygen	Louis-Paul Cailletet and Raoul-Pierre Pictet
1880	Inoculation	Louis Pasteur
1882	Tuberculosis germ	Robert Koch
1884	Local anesthesia (cocaine)	K. Koller
	Gram bacteria test	Hans Christian Joachim Gram
1885	Ammonium picrate (explosive)	Eugene Turpin
1886	Aluminum electrolysis process	Paul Louis Toussaint Heroult and Charles Martin Hall
1889	Active molecules	Svante August Arrhenius
	Cordite	James Dewar and Frederick Augustus Abel
	Lysine (amino acid)	Edmund Drechsel
1890	Diphtheria antitoxin	Emil Adolf von Behring and Shibasaburo Kitasato
1891	Silicon carbide	Eduard Goodrich Acheson
1892	Cholera vaccine	Waldemar Mordecai Wolff Haffkine
	Phagocytes	Ilya Mechnikov
	Viruses	Dmitri Iosifovich Ivanovsky

Year	Discovery	Discoverer/Origin
1893	Photoelectric cell	Julius Elster and Hans F. Geitel
1894	Argon gas	John William Strutt and William Ramsay
	Helium	William Ramsay
1895	X rays	Wilhelm Konrad von Roentgen
1896	Electron	Joseph John Thomson
	Histidine (amino acid)	Albrecht Kossel and Sven A. Hedin
1897	Digestion physiology	Ivan Petrovic Pavlov
1898	Antineuritic vitamin B	Christiaan Eijkman
	Krypton	William Ramsay and Morris William Travers
	Neon	William Ramsay and Morris William Travers
	Xenon	William Ramsay and Morris William Travers
1899	Aspirin	Felix Hoffman
1900	Quantum theory	Max Karl Ernst Planck
	Radon	Friedrich Ernst Dorn
	Tryptophan (amino acid)	Frederick Gowland Hopkins
1901	Blood groups	Karl Landsteiner
	Valine and proline (amino acids)	Emil Hermann Fischer
1902	Hormones	William Maddock Bayliss and Ernest H. Starling
	Ionosphere	Arthur Edwin Kennelly and Oliver Heaviside
	Radium	Pierre and Marie Curie
1903	Barbiturates	Emil Hermann Fischer and Emil Adolf Behring
1905	Theory of relativity	Albert Einstein
	Silicones	Frederic S. Kipping
1909	Synthetic ammonia	Fritz Haber
	Typhus fever body louse	Charles Jules Henri Nicolle
1910	Tumor virus	Francis Peyton Rous
1911	Cosmic rays	Victor Franz Hess
	Theory of atomic structure	Ernest Rutherford
1912	Diffraction of X rays	Max Theodor Felix von Laue
	Thiamine (vitamin B_1)	Casimir Funk
1913	Vitamin A	Thomas B. Osborne, Lafayette B. Mendel, Elmer V. McCollum, and M. Davis
1918	Vitamin D	Edward Mellanby
	Insulin	Frederick G. Banting and Charles H. Best
1922	Vitamin E	Herbert McLean Evans
1925	Quantum mechanics	Max Born and Werner Karl Heisenberg
	Masurium and rhenium	Ida Eva Noddack
1927	Sex hormones	Bernhard Zondek and Selmar Ascheim
1928	Penicillin	Alexander Fleming
	Vitamin C	Albert von Nagyrapolt Szent-Györgyi
	Tomography	Andre Bocage
1930	Pluto	Clyde Tombaugh
	Pepsin	John Howard Northrup

Year	*Discovery*	*Discoverer/Origin*
1931	Neutrino	Wolfgang Pauli
1932	Neutron	James Chadwick
	Proton bombardment (lithium disintegration)	John Douglas Cockcroft and Ernest Thomas Sinton Walton
	Positron	Carl David Anderson and Patrick M. Stuart Blackett
1933	Riboflavin (vitamin B_2)	Richard Kuhn
	Pantothenic acid	Roger J. Williams
1934	Cerenkov effect.	Pavel Alekseevich Cerenkov
	Vitamin K	Carl Peter Henrik Dam
	Progesterone	Adolf Friedrich Johann Butenandt
1935	Meson	Hideki Yukawa
1936	Vitamin B_6	T. W. Birch and Albert von Nagyrapolt Szent-Györgyi
1937	Citric acid cycle	Hans Adolf Krebs
	Niacin	Conrad A. Elvehjem
1938	Cortisone	Edward C. Kendall, Philip S. Hench, and Tadeus Reichstein
	Folic acid	P. L. Day
1939	Betatron	Donald W. Kerst
1940	Plutonium	Glenn Theodore Seaborg and Edwin Mattison McMillan
	Vitamin H (biotin)	Vincent du Vigneaud
1943	LSD	Arthur Stoll
	Streptomycin	Selman A. Waksman
1944	Americium	Glenn T. Seaborg and Albert Ghiorso
	Curium	Glenn T. Seaborg and Albert Ghiorso
1947	Coenzyme A	Fritz A. Lipmann
	Vitamin B_{12} as cure for pernicious anemia	Karl A. Folkers
	Radiocarbon dating	Willard Frank Libby
1949	Berkelium	Glenn T. Seaborg and Stanley G. Thompson
1950	Chlorpromazine (tranquilizer)	Paul Charpentier
	Radioimmunoassay	Rosalyn Sussman Yalow
1951	Oral contraceptive pill	Gregory Goodwin Pincus, Min Chuch Chang, John Rock, Carl Djerassi
1953	DNA	Francis H. Compton Crick and James D. Watson
	Fermium	Albert Ghiorso and Stanley G. Thompson
	Measles vaccine	John F. Enders and Thomas Peebles
	Reperine (antidepressant drug)	Nathan S. Kline
1955	Fiber optics	Narinder S. Kapany
	Mendelevium	Albert Ghiorso
	RNA synthesis	Severo Ochoa
	Ultrasound (to observe heart)	Leskell, U.S.
1956	Amniocentesis	St. Mary's Hospital, England
	Human growth hormone	Choh Hao Li
1957	BCS theory (superconductivity)	John Bardeen, Leon N. Cooper, and J. Robert Schrieffer
	Interferon (protein)	Alick Isaacs and Jean Lindeman
	Mossbauer effect (gamma radiation)	Rudolph Ludwig Mossbauer
	Polio vaccine	Albert B. Sabin

Year	Discovery	Discoverer/Origin
1958	Nobelium	Albert Ghiorso
	Van Allen radiation belts	James A. Van Allen
1961	Kenyapithecus Wickeri (upper jawbone)	Louis S. B. Leakey
	Valium	Hoffmann-LaRoche Laboratories, Switzerland
1962	Muon neutrino	Leon Max Lederman
1963	Anti-xi-zero (atomic particle)	Unknown
	Quarks	Murray Gell-Mann
	Quasars	Marten Schmidt
1964	Laser eye surgery	H. Vernon Ingram
1965	Rubella vaccine	Paul D. Parkman and Harry M. Meyer, Jr.
1968	Hemoglobin molecule structure (complete)	Max Ferdinand Perutz
1969	Antibody chemical and molecular structure	Rodney Robert Porter
1972	Enkephalin (brain chemical)	John Hughes
	Antimatter particles	Yuri Dmitriyevich Prokoshkin
	Black holes	Robert L. F. Boyd
1974	Psi atomic particle	Burton Richter and Samuel Chao Chung Ting
1975	Hybrid cells	Jack Lucy and Ted Cocking
1976	Charm subatomic particle	Stanford Linear Accelerator Center, U.S.
1978	Cyclosporin A	Tony Allison and Roy Calne
	Human insulin	Genetech, San Francisco
	Charon (Pluto's moon)	James Walter Christy
1979	Single-cell protein process	ICI Agricultural Division, England
1981	Anti-interferon	Medical Research Council's Molecular Biology Laboratory, England
1982	Abnormal cancer-causing genes	Robert Weinberg and Mariano Barbacid
1984	Gene cloning	National Institutes of Health, U.S.; Transgene, France; and Otago University, New Zealand
	Genetically engineered blood-clotting factor	Genetech, San Francisco, and Genetics Institute, Boston
	Top quark (subatomic particle)	Carlo Rubbia
1985	Cloned leprosy genes (for vaccines)	Ron Davis
	Anxiety chemical (human brain)	Alessandro Guidotti and Erminio Costa
1986	DNA fingerprinting	Alec Jeffreys
	Diminished ozone shield	Susan Solomon, National Oceanic and Atmospheric Administration, U.S.
1987	Alzheimer's disease gene	National Institutes of Health, U.S.; University of Cologne, Germany
	Gene-altered bacteria	Advanced Genetic Sciences, U.S.
	Superconductivity confirmed	Paul Wu, IBM, U.S.

Additional Sources of Information

Asimov, Isaac, ed. *Biographical Encyclopedia of Science and Technology*, 2nd ed. Doubleday, 1982.

Boorstin, Daniel J. *The Discoverers*. Random House, 1985.

Bronowski, Jacob. *The Ascent of Man*. Little, Brown, 1974.

Clark, Ronald W. *Works of Man*. Viking, 1985.

Cooke, David Coxe. *Inventions That Made History*. G. P. Putnam, 1968.

De Bono, Edward. *Eureka!: An Illustrated History of Inventions from the Wheel to the Computer*. Holt, Rinehart and Winston, 1974.

Gies, Joseph. *The Ingenious Yankees*. Crowell, 1976.

Giscard d'Estaing, Valerie-Anne. *The Second World Almanac Book of Inventions*. World Almanac, 1986.

Mount, Ellis, and List, Barbara A. *Milestones in Science and Technology: The Ready Reference Guide to Discoveries, Inventions and Facts*. Oryx Press, 1987.

The Smithsonian Book of Inventions. Smithsonian Exposition Books, 1978.

Strandh, Sigvard. *A History of the Machine*. A & W Publisher, 1979.

Williams, Trevor. *History of Invention: From Stone Axes to Silicon Chips*. Facts on File, 1986.

7

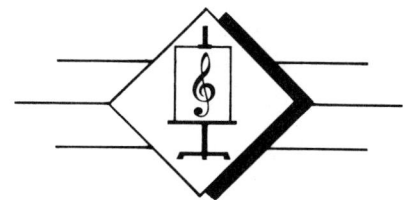

The Arts

Major Composers

American

Barber, Samuel (1910–81), b. Pennsylvania. Winner, Pulitzer Prize, for the opera *Vanessa* (1957) and Piano Concerto (1963). His works also include two symphonies, the overture to *The School for Scandal, Dover Beach,* and the popular *Adagio for Strings.*

Bernstein, Leonard (1918–   ), b. Massachusetts. Conductor and music director of the New York Philharmonic 1958–69. He has composed symphonies, songs, ballets, and musicals, including *West Side Story* (1957).

Blitzstein, Marc (1905–64), b. Pennsylvania. Pianist, composer, librettist. Among his most important works are orchestral variations; a piano concerto; operas, including the choral opera *The Condemned;* ballets; and film music.

Bloch, Ernest (1880–1959), b. Switzerland. Director of the Cleveland Institute of Music 1920–25 and the San Francisco Conservatory 1925–30. He composed symphonies, including *Hivers–Printemps, Israel, Trois poèmes juifs, America, Voice in the Wilderness,* and *Evocations;* chamber music; choral works; a piano sonata; songs; and the opera *Macbeth.*

Cage, John (1912–   ), b. California. Originator of controversial and experimental theories, performances, and compositions, including the *Music of Changes,* derived from the ideas of *I Ching, 4'33",* and *Imaginary Landscape No. 4* for 12 radios tuned randomly. Cage has collaborated with dancer Merce Cunningham, artist Marcel Duchamp, and others.

Copland, Aaron (1900–   ), b. New York State. Composer of three symphonies, a piano concerto, other orchestral works, chamber music, and ballets. The developer of a distinctly American music, Copland received the Pulitzer Prize in 1945.

Cowell, Henry Dixon (1897–1965), b. California. Pianist; composer of symphonies, an opera, and a piano concerto. Cowell founded the New Musical Society (1927); he invented (with Leon Thoremin) the "rhythmicon," an electronic instrument, and a method of playing the piano with forearm, elbow, and fist. His books on music include *New Musical Resources* (1931) and *Charles Ives and His Music* (1955).

Dello Joio, Norman (1913–   ), b. New York State. Concert pianist, organist, and award-winning composer. His works include three piano sonatas, chamber music, chamber concertos, orchestral and choral pieces, and ballets.

Gershwin, George (1898–1937), b. New York State. Composer of music in a distinct blend of classical, popular, and jazz styles. Gershwin's works include numerous popular songs and musical comedies and more ambitious concert pieces—*Rhapsody in Blue* (1924), *An American in Paris* (1928), and the jazz opera *Porgy and Bess* (1935).

Hanson, Howard (1896–1981), b. Nebraska. Conductor and composer of Romantic works, including symphonies, piano music, and the opera *Merry Mount* (1933). He served as director of the Eastman School of Music (1924–64) in Rochester, New York.

Ives, Charles (1874–1954), b. Connecticut. Composer of advanced and innovative works and winner of the Pulitzer Prize in 1947. Ives wrote four symphonies, chamber and choral music, songs, and piano works.

MacDowell, Edward (1860–1908), b. New York State. Best known as a composer of piano works. MacDowell also wrote orchestral works, symphonic poems, and a suite that appropriates melodies of the North American Indians. He was the first head of the Department of Music, Columbia University (1896–1904).

Menotti, Gian Carlo (1911–   ), b. Italy. Composer of ballets, a piano concerto, and the operas *Amelia Goes to the Ball, The Island God, The Medium, Amahl and the Night Visitors* (1951), and *The Saint of Bleecker Street* (1954). He founded the Festival of Two Worlds in Spoleto, Italy.

Moore, Douglas (1893–1969), b. New York State. Composer of works noted for their use of the American vernacular, including the opera *The Devil and Daniel Webster,* the children's opera *The Headless Horseman,* and *Moby Dick,* for orchestra. He was the author of *Listening to Music* (1931) and *From Madrigal to Modern Music* (1942).

Piston, Walter (1894–1976), b. Maine. Professor at Harvard and neoclassical composer of orchestral works, string quartets, sonatas, chamber music, and the ballet *The Incredible Flautist.* Piston wrote studies of harmony and counterpoint.

Schoenberg, Arnold (1874–1951), b. Austria. Originator of the revolutionary 12-tone system. The theory is exemplified in his works of 1921–33, including the *Five Pieces* for piano, the *Serenade* for seven instruments and bass baritone, and the *Variations* for orchestra.

Schuman, William (1910–), b. New York State. President of the Juilliard School of Music 1945–61 and Lincoln Center 1962–69. Schuman composed ballets, concertos, and chamber, orchestral, and choral works. He was the winner of the first Pulitzer Prize for music, 1943.

Sessions, Roger (1896–1985), b. New York State. Composer of eight symphonies, a violin concerto, piano works, organ pieces, and songs. His several books on music include *Reflections on Musical Life in America.*

Thomson, Virgil (1896–), b. Missouri. Music critic and composer. His works include two operas (with librettos by Gertrude Stein), a ballet, choral and chamber music, pieces for theater and film (among them *The River,* 1937), keyboard music, and songs. He is the author of *The State of Music* (1939), *The Musical Scene* (1945), and *The Art of Judging Music* (1948).

Varèse, Edgar (1883–1965), b. France. Founder and conductor of the New Symphony Orchestra, New York (1919) and founder of the International Composers Guild (1921). Varèse composed nontraditional works for orchestra with electronic music.

Austrian

Berg, Alban (1885–1935). Composer in Arnold Schoenberg's 12-tone system. Principal works are the operas *Wozzeck* (1922) and *Lulu* (1934), orchestral pieces, concertos, string quartets, *Lyric Suite,* and a piano sonata.

Bruckner, Anton (1824–96). Organist and composer of Romantic music. Much revised by his friends, his original compositions were published in 1929. Principal works include nine symphonies, choral works, and chamber music for string quintet.

Czerny, Karl (1791–1857). Virtuoso pianist and composer of many works for piano. Best known for his technical studies, Czerny was a pupil of Beethoven and a teacher of Liszt.

Haydn, Franz Joseph (1732–1809). Consummate artist of the classical style in music. Among his works are more than 100 symphonies, numerous concertos, 20 operas (five are lost), marionette operas, oratorios, church music, string quartets, piano trios, keyboard sonatas and variations, songs, and 377 arrangements of Scottish and Welsh airs.

Haydn, Johann Michael (1737–1806). Brother of Franz Joseph Haydn; composer of oratorios and church music, symphonies, concertos, divertimenti, quintets, and other instrumental works.

Mahler, Gustav (1860–1911). Conductor of the Hamburg and Vienna operas and the Metropolitan Opera in New York. He composed nine symphonies, as well as songs, in a late Romantic style, including the *Resurrection Symphony* (1894) and *Symphony of a Thousand* (1907). His orchestral works display powerful intensity and depth.

Mozart, Wolfgang Amadeus (1756–91). Master of the classical style in all its forms of his time. Mozart began to compose and perform at the age of six; at 11 he had composed three symphonies and 30 other works and arranged some piano concertos of J. S. Bach. His principal works include the operas *Le Nozze di Figaro* (1786), *Don Giovanni* (1787), and *The Magic Flute* (1791); chamber music; piano sonatas and fantasias; symphonies; and church music, including the *Requiem* (1791). Mozart's works are noted for lyrical charm.

Schubert, Franz Seraph Peter (1797–1828). Composer of numerous symphonies, masses, quartets, and sonatas, but most notably of songs in the spirit of early Romantic poetry. His works after 1823 consummate his lyrical, melodic style, as in the No. 9 C Major Symphony ("The Great") (1825), the piano sonatas, the A Minor (1824) and G Major Quartets (1826), and the Trios in B-flat (1826) and E-flat (1827).

Strauss, family of Viennese musicians. *Johann I* (1804–49) was the composer of waltzes famous throughout Europe. He was the father of *Johann II* (1825–99), who became his rival, composer of over 400 waltzes, including *The Blue Danube* (1866) and *Tales from the Vienna Woods* (1868), as well as operettas. His brothers, *Josef* (1827–70) and *Eduard I* (1835–1916), were also successful composers and conductors.

Webern, Anton von (1883–1945). Editor, conductor, and composer in the 12-tone system of Arnold Schoenberg. Webern wrote a symphony for small orchestra, three cantatas, a string quartet, a concerto for nine instruments, songs, and other works.

British

Britten, (Edward) Benjamin (1913–76). Major twentieth-century composer. His operas include *Peter Grimes, The Rape of Lucretia, Billy Budd,* and *The Turn of the Screw.* Among his most popular works are *A Ceremony of Carols* (1942), *A Young Person's Guide to the Orchestra* (1945), and the *War Requiem* (1962).

Byrd, William (1543–1623). Organist and composer. A master of sixteenth-century polyphony, Byrd excelled in composition of church music.

Delius, Frederick (1862–1934). Composer of orchestral works, including *Paris* (1899), *Appalachia* (1896), and *Brigg Fair* (1907); choral works, including *Sea Drift;* and the operas *A Village Romeo and Juliet* (1901) and *Fennimore and Gerda* (1910).

Dowland, John (c. 1563–1626). Lutenist and composer of the most important English collection of songs for lute. His most famous work is *Lachrimae* (1604).

Elgar, Sir Edward (1857–1934). Composer in a distinctly personal style. His works include *The Light of Life* (1896), *Scenes from the Bavarian Highlands* (1896), and *King Olaf* (1896), for chorus; orchestral works, including *Froissart* (1890), *Serenade for Strings* (1893), two symphonies, and concertos; and music for brass band, chamber music, organ sonatas, and songs.

Gibbons, Orlando (1583–1625). Organist and composer of anthems, madrigals, chamber music, and keyboard pieces.

Holst, Gustav (1874–1934). Composer who combined an interest in folk music with a knowledge of Hindu scales and Sanskrit literature. His later music experimented with harmony and polytonality. Principal works include the operas *Savitri, The Perfect Fool,* and *At the Boar's Head;* for orchestra, *Somerset Rhapsody* and *The Planets;* and for chorus, *Hymns from the Rig-Veda, The Cloud Messenger,* and *Ode to Death.*

Morley, Thomas (1557–1602). Composer, theorist, and organist at St. Paul's Cathedral. Morley was granted a monopoly on music printing (1598). He introduced the ballet into England and wrote the first comprehensive treatise on composition in English (1597).

Purcell, Henry (c. 1659–95). Organist at Westminster Abbey and composer of music for more than 40 plays, including *The Fairy Queen* (1692) and *The Tempest* (1695); and odes, songs, cantatas, church music, chamber music, and keyboard works.

Sullivan, Sir Arthur (1842–1900). Conductor, organist, and composer. His works include the grand opera *Ivanhoe* (1891); ballads; oratorios; cantatas, including *The Golden Legend;* church music; a symphony; songs; and works for piano. He is best known for his light operas to librettos by W. S. Gilbert.

Tallis, Thomas (c. 1505–85). Organist and composer. He was granted a monopoly in music printing with William Byrd (1575). Tallis's works include church music and secular pieces for vocals and keyboard.

Vaughan Williams, Ralph (1872–1958). Composer noted for his adaptations of folk music. Principal compositions include *A London Symphony* (1913), *Norfolk Rhapsodies* (1906), and *The Lark Ascending*

(1914), all for orchestra; *A Sea Symphony* (1911) and *Five Mystical Songs* (1911) for chorus; the operas *Hugh the Drover* (1914), *Riders to the Sea* (1932), and *The Pilgrim's Progress* (1951); and works for stage, chamber music, and songs.

Walton, William (1902–83). Composer best known for the opera *Troilus and Cressida* (1954); a setting for poems by Edith Sitwell, *Façade;* and the choral *Belshazzar's Feast*. Walton also wrote coronation marches, two symphonies, and chamber music.

French

Berlioz, Hector (1803–69). Conductor and composer of Romantic works. Berlioz is best known for the *Symphonie fantastique* (1830). He also wrote the symphonic work *Harold in Italy*, the opera *Damnation of Faust*, and the oratorio *Childhood of Christ* (1850–54).

Bizet, Georges (1838–75). Composer best known for the operas *The Pearlfishers* (1836), *The Young Maid of Perth* (1867), *Djmileh* (1872), and *Carmen* (1875). His Symphony in C Major (1868) is highly regarded.

Boulez, Pierre (1925–). Composer of works using the serial technique, including *Pli selon pli* (1962) and *Memoriales* (1975). He served as music director of the New York Philharmonic 1971–77.

Couperin, François (1668–1733). Member of a family of distinguished organists. Organist to the king at Versailles, he composed music for organ and harpsichord, instrumental ensembles, secular songs, and church music.

Debussy, Claude (1862–1918). Composer noted for his Impressionist style. Orchestral works include *La Mer* (1905) and *Nocturnes* (1899); piano works include *Clair de lune*, preludes, études, arabesques, and *The Children's Corner*. Debussy also wrote choral works, an opera, and the well-known tone poem *Prelude to the Afternoon of a Faun* (1894).

Delibes, (Clément Philibert) Léo (1836–91). Composer of operas, including *Le Roi l'a dit* (1873) and *Lakmé* (1883), and ballets, including *Coppélia* (1870) and *Sylvia* (1876).

Dukas, Paul (1865–1935). Composer best known for his orchestral scherzo *Sorcerer's Apprentice* (1897), the opera *Ariane et barbe-Bleue* (1907), and the ballet *La Peri*.

Fauré, Gabriel (1845–1924). Organist and composer who excelled in song writing. He wrote the operas *Prométheé* (1900) and *Pénélope* (1913), orchestral music, chamber works, and piano and church music. Fauré was the teacher of Maurice Ravel.

Franck, César (1822–90). A teacher who influenced an entire generation of composers. Distinctive compositions include Symphony in D Minor (1886–88), the *Symphonic Variations* for piano and orchestra, the oratorios *Ruth* (1846) and *Babel* (1865), and the operas *Hulda* (1895) and *Ghiselle* (1896).

Gounod, Charles (1818–93). Composer of the operas *Faust* (1859) and *Romeo and Juliet* (1867). Gounod also wrote church music, symphonies, and cantatas.

Honegger, Arthur (1892–1955). Founding member of the Parisian group ''The Six'' in 1916 with Erik Satie, Darius Milhaud, and Jean Cocteau. Honneger is best known for the oratorio *King David* (1921) and *Pacific 231* for orchestra.

Ibert, Jacques François Antoine (1890–1962). Ibert's colorful works include a suite for orchestra, *Escales* (1922); *Divertissement* (1930); music for theater and film; chamber music; and works for piano and organ. He served as director of the Academie de France in Rome (1937) and the Paris Opera (1955).

Lully, Jean-Baptiste (orig. Lulli, Giambattista) (1632–87). Lully composed for the comedy ballets of Molière and was the founder of the French opera (tragedie lyrique). He also composed court ballets, divertissements, church music, and two instrumental suites.

Massenet, Jules Emile Frédéric (1842–1912). Best known for his pop operas *Le Roi de Lahore* (1877), *Manon* (1884), *Werther* (1892), and *Le Jongleur de Notre-Dame* (1902). Massenet also wrote oratorios, orchestral works, concertos, and songs.

Massiaen, Oliver Eugène Prosper Charles (1908–). Organist and composer of symphonic poems and works for piano, organ, and vocals. Massiaen formed *Le Jeune France* with Yves Baudrier, Daniel Lesur, and Andre Jolivet in 1936 and wrote a treatise on composition.

Milhaud, Darius (1892–1974). A member of the Parisian group "The Six." Milhaud composed works that combine jazz, polytonality, and Brazilian elements. He is well known for his operas *Le Pauvre Matelot* (with libretto by Jean Cocteau, 1927) and for ballets, including the *Creation of the World* (1923).

Offenbach, Jacques (1819–80). Composer of 90 operettas, including the popular *Orpheus in the Underworld* (1858), *La Belle Hélène* (1864), and *La Vie Parisienne* (1866). His best work is thought to be *The Tales of Hoffmann* (1881).

Poulenc, Francis (1899–1963). Member of the Parisian circle "The Six." Poulenc composed ballets, including *Les Biches* (1924); chamber music; a concerto for two pianos; songs; choral works; a cantata; and operas, among them *Dialogues of the Carmelites* (1957).

Rameau, Jean-Philippe (1683–1764). Theorist and important composer of French opera. His works include the operas *Castor et Pollux* (1737) and *Dardamus* (1739), the opera-ballets *Les Indes galantes* (1735) and *Les Fêtes d'Hébé* (1739), and the ballet-bouffon *Platée* (1745). His treatises laid the foundation for the modern theory of harmony.

Ravel, Maurice, (1875–1937). Leading exponent of Impressionism. Ravel's principal works include *Rhapsodie espagnole* (1908) and *Bolero* (1928), for orchestra, and *Valse Nobles et Sentimentales* (1911) and *Le Tombeau de Couperin* (1917), for piano.

Saint-Saëns, Charles Camille (1835–1921). Pianist and composer. Saint-Saëns began performing at the age of 10 and later composed symphonic poems under the influence of Franz Liszt; operas, including *Samson et Dalila* (1877); and concertos.

Satie, Erik (1866–1925). Composer noted for his ironic, humorous style. Satie composed three ballets, including *Parade,* produced by Satie, Jean Cocteau, and Pablo Picasso (1917); operettas; a symphonic drama; songs; and piano pieces.

German

Bach, Johann Sebastian (1695–1750). Baroque organist and composer, and one of the greatest creators of Western music. In his early years as an organist, Bach wrote mostly keyboard music, such as his two- and three-part inventions, *The Well-Tempered Clavier,* and his many fugues and suites. Later he composed instrumental works, including the *Brandenburg* concertos, and superb religious works, such as *The St. Matthew Passion.* He had 20 children, 10 of whom survived, including *Wilhelm Friedemann* (1710–84), organist and composer; *Johann Christoph Friedrich* (1732–94), composer; and *Johann Christian* (1735–82), composer of 11 operas, church music, symphonies, piano concertos, chamber music, and songs.

Beethoven, Ludwig van (1770–1827). Composer of instrumental works, particularly symphonies. Beethoven was a student of Mozart and Haydn, whose influence permeates his early works. By 1824 he had lost his hearing, but he continued to compose under the sponsorship of aristocratic patrons. His works include *Fidelio,* an opera; a violin concerto and five piano concertos; the *Egmont* overture; 32 piano sonatas, including the *Apassionata;* 16 string quartets; the Mass in D *(Missa Solemnis);* and nine symphonies, the best known of which are the Third *(Eroica),* the Fifth *(Victory),* the Sixth *(Pastoral),* and the Ninth *(Choral).* The Ninth, completed in 1823, is considered the greatest of his works.

Brahms, Johannes (1833–97). Developer of a Romantic style, both lyrical and classical. His principal works include the *Tragic Overture,* two piano concertos, and serenades, for orchestra; *Renaldo* and *Song of Destiny,* for chorus; chamber music; piano solos, including variations on themes by Paganini and George Frideric Handel; rhapsodies; ballades; piano duets; waltzes; Hungarian dances; songs; folk song arrangements; and 11 choral preludes for organ.

Bruch, Max (1838–1920). Famous for his setting of the Hebrew melody *Kol Nidre* (1881), for cello and orchestra. His works also include three symphonies, three operas, an operetta, choral works, and chamber music.

Gluck, Christoph Willibald von (1714–87). Composer of more than 100 operas, among them *Orfeo ed Euridice* (1762) and *Alceste* (1767), which established a new style of Italian opera; 11 symphonies; instrumental trios; seven odes by Friedrich Klopstock for solo voice and keyboard; and a flute concerto.

Handel, George Frideric (1685–1759). Baroque composer most famous for the oratorio *Messiah* (1742). Trained in law and music in Germany, Handel produced his operas in Italy and London, incorporating German, Italian, and English styles. Among his works are many operas, including *Almira* (1705), *Flavio* (1723), and *Orlando* (1733); *Music for the Royal Fireworks* (1749) and the *Water Music* (1717); suites for harpsichord; chamber music; and many Italian cantatas.

Hindemith, Paul (1895–1963). Composer, teacher, theorist, performer, and conductor. Early works, such as the opera *Murder, Hope of Women* (1921), reflect the Expressionism of the period. Later works, including *Ludus Tonalis* (1942), exemplify his new theory of tonality expounded in *The Craft of Musical Composition*. Hindemith was banned by the Nazis for his modernity. His best-known work is a symphony from his opera *Mathis the Painter* (1938).

Humperdinck, Engelbert (1854–1921). Composer of six operas, including the popular *Hansel and Gretel* (1893); incidental music; vocal works; and songs.

Mendelssohn, Felix (1809–47). Composer of orchestral works, including five symphonies and the overture *A Midsummer Night's Dream* (1826); choral works, including the oratorios *St. Paul* (1836) and *Elija* (1846); operas, including *Son and Stranger* (1829); incidental music; piano works; and songs.

Meyerbeer, Giacomo (1791–1864). Composer of operas in a spectacular style that influenced Richard Wagner. His works include *Robert le Diable* (1831), *Les Huguenots* (1836), and *Le Prophète* (1849).

Orff, Carl (1895–1982). Composer of stage works, including the cantata *Carmina Burana* (1936); the opera *Der Mond* (1938); and musical plays, such as *Die Bernauerin* (1947). Orff developed a widely used system for teaching music to children.

Schumann, Clara Josephine née Wieck (1819–96). Pianist and composer of piano works and songs. She was a renowned interpreter of music, particularly the works of her husband, Robert Schumann.

Schumann, Robert (1810–56). Composer of piano music, including sonatas and impromptus, and of orchestral works. His piano compositions include *Scenes from Childhood, Album for the Young,* and Piano Concerto in A Minor (1845). The *Rhemish Symphony* (1850) combined classical and Romantic elements.

Strauss, Richard (1864–1949). Composer of numerous operas, many with librettos by Hugo von Hoffmansthal, including the famous *Der Rosenkavalier* (1909); two ballets; tone poems for orchestra; concertos; *Metamorphosen* for 23 solo strings; chamber music; songs; and piano works.

Wagner, Richard (1813–83). Composer of operas and architect of a theory of the ''total'' work of art, in which drama, spectacle, and music are fused. Principal works include *Der Ring des Nibelungen* (1853–74), which was made up of four operas—*Das Rheingold, Die Walküre, Siegfried,* and *Götterdämmerung; Tristan und Isolde* (1859); and *Parsifal* (1882). Exiled for his role in the revolution of 1848, Wagner resettled in Bavaria in 1864, where he constructed his theater at Bayreuth.

Weber, Carl Maria von (1786–1826). Composer, conductor, pianist, critic, and virtual creator of Romantic German opera. Principal works include the operas *Der Freischutz* (1821) and *Oberon* (1826), choral and orchestral pieces, piano sonatas, concertos, dances, and songs.

Italian

Bellini, Vincenzo (1801–35). Composer of operas, including *La Straniera* (1829), *La Sonnambula* (1831), *Norma* (1831), and *I Puritani* (1835).

Boccherini, Luigi (1743–1805). Cellist and composer. His principal compositions are for chamber music. Boccherini also wrote symphonies, concertos, and vocal music.

Boito, Arrigo (1842–1918). Poet and composer of operas, including *Mefistofele* (1868) and *Nerone* (1918). Boito is known chiefly for his librettos, notably for *Otello* and *Falstaff* by Giuseppe Verdi.

Cherubini, Maria Luigi (1760–1842). Composer of 24 operas, among them the classic "rescue" opera *The Water Carrier;* church music; string quartets; and piano sonatas. He served as director of the Paris Conservatory (1822).

Clementi, Muzio (1752–1832). Pianist and composer of symphonies, piano sonatas, and piano studies, including *Gradus ad Parnassum.*

Corelli, Arcangelo (1653–1713). Violinist and composer. His trio sonatas, solo violin sonatas, and concerti grossi established a style of composition for the violin.

Dallapiccola, Luigi (1904–75). Composer of atonal music. He is most noted for his operas *The Prisoner* (1944) and *Odysseus* (1968), the oratorio *Job* (1950), and the *Christmas Concerto* (1956).

Donizetti, Gaetano (1797–1848). Prolific composer of operas. His best-known works included *Lucrezia Borgia* (1833), *La Favorite* (1840), and the comic operas *L'Elisir d'amore* (1832) and *Don Pasquale* (1843).

Leoncavallo, Ruggiero (1857–1919). Composer of operas. His most successful was *Pagliacci* (1892). He wrote his own librettos, a ballet, and a symphonic poem.

Mascagni, Pietro (1863–1945). Opera composer and conductor. His most famous work is *Cavalleria Rusticana* (1890).

Monteverdi, Claudio (1567–1643). Ordained priest and composer of church music, including Masses, vespers, madrigals, magnificats, and motets. He also wrote secular vocal music, at least 12 operas, and ballets.

Palestrina, Giovanni Pierluigi da (Johannes Praenestinus) (c.1525–94). Organist, choirmaster, and composer of church music, including Masses, motets, and lamentations. He also wrote both sacred and secular madrigals.

Pergolesi, Giovanni Battista (1710–36). Composer of operas and comic intermezzos that became the prototype of the *opera buffa;* church music, including his renowned *Stabat Mater;* and sonatas, which contributed to the development of the form.

Puccini, Giacomo (1858–1924). Composer of many operas. Best known are *La Bohème* (1896), *Tosca* (1899), and *Madame Butterfly* (1904). *Turandot* was completed after his death by Franco Alfano.

Respighi, Ottorino (1879–1936). Composer of operas, tone poems, and other orchestral works, chamber music, concertos, and songs. Among his most popular works are *The Fountains of Rome* (1917) and *The Pines of Rome* (1924), both symphonic poems.

Rossini, Gioacchino (1792–1868). Composer of operas. The best known are *William Tell* and *The Barber of Seville.* Rossini also wrote cantatas, songs, piano pieces, and woodwind quintets.

Scarlatti, Alessandro (1660–1725). Conductor and the most prolific composer of Italian operas of his time. Besides 115 operas, he wrote 20 oratorios, some 600 cantatas, 10 Masses, a Passion, motets, and other church music, chamber pieces, concertos, and works for harpsichord.

Scarlatti, (Giuseppe) Domenico (1685–1757). Son of Alessandro Scarlatti and greatest Italian composer for harpsichord of his time. He wrote 550 pieces, now called sonatas, as well as concertos, operas, cantatas, Masses, a *Stabat Mater,* and two *Salve Reginas.*

Tartini, Giuseppe (1692–1770). Violinist, teacher, composer, and theorist. He composed over 100 violin concertos and symphonies, solo sonatas, trio sonatas, and church music; published treatises on violin playing and acoustics; and established a violin school in Padua (1728).

Verdi, Giuseppe (1813–1901). Foremost composer of operas. They include *Rigoletto* (1851), *La Traviata* (1853), and the supreme *Otello* (1887) and *Falstaff* (1893). Verdi also composed church music, including the *Requiem* (1874), *Ave Maria* (1889), *Stabat Mater* (1898), and *Te Deum* (1898).

Vivaldi, Antonio (1678–1741). Violinist, composer, and ordained priest. Master of the Italian Baroque, Vivaldi is best known for his instrumental music and the concertos *The Four Seasons*. He also wrote church music, an oratorio, and operas.

Russian

Borodin, Aleksandr (1833–87). Composer and scientist. His works include three symphonies; *In the Steppes of Central Asia* for orchestra; string quartets; and the opera *Prince Igor,* completed after his death by Nicolai Rimsky-Korsakov and Aleksandr Glazunov.

Glinka, Mikhail (1804–57). Composer of two operas and other works. *A Life for the Czar* (1836) and *Russlan and Ludmilla* (1842) established a Russian style against the conventions of Italian opera. Glinka introduced folk song into instrumental composition in the orchestral fantasia *Kamarinskaya*.

Khachaturian, Aram (1903–78). Armenian composer whose works are distinguished for their incorporation of oriental folk elements. He is best known for the ballet *Gayané* (1942) and its popular *Sabre Dance*.

Moussorgsky, Modest (1839–81). Composer of operas and orchestral works. Moussorgsky is best known for his outstanding operas *Boris Gudunov* (1868) and *Khovanschina* (1886), as well as for *Pictures at an Exhibition* (1874) for piano and *Night on Bald Mountain* (1860–66) for orchestra.

Prokofiev, Sergei (1891–1953). Composer, pianist, and conductor. His principal compositions are the operas *Love for Three Oranges* (1921) and *War and Peace* (1942); *Peter and the Wolf* (1936), for orchestra and narrator; and seven symphonies, piano concertos, ballets, and piano sonatas.

Rachmaninoff, Sergei (1873–1943). Composer, pianist, and conductor. Rachmaninoff emigrated to the United States at age 17. His compositions include three operas; orchestral works, including the tone poem *Isle of the Dead* (1907); four concertos; choral works; chamber music; and songs.

Rimsky-Korsakov, Nicolai (1844–1908). Composer of operas and orchestral works. His greatest works are the operas *Mlada* (1890), *Christmas Eve* (1895), *Sadko* (1896), and *The Golden Cockerel* (1907). His orchestration influenced the work of Igor Stravinsky and others.

Rubinstein, Anton (1829–94). Pianist and composer; founder of the Conservatory in St. Petersburg (1862). A representative of traditional Western ideas against the current of nationalism, his works include *Musical Portraits (Faust, Ivan the Terrible, Don Quixote)* for orchestra, 20 operas, six symphonies (including *The Ocean*), chamber music, and other works.

Scriabin, Aleksandr (1872–1915). Composer and pianist. Scriabin experimented with esoteric harmonies related to theosophical ideas in *The Divine Poem* (1904) and *Poem of Ecstasy* (1909–10) for orchestra; he wrote sonatas, preludes, and *Prometheus*, which includes the use of a "color organ" for slide projection.

Shostakovich, Dmitri (1906–75). Composer of chamber and symphonic works. Shostakovich alternated between political and satirical composition, later trying to bring his work closer to official prescriptions. His works include 11 symphonies, among them *May the First* (1930) and the outstanding *Ninth Symphony* (1940); operas; the ballet *The Golden Age* (1930); piano works; sonatas; and string quartets.

Stravinsky, Igor (1882–1971). Composer of the epochal ballet *Rite of Spring*. Later works, such as *The Soldier's Tale,* for narrator and instruments, and the ballet suite *Apollon Musagete,* are more austere and neoclassical. Stravinsky settled in the United States in 1941, where he experimented with 12-tone composition, as in the *Cantata* (1952).

Tchaikovsky, Peter Ilyich (1840–93). One of the most important Russian composers. Tchaikovsky is best known for his ballet music, including *Swan Lake* (1876) and *The Sleeping Beauty* (1889), and his operas *Eugene Onegin* (1878) and *Queen of Spades* (1890). He also wrote symphonies, including the popular Fifth Symphony (1888), chamber music, and choral works, and published books on harmony, autobiographical essays, and translations.

Other

Albéniz, Isaac (1860–1909). Spanish composer and pianist. Albéniz is known for his later piano works, notably *Iberia* (1906–09); he also wrote operas, including *The Magic Opal* (1893).

Bartók, Béla (1881–1945). Hungarian pianist and composer who studied and collected Hungarian folk music. His principal works include orchestral pieces; the opera *Duke Bluebeard's Castle;* the ballet *The Wooden Prince;* the pantomime *The Miraculous Mandarin;* chamber music; piano works, including the *Mikrokosmos;* and arrangements of folk songs. He emigrated to the United States in 1940.

Chávez, Carlos (1899–1978). Mexican composer of works using the idioms of Indian folk music, including *Xochipilli Macuilxochitl* (1940). Well-known works are the ballet symphony *H.P.* (1926) and *Sinfonía Antigona* (1933).

Dvořák, Antonín (1841–1904). Czech composer of works in a nationalist spirit, including the *Symphonic Variations, Slavonic Rhapsodies,* and the opera *The Peasant Rogue* (1877). His best-known work, the symphony *From the New World* (1893), contains elements of both Czech and American music.

Falla, Manuel de (1876–1946). Spanish composer and pianist. He published little but was the outstanding Spanish composer of his time. Principal works are the operas *La Vida Breve* (1905) and *El Retablo de Maese Pedro* (1923), the ballets *El Amor Brujo* (1915) and *The Three-Cornered Hat* (1919), and the *Fantasia Béticu* (1919) for piano.

Grainger, Percy Aldridge (1882–1961). Australian pianist and composer who settled in the United States in 1914. He was head of the Music Department at New York University and was known for his arrangements of traditional tunes from a variety of sources.

Granados, Enrique (1867–1916). Spanish pianist and composer, born in Cuba. Granados founded and directed the Academía Granados (1901) and composed seven operas, orchestral works, chamber music, a collection of *tonadillas,* and *Goyescas* (1915), based on the paintings of Goya. He died at sea in a torpedoed ship during World War I.

Grieg, Edvard (1843–1907). Norwegian composer, conductor, and pianist. Principal works include the overture *I Host* (1866), two suites from *Peer Gynt* (1888, 1891), *At a Southern Convent Gate* (1871) for chorus, and *Lyric Pieces* for piano.

Janáček, Leoš (1854–1928). Czech composer. Janáček wrote 10 operas, including *Jenůfa* (1904); orchestral, choral, and piano works; chamber music; and songs. He published collections of Moravian folk music and a treatise on harmony.

Kodály, Zoltán (1882–1967). Hungarian composer whose works are distinguished by the influence of native folk music. His best-known works are the opera *Háry János* (1926) and *Psalmus Hungaricus* (1923). Kodály developed a widely used method of teaching music.

Lasso, Orlando di (Roland de Lassus) (1532–94). Belgian composer. Among his many works are Masses, motets, magnificats, and other church music. The complete edition of his works comprises 60 volumes of nearly 2,000 works.

Liszt, Franz (1811–86). Hungarian composer who spent time in Paris and Rome. He was an unsurpassed virtuoso pianist and a composer of symphonies, including *Faust* (1853); symphonic poems; piano works, including concertos, études, and 19 *Hungarian Rhapsodies;* choral pieces; fantasia and fugues for organ; and songs.

Nielsen, Carl (1865–1931). Danish composer of operas, symphonies, string quartets, piano pieces, and songs. Nielsen served as director of the Copenhagen Conservatory (1915–27).

Paderewski, Ignace (1860–1941). Polish pianist and composer. One of the most renowned pianists of modern times, in 1919 Paderewski was prime minister of Poland. He composed many piano works, an opera, a symphony, a concerto, and songs.

Sibelius, Jean (1865–1957). Finnish composer. Sibelius attempted a national music, as in *En Saga* (1892) and *The Return of Lemminkäinen* (1895), based on the Finnish epic the *Kalevala*. Notable works include the symphonic poems *Pohjola's Daughter* (1906), *Night Ride and Sunrise* (1907), and *The Oceanides* (1914).

Smetana, Bedřich (1824–84). Czech composer. Among his operas on national subjects, the best known is *The Bartered Bride* (1866). Smetana wrote his best instrumental works despite deafness, especially *My Country* (1879) and the string quartets *From My Life* (1876).

Villa-Lobos, Heitor (1887–1959). Brazilian composer. His works show the influence of Indian music and Brazilian folk songs; they include five operas, six symphonies, symphonic poems, serenades, choral music, piano solos, and songs.

Wieniawski, Henri (1835–80). Polish violinist and composer. Wieniawski's compositions include two concertos and popular pieces.

Terms Used in Music

a cappella   Choral music without accompaniment (literally, "in the church style").

accelerando   A direction to increase the speed gradually.

accent   The stress given to one tone over another. In symmetrical music, the accent falls at regular intervals. Irregular accents fall on normally unstressed beats.

accidental   Term for a *sharp, double sharp, flat, double flat,* or *natural* prefixed to single notes.

accompaniment   Secondary instrument or background vocal added to the principal instrument or soloist.

acoustics   The science of sound, which deals with intensity, quality, resonance, pitch, tone, etc.

adagietto   A direction to play slightly faster than adagio.

adagio   A direction to play slowly.

adagissimo   A direction to play very slowly.

ad libitum   A direction to interpret, improvise, or omit, according to the player's preference.

affettuoso   A direction to play affectionately, with warmth.

agitato   A direction to play in an "agitated," restless, hurried manner.

air   A tune or melody. The French eighteenth-century term for song; also, an instrumental piece whose melodic style is similar to that of a solo song.

alla breve   A direction to play twice as fast as the notation signifies.

allargando   A direction to play slower, louder.

allegretto   A direction to play with moderately quick movement, slower than allegro but quicker than largo.

allegro   A direction to play quickly, briskly.

allemande   A moderately slow dance of German origin.

allentando   A direction to slow down.

Alto   The highest adult male voice, or lowest female voice; also, a tenor violin or viola.

andante   A direction to play in moderate tempo, inclining to slowness, flowing with ease.

andantino   A direction to play in a tempo slightly quicker than andante.

animato   A direction to play with animation.

answer   In a fugue, the transposition of a subject.

anthem   A choral piece for use in church services.

a poco   A direction signifying gradualness.

a poco a poco A direction signifying little by little.

appasionato A direction to play passionately.

appogiatura An inharmonious note preceding a principal note, marked with a diagonal line through it, of short or long duration.

arabesque A lyrical piece in a fanciful style; a term first used by Schumann and later by Debussy.

aria An extended vocal solo in an opera or oratorio.

arioso A piece of recitative song, but more songlike.

arpeggio The technique of playing the notes of a chord successively rather than simultaneously.

assai A direction to play very quickly.

a tempo A direction to play in time, following a deviation from the regular tempo.

aubade Morning music, in contrast to *serenade,* or evening music.

augmentation Presentation of a theme in notes of doubled value. It is the opposite of *diminution.*

auxiliary note Usually, a grace note one degree above or below a principal note.

ballad A narrative song, originally accompanied by dancing; also, an instrumental piece in ballad style.

bar A line drawn vertically across the staff to divide into measures.

baritone A high bass voice; also, any musical instrument intermediary between bass and tenor.

bass The lowest male voice, or lowest part in a musical composition; also, short for the double bass or bass tuba.

beat A unit of measurement indicated by the conductor's gesture; each unit of a measure with respect to accent.

berceuse A cradle song.

bolero A Spanish dance accompanied by castanets.

bowing A method of playing notes or passages indicated by signs for down bow (⊓) or up bow (∨).

brace A vertical line used to join two or more staves.

buffa In the comic style.

buffo The singer of a comic part.

cadence A progression that seems to arrive at a conclusion. *Perfect c:* full close, progression from dominant to tonic. *Imperfect c:* half close, progression from tonic to dominant. *Plagal c:* progression from subdominant to tonic. *Authentic c:* perfect cadence in which the final tonic chord is preceded by dominant. *Interrupted c:* progression from dominant to a chord other than the tonic. *Deceptive c:* progression in which dominant is followed not by the expected tonic but by the sixth tone.

cadenza An ornamental passage near the end of a composition.

canceling sign The natural sign (♮) used to reverse the effect of a previous sharp or flat sign.

canon A contrapuntal composition in which one part is imitated by one or more other parts, so that the successive statements overlap.

cantata A piece that is sung, in contrast to a *sonata,* which is played. The term now refers to secular or sacred choral works accompanied by orchestra, similar to the oratorio but shorter.

canto The part of a choral work that carries the melody.

canzona A form of Italian lyric poetry corresponding to the ode, set to music, in a style similar to a madrigal, though simpler; also, an instrumental piece in the style of a song.

capo The beginning.

capriccio A short composition in free form.

catch A round for three or more voices.

chaconne Originally, a Spanish dance; an instrumental composition with variations on a ground bass or stereotyped harmonic progression.

chamber music Music suitable for a small hall; instrumental music in the sonata form.

chanson A song for solo voice or vocal ensemble; also, an instrumental piece of vocal character.

chant A sacred song, used in accordance with prescribed ritual. It is the oldest form of choral music.

chorale. A psalm or hymn tune sung in church; also, a harmonization of a chorale melody.

chord The combination of three or more tones played at once. *Diatonic c.* uses only notes proper to the key. A *triad* is a chord of three notes in which the lowest is combined with the third and fifth above it. *Common c.* is a triad in root position. *Dominant c.* is founded on the dominant of the key. An *inverted c.* uses a tone other than the root as its lowest tone. *Harmony* is the study of chords and their relations.

chromatic Progression by semitones. It refers to music that contains tones outside the diatonic scale. A *c. chord* contains one or more notes foreign to the key. A *c. scale* consists of successive semitones.

clef A character that indicates the pitch of a particular line on a stave.

coda A passage at the end of a piece or movement that brings it to a conclusion.

Coll' arco With the bow.

Colla voce A direction indicating that the accompaniment should follow the voice for tempo.

comma The smallest difference in pitch recognizable by the ear, ⅑ of a whole step.

common time Four-four (⁴⁄₄) time—that is, four quarter notes to a measure.

compound interval An interval that extends beyond an octave.

compound time Time in which each beat of the bar is divisible into three, in contrast to *simple time,* in which each beat is divisible into two.

con bravura A direction to play with boldness.

concert master The leader of the first violins, next in rank to the conductor.

concerto A composition for solo instrument, usually with orchestral accompaniment.

concerto grosso. A composition for orchestra with passages for a group of solo instruments.

con fuoco A direction to play "with fire," or with great animation.

consecutive interval The progression of two like intervals between two parts.

console The part of the organ from which the player controls the instrument—the keyboard, pedals, etc., as distinguished from the pipes.

consort A chamber ensemble; also, music written for such a group.

con spirito A direction to play in a lively manner.

continuo The bass, or lowest, line of a composition.

contralto The range of a low female voice; alto.

contrapuntal In counterpoint.

counterpoint The combination of two or more parts, melodically and rhythmically independent.

countersubject The contrasting part to the subject of a fugue.

countertenor The highest male voice.

courante A lively dance in triple time; also, the second part of a suite.

crescendo A direction to increase the volume.

da capo A direction to repeat from the beginning.

decrescendo A direction to decrease the volume.

descant A contrasted melody to be sung simultaneously with an existing melodic line. It is the earliest form of polyphony, with contrasting motions between the parts.

development The extension of a theme through contrapuntal elaboration, modulation, rhythmical variation, etc.

diatonic Notes proper to a key. *D. harmony* is formed by the tones of a single minor or major scale; a *d. interval* is formed by two tones of the major or minor scale.

diminished chord A chord in which the highest and lowest tones form a diminished interval.

diminished interval A perfect or minor interval reduced by a semitone.

diminuendo Diminishing; getting softer.

diminution The presentation of a theme in notes of smaller time value.

discord, dissonance A combination of tones that are unresolved, jarring.

divertimento Originally, a suite of movements for chamber ensemble, designed for entertainment; a diminutive symphony.

divertissement A fantasia on well-known tunes.

divisi An indication in orchestral music that a group of players who play the same parts are to play two or more separate parts.

do The note C.

dolce A direction to play softly, sweetly.

dolcissimo A direction to play very sweetly.

dolente, doloroso Sorrowful.

dominant The fifth tone of the major or minor scale. A *D. chord* or *triad* has the dominant as its root.

doppio movimento Twice as fast.

Dorian mode A church mode represented on the white keys of a keyboard instrument by an ascending scale from D to D.

dot Written after a note, an indication of the prolongation of its length by ½; the double dot indicates by ¾. Above the note, the dot indicates staccato.

double stop A chord of two notes played on a bowed string instrument, obtaining a two-part harmony.

doxology In Christain worship, a hymn of praise to God.

duet A composition for two players or two voices, with or without accompaniment.

dynamics Degrees of loudness; the branch of musical science that deals with loudness.

eighth A note whose value is ⅛ of a whole note.

enharmonic Tones that have the same pitch when played on tempered instruments but that are different in notation, such as C♯ and D♭.

estinto So soft that it can hardly be heard.

etude A study; an exercise in technique.

exposition The statement of the musical material on which a movement is based.

expression marks Marks used to help the interpretation of a work; they are concerned with dynamics, tempo, and mood and indicate forte, allegro, con spirito, etc.

fa The note F.

falsetto The false voice; used to achieve notes above the normal range.

fantasia A piece in which the composition follows the fancy rather than any conventional form; of an improvisational character.

fifth The interval between the root and the fifth tone above it.

figuration The extended use of a particular melodic or harmonic figure; the ornamental treatment of a passage.

finale The last movement of a work of several movements; for example, the conclusion of a concerto or the last act of an opera.

flat The sign ♭, indicating the pitch is to be lowered by one semitone.

form The pattern of design of a work; its basic elements are repetition, variation, and contrast in the areas of harmony, rhythm, and tone.

forte   A direction to play loudly.

forte piano   A direction to play loudly, then softly.

fortissimo   A direction to play very loudly.

forza   A direction to play with force.

forzando   Strongly accenting. Also *sforzando*.

fourth   An interval reached by ascending three steps from the root in a diatonic scale.

fox-trot   A dance of American origin in duple time.

fugue   A contrapuntal composition in which two or more themes are interwoven by the various parts at different intervals of pitch.

fundamental   The lowest tone of a chord when the chord is founded on that tone; also, the lowest note in the harmonic series.

galop   A quick dance in ²⁄₄ time popular in the nineteenth century.

giocoso   Jocose; merry.

glee   A simple partsong, generally for male voices.

glissando   Sliding the finger rapidly across keys or strings.

grace note   An ornamental note not essential to the melody and not counted as part of the measure.

grandezza   Grandeur.

grave   A direction to play slowly, solemnly.

grazioso   A direction to play gracefully.

Gregorian chant   A style of church music for unaccompanied voices, without definite rhythm, in one of the eight church modes.

half note   A note having half the time value of a whole note and twice that of a quarter note.

harmonics   Sounds produced on a stringed instrument or harp by touching the strings at an exact fractional point corresponding to the upper partials of the strings; indicated by the *harmonic mark* (○).

harmony   The structure and relationships of chords and their successions.

homophonic   Single-voiced; music in which one melody or part is supported by chords; the opposite of *polyphonic*.

imitation   The use of the same or similar melodic material in different voices successively.

impresario   The conductor or manager of an opera or concert company.

impromptu   An improvised composition without fixed form.

incidental music   Music for performance during the action of a play.

interlude   A short piece played between the acts of a drama; the verses of a song, parts of a church service, or sections of a cantata.

intermezzo   A play with music performed between the acts of an opera or drama that gave rise to opera buffa; an interlude; a short movement in a symphony.

interval   The distance in pitch between two notes, harmonic if they are played together, melodic if they are played in succession. *Perfect i:* the prime, fourth, fifth, and octave. *Major i:* the second, third, sixth, and seventh of the major scale. *Minor i:* a chromatic half step smaller. *Augmented i:* a chromatic half step larger than perfect and major. *Diminished i:* a chromatic half step smaller than perfect and minor.

intonation   The production of tone with voice or instrument.

inversion   The transposition of the lower and upper notes of an interval. In an inverted chord, the lowest tone is not its root; an inverted melody is one in which its intervals are inverted.

Ionian mode   A mode of church music represented on the white keys of a keyboard by an ascending scale from C to C.

key   A series of notes forming a major or minor scale; tonality; also, the levers on a keyboard instrument.

key signature Sharps or flats placed at the beginning of a composition to indicate its key.

la The note A.

larghetto Diminutive of largo.

largo A direction to play broadly, more slowly than adagio but not as slowly as a grave.

leading tone The major seventh of any scale.

legato A direction to play smoothly and continuously.

lento A direction to play slowly, but not as slowly as largo.

libretto The text of an opera or oratorio.

litany A song of invocation to God.

madrigal An unaccompanied song for three or more voices using counterpoint and imitation.

maestoso A direction to play in a majestic, stately manner.

magnificat Canticle of the Virgin sung as part of the evening service in Reformed churches and at vespers in the Catholic church.

major Applied to chords, intervals, scales, and keys, a standard in contrast to diminished, augmented, or minor.

major scale A scale in which the half steps occur between the third and fourth and the seventh and eighth tones.

march A composition with strong rhythms for a procession or parade.

Mass A musical setting of the liturgy of the Eucharist.

mazurka The Polish national dance in triple time, often with a strong accent on the third beat.

me The note E.

measure A unit of rhythm, indicated by bars.

mediant The third note of a diatonic scale.

melody A succession of single tones, in contrast to *harmony*, which refers to simultaneous tones.

mensural music A medieval term for music with definite note values, as distinguished from plainsong.

meter A scheme of accents; a grouping of beats into units of measure.

mezzo Medium, half; moderate.

mezzo forte A direction to play moderately loudly.

mezzo soprano The female voice between soprano and alto.

middle C The C note that is nearest the middle of the piano keyboard.

minor Intervals, scales, keys, and chords having intervals a semitone less than major.

minor scale Natural minor has half steps between two and three and between five and six. Harmonic minor has half steps between two and three and between seven and eight, ascending; in descending it usually is natural.

minuet A slow, graceful dance of French origin in triple time; a composition in this rhythm.

mode A system of scales in ancient Greek and early church music made up of octaves and using only the notes represented by the white keys of the piano.

modulation The transition from one key to another through a succession of chords.

molto Very.

monophony Music consisting of melody only, without accompaniment, as in plainsong or folk song.

mordent An ornament played by quickly alternating a note with the note below it.

morendo A final cadence.

motet An unaccompanied vocal composition with sacred lyrics from the thirteenth century.

motif, motive The subject of a composition.

motion Melodic progression.

movement A distinct division of a composition with its own key, themes, rhythm, and character.

natural The interval between a fundamental tone and the ninth tone above it.

nocturne A serenade; a cantabile melody over a chordal accompaniment.

note A tone of definite pitch.

obbligato Indispensable; the opposite of *ad libitum*.

octave The interval between a fundamental tone and the eighth above it; all the tones within the interval.

octet A composition of eight parts or voices; also, the group of its performers.

opera A drama set to music performed with scenery and costumes; among its elements are arias, recitatives, duets, and choruses.

operetta A short opera.

opus A musical work or composition.

oratorio A musical setting of a scriptural text set without costumes, scenery, or action.

orchestra A group of musicians playing various instruments.

overture An introduction to a large composition such as an opera or oratorio; however, it can be independent or the predecessor of a symphonic poem.

parallel motion The movement of two or more parts by the same interval.

part A series of notes for voice, instrument, or group, to be performed with other parts or in solo.

partita A suite; a collection of dance tunes.

partsong A contrapuntal composition for three or more voices, unaccompanied.

passion music A musical setting for the story of the suffering and death of Christ.

pasticcio A medley; an opera made up of selections from other operas.

pastorale A musical composition suggestive of rural life.

pentatonic scale A five-toned scale; the diatonic scale with fourth and seventh tones omitted.

phrasing The emphasis and grouping of musical phrases; notation for proper phrasing.

pianissimo A direction to play very softly.

piano quartet A term usually applied to quartets for piano, violin, viola, and cello.

piano quintet A combination of piano with string quartet.

pizzicato A term indicating that strings should be plucked, not bowed.

plainsong A nonmetrical chant in one of the church modes.

poco Little.

poco a poco Little by little.

polka A lively dance in 2/4 time that originated in Bohemia c.1830.

polonaise A Polish dance in a stately rhythm adopted as a musical form by Chopin.

polyphony Contrapuntal music; a style in which melodically independent though harmonic parts are interwoven; the opposite of *homophony*.

precipitato Hurried.

preciso Precise.

prelude An introductory movement complete in itself, as opposed to an introduction, which leads directly into the principal section; a short piano piece in one movement.

program music Music intended to depict the concrete elements of a story or image.

progression   *Melodic:* the passage from tone to tone; *harmonic:* the passage from chord to chord.

quartet   A composition of four parts or voices; the performers of a four-part composition.

quintet   A composition of five voices or instruments; also, the performers of a five-part composition.

recitative   A style of singing resembling dramatic speech.

reel   A popular dance in Scotland for two couples. The Virginia reel is a variant for a large group of dancers.

refrain   Repeated lines that occur at the end of each stanza of a poem.

requiem   A Mass for the dead; also, a musical setting for such a Mass.

resolution   The progression from dissonance to consonance.

rest   A character indicating pause or silence.

retard, ritardando   A direction to gradually slow the speed.

rhapsody   A title given to compositions of a heroic or rhetorical character; an instrumental fantasy based on folk song.

rinforzando   Reinforcing.

ritenato   Immediately slower.

rogoroso   Exact.

romance   A vocal or instrumental composition of a romantic character without fixed form.

rondo   A form of instrumental composition with a recurring leading theme.

root   The fundamental tone of a chord; the lowest tone, unless the chord is inverted.

round   A canon for three or more voices.

scale   A series of tones arranged according to rising pitches.

scherzo   A playful, humorous instrumental composition.

second   The interval between a fundamental tone and the diatonic tone above.

semitone   Half a whole note.

septet   A composition for seven voices or instruments.

sequence   Repetition of a figure at different intervals.

serenade   An inpromptu or unsolicited vocal or instrumental performance, often outdoors; an instrumental composition in several movements for a small group, between the symphony and the suite.

signature   Indications placed on the staff at the beginning of a piece that show the key and the rhythm.

sixth   The sixth diatonic tone above a fundamental; an interval composed of the fundamental and the sixth tone above it.

slur   A curved line over a series of notes indicating the smooth transition between them.

solo   Performed alone.

sonata   An instrumental composition of three or four movements in related keys and in different forms and character.

sonatina   A short, simple sonata.

soprano   The highest female or boy's voice; the treble.

sostenuto   Sustained.

sotto voce   In a low voice.

staccato   Distinct, detached; the opposite of *legato*.

staff   The five horizontal lines on and between which notes are written.

stretto   Compressed; in a fugue, the overlapping of subject and answer.

subdominant   The dominant below; the fourth tone of the diatonic scale, in the same relation to the key note from below as the dominant is from above.

subito Suddenly.

subject A theme used as the basis of a musical form.

submediant The sixth tone of a diatonic scale.

subtonic Under the tone; the seventh tone of the diatonic scale.

suite An instrumental composition consisting of a series of movements or distinct compositions; originally, a cycle of dance tunes.

supertonic The tone one degree above the tonic.

symphonic poem Originated by Franz Liszt, a large narrative orchestral work in one movement.

symphony A sonata for orchestra, usually in four movements.

syncopation A shift from the normally strong to a weak beat.

tempo The speed at which a piece is played, indicated by terms such as *adagio*.

tenor A high male voice; also, the instrument of corresponding range.

tenuto Sustained; held.

theme A musical subject.

third The interval between a fundamental tone and the third diatonic tone above.

time Used synonymously with measure or rhythm.

toccata A composition popular in the sixteenth century, for organ or harpsicord, resembling the capriccio.

tonality Chords grouped around the central tonic chord.

tone A sound of definite duration and pitch; a note.

tone cluster A group of notes played simultaneously with forearm, elbow, and fist in a method introduced by Henry Cowell.

tono Thunder.

transpose To change the key of a composition.

treble The highest voice in a choir or part; soprano; G clef.

tremolo Rapid repetition of a note to resemble trembling.

triad A chord composed of a fundamental tone and a third and fifth above.

trio A composition for three parts or voices; the second part of a minuet or march.

triplet A group of three notes played in the time value of two.

triple time Time in which there are three beats to a measure.

turn An embellishment consisting of the rapid alternation between the written note, the note above it, and the note a half step below.

tutti All; a full orchestra or chorus.

twelve-tone music A method of composition based on a chromatic scale of 12, rather than 8, tones, developed by Arnold Schoenberg.

unison Equal pitch; performance of the same part by all voices.

variation Development of a theme through a variety of forms; differences in rhythm, key, harmony, etc.

vivace A direction to play in a lively manner.

volume Fullness of a tone.

waltz A round dance in triple rhythm performed by couples; also, music in this rhythm.

whole note The longest note in common use.

whole tone An interval of a major second; the interval of two semitones.

> ## THE MAKEUP OF A SYMPHONY ORCHESTRA
>
> **Strings:**   12 to 14 first violins, 10 to 12 second violins, 8 to 10 violas, 6 to 8 cellos, 4 to 6 double basses.
>
> **Woodwinds:**   2 flutes, 2 oboes, 2 clarinets, 2 bassoons.
>
> **Brass:**   2 trumpets, 2 or 4 horns, 2 or 3 trombones, 1 tuba.
>
> **Percussion:**   2 or 3 kettledrums and various instruments of definite pitch (glockenspiel, bells, xylophone) and indefinite pitch (snare drum, bass drum, cymbals, triangle).
>
> **Harps:**   1 or 2 (2 are called for more often than 1).
>
> A larger orchestra would have this typical composition:
>
> **Strings:**   16 first violins, 14 second violins, 12 violas, 10 cellos, 8 double basses.
>
> **Woodwinds:**   2 flutes and piccolo, 2 oboes and English horn, 2 clarinets and bass clarinet, 2 bassoons and contrabassoon.
>
> **Brass:**   3 trumpets, 4 horns, 3 trombones, 1 tuba.
>
> **Percussion and harps:**   As above.

> ## MUSICAL NOTES
>
>
>
> | | | | | | | |
> |---|---|---|---|---|---|---|
> | A | B | C | D | E | F | G |
>
> **Note:** A tone of definite pitch.
>
> The symbols above correspond to the following musical notes:
>
> A. whole note   E. sixteenth note
> B. half tone   F. thirty-second note
> C. quarter note   G. sixty-fourth note
> D. eighth note
>
> A dotted note such as a dotted half note (♩.) means that the note gets one added beat.

Major Dancers and Choreographers of the Twentieth Century

Ailey, Alvin (1931–   ). American choreographer. Ailey formed the American Dance Theater and is noted for dramatic works and use of African elements, as in *Creation of the World* (1954) and *Revelations* (1960).

Alonso, Alicia (1921–   ). Cuban dancer and choreographer. Alonso soloed with companies including the American Ballet Theater (1939) and danced on Broadway. She has formed her own company, now the National Ballet of Cuba.

Ashton, Sir Frederick (1906–88). British choreographer and director of Sadler's Wells (now Royal) Ballet (1935–70). His works include *Cinderella, Ondine*, and *A Month in the Country*.

Astaire, Fred (1899–1987). American actor and dancer in numerous musical comedies, such as *Over the Top* and *The Bandwagon*, and films, including *Top Hat* (1935) and *Shall We Dance?* (1937). Astaire co-starred with Judy Garland, Rita Hayworth, and Ginger Rogers and was distinguished by his original and graceful tap dancing.

Balanchine, George (1904–83). American choreographer and dancer (b. Russia). Balanchine danced with Sergei Diaghilev's Ballet Russe (1924–28); was ballet master, Royal Opera, Copenhagen; organized the Ballet Russe de Monte Carlo (1934); directed the Metropolitan Opera Ballet (1934–37); and served as principal artistic director and choreographer of the New York City Ballet (1948–82). His works, such as *Serenade* and *Agnon*, are often abstract and formal.

Baryshnikov, Mikhail (1948–   ). Soviet choreographer and dancer who emigrated to the West. Baryshnikov was a soloist with the Kirov Ballet (1969–74), a member of the American Ballet Theater (1974–78), and later its director (1980–   ). A leading male dancer of the early 1980s, he appeared in the film *The Turning Point* (1977).

Béjart, Maurice (1928–   ). French director of the Ballets de l'Étoile, Paris (1954–   ). Béjart organized the influential Ballet of the 20th Century, Brussels. His works incorporate nontraditional elements, such as jazz, avant-garde music, and acrobatics.

Bournonville, Auguste (1805–79). Member of the Royal Danish Ballet. Bournonville was a soloist and choreographer of more than 50 works in a distinctive Romantic style.

Bruhn, Erik (1929–   ). Member and director of the Royal Danish Ballet. Bruhn is noted for his precise, dramatic style in such works as *Swan Lake* and *Giselle*.

Cunningham, Merce (1922–   ). American dancer and choreographer. A soloist with the Martha Graham Company, Cunningham formed his own company and experimented in multimedia works, with music by John Cage and others. His works include *Symphony by Chance* and *Square Game*.

d'Amboise, Jacques (1934–   ). American soloist with the New York City Ballet and choreographer. D'Amboise is known for his roles in American-theme works, such as *Western Symphony*. His own works include the ballets *The Chase* and *Irish Fantasy*.

Danilova, Alexandra (c. 1906–   ). Russian-American dancer. Danilova was prima ballerina with the Ballet Russe de Monte Carlo (1939–58) and appeared in the film *The Turning Point* (1977).

De Mille, Agnes (c. 1908–   ). American choreographer and dancer. De Mille created the first American ballet, *Rodeo* (1942), and *Fall River Legend* (1948), and brought ballet techniques to musicals such as *Oklahoma!* (1943).

Diaghilev, Sergei Pavlovich (1872–1929). Russian impresario and founder of the Ballet Russe, Paris (1909), whose productions revolutionized ballet.

Dolin, Anton (1904–   ). English dancer with Diaghilev's Ballet Russe (1924). He was a partner of Alicia Markova in the formation of dance schools (1935, 1949) and danced principal roles at the New York City Ballet Theater.

Duncan, Isadora (1878–1927). American dancer who greatly influenced modern dance. Her works, based on Greek classical art, used free-flowing movements and barefoot dancers. Duncan founded schools in Berlin (1904), Paris (1914), and Moscow (1921).

Eglevsky, André (1917–77). Russian-American member of the Ballet Russe de Monte Carlo 1939–42; premier dancer with the New York City Ballet 1951–59.

Elssler, Fanny (1810–84). Austrian daughter of an assistant to Franz Josef Haydn, Elssler was a favorite in London and Paris, specializing in ballet and forte folk dance.

Fokine, Michel (1880–1942). Russian-American choreographer for Nijinsky and Diaghilev. Fokine is considered the founder of modern ballet. His works include *Firebird* and *Petrouchka*.

Fonteyn, Dame Margot (1919–   ). English star of the Royal Ballet. Her major roles were in *Sleeping Beauty, Firebird,* and *Petrouchka*. Fonteyn was the partner of Rudolf Nureyev after 1962.

Graham, Martha (1895–   ). American dancer and choreographer. Graham formed her own company in 1929. Her works include *Appalachian Spring* and *Archaic Hours*. Her technique is noted for austerity and technical rigor.

Helpmann, Robert (1909–   ). Australian member of the Sadler's Wells Ballet (1933) and partner to Margot Fonteyn. Among his notable works is *Miracle in the Gorbals*.

Horton, Lester (1906–58). American soloist with the Denishawn schools and pioneer of modern dance. His works include *Water Study* and *Theater Piece No. 2*.

Ivanov, Lev (1834–1905). Russian choreographer of the *Nutcracker* (1892) and leading figure of Russian Romanticism.

Joffrey, Robert (1930–88). American choreographer. Joffrey formed his own company, the City Center Joffrey Ballet, in 1954. He choreographed works for the New York City Opera, including Douglas Moore's *The Devil and Daniel Webster* and Marc Blitzstein's *Regina*.

Jooss, Kurt (1901–79). German artist noted for his antiwar *Green Table*. Jooss worked in England with the Ballet Jooss during the Hitler era. He is noted for introducing psychological themes into ballet.

Karsavina, Tamara (1885–1978). Russian member of Diaghilev's Ballet Russe. Karsavina created principal roles in *Firebird* and *Petrouchka* with her partner Nijinsky. She espoused the theories of Fokine.

Kirstein, Lincoln (1907–   ). American co-founder, with Balanchine, of the School of American Ballet (1934). Kirstein was the director of the New York City Ballet (1948–   ) and a promoter of an authentic American style.

Lifar, Serge (1905–   ). Russian member of Diaghilev's company (1923–29). Lifar created the title role for Balanchine's *Prodigal Son* and revolutionized French ballet in works such as *Phèdre*.

Makarova, Natalia (1940–   ). Russian member of the Kirov Ballet (1959–70) and the American Ballet Theater (1970–72). Makarova is noted for outstanding dramatic technique.

Massine, Léonide (1896–1979). Russian-American principal dancer and choreographer of Diaghilev's company (1914–20) and the Ballet Russe de Monte Carlo (1932–42). His choreographed works include *Parade* and the film *The Red Shoes* (1948).

Mitchell, Arthur (1934–   ). American soloist with the New York City Ballet and founder of the Dance Theater of Harlem (1968), the first black classical dance company.

Moiseyev, Igor A. (1906–   ). Soviet ballet master. His company, formerly the State Folk Dance Ensemble, uses classically trained dancers to perform adaptations of folk dances of the Soviet Republics.

Nijinsky, Vaslav (1890–1950). Russian premier dancer with Diaghilev's Ballet Russe. Nijinsky created some of the greatest ballet roles, as in *Petrouchka* and *Afternoon of a Faun*. He is considered by many to be the greatest dancer of the twentieth century.

Nikolais, Alwin (1912–   ). American choreographer of abstract works, including *Kaleidoscope* and *Illusion*. Nikolais formed his own company in New York City in 1949.

Nureyev, Rudolf (1938–   ). Russian soloist with the Kirov Ballet (1958) and leading classical dancer of his generation. Nureyev, often partner to Dame Margot Fonteyn in the Royal Ballet, defected to the West in 1961.

Pavlova, Anna Matreyevna (1881–1931). Russian member of Diaghilev's Ballet Russe. Pavlova toured widely and was considered the greatest ballerina of her generation. She is noted for her role in *Dying Swan*.

Perrot, Jules (1810–1910). French dancer with the Imperial Theater, St. Petersburg (1848–59). His ballets include *Esmeralda* and *Ondine*.

Petipa, Marius (1822–1910). French creator of modern classical ballet. Petipa introduced European technique to the St. Petersburg Imperial Theater. His works include *La Bayadère* (1874) and *Sleeping Beauty* (1890).

Petit, Roland (1924–   ). French founder of the Ballets de Paris de Roland Petit (1948) and director of the Ballets de Marseilles (1972–   ).

Robbins, Jerome (1918–   ). American dancer and choreographer of musical comedies; member of the American Ballet Theater and the New York City Ballet (1969–   ). Robbins is noted for his roles in *Fancy Free* and *West Side Story*. His works include *Dances at a Gathering*.

St. Denis, Ruth (1877–1968). American choreographer and dancer. St. Denis founded the Denishawn schools with her husband, Ted Shawn (1920). Her works include *Radha, Cobras,* and *Incense*.

Taglioni, Maria (1804–84). Italian major ballerina of the Romantic period, noted for her ethereal style and outstanding performances, as in *La Sylphide*, Paris Opera (1832).

Tallchief, Maria (1925–   ). American prima ballerina with the Ballet Russe de Monte Carlo (1942–47) and the New York City Ballet. She promoted American ballet through television appearances and tours.

Taylor, Paul (1930–   ). American dancer with Merce Cunningham and Martha Graham. Taylor formed his own company of innovative modern dance in 1954.

Tharp, Twyla (1941–   ). American innovative dancer (1962–65) and choreographer. Tharp was the director of the Netherlands Dance Theater (1969) and the Stuttgart Ballet (1974–76). She subsequently formed her own company.

Tudor, Anthony (1909–   ). English creator of psychological dramas for the American Ballet Theater and other companies, including *Romeo and Juliet* and *Tiller in the Fields*.

Valois, Dame Ninette de (1898–   ). English choreographic director of the Abbey Theatre, Dublin, and the Old Vic Theatre, London. She established the Sadler's Wells Ballet (1931), London, and became its director.

Vestris, Gaetan (1729–1808). Italian dance master to Louis XVI; considered the greatest dancer of his time. He was the first to discard the mask in mime.

Weidman, Charles (1901–75). American member of the Denishawn company (1920–27). Weidman founded a company with Doris Humphrey in 1927 and his own school in 1945.

Terms Used in Dance

abstract dance A composition of pure or absolute dance movements with no implied meaning beyond that of the movements themselves.

agitando Heel work used in non-Flamenco Spanish dance.

air, en l' In ballet, a step done off the ground—for instance, tour en l'air, rond de jambe. It is the opposite of *par terre*.

alegrias One of the oldest of Flamenco dances, considered the purest and most dignified.

allongé In ballet, an elongated line; the term usually refers to the extension of arms in an arabesque.

arabesque In ballet, the extension of one leg straight in back, while the position of arms and body may vary.

assemblé In ballet, a jump taken with both feet together, usually in fifth position.

attitude In ballet, a pose in which one leg is raised in back with knee bent, usually with arm raised.

axial movement Movement around an axis—for instance, an arm around a body or a group of dancers around another group or individual.

balance A balancing step performed in place, usually in ¾ time.

ballet Classical theatrical dancing; its basic law is aplomb, or perfect balance. Dances are based on five classic positions of the feet.

ballet d'action Ballet with a plot, usually tragic.

balletomane A ballet enthusiast.

ballet de cours, les (court ballets) Spectacles for entertainment produced during the sixteenth and seventeenth centuries, including verse, vocal music, and danced entrées.

ballo Standard Italian dances and their music of the fifteenth and sixteenth centuries.

ballon In ballet, the ability of a dancer to remain suspended in air during a jump; elasticity in jumping.

ballroom dances Social dances usually performed by couples, including the fox-trot, waltz, tango, rumba, and cha cha.

bas In ballet, low, as in the position of arms.

basic movement In ballroom dance, a characteristic figure that remains constant.

basse danse A court dance, precursor of the minuet.

battement A beating movement.

beat In ballet, a beating movement of one leg against the other, or crossing, while in the air.

bergamasque A rustic dance in ¾ time.

bocane A sedate dance for two in ¾ time, named after Bocan, c. 1640.

bourrée A court dance of the sixteenth century, related to the polka.

brisé In ballet, a broken movement.

cabriole In ballet, a movement in the air in which the legs are at an angle to the floor and one leg beats against the other.

cachucha A Spanish dance in ¾ time with castanets.

cambré In ballet, bending back or to the side.

can-can A raucous dance, originated in Paris c. 1830, featuring high leg kicks.

chassé In ballet, a sliding step in which one foot "chases" and displaces the other.

ciseaux A jump in which both legs open while in the air, resembling a scissors.

closed positions In ballet, positions in which the feet are closed: the first, third, and fifth positions.

coda The third part of the pas de deux; the finale of a classic ballet in which all principals appear.

conga A ballroom dance of Afro-Cuban origin in ⁴⁄₄ time in which dancers step to the first three beats and kick to the fourth.

contretemps In ballet, a step in counter time.

corps de ballet The members of a ballet company who do not perform solo.

country dance A traditional English dance in which dancers form two facing lines.

coupé In ballet, a step in which one foot cuts or displaces the other.

couru In ballet, a running step, usually in preparation for a grand jeté.

danseuse étoile The star female dancer of a ballet company.

de face Facing the audience.

dégagé In ballet, to free the foot in preparation for a step.

demi A movement or position executed in less than full measure or force.

demi-plié A half plié; a pose with knees half bent and heels on the floor in any of the five positions.

demi-point On the half toes.

detourné Turning on both feet in a backward direction.

effacé A pose in which the body is at an angle to the audience and the working leg is extended away from the body.

en l'air *See* air, en l'.

entrechat A ballet movement in which the dancer repeatedly crosses his or her legs in the air.

fermé In closed position.

flamenco A Sevillian gypsy dance; also, all nonformal Spanish dances.

fondu In ballet, a lowering of the body by bending the knee.

fouetté en tournant A spectacular movement in which the dancer propels himself or herself around a supporting leg with rapid circular movements of the other leg while remaining in a fixed spot.

foxtrot A dance of American origin in duple time.

galop A quick dance in ¾ time popular in the nineteenth century.

jeté A thrown step; a jump to the side; the *grand jeté:* a large leap forward.

jitterbug A social dance, especially popular in the 1940s, to syncopated music in ⁴⁄₄ time.

kabuki An indigenous Japanese theater dance form, featuring stylized narrative choreographic movements.

mazurka A Polish national dance in triple time, often with a strong accent on the third beat.

minuet A slow, graceful dance of French origin in triple time.

ouvert In ballet, open positions: second and sixth.

pantomime ballet An aspect of ballet movement intended to convey action through the conventional or expressive gesture.

par terre Steps performed on the floor. It is the opposite of *en l'air.*

pas In ballet, a step; usually prefixed to the name of a step, as in *pas allé,* walking step, and *pas couru,* turning step; also, a dance or dance sequence such as *pas seul,* a solo dance.

pas de deux A dance for two people; in classic ballet, a choreographic poem in three parts: the adagio, variations, and the coda.

penché In ballet, leaning forward.

percussive movement In modern dance, a type of movement similar to staccato: the original force of the movement is greater than what is carried through; used particularly in the early works of Martha Graham.

petit tours In ballet, short fast turns in which the dancer progresses in a straight line or circle.

piqué Stepping directly onto the point of a supporting foot.

pirouette A turn on one foot propelled by the swing of the arm.

plié In ballet, bending the knees; *grand plié:* a deep bend in which heels are raised; *demi plié:* a bend with heels remaining on the floor.

polka A Bohemian folk dance in ¾ time, c. 1830, popular throughout central and Eastern Europe.

port de bras Movement of the arms.

premier danseur The principal male dancer of a ballet company.

premier danseuse The ballerina next in rank below *danseuse etoile.*

promenade In ballet, a slow turn of the body on the whole foot in adagio movements.

reel A popular dance in Scotland for two couples. The *Virginia reel* is a variant for a large group of dancers.

relevé In ballet, rising with a spring movement to point or demi-point.

revue A theatrical production of musical numbers, dances, and sketches, without plot or story.

révérence A ballet bow or curtsy.

specialty A solo or duet in a musical, generally prepared by the dancers themselves rather than the choreographer.

spotting Movement of the head during fast turns in which the eyes of the dancer fix on a single spot.

square dance An American folk dance in which an even number of dancers participate, arranged in the formation of a square.

temps In ballet, a step in which there is no transfer of weight from one foot to the other.

tour In ballet, a turn.

two-step A ballroom dance in ¾ time; the precursor of the fox-trot.

variation The second part of the pas de deux; any solo performance in a ballet.

waltz A basic dance in classical and romantic ballets, usually for large ensembles; also, a ballroom dance in ¾ time.

Major Painters and Sculptors

American

Albers, Josef (1888–1976), b. Germany. Artist and designer, teacher at the Bauhaus and director of the Yale School of Art. Albers is best known for the *Homage to the Square* series and for his widely studied color theories.

Calder, Alexander (1898–1976), b. Pennsylvania. Artist best known for his mobiles and his witty wire portraits and constructions of zoos and circuses.

Davies, Arthur Bowen (1862–1928), b. New York State. Member of "The Eight"; organizer of the historic 1913 Armory Show.

Davis, Stuart (1894–1964), b. Pennsylvania. Painter of bright, vibrant works. Davis developed a distinctly American interpretation of Cubism, as in *Colonial Cubism*.

de Kooning, Willem (1904–   ), b. The Netherlands. Leader of U.S. Abstract Expressionism, best known for his monumental series, *Woman*.

Demuth, Charles (1883–1935), b. Pennsylvania. One of the first to incorporate geometric shapes of modern technology into painting. His best-known work is *I Saw the Figure 5 Receding*.

Dove, Arthur (1880–1946), b. New York State. Forerunner of Abstract Expressionism; painter of abstracted natural forms.

Feininger, Lyonel (1871–1956), b. New York State. Teacher at the Bauhaus (1919–32). Feininger developed a geometric style of painting, often representing sailboats or skyscrapers.

Frankenthaler, Helen (1928–   ), b. New York City. Teacher and artist influenced by de Kooning and Pollock. Her works are recognizable for their use of vertical rectangles and square areas creating a sense of distance.

Gorky, Arshile (1904–48), b. Armenia. Painter of abstractions of mysterious organic forms. Gorky influenced the development of Abstract Expressionism.

Hartley, Marsden (1877–1943), b. Maine. Painter of brightly colored works. Hartley developed a distinctly American blend of modernism.

Henri, Robert (1865–1929), b. Ohio. Influential teacher; member of "The Eight." A leader in the rebellion against academicism, Henri is best known for his dramatic portraits.

Hofmann, Hans (1880–1966), b. Germany. Founder of two U.S. art schools important to the development of Abstract Expressionism. His paintings are distinguished by their rough, dissonantly colored rectangular forms.

Homer, Winslow (1836–1910), b. Massachusetts. Probably the most prominent nineteenth-century American painter. A watercolorist, Homer is best known for his dramatic seascapes such as *Breaking Storm* and *The Hurricane*.

Hopper, Edward (1882–1967), b. New York State. Painter of lonely street scenes and stark interiors in vibrant and muted colors, including *Early Sunday Morning*.

Indiana, Robert (1928–   ), b. New Castle, Indiana. Pop artist best known for his *LOVE* paintings and sculpture, which are boldly lettered, vividly colored pieces.

Johns, Jasper (1930–   ), b. Georgia. A founder of the Pop Art movement. Johns used common signs and symbols in his art, such as numbers, flags, and targets, as playful enigmas.

Kent, Rockwell (1882–1971), b. New York State. Painter, writer, and social critic. His major paintings include *Toilers of the Sea* and *Winter*.

Kline, Franz (1910–62), b. Pennsylvania. Painter of large canvases with dynamic black and white brushstrokes. His work exemplifies Abstract Expressionism.

Lichtenstein, Roy (1932–), b. New York City. Painter associated with Pop Art, known for his paintings derived from comic strips, such as *Preparedness*.

Louis, Morris (1912–62), b. Baltimore, Maryland. Painter whose major and later life works used open color technique, which creates an effect where paint and canvas become one in the manner of a dyed cloth.

Marsh, Reginald (1898–1954), b. France. Illustrator and painter known for his depictions of city street life, including *Why Not Use the 'L'?*

Moses, Grandma (Anna Mary Robertson Moses) (1860–1961), b. New York State. A farmer's wife who began painting in her 70s. Her primitive-style, colorful paintings of farm life, such as *Sugaring-Off*, achieved wide popularity.

Motherwell, Robert (1915–), b. Washington State. Painter, writer, and important theoretician of Abstract Expressionism. His works are characterized by amorphous shapes in austere colors; best known is the series *Elegy for the Spanish Republic*.

Nevelson, Louise (1900–88), b. Russia. Sculptor known for her large works of painted wood.

Newman, Barnett (1905–71), b. New York State. Painter whose works bridged Abstract Expressionism and the Color Field movement. His canvases are typically large planes of flat color with thin vertical stripes.

O'Keeffe, Georgia (1887–1987), b. Wisconsin. Painter whose most characteristic images are abstract organic forms. She lived in New Mexico and often used elements of the Southwestern landscape, as in *Cow's Skull, Red, White and Blue*.

Oldenberg, Claes (1929–), b. Sweden. Leader of the Pop Art movement, known for his giant sculptures of common objects, including *Lipstick*.

Parrish, Maxfield (1870–1966), b. Pennsylvania. Creator of posters, magazine covers, and book illustrations in a distinctive, decorative style.

Pollock, Jackson (1912–56), b. Wyoming. Pioneer of Abstract Expressionism. Pollock developed a method of "action paintings." His works are typically large, of dripped and thrown paint in complex, dense rhythms.

Prendergast, Maurice (1859–1924), b. Canada. Member of "The Eight" and painter of landscapes and figurative works in a Post-Impressionist style, including *Promenade* and *Gloucester*.

Pyle, Howard (1853–1911), b. Delaware. Illustrator and writer. His illustrations for children's books display both realism and charm.

Rauschenberg, Robert (1925–), b. Texas. Painter of collages ("combines") appropriating everyday images and objects. The works emphasize their sculptural transformation.

Rivers, Larry (1923–), b. New York State. Painter of Abstract Expressionist works in the 1950s. Later Rivers returned to realistic figures in a style that came to be known as Pop Art.

Rockwell, Norman (1894–1978), b. New York State. Illustrator best known for his *Saturday Evening Post* covers. His popular works portray anecdotal scenes of small-town America.

Rothko, Mark (1903–70), b. Russia. Leader of Abstract Expressionism. His typical canvases contain blurred rectangular forms.

Sargent, John Singer (1856–1925), b. Italy. Painter known for his portraits of celebrities. He also produced impressionistic watercolor landscapes.

Segal, George (1924–), b. New York City. Sculptor known for his life-sized human figures in plaster. Segal is associated with the Pop Art movement.

Shahn, Ben (1898–1969), b. Lithuania. Versatile artist of social-realistic work that often tells a story without the effect of preaching.

Sheeler, Charles (1883–1965), b. Pennsylvania. Photographer and painter known for his depictions of industrial forms reduced to cool, formal simplification.

Smith, David (1906–65), b. Indiana. Renowned abstract sculptor whose works are of wrought iron and cut steel in tomblike form.

Stella, Frank (1936–   ), b. Massachusetts. Painter and sculptor whose works, often wildly exuberant, typically employ sweeping arched forms and concentric angular strips.

Sully, Thomas (1783–1872), b. England. Romantic portraitist of national figures. His most famous work is the historical scene *Washington's Passage of the Delaware*.

Warhol, Andy (1930–87), b. Pennsylvania. Leader of the Pop Art movement. His works are notable for the repetition of everyday images, such as Campbell's soup cans.

Wood, Grant (1891–1942), b. Iowa. Painter best known for his stylized landscapes of the rural Midwest. *American Gothic* is a quintessential American work.

Wyeth, Andrew (1917–   ), b. Pennsylvania. Popular painter of rural landscapes in a meticulous, naturalistic style. His best-known work is *Christina's World*. In the mid-1980s, Wyeth astonished the public with the appearance of the previously secret series the *Helga* paintings.

Belgian: See *Flemish, Belgian*

British

Bacon, Francis (1910–   ), b. Ireland. Painter of horrifying, hallucinatory images, as in *Crucifixion*.

Blake, William (1757–1827). Painter, engraver, and poet. Blake illustrated the works of Milton, the Book of Job, and his own poetic works. In the works of this mystic and visionary, human and natural forms become mythological figures in a spiritual drama.

Constable, John (1776–1837). Leading English Romantic landscape painter. His works include *View on the Stour* and *The Hay Wain*.

Gainsborough, Thomas (1727–88). Portraitist and landscape painter. His well-known works include *The Mall*, *Perdition*, and *The Blue Boy*.

Hogarth, William (1697–1764). Painter of satirical works, often on moralistic themes, especially *The Harlot's Progress* and his masterpiece, *Marriage à la Mode*.

Moore, Henry (1898–1986). Sculptor whose works of reclining women were followed by abstract sculptures with smooth, organic shapes and frequent hollows or voids.

Turner, Joseph Mallord William (1775–1851). Foremost English landscape painter. Turner's works became increasingly abstract in his attempt to represent light, atmosphere, space, and the elemental forces of nature, as in *The Grand Canal* and *Approach to Venice*.

Dutch

Bosch, Hieronymus (Jerom Bos) (c. 1450–1516). Painter whose works depicted ordinary objects, figures, and events in an eerie, surreal fashion.

De Hooch (Hoogh), Pieter (c. 1629–77). Genre painter of intimate interiors. His works show a deft handling of lighting, as in *Courtyard of a Dutch House*.

Mondrian, Piet (1872–1944). Co-founder of the Stijl group and the magazine *De Stijl*. Mondrian developed a geometric style, "Neoplasticism"; typical works are composed of primary-color squares in highly kinetic patterns.

Rembrandt Harmenszoon van Rijn (Ryn) (1606–69). Master of the Dutch school and one of the great Western painters of all time. Rembrandt became established as a portrait painter with his *Anatomy Lesson of Dr. Tulp* (1632). He produced some 600 paintings, including over 100 self-portraits, 300 etchings, and 2,000 drawings, all distinguished by their profound humanity.

Van Gogh, Vincent (1853–90). Perhaps the greatest known of all painters. The majority of Van Gogh's vibrant paintings were produced in a 29-month period of frenzied work that culminated in his suicide. Among his most famous works are *The Potato Eaters, Starry Night, Irises*, and numerous self-portraits.

Vermeer, Jan (Johannes) (1632–75). Genre and landscape painter. Vermeer was a major colorist and painter of intimate interiors, often with a solitary female figure. *Young Woman with a Water Jug* is among his best-known pieces.

Flemish, Belgian

Bruegel, Pieter, the Elder (c. 1525–69). Painter of peasant life in fields and forests, as in *The Harvesters*, and of religious histories and rhythmic landscapes.

Ensor, James (Baron) (1860–1949). Painter and etcher. Ensor created innovative, bizarre, and grotesque compositions, opening the way for the Surrealist movement.

Magritte, René (1898–1967). Early Cubist painter who succumbed to the influence of Surrealist works, as in *The Red Model*.

Rubens, Peter Paul (1577–1640). Foremost Flemish painter of the seventeenth century. Rubens organized a large workshop that produced more than 2,000 works, including *Raising the Cross* and paintings depicting the life of Marie de Médici. His most joyous works, among them *Three Graces* and *Venus and Adonis*, were painted in the last 10 years of his life.

Van Dyck (Vandyke), Sir Anthony (1599–1641). Portraitist, religious painter, and etcher, and assistant to Rubens, later his rival. Van Dyck's portraits include those of James Stuart and Marchesa Durazzo; among his masterpieces is *Lamentation*.

Van Eyck, Jan (c. 1370–c.1440). Known as the father of Flemish painting, Van Eyck established a style of portrait painting that was to become the standard for centuries.

French

Arp, Jean (Hans) (1887–1966). Creator of witty organic abstract works in various media, including *Navel* and *Human Concretion*. Arp was associated with the Dadaists and Surrealists.

Bonnard, Pierre (1867–1947). Painter, lithographer, and illustrator who excelled at domestic interiors. His subtle light effects, as in *Bowl of Fruit*, were reminiscent of Impressionism.

Braque, Georges (1882–1963). Exponent of Fauvism and founder of Cubism with Picasso. His works include *Nude*, *The Table*, and *Woman with a Mandolin*.

Cézanne, Paul (1839–1906). Impressionist painter who moved toward abstraction and Expressionism, as in *Mont Sainte-Victoire*. Cézanne had a profound influence on modern art, especially Cubism.

Chardin, Jean-Baptiste-Siméon (1699–1779). Painter of still lifes and domestic interiors as well as abstract compositions. His works include *Benediction* and *Return from Market*.

Corot, Jean-Baptiste Camille (1796–1875). Influential landscape painter whose works include *The Coliseum*, *Femme à la Perle*, and *Interrrupted Reading*.

Courbet, Gustave (1819–77). Painter of subjects from everyday life. Courbet's work was rejected in his lifetime but later proved highly influential.

Daumier, Honoré (1808–79). Caricaturist, painter, and sculptor. The greatest social satirist of his time, Daumier produced some 4,000 lithographs as well as small canvases in a similar style.

David, Jacques-Louis (1748–1825). Painter and authority on French art who introduced modern art through works inspired by the ideals of the French Revolution.

Degas, Edgar (1834–1917). Painter who favored ballet dancers as subjects. Degas introduced daring compositional innovations, such as cut-off views and unusual angles, as in *Woman with Chrysanthemums* and *Foyer of the Dance*.

Delacroix, Eugène (1798–1863). Foremost French Romantic painter, leader of the opposition to the Neoclassical School of David. His works include *Woman of Algiers* and *Tiger Attacking a Horse*.

Dubuffet, Jean (1901–85). Painter and sculptor of playful, childlike works, typically of asphalt, pebbles, and glass.

Duchamp, Marcel (1887–1968). Painter and sculptor. His *Nude Descending a Staircase* is perhaps the most well known and epochal of Cubist works. Duchamp revolutionized the art world with his "ready mades." His works are characterized by humor, enigma, and complexity.

Dufy, Raoul (1887–1953). Painter, illustrator, and decorator known for his Fauvist landscapes, seascapes, and portraits of society people.

Gauguin, Paul (1848–1903). Painter and woodcutter. At 35 Gauguin left his career as a stockbroker to devote himself to painting. His best-known work, using flat planes, abstracted figures, and bright colors, was executed while he lived on the island of Tahiti.

Ingres, Jean Auguste Dominique (1780–1867). Hailed as an exemplar of Davidian Classicism, Ingres was also deeply influenced by the work of Raphael. His works are both rigidly academic and richly sensual.

Lorrain, Claude (Claude Gelée) (1600–82). French landscape painter who used unlimited vistas and panoramas. Lorrain had a marked impact on Romantic painting.

Manet, Édouard (1832–83). Painter who profoundly influenced Impressionism through the immediacy of his perception. His major works include *The Balcony* and *The File Player*.

Matisse, Henri (1869–1954). Painter, sculptor, lithographer, and major artist of the modern era. Matisse executed significant Impressionist works, including *The Dinner Table*. He used color for abstract, expressive effects and reintroduced the decorative in art.

Millet, Jean François (1814–75). Realist painter associated with the Barbizon School. His works include *The Gleaners* and *The Angelus*.

Monet, Claude (1840–1926). Major figure in the history of landscape painting and a founder of Impressionism. His works are characterized by their intense observation of subtle changes in light and atmosphere, as in the *Haystack* series and the incomparable *Water Lilies*.

Pissarro, Camille (1830–1903), b. Virgin Islands. Impressionist landscape painter who experimented with color theories before developing his own vital interpretation of nature, as in *Bather in the Woods*.

Poussin, Nicolas (1594–1665). Painter who lived most of his life in Italy yet developed the standard for French Classicism. His contemplative, precise clarity had a profound influence on nineteenth-century art.

Renoir, Pierre Auguste (1841–1919). Impressionist painter of sensuous, joyous, light-filled works, such as *Luncheon of the Boating Party*.

Rouault, Georges (1871–1958). Expressionist painter of sad clowns, corrupt judges, prostitutes, and, especially, the suffering Christ.

Rousseau, Henri (1844–1910). Self-taught painter known for his primitive, haunting landscapes.

Seurat, Georges (1859–91). Neo-Impressionist painter who developed the pointillist technique of using small dots of pure color. His works include *A Sunday Afternoon on the Island of La Grande Jatte*.

Toulouse-Lautrec, Henri de (1864–1901). Painter and lithographer influenced by Degas. Music halls, cabarets, and circuses were among his favorite subjects.

Vuillard, Édouard (1868–1940). Painter, lithographer, and member of the Nabis, known for his scenes of Montmartre and his domestic paintings.

German

Dürer, Albrecht (1471–1528). Painter, engraver, and most influential artist of the German School. Dürer is known for his technical mastery, his theoretical contributions, and his adoption of the principles of the Italian Renaissance. His works include the series *Apocalypse* and the humanistic *St. Jerome in His Cell*.

Ernst, Max (1891–1976). Dadaist and a founder of Surrealism. His works include *Two Children Are Threatened by a Nightingale*.

Grosz, George (1893–1959). Artist known for his savage caricatures of post-World War I bourgeois society. Grosz fled Germany for the United States in 1932.

Grünewald, Mathias (Mathis Gothart Neithart) (c. 1475–1528). Religious painter of unusually expressive works, most frequently of the Crucifixion of Christ. His masterpiece is the Isenheim Altarpiece.

Holbein, Hans, the Younger (c. 1497–1543). Outstanding portrait and religious painter of the Northern Renaissance. His works include the famous *Madonna of the Burgomaster Meyer*, *Dead Christ*, and his portrait of Christine of Denmark.

Kollwitz, Käthe Schmidt (1867–1945). Graphic artist and sculptor known for her woodcuts and lithographs. Kollwitz's work reflected her socialist and pacifist views.

Italian

Bellini, family of Venetian painters of the Renaissance. *Gentile Bellini* (1429–1507) painted contemporary Venetian life. His brother *Giovanni* (c. 1430–1516) painted serene and luminous works such as *St. Job* and *St. Francis in Ecstasy*. Giovanni was the teacher of Titian and Giorgione.

Bernini, Giovanni Lorenzo (Gianlorenzo) (1598–1680). Sculptor, painter, architect, and leading figure of Italian Baroque art. Bernini produced dynamic works, such as *Rape of Proserpine* and *Apollo and Daphne*, in reaction to the Mannerist works of his time.

Boccioni, Umberto (1882–1916). Painter, sculptor, and major figure of Futurist art. His works include the painting *The City Rises* and the sculpture *Unique Forms of Continuity in Space*.

Botticelli, Sandro (Alessandro di Mariano Filipepi) (c. 1444–1510). Renaissance painter, favorite of the Medici, supreme colorist, and master of the rhythmic line. Botticelli is known for his mythological scenes, as in *Spring* and *Birth of Venus*.

Caravaggio, Michelangelo (Michelangelo Merisi) (c. 1565–1609). Painter whose placement of sacred figures in commonplace settings was thought irreverent in his time but who ultimately influenced such figures as Rembrandt and Ribera.

Cellini, Benvenuto (1500–71). Sculptor, metalsmith, and author. His late Florentine sculptures include *Perseus with the Head of Medusa* and the bust of Cosimo I.

Chirico, Giorgio de (1888–1978), b. Greece. Forerunner of Surrealism. His "metaphysical paintings" are characterized by deep perspective, mannequin figures, and forms unrelated to their contexts.

Correggio (Antonio Allegri) (c. 1494–1534). Baroque painter of mythological scenes. His most famous piece is *Assumption of the Virgin*.

Da Vinci, Leonardo *See* Leonardo da Vinci.

della Robbia, Florentine family of sculptors and ceramicists known for their enameled terra cotta. *Luca della Robbia* (c. 1400–82) founded a workshop and perfected a method of ceramics continued by his nephew *Andrea della Robbia* (1435–c. 1525) and Andrea's sons, *Luca II, Giovanni,* and *Girolamo.*

Donatello (c. 1386–1466). Foremost sculptor of the Renaissance. Donatello headed a vast workshop in Padua. His masterpieces include *Magdalen* of San Lorenzo and the expressive *St. Mark.*

Fra Angelico (Guido or **Guidolino de Pietro,** also known as **Giovanni da Fiesole)** (c. 1400–55). Religious painter whose works include the frescos *Annunciation* and *Noli Mi Tangere,* distinguished for their sense of spatial depth.

Giotto (Giotto di Bondone) (c. 1266–c. 1337). Florentine painter and architect said to have determined the course of painting in Europe. Giotto turned from Byzantine formulas to the study of nature. He painted dramatic narrative frescos, such as *Life of the Virgin* and *Last Judgment,* which achieved a remarkable representation of space without the use of a system of perspective.

Leonardo da Vinci (1452–1519). Painter, sculptor, musician, engineer, scientist, and supreme figure of the Renaissance. His studies of perspective and anatomy contributed greatly to the course of painting. Among Leonardo's paintings are some of Europe's greatest masterpieces, including the sublime *Last Supper.*

Lippi, Fra Filippo (c. 1406–69). Foremost Florentine Renaissance painter, best known for his easel paintings, including *Virgin Adoring the Christ Child.*

Michelangelo Buonarroti (1475–1564). Sculptor, painter, poet, architect, and foremost figure of the Renaissance. His master works include the well-known statue *David* in Florence; the scenes from Genesis on the ceiling of the Sistine Chapel; his statues of the Medici; and the allegorical *Dawn, Evening, Night and Day.*

Modigliani, Amedeo (1884–1920). Sculptor, painter, and early Cubist. African influences are evident in his later style, distinguished by the use of long faces drawn in pure lines.

Piero della Francesca (c. 1420–92). Major Renaissance painter who enjoyed the play of mathematical ratios, as in *The Story of the True Cross,* depicting scenes from the *Golden Legend.*

Pisano, Nicola (c. 1220–c. 1280). Sculptor and founder of a school of sculpture. His greatest works include the pulpit with scenes from the life of Christ for the baptistry in Pisa and the reliefs for the fountain at Perugia.

Raphael (Santi or **Sanzio)** (1483–1520). High Renaissance painter emulated far into the nineteenth century. His works include *The Knight's Dream, Agony in the Garden,* numerous madonnas, and *The Deliverance of St. Peter.*

Titian (Tiziano Vecellio) (c. 1490–1576). Venetian Renaissance painter. His masterpieces include the altarpiece of the Assumption of the Virgin, *La Gloria,* and the *Rape of Europa.*

Uccello, Paolo (c. 1396–1475). Florentine painter and early master of perspective. His scenes from *Battle of San Romano* are notable for their experiments with foreshortening.

Verrocchio, Andrea del (Andrea di Michele di Francesco di Lioni) (1435–88). Florentine sculptor and painter. Verrocchio was a figure of the early Renaissance. His sculptures include *Boy with a Dolphin* and the imposing figure for the equestrian monument of Bartolomeo Colleoni in Venice.

Mexican

Kahlo, Frida (1907–54). Crippled painter of self-portraits and works that convey physical and psychic pain.

Orozco, José Clemente (1883–1949). Muralist and one of the leaders of the Mexican Renaissance. Orozco is known for his frescos, including *Mankind's Struggle*.

Rivera, Diego (1886–1957). Muralist whose works typically portray his socialist ideals and the hope for a Mexican socio-political renaissance.

Tamayo, Rufino (1899–   ). Foremost modern Mexican painter of formal and decorative works, influenced by Cubism and Fauvism.

Spanish

Dali, Salvador (1904–89). Surrealist painter working in a precise style, typically on small canvases. His nightmarish effects can be seen in *Persistence of Memory*.

El Greco *See* Greco, El.

Goya y Lucientes, Francisco José de (1746–1828). Painter known for his savage satires and bleak outlook. Among his best-known works are *Disasters of War*, *Black Painting*, and *Satan Devouring His Children*.

Greco, El (Domenicos Theotocopoulos) (c. 1541–1614), b. Crete. Visionary painter who produced dynamic representations of religious ecstasy. Among his masterpieces are *Baptism, Crucifixion*, and *Resurrection*.

Gris, Juan (José Victoriáno Gonzalez) (1887–1972). Painter of still lifes in oil and collages. Gris used simple, architectural forms and was a developer of Synthetic Cubism.

Miró, Joan (1893–1983). Surrealist painter in a lyrical style characterized by brilliant colors and the free play of abstract shapes.

Murillo, Bartolemé Estéban (1617–82). Religious and portrait painter. Among his greatest works are *Knight of the Collar* and *Girl and Her Duenna*.

Picasso, Pablo (1881–1973). Painter, sculptor, graphic artist, and ceramicist. Picasso's versatile works fall into varied periods of style, personal rather than historical, such as his blue period and his rose period. His landmark *Guernica* is a large-scale work on the agony of war.

Velázquez, Diego Rodriguez de Silva y (1599–1660). Most celebrated painter of the Spanish School. From his early monumental chiaroscuro works evolved consummate art based on color values. Velázquez' paintings include *Venus and Cupid*, *Coronation of the Virgin*, and *The Maids of Honor*.

Zurbarán, Francisco de (1598–1664). Baroque painter who produced large narrative works as well as portraits of devotional figures.

Other

Brancusi, Constantin (1876–1957). Rumanian sculptor whose economical, simple style was radically innovative. His best-known work is the elegant *Bird in Space*.

Chagall, Marc (1889–1985). Russian painter who lived most of his life in France. His works, such as *I and the Village* and *Rabbi of Vitebsk*, explored Jewish life and folklore, often in a fantastic and symbolic way.

Gabo, Naum (1890–1977). Russian Constructivist sculptor and theorist. Gabo wrote the *Realist Manifesto*, in which he proposed that modern concepts of time and space be incorporated into art.

Giacometti, Alberto (1901–66). Swiss sculptor and painter known for his bronze sculptures of elongated figures, such as *Man Walking*.

Kandinsky, Wassily (1866–1944). Russian painter considered the originator of abstract art. Kandinsky was the author of *Concerning the Spiritual in Art* (1912), a founder of the avant-garde *Blaue Reiter* group, and a teacher at the Bauhaus.

Klee, Paul (1879–1940). Swiss painter whose works, such as *Twittering Machine* and *Revolutions of the Viaducts*, combined sophisticated theories of abstraction with playful, childlike inventiveness. Klee was associated with the *Blaue Reiter* group.

Klimt, Gustav (1862–1918). Austrian figure of the Art Nouveau movement, creator of extravagant exotic and erotic works with symbolic themes.

Kokoschka, Oskar (1886–1980). Austrian Expressionist painter. His well-known works include the portrait of Hans Tietze and his wife and the landscape *Jerusalem.*

Munch, Edvard (1863–1944). Norwegian painter and graphic artist. Munch forwarded Expressionism through his emotionally charged images of fear, anxiety, and isolation, as in *The Shriek, The Kiss*, and *The Vampire.*

Phidias (Pheidias) (c. 500–c. 432 B.C.). One of the greatest of ancient Greek sculptors, although none of his works survive. Phidias was the creator of the famed sculpture of Zeus at Olympus, one of the Seven Wonders of the Ancient World.

Praxiteles (c. 370–330 B.C.). Greek sculptor considered the greatest of his time. His *Hermes with the Infant Dionysus* is the only extant sculpture by an ancient master.

Tatlin, Vladmir Evagofovitch (1885–1956). Russian founder of Constructivism. His works include the *Constructions* of 1913–14 in wood, metal, and glass.

Terms Used in Art

appliqué An alien material applied to the surface of an art object or painting for ornamentation.

bas-relief Low relief; sculpture in which figures project slightly from the background.

cameo A gem on which a design has been engraved in relief.

caricature A picture ludicrously exaggerating the qualities, defects, or peculiarities of a person or idea.

cartoon A humorous sketch or drawing usually telling a story or caricaturing some person or action. In fine arts, a preparatory sketch or design for a picture or ornamental motif to be transferred to a fresco or tapestry.

chiaroscuro The rendering of light and shade in painting; the subtle gradations and marked variations of light and shade for dramatic effect; also, a woodcut print produced from two blocks, each of a different tone of the same color.

colors, complementary Two colors at opposite points on the color scale, for example, orange and blue, green and red.

colors, primary Red, yellow, and blue, the mixture of which will yield all other colors in the spectrum but which themselves cannot be produced through a mixture of other colors.

colors, secondary Orange, green, and purple, colors produced by mixing two primary colors.

composition The organization of the parts of a work into a unified whole.

dry point A technique of engraving, using a sharp-pointed needle, that produces a furrowed edge resulting in a print with soft, velvety lines.

engraving The art of producing printed designs through various methods of incising on wood or metal blocks, or through photographic processes.

etching The technique of engraving designs on metal blocks through the corrosive action of acids.

figure A representation of a human or an animal form.

foreshortening Reducing or distorting in order to represent three-dimensional space as perceived by the eye, according to the rules of perspective.

fresco The technique of painting on most lime plaster with colors ground in water or a limewater mixture.

genre painting A realistic style of painting in which everyday life forms the subject matter, as distinguished from religious or historical painting.

highlight On a represented form, a point of most intense light.

high relief Sculptured relief in which areas strongly project from the background, almost becoming a sculpture in the round.

impasto In painting, the thick application of paint; in ceramics, the application of enamel or slip to a ceramic object to form a decoration in low relief.

inlaying The decoration of an object with fine materials set into its surface.

landscape The genre of painting in which natural scenery is the subject.

lithography A printing process in which ink impressions are taken from a flat stone or metal plate prepared with some greasy or oily substance.

middle distance (middle ground) The represented space in a picture between background and foreground.

modeling The formation of an image in clay, wax, etc., to be reproduced in some more durable material, such as bronze; also, the representation of a structure, such as a building.

monochrome A painting or drawing with a single color in different shades.

monotype A single print made from a metal or glass plate on which has been painted an image in paint, ink, etc.

palette A flat surface used by a painter to mix colors, traditionally oblong with a hole for the thumb; also, a range of colors used by a particular painter.

paste A soft, subdued color; a dry paste made of ground pigments, chalk, and gum water formed into a stick; also, a drawing made with such a stick.

perspective A method of representing three-dimensional volumes and spatial relationships on a flat surface.

photoengraving A photographic process of preparing plates in relief for letterpress printing.

polychrome Of many or various colors.

primary colors *See* colors, primary.

relief The projection of an image or form from its background. In painting or drawing, the apparent projection of parts conveying the illusion of three dimensions; in printing, any process in which ink impressions are produced from the high areas of a prepared printing block.

scumbling A painting technique in which parts are overlayed with opaque or semiopaque color applied lightly with an almost dry brush.

secondary colors *See* colors, secondary.

stenciling A method of producing images or letters from sheets of cardboard, metal, or other materials from which images or letters have been cut away.

still life The representation of inanimate objects in painting, drawing, or photography.

tempera A painting technique in which an emulsion of water and egg yolk, or egg and oil, is used as a binding medium.

texture The visual and tactile quality of a work of art effected through the particular way the materials are worked; also, the distribution of tones or shades of a single color.

tone The effect of the harmony of color and values in a work, for example, warm or cold tones.

trompe l'oeil In painting, the fine, detailed rendering of objects to convey the illusion of spatial and tactile qualities.

values In painting, the degree of lightness or darkness in a color.

Art Movements

Abstract Expressionism A movement in painting, also called action painting, originating in New York City in the 1940s. Propelled by the work of Arshile Gorky, its focus is on surface qualities and on the act of painting itself, with the admission of the accidental. It was the first important school of American painting to develop independently of European styles.

Art Deco Design prevalent during the 1920s and 1930s, characterized by a sleek use of straight lines and slender forms.

Art Nouveau A decorative art movement that emerged at the turn of the century. It is characterized by dense ornamentation in sinuous forms, as in twining plant tendrils, and is often symbolic and of an erotic nature.

Ash Can ("The Eight") A group of American artists, founded in 1908, bound by their opposition to academicism, so called because of their portrayal of everyday American life.

Barbizon School An association of French landscape painters c. 1830–70, led by Théodore Rousseau.

Baroque A movement in painting of the seventeenth and eighteenth centuries characterized by deep perspective and strong compositional unity, with attention to the treatment of three-dimensional volumes in space. It is exemplified in the work of Caravaggio and Rubens.

Byzantine A style of art of the Byzantine Empire and its provinces, characterized by the use of iconography, rich colors, tight formalism, and shallow pictorial space.

classical Referring to the principles of the Greek art of antiquity with its emphasis on harmony and proportion; also, describing works in which the emphasis is on structure and form.

Conceptual Art A radical movement in the United States of the 1960s and 1970s that emphasized the art concept over the art object. It attempted to free art from the confines of the gallery and the pedestal.

Constructivism A Russian movement founded by Vladimir Tatlin (c. 1913) related to Suprematism; free geometric constructions in space were created using materials of the machine age.

Cubism A movement in painting, originated in Paris, 1907, that presents objects analytically, typically in fragmented planes, as the mind—not the eye—perceives them, following the principles of modern science.

Dadaism A nihilist movement (1916–22) originated in Europe by the French poet Tristan Tzara and continued in the United States by Duchamp, Arp, and Ernst. Dadaism laid the foundation for Surrealism.

The Eight *See* Ash Can.

Expressionism A style of painting in which the communication of an inner vision or feeling is achieved through the distorted rendering of external reality.

Fauvism Literally, "wild beast," a name used derisively yet adopted by a group of French painters, including Matisse, Braque, and Dufy, who used distorted forms and abstract or expressive color.

folk art Works of a culturally homogeneous people without formal training, generally according to nationalistic traditions and involving crafts.

Futurism An Italian school of painting (1909–19) that conveys the dynamism of the twentieth century, the machine age, and the glories of war. It heralded the emergence of fascism.

Impressionism A late nineteenth-century French school of painting characterized by the direct yet analytical observation of nature and the rendering of transitory visual impressions, with an emphasis on light.

Mannerism A style in art and architecture (c. 1520–1600) that arose in reaction to the harmony of form and proportion of the High Renaissance, featuring strange, unbalanced forms, tunnel-like spaces, arbitrary arrangements, and harsh lighting.

Minimalism A movement in American painting and sculpture that originated in New York City in the early 1960s. It emphasized pure, reduced forms and colors without references beyond themselves, as exemplified in the works of Joel Shapiro and Frank Stella.

pointillism A systematic method of painting developed by Georges Seurat and Paul Signac using dabs of pure color to produce intense color effects.

Pop Art An American movement that arose in the 1950s in opposition to seriousness in art. It used common objects and the repetition of commercial imagery, as in the soup cans of Andy Warhol.

Post-Impressionism A term used by Roger Fry to refer to a group of nineteenth-century painters, including Cézanne, Van Gogh, Gauguin, Matisse, and Picasso, who rejected Impressionism.

Pre-Raphaelites English painters and poets (c. 1848) who imitated the style of Italian painters prior to Raphael in rejection of the materialism of industrialized England.

Realism The direct representation of natural forms; the nineteenth-century French movement that sprang up in reaction to academicism.

Romanticism A movement in painting of the late eighteenth and nineteenth centuries that arose in opposition to Classical Formalism and Rationalism. It emphasized nature and atmosphere.

Suprematism A Russian movement in painting originated by Kazimir Malevich in 1913 parallel to Constructivism in sculpture. It was characterized by flat geometrical shapes on pure canvases and emphasized the spiritual value of pure form.

Surrealism A movement in art of the 1920s and 1930s that emphasized the unconscious, often using images from dreams. Images were arranged either without rational connections or in abstract, amorphous forms.

Major Playwrights and Their Best-Known Works

Greek

Aeschylus (525–456 B.C.) Athenian tragic poet and the originator of tragic drama. Aeschylus authored some 90 plays, including the trilogy the *Oresteia* and the famous *Prometheus Bound*.

Aristophanes (c. 448–c. 388 B.C.). Athenian comic poet, greatest of the ancient writers of comedy. His 11 surviving plays, social, political, and literary satires, are the only complete extant examples of ancient Greek comedy. Among them are *The Clouds, The Wasps, Lysistrata, The Frogs,* and *Plutus.*

Euripides (c. 480–406 B.C.). Greek tragic poet. One of the three great Greek tragedians, Euripides' work is characterized by his rationalism. He authored some 92 plays, 19 of which survive. Among them are *Alcestis, Medea, Electra, Iphigenia in Tauris, The Phoenician Women, Orestes,* and *The Bacchae.*

Sophocles (c. 496–c. 406 B.C.). Greek tragic poet. One of the three great Greek tragedians, Sophocles was the innovator of dramatic form. Seven of his plays survive, including *Ajax* (perhaps his earliest), *Antigone, Oedipus Rex,* and *Electra.*

Roman

Seneca (3 B.C.–A.D. 65.) Roman philosopher, dramatist, and statesman. His nine extant tragedies, characterized by their lofty, moralistic tone, are modeled on Greek tragedies. His plays include *Phaedra, Agamemnon,* and *Medea.*

English

Beaumont, Francis (c. 1584–1616). Dramatist who collaborated with John Fletcher on many plays. Beaumont wrote as sole author *The Knight of the Burning Pestle* (1607–10), *The Masque of the Inner Temple, Gray's Inn* (1613), and *The Theatre of Apollo*.

Dekker (Decker), Thomas (c. 1572–1632). Dramatist and pamphleteer. His most significant plays are *The Shoemaker's Holiday* (1600), *Old Fortunatus* (1600), *The Honest Whore* (with Thomas Middleton, 1604; part II, 1630), *The Roaring Girl* (with Thomas Middleton, 1611), and *The Virgin Martyr* (with Philip Massinger, 1622). Dekker was imprisoned for debt from 1613 to 1619.

Fletcher, John (1579–1625). Prolific and immensely popular playwright who collaborated with Francis Beaumont and many other dramatists, apparently including Shakespeare (*The Two Noble Kinsmen*, 1613–16, and *Henry VIII*, 1613). Among Fletcher's solo plays are two early tragedies, *Valantinian* (1610–14) and *Bonduca* (1609–14), and the comedies *Wit Without Money* (1614–20), *The Woman's Prize* (1604–17), and *Rule a Wife and Have a Wife* (1624), his sequel to Shakespeare's *The Taming of the Shrew*.

Jonson, Ben (1572–1637). Dramatist and poet tried for killing another actor in a duel and imprisoned in 1598. His masterpieces are *Volpone, Epicone, The Alchemist,* and *Bartholomew Fair*.

Kyd (Kid), Thomas (1558–94). Author of *The Spanish Tragedy* (1592), which may have been the source for the ghost and play-within-the-play of Shakespeare's *Hamlet*. Kyd was the major playwright of the English Renaissance and the best-known representative of the "tragedy of the blood" genre.

Marlowe, Christopher (1564–93). Elizabethan playwright second only to Shakespeare. Marlowe established the use of blank verse in English drama. His most important plays are *Tamburlaine* (c. 1587), *Dr. Faustus* (c. 1588), *The Jew of Malta* (c. 1589), and a history, *Edward II*.

Middleton, Thomas (1570–1627). Dramatist and pamphleteer known for his satiric plays. Among the most outstanding are *A Trick to Catch the Old One* (1608), *A Chaste Maid in Cheapside* (c. 1612), and *No Wit, No Help Like a Woman's* (c. 1617). His powerful tragedies include *The Changeling* (1653) and *The Spanish Gipsy* (1653).

Rowley, William (c. 1585–c. 1642). Dramatist and actor best known for his works written with Thomas Middleton, including *The Spanish Gipsy* (1653) and *The Changeling* (1653). His solo plays include *A New Wonder* (1632), *A Watch at Midnight* (1633), and *All's Lost by Lust* (1633).

Shakespeare, William (1564–1616). Poet, dramatist, and the most influential writer in the history of English literature. His career may be divided into four periods. The first (1589–94) includes *The Comedy of Errors*, the three parts of *Henry VI, Titus Andronicus, The Two Gentlemen of Verona, Richard II, Love's Labour's Lost, The Taming of the Shrew,* and *King John*. The second (1595–1600), referred to as Shakespeare's lyrical period, includes his best comedies and history plays, as well as most of his poems and sonnets: *Richard II, A Midsummer Night's Dream, The Merchant of Venice, Romeo and Juliet,* parts I and II of *Henry IV, The Merry Wives of Windsor, Much Ado About Nothing, Henry V, Julius Caesar, As You Like It,* and *Twelfth Night*. The third period (1601–09) includes his greatest tragedies: *Hamlet, Measure for Measure, Othello, King Lear, Macbeth, Antony and Cleopatra, Timon of Athens,* and *Pericles, Prince of Tyre*. The fourth period (1609–13) includes *The Tempest, The Winter's Tale, Cymbeline,* and two plays that appear to have been written with John Fletcher, *Henry VIII* and *The Two Noble Kinsmen*.

Sheridan, Richard Brinsley (Irish-English, 1751–1816). Dramatist. His works include *The Rivals* (1775), *The School for Scandal* (1777), and *The Critic* (1779).

Webster, John (1580–1625). Playwright best known for two tragedies, *The White Devil* (1612) and *The Duchess of Malfi* (1614). Webster collaborated with numerous playwrights, including Thomas Dekker, with whom he wrote *Westward Ho!* (1604) and *Northward Ho!* (1605).

Spanish

Calderón de la Barca, Pedro (1600–81). Writer of a masterful series of one-act religious plays as well as philosophical dramas, including his masterpiece, *Life Is a Dream*.

Tirso de Molina (Gabriel Tellez) (1571–1648). Author of *The Love Rogue*, probably the original version of the Don Juan legend, and the outstanding playwright of the Golden Age. Tirso authored some 300 to 400 plays, among them *The Man Damned by Jealousy, Prudence in a Woman,* and *Pious Martha.*

Vega, Lope de (Lope Félix de Vega Carpio) (1652–35). Member of the Spanish Armada and outstanding figure of Spanish literature. His disregard for neoclassical models had a market impact on European drama. Vega's works include *The Star of Seville, King Peter in Madrid,* and *The Golden Fleece.*

French

Corneille, Pierre (1606–84). Playwright whose early masterpiece *Le Cid* (1637) received such harsh criticism from the French Academy that his subsequent works were stifled by adherence to classical models. Corneille continued to produce a score of tragedies, among them *Horace* (1640), *Cinna* (1640), and *Polyeucte* (1643).

Molière, Jean Baptiste Poquelin (1622–73). Dramatist and actor. In his youth Molière joined the Béjart troupe of actors, with whom he remained. His comedies are distinguished for their caricatures and satire. Among them are *Le Misanthrope* (1664), *L'Avare* (1668), and *Le Bourgeois Gentilhomme* (1670).

Racine, Jean (1639–99). Exemplar of French Classicism, master of the Alexandrian line. His early plays were imitative of Pierre Corneille, whose status as the leading French dramatist Racine was to rival with the appearance of his tragedy *Andromaque* (1667). His subsequent tragedies include *Britannicus* (1669), *Berenice* (1670), *Mithradate,* and *Phedre.*

Nineteenth-Century

Chekhov, Anton Pavlovich (1860–1904). Russian dramatist and short-story writer. His outstanding plays are *Ivanov, The Sea Gull, Uncle Vanya* (1899), *The Three Sisters* (1901), and *The Cherry Orchard* (1904).

Gorky, Maxim (Aleksey Maximovich Pyeshkov) (1868–1936). Russian novelist, short-story writer, and playwright. Gorky won his international reputation for his drama of the slums, *The Lower Depths* (1902).

Hugo, Victor Marie (1802–85). French poet, dramatist, novelist, and outstanding figure of nineteenth-century French literature. His dramatic works include the tragedy *Hernani* (the source for Verdi's opera *Ernani*) and *Le roi s'amuse* (1832) (the source for Verdi's *Rigoletto*). Other plays include *Marione de lorme* and *Les burgraves* (1843).

Ibsen, Henrik (1828–1906). Norwegian poet and dramatist. His plays characteristically deal with the conflict between the individual and society. Among his masterpieces are *A Doll's House* (1879), *Ghosts* (1881), *An Enemy of the People* (1882), *The Wild Duck* (1884), *The Lady From the Sea* (1888), *Hedda Gabler* (1894), and *When We Dead Awaken* (1899).

Rostand, Edmond (1868–1918). French poet and dramatist, author of the masterly *Cyrano de Bergerac* (1897), a tour de force of dramatic poetry.

Shaw, George Bernard (1856–1950). British (b. in Ireland) dramatist, journalist, music critic, and drama critic. Among his best-known plays are *Man and Superman* (1903), *Major Barbara* (1905), *Androcles and the Lion* (1911), *Pygmalion* (1912), and his masterpiece, *Saint Joan* (1924).

Strindberg, Johan August (1849–1912). Swedish dramatist and novelist known for his plays about the misery of domestic life. Of some 70 plays, the best-known are *The Father* (1887), *Comrades* (1888), *Miss Julie* (1888), and *After the Fire* (1907).

Wilde, Oscar (1854–1900), British (b. in Ireland) dramatist, novelist, and poet. Wilde was distinguished for his wit and versatility as well as his eccentricity in dress and life style. His dramatic works include a verse tragedy, *The Duchess of Padua* (1891), as well as drawing-room comedies such as *A Woman of No Importance* (1893) and *The Importance of Being Earnest* (1895).

Twentieth-Century

Albee, Edward (1928–   ). American writer, producer, director. He is best known for a skillful sense of dialogue and the plays *The Zoo Story* (1959), *Who's Afraid of Virginia Woolf?* (1962), and *Tiny Alice* (1964).

Anouilh, Jean (1910–   ). French dramatist. Among his innovative dramas are *Antigone* (1944) and *The Waltz of the Toreadors* (1952).

Beckett, Samuel (1906–   ). French (b. in Ireland) novelist and playwright. His most significant plays, *Waiting for Godot* (1952) and *Endgame* (1957), typify his theater of the absurd technique, combining humor and pathos with existential anguish and vacuity.

Brecht, Bertolt (1898–1956). German playwright and poet, innovator of the revolutionary "epic theater," and committed Marxist. His best-known plays in English translation are *The Threepenny Opera* (with music by Kurt Weill, 1928), *Galileo* (1939), and *Mother Courage* (1941).

Coward, Sir Noel (1899–1973). English dramatist, actor, producer, composer, and director. Coward was best known for his highly successful comedies and musicals, including *Private Lives* (1930), *Blithe Spirit* (1941), and *Bitter Sweet* (1929).

Eliot, Thomas Stearns (T.S.) (1888–1965). English author. His plays, including *Murder in the Cathedral* (1935) and *The Cocktail Party* (1950), are outstanding examples of modern verse drama.

Genet, Jean (1919–86). French dramatist and preeminent playwright of the theater of the absurd. His best-known plays in English translation include *The Balcony* (1956), *The Blacks* (1958), and *The Screens*.

Giraudoux, Jean (1882–1944). French novelist and dramatist. His plays, such as *Tiger at the Gates* (1935) and *Electra* (1937), are mostly reinterpretations of Greek myths.

Hellman, Lillian (1905–84). American dramatist. Her best-known plays, often indictments of injustice, include *The Children's Hour* (1934), *The Little Foxes* (1939), and *Watch on the Rhine* (1941).

Ionesco, Eugene (1912–   ). French (b. in Rumania) playwright, author of classic plays of the theater of the absurd. His plays include *The Bald Soprano* (1950), *The Chairs* (1952), and *Rhinoceros* (1959).

Lorca, Federico Garcia (1899–1936). Spanish poet and playwright. Among his best-known plays in English translation are *Blood Wedding* (1939), *Yerma* (1934), and *The House of Bernarda Alba* (1936). He was shot dead by Franco's soldiers soon after the outbreak of the Spanish Civil War.

Mamet, David (1947–   ). American playwright best known for *American Buffalo* (1975).

Miller, Arthur (1915–   ). Outstanding American playwright. His plays include *The Crucible* (1953), *A View from the Bridge* (1955), and his masterpiece, *Death of a Salesman* (1949).

Odets, Clifford (1906–63). American playwright. His plays of social and political protest include *Waiting for Lefty* (1935) and *Awake and Sing* (1935). Among his other plays are *Golden Boy* (1937) and *The Big Knife* (1949).

O'Neill, Eugene (1888–1953). American playwright and four-time winner of the Pulitzer Prize, in 1920 for *Beyond the Horizon;* in 1922 for *Anna Christie;* in 1928 for *Strange Interlude;* and in 1956 for *A Long Day's Journey into Night.* O'Neill also won the 1936 Nobel Prize for literature. Among his other outstanding plays are *The Iceman Cometh* (1946) and the trilogy *Mourning Becomes Electra* (1931), based on Aeschylus' trilogy.

Pinter, Harold (1930–   ). English dramatist. His best-known plays include *The Dumbwaiter* (1957), *The Birthday Party* (1958), *The Caretaker* (1960), and *The Homecoming* (1965). Pinter's works are characterized by silences and the use of inaction.

Pirandello, Luigi (1867–1936). Italian dramatist and novelist, winner of the 1934 Nobel Prize for literature. Among his plays in English translation are *Right You Are If You Think You Are* (1922), *Henry IV* (1922), and *The Pleasure of Honesty* (1923). Pirandello's best-known work outside of Italy is *Six Characters in Search of an Author* (1921).

Saroyan, William (1908–81). American author of the Pulitzer prize-winning *The Time of Your Life* (1939). Saroyan refused the award.

Sartre, Jean-Paul (1905–80). French philosopher, novelist, and playwright. His plays in English translation include *The Flies* (1947), *No Exit* (1947), *The Victors* (1948), and *The Dirty Hands* (1949), all of which embody his Existentialist philosophy. In 1964 Sartre won the Nobel prize for literature.

Shepard, Sam (1943–   ). American writer of surrealistic, allegorical plays that include *Operation Sidewinder* (1970); *The Curse of the Starving Class* (1976), a Pulitzer Prize winner; *Buried Child* (1978); and *Fool for Love* (1984).

Stoppard, Tom (1937–   ). Czech-born English dramatist best known for *Rosencrantz and Guilderstein Are Dead* (1967).

Synge, John Millington (1871–1909). Irish poet and dramatist best known for his plays about Irish peasant life. Synge was co-founder of the Abbey Theatre with William Butler Yeats. Among his works are *In the Shadow of the Glen* (1903), *Riders to the Sea* (1904), and *Playboy of the Western World* (1907), which created a furor.

Wilder, Thornton (1897–1975). American novelist and playwright. His plays *Our Town* (1938) and *The Skin of Our Teeth* (1942) were both winners of the Pulitzer Prize. Other plays are included in *The Long Christmas Dinner and Other Plays* (1931).

Williams, Tennessee (1911–83). American dramatist. Among his outstanding plays are *The Glass Menagerie* (1945), which won the New York Drama Critics Circle Award; *A Streetcar Named Desire* (1947), winner of the Pulitzer Prize; *Summer and Smoke* (1949); *Cat on a Hot Tin Roof,* winner of the 1955 Pulitzer Prize; and *Night of the Iguana* (1961).

Significant Architects and Their Works

Adam, Robert (1728–92). Scottish architect. Adam designed, with his brother James, numerous public and private buildings in England and Scotland in a distinctive style that combined Palladian, Renaissance, and antique elements. Notable examples are Osterley Park (1761–80) and Syon House (1762–69), near London.

Alberti, Leon Battista (1404–72). Italian architect, painter, author, and pioneering theoretician of Renaissance architecture. Alberti's buildings include the Rucellai Palace in Florence; the Church of San Francesco in Rimini, which he redesigned as a Roman temple; and the Church of Sant'Andrea at Mantua.

Behrens, Peter (1868–1940). German architect. Behrens is known for his factory buildings, which show a simple, utilitarian approach. Le Corbusier, Mies van der Rohe, and Walter Gropius were his students.

Berlage, Hendrik Petrus (1856–1934). Dutch architect, town planner, and furniture designer. His most significant work is the red brick Amsterdam Exchange, which introduced a new tradition in Dutch architecture.

Bernini, Giovanni Lorenzo (Gianlorenzo) (1598–1680). Italian architect and sculptor. Bernini was the dominant figure of the Italian Baroque period and the designer of many churches, chapels, fountains, tombs, and statues for the popes. He designed the great piazza in front of St. Peter's, as well as many of its interior details. His other Roman works include the fountains of the Piazza Navona and the churches of Santa Maria della Vittoria.

Bramante (Donato d'Agnolo) (1444–1514). One of the greatest architects of the Italian High Renaissance. Bramante's works include the churches of San Satiro and Santa Maria delle Grazie in Milan and the

Cancelleria Palace in Rome. He constructed a corridor at the Vatican and designed the new St. Peter's. Most of his plans were executed after his death.

Brunelleschi, Filippo (1377–1446). Florentine architect and the first great architect of the Italian Renaissance. Brunelleschi designed the celebrated octagonal dome for the cathedral in Florence. His other works include the small Pazzi chapel (1420), the churches of San Lorenzo and Santo Spirito, and the Pitti Palace, all in Florence.

Bulfinch, Charles (1763–1844). American (b. in Massachusetts) architect. Bulfinch designed the first theater in New England, the Federal Street Theatre (1794), as well as the Boston statehouse (1799), University Hall at Harvard (1815), Massachusetts General Hospital (1820), and, most significantly, the Washington Capitol, which served as a model for state capitols throughout the United States.

Burnham, Daniel Hudson (1846–1912). American (b. in New York State) architect and city planner. He designed the first important skeleton skyscraper, the Masonic Temple Building in Chicago (1892). His other important buildings include the Flatiron Building in New York City and Union Station in Washington, D.C. With John Root he designed the general plan for the Columbian Exposition in Chicago.

Butterfield, William (1814–1900). English architect. His many churches include St. Matthais, Stoke Newington; St. Albans, Holborn; and his greatest achievement, the "model" Church of All Saints, Margaret Street, London (1849). He also designed Keble College, Oxford (1867).

Chambers, Sir William (1723–96). English architect, the most prominent official architect of his day. Chambers designed decorative structures for Kew Gardens as well as the neo-Palladian Somerset House (1776).

Da Vinci, Leonardo *See* Leonardo da Vinci.

Fuller, (Richard) Buckminster (1895–1983). American (b. in Massachusetts) architect and engineer. He developed revolutionary designs aimed at maximum ecological efficiency, notably the Dymaxion automobile (1933) and the geodesic dome.

Garnier, Jean Louis Charles (1825–98). French architect. His principal work is the Opéra in Paris (1863–75). Garnier also built the Casino at Monte Carlo and the Observatory at Nice.

Gaudí i Cornet, Antonio (1852–1926). Spanish architect whose sculptural style paralleled the development of Art Nouveau, or Modernismo. His work is exemplified in Casa Milá, Barcelona, and his masterpiece, the Expiatory Church of the Holy Family.

Giotto (c. 1266–c. 1337). Florentine architect and painter. Giotto was the director of the works at Santa Maria del Fiore, Rome, where he designed the west front of the cathedral and the campanile, called Giotto's Tower.

Gropius, Walter (1883–1969). German-American architect. Gropius, a great modern functionalist, was director of the Weimar School of Art, which he reorganized as the Bauhaus. He designed the glass Fagus factory buildings at Alfeld (1910–11), the Bauhaus buildings in Dessau, the Staattheater in Jena (1923), the Pan Am building in New York City, and many homes and industrial buildings. Gropius taught at Harvard from 1937 to 1952.

Hoffmann, Josef (1870–1956). Austrian designer of the Palais Stoclet (1905–11), Brussels, and leader of the modern Viennese style. Hoffmann is known for his use of rectilinear units.

Hunt, Richard Morris (1828–95). American (b. in Vermont) architect. His work exemplifies nineteenth-century eclecticism in imitation of historical styles. Hunt designed the Lenox Library in New York City and numerous mansions in New York and Rhode Island.

Jenny, William Le Baron (1832–1907). American (b. in Massachusetts) architect and engineer. His Home Insurance Building in Chicago, 10 stories high, is considered to have been the first skyscraper. It was the first building in which a metal skeletal frame was used.

Johnson, Philip Cortelyou (1906–   ). American (b. in Ohio) architect noted for his glass-walled New Canaan House (1949), Connecticut, and the New York State Theater at Lincoln Center (1962–64).

Johnson co-authored *The International Style* (1932); collaborated on the Seagram Building, New York, with Miës van der Rohe (1958); and won the Pritzer Architecture Prize (1979).

Jones, Inigo (1573–1652). One of the first great English architects. Jones broke from the Jacobean style, thus beginning the Renaissance and Georgian periods in English architecture.

Kahn, Louis Isador (1901–74). Estonian-American architect. A highly influential theorist, Kahn's significant works include the Yale University Art Gallery and the Kimbell Art Museum, Fort Worth, Texas, as well as many housing projects, such as Carver Court, Coatsville, Pennsylvania (1944).

Labrouste, Henri (1801–75). French architect. He was among the first to successfully use metal construction in architecture, as in the reading room of the Bibliothèque St. Geneviève (1843–50), Paris, He also worked extensively on the Bibliothèque Nationale.

Latrobe, Benjamin Henry (1766–1820). British-American architect. Considered the first professional architect in the United States, Latrobe produced some of the best monumental architecture of his time in Classical Revival style. His works include the Bank of Pennsylvania, Philadelphia (1799); the Bank of the United States, now the old Philadelphia Custom House (completed by William Strickland, 1819–24); the Roman Catholic Cathedral, Baltimore, the first cathedral built in the United States (1805–18); and St. John's Church in Washington, D.C. (1816).

Le Corbusier (Charles Édouard Jeanneret) (1887–1965). Swiss architect. His buildings as well as his writings expressed a radical attitude toward aesthetic and technological architectural problems. Le Corbusier's works include studio houses at Boulogne-sur-Seine, a housing development at Pessac, and the Swiss Building at Cité Universitaire, Paris.

Leonardo da Vinci (1452–1519). Italian painter, sculptor, architect, musician, engineer, and scientist. In 1490 Leonardo was consulting engineer on the restoration of the cathedral at Pavin and later on the cathedral at Piacenza. In 1506 he served as architect and engineer in Milan for the French king Louis XII. In Rome in 1513 he worked on several architectural and engineering projects for the Vatican.

Loos, Adolf (1870–1933). Austrian architect. His best-known work is the office building on Michaelerplatz (1910). His purity of form had a pronounced impact on the development of modern architecture.

Lutyens, Sir Edwin Landseer (1869–1944). English architect. His outstanding achievement was the plan for the city of New Delhi, India. Lutyens also designed many war memorials, including the Cenotaph in London and those in Manchester, England, and Johannesburg, South Africa. He also designed the Hampton Court Bridge and the British Embassy in Washington, D.C.

Mendelsohn, Erich (1887–1953). German-Israeli architect. In Germany he designed the Steinberg hat factory, near Berlin (1923); a Berlin department store; and the highly original concrete Potsdam Observatory, also called the Einstein Tower (1927). In 1937 he emigrated to Israel, where he built the Hebrew University on Mt. Scopus, a government hospital in Haifa, and a trade school at Yagur.

Michelangelo Buonarroti (1475–1564). Italian sculptor, painter, architect, and poet. After finishing the frescos of the Pauline Chapel (1541–50), Michelangelo devoted himself primarily to architecture. In 1546 he became the chief architect of St. Peter's in Rome. He also remodeled the tepidarium of the Baths of Diocletian into the Church of Santa Maria degli Angeli and the facades and court of the palace group on Capitoline Hill.

Miës van der Rohe, Ludwig (1886–1969). German-American architect and director of the Bauhaus (1930–33). Mies perfected the simple, unornamented skyscraper. His outstanding works include the Farnsworth House, Illinois (1950), Chicago's Lake Shore Drive Apartments (1950), and his crowning work, the Seagram Building, New York (1958).

Mills, Robert (1781–1855). American (b. in South Carolina) architect. Mills was an exponent of the Classic Revival School. He was the presidentially appointed architect of public buildings in Washington, D.C., including the Treasury Building (1836), the Patent Office and Old Post Office (1839), and the Washington Monument (1833–84). Mills also designed the Bunker Hill monument.

Palladio, Andrea (1508–80). Italian architect. In his greatest work, the basilica at Vicenza, appear the much imitated arch-and-column compositions known as the Palladian motif. Palladio's other highly original and influential works include the Teatro Olimpico (1580); the Villa Capra, or Rotunda, near Vicenza; and the San Giorgio Maggiore and the Church of the Rendenfore in Venice.

Paxton, Sir Joseph (1801–65). English architect and horticulturist. After erecting a great conservatory for the Duke of Devonshire in Derbyshire, Paxton was commissioned to erect a similar structure, the Crystal Palace, for the Great Exhibition of 1851 in London.

Pei, I(eou) M(ing) (1917–   ). Chinese-American architect. Among his major works are the John Fitzgerald Kennedy Library in Cambridge, Massachusetts, the Mile High Center in Denver, the Johnson Museum of Art at Cornell University, and a pyramidal addition to the Louvre Museum. Pei is the winner of several awards for excellence in design.

Pugin, Augustus Welby Northmore (1812–52). English architect and author. Pugin played a prominent role in the Gothic Revival and erected numerous churches, monasteries, and convents; however, his writings proved more influential than his buildings. Pugin executed a cathedral in St. George's Fields, London, and worked on details of the House of Parliament. He wrote the classic book on Gothic Revival architecture, *The True Principles of Pointed or Christian Architecture* (1841), as well as *Gothic Furniture in the Style of the 15th Century* (1835) and *Glossary of Ecclesiastical Ornament and Costume* (1844).

Richardson, Henry Hobson (1838–86). American (b. in Louisiana) architect. His monumental work, Trinity Church, Boston (1822–27), exemplifies the "Richardson Romanesque" style. Among his other buildings is the Marshall Field department store, Chicago.

Saarinen, Eliel (1873–1950). Finnish city planner, architect, and author. In Finland Saarinen designed the National Museum and the railway station in Helsinki. In America, where he resided after 1923, he designed many of the performance halls at the Berkshire Music Center, as well as several buildings of the Cranbrook Foundation, where he was head of the Academy of Art. Saarinen wrote *The City: Its Growth, Its Decay, Its Future* (1943) and *Search for Form* (1948).

Smirke, Sir Robert (1781–1867). English architect and notable exponent of the Classical Revival School. His best-known work is the main facade of the British Museum (1823–47). Other achievements include the General Post Office and the Royal College of Physicians, both in London.

Smirke, Sydney (1798–1877). English architect, brother of Robert Smirke. Upon his brother's retirement, Smirke took over his work at the British Museum, where he erected the new reading room and the western side of the quadrangle (1854–57). He also built the Carlton Club (1857) and the exhibition galleries for the Royal Academy at Burlington House (1866).

Soufflot, Jacques Germain (1713–80). French architect. Best known as the designer of the Panthéon in Paris, his other works include the Hôtel-Dieu, Lyons, and the École de Droit, Paris.

Strickland, William (1787–1854). American (b. in Pennsylvania) architect. A student of Latrobe, Strickland completed Latrobe's Bank of the United States after his death. His most outstanding work is the Merchant's Exchange (1834). He also restored Independence Hall (1828) and built the Naval Asylum and the Mint (1829–33), as well as the state capitol in Nashville, Tennessee. Strickland was a founder and first president of the American Institute of Architects and the author of *Reports on Canals, Railways, Roads and Other Subjects* (1826).

Sullivan, Louis Henry (1856–1924). American (b. in Massachusetts) architect. A prominent figure in the development of modern architecture, Sullivan was an exponent of the form-follows-function school. He designed the Wainwright Building, St. Louis (1890), and the Transportation Building at the Columbian Exposition, Chicago (1893).

Vanbrugh, Sir John (1664–1726). English architect and dramatist. He designed Castle Howard in 1699, a masterpiece of Palladian architecture, initiating his successful career, mainly as an architect of country houses. Vanbrugh became the architect of the palace at Blenheim Park in 1705 and in 1716 became the architect for Greenwich Hospital.

Wagner, Otto (1841–1918). Austrian architect. A pioneer of modern architecture, Wagner's most significant work was the Postal Savings Bank, Vienna (1904–06). He also designed buildings for the Vienna tramways and the church at Steinhof, near Vienna (1894).

Walter, Thomas Ustick (1804–87). American (b. in Pennsylvania) architect. Walter designed extensions of government buildings, including the Senate and House wings of the Capitol and its iron dome. His main building of Girard College, Philadelphia (1833) was a significant work of Classical Revival.

White, Stanford (1853–1906). American (b. in New York City) architect. Most interested in the decorative aspects of building, his long-term partnership with C. F. McKim and William R. Mead produced significant works. White designed the Washington Square Arch and the Century Club in New York.

Wren, Sir Christopher (1632–1723). English architect, astronomer, and mathematician. His redesign of the city of London after the Great Fire of 1666 was never executed, yet Wren is known for some of England's most outstanding structures: St. Paul's Cathedral, among 52 other London churches; the Chelsea Hospital; the Sheldonian Theatre in Oxford; and the Trinity College Library in Cambridge.

Wright, Frank Lloyd (1869–1959). American (b. in Wisconsin) architect. His innovative approach integrated modern technology into architectural aesthetics. Wright's most significant and pace-setting works include the Larkin Building, Buffalo (1904); the Oak Park Unity Temple, near Chicago (1906); the Imperial Hotel, Tokyo (1916–23); the Kaufman house, "Falling Water," Bear Run, Pennsylvania (1936–37); and the Guggenheim Museum, New York City (1959).

Architectural Terms

abacus A tablet placed horizontally on the capital of a column, aiding the support of the architrave.

abutment A solid piece of masonry used to support a projecting part of a structure, for example, the supports that connect a bridge with a river bank.

acropolis The citadel in ancient Greek towns.

adobe Sun-dried brick used in places with warm, dry climates, such as Egypt and Mexico; the clay from which bricks are made; the structures built out of adobe bricks.

ambulatory A continuous aisle in a circular building, as in a church.

apse A semicircular area; in most churches it contains the altar.

arabesque Ornament consisting of garlands of foliage with figures, fancifully interlaced to form graceful curves and painted, inlaid, or carved in low relief.

arcade A series of arches supported by columns or piers, or a passageway formed by these arches.

arch A curved structure that supports the weight of the material above it.

architrave The lowest part of an entablature resting on the capital of a column; also, the holdings around a doorway.

ashlar Stones hewn and squared for use in building, as distinguished from rough stones.

atrium In an ancient Roman structure, a central room open to the sky, usually having a pool for the collection of rainwater. In Christian churches, a courtyard flanked by porticos.

attic The part of the entablature above the cornice, serving to hide the roof.

baldachin A richly ornamented canopy structure supported by columns, suspended from a roof, or projected from a wall, as over an altar.

Baroque A style that flourished in the seventeenth and eighteenth centuries, characterized by exuberant decoration, curvaceous forms, and a grand scale generating a sense of movement; later developments show greater restraint.

basilica The early Greek name for a royal palace; a large oblong building with double columns and a semicircular apse at one end, frequently used by Christian emperors of Rome for religious purposes.

Bauhaus The style of the Bauhaus School, founded in Germany by Walter Gropius in 1919, emphasizing simplicity, functionalism, and craftsmanship.

buttress A projecting support built into or against the external wall of a building, typically used in Gothic buildings.

Byzantine A style dating from the fifth century, characterized by masonry construction around a central plan, with domes on penditives, typically depicting the figure of Christ; foliage patterns on stone capitals; and interiors decorated with mosaics and frescos.

campanile A bell tower usually not actually attached to a church; also, lofty towers that form parts of buildings.

cantilever A horizontal projection, such as a balcony or beam, supported at one end only.

classicism A tradition of Greek and Roman antiquity, distinguished by the qualities of simplicity, harmony, and balance.

Classical Revival The Italian Renaissance or neoclassical movements in England and the United States in the nineteenth century that looked to the traditions of Greek and Roman antiquity.

clerestory Part of an interior rising above adjacent rooftops, permitting the passage of light.

cloister In religious institutions, a courtyard with covered walks.

colonnade A row of columns, usually equidistant.

column A vertical support; in an order it consists of a shaft and capital, often resting on a base.

Composite Order A Roman order; its capital combines the Corinthian acanthus leaf decoration with volutes from the Ionic Order.

Corinthian Order The last of the three Greek orders, similar to the Ionic, but with the capital decorated with carvings of the acanthus leaf.

cornice The upper part of an entablature, extending beyond the frieze.

dome A roof formed by a series of arches, roughly forming a semicircle.

Doric Order The first and simplest of the three Greek orders and the only one that normally has no base.

entablature The upper horizontal part of an order, between a capital and the roof; it consists of the architrave, frieze, and cornice.

facade Any important face of a building, usually the principal front with the main entrance.

frieze The middle part of an entablature, often decorated with spiral scrolls (volutes).

gargoyle A spout placed on the roof gutter of a Gothic building to carry away rainwater, commonly carved fancifully as in the shapes of animal heads.

Georgian The prevailing style of English architecture during the reigns of George I, II, and III (1714–1820), based on the principles of the Italian Renaissance architect Andrea Palladio. The style was transported to England by Inigo Jones and Sir Christopher Wren. It became the prototype for the colonial style in America.

Gothic A style employed in Europe during the thirteenth, fourteenth, and fifteenth centuries; also called *pointed*. It is characterized by the use of pointed arches and ribbed vaults, piers, and buttresses in the support of its stone construction. The style is best exemplified by the Notre Dame in Paris and the cathedrals of Amiens and Bourges.

Ionic Order Second of the three Greek orders. Its capital is decorated with spiral scrolls (volutes).

lintel *See* post and lintel.

loggia A rostrum developed in medieval Italian towns, roofed, slightly elevated, and open on three sides, from which orators could address crowds.

minaret A slender, lofty tower with balconies attached to a Muslim mosque.

module The measurement that architects use to determine the proportions of a structure, for example, the diameter of a column.

narthex An enclosed passage from the nave to the main entrance of a church.

nave The principal area of a church, extending from the main area to the transept.

Norman A style of buildings erected by the Normans (1066–1154) based on the Italian Romanesque. It was used principally in castles, churches, and abbeys of massive proportions. Sparsely decorated masonry and the use of the round arch are characteristic.

order A term applied to the three styles of Greek architecture, the Dorian, Corinthian, and Ionic, referring to the style of columns and their entablatures; it also refers to the Composite and the Tuscan, developed from the original three orders.

pagoda A temple or sacred building, typically in an Asian nation, usually pyramidal, forming a tower with upward curving roofs over the individual stories.

pediment In a classical-style building, the triangular segment between the horizontal entablature and the sloping roof.

pendentive A curved support shaped like an inverted triangle, used to support a dome.

pier A large pillar used to support a roof.

portico A structure usually attached to a building, such as a porch, consisting of a roof supported by piers or columns.

post and lintel A method of construction in which vertical beams (posts) are used to support a horizontal beam (lintel).

pyramid In ancient Egypt, a quadrilateral masonry mass with steeply sloping sides meeting at an apex, used as a tomb.

relief Moldings and ornamentation projecting from the surface of a wall.

Renaissance Styles existing in Italy in the fifteenth and sixteenth centuries; adaptations of ancient Roman elements to contemporary uses, with attention to the principles of Vitruvius and to existing ruins. Symmetry, simplicity, and exact mathematical relationships are emphasized.

Rococo A style originating in France c. 1720, developed out of Baroque types, and characterized by its ornamentation of shellwork, foliage, etc., and its refined use of different materials, such as stucco, metal, or wood for a delicate effect.

Romanesque A style developed in western and southern Europe after 1000 characterized by heavy masonry and the use of the round arch, barrel and groin vaults, narrow openings, and the vaulting rib, the vaulting shaft, and central and western towers.

spire A tall, tapering, acutely pointed roof to a tower, as in the top of a steeple.

tracery Ornament of ribs, bars, etc., in panels or screens, as in the upper part of a Gothic window.

transept A structure that forms the arms of a T- or cross-shaped church.

Tudor A style of English architecture prevalent during the reigns of the Tudors (1485–1558), transitional between Gothic and Palladian, with emphasis on privacy and interiors.

turret A small tower, usually starting at some distance from the ground, attached to a building such as a castle or fortress.

Tuscan Order A Roman order resembling the Doric without a fluted shaft.

vault An arched brick or stone ceiling or roof. The simplest form is the *barrel vault,* a single continuous arch; the *groined vault* consists of two barrel vaults joined at right angles; a *ribbed vault* has diagonal arches projecting from the surface.

westwork In German Romanesque, a monumental entrance to a church consisting of porches and towers, with a chapel above.

Illustrations of Architectural Styles and Elements

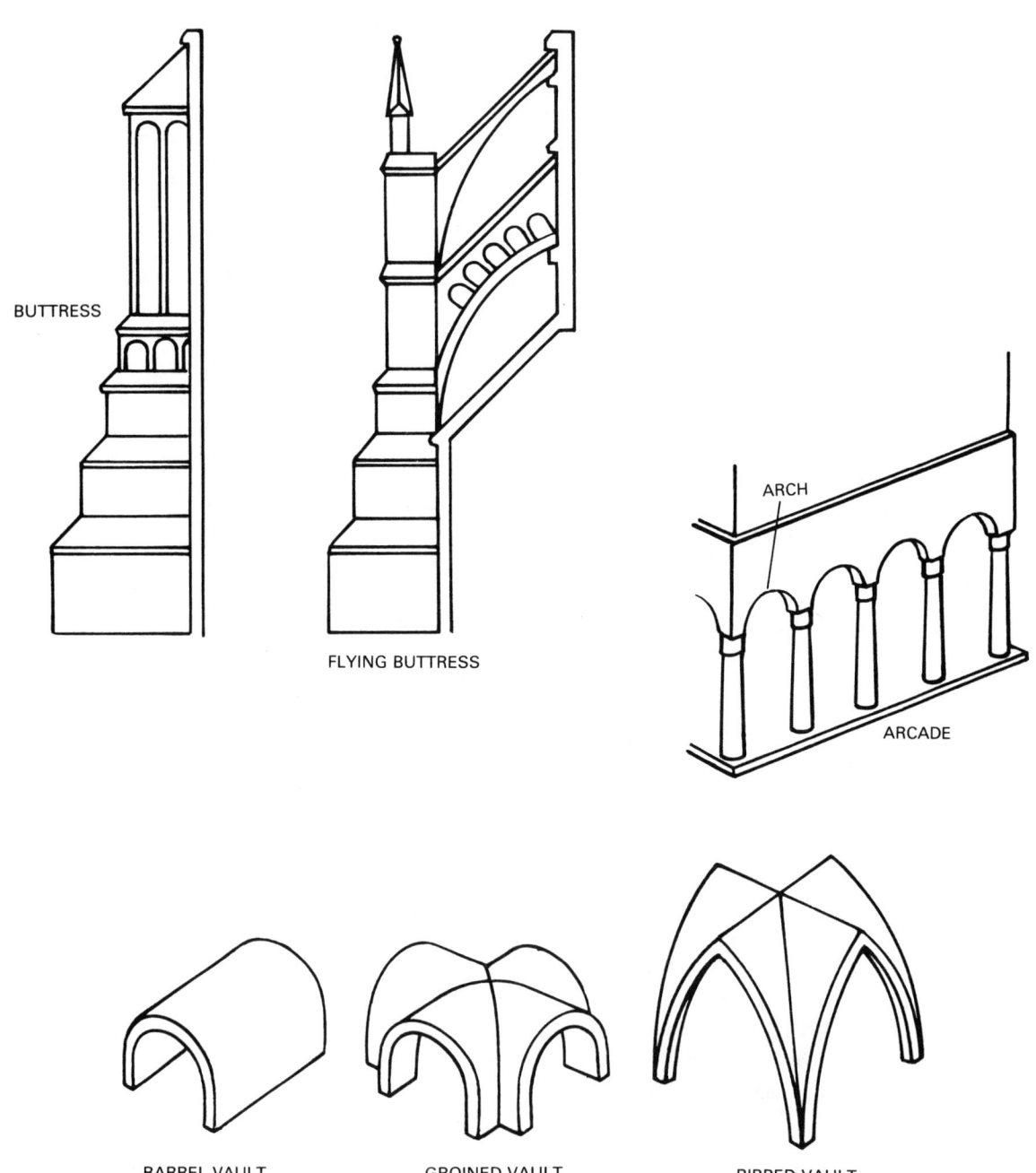

BUTTRESS

FLYING BUTTRESS

ARCH

ARCADE

BARREL VAULT

GROINED VAULT

RIBBED VAULT

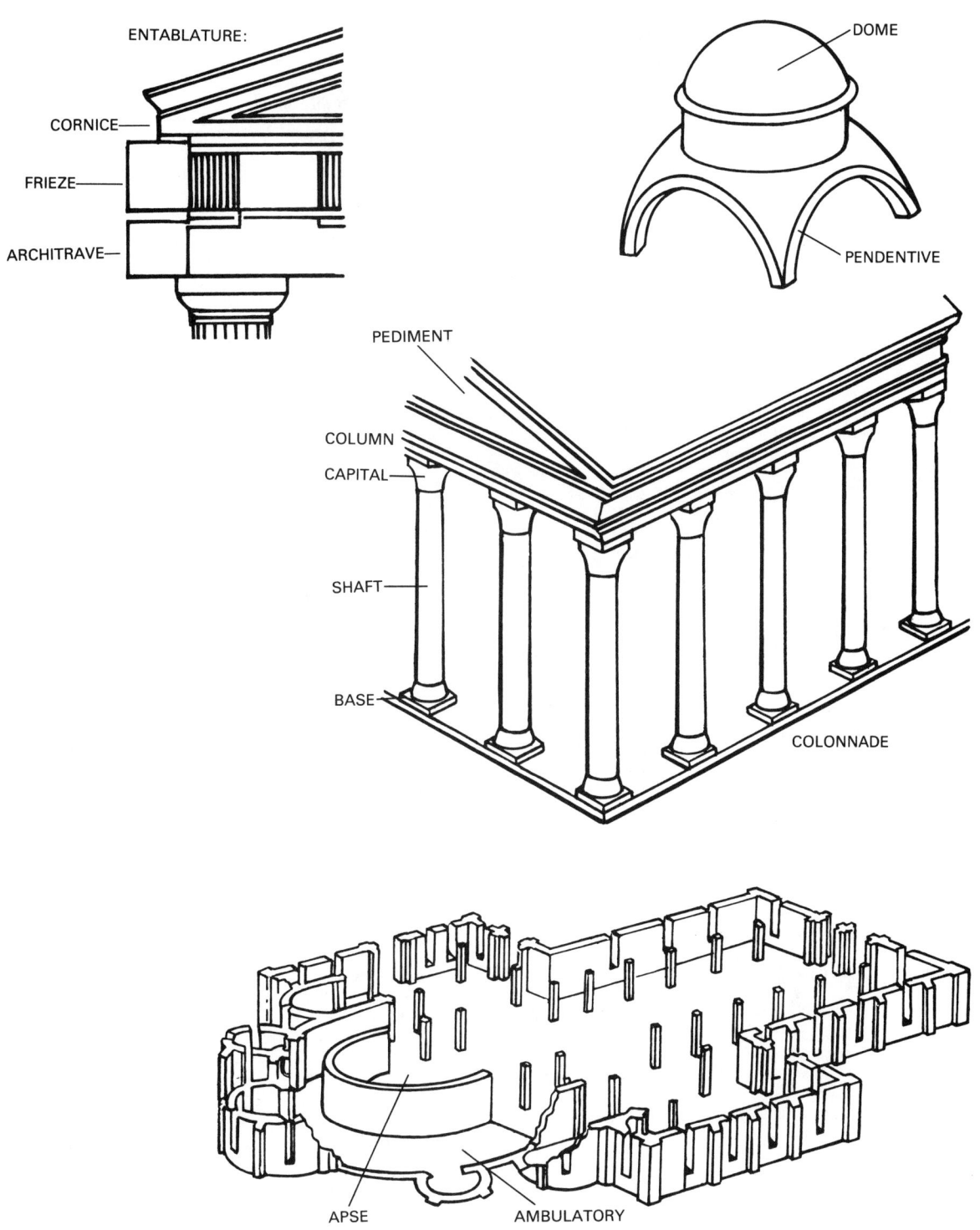

ENTABLATURE:

CORNICE

FRIEZE

ARCHITRAVE

DOME

PENDENTIVE

PEDIMENT

COLUMN

CAPITAL

SHAFT

BASE

COLONNADE

APSE

AMBULATORY

The Academy Awards, 1927–88

	Best actor	Best actress	Best director	Best picture
1927–28	Emil Jannings (*The Way of All Flesh*)	Janet Gaynor (*Seventh Heaven*)	Frank Borzage (*Seventh Heaven*)	*Wings*
1928–29	Warner Baxter (*In Old Arizona*)	Mary Pickford (*Coquette*)	Frank Lloyd (*The Divine Lady*)	*Broadway Melody*
1929–30	George Arliss (*Disraeli*)	Norma Shearer (*The Divorcee*)	Lewis Milestone (*All Quiet on the Western Front*)	*All Quiet on the Western Front*
1930–31	Lionel Barrymore (*A Free Soul*)	Marie Dressler (*Min and Bill*)	Norman Taurog (*Skippy*)	*Cimarron*
1931–32	Frederic March (*Dr. Jekyll and Mr. Hyde*) Wallace Berry (*The Champ*)	Helen Hayes (*The Sin of Madelon Claudet*)	Frank Borzage (*Bad Girl*)	*Grand Hotel*
1932–33	Charles Laughton (*The Private Life of Henry VIII*)	Katharine Hepburn (*Morning Glory*)	Frank Lloyd (*Cavalcade*)	*Cavalcade*
1934	Clark Gable (*It Happened One Night*)	Claudette Colbert (*It Happened One Night*)	Frank Capra (*It Happened One Night*)	*It Happened One Night*
1935	Victor McLaglen (*The Informer*)	Bette Davis (*Dangerous*)	John Ford (*The Informer*)	*Mutiny on the Bounty*
1936	Paul Muni (*The Story of Louis Pasteur*)	Luise Rainer (*The Great Ziegfeld*)	Frank Capra (*Mr. Deeds Goes to Town*)	*The Great Ziegfeld*
1937	Spencer Tracy (*Captains Courageous*)	Luise Rainer (*The Good Earth*)	Leo McCarey (*The Awful Truth*)	*The Life of Emile Zola*
1938	Spencer Tracy (*Boys Town*)	Bette Davis (*Jezebel*)	Frank Capra (*You Can't Take It with You*)	*You Can't Take It with You*
1939	Robert Donat (*Goodbye Mr. Chips*)	Vivien Leigh (*Gone with the Wind*)	Victor Fleming (*Gone with the Wind*)	*Gone with the Wind*
1940	James Stewart (*The Philadelphia Story*)	Ginger Rogers (*Kitty Foyle*)	John Ford (*The Grapes of Wrath*)	*Rebecca*
1941	Gary Cooper (*Sergeant York*)	Joan Fontaine (*Suspicion*)	John Ford (*How Green Was My Valley*)	*How Green Was My Valley*
1942	James Cagney (*Yankee Doodle Dandy*)	Greer Garson (*Mrs. Miniver*)	William Wyler (*Mrs. Miniver*)	*Mrs. Miniver*
1943	Paul Lukas (*Watch on the Rhine*)	Jennifer Jones (*The Song of Bernadette*)	Michael Curtiz (*Casablanca*)	*Casablanca*
1944	Bing Crosby (*Going My Way*)	Ingrid Bergman (*Gaslight*)	Leo McCarey (*Going My Way*)	*Going My Way*
1945	Ray Milland (*The Lost Weekend*)	Joan Crawford (*Mildred Pierce*)	Billy Wilder (*The Lost Weekend*)	*The Lost Weekend*
1946	Frederic March (*The Best Years of Our Lives*)	Olivia de Havilland (*To Each His Own*)	William Wyler (*The Best Years of Our Lives*)	*The Best Years of Our Lives*
1947	Ronald Coleman (*A Double Life*)	Loretta Young (*The Farmer's Daughter*)	Elia Kazan (*Gentleman's Agreement*)	*Gentleman's Agreement*
1948	Laurence Olivier (*Hamlet*)	Jane Wyman (*Johnny Belinda*)	John Huston (*Treasure of the Sierra Madre*)	*Hamlet*

	Best actor	Best actress	Best director	Best picture
1949	Broderick Crawford (*All the King's Men*)	Olivia de Havilland (*The Heiress*)	Joseph L. Mankiewicz (*A Letter to Three Wives*)	*All the King's Men*
1950	Jose Ferrer (*Cyrano de Bergerac*)	Judy Holliday (*Born Yesterday*)	Joseph L. Mankiewicz (*All About Eve*)	*All About Eve*
1951	Humphrey Bogart (*The African Queen*)	Vivien Leigh (*A Streetcar Named Desire*)	George Stevens (*A Place in the Sun*)	*An American in Paris*
1952	Gary Cooper (*High Noon*)	Shirley Booth (*Come Back, Little Sheba*)	John Ford (*The Quiet Man*)	*The Greatest Show on Earth*
1953	William Holden (*Stalag 17*)	Audrey Hepburn (*Roman Holiday*)	Fred Zinnemann (*From Here to Eternity*)	*From Here to Eternity*
1954	Marlon Brando (*On the Waterfront*)	Grace Kelly (*The Country Girl*)	Elia Kazan (*On the Waterfront*)	*On the Waterfront*
1955	Ernest Borgnine (*Marty*)	Anna Magnani (*The Rose Tattoo*)	Delbert Mann (*Marty*)	*Marty*
1956	Yul Brynner (*The King and I*)	Ingrid Bergman (*Anastasia*)	George Stevens (*Giant*)	*Around the World in Eighty Days*
1957	Alec Guinness (*The Bridge on the River Kwai*)	Joanne Woodward (*The Three Faces of Eve*)	David Lean (*The Bridge on the River Kwai*)	*The Bridge on the River Kwai*
1958	David Niven (*Separate Tables*)	Susan Hayward (*I Want to Live*)	Vincente Minnelli (*Gigi*)	*Gigi*
1959	Charlton Heston (*Ben-Hur*)	Simone Signoret (*Room at the Top*)	William Wyler (*Ben-Hur*)	*Ben-Hur*
1960	Burt Lancaster (*Elmer Gantry*)	Elizabeth Taylor (*Butterfield 8*)	Billy Wilder (*The Apartment*)	*The Apartment*
1961	Maximillian Schell (*Judgment at Nuremberg*)	Sophia Loren (*Two Women*)	Jerome Robbins, Robert Wise (*West Side Story*)	*West Side Story*
1962	Gregory Peck (*To Kill a Mockingbird*)	Anne Bancroft (*The Miracle Worker*)	David Lean (*Lawrence of Arabia*)	*Lawrence of Arabia*
1963	Sidney Poitier (*Lilies of the Field*)	Patricia Neal (*Hud*)	Tony Richardson (*Tom Jones*)	*Tom Jones*
1964	Rex Harrison (*My Fair Lady*)	Julie Andrews (*Mary Poppins*)	George Cukor (*My Fair Lady*)	*My Fair Lady*
1965	Lee Marvin (*Cat Ballou*)	Julie Christie (*Darling*)	Robert Wise (*The Sound of Music*)	*The Sound of Music*
1966	Paul Scofield (*A Man for All Seasons*)	Elizabeth Taylor (*Who's Afraid of Virginia Woolf?*)	Fred Zinnemann (*A Man for All Seasons*)	*A Man for All Seasons*
1967	Rod Steiger (*In the Heat of the Night*)	Katharine Hepburn (*Guess Who's Coming to Dinner*)	Mike Nichols (*The Graduate*)	*In the Heat of the Night*
1968	Cliff Robertson (*Charly*)	Katharine Hepburn (*The Lion in Winter*); Barbra Streisand (*Funny Girl*)	Sir Carol Reed (*Oliver!*)	*Oliver!*
1969	John Wayne (*True Grit*)	Maggie Smith (*The Prime of Miss Jean Brodie*)	John Schlesinger (*Midnight Cowboy*)	*Midnight Cowboy*
1970	George C. Scott (*Patton; refused*)	Glenda Jackson (*Women in Love*)	Franklin Schaffner, Frank McCarthy (*Patton*)	*Patton*
1971	Gene Hackman (*The French Connection*)	Jane Fonda (*Klute*)	William Friedkin (*The French Connection*)	*The French Connection*

	Best actor	Best actress	Best director	Best picture
1972	Marlon Brando (*The Godfather*; refused)	Liza Minnelli (*Cabaret*)	Bob Fosse (*Cabaret*)	*The Godfather*
1973	Jack Lemmon (*Save the Tiger*)	Glenda Jackson (*A Touch of Class*)	George Roy Hill (*The Sting*)	*The Sting*
1974	Art Carney (*Harry and Tonto*)	Ellen Burstyn (*Alice Doesn't Live Here Anymore*)	Francis Ford Coppola (*The Godfather, Part II*)	*The Godfather, Part II*
1975	Jack Nicholson (*One Flew over the Cuckoo's Nest*)	Louise Fletcher (*One Flew over the Cuckoo's Nest*)	Milos Forman (*One Flew over the Cuckoo's Nest*)	*One Flew over the Cuckoo's Nest*
1976	Peter Finch (*Network*)	Faye Dunaway (*Network*)	John G. Avildsen (*Rocky*)	*Rocky*
1977	Richard Dreyfuss (*The Goodbye Girl*)	Diane Keaton (*Annie Hall*)	Woody Allen (*Annie Hall*)	*Annie Hall*
1978	Jon Voight (*Coming Home*)	Jane Fonda (*Coming Home*)	Michael Cimino (*The Deer Hunter*)	*The Deer Hunter*
1979	Dustin Hoffman (*Kramer vs. Kramer*)	Sally Field (*Norma Rae*)	Robert Benton (*Kramer vs. Kramer*)	*Kramer vs. Kramer*
1980	Robert De Niro (*Raging Bull*)	Sissy Spacek (*Coal Miner's Daughter*)	Robert Redford (*Ordinary People*)	*Ordinary People*
1981	Henry Fonda (*On Golden Pond*)	Katharine Hepburn (*On Golden Pond*)	Warren Beatty (*Reds*)	*Chariots of Fire*
1982	Ben Kingsley (*Gandhi*)	Meryl Streep (*Sophie's Choice*)	Richard Attenborough (*Gandhi*)	*Gandhi*
1983	Robert Duvall (*Tender Mercies*)	Shirley MacLaine (*Terms of Endearment*)	James L. Brooks (*Terms of Endearment*)	*Terms of Endearment*
1984	F. Murray Abraham (*Amadeus*)	Sally Field (*Places in the Heart*)	Milos Forman (*Amadeus*)	*Amadeus*
1985	William Hurt (*Kiss of the Spider Woman*)	Geraldine Page (*The Trip to Bountiful*)	Sydney Pollack (*Out of Africa*)	*Out of Africa*
1986	Paul Newman (*The Color of Money*)	Marlee Matlin (*Children of a Lesser God*)	Oliver Stone (*Platoon*)	*Platoon*
1987	Michael Douglas (*Wall Street*)	Cher (*Moonstruck*)	Bernardo Bertolucci (*The Last Emperor*)	*The Last Emperor*
1988	Dustin Hoffman (*Rain Man*)	Jody Foster (*The Accused*)	Barry Levinson (*Rain Man*)	*Rain Man*

Additional Sources of Information

Apel, Willi, ed. *The Harvard Dictionary of Music.*, rev., enl. Harvard University Press, 1969.

Chujoy, Anatole, and Manchester, P. W., eds. *The Dance Encyclopedia.* Simon & Schuster, 1967.

Fleming, John, ed. *The Penguin Dictionary of Architecture*, 1972.

Gassner, John, and Quinn, Edward, eds. *The Reader's Encyclopedia of World Drama.* Crowell, 1969.

Gloag, John. *Guide to Western Architecture.* Macmillan, 1958.

Hartnoll, Phyllis, ed. *The Oxford Companion to the Theatre*, 4th ed. Oxford University Press, 1983.

Janson, Horst W. *History of Art*, 3rd ed. Prentice-Hall, 1986.

Kennedy, Michael. *The Oxford Dictionary of Music*. Oxford University Press, 1985.

Kobbe, Gustave. *The Definitive Kobbe's Opera Book*. Putnam, 1987.

Koegler, Horst. *Concise Oxford Dictionary of Ballet*. Oxford University Press, 1982.

Murphy, Howard. *Music Fundamentals, A Guide to Musical Understanding*. Sam Fox, 1962.

Musgrove, John, ed. *A History of Architecture: Sir Banister-Fletcher's*, 19th ed. Butterworth, 1987.

Peltz, Mary Ellis, ed. *Introduction to Opera, A Guidebook Sponsored by the Metropolitan Opera Guild.* Barnes & Noble, 1962.

Sadie, Stanley, ed. *The New Grove Dictionary of Music and Musicians*. 20 vols. Macmillan, 1980.

Shipley, Joseph T. *Crown Guide to the World's Great Plays,* rev. ed. Crown, 1984.

Slonimsky, Nicolas. *Bakers Biographical Dictionary of Musicians,* 7th rev. ed. G. Schirmer, 1984.

Upjohn, E. M. *A History of World Art*. Oxford University Press, 1958.

Vinson, James, ed. *Contemporary Dramatists*, St. Martin's Press, 1973.

Vinton, John, ed. *Dictionary of Contemporary Music*. Dutton, 1974.

8

Literature

Important U.S. and Canadian Authors

Any list of "important" authors is subject to debate. The following list includes writers who have had a substantial impact on American and Canadian literature, whether as a result of a single work or an entire oeuvre. This list is not all-inclusive, but it does contain most of the authors who are generally considered to have made a substantial contribution to American and Canadian literature.

The titles and dates of first publication of each author's major works are given. An asterisk (*) designates a book that was awarded a Pulitzer Prize in literature; a plus sign (+) indicates that the work was awarded a National Book Award. In those instances where an author is known by a pseudonym, he or she is listed by that pseudonym with the real name in brackets.

Note: *See also* Chapter 7 for major playwrights.

Agee, James (1909–55): *Let Us Now Praise Famous Men* (1941),* *A Death in the Family* (1957), *Agee on Film* (1958)

Aiken, Conrad (1889–1973): *The House of Dust: A Symphony* (1920), *Selected Poems* (1929), *Conversation; or, Pilgrim's Progress* (1940), *The Soldier* (1944), *The Kid* (1947)

Alcott, Louisa May (1832–88): *Little Women* (1868–69), *Little Men* (1871), *Silver Pitchers and Independence* (1876), *Spinning-Wheel Stories* (1884)

Algren, Nelson (1909–81): *The Man with the Golden Arm* (1949), *A Walk on the Wild Side* (1956)

Anderson, Sherwood (1876–1941): *Winesburg, Ohio* (1919), *The Triumph of the Egg* (1921), *A Story Teller's Story* (1924), *Dark Laughter* (1925), *Beyond Desire* (1932)

Asimov, Isaac (1920–): *Foundation* (1951), *Foundation and Empire* (1952), *Second Foundation* (1953), *Opus 200* (1979)

Atwood, Margaret (1939–): *The Circle Game* (1966), *Surfacing* (1972), *Selected Poems* (1976), *Dancing Girls* (1977), *Bodily Harm* (1981), *The Handmaid's Tale* (1985), *Cat's Eye* (1988)

Auchincloss, Louis [Stanton] (1917–): *Portrait in Brownstone* (1962), *The Winthrop Covenant* (1976), *Life, Law and Letters* (1979), *Diary of a Yuppie* (1987)

Auden, W(ystan) H(ugh) (1907–73): *Spain* (1937), *For the Time Being* (1945), *The Age of Anxiety: A Baroque Eclogue* (1948), *Collected Shorter Poems, 1930–44* (1950), *Making, Knowing and Judging* (1956), *The Dyer's Hand* (1962), *Collected Poems* (1976)

Audubon, John James (1785–1851): *The Birds of America* (1827–38)

Austin, Mary (1868–1934): *Isidro* (1905), *A Woman of Genius* (1912), *The Ford* (1917), *Earth Horizon* (1932)

Baldwin, James (1924–87): *Go Tell It on the Mountain* (1953), *Notes of a Native Son* (1955), *Nobody Knows My Name* (1961), *Another Country* (1962), *Just Above My Head* (1979)

Baraka, Imamu Amiri (formerly LeRoi Jones, 1934–): *Dutchman* (1964), *The Slave* (1964), *The Toilet* (1964), *Black Music* (1967), *Black Magic . . .* (1969), *Selected Plays and Prose* (1979), *Selected Poetry* (1979)

Barth, John [Simmons] (1930–): *The Sot-Weed Factor* (1960), *Giles Goat-Boy* (1966), *Chimera* (1972)

Barthelme, Donald (1931–): *Come Back, Dr. Caligari* (1964), *Snow White* (1967), *City Life* (1970), *Sixty Stories* (1982)

Bartlett, John (1820–1905): *Familiar Quotations* (1855)

Baum, Lyman Frank (1856–1919): *The Wonderful Wizard of Oz* (1900)

Beattie, Ann (1947–   ): *Distortions* (1976), *Chilly Scenes of Winter* (1976)

Bellow, Saul (1915–   ): *Dangling Man* (1944), + *The Adventures of Augie March* (1953), *Henderson the Rain King* (1959), *Herzog* (1964), **Humboldt's Gift* (1975), *The Dean's December* (1982)

Benchley, Robert (1889–1945): *Love Conquers All* (1922), *My Ten Years in a Quandary* (1936), *Benchley Beside Himself* (1943)

Benét, Stephen Vincent (1898–1943): **John Brown's Body* (1928), *Ballads and Poems, 1915–30* (1931), **Western Star* (1943)

Benét, William Rose (1886–1950): *Oxford Anthology of American Literature* (editor, 1938), **The Dust Which Is God* (1941)

Bierce, Ambrose (1842–1914?): *Tales of Soldiers and Civilians* (1891), *Can Such Things Be?* (1893), *The Devil's Dictionary* (1911)

Bontemps, Arna (1902–73): *God Sends Sunday* (1931), *Drums at Dusk* (1939), *Sam Patch* (1951), *One Hundred Years of Negro Freedom* (1961)

Boyle, Kay (1903–   ): *Wedding Day* (1930), *Plagued by the Nightingale* (1931), *Death of a Man* (1936), *Thirty Stories* (1946), *The Underground Woman* (1975), *Fifty Stories* (1980)

Bradbury, Ray (1920–   ): *The Martian Chronicles* (1950), *The Illustrated Man* (1951), *Fahrenheit 451* (1953), *Something Wicked This Way Comes* (1963), *I Sing the Body Electric* (1969)

Bradstreet, Anne (c. 1612–72): *The Tenth Muse Lately Sprung Up in America* (1650)

Brooks, Gwendolyn (1917–   ): *Annie Allen* (1949), *In the Mecca* (1968), *Family Pictures* (1970)

Buck, Pearl (1892–1973): **The Good Earth* (1931), *My Several Worlds* (1954), *Imperial Woman* (1956), *Command the Morning* (1959), *A Bridge for Passing* (1962)

Burroughs, Edgar Rice (1875–1950): *Tarzan of the Apes* (1914)

Burroughs, William S. (1914–   ): *The Naked Lunch* (1959), *Nova Express* (1964), *Cities of the Red Night* (1981)

Cather, Willa (1873–1947): *O Pioneers!* (1913), *The Song of the Lark* (1915), *My Antonia* (1918), **One of Ours* (1922), *Shadows on the Rock* (1931)

Chandler, Raymond (1888–1959): *The Big Sleep* (1939), *Farewell, My Lovely* (1940), *The Long Goodbye* (1954)

Cheever, John (1912–82): + *The Wapshot Chronicle* (1957), *The Wapshot Scandal* (1964), *Falconer* (1977)

Chopin, Kate (1851–1904): *Bayou Folk* (1894), *the Awakening* (1899)

Cooper, James Fenimore (1789–1851): *The Spy* (1821), *The Pioneers* (1823), *The Pilot* (1823), *The Last of the Mohicans* 1826), *The Prairie* (1827), *The American Democrat* (1838), *The Pathfinder* (1840), *The Deerslayer* (1841)

Crane, Stephen (1871–1900): *Maggie: A Girl of the Streets* (1893), *The Red Badge of Courage* (1895), *The Black Riders* (1895), *The Open Boat* (1898), *The Monster* (1899)

cummings, ee [Edward Estlin] (1894–1962): *The Enormous Room* (1922), *&* (1925), *is 5* (1926), *50 Poems* (1940), *I × I* (1944), *95 Poems* (1958)

Davies, Robertson (1913–   ): *A Mixture of Frailties* (1958), *Fifth Business* (1970), *The Rebel Angels* (1981), *What's Bred in the Bone* (1985)

Dickinson, Emily (1830–86): *Poems* (1890), *Poems: Second Series* (1891), *Poems: Third Series* (1896), *The Single Hound* (1914)

Didion, Joan (1934–   ): *Slouching towards Bethlehem* (1968), *The White Album* (1970), *Play It As It Lays* (1970)

Dillard, Annie (1945–   ): **Pilgrim at Tinker Creek* (1974), *Teaching a Stone To Talk* (1982)

Doctorow, E(dgar) L(awrence) (1931–   ): *The Book of Daniel* (1971), *Ragtime* (1975), *Loon Lake* (1980), *World's Fair* (1986)

Dos Passos, John (1896–1970): *Manhattan Transfer* (1925), *The 42nd Parallel* (1930), *1919* (1932), *The Big Money* (1936)

Dreiser, Theodore (1871–1945): *Sister Carrie* (1900), *The Financier* (1912), *The Titan* (1914), *The Genius* (1915), *An American Tragedy* (1925)

Edel, Leon (1907–   ): *The Untried Years* (1953), *The Conquest of London* (1962), *The Middle Years* (1962), *The Treacherous Years* (1969), *The Master* (1972), *Bloomsbury: A House of Lions* (1979)

Eliot, T(homas) S(tearns) (1888–1965): *Prufrock and Other Observations* (1917), *The Waste Land* (1922), *Murder in the Cathedral* (1935), *Four Quartets* (1943)

Ellison, Ralph (1914–   ): + *The Invisible Man* (1952)

Emerson, Ralph Waldo (1803–82): *Self-Reliance* (1834), *Nature* (1836), *The American Scholar* (1837), *May-Day and Other Pieces* (1867), *Society and Solitude* (1870)

Faulkner, William (1897–1962): *Soldier's Pay* (1926), *Sartoris* (1929), *The Sound and the Fury* (1929), *As I Lay Dying* (1930), *Absalom, Absalom!* (1936), *The Hamlet* (1940), *A Fable* (1954), *The Reivers* (1962)

Fitzgerald, F. Scott (1896–1940): *Tales of the Jazz Age* (1922), *The Great Gatsby* (1925), *Tender Is the Night* (1934), *The Last Tycoon* (1941)

Franklin, Benjamin (1706–90): *Poor Richard's Almanack* (1733–58), *Autobiography* (1771–88)

Frost, Robert (1874–1963): *North of Boston* (1914), *Mountain Interval* (1916), *New Hampshire* (1923), *Collected Poems* (1930), *A Further Range* (1936), *A Witness Tree* (1942), *In the Clearing* (1962)

Frye, Northrop (1912–   ): *Fearful Symmetry: A Study of William Blake* (1947), *Anatomy of Criticism* (1957), *The Great Code: Literature and the Bible* (1982)

Gardner, John (1933–82): *Grendel* (1971), *October Light* (1976), *Freddy's Book* (1980)

Ginsberg, Allen (1926–   ): *Howl and Other Poems* (1956), *Kaddish and Other Poems* (1961), *Collected Poems 1947–1980* (1984)

Gordon, Charles William [Ralph Connor] (1860–1937): *Black Rock: A Tale of the Selkirks* (1898), *The Sky Pilot: A Tale of the Foothills* (1899), *The Men from Glengarry: A Tale of the Ottawa* (1901), *Glengarry School Days: A Story of Early Days in Glengarry* (1902), *The Foreigner: A Tale of Saskatchewan* (1909), *The Sky Pilot in No Man's Land* (1919)

Hammett, Dashiell (1894–1961): *The Maltese Falcon* (1930), *The Thin Man* (1932)

Hawkes, John [Clendennin Burne, Jr.] (1925–   ): *The Lime Twig* (1961), *The Blood Oranges* (1971), *Death, Sleep and the Traveler* (1974)

Hawthorne, Nathaniel (1804–64): *Twice-Told Tales* (1837; enlarged 1842), *The Scarlet Letter* (1850), *The House of the Seven Gables* (1851)

Heinlein, Robert A. (1907–   ): *Stranger in a Strange Land* (1961), *Time Enough for Love* (1973)

Heller, Joseph (1923–   ): *Catch-22* (1961), *Something Happened* (1974)

Hellman, Lillian (1905–84): *An Unfinished Woman* (1969), *Pentimento* (1973), *Scoundrel Time* (1976)

Hemingway, Ernest (1899–1961): *The Sun Also Rises* (1926), *A Farewell to Arms* (1929), *To Have and Have Not* (1937), *For Whom the Bell Tolls* (1940),* *The Old Man and the Sea* (1952), *A Moveable Feast* (1964)

Henry, O. (William Sydney Porter 1862–1910): *Cabbages and Kings* (1904), *The Four Million* (1906), *The Trimmed Lamp* (1907), *The Voice of the City* (1908), *Whirligigs* (1910), *Strictly Business* (1910), *Sixes and Sevens* (1911), *Rolling Stones* (1913), *Postscripts* (1923)

Hersey, John [Richard] (1914–   ):* *A Bell for Adano* (1944), *Hiroshima* (1946), *The Wall* (1950)

Howells, William Dean (1837–1920): *The Rise of Silas Lapham* (1885), *A Traveler from Altruria* (1894)

Hughes, Langston (1902–67): *The Weary Blues* (1926), *The Ways of White Folks* (1934), *Shakespeare in Harlem* (1941), *Ask Your Mama* (1961)

Hurston, Zora Neale (1901–60): *Mules and Men* (1935), *Their Eyes Were Watching God* (1937), *Dust Tracks on a Road* (1942)

Irving, Washington (1783–1859): *History of New York* (1809), *The Sketch Book* (1819–20), *The Crayon Miscellany* (3 vols., 1835)

Jackson, Shirley (1919–65): *The Lottery; or, the Adventures of James Harris* (1949), *We Have Always Lived in the Castle* (1953), *The Bird's Nest* (1954), *The Haunting of Hill House* (1959)

James, Henry (1843–1916): *The American* (1877), *The Europeans* (1878), *Daisy Miller* (1879), *The Portrait of a Lady* (1881), *The Bostonians* (1886), *Embarrassments* (1896), *The Two Magics* (1898), *The Awkward Age* (1899), *The Ambassadors* (1903), *The Golden Bowl* (1904)

Jong, Erica (1942–   ): *Fear of Flying* (1973), *Fanny* (1987)

Kerouac, Jack (1922–69): *On the Road* (1957), *The Dharma Bums* (1958), *Desolation Angels* (1965)

Kosinski, Jerzy (1933–   ): *The Painted Bird* (1965), *Steps* (1968), *Being There* (1971)

Lardner, Ring (1885–1933): *You Know Me, Al: A Busher's Letters* (1916), *How to Write Short Stories* (1924)

Leacock, Stephen (1869–1944): *Literary Lapses* (1910), *Nonsense Novels* (1911), *Sunshine Sketches of a Little Town* (1912), *Arcadian Adventures with the Idle Rich* (1914), *My Discovery of the West* (1937)

Lewis, Sinclair (1885–1951): *Main Street* (1920), *Babbitt* (1922), *Arrowsmith* (1925), *Dodsworth* (1929)

London, Jack (1876–1916): *The Call of the Wild* (1903), *The Sea-Wolf* (1904), *White Fang* (1906), *The Iron Heel* (1908), *Martin Eden* (1909)

Longfellow, Henry Wadsworth (1807–82): *Voices of the Night* (1839), *Ballads and Other Poems* (1841), *Hiawatha* (1855), *The Courtship of Miles Standish* (1858), *The Tales of a Wayside Inn* (1863)

Lowry, Malcolm (1909–57): *Ultramarine* (1933), *Under the Volcano* (1947), *Hear Us O Lord from Heaven Thy Dwelling Place* (1961)

Mailer, Norman (1923–   ): *The Naked and the Dead* (1948), *An American Dream* (1965), *The Armies of the Night* (1968), *The Executioner's Song* (1979)

McCarthy, Mary (1912–   ): *The Groves of Academe* (1952), *Memories of a Catholic Girlhood* (1957), *The Group* (1963)

Melville, Herman (1819–91): *Typee* (1846), *Omoo* (1847), *White-Jacket* (1850), *Moby-Dick* (1851)

Mencken, H(enry) L(ouis) (1880–1956): *The American Language* (1919, revised 1921, 1923, 1936; supplements in 1945, 1948)

Michener, James (1907–   ): *Tales of the South Pacific* (1947), *Hawaii* (1959), *The Drifters* (1971), *Chesapeake* (1978)

Miller, Henry (1891–1980): *Tropic of Cancer* (1934), *Tropic of Capricorn* (1939)

Mitchell, Margaret (1900–49): *Gone with the Wind* (1936)

Montgomery, Lucy Maude (1874–1942): *Anne of Green Gables* (1908), *Emily of New Moon* (1923), *The Blue Castle* (1926), *A Tangled Web* (1931), *Jane of Lantern Hill* (1937)

Morrison, Toni [Chloe Anthony Wofford] (1931–   ): *The Bluest Eye* (1969), *Sula* (1973), *Song of Solomon* (1977), *Tar Baby* (1981), *Beloved* (1987)

Oates, Joyce Carol (1938–   ): *A Garden of Earthly Delights* (1967), *Expensive People* (1968), *them* (1969), *Bellefleur* (1980), *On Boxing* (1987), *You Must Remember This* (1988)

Paine, Thomas (1737–1809): *Common Sense* (1776), *The Age of Reason* (1794–95)

Percy, Walker (1916–   ): *The Moviegoer* (1961), *The Last Gentleman* (1966), *Love in the Ruins* (1971), *The Thanatos Syndrome* (1987)

Plath, Sylvia (1932–63): The Colossus (1960), *The Bell Jar* (1963), *Ariel* (1965)

Poe, Edgar Allan (1809–1849): *Poems by Edgar A. Poe* (1831), *Tales of the Grotesque and the Arabesque* (1840), *Tales* (1845), *The Raven and Other Poems* (1845)

Porter, Katherine Anne (1890–1980): *Flowering Judas* (1930), *Pale Horse, Pale Rider* (1939), *Noon Wine* (1937), *Ship of Fools* (1962), *Collected Stories* (1965)

Pound, Ezra (1885–1972): *Cantos* (1970)

Pratt, E. J. (1882–1964): *The Witches' Brew* (1925), *Titans: Two Poems* (1926), *The Fable of the Goats and Other Poems* (1932), *The Titanic* (1935), *Brebeuf and His Brethren* (1940), *Towards the Last Spike* (1952), *The Collected Poems of E. J. Pratt* (1958)

Pynchon, Thomas (1937–   ); *V* (1963), *+Gravity's Rainbow* (1973)

Richler, Mordecai (1931–   ): *A Choice of Enemies* (1957), *The Apprenticeship of Duddy Kravitz* (1959), *Cocksure* (1968), *St. Urbain's Horseman* (1971)

Roberts, Sir Charles G. D. (1860–1943): *Orion, and Other Poems* (1880), *In Divers Tones* (1886), *Songs of the Common Day* (1893), *Earth's Enigmas* (1896), *The Vagrant of Time* (1927), *The Iceberg, and Other Poems* (1934), *Further Animal Stories* (1936)

Ross, Sinclair (1908–   ): *As for Me and My House* (1941), *The Well* (1958), *The Lamp at Noon and Other Stories* (1968), *Whir of Gold* (1970), *Sawbones Memorial* (1974)

Roth, Philip (1933–   ): *+Goodbye, Columbus* (1959), *Letting Go* (1962), *Portnoy's Complaint* (1969), *The Great American Novel* (1973), *The Ghost Writer* (1979), *The Facts: A Novelist's Autobiography* (1988)

Salinger, J. D. (1919–   ): *The Catcher in the Rye* (1951), *Franny and Zooey* (1961)

Sandburg, Carl (1878–1967): *Chicago Poems* (1916), *Cornhuskers* (1918), *Complete Poems* (1950)

Saroyan, William (1908–81): *The Daring Young Man on the Flying Trapeze* (1934), *The Human Comedy* (1943), *One Day in the Afternoon of the World* (1964)

Singer, Isaac Bashevis (1904–   ): *Satan in Goray* (1935), *The Family Moskat* (1950), *Gimpel the Fool* (1957), *The Spinoza of Market Street* (1961), *Old Love* (1979)

Stein, Gertrude (1874–1946): *Three Lives* (1909), *The Autobiography of Alice B. Toklas* (1933), *Yes Is for a Very Young Man* (1946)

Steinbeck, John (1902–68): *Tortilla Flat* (1935), *Of Mice and Men* (1937), *The Long Valley* (1938), *The Grapes of Wrath* (1939), *East of Eden* (1952)

Stowe, Harriet Beecher (1811–96): *Uncle Tom's Cabin* (1852)

Styron, William (1925–   ): *Lie Down in Darkness* (1951), *The Confessions of Nat Turner* (1967), *Sophie's Choice* (1979)

Thoreau, Henry David (1817–62): *Civil Disobedience* (1849), *Walden* (1854), *The Maine Woods* (1864)

Twain, Mark [Samuel Langhorne Clemens] (1835–1910): *The Innocents Abroad* (1869), *Roughing It* (1872), *The Adventures of Tom Sawyer* (1876), *The Adventures of Huckleberry Finn* (1884), *Following the Equator* (1897)

Tyler, Anne (1941–   ): *A Slipping-Down Life* (1970), *Searching for Caleb* (1976), *Morgan's Passing* (1980), *Dinner at the Homesick Restaurant* (1982), *The Accidental Tourist* (1985), *Breathing Lessons* (1988)

Updike, John (1932–   ): *Rabbit, Run* (1960), *Couples* (1968), *Rabbit Is Rich* (1981), *The Witches of Eastwick* (1984)

Vonnegut, Kurt Jr., (1922–   ); *Cat's Cradle* (1963), *Slaughterhouse-Five; or The Children's Crusade* (1969)

Walker, Alice (1944–   ): *Meridian* (1976), *The Color Purple* (1982)

Warren, Robert Penn (1905–   ): *All the King's Men* (1946), *Promises* (1957), *The Cave* (1959)

Webster, Noah (1758–1843): *An American Dictionary of the English Language* (2 vols., 1828)

Welty, Eudora (1909–   ): *The Bride of the Innisfallen* (1955), *Thirteen Stories* (1965), *The Optimist's Daughter* (1970), *The Collected Stories of Eudora Welty* (1980), *One Writer's Beginnings* (1984)

Wharton, Edith (1862–1937): *Ethan Frome* (1911), *Xingu and Other Stories* (1916), *The Age of Innocence* (1920)

White, E. B. (1899–1985): *One Man's Meat* (1942), *Here Is New York* (1949), *Charlotte's Web* (1952), *The Elements of Style* (1959)

Whitman, Walt (1819–92): *Leaves of Grass* (1855), *Drum-Taps* (1865), *Passage to India* (1871), *Two Rivulets* (1876), *November Boughs* (1888)

Wilson, Edmund (1895–1972): *Axel's Castle* (1931), *The Wound and the Bow* (1940), *Patriotic Gore* (1962)

Wolfe, Thomas (1900–38): *Look Homeward, Angel* (1929), *Of Time and the River* (1935), *The Web and the Rock* (1939)

Wolfe, Tom [Thomas Kennerly, Jr.] (1931–   ): *The Pump House Gang* (1968), *The Electric Kool-Aid Acid Test* (1968), *The Right Stuff* (1975), *The Bonfire of the Vanities* (1988)

Wouk, Herman (1915–   ): *The Caine Mutiny* (1951), *Marjorie Morningstar* (1955), *The Winds of War* (1971), *War and Remembrance* (1978)

Wright, Richard (1908–60): *Native Son* (1940), *Black Boy* (1945), *The Outsider* (1953)

Important European and Russian Authors

This list of important European authors is not meant to be comprehensive. It includes most European writers who have made substantial contributions to the literature of their countries, their continent, and the world at large. Some of their most significant works appear here.

The years of first publication are given in parentheses. Authors known by their pseudonyms are so listed, with their real names given in brackets.

Note: *See also* Section 7 for major playwrights.

Andersen, Hans Christian (Danish, 1805–75): *Fairy Tales for Children* (1835–42), *Tales and Stories* (1839), *New Fairy Tales* (1843–47), *New Tales and Stories* (1858–67)

Austen, Jane (English, 1775–1817): *Sense and Sensibility* (1811), *Pride and Prejudice* (1813), *Emma* (1816), *Persuasion* (1818)

Balzac, Honoré de (French, 1799–1850): *Droll Tales* (1832–37), *The Human Comedy* (1830–50)

Baudelaire, Charles Pierre (French, 1821–67): *Les fleurs du mal* (1857), *Les paradis artificiels* (1860), *Les epaves* (1861), *Nouveles fleurs du mal* (1866), *Petits poemes en prose* (1869)

Belloc, Joseph Hilaire Peter (English, 1870–1914): *The Bad Child's Book of Beasts* (1896), *On Nothing* (1908), *Cautionary Tales for Children* (1908), *On Everything* (1909), *On Anything* (1910)

Blake, William (English, 1757–1827): *Poetical Sketches* (1783), *Songs of Innocence* (1789), *The Marriage of Heaven and Hell* (1793), *The Visions of the Daughters of Albion* (1793), *Songs of Experience* (1794), *Milton* (1804)

Blasco Ibañez, Vicente (Spanish 1867–1928): *Flor de Mayo* (1896), *La barraca* (1898), *Cañas y barro* (1902), *La bodega* (1905), *Sangre y arena* (1908)

Blok, Alexander Alexandrovich (Russian, 1880–1921): *Verses About the Beautiful Lady* (1904), *The Puppet Show* (1906), *A Frightful World* (c. 1910), *Dances of Death* (c. 1910), *Black Blood* (c. 1910), *The Twelve* (1917)

Boccaccio, Giovanni (Italian, 1313–75): *Decameron* (1349–53)

Böll, Heinrich (German, 1917–   ): *Traveler, If You Come to Spa* (1950), *Adam, Where Art Thou?* (1951), *Billiards at Half-past Nine* (1959), *The Clown* (1965), *Group Portrait with Lady* (1971), *The Lost Honor of Katharina Blum* (1974)

Boswell, James (English, 1740–95): *The Life of Samuel Johnson* (1791)

Brontë, Charlotte (English, 1816–55): *Jane Eyre* (1847)

Brontë, Emily (English, 1818–48): *Wuthering Heights* (1847)

Browning, Elizabeth Barrett (English, 1806–61): *The Seraphim and Other Poems* (1838), *Sonnets from the Portuguese* (1850), *Aurora Leigh* (1856), *Last Poems* (1862)

Browning, Robert (English, 1812–89): *Bells and Pomegranates* (1841–46), *Dramatic Lyrics* (1842), *Dramatic Romances and Lyrics* (1845), *Christmas Eve and Easter Day* (1850), *Men and Women* (1855), *Dramatis Personae* (1864)

Burgess, Anthony (English, 1917–   ): *A Clockwork Orange* (1962), *Napoleon Symphony: A Novel in Four Movements* (1974)

Burns, Robert (Scottish, 1759–96): *Poems, Chiefly in the Scottish Dialect* (1786), *The Scots Musical Museum* (1787–96)

Byron, Lord [George Gordon] (English, 1788–1824): *Childe Harold's Pilgrimage,* Cantos I and II (1812), *Childe Harold,* Cantos III and IV (1816, 1817), *The Prisoner of Chillon* (1816), *Manfred* (1817), *Don Juan* (1819–24)

Calvino, Italo (Italian, 1923–   ): *The Path of the Nest of Spiders* (1947), *The Watcher and Other Stories* (1958), *Cosmicomics* (1965), *T Zero* (1967), *Italian Folktales* (1971), *Invisible Cities* (1974), *If on a Winter's Night a Traveler* (1979), *Mr. Palomar* (1985)

Camus, Albert (French, 1913–60): *The Stranger* (1942, revised 1953), *The Myth of Sisyphus and Other Essays* (1942), *Caligula* (1944), *The Plague* (1948), *The Rebel* (1951), *The Fall* (1956), *Exile and the Kingdom* (1957)

Canetti, Elias (German, 1905–   ): *Auto-da-Fe* (1936), *Crowds and Power* (1960)

Capek, Karel (Czech, 1890–1938): *R.U.R.* (1921), *Tales from One Pocket* (1929), *Tales from the Other Pocket* (1929), *Hordubal* (1933), *Meteor* (1934), *An Ordinary Life* (1934)

Carroll, Lewis [Charles Lutwidge Dodgson] (English, 1832–98): *Alice's Adventures in Wonderland* (1865), *Through the Looking Glass* (1872)

Catullus (Roman, c. 84 B.C.–54 B.C.): verse

Cervantes Saavedra, Miguel de (Spanish, 1547–1616): *Don Quixote* (1605–15), *Exemplary Novels* (1613)

Chaucer, Geoffrey (English, c. 1340–1400): *The Canterbury Tales* (after 1387)

Chekhov, Anton Pavlovich (Russian, 1860–1904): *The Shooting Party* (1884), *Motley Tales* (1886), *The Duel* (1892), *Uncle Vanya* (1896), *The Seagull* (1896), *Three Sisters* (1900), *The Cherry Orchard* (1904)

Christie, Agatha (English, 1891–1976): *The Murder of Roger Ackroyd* (1926), *Murder at the Vicarage* (1930), *The Body in the Library* (1942), *Passenger to Frankfurt* (1970)

Coleridge, Samuel Taylor (English, 1772–1834): *Lyrical Ballads* (1798), *The Poetical Works* (1834)

Colette [Sidonie-Gabrielle Colette] (French, 1873–1954): *Claudine* (1900–03), *The Vagrant* (1910), *Mitsou* (1919), *Cheri* (1920), *A Lesson in Love* (1928), *Gigi* (1944)

Conrad, Joseph (English, 1857–1924): *The Nigger of the "Narcissus"* (1897), *Lord Jim* (1900), *Typhoon* (1903), *Nostromo* (1904), *Chance* (1914)

Dante Alighieri (Italian, 1265–1321): *Divine Comedy* (c. 1310–20)

Defoe, Daniel (English, c. 1660–1731): *Robinson Crusoe* (1719), *Moll Flanders* (1722), *The Fortunate Mistress: Roxanna* (1724)

Dickens, Charles (English, 1812–70): *Oliver Twist* (1838), *Nicholas Nickleby* (1839), *A Christmas Carol* (1843), *David Copperfield* (1850), *Bleak House* (1853), *A Tale of Two Cities* (1859), *Great Expectations* (1861), *Edwin Drood* (1870)

Dinesen, Isak [Karen Blixen] (Danish, 1885–1962): *Seven Gothic Tales* (1934), *Out of Africa* (1937), *Winter's Tales* (1942), *Last Tales* (1957)

Donne, John (English, 1572–1631): *The Anniversaries* (1611, 1612), *Songs and Sonnets* (1633)

Dostoyevsky, Fyodor Mikhaylovich (Russian, 1821–81): *Notes from the Underground* (1864), *Crime and Punishment* (1866), *The Idiot* (1869), *The Possessed* (1871–72), *The Brothers Karamazov* (1880)

Doyle, Sir Arthur Conan (English, 1858–1930): *Study in Scarlet* (1887), *The Sign of the Four* (1889), *The Adventures of Sherlock Holmes* (1904), *The Valley of Fear* (1915), *The Case Book of Sherlock Holmes* (1927)

Dryden, John (English, 1631–1700): *All for Love* (1678), *Absalom and Achitophel* (1681), *The Medal* (1682), *MacFlecknoe* (1682)

Dumas, Alexandre, pere (French, 1802–70): *The Count of Monte-Cristo* (1844–45), *The Three Musketeers* (1844), *The Corsican Brothers* (1844)

Eliot, George [Mary Ann Evans] (English, 1819–80): *Silas Marner* (1861), *Middlemarch* (1871–72)

Fielding, Henry (English, 1707–54): *The Tragedy of Tragedies; or, The Life and Death of Tom Thumb the Great* (1731), *Joseph Andrews* (1742), *Tom Jones* (1749)

Flaubert, Gustave (French, 1821–80): *Madame Bovary* (1857), *Sentimental Education* (1869)

García Lorca, Federico (Spanish, 1898–1936): *Canciones* (1927), *Ode to Walt Whitman* (1933), *Llanto por la muerte de Ignacio Sanchez Mejias* (1935), *Poet in New York* (1940)

Gide, André (French, 1869–1951): *The Immortalist* (1902), *Straight is the Gate* (1909), *The Pastoral Symphony* (1919)

Goethe, Johann Wolfgang von (German, 1749–1832): *Wilhelm Meister's Apprenticeship* (1795–96), *Faust*, Part I (1819), Part II (1821)

Gogol, Nikolai (Russian, 1809–52): *Arabesques* (1835), *Mirgorod* (1835), *The Inspector General* (1836), *Dead Souls* (1842), *Collected Works* (1842)

Golding, William (English, 1911–   ): *Lord of the Flies* (1954)

Gombrowicz, Witold (Polish, 1904–69): *Memoir from Adolescence* (1933), *Ferdydurke* (1937), *Pornografia* (1960)

Gorky, Maxim (Russian, 1868–1936): *Foma Gordeyev* (1899), *Twenty-Six Men and a Girl and Other Stories* (1902), *The Lower Depths* (1902), *Mother* (1906)

Grass, Günter (German, 1927–   ): *The Tin Drum* (1959), *The Flounder* (1977)

Grimm, Wilhelm (German, 1786–1859); **Grimm, Jakob** (German, 1785–1863): *Fairy Tales* (3 vols., 1812, 1815, 1822), *Fairy Tales* (2 vols., 1816, 1818)

Hamsun, Knut (Norwegian, 1859–1952): *Hunger* (1890), *Mysteries* (1892), *The Growth of the Soil* (1917)

Hardy, Thomas (English, 1840–1928): *Far from the Madding Crowd* (1874), *The Return of the Native* (1878), *Tess of the D'Urbervilles* (1891), *Jude the Obscure* (1896)

Hasek, Jaroslav (Czech, 1883–1923): *The Good Soldier Svejk and Other Strange Stories* (1912), *The Good Soldier Svejk and His Fortunes in the World War* (4 vols., 1921–23)

Hesse, Hermann (German, 1877–1962): *Demian* (1919), *Siddhartha* (1922), *Steppenwolf* (1927)

Homer (Greek, c. 700 B.C.): *The Iliad, The Odyssey*

Hugo, Victor Marie (French, 1802–85): *The Hunchback of Notre-Dame* (1831), *Lucretia Borgia* (1833), *Les Miserables* (1862)

Ibsen, Henrik Johan (Norwegian, 1828–1906): *Peer Gynt* (1867), *A Doll's House* (1879), *An Enemy of the People* (1882), *The Wild Duck* (1884), *Hedda Gabler* (1890)

Johnson, Samuel (English, 1709–84): *A Dictionary of the English Language* (1755)

Joyce, James (Irish, 1882–1941): *Dubliners* (1914), *Portrait of the Artist as a Young Man* (1916), *Ulysses* (1922), *Finnegan's Wake* (1939)

Kafka, Franz (German, 1883–1924): *Metamorphosis* (1916), *The Judgment* (1916), *In the Penal Colony* (1919), *The Trial* (1925), *The Castle* (1926), *Amerika* (1927)

Keats, John (English, 1795–1821): *The Poems of John Keats* (1817), *Endymion* (1818), *The Fall of Hyperion* (1819–21), *Lamia, Isabella, and The Eve of St. Agnes and Other Poems* (1820)

Kipling, Rudyard (English, 1865–1936): *Plain Tales from the Hills* (1888), *The Phantom Rickshaw* (1889), *Barrack-Room Ballads* (1892), *The Jungle Book* (1894), *The Second Jungle Book* (1895), *Captains Courageous* (1897), *Kim* (1901), *Just So Stories* (1902)

Lawrence, D(avid) H(erbert) (English, 1885–1930): *Sons and Lovers* (1913), *Women in Love* (1920), *Lady Chatterley's Lover* (1928)

Lessing, Doris (British, 1919–   ): *The Grass Is Singing* (1950), *Martha Quest* (1952), *The Golden Notebook* (1962), *Briefing for a Descent into Hell* (1971), *The Good Terrorist* (1986)

Malory, Sir Thomas (English, ?–1471): *Le Morte d'Arthur* (1485)

Malraux, André (French, 1901–76): *Man's Fate* (1933), *Man's Hope* (1937)

Mandelstam, Osip Emilevich (Russian, 1891–1938): *Kamen* (1913), *Tristia* (1922), *Journey to Armenia* (1933)

Mann, Thomas (German, 1875–1955): *Buddenbrooks* (1900), *Death in Venice* (1913), *The Magic Mountain* (1924)

Manzoni, Alessandro (Italian, 1785–1873): *The Betrothed* (1827)

Maugham, William Somerset (English, 1874–1965): *Of Human Bondage* (1915), *Cakes and Ale* (1930), *The Summing Up* (1938), *The Razor's Edge* (1944)

Maupassant, Henri Rene Albert Guy de (French, 1850–93): *Boule de suif* (1880), *La Maison Tellier* (1881), *Bel-Ami* (1885), *Pierre et Jean* (1888)

Mauriac, François Charles (French, 1885–1970): *The Family* (1923), *Thérèse* (1927), *The Desert of Love* (1929), *A Woman of the Pharisees* (1941)

Milton, John (English, 1608–74): *Paradise Lost* (1667), *Paradise Regained* (1671)

Montaigne, Michel de (French, 1533–92): *Essais* (1580)

Nabokov, Vladimir Vladimirovich (Russian, 1899–1977): *Lolita* (1955), *Invitation to a Beheading* (1959), *Pale Fire* (1962), *Speak, Memory* (1969)

Orwell, George [Eric Blair] (English, 1903–50): *Animal Farm* (1945), *1984* (1949)

Ovid (Roman, 43 B.C.–A.D. 17): *Amores* (c. 16 B.C.), *Heroines, Metamorphoses*

Pasternak, Boris Leonidovich (Russian, 1890–1960): *My Sister—Life* (1922), *Doctor Zhivago* (1957)

Petronius (Roman, ?–66): *Satyricon* (c. 50)

Plato (Greek, c. 428–347 B.C.): *Parmenides* (c. 370 B.C.), *The Republic, Apologia* (c. 399 B.C.)

Plutarch (Greek, c. 48–122): *Moralia, Parallel Lives*

Pope, Alexander (English, 1688–1744): *An Essay on Criticism* (1711), *The Rape of the Lock* (1712)

Proust, Marcel (French, 1871–1922): *Remembrance of Things Past* (7 vols., 1913–27)

Rabelais, François (French, 1494?–1553): *Gargantua and Pantagruel* (1532–64)

Racine, Jean (French, 1639–99): *Bajazet* (1672), *Mithridate* (1673), *Iphigénie en Aulide* (1674), *Phèdre* (1677)

Rilke, Rainer Maria (German, 1875–1926): *Das Buch der Bilder* (1902), *New Poems* (2 vols., 1907–08), *Duino Elegies* (1923), *Sonnets to Orpheus* (1923)

Rostand, Edmond (French, 1868–1918): *Cyrano de Bergerac* (1897), *The Princess Faraway* (1921)

Sand, George [Amandine-Aurore-Lucie Dupin] (French 1804–76): *Indiana* (1832), *Lelia* (1833), *The Companion of the Tour of France* (1841), *Consuelo* (1842–43), *He and She* (1859), *The Marquis of Villemer* (1860–61)

Sappho (Greek, c. 612 B.C.–?): verse

Sartre, Jean-Paul (French, 1905–80): *Nausea* (1938), *The Flies* (1943), *Being and Nothingness* (1943), *No Exit* (1944), *The Condemned of Altona* (1961)

Scott, Sir Walter (Scottish, 1771–1832): *The Heart of Midlothian* (1818), *The Bride of Lammermoor* (1819), *Ivanhoe* (1819), *Kenilworth* (1821)

Shakespeare, William (English, 1564–1616): *Richard III* (1592–93), *Romeo and Juliet* (1594–95), *The Two Gentlemen of Verona* (1594–95), *A Midsummer Night's Dream* (1595–96), *Hamlet* (1600–01), *Macbeth* (1605–06), *Sonnets* (1609), *The Winter's Tale* (1610–11), *Henry VIII* (1612–13)

Shaw, George Bernard (Irish, 1856–1950): *Plays Pleasant and Unpleasant* (1898), *Man and Superman* (1901–03), *Major Barbara* (1905), *Pygmalion* (1912)

Shelley, Mary Wollstonecraft (English, 1797–1851): *Frankenstein, or the Modern Prometheus* (1818)

Shelley, Percy Bysshe (English, 1792–1822): *Prometheus Unbound* (1820), *Adonais* (1821)

Solzhenitsyn, Aleksandr I. (Russian, 1918–   ): *One Day in the Life of Ivan Denisovich* (1962), *The Cancer Ward* (1968), *The Gulag Archipelago* (1973–76)

Spenser, Edmund (English, c. 1552–99): *The Faerie Queene* (1590)

Stevenson, Robert Louis (Scottish, 1850–94): *Treasure Island* (1883), *The Stange Case of Dr. Jekyll and Mr. Hyde* (1886)

Strindberg, August (Swedish, 1849–1912): *Master Olof* (1874), *Married* (1884–86), *The Father* (1887), *Comrades* (1888), *Miss Julie* (1888)

Swift, Jonathan (Irish, 1667–1745): *Gulliver's Travels* (1726)

Swinburne, Algernon Charles (English, 1837–1909): *Atalanta in Calydon* (1865), *Poems and Ballads: First Series* (1866), *Poems and Ballads: Second Series* (1878), *Astrophel* (1894), *A Tale of Balen* (1896)

Synge, John Millington (Irish, 1871–1909): *Riders to the Sea* (1904), *The Playboy of the Western World* (1907)

Tennyson, Alfred (Lord) (English, 1809–92): *Poems, Chiefly Lyrical* (1830), *Poems* (1832), *Poems* (1842), *Locksley Hall* (1842), *In Memoriam* (1833–50), *Maud, and Other Poems* (1855), *Idylls of the King* (1859–85)

Thackeray, William Makepeace (English, 1811–63): *Barry Lyndon* (1844), *Vanity Fair* (1847–48)

Thomas, Dylan Marlais (English-Welsh, 1914–53): *Eighteen Poems* (1934), *Twenty-five Poems* (1936), *A Child's Christmas in Wales* (1952), *Under Milk Wood* (1954)

Tocqueville, Alexis de (1805–1859): *De la democratie en Amerique* (2 vols., 1835; 2 supplementary vols., 1840)

Tolstoy, Leo [Count Lev Nikolayevich] (Russian, 1828–1910): *War and Peace* (1863–69), *Anna Karenina* (1875–77)

Trollope, Anthony (English, 1815–82): *The Warden* (1855), *Barchester Towers* (1857)

Turgenev, Ivan (Russian, 1818–83): *A Month in the Country* (1850), *A Sportsman's Sketches* (1852), *A Nest of Gentlefolk* (1858), *On the Eve* (1860), *Fathers and Sons* (1862), *Smoke* (1867)

Undset, Sigrid (Norwegian, 1882–1949): *Kristin Lavransdatter* (1920–22), *Olaf Andunsson* (1925–27)

Verne, Jules (French, 1828–1905): *A Voyage to the Center of the Earth* (1864), *Twenty Thousand Leagues Under the Sea* (1870), *Around the World in Eighty Days* (1873)

Virgil [Publius Vergilius Maro] (Roman, 70–19 B.C.): *Georgics* (37–30 B.C.), *Bucolics* (37 B.C.), *Aeneid* (30–19 B.C.)

Voltaire (François-Marie Arouet, French, 1694–1778): *Candide* (1759)

Wilde, Oscar (Irish, 1854–1900): *The Portrait of Dorian Gray* (1891), *Salome* (1893), *The Importance of Being Earnest* (1899)

Wordsworth, William (English, 1770–1850): *Lyrical Ballads* (1798), *Poems Chiefly of Early and Late Years* (1842)

Yeats, William Butler (Irish, 1865–1939): *The Wind Among the Reeds* (1899), *The Wild Swans at Coole* (1919), *The Winding Stair* (1933), *Collected Poems* (1933)

Zola, Emile Edouard Charles Antoine (French, 1840–1902): *Thérèse Raquin* (1867), *Nana* (1880), *Germinal* (1885)

Important Asian, African, and Latin American Authors

Armah, Ayi Kweh (Ghanaian, 1939–   ): *The Beautiful Ones Are Not Yet Born* (1968), *Why Are We So Blest?* (1972)

Bashō [Matsuo Munefusal] (Japanese, 1644–94): *The Narrow Road to the Deep North* (1694)

Beti, Mongo [Alexandre Biyidi] (Cameroonian, 1932–   ): *Le pauvre Christ de Bomba* (1956), *Mission terminée* (1957), *Le roi miraculé* (1958)

Borges, Jorge Luis (Argentinian, 1899–1987): *A Universal History of Infamy* (1935), *Six Problems for Don Isidro Parodi* (1942), *Ficciones* (1935–44), *The Aleph and Other Stories* (1949), *Labyrinthe* (1962), *The Book of Sand* (1975)

Cesaire, Aimé (West Indian, 1913–   ): *Return to My Native Land* (1939), *State of the Vinou* (1946), *The Tragedy of King Christophe* (1963)

Chatterje, Bankim-Chandra (Indian, 1838–94): *The Chieftain's Daughter* (1880), *Kopal-Kundala: A Tale of Bengali Life* (1885), *Krishna Kante's Will* (1895)

Confucius (Chinese, c. 551–479 B.C.): *The Analects of Confucius*

Fuentes, Carlos (Mexican, 1929–   ): *The Death of Artemio Cruz* (1962), *Distant Relations* (1980)

García Márquez, Gabriel (Colombian, 1928–   ): *One Hundred Years of Solitude* (1968), *The Autumn of the Patriarch* (1975), *Love in the Time of Cholera* (1988)

Guzmán, Martín Luis (Mexican, 1887–1976): *The Eagle and the Serpent* (1928), *Memorias de Pancho Villa* (4 vols., 1938–40)

Kawabata, Yasunari (Japanese, 1899–1972): *Snow Country* (1937), *Thousand Cranes* (1952), *Beauty and Sadness* (1965)

Lao-tzu (Chinese, c. 6th century B.C.): *Tao-te-ching*

Laye, Camara (Guinean, 1928–   ): *The African Child* (1953), *The Radiance of the King* (1954), *The Guardian of the Word* (1980)

Li Po (Chinese, 701–762): *Complete Works*

Machado de Assis, Joaquim Maria (Brazilian, 1839–1908): *The Posthumous Memoirs of Braz Cubas* (1881), *Philosopher or Dog?* (1891), *Dom Casmurro* (1899)

Marquéz, Gabriel García *See* García Márquez, Gabriel.

Mishima, Yukio (Japanese, 1925–70): *Confession of a Mask* (1948), *Forbidden Colors* (2 vols., 1951–53), *The Sailor Who Fell from Grace with the Sea* (1963), *The Sea of Fertility* (4 vols., 1969–71)

Murasaki, Shikibu (Japanese, c. 978–1026): *The Tale of the Genji* (c. 1010)

Naipaul, V. S. (Trinidadian, 1932–   ): *The Mystic Masseur* (1957), *A House for Mr. Biswas* (1961), *The Middle Passage* (1962), *In a Free State* (1971)

Natsume Sōseki (Japanese, 1867–1916): *I Am a Cat* (1905–07), *The Three-Cornered World* (1907), *And Then* (1910)

Neruda, Pablo [Neftali Ricardo Reyes Basoalto] (Chilean, 1904–73): *Twenty Love Poems and a Story of Despair* (1924), *Canto General* (1950), *Elementary Odes* (3 vols., 1954–57), *We Are Many* (1967), *End of the World* (1969)

Omar Khayyam (Persian, 1048–1131): *Rubaiyat* (1859)

Paton, Alan Stewart (South African, 1903–88): *Cry the Beloved Country* (1948)

Paz, Octavio (Mexican, 1914–   ): *The Labyrinth of Solitude* (1950), *Sun-Stone* (1957), *Salamandra 1958–1961* (1962), *Ladera esta 1962–1968* (1969), *Vuelta* (1976)

Sembene, Ousmane (Senegalese, 1923–   ): *Le docher noir* (1956), *L'Harmattan* (1964), *The Money Order* (1965)

Senghor, Leopold Sedar (Senegalese, 1906–   ): *Chants d'ombre* (1945), *Nocturnes* (1961), *Liberte I. Negritude et Humanisme* (1964)

Soyinka, Wole (Nigerian 1934–   ): *Three Plays* (1963), *The Road* (1965), *The Forest of a Thousand Daemons* (1968)

Tanizaki Junichiro (Japanese, 1886–1965): *Tattoo* (1911), *The Secret History of the Lord Musashi* (1935), *The Key* (1956), *Seven Japanese Tales* (1963)

Ts'so Hsueh-ch'in (Chinese, c. 1715–63): *The Dream of Red Chamber* (c. 1763)

Vargas Llosa, Mario (Peruvian, 1936–   ): *The Green House* (1966), *Conversations in the Cathedral* (1969)

Literary Terms

allegory A story with an underlying meaning symbolized by the characters and action.

alliteration The use of a repeated consonant, usually at the start of a word.

allusion Reference to a familiar person or event, often from literature.

anachronism A chronological error in literature that places a person, event, or object in an impossible historical context.

anagram A word created by transposing the letters of another word.

analogy The relation of one thing to something familiar.

antagonist The major character opposing a hero or a protagonist.

anthropomorphism The assigning of human characteristics and feelings to animals and nonhuman things.

anticlimax Something that works against a climax, such as humor; a sudden descent from the lofty to the trivial.

antihero A protagonist lacking in heroic qualities like courage, idealism, and honesty.

autobiography The story of one's life as written by oneself.

ballad A poem, often meant to be sung, that tells a story.

bathos A sudden descent from the lofty to the ordinary or ridiculous.

belles-lettres Literature.

bibliography A list of books on a similar subject or by a given author or authors.

biography The story of someone's life as written by another.

blank verse Unrhymed poetry, especially poetry written in iambic pentameter.

cacophony Discordant sounds, sometimes used in poetry for effect.

caesura A pause in a line of verse, usually in the middle of a line, caused when a word ends within a metrical foot.

climax The point of high emotional intensity at which a story or play reaches its peak.

couplet Two successive lines of poetry, usually rhymed.

denouement The events following a climax.

doggerel Crudely written poetry.

elegy A poetic lament.

epic An extended narrative poem.

epistolary novel A novel written in the form of correspondence.

essay A short written work of nonfiction, usually on one topic.

euphony Harmonious sounds, often used in poetry for effect.

fable A prose or poetic story that illustrates a moral.

fiction An invented work of prose, verse, or drama.

free verse A poem without regular meter or line length.

haiku An unrhymed poem form, originated by the Japanese, consisting of three lines of five, seven, and five syllables that record the essence of a moment.

hero A character, often the protagonist, who exhibits qualities such as courage, idealism, and honesty.

high comedy Comedy that is characterized by intellect or wit.

historical novel A narrative that places fictional characters or events in historically accurate surroundings.

hyperbole A deliberate overstatement.

iamb A metrical foot that contains one short or unstressed syllable preceding one long or stressed syllable.

iambic pentameter Poetry consisting of five parts per line, each part having one short or unstressed syllable and one long or stressed syllable.

imagery Figurative language used to evoke particular mental pictures.

irony An expression of a meaning that contradicts the literal meaning.

literature Novels, stories, poems, and plays of high standards that entertain, inform, stimulate, or provide aesthetic pleasure.

low comedy Humorous material that employs physical actions or jokes of questionable taste.

malapropism A mistaken substitution of one word for another that sounds similar, generally with humorous effect.

metaphor A comparison between two unlike things.

meter The pattern of stressed and unstressed syllables in poetry.

motif A recurring or central theme that runs throughout a work or series of works.

myth A legend, usually made up in part of historical events, that helps define the beliefs of a people and that often has evolved as an explanation for rituals and natural phenomena.

nonfiction A historically accurate narrative.

novel A long work of fictional prose.

novella A short novel; also, the early tales or short stories of French and Italian writers.

ode A lyric poem marked by strong feelings and an involved style.

onomatopoeia Formation of a word by imitating the natural sound associated with the object or action involved; the use of words that are so named.

oxymoron A figure of speech that employs two contradictory terms.

palindrome A word, a sentence, or a group of sentences (sometimes in verse) that reads the same backward and forward.

parable A short story that illustrates a moral.

paradox An apparently contradictory statement that contains a truth that reconciles the contradiction.

parody A humorous, often exaggerated, imitation of a serious literary work.

pathetic fallacy The assigning of human attributes to nature.

pathos An element that evokes feelings of pity, tenderness, and sympathy.

personification The assigning of human attributes to abstractions, objects, and other nonhuman things.

plot The orginization of individual incidents in a narrative or play.

poem A rhythmic expression of feelings or ideas, often using metaphor, meter, and rhyme.

poetic license The practice of violating rules, expectations, or conventions to achieve a desired effect.

prologue An introductory speech or monologue, given by an actor or actress before a play, which helps to set the stage for what is to come.

prose As distinguished from poetry, literary writing that varies in rhythm and is more like ordinary speech.

protagonist The main character of a play, novel, or story, usually the hero.

pun A humorous and often clever play on words in which one word evokes another with a similar sound but a different meaning.

refrain A phrase or verse that is repeated throughout a poem or song.

rhetorical question A question put forth to achieve an effect or make a point, to which an answer is not expected.

rhyme The repetition of similar or identical sounds at the ends of lines of verse.

rhythm The pattern of stressed and unstressed syllables in a line of poetry or prose.

satire Ridicule of a subject; the work in which it is contained.

short story A brief work of narrative prose.

simile A comparison of two unlike things that usually employs *like* or *as.*

soliloquy A dramatic monologue meant to convey the thoughts of a character in a play.

sonnet A poem consisting of fourteen iambic pentameter lines with a rigidly prescribed rhyming scheme.

spondee A type of metrical foot with two stressed syllables.

spoonerism The transposition of the initial sounds of two or more words, often with humorous results. Named for a Professor Spooner of Oxford, who was famous for such transpositions.

style An author's individual method and tone.

subplot A secondary plot in a story.

symbol In literature, something that stands for, or means, something else.

theme The central idea or thesis of a work.

trochee A metrical foot that contains one long or stressed syllable preceding one short or unstressed syllable.

verse Lines of writing arranged in metrical patterns, or a single such line.

Pseudonyms of Famous Authors

Most of the authors in this list published under both their real names and pseudonyms.

Real Name	*Pseudonym or Pen Name*
Kingsley Amis	Robert Markham
Hans Christian Andersen	Villiam Christian Walter
Isaac Asimov	Dr. A. Paul French
Louis Auchincloss	Andrew Lee
L. Frank Baum	Edith Van Dyne
Robert Benchley	Guy Fawkes
Ambrose Bierce	Dod Grile
Eric Arthur Blair	George Orwell
Anne Brontë	Acton Bell, Lady Geralda, Olivia Vernon, Alexandria Zenobia
Charlotte Brontë	C. B., Currer Bell, Marquis of Douro, Genius, Lord Charles Wellesley

Emily Jane Brontë	R. Alcon, Ellis Bell
William S. Burroughs	William Lee
Barbara Cartland	Barbara Hamilton McCorquodale
Agatha Christie	Agatha Christie Mallowen, Mary Westmacott
Samuel Langhorne Clemens	Mark Twain
Howard Fast	E. V. Cunningham
Erle Stanley Gardner	A. A. Fair, Charles M. Green, Carleton Kendrake, Charles J. Kenny
Theodor Seuss Geisel	Theo LeSieg, Dr. Seuss
Edward St. John Gorey	Eduard Blutig, Mrs. Regera Dowdy, Redway Grode, O. Mude, Hyacinthe Phypps, Ogdred Weary, Dreary Wodge
Dashiell Hammett	Peter Collinson
Robert A. Heinlein	Anson MacDonald
Eleanor Alice Burford Hibbert	Eleanor Burford, Philippa Carr, Elbur Ford, Victoria Holt, Kathleen Kellow, Jean Plaidy, Ellalice Tate
L. Ron Hubbard	Elron, Tom Esterbrook, Rene La Fayette, Capt. B. A. Northrop, Kurt von Rachem
Ford Madox Hueffer	Ford Madox Ford
E. Howard Hunt	John Baxter, Gordon Davis, Robert Dietrich, David St. John
Evan Hunter	Hunt Collins, Richard Marsten, Ed McBain
LeRoi Jones	Imamu Amiri Baraka
Teodor Jozef Konrad Korzeniowski	Joseph Conrad
Louis L'Amour	Tex Burns
T. E. Lawrence	J. H. Ross, T. E. Shaw
Manfred Lee and Frederic Dannay	Ellery Queen, Barnaby Ross
Kenneth Millar	John Ross Macdonald, Ross Macdonald
Edna St. Vincent Millay	Nancy Boyd
Mystery Writers of America, California chapter	Theo Durrant
Conor Cruise O'Brien	Donat O'Donnell
Dorothy Parker	Constant Reader
Eric Partridge	Vigilans
William Sydney Porter	O. Henry
William Saroyan	Sirak Goryan
Terry Southern	Maxwell Kenton
Irving Stone	Irving Tannenbaum
Gore Vidal	Edgar Box
Nathan Wallenstein Weinstein	Nathaniel West
J. A. Wight	James Herriot
John Burgess Wilson	Anthony Burgess, Joseph Kell
Willard Huntington Wright	S. S. Van Dine

Poet Laureates

In 1616 Ben Jonson was named England's first poet laureate; however, the title did not become an official royal office until 1668, when John Dryden assumed the honored post. Since that time, the office has been awarded for life. The poet laureate is responsible for composing poems for court and national occasions. At the time of each laureate's death, it is the duty of the prime minister to nominate successors from which the reigning sovereign will choose. It is the Lord Chamberlain who appoints the poet laureate by issuing a warrant to the laureate-elect. The life appointment is always announced in the *London Gazette*.

Laureateship	Poet	Birth and Death Dates
1668–88	John Dryden	1631–1700
1688–92	Thomas Shadwell	1643?–92
1692–1715	Nahum Tate	1652–1715
1715–18	Nicholas Rowe	1674–1718
1718–30	Laurence Eusden	1688–1730
1730–57	Colley Cibber	1671–1757
*1757–85	William Whitehead	1715–85
1785–90	Thomas Warton	1728–90
1790–1813	Henry James Pye	1745–1813
1813–43	Robert Southey	1774–1843
1843–50	William Wordsworth	1770–1850
†1850–92	Alfred, Lord Tennyson	1809–92
1896–1913	Alfred Austin	1835–1913
1913–30	Robert Bridges	1844–1930
1930–67	John Masefield	1878–1967
1968–72	Cecil Day-Lewis	1904–72
1972–84	Sir John Betjeman	1906–84
1984–	Ted Hughes	(b. 1930)

* The 1757 appointment was declined by Thomas Gray.

† The 1850 appointment was declined by Samuel Russell.

Book Awards and Their Recipients

Nobel Prize in Literature

1901	René F.A. Sully-Prudhomme, France		1916	Verner von Heidenstamm, Sweden
1902	Theodor Mommsen, Germany		1917	Karl A. Gjellerup, Denmark
1903	Bjornsterne Björnson, Norway			Henrik Pontoppidan, Denmark
1904	Frederic Mistral, France		1918	*No award*
	José Echegaray, Spain		1919	Carl F. G. Spitteler, Switzerland
1905	Henryk Sienkiewicz, Poland		1920	Knut Hamsun, Norway
1906	Giosue Carducci, Italy		1921	Anatole France, France
1907	Rudyard Kipling, Great Britain		1922	Jacinto Benavente y Martinez, Spain
1908	Rudolph C. Eueken, Germany		1923	William Butler Yeats, Ireland
1909	Selma Lagerlöf, Sweden		1924	Wladyslaw S. Reymont, Poland
1910	Paul J.L. Heyse, Germany		1925	George Bernard Shaw, Great Britain
1911	Maurice Maeterlinck, Belgium		1926	Grazia Deledda, Italy
1912	Gerhart Hauptmann, Germany		1927	Henri Bergson, France
1913	Rabindranath Tagore, India		1928	Sigrid Undset, Norway
1914	*No award*		1929	Thomas Mann, Germany
1915	Romain Rolland, France		1930	Sinclair Lewis, U.S.

1931	Erik A. Karlfeldt, Sweden	1962	John Steinbeck, U.S.

1931 Erik A. Karlfeldt, Sweden
1932 John Galsworthy, Great Britain
1933 Ivan A. Bunin, France
1934 Luigi Pirandello, Italy
1935 *No award*
1936 Eugene O'Neill, U.S.
1937 Roger Martin de Gard, France
1938 Pearl S. Buck, U.S.
1939 Frans E. Sillanpää, Finland
1940 *No award*
1941 *No award*
1942 *No award*
1943 *No award*
1944 Johannes V. Jensen, Denmark
1945 Gabriela Mistral, Chile
1946 Hermann Hesse, Switzerland
1947 André Gide, France
1948 T.S. Eliot, Great Britain
1949 William Faulkner, U.S.
1950 Bertrand Russell, Great Britain
1951 Pär F. Lagerkvist, Sweden
1952 François Mauriac, France
1953 Sir Winston Churchill, Great Britain
1954 Ernest Hemingway, U.S.
1955 Halldor K. Laxness, Iceland
1956 Juan Ramón Jiménez, Puerto Rico
1957 Albert Camus, France
1958 Boris L. Pasternak, U.S.S.R. (prize declined)
1959 Salvatore Quasimodo, Italy
1960 Saint-John Perse, France
1961 Ivo Andric, Yugoslavia

1962 John Steinbeck, U.S.
1963 Giorgos Seferis, Greece
1964 Jean-Paul Sartre, France (prize declined)
1965 Mikhail Sholokhov, U.S.S.R.
1966 Samuel Joseph Agnon, Israel
      Nelly Sachs, Sweden
1967 Miguel Angel Asturias, Guatemala
1968 Yasunari Kawabata, Japan
1969 Samuel Beckett, Ireland
1970 Aleksandr I. Solzhenitsyn, U.S.S.R.
1971 Pablo Neruda, Chile
1972 Heinrich Böll, Federal Republic of Germany
1973 Patrick White, Australia
1974 Eyvind Johnson, Sweden
      Harry Edmund Martinson, Sweden
1975 Eugenio Montale, Italy
1976 Saul Bellow, U.S.
1977 Vicente Aleixandre, Spain
1978 Isaac Bashevis Singer, U.S.
1979 Odysseus Elytis, Greece
1980 Czeslaw Milosz, Poland–U.S.
1981 Elias Canetti, Bulgaria–Great Britain
1982 Gabriel García Márquez, Colombia–Mexico
1983 William Golding, Great Britain
1984 Jaroslav Siefert, Czechoslovakia
1985 Claude Simon, France
1986 Wole Soyonka, Nigeria
1987 Joseph Brodsky, U.S.
1988 Naguib Mahfouz, Egypt

Pulitzer Prize in Letters

Fiction

1918 Ernest Poole, *His Family*
1919 Booth Tarkington, *The Magnificent Ambersons*
1920 *No award*
1921 Edith Wharton, *The Age of Innocence*
1922 Booth Tarkington, *Alice Adams*
1923 Willa Cather, *One of Ours*
1924 Margaret Wilson, *The Able McLaughlins*
1925 Edna Ferber, *So Big*
1926 Sinclair Lewis, *Arrowsmith* (prize declined)
1927 Louis Bromfield, *Early Autumn*
1928 Thornton Wilder, *Bridge of San Luis Rey*
1929 Julia M. Peterkin, *Scarlet Sister Mary*
1930 Oliver LaFarge, *Laughing Boy*

1931 Margaret Ayer Barnes, *Years of Grace*
1932 Pearl S. Buck, *The Good Earth*
1933 T.S. Stribling, *The Store*
1934 Caroline Miller, *Lamb in His Bosom*
1935 Josephine W. Johnson, *Now in November*
1936 Harold L. Davis, *Honey in the Horn*
1937 Margaret Mitchell, *Gone with the Wind*
1938 John P. Marquand, *The Late George Apley*
1939 Marjorie Kinnan Rawlings, *The Yearling*
1940 John Steinbeck, *The Grapes of Wrath*
1941 *No award*
1942 Ellen Glasgow, *In This Our Life*
1943 Upton Sinclair, *Dragon's Teeth*

1944 Martin Flavin, *Journey in the Dark*
1945 John Hersey, *A Bell for Adano*
1946 *No award*
1947 Robert Penn Warren, *All the King's Men*
1948 James A. Michener, *Tales of the South Pacific*
1949 James Gould Cozzens, *Guard of Honor*
1950 A.B. Guthrie, Jr., *The Way West*
1951 Conrad Richter, *The Town*
1952 Herman Wouk, *The Caine Mutiny*
1953 Ernest Hemingway, *The Old Man and the Sea*
1954 *No award*
1955 William Faulkner, *A Fable*
1956 MacKinlay Kantor, *Andersonville*
1957 *No award*
1958 James Agee, *A Death in the Family*
1959 Robert Lewis Taylor, *The Travels of Jaimie McPheeters*
1960 Allen Drury, *Advise and Consent*
1961 Harper Lee, *To Kill a Mockingbird*
1962 Edwin O'Connor, *The Edge of Sadness*
1963 William Faulkner, *The Reivers*
1964 *No award*
1965 Shirley Ann Grau, *The Keepers of the House*
1966 Katherine Anne Porter, *Collected Stories of Katherine Anne Porter*

1967 Bernard Malamud, *The Fixer*
1968 William Styron, *The Confessions of Nat Turner*
1969 N. Scott Momaday, *House Made of Dawn*
1970 Jean Stafford, *Collected Stories*
1971 *No award*
1972 Wallace Stegner, *Angle of Repose*
1973 Eudora Welty, *The Optimist's Daughter*
1974 *No award*
1975 Michael Shaara, *The Killer Angels*
1976 Saul Bellow, *Humboldt's Gift*
1977 *No award*
1978 James Alan McPherson, *Elbow Room*
1979 John Cheever, *The Stories of John Cheever*
1980 Norman Mailer, *The Executioner's Song*
1981 John Kennedy Toole, *A Confederacy of Dunces*
1982 John Updike, *Rabbit Is Rich*
1983 Alice Walker, *The Color Purple*
1984 William Kennedy, *Ironweed*
1985 Alison Lurie, *Foreign Affairs*
1986 Larry McMurtry, *Lonesome Dove*
1987 Peter Taylor, *A Summons to Memphis*
1988 Toni Morrison, *Beloved*
1989 Anne Tyler, *Breathing Lessons*

General Nonfiction

1962 Theodore White, *The Making of the President 1960*
1963 Barbara W. Tuchman, *The Guns of August*
1964 Richard Hofstadter, *Anti-Intellectualism in American Life*
1965 Howard Mumford Jones, *O Strange New World*
1966 Edwin Way Teale, *Wandering Through Winter*
1967 David Brion Davis, *The Problem of Slavery in Western Culture*
1968 Will and Ariel Durant, *Rousseau and Revolution*
1969 Norman Mailer, *The Armies of the Night*
René Jules Dubois, *So Human an Animal: How We are Shaped by Surroundings and Events*
1970 Eric H. Erikson, *Gandhi's Truth*
1971 John Toland, *The Rising Sun*

1972 Barbara W. Tuchman, *Sitwell and the American Experience in China, 1911–1945*
1973 Frances FitzGerald, *Fire in the Lake*
Robert Coles, *Children in Crisis* (vols. 2 and 3)
1974 Ernest Becker, *The Denial of Death*
1975 Annie Dillard, *Pilgrim at Tinker Creek*
1976 Robert N. Butler, *Why Survive? Being Old in America*
1977 William W. Warner, *Beautiful Swimmers*
1978 Carl Sagan, *The Dragons of Eden*
1979 Edward O. Wilson, *On Human Nature*
1980 Douglas R. Hofstadter, *Gödel, Escher, Bach: An Eternal Golden Braid*
1981 Carl E. Schorske, *Fin-de-Siecle Vienna: Politics and Culture*
1982 Tracy Kidder, *The Soul of a New Machine*
1983 Susan Sheehan, *Is There No Place on Earth for Me?*

1984   Paul Starr, *Social Transformation of American Medicine*
1985   Studs Terkel, *The Good War*
1986   Joseph Lelyveld, *Move Your Shadow*
        J. Anthony Lukas, *Common Ground*

1987   David K. Shipler, *Arab and Jew*
1988   Richard Rhodes, *The Making of the Atomic Bomb*
1989   Neal Sheehan, *A Bright Shining Lie*

Additional Sources of Information

Atkinson, Frank. *Dictionary of Literary Pseudonyms,* 4th ed. American Library Association, 1987.

Bauer, Andrew. *The Hawthorn Dictionary of Pseudonyms.* Hawthorn Books, 1971.

Beckson, Karl, and Ganz, Arthur. *Literary Terms: A Dictionary.* Farrar, Straus & Giroux, 1975.

Bede, Jean-Albert, and Edgerton, William B., eds. *Columbia Dictionary of Modern European Literature.* Columbia University Press, 1980.

Benet's Reader's Encyclopedia, 3rd ed. Harper & Row, 1987.

Drabble, Margaret, ed. *The Oxford Companion to English Literature,* 5th ed. Oxford University Press, 1985.

Frye, Northrop; Baker, Sheridan; and Perkins, George. *The Harper Handbook to Literature.* Harper & Row, 1985.

Hart, James D. *The Concise Oxford Companion to American Literature.* Oxford University Press, 1986.

Holman, Clarence Hugh. *A Handbook to Literature,* 5th ed. Macmillan, 1986.

O'Neal, Robert. *Teachers' Guide to World Literature for the High School.* National Council of Teachers of English, 1966.

Toye, William, ed. *The Oxford Companion to Canadian Literature.* Oxford University Press, 1983.

Vinson, James, and Kirkpatrick, Daniel, eds. *Great Foreign Language Writers.* St. Martin's Press, 1984.

Religions

The World's Major Religions

Religious beliefs of one sort or another are an intrinsic aspect of virtually every society that has ever existed on this planet. Many of these beliefs are organized and codified, often based on the teachings and writings of one or more founders. Other belief systems are less rigid in their external structures and may be transmitted orally from one generation to the next, whether by family members or by religious leaders within the community.

While all religious beliefs are of vital importance to those who hold them, the less formalistic belief systems—variously referred to as animist or tribal religions, and adhered to by peoples all over the world—have proven somewhat enigmatic to Western minds. This section, therefore, deals only with those religions that are recognizable as such to Westerners, ones that employ certain readily identifiable tenets, beliefs, and doctrines.

Bahá'í

Bahá'í, which has 4.5 million followers, was founded by Mirza Husayn 'Ali Nuri, who took the name Baha'Ullah (Glory of God) in 1863 while in exile in Baghdad. Baha'Ullah's coming had been foretold by Mirza Ali Muhammad, known as al-Bab, who founded Babism in 1844, from which the Bahá'í faith grew. The Bahá'í faith emphasizes the unity of all religious teachings that share the same spiritual truths and promotes universal education, equality between the sexes, world peace, and world government.

Buddhism

Buddhism has 307 million followers. It was founded by Siddhartha Gautama, known as the Buddha (Enlightened One), in southern Nepal in the sixth and fifth centuries B.C. The Buddha achieved enlightenment through meditation and gathered a community of monks to carry on his teachings. Buddhism teaches that meditation and the practice of good religious and moral behavior can lead to Nirvana, the state of enlightenment, although before achieving Nirvana one is subject to repeated lifetimes that are good or bad depending on one's actions (*karma*). The doctrines of the Buddha describe temporal life as featuring "four noble truths": existence is a realm of suffering; desire, along with the belief in the importance of one's self, causes suffering; achievement of Nirvana ends suffering; and Nirvana is attained only by meditation and by following the path of righteousness in action, thought, and attitude.

Confucianism

A faith with 5.6 million followers, Confucianism was founded by Confucius, a Chinese philosopher, in the sixth and fifth centuries B.C. Confucius's sayings and dialogues, known collectively as the *Analects*, were written down by his followers. Confucianism, which grew out of a strife-ridden time in Chinese history, stresses the relationship between individuals, their families, and society, based on *li* (proper behavior) and *jen* (sympathetic attitude). Its practical, socially oriented philosophy was challenged by the more mystical precepts of Taoism and Buddhism, which were partially incorporated to create neo-Confucianism during the Sung dynasty (A.D. 960–1279). The overthrow of the Chinese monarchy and the Communist revolution during the twentieth century have severely lessened the influence of Confucianism on modern Chinese culture.

Ethical Culture

Ethical Culture, which has 7,000 followers, was founded as the Society for Ethical Culture in 1876 in New York City by Felix Adler. The International Union of Ethical Societies was formed in 1896. It joined other humanist organizations in 1952 to form the International Humanist and Ethical Union, based in Utrecht, The Netherlands. The Ethical Culture movement stresses the importance of ethics and morality in human interaction, although it offers no system of ethics or other religious beliefs of its own.

Hinduism

A religion with 648 million followers, Hinduism developed from indigenous religions of India in combination with Aryan religions brought to India c. 1500 B.C. and codified in the Veda and the Upanishads, the sacred scriptures of Hinduism. Hinduism is a term used to broadly describe a vast array of sects to which most Indians belong. Hindu beliefs include the acceptance of the caste system, which ranks people from birth based on religious practice, employment, locale, and tribal affiliation, among other categories, and classifies society at large into four groups: the Brahmins or priests, the rulers and warriors, the farmers and merchants, and the peasants and laborers. The goals of Hinduism are release from repeated reincarnation through the practice of yoga, adherence to Vedic scriptures, and devotion to a personal guru. Various deities are worshiped at shrines; the divine trinity, representing the cyclical nature of the universe, are Brahma the creator, Vishnu the preserver, and Shiva the destroyer.

Islam

Islam has 840 million followers. It was founded by the prophet Muhammad, who received the holy scriptures of Islam, the Koran, from Allah (God) c. A.D. 610. Islam (Arabic for "submission to God") maintains that Muhammad is the last in a long line of holy prophets, preceded by Adam, Abraham, Moses, and Jesus. In addition to being devoted to the Koran, followers of Islam (Muslims) are devoted to the worship of Allah through the Five Pillars: the statement "There is no god but God, and Muhammad is his prophet"; prayer, conducted five times a day while facing Mecca; the giving of alms; the keeping of the fast of Ramadan during the ninth month of the Muslim year; and the making of a pilgrimage at least once to Mecca, if possible. Consumption of pork and alcohol, as well as usury, slander, and fraud, are prohibited. The two main divisions of Islam are the Sunni and the Shiite; the Wahabis are the most important Sunni sect, while the Shiite sects include the Assassins, the Druses, and the Fatimids, among countless others.

Judaism

Stemming from the descendants of Judah in Judea, Judaism was founded c. 2000 B.C. by Abraham, Isaac, and Jacob and has 18 million followers. Judaism espouses belief in a monotheistic God, who is creator of the universe and who leads His people, the Jews, by speaking through prophets. His word is revealed in the Hebrew Bible (or Old Testament), especially in that part known as the Torah. Jews believe that the human condition can be improved, that the letter and the spirit of the Torah must be followed, and that a Messiah will eventually bring the world to a state of paradise. Judaism promotes community among all people of Jewish faith, dedication to a synagogue or temple (the basic social unit of a group of Jews, led by a rabbi), and the importance of family life. Religious observance takes place both at home and in temple. Judaism is divided into three main groups who vary in their interpretation of those parts of the Torah that deal with personal, communal, international, and religious activities: The Orthodox community, which views the Torah as derived from God, and therefore absolutely binding; the Reform movement, which follows only its ethical content; and the Conservative Jews, who follow most of the observances set out in the Torah but allow for change in the face of modern life.

Orthodox Eastern Church

With 158 million followers, the Orthodox Eastern Church is the second largest Christian community in the world. It began its split from the Roman Catholic Church in the fifth century; the break was finalized in 1054. The followers of the Orthodox Church are in fact members of many different denominations, including the Church of Greece, the Church of Cyprus, and the Russian Orthodox Church. Orthodox religion holds biblical Scripture and tradition, guided by the Holy Spirit as expressed in the consciousness of the entire Orthodox community, to be the source of Christian truth. It rejects doctrine developed by the Western churches. Doctrine was established by seven ecumenical councils held between 325 and 787 and amended by other councils in the late Byzantine period. Relations between the Orthodox churches and Roman Catholicism have improved since Vatican Council II (1962–65).

Protestantism

Major Protestant Denominations in the United States

Name	Founder	Followers	Tenets
Amish Mennonites	Founded in Switzerland in the 1500s after secession from the Zurich state church; the followers of Jacob Ammann broke from the other Mennonites in Switzerland and Alsace in 1693; most Amish Mennonites emigrated to Pennsylvania in the eighteenth century when others rejoined the main Mennonite group.	40,000 Amish Mennonites; 180,000 Mennonites	The Bible is the sole rule of faith; beliefs are outlined in the *Dordrecht Confession of Faith* (1632); Mennonites shun worldly ways and modern innovation (education and technology); the sacraments are adult baptism and communion.

Name	*Founder*	*Followers*	*Tenets*
Baptists	Founded by John Smyth in England in 1609 and Roger Williams in Rhode Island in 1638.	31 million	No creed; authority stems from the Bible; most Baptists oppose the use of alcohol and tobacco; baptism is by total immersion.
Church of Christ	Organized by Presbyterians in Kentucky in 1804 and in Pennsylvania in 1809.	1.6 million	The New Testament is believed in and what is written in the Bible is followed without elaboration; rites are not ornate; baptism is of adults.
Church of England	King Henry VIII of England broke with the Roman Catholic Church; he issued the Act of Supremacy in 1534, which declared the king of England to be the head of the Church of England.	6,000 in Anglican Orthodox Church in the United States	Supremacy of the Bible is the test of doctrine; emphasis is on the most essential Christian doctrines and creeds; the *Book of Common Prayer* is used; the Church of England is part of the Anglican community, which is represented in the United States mainly by the Episcopal Church.
Episcopal Church	U.S. offshoot of the Church of England; it installed Samuel Seabury as its first bishop in 1784 and held its first General Convention in 1789; the Church of England, headed by King Henry VIII, broke with the Roman Catholic Church in 1534.	2.7 million	Worship is based on the *Book of Common Prayer* and interpretation of the Bible using a modified version of the Thirty-Nine Articles (originally written for the Church of England in 1563); services range from spartan to ornate, from liberal to conservative; baptism is of infants.
Jehovah's Witnesses	Founded by Charles T. Russell in the United States in the late nineteenth century.	700,000	Belief is in the imminent second coming of Christ and the potential salvation of mortal souls during the millennium; all members are ministers who proselytize their faith with door-to-door missionary work; members refuse service in the armed forces, will not salute national flags or participate in government, will not accept blood transfusions, and discourage smoking, drinking, card-playing, and dancing.
Lutheran Church	Based on the writings of Martin Luther, who broke (1517–21) with the Roman Catholic Church and led the Protestant Reformation; the first Lutheran congregation in North America was founded	8 million	Faith is based on the Bible, the principles of Martin Luther, and the Augsburg Confession (written in 1530); salvation comes through faith alone; simple services include the Lord's Supper (communion);

Name	Founder	Followers	Tenets
	in 1638 in Wilmington, Delaware; the first North American regional synod was founded in 1748 by Heinrich Melchior Mühlenberg.		Lutherans are mostly conservative in religious and social ethics; infants are baptized, the church is organized in synods; the three largest synods in the United States are the Lutheran Church in America, the American Lutheran Church, and the Lutheran Church-Missouri Synod.
Mennonites *See* Amish Mennonites.			
Methodist Church	Reverend John Wesley began evangelistic preaching within the Church of England in 1738; a separate Wesleyan Methodist Church was established in 1791; the Methodist Episcopal Church was founded in the United States in 1784.	13.5 million	The name derives from the founders' desire to study religion "by rule and method" and follow the Bible interpreted by tradition and reason; worship varies by denomination within Methodism (the United Methodist Church is the largest congregation); the church is perfectionist in social dealings; communion and the baptism of infants and adults are practiced.
Mormons (Church of Jesus Christ of Latter-Day Saints)	Joseph Smith, in 1827, had visions in which were revealed golden tablets with *The Book of Mormon* inscribed on them; church headquarters were established in Ohio in 1831; after two attempts to establish a permanent home for the church (the second resulting in Smith's death at the hands of a mob), Salt Lake City, Utah, was founded in 1847 under the leadership of Brigham Young.	2.8 million	Faith is based on the Bible, *The Book of Mormon*, other writings by Smith, and sayings collected in *The Pearl of Great Price;* stress is placed on revelation through the connection of spiritual and physical worlds and through proselytizing; members abstain from alcohol and tobacco and believe in community self-reliance; public services are conservative; there is adult baptism, laying on of hands, and communion; a secret temple holds other ceremonies, including baptism for the dead.
Pentecostal churches	The churches grew out of the "holiness movement" that developed among Methodists and other Protestants in the first decade of the twentieth century.	3.5 million	Baptism in the Holy Spirit, speaking in tongues, faith healing, and the second coming of Jesus are believed in; of the various Pentecostal churches, the Assemblies of God is the largest; a perfectionist attitude toward secular affairs is common; services feature enthusiastic sermons and hymns; adult baptism and communion are practiced.

Name	*Founder*	*Followers*	*Tenets*
Presbyterian Church	Grew out of Calvinist churches of Switzerland and France; John Knox founded the first Presbyterian church in Scotland in 1557; the first presbytery in North America was established by Irish missionary Francis Makemie in 1706.	3.2 million	Faith is in the Bible; the sacraments are infant baptism and communion; the church is organized as a system of courts in which clergy and lay members (presbyters) participate at local, regional, and national levels; services are simple, with emphasis on the sermon.
Religious Society of Friends (Quakers)	George Fox in England in the seventeenth century began preaching against organized churches, professing a doctrine of the Inner Light.	113,000	Reliance is on the Inner Light, the voice of God's Holy Spirit experienced within each person; meetings are characterized by quiet meditation without ritual or sermon; Quakers are active in peace, education, and social welfare movements; they refuse to bear arms or take oaths; earlier schisms are still reflected in three main affiliations of Friends.
Unitarian Universalist Association	The denomination resulted from the merger of the Universalist Church of America (organized in 1779) and the American Unitarian Association (founded in 1825).	171,000	Members profess no creed; strong social, ethical, and humanitarian concerns are manifest in the search for religious truth through freedom of belief; theists, humanists, and agnostics are accepted in religious fellowship; efforts are aimed at the creation of a worldwide interfaith religious community; many members come from other denominations and religions.
United Church of Christ	Formed in 1957 by the union of the General Council of Congregational Christian Churches with the Evangelical and Reformed Churches.	1.7 million	Belief in the Bible is guided by the *Statement of Faith* (written in 1959); the church is organized by congregations, which are represented at a general synod that sets policy; services are simple, with emphasis on the sermon; infant baptism and communion are practiced.

Roman Catholicism

The Roman Catholic church, with 900 million followers, is the largest Christian church in the world. It claims direct historical descent from the church founded by the apostle Peter. The Pope in Rome is the spiritual leader of all Roman Catholics. He administers Church affairs through bishops and priests. Members accept the gospel of Jesus Christ and the teachings of the Bible, as well as the Church's interpretations of these. God's grace is conveyed through the sacraments, especially the Eucharist or communion that is celebrated at Mass, the regular service of worship. Redemption through Jesus Christ is professed as the sole method of obtaining salvation, which is necessary to ensure a place in Heaven after life on earth.

Rosicrucianism

Rosicrucianism is a modern movement begun in 1868 by R. W. Little that claims ties to an older Society of the Rose and Cross that was founded in Germany in 1413 by Christian Rosencreuz. The number of its followers is uncertain. The Ancient Mystical Order Rosae Crusis (AMORC) was founded in San Jose, California, in 1915 by H. Spencer Lewis. The Rosicrucian Brotherhood was established in Quakertown, Pennsylvania, by Reuben Swinburne Clymer in 1902. Both sects could be classified as either fraternal or religious organizations, although they claim to empower members with cosmic forces by unveiling secret wisdom regarding the laws of nature.

Shinto

Shinto, with 3.5 million followers, is the ancient native religion of Japan, established long before the introduction of writing to Japan in the fifth century A.D. The origins of its beliefs and rituals are unknown. Shinto stresses belief in a great many spiritual beings and gods, known as *kami,* who are paid tribute at shrines and honored by festivals, and reverence for ancestors. While there is no overall dogma, adherents of Shinto are expected to remember and celebrate the *kami,* support the societies of which the *kami* are patrons, remain pure and sincere, and enjoy life.

Taoism

Both a philosophy and a religion, Taoism was founded in China by Lao-tzu, who is traditionally said to have been born in 604 B.C. Its number of followers is uncertain. It derives primarily from the *Tao-te-ching,* which claims that an ever-changing universe follows the Tao, or path. The Tao can be known only by emulating its quietude and effortless simplicity; Taoism prescribes that people live simply, spontaneously, and in close touch with nature and that they meditate to achieve contact with the Tao. Temples and monasteries, maintained by Taoist priests, are important in some Taoist sects. Since the Communist revolution, Taoism has been actively discouraged in the People's Republic of China, although it continues to flourish in Taiwan.

Significant Dates in the History of Religion

B.C.

c. 2000?	Abraham, founder of Judaism, is alive
c. 13th century	Moses, Hebrew lawgiver, is alive
c. 1200–c. 900	The *Rig-Veda*, sacred texts of the Hindus, are compiled
604	Traditional birth date of Lao-tzu, founder of Taoism
588	Traditional date of Zoroaster's revelation
c. 563–c. 483	Buddha, founder of Buddhism, is alive
551–479	Confucius, founder of Confucianism, is alive
c. 540–c. 468	Mahavira, founder of the Jains, is alive
c. 400	The *Bhagavad Gita*, important Hindu text, is written
6 or 4–c. A.D. 30	Jesus of Nazareth, founder of Christianity, is alive

A.D

33?	The Crucifixion and death of Jesus Christ
64?	Peter, disciple of Jesus and, according to tradition, first bishop of Rome, dies
c. 70–c. 100	First four books of the New Testament—Matthew, Mark, Luke, and John—are written
5th century	Two Buddhist sects—Zen and Pure Land (or Amidism)—are established
c. 570–632	Muhammad the prophet—whose teachings, recorded in the Koran, form the basis of Islam—is alive
622	Muhammad flees persecution in Mecca and settles in Yathrib (later Medina); the first day of the lunar year in which this event, known as the Hegira, takes place marks the start of the Muslim era
936	Traditional date of the arrival from Iran of the first Parsis (followers of Zoroastrianism) in India
1054	Catholic Pope Leo IX condemns the patriarch of Constantinople, finalizing the split between the Eastern Orthodox Church and the Roman Catholic Church
c. 1224–74	Saint Thomas Aquinas, Italian philosopher and Roman Catholic theologian, is alive
1309–77	The Roman Catholic papacy is seated in Avignon, France
1483–1546	Martin Luther, leader of the Protestant Reformation in Germany and author of "95 Theses" (1517), is alive
1491–1556	Ignatius Loyola, founder of the Jesuit Order of Roman Catholic priests, is alive
1509–64	John Calvin, leader of the Protestant Reformation in France, is alive
1549	The first Christian mission in Japan is established
1582	Jesuit Matteo Ricci is the first missionary to be sent to China
1620	Plymouth Colony in North America is founded in December by 102 English Puritan separatists, known as Pilgrims
1624–91	George Fox, English founder of the Protestant Society of Friends (the Quakers), is alive
1703–91	John Wesley, English founder of the Protestant movement that later became the Methodist Church, is alive
1859	Charles Darwin, English naturalist, publishes *Origin of Species*, which elucidates his theory of organic evolution

1869–70	The first Roman Catholic Vatican Council, at which the dogma of papal infallibility is promulgated, is convened by Pope Pius IX
1869–1948	Mohandas K. Gandhi, Indian spiritual and political leader who helped his country achieve independence from Britain and sought rapprochement between Hindus and Muslims, is alive
1933–45	The systematic persecution and attempted extermination of European Jews, known as the Holocaust, by Adolf Hitler's Nazi party takes place
1948	The independent Jewish state of Israel is declared
1962–65	The second Roman Catholic Vatican Council, at which changes were made in the liturgy and greater participation in services by lay church members was encouraged, is convened by Pope John XXIII and concluded by Pope Paul VI

Major Religious Holidays in the United States

January 6	*Feast of the Epiphany* (Christian) marks the arrival of the Three Wise Men who sought the newborn baby Jesus and the Twelfth Night, or end, of the Christmas season
February 2	*Candlemas* (Christian) celebrates the presentation of the Christ child in the temple and the purification of the Blessed Virgin Mary 40 days after she gave birth to Jesus; mostly observed in Roman Catholic, Orthodox Eastern, and Anglican churches
February 14	*St. Valentine's Day* (Roman Catholic) celebrates the feast day of the patron saint of lovers, engaged couples, and anyone wishing to marry; it has, by tradition, become an ecumenical day celebrating love and affection
February or March	*Purim* (Jewish), the Feast of Lots, memorializes Queen Esther's prevention of the annihilation of the Persian Jews with a celebratory festival of food, entertainment, and costumes; held on the 14th day of the lunar year of Adar
	Shrove Tuesday (Christian), or Mardi Gras, is the last day before Lent; it is celebrated by eating rich foods forbidden during Lent and by carnivals in such cities as New Orleans, Rio de Janeiro, and Nice
February, March, or April	*Lent* (Christian) is a 40-day period of fasting and penitence in preparation for Easter that begins on Ash Wednesday in Western churches and on the Monday 42 days before Easter in the Orthodox Eastern Church
March 17	*St. Patrick's Day* (Roman Catholic) celebrates the feast day of the patron saint of Ireland; by tradition, it has become a day to celebrate the Irish and their contributions to U.S. culture
March or April	*Passover* (Jewish), or Pesach, commemorates the time when Moses led the Jews out of Egypt; it is celebrated for seven days by Reform and Israeli Jews and for eight days by Orthodox and Conservative Jews, starting on the fourteenth day of the lunar month Nisan with a meal of remembrance called a seder
	Palm Sunday (Christian) celebrates Jesus's triumphal ride into Jerusalem and the start of Holy Week; it is observed the Sunday before Easter
	Maundy Thursday (Christian), the Thursday before Easter, marks the Last Supper, the Agony in the Garden, and the arrest of Jesus
	Good Friday (Christian), the Friday before Easter, commemorates Jesus's Crucifixion

	Holy Saturday (Christian), the Saturday before Easter, is observed primarily in Roman Catholic, Orthodox Eastern, and Anglican churches
	Easter Sunday (Christian) celebrates the day Jesus Christ rose from the dead
May or June	*Ascension Day* (Christian) celebrates Christ's ascent to Heaven; it is held 40 days after Easter
	Shavuot (Jewish) celebrates the harvest of grain while also observing the receipt of the Ten Commandments by Israel; it is held for one day by Reform and Israeli Jews or for two days by Orthodox and Conservative Jews, starting the sixth day of the lunar month of Sivan
	Pentecost (Christian), or Whitsunday, marks the descent of the Holy Spirit on the Apostles; it is held 50 days after Easter
August 15	*The Assumption of the Blessed Virgin Mary* (Roman Catholic and Orthodox Eastern) is the principal feast day in honor of Mary, celebrating her assumption, body and soul, into Heaven after her death
September or October	*Rosh Hashanah* (Jewish) marks the start of the new year with solemn prayer and the blowing of the shofar, a ram's horn; it is observed for one day by Reform and Israeli Jews or for two days by Orthodox and Conservative Jews, starting the first day of the lunar month of Tishri
	Yom Kippur (Jewish), the Day of Atonement, is a day of fasting and repentance for the previous year's sins; it follows the 10 days of penitence that began on Rosh Hashanah; it is observed on the tenth day of the lunar month of Tishri
	Sukkoth (Jewish), the Feast of the Tabernacles, is an autumn harvest festival that recalls the wandering of the Jews in the wilderness; it is celebrated for eight days (seven in Israel) starting on the fifteenth day of the lunar month of Tishri
Sunday nearest October 31	*Reformation Sunday* (Protestant) celebrates the day Martin Luther nailed his "95 Theses" to a church door, heralding the start of the Protestant Reformation
November 1	*All Saints' Day* (Christian) is the feast day honoring all martyrs and the Virgin Mary; it is celebrated by Roman Catholic, Orthodox Eastern, and Anglican churches; it is also known as All Hallows' Day and is preceded by Halloween on October 31
Sunday nearest November 30 through Christmas Eve	*Advent* (Christian) is the period of repentance in preparation for the anniversary of the birth of Christ
December	*Hanukkah* (Jewish), the Festival of Lights, is marked by the lighting of eight candles in a menorah; it commemorates the restoration of traditional worship and the rededication of the temple in Jerusalem as well as the rededication of the Jews to their religious ancestry; it is held for eight days beginning on the twenty-fifth day of the lunar month of Kislev
December 8	*Feast of the Immaculate Conception* (Roman Catholic) honors the Virgin Mary's state of freedom from original sin from the time of her conception
December 9	*Feast of the Conception of St. Anne* (Orthodox Eastern) celebrates the conception of the Virgin Mary
December 25	*Christmas Day* (Christian) celebrates the birth of Jesus Christ; in many Western countries it has become a nonsectarian winter holiday

Roman Catholic Patron Saints

Protector of	*Saint*
Accountants	Matthew
Actors	Genesius
Air travelers	Joseph of Cupertino

Protector of	*Saint*
Altar boys	John Berchmans
Architects	Barbara
Art	Catherine of Bologna
Artists	Luke
Astronomers	Dominic
Athletes	Sebastian
Authors	Francis de Sales
Bakers	Elizabeth of Hungary
Bankers	Matthew
Barren women	Antony of Padua
Beggars	Alexius, Giles
Blind	Raphael
Bookbinders	Peter Celestine
Bookkeepers	Matthew
Booksellers	John of God
Boy Scouts	George
Bricklayers	Stephen
Brides	Nicholas of Myra
Broadcasters	Archangel Gabriel
Builders	Vincent Ferrer
Cab drivers	Fiacre
Cancer victims	Peregrine Laziosi
Carpenters	Joseph
Charitable societies	Vincent de Paul
Childbirth	Gerard Majella
Children	Nicholas of Myra
Church	Joseph
Comedians	Vitus
Cooks	Martha
Cripples	Giles
Dancers	Vitus
Deaf	Francis de Sales
Dentists	Apollonia
Desperate situations	Jude
Domestic animals	Antony
Dying	Joseph
Ecologists	Francis of Assisi
Editors	John Bosco
Emigrants	Frances Xavier Cabrini
Falsely accused	Raymund Nonnatus
Farmers	Isidore the Farmer
Fathers	Joseph
Fire fighters	Florian
Fire prevention	Catherine of Siena
Fishermen	Andrew, Peter
Foundlings	Holy Innocents
Funeral directors	Joseph of Arimathea
Gardeners	Adelard
Girls	Agnes
Glassworkers	Luke
Gravediggers	Antony the Abbot
Grocers	Michael
Hairdressers	Martin de Porres

Protector of	Saint
Heart patients	John of God
Hospitals	Camillus de Lellis, John of God
Hotelkeepers	Amand
Invalids	Roch
Jewelers	Eligius
Journalists	Francis de Sales
Laborers	Isidore
Lawyers	Thomas More, Yves
Learning	Ambrose
Librarians	Jerome
Lost articles	Antony of Padua
Lovers	Valentine
Mariners	Nicholas of Tolentine
Married women	Monica
Mentally ill	Dympna
Messengers	Gabriel
Midwives	Raymund Nonnatus
Missions	Francis Xavier, Thérèse of Lisieux, Leonard of Port Maurice
Mothers	Monica
Musicians	Cecelia, Gregory
Nurses	Agatha, Camillus de Lellis, John of God
Orators	John Chrysostom
Orphans	Jerome Emiliani
Painters	Luke
Pawnbrokers	Nicholas of Myra
Philosophers	Catherine of Alexandria, Justin
Physicians	Cosmas and Damian, Luke
Plasterers	Bartholomew
Poets	David
Police officers	Michael
Poor	Antony of Padua
Postal workers	Gabriel
Preachers	Catherine of Alexandria, John Chrysostom
Pregnant women	Gerard Majella
Priests	John Vianney
Printers	Augustine, Genesius, John of God
Prisoners	Dismas
Radio workers	Gabriel
Rheumatism	James the Greater
Sailors	Brendan, Erasmus
Scholars	Brigid
Scientists	Albert the Great
Sculptors	Claude
Secretaries	Genesius
Servants	Martha
Sick	John of God, Camillus de Lellis
Skaters	Lidwina
Skiers	Bernard
Social justice	Joseph
Social workers	Louise de Marillac
Soldiers	George, Martin of Tours
Students	Catherine of Alexandria, Thomas Aquinas
Surgeons	Cosmas and Damian, Luke
Tax collectors	Matthew

Protector of	Saint
Teachers	Gregory, John Baptist de la Salle
Television	Clare of Assisi
Theologians	Alphonsus Liguori, Augustine
Throat ailments	Blaise
Travelers	Christopher
Vintners	Amand, Morand, Vincent
Vocations	Alphonsus
Widows	Paula
Women in labor	Anne
Writers	Francis de Sales
Youth	Aloysius Gonzaga

Holy Books of the World

Bhagavad-Gita A Sanskrit poem that is part of the Indian epic known as the *Mahabharata*. It describes, in a dialogue between Lord Krishna and Prince Arjuna, the Hindu path to spiritual wisdom and the unity with God that can be achieved through *karma* (action), *bhakti* (devotion), and *jnana* (knowledge). The *Bhagavad-Gita* was probably written sometime between 200 B.C. and A.D. 200.

Five Classics Five works traditionally attributed to Confucius that form the basic texts of Confucianism. They are the *Spring and Autumn Annals,* a history of Confucius's native district; the *I Ching* (or *Book of Changes*), a system of divining the future; the *Book of Rites,* which outlines ceremonies and describes the ideal government; the *Book of History;* and the *Book of Songs,* a collection of poetry. Together they promulgate a system of ethics for managing society based on sympathy for others, etiquette, and ritual. Although the dates of these books are uncertain, they were probably written before the third century B.C.

Koran (Arabic, **al-Qur'ân**) The primary holy book of Islam. It is made up of 114 *suras,* or chapters, which contain impassioned appeals for belief in God, encouragement to lead a moral life, portrayals of damnation and beatitude, stories of Islamic prophets, and rules governing the social and religious life of Muslims. Believers maintain that the Koran contains the verbatim word of God, revealed to the prophet Muhammad through the Angel Gabriel. Some of the *suras* were written during Muhammad's lifetime, but an authoritative text was not produced until c. A.D. 650.

New Testament The second portion of the Christian Bible, which contains 27 books that form the basis of Christian belief. These books include the sayings of Jesus, the story of his life and work, the death and resurrection of Jesus now celebrated as Easter, the teachings and writings of the apostles, and instruction for converting nonbelievers and for performing baptisms, blessings, and other rituals. The New Testament is believed to have been written c. A.D. 100, some 70 to 90 years after the death of Jesus.

Old Testament The Christian name for the Hebrew Bible. It is the sacred scripture of Judaism and the first portion of the Christian Bible. According to Jewish teachings, it is made up of three parts: *the Law* (also known as the Torah or Pentateuch), comprising the first five books (Genesis, Exodus, Leviticus, Numbers, and Deuteronomy), which describes the origins of the world, the covenant between the Lord and Israel, the exodus and entry into the promised land, and the various rules governing social and religious behavior; *the Prophets,* including the former prophets (Joshua, Judges, Samuel 1-2, Kings 1-2) and the latter prophets (Isaiah, Jeremiah, Ezekiel, and the 12 minor prophets), which describes the history of the Israelites, the stories of heroes, kings, judges, and wars, and the choosing of David as leader of the Israelites; and *the Writings* (including Psalms, Job, Song of Solomon, and Ruth, among others), which describes the reactions of the people to the laws and covenants, as well as prayers and praises of the covenant. Some books of the Old Testament regarded as sacred by the Jews are not accepted as such by Christians; among Christians there are differences between Roman Catholics and

Protestants about the inclusion of some books, the order of the books, and the original sources used in translating them. Scholars generally agree that the Old Testament was compiled from c. 1000 B.C. to c. 100 B.C.

Talmud A compilation of Jewish oral law and rabbinical teachings that is separate from the scriptures of the Hebrew Bible, or Old Testament. It is made up of two parts: the *Mishna,* which is the oral law itself, and the *Gemara,* a commentary on the *Mishna.* The Talmud contains both a legal section (the *Halakah*) and a portion devoted to legends and stories (the *Aggada*). The authoritative Babylonian Talmud was compiled in the sixth century.

Tao-te-ching (The Way and Its Power) The basic text of the Chinese philosophy and religion known as Taoism. It is made up of 81 short chapters or poems that describe a way of life marked by quiet effortlessness and freedom from desire. This is thought to be achieved by following the creative, spontaneous life force of the universe, called the Tao. The book is attributed to Lao-tzu, but it was probably written in the third century B.C.

Upanishads The basis of Hindu religion and philosophy that form the final portion of the *Veda.* The 112 Upanishads describe the relationship of the *Brahman,* or universal soul, to the *atman,* or individual soul; they also provide information about Vedic sacrifice and yoga. The original texts of the Upanishads come from various sources and were written beginning c. 900 B.C.

Veda The sacred scripture of Hinduism. Four Vedas make up the *Samhita,* a collection of prayers and hymns that are considered to be revelations of eternal truth written by seer-poets inspired by the gods. The *Rig-Veda,* the *Sama-Veda,* and the *Yajur-Veda* are books of hymns; the *Atharva-Veda* compiles magic spells. These writings maintain that the Brahman, or Absolute Self, underlies all reality and can be known by invoking gods through the use of hymns or mantras. The Vedic texts were compiled between c. 1000 B.C. and c. 500 B.C., making them the oldest known group of religious writings.

The Greek and Roman Deities

The gods and goddesses of ancient Greece and Rome have had a lasting impact on Western religious thought. They have also played an important part in the development of the arts, philosophy, and psychology. The following lists give the names of these ancient deities as well as the spheres of influence ascribed to them.

Greek Deities

Adonis	Symbolizes the death of nature each autumn and its rebirth in the spring
Aeolus	God of the winds
Aesculapius	God of medicine
Aphrodite	Goddess of love and beauty
Apollo	God of beauty, youth, poetry, music, prophecy, and archery
Ares	God of war
Artemis	Goddess of the hunt, the moon, and nature
Athena	Goddess of wisdom
Chaos	God of the shapeless void that preceded creation of the Earth
Chloris	Goddess of flowers
Cronus	Leader of the Titans who ruled the heavens after overthrowing his father, Uranus
Demeter	Goddess of the earth, grain, and harvests
Dionysus	God of wine
Eos	Goddess of dawn
Eris	Goddess of strife and discord
Eros	God of love

Gorgones	Three winged sisters—Euryale, Medusa, and Stheno—the sight of whom turned mortals to stone
Hades	God of the underworld
Hephaestus	God of fire
Hera	Sister and wife of Zeus; queen of the goddesses
Herakles	Son of Zeus; greatest of Greek heroes, who performed 12 labors and was eventually granted immortality
Hermaphroditus	Son of Hermes and Aphrodite who was joined forever to the nymph of the fountain of Salmacis, creating one body with the sexual characteristics of both males and females
Hermes	Messenger of the gods; patron of thieves
Hestia	Goddess of the hearth
Hygeia	Goddess of health
Hymen	God of marriage
Hypnus	God of sleep
Metis	First wife of Zeus, who helped him become king of gods; personification of prudence
Morpheus	God of dreams
Muses	Nine sisters, daughters of Zeus, who are goddesses of the arts and sciences: Clio (history), Euterpe (lyric poetry), Thalia (comedy), Melpomene (tragedy), Terpsichore (dance), Erato (erotic poetry), Polyhymnia (sacred poetry), Urania (astronomy), and Calliope (chief of the Muses)
Nemesis	Goddess of vengeance
Nike	Goddess of victory
Nymphs	Nature spirits who oversee water, trees, mountains, valleys, and particular locations
Nyx	Goddess of night
Pan	God of flocks and shepherds
Persephone	Goddess of the underworld; symbol of the death of nature each autumn and its rebirth each spring
Plutus	God of wealth
Poseidon	God of the oceans
Priapus	God of fertility
Rhea	Wife of Cronus; mother of the Olympian gods and goddesses Demeter, Hades, Hera, Hestia, Poseidon, and Zeus
Satyrs	Field and forest gods who represent nature's bounty
Selene	Goddess of the moon
Sirens	Sea nymphs whose singing enchanted those who heard it
Thanatos	God of death
Titans	Sons and daughters of Uranus, who took power when Cronus overthrew their father: Atlas, Coeus, Crius, Dione, Epimetheus, Eurynome, Hyperion, Iapetus, Leto, Maia, Mnemosyne, Oceanus, Ophion, Pallas, Phoebe, Prometheus, Rhea, Tethys, Themis, and Thia
Tyche	Goddess of fortune or fate
Uranus	God of heaven; father of the Titans
Zeus	Chief god of Olympus; ruler of heaven, who wielded thunder and lightning

Roman Deities

Aurora	Goddess of the dawn
Bacchus	God of wine
Cerberus	Guardian of the gates of hell
Ceres	Goddess of the earth, grain, and harvests

Coelus	God of heaven
Cupid	God of love
Diana	Goddess of the hunt, the moon, and nature
Dis	God of the underworld
Faunus	God of fields and shepherds
Flora	Goddess of flowers
Graces	Three sisters—Aglaia, Euphrosyne, and Thalia—who were goddesses of banquets, dances, social enjoyments, and the arts
Hercules	Roman name for Herakles
Janus	God of beginnings, responsible for the new year and the seasons
Juno	Queen of the gods; wife of Jupiter
Jupiter (Jove)	The supreme god; ruler of heaven
Juventas	Goddess of youth
Lares	Spirits of ancestors who watch over homes and cities
Lemures	Spirits of the dead, both good and bad
Liber	Another name for Bacchus
Luna	Goddess of the moon
Mars	God of war
Mercury	Messenger of the gods
Minerva	Goddess of wisdom
Mors	God of death
Neptune	God of the oceans
Nox	Goddess of night
Orcus	God of the underworld
Picus	God who could foresee the future
Pomona	Goddess of fruit trees and gardens
Proserpina	Goddess of the underworld
Psyche	Goddess of the soul, who was united with Cupid
Romulus	Founder of the city of Rome; raised by a wolf with his twin brother, Remus
Salacia	Goddess of the oceans
Saturn	Roman name for the Greek god Cronus
Somnus	God of sleep
Tartarus	God of the underworld
Venus	Goddess of love and beauty
Vesta	Goddess of the hearth
Victoria	Goddess of victory

The Roman Catholic Popes

The religious head of the Roman Catholic Church is known as the Pope or the bishop of Rome. He is elected by the College of Cardinals, who as a group rank next to the Pope in ecclesiastical authority. New Popes are elected on the death or retirement of a current Pope. To be elected, a new Pope must be named on two-thirds of the ballots cast, and each member of the College of Cardinals must vote. Once elected, a Pope must be asked by the dean of cardinals if he accepts the post. If he does, he is then asked to choose a name. The custom of a Pope changing his name upon election originated shortly before the year 1000.

    The following list includes all the Popes of the Roman Catholic Church, beginning with St. Peter the Apostle, who is traditionally considered to be the first Pope because of his appointment by Jesus and his role in organizing the Church. Also included in this list are the so-called antipopes, those who were elected or claimed to be pope at various times during Church history but whose positions were later invalidated; their names appear in brackets. The list gives the names of the Popes, the years of their papacies, and the original names of those who changed their names upon election. Alternate spellings of names are given in parentheses.

Pope	*Reign*	*Original Name*
St. Peter the Apostle	died c. 64	Symeon (Simon)
St. Linus	c. 66–c. 78	
St. Anacletus (Cletus)	c. 79–c. 91	
St. Clement I	c. 91–c. 100	
St. Evaristus	c. 100–c. 109	
St. Alexander I	c. 109–c. 116	
St. Sixtus I	c. 116–c. 125	
St. Telesphorus	c. 125–c. 136	
St. Hyginus	c. 136–c. 142	
St. Pius I	c. 142–c. 155	
St. Anicetus	c. 155–c. 166	
St. Soter	c. 166–c. 174	
St. Eleutherius (Eleutherus)	c. 174–189	
St. Victor I	189–98	
St. Zephyrinus	198–217	
St. Callistus (Calixtus) I	217–222	
[St. Hippolytus]	217–235	
St. Urban I	222–30	
St. Pontianus (Pontian)	July 21, 230–September 29, 235	
St. Anterus	November 21, 235–January 3, 236	
St. Fabian	January 10, 236–January 20, 250	
St. Cornelius	March 251–June 253	
[Novatian]	March 251–c. 258	
St. Lucius I	June 25, 253–March 5, 254	
St. Stephen I	May 12, 254–August 2, 257	
St. Sixtus II	August 30, 257–August 6, 258	
St. Dionysius	July 22, 260–December 26, 268	
St. Felix I	January 3, 269–December 30, 274	
St. Eutychian	January 4, 275–December 7, 283	
St. Gaius (Caius)	December 17, 283–April 22, 296	
St. Marcellinus	June 30, 296–c. 304	
St. Marcellus I	November/December, 306–January 16, 308	
St. Eusebius	April 18, 310–October 21, 310	
St. Miltiades (Melchiades)	July 2, 311–January 11, 314	
St. Silvester I	January 31, 314–December 31, 335	
St. Mark	January 18, 336–October 7, 336	
St. Julius I	February 6, 337–April 12, 352	
Liberius	May 17, 352–September 24, 366	
[Felix II]	c. 355–November 22, 365	
St. Damasus I	October 1, 366–December 11, 384	
[Ursinus]	September 366–November 367	
St. Siricius	December 384–November 26, 399	
St. Anastasius I	November 27, 399–December 19, 401	

Pope	*Reign*	*Original Name*
St. Innocent I	December 22, 401–March 12, 417	
St. Zosimus	March 18, 417–December 26, 418	
St. Boniface I	December 28, 418–September 4, 422	
[Eulalius]	December 27, 418–April 3, 419	
St. Celestine I	September 10, 422–July 27, 432	
St. Sixtus III	July 31, 432–August 19, 440	
St. Leo I	August/September, 440–November 10, 461	
St. Hilary (Hilarus)	November 19, 461–February 29, 468	
St. Simplicius	March 3, 468–March 10, 483	
St. Felix III (II)	March 13, 483–March 1, 492	
St. Gelasius I	March 1, 492–November 21, 496	
Anastasius II	November 24, 496–November 19, 498	
St. Symmachus	November 22, 498–July 19, 514	
[Lawrence]	November 22, 498–February 499; 501–506	
St. Hormisdas	July 20, 514–August 6, 523	
St. John I	August 13, 523–May 18, 526	
St. Felix IV (III)	July 12, 526–September 22, 530	
Boniface II	September 22, 530–October 17, 532	
[Dioscorus]	September 22, 530–October 14, 530	
John II	January 2, 533–May 8, 535	Mercury
St. Agapitus I	May 13, 535–April 22, 536	
St. Silverius	June 8, 536–November 11, 537	
Vigilius	c. 538–June 7, 555	
Pelagius I	April 16, 556–March 3, 561	
John III	July 17, 561–July 13, 574	Catelinus
Benedict I	June 2, 575–July 30, 579	
Pelagius II	November 26, 579–February 7, 590	
St. Gregory I	September 3, 590–March 12, 604	
Sabinian	September 13, 604–February 22, 606	
Boniface III	February 19, 607–November 12, 607	
St. Boniface IV	September 15, 608–May 8, 615	
St. Deusdedit I	October 19, 615–November 8, 618	
Boniface V	December 23, 619–October 25, 625	
Honorius I	October 27, 625–October 12, 638	
Severinus	May 28, 640–August 2, 640	
John IV	December 24, 640–October 12, 642	
Theodore I	November 24, 642–May 14, 649	
St. Martin I	July 5, 649–June 17, 653	
St. Eugene I	August 10, 654–June 2, 657	
St. Vitalian	July 30, 657–January 27, 672	
Deusdedit III (Adeodatus II)	April 11, 672–June 17, 676	
Donus	November 2, 676–April 11, 678	
St. Agatho	June 27, 678–January 10, 681	
St. Leo II	August 17, 682–July 3, 683	
St. Benedict II	June 26, 684–May 8, 685	
John V	July 23, 685–August 2, 686	
Conon	October 21, 686–September 21, 687	
[Theodore]	687	
[Paschal]	687	
St. Sergius I	December 15, 687–September 9, 701	
John VI	October 30, 701–January 11, 705	
John VII	March 1, 705–October 18, 707	

Pope	*Reign*	*Original Name*
Sisinnius	January 15, 708–February 4, 708	
Constantine	March 25, 708–April 9, 715	
St. Gregory II	May 19, 715–February 11, 731	
St. Gregory III	March 18, 731–November 28, 741	
St. Zachary (St. Zacharius)	December 3, 741–March 15, 752	
Stephen	March 22 or 23, 752–March 25 or 26, 752	
Stephen II (III)	March 26, 752–April 26, 757	
St. Paul I	May 29, 757–June 28, 767	
[Constantine]	July 5, 767–August 6, 768	
[Philip]	July 31, 768	
Stephen III (IV)	August 7, 768–January 24, 772	
Adrian I (Hadrian I)	February 1, 772–December 25, 795	
St. Leo III	December 26, 795–June 12, 816	
Stephen IV (V)	June 22, 816–January 24, 817	
St. Paschal I	January 24, 817–February 11, 824	
Eugene II	February 824–August 827	
Valentine	August 827–September 827	
Gregory IV	827–January 25, 844	
[John]	January 844	
Sergius II	January 844–January 27, 847	
St. Leo IV	April 10, 847–July 17, 855	
Benedict III	September 29, 855–April 17, 858	
[Anastasius (Bibliothecarius)]	August 855–September 855	
St. Nicholas I	April 24, 858–November 13, 867	
Adrian II (Hadrian II)	December 14, 867–November or December 872	
John VIII	December 14, 872–December 16, 882	
Marinus I	December 16, 882–May 15, 884	
St. Adrian III (St. Hadrian III)	May 17, 884–September 885	
Stephen V (VI)	September 885–September 14, 891	
Formosus	October 6, 891–April 4, 896	
Boniface VI	April 896	
Stephen VI (VII)	May 896–August 897	
Romanus	August 897–November 897	
Theodore II	November 897	
John IX	January 898–January 900	
Benedict IV	May/June 900–August 903	
Leo V	August 903–September 903	
[Christopher]	September 903–January 904	
Sergius III	January 29, 904–April 14, 911	
Anastasius III	c. June 911–c. August 913	
Lando	c. August 913–c. March 914	
John X	March 914–May 928	
Leo VI	May 928–December 928	
Stephen VII (VIII)	December 928–February 931	
John XI	February or March 931–December 935 or January 936	
Leo VII	January 3, 936–July 13, 939	
Stephen VIII (IX)	July 14, 939–October 942	
Marinus II	October 30, 942–May 946	
Agapetus (Agapitus) II	May 10, 946–December 955	

Pope	Reign	Original Name
John XII	December 16, 955–May 14, 964	Octavian
Leo VIII	December 4, 963–March 1, 965	
Benedict V	May 22, 964–June 23, 964	
John XIII	October 1, 965–September 6, 972	
Benedict VI	January 19, 973–July 974	
[Boniface VII]	June 974–July 974; August 984–July 20, 985	Franco
Benedict VII	October 974–July 10, 983	
John XIV	December 983–August 20, 984	Peter Canepanova
John XV	August 985–March 996	
Gregory V	May 3, 996–February 18, 999	Bruno
[John XVI]	February 997–May 998	John Philagathos
Silvester II	April 2, 999–May 12, 1003	Gerbert
John XVII	May 16, 1003–November 6, 1003	John Sicco
John XVIII	December 25, 1003–July 1009	John Fasanus
Sergius IV	July 31, 1009–May 12, 1012	Peter
Benedict VIII	May 17, 1012–April 9, 1024	Theophylact
[Gregory]	1012	
John XIX	April 19, 1024–October 20, 1032	Romanus
Benedict IX	October 21, 1032–September 1044;	Theophylact
	March 10, 1045–May 1, 1045;	
	November 8, 1047–July 16, 1048	
Silvester III	January 20, 1045–May 10, 1045	John of Sabina
Gregory VI	May 1, 1045–December 20, 1046	John Gratian
Clement II	December 24, 1046–October 9, 1047	Suidger
Damasus II	July 17, 1048–August 9, 1048	Poppo
St. Leo IX	February 12, 1049–April 19, 1054	Bruno
Victor II	April 13, 1055–July 28, 1057	Gebhard
Stephen IX (X)	August 2, 1057–March 29, 1058	Frederick of Lorraine
[Benedict X]	April 5, 1058–January 24, 1059	John Mincius
Nicholas II	December 6, 1058–July 19 or 26, 1061	Gerard
Alexander II	September 30, 1061–April 21, 1073	Anselm
[Honorius II]	October 28, 1061–May 31, 1064	Peter Cadalus
St. Gregory VII	April 22, 1073–May 25, 1085	Hildebrand
[Clement III]	June 25, 1080; March 24, 1084–September 8, 1100	Guibert
Victor III	May 24, 1086; May 9, 1087–September 16, 1087	Daufer (Daufari)
Urban II	March 12, 1088–July 29, 1099	Odo (Eudes)
Paschal II	August 13, 1099–January 21, 1118	Rainerius
[Theodoric]	September 1100–January 1101	
[Albert (Adalbert)]	1101	
[Silvester IV]	November 18, 1105–April 12, 1111	Maginulf
Gelasius II	January 24, 1118–January 29, 1119	John of Gaeta
[Gregory VIII]	March 8, 1118–April 1121	Maurice Burdinus
Calistus II	February 2, 1119–December 14, 1124	Guido
Honorius II	December 21, 1124–February 13, 1130	Lamberto of Ostia
[Celestine II]	December 15–16, 1124	Teobaldo Boccapecci
Innocent II	February 14, 1130–September 24, 1143	Gregorio Papareschi
[Anacletus II]	February 14, 1130–January 25, 1138	Pietro Pierleoni
[Victor IV]	March 1138–May 29, 1138	Gregorio Conti
Celestine II	September 26, 1143–May 8, 1144	Guido of Citta di Castello
Lucius II	March 12, 1144–February 15, 1145	Gherardo Caccianemici
Eugene III	February 15, 1145–July 8, 1153	Bernardo Pignatelli
Anastasius IV	July 8, 1153–December 3, 1154	Corrado

Pope	*Reign*	*Original Name*
Adrian IV (Hadrian IV)	December 4, 1154–September 1, 1159	Nicholas Breakspear
Alexander III	September 7, 1159–August 30, 1181	Orlando (Roland) Bandinelli
[Victor IV]	September 7, 1159–April 20, 1164	Ottaviano
[Paschal III]	April 22, 1164–September 20, 1168	Guido of Crema
[Calistus III]	September 1168–August 29, 1178	Giovanni
[Innocent III]	September 29, 1179–January 1180	Lando
Luicius III	September 1, 1181–November 25, 1185	Ubaldo Allucingoli
Urban III	November 25, 1185–October 20, 1187	Umberto Crivelli
Gregory VIII	October 21, 1187–December 17, 1187	Alberto de Morra
Clement III	December 19, 1187–March 1191	Paolo Scolari
Celestine III	March/April 1191–January 8, 1198	Giacinto Bobo
Innocent III	January 8, 1198–July 16, 1216	Lotario
Honorius III	July 18, 1216–March 18, 1227	Cencio Savelli
Gregory IX	March 19, 1227–August 22, 1241	Ugo (Ugolino)
Celestine IV	October 25, 1241–November 10, 1241	Goffredo da Castiglione
Innocent IV	June 25, 1243–December 7, 1254	Sinibaldo Fieschi
Alexander IV	December 12, 1254–May 25, 1261	Rinaldo, Count of Segni
Urban IV	August 29, 1261–October 2, 1264	Jacques Pantaléon
Clement IV	February 5, 1265–November 29, 1268	Guy Foulques
Gregory X	September 1, 1271–January 10, 1276	Tedaldo Visconti
Innocent V	January 21, 1276–June 22, 1276	Pierre of Tarentaise
Adrian V (Hadrian V)	July 11, 1276–August 18, 1276	Ottobono Fieschi
John XXI	September 8, 1276–May 20, 1277	Pedro Julião (Peter of Spain)
Nicholas III	November 25, 1277–August 22, 1280	Giovanni Gaetano
Martin IV	February 22, 1281–March 28, 1285	Simon de Brie (Brion)
Honorius IV	April 2, 1285–April 3, 1287	Giacomo Savelli
Nicholas IV	February 22, 1288–April 4, 1292	Girolamo Masci
St. Celestine V	July 5, 1294–December 13, 1294	Pietro del Morrone
Boniface VIII	December 24, 1294–October 11, 1303	Benedetto Caetani
Benedict XI	October 22, 1303–July 7, 1304	Niccolò Boccasino
Clement V	June 5, 1305–April 20, 1314	Bertrand de Got
John XXII	August 7, 1316–December 4, 1334	Jacques Duèse
[Nicholas V]	May 12, 1328–July 25, 1330	Pietro Rainalducci
Benedict XII	December 20, 1334–April 25, 1342	Jacques Fournier
Clement VI	May 7, 1342–December 6, 1352	Pierre of Rosier d'Egleton
Innocent VI	December 18, 1352–September 12, 1362	Étienne Aubert
Urban V	September 28, 1362–December 19, 1370	Guillaume de Grimoard
Gregory XI	December 30, 1370–March 27, 1378	Pierre Roger de Beaufort
Urban VI	April 8, 1378–October 15, 1389	Bartolomeo Prignano
[Clement VII]	September 20, 1378–September 16, 1394	Robert of Cambrai
Boniface IX	November 2, 1389–October 1, 1404	Pietro Tomacelli
[Benedict XIII]	September 28, 1394–July 26, 1417	Pedro de Luna
Innocent VII	October 17, 1404–November 6, 1406	Cosimo Gentile de'Migliorati
Gregory XII	November 30, 1406–July 4, 1415	Angelo Correr
[Alexander V]	June 26, 1409–May 3, 1410	Pietro Philarghi (Peter of Candia)
[John XXIII]	May 17, 1410–May 29, 1415	Baldassare Cossa
Martin V	November 11, 1417–February 20, 1431	Oddo Colonna
[Clement VIII]	June 10, 1423–July 26, 1429	Gil Sanchez Muñoz
[Benedict XIV]	November 12, 1425–?	Bernard Garnier

Pope	Reign	Original Name
Eugene IV	March 3, 1431–February 23, 1447	Gabriele Condulmaro
[Felix V]	November 5, 1439–April 7, 1449	Amadeus VIII, Duke of Savoy
Nicholas V	March 6, 1447–March 24, 1455	Tommaso Parentucelli
Callistus III	April 8, 1455–August 6, 1458	Alfonso de Borja (Borgia)
Pius II	August 19, 1458–August 15, 1464	Enea Silvo
Piccolomini (Paul II)	August 30, 1464–July 26, 1471	Pietro Barbo
Sixtus IV	August 9, 1471–August 12, 1484	Franceso della Rovere
Innocent VIII	August 29, 1484–July 25, 1492	Giovanni Battista Cibò
Alexander VI	August 11, 1492–August 18, 1503	Rodrigo de Borja y Borja (Borgia)
Pius III	September 22, 1503–October 18, 1503	Francesco Todeschini
Julius II	November 1, 1503–February 21, 1513	Giuliano dell Rovere
Leo X	March 11, 1513–December 1, 1521	Giovanni de' Medici
Adrian VI (Hadrian VI)	January 9, 1522–September 14, 1523	Adrian Florensz Dedal
Clement VII	November 19, 1523–September 25, 1534	Giulio de' Medici
Paul III	October 13, 1534–November 10, 1549	Alessandro Farnese
Julius III	February 8, 1550–March 23, 1555	Giovanni Maria Ciocchi del Monte
Marcellus II	April 9, 1555–May 1, 1555	Marcello Cervini
Paul IV	May 23, 1555–August 18, 1559	Giampietro Carafa
Pius IV	December 25, 1559–December 9, 1565	Giovanni Angelo Medici
St. Pius V	January 7, 1566–May 1, 1572	Michele Ghislieri
Gregory XIII	May 14, 1572–April 10, 1585	Ugo Boncompagni
Sixtus V	April 24, 1585–August 27, 1590	Felice Peretti
Urban VII	September 15, 1590–September 27, 1590	Giambattista Castagna
Gregory XIV	December 5, 1590–October 16, 1591	Niccolò Sfondrati
Innocent IX	October 29, 1591–December 30, 1591	Giovanni Antonio Fachinetti
Clement VIII	January 30, 1592–March 5, 1605	Ippolito Aldobrandini
Leo XI	April 1, 1605–April 27, 1605	Alessandro Ottaviano de' Medici
Paul V	May 16, 1605–January 28, 1621	Camillo Borghese
Gregory XV	February 9, 1621–July 8, 1623	Alessandro Ludovisi
Urban VIII	August 6, 1623–July 29, 1644	Mafeo Barberini
Innocent X	September 15, 1644–January 1, 1655	Giambattista Pamfili
Alexander VII	April 7, 1655–May 22, 1667	Fabio Chigi
Clement IX	June 20, 1667–December 9, 1669	Giulio Rospigliosi
Clement X	April 29, 1670–July 22, 1676	Emilio Altieri
Innocent XI	September 21, 1676–August 12, 1689	Benedetto Odescalchi
Alexander VIII	October 6, 1689–February 1, 1691	Pietro Ottoboni
Innocent XII	July 12, 1691–September 27, 1700	Antonio Pignatelli
Clement XI	November 23, 1700–March 19, 1721	Giovanni Francesco Albani
Innocent XIII	May 8, 1721–March 7, 1724	Michelangelo dei Conti
Benedict XIII	May 29, 1724–February 21, 1730	Pietro Francesco Orsini
Clement XII	July 12, 1730–February 6, 1740	Lorenzo Corsini
Benedict XIV	August 17, 1740–May 3, 1758	Prospero Lorenzo Lambertini
Clement XIII	July 6, 1758–February 2, 1769	Carlo della Torre Rezzonico
Clement XIV	May 19, 1769–September 22, 1774	Lorenzo Ganganelli
Pius VI	February 15, 1775–August 29, 1799	Giovanni Angelo Brachi

Pope	*Reign*	*Original Name*
Pius VII	March 14, 1800–July 20, 1823	Luigi Barnabà Chiaramonte
Leo XII	September 28, 1823–February 10, 1829	Annibale Sermattei della Genga
Pius VIII	March 31, 1829–November 30, 1830	Francesco Saverio Castiglione
Gregory XVI	February 2, 1831–June 1, 1846	Bartolomeo Albert Cappellari
Pius IX	June 16, 1846–February 7, 1878	Giovanni Maria Mastai-Ferretti
Leo XIII	February 20, 1878–July 20, 1903	Gioacchino Vincenzo Pecci
St. Pius X	August 4, 1903–August 20, 1914	Giuseppe Melchiorre Sarto
Benedict XV	September 3, 1914–January 22, 1922	Giacomo Della Chiesa
Pius XI	February 6, 1922–February 10, 1939	Ambrogio Damiano Achille Ratti
Pius XII	March 2, 1939–October 9, 1958	Eugenio Maria Giuseppe Giovanni Pacelli
John XXIII	October 28, 1958–June 3, 1963	Angelo Giuseppe Roncalli
Paul VI	June 21, 1963–August 6, 1978	Giovanni Battista Montini
John Paul I	August 26, 1978–September 28, 1978	Albino Luciani
John Paul II	October 16, 1978–	Karol Wojtyla

"THE SEVEN . . ."

The number seven (7) is one of many numbers that are considered to have mystical properties. It appears with special frequency in Christian and other religious writings and doctrines. The following are some of the more well-known appearances of this "magic" number.

Seven Apostles of Spain. Seven missionaries sent by St. Peter in A.D. 64–65 to Betica to found churches.

Seven Churches of Asia. Seven churches in Asia Minor referred to by St. John in the Book of Revelation. They are located in Ephesus, Smyrna, Pergamum, Thyatira, Sardis, Philadelphia, and Laodicea.

Seven Churches of Rome. The basilicas of St. John Lateran, St. Peter, St. Mary Major, St. Paul-outside-the-Walls, St. Lawrence-outside-the-Walls, St. Sebastian-outside-the-Walls, and Holy Cross-in-Jerusalem. They were visited by early pilgrims as penance.

Seven Councils. The first seven ecumenical councils held by the church before the break between Eastern churches and Rome.

Seven Days of Creation. The time, according to the biblical account of creation, in which God created the universe from the void.

Seven Deacons. The first seven assistants ordained by the Apostles to minister to the poor.

Seven Deadly Sins. Pride, covetousness, lust, anger, gluttony, envy, and sloth.

Seven Gifts. Wisdom, understanding, counsel, fortitude, knowledge, piety, and fear of the Lord. All are said to be infused into the soul upon baptism.

Seven Heavens. Heaven's division into seven levels of beatitude, a belief popularly held by Roman Catholics and Jews and forming a part of Islamic doctrine; seventh heaven is the highest level.

Seven Last Words. The seven last statements made by Christ from the cross: "Father, forgive them for they do not know what they are doing"; "Indeed, I promise you, today you will be with Me in paradise"; "Woman, this is your son"; "This is your mother"; "My God, my God, why have you deserted me?"; "I am thirsty"; and "It is accomplished."

Seven Sacraments. Baptism, confirmation, the Eucharist, penance, holy orders, matrimony, and anointing the sick: the seven rites that confer grace in the Roman Catholic Church.

Additional Sources of Information

Bulfinch's Mythology. Spring Books, 1964.

Cavendish, Richard, ed. *Man, Myth and Magic: The Illustrated Encyclopedia of Mythology, Religion and the Unknown*, 2nd ed. Marshall Cavendish, 1983.

Directory of Religious Organizations in the United States of America. McGrath, 1977.

Ickis, Marguerite. *The Book of Religious Holidays and Celebrations.* Dodd, Mead, 1966.

Kelly, J. N. D. *The Oxford Dictionary of Popes.* Oxford University Press, 1986.

Meagher, Paul Kevin, O'Brien, Thomas C., and Aherne, Sister Consuelo Maria, eds. *Encyclopedic Dictionary of Religion.* 3 vols. Corpus Publications, 1979.

New Catholic Encyclopedia. McGraw-Hill, 1967.

Parrinder, Geoffrey, ed. *Religions of the World.* Grosset & Dunlap, 1971.

Walsh, Michael, ed. *Butler's Lives of the Saints*, concise ed. Harper & Row, 1985.

10

Philosophy

Major World Philosophers

Abelard, Peter (1079–1142). French philosopher. One of the most influential medieval logicians and theologians. Around 1113, while teaching theology in Paris, Abelard fell in love with his student Heloise, whom he secretly married; he was condemned for heresy a few years later because of his nominalist views about universals.

Anaxagoras (c. 500–428 B.C.). Greek Presocratic philosopher who is said to have made Athens the center of philosophy and to have been Socrates' teacher; he rejected the four elements theory of Empedocles and posited instead an infinite number of unique particles of which all objects are composed.

Anaximander (c. 611–547 B.C.). Greek Presocratic thinker who believed the universal substance to be "the boundless" or "the indefinite," rather than something resembling familiar objects. Unlike Thales (his teacher) and Anaximenes, he did not believe that a single element underlies all things.

Anaximenes (6th century B.C.). One of the Presocratics and an associate of Anaximander. He agreed with Thales that one type of substance underlies the diversity of observable things. Anaximenes believed that air was that universal substance and that all things are made of air in different degrees of density.

Anselm, St. (1033–1109). Italian monk and Scholastic theologian who became archbishop of Canterbury. St. Anselm founded Scholasticism, integrated Aristotelian logic into theology, and believed that reason and revelation are compatible. He is most famous for his influential ontological argument for God's existence.

Aquinas, St. Thomas (1225–74). The greatest thinker of the Scholastic School. His ideas were, in 1879, made the official Catholic philosophy. He incorporated Greek ideas into Christianity by showing Aristotle's thought to be compatible with church doctrine. In his system, reason and faith (revelation) form two separate but harmonious realms whose truths complement rather than oppose one another. He presented influential philosophical proofs for the existence of God.

Aristotle (384–322 B.C.). Greek philosopher, scientist, logician, and student of many disciplines. Aristotle studied under Plato and became the tutor of Alexander the Great. In 335 he opened the Lyceum, a major philosophical and scientific school in Athens. Aristotle emphasized the observation of nature and analyzed all things in terms of "the four causes." In ethics, he stressed that virtue is a mean between extremes and that man's highest goal should be the use of his intellect. Most of Aristotle's works were lost to Christian civilization from the fifth through the twelfth centuries.

Augustine of Hippo, St. (354–430). The greatest of the Latin church fathers and possibly the most influential Christian thinker after St. Paul. St. Augustine emphasized man's need for grace. His *Confessions* and *The City of God* were highly influential.

Averroes (1126–98). Spanish-born Arabian philosopher, lawyer, and physician whose detailed commentaries on Aristotle were influential for over 300 years. He emphasized the compatibility of faith and reason but believed philosophical knowledge to be derived from reason. The Church condemned his views.

Avicenna (980–1037). Islamic medieval philosopher born in Persia. His Neoplatonist interpretation of Aristotle greatly influenced medieval philosophers, including St. Thomas Aquinas. Avicenna was also a physician; his writings on medicine were important for nearly 500 years.

Bacon, Sir Francis (1561–1626). English statesman, essayist, and philosopher, one of the great precursors of the tradition of British empiricism and of belief in the importance of scientific method. He emphasized the use of inductive reasoning in the pursuit of knowledge.

Bentham, Jeremy (1748–1832). English philosopher and lawyer, and one of the founders of utilitarianism. Bentham was a highly influential reformer of the British legal, judicial, and prison systems.

Berkeley, George (1685–1753). Irish philosopher and an Anglican bishop, one of the British empiricists. Berkeley held to a "subjective idealism." He believed that everything that exists is dependent on being perceived by a mind. According to this view, material objects are simply collections of sensations or "ideas" in the mind of a person or of God.

Boethius (c. 475–535). Roman statesman, philosopher, and translator of Aristotle, whose *Consolation of Philosophy* (written in prison) was widely read throughout the Middle Ages; it showed reason's role in the face of misfortune and was the link between the ancient philosophers and the Scholastics.

Buber, Martin (1878–1965). German-Israeli philosopher influenced by Jewish mysticism and existentialism, a major force in twentieth-century Jewish thought and philosophy of religion. His *I and Thou* held that God and man can have a direct and mutual "dialogue."

Comte, Auguste (1798–1857). French founder of Positivism and social reformer. Comte put forth a "religion of humanity" that replaced the notion of God with the notion of mankind as a whole. He invented the term *sociology*.

Democritus (c. 460–c. 370 B.C.). Greek philosopher who proposed a mechanistic theory of the world that required no supernatural forces, only the constant motion of the indestructible atoms of which everything is composed. He held that perception is an unreliable source of knowledge and knowledge can be obtained through reason only.

Descartes, René (1596–1650). French philosopher and scientist, considered the father of modern philosophical inquiry. Descartes tried to extend mathematical method to all knowledge in his search for certainty. Discarding the medieval appeal to authority, he began with "universal doubt," finding that the only thing that could not be doubted was his own thinking. The result was his famous "Cogito, ergo sum," or "I think, therefore I am."

Dewey, John (1859–1952). Leading American philosopher, psychologist, and educational theorist. Dewey developed the views of Charles S. Peirce (1839–1914) and William James into his own version of pragmatism. He emphasized the importance of inquiry in gaining knowledge and attacked the view that knowledge is passive.

Diderot, Denis (1713–84). Materialist thinker of the French Enlightenment and originator of the *Encyclopédie*.

Diogenes (c. 400–325 B.C.). Greek founder of Cynicism who rejected social conventions and supposedly lived in a tub in defiance of conventional comforts.

Empedocles (c. 495–c. 435 B.C.). Greek Presocratic philosopher who believed the universe to consist of the four elements, air, fire, water, and earth. Empedocles held that the interaction between love and hate causes the mixing of the elements.

Engels, Friedrich (1820–95). German socialist thinker and historian, and the co-founder of Marxism; Marx's lifelong collaborator; and an originator of the philosophy of dialectical materialism.

Epictetus (c. 50–c. 138). Stoic moral philosopher who established a school of philosophy after being freed as a slave. His *Manual* teaches that only by detaching ourselves from what is not in our power can we attain inward freedom.

Epicurus (341–270 B.C.). Founder of the Epicurean philosophy and a follower of Democritus, founder of atomism. Virtually all of Epicurus' writings are lost.

Hegel, Georg Wilhelm Friedrich (1770–1831). German philosopher whose idealistic system of metaphysics was highly influential; it was based on a concept of the world as a single organism developing by its own inner logic through trios of stages called "thesis, antithesis, and synthesis" and gradually coming to embody reason. Hegel held the monarchy to be the highest development of the state.

Heidegger, Martin (1889–1976). German philosopher who studied with Husserl. Heidegger's own philosophy, which was influenced by Kierkegaard, emphasized the need to understand "being," especially the unique ways that humans act in and relate to the world.

Heraclitus (c. 535–c. 475 B.C.). Presocratic philosopher opposed to the idea of a single ultimate reality. Heraclitus believed that all things are in a constant state of change.

Hobbes, Thomas (1588–1679). English materialist and empiricist, one of the founders of modern political philosophy. In the *Leviathan,* Hobbes argued that because men are selfish by nature, a powerful absolute ruler is necessary. In a "social contract," men agree to give up many personal liberties and accept such rule.

Hume, David (1711–76). British empiricist whose arguments against the proofs for God's existence are still influential. Hume held that moral beliefs have no basis in reason, but are based solely on custom.

Husserl, Edmund (1859–1938). German philosopher who founded the Phenomenology movement. He aimed at a completely accurate description of consciousness and conscious experience.

James, William (1842–1910). American philosopher and psychologist, one of the founders of Pragmatism, and one of the most influential thinkers of his era. James viewed consciousness as actively shaping reality, defined truth as "the expedient" way of thinking, and held that ideas are tools for guiding our future actions rather than reproductions of our past experiences.

Kant, Immanuel (1724–1804). German philosopher, possibly the most influential of modern times. He synthesized Leibniz's rationalism and Hume's skepticism into his "critical philosophy": that ideas do not conform to the external world, but rather the world can be known only insofar as it conforms to the mind's own structure. Kant claimed that morality requires a belief in God, freedom, and immortality, although these can be proved neither scientifically nor by metaphysics.

Kierkegaard, Søren (1813–55). Danish philosopher, religious thinker, and extraordinarily influential founder of existentialism. Kierkegaard held that "truth is subjectivity," that religion is an individual matter, and that man's relationship to God requires suffering.

Leibniz, Gottfried Wilhelm (1646–1716). German philosopher, diplomat, and mathematician, one of the great minds of all time. Leibniz was an inventor (with Sir Isaac Newton) of the calculus and a forefather of modern mathematical logic. He held that the entire universe is one large system expressing God's plan.

Locke, John (1632–1704). Highly influential founder of British empiricism. Locke believed that all ideas come to mind from experience and that none are innate. He also held that authority derives solely from the consent of the governed, a view that deeply influenced the American Revolution and the writing of the U.S. Constitution.

Lucretius (c. 99–c. 55 B.C.). Roman Epicurean philosopher and poet. In *De Rerum Natura* (On the Nature of Things), Lucretius depicted the entire world, including the soul, as composed of atoms.

Machiavelli, Niccolò (1469–1527). Italian Renaissance statesman and political writer. In *The Prince,* one of the most influential political books of modern times, Machiavelli argues that any act of a ruler designed to gain and hold power is permissible. The term *Machiavellian* is used to refer to any political tactics that are cunning and power-oriented.

Maimonides (1135–1204). Spanish-born medieval Jewish philosopher and thinker. Maimonides tried to synthesize Aristotelian and Judaic thought. His works had enormous influence on Jewish and Christian thought.

Marcus Aurelius (121–180). Roman emperor from A.D. 161, and a proponent of the Stoic philosophy. His *Meditations* held that death is as natural as birth and that the world is rational and orderly. Although a great humanitarian, Marcus Aurelius persecuted the Christians of his time.

Marx, Karl (1818–83). German revolutionary thinker, social philosopher, and economist. His ideas, formulated with Engels, laid the foundation for nineteenth-century socialism and twentieth-century communism. Although Marx was initially influenced by Hegel, he soon rejected Hegel's idealism in favor of materialism. His *Communist Manifesto* and *Das Kapital* are among the most important writings of the last 200 years.

Mill, John Stuart (1806–73). English empiricist philosopher, logician, economist, and social reformer. His *System of Logic* described the basic rules for all scientific reasoning. As a student of Jeremy Bentham, he elaborated on utilitarian ethics; in *On Liberty,* he presented a plea for the sanctity of individual rights against the power of any government.

Montesquieu, Baron de (Charles-Louis de Secondat) (1689–1755). French political philosopher, influenced by Locke. In *Spirit of the Laws,* Montesquieu put forth the theory of separation of powers that strongly influenced the writing of the U.S. Constitution.

Moore, G. E. (George Edward) (1873–1958). British philosopher who emphasized the "common sense" view of the reality of material objects. In ethics, Moore held that goodness is a quality known directly by moral intuition and that it is a fallacy to try to define it in terms of anything else.

More, Sir Thomas (1478–1535). A leading Renaissance humanist and statesman, Lord Chancellor of England. More was beheaded for refusing to accept the king as head of the Church. Influenced by Greek thinking, he believed in social reform and drew a picture of an ideal peaceful state in his *Utopia*.

Nietzsche, Friedrich Wilhelm (1844–1900). German philosopher, philologist, and poet. As a moralist, he rejected Christian values and championed a "Superman" who would create a new, life-affirming, heroic ethic by his "will to power."

Parmenides (b. c. 515 B.C.). The founder of Western metaphysics. This Presocratic thinker held that "being" is the basic substance and ultimate reality of which all things are composed and that motion, change, time, difference, and reality are illusions of the senses.

Pascal, Blaise (1623–62). French philosopher, mathematician, scientist, and theologian. His posthumous *Pensées* ("Thoughts") argues that reason is by itself inadequate for man's spiritual needs and cannot bring man to God, who can be known only through mystic understanding.

Plato (c. 428–c. 348 B.C.). Athenian father of Western philosophy and student of Socrates, after whose death he traveled widely. On returning to Athens, he founded an Academy, where he taught until he died. His writings are in the form of dialogues between Socrates and other Athenians. Many of Plato's views are set forth in *The Republic*, where an ideal state postulates philosopher kings, specially trained at the highest levels of moral and mathematical knowledge. Plato's other works analyzed moral virtues, the nature of knowledge, and the immortality of the soul. His views on cosmology strongly influenced the next two thousand years of scientific thinking.

Plotinus (205–270). Egyptian-born founder of Neoplatonism, who synthesized the ideas of Plato and other Greek philosophers. Plotinus believed all reality is caused by a series of outpourings (called emanations) from the divine source. Although not himself a Christian, he was a major influence on Christianity.

Pythagoras (c. 582–c. 507 B.C.). Greek philosopher, mathematician, and mystic, founder of a religious brotherhood that believed in the immortality and the transmigration of the soul. Pythagoras may have been the first thinker to assert that numbers constitute the true nature of all things; he also may have coined the term *philosophy*.

Rousseau, Jean Jacques (1712–78). Swiss-French thinker, born in Geneva. Rousseau has been enormously influential in political philosophy, educational theory, and the Romantic movement. In *The Social Contract* (1762), he viewed governments as being expressions of the people's "general will," or rational men's choice for the common good. Rousseau emphasized man's natural goodness.

Russell, Bertrand (1872–1970). English philosopher and logician influential as an agnostic and a pacifist. Early work with Alfred North Whitehead gave birth to modern logic. Russell changed his views numerous times but always sought to establish philosophy, especially epistemology, as a science.

Santayana, George (1863–1952). Spanish-born American philospher and poet; a student of William James. Santayana attempted to reconcile Platonism and materialism, studied how reason works, and found "animal faith," or impulse, to be the basis of reason and belief.

Sartre, Jean-Paul (1905–80). French philosopher, novelist, and dramatist; one of the founders of existentialism. Sartre was a Marxist through much of his life. He held that man is "condemned to be free" and to bear the responsibility of making free choices.

Schopenhauer, Arthur (1788–1860). German post-Kantian philosopher who held that although irrational will is the driving force in human affairs, it is doomed not to be satisfied. He believed that only art and contemplation could offer escape from determinism and pessimism. Schopenhauer strongly influenced Nietzsche, Freud, Tolstoy, Proust, and Thomas Mann.

Scotus, John Duns (c. 1266–1308). Scottish-born Scholastic philosopher who tried to integrate Aristotelian ideas into Christian theology. Scotus emphasized that all things depend not just on God's intellect but on divine will as well.

Smith, Adam (1723–1790). Scottish philosopher and economist. He believed that if government left the marketplace to its own devices, an "invisible hand" would guarantee that the results would benefit the populace. Smith has had enormous influence on economists into the present day.

Socrates (464–399 B.C.). Athenian philosopher who allegedly wrote down none of his views, supposedly from his belief that writing distorts ideas. His chief student, Plato, is the major source of knowledge of what is known of his life. Socrates questioned Athenians about their moral, political, and religious beliefs, as depicted in Plato's dialogues; his questioning technique, called dialectic, has greatly influenced western philosophy. Socrates is alleged to have said that "the unexamined life is not worth living." In 399 B.C., he was brought to trial on charges of corrupting the youth and religious heresy. Sentenced to die, he drank poison.

Spinoza, Benedict (Baruch) (1623–77). Dutch-born philosopher expelled from the Amsterdam Jewish community for heresy in 1656; he was attacked by Christian theologians 14 years later. In *Ethics*, Spinoza presents his views in a mathematical system of deductive reasoning. A proponent of monism, he held—in contrast to Descartes—that mind and body are aspects of a single substance, which he called God or nature.

Thales of Miletus (c. 636–c. 546 B.C.). Regarded as the first Western philosopher, this Presocratic monist thinker is said to have believed that the fundamental principle of all things, or universal substance, is water. All of his writings are lost.

Unamuno, Miguel de (1864–1936). The major Spanish philosophical thinker of his time. Unamuno criticized philosophical abstractions such as "man" for ignoring concrete men. He held that reason by itself is virtually useless and cannot reveal the basic fact of human immortality.

Voltaire (François Marie Arouet) (1694–1778). French philosopher, essayist, and historian; one of the major thinkers of the Enlightenment. A Deist who was anti-Christian, Voltaire widely advocated tolerance of liberal ideas and called for positive social action. His novel *Candide* is a parody of the optimism of Leibniz.

Whitehead, Alfred North (1861–1947). British philosopher and mathematician who worked with Bertrand Russell. Whitehead tried to integrate twentieth-century physics into a metaphysics of nature.

William of Ockham (Occam) (c. 1285–c. 1349). Franciscan monk and important English theologian and philosopher. In his nominalism, he opposed much of the thought of St. Thomas Aquinas and of medieval Aristotelianism; he also rejected the Pope's power in the secular realm.

Wittgenstein, Ludwig (1889–1951). Austrian-born philosopher who spent the last 20 years of his life in England. Wittgenstein was one of the most influential philosophers of the century, primarily through his emphasis on the importance of the study of language. His early writings influenced analytic philosophy. His later views emphasized that philosophic problems are often caused by linguistic confusions.

Zeno of Elea (c. 490–c. 430 B.C.). Presocratic philosopher and disciple of Parmenides. Zeno argued that motion, change, and plurality are logical absurdities and that only an unchanging being is real. His four arguments against motion (Zeno's paradoxes) attempted to demonstrate logically that the notions of time and motion are erroneous.

Zeno (of Citium) the Stoic (c. 334–c. 262 B.C.). Greek philosopher born in Cyprus; the founder of Stoicism.

Philosophical Terms

Entries in this glossary include terms used by philosophers (for instance, *a priori*); "isms" that describe philosophical viewpoints or positions (for example, pantheism); and specific historical movements (such as Existentialism) and schools (Cartesianism). Names of philosophers referred to in the glossary who are listed under "Major World Philosophers" are marked with an asterisk *.

absolutism The doctrine that there is one explanation of all reality—the absolute—that is unchanging and objectively true. Absolutists (such G. W. F. Hegel*) hold that this absolute, such as God or mind, is eternal and that in it all seeming differences are reconciled.

aesthetics (esthetics) The philosophical study of art, or of beauty in general. It attempts to systematically answer such questions as, What is beauty? How do we evaluate works of art? Are aesthetic judgments objective or subjective? How does art embody truth and convey knowledge? How does beauty in art relate to beauty in nature?

agnosticism The belief that it is impossible to know whether God exists, or to have any other theological knowledge. English thinkers T. H. Huxley (1825–95) and Bertrand Russell* were influential agnostics.

altruism The ethical theory that morality consists of concern for and the active promotion of the interests of others. Altruists strongly disagree with the doctrine of egoism, which states that individuals act only in their own self-interest.

analytical philosophy An influential twentieth-century movement whose major proponents include Bertrand Russell,* Ludwig Wittgenstein,* and such logical positivists as Rudolph Carnap (1891–1970) and Willard Van Orman Quine (1908–). This school of thought emphasizes restating philosophical problems in highly structured terms based on modern logic.

analytic statement A statement true by definition, such as ''All triangles have three sides.''

anarchism A political philosophy that advocates the abolition of an organized state as the ruling government. Its advocates believe that individuals should be free to organize themselves in the ways that best enable them to fulfill their needs and ideals. The Russian thinker Mikhail Bakunin (1814–76) was an influential anarchist.

angst A German word meaning anxiety, anguish, or dread. The term was used by Heidegger* and other adherents of Existentialism to express their belief that anxiety characterizes the human condition and that dread arises from our realization that we are totally responsible for all of our choices.

anthroposophy The philosophy of Rudolf Steiner (1861–1925), an Austrian-born thinker who held that cultivating man's spiritual development is humanity's most important task. His followers founded a large number of schools worldwide based on his philosophy.

a posteriori knowledge Knowledge based on or derived from sensory experience.

a priori knowledge Knowledge acquired by the mind or reasoning alone, without any specific basis in experience—for instance, $2 + 2 = 4$.

argument An attempt to relate one set of statements, called the premises or the starting point, to another set, called the conclusion or the end point, by valid means. Arguments are either inductive or deductive. *See also* syllogism.

Aristotelianism The thinking and writings of Aristotle,* influential until the fall of Rome, when all but his writings on logic were lost to Christian civilization in Europe. However, his works were preserved in Syrian and Arabic cultures and were revived at the end of the twelfth century.

asceticism The view that attention to the body's needs is evil, an obstacle to moral and spiritual development, and displeasing to God. According to this view, humans are urged to withdraw into an inner spiritual world to reach the good life.

associationism A philosophical theory of the mind that holds that all mental states can be analyzed as separate component items and that all mental activity can be explained by the combining and recombining of these items, often called ideas. David Hume* and John Stuart Mill* were prominent advocates of this view. *See also* association of ideas.

association of ideas (laws of association) The principles by which the mind connects ideas. Aristotle* included similarity, contrast, and closeness; David Hume* held the basic laws to be resemblance, closeness in time or place, and causality. Hume and John Stuart Mill* are the two most prominent philosophers who emphasized association as the basic principle of the mind. *See also* associationism.

atheism The rejection of the belief in God. Some atheists have held that there is nothing in the world that requires a God in order to be explained. Atheism is not the same as agnosticism, which holds that we can have knowledge neither of the existence nor of the nonexistence of God.

atomism The theory that reality is composed of simple and indivisible units (atoms) that are completely separate from and independent of one another. Philosophers have differed as to the nature of atoms; for instance, the Greek thinkers Leucippus and Democritus* (fifth century B.C.) held that the atoms are different-shaped bits of matter.

bad faith Term used by Jean-Paul Sartre* for self-deception and the deception of others caused by denying one's freedom of choice and one's responsibility for making decisions.

becoming That which changes from one form to another, or, in Plato,* that which is known only by experience and exists only temporarily. *See also* being.

being Frequently used in metaphysics to contrast with appearance or nonexistence; often synonymous with unchanging substance, ultimate reality, God, infinity, or all that exists. Aristotle held that being is the subject matter of metaphysics. *See also* becoming.

bioethics A branch of philosophy that studies ethical issues that arise from conflicts between human rights and medical and biological research and the technology they use. Areas of concern are genetic manipulation, euthanasia, and brain control.

British empiricism The empiricism of Locke,* Berkeley,* and Hume* in the seventeenth and eighteenth centuries. They share the axiom that our knowledge of the world derives from experience or sensation rather than from reason. This view is opposed to rationalism, as well as to the Platonic notion of Forms as the source of knowledge.

British idealism (neo-Hegelianism) The philosophy of Hegel* as revived in England and Scotland in the mid-nineteenth century. The most prominent members of this school were T. H. Green (1836–82), Bernard Bosanquet (1848–1923), and F. H. Bradley (1846–1924). They were united in their opposition to empiricism and utilitarianism and in their emphasis on mind and spirit as primary.

Buridan's ass A story, falsely attributed to the fourteenth-century thinker John Buridan, in which an ass, faced with two equally desirable bales of hay, starves to death because he cannot find a good reason for preferring one bale to the other.

Cambridge Platonists A group of seventeenth-century English philosophers and theologians who tried to provide Christian theology with a philosophical defense based on Platonic and Neoplatonic theories. Ralph Cudworth (1617–88) was the most prominent member.

Cartesianism The views of Descartes* as interpreted by rationalistic, dualistic, and theistic philosophers. Nicolas Malebranche (1638–1715) was the most prominent of the group.

categorical imperative Kant's* term for the absolutely binding law of morality, in which a rational person must act whether he or she wishes to or not.

cause Whatever is responsible for change, action, or motion. Historically, Aristotle's* analysis of cause falls into four types: material cause, the substance a thing is made of; formal cause, the design of the thing; efficient cause, the maker of the thing; and final cause, its purpose or function. Hume* argued that all knowledge of cause comes from our actual experience of observed regularities.

certainty According to Descartes,* a condition of knowing that anything is true; various types of statements that are certain, for example, $1 + 1 = 2$, or all widows are female.

chain of being An idea, originating with Plato* and very influential in Western thought into the Renaissance, that all possible things are realized in the world in an ordered chain of diminishing complexity and richness, from God down to the tiniest, humblest bit of matter. The view captures the concept of the universe as an ordered hierarchy.

conceptualism The theory that general ideas, such as the idea of man or of redness, exist as entities produced by the human mind and that they can exist in the minds of all men. This view is typically contrasted with nominalism and realism.

cosmogony A theory or story about the origin of the universe, either scientific or mythological. Cosmogonies are also called creation myths.

cosmology The systematic study of the origin and structure of the universe as a whole. In such philosophers as Plato,* Aristotle,* and Kant,* cosmology was based on metaphysical speculation; today cosmology is a branch of the physical sciences.

counterexample A specific fact that refutes or negates a generalization; for instance, a black swan is a counterexample to the statement "All swans are white."

Cynics A school of Greek philosophers founded by Diogenes.* According to legend, Diogenes walked around night and day with a lighted lantern seeking an honest man but could not find one. The Cynics held that men should live in a simple state of nature with as few desires and needs as possible. They advocated moderation, self-discipline, and training of the mind as well as the body.

Cyrenaics A school of philosophy of the fourth century B.C. in Athens founded by Cyrene, a disciple of Socrates. Cyrenaics believed that only momentary feelings of pleasure or pain can be known; they held that the good life is one that maximizes pleasure derived from satisfying one's bodily desires. *See also* hedonism.

deductive reasoning Reasoning from a general statement to a particular or specific example; for example, "All cats are mortal; William is a cat; therefore, William is mortal." *See also* syllogism.

deism A philosophical viewpoint appearing in England in the seventeenth and eighteenth centuries and in France in the eighteenth century. Deists hold that although God created the universe and its laws, He then removed Himself from any ongoing interaction with the material world.

deontology The ethical philosophy that makes duty the basis of all morality. According to deontological theorists, such as Kant,* some acts—such as keeping a promise or telling the truth—are moral obligations regardless of their consequences.

determinism The view that every event has a cause and that everything in the universe is absolutely dependent on and governed by causal laws. Since determinists believe that all events, including human actions, are predetermined, determinism is typically thought to be incompatible with free will.

dialectic A term with different meanings for different philosophers. It derives from the Greek word meaning "to converse" and is used to describe Socrates'* method of teaching by question-and-answer technique. Plato* used the word to mean the study of the Forms. In Kant,* it refers to a method of criticizing claims of knowledge going beyond experience. Hegel* means by it the necessary pattern of thinking.

dialectical materialism The philosophy of Karl Marx* and many of his followers. It holds that matter is the primary reality and that it obeys the dynamic laws of change. The most fundamental of these laws is that progress occurs through conflict and struggle between opposing forces, such as between different classes and between capitalism and communism. *See also* Marxism.

doubt According to Descartes,* the argument that nothing can be considered true unless it can never be doubted under any conditions. Descartes doubted everything "systematically" to find out if anything is indubitable; his "Cogito, ergo sum" ("I think, therefore I am") survived his test.

dualism Any philosophical theory holding that the universe consists of, or can only be explained by, two independent and separate forces, such as matter and spirit, the forces of good and evil, or the supernatural and natural. *See also* mind-body problem.

duty According to many ethical theories, the basis of the virtuous life. The Stoics held that man has a duty to live virtuously and according to reason; and Kant* held that his categorical imperative is the highest law of duty, no matter what the consequences.

egocentric predicament The belief that each of us is limited to, and by, our unique pattern of perceptions. Any knowledge of the world outside our minds would thus be colored by our perceptions. *See also* solipsism.

egoism The ethical theory that each person should forward his or her own self-interest. Egoists sometimes argue that this is not selfishness, but that self-interest is compatible with helping others as well. Some egoists also argue that, psychologically speaking, human beings always in fact seek their own well-being.

élan vital *See* vitalism.

Eleatics A school of Presocratic philosophers from Elea in southern Italy, of whom Parmenides* and Zeno of Elea* are the best known. The Eleatics denied the reality of what is known to the senses, holding that the ultimate reality is an undifferentiated and unchanging "being."

empirical Based on experience, observation, or facts—in short, describing any knowledge derived from or validated by sensory experience.

empiricism The view that all knowledge of the world derives solely from sensory experience, using observation and experimentation if needed; empiricism also holds that reason on its own can never provide knowledge of reality unless it also utilizes experience. *See also* British empiricism.

Encyclopedists A group of eighteenth-century French writers who combined to produce an encyclopedia of philosophy, art, and science (1751–65) edited by Diderot* and D'Alembert. The work was skeptical about religion and advocated liberal, democratic political views. At the time, it was the largest compendium of human knowledge that had ever been produced.

Enlightenment (Age of Reason) A period that stretched from the early seventeenth to the early nineteenth century, especially in France, England, and Germany. Its thinkers strove to make reason the ruler of human life; they believed that all men could gain knowledge and liberation. Major Enlightenment figures include Voltaire,* Rousseau,* Diderot,* and Montesquieu* in France; Bacon*, Hobbes,* and Locke* in England; and Leibniz,* Lessing (1729–81), and Herder (1744–1803) in Germany.

Epicureanism A school founded by Epicurus* about 306 B.C. that taught that pleasure and happiness should be man's supreme goals. Epicureans sought mental pleasures over bodily ones.

epistemology The branch of philosophy that studies how knowledge is gained, how much we can know, and what justification there is for what is known.

eschatology In theology, the study of "final things," such as death, resurrection, immortality, the second coming of Christ, and the day of judgment.

essence That which makes a specific thing what it is and not something else; its nature. While the Greek philosophers viewed essence and substance as basically the same, St. Thomas Aquinas* and the philosophy of Scholasticism held that even nonexistent things have natures or essences distinguishable from the fact of their existence.

esthetics *See* aesthetics.

euthanasia The act of allowing a terminally ill person to freely choose when and how he or she will die; mercy killing.

existentialism A philosophy of the nineteenth and twentieth centuries. The dogma holds that since there are no universal values, man's essence is not predetermined but is based only on free choice; man is in a state of anxiety because of his realization of free will; and there is no objective truth. Major existentialists were Kierkegaard,* Nietzsche,* Sartre,* Heidegger,* Karl Jaspers (1883–1969), and the religious existentialists Martin Buber* and Gabriel Marcel (1889–1973).

fatalism The belief that "what will be will be," since all past, present, and future events have already been predetermined by God or another all-powerful force. In religion, this view may be called predestination; it holds that whether our souls go to Heaven or Hell is determined before we are born and is independent of our good deeds.

Forms According to Plato,* all existing things are merely imperfect copies of eternal, unchanging, immaterial, and perfect archetypes called Forms or Ideas.

four elements According to many early Greek philosophers, the four basic constituents of the physical world: earth, air, fire, and water.

free will The theory that human beings have freedom of choice or self-determination; that is, that given a situation, a person could have done other than what he did. Philosophers have argued that free will is incompatible with determinism. *See also* indeterminism.

golden mean The ethical doctrine, originating with Aristotle, that virtuous actions fall exactly between too much of some quality, such as impulsive behavior, and too little of it, such as timidity. It is associated with ethics calling for moderation.

golden rule The fundamental moral rule of most religions, especially Christianity, that states, "Do unto others as you would have others do unto you."

greatest happiness principle *See* principle of utility; Utilitarianism.

hedonism A philosophy of ethics holding that pleasure is the highest or the only good in life, and that men should strive for pleasure and the avoidance of pain. Among the chief proponents of hedonism were the Epicureans and the utilitarians.

Hegelianism (neo-Hegelianism) A school of thought associated with Hegel* in the nineteenth and early twentieth centuries, especially in England, America, France, and Italy. F. G. Bradley (1846–1924), Josiah Royce (1855–1916), and Benedetto Croce (1866–1952) were prominent members; they emphasized the importance of spirit and the belief that ideas and moral ideals are fundamental.

Hobson's choice A choice offered without any real alternative—therefore, not really a choice at all.

humanism Any philosophic view that holds that mankind's well-being and happiness in this lifetime are primary and that the good of all humanity is the highest ethical goal. Twentieth-century humanists tend to reject all beliefs in the supernatural, relying instead on scientific methods and reason. The term is also used to refer to Renaissance thinkers, especially in the fifteenth century in Italy, who emphasized knowledge and learning not based on religious sources.

idealism A term applied to any philosophy holding that mind or spiritual values, rather than material things or matter, are primary in the universe. *See also* British idealism.

immortality The view that the individual soul is eternal, and thus survives the death of the body it resides in. *See also* transmigration of souls.

indeterminism The view that there are events that do not have any cause; many proponents of free will believe that acts of choice are capable of not being determined by any physiological or psychological cause.

inductive reasoning Any process of reasoning from something particular to something general, or from a part to a whole. Inductive reasoning can be valid or invalid.

innate ideas Ideas that are inborn and part of the mind at birth, rather than based on specific experiences. Descartes* believed there are "clear and distinct" ideas that are innate and that form the basis of all knowledge. Plato* believed that knowledge of the Forms derives from innate ideas.

instrumentalism A theory that holds that ideas and concepts should be regarded as tools or instruments to be used in specific situations. As such, they cannot be described as true or false, but only as effective or ineffective. This theory was first put forth by John Dewey.*

intuitionism Any philosophy holding that intuition is the basis of knowledge or of philosophy. French philosopher Henri Bergson (1859–1941) was a prominent advocate. In particular, intuitionism refers to a British school of thought that maintains that all ethical knowledge rests on moral intuition.

justice According to most philosophers, starting with Plato,* the harmonious balance between the rights of the various members of a society. Justice is usually understood as including such social virtues as fairness, equality, and correct and impartial treatment.

language *See* philosophy of language.

language game A concept introduced by Ludwig Wittgenstein,* who drew an analogy between how we use language and how we play games: both have rules and moves that make sense only in the context of a particular game. Wittgenstein and his followers used this concept to point out that philosophers frequently try to make moves in one context that make sense only in another, as when they try to verify religious statements as if they were a part of science.

linguistic philosophy (linguistic analysis) The twentieth-century school of thought whose key tenet is that philosophical problems are best approached by asking questions about the use of words and by analyzing how language works in specific social contexts.

logic The study of the rules and the nature of reasoning and of valid or sound patterns of thought. Aristotle* classified many of the rules of reasoning. In the late nineteenth and early twentieth centuries, logic was advanced into a branch of mathematics. Currently, mathematical logic is a growing field independent of philosophy. *See also* syllogism.

logical positivism A twentieth-century school founded in the 1920s in Europe that was extremely influential for

American and English philosophers. It advocated the principle of verifiability, according to which all statements that could be validated empirically were meaningless. Logical positivism held that this principle showed that all of metaphysics, religion, and ethics was incapable of being proved either true or false. *See also* Vienna Circle.

Manichaeanism A religious-philosophical doctrine that originated in Persia in the third century and reappeared throughout the next 1300 years. It holds that the entire universe, especially human life, is a struggle between the opposing forces of good and evil (light and darkness).

Marxism The political, economic, and philosophical theories developed by Karl Marx* and Friedrich Engels* in the second half of the nineteenth century. The philosophical side of Marxism is called dialectical materialism; it emphasizes economic determinism. *See also* dialectical materialism.

materialism The theory that holds that the nature of the world is dependent on matter, or that matter is the only fundamental substance; thus, spirit and mind either do not exist or are manifestations of matter.

mathematical logic *See* logic.

mathematics *See* philosophy of mathematics.

mechanism The philosophical theory that states that living organisms, including man, are complex machines, since they are composed of matter.

meta-ethics A branch of philosophy that analyzes ethics. It is concerned with such issues as, How are moral decisions justified? What is the foundation of any ethical view? What language is used to state moral beliefs?

metaphysics The branch of philosophy concerned with the ultimate nature of reality and existence as a whole. Metaphysics also includes the study of cosmology and philosophical theology. Aristotle* produced the first ''system'' of metaphysics.

metempsychosis *See* transmigration of souls.

Miletian School The Presocratics from Miletus in Greece—Thales* and his two best-known pupils, Anaximander* and Anaximenes.*

mind *See* philosophy of mind.

mind-body problem A central problem of modern philosophy that originated with Descartes.* It asks how the mind and the body are related.

monad According to Leibniz,* the ultimate and indivisible units of all existence. Monads are not material, like atoms; each monad is self-activating, a unique center of force. All monads are in a ''pre-established harmony'' with each other and with God, the supreme monad.

monism The theory that everything in the universe is composed of, or can be explained by or reduced to, one fundamental substance, energy, or force.

mysticism Any philosophy whose roots are in mystical experiences, intuitions, or direct experiences of the divine. In such experiences, the mystic believes that his or her soul has temporarily achieved union with God. Mystics believe reality can be known only in this manner, not through reasoning or everyday experience.

myth of Er A parable at the end of Plato's *Republic* about the fate of souls after bodily death; according to Plato,* the soul must choose wisdom in the afterlife to guarantee a good life in its next cycle of incarnation.

naturalism A philosophic view stating that all there is in reality is what the physical and human sciences (for example, physics or psychology) study and that there is no need to posit any supernatural forces or being, such as God, mind, or spirit.

naturalistic fallacy A belief of many twentieth-century philosophers in England and America that it is invalid to infer any statements of morality (for example, ''Men ought to act kindly'') from factual statements (for example, ''Kindness is a natural quality''). The notion tries to derive *ought* from *is* and was first described by Hume.*

natural law The theory that there is a higher law than the manmade laws put forth by specific governments. This law is universal, unchanging, and a fundamental part of human nature. Advocates of this view believe that natural law can be discovered by reason alone. The theory originated with the Stoics and was elaborated on by St. Thomas Aquinas,* among others.

natural rights Certain freedoms or privileges that are held to be an innate part of the nature of being a human being and that cannot be denied by society. These are different from civil rights, which are granted by a specific nation or government. Philosophers have differed on which rights are natural, but usually included are life, liberty, equality, equal treatment under the law, the pursuit of happiness, and equality of opportunity. Locke's* influential views on natural rights inspired the writers of the American Constitution.

necessary and contingent truth Terms used by philosophers to contrast two types of statements, such as ''All widowers are male,'' which is necessarily true, and ''All widowers are over 20 years old,'' which may be true but is not necessarily true.

Neoplatonism A school of philosophy that flourished from the second to the fifth centuries A.D. It was founded by Plotinus* and was influential for the next thousand years.

nihilism A term first used in *Fathers and Sons* (1862) by the Russian novelist Turgenev. *Ethical nihilism* is the theory that morality cannot be justified in any way and that all moral values are, therefore, meaningless and irrational. *Political nihilism* is the social philosophy that society and its institutions are so corrupt that their complete destruction is desirable. Nihilists may, therefore, advocate violence and even terrorism in the name of overthrowing what they believe to be a corrupt social order.

nominalism The view that general terms, such as "table," do not refer to essences, concepts, abstract ideas, or anything else; "table" makes sense only because all tables resemble each other. According to this view, such general terms do not have any independent existence.

non sequitur A Latin phrase meaning "it does not follow"; any argument where the conclusion drawn has not even the slightest connection to the premises offered.

objectivism The view that there are moral truths that are valid universally and that it is wrong to knowingly gain pleasure from causing another pain.

obligation In ethics, a moral necessity to do a specific deed. Some ethicists, following Kant,* hold that moral obligations are absolute. *See also* categorical imperative.

Ockham's razor A principle attributed to the fourteenth-century English philosopher William of Ockham.* It states that entities should not be multiplied beyond necessity, or that one should choose the simplest explanation, the one requiring the fewest assumptions and principles.

ontology A branch of metaphysics that studies the nature of existence or reality, as such, as opposed to specific types of existing entities.

operationalism (operationism) A philosophy of science according to which any scientific concept must be definable in terms of concrete, observable activities or the operations to which it refers.

optimism The philosophic attitude that this is the best of all possible worlds, that hope and joy are justified, and that all things are ordered for the best. According to optimists, such as Leibniz,* evil either is an illusion or will be compensated for by an even greater good.

Ordinary Language Philosophy The twentieth-century school advocating that we can best understand and resolve philosophic problems by analyzing how people other than philosophers ordinarily use language and the presuppositions underlying such use; the school holds that everyday language is adequate for philosophy. Wittgenstein,* Gilbert Ryle (1900–76), and John L. Austin (1911–60) were the most influential members of this school.

pantheism The belief that God and the universe are identical; among modern philosophers, Spinoza* is considered to be a pantheist.

particulars *See* universals.

Pascal's wager An argument made by Blaise Pascal* for believing in God. Pascal said that either the tenets of Roman Catholicism are true or they are not. If they are true, and we wager that they are true, then we have won an eternity of bliss; if they are false, and death is final, what has the bettor lost? On the other hand, if one wagers against God's existence and turns out to be wrong, there is eternal damnation.

personalism A term applied to any philosophy that makes personality (whether of people, God, or spirit) the supreme value or the source of reality. Personalism as a movement flourished in England and America in the nineteenth and twentieth centuries. Personalists are usually idealists.

pessimism The philosophic attitude holding that hope is unreasonable, that man is born to sorrow, and that this is the worst of all possible worlds. Schopenhauer's* philosophy is an example of extreme pessimism.

phenomenalism The doctrine that the only knowledge we can ever have is of appearances, and thus that we can never know the nature of ultimate reality. Major adherents of the philosophy were John Stuart Mill* and some members of the Vienna Circle.

Phenomenology A school founded by Edmund Husserl,* and an important influence on Existentialism. This school developed its own philosophical "method" of using intuition for describing consciousness and experience. Phenomenologists claim that this method can be used to study the inherent qualities of phenomena as they appear to the mind.

philosopher king In Plato's* *Republic*, a philosopher trained by formal study in disciplines including mathematics and philosophy. Plato emphasized that philosopher kings' leadership would be shown by their ability to see the Forms, or universal ideals. *See also* Forms.

philosophies Term applied to eighteenth-century French Enlightenment thinkers such as Rousseau,* Diderot,* and Voltaire.*

philosophy of language The area of philosophic study whose subject matter is the nature and workings of language. Detailed discussions of such topics as meaning, reference, grammar, and symbols infuse this branch of philosophy.

philosophy of mathematics A branch of philosophy that studies such questions as, What are mathematical statements about? Why is mathematics true? How do we come to have mathematical knowledge? Why is mathematics so useful in studying reality?

philosophy of mind The area of philosophy that studies the mind, consciousness, and mental functions such as thinking, intention, imagination, and emotion. It is not one specific branch of philosophy, but rather an aspect of most traditional branches, such as metaphysics, epistemology, and aesthetics.

philosophy of religion A branch of philosophy concerned with such questions as, What is religion? What is God? Can God's existence be proved? Is there immortality? What is the relationship between faith, reason, and revelation? Is there a divine purpose in the world?

philosophy of science The branch of philosophy that studies the nature of science. It is particularly concerned with the methods, concepts, and assumptions of science, as well as with analyzing scientific concepts such as space, time, cause, scientific law, and verification.

physicalism A theory about knowledge that originated within the Vienna Circle. It holds that all factual statements can be reduced to observations of physical objects and events. *See also* operationalism.

Platonism Thoughts and writings developed in the fifth century B.C. in Athens by Plato,* the greatest student of Socrates.* Platonism's chief tenet is that the ultimate reality consists of unchanging, absolute, eternal entities called Ideas or Forms; all earthly objects are not truly real but merely partake in the Forms.

Plato's cave An analogy in Plato's* *Republic* between reality and illusion. The main image is of men who see on the walls of a cave only the shadows of the real objects moving around outside the cave. When these men leave the cave and see the real objects, they cannot, upon returning to the cave, convince those who have never left of the reality of the objects.

pluralism The view that there are more than two kinds of fundamental, irreducible realities in the universe, or that there are many separate and independent levels of reality.

political philosophy The branch of philosophy that studies man as a political animal. It is concerned with such questions as, What obligations do I have to my government? How is political power justified? Under what conditions is war justified? It also studies the nature of property, justice, freedom, liberty, and political rights.

positivism A theory originated by French philosopher Auguste Comte.* It holds that all knowledge is defined by the limits of scientific investigation; thus, philosophy must abandon any quest for knowledge of an ultimate reality or any knowledge beyond that offered by science. *See also* Logical Positivism.

Pragmatism An American philosophy developed in the nineteenth century by Charles Sanders Peirce* (1839–1914) and William James,* and elaborated on in the twentieth century by John Dewey.* Its central precepts are that thinking is primarily a guide to action and that the truth of any idea lies in its practical consequences.

predestination *See* fatalism.

premises *See* argument.

Presocratics Name given to all Greek "theorists of nature" or philosophers who lived before Socrates. Among the Presocratics are Anaximander,* Pythagoras,* and Thales.*

principle (or law) of noncontradiction Dating back to Aristotle, this universally accepted "law of thought" has two parts: a statement cannot be both true and false; nothing can both have a quality, like red, and not have it, at the same time.

principle of sufficient reason The philosophical doctrine of Leibniz* that asserts that for every fact there is a reason for its being the way it is rather than another way, even though we may not know that reason.

principle of utility (greatest happiness principle) The basic tenet of utilitarianism. It states that the highest ethical good provides the greatest happiness for the greatest number of people.

psychologism A view of philosophy holding that all philosophic concepts and problems are explainable based on psychological principles and that they should be treated by some form of psychological analysis. Advocates of this view may disagree on the type of psychological approach that is appropriate.

Pythagoreans Followers of Pythagoras.* The group flourished until about 400 B.C. and were influential in philosophy, religion, mathematics, and science. They strongly influenced the thinking of Plato* and Neoplatonists.

QED Latin for *quod erat demonstrandum* ("that which was to be demonstrated"). This abbreviation is often used right before or after stating a conclusion, as a synonym for *therefore, thus,* or *as was to be shown.*

rationalism The philosophic approach that holds that reality is knowable by the use of reason or thinking alone, without recourse to observation or experience. *See also* seventeenth-century rationalists.

realism The major medieval and modern view on the problem of universals other than nominalism. *Extreme realism,* which is close to Plato's* theory of Forms, holds that universals exist independently of both particular things and the human mind; *moderate realism* holds that they exist as ideas in God's mind, through which He creates things.

reincarnation *See* transmigration of souls.

relativism The precept that people's ideas of right and wrong vary considerably from place to place and time to time; therefore, there are no universally valid ethical standards.

religion *See* philosophy of religion.

Scholasticism A general term referring to the Christian philosophy of the Middle Ages, especially at the medieval universities. The Scholastics basically followed Aristotle's* empiricism, using highly analytical logical and linguistic methods of argumentation, especially with respect to the problem of universals.

science *See* philosophy of science.

sensationalism An empiricist theory of knowledge that holds that sensations are both the source of all knowledge and the ultimate verification of any statements. Hobbes* originated the view; Étienne Condillac (1715–1880) and Ernst Mach (1838–1916) developed it.

sense data The sensory qualities or feelings we experience directly, such as shapes, colors, and smells, without any interpretation of the material objects that may be causing them. Some empiricists and sensationalist philosophers make sense data the foundation of all factual knowledge.

seventeenth-century rationalists A broad term referring to the rationalism shared by Descartes,* Leibniz,* and Spinoza.* It held that reason and deduction could provide knowledge of the world independent of experience.

skepticism The philosophic theory that no certain knowledge can be attained by man. Broadly speaking, skepticism states that all knowledge should be questioned and tested, for instance, by the scientific method.

social contract That concept of an agreement between people, or between people and government or ruler, in which it is agreed that some personal liberties will be given up in exchange for the security of stable political rule. The term is used in the political philosophy of Hobbes,* Locke,* and Rousseau* to justify a form of political authority.

solipsism The theory that one cannot know anything other than his or her own thoughts, feelings, or perceptions; therefore, other people and the real world must be projections of one's own mind with no existence in and of themselves. *See also* egocentric predicament.

Sophists Wandering teachers in the fourth and fifth centuries in ancient Greece who taught any subjects that their paying students wished to learn, from grammar to public speaking. They were strongly ridiculed by Plato,* who held that they were less interested in truth than in pleasing their students for a fee.

spiritism A term referring to the belief that spirits of the dead communicate with the living, for instance, at seances or through a medium.

spiritualism The view that the ultimate reality in the universe is the spirit. Advocates of this view may disagree about the nature of the spirit.

state of nature A term used by seventeenth- and eighteenth-century social philosophers such as Hobbes,* Locke,* and Rousseau.* It referred to the condition of man without political organization, or before government.

Stoicism A Greek school founded by Zeno* in the third century B.C. Stoics held that men should submit to natural law and that a man's chief duty is to conform to his destiny. They also believed the soul to be another form of matter, and thus not immortal.

subjectivism The theory that all moral values are completely dependent on the personal tastes, feelings, or inclinations

of the individual and have no source of validity outside of such human subjective states of mind.

substance A changeless, self-subsistent entity, not dependent on anything else, that underlies being in all its forms. It has been identified with God, mind, matter, and self-contained ultimate realities. *See also* monad.

supernaturalism The belief that there are forces, energies, or beings beyond the material world—such as God, spirit, or occult forces—that affect events in our world.

syllogism A kind of deductive reasoning or argument. As defined by Aristotle, it was considered the basis of reasoning for over two thousand years. In every syllogism, there are two statements (premises) from which a conclusion follows necessarily. Syllogisms are of three basic logical types, as illustrated by these examples:
1. If a broom is new, it sweeps clean; the broom is new; therefore, it sweeps clean.
2. Either the horse is male or female; the horse is not female; therefore, it is male.
3. All philosophers are men; all men are mortal; therefore, all philosophers are mortal.

synthetic statement A factual statement describing a state of affairs, such as "Triangles are used in architectural studios."

tabula rasa A Latin phrase meaning "blank slate," used by Locke* to describe the state of the human mind at birth. Locke believed there are no innate ideas and that the mind gets all of its ideas from experience.

tautology Any statement that is necessarily true merely because of its meaning, such as "Bachelors are unmarried males," or "Every green object is colored." *See also* necessary and contingent truth.

teleological ethics In contrast with deontological ethics, this moral theory holds that whether an action is morally right depends solely on its expected consequences. *See also* utilitarianism.

Thomism The philosophical and theological system developed by St. Thomas Aquinas* in the thirteenth century. One of its chief principles is that philosophy seeks truth through reason while theology seeks it through revelation from God; therefore, the two are compatible.

transcendent Beyond the realm of sense experience. In many religious views, God is held to be transcendent.

Transcendentalism A nineteenth-century movement developed in New England and expounded by Ralph Waldo Emerson (1803–82) and Henry David Thoreau (1817–62). It maintains that beyond our material world of experience is an ideal spiritual reality that can be grasped intuitively.

transmigration of souls (metempsychosis; reincarnation) The belief that the same soul can, in different lifetimes (incarnations), reside in different bodies, human or animal. While typically a part of most Eastern religions, the doctrine came into Western philosophy from Pythagoras* and his contemporaries in the sixth century B.C. and especially through Plato.

universals The properties, or the abstract or general words, that apply to many individual things, called particulars. Redness, for instance, is a universal that applies to all red things.

utilitarianism A theory of morality holding that all actions should be judged for rightness or wrongness in terms of their consequences; thus, the amount of pleasure people derive from those consequences becomes the measure of moral goodness. Jeremy Bentham* and John Stuart Mill,* in the nineteenth century, were the chief proponents of this view. *See also* principle of utility.

utopianism The belief in the possibility or desirability of not just a better but a perfect society. The term derives from Sir Thomas More's* *Utopia* (1516), which depicts an ideal state. Utopian states also appear in the writings of Plato* and Bacon.*

verifiability *See* Logical Positivism.

Vienna Circle A major school of Logical Positivism founded by Moritz Schlick (1882–1936) in the 1920s. It was known for its hostility to metaphysics and theology and for its belief that physics is the model for all knowledge of the world. Other leading members of the school were Rudolph Carnap (1891–1970) and Otto Neurath (1882–1945).

vitalism The theory that living organisms are inherently different from inanimate bodies; thus, life cannot be explained fully by materialistic theories as it is based on a vital force that is unlike other physical forces. Aristotle,* Hans Driesch (1867–1941), and Henri Bergson (1859–1941) were prominent vitalists. In Bergson's view, the "élan vital" is the evolutionary force in organisms that propels life to achieve higher levels of structure.

will to believe A phrase made famous by William James.* He held that in the absence of decisive evidence, the mind may create belief in order to act, often resulting in discovery. He also maintained that believing in such situations is a human right that should not be backed away from.

will to power The view, expounded by Nietzsche,* that power is the chief motivating force in human nature. The view was influential in twentieth-century psychology and social science.

Young Hegelians A group of thinkers in Germany in the first half of the nineteenth century whose views strongly influenced Karl Marx.* They were followers of Hegel* who believed that the political conditions under which they lived were irrational. They held that the goal of philosophy should be to promote a revolution of ideas and critical thinking about the world. Ludwig Feuerbach (1804–72) was the most important of the Young Hegelians.

PROOFS FOR THE EXISTENCE OF GOD

While theology may take God's existence as absolutely necessary on the basis of authority, faith, or revelation, many philosophers—and some theologians—have thought it possible to demonstrate by reason that there must be a God.

St. Thomas Aquinas, in the thirteenth century, formulated the famous "five ways" by which God's existence can be demonstrated philosophically:

1. *The "unmoved mover" argument.* We know that there is motion in the world; whatever is in motion is moved by another thing; this other thing also must be moved by something; to avoid an infinite regression, we must posit a "first mover," which is God.

2. *The "nothing is caused by itself" argument.* For example, a table is brought into being by a carpenter, who is caused by his parents. Again, we cannot go on to infinity, so there must be a first cause, which is God.

3. *The cosmological argument.* All physical things, even mountains, boulders, and rivers, come into being and go out of existence, no matter how long they last. Therefore, since time is infinite, there must be some time at which none of these things existed. But if there were nothing at that point in time, how could there be anything at all now, since nothing cannot cause anything? Thus, there must always have been at least one necessary thing that is eternal, which is God.

4. *Objects in the world have differing degrees of qualities such as goodness.* But speaking of more or less goodness makes sense only by comparison with what is the maximum goodness, which is God.

5. *The teleological argument (argument from design).* Things in the world move toward goals, just as the arrow does not move toward its goal except by the archer's directing it. Thus, there must be an intelligent designer who directs all things to their goals, and this is God.

Two other historically important "proofs" are the ontological argument and the moral argument. The former, made famous by St. Anselm in the eleventh century and defended in another form by Descartes, holds that it would be logically contradictory to deny God's existence. St. Anselm began by defining God as "that [being] than which nothing greater can be conceived." If God existed only in the mind, He then would not be the greatest conceivable being, for we could imagine another being that is greater because it would exist both in the mind and in reality, and that being would then be God. Therefore, to imagine God as existing only in the mind but not in reality leads to a logical contradiction; this proves the existence of God both in the mind and in reality.

Immanuel Kant rejected not only the ontological argument but the teleological and cosmological arguments as well, based on his theory that reason is too limited to know anything beyond human experience. However, he did argue that religion could be established as presupposed by the workings of morality in the human mind ("practical reason"). God's existence is a necessary presupposition of there being any moral judgments that are objective, that go beyond mere relativistic moral preferences; such judgments require standards external to any human mind—that is, they presume God's mind.

ARGUMENTS AGAINST GOD'S EXISTENCE

Arguments against God's existence have been given by philosophers, atheists, and agnostics. Some of these arguments find God's existence incompatible with observed facts; some are arguments that God does not exist because the concept of God is incoherent or confused. Others are criticisms of the proofs offered *for* God's existence.

One of the most influential and powerful "proofs" that there is no God proceeds from "The Problem From Evil." This argument claims that the following three statements cannot *all* be true: (a) evil exists; (b) God is omnipotent; and (c) God is all-loving. The argument is as follows:

- if God can prevent evil, but *doesn't*, then He isn't all-loving.

- if God intends to prevent evil, but *cannot*, then He isn't omnipotent.

- if God *both* intends to prevent evil and is capable of doing so, then how can evil exist?

Another argument claims that the existence of an all-knowing God is incompatible with the fact that humans do make choices. If God is omniscient, He must know beforehand exactly what a person will do in a given situation. In that case, a person is not in fact free to do the alternative to what God knows he or she will do, and free will must be an illusion. To take this one step further, if one chooses to commit a sin, how can it then be said that one sinned freely?

Hume provided powerful critiques of the main arguments for God's existence. Against the cosmological argument (Aquinas' third argument), he argued that the idea of a necessarily existing being is absurd. Hume stated, "Whatever we can conceive as existent, we can also conceive as nonexistent." He also asked why the ultimate source of the universe could not be the entire universe itself, eternal and uncaused, without a God?

Hume also criticized the argument from design (Aquinas' fifth argument). In particular, he emphasized that there is no legitimate way we can infer the properties of God as the creator of the world from the qualities of His creation. For instance, Hume questioned how we can be sure that the world was not created by a team; or that this is not one of many attempts at creations, the first few having been botched; or, on the other hand, that our world is not a poor first attempt "of an infant deity who afterwards abandoned it, ashamed of his lame performance."

FAMOUS QUOTES

Aristotle (384–322 B.C.): "Man is by nature a political animal."

Francis Bacon (1561–1626): "Knowledge is power."

Jeremy Bentham (1748–1832): "The greatest happiness of the greatest number is the foundation of morals and legislation."

Confucius (551–479 B.C.): "Hold faithfulness and sincerity as first principles."

René Descartes (1596–1650): "Cogito, ergo sum" (Latin for "I think, therefore I am").

Ralph Waldo Emerson (1803–82): "Nature is a mutual cloud, which is always and never the same."

Friedrich Engels (1820–95): "The state is not 'abolished,' it withers away."

Georg Hegel (1770–1831): "What experience and history teach us is this—that people and governments have never learned anything from history, or acted on principles deduced from it."

Thomas Hobbes (1588–1679): "The life of a man (in a state of nature) is solitary, poor, nasty, brutish, and short."

Immanuel Kant (1724–1804): "Happiness is not an ideal of reason but of imagination."

John Locke (1632–1704): "No man's knowledge here can go beyond his experience."

Niccolò Machiavelli (1469–1527): "God is not willing to do everything, and thus take away our free will and that share of glory which belongs to us."

Karl Marx (1818–83): "The proletarians have nothing to lose (in this revolution) but their chains. They have a world to win. Workers of the world, unite!"
"Religion is the opium of the people."
"The class struggle necessarily leads to the dictatorship of the proletariat."

John Stuart Mill (1806–73): "Liberty consists in doing what one desires."

Friedrich Nietzsche (1844–1900): "I teach you the Superman. Man is something to be surpassed."

Thomas Paine (1737–1809): "Suspicion is the companion of mean souls, and the bane of all good society."

Plato (428–348 B.C.): "The life which is unexamined is not worth living."

Jean Jacques Rousseau (1712–78): "Man was born free, and everywhere he is in chains."

Bertrand Russell (1872–1970): "It is undesirable to believe a proposition when there is no ground whatever for supposing it true."

Seneca (c. 4 B.C.–A.D. 65): "Even while they teach, men learn."

Socrates (c. 470–399 B.C.): "There is only one good, knowledge, and one evil, ignorance."

Voltaire (1694–1778): "If God did not exist, it would be necessary to invent Him."

HOW TO ARGUE LOGICALLY

We like to think that we speak logically all the time, but we are aware that we sometimes use illogical means to persuade others of our point of view. In the heat of an impassioned argument, or when we are afraid our disputant has a stronger case, or when we don't quite have all the facts we'd like to have, we are prone to engage in faulty processes of reasoning, using arguments we hope will appear sound.

Such defective arguments are called *fallacies* by philosophers who, starting with Aristotle, have catalogued and classified these fallacious arguments. There are now over 125 separate fallacies, most with their own impressive-sounding names, many of them in Latin.

Some arguments have easily recognizable defects. For instance, in the *argument ad hominem*, a person's views are criticized because of a logically irrelevant personal defect: "You can't take Smith's advice on the stock market; he's a known philanderer." In the *genetic fallacy*, something is mistakenly reduced to its origins: "We know that emotions are nothing more than physiology; after all, medical research has shown emotions involve the secretion of hormones." Another illogical argument is named for the erroneous thinking a wagering person may fall prey to, the *gambler's fallacy* (also called the *Monte Carlo fallacy*): "I'm betting on heads; it's got to come up since we've just had nine straight tails."

Some fallacies may not be recognized as erroneous reasoning because they are such commonly used forms of argument. For instance, if we say, "I'm sure my cold is due to the weather; I started sneezing right after it went from 60 degrees to 31 degrees in three hours," we are committing the fallacy with the Latin name of *post hoc ergo propter hoc* ("after this, therefore because of this"). Many a political argument exemplifies the fallacy of *arguing in a circle*; for instance: "Only wealthy men are capable of leading the country; after all, leadership can be learned only if you have had money to exercise power." Many prejudicial or stereotypical arguments commit the *fallacy of division*, or of applying to the part what may be true of the whole: "North Dakota has wide-open spaces; since Jack's farm is there, it must be quite large." The converse of this is the *fallacy of composition*, where properties of the parts are erroneously attributed to the whole: "Every apple on this tree is rotten; therefore, the tree itself is hopelessly diseased."

It may be a surprise to realize that some widely accepted forms of argument are just as fallacious as the most logically defective reasoning. When we appeal to the beliefs or behavior of the majority to prove the truth of something, we are committing the *fallacy of consensus gentium*: "Imbibing alcohol cannot be bad for people, since all cultures studied have used alcohol." Or consider the person who argues that "Tragedy is the highest form of literature; after all, didn't Aristotle consider it such?" This is a form of the *fallacy of arguing from authority*. There is also the *fallacy of ignoratio elenchus*, which has nothing to do with ignorance; its name means that the point made is irrelevant to the issue at hand, as in the untenable view of a lawyer who says, "Ladies and gentlemen of the jury, you cannot convict my client of manslaughter while driving under the influence; after all, advertisements for alcohol exist everywhere in our culture."

MORE THAN JUST PHILOSOPHERS

Before knowledge was as specialized as it is today, many of the greatest philosophers followed their other interests while creating or studying philosophical systems. They did groundbreaking work in areas as far afield from philosophy proper as geometry, zoology, literary criticism, and calculus.

Perhaps Aristotle was the model for some of these thinkers, since he was regarded not only in his own time but throughout most of the Middle Ages as a universal genius whose knowledge on any subject he had written on could hardly be questioned. His nonphilosophical writings were astonishingly broad; even a partial list of his subjects, which include physics, zoology, botany, sociology, political theory, and economics, is testimony to one of the greatest minds of all time.

Even medicine and the law were not too far afield for some of the great philosophers. Avicenna, Averroes, and John Locke were trained in medicine; Avicenna's *Canon of Medicine* was the most influential medieval medical treatise. And Jeremy Bentham, a founder of utilitarianism, was one of the most influential jurists and lawyers of the nineteenth century; his work deeply influenced reform of the British penal, judicial, and parliamentary systems.

History, too, is a philosopher's domain. *History of England*, not his philosophy books, brought David Hume success and renown in mid-eighteenth-century England.

Both mathematics and logic were fruitfully developed by philosophers when they were not writing philosophical works. Leibniz is the co-inventor of calculus, along with Sir Isaac Newton;

Pascal is one of the fathers of the modern theory of probability; and Descartes invented analytical geometry almost single-handedly.

Logic, although now a separate discipline, was a part of philosophy until a hundred years ago. Aristotle was the founder of logic, but many other philosophers have invented or organized entire sections of the field. Mill formulated the "rules" of scientific experimentation that are now called Mill's methods; and Russell and Whitehead wrote *Principia Mathematica*, probably the most important work in modern logic.

The list of philosophers engaged in other fields is seemingly endless. Examples include Nietzsche, whose *On the Birth of Tragedy* is a classic in Greek studies and literary criticism; William James, whose *Principles of Psychology* deeply influenced decades of thinking in that field; and John Dewey, the father of the American progressive education movement.

Additional Sources of Information

Organizations and Services

The Philosophy Documentation Center is a key source of information. Its publications include U.S. and international directories of philosophers and *The Philosopher's Index*, a bibliographic journal and a series of cumulative bibliographies dating to 1940, arranged by author and subject.

Philosophy Documentation Center
Bowling Green State University
Bowling Green, OH 43403

Books

Copleston, Frederick C. *History of Philosophy.* 9 vols. Doubleday, 1985.

deGeorge, Richard T. *The Philosopher's Guide to Sources, Research Tools, Professional Life, and Related Fields.* Regents Press of Kansas, 1980.

Durant, Will. *The Story of Philosophy.* Washington Square Press, 1969.

Edwards, Paul, ed. *The Encyclopedia of Philosophy.* 4 vols. Free Press, 1973.

Ferm, Vergilius. *A History of Philosophical Systems.* Philosophical Library, 1950.

Lacey, A. R. *A Dictionary of Philosophy.* Routledge, Chapman & Hall, 1976.

Magill, Frank N., ed. *Masterpieces of World Philosophy in Summary Form.* Harper & Brothers, 1961.

O'Connor, D. J. *A Critical History of Western Philosophy.* Free Press, 1985.

Reese, William L., ed. *Dictionary of Philosophy and Religion: Eastern and Western Thought.* Humanities Press, 1980.

Runes, Dagobert D., ed. *Dictionary of Philosophy.* Rowman & Allanhead, 1984.

Urmson, James O. *A Concise Encyclopedia of Western Philosophy and Philosophers.* Hutchinson, 1975.

Weiner, Philip P., ed. *Dictionary of the History of Ideas: Studies of Selected Pivotal Ideas.* 5 vols. Scribner's, 1985.

The Libraries and Museums

Major Libraries of the United States and Canada and Their Special Collections

United States

Arizona

University of Arizona Library
Tuscon, AZ 85721
602-621-2101

Established in 1891, the University of Arizona has more than 2.7 million volumes, with special collections on photography as an art form, fine arts, drama, private presses, Southwestern Americana, Arizona, science history, science fiction, and Mexican colonial history.

California

Los Angeles County Public Library System
7400 East Imperial Highways
Downey, CA 90241
213-922-8131

Founded in 1912, this library system contains more than 5.1 million volumes, with special collections on Afro-American studies, Asian-Pacific studies, California, multimedia, mountaineering, Hispanic-Americans, Native Americans, and poetry. The collection is dispersed among 114 community, mobile, and institutional libraries.

Los Angeles Public Library System
630 West 5th Street
Los Angeles, CA 90071
213-612-3200

Founded in 1872, this public library system has 62 branches with more than 5.3 million volumes. Its special collections are on California studies, children's literature, cooking, genealogy, North American Indians studies, modern languages, orchestral scores, U.S. patents, and standards and specifications.

Stanford University Libraries
Stanford, CA 94305
415-723-9108

Founded in 1892, Stanford's libraries contain 5.4 million volumes. Its special collections cover transportation, music, science, California, Irish literature, engineering mechanics, children's literature, Chicano studies, theater, and Hebraica and Judaica.

University of California Los Angeles Library
405 Hilgard Avenue
Los Angeles, CA 90024
213-825-1201

Founded in 1919, the University of California Los Angeles Library has holdings of more than 5.4 million books. It has special collections on British Commonwealth history, contemporary Western writers, early English children's books, folklore, Latin American studies, Mazarinades, mountaineering, and Western Americana.

University of Southern California
Edward L. Doheny Memorial Library
University Park
Los Angeles, CA 90089
213-743-2543

Founded in 1880, the University of Southern California has more than 2.4 million volumes, with a number of independent departmental libraries whose subject matter ranges from architecture and fine arts to gerontology. Its special collections include American-Indian ethnopharmacology, American literature, cinema, dentistry, international relations, Latin American studies, and philosophy.

Colorado

University of Colorado, Boulder
University Libraries Campus Box 184
Boulder, CA 80309
303-492-7511

Founded in 1876, the University of Colorado maintains holdings of more than 2 million volumes, with special collections on juvenile literature, the history of silver, mountaineering, and Western U.S. history.

Connecticut

Yale University Library
120 High Street
P.O. Box 1603A, Yale Station
New Haven, CT 06520
203-432-1775

The second largest university library in the United States, Yale has 8.8 million volumes in its collection.

Its rare books total more than 500,000. Yale's special collections are numerous; they include works by James Boswell, the Aaron Burr family, Daniel Defoe, John Dryden, James Joyce, D. H. Lawrence, the Lindbergh family, Marcus Aurelius, H. L. Mencken, Napoleon, Mark Twain, and Edith Wharton. The *American Library Directory* lists more than 50 subjects of special strength for Yale, including Babylonian tablets, futurism, legal thought, playing cards, sporting books, urban and regional planning, and Western Americana. Founded in 1701.

District of Columbia

The Library of Congress
Washington, DC 20540
202-287-5000

The nation's largest single library, the Library of Congress, established in 1800, contains over 80 million items, including about 20 million books and pamphlets. Its collections include over 1 million volumes on Hispanic and Portuguese culture and the largest collection of Russian literature outside the Soviet Union. Special collections include books for the blind and physically handicapped, cartography, folk music, law books, manuscripts, microforms, motion pictures, music, the Orient, prints and photographs, and more than half a million rare books. The library's first priority is service to the Congress of the United States. It also registers creative work for copyright and provides services to both the public and libraries throughout the country.

Florida

University of Florida Libraries
210 Library West
Gainesville, FL 32611
904-392-0341

Founded in 1905, this system contains more than 2.5 million volumes, with special collections on Florida history, Latin America, Judaica, aerial photographs, coastal engineering, New England literature, Brazilian law, and Florida newspapers.

Georgia

University of Georgia Libraries
Athens, GA 30602
404-542-2716

Founded in 1800, this library system contains more than 2.4 million volumes, with special collections on music, theater, Georgia, Confederate imprints, Georgia authors, nineteenth- and twentieth-century politics, and Georgia newspapers.

Hawaii

Hawaii State Library System
Office of Library Services
Department of Education
Kekuannoa Building, Room B-1, 465 South King Street
Honolulu, HI 96813
808-548-5596

Founded in 1852, Hawaii's libraries contain more than 2.1 million volumes, with a special collection devoted to Hawaiian history.

Illinois

Chicago Public Library
425 North Michigan Avenue
Chicago, IL 60611
312-269-2900

Founded in 1872, Chicago's libraries offer more than 4.3 million volumes with special collections of national, U.S., foreign, and trade bibliographies; Chicago information; foreign language encyclopedias; Abraham Lincoln papers; miniature books; early American newspapers; and World War I and II posters.

Northwestern University Library
1935 Sheridan Road
Evanston, IL 60201
312-491-7658

Founded in 1856, Northwestern holds more than 2.4 million volumes and bound periodicals, with special collections on Africa, architecture, contemporary music scores, feminism, German classics, Italian futurism, manuscripts, and printing.

University of Chicago
Joseph Regenstein Library
1100 East 57th Street
Chicago, IL 60637
312-962-7874

The University of Chicago, founded in 1891, contains more than 4.6 million volumes. It maintains special collections of English Bibles, Lincolniana, modern poetry, anatomical illustrations, and Kentucky and Ohio River Valley history; children's books; early theology and Bible criticism; German fiction, 1790–1850; and books on ophthalmology.

University of Illinois Library at Urbana–Champaign
1408 West Gregory Drive
Urbana, IL 61801
217-333-0790

This library's collection includes more than 7 million volumes, with special collections on American humor and folklore, freedom of expression, sixteenth- and seventeenth-century Italian drama, nineteenth-century publishing, Carl Sandburg, and H.G. Wells. Founded 1868.

Indiana

Indiana University at Bloomington
Tenth Street and Jordan Avenue
Bloomington, IN 47405
812-335-3403

Founded in 1824, Indiana University has amassed a collection of more than 4.2 million volumes, with special collections of English and American literature, nineteenth-century British plays, English history, scientific and medical history, the works of Aristotle, and nineteenth-century French opera.

Iowa

University of Iowa Libraries
Iowa City, IA 52242
319-353-4450

Established in 1855, Iowa's libraries contain more than 2.5 million volumes, with special collections on Leigh Hunt and his friends, Abraham Lincoln, American Indians, Iowa authors, typography, the Union Pacific Railroad, editorial cartoons, the French Revolution, and the history of medicine.

Kansas

University of Kansas Libraries
Watson Library
Lawrence, KS 66045
913-864-3347

Established in 1866, Kansas' libraries contain in excess of 2.4 million volumes, with special collections on Anglo-Saxons, botany, children's books, Chinese classics, Colombia, the Continental Renaissance, economics, historical cartography, Irish history and literature, Kansas history, poetry, opera, ornithology, sound recordings, travel, and women.

Maryland

Enoch Pratt Free Library
400 Cathedral Street
Baltimore, MD 21201
301-396-5430

Founded in 1886, Enoch Pratt's 1.9-million-volume collection has a special H.L. Mencken section and a Maryland history collection.

Johns Hopkins University
Milton S. Eisenhower Library
Baltimore, MD 21218
301-338-8000

Established in 1876, Johns Hopkins has more than 2.4 million volumes, with special collections on economics, Lord Byron, French drama, modern German drama, German literature, sheet music, slavery, and trade unions.

Massachusetts

Boston Public Library and Eastern Massachusetts Regional Public Library System
Copley Square
Boston, MA 02117
617-536-5400

Founded in 1852, the Boston library system is believed to be the oldest free municipal library system supported by taxation anywhere in the world. It has 4.1 million volumes, with the following special collections: the library of John Quincy Adams; military science, history, and the Civil War; astronomy, mathematics, and navigation; Robert and Elizabeth Browning; Daniel Defoe; drama; genealogy; government documents; heraldry; music; patents; Christian Science; the Sacco-Vanzetti papers; Walt Whitman; and World War I.

Harvard University Library
Cambridge, MA 02138
617-495-3650

With more than 11 million volumes, the Harvard Library, founded in 1638, is the largest university library in the United States. Its special collections are numerous. They include the Trotsky archive; the Theodore Roosevelt collection; and works by such authors as Dante, T. S. Eliot, Faulkner, Goethe, Kipling, Longfellow, Milton, Petrarch, Rousseau, Shakespeare, Steinbeck, and Thomas Wolfe. Some of its branches are located outside of Massachusetts, such as the Harvard Library in New York and the Dumbarton Oaks Research Library and Collection in Washington, DC. Others specialize in topics ranging from music to divinity and include Harvard's famed law library and the fine arts library at the Fogg Art Museum.

Massachusetts Institute of Technology (MIT) Libraries
Room 14S-216
Cambridge, MA 02139
617-253-5651

Founded in 1862, MIT's library holdings total approximately 2 million volumes, with special collections devoted to the early history of aeronautics, architecture and planning, civil engineering, nineteenth-century U.S. glass manufacturers, early works in mathematics and physics, shipbuilding and naval history, and spectroscopy.

University of Massachusetts at Amherst Library
Amherst, MA 01003
508-545-0284

Founded in 1865, this university system maintains holdings in excess of 2 million volumes, with special collections on slavery and antislavery pamphlets; county atlases of New England, New York, and New Jersey; and the French Revolution.

Michigan

Detroit Public Library
5201 Woodward Avenue
Detroit, MI 48202
313-833-1000

Founded in 1865, Detroit's library contains more than 2.5 million volumes, with special collections on automotive history, labor history, and black music, dance, and drama.

Michigan State University Library
East Lansing, MI 48824
517-355-2344

Established in 1855, Michigan State has holdings of more than 3 million volumes, with special collections on American popular culture, American radical history, apiculture, cookery, criminology, fencing, illuminated manuscripts in fascimile, natural science, and veterinary history.

Wayne State University Libraries
Detroit, MI 48202
313-577-4020

Wayne State has more than 2 million volumes, with special collections on nineteenth-century Spanish history, social studies, women and the law, law, and children and young people.

Minnesota

University of Minnesota Libraries–Twin Cities
499 O. Meredith Wilson Library
309 19th Avenue South
Minneapolis, MN 55455
612-373-3097

Founded in 1851, this university system contains more than 3.6 million volumes, with special collections on American and English literature, the history of quantum physics, ballooning, dime novels, information processing, Sherlock Holmes, children's literature, performing arts, private presses, August Strindberg, and the history of biology and medicine.

Missouri

Kansas City Public Library
311 East 12th Street
Kansas City, MO 64106
816-221-2685

Founded in 1873, this library's collection numbers more than 2 million volumes, with special collections on black history and Missouri Valley history and genealogy.

University of Missouri-Columbia
Elmer Ellis Library
Columbia, MO 65201
314-882-4701

Established in 1839, this library holds more than 2.2 million volumes, with special collections devoted to American bestsellers, criminal law, philosophy, World War I and II posters, cartoons, and Fourth of July orations.

Washington University Libraries
Skinker and Lindell Boulevards
St. Louis, MO 63130
314-889-5400

Founded in 1853, this system maintains more than 2 million volumes, with special collections on German language and literature, Romance languages and literature, classical archeology and numismatics, architecture, musicology, history of the Russian Revolution and the Soviet Union, American and New York Stock Exchange reports, printing, and early history of communications-semantics.

New Jersey

Princeton University Library
Princeton, NJ 08540
609-452-3180

Founded as the College of New Jersey, Elizabeth, in 1746, the library's principal building is the Harvey S. Firestone Memorial Library, constructed in 1948. Princeton has approximately 4 million volumes, with special collections devoted to the Brontës, Disraeli, aeronautics, American historical manuscripts, chess, civil rights, coins, Emily Dickinson, emblem books, fishing and angling, graphic arts, Mormon history, mountaineering, papyrus manuscripts, publishing, sports, women, and famous individuals.

Rutgers, The State University of New Jersey
University Libraries
169 College Avenue
New Brunswick, NJ 08903
201-932-7505

Established in 1766, this venerable library contains more than 2.2 million volumes. It has a special collection of New Jersey public-sector collective bargaining contracts.

New York

Brooklyn Public Library System
Grand Army Plaza
Brooklyn, NY 11238
718-780-7700

Founded in 1896 and consolidated with the Brooklyn Library in 1902, the library system now has 58 branches with a total of more than 4.1 million books.

Special collections cover Brooklyn history, chess and checkers, the Civil War, costumes, fire protection, and Walt Whitman.

Columbia University
University Libraries
535 West 114th Street
New York, NY 10027
212-280-2271

Founded in 1761, Columbia offers more than 5.4 million volumes, with special collections on anatomy, architecture, cancer research, fine arts, physiology, and plastic surgery.

Cornell University Libraries
Ithaca, NY 14853
607-255-4144

With approximately 5 million volumes, the Cornell libraries include special collections on Southeast Asia, civil engineering, medical dissertations, field recordings, early sixteenth-century music, beekeeping, food and beverages, and labor history.

New York Public Library
Fifth Avenue at 42nd Street
New York, NY 10018
212-930-0800

Established in 1895 by the consolidation of the Astor and Lenox libraries and the Tilden Trust, the New York Public Library contains more than 30 million catalogued items: books, manuscripts, microfilm, prints, maps, recordings, photographs, and sheet music. It has special collections on black history and culture, performing arts, English and American literature, bindings and illustrated books, Japanese prints, tobacco, early Bibles including the Gutenberg, voyages and travels, and Jewish, Oriental, Slavonic, and local history and genealogy. The Library's 82 branches have 3.2 million circulating volumes and 5 million nonbook items.

New York State Library
State Department of Education, Cultural Education Center
Empire State Paza
Albany, NY 12230
518-474-5930

Founded in 1818, New York State's library contains more than 1.9 million volumes, with special collections on Dutch colonial records, New York State political and social history, and the Shakers.

New York University
Elmer Holmes Bobst Library
70 Washington Square South
New York, NY 10012
212-598-2484

Established in 1831, New York University's holdings total approximately 2 million volumes, with special

collections on Lewis Carroll, Robert Frost, rare Judaica and Hebraica, mathematics, and the history of dentistry.

Queens Borough Public Library System
8911 Merrick Boulevard
Jamaica, NY 11432
718-990-0700

Organized in 1896, this library system contains more than 4.6 million volumes and has 59 branches. It maintains special collections of Long Island history and genealogy and a collection of over 1.5 million pictures.

State University of New York at Buffalo
University Libraries
432 Capen Hall
Buffalo, NY 14260
716-636-2965

Founded in 1922, the State University libraries hold more than 1.8 million volumes, with special collections of poetry, the works of J. Frank Dobie, New York State governors' autographs, and books on science and engineering and the history of medicine.

Syracuse University Libraries
E.S. Bird Library
222 Waverly Avenue
Syracuse, NY 13244
315-423-2573

Established in 1871, Syracuse University has holdings of more than 1.3 million volumes, with special collections on Stephen Crane, Loyalists in the American Revolution, economic history, Margaret Bourke-White, Rudyard Kipling, and cartoonists; science fiction books and manuscripts; and the papers of Averell Harriman, Dorothy Thompson, and Benjamin Spock.

University of Rochester
Rush Rhees Library
Rochester, NY 14627
716-275-4461

Founded in 1850, the Rochester library's holdings include more than 2 million volumes, with special collections on nineteenth- and twentieth-century public affairs, nineteenth-century botany and horticulture, American literature, regional history, and Leonardo da Vinci.

North Carolina

Duke University
William R. Perkins Library
Durham, NC 27706
919-684-2034

Founded in 1838, Duke's library contains more than 2.9 million volumes, with special collections on American almanacs, architecture, city directories,

Samuel Taylor Coleridge, Confederate imprints, Ralpho Waldo Emerson, Latin American history, manuscripts, the Methodist Church, newspapers, the Philippines, utopias, and Wesleyana.

University of North Carolina at Chapel Hill
Walter Royal Davis Library
Chapel Hill, NC 27514
919-962-1301

Founded in 1795, North Carolina's library contains more than 3.1 million volumes, with special collections on North Carolina and Southern history.

Ohio

Cleveland Public Library
325 Superior Avenue
Cleveland, OH 44114
216-623-2800

Founded in 1869, the Cleveland Public Library contains 2.5 million volumes. Its special collections are devoted to folklore, the Orient, and chess.

Ohio State University Libraries
William Oxley Thompson Memorial Library
1858 Neil Avenue Mall
Columbus, OH 43210
614-422-6151

Established in 1873, Ohio State offers approximately 4 million volumes and bound periodicals. Special collections include those on the American Association of Editorial Cartoonists, American fiction to 1925, American sheet music, Australia, daguerreotypes and ambrotypes, dance notation, Reformation history, and science fiction magazines.

Public Library of Cincinnati and Hamilton County
800 Vine Street
Library Square
Cincinnati, OH 45202
513-369-6900

Founded in 1853, Cincinnati's library has more than 3.5 million volumes, with 139,337 maps and special collections on local history, genealogy, theology, art, music, theater, and oral history.

Oklahoma

University of Oklahoma
University Libraries
410 West Brooks
Norman, OK 73019
405-325-2611

Founded in 1895, the University of Oklahoma's library holds more than 2.2 million volumes, with special collections devoted to early science, Western history, Indian papers, political speeches, theater, film, and dance.

Pennsylvania

Carnegie Library of Pittsburgh
4400 Forbes Avenue
Pittsburgh, PA 15213
412-622-3100

Founded in 1895, the Carnegie Library collection contains more than 2.4 million volumes, with approximately 69,000 in foreign languages. It maintains special collections on architecture and design, the Atomic Energy Commission, cartoons, local history, U.S. patents, World War I, and nineteenth-century American and German music journals.

Free Library of Philadelphia
Logan Square
Philadelphia, PA 19103
215-686-5322

Founded in 1891, the Free Library contains 3.1 million volumes, with special collections on orchestral music, common law, automobile history, Americana, cuneiform tablets, Charles Dickens, Edgar Allan Poe, Beatrix Potter, Arthur Rackham, theater, and maps (including over 130,000 single-sheet maps, atlases, and geographies).

Pennsylvania State University
Fred Lewis Pattee Library
University Park, PA 16802
814-865-0401

Established in 1857, Penn State's library has approximately 2 million volumes, with special collections on American sociology, anthropology, art, architecture, Australia, Bibles, black literature, the Columbus family papers, English literature, photography, Pennsylvania, science fiction, Surrealism, and the United Steelworkers of America.

University of Pennsylvania Libraries
Van Pelt Library
3420 Walnut Street-CH
Philadelphia, PA 19104
215-898-7091

Founded in 1749, the University of Pennsylvania's libraries hold more than 3.2 million volumes, with special collections on church history, the Spanish Inquisition, canon law, witchcraft, Shakespeare, alchemy and chemistry, Aristotle, Bibles, Jonathan Swift, Sanskrit manuscripts, Theodore Dreiser, Washington Irving, and the Spanish Golden Age of literature, as well as Benjamin Franklin imprints.

University of Pittsburgh
University Libraries
Pittsburgh, PA 15260
412-624-4437

Founded in 1873, the University of Pittsburgh has holdings of more than 2.5 million volumes, with special collections on ballet, nineteenth- and twentieth-century American and English theater, popular culture, early history and travel, children's literature, Mr. Rogers' Neighborhood videos, and ethnic organizations.

South Carolina

University of South Carolina
Thomas Cooper Library
Columbia, SC 29208
803-777-3142

Founded in 1801, South Carolina's system contains more than 1.8 million volumes, with special collections on archeology, ornithology, aerial photography, and rare medical books.

Texas

Dallas Public Library
1515 Young Street
Dallas, TX 75201
214-749-4100

Founded in 1901, Dallas' library contains over 3 million volumes. Special collections cover business histories, children's literature, classical literature, classical recordings, Dallas black history, diaries and manuscripts on dance, fashion, genealogy, grants, printing, and Texas.

Houston Public Library
500 McKinney Avenue
Houston, TX 77002
713-224-5441

Founded in 1901, the Houston Public Library has more than 3.1 million volumes, with special collections of Bibles; books on the Civil War, genealogy, Texas, and petroleum; Salvation Army posters; early Houston photographs; early printing and illuminated manuscripts; juvenile literature; and sheet music.

University of Texas Libraries
Box P
Austin, TX 78713
512-471-3811

Founded in 1883, this university library system serves a student body of more than 46,000. With more than 5.5 million volumes, its holdings are divided among individual libraries devoted to Asia; film; the Middle East; Latin America; public affairs; architecture and planning; chemistry; classics; engineering; fine arts; geology; physics, math, and astronomy; science; business research; humanities; population research; and law. Its special collections cover Southern history, Canada, British Commonwealth literature, the U.S. Volleyball Association, and oral histories.

Utah

University of Utah
Marriott Library
Salt Lake City, UT 84112
801-581-8558

Founded in 1850, Utah's library contains in excess of 2 million volumes, with special collections on the Middle East, Western Americana, and the history of medicine.

Virginia

University of Virginia
Alderman Library
Charlottesville, VA 22903
804-924-3026

Established in 1819, Virginia's library holds more than 2.6 million volumes, with special collections devoted to American literature, the American Revolution, Americana, the Civil War and Reconstruction, political cartoons, Ceylon, classical studies, Stephen Crane, Oliver Cromwell, John Dos Passos, evolution, William Faulkner, finance, Rober Frost, Gothic novels, Bret Harte, Nathaniel Hawthorne, international law, Washington Irving, Thomas Jefferson, modern art, Mark Twain, typography and printing, Virginia, voyages and travels, and Walt Whitman.

Washington

University of Washington Libraries
FM-25
Seattle, WA 98195
206-543-9153

Founded in 1862, this university's holdings exceed 4.3 million volumes, with special collections devoted to East Asia, fisheries, forest resources, oceanography, and the Pacific Northwest.

Wisconsin

Milwaukee Public Library
814 West Wisconsin Avenue
Milwaukee, WI 53233
414-278-3000

Founded in 1878, the Milwaukee Public Library has more than 2.3 million volumes, with special collections on the Great Lakes, H. G. Wells, British and American authors, genealogy, and cookbooks.

University of Wisconsin–Madison
Memorial Library
728 State Street
Madison, WI 53706
608-262-3521

The University of Wisconsin has amassed a collection of more than 4.5 million volumes since its founding in 1850. Special collections include those on alchemy, American gifts, book plates, Brazilian positivism, Buddhism, children's literature, C. S. Lewis' letters, Calvinist theology and Dutch history, chess, early American women authors, history of chemistry, medieval history, Mexican pamphlets, Polish literature and history, Tibetan studies, Mark Twain, and Welsh theology.

Canada

Alberta

University of Alberta
University Library
Edmonton, Alberta T6G 2J8
403-432-3790

Established in 1909, Alberta's university system contains more than 2.8 million volumes, with special collections on literature, South American and North American Indians, Victorian book arts, western Canada, and theology and canon law.

Ontario

University of Toronto Library System
Toronto, Ontario M5S 1A5
416-978-2282

Founded in 1827, the University of Toronto has holdings of more than 6.3 million volumes, with extensive sections of sheet music, films, slides, maps, and photographs. Its special collections include those on Shakespeare, the history of science, Darwin, Victorian natural history, ornithology, medical and related sciences, Italian plays, juvenile drama, Canada, and Canadian authors.

British Columbia

University of British Columbia Library
1956 Main Mall
Vancouver, British Columbia V6T 1Y3
604-228-3871

Established in 1915, British Columbia's library holds more than 2.4 million volumes, with special collections on Pacific Northwest history, Canada, the Orient, the history of science, English literature, and Canadian and Japanese maps.

Quebec

McGill University Libraries
3459 McTavish Street
Montreal, Quebec H3A 1Y1
514-392-4948

Founded in 1821, this university system serves an enrollment of about 24,000 students and has holdings of 1.3 million volumes. Its special collections cover architecture, William Blake, Canada, entomology, early geology, the history of science and medicine, natural history and ornithology, printing, Shakespeare, and sixteenth- and seventeenth-century tracts.

Major Museums of the United States and Canada and Their Special Collections

United States

Arizona

Arizona State University Art Collections
Matthews Center, Arizona State University
Tempe, AZ 85287
602-965-2874

Founded in 1950, Arizona State's collection includes American paintings of the eighteenth and nineteenth centuries; a fine print collection with Rembrandts, Whistlers, and Dürers; fine Americana and decorative arts, particularly pottery; European painting and sculpture; Latin American arts; and crafts.

California

California Palace of the Legion of Honor
Lincoln Park
San Francisco, CA 94121
415-221-4811

The Fine Arts Museums of San Francisco
M.H. deYoung Museum
Golden Gate Park
San Francisco, CA 94118
415-558-2887

These museums are run by a joint administration, although they are not located near each other. Founded in 1924 and 1895, respectively, each museum has extensive collections. The deYoung includes the Hearst collection of Flemish Gothic tapestries; fine primitive pre-Columbian artifacts; Northwest Coast Indian, African, and Oceanic arts collections; and Renaissance and Baroque art. The California Palace is noted for its eighteenth-century French furniture and decorative arts; its French paintings, including those of Monet, Renoir, Fragonard, Boucher, Manet, and Corot; Rodin sculptures; and an extraordinary collection of prints and drawings of all periods.

J. Paul Getty Museum
17985 Pacific Coast Highway,
Malibu, CA 90265
213-459-2306

The world's best-endowed museum, the Getty was created in 1953. This popular museum is housed in a re-creation of the first-century B.C. Villa dei Paryri at Herculaneum, complete with elaborate gardens. The Getty has acquired extraordinary classical collections, including illuminated manuscripts and French decorative arts.

Huntington Library, Art Gallery, and Botanical Garden
1151 Oxford Road
San Marino, CA 91108
818-405-2100

In the Huntington complex, established in 1919, a beautiful garden setting enhances the extraordinary collections of eighteenth-century British paintings, including Gainsborough's *Blue Boy* and Lawrence's *Pinkie*; Renaissance bronzes and eighteenth-century marbles; early editions of Shakespeare and Chaucer in the extensive library; and prints and drawings. The setting includes a Japanese garden and sixteenth-century samurai's house.

Los Angeles County Museum of Art
5905 Wilshire Boulevard
Los Angeles, CA 90036
213-857-6111

Established in 1910, this museum houses a general collection in three pavilions surrounded by a sculpture garden with works from Rodin's time to the present. Its acquisitions include early Near and Middle Eastern antiquities; Roman, Greek, Western, and modern art; Far Eastern collections; textiles; costumes; Indian arts; pottery; Italian mosaics; pre-Columbian, African, and Oceanic arts; and nineteenth- and twentieth-century American and European paintings.

Norton Simon Museum
Colorado and Orange Grove Boulevards
Pasadena, CA 91106
213-449-6840

Established in 1924 as the Pasadena Museum of Modern Art, this museum has developed worldwide prominence through the loans of collector Norton Simon. His collections include European art from the Renaissance to recent times, with Old Masters of the highest quality.

Colorado

The Denver Art Museum
100 West 14th Avenue Parkway
Denver, CO 80204
303-575-2793

The Denver Art Museum is noted for its collection of primitive African, Oceanic, American, Native American, and Northwest Indian arts; its Peruvian art;

its collection of the arts of China, Japan, Korea, India, Southeast Asia, Tibet, and the Middle and Near East; period rooms; Impressionist, Post-Impressionist, and modern paintings; prints, drawings, and photographs; and the Neusteter Institute of Fashion, Costume, and Textiles.

Connecticut

The New Britain Museum of American Art
56 Lexington Street
New Britain, CT 06052
203-229-0257

The New Britain collection, established in 1903, focuses on outstanding American paintings from colonial times to the present. It includes Hudson River School painters and the Low memorial collection of American illustration, with N. C. Wyeth classics.

Yale Center for British Art
1080 Chapel Street
Box 2120
New Haven, CT 06520
203-432-4594

This collection of British watercolors, drawings, paintings, books, and prints is the largest of its kind outside of Great Britain. Established in 1977, the center was the gift of Paul Mellon, a lifelong collector of British art.

Yale University Art Gallery
1111 Chapel Street
New Haven, CT 06520
203-436-0574

This outstanding world art collection has been built up since the gallery's founding in 1832. It includes the Jarves collection of early Italian paintings; collections of American silver, painting, and decorative arts; modern art; Greek and Roman vases; manuscripts; prints and drawings; and primitive arts.

Delaware

Delaware Art Museum
2301 Kentmere Parkway
Wilmington, DE 19806
302-571-9590

The Delaware Art Museum, founded in 1912, specializes in American paintings, with examples by Hudson River School painters such as John Sloan, Howard Pyle, and the Wyeth family. There is an extensive collection of English Pre-Raphaelites; a research library on American arts; and prints and drawings.

Henry Francis Du Pont Winterthur Museum
Kennett Pike (Route 52)
Winterthur, DE 19735
302-888-4600

Founded in 1930, Winterthur has an outstanding collection of American furniture, furnishings, and decorative arts from the colonial period to the mid-nineteenth century. Period rooms display extensive collections of ceramics, glass, Chinese porcelain, fabrics, lighting fixtures, and carpets.

District of Columbia

Freer Gallery of Art, Smithsonian Institution
12th Street and Jefferson Drive, SW
Washington, DC 20560
202-357-2104

Established in 1906, the Freer has one of the world's best collections of Oriental art and a comprehensive collection of Whistler paintings (his close friend Charles Freer gathered the collection and donated it).

Hirshhorn Museum and Sculpture Garden, Smithsonian Institution
Independence Avenue at 8th Street, SW
Washington, DC 20560
202-357-3091

Created in 1966 to specialize in modern art, the Hirshhorn's collection is so vast that only a small portion can be displayed at any time.

National Air and Space Museum, Smithsonian Institution
Sixth Street and Independence Avenue, SW
Washington, DC 20560
203-357-2700

Founded in 1946, this museum houses a definitive collection of aeronautical and astronautical items; air and space craft; and instruments, equipment, art, uniforms, and personal memorabilia related to air and space.

National Gallery of Art
Constitution Avenue and 4th Street, NW
Washington, DC 20565
202-737-4215

The National Gallery was endowed by Andrew Mellon in 1937 and continues to benefit from his children's donations. It includes paintings and sculptures of all schools of Western art, decorative arts, and drawings and prints, with all the classic masters represented.

National Museum of American Art, The Smithsonian Institution
8th and G Streets, NW
Washington, DC 20560
202-357-3176

Housed in the historic Greek Revival Old Patent Office, the museum has a definitive collection of American arts, including graphic and decorative arts, from colonial times to the present.

Hawaii

Honolulu Academy of Arts
900 South Beretania Street
Honolulu, HI 96814
808-538-3693

The academy, founded in 1927, has a general collection representing everything from ancient Near Eastern and Mediterranean arts to European and American arts. Medieval art, the Michener collection of Japanese prints, Monet's *Water Lilies,* and the arts of Africa, Oceania, and the Americas are also included.

Illinois

The Art Institute of Chicago
Michigan Avenue at Adams Street
Chicago, IL 60603
312-443-3600

Founded in 1879, the Art Institute of Chicago has excellent collections in all areas of art. It is noted for the works of Old Masters, Impressionists, and American and Far Eastern artists; graphics; and Thorne miniature rooms. Famed works include Seurat's *Sunday Afternoon on the Island of la Grande Jatte,* Rembrandt's *Young Girl at an Open Half-Door,* and Mary Cassatt's *The Bath.*

The Field Museum of Natural History
Roosevelt Road at Lake Shore Drive
Chicago, IL 60605
312-922-9410

Founded in 1893, the Field Museum contains definitive collections on anatomy, anthropology, costumes, ethnology, geology, Indian artifacts, science, textiles, and zoology. Among its highlights are a full-scale replica of a Pawnee Earth Lodge and a herbarium.

**University of Chicago
Oriental Institute Museum**
1155 East 58th Street
Chicago, IL 60637
312-962-9520

Founded in 1919, the Oriental Institute houses a top collection of archeology and art of the ancient Near East, Babylonia, Egypt, early Christian cultures, and Islamic civilization.

Indiana

Indiana University Art Museum
Fine Arts Building
Bloomington, IN 47405
812-335-5445

This fine general collection, founded in 1941, includes everything from ancient to contemporary art, with Egyptian, Greek, and Roman sculpture; coins and glass; Western fine and decorative arts from the fourteenth to the twentieth centuries; and Far Eastern arts.

Indianapolis Museum of Art
1200 West 38th Street
Indianapolis, IN 46208
317-923-1331

Noted for its Chinese, primitive, and American art, this museum, founded in 1883, has an outstanding general collection of Old Masters, Turner watercolors, and European and American decorative arts.

Kansas

Wichita Art Museum
619 Stackman Drive
Wichita, KS 67203
316-268-4621

Established in 1935, this museum's outstanding collection ranges from art of the Old West by Charles M. Russell to Eakins' *Starting Out After Rail*. It is noted for its American paintings, sculptures, prints, and drawings.

Kentucky

J.B. Speed Art Museum
2035 South Third Street
Louisville, KY 40208
502-636-2893

This extensive collection, founded in 1925, includes European painting, sculpture, and decorative arts from the Middle Ages to the present; French and Flemish tapestries; and Kentuckiana.

Maryland

The Baltimore Museum of Art
Art Museum Drive
Baltimore, MD 21218
301-396-7101

Best known for its classic modern collections, this outstanding museum, established in 1914, displays contemporary drawings, period rooms illustrating stylistic development in Maryland, Old Masters paintings, and Far Eastern art.

Walters Art Gallery
600 North Charles Street
Baltimore, MD 21201
301-547-9000

Assembled by father and son, the Walters Art Gallery opened in 1931 with exquisite medieval treasures and Byzantine and Islamic art; early Christian liturgical vessels, Renaissance enamels, and jewelry; paintings from various periods; and Greek, Roman, and Etruscan art.

Massachusetts

Isabella Stewart Gardner Museum
280 The Fenway
Boston, MA 02115
617-566-1401

This personal collection, founded in 1900, covers a wide range of world art, with masterpieces such as Titian's *The Rape of Europa*, Giotto's *Presentation of the Child Jesus in the Temple*, and Botticelli's *Madonna of the Eucharist*.

Museum of Fine Arts
465 Huntington Avenue
Boston, MA 02115
617-267-9300

This collection, founded in 1870, includes masterpieces from around the world. It is noted for its Far Eastern, ancient, Egyptian, Greek, and Roman collections, as well as Old Masters, Impressionist, and Post-Impressionist works, and American paintings and decorative arts. It also has American silver, prints and drawings, ancient musical instruments, and ship models. Famed works include Paul Revere's Liberty Bowl, Renoir's *Le Bal à Bougival*, and a Greek marble *Head of Aphrodite*.

Fogg Art Museum
32 Quincy Street
Harvard University
Cambridge, MA 02138
617-495-7768

With the largest and most extensive art collection of any university in the United States, the Fogg, opened in 1895, is particularly noted for its drawings and prints of all periods. It also has a fine collection of Chinese sculptures, stones and bronzes, jades, and ceramics.

Old Sturbridge Village
Sturbridge, MA 01566
617-347-3362

Set up in 1938 as a living history museum, Old Sturbridge has a considerable collection of tools, crafts, arts and artifacts, decorative arts, and more than 100 period buildings of the eighteenth and nineteenth centuries.

Michigan

The Detroit Institute of Arts
5200 Woodward Avenue
Detroit, MI 48202
313-833-7900

Founded in 1885, this institute is renowned for its comprehensive collection of world arts, especially its Old Master paintings of Northern Europe, French eighteenth-century decorative arts, art of the ancient world, period rooms, prints and drawings, and American arts since colonial times.

Henry Ford Museum and Greenfield Village
20900 Oakwood Boulevard
Dearborn, MI 48121
313-271-1620

Described as a ''Disneyland of Americana,'' the indoor/outdoor facilities, established in 1929, of the museum and village offer demonstrations of crafts and manufacturing techniques that complement its extensive collections of arts, crafts, artifacts, and technology. Activities include everything from antique car rallies to country fairs on its 14 acres.

Minnesota

The Minneapolis Institute of Arts
2400 Third Avenue
South Minneapolis, MN 55404
612-870-3046

This outstanding general collection is strongest in European paintings from Old Masters to the present. Founded in 1912, the institute also houses the Pillsbury collection of Chinese bronzes, Japanese prints and paintings, textiles, and photographs.

New Jersey

The Art Museum
Princeton University
Princeton, NJ 08544
609-452-3788

Opened in 1882, this comprehensive collection contains a wide spectrum of world art, including Chinese paintings and bronzes, classical antiquities, and French paintings and sculptures.

New Mexico

The University of New Mexico Art Museum
Fine Arts Center
Albuquerque, NM 87131
505-277-4001

Established in 1963, the museum has important collections of nineteenth- and twentieth-century prints and photographs and American painting of the twentieth century, with emphasis on artists who worked in New Mexico.

New York

Albany Institute of History and Art
125 Washington Avenue
Albany, NY 12210
518-463-4478

Founded in 1791, the institute's collection focuses on the fine and decorative arts of Albany and Hudson River artists, with portraits, silver, furniture, and period rooms.

American Museum of Natural History
Central Park West at 79th Street
New York, NY 10024
212-873-1300

One of the world's largest natural history museums, opened in 1869, it has exceptional collections on American Indians, Eskimos, dinosaurs, wildlife, minerals, and fossil specimens.

The Brooklyn Museum
188 Eastern Parkway
Brooklyn, NY 11238
718-638-5000

The Brooklyn Museum was founded in 1823 and has amassed comprehensive collections of Egyptian and classical arts; American arts; European and American graphics; and Pre-Columbian, African, American Indian, and other primitive arts.

The Cloisters
Fort Tryon Park, NY
212-973-3700

A branch of the Metropolitan Museum devoted exclusively to medieval art, the Cloisters was built on a four-and-a-half acre site overlooking the Hudson. It was opened in 1938 and incorporates four medieval cloisters, an arcade, a chapel, and exhibition rooms. The museum features 12th- and 13th-century Byzantine and Romanesque art from France and Spain.

Cooper-Hewitt Museum, The Smithsonian Institution's National Museum of Design
2 East 91st Street
New York, NY 10128
212-860-6868

Established in 1897, the Cooper-Hewitt is housed in the Carnegie mansion. Its excellent collection of decorative arts includes furniture, fabrics, wallpaper, ceramics, drawings, prints, architecture and design publications, and metalwork. It boasts the world's largest collection of Winslow Homer drawings and sketches by other late nineteenth-century artists.

The Frick Collection
1 East 70th Street
New York, NY
212-288-0700

The former home of Henry Clay Frick, built in 1914 as an eighteenth-century model, still has most of its original furnishings intact, including excellent European paintings from the fourteenth through the eighteenth centuries.

Guggenheim Museum
See Solomon R. Guggenheim Museum.

The Metropolitan Museum of Art
Fifth Avenue at 82nd Street
New York, NY 10028
212-879-5500

One of the world's major museums, founded in 1870, the Metropolitan houses definitive collections covering about 5,000 years of art. A few of the highlights include medieval armor collections, Tiffany stained-glass windows, the complete Temple of Dendur (an early Christian structure from Egypt), extensive painting collections, sculpture, decorative arts, and a re-creation of a classic Ming dynasty Chinese garden court.

Museum of American Folk Art
2 Lincoln Square
New York, NY 10023
212-977-7170

This museum, established in 1961, elevates the crafts of the past to fine-art status. It includes collections of quilts, weathervanes, folk paintings, sculptures, weavings, and needlework from the colonial period to the early twentieth century.

The Museum of Modern Art
11 West 53rd Street
New York, NY 10019
212-708-9400

Begun in 1929, this exceptional collection traces the evolution of art from the Impressionist period forward. It represents a variety of disciplines, including drawings and prints, industrial design, architecture, paintings, sculpture, and decorative arts.

The Solomon R. Guggenheim Museum
1071 Fifth Avenue
New York, NY 10028
212-360-3500

Founded in 1937, this excellent collection of modern drawings, prints, paintings, and sculpture emphasizes abstract and nonobjective subjects. It is housed in a stunning Frank Lloyd Wright building.

Whitney Museum of American Art
Madison Avenue at 75th Street
New York, NY
212-530-3676

Opened in 1966, the Whitney houses New York's largest collection of twentieth-century art, with changing exhibitions of drawings, paintings, sculpture, and architecture. It shows contemporary avant-garde film and video and holds the Biennial of Contemporary American Art, a major showcase of the best recent work.

Ohio

Cincinnati Art Museum
Eden Park, OH 45202
513-721-5204

Founded in 1886, this major museum has an excellent, comprehensive general collection noted for its Near Eastern and American arts, Old Masters, medieval art, musical instruments, and drawings and prints. It includes works by Corot, Titian, Grant Wood, Gainsborough, Goya, and Velazquez.

Cleveland Museum of Art
11150 East Boulevard
Cleveland, OH 44106
216-421-7340

This excellent museum, founded in 1913, has a wide-ranging collection representing the artistic accomplishments of cultures throughout the world. It is recognized for one of the best Far Eastern collections and for its medieval art, Old Masters, classical antiquities, and American arts from the colonial time forward.

Oklahoma

Thomas Gilcrease Institute of American History and Art
1400 North 25 West Avenue
Tulsa, OK 74127
918-482-3122

This exceptional art collection, founded in 1942, captures the saga of America from prehistoric to modern times; the Gilcrease's art of the Old West is rivaled only by that of the Smithsonian. The institute also has maps, books, documents, artifacts, and manuscripts.

Oregon

Portland Art Museum
1219 South West Park Avenue
Portland, OR 97205
503-226-2811

The Portland, founded in 1892, focuses on Native American arts of the Northwest. It also includes a unique collection of Cameroon art, Pre-Columbian arts, Renaissance painting and sculpture, Ethiopian crosses, and European and American painting and sculpture.

Pennsylvania

Franklin Institute Science Museum and Planetarium
20th and Benjamin Franklin Parkway
Philadelphia, PA 19103
215-448-1200

Founded in 1824, this comprehensive museum offers collections featuring science, history, industry, technology, aeronautics, astronomy, space exploration, and stamps and coins.

Museum of Art, Carnegie Institute
4400 Forbes Avenue
Pittsburgh, PA 15213
412-622-3200

This museum, founded in 1896, displays art from around the world, including American art since the colonial period; ancient and classical art; African, Pre-Columbian, and Native American art; and European painting, sculpture, and decorative arts from the Renaissance forward. Works by Van Gogh, Cézanne, and Monet are included.

Pennsylvania Academy of the Fine Arts
Broad and Cherry Streets
Philadelphia, PA 19102
215-972-7600

Founded in 1805, the Pennsylvania Academy offers an excellent collection of American art from the eighteenth century to the present, with major works by Thomas Eakins, Charles Willson Peale, and William Rush.

Philadelphia Museum of Art
26th Street and Benjamin Franklin Parkway
Box 7646
Philadelphia, PA 19101
215-763-8100

This museum, established in 1876, is noted for its masterpieces from the twelfth to the nineteenth centuries; Barberini tapestries designed by Rubens; arms and armor; glass; European and American period rooms; folk, decorative, and primitive art; and the Stieglitz Center collection of photographs.

The University Museum, University of Pennsylvania
33rd and Spruce Streets
Philadelphia, PA 19104
215-898-4000

Founded in 1887, the museum is renowned for its worldwide acquisitions of ancient and primitive art, its collection of Native American gold, and the largest grouping of West African art in the Americas. It has sponsored more than 275 expeditions to gather outstanding artifacts from the ancient Near, Middle, and Far East, Southeast Asia, the Mediterranean, the Pacific, Europe, Africa, and the Americas.

Texas

Amon Carter Museum of Western Art
3501 Camp Bowie Boulevard
Fort Worth, TX 76107
817-738-1933

Housed in an impressive building designed by Philip Johnson since its founding in 1961, this museum concentrates on American paintings and sculptures from the nineteenth century forward, specializing in the works of the Old West. It also has a fine print collection and excellent Remingtons and Russells.

Kimbell Art Museum
3333 Camp Bowie Boulevard
Box 9440
Fort Worth, TX 76107
817-332-8451

Noted for its masterpieces from around the world, this collection, founded in 1972, ranges from twelfth-century panel paintings to J.M.W. Turner landscapes, Gainsboroughs, and Goyas.

The Museum of Fine Arts
1001 Bissonet Street
Box 6826
Houston, TX 77265
713-526-1361

This wide-ranging collection of world art, established in 1900, is especially strong in contemporary art; Pre-Columbian and American Indian art; Old Masters; and later European and American paintings and sculptures.

Virginia

Colonial Williamsburg
P.O. Box C
Williamsburg, VA 23187
804-220-7285

This village-style museum, founded in 1926, showcases American arts from colonial times forward. Colonial Williamsburg has 88 preserved and restored buildings dating from 1693 to 1837 and 50 reconstructed eighteenth-century buildings surrounded by gardens.

Wisconsin

Elvehjem Museum of Art, University of Wisconsin
800 University Avenue
Madison, WI 53706
608-263-2246

Established in 1962, this is one of the three largest university museums in the United States. Its wide-ranging collection of world art dates back to ancient times, with fine examples of classical coins and marbles; American painting, sculpture, and decorative arts from the eighteenth century forward; Indian miniatures; and Socialist Realist (propagandist) paintings from Russia.

Canada

Ontario

Art Gallery of Hamilton
123 King Street West
Hamilton, Ontario L8P 4S8
416-527-6610

A major North American museum, this gallery was established in 1914. It is noted for its collection of Canadian art; twentieth-century British and American painting, sculpture, drawings, and prints; and French Impressionist works.

Museum of Civilization
Victoria Memorial Museum Building
Metcalfe and McLeod Streets
Ottawa, Ontario K1A 0M8
613-992-3497

Opened in 1845, this museum specializes in history and folk culture, with excellent collections of the arts and crafts of Native Americans, particularly Eskimos and Northwest Coast Indians.

Children's Museums

There are more than 90 museums located throughout the United States devoted to children. While most museums offer at least a few special programs for children, those listed here focus almost exclusively on young visitors. A representative group is described in detail. For additional information, see the listing ''Children's and Junior Museums'' in *The Official Museum Directory*, published annually by the American Association of Museums.

Brooklyn Children's Museum
145 Brooklyn Avenue
Brooklyn, NY 11213
718-735-4400

Founded in 1899, this was the world's first children's museum. Its teaching collection includes more than 50,000 items, with exhibits on cultural history, natural history, and technology. It houses a greenhouse, a steam engine, and a gristmill. Children may attend workshops in school classes or groups. A portable loan collection and children's resource library is also available.

Capital Children's Museum
800 Third Street NE
Washington, DC 20002
202-543-8600

Founded in 1974, Capital Children's International Hall has a hands-on exhibit on Mexico where children learn to make their own tortillas, weave, and do other Mexican arts and crafts. Additional facilities include a living room, a metric exhibit, a simple machines display, a computer classroom, a communications exhibit, and a futuristic center.

Children's Museum
Museum Wharf
300 Congress Street
Boston, MA 02210
617-426-6500

Located on Boston's picturesque waterfront, Children's Museum was founded in 1913. It offers special collections of Native American and Japanese art; Americana; games, toys, dolls, and doll houses; and bird, insect, shell, and mineral specimens. The Exhibit Center presents participatory and cased exhibitions on child development, natural history, science and technology, careers, handicaps, and cross-cultural understanding. Its Resource Center makes available over 10,000 books, games, and other items to teachers, parents, students, and visitors.

Eugene Field House and Toy Museum
634 South Broadway
St. Louis, MO 63102
314-421-4689

Founded in 1936, this museum is housed in the birthplace of Eugene Field. It contains a collection of antique toys and dolls, along with a library on the works of Field.

The Exploratorium
3601 Lyon Street
San Francisco, CA 94123
415-563-7337

Housed in the Palace of Fine Arts, this science museum offers 500 participatory exhibits and art works illustrating the physical nature of the world and the sensory mechanisms through which we perceive it. Founded in 1969, it hosts field trips, concerts, lectures, and school groups.

Kidspace—A Participatory Museum
390 South El Molino
Pasadena, CA 91101
213-449-9143

Kidspace offers creative learning experiences for children, as in a mock television studio that children operate, a radio booth for broadcasting, and a medical clinic. There is even a robot who talks to visitors. Parents may host birthday parties in the museum.

Los Angeles Children's Museum
310 North Main Street
Los Angeles, CA 90012
213-687-8801

Children participate in a variety of activities at this museum in such places as Sticky City, with giant foam blocks for construction fun; City Streets, with city vehicles and street signs; TV Studios, where children create their own news broadcasts; and Workshop Place, which fosters creativity in arts and crafts.

Perelman Antique Toy Museum
270 South 2nd Street
Philadelphia, PA 19106
215-922-1070

Founded in 1962, Perelman's toy museum was first housed in 1758 in the Abercrombie House. Its special collections include antique toys, mechanical banks, toy pistols, and automatic toys.

Please Touch Museum
210 North 21st Street
Philadelphia, PA 19103
215-963-0667

Founded in 1976, the Please Touch Museum issues a children's newspaper and offers special exhibits on cultural artifacts of daily life, folk art and sculpture, natural science, technology, musical instruments, games, registered toys, costumes, masks, foot gear, and hats.

Reference Works for General Information

The following lists are not meant to be comprehensive but are intended to serve as wide-ranging sources for the subjects. A library will provide further reference materials and works on each of the subjects.

General Reference Works

American Reference Books Annual. Libraries Unlimited, 1970—.
This annual volume covers 1,300 to 1,800 new titles each year, reviewing about 300 categories of reference books. The most recent works in many disciplines are listed.

Bartlett's Familiar Quotations: A Collection of Passages, Phrases and Proverbs Traced to Their Sources in Ancient and Modern Literature, 15th ed. Little Brown, 1980.
This work lists more than 22,500 familiar and world-famous quotations along with a 600-page keyword subject index.

Books in Print. Bowker, 1947—.
This annual listing of books now in print or slated for publication by January 31 of the following year currently contains well over 700,000 titles.

Carruth, Gorton, ed. *The Volume Library*. The Southwestern Company, 1917—.
This two-volume, 2.5-million-word family encyclopedia is revised annually. It covers subjects of interest to students and their families and is illustrated and thoroughly indexed.

Chambers's Biographical Dictionary, rev. ed. Cambridge University Press, 1986.
Introduced in 1897, *Chambers's* currently lists more than 15,000 biographies spanning the history of the world.

Encyclopaedia Britannica, 17th ed. Encyclopaedia Britannica, 1987.
A major comprehensive reference tool for any library.

Ethridge, James M., ed. *The Directory of Directories: An Annotated Guide to Business and Industrial Directories, Professional and Scientific Rosters, and Other Lists and Guides of All Kinds,* 2nd ed. Information Enterprises, 1982.
The work lists 5,200 directories with categories such as business, education, and leisure, providing full details on each publication.

Guinagh, Kevin, ed. *Dictionary of Foreign Phrases and Abbreviations,* 3rd ed. H. W. Wilson, 1982.
This helpful dictionary defines more than 5,000 French, German, Greek, Italian, Latin, and Spanish abbreviations, phrases, proverbs, and quotations.

Guinness Book of World Records. Sterling, 1955—.
An annual guide to "the biggest, largest, longest, most" achieved all-time records.

Information Industry Market Place: An International Directory of Information Products and Services. Bowker, 1978–79—.
This international directory describes information collection centers, database and abstract publishers, information brokers, support services and suppliers, conferences, associations, periodicals, and reference books.

Readers' Guide to Periodical Literature. H. W. Wilson, 1900—.
The Readers' Guide provides a quick overview of current events through indexing of 174 general-interest U.S. magazines in a range of subject areas.

Sheehy, Eugene P., ed. *Guide to Reference Books*. American Library Association, 1986.
Found on nearly every reference librarian's basic bookshelf, Sheehy's *Guide* is grouped into five main categories: general reference works; humanities; social and behavioral sciences; history and area studies; and science, technology, and medicine.

Who's Who in America. Marquis Who's Who, 1899—.
The individuals listed in *Who's Who* provide the data to be included, so entries vary in completeness and accuracy. The work includes biographical details on approximately 72,000 Americans and others prominently linked to America.

World Almanac and Book of Facts. Newspaper Enterprise Association, 1868—.
A handy and easy-to-use reference, the *World Almanac* is updated annually. It provides statistics and factual data on economic, educational, industrial, political, religious, and social issues.

World Book Encyclopedia. World Book-Childcraft International, 1983.
Easy to use, the *World Book* is targeted at elementary through high school students, providing general reference information.

Anthropology and Ethnology. See also *Social Science*

Brace, C. Loring, et al. *Atlas of Human Evolution,* 2nd ed. Holt, Rinehart & Winston, 1979.
This book offers a discussion of the evolution of man for high school students and adults, using drawings and text to chronicle the important discoveries in this field.

Hawkes, Jacquetta. *The Atlas of Early Man.* St. Martin's, 1976.
This well-written and well-organized atlas covers developments in the ancient world from 35,000 B.C. to A.D. 500. It provides a complete description of the architecture, art, people, important events, and religions of each period.

Hunter, David E., and Whitten, Philip, eds. *Encyclopedia of Anthropology.* Harper & Row, 1976.
The first English-language encyclopedia in anthropological studies, this volume is compact, comprehensive, and accessible. It includes some 1,400 articles on pertinent topics, supplemented by generous illustrations, maps, diagrams, and photographs.

Applied Arts

Bernasconi, John R. *Collectors' Glossary of Antiques and Fine Arts,* 3rd ed. Transatlantic Arts, 1971.
A guide for the collector, layperson, and professional to terminology of the antiques and fine arts worlds. A thorough explanation of classical, heraldic, and religious symbols is provided.

Bond, Harold Lewis. *An Encyclopedia of Antiques.* Gale Research, 1975.
This classic reference reprints the 1945 original edition to offer definitions, history, and a field guide to furniture, glass, metals, pottery and porcelain, and textiles. It includes biographical information on important individuals in the field and bibliographic references.

Liman, Ellen. *The Collecting Book.* Penguin, 1980.
This book thoroughly describes individual collecting areas such as advertising memorabilia, comic books, tobacco items, clothing, boxes and tins, pottery, glass, and toys. It includes chapters on buying, preserving, and displaying collectibles, as well as numerous black-and-white photographs and extensive references to related publications and organizations.

Art and Architecture

American Art Directory. Bowker, 1898—.
A biennial guide to the thousands of art councils, museums, art libraries, and art schools in the United States, Canada, and abroad.

Artist's Market. Writer's Digest, 1974—.

This annual publication details names, addresses, contacts, payments, and other data for 4,000 purchasers of cartoons, illustrations, and photographs. It is considered a standard in its field.

Bell, Doris L. *Contemporary Art Trends: A Guide to Sources, 1960–1980*. Scarecrow Press, 1981.

This work identifies 41 contemporary art trends with listings of appropriate books and museum catalogs. It also contains a listing of 200 contemporary art journals and a bibliography.

Gardner, Helen. *Art Through the Ages*, 6th ed. Harcourt Brace Jovanovich, 1980.

A standard resource for librarians, students, and art aficionados, this volume surveys Western art from ancient through modern works.

Mayer, Ralph. *A Dictionary of Art Terms and Techniques*. Crowell, 1969.

This book defines more than 3,200 terms used in the fields of ceramics, drawing, painting, printmaking, and sculpture.

Phaidon Dictionary of Twentieth-Century Art, 2nd ed. Dutton, 1977.

This concise and thorough survey covers international art movements and artists in depth from 1900.

Richards, J. M., ed. *Who's Who in Architecture from 1400 to the Present*. Holt, Rinehart & Winston, 1977.

With more than 600 entries, this compendium describes the history of Western architecture. It lists important architects, engineers, landscape architects, and town planners whose works have advanced the field of architecture.

Astronomy

Menzel, Donald H. *A Field Guide to the Stars and Planets: Including the Moon, Satellites, Comets and Other Features of the Universe*, 2nd ed. Houghton-Mifflin, 1983.

This guide contains detailed sets of star maps for the southern and northern hemispheres as seen through amateur telescopes; 12 maps of the moon; and more than 50 photographic atlas charts. It also provides a helpful index of Latin and English names of stars, a bibliography, and a glossary.

Communications

Barnouw, Eric, ed. *International Encyclopedia of Communications*. 4 vols. Oxford University Press, 1988.

This comprehensive, illustrated encyclopedia covers the entire spectrum of communications studies. Most articles are followed by brief bibliographies, and the work is extensively cross-referenced.

Brown, Les. *Les Brown's Encyclopedia of Television*. Zoetrope, 1982.

This reference work covers television terminology, notable television programs, and profiles of important television personalities, including actors, directors, producers, and writers.

Representative American Speeches Series. H. W. Wilson, 1967—.

This annual publication includes selected major speeches with biographical notes on the speaker.

Writers Market: Where to Sell What You Write. Writer's Digest, 1929—.

An essential annual reference for freelance writers that gives the pertinent data on more than 4,500 publishers of books, periodicals, audiovisual materials, greeting cards, plays, and other materials. It includes basics of copyright law and authors' rights.

Economics and Business

Brownstone, David M., and Carruth, Gorton. *Where to Find Business Information: A World Guide for Everyone Who Needs the Answers to Business Questions* (A Hudson Group book), 2nd ed. Wiley, 1982.

More than 5,000 English-language publications from around the world are listed and briefly described, with concentration on current periodical publications and services, especially magazines, newsletters, computerized databases, printouts, and microforms. The compendium deals with all subjects of interest to business.

Business Periodicals Index: A Cumulative Subject Index to Periodicals in the Fields of Accounting, Advertising, Banking and Finance, General Business, Insurance, Labor and Management, Marketing and Purchasing, Office Management, Public Administration, Taxation, Specific Businesses, Industries, and Trades. H. W. Wilson, 1958—.
This monthly index provides data on approximately 250 periodicals and certain U.S. government documents.

Consumers Index to Product Evaluations and Information Sources. Pierian Press, 1973—. Quarterly; annual cumulation.
A quarterly guide to consumer magazine articles in 14 subject areas.

Consumer Reports Buying Guide. Consumers Union, 1936—.
Issued annually as the December issue of *Consumer Reports,* this guide is a starting point for a comparative analysis of all types of products. It contains test results, brand and model ratings and rankings, and general buying advice on products as diverse as stereos and orange juice. It also provides a subject index to evaluations from the previous five years of *Consumer Reports.*

Dow Jones–Irwin Business Almanac. Dow Jones-Irwin, 1977—.
This annual almanac provides business, financial, and tax statistics. It includes a short business directory and a review of the previous year's significant business news.

Dun and Bradstreet Million Dollar Directory. Dun and Bradstreet, 1959—.
This annual directory offers alphabetical listing of industries and businesses with a net worth of at least $1 million. It includes the name, address, corporate officers, Standard Industrial Classification (SIC) number, approximate sales, and number of employees for approximately 39,000 U.S. companies.

Dun and Bradstreet's Guide to Your Investments. Crowell, 1973—.
An introductory guide for amateur stock market investors, this annual explains basic concepts for all types of investments: common and preferred stocks; bonds; real estate; stock options; small business investment companies; and formula investing.

Fortune World Business Directory. Time, Inc., 1957—.
Taken from the annual listing in the May issue of *Fortune* magazine ranking the 500 largest U.S. industrial corporations, this directory includes the "Fortune 500" plus the 50 largest banks.

Franchise Opportunities Handbook. U.S. Bureau of Industrial Economics and Minority Business Development Agency, 1972—.
One of the best publications on franchising, this annual guide provides details on equity capital needed to buy specific franchises, available training, and support services.

Garcia, F. L., ed. *Encyclopedia of Banking and Finance,* 7th ed. Bankers Publishing, 1973.
This classic volume's 4,000 entries are arranged alphabetically. They describe basic terms as well as the mechanics and philosophy of banking practices, credit, insurance, investment, and money management.

Help: (Washington): The Useful Almanac. Everest House, 1977—.
This annual almanac offers up-to-date information for consumers. It is arranged topically, with material on health, real estate, nutrition, energy, education, insurance, and numerous other subjects.

Lesko, Matthew. *Something for Nothing.* Associated Press, 1980.
This book describes hotlines, consumer groups and agencies, government and private information resources, and various other free and inexpensive information sources.

Moody's Handbook of Common Stocks. Moody's Investors Service, 1965—.
Described as a quick-reference tool, Moody's quarterly publishes data on approximately 1,000 stocks, outlining capitalization, earnings, and projected outlook for each.

Moskowitz, Milton, ed. *Everybody's Business: An Almanac: The Irreverent Guide to Corporate America.* Harper & Row, 1980.
This almanac describes the inner workings of 317 major American businesses with details on the founding and reputation of each.

Standard and Poor's Register of Corporations, Directors and Executives. Standard and Poor's, 1928—.
A standard in the field, Standard and Poor's *Register* offers three volumes each year with current information on about 46,000 U.S. and Canadian companies. The volumes include biographies of executives as well as separate listings of newly added individuals and companies, obituaries for the previous year, and complete data on each company.

Standard Directory of Advertisers. National Register Publishing, 1907—.
This annual directory lists over 17,000 companies that advertise nationally through various media. The directory provides details on officers and sales personnel, product lines, advertising agencies, and media.

Thomas Register of American Manufacturers and Thomas Register Catalog File. Thomas Publications, 1905—.
This annual authoritative listing of manufacturers is grouped by more than 70,000 product classifications. Its 17 volumes contain lists of products and services; company names, addresses, and phone numbers; names of executives; and ratings, as well as a brand-name index and company catalogs.

U.S. Master Tax Guide. Commerce Clearing House, 1917—.
Using information on the Internal Revenue Code regulations and court and tax court decisions, this annual handbook covers all aspects of preparing federal income taxes for corporations, estates and trusts, individuals, and partnerships. It is considered a standard in its field.

Education

American Council on Education. *American Universities and Colleges,* 13th ed. Walter de Gruyter, 1987.
This comprehensive directory provides information about the structure of higher education in the United States, as well as complete details on each of the more than 1,700 institutions granting baccalaureate or higher degrees.

Durnin, Richard G. *American Education: A Guide to Information Sources.* Gale, 1982.
This bibliography covers books relating to American education, with 107 topical chapters listing works on childhood through higher education. Most works included are recent publications, but classic works also are described.

Weber, J. Sherwood, ed. *Good Reading: A Guide for Serious Readers,* 21st ed. Bowker, 1978.
This volume covers historical and regional works, literary forms (biography, the novel, drama, criticism), and the humanities (social sciences and sciences). It is helpful in its listing of classic works and important works on contemporary issues.

The World of Learning. Europa Publications, 1947—.
This annual directory of international institutions includes educational and scientific institutions and organizations listed by country.

Ethnic Studies

Thernstrom, Stephan, ed. *Harvard Encyclopedia of American Ethnic Groups.* Harvard University Press, 1980.
Essays describe the cultural, economic, political, religious, and social history of approximately 100 American ethnic groups.

Wynar, Lubomyr R. *Encyclopedic Directory of Ethnic Organizations in the United States.* Libraries Unlimited, 1975.
Some 73 ethnic groups are represented in the 1,475 organizations listed in this directory. They include major cultural, educational, fraternal, political, professional, religious, and scholarly groups.

Film

Halliwell, Leslie. *Halliwell's Complete Guide to Film.* Macmillan, 1987. This regularly revised comprehensive work covers a wide range of popular film lore.

Michael, Paul, ed. *The Great American Movie Book*. Prentice-Hall, 1980.
This alphabetical listing of 1,000 of the most popular films of the sound era includes data on cast, credits, and running time, with black-and-white photographs. It also lists Academy Award winners and indexes of players, directors, and producers.

Genealogy and Heraldry

Doane, Gilbert H., and Bell, James B. *Searching for Your Ancestors: The How and Why of Genealogy*, 5th ed. University of Minnesota Press, 1980.
This introductory guide to genealogical research covers both techniques and sources for locating genealogical data.

Fox-Davies, Arthur Charles. *A Complete Guide to Heraldry*. Barnes & Noble, 1969.
This guide includes information on how to apply for a coat of arms, as well as comprehensive details on the history of armory. It discusses regalia, seals, badges, cadency, and the law of armorial bearings.

Geography and Travel Guides

Rand McNally Cosmopolitan World Atlas. Rand McNally, rev. ed., 1987.
This atlas includes 350 color maps and map inserts, with individual maps of each U.S. state and Canadian province. It also provides a list of 1980 census totals for about 20,000 U.S. political subdivisions. The main index contains 82,000 entries.

Rand McNally Road Atlas, 1989: United States, Canada, and Mexico. Rand McNally.
This annual publication offers maps of all 50 states, each Canadian province, Central America, Mexico, and Puerto Rico, plus a 23,000-item place-name index. It also includes information on population, national park areas, mileage, recreational and historical sites, area codes, time zones, and how to compute miles per gallon.

Stamp, Dudley, and Clark, Audrey N., eds. *A Glossary of Geographical Terms*, 3rd ed. Longman, 1979.
This glossary is useful to both the specialist and layman with its generous cross-referencing and concise definitions.

History

Barraclough, Geoffrey, ed. *The Times Atlas of World History*, rev. ed. Hammond, 1984.
Seven sections detail the history of the world, beginning with "The World of Early Man" and concluding with "The Age of Global Civilizations." This work contains approximately 600 maps and illustrations depicting the rise and fall of major civilizations, as well as significant religious and historical events.

Barzun, Jacques, and Graff, Henry G. *The Modern Researcher*, 4th ed. Harcourt Brace Jovanovich, 1985.
This essential reference stresses historical research and provides methodologies useful to those in the humanities and social sciences. New material for the 4th edition covers the use of computers, word processors, and databases.

Carruth, Gorton. *The Encyclopedia of American Facts & Dates*. Harper & Row, 1987.
This chronologically arranged encyclopedia of American history has become a standard reference book for students and others seeking basic information. It covers explorations, treaties, battles, politics, literature, and science, among other topics.

Palmer, Alan. *Who's Who in Modern History, 1860–1980*. Holt, Rinehart & Winston, 1980.
Biographies of approximately 600 prominent individuals from the fields of politics, society, and literature.

Law

Black, Henry Campbell. *Black's Law Dictionary: Definitions of the Terms and Phrases of American and English Jurisprudence, Ancient and Modern,* 5th ed. West, 1979.
A standard reference in the field, *Black's* gives detailed definitions in all aspects of law, including criminal procedure, estate planning, accounting, taxes, and commercial transactions.

Cohen, Morris L., and Berring, Robert C. *How to Find the Law,* 7th ed. West, 1985.
A basic text for law students, as well as a helpful tool for the layman investigating resources and methodologies of legal research.

Dobelis, Inge N., ed., *Reader's Digest Family Legal Guide: A Complete Encyclopedia of Law for the Layman.* Reader's Digest, 1981.
Cross-referenced definitions give the layman an understanding of legal situations commonly encountered in everyday life, such as writing a will or buying a house.

Linguistics

Guinagh, Kevin, ed. *Dictionary of Foreign Phrases and Abbreviations,* 3rd ed. H. W. Wilson, 1983.
This dictionary contains definitions for more than 5,000 French, German, Greek, Italian, Latin, and Spanish abbreviations, phrases, quotations, and proverbs that appear in the English language. Similar expressions are cross-referenced.

Roget's International Thesaurus, 4th ed. Crowell, 1977.
Topical listings of more than 250,000 words are provided, with an alphabetical index for easy use.

Strunk, William, Jr., and White, E. B. *The Elements of Style,* 3rd ed. Macmillan, 1979.
A classic book noted for its simplicity and directness, *Elements* consists of only five chapters: "Elementary Rules of Usage," "Elementary Principles of Composition," "A Few Matters of Form," "Words and Expressions Commonly Misused," and "An Approach to Style."

Webster's New World Dictionary, 3rd College Edition. Simon & Schuster, 1988.
This authoritative dictionary provides over 170,000 entries, with in-depth etymologies, pronunciations, foreign expressions, a syllabification system, and over 11,000 Americanisms.

Webster's Ninth New Collegiate Dictionary. G. & C. Merriam, 1983.
Almost 160,000 entries are offered, with pronunciations, functional labels, inflected forms, word histories, usage, and word divisions. Also included are first known date of use for each word. The dictionary contains sections with biographical and geographical entries, foreign words and phrases, degree-granting colleges and universities, signs and symbols, and a style manual.

Literature

Carrier, Warren, ed. *Guide to World Literature.* National Council of Teachers of English, 1980.
This work focuses on cultures and literary works outside the Anglo-American tradition for American literature students. It discusses some 200 literary classics and their authors in the context of their contribution to world literature and their relationship to classics of other cultures.

Granger, Edith. *Granger's Index to Poetry.* Columbia University, 1986. This standard work is indexed by title, first line, author, and subject.

MLA International Bibliography of Books and Articles on the Modern Languages and Literatures. Modern Language Association of America, 1921—. Annual.
This useful reference covers articles and books in English, French, German, Spanish, Italian, Portuguese, Rumanian, and other languages.

Reader's Adviser. 6 vols. Bowker, 1986.
This basic guide to literature covers the best in English and American fiction, poetry, essays, biographies, and other areas in the fields of reference, history, philosophy, and science.

Medical Science

Physicians' Desk Reference to Pharmaceutical Specialties and Biologicals. Medical Economics, 1947—.
   This compendium, commonly referred to as the PDR, is a standard reference work for physicians and other health professionals. It offers details on dosage, contraindications, side effects, precautions, and undesirable interactions of pharmaceutical products.

Music

Abraham, Gerald. *The Concise Oxford History of Music.* Oxford University Press, 1980.
   This scholarly survey of Western music from ancient to modern times is presented chronologically. It describes the musical styles of each period and region, with extensive bibliographies.

Bayne, Pauline S., ed. *A Basic Music Library: Essential Scores and Books.* American Library Association, 1978.
   Created as a buying guide for small and medium-sized libraries, this reference work emphasizes books and music scores necessary to a core collection.

Havlice, Patricia Pate. *Popular Song Index.* Scarecrow Press, 1975. Supplement, 1978.
   More than 300 songbooks from the period 1940 to 1972, including children's songs, folk songs, hymns, and popular music, are anthologized. The Supplement includes another 72 anthologies from the period 1970 to 1975.

Randel, Don Michael. *New Harvard Dictionary of Music.* Harvard University Press, 1986.
   This comprehensive dictionary includes definitions and brief articles on music history, aesthetics, and theory.

Sadie, Stanley, ed. *The New Grove Dictionary of Music and Musicians*, 6th ed. 20 vols. Grove's Dictionaries of Music, 1980.
   This comprehensive dictionary includes entries and articles on composers, performers, theorists, music publishers, scholars, terminology, genres, and orchestras, with exhaustive bibliographies.

Mythology, Folklore, and Popular Customs

Thompson, Stith. *The Folktale.* University of California Press, 1977.
   Considered a standard in the field, this work discusses the form and development of folk stories, with summaries of the most popular folk tales of Europe, western Asia, and the North American Indians. It also covers various methods of researching and studying folk tales and folklore.

Philosophy

Magill, Frank N., ed. *Masterpieces of World Philosophy in Summary Form.* Harper & Row, 1961.
   This volume comprises more than 200 classic works, each described briefly in chronological order. It covers Western philosophy from ancient to modern times and includes a summary of each important philosopher's principal ideas and the important influences on his development.

The Philosopher's Index: An International Index to Philosophical Periodicals and the Philosophy Research Archives. Bowling Green State University, 1967—.
   This international quarterly index to philosophical periodicals provides listings in English, French, German, Italian, Portuguese, and Spanish.

Political Science

Congressional Quarterly's Guide to Congress, 3rd ed. Congressional Quarterly, 1982.
This accurate, nonpartisan guide to the history, power, structure, and workings of Congress includes the texts of the Articles of Confederation, Constitution, Declaration of Independence, and important pre-Constitutional documents.

Lesko, Mathew. *Information U.S.A.* Viking Press, 1983.
This book bills itself as "the ultimate guide to the largest source of information on earth," the U.S. government. It includes names, addresses, and phone numbers to locate information about hundreds of subjects, including consumer products, child care, medical services, educational opportunities, grants and loans, databases, marketing surveys, and government services.

Robert, Henry M. *Robert's Rules of Order,* rev. ed. Power Books, 1980.
This completely revised edition provides the authoritative guide to parliamentary procedure.

Washington Information Directory. Congressional Quarterly, 1975—.
This annual publication describes 5,000 congressional, executive, and nongovernmental agencies, committees, and organizations. It is considered an indispensable guide to both official and unofficial Washington.

Recreation and Sports

Carruth, Gorton, and Eugene Ehrlich. *Facts and Dates of American Sports.* Harper & Row, 1988.
Arranged chronologically, this thoroughly indexed reference book covers the main events in more than 90 sports from colonial times to the present. Records and statistics and biographies of well-known sports figures are included.

McWhirter, Norris. *Guinness Book of Sports Records Winners and Champions.* Sterling, 1982.
A handy reference to record-setting facts and figures for men's and women's sports.

Webster's Sports Dictionary. G. & C. Merriam, 1976.
This authoritative sports reference book defines terms for all popular spectator sports (baseball, basketball, football), international games (cricket, soccer), and recreational pursuits (hunting, mountain climbing). Diagrams and drawings further illuminate the subject.

Religion

Adams, Charles J., ed. *A Reader's Guide to the Great Religions,* 2nd ed. The Free Press, 1977.
Through bibliographic essays, this work covers major religions as well as ancient beliefs, religions of Mexico and Central and South America, the Sikh religion, and the Jains. It includes a subject index and an index of authors, compilers, translators, and editors for the serious researcher.

Attwater, Donald. *The Penguin Dictionary of Saints.* Penguin, 1975.
This book provides brief biographical sketches of 750 of the best-known saints. The selections are worldwide but emphasize those in Great Britain.

Brandon, S. G. F., ed. *Dictionary of Comparative Religions.* Scribner's, 1970.
Thorough and concise, this volume defines anthropology, iconography, philosophy, and the psychology of primitive, ancient, Asian, and Western religions. Articles describe practices and philosophies of specific religions, with terminology for each and pertinent bibliographies.

The Illustrated Bible Dictionary. 3 volumes. Tyndale House, 1980.
Comprehensive and well organized, this dictionary is based on the revised standard version. It offers definitions from all aspects of books of the Bible; major works and doctrines; and history, geography, customs, and cultures of biblical times. Extensive photographs, charts, diagrams, cross-references, and a useful index are included.

Morrison, Clinton. *An Analytical Concordance to the Revised Standard Version of the New Testament.* Westminster Press, 1979.
This massive work contains both a concordance and an index-lexicon. Entries give the English word followed by a subtitle line with three elements: definition, Greek word, and an English transliteration of the Greek word. Included are complete listings of each passage in which the subject word appears, with an explanation of its use in context.

Science and Technology

Chambers Science and Technology Dictionary. W.R. Chambers Ltd and Cambridge University Press, 1988.
A revision and expansion of a classic work, the *Chambers Dictionary* provides 45,000 understandable, alphabetical definitions of terms used in a variety of scientific disciplines.

Social Science. See also *History; Sociology.*

UNESCO Dictionary of the Social Sciences. Julius Gould and William L. Kolb, eds. The Free Press, 1964.
This excellent reference includes about 2,000 signed articles defining terminology in anthropology, economics, political science, sociology, and other social science specialties.

Sociology

Directory of Counseling Services. International Association of Counseling Services, 1969—.
This annual publication lists members of the American Personnel and Guidance Association who offer public and private counseling dealing with education, family, marriage, personal problems, rehabilitation, and vocational guidance.

Statistics and Demography

Bureau of the Census Catalog. U.S. Bureau of the Census, 1946—.
This catalog provides listings of all published and unpublished material (tape, cards, or microform) created by the Census Bureau during the period covered.

United Nations Statistical Yearbook. United Nations, 1949—.
This annual publication is considered the best source for international statistics. It offers data on such topics as agriculture, balance of payments, communications, construction, energy, population, transport, and wages and prices in 150 countries and territories.

Theater and Performing Arts

Encyclopedia of World Theater: With 420 Illustrations and an Index of Play Titles. Scribner's, 1977.
Based on the German compendium *Friedrichs Theaterlexicon* (1969), this one-volume work outlines both the history of theater and its contemporary state.

Guide to the Performing Arts. Scarecrow Press, 1960—.
This compendium contains an index to periodical reviews and articles pertaining to all areas of the performing arts.

Hughes, Catherine. *American Theater Annual.* Gale Research, 1976—.
All plays opening on and off Broadway during the year are listed, with details of cast members, opening and closing dates, plot summaries, and review excerpts.

Koegler, Horst. *The Concise Oxford Dictionary of Ballet*, 2nd ed. Oxford University Press, 1982.
This book contains more than 5,000 alphabetically arranged entries covering all areas of ballet: choreographers, composers, dancers, history, schools and companies, and basic definitions.

Notable Names in the American Theater. James T. White, 1976.
This major work is divided into nine sections: "New York Productions"; "Premieres in America"; "Premieres of American Plays Abroad"; "Theater Group Biographies"; "Theater Building Biographies"; "Awards"; "Bibliographical Biography"; "Necrology"; and, most valuable, "Notable Names in the American Theater." The sections cover administrators, agents, archivists, authors, casting directors, composers, conductors, critics, designers, directors, educators, historians, lyricists, performers, playwrights, producers, and teachers.

The Dewey Decimal System and How to Use It

Melvil Dewey (1851–1931) was a man who believed in organization. Even as a child he was busy devising a way to arrange his family's pantry to make it more efficient. Before his system of classifying library books was adopted, many libraries relied on systems that filed books by size or color—cumbersome and not very useful methods at best. While working as a librarian at Amherst College, Dewey developed a system that is used by most school and small public libraries today. Published anonymously in 1876, his classifications divide nonfiction books into ten broad categories:

000–099   General works (encyclopedias and similar works)

100–199   Philosophy (how people think and what they believe)

200–299   Religion (including mythology and religions of the world)

300–399   Social sciences (folklore and legends, government, manners and customs, vocations)

400–499   Language (dictionaries, grammars)

500–599   Pure science (mathematics, astronomy, chemistry, nature study)

600–699   Technology (applied sciences—aviation, building, engineering, homemaking)

700–799   Arts (photography, drawing, painting, music, sports)

800–899   Literature (plays, poetry)

900–999   History (ancient and modern, geography, travel)

Each of these sections is further divided for accuracy in classification. For example, the numbers 500–599 cover the pure sciences, such as astronomy, chemistry, mathematics, paleontology, and physics. Each of these areas has its own division and section number. All books on mathematics are assigned numbers in the 510 to 519 range; mathematics is then broken down into types, such as algebra, arithmetic, and geometry. Geometry's specific number is 513, which can be subdivided through the use of decimal points to provide ten basic categories. Additional digits can be added, creating an ever more precise categorization system.

Books are arranged alphabetically within each classification by the first letters of the author's last name. Therefore, a library that has several books on American history of the colonial period will assign the same basic number (973.2) to all the books and shelve them alphabetically.

Dewey's aim was to create a system that would be simple enough for even casual users to understand, but complex enough to meet a library's expanding needs. His system was developed to meet the needs of many libraries. A second popular system was created to fit the requirements of a specific library, the Library of Congress. This system, now in wide use, is even more detailed and has the advantage of being able to accommodate growth of knowledge in unexpected areas.

The Library of Congress Classification System

The Library of Congress Classification System is used in most large public and university libraries today. A Library of Congress (LC) classification number contains three lines, a letter at the top, a number in the middle, and a letter/number combination at the bottom.

The Library of Congress went through several systems before devising its own method. Because the Library of Congress contains almost every book ever published in the United States, as well as valuable tapes and research materials, it needs a highly flexible system. The Library of Congress Classification System contains 20 classes:

    A: General works

    B: Philosophy and religion

    C: History—auxiliary sciences

    D: History and topography (except America)

E–F: American history

    G: Geography, anthropology, folklore, manners and customs, recreation

    H: Social sciences

    J: Political sciences

    K: Law of the United States

    L: Education

    M: Music and books on music

    N: Fine arts

    P: Language and literature

    Q: Science

    R: Medicine

    S: Agriculture and plant and animal industry

    T: Technology

    U: Military science

    V: Naval science

    Z: Bibliography and library science

Each of these classes can be divided into a subclass with the addition of a second letter. By adding numbers, the category becomes even more specific. The flexibility of the system becomes apparent when one sees that the alphabet permits 26 subdivisions of any one class. Each of the subdivisions can be broken down further by using the numbers 1 to 9999.

Librarians recommend that researchers turn to *Subject Headings Used in the Dictionary Catalog of the Library of Congress* for assistance. Because the LC system groups related topics together, a researcher may discover unexpected, related avenues to pursue.

CATALOGING PUBLICATION DATA

On the copyright page of most books, under the heading "Cataloging in Publication Data," are numbers and abbreviations that help librarians to index new acquisitions for the card catalog. This data can be helpful to readers as well. A typical entry is shown below with an explanation of each part of the entry:

Library of Congress Cataloging in Publication Data

[Author]	McLanathan, Richard B.K.
[Title]	World art in American museums.

[Possible subject card headings, in order of importance]

    1. Art—United States—Guide-books. 2. Art museums—United States—Guide-books. 3. Museums—United States—Guide-books. 4. Art—Canada—Guide-books. 5. Art—museums—Canada—Guide-books. 6. Museums—Canada—Guide-books.

    I. Title.

[Library of Congress No.]   N510.M34 1983 708.13 (Dewey Decimal No.)

ISBN 0-385-18515-14 (International Standard Book Number: country number; publisher number; title number; and check digit. The ISBN was started by the British in 1967 and adopted in the United States a year later.)

    Cataloging in Publication Data might also include information on a book's illustrator, whether a book has an index or bibliography, and number of pages.

HOTLINES AND INFORMATION SERVICES

AIDS hotline	800-342-AIDS
Alzheimer's Disease and Related Disorders Association	800-621-0379
Auto safety hotline	800-424-9393
	202-426-0123 in Washington, DC
Cancer hotline	800-422-6237
Child abuse hotline	800-4-A-CHILD
Child support hotline	800-252-3515
Cocaine hotline	800-COCAINE
College money hotline	800-638-6700
	800-492-6602 in Maryland
Dial-a-hearing screening test	800-222-EARS
	800-345-EARS in Pennsylvania
Drug hotline	800-662-HELP
Heart disease hotline	800-241-6993
Insurance Information Institute	800-221-4954
IRS Taxpayer assistance	800-424-1040
National Center for Missing and Exploited Children	800-843-5678
Parents Anonymous/Abuse prevention hotline	800-421-0353
Parents who have kidnapped their children hotline	800-A-WAY-OUT
Product safety hotline—Consumer Product Safety Commission	800-638-2772
Runaway hotline	800-621-4000
	800-972-6004 in Illinois
Shriner's Hospital free children's hospital care referral line	800-237-5055
Surgical opinion hotline	800-638-6833

GETTING STARTED IN GENEALOGY

The search for a greater understanding of our ancestors has boomed in the United States since the American Bicentennial celebration and the publication of Alex Haley's immensely popular *Roots*. Genealogists lament that too many of us live in historical vacuums, unable to name more than a generation or two of our closest relatives. To join this search for a history that extends beyond the last few generations, experts offer several tips:

1. Begin with your closest family members, recording basic information that is already known to you and working backward. This part of the investigation can be quite far-reaching if you contact distant relatives and check sources that they suggest. You may be fortunate enough to have access to family Bibles, letters, and diaries. Vital records such as birth and death certificates can yield a wealth of information at this stage.

2. Consult popular references for research techniques. Some of the best follow.

    Andereck, Paul A., and Pence, Richard A. *Computer Genealogy: a Guide to Research Through High Technology.* Ancestry, 1985.

    Crandall, Ralph. *Shaking Your Family Tree.* Yankee Publishing, 1986.

    Doane, Gilbert Harry, and Bell, James B. *Searching for Your Ancestors: The How and Why of Genealogy,* 5th ed. University of Minnesota Press, 1980.

    Jacobus, Donald Lines. *Genealogy as Pastime and Profession,* 2nd ed. Genealogical Publishing Co., 1978.

3. Check out the libraries. Extensive genealogical collections exist at the Library of Congress, the New York Public Library, the Los Angeles Public Library, the Newberry Library in Chicago, and the Allen County Public Library in Fort Wayne, Indiana. Specialized libraries, such as the famed Genealogical Library of the Church of Jesus Christ of Latter-Day Saints in Salt Lake City, Utah, can be extremely helpful. This particular library offers more than 1.3 million reels of microfilm of all types of documents useful to genealogists. Also visit or contact local libraries in areas where your ancestors are known to have lived.

    ### Major Genealogical Libraries

    Burton Collection, Detroit Public Library, 5201 Woodward Avenue, Detroit, MI 48202

    Dallas Public Library, 1515 Young Street, Dallas, TX 75201

    Daughters of the American Revolution Library, 1776 D Street NW, Washington, DC 20006 (to be used with the Library of Congress and National Genealogical Society Library, 4527 17th Street N, Arlington, VA 22207)

    Genealogical Society Library, 50 East North Temple Street, Salt Lake City, UT 84150

    Los Angeles Public Library, 630 West 5th Street, Los Angeles, CA 90071

    Newberry Library, 60 West Walton Street, Chicago, IL 60610

    New England Genealogical Society, 101 Newbury Street, Boston, MA 02116

    New York Genealogical and Biographical Society, 122-6 East 58th Street, New York, NY 10022

    New York Public Library, 5th Avenue and 42nd Street, New York, NY 10018

    Public Library of Fort Wayne and Allen County, 301 West Wayne Street, Fort Wayne, IN 46802

    State Historical Society of Wisconsin, 816 State Street, Madison, WI 53703

    Western Reserve Historical Society, 10825 East Boulevard, Cleveland, OH 44106

4. Consider contacting the American Archives Association if your search involves identifying and locating missing and unknown heirs to estates. The association charges a percentage fee for successful searches. Call any weekday between 8:30 A.M. and 4:30 P.M., EST.

    American Archives Association

    1350 New York Avenue NW

    Washington, DC 20005

    202-737-6090

Additional Sources of Information

Organizations and Services

American Crafts Council Library
44 West 53rd Street
New York, NY 10019
212-869-9462

Questions about the history of crafts, or about learning how to pursue a particular craft, such as weaving or pottery, are answered. Calls may be made Tuesday through Friday between 10 A.M. and 5 P.M., EST.

American Museum of Natural History Library
79th Street and Central Park West
New York, NY 10024
212-873-4225

Founded in 1869, this special library has 400,000 volumes devoted to subjects ranging from anthropology to travel and expedition, with sections on biology, ethology, entomology, geology, herpetology, history of science, ichthyology, living and fossil invertebrates, mammalogy, mineralogy, museology, ornithology, and paleontology. Its special collections are devoted to astronomical instruments, rare books and manuscripts, rare films, and many other areas. The museum's librarians offer assistance in all areas.

Consumer Information Center
Pueblo, CO 81009

This federal government agency provides a wide selection of free publications such as its monthly *National Consumer Buying Alert* and guides to solar energy, tire buying, nutrition, budgeting, housing, and gardening. Write for a free catalog, or specify your area of interest.

Educational Film Library Association
45 John Street
New York, NY 10038
212-227-5599

Information is provided about animation, business films, documentary and educational films, films as art, and independent films. Questions about film schools and film vocabulary can also be answered. The library contains over 1,300 books and has special files on film festivals, library administration, grants, filmmakers, and film centers in the United States. Calls may be made weekdays, from 2 P.M. to 6 P.M., EST.

Educational Resources Information Center (ERIC)
1200 19th Street NW
Washington, DC 20208
202-254-5500

The National Institute of Education within the U.S. Department of Education sponsors ERIC, the educational information system, to provide literature pertaining to various aspects of education. General questions about education are also answered. If a computer search is necessary, a charge will be imposed; otherwise, the information is free. ERIC also provides referrals to other organizations, including its own clearinghouses on adult, career, and vocational education; counseling and personnel services; educational management; elementary and early childhood education; handicapped and gifted children; higher education; information resources; junior colleges; languages and linguistics; reading and communications skills; rural education and small schools; science, mathematics, and environmental education; social studies/social science education; teacher education; tests, measurements, and evaluation; and urban education. Calls are accepted 8 A.M. to 5:30 P.M., EST, weekdays.

Federal Information Center
26 Federal Plaza
New York, NY 10278
212-264-4464

This government-sponsored answer center will respond to general information questions or will refer you to a likely source of information. It also provides names, addresses, and telephone numbers of various government agencies and offers a free brochure listing all Federal Information Centers across the country.

Museum of Broadcasting
1 East 53rd Street
New York, NY 10022
212-752-4690

Founded in 1976, this museum has collected more than 10,000 radio and 8,000 TV tapes from the 1920s to the present and 2,400 radio scripts, with 1,600 available on microfiche. Its staff is knowledgeable about all aspects of broadcasting and has access to a thousand-volume library of books and magazines.

The National Archives
Central Reference Service Division
Washington, DC 20408
202-523-3218

This federal government agency is responsible for keeping the permanent records of the U.S. government. Its holdings include maps, photographs, films, U.S. Census records, and all types of correspondence generated and received by government officials. The archives also contain ship passenger records dating as far back as 1820 and military records from the Revolutionary War. Some of its holdings occasionally overlap those of the Library of Congress. Call between 8:45 A.M. and 5:15 P.M., EST, weekdays.

Nutrition Information Center
The New York Hospital–Cornell Medical Center
Room 904
Memorial Sloan-Kettering Cancer Center
515 East 71st Street
New York, NY 10021
212-472-6958

Advice is provided on clinical nutrition, nutrition research, and general nutrition. The staff will also furnish educational materials, make referrals, and assist in program planning. Calls may be made weekdays between 9 A.M. and 5 P.M., EST.

The Performing Arts Library
Roof Terrace Level
John F. Kennedy Center for the Performing Arts
Washington, DC 20566
202-287-6245 or 202-254-9803

Both the public and professional artists may call the library for information and reference assistance on broadcasting, dance, film, music, theater, and related areas. The library is a joint project of the Kennedy Center and the Library of Congress.

United Nations
United Nations Publications
Room 1059
New York, NY 10017
212-963-1234

This international organization's publications cover a wide range of topics, including human rights, public finance, atomic energy, treaties, and international statistics. The UN makes materials available in hardbound and paperback books, pamphlets, bulletins, periodicals, and official records—all in English, and frequently also in Spanish, French, and Russian. Write for a catalog and details of current offerings.

United States Military Academy Library
West Point, NY 10996
914-938-2209

Founded in 1802, the academy's library contains 400,000 volumes pertaining to the history of the military as well as government documents.

Data Banks Available for Computer Research

BRS Information Technologies
1200 Route 7
Latham, NY 12110
800-345-4BRS   518-783-1161

BRS provides online access to bibliographic and full-text databases covering diverse subjects, among them agriculture, books in print, chemistry, energy, medicine, dentistry, mental health, and social sciences. Its clients represent Canada, Europe, and the Middle East, as well as the United States.

CompuServe, Inc.
Information Services
P.O. Box 20212
5000 Arlington Centre Boulevard
Columbus, OH 43220
800-848-8199
614-457-0802 in Ohio or Canada

This online system offers forums for users of various computers, with electronic editions of newspapers and computer magazines, an international newswire, conferences, and message boards. CompuServe provides remote computing services, a videotex information service, and a value-added network service, as well as games, entertainment, and personal finance services.

DIALOG Information Services, Inc.
3460 Hillview Avenue
Palo Alto, CA 94304
800-334-2564   415-858-2700

This online system provides access to approximately 280 databases, making it possible to search through thousands of newspapers, general-interest and trade magazines, and other publications in seconds. It

includes databases compiled by Dun & Bradstreet, Moody's Investor's Service, and Standard & Poor's.

Dow Jones News/Retrieval
P.O. Box 300
Princeton, NJ 08534
609-452-2000

This online computer service offers an interactive information service with up-to-the-minute news and information to the business and financial community. Stories from the *Wall Street Journal, Barron's,* and the *Dow Jones News Service* appear as quickly as 90 seconds after filing and go back as far as 90 days. Dow Jones also offers online stock trading and portfolio management services.

ORBIT Search Service
800 Westpark Drive
McLean, VA 22102
800-421-7229   703-442-0900

This bibliographic database provides online services. Users may request copies of full-text documents from any of the available services.

WILSONLINE
The H. W. Wilson Company
950 University Avenue
Bronx, NY 10452
212-588-8400

WILSONLINE provides online access to *The Readers' Guide to Periodical Literature,* the *Business Periodicals Index,* the *Index to Legal Periodicals,* the *Education Index,* and numerous other periodical resources. It is used widely by corporations, government agencies, libraries, schools, and universities. Its database covers more than 3,000 periodicals and 500,000 books.

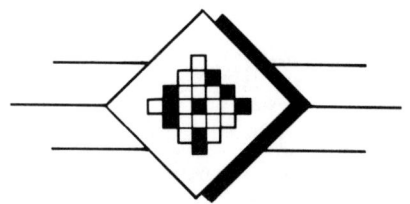

Words

Common Abbreviations

Note: *See also* Acronyms section.

An abbreviation is a shortened form of a word or phrase. Some abbreviations, such as Mr. and Mrs., always substitute for the longer form. Abbreviations are not limited to, but frequently are used for, titles, academic degrees, organizations, measurements, and scientific words.

a	acre
AAA	American Automobile Association
A.B.	*artium baccalaureus* (Latin, bachelor of arts)
A.D.	*anno domini* (Latin, in the year of our Lord)
ae.	*aetate* (Latin, aged)
AEF	American Expeditionary Force (World War I)
AFL	American Federation of Labor
AIDS	acquired immune deficiency syndrome
A.M.	*ante meridiem* (Latin, before noon)
AMA	American Medical Association
anon.	anonymous
A.R.A.	Associate of the Royal Academy
ASAP	as soon as possible
B.A.	bachelor of arts
Bart., Bt.	baronet
BBB	Better Business Bureau
bbl.	barrel(s)
B.C.	before Christ
B.C.E.	before the Christian era
B.D.	bachelor of divinity
B.P.O.E.	Benevolent and Protective Order of Elks
B.S.	bachelor of science
B.S.A.	Boy Scouts of America
bu.	bushel
B.V.M.	Blessed Virgin Mary
C	centigrade, Celsius
c., ca.	*circa* (Latin, about)
CAB	Civil Aeronautics Board
Cantab.	*Cantabrigiensis* (Latin, of Cambridge)
CARE	Cooperative for American Relief Everywhere
CCC	Civilian Conservation Corps
CEO	chief executive officer
cf.	*confer* (Latin, compare)
CIA	Central Intelligence Agency
CIO	Congress of Industrial Organizations
cm	centimeter
c/o	in care of
COD	cash on delivery
COO	chief operating officer
CORE	Congress of Racial Equality
CP	Communist Party

C.P.A.	certified public accountant
CPR	cardiopulmonary resuscitation
CPU	central processing unit (computers)
C.S.A.	Confederate States of America
CST	Central Standard Time
cu.	cubic
D.A.	district attorney
D.A.R.	Daughters of the American Revolution
D.D.	doctor of divinity
D.D.S.	doctor of dental surgery
DOA	dead on arrival
doz.	dozen
D.S.M.	Distinguished Service Medal
D.S.O.	Distinguished Service Order
DST	daylight saving time
DTs	delerium tremens
D.V.M.	doctor of veterinary medicine
EEO	equal employment opportunity
e.g.	*exempli gratia* (Latin, for example)
EPA	Environmental Protection Agency
Esq.	esquire
EST	eastern standard time
et. al.	*et alii* (Latin, and others)
etc.	*et cetera* (Latin, and others)
F	Fahrenheit
FAA	Federal Aviation Administration
ff.	and following
FBI	Federal Bureau of Investigation
FCC	Federal Communications Commission
FDA	Food and Drug Administration
FDIC	Federal Deposit Insurance Corporation
FHA	Federal Housing Administration
f.o.b.	freight on board
FRS	Federal Reserve System
F.R.S.	Fellow of the Royal Society
f/t	full time
ft.	foot
FTC	Federal Trade Commission
f/x	special effects (movies)
FYI	for your information
GAO	General Accounting Office
G.A.R.	Grand Army of the Republic
GMT	Greenwich mean time
GOP	Grand Old Party (Republican party)
GPO	Government Printing Office; general post office
G.S.A.	Girl Scouts of America
H.M.S.	his/her majesty's ship
HQ	headquarters
H.R.	House of Representatives

H.R.H.	his/her royal highness
HUD	(Department of) Housing and Urban Development
ibid.	*ibidem* (Latin, in the same place)
ICC	Interstate Commerce Commission
i.e.	*id est* (Latin, that is)
IHS	Jesus (Greek contraction)
in.	inch
I.N.R.I.	*Iesus Nazarenus Rex Iudaeorum* (Latin, Jesus of Nazareth, King of the Jews)
INS	Immigration and Naturalization Service
I.O.U.	I owe you
I.Q.	intelligence quotient
IRS	Internal Revenue Service
ISBN	international standard book number
J.D.	*jurum doctor* (Latin, doctor of laws)
K	1,000
k.	karat
kg	kilogram
K.G.B.	*Komitet Gosudarstvennoi Bezopasnosti* (Russian, State Security Committee)
km	kilometer
kt.	knight
kw.	kilowatt
kwh.	kilowatt-hour
l	liter
lat.	latitude
lb.	pound
l.c.	lower case (printing)
L.C.	Library of Congress
L.H.D.	*litterarum humaniorum doctor* (Latin, doctor of humane letters)
Litt.D.	*litterarum doctor* (Latin, doctor of literature)
LL.B.	*legum baccalaureus* (Latin, bachelor of laws)
LL.D.	*legum doctor* (Latin, doctor of laws)
long.	longitude
L.P.N.	licensed practical nurse
m	meter
m.	married
MC	master of ceremonies
M.D.	*medicinae doctor* (Latin, doctor of medicine)
mi.	mile
ml	milliliter
mm	millimeter
M.O.	money order; *modus operandi* (Latin, mode of operation)
M.P.	member of Parliament; military police
mph	miles per hour
M.S.	master of science
ms., mss.	manuscript, manuscripts
MSG	monosodium glutamate

N/A	not applicable
N.A.	North America
NAACP	National Association for the Advancement of Colored People
NASA	National Aeronautics and Space Administration
NATO	North Atlantic Treat Organization
N.B.	*nota bene* (Latin, note well)
NOW	National Organization for Women
NP	notary public
NRA	National Recovery Administration; National Rifle Association
NRC	National Regulatory Commission
N.S.	New Style (Russian dating)
NSC	National Security Council
O.B.E.	Order of the British Empire
op. cit.	*opere citato* (Latin, in the work cited)
O.S.	Old Style (Russian dating)
OSHA	Occupational Safety and Health Administration
o/t	overtime
Oxon.	*Oxoniensis* (Latin, of Oxford)
oz.	ounce
PA	public address
PC	personal computer
P & I	principal and interest
pk.	peck
P & L	profit and loss
P.M.	*post meridiem* (Latin, after noon); prime minister
pro tem.	*pro tempore* (Latin, for the time being)
P.S.	postscript
p/t	part time
pt.	pint
PTA	Parent-Teacher Association
PX	post exchange (commissary)
Q.E.D.	*quod erat demonstrandum* (Latin, which was to be proved)
qt.	quart
q.v.	*quod vide* (Latin, which see)
R.	*rex, regina* (Latin, king, queen)
R.A.	Royal Academy
rbi	runs batted in (baseball)
R & D	research and development
REM	rapid eye movement
RFD	rural free delivery
RIP	*requiescat in pace* (Latin, rest in peace)
RN	registered nurse
ROTC	Reserve Officers' Training Corps
rpm	revolutions per minute
RR	railroad
R & R	rest and relaxation (military)
R.S.V.	Revised Standard Version (Bible)
R.S.V.P.	*répondez s'il vous plaît* (French, respond if you please)
Rx	prescription

s	seconds
S.A.	South America; Salvation Army
SAC	Strategic Air Command
S.A.S.E.	self-addressed stamped envelope
s.c.	small capitals (printing)
SDI	Strategic Defense Initiative
SDS	Students for a Democratic Society
SEC	Securities and Exchange Commission
Sen.	Senate
seq.	*sequentes* (Latin, the following)
S.J.	Society of Jesus (Jesuits)
S.O.S.	international distress signal, often wrongly thought to stand for "Save Our Ship"
SPCA	Society for the Prevention of Cruelty to Animals
SPQR	*Senatus Populusque Romanus* (Latin, the Senate and the Roman people)
sq.	square
SS.	saints
SS	Social Security; steamship
T	ton
TD	touchdown (football)
T.N.T.	trinitrotoluene
TVA	Tennessee Valley Authority
u.c.	upper case (printing)
U.K.	United Kingdom
UFO	unidentified flying object
U.N.	United Nations
UNESCO	United Nations Educational, Scientific, and Cultural Organization
UNICEF	United Nations International Children's Emergency Fund
U.S.	United States
U.S.A.	United States of America; United States Army
U.S.A.F.	United States Air Force
U.S.C.G.	United States Coast Guard
U.S.I.A.	United States Information Agency
U.S.M.C.	United States Marine Corps
U.S.N.	United States Navy
U.S.S.	United States ship
U.S.S.R.	Union of Soviet Socialist Republics
VA	Veterans Administration
V.F.W.	Veterans of Foreign Wars
V.I.P.	very important person
viz.	*videlicet* (Latin, namely)
V.P.	vice-president
w	watt
WAC	Women's Army Corps
WAVES	Women Appointed for Volunteer Emergency Service (U.S. Navy)
W.C.T.U.	Women's Christian Temperance Union
Xmas	Christmas
yd.	yard
Y.M.C.A., Y.W.C.A.	Young Men's (Women's) Christian Association
Y.M.H.A., Y.W.H.A.	Young Men's (Women's) Hebrew Association
yr.	year

U.S. Postal Service Abbreviations

Two-Letter State and Territory Abbreviations

Alabama	AL	Kansas	KS	Northern Mariana Islands	CM
Alaska	AK	Kentucky	KY	Ohio	OH
Arizona	AZ	Louisiana	LA	Oklahoma	OK
Arkansas	AR	Maine	ME	Oregon	OR
American Samoa	AS	Marshall Islands	TT	Palau	TT
California	CA	Maryland	MD	Pennsylvania	PA
Colorado	CO	Massachusetts	MA	Puerto Rico	PR
Connecticut	CT	Michigan	MI	Rhode Island	RI
Delaware	DE	Minnesota	MN	South Carolina	SC
District of Columbia	DC	Mississippi	MS	South Dakota	SD
Federated States of		Missouri	MO	Tennessee	TN
Micronesia	TT	Montana	MT	Texas	TX
Florida	FL	Nebraska	NE	Utah	UT
Georgia	GA	Nevada	NV	Vermont	VT
Guam	GU	New Hampshire	NH	Virginia	VA
Hawaii	HI	New Jersey	NJ	Virgin Islands	VI
Idaho	ID	New Mexico	NM	Washington	WA
Illinois	IL	New York	NY	West Virginia	WV
Indiana	IN	North Carolina	NC	Wisconsin	WI
Iowa	IA	North Dakota	ND	Wyoming	WY

Geographic Directional Abbreviations

North	N	West	W	Southwest	SW
East	E	Northeast	NE	Northwest	NW
South	S	Southeast	SE		

Street Designators (Street Suffixes)

Word	Abbreviation	Word	Abbreviation	Word	Abbreviation
Alley	ALY	Camp	CP	Crescent	CRES
Annex	ANX	Canyon	CYN	Crossing	XING
Arcade	ARC	Cape	CPE	Dale	DL
Avenue	AVE	Causeway	CSWY	Dam	DM
Bayou	BYU	Center	CTR	Divide	DV
Beach	BCH	Circle	CIR	Drive	DR
Bend	BND	Cliffs	CLFS	Estates	EST
Bluff	BLF	Club	CLB	Expressway	EXPY
Bottom	BTM	Corner	COR	Extension	EXT
Boulevard	BLVD	Corners	CORS	Fall	FL
Branch	BR	Course	CRSE	Falls	FLS
Bridge	BRG	Court	CT	Ferry	FRY
Brook	BRK	Courts	CTS	Field	FLD
Burg	BG	Cove	CV	Fields	FLDS
Bypass	BYP	Creek	CRK	Flats	FLT

Word	Abbreviation	Word	Abbreviation	Word	Abbreviation
Ford	FRD	Lodge	LDG	Row	ROW
Forest	FRST	Loop	LOOP	Run	RUN
Forge	FRG	Mall	MALL	Shoal	SHL
Fork	FRK	Manor	MNR	Shoals	SHLS
Forks	FRKS	Meadows	MDWS	Shore	SHR
Fort	FT	Mill	ML	Shores	SHRS
Freeway	FWY	Mills	MLS	Spring	SPG
Gardens	GDNS	Mission	MSN	Springs	SPGS
Gateway	GTWY	Mount	MT	Spur	SPUR
Glen	GLN	Mountain	MTN	Square	SQ
Green	GRN	Neck	NCK	Station	STA
Grove	GRV	Orchard	ORCH	Stream	STRM
Harbor	HBR	Oval	OVAL	Street	ST
Haven	HVN	Park	PARK	Summit	SMT
Heights	HTS	Parkway	PKY	Terrace	TER
Highway	HWY	Pass	PASS	Trace	TRCE
Hill	HL	Path	PATH	Track	TRAK
Hills	HLS	Pike	PIKE	Trail	TRL
Hollow	HOLW	Pines	PNES	Trailer	TRLR
Inlet	INLT	Place	PL	Tunnel	TUNL
Island	IS	Plain	PLN	Turnpike	TPKE
Islands	ISS	Plains	PLNS	Union	UN
Isle	ISLE	Plaza	PLZ	Valley	VLY
Junction	JCT	Point	PT	Viaduct	VIA
Key	KY	Port	PRT	View	VW
Knolls	KNLS	Prairie	PR	Village	VLG
Lake	LK	Radial	RADL	Ville	VL
Lakes	LKS	Ranch	RNCH	Vista	VIS
Landing	LNDG	Rapids	RPDS	Walk	WALK
Lane	LN	Rest	RST	Way	WAY
Light	LGT	Ridge	RDG	Wells	WLS
Loaf	LF	River	RIV		
Locks	LCKS	Road	RD		

Common Crossword Puzzle Words

Certain words frequently appear in crossword puzzles. Following is a list of such words, particularly ones not used regularly in everyday speech. Many of these words will be recognized by avid crossword puzzle solvers. People new to crosswords will find familiarity with the list helpful in checking and building a crossword vocabulary.

aalii	tree; wood	abele	white poplar
Aare	Swiss river	abet	aid; assist
abbé	monk; cleric	abou	father (Arabic)

acer	maple genus	artel	union; cooperative
Acre	Israeli city	arum	cuckoopint; flowering plant
acta	deeds	Asgard	abode of Norse gods
Adah	wife of Lamech	Astarte	Phoenician love goddess
Adak	Alaskan island	atap	palm; nipa
Adar	Jewish month	ates	sweetsop
adit	mine entrance	Atka	Aleutian tribe
adze	shaping tool	atle	Tamarisk salt tree
Aeolus	Greek god of wind	Atli	Norse king
aga	Muslim chief	Aton	Egyptian solar deity
agar	moss; culture medium	atri	Italian commune
agee	awry; askew	Attica	Greek district; New York State
agha	Muslim leader		prison
agora	assembly	Attu	Alaskan island
Agra	site of Taj Mahal	Aude	French river
aile	winged (heraldry)	Auk	diving bird
Aino, Ainu	Japanese aborigine	aune	French length
Aire	French river	aux	French commune
ait	river island	ava	Pepper shrub; hummingbird
alae	winglike part	avocet	bird; plover
alar	winged	awn	beard on grain
alef	Hebrew letter	axil	leaf angle
alen	Danish length	axon	nerve-cell process
Aleut	Alaskan Indian		
Alma	Crimean river	Baal	god; idol
aloe	bitter herb; lily	baft	astern
alop	askew	Bahia	Brazilian state; bay
ama	cup; candlenut	baht	Siamese coin
amah	Oriental nurse	Baku	Caspian harbor
ameer	Arab chieftain	Bali	Indonesian island
amir	Arab chieftain	Balt	Lett; Lithuanian
Amos	biblical prophet	banc	judge's bench
ana	collection; anthology	bane	evil; scourge
anas	duck genus	bani	Rumanian money
ani	blackbird; cuckoo	Bann	Irish river
anil	indigo shrub	Barre	Vermont city
anile	old-womanish; feeble	Baya	Bantu tribe
anion	ion; particle	Beda	Arabian city
anise	fragrant seed	beka	biblical money; Hebrew weight
anoa	wild Celebes ox	Belem	Brazilian city
ans	Belgian commune	Benares	Indian city
ansa	loop; handle	Bera	Arabian city
ante	poker stake; before	berm	bank; lodge
anti	opposed	Berne	Swiss city
A one	first-rate; tops	bes	ancient Roman weight
apa	wallaba tree	besa	Abyssinian money
apis	bee; Egyptian sacred bull	besant	old French money
apod	footless	bezant	circle (heraldry)
Apollo	sun god	bhar	Indian weight
Aral	Soviet sea	bilk	cheat
Aran	Irish island	binh	Annam weight
Ares	Greek god of war	bisse	snake (heraldry)
aria	opera solo	Blanc	peak in Alps
aril	seed covering	boa	feathered scarf; constrictor

bole	friable clay
bolo	knife; machete
Bonn	West German city
brae	Scottish hillside
brut	dry wine
cabal	secret group; junta
Caen	French city
Caddo	Indian tribe
cadi	Muslim judge
Cain	Abel's brother
calp	limestone
cam	gear
Carib	South American Indian
carr	pool
cava	pepper shrub; vein
Cayuga	Iroquoian tribe
cere	wax; wrap
Ceres	grain goddess
Clare	Irish county
Clio	muse of history
Comus	god of mirth
Coos	Oregon tribe
copa	Spanish measure
cor	heart; brightest star
corium	dermis; layer
cos	lettuce
Cree	Indian tribe
Crimea	Russian peninsula
cuir	leather (French)
cull	choose; assort
cuya	Cuban timber tree
dace	carplike fish
Dade	Florida county
dado	groove
Dail	Irish parliament
daler	Dutch money
Davos	Swiss resort
Dee	English river
dhai	Midwife
dhak	East Indian dye tree
dhal	lentil
dhan	cattle; property
dhow	Oriental sailing ship
dinar	Bulgarian or Yugoslav money
dop	diamond holder
dopp	dip
Duma	Russian council
durn	gatepost
dyad	pair
Dyak	Borneo tribe
dyne	unit of force

ebon	black
Edda	Icelandic saga; Norse prose
ede	Dutch commune
Eder	German river
Edo	Tokyo
Eger	German river
Ela	highest note; Guido's note
Elam	biblical kingdom
elan	dash; ardor
Elbe	German river
Elul	Jewish month
emir	Muslim chieftain
emu	ostrichlike bird
Enna	Sicilian city
Enns	Austrian river
Enos	Seth's son
ente	grafted (heraldry)
ento	inner (prefix)
Enyo	Ares' mother
Eolus	Colorado mountain
epee	fencing blade
ephah	Hebrew measure
epi	finial; spire
Erda	Norse earth goddess
eri	silkworm
Eris	goddess of discord
Erlau	Hungarian commune
ern	sea eagle
erne	sea eagle; Irish river
Erse	Gaelic
esker	glacial ridge
esne	serf
esse	existence; abstract being
Este	Italian commune
Estes	Colorado park
estop	prevent by law
et al	and others (Latin abbreviation)
etui	vanity case; needle case
evoe	bacchanals' cry
ewer	pitcher
exe	English river
fane	temple
fanon	cape; orale
faro	card game
Faroe	danish islands
fass	Austrian measure
faun	satyr; Roman half goat
Faunus	rural deity
fels	Indian money
fete	festival
fiat	command; decree
fief	feudal estate
fils	son (French)

flak	antiaircraft bursts	hod	brick tray; coal scuttle
flan	custard	Hood	Oregon mountain
flay	skin	hora	Israeli dance
fosse	moat; pit	Horeb	biblical mountain
Frey	Norse god	Hosea	biblical prophet
Frigg	Odin's wife	Hoth	Norse god
		huk	Philippine guerrilla
gad	rove	hula	Hawaiian dance
Gael	Celt	Hun	barbarian; vandal
gam	mouth; leg	Hydra	nine-headed monster
gaol	prison		
gar	needlefish	iamb	verse foot
gard	French department	ibex	wild goat
gare	railway station (French)	Ibid	same place (abbreviation)
Gaspé	Canadian peninsula	ibis	wading bird
gata	shark	Ibo	West African tribe
Gaza	biblical city	ici	here (French)
Gerd	Frey's wife	icon	religious image
Geri	Odin's wolf	Ida	Asia Minor range; Crete mountain
ghat	range; pass		
gila	lizard	Idas	killer of Castor
Gilead	biblical mountain	ideo	idea (prefix)
gnu	antelope; wildebeest	ides	Roman date
Goa	former Portuguese colony	iglu	Eskimo hut
Golo	Bantu tribe	ilex	holly
Goshen	biblical land of plenty	ilia	hip bones
gowl	monster	imam	caliph
gradus	ancient Roman length	immi	Swiss measure
graf	German count	Indus	Indian river
grao	Portuguese weight	inee	arrow poison
gulden	Dutch money	Inez	Don Juan's mother
		Inga	shrub genus
Hades	Greek underworld	Iole	Hercules' captive
hadj	pilgrimage	Iona	Scottish isle
haft	handle	Ionia	Asia Minor district
ha ha	laugh; sunken fence	iota	Greek letter; bit
haka	dance	Irra	Babylonian god
Hamar	city in Norway	Isar	Bavarian river
Hamite	biblical tribe	Iser	Czech river
Han	river in China	Isere	French river
hart	stag	Isis	Egyptian goddess; sister and wife of Osiris
hemo	blood (prefix)		
Hera	queen goddess	itea	Virginia willow
Herat	Afghanistan city	ixia	iris
Hermes	Greek god		
Herod	biblical ruler	jako	parrot
Herr	Mister (German)	jama	tunic
Hesse	German state	jami	mosque
Hilo	Hawaiian city	jann	genie
hin	Hebrew measure	jara	palm
Hiram	biblical ruler	Jebu	West African tribe
hiro	Japanese length	Jehu	biblical ruler
Hler	Norse god	Jena	German city
hoar	frost	jeté	ballet jump

jhow	Tamarisk shrub	lait	milk (French)
jib	triangular sail	lama	Buddhist monk; Tibetan priest
jilt	cheat; reject	Lamech	biblical patriarch
jinn	demon	lar	gibbon
Joad	English philosopher	lath	strip of wood
Joshua	biblical ruler	lave	bathe
Jove	chief Roman god	lea	meadow
juba	African dance	Leda	Castor's mother; swan
Jung	psychiatrist	lees	dregs
Juno	Roman queen of gods	Lena	Asian river
junu	charm	Lenape	Indian tribe
jura	French department	Leto	Apollo's mother
		Levi	Jacob's son; Hebrew tribe
kabul	Indian river	Leyte	Pacific island
kadi	judge	libra	Mexican weight
Kafir	Bantu tribe	Lido	Adriatic resort
kana	Japanese writing	limn	portray
Kano	Nigerian walled city	limu	edible seaweed
kaph	Hebrew letter	Linz	Austrian city
Kara	Arabian sea	liss	fleur-de-lis
kava	Polynesian beverage	lobo	timber wolf
kawa	Pepper shrub	loch	Scottish lake
kela	Arabian weight	Loki	Norse god
keno	lotto; bingolike game	loup	half-mask (French)
Kent	English county	luff	sail into wind
kepi	military cap	Luna	moon goddess
kerf	notch	Lys	Belgian river
khat	Turkish length		
Kiel	German canal	Maas	Dutch river
Kiev	Russian city	mage	magician
kil	monk's cell; Irish church;	Maia	Hermes' mother
	kilometer (abbreviation)	Main	German river
kiln	oven	mani	peanut
Kiowa	Indian tribe	mano	hand grinding stone
kipe	basket	marl	clayey soil
kiri	Kaffir war club	Maui	Hawaiian island
kiwi	flightless bird	Mayo	Irish county; mayonnaise
Kobe	Honshu port	Mede	ancient Persian
Koko	Lord High Executioner	Medusa	Gorgon
kola	nut	mega	great (prefix)
kopek	Russian money	meld	declare, in cards
koss	Indian length	Melos	Aegean island
kraal	Enclosure	merl	blackbird
kris	dagger	Metz	French city
Krishna	Hindu god	mil	wire measure
krona	Icelandic money	Milo	Greek island
Kronos	Titan	Minos	Greek king
kudu	African antelope	moa	flightless bird; ostrich
Kurd	Turkish tribe	Moab	biblical tribe
kvas	Russian sour beer	moho	honey-eating bird
		mohr	gazelle
lac	resin	mojo	voodoo charm
lact	milk (prefix)	moki	New Zealand raft
Lagos	capital of Nigeria	Moro	Philippine Muslim

Mors	Roman god of death	orne	French department
Morta	goddess of fate	ort	morsel; leftover
Muir	Alaska glacier	osier	willow tree
mumm	disguise	Ossa	Greek mountain
		otic	pertaining to the ear
nacre	mother-of-pearl	Otoe	Oklahoma tribe
nae	no (Scottish)	oyez	attention; court cry
Nahor	biblical patriarch		
naif	lustrous	paal	Javanese length
Namur	Belgian commune	pac	boot, moccasin
nard	anoint; spice	paca	rodent
neap	tide	padre	priest; cleric
neb	beak; nose	pala	Indian weight
Nebo	biblical mountain	palp	tentacle; feeler
nee	born (French)	Panay	Philippine island
Nene	English river	pard	leopard
nep	catnip	parr	young fish
Nereid	sea nymph	pas	dance step
ness	promontory	pavis	shield; cover
Nestor	Greek king	Pelée	Martinique volcano
neve	glacier; snow	pelu	hardwood tree
newt	eft	peri	fairy
nez	nose (French)	phon	loudness
nimb	halo	phot	light unit
nipa	drink; East Indian palm	pica	type measure
		Pico	Azores volcano
oast	kiln; oven		
obi	Oriental sash	rale	rattle; breathing noise
obit	death notice	Rama	incarnation of Vishnu
oca	edible tuber	rame	branch
octo	eight (prefix)	rana	Indian prince
oda	harem room	rani	Indian queen
odea	music hall	rati	Indian weight
Oder	Baltic river	Remi	ancient people of Gaul
oeuf	egg (French)	rena	rockfish
ogee	arch; molding	ret	soak flax
Okie	migratory worker	rete	network
okra	gumbo	Rhea	Titan; Cronos' wife
ola	palm leaf	Rhus	Sumac genus
olay	palm leaf	ria	narrow inlet; estuary
olio	medley	rial	Iranian coin
olla	jar; meat dish	rien	nothing (French)
Olor	swan genus	Riga	Baltic city
Omei	China mountains	rime	frost
omni	all (prefix); Atlanta arena	ripa	riverbank
Omsk	Russian city	rom	gypsy husband
oner	individual; corker	rood	crucifix
onus	burden	Rosa	shrub genus
opah	colorful fish	Ross	Antarctic sea
ope	unlock (poetic)	roti	roasted (French)
orca	killer whale	rotl	Muslim weight
Orel	Russian port	Ruhr	German river; industrial area
orle	heraldic bearing	rune	mysterious sign; old alphabet
Orly	French airport		character

rupee	Indian money
Saar	European river
Sac	Algonquin Indian; pouch
sago	starch; pudding
samp	cereal; maize; pudding
sans	without (French)
sari	Indian dress
sego	edible bulb
sera	antitoxins; evening (Italian)
serac	glacial ridge; white cheese
sere	dry; parched
serif	part of printer's letter
seta	bristle
Seth	biblical patriarch; Adam's son
shay	carriage
Shem	biblical patriarch
shiv	knife
Sikh	Hindu soldier
sine	trigonometry function
sire	lord; father; beget
Siva	Hindu god
skag	part of ship's keel
skew	twist
Skye	Hebrides island
sloe	plum; blackthorn
Smee	Captain Hook's assistant; pintail duck
snee	dirk; knife
soir	evening (French)
Sol	sun god
sora	marsh bird
Spad	biplane; nail
Spes	Roman goddess of hope
Sri	Hindu goddess
SRO	box-office sign
stere	dry measure
stet	let it stand
stile	wall step; set of steps
stoa	portico
suet	hard fat
Suva	Fiji capital
Taal	Afrikaans
Tabor	biblical mountain
tabu	forbidden
tace	body armor
tael	Oriental weight
tamp	pack; ram
Taos	New Mexico town
tapa	bark cloth
Tara	Irish capital; plantation in *Gone with the Wind*
tare	biblical weed; allowance
tarn	lake; pool
taro	edible root
tat	make lace; crochet
tec	detective
tela	membrane; tissue
tele	from a distance (prefix)
tern	gull
Terra	earth goddess
Thalia	One of the Graces
Thetis	Achilles' mother
tia	aunt (Spanish)
tic	spasm
tio	uncle (Spanish)
Tioga	New York county
toga	Roman cloak
tole	lacquered metalware
Toltec	Mexican tribe
tome	large volume
tong	Chinese secret society
tor	craggy hill; pea
tort	civil wrong
torte	rich cake
tret	waste allowance
Triton	Greek god of sea
Truk	Island in Carolines
tsar	Russian despot
tsun	Chinese length
tun	vat; cask
tutu	New Zealand shrub; ballet skirt
tyro	novice
über	over (German)
uca	crab
uke	ukelele
ule	rubber tree
ulex	spine shrub
Ulm	German city
ulna	elbow bone
unde	lines (heraldry)
ungula	hoof; claw
Ural	Russian river; range
Urd	Norse goddess of destiny
urde	key-shaped (heraldry)
Uri	Swiss commune
Uria	Bathsheba's husband
ursa	bear
urus	ox; aurochs
Ute	Colorado Indian
Utu	Babylonian god
uvea	iris layer
uvic	grapelike
Vaal	South African river
vair	heraldic tincture

vale	valley; glen; farewell	xema	Arctic gull
vari	diverse (prefix)	Xenia	Ohio city
vasa	ducts	xeno	foreign (prefix)
Veda	Hindu bible	xeres	wine; sherry
vega	meadow	Xosa	Kaffir tribe
veld	South African grassland	Xtian	Christian
Venus	Roman goddess of love		
vert	green	yaba	cabbage tree
Vesta	goddess of hearth	yak	ox
Vishnu	Hindu god	Yalu	Korean river
vita	life (Latin)	yamp	tuber
vite	quick (French)	yapa	palm-leaf mat
vivo	lively (music)	yegg	burglar
viz	namely	Yemen	Arabian state
voce	voice (Italian)	yen	Japanese money; urge
vole	rodent	yin	Chinese weight
		Ymir	Norse giant
		Yser	Belgian river
WAC	female GI		
Waco	Texas city	zak	Dutch measure
wadd	black ocher	zany	nutty; crazy
wadi	dry river bed	Zara	Italian province
wale	cloth ridge	zee	final letter; zed
wang	Dutch East Indies weight	Zen	Buddhist sect
weel	fish trap	zero	nothing; cipher
weft	web; yarn	zeta	Greek letter
wen	cyst; old English letter	Zeus	chief Olympian god
woad	dyestuff	Zion	hill; heaven
Wodan	Norse god	Zulu	Bantu tribe
Woden	Norse god	Zuni	Pueblo Indian
Wotan	Norse god	zwei	two (German)

Commonly Misspelled Words

See also ''Commonly Misused Words'' on page 305.

See also ''Commonly Misused Words'' on page 305.

abscess	aisle/isle	arithmetic	battalion
accept/except	allege	asparagus	bazaar
accessory	all right	asthma	beginning
accidentally	already	athletic	believe
accommodate	amateur	attendance	benign
accompany	analogous	attorney	biscuit
accrue	antarctic	auxiliary	bizarre
acquaintance	antecedent		bookkeeper
acquire	apparent	banana	buoyant
address	arctic	baptize	bureau
affect/effect	argument	bargain	burglar

calendar
cantaloupe
capital/capitol
cashmere
caterpillar
ceiling
cellar
cemetery
cereal/serial
chamois
chandelier
changeable
chaperon(e)
chauffeur
chief
cinnamon
circuit
circumference
cocoa
colonel/kernel
committee
compliment/complement
comptroller
concede
conceive
conscientious
conscious
consensus
consignment
convenient
coquette
corduroy
correspondent
cough
counterfeit
crucifixion

debt
definite
dependent
design
desirable
desperately
dessert/desert
devise
diaphragm
diarrhea
dictionary
diphtheria
disappear
disappoint
dispel
dissatisfied

effect/affect
eighth
embarrass
embezzle
environment
equipped
erroneous
especially
etiquette
exaggerate
exceed
excel
existence
expense

familiar
fascinate
fatigue
February
fiancé
fiancée
financier
foreclosure
forehead
foreign
foreword/forward
formerly/formally
forth/fourth
fragile
freight

gauge
gingham
glacier
government
grammar
grease
guarantee
guess
guest

handkerchief
harass
height
heir
hemorrhage
hygiene
hypocrisy

idol/idle
incite/insight
independence
indict
indispensable

infinitesimal
irresistible
isthmus
its/it's

judgment

khaki

laboratory
larynx
laugh
league
library
license
licorice
literature
lose/loose
lying

mackerel
maintenance
malign
maneuver
manual
mathematics
mattress
minuscule
mischief
missionary
misspell
misstate
molasses
mortgage
mosquitoes

necessary
neighbor
niece
noticeable
nuisance

obedience
occasion
occur
occurred
o'clock
offense
omitted

parallel
parliament
phenomenon
physician

plaid
pneumonia
politically
porcelain
possess
potatoes
prairie
precede/proceed
preferred
principle/principal
privilege
probably
protégé
protégée
pseudonym
psychology
ptomaine

quiet/quite

rarefy
raspberry
receipt
receive
recess
recognize
recommend
reference
remittance
rendezvous
repellent
repentance
resemblance
reservoir
résumé
reverence
rhythm
ridiculous

sacrilege
sacrilegious
sandwich
satire/satyr
scissors
secretary
seize
separately
siege
sieve
similar
sincerely
soliloquy
special
squirrel

stationary/stationery	tariff	Tuesday	weird
straight/strait	temperance		wholly
strengthen	tenement	usually	whose/who's
succeed	than/then		withhold
success	their/there	vaccinate	
suit/suite	threshold	vacuum	yolk
superintendent	tobacco	villain	your/you're
supersede	tomatoes	vinegar	
susceptible	to/too/two		zephyr
synagogue	tragedy	warrant	
syringe	truly	Wednesday	

COMMON PHRASES: MAJOR EUROPEAN LANGUAGES

English	French	German	Italian	Spanish
Hello/good day	Bon jour	Guten tag	Buon giorno	Buenas días
Please	S'il vous plaît	Bitte	Prege per favere	Con su permiso; por favor
Thank you	Merci	Danke schön	Grazie	Gracias
Excuse me/ pardon me	Excuser moi/ pardonner moi	Entschuldigen sie mir	Perdonne me	Perdóname
Yes	Oui	Ja	Si	Sí
No	Non	Nein	No	No
Goodbye/ so long	Au révoir/ à bientôt	Auf wiedersehen	Arrivederci	Adiós; hasta la vista

Frequently Used Foreign Words and Phrases

à bas (F)	down with
ab initio (L)	from the beginning
ab ovo usque ad mala (L)	from soup to nuts (lit., "from the egg to the apples")
ab urbe condita (L)	from the founding of the city (Rome, 753 B.C.)
a capella (It)	in the church style (vocally)
ad astra per aspera (L)	to the stars through difficulties
adagio (It)	slowly
ad eundum (L)	to the same degree
ad hoc (L)	for a particular purpose (lit., "to this")
ad infinitum (L)	forever
ad libitum (L)	ad lib, freely (lit., "to pleasure")
ad nauseum (L)	to the point of disgust
aere perennius (L)	more durable than bronze
aficionado (Sp)	enthusiast, fan
alea jacta est (L)	the die is cast
alfresco (It)	in the open air
alma mater (L)	old school (lit., "fostering mother")

aloha (Hw)	greeting or farewell
amor con amor se paga (Sp)	one good turn deserves another (lit., "love is repaid with love")
amor vincit omnia (L)	love conquers all
ancien régime (Fr)	the old regime (pre-French revolution)
anno domini; A.D. (L)	in the year of the Lord
annus mirabilis (L)	wonderful year
a posteriori (L)	inductive (lit., "from what comes after")
après moi, le déluge (Fr)	after me, the deluge
a priori (L)	deductive (lit., "from what comes before")
arma virumque cano (L)	I sing of arms and the man (Virgil)
ars gratia gratis (L)	art for art's sake
ars longa, vita brevis (L)	art is long, life is short
au contraire (Fr)	on the contrary
au courant (Fr)	up to date, contemporary
au naturel (Fr)	nude, plain
aurea mediocritas (L)	golden mean
autre temps, autre mœurs (Fr)	other times, other customs
avant-garde (Fr)	forward, advanced; vanguard
ave atque vale (L)	hail and farewell
beau geste (Fr)	noble gesture
beau idéal (Fr)	highest ideal
bête noire (Fr)	pet peeve (lit., "black beast")
bienséance (Fr)	decorum, mannerliness
billet doux (Fr)	love letter
Blitzkrieg (Gr)	lightning war
bon marché (Fr)	inexpensive (lit., "good market")
bon mot (Fr)	clever turn of phrase
bonne chance (Fr)	good luck
bon vivant (Fr)	partygoer; one who enjoys life
bon voyage (Fr)	good journey
campesino (Sp)	peasant, farmer
canard (Fr)	insult, hoax (lit., "duck")
carpe diem (L)	seize the day
carte blanche (Fr)	free hand, no restrictions (lit., "white card")
cause célèbre (Fr)	scandal; notorious incident
caveat emptor (L)	let the buyer beware
c'est la vie (Fr)	that's life
ceteris paribus (L)	other things being equal
chacun à son gout (Fr)	each to his own taste
chef d'œuvre (Fr)	masterpiece
cherchez la femme (Fr)	look for the woman
chutzpah (Y)	gall, daring
ciao (It)	goodbye, so long
circa (c., ca.)	about, approximately
cogito ergo sum (L)	I think, therefore I am
cognoscenti (It)	intellectuals; those in the know
comédie de mœurs (Fr)	comedy of manners
comme il faut (Fr)	proper, appropriate
con mucho gusto (Sp)	with pleasure
corpus delicti (L)	evidence (lit., "body of the crime")
coup de grâce (Fr)	final blow

coup d'état (F)	overthrow of government
credo quia absurdum (L)	I believe because it is absurd
cui bono? (L)	to whose benefit?
cul de sac (Fr)	dead end (lit., "end of the bag")
cum grano salis (L)	with a grain of salt
de capo (It)	from the top
déclassé (Fr)	fallen in social standing
décolletage (Fr)	low-cut style
de facto (L)	in fact
de gustibus non est disputandum (L)	there is no arguing about taste
de jure (L)	in law
demi-monde (Fr)	underworld; other side of the tracks
de mortuis nil nisi bonum (L)	of the dead [say nothing] but good
Deo gratias (L)	thanks be to God
Deo volente (L)	God willing
dernier cri (Fr)	the last word
déshabillé (Fr)	disheveled, slovenly
deus ex machina (L)	desperate or contrived solution (lit., "god from the machine")
Ding an sich (Gr)	the thing in itself
dolce far niente (It)	sweet idleness
Doppelgänger (Gr)	phantom double
Drang nach Osten (Gr)	drive toward the east
dum spiro spero (L)	while there's life, there's hope
embarras de richesse (Fr)	embarrassment of riches
enfant terrible (Fr)	prodigy
en passant (Fr)	in passing; by the way
entre nous (Fr)	privately, between us
épater le bourgeois (Fr)	shock the middle class
e pluribus unum (L)	from many, one
ersatz (Gr)	fake, imitation
et cetera (etc.) (L)	and others
Eureka! (Gk)	I've found it!
ex cathedra (L)	with high authority (lit., "from the chair")
exempli gratia (e.g.) (L)	by way of example
ex post facto (L)	after the fact
fait accompli (Fr)	accomplished fact
faute de mieux (Fr)	for want of something better
faux pas (Fr)	social error (lit., "false step")
femme fatale (Fr)	alluring, dangerous woman
fin de siècle (Fr)	end of century; decadent
flagrante delicto (L)	caught in the act (lit., "with the crime blazing")
gaudeamus igitur (L)	let us therefore rejoice
glasnost (R)	openness
gnothi seauton (Gk)	know yourself
gonif (Y)	thief
goy (Y)	gentile
habeas corpus (L)	writ requiring a court appearance (lit., "[that] you have the body")

haut monde (Fr)	high society
hoi polloi (Gk)	common people, mob
homo lupus homini (L)	man is a wolf to man
honi soi qui mal y pense (Fr)	shame to him who thinks evil of it
hubris (Gk)	overweening pride, arrogance
idée fixe (Fr)	fixed idea, obsession
id est (i.e.) (L)	that is
infra dignitatem (infra dig.) (L)	beneath one's dignity
in loco parentis (L)	in the place of parents
in medias res (L)	in the middle of things
in vino veritas (L)	in wine, truth
ipso facto (L)	by the fact itself
joie de vivre (Fr)	good spirits, exuberance (lit., "joy of living")
jus gentium (L)	the law of nations
kamikaze (J)	suicide pilot (lit., "divine wind")
klutz (Y)	clumsy person
kvetch (Y)	complain, carp
la belle dame sans merci (Fr)	the beautiful woman without mercy
laissez-faire (Fr)	noninterference (lit., "let [people] do [as they wish]")
lapsus linguae (L)	slip of the tongue
Lebensraum (Gr)	living room; elbow room
lèse majesté (Fr)	treason
l'état, c'est moi (Fr)	I am the state
lingua franca (L)	common language (lit., "French tongue")
macher (Y)	celebrity, big shot
magnum opus (L)	major work
mañana (Sp)	tomorrow
manqué (Fr)	failed
maven (Y)	expert, authority
mazel tov (Y)	congratulations
mea culpa (L)	my fault
memento mori (L)	reminder of death
mens sana in corpore sano (L)	a sound mind in a sound body
meshuggah (Y)	crazy
mirabile dictu (L)	amazingly (lit., "remarkable to say")
modus operandi (M.O.) (L)	method of operation
morituri te salutamus (L)	we who are about to die salute you
mutatis mutandis	with the needed changes made
ne plus ultra (L)	the best
n'est-ce pas? (Fr)	isn't that true?
noblesse oblige (Fr)	the responsibility of noble birth
nom de plume (Fr)	pen name
non sequitur (L)	something that does not follow
nosh (Y)	nibble, eat
nota bene (N.B.) (L)	note well
nunc aut nunquam (L)	now or never
obiter dictum (L)	something said in passing; a peripheral comment
o tempora, o mores! (L)	o the times, o the customs!

panem et circenses (L)	bread and circuses
par excellence (Fr)	above all, preeminently
par exemple (Fr)	for example
pari passu (L)	at an equal pace
parvenu (Fr)	newcomer, upstart; nouveau riche
passim (L)	here and there
per diem (L)	by the day
per favore (It)	please
persona non grata (L)	unwanted person
pièce de résistance (Fr)	showpiece item
pied à terre (Fr)	in-town apartment; temporary lodging
plus ça change, plus c'est la même chose (Fr)	the more things change, the more they are the same
pons asinorum (L)	insoluble problem (lit., "bridge of asses")
por favor (Sp)	please
prego (It)	please
prima facie (L)	on the face of it; at first sight
primus inter pares (L)	first among equals
prix fixe (Fr)	fixed price
pro bono publico (L)	for the public good
quid pro quo (L)	fair exchange; tit for tat
quién sabe? (Sp)	who knows?
quod erat demonstrandum (Q.E.D.) (L)	as has been demonstrated
quod vide (q.v.) (L)	which see (used as cross-reference)
raison d'être (Fr)	reason for being
rara avis (L)	rarity (lit., "rare bird")
reductio ad absurdum (L)	reduction to absurdity (in logical argument)
répondez s'il vous plaît (R.S.V.P.) (Fr)	respond if you please
requiescat in pace (R.I.P.)	rest in peace
salaam aleicham (A)	peace
sancta sanctorum (L)	holy of holies
sangfroid (Fr)	aplomb; composure
savoir faire (Fr)	social savvy (lit., "to know what to do")
schlemiel (Y)	unlucky person, loser
schmaltz (Y)	excessive sentimentality
schtick (Y)	gimmick; a performer's idiosyncracy
semper fidelis (L)	always faithful
shalom (H)	greeting or farewell (lit., "peace")
sic (L)	thus
sic semper tyrannis (L)	thus always to tyrants
sic transit gloria mundi (L)	thus passes the glory of the world
sine qua non (L)	something indispensable (lit., "without which not")
sotto voce (It)	softly (lit., "in a soft voice")
status quo (L)	current state of affairs
Sturm und Drang (Gr)	storm and stress
sui generis (L)	one of a kind, unique
tabula rasa (L)	clean slate (lit., "erased tablet")
tant mieux (Fr)	all the better
tant pis (Fr)	all the worse

tempus fugit (L)	time flies
terra firma (L)	solid ground
terra incognita (L)	unknown territory
tête-à-tête (Fr)	intimate conversation (lit., ''head to head'')
tout de suite (Fr)	immediately
tout le monde (Fr)	everyone
tovarish (R)	comrade
trompe-l'œil (Fr)	illusionary (lit., ''fool the eye'')
vade mecum (L)	handbook, guide (lit., ''go with me'')
vaya con Dios (Sp)	go with God
veni, vidi, vici (L)	I came, I saw, I conquered
verboten (Gr)	forbidden
verbum sapienti sat (L)	a word to the wise is enough
volte-face (Fr)	about face, reversal
vox clamantis in deserto (L)	a voice crying in the desert
vox populi, vox Dei (L)	the voice of the people, the voice of God
Wanderjahre (Gr)	year of travel
Wanderlust (Gr)	desire to travel
Weltanschauung (Gr)	philosophy, outlook
Weltschmerz (Gr)	world-weariness (lit., ''world pain'')
Wunderkind (Gr)	prodigy
yenta (Y)	gossip or busybody
Zeitgeist (Gr)	spirit of the times

Key to abbreviations:

A	Arabic	H	Hebrew	lit.	literally
Fr	French	Hw	Hawaiian	Sp	Spanish
Gk	Greek	It	Italian	R	Russian
Gr	German	L	Latin	Y	Yiddish

86 Acceptable Two-Letter Scrabble™ Words

aa	ba	er	is	no	oy	us
ad	be	es	it	nu	pa	ut
ae	bi	et	jo	od	pe	we
ah	bo	ex	ka	oe	pi	wo
ai	by	fa	la	of	re	xi
am	da	go	li	oh	sh	xu
an	de	ha	lo	om	si	ya
ar	do	he	ma	on	so	ye
as	ef	hi	me	op	ta	
at	eh	ho	mi	or	ti	
aw	el	id	mu	os	to	
ax	em	if	my	ow	un	
ay	en	in	na	ox	up	

RECURRENT LETTERS OF THE ALPHABET

The normal frequencies with which letters of the alphabet occur from most to least frequent: E, T, A, O, I, N, S, H, R, D, L, U, C, M, P, F, Y, W, G, B, V, K, J, X, Z, Q.

OXYMORON: A PAIRING OF CONTRADICTORY OR INCONGRUOUS WORDS

acute dullness	home office	player coach
almost perfect	idiot savant	pretty ugly
bad health	instant classic	qualified success
bittersweet	intense apathy	randomly organized
blameless culprit	jumbo shrimp	real potential
cardinal sin	justifiably paranoid	rock opera
clearly confused	larger half	rolling stop
conservative liberal	least favorite	same difference
constant variable	linear curve	silent scream
definite maybe	liquid gas	simply superb
deliberately thoughtless	mild interest	sweet sorrow
divorce court	minor miracle	taped live
even odds	modern history	terribly enjoyable
exact estimate	nonalcoholic beer	tragic comedy
extensive briefing	nondairy creamer	unbiased opinion
fish farm	normal deviation	uncrowned king
freezer burn	old news	unsung hero
friendly takeover	only choice	vaguely aware
genuine imitation	open secret	war games
good grief	original copies	working vacation
holy war	passively aggressive	

Acronyms

Acronyms are pronounceable formations made by combining the initial letters or syllables of a string of words.

ACTION	American Council to Improve Our Neighborhoods
AID	Agency for International Development; American Institute of Decorators; Army Intelligence Department
AIDS	acquired immune deficiency syndrome
ALCOA	Aluminum Company of America
AMEX	American Express Company
AMOCO	American Oil Company
ARC	AIDS-related complex
ARCO	Atlantic Richfield Company
ASCAP	American Society of Composers, Authors and Publishers
AWOL	absent without leave
BAM	Brooklyn Academy of Music; Basic Access Method
BART	Bay Area Rapid Transit
BASE	Bank-Americard Service Exchange

BASIC	Beginner's All-purpose Symbolic Instruction Code (computer language)
BASS	Bass Anglers Sportsman Society
BIB	Bureau of International Broadcasting
BIZNET	American Business Network (database of Chamber of Commerce)
BOLD	Bibliographic On-Line Display (document retrieval system)
CALM	Citizens Against Legalized Murder
CARE	Cooperative for American Relief Everywhere
CAT (scan)	computerized axial tomography
CLASSMATE	Computer Language to Aid and Stimulate Scientific, Mathematical and Technical Education
COBOL	Common Business-Oriented Language
COMEX	Commodity Exchange (New York)
CONOCO	Continental Oil Company
CONUS	Continental United States
CORE	Congress of Racial Equality
CURE	Citizens United for Racial Equality
DAM	Dayton Art Museum; Denver Art Museum
DELCO	Dayton Engineering Laboratory Company
DISCO	Defense Industrial Security Clearing Office
DOS	disk operating system; digital operating system
DYNAMO	Dynamic Action Management Operation
EARS	Electronic Airborne Reaction System; Electronically Agile Radar System; Emergency Airborne Reaction System
ELECTRA	Electrical, Electronics and Communications Trade Association
ENDEX	Environmental Data Index
EPCOT	Experimental Prototype Community of Tomorrow
EXIMBANK	Export-Import Bank of the United States
FEDLINK	Federal Library Information Network
FEW	Federally Employed Women
FICA	Federal Insurance Contributions Act (Social Security)
FLIP	Flexible Loan Insurance Program; floating instrument platform
FORTRAN	formula translation (programming language)
GAG	Graphic Artists Guild
GARB	Garment and Allied Industries Requirements Board
GIPSY	General Information Processing System
GLAD	Gay and Lesbian Advocates and Defenders
GMAT	Graduate Management Admission Test
GRAD	Graduate Resume Accumulation and Distribution
GUPCO	Gulf Petroleum Corporation
HALF	Human Animal Liberation Front
HART	Honolulu Area Rapid Transit
HEAL	Health Education Assistance Loans
HOBOL	homing bomb
INLAW	infantry laser weapon
INTERMARC	International Machine-Readable Catalog
INTERPOL	International Criminal Police Organization
INTERTELL	International Intelligence Legion
IRA	individual retirement account; Irish Republican Army
JOBS	Job Opportunities in the Business Sector
JUMPS	Joint Uniform Military Pay System
LEAP	Loan and Educational Aid Program
LILCO	Long Island Lighting Company
LORAN	Long-range Aid to Navigation
LSAT	Law School Admission Test

MACOM	major Army command
MAD	mutually assured destruction
MADD	Mothers Against Drunk Driving
MARC	machine-reading cataloging
MASH	mobile Army surgical unit
MOMA	Museum of Modern Art (New York)
NAM	Network access machine; National Association of Manufacturers; National Air Museum
NAPA	National Automotive Parts Association; National Police Officers' Association of America
NARAD	Navy Research and Development
NARCO	United Nations Narcotics Commission
NASA	National Aeronautics and Space Administration
NASCAR	National Association of Sports Car Racing
NATO	North Atlantic Treaty Organization
NECCO	New England Confectionary Company
NOMAD	Navy oceanographic and meteorological device
NORAD	North American Air Defense
NOW	National Organization for Women
OASIS	Overseas Access Service for Information Systems
ODECO	Ocean Drilling and Exploration Company
ODESY	On-Line Data Entry System
OPEC	Organization of Petroleum Exporting Countries
OXFAM	Oxford Famine Relief
PAC	political action committee; Pacific Air Command
PATCO	Port Authority Transit Corporation
PATH	Port Authority Trans-Hudson
PEN	Poets, Playwrights, Editors, Essayists, and Novelists
PERT	program evaluation and review technique
PET	parent effectiveness training
PIN	personal identification number; Police Information Network
PIRG	public interest research group
QUICKTRAN	Quick FORTRAN (computer language)
RADAR	radio detecting and ranging
RAM	random-access memory
READ	real-time electronic access and display
RIF	Reading Is Fundamental
ROM	read-only memory
ROTC	Reserve Officer's Training Corps
SADD	Students Against Drunk Driving
SAFE	system for automated flight efficiency
SALT	strategic arms limitation talks
SUNOCO	Sun Oil Company
SEATO	Southeast Asia Treaty Organization
TAC	Tactical Air Command
UNESCO	United Nations Educational, Social, and Cultural Organization
UNICEF	United Nations International Children's Emergency Fund (now shortened to United Nations Children's Fund)
UNIVAC	universal automatic computer
VISTA	Volunteers in Service to America
WAC	Women's Army Corps
WASP	white Anglo-Saxon Protestant
WAVES	Women Accepted for Volunteer Emergency Service (Navy)
WHO	World Health Organization

WIN	work incentive program
WISE	World Information Systems Exchange
WUDO	Western European Defense Organization
YUPPIE	young urban professional
ZIP	zone improvement plan (U.S. Postal Service)

PALINDROMES

A palindrome can be a single word, a verse, a sentence, a series of sentences, or a number that reads the same forward and backward. People have been creating palindromes in all languages since at least as early as the third century B.C. Palindromic sentences often become jokes when meanings are ascribed to them and when punctuation is added. For example, the two best-known English palindromes are "Able was I ere I saw Elba," which was not written by but could have been uttered by Napoleon, and "Madam, I'm Adam," which is fun to think of as the first introduction. Note that "madam" alone is a palindromic word, but sentences are more amusing:

> Enid and Edna dine.
> A man, a plan, a canal, Panama!
> Draw, O Caesar, erase a coward.
> Al lets Della call Ed Stella.
> Dennis sinned.
> Ma is a nun, as I am.
> Naomi, did I moan?
> Niagara, O roar again!
> He lived as a devil, eh?

And here is a palindromic conversation between two owls:

> "Too hot to hoot!"
> "Too hot to woo!"
> "Too wot?"
> "Too hot to hoot!"
> "To woo!"
> "Too wot?"
> "Too hoot! Too hot to hoot!"

Greek Prefixes

Prefix	Meaning in English	Prefix	Meaning in English
a	not	an	not
acantho	spiny, thorny	ana	again, thorough, thoroughly
acous	hearing		
acro	top, tip	andro	man
adeno	gland	anem(o)	wind
aero	air, gas	anthropo	man
allo	other	anti	against
amphi	both, around	apo	away
amylo	starch	arch(i)	chief

Prefix	*Meaning in English*	*Prefix*	*Meaning in English*
arche(o), archae(o)	old, ancient	dermo, dermato	skin
arthro	joint	deutero	second
aster, astro	star	di(s)	apart
atmo	vapor	dia	through
auto	self	dino	terrible
azo	nitrogen	diplo	double
		dodeca	twelve
baro	weight	dyna, dynamo	force, power
batho, bathy	deep	dys	evil, difficult
biblio	book		
bio	life	echino	spiny
blepharo	eyelid	ecto	outside, external
bracchio	arm	ef	out
brachy	short	el, em, en	in, into
branchio	gills	encephalo	brain
broncho	throat	ennea	nine
		entero	gut
caco	evil	ento	inside, interior
cardio	heart	entomo	insect
carpo	fruit	eo	dawn, early
cath, cato	down, thorough, thoroughly	eph, epi	on
		ergo	work
ceno	common	erythro	red
cephalo	head	ethno	race, nation
cero	wax	eu	good
chilo	lip	ex	out
chiro	hand	exo	outside, external
chloro	green		
chole, cholo	bile	galacto	milk
chondro	cartilage	gam(o)	copulation, together
choreo	dance	gastro	stomach
choro	country	geo	earth, land
chrom(at)o	color	geronto	old age
chrono	time	glosso	tongue
chryso	gold	gluc, glyc	sweet
cleisto	closed	glypto, glyph	carving
clino	slope	gnath(o)	jaw
cocci	berry-shaped	gon(o)	reproduction (sexual)
coela	stomach	grapho	writing
conio	dust	gymno	nude, naked
coppro	excrement	gynec(o), gynaec(o)	woman
cosmo	universe		
cranio	skull	haemato	blood
cryo	cold	hagio	holy
crypto	hidden	halo	salt, sea
cteno	comb, rake	haplo	simple
cymo	wave	hecto	hundred
cysto	bladder	helico	spiral
cyto	cell	helio	sun
		hema	blood
dactylo	finger	hemi	half
deca	ten	hepato	liver
dendro	three	hepta	seven

Prefix	*Meaning in English*	*Prefix*	*Meaning in English*
hetero	different	noto	back (of body)
hexa	six	nycto	night
histo	tissue		
hodo	path, way	octa, octo	eight
holo	whole, complete	odonto	tooth
homeo	similar, like	oligo	few
homo	same	ombro	rain
hydro	water	oneiro	dream
hyeto	rain	onto	being
hygro	wet	oo	egg
hylo	matter	ophio	snake
hymeno	membrane	ophthalm(o)	eye
hyper	above	ornitho	bird
hypno	sleep	oro	mouth
hypo	under	ortho	straight
hypso	high	osteo	bone
hystero	womb	oto	ear
		oxy	sharp
iatro	medicine		
ichthyo	fish	pachy	thick
iso	equal	paleo, palaeo	ancient, old
		pan	all
kerato	horn	para	close, beside
kinesi, kineto	movement	patho	suffering, disease
		pedo	child
lepto	slender	penta	five
leuko	white	peri	around, very
litho	stone	petro	stone
logo	word, oral	phago	eating
lyo, lysi	dissolving	phlebo	vein
		phono	sound
macro	large	photo	light
malaco	soft	phreno	brain
mega, megalo	great	phyco	seaweed
melano	black	phyllo	leaf
mero	part	phylo	species
meso	middle	physio	nature
meta	beyond, after, changed	phyto	plant
metro	measure	picro	bitter
micro	small	piezo	pressure
miso	hatred	pleuro	side (of body)
mono	one, single	pluto	riches
morpho	shape	pneumato	breath, spirit
myelo	spinal cord	pneumo	lung
mylo	fungus	polio	gray matter
myo	muscle	poly	many
		pro	before, forward
necro	dead body	proto	first
neo	new	pseudo	false
nepho	cloud	psycho	mind, spirit, soul
nephro	kidney	psychro	cold
neuro	nerve	ptero	wing
noso	sickness	pyo	pus

Prefix	Meaning in English	Prefix	Meaning in English
pyro	fire	stomato	mouth
		stylo	pillar
rheo	flow	sy, syl, sym, syn	with
rhino	nose		
rhizo	root	tachy	rapid
		tauto	same
sacchro	sugar	tele	distant
sapro	decompose	teleo	final
sarco	flesh	telo	distant, final
scato	excrement	thalasso	sea
scelero	hard	thanato	death
schisto, schizo	split	theo	god
seleno	moon	thermo	heat
sidero	iron	thio	sulfur
somato	body	toco	child, birth
speleo	cave	topo	place
spermato	seed	toxico	poison
sphygmo	pulse	trachy	rough
splanchno	guts		
stato	position	xeno	foreign
stauro	cross		
steno	short, narrow	zoo	living
stereo	solid	zygo	double

Greek Suffixes

Suffix	Meaning in English	Suffix	Meaning in English
algia	pain	gamy	marriage
androus	man	gen(ous), geny, gony	giving birth to, bearing
archy	rule, government	gnathous	jaw
		gnomy, gnosis	knowledge
biosis	life	gon	angle
blast	bud	gonium	seed
branch	gills	gram, graph(y)	writing
carpous	fruit	hedral, hedron	side, sided
cele	hollow		
cephalic, cephalous	head	iasis	disease
chrome	color	iatrics, iatry	medical treatment
coccous	berry-shaped	itis	inflammation
cracy, crat	rule, government		
		kinesis	movement
dendron	tree		
derm	skin	lepsy	seizure, fit
drome, dromous	run (race)	lith	stone
		logy	science of, list
emia	blood	lysise, lyte	dissolving

Suffix	*Meaning in English*	*Suffix*	*Meaning in English*
machy	battle, fight	phyllous	leaf
mancy, mantic	foretelling	phyte	plant
mania(c)	craving	plasia, plasis	growth
mere, merous	part	plasm	matter
meter, metry	measure	plast	cell
morphic, morphous	shape	plegia	paralysis
mycete	fungus	plerous	wing
nomy	science of, law of	rrhagia, rrhagic, rrhea	flow
odont	tooth	saur	lizard
odynia	pain	scope, scopy	observation
oid	like, similar	sect, section	cutting
oma	tumor	soma, some	body
opia	eye, sight	sophy	wisdom
opsia	sight	sperm, spermous	seed
opsis	appearance	stichous	row
		stome, stomous	mouth
pathy	suffering, disease		
phage, phagous	eating	taxis, taxy	order
phany	manifestation	tomy	cutting
phobe, phobia	fear	trophy	feed
phone, phony	sound	tropous, tropy	turned

Latin Prefixes

Prefix	*Meaning in English*	*Prefix*	*Meaning in English*
a, abs	from	cis	near, on the near side of
ac, ad, af, ag, al, an, ap, as, at	to, toward	co, col, com, con, cor	with, thorough, thoroughly
		contra	against
alti, alto	high	costo	rib
ambi	both	cruci	cross
ante	before	cupro	copper, bronze
api	bee		
aqui	water	de	not, down
arbori	tree	deci	tenth
audio	hearing	demi	half
avi	bird	denti	tooth
		di(s)	apart
bacci	berry	digit(i)	finger
brevi	short	dorsi, dorso	back (of body)
calci	lime		
centi	hundred		
cerebro	brain	e, ec, ef	out
cervico	neck	equi	equal
circum	around	ex	out
cirro	curl	extra	outside, external

Prefix	Meaning in English	Prefix	Meaning in English
febri	fever	per	through, very
ferri, ferro	iron	pinni	fin, web
fissi	split	pisci	fish
fluvio	river	plano	flat
		plumbo	lead (metal)
gemmi	bud	pluvio	rain
		post	after
igni	fire	pre	before
il, im, in	not, against, in, into, on	preter	beyond
inguino	groin	primi	first
inter	between	pro	for, forward
intra, intro	inside, interior	pulmo	lung
ir	not, against, in, into, on		
		quadri	four
juxta	close, near, beside	quinque	five
labio	lip	re	again
lacto	milk	recti	straight
ligni	wood	reni	kidney
luni	moon	retro	backward
magni	great	sacro	dedicated
mal(e)	bad, evil	sangui	blood
multi	many	se	apart
		sebi, sebo	fatty
naso	nose	septi	seven
nati	birth	sidero	star
nocti	night	somni	sleep
		spiro	breath
ob, oc	against	stelli	star
octa, octo	eight	sub, suc, suf, sum, sup	under
oculo	eye		
of, op	against	super, supra	above
oleo	oil		
omni	all	terri	land, earth
oro	mouth	trans	through, on the far side of
ossi	bone		
ovi, ovo	egg	ultra	beyond
		uni	one, single
pari	equal	vari(o)	different

Latin Suffixes

Suffix	Meaning in English	Suffix	Meaning in English
cidal, cide	kill	grade	walking
fid	split	pennale	wing
fugal, fuge	run away from	vorous	eating

Additional Sources of Information

Berlitz, Charles. *Native Tongues.* Putnam Publishing Group, 1984.

Betteridge, Harold T. *Cassell's German Dictionary*, rev. ed. New York: Macmillan, 1978.

Bremner, John B. *Words, Words, Words: A Dictionary for Writers and Others Who Care About Words.* Columbia University Press, 1980.

Buchanan-Brown, John, et al. *Le Mot Juste: A Dictionary of Classical and Foreign Words and Phrases.* Vintage Books, 1981.

Byrne, Josefa Heifetz. *Mrs. Byrne's Dictionary of Unusual, Obscure and Preposterous Words.* Lyle Stuart, 1974.

Cassell's Italian Dictionary. Macmillan, 1977.

Chapman, Robert L., ed. *New Dictionary of American Slang.* Harper & Row, 1986.

Chapman, Robert L., ed. *Roget's International Thesaurus*, 4th ed. Harper & Row, 1977.

Ciardi, John. *The Complete Browser's Dictionary: The Best of John Ciardi's Two Browser's Dictionaries in a Single Compendium of Curious Expressions and Intriguing Facts.* Harper & Row, 1988.

De Sola, Ralph. *Abbreviations Dictionary*, 7th ed. Elsevier, 1986.

Ehrlich, Eugene, and Hand, Raymond, Jr. *NBC Handbook of Pronunciation*, 4th ed. Harper & Row, 1984.

Girard, Denis, ed. *Cassell's French Dictionary.* Macmillan, 1977.

Grambs, David. *Words About Words.* McGraw-Hill, 1984.

Laird, Charlton, ed. *Webster's New World Thesaurus*, rev. ed. Simon & Schuster, 1985.

McCrum, Robert, et al. *The Story of English.* Sifton/Viking, 1986.

Oxford English Dictionary, 2d ed. 20 vols. Oxford University Press, 1989.

Peers, Edgar A., ed. *Cassell's Spanish Dictionary.* Macmillan, 1977.

Random House College Dictionary, rev. ed. Random House, 1982.

Random House Dictionary of the English Language, 2nd ed. Random House, 1987.

Safire, William. *I Stand Corrected: More on Language.* Times Books, 1984.

Safire, William. *On Language.* Avon, 1981.

Safire, William. *What's the Good Word?* Times Books, 1982.

Simpson, D.P., ed. *Cassell's Latin Dictionary.* Macmillan, 1977.

Skillin, Marjorie E., and Gay, R. *Words Into Type*, 3rd ed. Prentice-Hall, 1978.

Spears, Richard A. *Dictionary of American Idioms.* National Textbook Company, 1987.

Stein, Jess, and Flexner, Stuart Berg, eds. *Random House Thesaurus: College Edition.* Random House, 1984.

Urdang, Laurence. *A Basic Dictionary of Synonyms and Antonyms.* Lodestar Books, 1979.

Urdang, Laurence, ed. *The New York Times Everyday Reader's Dictionary of Misunderstood, Misused and Mispronounced Words*, rev. ed. Times Books, 1985.

Webster's Compact Rhyming Dictionary. Merriam-Webster, 1987.

Webster's Third New International Dictionary, Unabridged. Merriam-Webster, 1986.

Webster's New World Crossword Puzzle Dictionary. Simon & Schuster, 1983.

Webster's New World Dictionary, 3d College Ed. Simon & Schuster, 1988.

Webster's Ninth New Collegiate Dictionary. Merriam-Webster, 1985.

Zinsser, William. *On Writing Well: An Informal Guide to Writing Nonfiction*, rev. ed. Harper & Row, 1985.

13

Grammar and Punctuation

The purpose of language is to communicate thoughts and ideas from one person to another. To do this effectively, all those using a given language must do so in the same way, putting words and sentences together in similar fashion so they are readily understood by anyone familiar with that language.

This is not to say that everyone must write the same sentence to communicate the same concept. On the contrary, American English is so varied, it is possible to express the same basic idea in any number of ways. And each of those ways can be equally correct.

What makes a variety of different sentences equally valid is grammar. Grammar is a set of rules that define the ways words can and cannot be used. These rules are not arbitrarily imposed on the language by English teachers or grammarians; they have, instead, grown out of the language itself and can be observed in action in the everyday speech and writing of those who grew up speaking and writing it.

Much of grammar is intuitive and can be understood by anyone who has spoken American English for any length of time, even without a knowledge of the rules. For instance, the sentence *You be not home go yet* is readily recognized as incorrect even without knowledge of the rules of word order.

But because American English is a complex and difficult language, it is sometimes helpful to have the rules at hand in case logic and intuition fail. What follows, then, are the basics of grammar, spelling, punctuation, and alphabetization for American English. The information presented here is by no means exhaustive, and, because language is a constantly changing thing, there can never be a "final word" as to what is correct and what is incorrect. Still, this guide should help provide a start in understanding grammar, usage, and punctuation.

The Parts of Speech

The parts of speech define the ways words can be used in various contexts. Every word in the English language functions as at least one part of speech; many words can serve, at different times, as two or more parts of speech, depending on the context.

adjective A word that modifies a noun (*blue-green, central, half-baked, temporary*).

adverb A word that modifies a verb, an adjective, or another adverb (*slowy, obstinately, much*).

article Any of three words used to signal the presence of a noun. *A* and *an* are known as indefinite articles; *the* is the definite article.

conjunction A word that connects other words, phrases, or sentences (*and, but, or, because*).

interjection A word, phrase, or sound used as an exclamation and capable of standing by itself (*oh, Lord, damn, my goodness*).

noun A word or phrase that names a person, place, thing, quality, or act (*Fred, New York, table, beauty, execution*). A noun may be used as the subject of a verb, the object of a verb, an identifying noun, the object of a preposition, or an appositive (an explanatory phrase coupled with a subject or object).

preposition A word or phrase that shows the relationship of a noun to a verb, an adjective, or another noun (*at, by, in, to, from, with*).

pronoun A word that substitutes for a noun and refers to a person, place, thing, idea, or act that was mentioned previously or that can be inferred from the context of the sentence (*he, she, it, that*).

verb A word or phrase that expresses action, existence, or occurrence (*throw, be, happen*). Verbs can be transitive, requiring an object (*her* in *I met her*), or intransitive, requiring only a subject (*The sun rises*). Some verbs, like *feel*, are both transitive (*Feel the fabric*) and intransitive (*I feel bad*, in which *bad* is an adjective and not an object).

Turning Words into Sentences

Individual words, even once their parts of speech are identified, do not communicate very much by themselves. They must be combined in such a way that they can convey meaning. This is done by forming sentences that combine words that have meaning in and of themselves (nouns, verbs, adjectives, adverbs, and pronouns) with those that are solely functional (conjunctions, prepositions, interjections, and articles).

There are three main types of sentences that can be constructed from these parts. Statements are sentences that tell of a fact, an occurrence, or an opinion; they provide information *(My daughter is almost three years old)*. Questions are sentences that seek out information *(How old is your daughter?)*. Commands are sentences that make a demand *(Tell your daughter to keep her hands off the cookies)*. In addition, there are exclamations *(You're a fool!)*, answers to questions *(Fine, thank you)*, sounds or cries *(Yipes!)*, and calls to others *(Yoo-hoo, Buzzy!)*.

Once the type of sentence has been selected, the subject, verb, and identifying noun or direct and indirect objects of the sentence can be determined. Their placement within the sentence goes along with the function they perform.

Subject

A subject is a noun or pronoun that is generally the doer of the verb's action *(Herb* in the sentence *Herb kicked the ball)* or the thing being described *(The painting* in the sentence *The painting is beautiful)*. It appears before the verb. In some cases more than one noun appears before the verb. This signifies a compound subject *(Paul and Carol* in the sentence *Paul and Carol argue only about money)*. A noun can function as an adjective *(man's* in the sentence *The man's car jumped the curb)*, an appositive *(gentlemen* in the sentence *The butler, a tall gentleman, came in)*, or as a preposition *(night* in the sentence *At night his hair grows long)*.

Verb

Subject–Verb Agreement

The verb generally follows the subject in statements *(are* in the sentence *We are happy)* and commands *(come* in *Come over here)*. It precedes the subject in questions *(Am* in *Am I blue?)*. The verb and the subject must agree in number if the verb is one that can show number. Verbs that show number are *am, is, are, was, were,* and the third-person singular present tense form of verbs, which usually end in -s *(he shops,* but *they shop* for plural form). Both the subject and verb must be either singular *(I am)* or plural *(we are)*.

A few subjects pose particularly tricky problems of subject–verb agreement. *Either* and *neither* are frequently misconstrued as plural subjects, although they should always be paired with singular verbs *(Neither of us is ready)*. Other subjects, such as *none* and *pair,* can be used in singular or plural constructions, depending on their meaning. For instance, when *none* means "not one," is it singular *(None of the guests is here)*; when it means "not any," it is plural *(None are more beautiful than a rose)*.

Compound subjects can also pose agreement difficulties. Most of the time a compound subject is plural (*Paul and Carol are ready for vacation*). But when a compound subject expresses a thought or concept that is definitely singular, it should be followed by a singular verb (*Hitting a ball and driving it over the outfield wall is a skill few can master*).

Tense

Tense is also indicated by the verb; but with the exception of the verb *to be*, past tense forms do not show the number involved. For the verb *to be*, *was* is used for the singular in the first and third person (*I was, she was*) and *were* is employed for plurals (*they were*) and for the second person singular (*you were*). The majority of other verbs are made into past tense forms by adding *-ed*, regardless of whether the verb's action is performed by the subject (*My dog walked*). In past participles (parts of a verb that express completed action, usually in the passive voice), the verb's action is performed on the subject (*My dog was walked*).

However, a number of verbs are made into past tense forms in ways that follow no general rule at all. *Bite* becomes *bit, fight* becomes *fought, go* becomes *went*, and so on. The only rule that can be applied is the age-old maxim "when in doubt, consult a dictionary."

Objects and Identifying Nouns

There are three types of nouns that can follow the verb in most sentence constructions: direct objects, indirect objects, and identifying nouns. Each operates somewhat differently; again, relative position within the sentence is a determining factor in choosing the appropriate noun.

The most straightforward is the identifying noun. It indicates the same person or thing as the subject of the sentence and generally stands alone, without another noun present on its "side" of the verb. In the sentence *The painting is a watercolor, watercolor* is the identifying noun.

When a single noun appears after the verb but does not refer to the same thing as the sentence's subject, it is called the direct object. The direct object is the recipient of the verb's action. In the sentence *She repaired the radio, radio* is the direct object.

In sentences with two nouns following the verb, the first is generally the indirect object, the word that tells to whom or for whom the action was done. The second is the direct object, the actual recipient of the action. In the sentence *Carol gives Tyler a bath*, a *bath* is what is given (the direct object) and *Tyler*, its recipient, is the indirect object.

Modifiers

There are two basic types of modifiers: single-word modifiers, which are generally adverbs or adjectives, and phrases, which are usually introduced by prepositions. Once more, position within a sentence goes along with the function of a modifier.

Adjectives, which modify nouns, often precede the nouns they modify. They serve to restrict, characterize, or further define the nouns immediately following. Thus, *great* in the sentence *You did a great job* is an adjective modifying the noun *job*.

Nouns can also be used to modify nouns. They, too, appear immediately before the noun being modified, and only their position in the sentence indicates that they are acting as modifiers rather than nouns. The noun *telephone* works as a modifier of the noun *booth* when it appears in the phrase *a telephone booth*.

When two or more adjectives each modify the noun independently, they are separated by commas (*a silly, cheerful mood*). When the first adjective modifies an idea expressed by the combination of the second adjective and the noun, no comma is used (*a pretty oil painting*). In some cases, two or more adjectives are combined, often with a hyphen, so that they function as a single adjective. In these compound adjectives, the first term modifies the second, which modifies the noun (*a high-flying airplane*).

Adverbs modify verbs, adjectives, or other adverbs or phrases. They can often be recognized by their characteristic *-ly* ending. When modifying verbs, adverbs generally appear immediately after the verbs (*quickly* in the sentence *He walked quickly through the room*). When used to modify an adjective, the adverb will immediately precede the adjective (*a swiftly moving deer*); such compounds are not hyphenated.

Phrases that modify nouns are often introduced by prepositions or pronouns. They immediately follow the nouns they modify and form an entity known as a dependent clause. While useful in defining the nouns to which they are attached, they are not essential to the sentence in the way a subject, verb, and object are. Examples of modifying phrases are *in the corner* in the sentence *The dog in the corner wagged her tail* and *who wants to know* in the sentence *Anyone who wants to know can get the information*.

Punctuation

Punctuation helps to make sense of the various parts constituting a sentence. It shows where to pause or stop, defines possession and contraction, sets off nonessential modifiers and asides, indicates excitement or interrogation, clarifies incompletion or continuation, and denotes dialogue and special terms.

Terminating Punctuation

There are four punctuation marks that signal the end of a sentence: the period (.), the question mark (?), the exclamation point (!), and the ellipsis (. . . .).

The **period** is used at the end of any sentence that is not a question or an exclamation. It shows that a sentence is finished and is followed by a space and a capital letter beginning the next sentence.

The **question mark** is used to terminate a sentence that is a question (*How much do you think this is worth?*), to terminate a question within quoted dialogue (*"Do you like my haircut?" he asked*), or to terminate a question within a sentence (*Will the Orioles lose every game this year? is the question on the minds of fans everywhere*). The question mark is not used to set off indirect questions (*Everyone wants to know whether the Orioles will continue losing*).

The **exclamation point** terminates sentences that convey excitement (*What a finish that play has!*) or are emphatic (*Leave me alone!*). It can also be used to terminate individual words used as interjections (*You'll get here today? Terrific!*), even when an interjection is within a sentence (*Take four parts gin, add one part vermouth, and, behold! you have a martini*).

The **ellipsis** indicates that one or more words are missing. When used at the end of an incomplete sentence, an ellipsis is made up of four dots (*I had hoped to go. . . .*). Four dots indicate that although what's there makes a complete sentence, one or more words have been omitted from the end of the sentence. A four-dot ellipsis can also indicate the omission of one or more sentences. When the middle portion of a sentence has been omitted, a three-dot ellipsis is used.

Pause Punctuation

The punctuation marks that can indicate a pause are the comma (,), the semicolon (;), the colon (:), the dash (—), and the ellipsis (. . .).

Comma

Commas are used to separate two main clauses set apart by a conjunction (such as *and, but,* or *or*) (*I'd hoped to be done this afternoon, but I'm not sure that's possible*). They can separate shorter clauses that do not have a conjunction between them (*I work, I sleep, I work some more*). They are also used to set off all manner of words and phrases, such as adverbial clauses (*When he was finished, he set down his knife*), transitional expressions (*Her remarks, on the other hand, were uncalled for*), conjunctions (*We are often late; however, we must be back by five o'clock*), illustrative expressions (*They were confused; that is, they felt bewildered and afraid*), and nonrestrictive clauses (*Your writing, although it is quite good, is not what we're looking for*).

In addition, commas are employed to separate a series of words or phrases (*Hope, charity, and faith were not enough to sustain her*); to set off direct address (*You know, son, that's a good idea*); to mark the beginning of a contrasting idea (*He likes to work, but he loves to party*); to set a direct quotation apart from the speaker (*"Don't quote me," he said*); and to set off a question being asked about the previous part of the sentence (*It was fun, wasn't it?*).

Finally, commas indicate the inference of a word not stated, especially one used earlier in the sentence (*For us it's money; for them, food*); set off the parts of an address, place name, or date (*They went to London, England, to conduct research*); and separate a name from a title following it (*Paul Fargis, president*).

Semicolon

The **semicolon** signals a more complete stop than is indicated by the comma. It is used to separate parts of a sentence that contain commas (*Our organization runs on the dedication, concern, and compassion of its staff; the generosity, moral support, and wisdom of its directors; and the gratitude, hope, and joy expressed by those it serves*). It can also join clauses that are not connected by a coordinating conjunction (*Those who can, do; those who can't, teach*) as well as those joined by conjunctive adverbs (*It's easy to lie; however, lying is a bad habit to get into*).

Colon

The **colon** represents the next closest thing to the full stop indicated by a period. It can mark the separation of an enumerated list or extract from the rest of a text (*The Ten Commandments are:*) or the introduction of an appositive (*She wanted only one thing: sleep*) or series (*It's easy to list the things money won't buy: love, health, happiness, and peace*). The colon also precedes an illustrative or explanatory phrase; many style guides recommend beginning such phrases with capital letters if they can function as sentences in and of themselves (*His Excellency demands satisfaction: He will expect you on the dueling field at dawn*).

Colons are frequently used in contexts other than sentences. They can separate book titles from their subtitles (*Curious Customs: The Stories Behind 296 Popular American Rituals*), set off the salutation in business correspondence (*Dear Mr. President:*) and the labels in memoranda (*To:*), and separate the elements of time (*8:45*), ratios (*a 3:5 mix of boys to girls*), and biblical references (*Deuteronomy 1:5*).

Dash

The **dash**, known as the em dash to compositors and editors, represents an abrupt shift within a sentence. It separates a clause or phrase from the rest of the sentence, whether for emphasis (*You want—my god, you need—an expert*) or to introduce a parenthetical remark (*He hopes to turn a profit—something I can't see happening any time soon—within six months*). Dashes also are used to separate quoted material from its author (*"I still find the Strunkian wisdom a comfort"—E. B. White*).

Ellipsis

The **ellipsis** is used in dialogue to indicate faltering speech (*"We want . . . that is, . . ."*).

Brackets and Parentheses

Brackets [ ] are specialized tools for setting off material from the rest of the text. They can be used with editorial comments: The *main point [emphasis mine] has been missed;* or as parentheses within parentheses: *It is hoped (some might say prayed [even atheists pray sometimes]) that she will pull through.* They should not be employed when simple parentheses will do.

Parentheses ( ) are used to set off explanatory words and phrases that demand more of a break than is shown by commas and less than that indicated by dashes: *We can't bear it (or so we believe)*; to surround numbers when enumerating points in a sentence: *He hopes (1) to be employed, and (2) to make lots of money*; to give abbreviations: *American Telephone & Telegraph (ATT)*; and to indicate potential plurals or other alternatives: *Please tell us which course(s) of action you wish to take.*

Apostrophes, Single Quotation Marks, and Double Quotation Marks

Apostrophes

Apostrophes are used to indicate a contraction (*didn't*) or a possessive by adding *'s* to most words (*Mr. Marx's humor*); an apostrophe alone is added to form the possessive of plurals (*the kittens' tails*). Apostrophes also appear in shortened forms of the year (*the '80s*) and for plurals of numbers, letters, and terms (*all at 6's and 7's*).

Single quotation marks

Single quotation marks are used for quotes within quotes (" *'I'm not sure,' is what I think he said,*" *she responded*) and for titles and special terms mentioned in dialogue ("*She said she doesn't read the 'His' column anymore,*" *he told his buddy*).

Double quotation marks

Double quotation marks are used for direct quotations and dialogue ("*What was she up to?*" *he asked*); to set off special terms (*soldiers are sometimes called* "*grunts*"); and to indicate the titles of stories, articles, songs, book chapters, TV and radio shows, poems, and lectures.

Punctuating a sentence that contains quotation marks can be tricky. Commas used to set off quoted material from the speaker are placed within the quotation marks ("*I hope it's finished,*" *she said*). A period is also placed within the quotation marks ("*We're done.*"). A question mark or exclamation point ending a sentence that ends in a quotation mark is placed within the quotation marks too ("*Will you marry me?*"). However, when quoted material is used in a question, but is not itself a question, the question mark is placed outside (*Do you think he really meant* "*till death do us part*"?).

Spelling Guidelines

Many words in American English are spelled just as they sound. That is, a long *a* sound is often spelled with an *a*. Aside from the old saw "*i* before *e* except after *c*, unless sounded as *a* as in *neighbor* and *weigh*," there are few easy ways of remembering the intricacies of correct spelling. The following table shows the ways in which various sounds common in English words can be spelled.

Sound	*Spellings*
a	s*a*t, m*e*ringue, s*a*lmon, l*au*gh
ah	f*a*ther, *au*nt, c*a*lm, s*e*rgeant, Afrik*aa*ns
aw	s*aw*, c*augh*t, *o*rder, *ou*ght, w*a*lk
ay	f*a*de, *ae*robic, pl*ai*n, c*ay*, br*ea*k, n*eigh*, wh*ey*, r*é*gime
ch	*c*ello, *ch*ip, ques*ti*on, na*t*ure
e	*a*ny, gu*e*ss, l*eo*pard, fr*ie*nd, br*ea*d
ee	m*e*, s*ee*, l*ea*, sk*i*, *ei*ther, *Ae*sop, ver*y*, bel*ie*ve, ph*oe*nix
er	*ear*th, j*er*k, st*ir*, t*ur*n, auth*o*r
f	*f*all, tele*ph*one, rou*gh*
ih	h*i*t, *E*nglish, w*o*men, b*u*sy, cabb*a*ge, b*ui*ld, carr*ia*ge, s*ie*ve
i	*i*ce, sl*y*, g*ey*ser, h*igh*, b*uy*, d*ie*, pap*a*ya, *eye*
j	*j*am, led*ge*, trage*d*y
k	*k*elp, *ch*aracter, sla*ck*, a*c*re, a*q*ua, a*cc*ount
n	*n*ap, *kn*ow, *p*neumonia, *g*naw
oh	b*o*ne, *oa*t, s*ou*l, *oh*, f*o*lk, br*oo*ch, cr*ow*, th*ough*, bure*au*
oo	d*o*, l*oo*, bl*ew*, s*u*e, y*ou*, cr*ui*se, bea*u*ty
ow	c*ow*, b*ough*, s*au*erkraut

sh	pu*sh*, o*c*ean, *ch*auffeur, spe*c*ial, fa*sc*ist, ti*ss*ue, compul*s*ion, na*t*ion, vi*c*ious, no*x*ious, nau*s*eous, *s*ure
uh	*u*p, *o*ven, tr*ou*ble, w*a*s, d*oe*s
v	lo*v*e, o*f*
z	*X*erox, *z*ebra, vi*s*ible
zh	re*g*ime, divi*s*ion, bra*z*ier

Alphabetization

There are two ways of alphabetizing a list of words, terms, or names. In both cases, lists can be compiled by comparing the first letter, then the second letter, and so forth. In a word-by-word list, only the first word of each entry is considered; hyphens are ignored. A letter-by-letter list is considered without regard for whether the entry consists of one word or more than one; spaces and hyphens are ignored.

The following list is arranged according to the word-by-word system:

> sea
> sea gull
> Sea Side Heights
> seafood
> seal
> seaside
> season ticket
> seasoning
> second best
> second name
> secondary

Now here is the same list compiled under the letter-by-letter system:

> sea
> seafood
> sea gull
> seal
> seaside
> Sea Side Heights
> seasoning
> season ticket
> secondary
> second best
> second name

Either method of alphabetization is acceptable, as long as it is scrupulously adhered to. While some lists may be better served by one approach or the other, it is not more correct to use one or the other.

Commonly Misused Words

See also "Commonly Misspelled Words" on page 278.

accept to receive; to respond positively
except to leave out (verb); with the exclusion of (preposition)

affect to influence; to pretend
effect a result, an influence, an impression; to bring about (verb)

anxious worried, unhappy
eager pleased but impatient

bathos triteness; an anticlimax
pathos sympathy

brake to stop
break to separate

capital a city; money; an uppercase letter
Capitol the building in which the U.S. Congress meets

compare to examine differences and similarities
contrast to examine differences

diagnosis the identification of a disease
prognosis the likely course of a disease

dinner the main meal of the day, at noontime or in the evening
supper the evening meal

dyeing coloring with dye
dying ceasing to live

emigrate to leave a country to live elsewhere
immigrate to enter a country to live there

flair skill, talent
flare a bright light; an outburst

guerrilla a warrior
gorilla an ape

hole a space, a void
whole complete, intact

illegible indecipherable
unreadable illegible; uninteresting, not worth reading

ingenious brilliant, clever
ingenuous simple, naive

its belonging to it
it's it is

lay to put; to set down
lie to rest in a horizontal position; to make an untrue statement

liable responsible, likely
libel a defamatory statement

majority more than half
plurality more votes than any other candidate; the margin of victory

notable worthy, impressive
notorious widely known and ill-regarded

peace harmony; the absence of war
piece part of a whole

personal intimate; having to do with a specific person
personnel the employees of a company or organization

pray to address God
prey a victim

principle a moral rule; a law
principal main (adjective); the person in charge; money lent or borrowed (noun)

protagonist the leading character
antagonist an adversary

put (someone) on to mislead someone
put (someone) down to make fun of someone

racket noise
racquet a stringed paddle

re-collect to collect again
recollect to remember

sail to ride in a wind-powered boat
sale a discounted offering

stationary not moving
stationery writing materials

talk to to address others
talk with to converse together

viral having to do with a virus
virile manly

whose of which
who's who is

your belonging to you
you're you are

American English and British English

It has been said that the United States and Great Britain are two nations divided by a single language. This is true in a number of ways. In the first place, spellings of the same words can be decidedly different. The following list shows some common examples of the variances between American and British spellings.

American	British	American	British
aluminum	aluminium	jail	gaol
center	centre	jewelry	jewellery
check (money)	cheque	labor	labour
color	colour	organization	organisation
connection	connexion	pajamas	pyjamas
curb	kerb	peddler	pedlar
diplomat	diplomatist	program	programme
gray	grey	realize	realise
honor	honour	recognize	recognise
inquire	enquire	theater	theatre

The two versions of the English language also diverge when it comes to the names for many everyday objects and events. It is easy for a visitor from across the Atlantic to provoke amusement from the natives by calling a cloth used to wipe one's mouth a *napkin* in England, or by asking an American waiter for the *W.C.* The following is a list of some common American terms and their counterparts in the United Kingdom.

American	British	American	British
apartment	flat	line	queue
bathroom	toilet, W.C., or loo	napkin	serviette
candy	sweets	oven	cooker
checkers	draughts	round-trip ticket	return ticket
closet	cupboard	suspenders	braces
corn	maize	truck	lorry
cracker	biscuit	trunk (of car)	boot
diaper	nappy	underpass	subway
drugstore	chemist's	undershirt	vest
faucet	tap	vacation	holiday
gas, gasoline	petrol	vest	waistcoat
hood (of car)	bonnet		

As if confusion about spelling and word choice were not enough, the quotation mark is also used in a substantially different way in the United States and Great Britain. While U.S. usage dictates the use of double quotation marks to indicate speech, British usage employs single quotes. And whereas Americans put periods and commas at the end of a quote within their double quotation marks, the British do just the opposite, placing them outside their single quotation marks.

Additional Sources of Information

Bernstein, Theodore M. *The Careful Writer: A Modern Guide to English Usage.* Atheneum, 1965.

The Chicago Manual of Style, 13th ed. University of Chicago Press, 1982.

Fowler, H. W. *A Dictionary of Modern English Usage,* 2d ed. (rev. by Sir Ernest Gowers). Oxford University Press, 1987.

Miller, Casey, and Swift, Kate. *The Handbook of Nonsexist Writing,* 2nd ed. Harper & Row, 1988.

MLA Handbook for Writers of Research Papers, Theses, and Dissertations. Modern Language Association, 1988.

Morris, William, and Morris, Mary. *Harper Dictionary of Contemporary Usage,* 2d ed. Harper & Row, 1985.

Strunk, W., Jr., and White, E. B. *The Elements of Style,* 3d ed. Macmillan, 1979.

Words into Type, 3d ed. Prentice-Hall, 1978.

Zinsser, William. *On Writing Well: An Informal Guide to Writing Nonfiction,* rev. ed. Harper & Row, 1985.

14

Etiquette

For most people, etiquette in everyday life has little to do with white gloves and raised pinkies, although this is a common image of what etiquette is all about. In fact, etiquette involves the use of good manners, consideration for others, and adherence to unspoken rules of behavior that are expected to be followed in certain situations.

This chapter explains the basic rules of conduct expected of late-twentieth-century Americans when they engage in a number of common business and social activities. It is hardly exhaustive—a great many books have been written on planning and organizing a wedding, for instance—and it does not cover the moral, psychological, or social implications of etiquette. But it does describe what can be expected to occur when one participates in certain activities and what is expected of those who participate.

Wedding Etiquette

Because weddings vary greatly in their level of formality and style, each component of a wedding—from the invitations to the reception—is flexible. The rule of thumb is that the various elements that make up a wedding should be compatible. That is, if a formal, evening church wedding is held, it should be preceded by formal, engraved invitations and followed by a formal, sitdown dinner; likewise, a wedding held in an open field in the countryside would call for an informal dining arrangement, perhaps a buffet.

Invitations and Announcements

Wedding invitations, like weddings themselves, come in two basic varieties: formal and informal. A formal, traditional invitation is engraved or printed in black ink on high-quality white or ivory paper. The size of the paper is either 5-by-7, folded in half before being put in an envelope, or 4-by-5, inserted into an envelope without folding.

The wording of a formal wedding invitation is written in the third person, and the date and time are written out in full. A typical example might read:

> Mr. and Mrs. Henry Appleton
> request the honor of your presence
> at the marriage of their daughter
> Carol June
> to
> Mr. Alan Hart
> Saturday, the fourth of February
> at eleven o'clock
> St. Albert's Church
> Bayonne, New Jersey

The invitation to the wedding ceremony itself can also invite the recipient to a reception afterward. If all those receiving invitations to the reception are not invited to the ceremony, or vice versa, a separate invitation to the reception is printed and, for those invited to both events, included with the wedding invitation. The reception invitation or the combined invitation should include the instructions "R.S.V.P."

Traditionally, the invitation is covered with a piece of tissue paper and enclosed with the reception invitation (and a response card and its envelope, if desired) in an inner envelope. The names of those invited, including a couple's children if they are also invited, are written out in full on the inner envelope. This inner envelope is then enclosed in an outer envelope that bears the handwritten names of all invited and their addresses, without abbreviations. Modern custom allows the bride's parents to forgo using an inner envelope altogether when sending out invitations.

Other enclosures that may be sent with the wedding invitation include cards designating reserved pews, "At-Home" cards that announce when the bride and groom will return from their honeymoon and where they will reside, and maps or other travel information.

Nontraditional, informal invitations can be designed and printed or handwritten in whatever style or form the bride and groom desire. They should, however, be in good taste—avoiding garish colors and bad poetry—and in harmony with the style of the wedding itself.

Wedding announcements usually are sent to people who would like to know about the wedding but who would not be expected to attend. They use the same paper and printing as the invitations. The wording is also similar, although the parents of both the bride and the groom are often mentioned and the words *announce the marriage of* replace *request the honor of your presence at the marriage of*. Wedding announcements are sent out the day of, or shortly after, the wedding day.

Response to a wedding invitation is dictated by the type of invitation. A formal invitation traditionally is answered with a third-person, handwritten note that might read:

Mr. and Mrs. Harold Sloane
accept with pleasure (or regret they will be unable to attend)
Mr. and Mrs. Appleton's
kind invitation for
Saturday, the fourth of February.

Of course, if a response card is enclosed, it may simply be filled out and returned. If the invitation is less formal, a handwritten response in more standard, informal English is correct.

Showers

Bridal or wedding showers can be given by any close friend of the bride. They should not be given by a member of the bride's immediate family.

There is no set rule for the number of showers that can be held before a wedding, although only members of the wedding party are invited to more than one shower. Neither is there a hard-and-fast rule for the types of parties they should be; serving anything from coffee and cake to cocktails to a light supper is appropriate.

Unless it is a surprise shower, the guest list is drawn up by the bride (or the bride and groom if both are to be present). The host for the party should set the limit on the number of guests. Guests invited to the shower should also be invited to the wedding, unless the wedding is to be very small.

Everyone attending a shower is expected to bring a present, which is opened at the party. The host or another friend of the bride should keep a list of who gave what, so that thank-you notes can be sent later on.

Bachelor Dinner

Several days before the wedding, a bachelor dinner can be given for the groom. It is usually held in a private room of a restaurant and hosted by the best man or the ushers, although a groom may give his own bachelor dinner.

Generally, the men drink and eat a great deal. At some point in the evening, the groom toasts his bride-to-be. It is rarely appropriate to break the glasses after such a toast, although this was once the custom. The only important rule regarding bachelor dinners is that they should not be held the night before the wedding, so that there is adequate time for the groom to recover from the festivities.

Ceremony

The wedding ceremony itself can be as formal or informal as the bride and groom wish it to be. Weddings are held in city halls, open fields, private homes, reception halls, restaurants, and churches and synagogues. For most weddings to which guests are invited, and especially church and synagogue weddings, a prescribed series of events will take place.

First comes the processional. In Christian and Reform Jewish weddings, the ushers come down the aisle first, arranged in height order, followed by any junior ushers. They are followed by junior bridesmaids, then bridesmaids, in height order, with the shortest first. Then comes the maid or matron of honor, the flower girls, the ring bearer, and, finally, the bride, holding the right arm of her father. The groom and the best man wait at the front of the room with the clergy.

Orthodox and Conservative Jewish processionals are led by the ushers, who are followed by the bridesmaids. Next come the rabbi and cantor followed by the best man and then the groom, accompanied by his mother and father. The maid of honor is next; she is followed by the bride, who walks between her mother and father.

The guests stand during the processional and remain standing until the clergy has asked them to sit, usually after opening remarks or a prayer. Once at the front of the room, the bride's father (or parents) step back or to one side and the groom steps forward to meet his bride. Bride and groom stand next to each other holding hands or with her hand on his arm, if they wish.

In Protestant ceremonies, the father of the bride gives her away before sitting down in the first pew. In Roman Catholic ceremonies, the father of the bride sits with his wife as soon as the bride is delivered to the groom. Orthodox and Conservative Jewish ceremonies require that the parents of the bride and groom remain at the front of the room; if there is space, they stand under the marriage canopy, known as a *chuppah*.

The actual events of the wedding ceremony differ widely among various denominations. Most Christian services include a blessing of the ring or rings. (If the bride is wearing an engagement ring, she should put it on her right hand for the service, then place it outside the wedding band afterward.) Orthodox Jewish services are mostly in Hebrew, and two glasses of wine are shared by the couple before the groom breaks the goblet at the end of the ceremony.

The recessional for Christian and Reform Jewish weddings is led by the bride and groom. They are followed by the flower girl, the best man and maid or matron of honor, and the ushers and bridesmaids; a line of bridesmaids follows the bride and a line of ushers follows the groom. Orthodox and Conservative Jewish recessionals are led by the bride and groom, followed by the bride's parents, the groom's parents, the maid of honor with the best man, the flower girl, and the rabbi and cantor. Bridesmaids and ushers bring up the rear. In Orthodox ceremonies, all the men are on one side and all the women on the other.

Reception

The style of the reception will follow from the style of the rest of the wedding. Ordinarily, photographs are taken immediately after the ceremony; they are ordered and paid for by the bride's family.

A receiving line, made up of the mothers of the bride and groom, the wedded couple, the maid of honor, and, at the discretion of those involved, the fathers of the couple, the bridesmaids, the best man, and the ushers, greets guests as they enter the room.

Formal receptions have assigned tables for those attending. The bridal party will generally be at the head table, and a parents' table will be nearby. Other guests should be assigned to tables with people whose company they will enjoy.

Almost all receptions include a toast to the bride and groom, which is proposed by the best man. The groom should reply with thanks after the toast has been drunk and offer a toast to his bride; other toasts may be offered as well. The toasts can be followed by dancing or a meal, if one is to be served. The wedding cake is cut just before dessert, or shortly before the bride and groom leave the reception if it is not a formal dinner. The bride cuts the first slice, with the help of her new husband, from the bottom tier of the cake, and the couple offer each other a bite. The top layer of the cake, with its decorations, is removed and saved for the bride and groom, while the remainder is cut up and served to the guests.

At the reception's end, the bride usually will toss her bouquet from stairs or a landing, turning her back and throwing it over her shoulder to her bridesmaids or other female friends; the one who catches it is supposed to marry next. Then the newlyweds change clothes, say goodbye to their families, and, led by the best man, leave in a shower of paper rose petals or rice.

Gifts and Thank-you Notes

Gifts can be sent to the address on the At-Home card, if one is enclosed with the invitation or to the home of the bride's mother. They also can be brought to the reception. Among some people, money is an appropriate wedding gift; it is usually presented to the bride in an envelope, which she will place in a special purse or in a box or basket put out for this purpose. Envelopes, and usually gifts as well, are not opened until after the reception.

Thank-you notes should be handwritten and should mention the gift that was given. They should be sent shortly after the couple's honeymoon is over.

DIVISION OF WEDDING EXPENSES

Today, the groom and his family often offer to share some of the wedding expenses that traditionally have been borne by the bride's family. This is a significant change of custom, as the costs of traditional weddings have become too prohibitive for many families to absorb. However, if the groom's family does not offer to share expenses, the bride's family should plan a wedding in accordance with their means.

The traditional division of expenses is listed below. In addition to the change noted above, it should be kept in mind that there are numerous exceptions and variations depending on religion, ethnicity, or local custom. Many items may be omitted without diminishing the ceremony in any way.

Expenses Paid by Bride's Family

Bridal consultant, if needed
Invitations and announcements
Flowers for the church and receptions, bouquets for the bridesmaids, bouquet for bride (sometimes given by groom)
Music for the ceremony, including organist or choir fee
Transportation of bridal party to church or synagogue and reception

Bride's presents to her bridesmaids
Bride's present to groom (optional)
Groom's wedding ring
Sexton's fee (church fee)
Accommodations for out-of-town bridesmaids
All expenses of reception, including music

Expenses Paid by Groom's Family

Bride's rings, both engagement and wedding
Groom's present to bride (optional)
Groom's presents to ushers and best man
Groom's boutonniere and boutonnieres for ushers
Ties and gloves for the ushers
Clergy member's fee; tips to altar boys
Corsages for immediate members of both families and bride's going-away corsage

Accommodations for out-of-town ushers
Bachelor dinner (optional, and often given by ushers)
Rehearsal dinner (optional, but becoming more standard)
Honeymoon

Expenses Paid by Bridesmaids

Dress and accessories
Transportation to and from town of wedding

Gift to the couple and contribution to a gift from all bridesmaids to the bride

Expenses Paid by Ushers

Transportation to and from town of wedding
Rental of wedding attire

Gift to the couple and contribution to a gift from all ushers to the groom
Bachelor dinner (optional, and often given by groom)

Expenses Paid by Out-of-Town Guests

Transportation and accommodations

Gift to the couple

Anniversary Gifts

Etiquette authorities differ on the appropriate gifts to be presented on the occasion of individual wedding anniversaries. The following list represents a modern consensus, with the eight oldest and most traditional gifts indicated in *italics*.

1	*Paper* or plastics	9 Pottery	35 Coral or jade
2	Cotton or calico	10 *Tin* or aluminum	40 Rubies or garnets
3	Leather	11 Steel	45 Sapphires or tourmalines
4	Linen, silk, or synthetics (rayon, nylon)	12 Silk or linen	50 *Gold*
5	*Wood*	13 Lace	55 Emeralds or turquoise
6	Iron	14 Ivory	60 *Diamonds* or gold
7	Copper, wool, or brass	15 *Crystal* or glass	75 Diamonds or gold
8	Bronze or electrical appliances	20 *China*	
		25 *Silver*	
		30 Pearls	

Business Etiquette

The business world is extraordinarily demanding and extremely competitive. In it, there are really only a few criteria on which members will be judged: competence, initiative, leadership, and how well one gets along with others. It is this last area in which manners plays a crucial role, for individuals must be able to present themselves well and deal well with others if they wish to succeed in business.

Appointments

Business life requires that people meet each other face-to-face to conduct transactions or exchange information. To do so, they schedule appointments. The first rule regarding business appointments is that they should be kept if at all possible; failing to show up for an appointment will be taken as a sign of disinterest, carelessness, and lack of professionalism. If an appointment cannot be kept, it should be cancelled as far in advance as possible. If an individual is unavoidably delayed, he or she should telephone the host or have someone else make the call.

When guests are shown into the office where the appointment will take place, the host should rise from his or her desk, shake hands, and greet them; if the host and guests have not met before, they should introduce themselves. The guests should be offered seats, and the host should either sit back down at the desk or sit with the visitors. Coffee or tea may be offered by the host but should not be requested by the guests.

Any business meeting should get to the business at hand as quickly as possible. It is just as important to listen as it is to talk, not simply to be polite but to get the most out of the meeting. It is also important not to interrupt others during meetings. Taking notes during a business meeting is acceptable.

The host usually will conclude a business meeting, either by making remarks that sum up the discussion or by suggesting outright that everything pertinent has now been discussed. It is important for guests to pick up on such cues, gather their belongings, thank the host, shake hands, and leave. A follow-up letter, thanking the host for the meeting and outlining whatever was agreed upon at the meeting, should be sent by the next business day.

Entertainment

Business entertaining generally takes place in an office; over breakfast, lunch, or dinner, at a restaurant; or over drinks after work. The purpose of business entertaining is to conduct business in a congenial setting that is less formal than an office.

The person initiating business entertainment acts as the host. That person is responsible for deciding on the setting, making reservations, and paying the bill. The site chosen for entertaining a client or colleague should be appropriate to the person being invited and the nature of the business relationship; a prestigious restaurant would be right for entertaining a major client, while drinks at a clubby bar might be a good choice for entertaining a vendor who regularly sells supplies to the company.

Regardless of setting, it should be kept in mind that business is the main purpose of the get-together. The host should endeavor to bring up the business at hand before the guest becomes impatient. However, business discussions should not interfere with the pleasure of enjoying the meal.

The host should pick up the check when it is brought to the table, look it over, and pay it. Because business entertaining should give both parties more or less equal status, it makes no difference whether the host is a man or a woman. There is no reason for a guest even to show a pretense of wanting to pick up the check; the guest can express his or her thanks to the host as they are leaving.

Gifts

Gift-giving is not at all unusual among people who work together. Bosses often give gifts to employees for birthdays, Christmas, or Secretaries Day; staff members may give the boss a present for holidays or birthdays; office colleagues sometimes give each other gifts; and executives can give presents to clients or vendors.

Such gifts are generally not lavish, although the type of gift is dictated by the nature of the relationship. Bosses tend to give larger presents to their employees than staff members give to the boss. Gifts to colleagues reflect the degree of friendship between them. Clients or vendors give and receive gifts appropriate to the amount of business transacted and the longevity of the relationship.

Business gifts should be less personal than gifts for a friend. A datebook or similar office accessory, costume jewelry, a tie, or a bottle of wine makes a good, inexpensive business gift. More lavish presents, like theater tickets, food baskets, or a case of wine can be given to longstanding clients or employees.

The Telephone

For many companies, the telephone is an essential tool for conducting business. Proper telephone manners can make it an effective tool.

Many people think that having a secretary or assistant place calls will enhance the image of an executive. In fact, having others place calls for oneself is an inconvenience, both for the secretary or assistant who must place the call and for the person receiving the call, who must wait for the executive to get on the line. People in business should place their own phone calls.

When the call goes through, the caller should identify himself or herself by name and company; if the nature of the call is not readily apparent, the caller should volunteer this information. With some companies, this process will have to be repeated two or three times— with the switchboard operator, a secretary, and the person being called.

A caller should not take offense if asked to identify the reason for the call, although this type of questioning is often a thinly disguised way of keeping a boss insulated from people he or she does not want to receive calls from. Screening phone calls is acceptable, but not if the caller is then asked to hold the line and finally is told that the person being called is not available. As with placing calls, the most convenient and least rude way of dealing with incoming calls is to answer them yourself; if you are too busy to answer the phone yourself, a secretary should keep the interrogation of a caller to a minimum.

People answering business phones should identify themselves and ask if they can help the caller. They should be attentive, organized, and unhurried. If answering someone else's phone, they should be ready to take a message.

Business phones should not be used for personal calls. If a personal call must be made, or if one is received, it should be kept as brief as possible. Similarly, business calls should be kept brief and to the point. Chattiness and rudeness are always to be avoided in business telephone calls.

Letter Writing

Like business phone calls, business letters should be brief and to the point. The first line below the letterhead should bear the date, with the name, company, and address of the recipient appearing two lines below it at the left margin. Two lines below the address, the salutation is given.

If the recipient is known personally, he or she can be greeted by first name ("Dear Fred:"). If the recipient is known casually or not at all, use *Mr.* or *Ms.* ("Dear Mr. Burrows:" or "Dear Ms. Johnston:"). When the addressee is unknown, "Dear Sir or Madam" or something like "Dear Sales Manager" can be employed.

The first paragraph of a business letter should clearly explain the purpose of writing. It should be straightforward and concise. If the letter is being written at the suggestion of someone else, this should be stated in the first paragraph along with the reason for writing.

The length of a business letter is determined by what needs to be said. If a reply is desired, the last paragraph should simply state, "I look forward to hearing from you at your earliest convenience." A response by a specific date should not be demanded unless there is a good reason for doing so.

Appropriate closings for a business letter include "Best wishes," "Sincerely," "Sincerely yours," or "Yours truly." Informal closings like "Yours" or "Cheers" should not be used. The signature can either be your full name ("Henry Wiggins") or, if the writer and the recipient are well acquainted, a first name alone ("Henry"). The writer's full name and company title should be typed below the signature unless they appear at the top of the letterhead.

How to Prepare a Résumé

A résumé is a tool that can be used to obtain a job interview. Along with a cover letter, it is the first impression a prospective employee makes on a potential employer. Therefore, it is important that a résumé provide as much relevant information as possible about the person being described in it: you. It is also important that the résumé be kept brief—no more than one full side of a sheet of 8½-by-11-inch paper.

A résumé must be neatly typed, with at least a ¾-inch margin on both sides, top, and bottom. Single-space all information in the résumé, leaving one line of space between blocks of information. Use underlining, capital letters, and asterisks to highlight important information.

Begin a résumé with your name, address, and home and business telephone numbers. They can be laid out on the page in any way you find visually pleasing, so far as space allows. Do not include your age, marital status, or other personal facts.

Many résumés then list a career goal, for example, "Career goal: Systems engineer responsible for monitoring, maintaining, and improving plant facilities" or "Objective: Position as illustrator/designer with opportunity to create book jackets from concept through mechanicals." This is a good tactic if you are looking for a specific type of job; however, job-hunters who would consider any of several possible careers are better off omitting any specific career goal.

Most résumés then present a chronological outline of work experience, starting with one's current or most recent job and working backward. For each job listed, the important duties and skills involved should be outlined or described. Depending on how much "real world" experience you have, relevant high school or college employment, internships, and part-time work can be included. Such a portion of a typical résumé might look like this:

WORK EXPERIENCE

1986–present   Vice President, Marketing, *Techno Corp.*

                Responsible for developing, implementing, and overseeing marketing of all services provided by this computer firm.

                —Created company's first five-year marketing plan

                —Developed continuing training program for sales force

                —Increased client billings by 25 percent

1983–1986   Marketing Director, *Numbercrunch, Inc.*

This section is followed by one outlining your educational background, again going from your most recent experience backward. List the date, school or course attended, and certificate or diploma obtained. Depending on the extent of your work experience, you may wish to give a more detailed description of your higher education. If you are a college student, you may wish to list your high school and any pertinent coursework or special achievements.

In the last part of your résumé, list any work you have done with civic or charitable organizations and any awards or certificates of recognition you have received. Place these under an appropriate heading, such as "COMMUNITY SERVICE." If you have no such background, leave this section out of your résumé.

Finally, it is unnecessary to write "References available upon request" at the bottom of a résumé. Anyone looking at it will assume you can provide references and will ask for them if and when they are needed.

Personal Letters

The demise of personal letter writing is considered by many to be a sad comment on the overall lack of civility in our society. Many people arrange their lives in such a way that they never need to write a letter outside of business situations. There are, however, several situations in which a note or letter is expected. And there are many other circumstances in which written communication will delight the recipient.

Thank-you notes should always be sent to the host and hostess of an overnight guest, for wedding presents, and for presents of any sort that the giver has not been thanked for personally. Thank-you notes to the host or hostess of a party or to someone who has done a favor are not required, but they will make the writer's gratitude clear and warm the heart of the person who gets them.

Other situations demand notes or letters as well. The death of someone in a friend's family is one such event. This is especially true if you cannot express your condolences personally at a wake or during *shiva*. A letter of condolence need not be long and involved, but it should be a personal, handwritten note, not just a printed sympathy card.

Formal invitations require a written response. For many, wedding invitations are the most common sort of formal invitation received. While response cards are frequently included with wedding invitations, a personal response in addition to or in place of the response card will be greatly appreciated.

When a friend or family member has something important to celebrate—a promotion or graduation, or receipt of an award or other honor—a congratulatory note will make the celebration even happier. Even the briefest of notes adds a warmth that cannot be conveyed by a phone call.

Personal letter writing can also be done for no good reason at all. Or rather, you may write letters to friends and family simply to keep in touch with them and to let them know that you are thinking of them. These are perhaps the most enjoyable letters to receive.

Personal letters, while not requiring a strict format, do have a few guidelines. The date should be written at the top, either in the center or the right-hand corner. The salutation, which may be a bit warmer than it would for a business letter ("My dearest Jeanne,") should be followed by a comma instead of a colon.

The body or text of a personal letter is, of course, a highly personal matter. It should be written with less of an eye to what would be stylistically or grammatically correct and more of an eye to expressing feelings and thoughts. A personal letter should sound like you, and techniques that would be out of place in a business letter, such as using dashes, ellipsis, and sentence fragments, can be employed in personal correspondence.

Closings for personal letters are also a matter of choice. "Love" is appropriate for those you do love; "Fondly" or "All my best" or "Affectionately" might be right for friends. As with the rest of the letter, the closing should express your own feelings.

Parties

Parties come in all shapes and sizes. They can be held for holidays, anniversaries, housewarmings, birthdays, weddings, or farewells or just to have some friends over. They range from sit-down dinners in banquet halls to tea and cookies in living rooms. But no matter the size or style of the party, certain aspects need to be tended to make it a success.

Invitations

Invitations can be given in writing, in person, or by telephone, depending on the sort of party they are for. Engraved invitations are sent for formal parties, like weddings and anniversary parties. Less formal events require less formal invitations; handwritten notes on personal stationery or printed invitation cards with blanks that can be filled in can be used. Invitations to small informal parties can be issued by telephone. Invitations should be sent out about three weeks before a party.

R.S.V.P.s

Your invitation should include a request that guests respond if you want to know in advance who will be coming. A formal invitation can include a response card or just "R.S.V.P." Informal invitations can include a statement like, "Unless we hear otherwise, we'll expect you on the third," or, "Please let us know if you can make it." Telephone invitations will usually get immediate responses; however, if you are invited by telephone and do not know whether you can attend, it is acceptable to put off a response. In any case, it is important to respond to an invitation as quickly as possible so the hosts can plan accordingly.

Formal Dinner Parties

Seating Arrangements

The host and hostess, as well as any guests of honor, are the people around whom seating arrangements are set at more formal dinner parties. The host and hostess will usually sit at either end of the table; a male guest of honor sits at the hostess' right and a female guest of honor at the host's right. Other guests are told where to sit by the host and hostess, either personally or by using place cards. While it is customary to alternate men and women at a sit-down dinner, this practice can be ignored if there are more members of one sex than of the other. Husbands and wives can be seated together or separated. Obviously, buffet dinner parties, cocktail parties, and other informal get-togethers do not require any sort of specific seating arrangement; guests can be expected to fend for themselves.

Tableware

A place setting at a formal dinner party can be somewhat intimidating to guests unfamiliar with such events. The arrangement of plates, glasses, and utensils is fairly standard, however, and fairly easy to deal with.

The basic setting should be in place when the guests sit down. A service plate is in the center, usually with the napkin on top of it. Flanking the plate will be the flatware: a dessert or salad fork to the immediate left of the plate, a dinner fork to the left of it, and a fish fork, if needed, on the outside. To the right of the plate are, from closest to furthest, the salad knife, the meat knife, the fish knife, a soup or fruit spoon (or both), and, if shellfish is being served, a shellfish fork. Utensils are used in order from the outside in.

Glasses are placed above the knives to the right of the plate. There will be a water goblet and, extending to the right from there, a champagne glass, one or two wine glasses, and a sherry glass.

In addition to the service plate, a butter plate is placed above the forks, to the left of the service plate. The butter knife is set across the butter plate.

Serving

Food at a formal dinner party is usually served by hired help. Guests are served from the left, and plates are cleared from the right. The female guest of honor is served first; if there is no guest of honor, women are served before men or, if this is hard to manage, a woman is served the first plate with the other guests served in order. The hostess is served last. Warmed dinner plates are usually brought out just before the entree is served. A clean service plate should be brought out for each of the other courses.

Formal Place Setting

a) *oyster or shellfish fork*
b) *soup spoon*
c) *fork and knife for fish*
d) *fork and knife for meat*
e) *fork and knife for salad and cheese*

f) *sherry glass (with soup)*
g) *white wine glass (with fish)*
h) *red wine glass (with meat)*
i) *water goblet*
j) *champagne glass (with dessert)*

Note: *Always use the outside silver first (after the oyster fork and soup spoon, just remember to use the fork farthest to the left and the knife farthest to the right).*

Deaths and Funerals

Plans for death should be discussed with family and loved ones before such plans are likely to be needed. A person's desires regarding the sort of funeral held, disposal of the body by burial or cremation, donation of organs, and so forth need to be known. Practical matters— where to find insurance papers, the will, bills, bank accounts, safety deposit boxes, or investment holdings—also should be dealt with in advance.

Funeral Arrangements

The details of funeral arrangements are handled by funeral directors. Placement of a death notice in the newspaper; selection of a coffin; travel to church, synagogue, and/or graveyard; and a variety of other services are provided. Many of these arrangements can be made in advance or at the time of death. The death notice would include the deceased's name and date of death, the names of immediate family members who survive, and the place and time of the wake and funeral if the funeral is not private.

Wakes

Traditionally, wakes were held at the dead person's home, but today wakes are usually held at a funeral home. They are strictly a Christian phenomenon; Jews sit *shiva* during a three- to seven-day period of mourning and remembrance immediately after burial. Anyone who wishes to may attend a wake, unless it is kept private. The hours and days are set and usually appear in the death notice in the newspaper. Nonfamily members should sign the guest book provided at the funeral home, stay just long enough to express sympathy to the bereaved family, then leave. Expressions of sympathy are best if they come from the heart; when at a loss for what to say, a simple "I'm sorry" is enough. Standing, kneeling, or praying at the coffin is optional.

Flowers

Sending flowers is a customary way of expressing sympathy, especially if attendance at the wake or funeral is not possible. They can be sent to either the funeral home or the church along with a card. Flowers are not appropriate for Jewish funerals or if the death notice requests donations to charity in lieu of them.

Funeral Services

Unless specified as private in the death notice, funeral services can be attended by anyone. They should be viewed not as an obligation but as an opportunity to publicly bid farewell to the person who died and to show concern for the survivors. Religious affiliation is unimportant; one may attend a funeral service regardless of faith. It is important to speak to the bereaved family at the funeral service; if sympathy has already been expressed at the wake, a positive comment about the service, the eulogy, or the church or synagogue would be appropriate.

Burial

For Jews, burial takes place within 24 hours, or as quickly as possible. Christians are buried two or more days after death. Close friends and family members are generally the only people expected to attend the actual interment.

A reception generally is held after the burial. The funeral director or a family member will invite those present to attend. It can be held at the home of a relative or at a catering hall or restaurant. Food and drink are provided by the bereaved family or arranged for by them.

Letters or Calls of Condolence

These are appropriate in lieu of attendance at a wake or funeral service. They should be brief and should focus on memories of the dead person, sympathy for the survivors, and offers of help to the survivors. Avoid pity in such communications or visits, and make clear that a response is not expected soon.

After Burial

It is important to be available to the grieving family after all ceremonies are over. If the family is Jewish, they will sit shiva for three to seven days; it is appropriate to drop by and bring food but not flowers. If the family is Christian, stop by a few days later to listen and talk. Whatever the religious affiliation, friends who are willing to listen and talk to bereaved family members are highly valued at this time.

Additional Sources of Information

Baldridge, Letitia. *The Amy Vanderbilt Complete Book of Etiquette: A Guide to Contemporary Living.* Doubleday, 1978.

Bryan, Dawn. *The Art and Etiquette of Gift Giving.* Bantam, 1987.

Ford, Charlotte. *Charlotte Ford's Book of Modern Manners.* Crown, 1988.

Mark, Lisbeth. *The Book of Hierarchies: A Compendium of Steps, Ranks, Orders, Levels, Classes, Grades, Tiers, Arrays, Degrees, Lines, Divisions, Categories, Precedents, Priorities & Other Distinctions.* William Morrow, 1984.

Martin, Judith. *Miss Manners' Guide to Excruciatingly Correct Behavior.* Atheneum, 1982.

Martin, Judith. *Miss Manners' Guide to Rearing Perfect Children.* Atheneum, 1984.

McCaffree, Maryjane, and Innis, Pauline. *Protocol: The Complete Handbook of Diplomatic, Official and Social Usage.* Devon, 1985.

Post, Elizabeth. *Emily Post On Entertaining: Answers to the Most Often Asked Questions about Entertaining at Home and in Business.* Harper & Row, 1987.

Post, Elizabeth. *Emily Post's Etiquette,* 14th ed. Harper & Row, 1984.

Post, Elizabeth. *Emily Post's Wedding Etiquette & Planner.* Harper & Row, 1982.

Rowland, Diana. *Japanese Business Etiquette: A Practical Guide to Business and Social Success with the Japanese.* Warner Books, 1985.

15

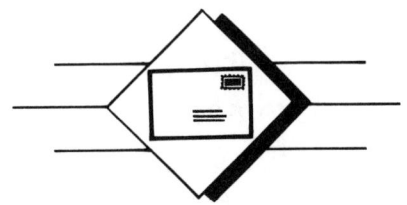

Forms of Address

Spoken and Written Forms of Address for U.S. Government Officials, Military Personnel, Foreign Officials, Nobility, and Religious Officials

This section gives the correct forms of address for United States public officials, diplomats, religious leaders, royalty, the British peerage, and military personnel. For each personage the chart gives the appropriate form or forms to be used in addressing letters, in letter salutations, in direct conversation, and in more formal introductions.

In diplomatic and other public circles, "Sir" is generally considered an acceptable alternative to the formal address in both written and spoken greetings; this does not apply to religious or titled persons. The use of "Madam" or "Ma'am" for a female addressee is less customary but still acceptable, especially for high officeholders ("Madam Governor"). This rule also holds for high officials of foreign countries.

For greetings in which "Mr." is used, the feminine equivalent may be "Madam" or, less formally, "Mrs.," "Miss," or "Ms." Although there is no formal rule for the use of "Ms.," the preference of the addressee should be respected.

Person	Letter Address	Letter Greeting	Spoken Greeting	Formal Introduction
President of the United States	The President The White House Washington, DC 20500	Dear Mr. President	Mr. President	The President or the President of the United States
former President	The Honorable John J. Jones Address	Dear Mr. Jones	Mr. Jones	The Honorable John J. Jones
Vice President	The Vice President Executive Office Building Washington, DC 20501	Dear Mr. Vice President	Mr. Vice President	The Vice President or the Vice President of the United States
Cabinet members	The Honorable John (or Jane) Jones The Secretary of _____ or The Postmaster General or The Attorney General Washington, DC	Dear Mr. (or Madam) Secretary	Mr. (or Madam) Secretary	The Secretary of _____
Chief Justice	The Chief Justice The Supreme Court Washington, DC 20543	Dear Mr. Justice or Dear Mr. Chief Justice	Mr. Chief Justice	The Chief Justice
Associate Justice	Mr. Justice Jones or Madam Justice Jones The Supreme Court Washington, DC 20543	Dear Mr. (or Madam) Justice	Mr. Justice or Mr. Justice Jones; Madam Justice or Madam Justice Jones	Mr. Justice Jones; Madam Justice Jones
United States Senator	The Honorable John (or Jane) Jones United States Senate Washington, DC 20001	Dear Senator Jones	Senator Jones	Senator Jones from Montana
Speaker of the House	The Honorable John (or Jane) Jones Speaker of the House of Representatives United States Capitol Washington, DC 20001	Dear Mr. (or Madam) Speaker	Mr. Speaker; Madam Speaker	The Speaker of the House of Representatives
United States Representative	The Honorable John (or Jane) Jones United States House of Representatives Washington, DC 20001	Dear Mr. (or Mrs., Ms.) Jones	Mr. (or Mrs., Ms.) Jones	Representative Jones from New Jersey

Person	Letter Address	Letter Greeting	Spoken Greeting	Formal Introduction
United Nations Representative	The Honorable John (or Jane) Jones / U.S. Representative to the United Nations / United Nations Plaza / New York, NY 10017	Dear Mr. (or Madam) Ambassador	Mr. (or Madam) Ambassador	The United States Representative to the United Nations
Ambassador	The Honorable John (or Jane) Jones / Ambassador of the United States / American Embassy / Address	Dear Mr. (or Madam) Ambassador	Mr. (or Madam) Ambassador	The American Ambassador
Consul-General	The Honorable John (or Jane) Jones / American Consul General / Address	Dear Mr. (or Mrs., Ms.) Jones	Mr. (or Mrs., Ms.) Jones	Mr. (or Mrs., Ms.) Jones
Foreign Ambassador	His (or Her) Excellency John (or Jean) Johnson / The Ambassador of ___ / Address	Excellency or Dear Mr. (or Madam) Ambassador	Excellency; or Mr. (or Madam) Ambassador	The Ambassador of ___
Secretary-General of the United Nations	His (or Her) Excellency Milo (or Mara) Jones / Secretary-General of the United Nations / United Nations Plaza / New York, NY 10017	Dear Mr. (or Madam) Secretary-General	Mr. (or Madam) Secretary-General	The Secretary-General of the United Nations
Governor	The Honorable John (or Jane) Jones / Governor of ___ / State Capitol / Address	Dear Governor Jones	Governor or Governor Jones	The Governor of Maine; Governor Jones of Maine
State legislators	The Honorable John (or Jane) Jones / Address	Dear Mr. (or Mrs., Ms.) Jones	Mr. (or Mrs., Ms.) Jones	Mr. (or Mrs., Ms.) Jones
Judges	The Honorable John J. Jones / Justice, Appellate Division / Supreme Court of the State of ___ / Address	Dear Judge Jones	Mrs. Justice or Judge Jones; Madam Justice or Judge Jones	The Honorable John (or Jane) Jones; Mr. Justice Jones or Judge Jones; Madam Justice Jones or Judge Jones

Mayor	The Honorable John (or Jane) Jones; His (or Her) Honor the Mayor / City Hall / Address	Dear Mayor Jones	Mayor Jones: Mr. (or Madam) Mayor; Your Honor	Mayor Jones; The Mayor
The Pope	His Holiness, the Pope or His Holiness, Pope John XII / Vatican City / Rome, Italy	Your Holiness or Most Holy Father	Your Holiness or Most Holy Father	His Holiness, the Holy Father; the Pope; the Pontiff
Cardinals	His Eminence, John Cardinal Jones, Archbishop of ____ / Address	Your Eminence or Dear Cardinal Jones	Your Eminence or Cardinal Jones	His Eminence, Cardinal Jones
Bishops	The Most Reverend John Jones, Bishop (or Archbishop) of ____ / Address	Your Excellency or Dear Bishop (Archbishop) Jones	Your Excellency or Bishop (Archbishop) Jones	His Excellency or Bishop (Archbishop) Jones
Monsignor	The Right Reverend Monsignor Harding / Address	Right Reverend Monsignor or Dear Monsignor Harding	Monsignor Harding or Monsignor	Monsignor Harding
Priest	The Reverend John Jones / Address	Reverend Father or Dear Father Jones	Father or Father Jones	Father Jones
Brother	Brother John or Brother John Jones / Address	Dear Brother John or Dear Brother	Brother John or Brother	Brother John
Sister	Sister Mary Luke / Address	Dear Sister Mary Luke or Dear Sister	Sister Mary Luke or Sister	Sister Mary Luke
Protestant Clergy	The Reverend John (or Jane) Jones* / Address	Dear Dr. (or Mr., Ms.) Jones	Dr. (or Mr., Ms.) Jones	The Reverend (or Dr.) John Jones
Bishop (Episcopal)	The Right Reverend John Jones* / Bishop of ____ / Address	Dear Bishop Jones	Bishop Jones	The Right Reverend John Jones, Bishop of Detroit
Rabbi	Rabbi Arthur (or Anne) Milgrom* / Address	Dear Rabbi (or Dr.) Milgrom	Rabbi Milgrom or Dr. Milgrom or Rabbi	Rabbi (or Dr.) Arthur Milgrom
King or Queen	His (Her) Majesty King (Queen) ____ / Address (letters traditionally are sent to reigning monarchs not directly but via the private secretary)		Your Majesty; Sir or Madam	Varies depending on titles, holdings, etc.

Person	Letter Address	Letter Greeting	Spoken Greeting	Formal Introduction
Other royalty	His (Her) Royal Highness, the Prince (Princess) of _____ Address	Your Royal Highness	Your Royal Highness; Sir or Madam	His (Her) Royal Highness, the Duke (Duchess) of Gloucester
Duke/Duchess	His/Her Grace, the D _____ of _____	My Lord Duke/Madam or Dear Duke of _____ Dear Duchess	Your Grace or Duke/Duchess	His/Her Grace, the Duke/Duchess of Bridgeport
Marquess/Marchioness	The Most Honorable the M _____ of Bridgeport	My Lord/Madam or Dear Lord/Lady Bridgeport	Lord/Lady Bridgeport	Lord/Lady Bridgeport
Earl	The Right Honorable the Earl of Franklin	My Lord or Dear Lord Franklin	Lord Franklin	Lord Franklin
Countess (wife of an earl)	The Right Honorable the Countess of Franklin	Madam or Dear Lady Franklin	Lady Franklin	Lady Franklin
Viscount/Viscountess	The Right Honorable the V _____ Tyburn	My Lord/Lady or Dear Lord/Lady Tyburn	Lord/Lady Tyburn	Lord/Lady Tyburn
Baron/Baroness	The Right Honorable Lord/Lady Austin	My Lord/Madam or Dear Lord/Lady Austin	Lord/Lady Austin	Lord/Lady Austin
Baronet	Sir John Jones, Bt.	Dear Sir or Dear Sir John	Sir John	Sir John Jones
Wife of baronet	Lady Jones	Dear Madam or Dear Lady Jones	Lady Jones	Lady Jones
Knight	Sir John Jones	Dear Sir or Dear Sir John	Sir John	Sir John Jones
Wife of knight	Lady Jones	Dear Madam or Dear Lady Jones	Lady Jones	Lady Jones

Military
Personnel

For commissioned officers in the United States armed services, the full rank is used as a title only in addressing letters and in formal introductions: one writes to Major General Ann Jones, U.S. Army, and introduces her as Major General Jones. In greetings the full rank is shortened to General: "Dear General Jones." Similar acceptable shortened greetings follow:

	Full Rank	*Greeting*
Army, Air Force, Marines	General of the Army	General
	Lieutenant General	General
	Brigadier General	General
	Lieutenant Colonel	Colonel
	First Lieutenant	Lieutenant
	Second Lieutenant	Lieutenant
Navy, Coast Guard	Fleet Admiral	Admiral
	Vice Admiral	Admiral
	Rear Admiral	Admiral
	Lieutenant Commander	Commander
	Lieutenant, Junior Grade	Lieutenant

For enlisted personnel, a similar principle applies. Sergeants—whether staff sergeants, gunnery sergeants, or first sergeants—are greeted simply as "Sergeant"; privates first class are referred to as "Private"; and, in the Navy and Coast Guard, chief petty officers are referred to as "Chief." Other noncommissioned officers are greeted by their ranks, although, informally, lower grades may be referred to generically as "Soldier" or "Sailor."

The universal terms of respect that lower ranks must use when addressing senior officers are "Sir" and "Madam." These terms are not applied to noncommissioned officers, however; the appropriate affirmative response to a sergeant, for example, is "Yes, Sergeant."

* If the cleric holds a doctorate in divinity, it is customary to add the designation D.D. after his or her name in the letter address.

Order of British Peerage

Titles of nobility, or peerages, are granted by the king or queen of Great Britain on the recommendation of the prime minister. In most *hereditary peerages,* the title passes on to a peer's oldest son, or to his closest male heir if the peer has no son (the other children are considered commoners). The title becomes extinct if there is no male heir. There are some ancient peerages that allow the title to be passed to a daughter if the holder leaves no male descendant. The last hereditary peerage was granted in 1964.

Life peerages are created each year by the British monarch for several distinguished persons. Life peers hold the rank for their own lives only; the titles do not pass on to their children. Both men and women may be granted life peerages, and the titles given to them are baron or baroness.

The following are the five grades of peers ranked from the highest to the lowest and the dates they were created. (Duke is the highest hereditary rank below that of prince.)

1.	duke	or	duchess (1337)
2.	marquess, marquis	or	marchioness (1385)
3.	earl	or	countess (c. 800–1000)
4.	viscount	or	viscountess (1440)
5.	baron	or	baroness (c. 1066)

Abbreviated Titles That Follow Names

An abbreviated title can tell more about a person than his or her name. It will identify a rank or position, membership in a monastic or secular order, academic degree, or military or civil honor. The following list includes some familiar as well as some obscure abbreviated titles.

Abbreviation	Title
A.B.	artium baccalaureus (bachelor of arts)
A.M.	artium magister (master of arts)
B.A.	bachelor of arts
B.D.	bachelor of divinity
B.S.	bachelor of science
D.B.	divinitatis baccalaureus (bachelor of divinity)
D.D.	divinitatis doctor (doctor of divinity)
D.D.S.	doctor of dental surgery
D.O.	doctor of osteopathy
D.S.O.	Distinguished Service Order
D.V.M.	doctor of veterinary medicine
Esq.	esquire
F.R.S.	fellow of the Royal Society
J.D.	juris doctor (doctor of law)
J.P.	justice of the peace
Kt.	knight
L.H.D.	litterarum humaniorum doctor (doctor of humanities)

Abbreviation	Title
Litt.D.	litterarum doctor (doctor of letters)
LL.B.	legum baccalaureus (bachelor of laws)
M.A.	master of arts
M.D.	medicinae doctor (doctor of medicine)
M.P.	member of Parliament
M.S.	master of science
Ph.B.	philosophiae baccalaureus (bachelor of philosophy)
Ph.D.	philosophiae doctor (doctor of philosophy)
Ph.G.	graduate in pharmacy
Psy.D	doctor of psychology
R.N.	registered nurse
S.B.	bachelor of science
S.J.	Society of Jesus
S.M.	master of science
S.T.B.	sacrae theologiae baccalaureus (bachelor of sacred theology)

Additional Sources of Information

Baldridge, Letitia. *Amy Vanderbilt's Complete Book of Etiquette,* rev. ed. Doubleday, 1978.

Blumenthal, Lassor A. *The Art of Letter Writing.* Putnam, 1986.

Crisp, Quentin, and Hofsess, Joseph. *Manners From Heaven: A Divine Guide to Good Behavior.* Harper & Row, 1985.

Lott, James E. *Practical Protocol: A Guide to International Courtesies.* Gulf, 1973.

Mark, Lisbeth. *The Book of Hierarchies: A Compendium of Steps, Ranks, Orders, Levels, Classes, Grades, Tiers, Arrays, Degrees, Lines, Divisions, Categories, Precedents, Priorities & Other Distinctions.* William Morrow, 1984.

Martin, Judith. *Miss Manners' Guide to Excruciatingly Correct Behavior.* Warner Books, 1983.

McCaffree, Maryjane, and Innis, Pauline. *Protocol: The Complete Handbook of Diplomatic, Official and Social Usage,* rev. ed. Devon, 1985.

Post, Elizabeth. *Emily Post's Etiquette,* 14th ed. Harper & Row, 1984.

Swartz, Oretha D. *Service Etiquette,* 4th ed. Naval Institute Press, 1988.

16

Legal Information

Federal Judicial System

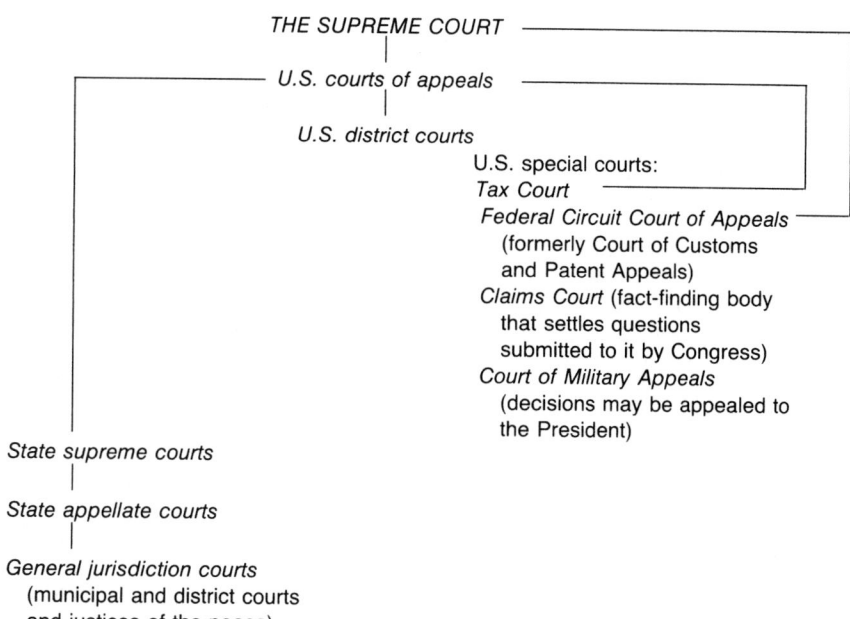

THE SUPREME COURT

U.S. courts of appeals

U.S. district courts

U.S. special courts:
Tax Court
Federal Circuit Court of Appeals
(formerly Court of Customs
and Patent Appeals)
Claims Court (fact-finding body
that settles questions
submitted to it by Congress)
Court of Military Appeals
(decisions may be appealed to
the President)

State supreme courts

State appellate courts

General jurisdiction courts
(municipal and district courts
and justices of the peace)

Supreme Court Justices

Justice	Term	Justice	Term
*John Jay	1789–95	Alfred Moore	1799–1804
John Blair	1789–96	*John Marshall	1801–35
William Cushing	1789–1810	William Johnson	1804–34
Robert H. Harrison	1789–90	Brockolst Livingston	1806–23
John Rutledge	1789–91	Thomas Todd	1807–26
James Wilson	1789–98	Joseph Story	1811–45
James Iredell	1790–99	Gabriel Duval	1812–35
Thomas Johnson	1791–93	Smith Thompson	1823–43
William Paterson	1793–1806	Robert Trimble	1826–28
*John Rutledge	1795 (Congress rejected his appointment as chief justice)	John McLean	1829–61
		Henry Baldwin	1830–44
		James M. Wayne	1835–67
		*Roger B. Taney	1836–64
*Oliver Ellsworth	1796–99	Philip P. Barbour	1836–41
Samuel Chase	1796–1811	John Catron	1837–65
Bushrod Washington	1798–1829	John McKinley	1837–52

Justice	Term	Justice	Term
Peter V. Daniel	1841–60	Louis D. Brandeis	1916–39
Samuel Nelson	1845–72	John H. Clarke	1916–22
Levi Woodbury	1845–51	*William H. Taft	1921–30
Robert C. Grier	1846–70	Pierce Butler	1922–39
Benjamin R. Curtis	1851–57	George Sutherland	1922–38
John A. Campbell	1853–61	Edward T. Sanford	1923–30
Nathan Clifford	1858–81	Harlan F. Stone	1925–41
David Davis	1862–77	*Charles E. Hughes	1930–41
Samuel F. Miller	1862–90	Owen J. Roberts	1930–45
Noah H. Swayne	1862–81	Benjamin N. Cardozo	1932–38
Stephen J. Field	1863–97	Hugo L. Black	1937–71
*Salmon P. Chase	1864–73	Stanley F. Reed	1938–57
Joseph P. Bradley	1870–92	William O. Douglas	1939–75
William Strong	1870–80	Felix Frankfurter	1939–62
Ward Hunt	1873–82	Frank Murphy	1940–49
*Morrison R. Waite	1874–88	*Harlan F. Stone	1941–46
John M. Harlan	1877–1911	James F. Byrnes	1941–42
Stanley Matthews	1881–89	Robert H. Jackson	1941–54
William B. Woods	1881–87	Wiley B. Rutledge	1943–49
Samuel Blatchford	1882–1903	Harold H. Burton	1945–58
Horace Gray	1882–1902	*Fred M. Vinson	1946–53
*Melville W. Fuller	1888–1910	Tom C. Clark	1949–67
Lucius Q. C. Lamar	1888–93	Sherman Minton	1949–56
David J. Brewer	1890–1910	*Earl Warren	1953–69
Henry B. Brown	1891–1906	John Marshall Harlan	1955–71
George Shiras, Jr.	1892–1903	William H. Brennan, Jr.	1956–
Howell E. Jackson	1893–95	Charles E. Whittaker	1957–62
Edward D. White	1894–1910	Potter Stewart	1958–81
Rufus W. Peckham	1896–1909	Arthur J. Goldberg	1962–65
Joseph McKenna	1898–1925	Byron R. White	1962–
Oliver W. Holmes	1902–32	Abe Fortas	1965–69
William R. Day	1903–22	Thurgood Marshall	1967–
William H. Moody	1906–10	*Warren E. Burger	1969–86
*Edward D. White	1910–21	Harry A. Blackmun	1970–
Charles E. Hughes	1910–16	Lewis F. Powell, Jr.	1972–87
Horace H. Lurton	1910–14	*William H. Renquist	1972–
Joseph R. Lamar	1911–16	John Paul Stevens, III	1975–
Willis Van Devanter	1911–37	Sandra Day O'Connor	1981–
Mahlon Pitney	1912–22	Antonin Scalia	1986–
James C. McReynolds	1914–41	Anthony Kennedy	1988–

* chief justice

Forms and Contracts

The wording of the documents in the following sections are fairly standard versions of simple agreements, requests, or statements. They are meant to demonstrate the content of such documents. Because laws vary from state to state, and because agreements can have their own special circumstances, terms, or other complexities, it is always a good idea to consult with a lawyer before drawing up or signing a contract.

Certificate of Notary

A certificate of notary often accompanies agreements or statements; it may be required in some localities. The certificate of notary might be useful with the following documents in this section:

Bill of Sale

Declaration of Gift

Request for Reason for Adverse Credit Action

Power of Attorney

Living Will

Privacy Act/Freedom of Information Act Request

CERTIFICATE OF NOTARY

STATE OF   )
) ss:
COUNTY OF   )

On this _____ day of _____, 19_____, before me personally came and appeared _____, known, and known to me, to be the individual described in and who executed the foregoing instrument, and who duly acknowledged to me that he/she executed same for the purpose therein contained.

IN WITNESS WHEREOF, I hereunto set my hand and official seal.

_____
Notary Public

My commission expires: _____

Leases

Lease Agreement—Unfurnished Apartment

Landlord _____

_____

                                                Address   *Phone*

Managing Agent _____

_____

                                                Address   *Phone*

Premises _____

                                                Address   *Apt. No.*

Tenant _____

Tenant _____

    1. The LANDLORD hereby leases to _____ (and) _____, hereinafter termed TENANT, the premises described above for a term of _____ beginning _____ _____ and ending _____, at a monthly rate of $_____, making a total rental amount payable under this lease of $_____.

    2. The tenant agrees to pay the rent herein provided subject to the terms and conditions set forth herein.

    3. Rent shall be payable in equal monthly installments to be paid in advance on the _____ day of each month.

    4. Rent shall be payable in the following manner:

(Specify above if payments are to be made by mail, and if so, to what address. If payments are to be made to the landlord or the landlord's agent in person, state the place where, and the person to whom, payments are to be made.)

5. Upon receiving any payment of rent in cash, the landlord agrees to issue a receipt stating the tenant's name, a description of the premises, the amount of rent paid, the date paid and the period for which rent is paid.

6. The landlord covenants that the leased premises are, to the best of his or her knowledge, clean, safe, sound, and healthful and that there exists no violation of any applicable housing code, law or regulation of which he or she is aware.

7. The tenant agrees to comply with all sanitary laws, ordinances and rules, and all orders of the Board of Health or other authorities affecting the cleanliness, occupancy, and preservation of the premises during the term of this lease.

8. The tenant shall use the leased premises exclusively as a private residence for no more than _____ persons, and the tenant will not make alterations therein without the written consent of the landlord.

9. The tenant shall keep fixtures in said apartment in good order and repair, and the tenant shall cause to be made, at the tenant's expense, all required repairs to heating and air-conditioning apparatus, refrigerator, range, electric and gas fixtures, and plumbing work whenever such damage shall have resulted from misuse, waste, or neglect, it being understood that the landlord is to have same in good order and repair when giving possession.

10. The tenant shall not keep or have in the leased premises any article or thing of a dangerous, inflammable, or explosive nature that might be pronounced "hazardous" or "extra hazardous" by any responsible insurance company.

11. The tenant shall give prompt notice to the landlord of any dangerous, defective, unsafe, or emergency condition in the leased premises, said notice being given by any suitable means. The landlord shall repair and correct said conditions promptly upon receiving notice thereof from the tenant.

12. The landlord covenants that all essential services are now provided and shall be provided at all times during the term of this lease and any extension, renewal, or continuation thereof, except where any interruption of essential services shall be for maintenance or for cause beyond control of the landlord such as strike, storm, civil insurrection, fire, or acts of God. "Essential services" hereunder are defined as heat, hot and cold running water, a properly functioning toilet, light in public areas, and suitable building security.

13. The _____ shall pay for gas and electricity except to the extent otherwise set forth herein.

14. The landlord covenants that consumption of electricity for the public halls and other common areas and use and consumption of gas for heat or hot water in public areas are recorded on separate meters, and that said electricity and gas are and will at all times be billed to and paid by the landlord.

15. The tenant covenants that during the last 30 days of this lease, or any renewal thereof, the landlord or his agents, with reasonable notice, and at reasonable hours, have the privilege of showing the premises to prospective buyers or tenants.

16. The tenant shall, at reasonable times, give access to the landlord or his agents for any reasonable and lawful purpose. Except in situations of compelling emergency, or to show the premises for rental or sale, the landlord agrees to give the tenant 24 hours' notice, stating the time and date when access will be sought, and the reason therefore.

17. The landlord covenants that the tenant and the tenant's family shall have, hold, and enjoy the leased premises for the term of this lease, subject to the provisions and conditions set forth herein.

18. The tenant covenants that he shall not commit nor permit a nuisance in or upon the premises, that he shall not maliciously or by reason of gross negligence damage the premises and that he shall not engage in conduct so as to interfere substantially with the comfort and safety of occupants of adjacent apartments or buildings.

19. The tenant agrees to place a security deposit with the landlord in the amount of $_____, to be used by the landlord for the cost of replacing and/or repairing damage, if any, to the premises caused by the intentional or negligent acts of the tenant.

20. The landlord agrees, within ten days of receiving said security deposit, to deposit same in an interest-bearing account in a banking organization, in which said deposit shall earn interest at a rate which shall be the prevailing rate earned by other such deposits made with banking organizations in such circumstances.

21. The landlord agrees, within ten days of making such deposit, to notify the tenant, in writing, of the name and address of the banking organization in which the deposit of security money has been made.

22. The landlord shall be entitled to receive, as administrative expenses, an amount equal to one percent per annum upon the security payment so deposited, which shall be in lieu of all other administrative and custodial expenses. The balance of the interest paid by the banking organization shall be the money of the tenant and shall be paid to the tenant on each anniversary of this lease or any extension or renewal thereof.

23. The landlord agrees to return said security deposit to the tenant within ten days of the tenant's vacating the leased premises subject to the terms and conditions set forth herein.

24. In the event of any breach by the tenant of any of the tenant's covenants or agreements herein, the landlord may give the tenant five days' notice to cure said breach, setting forth in writing which covenants or agreements have been breached. If any breach is not cured within said five-day period, or reasonable steps to effectuate said cure are not commenced and diligently pursued within said five-day period and thereafter until said breach has been cured, the landlord may terminate this lease upon five days' additional notice to the tenant, with said notice being in lieu of a Notice to Quit, which tenant hereby waives. The tenant shall then become liable for the cost of landlord's normal redecorating and cleaning expenses related to preparation of the premises for rental to a succeeding tenant.

Said termination shall be ineffective if the tenant cures said breach or commences and diligently pursues reasonable steps to effectuate such cure at any time prior to the expiration of said five-day termination. Upon terminating this lease as provided herein, the landlord or his agent may commence proceedings against the tenant for his removal as provided for by law.

25. In the event of any breach by the landlord of any of the landlord's covenants or agreements herein, the tenant may give the landlord ten days' notice to cure said breach, setting forth in writing the manner in which said covenants and agreements have been breached. If said breach is not cured within said ten-day period, or reasonable steps to effectuate said cure are not commenced and diligently pursued within said ten-day period and thereafter until said breach has been cured, rent hereunder shall be fully abated from the time at which said ten days' notice expired until such time as the landlord has fully cured the breach set forth in the notice provided for in this paragraph.

26. In no case shall any abatement of rent hereunder be effected where the condition set forth in the notice provided for herein was created by the intentional or negligent act of the tenant, but the landlord shall have the burden of proving that rent abatement may not be effected for the foregoing reason.

27. The landlord agrees to deliver possession of the leased premises at the beginning of the term provided for herein. In the event of the landlord's failure to deliver possession at the beginning of said term, the tenant shall have the right to rescind this lease and to recover any consideration paid under terms of this agreement.

28. The tenant agrees that this lease shall be subject to and subordinate to any mortgage or mortgages now on said premises or which any owner of said premises may hereafter at any time elect to place on said premises.

29. Unless otherwise provided for elsewhere in this lease, any notice required or authorized herein shall be given in writing, one copy of said notice mailed via U.S. certified mail, return receipt requested, and one copy of said notice mailed via U.S. first-class mail.

Notice to the tenant shall be mailed to him at the leased premises. Notice to the landlord shall be mailed to him, or to the managing agent, at their respective addresses as set forth herein, or at such new address as to which the tenant has been duly notified.

30. This lease constitutes the entire agreement between the parties hereto. No changes shall be made herein except by writing, signed by each party and dated. The failure to enforce any right or remedy hereunder, and the payment and acceptance of rent hereunder, shall not be deemed a waiver by either party of such right or remedy in the absence of a writing as provided for herein.

31. In the event legal action is required to enforce any provision of this agreement, the prevailing party shall be entitled to recover reasonable attorney's fees and costs.

32. The landlord and tenant agree that this apartment lease, when filled out and signed, is a binding legal obligation.

IN WITNESS WHEREOF, the parties hereto have executed this agreement.

_____

Landlord

By _____

_____
Witness as to landlord

_____
Witness as to landlord

_____

Tenant

_____
Witness as to tenant

_____
Witness as to tenant

_____

Tenant

_____
Witness as to tenant

_____
Witness as to tenant

Dated this _____ day of _____, 19_____.

Seasonal Lease Agreement—Furnished Country/Seashore House

Landlord _____

_____
Address   *Phone*

Managing Agent _____

_____
Address   *Phone*

Premises _____

_____

Tenant _____

_____
Address   *Phone*

Tenant _____

_____
Address   *Phone*

    1. The LANDLORD hereby leases to _____ (and) _____, hereinafter termed TENANT, the premises described above for a term of _____ beginning _____ and ending _____, at a monthly rate of $_____, making a total rental amount payable under this lease of $_____.

    2. The tenant agrees to pay the rent in the following manner:

(Landlord specify if payments are to be made by mail, and if so, to what address. If payments are to be made to the landlord or his agent in person, state the place where, and the person to whom, payments should be made.)

3. The tenant, in addition to rent, agrees to pay all charges for water, gas, fuel oil, and electricity used during the term of the lease, such charges to be paid monthly in addition to rent.

4. Upon receipt of any payment for rent or utilities in cash, the landlord agrees to issue a receipt stating the tenant's name, a description of the premises, the amount paid, the date paid, and the period for which rent or utilities is paid.

5. The tenant agrees to place a security deposit of $_____, to be used by the landlord at the termination of this lease for the cost of replacing or repairing damage, if any, to the premises or furnishings caused by the intentional or negligent acts of the tenant.

6. The landlord agrees to return said security deposit to the tenant upon the tenant's vacating the premises subject to the terms and conditions herein.

7. The tenant agrees to take good care of the premises and of the furnishings therein, and at the end of the term of this lease to deliver up to the landlord the premises and furnishings in good order, normal wear and tear excepted.

8. The landlord covenants that the leased premises are, to the best of his or her knowledge, clean, safe, sound, and healthful and that there exists no violation of any applicable housing code, law, or regulation of which he or she is aware, and that no such violation will be permitted to exist during the term of this lease or any extension thereof.

9. The tenant shall promptly comply with all laws, orders, ordinances and regulations pertaining to his or her use of the premises, and the tenant shall not keep therein any article or thing of a dangerous, flammable or explosive nature that might be pronounced "hazardous" or "extra hazardous" by any responsible insurance company.

10. The tenant shall, in case of fire, give immediate notice to the proper authorities and to the landlord who will cause the damage to be promptly repaired; but if the premises be so damaged that the landlord shall decide to terminate this lease, then upon ten days' personal or written notice to the tenant this lease shall terminate and the accrued rent shall be paid up to the time of the fire.

11. The tenant shall do no cooking in any room used for sleeping purposes, but shall have the right to use jointly with any other tenants a room set aside by the landlord for that purpose.

12. The tenant shall, at reasonable times, give access to the landlord or his agents for any reasonable and lawful purpose. Except in situations of compelling emergency, the landlord shall give the tenant at least 24 hours' notice of intention to seek access, the date and time at which access will be sought, and the reason therefore.

13. In the event of default by the tenant, the tenant shall remain liable for all rent due or to become due during the term of this lease. The landlord shall have the obligation to relet the premises in the landlord's name for the balance of the term, or longer, and will apply proceeds of such reletting toward the reduction of the tenant's obligations enumerated herein.

14. The tenant shall permit the landlord or his agents to show the premises at reasonable hours, to persons desiring to rent or purchase same, 30 days prior to the expiration of this lease, and will permit the notice "To Let" or "For Sale" to be placed on said premises and remain thereon without hindrance or molestation after said date.

15. The tenant shall not assign this lease, nor underlet or underlease the premises, or any part thereof, nor make any alterations to the premises, nor permit same to be used at any time during the term of this lease for any other purpose than a private residence.

16. This lease, and any attached List of Furnishings signed by both parties and dated, and incorporated herein by reference for all purposes, constitutes the entire agreement between the parties hereto. No changes shall be made herein except by writing, signed by each party and dated.

17. In the event legal action is required to enforce any provision of this agreement, the prevailing party shall be entitled to recover reasonable attorney's fees and costs.

18. This lease, when filled out and signed, is a binding legal obligation.

IN WITNESS WHEREOF, the parties hereto have executed this agreement.

_____
Landlord

By _____

_____
Witness as to landlord

_____
Tenant

_____
Tenant

_____
Witness as to tenant

_____
Witness as to tenant

Dated this _____ day of _____, 19_____.

"Open" Rental Agreement

THIS AGREEMENT is made this _____ day of _____ , 19_____ , between

_____ , of

| Street Address | City | State | Zip |

hereinafter called "Owner," and _____ , of

| Street Address | City | State | Zip |

hereinafter called "Renter."

Property

_____

_____

_____

_____

| Year | Make | Model/Type |

| Capacity | Horsepower | Serial No. |

The Owner warrants that to the best of his/her knowledge and belief the aforesaid property is free of any known faults or deficiencies which would affect its safe and dependable operation under normal and prudent usage.

Rental Period

The Owner agrees to rent the above-described property to the Renter for a period of _____ beginning _____ and ending _____ .

Use of Property

_____

_____

_____

_____

_____

The Renter further agrees that the rented property (A) shall not be used beyond any rated capacity; (B) shall not be used for any illegal purpose; (C) shall not be used in any manner for which it was not designed, built, or designated by the manufacturer; (D) will not be used in a negligent manner; (E) will not be operated by any other person without the written permission of the Owner; and (F) will not be removed from the designated area of use or operation.

Area of Use or Operation

The Renter agrees to operate/use the above-described property only at the following location or within the following described area(s):

_____

_____

_____

Insurance

The Renter hereby agrees that he/she shall fully indemnify the Owner for any and all damage to or loss of the rented property and any accessories or related equipment during the term of this Agreement whether caused by fire, theft, flood, vandalism, or any other cause, except that which shall be determined to have been caused by a fault or deficiency of the rented property, accessories, or equipment.

Rental Rate

The Renter hereby agrees to pay the Owner at the rate of $_____ per _____ for the use of said property and any accessories/equipment. Any fuel used shall be paid for by the Renter.

Deposit

The Renter further agrees to make a deposit of $_____ with the Owner, said deposit to be used, in the event of loss of or damage to the rented property and any accessories/equipment during the term of this Agreement, to defray fully or partially the cost of necessary repairs or replacement. In the absence of any damage or loss, said deposit shall be credited toward payment of the rental fee and any excess shall be returned to the Renter.

Return of Property to Owner

The Renter hereby agrees to return the rented property and any accessories/equipment to the Owner at _____
_____ no later than _____.

Termination of Agreement

It is mutually agreed that the Renter shall have the right to terminate this Agreement at any time by payment of one full day's rental for each 24-hour period or any part thereof, during which the Renter has retained possession of the property and any accessories/equipment during the term of this Agreement.

IN WITNESS WHEREOF, the parties hereto hereby execute this Agreement.

(Signed) _____
                                           Renter

(Signed) _____
                                           Owner

Contract

𝕬greement 𝕭etween 𝕺wner and 𝕮ontractor

THIS AGREEMENT is hereby entered into this _____ day of _____, 19 ____, between

_____, of

| _____ | _____ | _____ | _____ | _____ |
| *Street Address* | *City* | *Street* | *Zip* | *Phone* |

hereinafter called Owner, and _____, of

| _____ | _____ | _____ | _____ | _____ |
| *Street Address* | *City* | *Street* | *Zip* | *Phone* |

hereinafter called the Contractor.

The said parties, for the considerations hereinafter mentioned, hereby agree to the following:

Description of the Work

1. The Contractor shall provide all materials and labor required to perform all of the work for:

as shown on the drawing(s), and set forth in the specifications and/or description(s) prepared by _____, which drawing(s) and specifications and/or description(s) are identified by the signatures of the parties to this agreement, and which form a part of this agreement and are incorporated by reference herein for all purposes.

Payment

2. Under the terms of this agreement, the Owner agrees to pay the Contractor, for materials to be furnished and work to be done, the sum of _____ ($_____), subject to any additions or deductions as hereinafter provided for in this agreement, and to make the following payments:

and that the final payment shall be made subject to the hereinafter stated conditions of this agreement.

It is agreed that no payment made under this agreement shall be considered conclusive evidence of full performance of this contract, either wholly or in part by the Contractor, and that acceptance of payment shall not be considered by the Contractor to be acceptance by the Owner of any defective materials or workmanship.

Liens

3. Final payment shall not be due until such time as the Contractor has provided the Owner with a release of any liens arising from this agreement; or receipts for payment in full for all materials and labor for which a lien could be filed; or a bond satisfactory to the Owner indemnifying the Owner against any lien.

Timely Completion of the Work

4. The Contractor agrees that the various portions of the work shall be completed on or before the following dates:

and the entire work shall be completed on or before the _____day of _____, 19_____.

In the event the work is not completed by the aforementioned date, the Owner shall be entitled to receive as damages from the Contractor, the sum of _____ ($_____) per _____, it being agreed that the aforementioned sum is reasonable, taking into account the difficulty in determining the exact amount of damages the Owner would sustain in the event of said delay, and that the agreed sum shall be considered as liquidated damages.

If the Contractor is delayed in the completion of the work by any changes ordered in the work, by acts of God, fire, flood, or any other unavoidable casualties; or by labor strikes, late delivery of materials; or by neglect of the Owner, his agents or representatives; or by any subcontractor employed by the Contractor; the time for completion of the work shall be extended for the same period as the delay occasioned by any of the aforementioned causes.

Surveys and Easements

5. The Owner shall provide and pay for all surveys. All easements for access across the property of another, and for permanent changes, and for the construction or erection of structures shall also be obtained and paid for by the Owner.

Licenses, Permits, and Building Codes

6. The Contractor shall obtain and pay for all permits and licenses required for the prosecution and timely completion of the work. The Contractor shall comply with all appropriate regulations relating to the conduct of the work and shall advise the Owner of any specifications or drawings which are at variance therewith.

Materials and Equipment

7. The Contractor shall provide and pay for all materials, tools and equipment required for the prosecution and timely completion of the work. Unless otherwise specified in writing, all materials shall be new and of good quality.

Samples

8. Whenever the Owner may require, the Contractor will furnish for approval all samples as directed, and the work shall be in accordance with approved samples.

Labor and Supervision

9. In the prosecution of the work the Contractor shall at all times keep a competent foreman and a sufficient number of workers skilled in their trades to suitably perform the work.

The foreman shall represent the Contractor and, in the absence of the Contractor, all instructions given by the Owner to the foreman shall be binding upon the Contractor as though given to the Contractor. Upon request of the foreman, instructions shall be in writing.

Alterations and Changes

10. All changes and deviations in the work ordered by the Owner must be in writing, the contract sum being increased or decreased accordingly by the Contractor. Any claims for increases in the cost of the work must be presented by the Contractor to the Owner in writing, and written approval of the Owner shall be obtained by the Contractor before proceeding with the ordered change or revision.

In the event that additional work, not shown on the drawings and/or not described in the specifications, is required to comply with laws, regulations, or building codes, such additional work shall be considered as done under the terms of this agreement.

Correction of Deficiencies

11. The Contractor agrees to reexecute any work which does not conform to the drawings and specifications, warrants the work performed, and further agrees that he shall remedy any defects resulting from faulty materials or workmanship which shall become evident during a period of one year after completion of the work. This provision shall apply with equal force to all work performed by subcontractors as to work that is performed by direct employees of the Contractor.

Protection of the Work

12. It shall be the responsibility of the Contractor to reasonably protect the work, the property of the Owner, and adjacent property and the public, and the Contractor shall be responsible for any damage, injury or death resulting from his negligence or from any intentional act of the Contractor or the Contractor's employees, agents, or subcontractors.

Cleaning Up

13. The Contractor shall keep the premises free from the accumulation of waste and, upon completion of the work, shall remove all waste, equipment, and other materials and leave the premises in broom-clean condition.

Contractor's Liability Insurance

14. The Contractor shall obtain insurance to protect himself against claims for property damage arising out of his or any subcontractor's performance of this contract; and to protect himself against claims under provisions of Workman's Compensation and any similar employee benefit acts, and from claims for bodily injury, including death, due to performance of this contract by the Contractor or any subcontractor employed for the performance of this contract.

Owner's Liability Insurance

15. It shall be the responsibility of the Owner, at the Owner's option, to obtain insurance to protect himself from the contingent liability of claims for property damage and bodily injury, including death, that may arise from the performance of this contract.

Fire Insurance with Extended Coverage

16. The Owner shall obtain fire insurance with extended coverage at 100 percent of the value of the entire structure, including materials and labor related to the work described in this agreement. Certificates of insurance shall be filed with the Contractor if he so requests. The aforesaid fire insurance need not include tools, equipment, scaffolding, or forms owned or rented by the Contractor, any subcontractor, or their respective employees.

Owner's Right to Terminate the Agreement

17. In the event the Contractor shall fail to meet the provisions of this agreement, the Owner shall, after seven (7) days' written notice to the Contractor and his surety, have the right to take possession of the premises in order to complete the work as specified in the agreement. The Owner may deduct the cost thereof from any payment then and thereafter due to the Contractor or may, at his option, terminate the agreement, take possession of any materials, and complete the work as he deems appropriate. If the unpaid balance of the contracted sum exceeds the Owner's expenses of completing the work, such excess shall be paid to the Contractor. If such expense shall exceed the unpaid balance, the Contractor shall pay the difference to the Owner.

Contractor's Right to Terminate the Agreement

18. In the event the Owner shall fail to pay the Contractor within seven (7) days after the date upon which payment shall become due, the Contractor shall have the right, after seven (7) days' written notice to the Owner, to stop work and may, at his option, terminate the agreement and recover from the Owner payment for all work executed, plus any loss sustained, plus a reasonable profit, plus damages.

In the event the work is stopped by any court or other public authority for a period of thirty (30) days through no fault of the Contractor, the Contractor shall have the right to stop work and may, at his option, terminate the agreement and recover from the Owner payment for all work executed, plus any loss sustained, plus a reasonable profit, plus damages.

Assignment of Rights

19. Neither the Owner nor Contractor shall have the right to assign any rights or interest occurring under this agreement without the written consent of the other, nor shall the Contractor assign any sums due, or to become due, to him under the provisions of this agreement.

Access and Inspection

20. The Owner, Owner's representative, and public authorities shall at all times have access to the work.

An appropriately licensed representative of the Owner, whose authority shall be set forth in writing by the Owner, shall have the authority to direct the removal of any materials and the taking down of any portions of the work failing to meet drawings, specifications, laws, regulations, or building codes; the reexecution of said work deemed as being done under the provisions of Article 11 of this agreement.

Any other removal of materials or taking down of any portions of the work as directed by the Owner's representative shall be in writing and at the sole expense of the Owner.

Attorney Fees

21. Attorney fees and court costs shall be paid by the defendant in the event that judgment must be obtained, and is, to enforce this agreement or any breach thereof.

IN WITNESS WHEREOF, the parties hereto set their hands and seals the day and year written above.

_____   _____
Witness as to Owner   *Owner*

_____   _____
Witness as to Contractor   *Contractor*

Bill of Sale

𝕭𝖎𝖑𝖑 𝖔𝖋 𝕾𝖆𝖑𝖊
of

_____

STATE OF   )

)   ss:

COUNTY OF   )

KNOW YE ALL MEN BY THESE PRESENTS,

That I, _____ , of

_____ ,

   Street Address   *City*   *State*   *Zip*

for and in consideration of payment of the sum of $_____ , the receipt of which is hereby acknowledged, do hereby grant, bargain, sell, and convey to:

_____ , of

_____ ,

   Street Address   *City*   *State*   *Zip*

and his/her heirs, executors, administrators, successors, and assigns the following property:

I hereby warrant that I am the lawful owner of said property and that I have full legal right, power, and authority to sell said property. I further warrant said property to be free of all encumbrances and that I will warrant and defend said property hereby sold against any and all persons whomsoever.

IN WITNESS WHEREOF, I, the seller, have hereto set my hand and seal this _____ day of _____ , 19_____ .

(Signed) _____

                                         Seller

Declaration of a Gift

Declaration of Gift

TO ALL TO WHOM THESE PRESENTS SHALL COME OR MAY CONCERN, KNOW THAT on

this _____day of _____, 19_____ I, _____

_____, of _____ ,
         Street   *City*   *State*   *Zip*

being of sound and disposing mind and memory, do hereby irrevocably give, bestow, and deliver up to

_____ ,

of _____ ,
    Street   *City*   *State*   *Zip*

all of my right, title, and interest in the following described property valued at _____
($_____):

_____

_____

_____

_____

_____

_____

_____

_____

IN WITNESS WHEREOF, I hereunto set my hand and seal on the date above mentioned.

_____

Promissory Note

Promissory Note

$_____

Date _____

_____ after the above date I promise to pay to the order of _____
(number of days)

_____ the sum of _____
_____ ($_____), together with interest at _____ percent per annum,
payable at _____.

The maker and endorser of this note further agree to waive demand, notice of nonpayment and protest, and in case suit shall be brought for the collection hereof, or the same has to be collected upon demand of an attorney, to pay reasonable attorney's fees for making such collection. Deferred interest payments to bear interest from maturity at _____ percent per annum, payable semiannually.

(Signed) _____
Maker

(Signed) _____
Endorser

Due _____

Security Agreement

Security Agreement

STATE OF   )
)   ss:
COUNTY OF   )

KNOW YE ALL MEN BY THESE PRESENTS,

That I, _____, of

_____
Street Adress   *Apt. No.*   *City*   *State*   *Zip*

hereinafter called "Debtor," hereby grant to _____, of

_____
Street Address   *Apt. No.*   *City*   *State*   *Zip*

hereinafter called the "Secured Party," a security interest in the following described property as collateral to secure payment of the obligation described herein.

Collateral

_____

_____

_____

_____

Obligation

_____

_____

_____

Default in the payment of all or any part of the obligation described is a default under this Agreement. Upon such default the Secured Party may declare all of the above-described obligation(s) immediately due and payable and shall have the remedies of a secured party under provisions of the Uniform Commercial Code. In the event legal action is required to enforce any provision of this Agreement, the prevailing party shall be entitled to recover reasonable attorney's fees and costs.

The Debtor hereby agrees to exercise reasonable caution and care in use of the herein-described collateral; to adequately insure or keep insured the described collateral; not to attempt to sell, assign, or dispose of said collateral or his/her interest therein; not to encumber nor to permit any encumbrance against same; and not to remove said collateral from the county where the Debtor resides without written permission of the Secured Party.

EXECUTED this _____ day of _____, 19_____.

(Signed) _____
Debtor

(Signed) _____
Secured Party

Request for Reason for Adverse Credit Action

Date: _____

REQUEST FOR REASON FOR ADVERSE CREDIT ACTION

Dear

On _____, I was notified that my application for credit dated _____ _____was denied based upon information received by you from a source other than a consumer credit reporting agency.

Pursuant to my right under the Fair Credit Reporting Act, Title 15 USC, Sec. 1681m(b), I hereby request that the nature of the information received by you be disclosed to me.

Please forward such information to me at the above address.

Thank you for your prompt attention to this matter.

Sincerely,

Power of Attorney

Power of Attorney

STATE OF _____)
)   ss:
COUNTY OF _____)

KNOW YE ALL MEN BY THESE PRESENTS,

That I, _____, of

_____
Street Address   *Apt. No.*   *City*   *State*   *Zip*

do hereby make, constitute, and appoint _____, of

_____
Street Address   *City*   *State*   *Zip*

as my true and lawful Attorney-in-Fact, for me and in my name, place, and stead to:

_____

_____

_____

_____

I further give and grant to my said Attorney-in-Fact full power and authority to do and perform every act necessary and proper to be done in the exercise of any of the foregoing powers as fully as I might or could do if personally present, with full power of substitution and revocation, hereby ratifying and confirming all that my said Attorney-in-fact shall lawfully do, or cause to be done by virtue hereof.

This instrument may not be changed orally.

IN WITNESS WHEREOF, I have hereunto set my hand and seal this _____ day of _____ _____, 19_____.

(Signed) _____

Living Will

_____

𝕷𝖎𝖇𝖎𝖓𝖌 𝖂𝖎𝖑𝖑

Directive to Physicians:

I, _____, of

| _____ | _____ | _____ | _____ | _____ |
| Street Address | Apt. No. | City | State | Zip |

being of sound mind, do hereby willfully and voluntarily make known my desire that my life not be prolonged under any of the following conditions, and do hereby further declare:

1. If I should, at any time, have an incurable condition caused by any disease or illness, or by any accident or injury, and be determined by any two or more physicians to be in a terminal condition whereby the use of "heroic measures" or the application of life-sustaining procedures would only serve to delay the moment of my death, and where my attending physician has determined that my death is imminent whether or not such "heroic measures" or life-sustaining measures are employed, I direct that such measures and procedures be withheld or withdrawn and that I be permitted to die naturally.

2. In the event of my inability to give directions regarding the application of life-sustaining procedures or the use of "heroic measures," it is my intention that this directive shall be honored by my family and physicians as my final expression of my right to refuse medical and surgical treatment, and my acceptance of the consequences of such refusal.

3. I am mentally, emotionally, and legally competent to make this directive and I fully understand its import.

4. I reserve the right to revoke this directive at any time.

5. This directive shall remain in force until revoked.

IN WITNESS WHEREOF, I have hereunto set my hand and seal this _____ day of _____, 19_____.

(Signed) _____

Declaration of Witness

The declarant is personally known to me and I believe him/her to be of sound mind and emotionally and legally competent to make the herein-contained **Directive to Physicians**. I am not related to the declarant by blood or marriage, nor would I be entitled to any portion of the declarant's estate upon his/her decease, nor am I an attending physician of the declarant, nor an employee of the attending physician, nor an employee of a health care facility in which the declarant is a patient, nor a patient in a health care facility in which the declarant is a patient, nor am I a person who has any claim against any portion of the estate of the declarant upon his/her decease.

(Signed) _____
Witness

_____
Address

_____

(Signed) _____
Witness

_____
Address

_____

Privacy Act/Freedom of Information Act Request

Attn:

This is a request under provisions of Title 5 USC, Sec. 552, the Freedom of Information Act, and Title 5 USC, Sec. 552a, the Privacy Act.

Please furnish me with copies of all records on me retrievable by the use of an individual identifier and by the use of any combination of identifiers (e.g., name + date of birth + Social Security number, etc.) that are contained in the following systems of records:

In order to identify myself and to facilitate your search of records systems, I provide the following information:

Last Name	*First*	*Middle*

Street	*City*	*State*	*Zip*

Date of Birth	*Place of Birth*	*Sex*	*Social Security Number*

In the event that any part or all of my records are withheld, I request a complete list of all records being withheld and the specific exemption being claimed for the withholding of each.

In the event that search and copying fees are estimated to exceed \$_____, I request an opportunity to review such records, or to have a duly authorized representative review such records, in order to select those to be copied.

If you have any questions regarding this request, please telephone me at _____ weekdays between _____ and _____ or write to me at the above address.

As provided for by Sec. 552(a)(6)(i) of the Freedom of Information Act, I shall expect to receive a reply within ten (10) business days.

Sincerely,

Statute of Limitations

Federal Statute of Limitations

Capital Offenses

There is no limitation on prosecution in cases punishable by death and in the crime of murder, even when the death penalty is not prescribed.

Noncapital Offenses

The limitation on noncapital offenses is five years, although Congress may make specific exceptions.

State Statute of Limitations

Varies by crime and by state.

Copyrights

The copyright law protects works of authorship, published or unpublished, in any tangible medium of expression. Under this law, creators of, among other things, books, theatrical works, computer programs, videotapes, movies, music, lyrics, choreography, pantomimes, and recordings can secure exclusive rights to perform, display, or reproduce their works. These individuals have a property right in their work and may license it for reproduction or other use.

However, anyone may make "fair use" of copyrighted material. The definition of this term depends on who is using the material, how much is used, the percentage of the entire work that the excerpt used constitutes, the purpose of the use, and the effect such use may have on the ability of the copyright holder to derive income from his or her creation. For example, a teacher may be able to photocopy a few pages of a book for use in a classroom, but an advertising firm may be entitled to quote no more than a few lines from the same book in an ad without obtaining permission from the copyright holder. And while it may be lawful to quote 200 words from a novel without asking permission, the same would not be true in the case of a poem if the 200 words constituted the whole poem.

The most recent version of the copyright law took effect in 1978. Works created before 1973 are protected for 28 years from the time they were first published. The copyright may be renewed for an additional 47 years. Works created since the beginning of 1978 may be copyrighted for the life of the author plus 50 years after his or her death. For works made for hire, and for anonymous and pseudonymous works (unless the author's identity is revealed in Copyright Office records), the term is 100 years from creation or 75 years from first publication, whichever period is shorter.

Copyrighted works must display a notice of copyright. This includes the word "Copyright," or the abbreviation "Copr.," the year the work was first published, and the name of the copyright holder. The copyright symbol, a "C" in a circle © (except for recordings, which use a circled "P"), must also be displayed. A copy of a work published in the United States bearing this symbol must be deposited with the Library of Congress.

Displaying the notice of copyright is sufficient to establish exclusive rights to an original work. However, formal registration of a copyright claim is a prerequisite to filing suit for infringement. Subject to certain exceptions, the remedies of statutory damages and attorneys' fees are not available for those infringements occurring before registration.

The United States has copyright relations with more than 70 countries. Under this reciprocal agreement, works of American authors are protected in those countries and the works of their authors are protected in the United States. The basic feature of this protection is "national treatment," under which the alien author is treated by a country in the same manner that it treats its own authors.

Filing for copyright registration presently costs $10. For more information and application forms, write to:

Register of Copyrights
The Library of Congress
Washington, DC. 20557

Patents

Congressional grants of patents and copyrights are based on Article I, Section 8 of the Constitution, which reads "Congress shall have power . . . to promote the progress of science and useful arts, by securing for limited times to authors and inventors the exclusive rights to their respective writings and discoveries."

A patent is the grant of a property right to an inventor, excluding others from making, using, or selling his or her invention. The invention may consist of "any new and useful process, machine, manufacture, or composition of matter, or any new and useful improvements thereof . . . ." It also covers ornamental designs and plants and may soon include new forms of animal life. But no one can patent printed matter or a way of doing business.

In addition to being useful, the invention must be new. If the inventor describes the invention in a printed publication or uses the invention publicly, or places it on sale, he or she must apply for a patent before one year has gone by; otherwise, any right to a patent will be lost.

The Patent and Trademark Office currently receives about 100,000 applications for patents each year, and it has granted more than 4.5 million since 1790. The agency grants new patents only after a diligent search of the records to make sure that the patent is original. Inventors may use its Search Room (patent research library) in Washington or any of the many Patent Depository Libraries throughout the United States to conduct their own searches before filing.

Although inventors can handle their own applications, the agency advises that the process is complex enough to require a patent attorney—a lawyer who also has a degree in engineering or physical science.

Only the inventor may apply for a patent. If the inventor is dead or incapacitated, legal representatives or a guardian may apply. If two or more persons shared the ideas for the invention, they may apply jointly. But if one person had the idea and the other financed its development, only the person with the original idea may apply. "Small entities"—independent inventors, small businesses, and nonprofit organizations—pay a modest filing fee; others pay a higher one.

The application consists of a written description of the invention, with "claims" relating its distinguishing features—ways in which it does things in an entirely novel manner or improves significantly on previous inventions. If applicable, pen-and-ink or color drawings must accompany the description. Models are usually unnecessary. The Patent Office keeps all documents submitted in application for a patent strictly confidential while the application process runs it course.

It is not uncommon for some or all of the claims to be rejected on the first action by the patent examiner; relatively few applications are allowed as filed. The applicant responds to the examiner's objections with clarification and explanation. If the Patent Office finally rejects the application, the inventor can take the case to the Board of Patent Appeals and Interferences. If the board turns down the application, the inventor has recourse either to the Court of Appeals for the Federal Circuit or to a civil suit in U.S. District Court in Washington, D.C.

In about 1 percent of all applications, two or more applications are filed by different inventors claiming substantially the same patentable invention. Only one can receive a patent, and the procedure to determine that one is called an "interference." Each party to such a proceeding must submit evidence of facts proving when the invention was made. As in the case of the rejection of any other patent, the decision of the examiners can be appealed.

If the patent is granted, it is good for 17 years. The fee for granting a patent is presently $280 for small entities and $560 for large ones. Inventors also must pay maintenance fees after $3\frac{1}{2}$, $7\frac{1}{2}$, and $11\frac{1}{2}$ years. Currently, these fees for small entities are $225, $445, and $670; for large ones, they are $450, $890, and $1,340.

Once a patent is granted, all documents relating to it become available for public inspection. The Patent Office can, however, keep such information secret if its commissioner decides that such information is vital to the national security.

As with any other property, patents may be sold or assigned in whole or in part to someone else. The patent holder also may license others to use the process or produce the product under specific conditions. The Patent Office cautions that a part owner of a patent, no matter how small his or her interest, may make, use, and sell the invention for his or her own profit without regard to the other owner and may sell the interest or any part of it, or license others to use or make it. Therefore, inventors should be very careful when agreeing to sell a part interest in their patent.

Patented articles must be marked with the word "Patent" and the number of the patent. Some people use "Patent Pending" or "Patent Applied For" to inform others of the status of a patent claim, but such words have no legal effect. To combat infringement of a patent, a patentee may bring a civil suit.

Patents granted by the Patent and Trademark Office protect inventions in the United States only. However, the United States is a signatory of several treaties that facilitate applications for patent protection in other countries. For further information, write to:

Commissioner of Patents and Trademarks
Washington, DC 20231

Legal Terms

accessory An individual who helps another person commit or try to commit a crime before the fact, but who is not present at the commission of the crime. An accessory *during* the fact witnesses a crime but does not do what he or she could do to prevent it; one who helps another avoid arrest for the commission of a crime is an accessory after the fact.

accomplice An individual who joins with another to commit a crime. The accomplice bears equal responsibility under the law.

actus reus A wrongful act, as opposed to *mens rea*, or thoughts and intentions behind the act. For example, in a murder, homicide is the actus reus, and "malice aforethought" is the mens rea.

adjudication A final judgment in a legal proceeding.

affidavit A written statement sworn or affirmed to be true before a person legally authorized to administer an oath.

age of consent The minimum age for marrying without parental consent; also, the minimum age for consensual sexual relations. Sexual intercourse at an earlier age can result in a charge of assault or statutory rape, even if both people participate willingly.

amicus curiae Latin for "friend of the court." A person or organization not party to a case who submits information useful to the court in that proceeding. Amicus curiae briefs are generally submitted when the suit involves matters of wide public interest.

appeal A request to a superior court to reverse the decision of a lower court or government agency or to grant a new trial.

appellate court A court whose jurisdiction is confined to reviewing decisions of lower courts or agencies.

arraignment A court procedure in which formal charges are brought against a defendant, who is advised of his or her constitutional rights and may have the opportunity to offer a plea.

assault A threatened or attempted physical attack in which the attacker appears to have the ability to bring about bodily harm if not stopped; *aggravated assault* involves an attack perpetrated with recklessness and intent to injure seriously, or an assault with a deadly weapon. *Battery* is an assault in which the assailant makes contact.

attachment A court writ authorizing legal authorities to seize property that may be needed for the payment of a judgment in a judicial proceeding.

bail Security provided to ensure the presence of a defendant in court during the course of a case. Defendants raising this security are said to "make bail"; those fleeing and forfeiting the security have "jumped bail." The actual document securing the defendant's release is the bail bond.

battery *See* assault.

bench warrant A court order authorizing a public official to arrest a person and bring that individual to court.

bequest Personal property bequeathed (given as a gift) in a will. *Devise* is the term for real property handed down through a will.

bill of particulars The specific events to be dealt with in a criminal trial, presented to the defendant so that he or she may effectively prepare a defense.

bind over Action of a lower court shifting a case to a grand jury or superior court when the inferior court believes that a crime has been committed. Also, a court order to jail a defendant during the course of a proceeding.

boilerplate Language uniformly found in certain types of documents—for instance, the "small print" in a contract that people often neglect to read.

breach of contract Failure to do something required in a contract.

breaking and entering The illegal entrance into premises with criminal intent. Simply pushing a door open and walking in may constitute breaking and entering.

brief A document in which a lawyer makes his or her client's case by raising legal points and citing authorities.

burglary Unlawful presence in a building with the aim of committing a felony or taking something of value. *See also* robbery.

capacity The ability to understand the facts and significance of one's behavior. A defendant cannot be convicted of a crime in which he or she did not have the legal capacity to comprehend it.

cease and desist order A legal order preventing a person or organization from continuing a specific activity. A *mandatory injunction*, on the other hand, orders the performance of a specified act.

certiorari A writ in which a superior court commands an inferior court to deliver the records of a proceeding to the superior body so that it may decide whether there is basis for appeal.

character witness *See* witness.

chattel Personal, rather than real, property; a *chattel mortgage*, for example, is a loan to buy an expensive item, such as a car, in which the item, or chattel, is security for the debt.

circumstantial evidence Evidence based not on direct observation or knowledge but rather implied from things already known.

codicil An addition to a will altering it.

common-law marriage A relationship in which two people live together as husband and wife without formally getting married.

community property Property owned by husband and wife jointly.

competency hearing A procedure to determine legal capacity, for example, of a defendant in a criminal case, to understand the charges, and to cooperate with a lawyer in preparing a defense. *Compos mentis* is a finding of competence to stand trial; *noncompos mentis*, a lack of competence to go to trial.

complaint The first statement of facts (in a civil proceeding) or accusation (in a criminal case).

compos mentis *See* competency hearing.

consent decree An agreement between two parties sanctioned by the court, for example, between a company and the government involving alleged violations of antitrust laws. In the consent decree, the company would agree to cease such practices without formally admitting guilt.

conspiracy The plotting by two or more people to break the law.

contempt of court Anything done to hinder the work of the court. *Civil contempt* involves failure to follow a court order benefiting another party in a case, as in the failure to pay court-ordered damages; *criminal contempt* consists of the obstruction of justice.

contract A commitment between two or more parties, enforceable by law.

corpus delicti The object upon which a crime has been committed. The term does not necessarily refer to a body, although a corpse with a knife in its back would be an example in an alleged homicide.

corroborating evidence Additional evidence, or evidence different in kind, that backs up proof already offered in a proceeding.

criminal negligence *See* negligence.

cross-examination The interrogation of a witness to discredit or show in new light testimony already offered by that person in direct examination.

custody In a divorce case, the right to house, care for, and discipline a child.

damages A court-ordered monetary award to someone hurt by another.

decree A court's decision in a case; its judgment.

de facto A practice whose sanction is custom, as opposed to *de jure*, a practice formally backed by law.

defamation The damaging of another person's reputation through writing (libel) or speech (slander).

default judgment A court determination made against a defendant who fails to show up in court.

defendant A person or institution in a legal proceeding being sued or accused.

de jure *See* de facto.

deposition A pretrial interrogation of a witness, usually in a lawyer's office.

directed verdict A verdict in a civil trial declared by the court before the jury gets the case. Judges render this verdict when the facts and the law in a case point to a definite conclusion. There cannot be a directed verdict of guilty in a criminal trial, since that would violate a defendant's right to trial by jury.

discovery A pretrial process that enables one side in a litigation to elicit information from the other side relating to facts in the case.

disorderly conduct A broad spectrum of offenses, such as drunkenness or fighting, that disturb the public peace.

district attorney *See* prosecutor.

docket A list of cases to be tried by a court—its calendar; also, a summary of a court's activities.

double jeopardy The constitutional right not to be tried twice for the same criminal offense.

due process The general doctrine that legislation must promote the legitimate aims of government (substantive due process) and that nobody can be deprived of liberty or property through unfair procedures (procedural due process).

easement A right to use another person's land.

emancipation The parental yielding of authority over, control over, and responsibility for a minor.

eminent domain The right of the state to convert private property to public property.

entrapment A defense in which a defendant seeks to show that he or she would not have committed an unlawful act if not tricked into doing it by law enforcement officials.

estate Everything an individual owns.

eviction The dispossessing of a tenant from land or premises he or she has occupied.

evidence Testimony, documents, and objects used to prove matters of fact at a trial.

exclusionary rule A rule preventing introduction at a criminal trial of evidence obtained in violation of the Constitution's prohibition against unreasonable searches and seizures, even if that evidence would otherwise be admissable. *See also* search and seizure.

executor A person appointed to administer the provisions of a will.

eyewitness One who can testify as to what happened because he or she was there when it happened and saw it; technically, one who offers testimony of something overheard is an "earwitness."

fair hearing A special administrative procedure set up to ensure that a person will not be harmed or denied his or her rights without due process of law before a court can intervene; examples of extraordinary circumstances calling for a fair hearing include loss of welfare benefits and deportation.

fair use The conditions under which one can use material copyrighted by another.

false imprisonment *See* kidnapping.

false pretense Taking another's property through trickery. This crime involves intent to secure title to the property through some seemingly legal transaction. *See also* larceny.

fee Unencumbered ownership of property; *freehold* is land held in fee.

felony A serious crime, as opposed to a *misdemeanor*; the distinction is often made in terms of the applicable punishment, felonies being punishable by a certain minimum prison term—under federal law, a year.

felony murder Homicide committed in the course of another crime, such as a burglary.

fiduciary A person in a position of trust who acts for the benefit of another person; examples are executors, corporate directors, and infant guardians.

finding The basis in fact or law for a judgment. *See also* judgment.

fraud The injury of a person or group of persons through deceit.

freehold *See* fee.

frisk *See* stop and frisk.

garnishment Legal impoundment of funds owed by C to B to pay off B's debt to A; for example, the seizing of a person's pay at work to pay off a debt owed to another party.

grand jury A jury of from 12 to 23 people empowered to look into possible criminal activity in an area, report on it, and indict individuals when it finds evidence that they have committed crimes.

guardian A person entrusted to look out for the interests of a minor or an incompetent person. The specific fiduciary relationship is defined by law and court orders.

habeas corpus The order by a judge to have a prisoner brought to court to determine the legality of the imprisonment.

hearsay evidence Statements made outside of court attesting to some fact, where the person making the statements may not be cross-examined or otherwise scrutinized; for example, if A testifies in court that he or she heard B say something, in most cases, B's statement will not be admissible as evidence.

homicide An act in which one person causes the death of another. *See also* manslaughter; murder.

hung jury A jury that is unable to reach a verdict.

immunity from prosecution Exemption of a witness from prosecution to thwart a refusal to testify based on constitutional rights. The witness cannot be prosecuted on the basis of anything he or she says while testifying under such immunity.

in camera A judicial proceeding from which the public is excluded. Although the term literally means ''in chambers,'' the proceeding can be held anywhere outside of open court.

indictment A document, delivered to a grand jury, in which a public prosecutor accuses one or more persons of committing a crime. If the grand jury thinks the evidence submitted is sufficient to warrant a trial, it will endorse the indictment as a true bill.

infant A person who has not reached the age of majority (usually 18), at which he or she enjoys the full rights of citizenship and is legally responsible for his or her acts.

information A prosecuting attorney's written accusation of criminal activity, similar to an indictment but not presented to a grand jury. Information may be used to initiate proceedings against defendants in state, but not federal, courts.

injunction A court order preventing someone from doing a specific act.

injury The violation of a person's rights to the point where he or she suffers any kind of damage, including financial.

in loco parentis A person or institution acting toward a minor ''in place of parents'' without a formal adoption procedure; for example, the relationship between a school and a student.

inquest A coroner's investigation of the cause of death.

in rem A proceeding involving property without reference to the claims of people on that property.

insanity A mental state in which one lacks legal responsibility.

intestate Without a will.

judgment A court's final decision in a case.

jury A representative group of people who determine issues of fact at a trial. The Constitution guarantees the right to trial by jury for all crimes punishable by imprisonment for more than six months. In civil trials, juries range in number from six to twelve people. State trial juries do not need a unanimous vote to convict (with the exception of six-person juries), but federal juries do.

kidnapping The illegal seizure and removal of a person without his or her consent. *False imprisonment* involves illegally confining a person against his or her will without moving that person.

larceny The act of gaining the use or possession of property through an overtly illegal act, as in stealing a car. *Grand larceny* involves the theft of an object worth more than a specified amount. *See also* robbery.

leading question A lawyer's question to a witness that predetermines the answer, thus putting words in the witness' mouth. Such questions are legitimate during direct examination but not during cross-examination.

libel *See* defamation.

magistrate An official, such as a justice of the peace, who performs low-level judicial functions.

majority, age of *See* infant.

malfeasance Wrongful conduct by a public official. *Misfeasance* is the misperforming of a proper act; *nonfeasance,* the nonperformance of an act that a person has agreed to or is duty-bound to do.

malice aforethought An antisocial state of mind, often at issue in a murder trial, marked by cruelty and recklessness for which there is no justification. *See also* manslaughter.

malpractice Wrongful conduct by a professional, either through negligence or lack of ethics.

mandamus A writ commanding someone, often a public official, to perform some act. Mandamus is frequently issued when time is of the essence.

mandatory injunction *See* cease and desist order.

manslaughter Homicide without malice aforethought. *Voluntary manslaughter* is homicide with mitigating circumstances, for example, a fight in which one person kills another; *involuntary manslaughter,* killing through criminal negligence, as in drunk driving.

material witness *See* witness.

mens rea *See* actus reus.

Miranda rule The obligation of the police, when interrogating someone after an arrest, to read to that person his or her constitutional rights to a lawyer and to remain silent until advised by counsel, and to inform the suspect that anything he or she says may be used as evidence.

misdemeanor *See* felony.

misfeasance *See* malfeasance.

mistrial The ending of a trial before the rendering of a verdict. Possible causes include a hung jury or the incapacity of the judge, jurors, or attorneys.

mitigating circumstances Conditions under which a crime was committed that tend to reduce the punishment in a case, for example, the circumstances leading to a crime of passion.

moral turpitude Baseness, depravity, vileness, or extreme antisocial behavior.

murder Homicide with malice aforethought. Murder in the second degree generally involves less premeditation than the same crime in the first degree.

negligence Carelessness, acting without reasonable caution, putting another person at risk of injury, or not performing an act that one is obliged to do, with the same consequences. In *criminal negligence* there is the added element of recklessness.

next of kin Closest blood relatives or, lacking them, the next closest relations, even if they are related only by marriage.

nolo contendere A defendant's statement that the charges in a case will not be contested.

noncompos mentis *See* competency hearing.

nonfeasance *See* malfeasance.

notary public A person with the authority to administer oaths, witness documents, and accept depositions.

on the merits A court judgment resting on the facts in the case rather than on a legal technicality.

open court Judicial proceedings fully accessible to the public.

pardon An act by which a governor or the president can excuse a person from punishment and restore his or her civil rights; however, a pardon usually does not wipe out a conviction.

parole The release of a person from prison under controlled conditions. The parolee must fulfill certain requirements, such as reporting regularly to a parole officer.

plaintiff The person who initiates a lawsuit.

plea A defendant's answer to a complaint.

plea bargaining A deal between prosecutor and accused, in which the accused pleads guilty in return for lesser punishment than might be received at the end of a trial.

polling the jury A proceeding in which the judge asks each juror, after the verdict has been rendered, to restate his or her decision in the case.

power of attorney A document in which one person authorizes another to act as an agent on his or her behalf.

preliminary hearing A proceeding held after an arrest but before an indictment to see whether there is sufficient evidence to continue holding the prisoner and proceed with a case.

premeditation Calculation, often a factor in determining the degree of guilt in a murder case.

presentment A grand jury's accusation, based not on material presented to it by a prosecutor, but rather on its own investigation.

preventive detention The holding of a prisoner without bail; also accomplished by setting bail so high that the prisoner cannot meet it.

probable cause The rule under which police need to have a reasonable belief that someone has committed a crime before making an arrest, or that the object for which they are searching in connection with a crime is at a specific location before they search for and seize it. *See also* search and seizure.

probate The process in which the legitimacy of a will is established.

probation The procedure under which a court, rather than imprisoning a person convicted of a crime, leaves that individual at liberty but under court supervision.

pro bono Designating the taking of a case by an attorney without a fee. Pro bono cases are often defended on behalf of groups backing important causes.

process A writ requiring that a person appear in court.

prosecutor The person responsible for bringing the accused to justice. Depending on the level on which he or she functions, the prosecutor is usually called a district attorney, county prosecutor, federal prosecutor, or, if appointed by a legislature to conduct an investigation, special prosecutor.

protective custody The imprisonment of an individual for his or her own protection.

public defender A lawyer provided by the state to an accused person who cannot afford or who refuses counsel.

reasonable doubt The criteria against which jurors are told to weigh the evidence in a criminal case. The jurors must find the prosecution's case proven beyond the point at which a reasonable, average, prudent person would be convinced before returning a verdict of guilty.

release on one's own recognizance Release of the accused on a promise to appear in court rather than on bail.

restraining order A temporary order granted to prevent some action until a hearing can be held on that action.

robbery The use of violence or intimidation to seize another person's property. *See also* burglary.

search and seizure A law enforcement procedure involving the search of a person or premises when police have probable cause to suspect they will find and be able to seize criminal evidence. *See also* probable cause; search warrant.

search warrant A court order authorizing law enforcement officials to look for objects or people involved in the commission of a crime and to produce them in court; the order stipulates the places that the officials may search.

self-defense A plea by which a person may justify the use of force to ward off an attack if the attack was unprovoked, retreat was impossible, and the threat of harm seemed imminent.

self-incrimination An act in a legal proceeding by which a person says something that incriminates himself or herself; under the Fifth Amendment, a person cannot be forced to make such a statement.

show cause order A court order, issued at the request of one party, requiring a second party to convince the court, usually within a matter of days, that a specific act should not be carried out or allowed.

slander *see* defamation.

statute of limitations The time limitation for bringing a legal action.

statutory rape A criminal offense involving sex with a girl under the age of consent; the age differs in various states.

stay A court order preventing some act or proceeding until a specific condition is met or the stay is lifted.

stop and frisk A procedure in which police who believe a suspect may be carrying a weapon with intent to use it can stop that person and search the suspect's outer layer of clothing for a weapon.

subpoena A court writ requiring a person to appear to testify at a judicial proceeding at a specific time and place under penalty of law.

summons A notice to appear in court as a defendant in a suit.

testament *See* will.

tort A wrongful act, not involving a contract, that damages someone's interests, for example, injuries caused by the failure of a public official to perform his or her duties.

true bill *See* indictment.

verdict A judge or jury's finding of fact. The judgment, not the verdict, is the final determination in a case; for example, a judge can declare a jury's verdict "false"—that is, invalid because it is not based on the evidence.

voir dire examination A term usually applied to the interrogation of people to see whether they qualify as jurors. The term, which is French for "speak the truth," also describes a trial hearing without the jury present to determine a matter of fact or law, such as the validity of a confession.

waiver The conscious forgoing of a legal right.

warrant A court writ directing a public employee to do something, for example, to make an arrest.

will A document specifying the disposition of a person's property after his or her death. Most states require two or three people to witness a will. Although "will" generally means the same thing as "testament," the latter applies only to the distribution of personal, as opposed to real, property.

witness A person who testifies in court under oath. A *material witness* is one whose testimony is central to a case; a *character witness* testifies to the character of an individual.

writ A written order from a judicial body commanding a law enforcement officer to do something specified.

wrongful death statute A law that enables survivors or the person administering an estate to sue for money damages in a death caused by some person or persons. The law is based on the fact that the death deprives survivors or the estate of the services or income of the deceased.

youthful offender One who, at a judge's discretion, may be sentenced with special consideration given to his or her age. The category applies to defendants older than juveniles (no longer minors) but not yet, in the opinion of the judge, adults.

Supreme Court Decisions

The following Supreme Court decisions are among the most significant in the nineteenth and twentieth centuries.

1803 *Marbury v. Madison.* For the first time, the Supreme Court ruled an act of Congress unconstitutional, establishing the principle of judicial review.

1819 *McCullock v. Maryland.* The Court's ruling upheld the constitutionality of the creation of the Bank of the United States and denied to the states the power to tax such an institution because, as Justice John Marshall put it, "the power to tax is the power to destroy."

1819 *Trustees of Dartmouth College v. Woodward.* The Court ruled that a state could not arbitrarily alter the terms of a contract. Although this case applied to a college, its implications widened in later years when the same principle was used to limit states' ability to interfere with business contracts.

1857 *Dred Scott v. Sanford.* The Missouri Compromise was declared unconstitutional because it deprived a person of his property (a slave) without due process of law. This was only the second time that the Court had asserted the power of judicial review. The decision also stated that slaves are not citizens of any state or of the United States.

1877 *Munn v. Illinois.* States were allowed to regulate businesses when "a public interest" was involved. This principle was weakened by rulings in other cases in the late nineteenth century.

1895 *U.S. v. E. C. Knight Co.* In stating that manufacturing and commerce are not connected, and that the Sherman Anti-Trust Act could not be applied to manufacturers, the Court seriously impaired the government's ability to regulate monopolies.

1896 *Plessy v. Ferguson.* The Supreme Court ruled that state laws enforcing segregation by race are constitutional if accommodations are equal as well as separate. Subsequently overturned by Brown v. Board of Education of Topeka.

1904 *Northern Securities Co. v. U.S.* The High Court backed government action against big businesses that restrained trade, in effect, putting teeth in the Sherman Anti-Trust Act.

1908 *Muller v. Oregon.* The Court ruled that a state could legislate maximum working hours based on evidence compiled by attorney Louis Brandeis.

1911 *Standard Oil Co. of New Jersey Et Al. v. U.S.* The Court dissolved the Standard Oil Trust not because of its size but because of its unreasonable restraint of trade. The principle involved is called "the rule of reason."

1919 *Schenck v. U.S.* The Court upheld the World War I Espionage Act. In a landmark decision dealing with free speech, Justice Oliver W. Holmes said that a person who encourages draft resistance during a war is a "clear and present danger."

1935 *Schechter v. U.S.* Invalidating the National Industrial Recovery Act of the New Deal, the Court declared that Congress could not delegate its powers to the President.

1951 *Dennis Et Al. v. U.S.* The Supreme Court ruled the 1946 Smith Act constitutional; the act made it a crime to advocate the overthrow of the government by force. In its 1957 *Yates v. U.S.* decision, the Court tempered this ruling by permitting such advocacy in the abstract if it is not connected to action to achieve this goal.

1954 *Brown v. Board of Education of Topeka.* In an example of sociological jurisprudence, the Court held unconstitutional laws enforcing segregated schools; it called for desegregation of schools "with all deliberate speed."

1957 *Roth v. U.S.* The ruling based obscenity decisions on whether a publication appeals to "prurient interests." The Court also said that obscene material is that which lacks any "redeeming social importance."

1961 *Mapp v. Ohio.* The High Court extended the federal exclusionary rule to the states; this rule prevented prosecutors from using illegally obtained evidence in a criminal trial.

1962 *Baker v. Carr.* The Court held that state legislatures must be apportioned to provide equal protection under the law (Fourteenth Amendment). A follow-up decision applied the same principle to the size of congressional districts, insisting that they be approximately equal in population.

1966 *Miranda v. Arizona.* The case declared that before questioning suspects, police must inform them of their right to remain silent, that any statements they make can be used against them, and that they have the right to remain silent until they have an attorney, which the state will provide if they cannot afford to pay.

1972 *Furman v. Georgia.* The Court found unconstitutional all death penalty statutes then in force in the states, but held out the possibility that if they were rewritten so as to be less subjective and randomly imposed, they might be constitutional (as the Court has subsequently held in many instances).

1973 *Roe v. Wade.* The Court ruled state antiabortion laws unconstitutional, except as they apply to the last trimester of pregnancy.

1978 *University of California v. Bakke.* The ruling allowed a university to admit students on the basis of race if the school's aim is to combat discrimination. Subsequent decisions of the Court have filled in the details of how government and business may use quotas to make up for past racism.

1986 *Bowers v. Hardwick.* In a case involving enforcement of Georgia's law against sodomy, the Court ruled that states have the power to regulate sexual relations in private between consenting adults.

THE DEATH PENALTY

States That Have Capital Punishment	**States That Do Not Have Capital Punishment**

States That Have Capital Punishment

Alabama	Nevada
Arizona	New Hampshire
Arkansas	New Jersey
California	New Mexico
Colorado	North Carolina
Connecticut	Ohio
Delaware	Oklahoma
Florida	Oregon
Georgia	Pennsylvania
Idaho	Rhode Island
Illinois	South Carolina
Indiana	South Dakota
Kentucky	Tennessee
Louisiana	Texas
Maryland	Utah
Mississippi	Vermont
Missouri	Virginia
Montana	Washington
Nebraska	Wyoming

States That Do Not Have Capital Punishment

- Alaska
- Hawaii
- Iowa
- Kansas
- Maine
- Massachusetts
- Michigan
- Minnesota
- New York
- North Dakota
- Vermont
- Washington, D.C.
- West Virginia
- Wisconsin

Additional Sources of Information

Organizations and Services

American Bar Association (ABA)
Lawyers Referral and Information Service
1155 East 60th Street
Chicago, IL 60637
312-332-1111

A staff member will refer individuals or groups making inquiries to a local legal referral service that can advise them of their options. The ABA answers calls from 9 A.M. to 5 P.M., CST.

NAACP Legal Defense and Educational Fund
99 Hudson Street
16th Floor
New York, NY 10013
212-219-1900

The staff at the NAACP Legal Defense Fund will put individuals or groups who feel that they have been discriminated against in touch with an attorney who can help. The office is open weekdays from 9:30 A.M. to 5:30 P.M., EST.

National Center for Youth Law
1663 Mission Street
5th Floor
San Francisco, CA 94103
415-543-3307

Attorneys are available to help other attorneys who need to have fine points of the law cleared up. The office is open from 9 A.M. to 5 P.M., PST.

National Legal Aid and Defender Association
1625 K Street, NW
8th Floor
Washington, DC 20006
202-452-0620

This association acts as a clearinghouse of organizations, providing legal services for those without the means to pay. The office is open from 9 A.M. to 5:30 P.M., EST.

National Resource Center for Consumers of Legal Services
3254 Jones Court, NW
Washington, DC 20007
202-338-0714

This office is for people who need help in choosing a lawyer or who wish to complain about an incompetent one. A staff member offers help weekdays from 9 A.M. to 5 P.M., EST.

United States Department of Justice
Tenth Street and Constitution Avenue, NW
Washington, DC 20530
202-633-2000

Women's Legal Defense Fund
2000 P Street, NW
Washington, DC 20036
202-887-0364

This national organization is dedicated to securing women's rights through advocacy and litigation. Legal counseling is available on matters related to sexism, such as pregnancy discrimination, economic inequality, and problems with changing one's surname. Referrals are available. The office is open weekdays from 9 A.M. to 5 P.M., EST.

Books

Belli, Melvin, and Wilkinson, Allen P. *Everybody's Guide to the Law*. Harcourt Brace Jovanovich, 1986.

Black, Henry C. *Black's Law Dictionary*, 5th ed. West, 1979.

Gifis, Steven H. *Law Dictionary*. Barron's Educational Series, 1984.

Reader's Digest Family Legal Guide: A Complete Encyclopedia of Law for the Layman. Reader's Digest, 1981.

Ross, Martin J., and Ross, Jeffrey. *Handbook of Everyday Law,* 4th ed. Harper & Row, 1981.

17

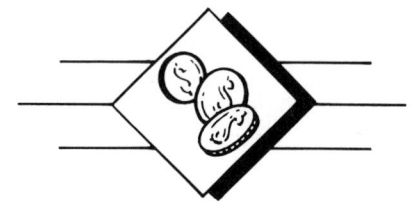

Personal Finances

Personal finances are often a mystifying subject. The objective of making more from your income than just enough to live on is shared by many. But faced with a huge assortment of possible investments, insurance plans, real estate ventures, and retirement plans, how can you, as an individual, decide on the best course of action?

This section provides a starting point. It contains information on making a budget, kinds of insurance available, loans, real estate and mortgages, Social Security and retirement planning, and glossaries of financial and real estate terms. However, consultation with books and periodicals devoted to financial planning or with professional financial planners is recommended before you create a master plan for your own personal finances.

Tables of Common Interest

Simple Interest

Simple interest is computed on the amount of the principal of a loan. That principal is multiplied by the rate of interest; the resulting figure is then multiplied by the time over which the loan will be repaid.

Simple Interest on a $100 Loan

Time	Annual rate			
	5%	10%	15%	20%
1 month	.4167	.8333	1.2500	1.6667
6 months	2.5000	5.0000	7.5000	10.0000
12 months	5.0000	10.0000	15.0000	20.0000
24 months	10.0000	20.0000	30.0000	40.0000
36 months	15.0000	30.0000	45.0000	60.0000

Compound Interest

Compound interest is computed by multiplying the sum of the principal and the accrued interest by the rate of interest. This calculation must be refigured each time the principal is compounded.

**Compound Interest on $100 Principal,
Compounded Annually**

Time	Annual rate			
	5%	7.5%	10%	12.5%
6 months	2.50	3.75	5.00	6.25
1 year	5.00	7.50	10.00	12.50
2 years	10.25	15.56	21.00	26.56
3 years	15.76	24.23	33.10	42.38
4 years	12.55	33.55	46.41	60.18
5 years	27.63	43.57	61.05	80.20

Making a Budget

The first step in personal financial planning is to get a clear picture of where you now stand. An inventory of expected income and expenses projected on both a monthly and an annual basis will allow individuals and families to create a budget. A budget helps to keep expenses within the boundaries of income while also showing what amount, if any, is available for investments.

Following are outlines of income and expense categories that should be included in any personal budget. Note that expenses include fixed obligations and flexible or discretionary outlays, which can be changed as circumstances and objectives change.

Income

Salaries (total in household)	_____	
Bonuses, tips	_____	
Investments (interest, dividends, capital gains, real estate income)	_____	
TOTAL INCOME		_____

Expenses

Housing (rent or mortgage payments)	_____	
Utilities (gas, electric, water, telephone)	_____	
Taxes (federal, state, and local income; local real estate; Social Security)	_____	
Interest payments (car, bank loan, credit card, other loans)	_____	
Principal payments (amounts of borrowed principal repaid)	_____	
Insurance (health, life, property)	_____	
Education (tuition, supplies, room and board)	_____	
Personal expenses	_____	
Contributions	_____	
Food	_____	
Transportation	_____	
TOTAL FIXED OUTLAYS		_____
Clothing	_____	
Entertainment	_____	
Vacations and recreation	_____	
Furniture, appliances, and home improvements	_____	
Health and beauty	_____	
Savings (general or specific for future purchases or objectives)	_____	
Miscellaneous	_____	
TOTAL VARIABLE OUTLAYS		_____
TOTAL EXPENSES		_____
AMOUNT AVAILABLE FOR INVESTING (total income minus total expenses)		_____

Budgets are useful only when the amounts specified in each category are not regularly exceeded. If you have trouble keeping a budget, you may want to make sure that your spending targets reflect your actual expenses and that the members of your household understand the ultimate benefits of budgeting income and expenses.

Insurance

Life is full of risks. One means of minimizing the effects of these risks is to obtain insurance. By insuring your health, your life, your property, and your car and getting coverage for loss of income in the event of a disability, you can assure yourself and your family of financial stability even if catastrophe strikes. Additionally, you can use some types of insurance to further your personal financial goals.

Health Insurance

Health insurance covers the costs of medical care. It is available to individuals and families through private insurance companies, Blue Cross–Blue Shield organizations, and health maintenance organizations (HMOs). While many Americans are covered by one of these plans—paid for or organized through employers, unions, or other groups—individual policies can be bought to provide additional coverage or to replace the group benefits. For the self-employed, individual policies are often the only choice available.

Private Insurance

Health insurance obtained from a private company can cover a wide variety of services, paying for them directly or through reimbursements to the insured individual.

Basic coverage usually includes hospital expenses such as room and board, surgeon's fees, diagnostic charges, anesthesia, operating or delivery room fees, drugs, and medical equipment. Also included in some basic policies are reasonable medical expenses for outpatient care, emergency room treatment, nursing care, and even prescription drugs and eyeglasses. The typical basic plan includes an annual deductible, generally around $200, which must be spent before coverage begins; the plan then pays a set percentage, usually 80 percent, of covered costs for specified illnesses and conditions. Such plans frequently pay according to a predetermined fee schedule; any amounts in excess of the scheduled fee are considered to be beyond the limits of "reasonable" expenses and will not be reimbursed or paid out. Basic plans without any supplemental insurance are considered insufficient because they often exclude common medical conditions; in addition, the limits of coverage are often too low to provide adequate protection.

Major medical coverage pays only for major medical expenses beyond those covered by basic insurance plans. There is a deductible, a co-insurance provision that requires the insured individuals themselves to pay a set percentage of medical costs up to a set amount, and a high ceiling on liability. There are generally few excluded conditions or fee schedules. Important provisions to look for in major medical policies include guaranteed renewability to age 65, a reasonable cutoff for the co-insurance provision, and full coverage for acute-care facilities.

Comprehensive medical coverage combines basic and major medical coverage in one package. It provides a set amount of basic coverage after a deductible and then coverage for charges beyond that amount and for other major medical expenses with a co-insurance provision coming into effect.

Blue Cross–Blue Shield

The basic difference between Blue Cross–Blue Shield plans and those offered by private companies is the way payments for covered expenses are handled. Blue Cross usually pays hospital costs directly to the care provider rather than reimbursing the insured individual. Blue Shield plans come in three varieties: full-service coverage that pays health-care providers directly for all covered conditions; indemnity coverage that reimburses the insured individual; and partial service benefits, which provide full coverage for those with incomes below a certain level and indemnity coverage for those whose incomes are above that level.

Health Maintenance Organizations (HMOs)

HMOs provide medical care to those who pay a quarterly fee. They are oriented toward preventive health care, and those paying the premium are entitled to medical, surgical, and hospital care; some plans also cover the costs of some prescription medicines and provide partial coverage of dental services. Some HMOs provide the services of several doctors at a single location connected with a hospital. Others allow subscribers to receive care from doctors in their individual offices; the doctors are then reimbursed by the HMO on a fee-for-service basis. Important aspects of an HMO that should be scrutinized are the patient-to-physician ratio, the services for which deductibles or additional fees are charged, the availability of maternity benefits, and the relationship of the HMO or participating doctor to a hospital.

Life Insurance

The purpose of life insurance is to provide future financial security for your family. It provides an immediate estate that will enable your family to maintain their household after you die. Life insurance can also be used to build up cash reserves for future expenses, such as retirement or college tuition.

By purchasing a life insurance policy, you are buying into a risk-sharing group. Although no one can predict with any reliability when any individual is going to die, it is possible to predict with great accuracy the number of nonsmoking 32-year-old women who exercise regularly and are not overweight who will die at any given point over the next 40 years. The costs of premiums for people of different ages in different risk categories can then be calculated on the basis of how much the insurance company will pay out in benefits to each group's beneficiaries.

There are six types of life insurance available.

Term insurance provides a death benefit to beneficiaries for a specified period of time. It can be renewable or convertible to whole life and features a low initial premium that rises with each new term. Term life typically has no cash value.

Whole life insurance offers protection for life at a fixed premium. It provides a fixed death benefit and a cash value that can be borrowed against and that increases over the years

Universal life insurance offers permanent protection, flexible premiums and death benefits, and a cash value based on premiums paid to date and current interest rates.

Excess interest whole life insurance provides permanent protection, a fixed premium that the insurer may adjust after the policy is issued, a fixed death benefit, a cash value that grows dependent on market conditions, and the possibility that premiums may be reduced or dispensed with for one or more years if investments are sufficiently profitable.

Variable life insurance offers permanent protection, fixed or flexible premiums, policyholder control over the investment of the policy's cash value, and variable death benefits and cash values depending on performance of the investments account.

Adjustable life insurance gives permanent protection that can be reduced to a shorter term if desired, a death benefit that can be raised or lowered, and premiums that can be increased or decreased.

The American Council of Life Insurance recommends that people evaluate their life insurance needs, buy from a company licensed in their state, select a trustworthy insurance agent, compare costs of similar policies, ask about lower premium rates for nonsmokers, and read their policies and understand them. After selecting coverage that is right for you, inform your beneficiaries about the kind and amount of life insurance you own, keep your policy in a safe place at home, keep the company's name and policy number in a safe deposit box, and check your coverage periodically to be sure it meets your current needs.

Disability Insurance

Disability insurance provides coverage for loss of income when an illness or injury prevents you from working. Temporary disability insurance is provided in California, Hawaii, New Jersey, New York, Rhode Island, and Puerto Rico. Social Security also provides disability coverage at varying levels depending on family size and the recipient's age.

In addition, there are three types of disability insurance available through private companies. *Noncancellable policies* protect your income as long as you continue to make premium payments; coverage may be increased as income increases. *Guaranteed renewable policies* are less expensive than noncancellable ones because insurers can increase premium rates. *Optionally renewable policies* can be renewed or not renewed each year, with variable premium rates. They are the least expensive private option.

Property and Liability Insurance

The purchase of a home is the largest investment most individuals will make in their lifetimes. The home also represents the largest portion of their total financial worth. It therefore makes sense to insure against its possible damage or loss. Even renters stand to lose a substantial amount of money if the uninsured contents of their apartments or houses are destroyed.

There is a wide array of homeowner's insurance policies, including coverage for renters and apartment dwellers. The type of coverage most appropriate for you depends on the sort of risks the property is exposed to and the value of the property. Some policies cover only specific causes of damage or loss, while others provide "all-risk" coverage that will pay for any loss or damage except that specifically excluded by the policy. The available homeowner's policies are as follows.

Homeowner's 1 covers fire, lightning, extended perils (such as windstorms, hail, smoke damage, explosions, riots, and vehicular and aircraft damage), vandalism, malicious mischief, theft, and personal liability.

Homeowner's 2 adds extended coverage for a variety of other potential problems, such as broken water pipes, freezing, and building collapse, to the coverage offered in Homeowner's 1.

Homeowner's 3 is an "all risks" policy for buildings that is more extensive than either 1 or 2; it also can cover personal property to a limited extent.

Homeowner's 4 covers personal property only; the extent of coverage is generally the same as in 2, but the policy is designed for renters.

Homeowner's 5 provides the most comprehensive "all risks" coverage for homes and personal property.

Homeowner's 6 is designed for condominium owners; it covers loss of personal property and loss of use of the dwelling.

Homeowner's 8 is more limited than Homeowner's 1; it is for homes that are below the standard underwriters use to determine eligibility for insurance.

Homeowner's policies cover more than just a home and its contents. Most types include the main dwelling, any other structures on the property, personal belongings that are kept either in the dwelling or elsewhere, costs of additional living expenses, and comprehensive personal liability, including medical payments and damage to others' property.

Comprehensive personal liability insurance protects against the loss of your home or property in the event someone is accidentally injured, whether the injury occurs at the home or elsewhere (such as on a golf course or during a softball game). It will pay up to a set amount for each occurrence of personal liability (injury and property damage) and up to set amounts for medical payments to others and damage to others' property. Excluded from comprehensive personal liability insurance provisions of most homeowners' policies are losses resulting from business or professional activities; use of boats, ships, and planes; intentional injury or damage; acts of war, or nuclear accidents; and liabilities covered by other insurance policies, such as workers' compensation. Additional liability insurance is available for these situations.

Automobile Insurance

When you are evaluating the risks to which you are regularly exposed, driving a car is one that must be considered. The possibility of an accident involving your car is so great that many states have made at least limited automobile insurance mandatory.

Automobile insurance covers three broad risk categories.

Liability insurance covers personal injuries and property damage resulting from ownership, maintenance, or use of a vehicle. Separate limits for payments apply to each person involved in an accident and to property damage incurred.

Medical insurance covers the medical costs incurred in an accident up to a set amount per person per accident.

Collision insurance pays the costs of having a car repaired after it has been damaged in an accident.

Additional automobile insurance is also available to pay for damages resulting from an uninsured driver, for towing and labor, and for transportation needed while a damaged car is being repaired. Many states mandate the inclusion of no-fault personal injury insurance in any automobile insurance policy; this provides benefits for those injured in an accident regardless of who was responsible for the accident.

The types of coverage and the monetary limits of the policy, the driver's age, the frequency of use of the vehicle, the driver's accident history, and the place where the vehicle is kept are considered in determining the cost of liability insurance. Costs for coverage of damage to a vehicle are calculated on the purchase price of the vehicle and its age. When evaluating insurance policies, it is important to compare what is not covered by a given policy—its exclusions—as well as what is covered and how much it will cost. Comparative shopping and a trustworthy insurance agent can help automobile owners to choose wisely when buying insurance for use of the their vehicles.

Credit and Loans

One key to enhancing personal finances is through credit. With loans, credit cards, revolving charge plans at department stores, and other methods of delaying payment, people obtain goods and services for which they otherwise would have to wait. Of course, use of credit results in debts and interest charges that must be paid to maintain a good credit rating and ensure the availability of more credit.

Getting credit is a fairly straighforward procedure. You can apply to a bank for a loan or a bank credit card, such as Visa or MasterCard, or to a department store or gasoline company for a revolving charge account, by filling out an application form. These companies will ask about your income, employment history, length and type of residence, credit history, and major assets (car, home, etc.) in order to determine your creditworthiness.

A positive credit history—meaning that you have received credit and made payments on time—is one of the strongest recommendations for further credit. If you have never had credit before, a good first step is to obtain a department store or gasoline company credit card, which is often easier to get, or to take out a small loan at a bank where you keep a savings and/or a checking account. Having a reasonably large amount of money in the bank also can help persuade issuers to provide you with credit.

When looking to obtain credit, especially once creditworthiness has been established, comparison shopping is very important. Different states have different limits on the amount of interest that can be charged on consumer loans and bank cards. Interest rates on loans can range from less than 2 percent per month to 36 percent per year or more; credit card rates range from under 15 percent to 30 percent or more per year. You do not need to be a resident of a state to get credit from lending institutions headquartered there, and you can apply by mail.

The amount of indebtedness you should assume is not easy to calculate. The credit-granting institution bases its decision on your gross income and expenses. Your own decision about how much credit you should use is harder to come by. Calculating the amount of money you have available from your income after deducting monthly expenses will give you some idea of what you can afford, although other factors—such as ever-decreasing balances in your checking and savings accounts, use of overdrafts or credit to cover regular expenses, and difficulty making payments on credit lines you already have—may suggest that additional credit is not a good idea.

Problems that can arise from credit, such as billing errors or unfair denial of credit, can be remedied under federal regulations. The Fair Credit Billing Act requires that, if you notify a creditor in writing about an error on a bill, your complaint must be acknowledged within 30 days and resolved within 90 days. The Equal Credit Opportunity Act requires creditors to give a reason if you are denied credit and prohibits discrimination based on race, sex, age, marital status, color, religion, national origin, or receipt of public assistance.

If you are denied credit on the basis of a negative report from a credit bureau, you can obtain the information that agency supplied to the creditor free of charge if you request it within 30 days of being turned down or for a small fee at any time. You can challenge the accuracy of any item in your credit file; this will force the credit bureau to investigate the item and remove it if it cannot be substantiated. Any item in your file also can be amended at your request to include a 100-word explanation that will be added to your file.

Real Estate and Mortgages

American society is geared toward home ownership. The desire to own a home, and the labyrinthine process of purchasing one, can have tremendous impact on an individual's or a family's finances. A home represents the single largest financial commitment most people will make in their lifetimes. It therefore requires a careful, reasoned decision based on a thorough examination of the steps involved in the purchase. What follows are some of the basics involved in buying a home and obtaining a mortgage. Potential home buyers are cautioned to seek out as much additional information as is practical from specialized books, real estate professionals, and friends who have made similar purchases.

The Decision to Buy a Home

Owning their own home is something most people believe to be desirable regardless of their financial circumstances. They think that owning a home is a perfect investment, and that renting is akin to throwing money away. This is not always the case. Home ownership often includes a great many hidden expenses, while renters take care of the basic need for shelter at a set monthly cost without having to deal with such headaches as taxes, sewage disposal, or sidewalk repairs.

A number of factors need to be considered when deciding whether you should buy your own home. First among these should be the way you lead your life. Home ownership can provide greater space, a chance to set down roots, the option to make any alterations you choose, the possibility of providing yard space and better schools for your children, and the pride of having a home of your own. Renters have greater flexibility about when they can move, pay less of their income for shelter, avoid the ancillary costs and added work of maintaining a residence, and can use any excess funds for investments that offer a guaranteed rate of return.

Also of great importance in the decision to buy a home is your current financial situation. Home ownership requires enough money to make a down payment (generally at least 10 percent of the purchase price, and often 20 or 25 percent), to obtain a mortgage, and to make payments on that mortgage for many years to come. Renters need to have enough money to pay the rent each month.

Affordability

It is best to shop for a mortgage before you shop for a home so as to know how much money is available to you. A long-standing rule of thumb is that the annual cost of a home should not exceed 25 percent of your gross income. If you can manage monthly payments that do not exceed 25 percent of your income, you will probably have little trouble obtaining a mortgage or making the payments.

But even if mortgage payments come to 25 percent of your income, the cost of a home will be substantially more. Funds to cover utilities, water and sewage costs, taxes, repairs, improvements, and even garbarge cans and yard equipment will be needed. Additional costs may include more costly commutation. It is wise to set aside an additional 10 percent of the basic annual costs for unseen expenses.

A careful evaluation of present and projected income and expenses—including money spent on nonessential interests, hobbies, and pastimes—will give you some idea of what you can afford to pay for a home on a monthly basis. From there, you can look at mortgage payment schedules to find out how much of a mortgage you can afford.

One thing to keep in mind when deciding what you can afford is that many experts recommend against buying the most expensive house in a given neighborhood. A lower-priced home in a higher-priced neighborhood offers greater security and a better likelihood of seeing the property value increase.

An Old Home or a New One?

If there is a choice between buying a new home or one that has been occupied before, you must weigh the pluses and minuses of each. The value of similar new and used homes in similar neighborhoods will go up about equally, but other aspects of each may make you choose one over the other.

New homes have more modern amenities, are often less likely to suffer system breakdowns (that is, plumbing, heating, and water supply), should not require much upkeep or many repairs, and often can be mortgaged for a greater percentage of the price over a longer term. Older homes frequently are less expensive, have larger rooms, are better built, have finished landscaping, and are closer to the center of town. The individual merits of the actual houses you look at will guide you in making a final choice.

The Down Payment

Among the many decisions to be made in the home-buying process is whether to make a large or small down payment.

While a higher down payment can reduce your monthly payments or the term of the mortgage, there are a number of advantages in making as small a down payment as possible: you retain access to your money; the money you pay in later years will be less valuable, because of inflation, than any spent now; and the interest included in your mortgage payments is tax deductible, so the more you borrow, the more you can deduct.

The Mortgage

At one time the only mortgages widely available in the United States were fixed-rate mortgages that required fixed monthly payments for a specific period, usually 25 or 30 years. Recently, however, a wide variety of different mortgage options have become available.

The *graduated payment mortgage* (GPM) has a fixed rate of interest but varying payments. Payments begin lower and are increased at a fixed rate each year, rising to a level higher than on a fixed-rate mortgage. Initial payments may be lower than the cost of interest, in which case the unpaid interest is added to the principal. This type is good for first-time buyers who expect their incomes to rise during the course of the mortgage.

The *pledged-account mortgage* (PAM) is a variation of the GPM that takes the difference between payments and the accrued interest from a savings account pledged to that purpose by the borrower.

The *adjustable rate mortgage* (ARM) has a flexible interest rate that varies according to a selected interest-rate index. It may go up when the index goes up and must go down when the index goes down; it may contain limitations on the maximum and minimum rates. The changing rate can affect the monthly payment, the term, or the outstanding principal. Some plans change the rate more frequently than they change the payments. This can result in underpayments on interest that are then added to the outstanding balance.

The *graduated-payment adjustable-rate mortgage* (GPARM) combines features of GPMs and ARMs. Some plans defer interest in the early years; others set rising payments during the first several years; and still others fix low payments early on. Countless variations are possible.

The *wraparound mortgage* allows the buyer to assume the balance of a lower-rate mortgage from the seller, making payments to amortize both that original mortgage and the additional amount being borrowed at prevailing rates. This mortgage reduces the overall interest rate on the total amount.

The *shared-appreciation mortgage* (SAM) is available from some lenders. In return for a reduced interest rate, the lender receives a set portion of the amount by which the home has appreciated when it is sold or the loan is paid. Because the final value of the home cannot be determined in advance, additional interest can be due if the value has not appreciated sufficiently.

A *reverse mortgage* really is not a mortgage at all, but a way of getting monthly payments in return for some of the equity in a house. It is advantageous for those over 75 with significant equity and insufficient cash.

In addition to the mortgage payments themselves, many lenders also charge "points." These additional amounts—each point is equal to 1 percent of the loan—are paid by the buyer at the time the mortgage goes into effect, at the closing.

Going to Contract

Anything and everything can and possibly will go wrong when it comes time to draw up a contract and close the deal to buy a home. No list of potential pitfalls could be considered all-inclusive. The best advice is to obtain a lawyer who is familiar with the kind of property purchase you are making and to read every word in every document presented to you with your lawyer.

Investments and Retirement

If you are like most people, your main source of income for the greater part of your life is the salary or fees you earn from working. This income may or may not be adequate to support the life-style you wish to maintain. If you would like to increase your income, you might consider making investments. Even if your earned income is enough for the present, you may want to invest now in order to plan for a secure retirement.

Setting Goals

There is little point in considering investments without developing the goals you hope to reach by making them. Investing is a means to an end. That end generally can be described as financial security—having enough income to live on after you retire. But a more specific set of goals is essential.

Short-term and long-term strategies must be developed. The amounts you have available to invest now, and those you can make available in the future, must be calculated. The rate of return you require from your investments must be figured, taking into account the amount of income you will need them to produce in the future after factoring in inflation. Your need for access to the principal or profit on short notice must be evaluated, too, along with whether you are willing to take greater risks for a potentially higher return or will accept lower profits in return for greater security.

Other aspects that should be considered in creating short- and long-term goals are diversification of your investments to reduce risks; the tax status of the income your investments produce; and the availability of loans using your investments as collateral.

Setting goals is a continual process. Your current goals should be based on how you envision your future.

Choosing Your Investments

Once you have decided on your investment goals, you must answer the most difficult question of all: What should you invest in? The possibilities are almost limitless.

It is unwise to select an investment without close scrutiny. Selecting a stock because someone—even a stockbroker—tells you "it's a good bet" is not a good way to handle your money. You can select the types of investments you believe will be most effective in helping you reach your short- and long-term goals. But professional assistance should then be sought from an appropriate source: bankers for information about money market accounts, individual retirement accounts, or certificates of deposit; or stockbrokers for stock and bonds.

Passbook savings are the first investments most people are exposed to. They are insured by the federal government, require no minimum deposit, offer set interest rates, and can be added to or withdrawn from at any time. *Time deposits* offer higher interest rates, require a minimum deposit of $2,500 in most cases, are available for varying lengths of time, and often provide free checking privileges. They penalize early withdrawals. *Money market accounts* generally require a minimum deposit of $1,000, pay interest rates comparable to those available on larger certificates of deposit, have no requirements for length of time of deposit, and allow withdrawals and transfers at any time.

Certificates of deposit (CDs) are available in varying amounts (usually from $500) for anywhere from 90 days to two years, pay high interest rates, and penalize early withdrawals.

Long-term certificates require deposits for two and a half years or more, compound interest for greater yields, and offer high interest rates.

Individual Retirement Accounts (IRAs) have varying minimum deposit requirements, provide interest that will not be taxed until it is withdrawn, have maximum individual deposit limits of $2,000 per year, and sometimes allow depositors to deduct the amounts of their deposits from their taxable income.

Mutual fund accounts come in a variety of types. Your choice will depend on whether your investment needs require growth of capital, substantial current flow of income, or a balance of reasonable capital growth, reasonable current income, and security of the principal. Minimum deposits vary, and deposits can be withdrawn at any time.

Bond funds allow investors to buy into a diversified portfolio of bonds. They can easily be resold but lose value if interest rates rise. Some funds can be exempt from federal income tax. *U.S. savings bonds* require a minimum $25 deposit, mature in five years, and provide virtually guaranteed security. *Corporate bonds* require a minimum deposit of $1,000, mature in 10 to 30 years, and can easily be cashed in. They provide the current market rate of return but can lose value if interest rates rise. *Zero-coupon bonds* provide a fixed yield when the bond matures, are sold at a large discount off face value, mature in six months to ten years or longer, and usually require a minimum deposit of $1,000.

Stock funds allow investors to diversify their stock holdings, require minimum investments, and change in value according to stock market price changes. *Common stocks* can provide dividend income and long-term growth of capital but require careful management to avoid loss or diminution of capital.

Treasury bills are six-month instruments available in $10,000 denominations. They offer market interest rates with high security, can be easily sold, and are not subject to state and local income taxes.

More detailed information about the common types of investments outlined here—as well as more "exotic" investments ranging from oil drilling ventures and real estate partnerships to precious metals, commodities, or a relative's new business—can be obtained from books, government publications, and the agencies that regulate such activities.

Planning for Retirement

Although few working people require income from their investments to meet routine expenses, most people will require income from outside sources in order to retire in security and comfort. There are three potential providers of retirement income: pension plans funded by an employer; government retirement funds; and an individual's own retirement fund. The best way to assure your own financial security after retirement is to arrange for retirement income from at least two or even all three of these sources.

Employer-funded retirement plans can be pension plans, profit-sharing plans, or a combination of the two. Most pension plans define the benefits due and eligibility qualifications required of each employee in advance. They are designed to provide employees with a guaranteed income after they reach a certain age, generally 65, and retire. Some plans allow for early retirement at reduced benefits. In addition to providing income after retirement, many plans also provide vested benefits for employees who stop working for the company before they reach the minimum retirement age, death benefits, medical benefits, and a pension for surviving spouses. *Profit-sharing plans* differ from pension plans in that an employer's contributions to the fund are dependent on company profits. Profit-sharing plans also may have provisions for vesting at an earlier age and withdrawal and loan privileges.

Social Security is the basic retirement plan provided by the government. More than 90 percent of the workers in the United States are earning benefits under Social Security through contributions they and their employers make in the form of Social Security taxes. Social Security provides monthly payments to qualified workers who retire at age 62 or older, health insurance for the elderly under Medicare, and monthly payments to disabled workers and to spouses and children of workers who retire, become disabled, or die. The dollar amount of benefits is dependent on the rate set by the government as well as on other sources of income the retiree has available. Qualification for Social Security benefits is earned on the basis of ''quarters of coverage.'' Workers earn one credit toward coverage for a set amount of income they earn, up to four credits each calendar year. Coverage for retirement benefits starts when a worker has earned 9.25 credits if he or she turns 62 in 1988; 9.5 credits in 1989; 9.75 credits in 1990; or 10 credits from 1991 on.

Individual retirement plans can be created according to needs and financial resources using many of the investments outlined above. The most popular individual plan, the Individual Retirement Account (IRA), allows some individuals to deduct contributions of up to $2,000 a year from their income taxes. Under rules that took effect in 1987, married couples with adjusted gross incomes under $40,000, and single people with gross incomes under $25,000, may deduct up to $2,000 in contributions to their IRAs, with deductions phased out over the next $10,000 of adjusted gross income.

Investment Terms

accrued interest Interest earned by a bond since the last payment was made.

AMEX The American Stock Exchange.

appreciation The increase in value of an investment.

asset Something owned by one or owed to one.

bear market A declining stock market.

bid and asked price The highest price offered for a security at a given time (*bid*) and the lowest price accepted for that security at that time (*asked*).

Big Board The New York Stock Exchange.

blue chip The stock of a top-rated company known for the quality of its products and the security and return on investment of its stock; also the company itself.

bond A corporation's note acknowledging indebtedness for a certain amount and promising to pay interest at a given rate on that amount as well as to pay back the principal on a certain date. *See also* Treasury bond.

book value The theoretical worth of a share of stock as shown on a company's balance sheet; this has little relationship to the stock's market value.

bull market A rising stock market.

capital gain or capital loss The gain or loss resulting from the sale of an asset.

capitalization All securities issued by a company, including bonds, common and preferred stock, and debentures.

capital stock All shares of stock in a company, both common and preferred.

collateral Property or securities used by a borrower to secure a loan.

convertible securities Securities that can be exchanged by the holder for common stock or another security.

coupon bond A bond with coupons attached that are clipped by the holder and presented for payment of interest due.

current assets The total amount of cash, securities, inventory, and receivables expected during the normal business cycle of a company.

current liabilities The total amount of debt and other payments that will be due during the normal business cycle of a company, usually one year.

debenture An unsecured promissory note backed by a company's general credit.

discount The amount of money below the issuing price of a stock or bond by which it sells.

discretionary account A securities account that leaves some or all decisions about purchases and sales to the discretion of a broker.

dividend A payment by a company equally divided among its stockholders. *See also* stock dividend.

Dow Jones average The average price of selected stocks, used as an indicator of the stock market's performance.

equity The interest stockholders have in a company, or the amount of property a propertyholder has actually paid for as opposed to the portion held by a mortgage.

ex-dividend A stock that does not pay a recently declared dividend to its new purchaser.

Federal Deposit Insurance Corporation (FDIC) The federal agency that insures amounts up to $100,000 deposited in qualified banks.

fiduciary Someone who acts on behalf of another in financial matters.

gilt-edged stock A high-grade preferred stock or bond issued by a company with a strong performance record.

income fund A mutual fund designed to provide current income.

Individual Retirement Account (IRA) A tax-deductible retirement plan.

interest The money paid by a borrower to a lender for the use of the borrowed money.

investment The use of money to make more money.

Keogh plan A tax-sheltered retirement plan for self-employed people with no pension plans.

liabilities All claims against and amounts owed by a company.

listed stock Stock traded on a securities exchange.

margin The portion of a stock's price paid by the buyer when the broker arranges for the remainder to be purchased on credit.

market order An order to buy or sell at the current market price of a security.

maturity The date on which a bond or loan is to be paid off.

money market fund A mutual fund that invests in short-term financial securities.

municipal bond A bond issued by a local government.

mutual fund An investment company that continually offers new stock and redeems outstanding shares on demand.

odd lot An amount of stock bought or sold in units other than 10 shares or 100 shares.

offer The price at which someone is willing to sell.

over-the-counter market The arena in which stocks not listed on exchanges are bought and sold.

par The issuing value of a share of common stock.

preferred stock Stock that must receive its share of earnings before payment is made on common stock.

premium The amount over par value by which a preferred stock is sold.

puts and calls Options that give the right to sell or buy a specified number of shares of stock at a specified price within a specified time.

red herring A preliminary prospectus issued to gauge interest in a new stock issue.

Securities and Exchange Commission (SEC) The federal agency that oversees securities trading.

stock Ownership shares in a company.

stock dividend Shares distributed to current shareholders in a company in proportion to those they hold.

stock split The division of currently outstanding shares into a larger number of shares.

tax shelter A way in which taxes on income may be legally decreased, eliminated, or deferred.

tender offer An offer by one company to purchase shares of stock in another company directly from its stockholders.

Treasury bill A short-term U.S. government security sold at discount in competitive bidding.

Treasury bond A long-term U.S. government bond issued in $1,000 denominations.

yield The amount of dividend or interest expressed as a percentage of the selling price.

zero-coupon bonds Bonds that are sold at a discount from their face value but that do not pay interest.

Real Estate Terms

amortization A gradual paying off of a mortgage by periodic installments.

appraisal An estimation of a property's value, often made by lenders before deciding the amount of a mortgage.

assessed valuation A value placed on a property as a basis for taxation.

assumable mortgage A mortgage taken over from the seller of a property by the buyer.

balloon payment The final payment on a loan or mortgage, usually larger than the previous payments.

binder An agreement by the buyer to cover the down payment on the purchase of real estate before a final contract is drawn up.

broker Usually a licensed agent who acts on behalf of the seller of a property, making arrangements for the sale.

closing The meeting of a buyer, a seller, a banker, and attorneys for all parties at which a real estate sale is completed with the writing of checks; it usually takes place 30 to 60 days after signing of the contract.

commission The amount paid to a real estate broker for services rendered.

condominium A form of individual ownership in a multiple-unit dwelling, townhouse, or detached house in which the owner buys title to a single unit and an interest in common areas.

contract A binding agreement between parties to transact real estate under agreed-upon terms.

cooperative apartment A form of individual ownership in a multiple-unit dwelling in which buyers purchase shares in a cooperative corporation that owns the building; the shares entitle the holder to a proprietary lease on an apartment in the building.

deed A written document that conveys ownership of real property.

equity The value of an owner's real property after deducting mortgages and liens.

escrow A written agreement to place money or property with someone else until it is due to be delivered to a designated party; often used for payment of taxes along with mortgage payments.

Fannie Mae The Federal National Mortgage Association, the largest secondary mortgage agency.

Federal Housing Administration (FHA) A division of the federal government's Department of Housing and Urban Development that insures mortgages.

Freddie Mac The Federal Home Loan Mortgage Corporation, which buys mortgages from lenders, allowing the lenders to make new mortgages.

Ginnie Mae The Government National Mortgage Association, which buys FHA-insured loans from lenders.

indexing A means of adjusting the interest rate on a loan or mortgage according to an agreed-upon index or indicator.

interest Money paid to a lender for use of borrowed principal.

lien An interest in a property granted as collateral for a loan or mortgage.

mortgage A written instrument that creates a lien on a given property in return for a loan.

point An amount equal to 1 percent of a loan, charged to the borrower by the lender.

prepayment penalty An additional fee charged for paying off a mortgage before it is due.

principal The amount of money borrowed from a lender for a mortgage, upon which interest is computed.

title A written document that gives evidence of property ownership.

Calculating Your Net Worth

Use the following chart to calculate your current net worth. Be sure to include amounts held individually and jointly to evaluate your family's net worth.

Assets

Cash on hand and liquid assets	
Checking and savings accounts	_____
Cash value of life insurance	_____
U.S. savings bonds	_____
Equity in pension funds	_____
Money market funds	_____
Brokerage funds	_____
Trusts	_____
Debts owed you	_____
Other	_____
TOTAL	_____

Personal holdings
    Car(s) (current value)   _____
    Home(s)   _____
    Boat(s)   _____
    Major appliances   _____
    Furs and jewelry   _____
    Antiques and collectibles   _____
    Art   _____
    Other   _____
    TOTAL   _____
Investments
    Common stocks   _____
    Preferred stocks   _____
    Corporate and municipal bonds   _____
    Mutual funds   _____
    Certificates of deposit   _____
    Business investments   _____
    Real estate investments   _____
    IRAs   _____
    Other   _____
    TOTAL   _____
TOTAL ASSETS   _____

Liabilities
    Bills due   _____
    Revolving charge and bank-card debts   _____
    Taxes due   _____
    Outstanding mortgage   _____
    Outstanding loans (bank, insurance, etc.)   _____
    Stock margin accounts payable   _____
    Other debts   _____
TOTAL LIABILITIES   _____

NET WORTH (Assets minus liabilities)   _____

Tipping

The following list suggests what are generally considered to be adequate amounts to tip various people for services rendered. It should be kept in mind that tips are a way of expressing satisfaction. Larger tips should be left for those who provide extraordinarily good service; smaller tips or no tip at all should be left when service is poor.

Location	Person	Amount
Restaurant	waiter or waitress	15% of bill
	headwaiter/maitre d'	none, unless special services are provided; then, about $5
	wine steward	15% of wine bill
	bartender	10–15% of bar bill
	busboy	none
	servers at counter	15% of bill
	coat check attendant	$1 for one or two coats
	restroom attendant	50 cents
	car park attendant	50 cents

Location	Person	Amount
Hotel	chambermaid	no tip for one-night stays; $1 a night or $5–$10 a week for longer stays
	room-service waiter	15% of bill
	bellhop	$1 per bag for bringing you to your room with luggage; 50 cents for opening and showing the room
	lobby attendant	none for opening door or calling taxi from stand; 50 cents or more for help with luggage or finding a taxi on the street
	desk clerk	none unless special service is given during long stay; then, $5
Train	dining car waiter	15% of bill
	stewards/bar-car waiters	15% of bar bill
	redcaps	posted rate plus 50 cents
Airport	skycaps	$1 or more for full baggage cart
	in-flight personnel	none
Cruise ship	cabin steward	2.5% to 4% of total fare
	dining-room steward	2.5% to 4% of total fare
	cabin boy, bath steward, bar steward, wine steward	5% to 7½% of total fare divided proportionately among them, paid at the end of each week
Taxi	driver	15% of fare, no less than 25 cents
Barbershop	haircutter	15% of the cost, generally a minimum of $1
Beauty shop	one operator	15% of bill
	several operators	10% of bill to person who sets hair; 10% divided among others
	manicurist	$1 or more, depending on cost
Sports arena	usher	50 cents to $1 per party if shown to your seat

Additional Sources of Information

Organizations and Services

Consult the following organizations for referrals to reputable financial planners.

Institute of Certified Financial Planners
Two Denver Highlands
Suite 320
10065 East Harvard Avenue
Denver, CO 80231
303-751-7600

International Association for Financial Planning
Two Concourse Parkway
Suite 800
Atlanta, GA 30328
404-395-1605

The following publications offer substantial coverage of events and trends that affect personal finances. Addresses are for subscriptions.

Barron's National Business Weekly
200 Burnett Road
Chicopee, MA 01020

Business Week
1221 Avenue of the Americas
New York, NY 10020

Changing Times (monthly)
Editors Park, MD 20782

Money (monthly)
P.O. Box 54429
Boulder, CO 80322

Books

Donoghue, William E. *William E. Donoghue's Lifetime Financial Planner: Straight Talk About Your Money Decisions*. Harper & Row, 1988.

Dowd, Merle E. *A Consumer's Guide to Financial Planning: How to Get the Best Plan for Your Money*. Franklin Watts, 1987.

Klein, Robert J. *The Money Book of Money: A Lifetime Guide to Family Finances*. Little, Brown, 1987.

Lerner, Joel J. *Financial Planning for the Utterly Confused*. McGraw-Hill, 1988.

Loeb, Marshall. *Marshall Loeb's Money Guide, 1989*. Little, Brown, 1988.

Passell, Peter. *Personalized Money Strategies: Fifteen No-Nonsense Investment Plans to Achieve Your Goals*. Warner Books, 1986.

Porter, Sylvia. *Love and Money*. Avon, 1986.

Porter, Sylvia. *Sylvia Porter's Your Own Money*. Avon, 1983.

Shane, Dorlene V. *Be Your Own Financial Planner: The 21 Day Guide to Financial Success*. Wiley, 1986.

Sheen, Brian J. *Nest Egg Investing: The Lifelong Program for Financial Independence*. Putnam, 1987.

Stribling, Catherine. *Growing Up Financially: A Money Management Guide*. Ballantine, 1986.

Thomsett, Michael C. *Homeowners Money Management Guide*. Rodale Press, 1987.

Tobias, Andrew P. *The Only Other Investment Guide You'll Ever Need*. Simon & Schuster, 1987.

18

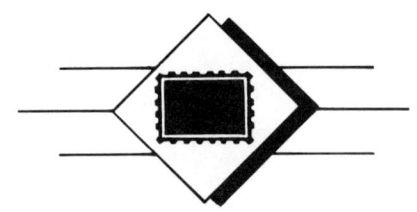

Useful Addresses

Aging

Private Organizations

American Association of Retired Persons
National Gerontology Resource Center
1909 K Street, NW
Washington, DC 20049
202-728-4880

American Association of Retired Persons
Widowed Persons Service
1909 K Street, NW
Washington, DC 20049
202-728-4370

American Society on Aging
833 Market Street
Suite 516
San Francisco, CA 94103
415-543-2617

Andrus Gerontology Center
University of Southern California
Los Angeles, CA 90089
213-743-6060

Asociacion Nacional por Personas Mayores
Library Resource Center
2727 West 6th Street
Suite 270
Los Angeles, CA 90057
203-487-1922

National Senior Citizens Law Center
1636 West 8th Street
Suite 201
Los Angeles, CA 90017
213-388-1381

Rehabilitation Research and Training Center on Aging
University of Southern California
c/o Rancho Los Amigos Hospital
7600 Consuelo Street
Downey, CA 90242
213-722-7402

Self-Help for the Elderly
640 Pine Street
San Francisco, CA 94108
415-982-9171

State Commissions and Offices

State commissions and offices on aging are responsible for coordinating services for older Americans. They can provide information on programs, services, and opportunities for the aging.

Alabama

Commission on Aging
502 Washington Avenue
Montgomery, AL 36130
205-261-5743

Alaska

Older Alaskans Commission
P.O. Box C
Juneau, AK 99811
907-465-3250

Arizona

Aging and Adult Administration
1400 West Washington Avenue
P.O. Box 6123—950A
Phoenix, AZ 85007
602-255-4446

Arkansas

Office on Aging and Adult Services
Department of Human Services
1428 Donaghey Building
7th and Main Streets
Little Rock, AR 72201
501-371-2441

California

Department of Aging
Health and Welfare Agency
1020 19th Street
Sacramento, CA 95814
916-322-5290

Colorado

Aging and Adult Services Division
Department of Social Services
1575 Sherman Street
Room 803
Denver, CO 80203
303-866-2586

Connecticut

Department on Aging
175 Main Street
Hartford, CT 06106
203-566-7728

Delaware

Division of Aging
Department of Health and Social Services
Delaware State Hospital
CT Building
1901 North DuPont Highway
New Castle, DE 19720
302-421-6791

District of Columbia

D.C. Office on Aging
Special Assignment of the Mayor's Office
1424 K Street, NW
2nd Floor
Washington, DC 20005
202-724-5623

Florida

Aging and Adult Services
Department of Health and Rehabilitative Services
1321 Winewood Boulevard
Building 2, Room 328
Tallahassee, FL 32301
904 488-2650

Georgia

Office of Aging
Department of Human Resources
878 Peachtree Street, NE
Atlanta, GA 30309
404-894-5333

Hawaii

Executive Office on Aging
Office of the Governor
State of Hawaii
1149 Bethel Street
Room 307
Honolulu, HI 96813
808-548-2593

Idaho

Idaho Office on Aging
Statehouse
Room 114
Boise, ID 83720
208-334-3833

Illinois

Department on Aging
421 East Capitol Avenue
Springfield, IL 62701
217-785-2870

Indiana

Department on Aging and Community Services
115 North Pennsylvania Street
1350 Consolidated Building
Indianapolis, IN 46204
317-232-7006

Iowa

Commission on Aging
914 Grand Avenue
Jewett Building
Suite 236
Des Moines, IA 50319
515-281-5187

Kansas

Department on Aging
610 West 10th Street
Topeka, KS 66612
913-296-4986

Kentucky

Division for Aging Services
Department for Social Services
275 East Main Street
6th Floor, West
Frankfort, KY 40621
502-564-6930

Louisiana

Governor's Office of Elderly Affairs
P.O. Box 80374
Baton Rouge, LA 70898
504-925-1700

Maine

Bureau of Maine's Elderly
Department of Human Services
State House, Station 11
Augusta, ME 04333
207-289-2561

Maryland

Office on Aging
301 West Preston Street
10th Floor
Baltimore, MD 21201
301-383-2100

Massachusetts

Department of Elder Affairs
38 Chauncey Street
2nd floor
Boston, MA 02111
617-727-7750, 51, 52

Michigan

Office of Services to the Aging
101 North Pine Street
P.O. Box 30026
Lansing, MI 48909
517-373-8230

Minnesota

Minnesota Board on Aging
204 Metro Square Building
121 East 7th Street
St. Paul, MN 55101
612-296-2544

Mississippi

Council on Aging
301 West Pearl Street
Jackson, MS 39201
601-949-2013

Missouri

Office of Aging
Department of Social Services
P.O. Box 1337
Broadway State Office Building
6th Floor
Jefferson City, MO 65102
314-751-2075

Montana

Aging Branch
Contracts Bureau
Department of Social and Rehabilitation Services,
Community Services Division
P.O. Box 4210
Room 204
Helena, MT 59604
406-444-5650

Nebraska

Nebraska Department of Aging
State House Station 95044
Lincoln, NE 68509
402-471-2307

Nevada

Division for Aging Services
Department of Human Resources
505 East King Street
Room 101
Carson City, NV 89710
702-885-4210

New Hampshire

Council on Aging
14 Depot Street
Concord, NH 03301
603-271-2751

New Jersey

Division on Aging
Department of Community Affairs
363 West State Street, CN 807
Trenton, NJ 08625
609-292-4833

New Mexico

State Agency on Aging
224 East Palace Avenue
La Villa Rivera Building
4th Floor
Santa Fe, NM 87501
505-827-7640

New York

New York State Office for the Aging
Agency Building 2
Empire State Plaza
Albany, NY 12223
518-474-5731

North Carolina

Division of Aging
Department of Human Resources
708 Hillsborough Street
Suite 200
Raleigh, NC 27603
919-733-3983

North Dakota

Aging Services
Department of Human Services
State Capitol Building
Bismarck, ND 58505
701-224-2310

Ohio

Ohio Commission on Aging
50 West Broad Street
9th Floor
Columbus, OH 43215
614-466-5500

Oklahoma

Special Unit on Aging
Department of Human Services
P.O. Box 25352
Oklahoma City, OK 73125
405-521-2281

Oregon

Senior Services Division
Human Resources Department
313 Public Service Building
Salem, OR 97310
503-378-4728

Pennsylvania

Department of Aging
Barto Building
231 State Street
Harrisburg, PA 17101
717-783-1550

Rhode Island

Department of Elderly Affairs
79 Washington Street
Providence, RI 02903
401-277-2880

South Carolina

Commission on Aging
915 Main Street
Columbia, SC 29201
803-758-2576

South Dakota

Office of Adult Services and Aging
Department of Social Services
700 North Illinois Street
Pierre, SD 57501
605-773-3656

Tennessee

Commission on Aging
703 Tennessee Building
535 Church Street
Nashville, TN 37219
615-741-2056

Texas

Texas Department on Aging
Capitol Station
P.O. Box 12786
Austin, TX 78711
512-475-2717

Utah

Division of Aging
Department of Social Services
P.O. Box 45500
Salt Lake City, UT 84145
801-533-6422

Vermont

Office on Aging
103 South Main Street
Waterbury, VT 05676
802-241-2400

Virginia

Department for the Aging
101 North 14th Street
18th Floor
Richmond, VA 23219
804-225-2271

Washington

Bureau of Aging and Adult Services
Department of Social and Health Services
Ob-43G
Olympia, WA 98504
206-753-2502

West Virginia

Commission on Aging
State Capitol
Charleston, WV 25305
304-348-3317

Wisconsin

Bureau on Aging
Department of Health and Social Services
Division of Community Services
One West Wilson Street
P.O. Box 7851
Madison, WI 53707
608-266-2536

Wyoming

Commission on Aging
Hathaway Building
Cheyenne, WY 82002
307-777-7986

American Samoa

Territorial Administration on Aging
Government of American Samoa
Pago Pago, American Samoa 96799
(written complaints only)

Guam

Office of Aging
Social Service Department of Public Health
Government of Guam
P.O. Box 2816
Agana, GU 96910
(written complaints only)

Puerto Rico

Gericulture Commission
Department of Social Services
P.O. Box 11398
Santurce, PR 00910
(written complaints only)

Virgin Islands

Commission on Aging
P.O. Box 539
Charlotte Amalie
St. Thomas, VI 00801
(written complaints only)

Alcoholism and Drug Abuse

Alcoholism

Alcohol and Drug Problems Association of North America
444 North Capitol Street
Suite 181
Washington, DC 20001
202-737-4340

Alcohol, Drug Abuse and Mental Health Administration
Public Health Service
Parklawn Building
5600 Fishers Lane
Room 12C-15
Rockville, MD 20857
301-443-3783

Alcohol Education for Youth and Community
362 State Street
Albany, NY 12210
518-436-9319

Alcoholics Anonymous World Services
P.O. Box 459
Grand Central Station
468 Park Avenue South
New York, NY 10163
212-686-1100

American Council on Alcohol Problems
2908 Patricia Drive
Des Moines, IA 50322
515-276-7752

Association of Halfway House Alcoholism Programs of North America
786 East 7th Street
St. Paul, MN 55106
612-771-0933

Boost Alcohol Consciousness Concerning Health of Students
124 Tigert Hall
University of Florida
Gainesville, FL 32611
904-392-1261

Center for Alcohol Studies
Rutgers University
New Brunswick, NJ 08903
609-452-4851

**Community Organization for Drug Abuse, Mental
    Health, and Alcohol**
124 West Thomas Road
No. 110
Phoenix, AZ 85013
602-234-0096

Do It Now Foundation
P.O. Box 5115
2050 East University Drive
Suite 7
Phoenix, AZ 85010
602-257-0797

Families Anonymous
P.O. Box 528
14617 Victory Boulevard
Suite 1
Van Nuys, CA 91408
818-989-7841

Hazelden Research Services
1400 Park Avenue South
Minneapolis, MN 55404
612-349-9400

National Association for Children of Alcoholics
31706 Coast Highway
Suite 201
San Laguna, CA 92677
714-499-3889

**National Association of State Mental Health Program
    Directors**
1001 Third Street, SW
Suite 115
Washington, DC 20024
202-554-7807

National Clearinghouse for Alcohol Information
P.O. Box 2345
1776 East Jefferson Street
Rockville, MD 20852
301-468-2600

National Nurses Society on Addictions
2506 Gross Point Road
Evanston, IL 60201
312-475-7300

Drug Abuse

American Council for Drug Education
6193 Executive Boulevard
Rockville, MD 20852
301-984-5700

**American Medical Society on Alcoholism and Other
    Drug Dependencies**
12 West 12th Street
New York, NY 10010
212-206-6770

Committees of Correspondence
P.O. Box 232
Topfield, MA 01983
617-774-2641

Division of Substance Abuse Medicine
Medical College of Virginia Hospital
P.O. Box 109
Richmond, VA 23298
804-786-9914

Do It Now Foundation
P.O. Box 5115
2050 East University Drive
Suite 7
Phoenix, AZ 85010
602-257-0797

Drug Abuse Warning Network
National Institute on Drug Abuse
Parklawn Building
5600 Fishers Lane
Room 11A-55
Rockville, MD 20857
301-443-6637

Drug and Alcohol Council
396 Alexander Street
Rochester, NY 14607
716-244-3190

Drug Information Center
462 Grider Street
Buffalo, NY 14215
716-898-3927

Families Anonymous
P.O. Box 528
14617 Victory Boulevard
Suite 1
Van Nuys, CA 91408
818-989-7841

Families in Action
National Drug Information Center
3845 North Druid Hills Road
Suite 300
Decatur, GA 30033
404-325-5799

**Institute for Studies of Destructive Behaviors
    and the Suicide Prevention Center**
1041 South Menlo Avenue
Los Angeles, CA 90006
213-386-5111

Narcotics Anonymous
World Service Office
16155 Wyandotte Street
Van Nuys, CA 91406
818-780-3951

National Association of Alcoholism and Drug Abuse
  Counselors
951 South George Mason Drive
Arlington, VA 22204
703-920-4644

National Association on Drug Abuse Problems
355 Lexington Avenue
New York, NY 10017
212-986-1170

National Cocaine Hotline
Fair Oaks Hospital
19 Prospect Street
Summit, NJ 07901
800-262-2463

National Federation of Parents for Drug-Free Youth
8730 Georgia Avenue
Suite 200
Silver Spring, MD 20910
301-585-5437

National Institute on Drug Abuse
Office of Science
5600 Fishers Lane
Room 10-16
Rockville, MD 20857
301-443-6480

NIDA Addiction Research Center
P.O. Box 5180
Baltimore, MD 21224
301-955-7502

Odyssey Institute Corporation
817 Fairfield Avenue
Bridgeport, CT 06604
203-334-3488

Operation PAR
6613 49th Street North
Pinellas Park, FL 33565
813-527-5866

Parent Resources Institute on Drug Education
100 Edgewood Avenue
Suite 1216
Atlanta, GA 30303
404-658-2548

PharmChem
3925 Bohannon Drive
Menlo Park, CA 94025
415-328-6200

Pills Anonymous
P.O. Box 473
Ansonia Station
New York, NY 10023
212-874-0700

Potsmokers Anonymous
316 East Third Street
New York, NY 10009
212-254-1777

PYRAMID
1777 North California Boulevard
Suite 200
Walnut Creek, CA 94596
415-939-6666

Therapeutic Communities of America
624 South Michigan Avenue
Chicago, IL 60605
312-663-1130

Women in Crisis
133 West 21st Street
Suite 11
11th Floor
New York, NY 10011
212-242-3081

Children

Child Abuse

American Association for Protecting Children
American Humane Association
P.O. Box 1266
Colorado Springs, CO 80910
303-596-6006

Children's Bureau Clearinghouse on Child Abuse
  and Neglect Information
Department of Health and Human Services
P.O. Box 1182
400 Sixth Street, SW
Washington, DC 20013
202-245-2856

Children's Legal Rights Information and Training Program
2008 Hillyer Place
Washington, DC 20009
202-332-6575

Kempe National Center for the Prevention and Treatment of Child Abuse and Neglect
Department of Pediatrics
Health Sciences Center
University of Colorado
1205 Oneida Street
Denver, CO 80220
303-321-3963

National Committee for Prevention of Child Abuse
332 South Michigan Avenue
Suite 1250
Chicago, IL 60604
312-663-3520

National Network of Youth Advisory Boards
P.O. Box 402036
Ocean View Beach
Miami, FL 33140
305-532-2607

Odyssey Institute Corporation
817 Fairfield Avenue
Bridgeport, CT 06604
203-334-3488

Parents Anonymous
7120 Franklyn Avenue
Los Angeles, CA 90046
213-876-9642

Handicapped Children

Association for Children with Retarded Mental Development
162 Fifth Avenue
11th Floor
New York, NY 10010
212-475-7200

Council for Exceptional Children
Department of Information Services
1920 Association Drive
Reston, VA 22091
703-620-3660

Foundation for Children with Learning Disabilities
99 Park Avenue
6th Floor
New York, NY 10016
212-687-7211

National Information Center for Handicapped Children and Youth
P.O. Box 1492
Washington, DC 20001
1555 Wilson Boulevard
Rosslyn, VA
703-522-3332

Runaways

American Youth Work Center
1522 Connecticut Avenue, NW
4th Floor
Washington, DC 20036
202-785-0764

Contact Center
P.O. Box 81826
Superior Industrial Park
Lincoln, NE 68501
402-464-0602

Metro-Help National Runaway Switchboard
2210 North Halsted Street
Chicago, IL 60614
312-880-9860
800-621-4000
800-972-6004 (in Illinois)

Missing Children Help Center
410 Ware Boulevard
Suite 400
Tampa, FL 33619
813-623-KIDS

Consumers

Better Business Bureaus

Better Business Bureaus (BBBs) are nonprofit organizations sponsored by local businesses. There are some 170 BBBs in the United States today. BBBs offer a variety of consumer education programs and materials, provide general information on companies, handle consumer inquiries, mediate and arbitrate complaints, and maintain records of consumer satisfaction or dissatisfaction with individual companies.

United States Bureaus

National Headquarters

Council of Better Business Bureaus
1515 Wilson Boulevard
Arlington, VA 22209
703-276-0100

Local Bureaus

Alabama

1214 South 20th Street
Birmingham, AL 32503
205-933-2893

108 Jefferson Street
Huntsville, AL 35801
205-533-1640

707 Van Antwerp Building
Mobile, AL 36602
205-433-5494

Union Bank Building
Commerce Street
Suite 810
Montgomery, AL 36104
205-262-5606

Alaska

417 Barrow
3605 Arctic Boulevard #BB
Anchorage, AK 99503
907-276-5901

Arizona

4428 North 12th Street
Phoenix, AZ 85013
602-264-1721

100 East Alameda Street
Suite 403
Tucson, AZ 85701
602-622-7651 (inquiries)
602-622-7654 (complaints)

Arkansas

1216 South University
Little Rock, AR 72204
501-664-7274

California

705 18th Street
Bakersfield, CA 93301
805-322-2074

1265 North La Cadena
Colton, CA 92324
714-825-7280

5070 North Sixth Street
Suite 176
Fresno, CA 93720
209-222-8111

639 South New Hampshire Avenue
3rd Floor
Los Angeles, CA 90005
213-383-0992

508 16th Street
Room 1500
Oakland, CA 94612
415-839-5900

1401 21st Street
Suite 305
Sacramento, CA 95814
916-443-6843

Union Bank Building
Suite 301
San Diego, CA 92101
619-234-0966

4310 Orange Avenue
San Diego, CA 92105
619-283-3927

2740 Van Ness Avenue #210
San Francisco, CA 94109
415-775-3300

P.O. Box 8110
1505 Meridian Avenue
San Jose, CA 95125
408-978-8700

P.O. Box 294
20 North San Mateo Drive
San Mateo, CA 94401
415-347-1251, 1252, 1253

P.O. Box 746
111 North Milpas Street
Santa Barbara, CA 93102
805-963-8657

1111 North Center Street
Stockton, CA 95202
209-948-4880

17662 Irvine Boulevard
Suite 15
Tustin, CA 92680
714-544-6942 (inquiries)
714-544-5842 (complaints)

Colorado

524 South Cascade
Suite 2
Colorado Springs, CO 80903
303-636-1155

1780 South Bellaire
Suite 700
Denver, CO 80222
303-758-2100

140 West Oak Street
Fort Collins, CO 80524
303-484-1348

Connecticut

Fairfield Woods Plaza
2345 Black Rock Turnpike
Fairfield, CT 06430
203-374-6161

P.O. Box 2068
100 South Turnpike Road
New Haven, CT 06473
203-269-2700 (inquiries)
203-269-4457 (complaints)

630 Oakwood Avenue
Suite 223 West Hartford, CT 06110
203-247-8700

Delaware

P.O. Box 300
20 South Walnut Street
Milford, DE 19963
302-856-6969

P.O. Box 4085
1901-B West 11th Street
Wilmington, DE 19807
302-652-3833

District of Columbia

1012 14th Street, NW
Prudential Building
14th Floor
Washington, DC 20005
202-393-8000

Florida

3969 Ulmerton Road
Clearwater, FL 33520
813-577-6040

8600 NE 2nd Avenue
Miami, FL 33138
305-757-3446

3080 Tamiami Trail North
Naples, FL 33940
813-261-0606

608 Gulf Drive West
Suite 3
New Port Richey, FL 33552
813-842-5459

132 East Colonial Drive
Orlando, FL 32801
305-843-8873

P.O. Box 1511
Pensacola, Florida 32597
904-433-6111

3015 Exchange Court
West Palm Beach, FL 33409
305-686-2200

Georgia

100 Edgewood Avenue
Suite 1012
Atlanta, GA 30303
404-688-4910

P.O. Box 2085
624 Ellis Street
Suite 106
Augusta, GA 30903
404-722-1574

8 13th Street
Columbus, GA 31901
404-324-0712, 0713

P.O. Box 13956
6822 Abercom Extension
Savannah, GA 31406
912-354-7521

Hawaii

677 Ala Moana Boulevard
Suite 614
Honolulu, HI 96813
808-531-8131, 8132, 8133

Idaho

409 West Jefferson
Boise, ID 83702
208-342-4649

Illinois

35 East Wacker Drive
Chicago, IL 60601
312-444-1188 (inquiries)
312-346-3313 (complaints)

109 Southwest Jefferson Street
Suite 305
Peoria, IL 61602
309-673-5194

3 West-Old Capitol Plaza
Room 14
Springfield, IL 62701
319-366-5401

Indiana

P.O. Box 405
118 South Second Street
Elkhart, IN 46515
219-293-5731

113 SE Fourth Street
Evansville, IN 47708
812-422-6879

1203 Webster Street
Fort Wayne, IN 46802
219-423-4433

4231 Cleveland Street
Gary, IN 46408
219-980-1511

22 East Washington Street
Suite 310
Indianapolis, IN 46204
317-637-0197

204 Iroquois Building
Marion, IN 46952
317-668-8954

Ball State University BBB
Whitinger Building
Room 192
Muncie, IN 47306
317-285-5666

Iowa

Alpine Center
2435 Kimberly Road
Suite 110 North
Bettendorf, IA 52722
319-355-6344

3 Irvine Building
417 First Avenue, SE
Suite 3
Cedar Rapids, IA 52401
319-366-5401

615 Insurance Exchange Building
Des Moines, IA 50309
515-243-8137

318 Badgerow Building
Sioux City, IA 51101
712-252-4501

Kansas

501 Jefferson
Suite 24
Topeka, KS 66607
913-232-0454, 0455

300 Kaufman Building
Wichita, KS 67202
316-263-3146

Kentucky

629 North Broadway
Lexington, KY 40508
606-252-4492

844 South Fourth Street
Louisville, KY 40203
502-583-6546

Louisiana

1407 Murray Street
Suite 101
Alexandria, LA 71306
318-473-4494

2055 Wooddale Boulevard
Baton Rouge, LA 70806
504-926-3010

300 Bond Street
Box 9129
Houma, LA 70360
504-868-3456

P.O. Box 3651
804 Jefferson Street
Lafayette, LA 70501
318-234-8341

P.O. Box 1681
1413 Ryan Street
Suite C
Lake Charles, LA 70602
318-433-1633

141 De Siard Street
ONB Building
Suite 114
Monroe, LA 71201
318-837-4600, 4601

301 Camp Street
Suite 403
New Orleans, LA 70130
504-581-6222

1407 North Market Street
Shreveport, LA 71107
318-221-8352

Maryland

401 North Howard Street
Baltimore, MD 21201
301-468-3405

6917 Arlington Road
Bethesda, MD 20814
301-468-3405

Massachusetts

8 Winter Street
Boston, MA 02108
617-482-9151 (inquiries)
617-482-9190 (complaints)

106 State Road
Suite 4
Dartmouth, MA 02747
617-999-6060

One Kendall Street
Suite 307
Framingham, MA 01701
617-872-5585

The Federal Building
Suite 1
78 North Street
Hyannis, MA 02601
617-771-3022

316 Essex Street
Lawrence, MA 01840
617-687-7666

293 Bridge Street
Suite 324
Springfield, MA 01103
413-734-3114

P.O. Box 379
32 Franklin Street (16108)
Worcester, MA 01601
617-755-2548

Michigan

150 Michigan Avenue
Detroit, MI 48226
313-962-7566 (inquiries)
313-962-6785 (complaints)

1 Peoples Building
Grand Rapids, MI 49503
616-744-8236

Holland/Zeeland 616-772-6063

Muskegon 616-722-0707

Minnesota

1745 University Avenue
St. Paul, MN 55104
612-646-4631

Mississippi

502 Edgewater Gulf Drive
Building C–Suite 10
Biloxi, MS 39531
601-388-9244

105 Fifth Avenue
Columbus, MS 39701
601-327-8594

P.O. Box 2090
510 George Street
Suite 107
Jackson, MS 39225
601-948-4732

601 22nd Avenue
Suite 313
Meridian, MS 39301
601-482-8752

Missouri

306 East 12th Street
Suite 1024
Kansas City, MO 64106
816-421-7800

Mansion House Center
440 North Fourth Street
St. Louis, MO 63102
314-241-3100

205 Park Central East
Suite 312
Springfield, MO 65806
417-862-9231

Nebraska

719 North 48th Street
Lincoln, NE 68504
402-467-5261

1613 Farnam Street
Room 417
Omaha, NE 68102
402-346-3033

Nevada

1829 East Charleston Boulevard
Suite 103
Las Vegas, NV 89104
702-322-0657

P.O. Box 2932
372-A Casazza Drive (39502)
Reno, NV 89505
702-735-6900

New Hampshire

One Pillsbury Street
Concord, NH 03301
603-224-1991

New Jersey

P.O. Box 303
836 Haddon Avenue
Collingswood, NJ 08108
609-854-8467

690 Whitehead Road
Lawrenceville, NJ 08648
609-396-1199 (Mercer County)
201-536-6306 (Monmouth County)
201-329-6854, 55 (Middlesex, Somer-
    set, and Hunterdon counties)

34 Park Place
Newark, NJ 07102
201-643-3025

2 Forest Avenue
Paramus, NJ 07652
201-845-4044

1721 Route 37 East
Toms River, NJ 06753
201-270-5577

New Mexico

4520 Montgomery, NE
Suite B-1
Albuquerque, NM 87109
505-884-0500

308 North Locke
Farmington, NM 87401
505-326-6501

Santa Fe Division
227 East Palace Avenue
Suite C
Santa Fe, NM 87501
505-988-3648

New York

775 Main Street
Buffalo, NY 14203
716-856-7180

266 Main Street
Farmingdale, NY 11735
516-420-0500 (Long Island)

257 Park Avenue South
New York, NY 10010
212-533-6200 (inquiries and complaints)
212-533-7500 (other)
212-533-6200 (Harlem)

1122 Sibley Tower
Rochester, NY 14604
716-546-6776

200 University Building
Syracuse, NY 13202
315-479-6635

209 Elizabeth Street
Utica, NY 13501
315-724-3129

158 Westchester Avenue
White Plains, NY 10601
914-428-1230, 1231

120 East Main
Wappinger Falls, NY 12590
914-297-6550

North Carolina

29½ Page Avenue
Ashville, NC 28801
704-253-2392

202 North Tryon Street
Charlotte, NC 28202
704-332-7151

3608 West Friendly Avenue
Greensboro, NC 27410
919-852-4240, 4241, 4242

Northwestern Bank Building
11 South College Avenue
Suite 203
Newton, NC 28658
704-464-0372

P.O. Box 95066
3120 Poplarwood Drive
Suite G-1 (27604)
Raleigh, NC 27625
919-872-9240

2110 Cloverdale Avenue
Suite 2-B
Winston-Salem, NC 27103
919-725-8348

Ohio

P.O. Box F 596
Akron, OH 44308
216-253-4590

1434 Cleveland Avenue North
Canton, OH 44713
216-454-9401

898 Walnut Street
Cincinnati, OH 45202
513-421-3015

1720 Keith Building
Cleveland, OH 44115
216-241-7678

527 South High Street
Columbus, OH 43215
614-221-6336

40 West Fourth Street
Suite 280
Dayton, OH 45402
513-222-5825

P.O. Box 1706
130 West Second Street (44902)
Mansfield, OH 44901
419-522-1700

405 North Huron Street
Toledo, OH 43604
419-241-6276

P.O. Box 1495
Mahoning Valley
Youngstown, OH 44501
216-744-3111

Oklahoma

606 North Dewey
Oklahoma City, OK 73102
405-239-6081, 82, 83

4833 South Sheridan
Suite 412
Tulsa, OK 74145
918-664-1266

Oregon

520 SW Sixth Avenue
Suite 600
Portland, OR 97204
503-226-3981

Pennsylvania

528 North New Street
Dodson Building
Bethlehem, PA 18018
215-866-8780

53 North Duke Street
Lancaster, PA 17602
717-291-1151
717-846-2700 (York County residents)

511 North Broad Street
Philadelphia, PA 19123
215-574-3600

610 Smithfield Street
Pittsburgh, PA 15222
412-456-2700

601 Connell Building
North Washington Avenue
Scranton, PA 18503
717-342-9129

Puerto Rico

155 José Padin Street
Huyke Urb.
Hato Rey, PR 00918
(packages, UPS)

G.P.O. Box 70212
San Juan, PR 00936
(general correspondence)
809-756-5400

Rhode Island

270 Weybosset Street
Providence, RI 02903
401-272-9800

South Carolina

1338 Main Street
Suite 500
Columbia, SC 29201
803-254-2525

608 East Washington Street
Greenville, SC 29601
803-242-5052

Tennessee

Park Plaza Building
1010 Market Street
Suite 200
Chattanooga, TN 37402
615-266-6144

P.O. Box 3608
124 West Summit Hill Drive
Knoxville, TN 37902
615-522-1300

P.O. Box 41406
1835 Union
Suite 312
Memphis, TN 38104
901-272-9641

506 Nashville City Bank Building
Nashville, TN 37201
615-254-5872

Texas

Bank of Commerce Building
Suite 320
Abilene, TX 79605
915-691-1533

1008 West 10th Street
Amarillo, TX 79101
806-374-3735

1005 American Plaza
Austin, TX 78701
512-476-6943

P.O. Box 2988
476 Oakland Avenue (77701)
Beaumont, TX 77704
713-835-5348

202 Varisco Building
Bryan, TX 77803
713-823-8148

109 North Chaparral
Suite 101
Corpus Christi, TX 78401
512-888-5555

2001 Bryan Street
Suite 850
Dallas, TX 75201
214-220-2000

6024 Gateway East
El Paso, TX 79905
915-778-7000

709 Sinclair Building
106 West 5th Street
Forth Worth, TX 76102
817-332-7585

2707 North Loop West
Suite 900
Houston, TX 77008
713-868-9500

910 East Marshall Street
Longview, TX 75601
214-236-3339

P.O. Box 1178
1015 15th Street
Lubbock, TX 79401
806-763-0459

P.O. Box 6006
Air Terminal Building
Room 216
Midland, TX 79711
915-563-1880 (inquiries)
915-563-1881 (complaints)

115 South Randolph
San Angelo, TX 76903
915-653-2318

1800 Northeast Loop 410
Suite 400
San Antonio, TX 78217
512-828-9441

P.O. Box 7203
608 New Road (76710)
Waco, TX 76714
817-772-7530

1106 Brook Avenue
Wichita Falls, TX 76301
817-723-5526

Utah

1588 South Main Street
Salt Lake City, UT 84115
801-487-4656

Virginia

105 East Annandale Road
Suite 210
Falls Church, VA 22046
703-533-1900

P.O. Box 11133
2019 Llewellyn Avenue
Norfolk, VA 23517
804-627-5651
804-851-9101 (peninsula area)

701 East Franklin
Suite 100
Richmond, VA 23219
804-648-0016

151 West Campbell Avenue, SW
Roanoke, VA 24011
703-342-3455

Washington

2200 Sixth Avenue
Seattle, WA 98121
206-622-8067, 8068

South 176 Stevens Street
Suite A
Spokane, WA 99204
509-747-1155

1101 Fawcett Avenue #222
Tacoma, WA 98401
206-383-5561

424 Washington Mutual Building
Yakima, WA 98907
509-248-1326

Wisconsin

740 North Plankinton Avenue
Milwaukee, WI 53203
414-273-1600

Canadian Bureaus

National Headquarters

2180 Steeles Avenue W #219
Concord, ON L4K 2Z5
416-669-1248

Local Bureaus

Newfoundland and Labrador
2 Forbes Street #9
Box 516
St. John's, NF A1C 5K4
709-722-2222

New Brunswick
236 St. George Street
Box 1002
Moncton, NB E1C 8P2
506-857-3255

Nova Scotia
1731 Barrington Street
Box 2124
Halifax, NS B3J 3B7
902-422-6581

Quebec
475 rue Richelieu
Quebec, QC G1R 1K2
418-523-2555

Montreal
2055 Peel Street
#460
Montreal, QC H3A 1V4
514-286-9281

Ottawa and Hull
Sovereign Building
71 Bank Street #503
Ottawa, ON K1P 5N2
613-233-3562

Metropolitan Toronto
1 St. John's Road #501
Toronto, ON M6P 4C7
416-766-5744

South Central Ontario
170 Jackson Street, E.
Hamilton, ON L8N 1L4
416-526-1111

London and District
304 York Street
Box 2153, Station A
London, ON N6A 4E3
519-673-3222

Mid-Western Ontario
58 Scott Street
Kitchener, ON N2H 2R1
519-579-3080

Windsor and District
500 Riverside Drive
West Windsor, ON N9A 5K6
519-258-7222

Winnipeg and Manitoba
365 Hargrave Street #204
Winnipeg, MB R3B 2K3
204-943-1486

Saskatchewan
2049 Lorne Street
Regina, SK S4P 2M4
306-352-7601

Calgary and Southern Alberta
630 8th Avenue SW #404
Calgary, AB T2P 1G6
403-269-3905

Central and Northern Alberta
600 Guardian Building
10240 124th Street
Edmonton, AB T5N 3W6
403-482-2341

British Columbia
#404
788 Beatty Street
Vancouver, BC V6B 2M1
604-682-2711

Vancouver Island
635 Humboldt Street
Victoria, BC V8W 1A7
604-386-6348

State, County, and City Government Consumer Protection Offices

Listed below are consumer protection offices that are part of state, county, and city governments. Some are located in governors' offices, state attorney generals' offices, or mayors' offices. Check in your state to see which office can help resolve complaints, furnish information or helpful publications, or provide other services. As a general rule, the first place to go for help with a consumer problem is the local office nearest your home. Since most offices require that complaints be in writing, you might save time by writing, rather than calling, with your initial complaint.

Alabama

State Office
Director
Office of Attorney General
Consumer Protection Division
560 South McDonough Street
Montgomery, AL 36104
205-261-4200
800-392-5658 (toll free—Alabama only)

Alaska

State Office
Chief
Office of Attorney General
Consumer Protection Section
1031 West Fourth Avenue
Suite 300
Anchorage, AK 99501
907-279-0428

Branch Offices
Office of Attorney General
First National Center
100 Cushman Street
Suite 400
Fairbanks, AK 99707
907-456-8588

Office of Attorney General
Consumer Protection Section
Pouch K
Juneau, AK 99811
907-465-3692

Arizona

State Office

Chief Counsel
Office of Attorney General
Financial Fraud Division
1275 West Washington Street
Phoenix, AZ 85007
602-255-5763 (fraud only)
800-352-8431 (toll free—Arizona only)

Branch Office
Office of Attorney General
Financial Fraud Division
402 West Congress Street
Suite 315
Tucson, AZ 85701
602-628-5501 (fraud only)

County Offices

Chief Investigator
Cochise County Attorney's Office
P.O. Drawer CA
Bisbee, AZ 85603
602-432-5703 (ext. 470)

Director
Pima County Attorney's Office
Consumer Protection/Economic Crime Unit
111 West Congress
Ninth Floor
Tucson, AZ 85701
602-792-8668

Yuma County Attorney's Office
P.O. Box 1048
Yuma, AZ 85364
602-782-4534 (ext. 55)

City Offices

Supervising Attorney
Tucson City Attorney's Office
P.O. Box 27210
2302 East Speedway
Room 202
Tucson, AZ 85726
602-791-4886

Arkansas

State Office

Director
Office of Attorney General
Consumer Protection Division
Justice Building
Little Rock, AR 72201
501-371-2341
800-482-8982 (toll free—Arkansas only)

California

State Offices

Office of Attorney General
Public Inquiry Unit
1515 K Street
Suite 511
Sacramento, CA 95814
916-322-3360
800-952-5225 (toll free—California only)

Director
California Department of Consumer Affairs
1020 N Street
Sacramento, CA 95814
916-445-0660 (complaints, 10:00–3:00 daily)
916-445-1254 (consumer information)

Consumer Advisory Council
1020 N Street
Room A603
Sacramento, CA 95814
916-322-0548

California Department of Consumer Affairs
Bureau of Automotive Repair
3116 Bradshaw Road
Sacramento, CA 95827
916-366-5050
800-952-5210 (toll-free—California only; auto repair only)

Branch Offices
California Department of Consumer Affairs
107 South Broadway
Room 8020
Los Angeles, CA 90012
213-620-4360

Complaint Assistance Unit
1020 N Street
Room 586
Sacramento, CA 95814
916-445-0660

County Offices

Chairperson
Alameda County Consumer Affairs Commission
10910 East 14th Street
Oakland, CA 94603
415-639-4812

Contra Costa County District Attorney
Special Operations Division
P.O. Box 670
725 Court Street
4th Floor
Martinez, CA 94553
415-372-4500 (ext. 4620)

Fresno County District Attorney's Office
Consumer Fraud Division
1100 Van Ness Avenue
Fresno, CA 93721
209-488-3141

District Attorney
Kern County District Attorney's Office
Consumer and Major Business Fraud Section
1215 Truxton Avenue
Bakersfield, CA 93301
805-861-2421

Deputy District Attorney
Los Angeles County District Attorney's Office
Consumer Protection Division
320 West Temple Street
Room 540
Los Angeles, CA 90012
213-974-3970

Director
Los Angeles County Department of Consumer Affairs
500 West Temple Street
Room B-96
Los Angeles, CA 90012
213-974-1452

Director
Madera County Weights and Measures
Consumer Protection Unit
902 North Gateway Drive
Madera, CA 93637
209-675-7809

District Attorney
Mendocino County District Attorney's Office
Consumer Division
P.O. Box 1000
Ukiah, CA 95482
707-463-4211

Coordinator
Monterey County Office of Consumer Affairs
P.O. Box 1369
Salinas, CA 93902
408-758-4626

Deputy District Attorney
Napa County District Attorney's Office
Consumer Affairs Division
1125 Third Street
Napa, CA 94559
707-253-4427

Deputy District Attorney
Orange County District Attorney's Office
Major Fraud Consumer Protection Unit
P.O. Box 808
700 Civic Center Drive West
Santa Ana, CA 92702
714-834-3600

Director
Orange County Office of Consumer Affairs
1300 South Grand Avenue
Building B
Santa Ana, CA 92711
714-834-6100

Deputy District Attorney
Riverside County District Attorney's Office
Economic Crime Division
4080 Lemon Street
Riverside, CA 92501
714-787-6372

Supervising Deputy District Attorney
Sacramento County District Attorney's Fraud Division
P.O. Box 749
Sacramento, CA 95804
916-440-6174

Director
San Diego County District Attorney's Office
Consumer Fraud Division
P.O. Box X-1011
San Diego, CA 92112
619-236-2474

Attorney in Charge
San Francisco County District Attorney's Office
Consumer Fraud/Economic Crime Unit
732 Brennan Street
San Francisco, CA 94103
415-552-6400

Deputy District Attorney in Charge
San Joaquin County District Attorney's Office
Consumer Fraud and Regulatory Agencies Division
P.O. Box 50
222 East Weber
Stockton, CA 95201
209-944-3811

District Attorney
San Luis Obispo County District Attorney's Office
Consumer Unit
Room 450
County Government Center
1050 Monterey Street
San Luis Obispo, CA 93408
805-549-5800

FLAGS OF THE NATIONS

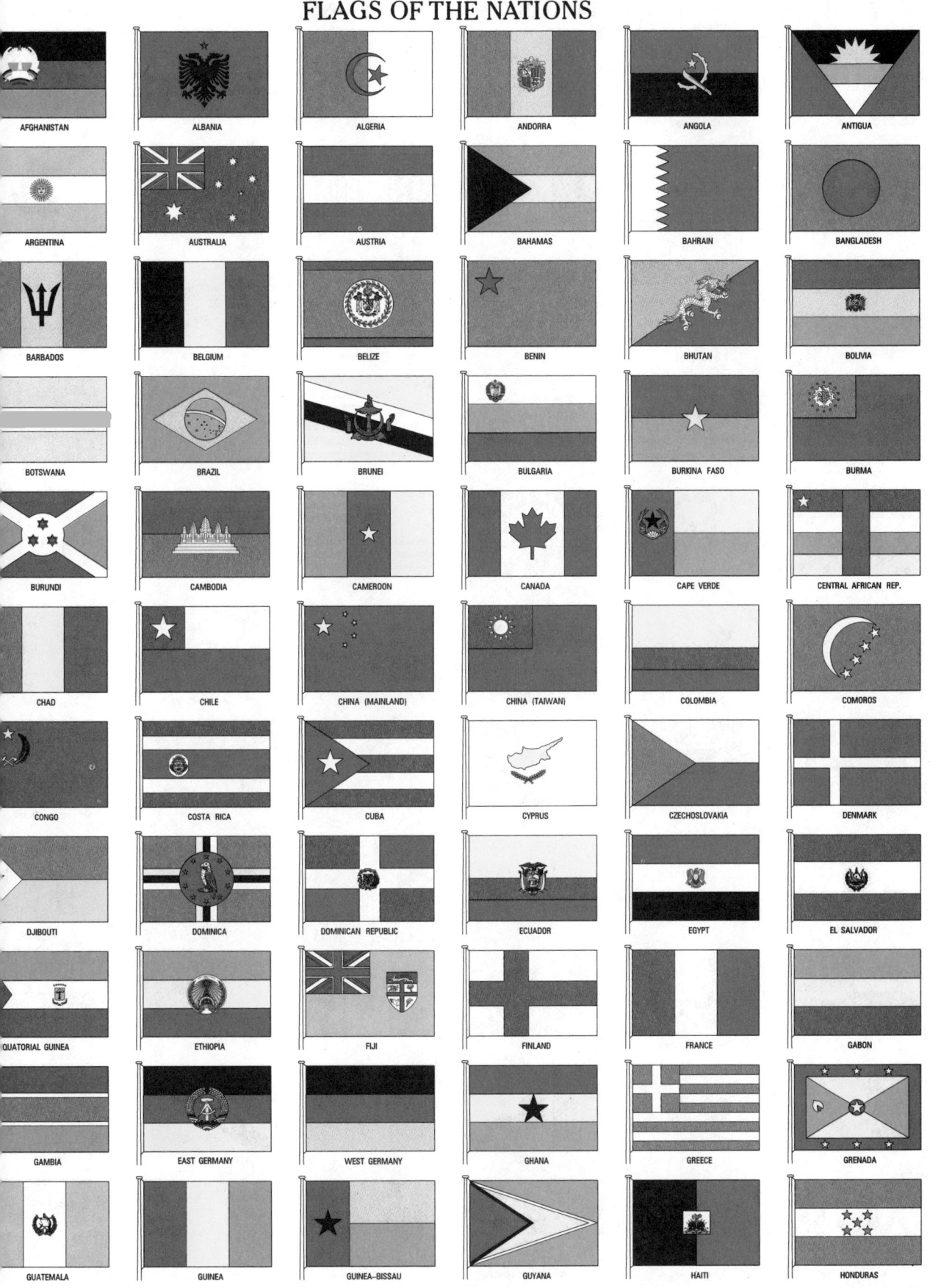

AFGHANISTAN	ALBANIA	ALGERIA	ANDORRA	ANGOLA	ANTIGUA
ARGENTINA	AUSTRALIA	AUSTRIA	BAHAMAS	BAHRAIN	BANGLADESH
BARBADOS	BELGIUM	BELIZE	BENIN	BHUTAN	BOLIVIA
BOTSWANA	BRAZIL	BRUNEI	BULGARIA	BURKINA FASO	BURMA
BURUNDI	CAMBODIA	CAMEROON	CANADA	CAPE VERDE	CENTRAL AFRICAN REP.
CHAD	CHILE	CHINA (MAINLAND)	CHINA (TAIWAN)	COLOMBIA	COMOROS
CONGO	COSTA RICA	CUBA	CYPRUS	CZECHOSLOVAKIA	DENMARK
DJIBOUTI	DOMINICA	DOMINICAN REPUBLIC	ECUADOR	EGYPT	EL SALVADOR
EQUATORIAL GUINEA	ETHIOPIA	FIJI	FINLAND	FRANCE	GABON
GAMBIA	EAST GERMANY	WEST GERMANY	GHANA	GREECE	GRENADA
GUATEMALA	GUINEA	GUINEA-BISSAU	GUYANA	HAITI	HONDURAS

FLAGS OF THE NATIONS

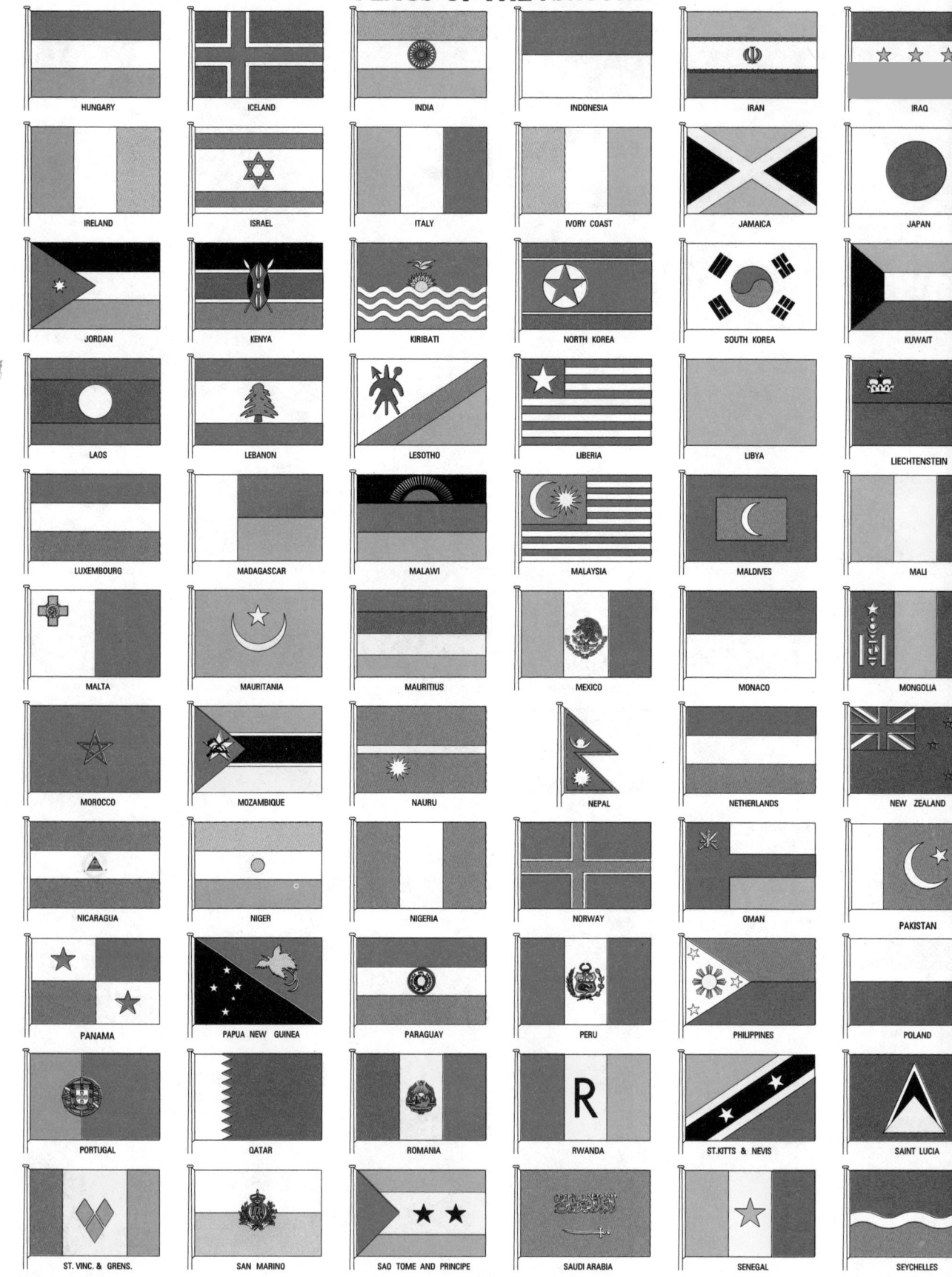

HUNGARY	ICELAND	INDIA	INDONESIA	IRAN	IRAQ
IRELAND	ISRAEL	ITALY	IVORY COAST	JAMAICA	JAPAN
JORDAN	KENYA	KIRIBATI	NORTH KOREA	SOUTH KOREA	KUWAIT
LAOS	LEBANON	LESOTHO	LIBERIA	LIBYA	LIECHTENSTEIN
LUXEMBOURG	MADAGASCAR	MALAWI	MALAYSIA	MALDIVES	MALI
MALTA	MAURITANIA	MAURITIUS	MEXICO	MONACO	MONGOLIA
MOROCCO	MOZAMBIQUE	NAURU	NEPAL	NETHERLANDS	NEW ZEALAND
NICARAGUA	NIGER	NIGERIA	NORWAY	OMAN	PAKISTAN
PANAMA	PAPUA NEW GUINEA	PARAGUAY	PERU	PHILIPPINES	POLAND
PORTUGAL	QATAR	ROMANIA	RWANDA	ST.KITTS & NEVIS	SAINT LUCIA
ST. VINC. & GRENS.	SAN MARINO	SAO TOME AND PRINCIPE	SAUDI ARABIA	SENEGAL	SEYCHELLES

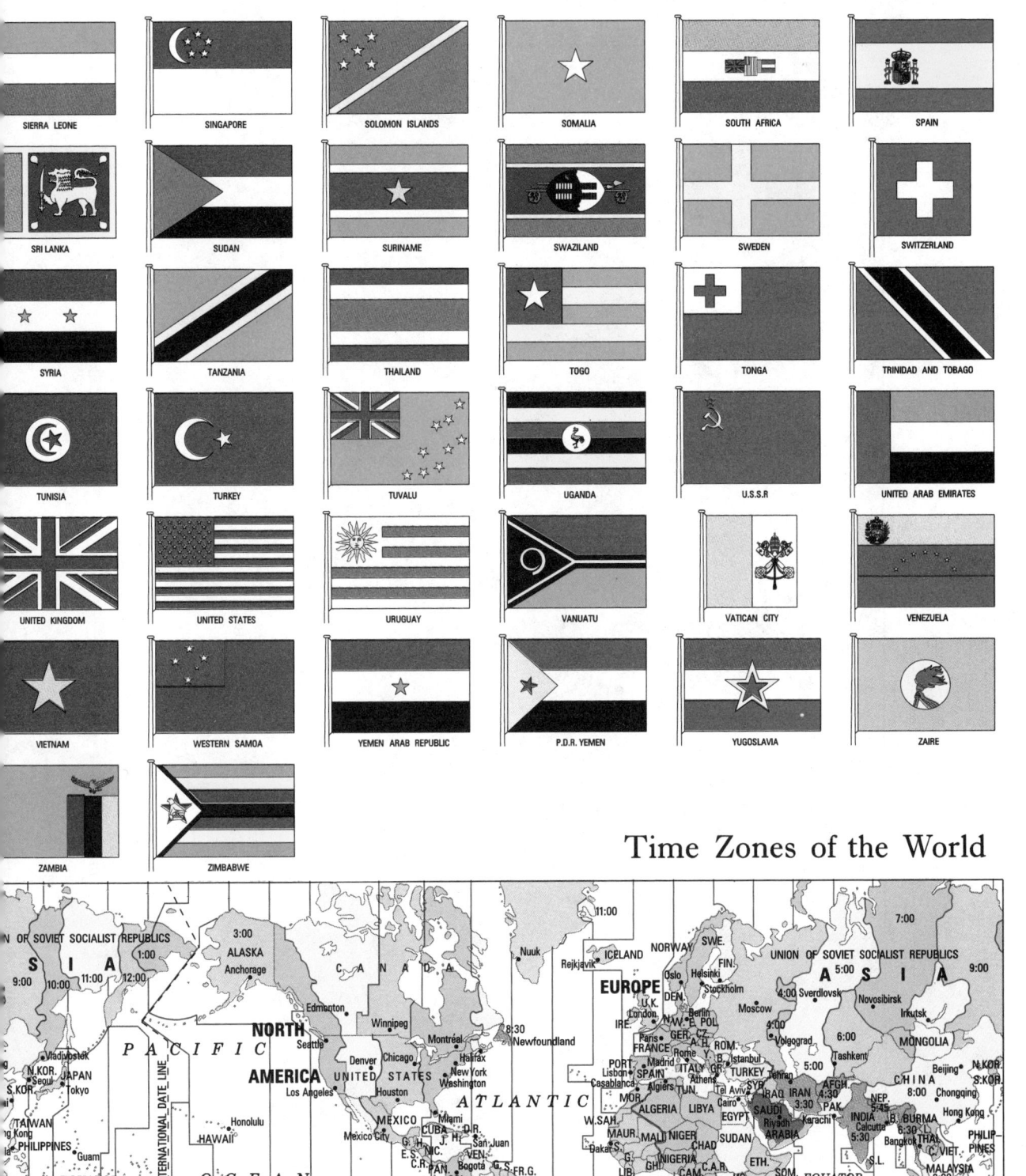

SIERRA LEONE

SINGAPORE

SOLOMON ISLANDS

SOMALIA

SOUTH AFRICA

SPAIN

SRI LANKA

SUDAN

SURINAME

SWAZILAND

SWEDEN

SWITZERLAND

SYRIA

TANZANIA

THAILAND

TOGO

TONGA

TRINIDAD AND TOBAGO

TUNISIA

TURKEY

TUVALU

UGANDA

U.S.S.R

UNITED ARAB EMIRATES

UNITED KINGDOM

UNITED STATES

URUGUAY

VANUATU

VATICAN CITY

VENEZUELA

VIETNAM

WESTERN SAMOA

YEMEN ARAB REPUBLIC

P.D.R. YEMEN

YUGOSLAVIA

ZAIRE

ZAMBIA

ZIMBABWE

Time Zones of the World

© Copyright by HAMMOND INCORPORATED, Maplewood, N.J.

Standard Time Zones

Areas Using Half Hour Deviations

Areas Not Using Zone System

| 9 P.M. | 10 P.M. | 11 P.M. | MIDNIGHT | 1 A.M. | 2 A.M. | 3 A.M. | 4 A.M. | 5 A.M. | 6 A.M. | 7 A.M. | 8 A.M. | 9 A.M. | 10 A.M. | 11 A.M. | NOON | 1 P.M. | 2 P.M. | 3 P.M. | 4 P.M. | 5 P.M. | 6 P.M. | 7 P.M. | 8 P.M. |

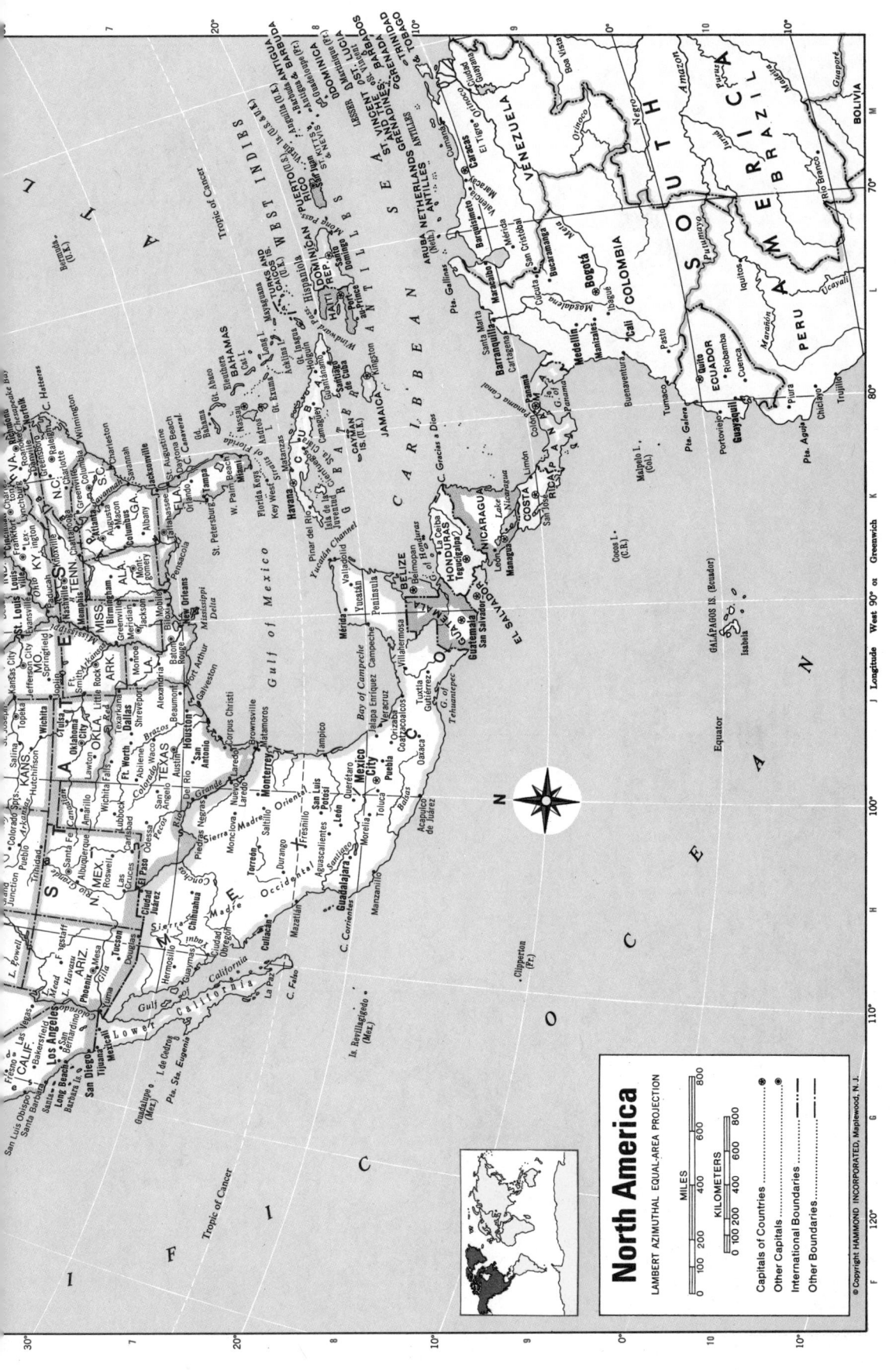

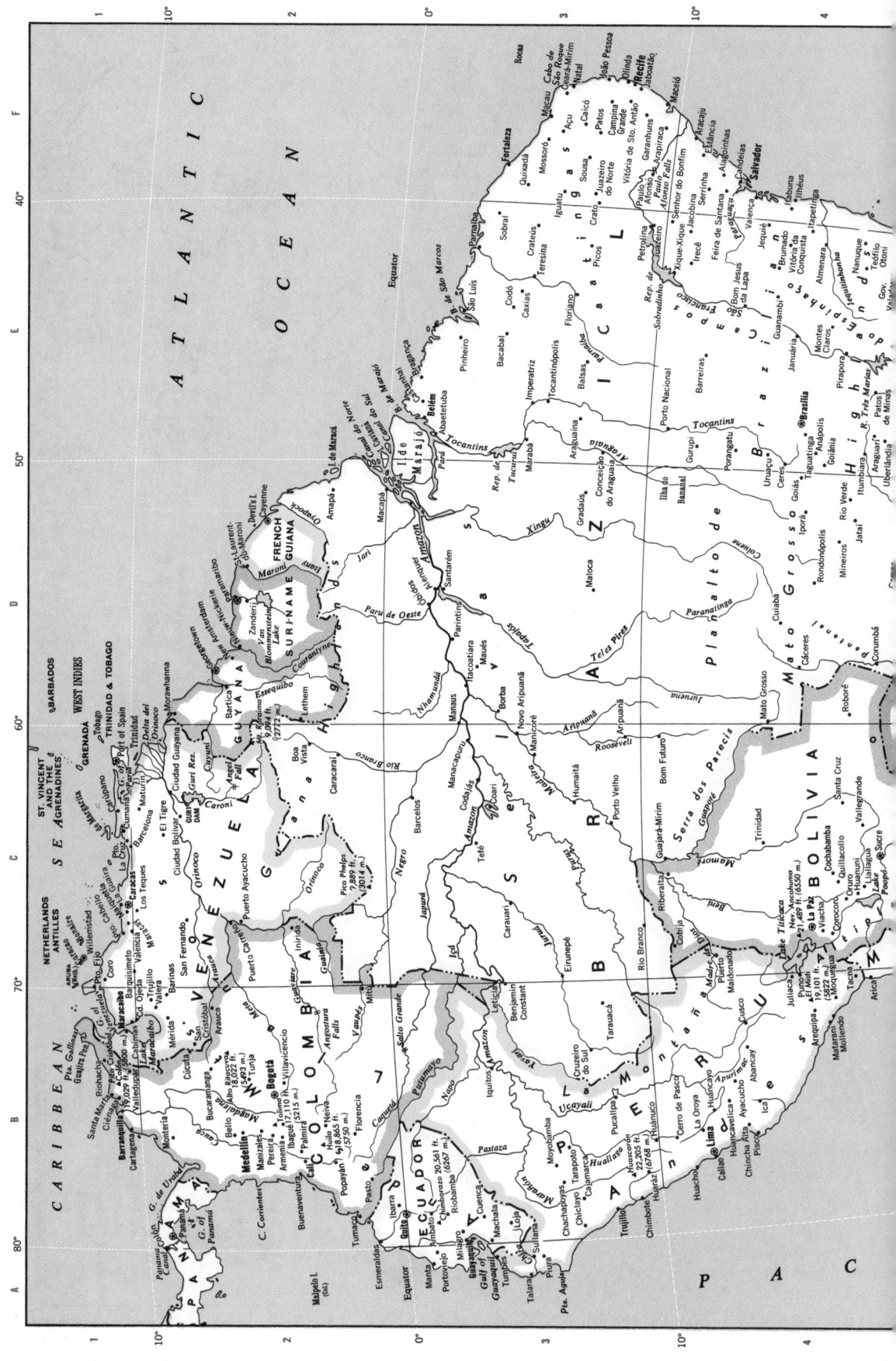

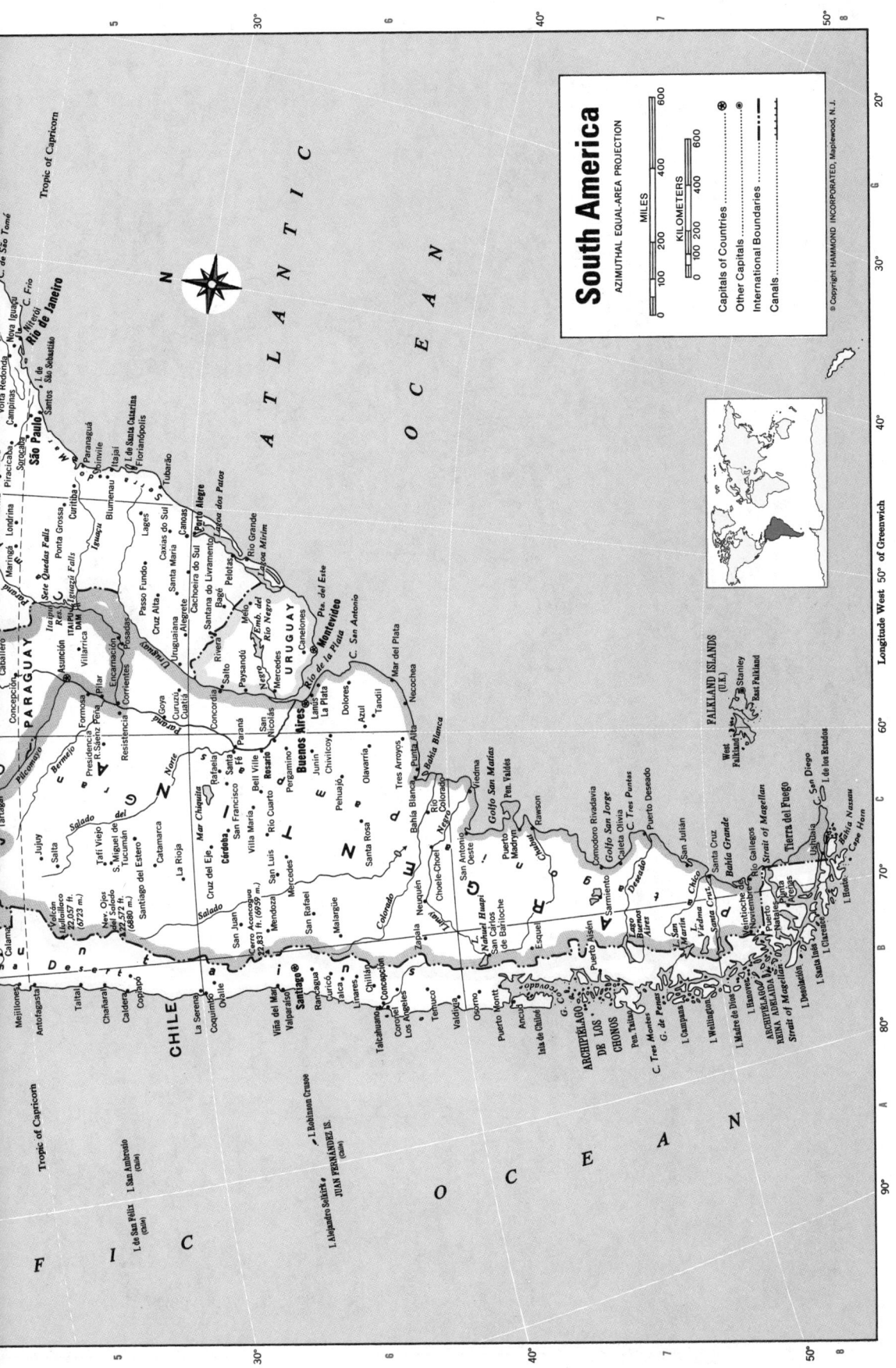

South America

AZIMUTHAL EQUAL-AREA PROJECTION

MILES
0   100   200   400   600

KILOMETERS
0   100 200   400   600

Capitals of Countries ....⊛
Other Capitals ....⊛
International Boundaries ....
Canals ....

® Copyright HAMMOND INCORPORATED, Maplewood, N.J.

Longitude West 50° of Greenwich

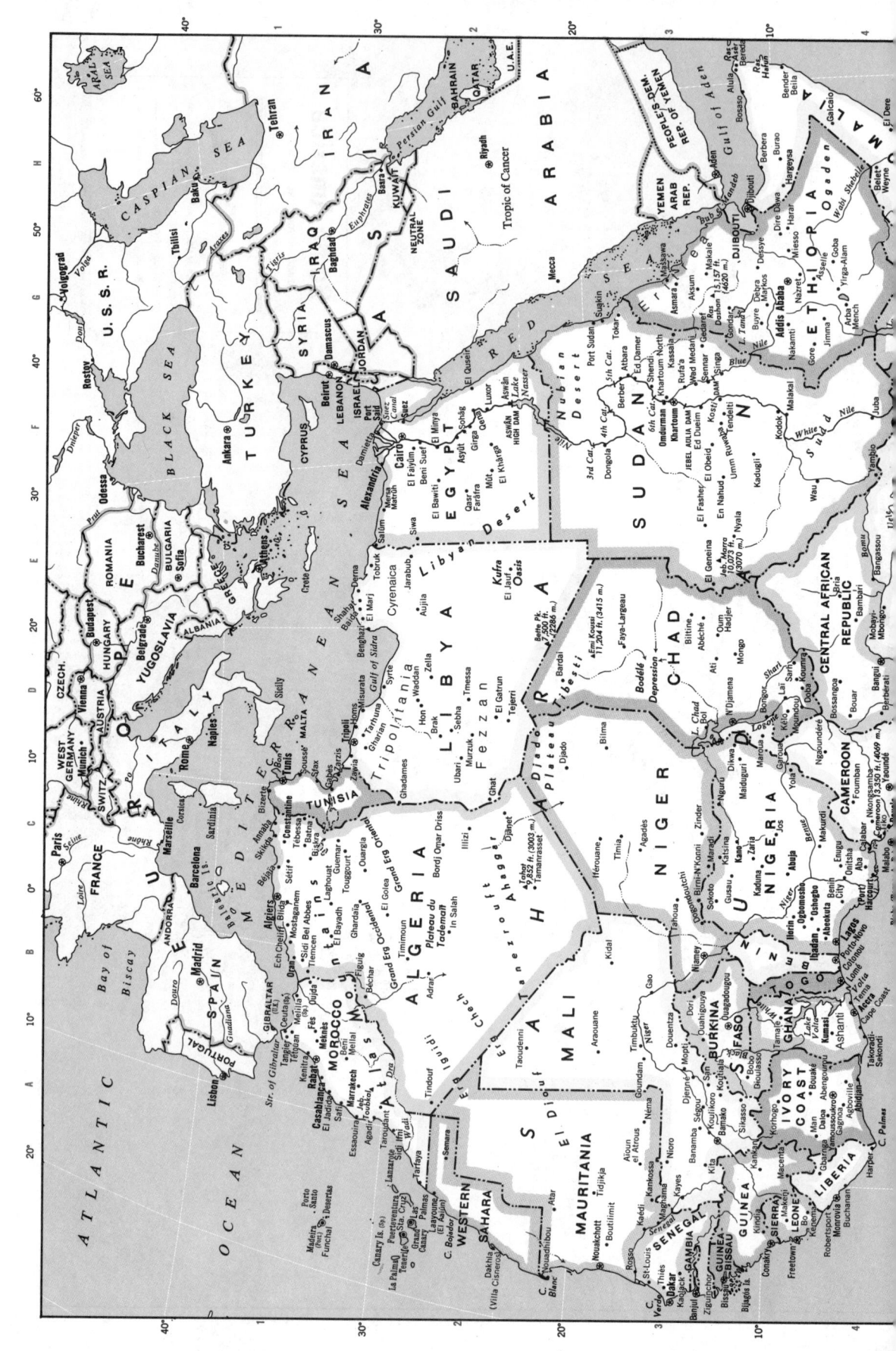

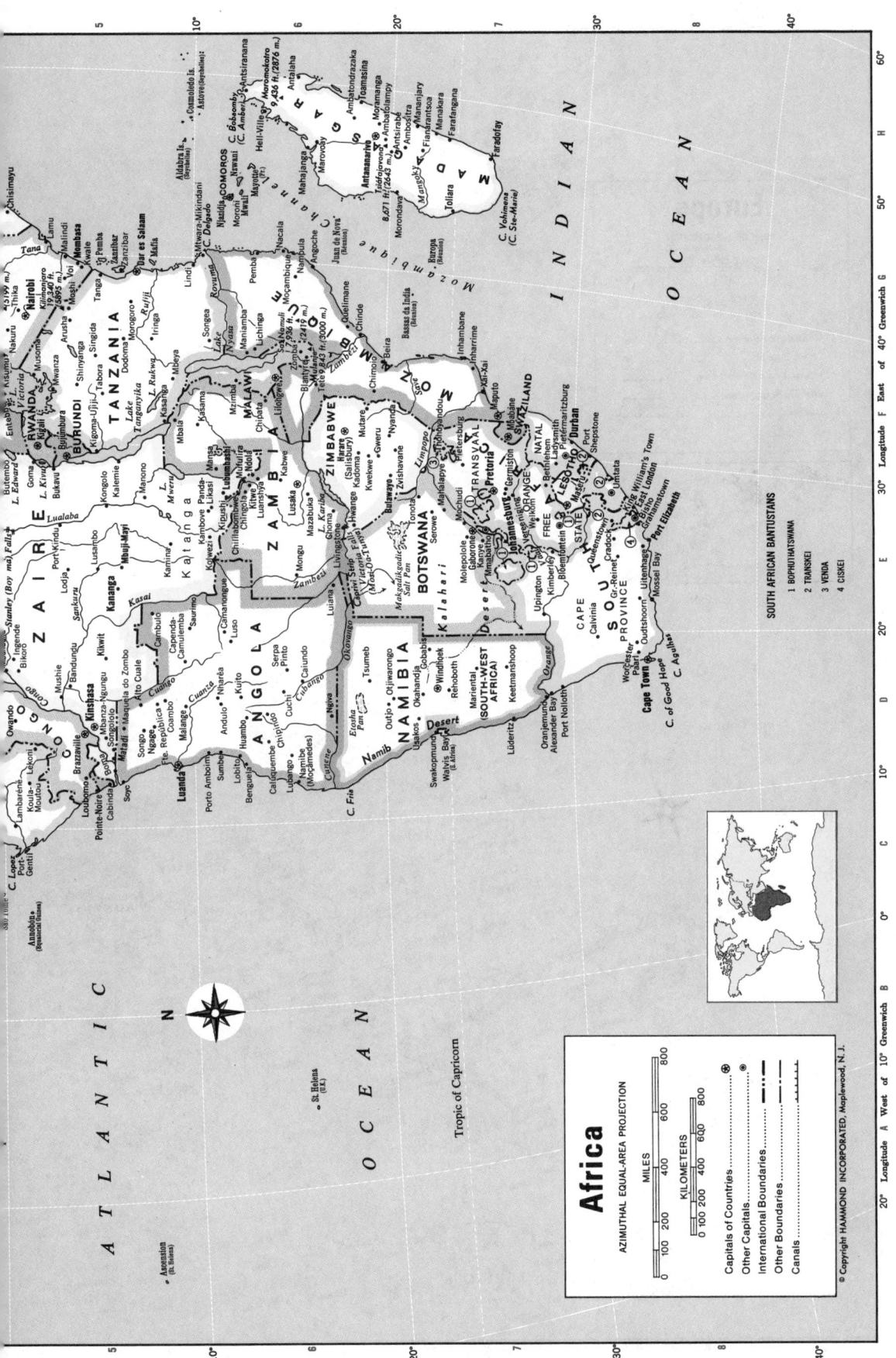

Europe

POLYCONIC PROJECTION

SCALE OF MILES

0 100 200 300 400

KILOMETERS

0 100 200 300 400

Capitals of Countries..........................⊛

Other Capitals.....................................◉

International Boundaries ....–·–·–·

Internal Boundaries ....–··–··–

Canals...

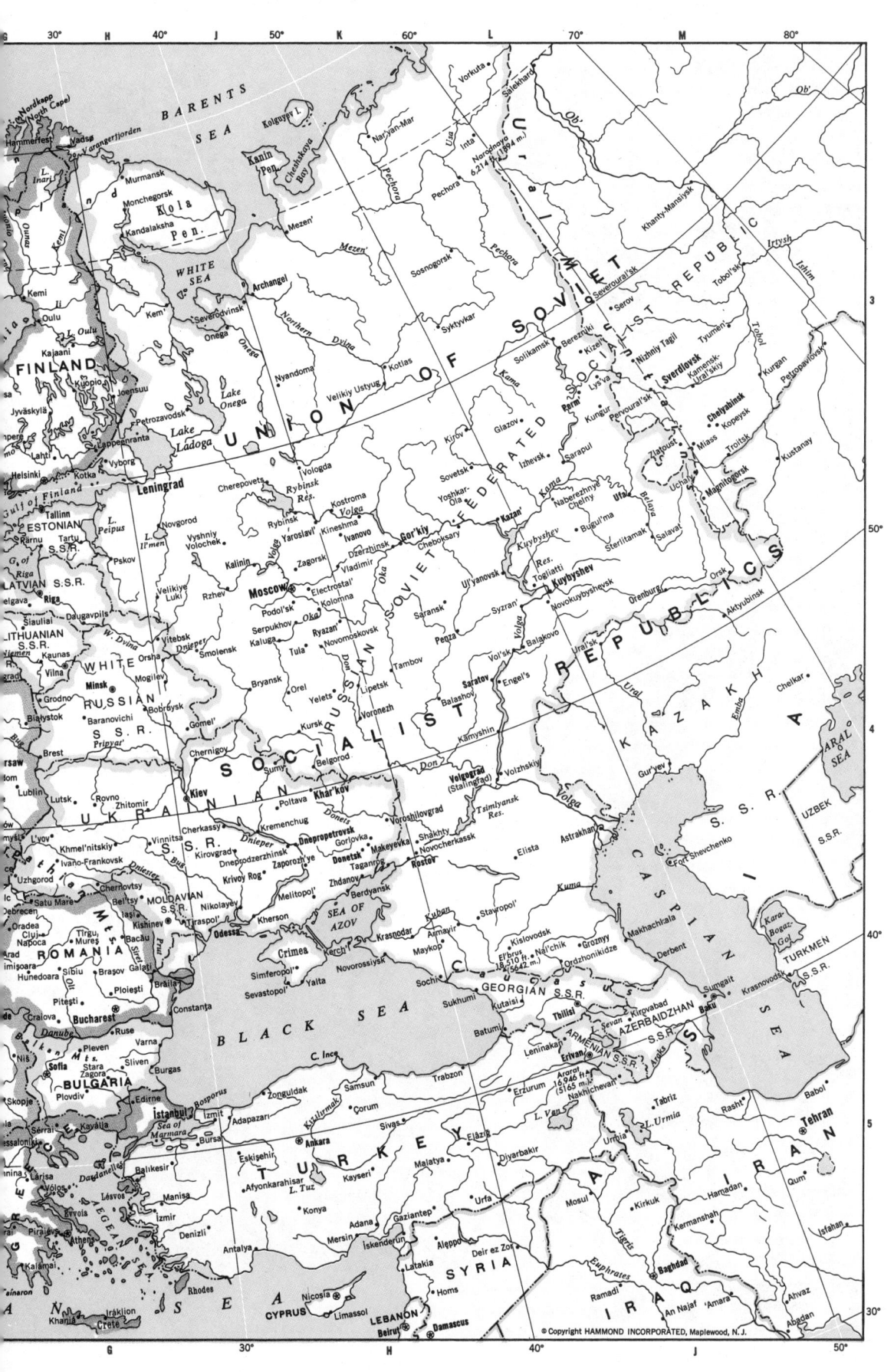

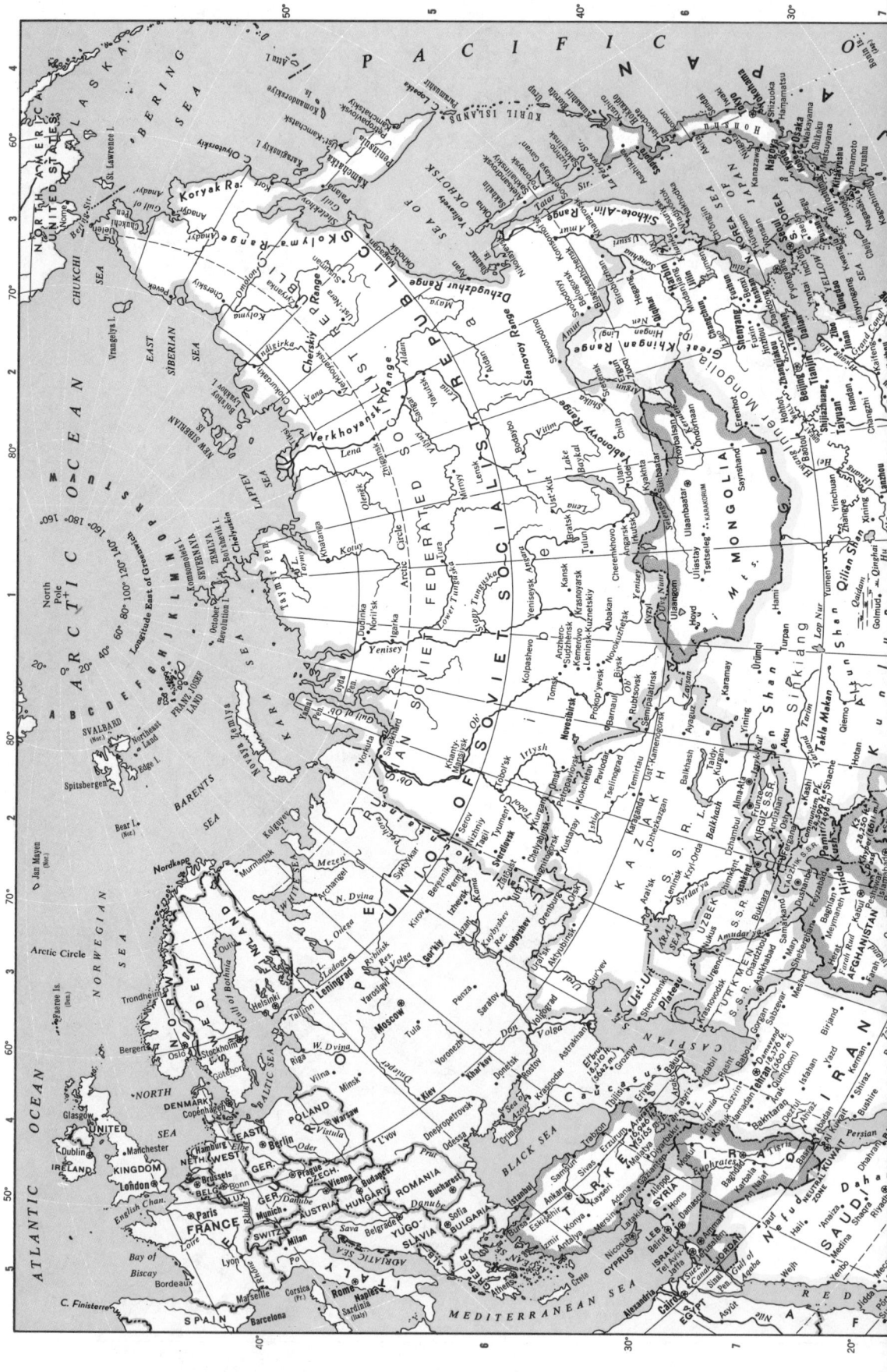

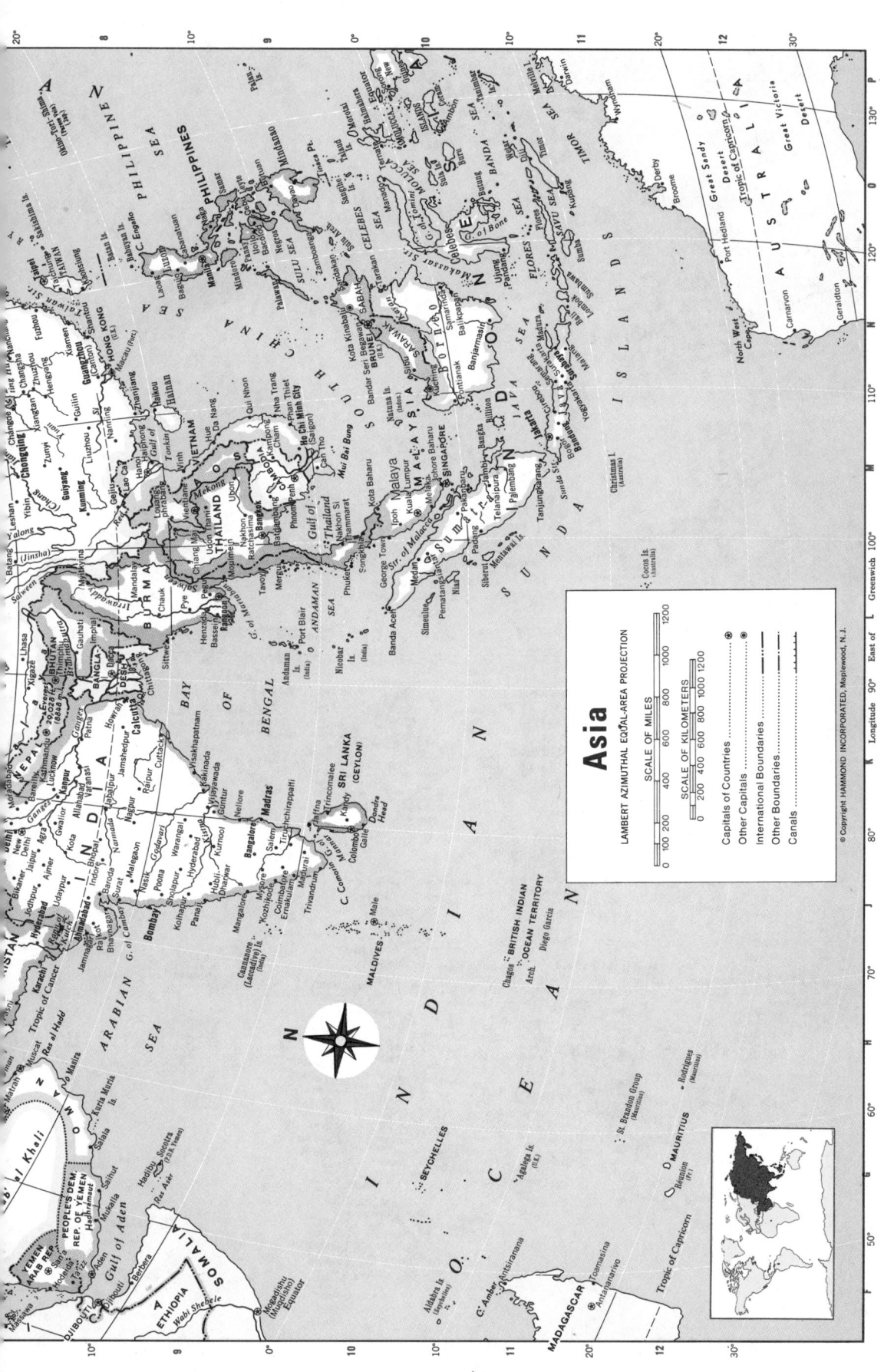

Asia

LAMBERT AZIMUTHAL EQUAL-AREA PROJECTION

SCALE OF MILES

0   100 200   400   600   800   1000 1200

SCALE OF KILOMETERS

0   200 400   600   800 1000 1200

Capitals of Countries .... ⊛
Other Capitals .... ⊛
International Boundaries ....
Other Boundaries ....
Canals ....

© Copyright HAMMOND INCORPORATED, Maplewood, N.J.

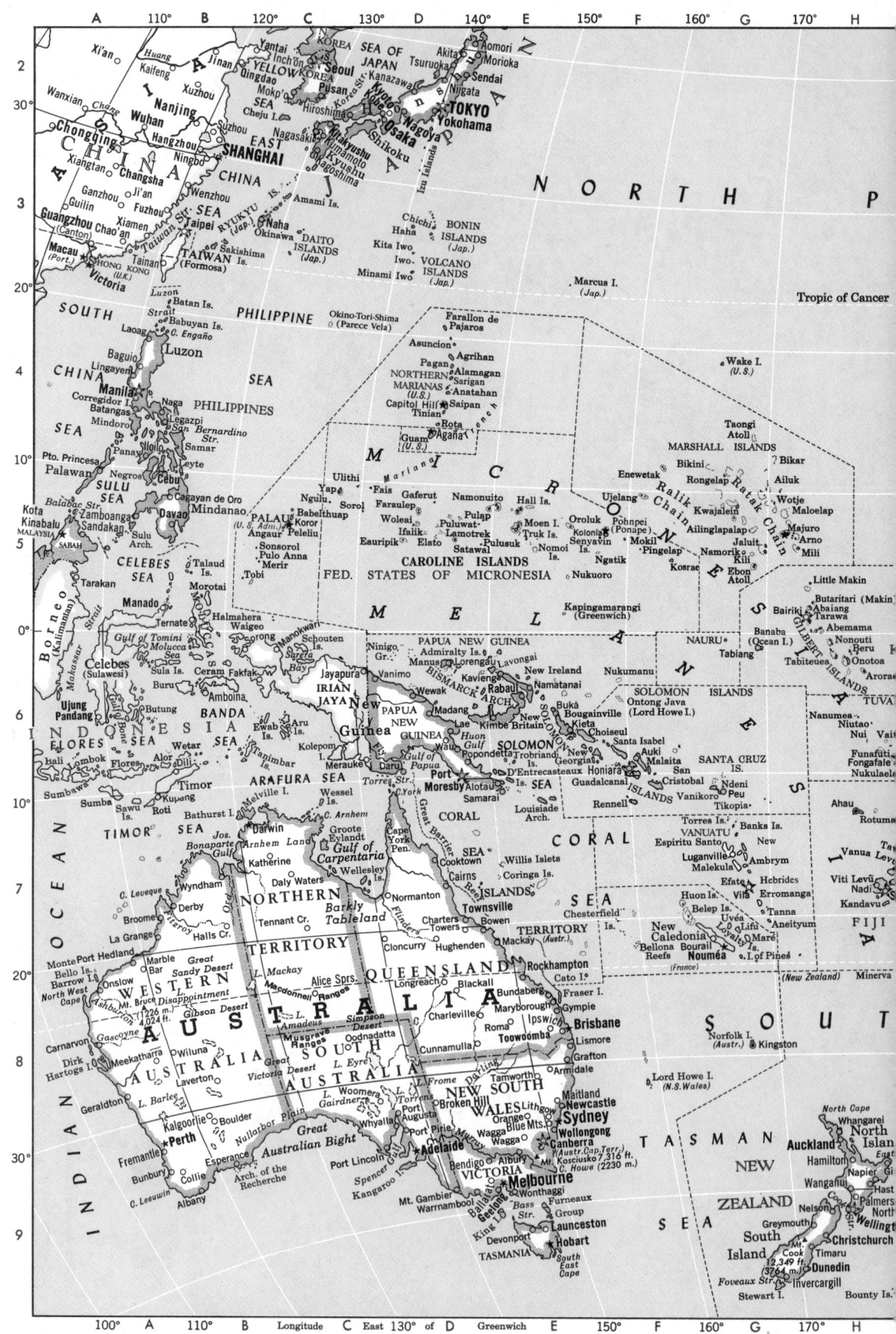

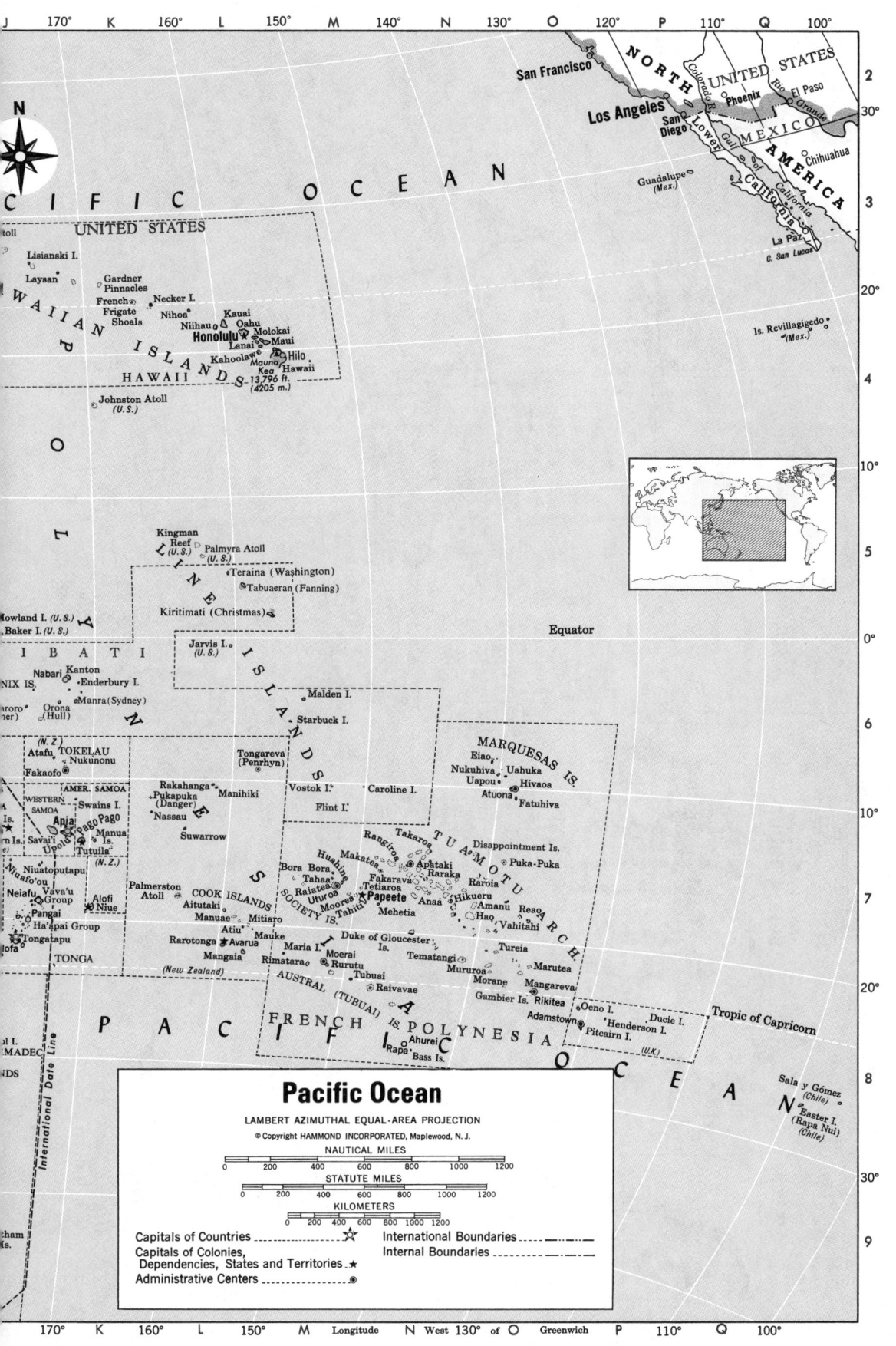

Pacific Ocean

LAMBERT AZIMUTHAL EQUAL-AREA PROJECTION

© Copyright HAMMOND INCORPORATED, Maplewood, N.J.

NAUTICAL MILES
0   200   400   600   800   1000   1200

STATUTE MILES
0   200   400   600   800   1000   1200

KILOMETERS
0   200   400   600   800   1000   1200

Capitals of Countries .... ☆
Capitals of Colonies,
  Dependencies, States and Territories .. ★
Administrative Centers .... ⊛

International Boundaries ___ ___ ___
Internal Boundaries ___ __ ___ __ ___

United States
POLYCONIC PROJECTION

SCALE OF MILES

Capitals of Countries ⊙
International Boundaries ---
State Capitals ⊚
State Boundaries ---
Copyright by C. S. HAMMOND & CO., N.Y.

Deputy District Attorney
San Mateo County District Attorney's Office
Consumer Fraud Unit
Hall of Justice and Records
401 Marshall Street
Redwood City, CA 94063
415-363-4656

Deputy District Attorney
Santa Barbara County District Attorney's Office
Consumer/Business Law Section
118 East Figueroa
Santa Barbara, CA 93101
805-963-6158

Director
Santa Clara County Department of Consumer Affairs
1553 Berger Drive
San Jose, CA 95112
408-299-4211

Deputy District Attorney
Santa Clara County District Attorney's Office
Consumer Fraud Unit
70 West Hedding Street, West Wing
San Jose, CA 95110
408-299-7435

Coordinator
Santa Cruz County District Attorney's Office
Division of Consumer Affairs
701 Ocean Street
Room 240
Santa Cruz, CA 95060
408-425-2054

Deputy District Attorney
Solano County District Attorney's Office
Consumer Affairs Unit
600 Union Avenue
Fairfield, CA 94533
707-429-6451

Consumer Affairs Director
Stanislaus County Office of Consumer Affairs
1100 H Street
2nd Floor
Modesto, CA 95354
209-571-6211

Deputy District Attorney
Stanislaus County District Attorney's Office
Consumer Fraud Unit
P.O. Box 442
Modesto, CA 95353
209-571-5550

Deputy District Attorney
Ventura County District Attorney's Office
Consumer and Environmental Protection Division
800 South Victoria Avenue
Ventura, CA 93009
805-654-3110

Deputy District Attorney
Yolo County District Attorney's Office
Consumer Fraud Division
P.O. Box 1247
Woodland, CA 95695
916-666-8180

City Offices
Supervising Deputy City Attorney
Los Angeles City Attorney's Office
Consumer Protection Section
200 North Main Street
1600 City Hall East
Los Angeles, CA 90012
213-485-4515

Deputy City Attorney
San Diego City Attorney's Office
Consumer Fraud Unit
Union Bank Building
525 B Street
Suite 2100
San Diego, CA 92101
619-236-6007

Consumer Affairs Specialist
Santa Monica City Attorney's Office
Consumer Division
1685 Main Street
Room 310
Santa Monica, CA 90401
213-458-8336

Colorado

State Offices
Office of Attorney General
Antitrust and Consumer Protection Enforcement Section
1525 Sherman Street
3rd Floor
Denver, CO 80203
303-866-3611

Consumer Specialist
Office of Attorney General
Consumer Protection Unit
1525 Sherman Street
Room 215
Denver, CO 80203
303-866-3611

Consumer and Food Specialist
Department of Agriculture
1525 Sherman Street
4th Floor
Denver, CO 80203
303-866-3561

County Offices

District Attorney
Archuleta, LaPlata and San Juan Counties District
Attorney's Office
P.O. Box 3455
Durango, CO 81302
303-247-8850

District Attorney
Boulder County District Attorney's Consumer Office
P.O. Box 471
Boulder, CO 80306
303-441-3700

Executive Director
Denver County District Attorney's Consumer Fraud
Office
303 West Colfax
Suite 1308
Denver, CO 80204
303-575-3555 (inquiries)
303-575-3557 (complaints)

Chief Deputy District Attorney
El Paso and Teller Counties District Attorney's
Consumer Office
Economic Crime Division
326 South Tejon
Colorado Springs, CO 80903
303-520-6002

Investigator
Larimer County District Attorney's Office
Rocky Mountain Bank Building
P.O. Box 1489
Fort Collins, CO 80522
303-221-7200

District Attorney
Pueblo County District Attorney's Consumer Office
Courthouse
Tenth and Main Streets
Pueblo, CO 81003
303-544-0075

District Attorney
Weld County District Attorney's Consumer Office
P.O. Box 1167
Greeley, CO 80632
303-356-4000 ext. 4734

Connecticut

State Offices

Commissioner
Department of Consumer Protection
State Office Building
165 Capitol Avenue
Hartford, CT 06106
203-566-4999
800-842-2649 (toll free—Connecticut only)

Assistant Attorney General
Office of Attorney General
Antitrust Consumer Protection
30 Trinity Street
Hartford, CT 06106
203-566-5374

City Office

Director
Middletown Office of Consumer Protection
City Hall
Middletown, CT 06457
203-344-3400

Delaware

State Offices

Director
Division of Consumer Affairs
Department of Community Affairs
820 North French Street
4th Floor
Wilmington, DE 19801
302-571-3250

Deputy in Charge
Economic Crime/Consumer Rights Division
820 North French Street
Wilmington, DE 19801
302-571-3849

District of Columbia

Director
District of Columbia
Department of Consumer and Regulatory Affairs
614 H Street, NW
Washington, DC 20001
202-727-7000

Florida

State Offices

Director
Division of Consumer Services
508 Mayo Building
Tallahassee, FL 32301
904-488-2221
800-342-2176 (toll free—Florida only)

Assistant Attorney General
Office of Attorney General
Consumer Protection Division
State Capitol
Tallahassee, FL 32301
904-488-9105

Branch Office
Consumer Counsel
Office of Attorney General
Consumer Protection Division
401 NW Second Avenue
Suite 450
Miami, FL 33128
305-377-5619

County Offices

Assistant State Attorney
Office of State Attorney
Brevard County Consumer Fraud Division
County Courthouse
Titusville, FL 32780
305-269-8112

Director
Broward County Consumer Affairs Division
115 South Andrews Avenue
Room 119
Fort Lauderdale, FL 33301
305-357-6030

Director
Metropolitan Dade County Consumer Protection
  Division
44 West Flagler Street
Suite 2303
Miami, FL 33130
305-579-4222

Consumer Advocate
Metropolitan Dade County
111 Northwest First Street
17th Floor
Miami, FL 33128
305-375-4206

Chief
Office of State Attorney
Dade County Economic Crime Unit
1351 NW 12th Street
Miami, FL 33125
305-547-7041

Consumer Affairs Officer
Duval County Division of Consumer Affairs
Department of Human Resources
614 City Hall
Jacksonville, FL 32202
904-633-3429, 3940

Director
Hillsborough County Department of Consumer Affairs
412 East Madison Street
Room 1001
Tampa, FL 33602
813-272-6750

State Attorney for Manatee, Sarasota and DeSoto
  Counties
Office of State Attorney
2002 Ringling Boulevard
Sarasota, FL 33577
813-955-9310

Chief
Investigative Unit
Orange County Consumer Fraud Unit
P.O. Box 1673
250 North Orange Avenue
Orlando, FL 32802
305-420-3880

Director
Palm Beach County Department of Consumer Affairs
301 North Olive Avenue
Suite 301
West Palm Beach, FL 33401
305-837-2670

Citizens Intake
Office of State Attorney
P.O. Drawer 2905
West Palm Beach, FL 33402
305-837-3560

Administrator
Pasco County Consumer Affairs Division
7530 Little Road
New Port Richey, FL 33553
813-847-8110

Director
Pinellas County Office of Consumer Affairs
P.O. Box 5145
Largo, FL 34294
813-586-5402

Coordinator
Seminole County Consumer Fraud Division
Office of State Attorney
P.O. Box 2112
Sanford, FL 32772-2114
305-322-7534

City Offices

Chairman
Lauderhill Consumer Affairs Committee
1176 NW 42nd Way
Lauderhill, FL 33313
305-583-1045

Chairman
Tamarac Board of Consumer Affairs
5811 NW 88th Avenue
Tamarac, FL 33321
305-722-5900 (ext. 26, 10:00–12:00 daily)

Georgia

State Offices

Administrator
Governor's Office of Consumer Affairs
2 Martin Luther King, Jr. Drive
Plaza Level—East Tower
Atlanta, GA 30334
404-656-3790
800-282-5808 (toll free—Georgia only)

Assistant Attorney General
Office of Attorney General
210 State Judicial Building
Atlanta, GA 30334
404-656-3345

Hawaii

State Office

Director
Department of Commerce and Consumer Affairs
Office of Consumer Protection
P.O. Box 3767
250 South King Street
Room 520
Honolulu, HI 96812
808-548-2560 (administrative and legal—Hawaii only)
808-548-2540 (complaints and investigations—Hawaii only)

Branch Office
Investigator
Department of Commerce and Consumer Affairs
Office of Consumer Protection
75 Aupuni Street
Hilo, HI 96720
808-961-7433

Illinois

State Offices

Special Assistant to the Governor
Governor's Office of Citizen's Assistance
100 West Randolph Street
Chicago, IL 60601
312-793-2773

Assistant Attorney General and Chief
Office of Attorney General
Consumer Protection Division
500 South Second Street
Springfield, IL 62706
217-782-9011

Chief
Consumer Protection Division
Office of Attorney General
100 West Randolph
12th Floor
Chicago, IL 60601
312-917-3580

Regional Offices
Assistant Attorney General
Office of Attorney General
Carbondale Regional Office
626A East Walnut Street
Carbondale, IL 62901
618-457-3505

Assistant Attorney General
Office of Attorney General
Champaign Regional Office
34 Main Street
Champaign, IL 61820
217-333-7691

Assistant Attorney General
Office of Attorney General
Decatur Regional Office
140 South Water Street
Decatur, IL 62523
217-428-5076

Assistant Attorney General
Office of Attorney General
East St. Louis Regional Office
8712 State Street
East St. Louis, IL 62203

Assistant Attorney General
Office of Attorney General
Granite City Regional Office
1314 Niedringhaus
Granite City, IL 62040
618-877-0404

Assistant Attorney General
Office of Attorney General
Kankakee Regional Office
270 East Court Street
Kankakee, IL 60901
815-935-8500

Assistant Attorney General
Office of Attorney General
LaSalle Regional Office
143 Gooding
LaSalle, IL 61301
815-224-4861

Assistant Attorney General
Office of Attorney General
Mt. Vernon Regional Office
718 East Main
Mt. Vernon, IL 62864
618-242-8200

Assistant Attorney General
Office of Attorney General
Peoria Regional Office
323 Main Street
Peoria, IL 61602
309-671-3191

Assistant Attorney General
Office of Attorney General
Quincy Regional Office
523 Main Street
Quincy, IL 62301
217-223-2221

Assistant Attorney General
Office of Attorney General
Rockford Regional Office
110 North Church
Rockford, IL 61101
815-987-7580

Assistant Attorney General
Office of Attorney General
Rock Island Regional Office
310 20th Street
Rock Island, IL 61201
309-793-0950

Assistant Attorney General
Office of Attorney General
West Frankfort Regional Office
222 East Main Street
West Frankfort, IL 62896
618-937-6453

Branch Offices
Assistant Attorney General
Office of Attorney General
Addison Regional Office
19 West 340 Lake Street
Addison, IL 60101
312-628-1912

Office of Attorney General
Community Center
1616 North Arlington Heights Road
Arlington Heights, IL 60004
312-259-7730 (Wednesdays only)

Special Assistant to the Attorney General
Office of Attorney General
Consumer Protection Division
McClean County Chamber of Commerce Building
210 Southeast Street
Bloomington, IL 61701
309-829-6344

Consumer Protection Division
Office of Attorney General
520 Jackson Street
Charleston, IL 61920
217-345-5651

Assistant Attorney General
Chicago North, Regional Office
Office of Attorney General
Office of Citizen Advocacy
2329 West Chicago Avenue
Chicago, IL 60622
312-278-0403

Office Director
Chicago South, Regional Office
Office of Attorney General
Office of Citizen Advocacy
7906 South Cottage Grove
Chicago, IL 60619
312-488-2600

Indiana

State Office

Chief Counsel and Director
Office of Attorney General
Consumer Protection Division
219 State House
Indianapolis, IN 46204
317-232-6330, 6331
800-382-5516 (toll free—Indiana only)

County Offices
Director
Lake County Prosecutor's Office
Consumer Protection Division
2293 North Main Street
Crown Point, IN 46307
219-738-9055

Marion County Prosecuting Attorney
560 City-County Building
Indianapolis, IN 46204
317-236-3522

Vanderburgh County Prosecuting Attorney
First Judicial Circuit
Courts Building
Civic Center Complex
Room 220
Evansville, IN 47708
812-426-5150

City Office
Director
Gary Office of Consumer Affairs
Annex East
1100 Massachusetts Street
Gary, IN 46407
219-886-0145

Iowa

State Offices

Assistant Attorney General
Office of Attorney General
Consumer Protection Division
1300 East Walnut Street
2nd Floor
Des Moines, IA 50319
515-281-5926

Iowa Citizens' Aide/Ombudsman
515 East 12th Street
Des Moines, IA 50319
515-281-3592
800-358-5510 (toll free—Iowa only)

Kansas

State Office

Deputy Attorney General and Chief
Office of Attorney General
Consumer Protection and Antitrust Division
Kansas Judicial Center
2nd Floor
Topeka, KS 66612
913-296-3751
800-432-2310 (toll free—Kansas only)

County Offices

Assistant District Attorney and Head
Johnson County District Attorney's Office Consumer
   Fraud Division
Johnson County Courthouse, Box 728
Olathe, KS 66061
913-782-5000 (ext. 318)

Director
Sedgwick County District Attorney's Office
Consumer Fraud and Economic Crime Division
Sedgwick County Courthouse
Wichita, KS 67203
316-268-7921

Assistant District Attorney
Shawnee County District Attorney's Office
Shawnee County Courthouse
Room 212
Topeka, KS 66603
913-295-4330

City Office

Assistant City Attorney
City Attorney's Office
Topeka Consumer Protection Division
215 East Seventh Street
Topeka, KS 66603–3979
913-295-3883

Kentucky

State Office

Director
Office of Attorney General
Consumer Protection Division
209 Saint Clair Street
Frankfort, KY 40601
502-564-2200
800-432-9257 (toll free—Kentucky only)

County Office

Administrator
Jefferson County Consumer Protection Department
517 Court Place
Room 606
Louisville, KY 40202
502-581-6280

Louisiana

State Offices

Director
State Office of Consumer Protection
P.O. Box 94455
Baton Rouge, LA 70804
504-925-4401
800-272-8478 (toll free—Louisiana only)

Chief
Office of Attorney General
Consumer Protection Section
1885 Wooddale Boulevard
Suite 1208
Baton Rouge, LA 70806
504-925-4181

Assistant Commissioner
Department of Agriculture
Office of Marketing
P.O. Box 44184
Capitol Station
Baton Rouge, LA 70804
504-292-3600

Branch Office

Assistant Attorney General
Office of Attorney General
Consumer Protection Section
234 Loyola Avenue
7th Floor
New Orleans, LA 70112
504-568-5575

County Office

Director
Jefferson Parish District Attorney's Office
Consumer Protection and Commercial Fraud Division
200 Huey P. Long Avenue
Gretna, LA 70053
504-361-8139

Maine

State Offices

Chief
Office of Attorney General
Consumer and Antitrust Division
State House Station No. Six
Augusta, ME 04333
207-289-3716 (9:00–10:00 A.M.)

Superintendent
Bureau of Consumer Credit Protection
Department of Business, Occupational, and Professional
  Regulation
State House Station No. 35
Augusta, ME 04333
207-289-3731

Maryland
State Offices
Director
Motor Vehicle Administration
Office of Licensing and Consumer Services
6601 Ritchie Highway, NE
Glen Burnie, MD 21062
301-768-7420

Director
Office of Attorney General
Consumer and Investor Affairs and Chief, Consumer
  Protection Division
Seven North Calvert Street
Baltimore, MD 21202
301-528-8662 (8:30–4:30)

Branch Offices
Director
Office of Attorney General
Western Maryland Branch Office
Consumer Protection Division
138 East Antietam Street
Suite 210
Hagerstown, MD 21740
301-791-4780

Consumer Specialist
Office of Attorney General
Eastern Shore Branch Office
Consumer Protection Division
State Office Complex
Salisbury, MD 21801
301-546-4407

County Offices
Administrator
Howard County Office of Consumer Affairs
Carroll Building
3450 Courthouse Drive
Ellicott City, MD 21043
301-922-2176

Executive Director
Montgomery County Office of Consumer Affairs
100 Maryland Avenue
3rd Floor
Rockville, MD 20850
301-251-7373

Executive Director
Prince George's County Consumer Protection
  Commission
1142 County Administration Building
Upper Marlboro, MD 20772
301-952-4700

Massachusetts
State Offices
Executive Office of Consumer Affairs and Business
  Regulation
One Ashburton Place
Room 1411
Boston, MA 02108
617-727-7780 (information and referral)

Chief
Department of Attorney General
Consumer Protection Division
One Ashburton Place
19th Floor
Boston, MA 02108
617-727-8400

Branch Offices
Assistant Attorney General
Department of Attorney General
Consumer Protection Division
436 Dwight Street
Springfield, MA 01103
413-785-1951

County Offices
District Attorney's Office
Franklin County Consumer Protection Agency
55 Federal Street
Greenfield, MA 01301
413-774-5102

Director
Hampden County Consumer Action Center
P.O. Box 1449
17 Wilbrahan Road
Springfield, MA 01101
413-737-4376

Director
Hampshire County District Attorney's Office
Consumer Protection Agency
Courthouse
15 Gothic Street
Northampton, MA 01060
413-584-1597

Project Coordinator
Worcester County Consumer Rights Project
332 Main Street
Suite 320
Worcester, MA 01608
617-752-3410 (Monday–Friday 1:00–4:00 P.M.)

City Offices
Commissioner
Boston Mayor's Office of Consumer Affairs
1 City Hall Plaza
Room 703
Boston, MA 02201
617-725-3320

Director
Consumer Division
Lowell Community Team Work, Inc.
167 Dutton Street
Lowell, MA 01852
617-452-0908

Michigan

State Offices

Assistant Attorney General
Office of Attorney General
Consumer Protection Division
670 Law Building
Lansing, MI 48913
517-373-1140

Executive Director
Michigan Consumers Council
414 Hollister Building
106 West Allegan Street
Lansing, MI 48933
517-373-0947

Director
Bureau of Automotive Regulation
Michigan Department of State
Lansing, MI 48918
517-373-7857
800-292-4204 (toll free—Michigan only)

County Offices

Prosecuting Attorney
Bay County Consumer Protection Unit
Bay County Building
Bay City, MI 48708
517-893-3594

Prosecuting Attorney
Office of Prosecuting Attorney
Genesee County Consumer Affairs Division
2065 South Center Road
Burton, MI 48529
313-257-3161

Chief
Macomb County Office of Prosecuting Attorney
Consumer Fraud Unit
Macomb Court Building
6th Floor
Mt. Clemens, MI 48043
313-469-5350

Director
Washtenaw County Consumer Services
4133 Washtenaw Road
Ann Arbor, MI 48107
313-971-6054

City Office
Director
City of Detroit Consumer Affairs Department
1600 Cadillac Tower
Detroit, MI 48226
313-224-3508

Minnesota

State Office

Director
Office of Attorney General
Office of Consumer Services
124 Ford Building
117 University Avenue
St. Paul, MN 55155
612-296-2331

Branch Office
Regional Supervisor
Office of Attorney General
Office of Consumer Services
320 West Second Street
Duluth, MN 55802
218-723-4891

County Office
Hennepin County Attorney's Office Citizen Protection Unit
Legal Services Adviser
C2000 County Government Center
Minneapolis, MN 55487
612-348-4528

City Office
Director
Minneapolis Department of Licenses and Consumer Services
Consumer Affairs Division
101A City Hall
Minneapolis, MN 55415
612-348-2080

Assistant Attorney General
Office of Attorney General
Skokie Regional Office
4738 West Dempster
Skokie, IL 60076
312-673-2540

Assistant Attorney General
Office of Attorney General
Waukegan Regional Office
32 North Utica
Waukegan, IL 60085
312-336-2207

County Offices

Supervisor
Consumer Fraud Division
Cook County Office of State Attorney
500 Daley Center
Room 303
Chicago, IL 60602
312-443-4364

State's Attorney
Madison County Office of State Attorney
103 Purcell Street
3rd Floor
Edwardsville, IL 62025
618-692-6280

Director
Consumer Protection Division
Rock Island County State Attorney's Office
County Court House
Rock Island, IL 61201
309-786-4451 (ext. 228)

City Offices
Commissioner
Chicago Department of Consumer Services
121 North LaSalle Street
Room 808
Chicago, IL 60602
312-744-4090

Administrator
Des Plaines Consumer Protection Commission
1420 Miner Street
Des Plaines, IL 60016
312-391-5363

Mississippi

State Offices

Assistant Attorney General and Chief
Office of Attorney General
Consumer Protection Division
P.O. Box 220
Jackson, MS 39205
601-359-3095

Director
Department of Agriculture and Commerce
Consumer Protection Division
P.O. Box 1609
High and President Streets
Jackson, MS 39215
601-359-3648
800-222-7622 (toll free—Mississippi only)

Missouri

State Offices

Director
Department of Economic Development
P.O. Box 1157
Jefferson City, MO 65102
314-751-4996

Chief Counsel
Office of Attorney General
Trade Offense Division
P.O. Box 899
Jefferson City, MO 65102
314-751-2616
800-372-8222 (toll free—Missouri only)

Branch Offices
Office of Attorney General
Trade Offense Division
Penn Tower
31 Broadway
Suite 609
Kansas City, MO 64111
816-531-4207

Assistant Attorney General
Office of Attorney General
Trade Offense Division
111 North Seventh Street
Suite 903
St. Louis, MO 63101
314-444-6815

Montana

State Office

Department of Commerce
Consumer Affairs Unit
1424 Ninth Avenue
Helena, MT 59620
406-444-4312

County Office

Missoula County Attorney
County Courthouse
Missoula, MT 59802
406-721-5700

Nebraska

State Office

Assistant Attorney General
Department of Justice
Consumer Protection Division
605 South 14th Street
Lincoln, NE 68509
402-471-2682

County Office

Director
Douglas County Attorney's Office
Consumer Fraud Division
909 Omaha-Douglas Civic Center
Omaha, NE 68183
402-444-7625

Nevada

State Office

Commissioner of Consumer Affairs
Department of Commerce
State Mail Room Complex
Las Vegas, NV 89158
702-386-5293

Branch Office
Investigator
Department of Commerce
Consumer Affairs Division
201 Nye Building
Capitol Complex
Carson City, NV 86710
702-885-4340
800-992-0900 (ext. 4340, toll free—Nevada only)

County Office

Investigator
Washoe County District Attorney's Office
P.O. Box 11130
Reno, NV 89520
702-785-5652

New Hampshire

State Office

Chief
Office of Attorney General
Consumer Protection and Antitrust Division
State House Annex
Concord, NH 03301
603-271-3641

New Jersey

State Offices

Director
Division of Consumer Affairs
Department of Law and Public Safety
1100 Raymond Boulevard
Room 504
Newark, NJ 07102
201-648-4010

Acting Public Advocate
CN 850
Justice Complex
Trenton, NJ 08625
609-292-7087

Deputy Attorney General
1100 Raymond Boulevard
Room 335
Newark, NJ 07102
201-548-8510

New Jersey Office of Consumer Protection
1100 Raymond Boulevard
Room 405
Newark, NJ 07102
201-648-4019

County Offices

Director
Atlantic County Consumer Affairs
1333 Atlantic Avenue
8th Floor
Atlantic City, NJ 08401
609-345-6700

Director
Bergen County Consumer Affairs
355 Main Street
Hackensack, NJ 07601
201-646-2650

Director
Burlington County Office of Consumer Affairs
49 Rancocas Road
Mount Holly, NJ 08060
609-261-5054

Director
Cape May County Consumer Affairs
DN-310 Central Mail Room
Cape May Court House
Cape May, NJ 08210
609-465-7111 (ext. 206)

Director
Cumberland County Consumer Affairs
788 East Commerce Street
Bridgeton, NJ 08302
609-451-8000

Director
Essex County Consumer Services
900 Bloomfield Avenue
Verona, NJ 07044
201-226-1571

Director
Gloucester County Consumer Affairs
The Cotton Building
One South Broad Street, Box 337
Woodbury, NJ 08096
609-853-3349

Counsel
Hudson County Consumer Affairs
County Administration Building
595 Newark Avenue
Jersey City, NJ 07306
201-795-6462, 6295, 6296, 6297

Director
Hunterdon County Consumer Affairs
P.O. Box 125
Stanton, NJ 08885
201-236-2249

Division Chief
Mercer County Consumer Affairs
640 South Broad Street
Trenton, NJ 08650
609-989-6671

Director
Middlesex County Consumer Affairs
841 Georges Road
North Brunswick, NJ 08902
201-745-4242

Director
Monmouth County Consumer Affairs
P.O. Box 1255
Hall of Records Annex
Main Street
Freehold, NJ 07728
201-431-7900

Director
Morris County Consumer Affairs
Court House
32 Washington Street
Morristown, NJ 07960
201-829-8123

Director
Ocean County Consumer Affairs
C.N. 2191, County Administration Building
Room 203-2
Toms River, NJ 08753
201-929-2105
609-693-5011

Director
Passaic County Consumer Affairs
County Administration Building
309 Pennsylvania Avenue
Paterson, NJ 07503
201-881-4499, 4549

Director
Somerset County Consumer Affairs
P.O. Box 3000
County Administration Building
Somerville, NJ 08876
201-231-7000 (ext. 7400)

Director
Union County Consumer Affairs
P.O. Box 186
300 North Avenue East
Westfield, NJ 07090
201-233-0502

Director
Warren County Consumer Affairs
Court House Annex
Belvedere, NJ 07823
201-475-5361 (ext. 353)

City Offices
Director
Belleville Consumer Affairs
Municipal Building
Belleville, NJ 07109
201-450-3399

Director
Brick Consumer Affairs
Municipal Building
401 Chambers Bridge Road
Brick, NJ 08723
201-477-3000 (ext. 260)

Cedar Grove Consumer Affairs
123 Tierney Drive
Cedar Grove, NJ 07009
201-239-8725

Director
Cinnaminson Consumer Affairs
Municipal Building
1621 Riverton Road
Cinnaminson, NJ 08077
(609)-829-6000

Director
Clark Consumer Affairs
Municipal Building
Westfield Avenue
Clark, NJ 07066
201-388-3600

Clifton Consumer Affairs
City Hall
900 Clifton Avenue
Clifton, NJ 07013
201-473-2600 (ext. 297)

Director
East Brunswick Consumer Affairs
Jean Walling Civic Center
East Brunswick, NJ 08816
201-390-6954

East Orange Community Development Corporation
490 Main Street
East Orange, NJ 07017
201-266-5315

Director
Edison Consumer Affairs
Municipal Building
Edison, NJ 08817
201-287-0900 (ext. 234)

Director
Elizabeth Consumer Affairs
City Hall
60 West Scott Place
Elizabeth, NJ 07201
201-820-4183

Director
Fort Lee Consumer Protection Board
Borough Hall
309 Main Street
Fort Lee, NJ 07024
201-592-3579
201-947-5235

Director
Freehold Consumer Affairs
Municipal Plaza
Schanck Road
Freehold, NJ 07728
201-431-7900

Director
Garwood Consumer Affairs
Borough Hall
Center Street
Garwood, NJ 07027
201-789-0689

Director
Glen Rock Consumer Affairs
Borough Hall
Harding Plaza
Glen Rock, NJ 07452
201-447-2555

Director
Hackensack Consumer Affairs
Municipal Building
65 Central Avenue
Hackensack, NJ 07602
201-342-3000 (ext. 216)

Director
Hoboken Consumer Affairs
City Hall
Washington Street
Hoboken, NJ 07030
201-420-2038

Jersey City Consumer Affairs
415 Marin Boulevard
Room 19
Jersey City, NJ 07302
201-547-4663

Director
Kearny Consumer Affairs
26 North Midland Avenue
Kearny, NJ 07032
201-991-9282

Director
Livingston Consumer Affairs
Township Hall
357 South Livingston Avenue
Livingston, NJ 07039
201-992-2244

Lodi Consumer Affairs
Borough Hall
1 Memorial Drive
Lodi, NJ 07644
201-365-4039 (ext. 234)

Director
Middlesex Borough Consumer Affairs
Middlesex, NJ 08846
201-356-8090

Montclair Neighborhood Development Corporation
228 Bloomfield Avenue
Montclair, NJ 07042
201-744-9094

Mountainside Consumer Affairs
Municipal Building
Mountainside, NJ 07092
201-232-6600

Manager
Newark Office of Consumer Services
City Hall
920 Broad Street
Room B-4
Newark, NJ 07102
201-733-8000

New Milford Consumer Affairs
Borough Hall
930 River Road
New Milford, NJ 07640
201-262-6100

Director
Nutley Consumer Affairs
City Hall
228 Chestnut Street
Nutley, NJ 07110
201-667-3300 (ext. 227)

Old Bridge Township
1 Old Bridge Plaza
Old Bridge, NJ 08857
201-721-5600 (ext. 202)

Director
Paramus Consumer Affairs
Borough Hall
Jockish Square
Paramus, NJ 07652
201-265-8129

Director
Parsippany Consumer Affairs
Municipal Building
1001 Parsippany Boulevard
Parsippany, NJ 07054
201-263-7152

Director
Perth Amboy Consumer Affairs
City Hall
44 Market Street
Perth Amboy, NJ 08861
201-826-0290 (ext. 61)

Director
**City of Plainfield, Division of Community Relations
   and Social Services**
City Hall Annex
510 Watchtung Avenue
Plainfield, NJ 07060
201-753-3519

Rochelle Park Township Consumer Affairs
127 Chestnut Street
Rochelle Park, NJ 07662
201-843-7862, 7866

Director
Secaucus Department of Consumer Affairs
Municipal Building
1203 Paterson Plank Road
Secaucus, NJ 07094
201-330-2000

CALA Officer
Summit Consumer Affairs
City Hall
512 Springfield Avenue
Summit, NJ 07901
201-273-6474

Director
Teaneck Consumer Affairs
Municipal Building
818 Teaneck Road
Teaneck, NJ 07666
201-837-1600 (ext. 14)

Director
Union City Consumer Affairs
507 26th Street
Union City, NJ 07087
201-330-3816

Director
Union Township Consumer Affairs
Municipal Building
1976 Morris Avenue
Union, NJ 07083
201-688-2800 (ext. 16)

Director
Wayne Township Consumer Affairs
Municipal Building
475 Valley Road
Wayne, NJ 07470
201-694-1800 (ext. 246)

Weehawken Consumer Affairs
City Hall
400 Park Avenue
Weehawken, NJ 07087
201-867-1715 (ext. 230)

Director
West New York Consumer Affairs
Municipal Building
428 60th Street
West New York, NJ 07093
201-861-7000 (ext. 230)

Director
West Orange Consumer Affairs
Municipal Building
66 Main Street
West Orange, NJ 07052
201-325-4121

Director
Wildwood Action Line
4400 New Jersey Avenue
Wildwood, NJ 08260
609-729-4444

Director
Willingboro Consumer Affairs
Municipal Complex
Salem Road
Willingboro, NJ 08046
609-877-2200 (ext. 221)

Woodbridge Township Consumer Affairs
Municipal Building
One Main Street
Woodbridge, NJ 07095
201-634-4500 (ext. 231)

New Mexico

State Office

Director
**Office of Attorney General
Consumer and Economic Crime Division**
P.O. Drawer 1508
Santa Fe, NM 87504
505-827-6910

County Office

Director
**Bernatillo County District
Consumer Affairs Division**
Attorney's Office
415 Tijeras, NW
Albuquerque, NM 87102
505-841-7200

New York

State Offices

Chairperson and Executive Director
New York State Consumer Protection Board
99 Washington Avenue
Albany, NY 12210
518-474-8583

Executive Director
New York State Consumer Protection Board
Two World Trade Center
Room 2508
25th Floor
New York, NY 10047
212-488-5666

Assistant Attorney General
Office of Attorney General
Bureau of Consumer Frauds and Protection
State Capitol
Albany, NY 12224
518-474-5481

Branch Offices
Assistant Attorney General
Office of Attorney General
Bureau of Consumer Frauds and Protection
59–61 Court Street
Binghamton, NY 13905
607-773-7798

Assistant Attorney General
Office of Attorney General
Bureau of Consumer Frauds and Protection
65 Court Street
Buffalo, NY 14202
716-847-7184

Assistant Attorney General
Office of Attorney General
Bureau of Consumer Frauds and Protection
State Office Building
Veterans Memorial Highway
Hauppauge, NY 11788
516-360-6196

Assistant Attorney General
Office of Attorney General
Bureau of Consumer Frauds and Protection
Two World Trade Center
New York, NY 10047
212-488-7450

Assistant Attorney General
Office of Attorney General
Bureau of Consumer Frauds and Protection
70 Clinton Street
Plattsburgh, NY 12901
518-563-8012

Assistant Attorney General
Office of Attorney General
Bureau of Consumer Frauds and Protection
235 Main Street
Poughkeepsie, NY 12601
914-485-3920

Assistant Attorney General
Office of Attorney General
Bureau of Consumer Frauds and Protection
900 Reynolds Arcade
16 East Main Street
Rochester, NY 14614
716-454-3412

Assistant Attorney General
Office of Attorney General
Bureau of Consumer Frauds and Protection
333 East Washington Street
Syracuse, NY 13202
315-428-4282

Assistant Attorney General
Office of Attorney General
Bureau of Consumer Frauds and Protection
207 Genesee Street
Utica, NY 13501
315-793-2225

County Offices

Consumer Affairs Specialist
Broome County Bureau of Consumer Services
P.O. Box 1766
Governmental Plaza
Binghamton, NY 13902
607-772-2168

Assistant District Attorney
Erie County District Attorney's Office
Consumer Fraud Bureau
25 Delaware Avenue
Buffalo, NY 14202
716-855-2424

Commissioner
Nassau County Office of Consumer Affairs
160 Old Country Road
Mineola, NY 11501
516-535-2600

Chief
Nassau County Commercial Frauds and Environmental Investigations Bureau
310 Old Country Road
Garden City, NY 11530
516-535-2164

Director
Oneida County Consumer Affairs
County Office Building
800 Park Avenue
Utica, NY 13501
315-798-5601

Director
Onondaga County Office of Consumer Affairs
County Civic Center
421 Montgomery Street
Syracuse, NY 13202
315-425-3479

Director
**Orange County Department of Weights and Measures
and Consumer Affairs**
Courthouse Annex
99 Main Street
Goshen, NY 10924
914-294-5151 (ext. 162)

District Attorney
**Orange County District Attorney's Office of Consumer
Affairs**
County Government Center
Goshen, NY 10924
914-294-5471

Director
Putnam County Department of Consumer Affairs
Two County Center
Carmel, NY 10512
914-225-3641 (ext. 275)

Director
Rockland County Office of Consumer Protection
County Office Building
18 New Hempstead Road
New City, NY 10956
914-638-5282

Director
**Steuben County Department of Weights and Measures
and Consumer Affairs**
40 East Steuben Street
Bath, NY 14810
607-776-4949

Commissioner
Suffolk County Department of Consumer Affairs
Suffolk County Center
Hauppauge, NY 11788
516-360-4618

Director
Ulster County Consumer Fraud Bureau
285 Wall Street
Kingston, NY 12401
914-339-5680 (ext. 240, 243, 244)

Director
Westchester County Department of Consumer Affairs
Michaelian Office Building
Room 104
White Plains, NY 10601
914-285-2155

Chief
Westchester County District Attorney's Office
Frauds Bureau
County Courthouse
111 Grove Street
White Plains, NY 10601
914-285-3303

City Offices

Chairman
Babylon Consumer Protection Board
200 East Sunrise Highway
Lindenhurst, NY 11757
516-957-3021

Town of Colonie Consumer Protection Board
Memorial Town Hall
Newtonville, NY 12128
518-783-2790

Director
Huntington Consumer Protection Board
100 Main Street
Huntington, NY 11743
516-351-3007

Ombudsman
Islip Town Citizens Action Bureau
Islip Town Hall
401 Main Street
Islip, NY 11751
516-224-5510

Commissioner
Mt. Vernon Office of Consumer Affairs
City Hall
Mt. Vernon, NY 10550
914-668-6000 (ext. 231)

Commissioner
New York City Department of Consumer Affairs
80 Lafayette Street
New York, NY 10013
212-577-0111

Branch Offices
New York City Department of Consumer Affairs
Bronx Neighborhood Office
1932 Arthur Avenue
Bronx, NY 10457
212-579-6766

New York City Department of Consumer Affairs
Brooklyn Neighborhood Office
209 Joralemon Street
Room 6
Brooklyn, NY 11201
718-596-4780

Director
New York City Department of Consumer Affairs
Harlem Neighborhood Office
227 East 116th Street
New York, NY 10029
212-348-0600

Director
New York City Department of Consumer Affairs
Queens Neighborhood Office
120-55 Queens Boulevard
Room 301A
Kew Gardens, NY 11424
718-261-2922

Director
New York City Department of Consumer Affairs
Staten Island Neighborhood Office
Staten Island Borough Hall
Room 422
Staten Island, NY 10301
718-390-5154

Director
**Oswego Office of Consumer Affairs, Weights and
  Measures**
City Hall
Oswego, NY 13126
315-342-5600 (ext. 66)

Chairperson
Ramapo Consumer Protection Board
Ramapo Town Hall
237 Route 59
Suffern, NY 10901
914-357-5100 (ext. 267)

Director
Schenectady Bureau of Consumer Protection
22 City Hall
Jay Street
Schenectady, NY 12305
518-382-5061

Director
Syracuse Consumer Affairs Office
422 City Hall
233 East Washington Street
Syracuse, NY 13202
315-473-3240

Director
White Plains Department of Weights and Measures
279 Hamilton Avenue
White Plains, NY 10601
914-682-4278

**Yonkers Office of Consumer Protection and Weights
  and Measures**
201 Palisade Avenue
Yonkers, NY 10703
914-964-3563, 3564, 3565

North Carolina

State Office

Special Deputy Attorney General and Chief
Office of Attorney General
Consumer Protection Division
P.O. Box 629
Department of Justice Building
Raleigh, NC 27602
919-733-7741

North Dakota

State Offices

Attorney General for the State of North Dakota
State Capitol Building
Bismarck, ND 58505
701-224-2210

Office of Attorney General
Consumer Fraud Division
State Capitol Building
Bismarck, ND 58505
701-224-3404
800-472-2600 (toll free—North Dakota only)

County Office

Executive Director
Quad County Community Action Agency
27½ South Third Street
Grand Forks, ND 58201
701-746-5431

Ohio

State Offices

Consumers' Counsel
137 East State Street
Columbus, OH 43215
614-466-9605
800-282-9448 (toll free—Ohio only)

Chief
Office of Attorney General
Consumer Frauds and Crimes Section
30 East Broad Street
15th Floor
Columbus, OH 43215
614-466-8831, 4986
800-282-0515 (toll free—Ohio only)

County Offices

Franklin County Office of Prosecuting Attorney
Economic Crime Division
Hall of Justice
369 South High Street
Columbus, OH 43215
614-462-3248

County Investigator
Lake County Office of Prosecuting Attorney
Consumer Protection Division
Lake County Court House
Painesville, OH 44077
216-357-2683

Assistant Prosecuting Attorney
Montgomery County Fraud Section
County Courts Building
41 North Perry
Dayton, OH 45422
513-225-5757

Prosecuting Attorney
Portage County Prosecutor's Office
Consumer Protection Division
466 South Chestnut Street
Ravenna, OH 44266
216-296-4593

Prosecuting Attorney
Summit County Bureau of Investigations
53 East Center Street
Akron, OH 44308
216-379-2784

City Offices

Akron Division of Consumer Protection
161 South High Street
Akron, OH 44308
216-375-2730

Director, Office of Consumer Affairs
218 Cleveland Avenue, SW
6th Floor
Room 605B
Canton, OH 44702

Cincinnati Office of Consumer Protection
Division of Human Services
City Hall
Room 105
Cincinnati, OH 45202
513-352-3971

Director
Cleveland Office of Consumer Affairs
1230 East Sixth Street
Cleveland, OH 44114
216-664-3200

Administrator
City of Columbus Community Human Services
50 West Gay Street
Room 601
Columbus, OH 43215
614-222-7144

Director
Youngstown Division of Consumer Affairs
City Hall
26 South Phelps Street
Youngstown, OH 44502
216-742-8700

Oklahoma

State Offices

Director
Department of Complaints, Investigation and Mediation
Oklahoma Corporation Commission
Jim Thorpe Building
Room 680
Oklahoma City, OK 73105
405-521-4113

Administrator
Department of Consumer Credit
B82 Jim Thorpe Building
Oklahoma City, OK 73105
405-521-3653

Assistant Attorney General for Consumer Protection
Office of Attorney General
112 State Capitol Building
Oklahoma City, OK 73105
405-521-3921

Oregon

State Office

Attorney in Charge
Department of Justice
Financial Fraud Section
Justice Building
Salem, OR 97310
503-378-4732
503-378-4320 (consumer hotline—Oregon only)

Pennsylvania

State Offices

Director
Office of Attorney General
Bureau of Consumer Protection
Strawberry Square
14th Floor
Harrisburg, PA 17120
717-787-9707

Consumer Advocate
Office of Attorney General
Office of Consumer Advocate—Utilities
1425 Strawberry Square
14th Floor
Harrisburg, PA 17120
717-783-5048 (utilities only)

Branch Offices
Deputy Attorney General
Office of Attorney General
Bureau of Consumer Protection
27 North Seventh Street
Allentown, PA 18101
215-821-6690

Deputy Attorney General
Office of Attorney General
Bureau of Consumer Protection
919 State Street
Room 203
Erie, PA 16501
814-871-4371

Deputy Attorney General
Office of Attorney General
Bureau of Consumer Protection
Strawberry Square
14th Floor
Harrisburg, PA 17120
717-787-7109

Deputy Attorney General
Office of Attorney General
Bureau of Consumer Protection
1009 State Office Building
1400 West Spring Garden Street
Philadelphia, PA 19130
215-560-2414

Deputy Attorney General
Office of Attorney General
Bureau of Consumer Protection
564 Forbes Avenue
Manor Building
4th Floor
Pittsburgh, PA 15219
412-565-5135

Deputy Attorney General
Office of Attorney General
Bureau of Consumer Protection
State Office Building
Room 358
100 Lackawanna Avenue
Scranton, PA 18503
717-963-4913

County Offices

Chairperson
Beaver County Alliance for Consumer Protection
699 Fifth Street
Beaver, PA 15009
412-728-7267

Director
Bucks County Bureau of Consumer Protection and
  Weights and Measures
Courthouse Annex
Broad and Union Streets
Doylestown, PA 18901
215-348-7442

Director
Chester County Bureau of Consumer Protection and
  Weights and Measures
F&M Building
5th Floor
High and Market Streets
West Chester, PA 19380
215-431-6150

Director
Cumberland County Bureau of Consumer Affairs
Courthouse
Carlisle, PA 17013
717-249-5802

Director
Delaware County Office of Consumer Affairs and
  Weights and Measures
Government Center Building
Second and Olive Streets
Media, PA 19063
215-891-4865

Director
Indiana County Bureau of Consumer Affairs
P.O. Box 187
Indiana, PA 15701
412-465-2657

Lancaster County Consumer Protection Commission
P.O. Box 3480
50 North Duke Street
Lancaster, PA 17603
717-299-7921

Director
Montgomery County Consumer Affairs Department
County Courthouse
Norristown, PA 19404
215-278-3565

City Offices

Division Chief
Action Center–Consumer Services
121 City Hall
Philadelphia, PA 19107
215-686-7595

Chief
Philadelphia District Attorney's Office
Economic Crime Unit
1300 Chestnut Street
Philadelphia, PA 19107
215-875-6036

Rhode Island

State Offices

Assistant Attorney General and Chief
Department of Attorney General
Consumer Protection Unit
72 Pine Street
Providence, RI 02903
401-274-3400

Executive Director
Rhode Island Consumers' Council
365 Broadway
Providence, RI 02909
401-277-2764

South Carolina

State Offices

Administrator
Department of Consumer Affairs
P.O. Box 5757
Columbia, SC 29250
803-758-2040
800-922-1594 (toll free—South Carolina only)

Assistant Attorney General
Office of Attorney General
Consumer Fraud and Antitrust Section
P.O. Box 11549
Columbia, SC 29211
803-758-3040

State Ombudsman
Office of Executive Policy and Program
1205 Pendleton Street
Room 412
Columbia, SC 29201
803-758-2249

South Dakota

State Office

Assistant Attorney General
Office of Attorney General
Division of Consumer Protection
Anderson Building
Pierre, SD 57501
605-773-4400
800-592-1865 (toll free—South Dakota only)

Tennessee

State Offices

Director
Department of Commerce and Insurance
Division of Consumer Affairs
206 State Office Building
Nashville, TN 37204
615-741-4737
800-342-8385 (toll free—Tennessee only)

Deputy Attorney General
Office of Attorney General
Antitrust and Consumer Protection Division
450 James Robertson Parkway
Nashville, TN 37219
615-741-2672

Texas

State Offices

Assistant Attorney General and Chief
Office of Attorney General
Consumer Protection Division
P.O. Box 12548
Capitol Station
Austin, TX 78711
512-475-1801

Branch Offices
Assistant Attorney General
Office of Attorney General
Consumer Protection Division
Renaissance Place
7th Floor
714 Jackson Street
Dallas, TX 75202
214-742-8944

Assistant Attorney General
Office of Attorney General
Consumer Protection Division
4824 Alberta Street
Suite 160
El Paso, TX 79905
915-533-3484

Assistant Attorney General
Office of Attorney General
Consumer Protection Division
1001 Texas Avenue
Suite 700
Houston, TX 77002-3111
713-223-5886

Assistant Attorney General
Office of Attorney General
Consumer Protection Division
806 Broadway
Suite 312
Lubbock, TX 79401
806-747-5238

Assistant Attorney General
Office of Attorney General
Consumer Protection Division
4309 North Tenth
Suite B
McAllen, TX 78501
512-682-4547

Assistant Attorney General
Office of Attorney General
Consumer Protection Division
200 Main Plaza
Suite 400
San Antonio, TX 78205
512-225-4191

County Offices

Dallas County Consumer Fraud Division
2720 Stemmons Expressway
400 Stemmons Tower South
Dallas, TX 75207
214-630-6300

Assistant District Attorney
Office of District Attorney
Harris County Consumer Fraud Division
201 Fannin
Suite 200
Houston, TX 77002
713-221-5836

Assistant District Attorney
Tarrant County Economic Crimes
200 West Belknap Street
Fort Worth, TX 76196
817-334-1111 (criminal consumer fraud)

City Offices

Director
Dallas Department of Consumer Services
1500 Marilla 1D South
Dallas, TX 75201
214-670-3168

Fort Worth Office of Consumer Affairs and Weights
  and Measures
1800 University Drive
Room 208
Fort Worth, TX 76107
817-870-7570

Utah

State Offices

Director
Department of Business Regulation
Division of Consumer Protection
P.O. Box 45802
Heber M. Wells Building
160 East 300 South
Salt Lake City, UT 84115
801-530-6619

Assistant Attorney General for Consumer Affairs
Office of Attorney General
130 State Capitol
Salt Lake City, UT 84114
801-533-5319

Vermont

State Offices

Assistant Attorney General and Chief
Office of Attorney General
Consumer Protection Division
109 State Street
Montpelier, VT 05602
802-828-3186
800-642-5149 (toll free—Vermont only)

Director
Weights and Measures Division
Department of Agriculture
116 State Street
Montpelier, VT 05602
802-828-2436

Virginia

State Offices

Senior Assistant Attorney General
Office of Attorney General
Division of Consumer Counsel
Supreme Court Building
101 North Eighth Street
5th Floor
Richmond, VA 23219
804-786-3433

Director
Department of Agriculture and Consumer Services
State Office of Consumer Affairs
Washington Building
1100 Bank Street
Room 110
Richmond, VA 23219
804-786-2042
800-552-9963 (toll free for complaints regarding state
agencies—Virginia only)

Branch Office

Coordinator
Department of Agriculture and Consumer Services
Northern Virginia Branch
State Office of Consumer Affairs
100 North Washington Street
Suite 412
Falls Church, VA 22046
703-532-1613

County Offices

Director
Arlington County Office of Consumer Affairs
1400 North Courthouse Road
Room 16
Arlington, VA 22201
703-558-2142

Director
Fairfax County Department of Consumer Affairs
3959 Pender Drive
Fairfax, VA 22030
703-691-3214

Administrator
Prince William County Office of Consumer Affairs
15960 Cardinal Drive
Woodridge, VA 22191
703-335-7370

City Offices

Director
Alexandria Office of Citizens Assistance
P.O. Box 178
City Hall
Alexandria, VA 22313
703-838-4350

Chief
Norfolk Division of Consumer Protection
804 City Hall Building
Norfolk, VA 23501
804-441-2821

Assistant to the City Manager
Roanoke Consumer Protection Division
353 Municipal Building
215 Church Avenue, SW
Roanoke, VA 24011
703-981-2583

Consumer Protection Officer
Virginia Beach Division of Consumer Protection
City Hall
Virginia Beach, VA 23456
804-427-8983

Washington

State Offices

Consumer Specialist (Agriculture)
Department of Agriculture
Office of Consumer Services
406 General Administration Building, AX41
Olympia, WA 98504
206-754-2195

Chief
Office of Attorney General
Consumer Protection/Antitrust Division
Temple of Justice
Olympia, WA 98504
206-753-6210

Assistant Attorney General Chief
Office of Attorney General
Consumer Protection/Antitrust Division
1366 Dexter Horton Building
Seattle, WA 98104
206-464-7744
800-551-4636 (toll free—Washington only)

Chief
Office of Attorney General
Consumer Protection/Antitrust Division
West 1116 Riverside Avenue
Spokane, WA 99201
509-456-3123

Chief
Office of Attorney General
Consumer Protection/Antitrust Division
949 Market Street
Tacoma, WA 98402
206-593-2904

County Office

Chief Deputy Prosecuting Attorney
Fraud Division
King County Prosecuting Attorney's Office
E531 King County Courthouse
Seattle, WA 98104
206-583-4513

City Offices

Inspector
Everett Weights and Measures Department
3200 Cedar Street
Everett, WA 98201
206-259-8745

Director
Seattle Department of Licenses and Consumer Affairs
102 Municipal Building
Seattle, WA 98104
206-625-2536 (inquiries)
206-625-5500 (complaints)

West Virginia

State Offices

Director
Office of Attorney General
Consumer Protection Division
1204 Kanawha Boulevard East
Charleston, WV 25301
304-348-8986

Director
Weights and Measures Capitol Complex
Department of Labor
1900 Washington Street East
Charleston, WV 25305
304-348-7890

City Office

Director
Charleston Consumer Protection Department
P.O. Box 2749
Charleston, WV 25330
304-348-8173

Wisconsin

State Offices

Assistant Attorney General
Department of Justice
Office of Consumer Protection
P.O. Box 7856
Madison, WI 53707
608-266-1852
800-362-8189 (toll free—Wisconsin only)

Administrator
Department of Agriculture, Trade, and Consumer
  Protection
Division of Trade and Consumer Protection
P.O. Box 8911
801 West Badger Road
Madison, WI 53708
608-266-9836
800-362-3020 (toll free—Wisconsin only)

Director
Department of Justice
Office of Consumer Protection
Milwaukee State Office Building
819 North 6th Street
Room 520
Milwaukee, WI 53203
414-224-1867

Branch Offices
Supervisor
Department of Agriculture, Trade, and Consumer
  Protection
Division of Trade and Consumer Protection
927 Loring Street
Altoona, WI 54720
715-836-2537

Regional Supervisor
Department of Agriculture, Trade, and Consumer
  Protection
Consumer Protection Bureau
200 North Jefferson Street
Suite 146A
Green Bay, WI 54301
414-497-4087

Supervisor
Department of Agriculture, Trade, and Consumer
  Protection
Division of Trade and Consumer Protection
10320 West Silver Spring Drive
Milwaukee, WI 53225
414-438-4844

County Offices

Consumer Investigator
Kenosha County District Attorney's Office
912 56th Street
Kenosha, WI 53140
414-656-6480

District Attorney
Marathon County District Attorney's Office
Consumer Fraud Unit
Marathon County Court House
Wausau, WI 54401
715-847-5555

Assistant District Attorney
Milwaukee County District Attorney's Office
Consumer Fraud Unit
821 West State Street
Room 412
Milwaukee, WI 53233
414-278-4792

District Attorney
Portage County District Attorney's Office
Consumer Fraud Unit
Portage County Court House
Stevens Point, WI 54481
715-346-1300

Consumer Fraud Investigator
Racine County Sheriff's Department
717 Wisconsin Avenue
Racine, WI 53403
414-636-3125

Wyoming

State Office

Senior Assistant Attorney General
Office of Attorney General
123 State Capitol Building
Cheyenne, WY 82002
307-777-7841, 6286

American Samoa

Assistant Attorney General
Consumer Protection Bureau
P.O. Box 7
Pago Pago. American Samoa 96799
684-633-4163, 1786

Puerto Rico

Department of Consumer Affairs
P.O. Box 41059
Manillas Governmental Center
Torre Norte Building
De Diego Avenue, Stop 22
Santurce, PR 00940
809-722-7555

Secretary
Department of Justice
P.O. Box 192
Old San Juan, PR 00902
809-721-2900
809-725-8158

Virgin Islands

Director
Consumer Services Administration
P.O. Box 5468
Charlotte Amalie, St. Thomas
U.S. Virgin Islands 00801
809-774-3130

Domestic Violence Hotlines

Alabama Coalition Against Domestic Violence
205-767-3076
Collect, 24 hours

Arkansas Coalition Against Violence to Women and Children
501-442-9811
Collect, 24 hours

Northern California Shelter Support Services
415-342-0850
Collect, 24 hours

Southern California Coalition on Battered Women
213-392-9874
Collect, 9 A.M. to 5 P.M., weekdays

Connecticut Task Force on Abused Women
203-524-5890
Collect, 24 hours

Delaware Families in Transition
302-422-8058
302-856-4919
Collect, 24 hours

Florida Women in Distress
305-467-6333
800-342-9152
24 hours

Georgia Network Against Domestic Violence
404-536-5860
Collect, 24 hours

Indiana Coalition Against Domestic Violence
812-334-8378
Collect, 8 A.M. to 5 P.M., weekdays

Kansas Association of Domestic Violence Programs
800-257-2255
24 hours

Kentucky Domestic Violence Association/Women's Crisis Center
606-491-3335
Collect, 24 hours

Maine Family Violence Assistance Project
207-623-3569
Collect, 24 hours

Massachusetts Coalition of Battered Women's Service Groups
617-426-8492
Collect, 9 A.M. to 5 P.M., weekdays

Michigan Coalition Against Domestic Violence: Harbor Hotline
800-292-3925
24 hours

Mississippi Coalition Against Domestic Violence
601-435-1968
Collect, 24 hours

New Hampshire Coalition Against Domestic and Sexual Violence
603-224-8893
800-852-3311
Collect, 9 A.M. to 5 P.M., weekdays

New Jersey Women's Referral Central
800-322-8092
24 hours

New Mexico Coalition Against Domestic Violence/La Casa
505-526-6661
Collect, 24 hours

New York State Domestic Violence Hotline
800-942-6906
24 hours

New York State Bilingual Domestic Violence Hotline—in Spanish
800-942-6908
9 A.M. to 5 P.M., weekdays

North Dakota Council on Abused Women's Services: Domestic Violence Hotline
800-472-2911
24 hours

Ohio Womanshelter
216-297-9999
Collect, 24 hours

Oklahoma Domestic Violence Safeline
800-522-7233
24 hours

Oregon Coalition Against Domestic and Sexual Violence/ Portland Women's Crisis Line
503-235-5333
Collect, 24 hours

Pennsylvania Coalition Against Domestic Violence
800-932-4632
9 A.M. to 5 P.M., weekdays

Rhode Island Council on Domestic Violence
401-723-3051
Collect, 24 hours

South Carolina Coalition Against Domestic Violence and Sexual Assault/Sistercare Crisis and Information Line
803-765-9428
Collect, 24 hours

South Dakota Coalition Against Domestic Violence
605-226-1212
Collect, 24 hours

Tennessee Coalition Against Domestic Violence: Safe Space Hotline
615-623-3125
Collect, 24 hours

Texas Council on Family Violence
512-482-8200
Collect, 9 A.M. to 5 P.M., weekdays

Washington Domestic Violence Hotline
800-562-6025
24 hours

Wyoming Family Violence and Sexual Assault Statewide Referral
800-442-8337
24 hours

Family Planning

Association for Voluntary Sterilization
122 East 42nd Street
18th Floor
New York, NY 10168
212-573-8350

Birth Control Institute
1242 West Lincoln Avenue
Suite 7–10
Anaheim, CA 92805
714-956-4630

Human Life and Natural Family Planning Foundation
5609 Broadmoor Street
Alexandria, VA 22310
703-836-3377

Institute for Family Research Education
Slocum Hall
Room 110
Syracuse, NY 13210
315-423-4584

International Planned Parenthood Federation
105 Madison Avenue
New York, NY 10016
212-679-2230

National Clearinghouse for Family Planning Information
P.O. Box 12921
1700 North Moore St.
Arlington, VA 22209
703-558-7932

Planned Parenthood Federation of America
Educational Resources Clearinghouse
810 Seventh Avenue
New York, NY 10019
212-541-7800

Planned Parenthood Federation of America
Katharine Dexter McCormick Library
810 Seventh Avenue
New York, NY 10019
212-603-4637

Population Institute
110 Maryland Avenue, NE
No. 207
Washington, DC 20002
202-544-3300

Resolve
P.O. Box 474
497 Common Street
Belmont, MA 02178
617-484-2424

Genealogy

American Archives Association
1350 New York Avenue, NW
Washington, DC 20005

Children of the American Revolution
1776 D Street, NW
Washington, DC 20006

Library of Congress
Local History and Genealogy Reading Room
10 First Street, SE
Washington, DC 20540

National Archives and Records Administration
Public Programs and Exhibits
8th Street and Pennsylvania Avenue, NW
Washington, DC 20408

National Archives and Records Administration
Reference Services Branch
8th Street and Pennsylvania Avenue, NW
Washington, DC 20408

National Genealogical Society
1921 Sunderland Place, NW
Washington, DC 20036

National Society of Colonial Dames of America
2715 Q Street, NW
Washington, DC 20007

National Society, Colonial Dames XVII Century
1300 New Hampshire Avenue, NW
Washington, DC 20036

National Society, Daughters of the American Revolution
2205 Massachusetts Avenue, NW
Washington, DC 20008

National Society, Daughters of the American Revolution
1776 D Street, NW
Washington, DC 20006

National Society, Daughters of Founders and Patriots of America
2540 Massachusetts Avenue, NW
Washington, DC 20008

National Society, Sons and Daughters of the Pilgrims
2540 Massachusetts Avenue, NW
Washington, DC 20008

National Society, U.S. Daughters of 1812
1461 Rhode Island Avenue, NW
Washington, DC 20036

Government Agencies and Bureaus

Agriculture Department
14th Street and Independence Avenue, SW
Washington, DC 20250

AMTRAK
Office of Customer Relations
400 North Capitol Street, NW
Washington, DC 20001

Auto Safety Hotline
Transportation Department
Washington, DC 20590
202-426-0123
800-424-9393

Civil Rights Commission
Congressional and Community Relations
1121 Vermont Avenue, NW
Washington, DC 20425

Commerce Department
Consumer Affairs
14th Street and Constitution Avenue, NW
Washington, DC 20230

Commodity Futures Trading Commission
Office of Governmental Affairs
2033 K Street, NW
Washington, DC 20581

Consumer Affairs Council
1725 I Street, NW
Washington, DC 20201

Consumer Information Center
Pueblo, CO 81009

Consumer Product Safety Commission
Office of the Secretary
Washington, DC 20207

Consumer Services Administration
Consumer Information Center
18th and F Streets, NW
Washington, DC 20405

Defense Department
Manpower, Installations, and Logistics
The Pentagon
Washington, DC 20301

Education Department
Consumer Affairs
400 Maryland Avenue, SW
Washington, DC 20202

Energy Department
1000 Independence Avenue, SW
Washington, DC 20585

Environmental Protection Agency
Public Affairs
401 M Street, NW
Washington, DC 20460

Federal Communications Commission
Public Affairs, Consumer Assistance, and Information
1919 M Street, NW
Washington, DC 20554

Federal Deposit Insurance Corporation
Consumer Programs
550 17th Street, NW
Washington, DC 20429

Federal Emergency Management Agency
Public Affairs
500 C Street, SW
Washington, DC 20472

Federal Home Loan Bank Board
Examination and Supervision
1700 G Street, NW
Washington, DC 20552

Federal Maritime Commission
Informal Inquiries and Complaints
1100 L Street, NW
Washington, DC 20573

Federal Reserve System
Consumer and Community Affairs
20th and C Streets, NW
Washington, DC 20551

Federal Trade Commission
Bureau of Consumer Protection
6th Street and Pennsylvania Avenue, NW
Washington, DC 20580

Food and Drug Administration
Health and Human Services Department
Consumer Affairs
5600 Fishers Lane
Rockville, MD 20857

Interior Department
Public Affairs
Main Interior Building
Washington, DC 20240

Interstate Commerce Commission
Compliance and Consumer Assistance
12th Street and Constitution Avenue, NW
Washington, DC 20423

Justice Department
Consumer Litigation
Washington, DC 20530

Labor Department
200 Constitution Avenue, NW
Washington, DC 20210

Merit Systems Protection Board
1120 Vermont Avenue, NW
Washington, DC 20419

National Bureau of Standards
Commerce Department
Route I-270 and Quince Orchard Road
Gaithersburg, MD 20899

National Credit Union Administration
Supervision and Examination
1776 G Street, NW
Washington, DC 20456

National Labor Relations Board
1717 Pennsylvania Avenue, NW
Room 701
Washington, DC 20570

Nuclear Regulatory Commission
Public Affairs
7735 Old Georgetown Road
Bethesda, MD
(mailing address: Washington, DC 20555)

Peace Corps
Volunteer Program Information
199 K Street, NW
Washington, DC 20526
800-424-8580
DC: 202-254-6886

Postal Rate Commission
Consumer Advocate
1333 H Street, NW
Washington, DC 20268

Postal Service
Consumer Affairs
475 L'Enfant Plaza, SW
Washington, DC 20260

Securities and Exchange Commission
Consumer Affairs
450 5th Street, NW
Washington, DC 20549

Small Business Administration
1441 L Street, NW
Washington, DC 20416

Transportation Department
Public Affairs and Public Liaison
Main Treasury Building
Washington, DC 20220

Veterans Administration
Public and Consumer Affairs
810 Vermont Avenue, NW
Washington, DC 20420

Federal Information Centers

Alabama

Birmingham: 205-322-8591
Mobile: 205-438-1421

Alaska

Anchorage: 907-271-3650

Arizona

Phoenix: 602-261-3313

Arkansas

Little Rock: 501-378-6177

California

Los Angeles: 213-894-3800
Sacramento: 916-551-2380
San Diego: 619-293-6030
San Francisco: 415-556-6600
Santa Ana: 714-836-2386

Colorado

Denver: 303-844-6575
Colorado Springs: 303-471-9491
Pueblo: 303-544-9523

Connecticut

Hartford: 203-527-2617
New Haven: 203-624-4720

Florida

Ft. Lauderdale: 305-522-8531
Jacksonville: 904-354-4756
Miami: 305-536-4155
Orlando: 305-422-1800
St. Petersburg: 813-893-3495
Tampa: 813-229-7911
West Palm Beach: 305-833-7566

Georgia

Atlanta: 404-331-6891

Hawaii

Honolulu: 808-546-8620

Illinois

Chicago: 312-353-4242

Indiana

Gary: 219-883-4110
Indianapolis: 317-269-7373

Iowa

800-532-1556

Kansas

800-432-2934

Kentucky

Louisville: 502-582-6261

Louisiana

New Orleans: 504-589-6696

Maryland

Baltimore: 301-962-4980

Massachusetts

Boston: 617-565-8121

Michigan

Detroit: 313-226-7016
Grand Rapids: 616-451-2628

Minnesota

Minneapolis: 612-349-5333

Missouri

St. Louis: 314-425-4106
Other cities: 800-392-7711

Nebraska

Omaha: 402-221-3353
Other cities: 800-642-8383

New Jersey

Newark: 201-645-3600
Trenton: 609-396-4400

New Mexico

Albuquerque: 505-766-3091

New York

Albany: 518-463-4421
Buffalo: 716-846-4010
New York: 212-264-4464
Rochester: 716-546-5075
Syracuse: 315-476-8545

North Carolina

Charlotte: 704-376-3600

Ohio

Akron: 216-375-5638
Cincinnati: 513-684-2801
Cleveland: 216-522-4040
Columbus: 614-221-1014
Dayton: 513-223-7377
Toledo: 419-241-3223

Oklahoma

Oklahoma City: 405-231-4868
Tulsa: 918-584-4193

Oregon

Portland: 503-221-2222

Pennsylvania

Philadelphia: 215-597-7042
Pittsburgh: 412-644-3456

Rhode Island

Providence: 401-331-5565

Tennessee

Chattanooga: 615-265-8231
Memphis: 901-521-3285
Nashville: 615-242-5056

Texas

Austin: 512-472-5494
Dallas: 214-767-8585
Fort Worth: 817-334-3624
Houston: 713-229-2552
San Antonio: 512-224-4471

Utah

Salt Lake City: 801-524-5353

Virginia

Norfolk: 804-441-3101
Richmond: 804-643-4928
Roanoke: 703-982-8591

Washington

Seattle: 206-442-0570
Tacoma: 206-383-5230

Wisconsin

Milwaukee: 414-271-2273

Handicapped

Operator Services

Hearing- and speech-impaired people who use a telecommunication device for the deaf (known as TDD or TTY) can get help with calls made from a TDD to a TDD by using the following service:

TDD/TTY Operator Services
800-855-1155

The TDD operator can help you if you have telecommunications devices for the deaf to make:

- Credit card calls (if you have a telephone credit card)
- Collect calls (calls paid for by the person you are calling)
- Third number telephone calls (calls billed to a number other than the one you are calling to or from)
- Person-to-person calls (calls to a specific person)
- Calls from a hotel or motel
- Calls from a coin phone (credit card, collect, or bill to third number calls only)

The TDD operator can also help you:

- Get the number if you have a problem with a call
- Get assistance for problems with calls
- Get telephone numbers that you cannot find in the telephone book
- Report problems with your telephone

The TDD operator cannot interpret voice to TDD or TDD to voice.

Remember, most calls made with the help of an operator are more expensive, so dial calls yourself when you can to save money.

Federal TDD Numbers

Many federal departments and agencies have telephone numbers for your use if you have a telecommunications device for the deaf (TDD).

Agriculture Department

Central Employment and Selective Placement Office
14th Street and Independence Avenue, SW
Room 1078 South
Washington, DC 20250
202-447-2436

Architectural and Transportation Barriers Compliance Board

MES Building
330 C Street, SW
Room 1010
202-245-1801   202-245-1591   202-472-2700

Equal Employment Opportunity Office
14th Street and Independence Avenue. SW
Auditors Building
Room 2405
Washington, DC 20250
202-447-7327

Meat and Poultry Hotline
Food Safety and Inspection Service
South Building
Room 1163
Washington, DC 20250
202-447-3333
800-535-4555

Commerce Department

14th Street and Constitution Avenue, NW
Room 1894
Washington, DC 20230
202-377-5588

Consumer Product Safety Commission

1111 18th Street, NW
Washington, DC 20207
800-492-8104 (toll free—Maryland)
800-638-8270 (toll free elsewhere)

Education Department

Captioning and Media Services
330 C Street, SW
Washington, DC 20202
202-732-1177

Handicapped Concerns Staff
330 C Street, SW
MES Building
Room 3124
Washington DC 20202
202-472-3731

National Institute of Handicapped Research
330 C Street, SW
MES Building
Room 3431
Washington, DC 20201
202-732-1198

Office for Civil Rights
Office of Program Review and Assistance
Division of External Technical Assistance
330 C Street, SW
MES Building
Room 5613
Washington, DC 20202
202-732-1467

Office of Deafness and Communicative Disorders (RSA)
330 C Street, SW
MES Building
Room 3414
Washington, DC 20202
202-245-0591, 0574, 0584

Office of Public Affairs
330 C Street, SW
MES Building
Room 5120
Washington, DC 20202
202-245-8717

Rehabilitation Services Administration
330 C Street, SW
Washington, DC 20202
202-732-1298 TDD

Education Department
Regional Offices

Region I–Connecticut, Maine, Massachusetts, New Hampshire, Rhode Island, Vermont
Office for Civil Rights
140 Federal Street
Boston, MA 02110
617-233-1111

Rehabilitation Services Administration
John F. Kennedy Federal Building
Room E—400
Boston, MA 02203
617-223-6820

Region II–New York, New Jersey, Puerto Rico, Virgin Islands
Office for Civil Rights
26 Federal Plaza
New York, NY 10278
212-264-9464

Rehabilitation Services Administration
26 Federal Plaza
New York, NY 10278
212-264-4714

Region III–Delaware, Maryland, Pennsylvania, Virginia, West Virginia, District of Columbia
Technical Assistance Office
Gateway Building
3535 Market Street
Philadelphia, PA 19101
215-596-6794

Rehabilitation Services Administration
Gateway Building
3535 Market Street
Room 3350
Philadelphia, PA 19101
215-596-0319

**Region IV—Alabama, Florida, Georgia, Kentucky,
  Mississippi, North Carolina, South Carolina, Tennessee**
Office for Civil Rights
101 Marietta Street
Atlanta, GA 30323
404-221-2910

Rehabilitation Services Administration
101 Marietta Street
Atlanta, GA 30323
404-221-2910

**Region V—Illinois, Indiana, Michigan, Minnesota,
  Ohio, Wisconsin**
Rehabilitation Services Administration
160 North LaSalle
Room 1020
Chicago, IL 60601
312-793-3040

**Region VI—Arkansas, Louisiana, New Mexico,
  Oklahoma, Texas**
Office for Civil Rights
1200 Main Tower
Dallas, TX 75202
214-767-6599

Rehabilitation Services Administration
1200 Main Tower
Dallas, TX 75202
214-767-2961

Region VII—Iowa, Kansas, Missouri, Nebraska
Office for Civil Rights
324 East 11th Street
24th Floor
Kansas City, MO 64106
816-374-5025

**Region VIII—Colorado, Montana, North Dakota, South
  Dakota, Utah, Wyoming**
Office for Civil Rights
1961 Stout Street
Denver, CO 80294
303-844-3417

Rehabilitation Services Administration
1961 Stout Street
Denver, CO 80294
303-844-2135

**Region IX—Arizona, California, Hawaii, Nevada,
  Guam, Trust Territory of Pacific Islands, American
  Samoa**
Office for Civil Rights
1275 Market Street
San Francisco, CA 94103
415-556-1933

Region X—Alaska, Idaho, Oregon, Washington
Office for Civil Rights
2901 Third Avenue
Mail Stop 106
Seattle, WA 98121
206-442-4542

Rehabilitation Services Administration
2901 3rd Avenue
Mail Stop 106
Seattle, WA 98121
206-442-4442

Environmental Protection Agency

Civil Rights Office
401 M Street, SW
Washington, DC 20460
202-382-4565 TDD

Equal Employment Opportunity Commission

1900 E Street, NW
Washington, DC 20415
202-632-6272 v/TDD

Executive Office of the President

The White House
1600 Pennsylvania Avenue, NW
Washington, DC 20500
202-456-6213

United States Senate
Washington, DC 20510
202-224-4049 TDD
202-224-4048 Voice

U.S. Congress
Washington, DC 20515
202-225-1904 v/TDD

Federal Bureau of Investigation

Technological Office
9th and Pennsylvania Avenue, NW
Washington, DC 20535
202-324-2333 TDD

Federal Communications Commission

Consumer Assistance Office
1919 M Street, NW
Washington, DC 20554
202-632-6999 TDD

Federal Trade Commission

Public Reference Branch
6th and Pennsylvania Avenue, NW
Washington, DC 20580
202-523-3638 TDD

General Services Administration

National Archives and Records Service
8th and Pennsylvania Avenue, NW
Washington, DC 20408
202-523-0774 TDD

Health and Human Services Department

Food and Drug Administration
200 C Street, SW
Room 1825
Washington, DC 20204
202-245-1284

Food and Drug Administration
5600 Fishers Lane
Parklawn Building
Room 12B03
Rockville, MD 20857
301-443-1818

Handicapped Employment Program
200 Independence Avenue, SW
Washington, DC 20201
202-245-6568

National Library of Medicine, NIH
8600 Rockville Pike
Rockville, MD 20857
301-496-5511 TDD

Office of Civil Rights
200 Independence Avenue, SW
Washington, DC 20201
202-472-2916

Public Health Service
5600 Fishers Lane
Parklawn Building
Room 5B07
Rockville, MD 20857
301-443-4229

Social Security Administration
6401 Security Boulevard
Baltimore, MD 21235
800-325-0788

Social Security Administration (Missouri only)
4300 Goodfellow Boulevard
St. Louis, MO 63120
800-325-0778 TDD
800-392-0812 TDD

Department of Housing and Urban Development

451 Seventh Street, SW
Washington, DC 20410
202-426-6030

Department of Interior

Clara Barton House
MacArthur Boulevard
Glen Echo, MD 20768
301-492-6296 v/TDD

Old Stone House
3051 M Street, NW
Washington, DC 20007
202-426-6851 v/TDD

Interstate Commerce Commission

Constitution Avenue and 12th Street, NW
Washington, DC 20011
202-275-1721 TDD

Catoctin Mountain Park
Fairmont, MD 21788
301-663-9330 v/TDD

Frederick Douglass Home
1411 W Street, SE
Washington, DC 20020
202-426-5963 v/TDD

National Park Service
Special Programs Branch
Washington, DC 20013
202-343-3679 v/TDD

National Park Service
George Washington Memorial Parkway
McLean, VA 22101
703-285-2620 v/TDD

Justice Department

Coordination and Review Section
320 1st Street, NW
Washington, DC 20530
202-724-7678 TDD

Equal Employment Opportunity Office
10th Street and Constitution Avenue, NW
Washington, DC 20530
202-633-3696

Library of Congress

1st Street and Independence Avenue, SE
Washington, DC 20540
202-287-6200

Merit Systems Protection Board

1120 Vermont Avenue, NW
Washington, DC 20419
202-653-8896 TDD

Office of Personnel Management

Federal Job Information Center
1900 E Street, NW
Washington, DC 20415
202-632-6063

Selective Placement Program Division
1900 E Street, NW
Room 7H17
Washington, DC 20415
202-632-9594

President's Committee on Employment of the Handicapped

1111 20th Street, NW
Suite 600
Washington, DC 20036
202-653-5112

Securities and Exchange Commission

Personnel
450 Fifth Street, NW
Room 1C45
Washington, DC 20549
202-272-2552

Small Business Administration

1441 L Street, NW
Washington, DC 20416
202-653-7561 TDD

Department of Transportation

400 Seventh Street, SW
Washington, DC 20590
202-755-7687

National Highway Traffic Safety Administration
400 Seventh Street, SW
Room 6125
Washington, DC 20590
202-426-2989

Department of the Treasury

15th Street and Pennsylvania Avenue, NW
Washington, DC 20226
202-287-4097

Bureau of the Public Debt
13th and C Street, SW
Washington, DC 20590
202-287-4087 TDD

Internal Revenue Service
1111 Constitution Avenue, NW
Washington, DC 20224
800-424-1040

Telecommunications Center
15th and Pennsylvania Avenue, NW
Washington, DC 20020
202-566-2673 TDD

United States Information Agency

Equal Opportunity
301 4th Street, SW
Washington, DC 20547
202-485-7157 v/TDD

Books for Blind and Physically Handicapped Persons

The **Library of Congress** has a free reading program for blind and physically handicapped individuals and offers publications in Braille and recorded books and magazines to persons who cannot hold a book or see well enough to read regular print. Special playback equipment is available on a loan basis from the Library of Congress, and cassettes and recordings on discs can be ordered from about 160 cooperating libraries. Anyone who is medically certified as unable to hold a book or read ordinary print because of a visual handicap can borrow these materials postage-free and return them in the same manner.

For more information, send name and address to:

> **National Library Service for the Blind and**
> **Physically Handicapped**
> The Library of Congress
> Washington, DC 20542

Recording for the Blind (RFB) is a national nonprofit service organization that provides free cassettes of educational textbooks to medically certified individuals. Eligibility extends to visually, physically, and perceptually handicapped individuals. One of RFB's special services is a collection of cassettes of a wide variety of consumer publications from the federal government.

For more information and an application, contact:

Student Services—CI
Recording for the Blind, Inc.
20 Roszel Road
Princeton, NJ 08540
609-452-0606
800-221-4792 (toll free outside New Jersey)

Services for Handicapped Children

Association for Children with Retarded Mental Development
162 Fifth Avenue
11th Floor
New York, NY 10010
212-475-7200

Council for Exceptional Children
Department of Information Services
1920 Association Drive
Reston, VA 22091
703-620-3660

Foundation for Children with Learning Disabilities
99 Park Avenue
6th Floor
New York, NY 10016
212-687-7211

National Information Center for Handicapped Children and Youth
P.O. Box 1492
Washington, DC 20001
1555 Wilson Boulevard
Rosslyn, VA 22209
703-522-3332

Health and Nutrition

AIDS Hotline
800-342-AIDS

Alzheimer's Disease and Related Disorders Association
70 East Lake Street
Chicago, IL 60601
312-853-3060

American Dietetic Association
430 North Michigan Avenue
Chicago, IL 60611
312-280-5000

American Health and Wellness Association
781 West Oakland Park Boulevard
Suite 273
Ft. Lauderdale, FL 33311
305-761-1279

American Institute of Nutrition
9650 Rockville Pike
Bethesda, MD 20814
301-530-7050

American Medical Association
Food and Nutrition Program
535 North Dearborn Street
Chicago, IL 60610
312-645-5070

American Prevention Institute
1425 Engracia Avenue
Torrance, CA 90501
213-328-6338

Cancer Hotline
800-638-6070 (toll free—Alaska)
800-4-CANCER (toll free elsewhere)
202-636-5700 (District of Columbia)
808-524-1234 (Hawaii)
212-794-7982 (New York City)

Center for Food Safety and Applied Nutrition
Food and Drug Administration
200 C Street, SW
Room 3321
Washington, DC 20204

Centers for Disease Control
Atlanta, GA 30333

Community Nutrition Institute
2001 S Street, NW
Washington, DC 20009
202-462-4700

Health and Human Services Department
U.S. Office of Consumer Affairs
1725 I Street, NW
Washington, DC 20201
202-634-4140

Health Care Financing Administration
Health and Human Services Department
6325 Security Boulevard
Baltimore, MD 21207
301-594-9086
TTY for the deaf: 301-594-9016

Health Maintenance Organizations
Division of Private Sector Initiatives
Parklawn Building
Room 17A55
5600 Fishers Lane
Rockville, MD 20857
301-443-2778

Human Nutrition Information Service
Food and Consumer Services
USDA
6505 Belcrest Road
Hyattsville, MD 20782
301-436-7725

National Gay Health Foundation
P.O. Box 784
New York, NY 10036
212-563-6313

National Health Information Clearinghouse
1555 Wilson Boulevard
Suite 600
Rosslyn, VA 22209
800-336-4979
703-522-2590 (District of Columbia)

Office of Information and Consumer Affairs
Occupational Safety and Health Administration
Labor Department
Washington, DC 20210
202-523-8151

Public Health Service
Centers for Disease Control
U.S. Public Health Service
1600 Clifton Road, NE
Atlanta, GA 30333
404-639-3534

Second Surgical Opinion Program
Health and Human Services Department
Hubert Humphrey Building
Room 313H
Washington, DC 20201
800-492-6603 (toll free Maryland)
800-638-6833 (toll free elsewhere)

Society for Nutrition Education
1736 Franklin Street
Suite 900
Oakland, CA 94612
415-444-7133

Vitamin Information Bureau
664 North Michigan Avenue
Chicago, IL 60611
312-751-2223

ZIP Codes

Five-digit ZIP (Zoning Improvement Plan) Codes were introduced in 1964 to identify each postal delivery area in the United States. In some communities, two cities may share a ZIP Code; in others, such as New York City, one geographic area may have many ZIP Codes, including separate ZIP Codes for each major office building. In this book, the ZIP Codes are representative rather than specific for the larger cities. In New York City, for example, the indicated ZIP Code is 10001, which is technically the ZIP Code for the Manhattan borough postmaster. For the ZIP Code for a specific address in any area served by the U.S. Postal Service, the reader should consult a copy of the *U.S. Postal Service National Five-Digit ZIP Code & Post Office Directory,* available at any local post office and revised yearly.

City	ZIP	City	ZIP	City	ZIP
Aberdeen, SD	57401	Bangor, ME	04401	Bowie, MD	20715
Abilene, TX	79604	Barberton, OH	44203	Bowling Green, KY	42101
Addison, IL	60101	Bartlesville, OK	74003	Bowling Green, OH	43402
Akron, OH	44309	Baton Rouge, LA	70821	Boynton Beach, FL	33435
Alameda, CA	94501	Battle Creek, MI	49016	Bradenton, FL	33506
Albany, GA	31706	Bay City, MI	48706	Brea, CA	92621
Albuquerque, NM	87101	Bayonne, NJ	07002	Bremerton, WA	98310
Alexandria, LA	71301	Baytown, TX	77520	Bridgeport, CT	06602
Alexandria, VA	22313	Beaumont, TX	77704	Bristol, CT	06010
Alhambra, CA	91802	Beavercreek, OH	45401	Brockton, MA	02403
Allen Park, MI	48101	Beaverton, OR	97005	Broken Arrow, OK	74012
Allentown, PA	18101	Bell, CA	90201	Brookfield, WI	53005
Alton, IL	62002	Belleville, IL	62220	Brooklyn Center, MN	55429
Altoona, PA	16603	Belleville, NJ	07109	Brooklyn Park, MN	55007
Amarillo, TX	79120	Bellevue, WA	98009	Brook Park, OH	44142
Ames, IA	50010	Bellflower, CA	90706	Brownsville, TX	78520
Anaheim, CA	92803	Bell Gardens, CA	90201	Brunswick, OH	44212
Anchorage, AK	99502	Bellingham, WA	98225	Bryan, TX	77801
Anderson, IN	46018	Beloit, WI	53511	Buena Park, CA	90622
Anderson, SC	29621	Bergenfield, NJ	07621	Buffalo, NY	14240
Annapolis, MD	21401	Berkeley, CA	94704	Burbank, CA	91505
Ann Arbor, MI	48106	Berwyn, IL	60402	Burbank, IL	60459
Anniston, AL	36201	Bessemer, AL	35020	Burlingame, CA	94010
Antioch, CA	94509	Bethel Park, PA	15102	Burlington, IA	52601
Appleton, WI	54911	Bethlehem, PA	18016	Burlington, NC	27215
Arcadia, CA	91006	Bettendorf, IA	52722	Burlington, VT	05401
Arlington, TX	76010	Beverly, MA	01915	Burnsville, MN	55337
Arlington Heights, IL	60004	Beverly Hills, CA	90213	Burton, MI	48502
Arvada, CO	80001	Billings, MT	59101	Butte, MT	59701
Asheville, NC	28810	Biloxi, MS	39530	Calumet City, IL	60409
Ashland, KY	41101	Binghamton, NY	13902	Camarillo, CA	93010
Athens, GA	30601	Birmingham, AL	35203	Cambridge, MA	02140
Atlanta, GA	30304	Bismarck, ND	58501	Camden, NJ	08101
Atlantic City, NJ	08401	Blacksburg, VA	24060	Campbell, CA	95008
Attleboro, MA	02703	Blaine, MN	55433	Canton, OH	44711
Auburn, AL	36830	Bloomfield, NJ	07003	Cape Coral, FL	33910
Auburn, NY	13021	Bloomington, IL	61701	Cape Girardeau, MO	63701
Auburn, WA	98002	Bloomington, IN	47401	Carbondale, IL	62901
Augusta, GA	30901	Bloomington, MN	55420	Carlsbad, CA	92008
Aurora, CO	80010	Blue Springs, MO	64015	Carlsbad, NM	88220
Aurora, IL	60507	Boca Raton, FL	33432	Carrollton, TX	75006
Austin, TX	78710	Bolingbrook, IL	60439	Carson, CA	90749
Azusa, CA	91702	Bossier City, LA	71111	Carson City, NV	89701
Bakersfield, CA	93302	Boston, MA	02205	Casper, WY	82601
Baldwin Park, CA	91706	Boulder, CO	80302	Cedar Falls, IA	50613
Baltimore, MD	21233	Bountiful, UT	84010	Cedar Rapids, IA	52401

Cerritos, CA	90701	Cumberland, MD	21502	Elmhurst, IL	60126
Champaign, IL	61820	Cupertino, CA	95014	Elmira, NY	14901
Chandler, AZ	85224	Cuyahoga Falls, OH	44222	El Monte, CA	91734
Chapel Hill, NC	27514	Cypress, CA	90630	El Paso, TX	79910
Charleston, SC	29423	Dallas, TX	75260	Elyria, OH	44035
Charleston, WV	25301	Daly City, CA	94015	Emporia, KS	66801
Charlottesville, VA	22906	Danbury, CT	06810	Englewood, CO	80110
Chattanooga, TN	37401	Danville, IL	61832	Enid, OK	73701
Chelsea, MA	02150	Danville, VA	24541	Erie, PA	16515
Chesapeake, VA	23320	Davenport, IA	52802	Escondido, CA	92025
Chester, PA	19013	Davis, CA	95616	Euclid, OH	44117
Cheyenne, WY	82001	Dayton, OH	45401	Eugene, OR	97401
Chicago, IL	60607	Daytona Beach, FL	32015	Evanston, IL	60204
Chicago Heights, IL	60411	Dearborn, MI	48120	Evansville, IN	47708
Chico, CA	95926	Dearborn Heights, MI	48127	Everett, MA	02149
Chicopee, MA	01021	Decatur, AL	35602	Everett, WA	98201
Chula Vista, CA	92010	Decatur, IL	62521	Fairborn, OH	45324
Cicero, IL	60650	Deerfield Beach, FL	33441	Fairfield, CA	94533
Cincinnati, OH	45234	De Kalb, IL	60115	Fairfield, OH	45014
Claremont, CA	91711	Del City, OK	73115	Fair Lawn, NJ	07410
Clarksville, TN	37041	Delray Beach, FL	33444	Fall River, MA	02722
Clearwater, FL	33575	Del Rio, TX	78840	Fargo, ND	58102
Cleveland, OH	44101	Denton, TX	76201	Farmington, NM	87401
Cleveland, TN	37311	Denver, CO	80202	Farmington Hills, MI	48024
Cleveland Heights, OH	44118	Des Moines, IA	50318	Fayetteville, AR	72701
Clifton, NJ	07015	Des Plaines, IL	60018	Fayetteville, NC	28302
Clinton, IA	52732	Detroit, MI	48233	Ferndale, MI	48220
Clovis, CA	93612	Dothan, AL	36303	Findlay, OH	45840
Clovis, NM	88010	Downers Grove, IL	60515	Fitchburg, MA	01420
College Station, TX	77840	Downey, CA	90241	Flagstaff, AZ	86001
Colorado Springs, CO	80901	Dubuque, IA	52001	Flint, MI	48502
Columbia, MO	65201	Duluth, MN	55806	Florence, AL	35631
Columbia, SC	29201	Duncanville, TX	75138	Florence, SC	29501
Columbia, TN	38401	Dunedin, FL	33528	Florisant, MO	63033
Columbus, GA	31908	Durham, NC	27701	Fond du Lac, WI	54935
Columbus, IN	47201	East Chicago, IN	46312	Fontana, CA	92335
Columbus, MS	39701	East Cleveland, OH	44112	Fort Collins, CO	80521
Columbus, OH	43216	East Detroit, MI	48021	Fort Dodge, IA	50501
Compton, CA	90220	East Lansing, MI	48823	Fort Lauderdale, FL	33450
Concord, CA	94520	Easton, PA	18042	Fort Lee, NJ	07024
Concord, NH	03301	East Orange, NJ	07019	Fort Myers, FL	33906
Coon Rapids, MN	55433	East Point, GA	30364	Fort Pierce, FL	33450
Coral Gables, FL	33114	East Providence, RI	02914	Fort Smith, AR	72901
Coral Springs, FL	33065	East St. Louis, IL	62201	Fort Wayne, IN	46802
Corona, CA	91720	Eau Claire, WI	54701	Fort Worth, TX	76101
Corpus Christi, TX	78408	Edina, MN	55424	Fountain Valley, CA	92728
Corvallis, OR	97333	Edmond, OK	73034	Frankfort, KY	40601
Costa Mesa, CA	92626	Edmonds, WA	98020	Frederick, MD	21701
Council Bluffs, IA	51501	El Cajon, CA	92020	Freeport, IL	61032
Covina, CA	91722	El Dorado, AR	71730	Freeport, NY	11520
Covington, KY	41011	Elgin, IL	60120	Fremont, CA	94538
Cranston, RI	02910	Elizabeth, NJ	07207	Fresno, CA	93706
Crystal, MN	55428	Elk Grove, IL	60007	Fridley, MN	55432
Culver City, CA	90230	Elkhart, IN	46515	Fullerton, CA	92631

Gadsen, AL	35901	Highland, IN	46322	Kennewick, WA	99336
Gainesville, FL	32602	Highland Park, IL	60035	Kenosha, WI	53141
Gaithersburg, MD	20877	Highland Park, MI	48203	Kent, OH	45429
Galesburg, IL	61401	High Point, NC	27260	Kentwood, MI	49508
Galveston, TX	77553	Hillsboro, OR	97123	Kettering, OH	45429
Gardena, CA	90247	Hilo, HI	96720	Killeen, TX	76541
Garden City, MI	48135	Hobbs, NM	88240	Kingsport, TN	37662
Garden Grove, CA	92640	Hoboken, NJ	07030	Kingston, NC	28501
Garfield, NJ	07026	Hoffman Estates, IL	60195	Kingsville, TX	78363
Garfield Heights, OH	44125	Holland, MI	49423	Kirkwood, MO	63122
Garland, TX	75040	Hollywood, FL	33022	Knoxville, TN	37901
Gary, IN	46401	Holyoke, MA	01040	Kokomo, IN	46902
Gastonia, NC	28052	Honolulu, HI	96820	La Crosse, WI	54601
Glendale, AZ	85301	Hopkinsville, KY	42240	Lafayette, IN	47901
Glendale, CA	91209	Hot Springs, AR	71901	Lafayette, LA	70501
Glendora, CA	91740	Houma, LA	70360	La Habra, CA	90631
Glenview, IL	60025	Houston, TX	77201	Lake Charles, LA	70601
Gloucester, MA	01930	Huber Heights, OH	45424	Lakeland, FL	33802
Goldsboro, NC	27530	Huntington, WV	25704	Lakewood, CA	90714
Grand Forks, ND	58201	Huntington Beach, CA	92647	Lakewood, CO	80215
Grand Island, NE	68801	Huntington Park, CA	90255	Lakewood, OH	44107
Grand Junction, CO	81501	Huntsville, AL	35813	Lake Worth, FL	33461
Grand Prairie, TX	75051	Hurst, TX	76053	La Mesa, CA	92041
Grand Rapids, MI	49501	Hutchinson, KS	67501	La Mirada, CA	90638
Granite City, IL	62040	Idaho Falls, ID	83401	Lancaster, CA	93534
Great Falls, MT	59403	Independence, MO	64501	Lancaster, OH	43130
Greeley, CO	80631	Indianapolis, IN	46206	Lancaster, PA	17604
Green Bay, WI	54301	Inglewood, CA	90311	Lansing, IL	60438
Greenfield, WI	53220	Inkster, MI	48141	Lansing, MI	48924
Greensboro, NC	27420	Iowa City, IA	52240	La Puenta, CA	91747
Greenville, MS	38701	Irvine, CA	92713	Laredo, TX	78041
Greenville, NC	27834	Irving, TX	75061	Largo, FL	33540
Greenville, SC	29600	Irvington, NJ	07111	Las Cruces, NM	88001
Gresham, OR	97030	Ithaca, NY	14850	Las Vegas, NV	89114
Gulfport, MS	39503	Jackson, MI	49201	Lauderdale Lakes, FL	33313
Hackensack, NJ	07602	Jackson, MS	39205	Lauderhill, FL	33313
Hagerstown, MD	21740	Jackson, TN	38301	Lawrence, IN	46226
Hallandale, FL	33009	Jacksonville, AR	72076	Lawrence, KS	66044
Haltom City, TX	76117	Jacksonville, FL	32203	Lawrence, MA	01842
Hamilton, OH	45012	Jamestown, NY	14701	Lawton, OK	73501
Hammond, IN	46320	Janesville, WI	53545	Leavenworth, KS	66048
Hampton, VA	23670	Jefferson City, MO	65101	Lebanon, PA	17042
Hanover Park, IL	60103	Jersey City, NJ	07303	Lee's Summit, MO	64063
Harlingen, TX	78551	Johnson City, TN	37601	Leominster, MA	01453
Harrisburg, PA	17105	Johnstown, PA	15901	Lewiston, ID	83501
Hartford, CT	06101	Joliet, IL	60436	Lewiston, ME	04240
Harvey, IL	60426	Jonesboro, AR	72401	Lexington, KY	40511
Hattiesburg, MS	39401	Joplin, MO	64801	Lima, OH	45802
Haverhill, MA	01830	Kalamazoo, MI	49001	Lincoln, NE	68501
Hawthorne, CA	90250	Kankakee, IL	60901	Lincoln Park, MI	48146
Hayward, CA	94544	Kansas City, KS	66110	Linden, NJ	07036
Hazelton, PA	18201	Kansas City, MO	64108	Lindenhurst, NY	11757
Hempstead, NY	11551	Kearny, NJ	07032	Little Rock, AR	72231
Hialeah, FL	33010	Kenner, LA	70062	Littleton, CO	80120

Livermore, CA	94550	Mentor, OH	44060	New Albany, IN	47150
Livonia, MI	48150	Merced, CA	95340	Newark, CA	94560
Lodi, CA	95240	Meriden, CT	06450	Newark, DE	19711
Logan, UT	84321	Meridian, MS	39301	Newark, NJ	07102
Lombard, IL	60148	Merrillville, IN	46410	Newark, OH	43055
Lompoc, CA	93436	Mesa, AZ	85201	New Bedford, MA	02741
Long Beach, CA	90809	Mesquite, TX	75149	New Berlin, WI	53151
Long Beach, NY	11561	Miami, FL	33152	New Britain, CT	06050
Long Branch, NJ	07740	Miami Beach, FL	33139	New Brunswick, NJ	08901
Longmont, CO	80501	Michigan City, IN	46360	New Castle, PA	16101
Longview, TX	75602	Middletown, CT	06457	New Haven, CT	06511
Longview, WA	98632	Middletown, OH	45042	New Iberia, LA	70560
Lorain, OH	44052	Midland, MI	48640	New London, CT	06320
Los Altos, CA	94022	Midland, TX	79702	New Orleans, LA	70113
Los Angeles, CA	90052	Midwest City, OK	73140	Newport, RI	02840
Los Gatos, CA	95030	Milford, CT	06460	Newport Beach, CA	92660
Louisville, KY	40231	Milpitas, CA	95035	Newport News, VA	23607
Loveland, CO	80537	Milwaukee, WI	53201	New Rochelle, NY	10802
Lowell, MA	01853	Minneapolis, MN	55401	Newton, MA	02158
Lubbock, TX	79408	Minnetonka, MN	55343	New York, NY	10001
Lufkin, TX	75901	Minot, ND	58701	Niagara Falls, NY	14302
Lynchburg, VA	24506	Miramar, FL	33023	Niles, IL	60648
Lynn, MA	01901	Mishawaka, IN	46544	Norfolk, VA	23501
Lynwood, CA	90262	Missoula, MT	59806	Normal, IL	61761
Macon, GA	31213	Mobile, AL	36601	Norman, OK	73070
Madison, WI	53707	Modesto, CA	95350	Norristown, PA	19401
Madison Heights, MI	48071	Moline, IL	61265	Northampton, MA	01060
Malden, MA	02148	Monroe, LA	71203	Northbrook, IL	60062
Manchester, NH	03103	Monroeville, PA	15146	North Charleston, SC	29406
Manhattan, KS	66502	Monrovia, CA	91016	North Chicago, IL	60064
Manhattan Beach, CA	90266	Montclair, NJ	07042	Northglenn, CO	80233
Manitowoc, WI	54220	Montebello, CA	90640	North Las Vegas, NV	89030
Mankato, MN	56001	Monterey, CA	93940	North Little Rock, AR	72114
Mansfield, OH	44901	Monterey Park, CA	91754	North Miami, FL	33161
Maple Heights, OH	44137	Montgomery, AL	36119	North Miami Beach, FL	33160
Maplewood, MN	55109	Moore, OK	73153	North Olmsted, OH	44070
Margate, FL	33063	Moorhead, MN	56560	North Richland Hills, TX	76118
Marietta, GA	30060	Morgantown, WV	26505	North Tonawanda, NY	14120
Marion, IN	46952	Mountain View, CA	94042	Norwalk, CA	90650
Marion, OH	43302	Mount Prospect, IL	60056	Norwalk, CT	06856
Marlborough, MA	01752	Mount Vernon, NY	10551	Norwich, CT	06360
Marshalltown, IA	50158	Muncie, IN	47032	Norwood, OH	45212
Mason City, IA	50401	Murfreesboro, TN	37130	Novato, CA	94947
Massillon, OH	44646	Murray, UT	84107	Nutley, NJ	07110
Maywood, IL	60153	Muskegon, MI	49440	Oak Forest, IL	60452
McAllen, TX	78501	Muskogee, OK	74401	Oakland, CA	94615
McKeesport, PA	15134	Nacogdoches, TX	75961	Oak Lawn, IL	60454
Medford, MA	02155	Nampa, ID	83651	Oak Park, IL	60301
Medford, OR	97501	Napa, CA	94558	Oak Park, MI	48237
Melbourne, FL	32901	Naperville, IL	60566	Oak Ridge, TN	37830
Melrose, MA	02176	Nashua, NH	03061	Ocala, FL	32678
Memphis, TN	38101	Nashville, TN	37202	Oceanside, CA	92054
Menlo Park, CA	94025	National City, CA	92050	Odessa, TX	79760
Menomonee Falls, WI	53051	Naugatuck, CT	06770	Ogden, UT	84401

Oklahoma City, OK	73125	Pleasanton, CA	94566	Rock Island, IL	61201
Olathe, KS	66061	Plum, PA	15239	Rockville, MD	20850
Olympia, WA	98501	Plymouth, MN	55447	Rockville Center, NY	11570
Omaha, NE	68108	Pocatello, ID	83201	Rocky Mount, NC	27801
Ontario, CA	91761	Pomona, CA	91766	Rome, GA	30161
Orange, CA	92667	Pompano Beach, FL	33060	Rome, NY	13440
Orange, NJ	07051	Ponca City, OK	74601	Rosemead, CA	91770
Orem, UT	84057	Pontiac, MI	48056	Roseville, MI	48066
Orlando, FL	32802	Portage, IN	46368	Roseville, MN	55113
Oshkosh, WI	54901	Portage, MN	49081	Rosewell, NM	88201
Ottumwa, IA	52501	Port Arthur, TX	77640	Royal Oak, MI	48068
Overland Park, KS	66204	Port Huron, MI	48060	Sacramento, CA	95813
Owensboro, KY	43201	Portland, ME	04101	Saginaw, MI	48065
Oxnard, CA	93030	Portland, OR	97208	St. Charles, MO	63301
Pacifica, CA	94044	Portsmouth, NH	03801	St. Clair Shores, MI	48080
Paducah, KY	42001	Portsmouth, OH	45662	St. Cloud, MN	56301
Palatine, IL	60067	Portsmouth, VA	23705	St. Joseph, MO	64501
Palm Springs, CA	92263	Poughkeepsie, NY	12601	St. Louis, MO	63155
Palo Alto, CA	94303	Prichard, AL	36610	St. Louis Park, MN	55426
Panama City, FL	32401	Providence, RI	02940	St. Paul, MN	55101
Paramount, CA	90723	Provo, UT	84603	St. Petersburg, FL	33730
Paramus, NJ	07652	Pueblo, CO	81003	Salem, MA	01970
Paris, TX	75460	Quincy, IL	62301	Salem, OR	97301
Parkersburg, WV	26101	Quincy, MA	02269	Salina, KS	67401
Park Forest, IL	60466	Racine, WI	53401	Salinas, CA	93907
Park Ridge, IL	60068	Rahway, NJ	07065	Salt Lake City, UT	84119
Parma, OH	44129	Raleigh, NC	27611	San Angelo, TX	76902
Pasadena, CA	91109	Rancho Cucamonga, CA	91730	San Antonio, TX	78284
Pasadena, TX	77501	Rancho Palos Verdes, CA	90274	San Bernardino, CA	92403
Pascagoula, MS	39567	Rapid City, SD	57701	San Bruno, CA	94066
Passaic, NJ	07055	Raytown, MO	64133	San Buenaventura	
Paterson, NJ	07510	Reading, PA	19603	(Ventura), CA	93002
Pawtucket, RI	02860	Redding, CA	96001	San Clemente, CA	92672
Peabody, MA	01960	Redlands, CA	92373	San Diego, CA	92199
Pembroke Pines, FL	33024	Redondo Beach, CA	90277	Sandusky, OH	44870
Pensacola, FL	32501	Redwood City, CA	94064	Sandy City, UT	84070
Peoria, IL	61601	Reno, NV	89510	San Francisco, CA	94188
Perth Amboy, NJ	08861	Renton, WA	98057	San Gabriel, CA	91776
Petaluma, CA	94952	Revere, MA	02151	San Jose, CA	95101
Petersburg, VA	23804	Rialto, CA	92376	San Leandro, CA	94577
Phenix City, AL	36867	Richardson, TX	75080	San Luis Obispo, CA	93401
Philadelphia, PA	15219	Richfield, MN	55423	San Mateo, CA	94402
Phoenix, AZ	85026	Richland, WA	99352	San Rafael, CA	94901
Pico Rivera, CA	90660	Richmond, CA	94802	Santa Ana, CA	94901
Pine Bluff, AR	71601	Richmond, IN	47374	Santa Barbara, CA	93102
Pinellas Park, FL	33565	Richmond, VA	23232	Santa Clara, CA	95050
Pittsburg, CA	94565	Ridgewood, NJ	07451	Santa Cruz, CA	95060
Pittsburgh, PA	15219	Riverside, CA	92507	Santa Fe, NM	87501
Pittsfield, MA	01201	Riviera Beach, FL	33404	Santa Maria, CA	93456
Placentia, CA	92670	Roanoke, VA	24022	Santa Monica, CA	90406
Plainfield, NJ	07061	Rochester, MN	55901	Santa Rosa, CA	95402
Plano, TX	75074	Rochester, NY	14692	Sarasota, FL	33578
Plantation, FL	33318	Rockford, IL	61125	Saratoga, CA	95070
Pleasant Hill, CA	94523	Rock Hill, SC	29730	Savannah, GA	31401

Sayreville, NJ	09972	Tamarac, FL	33320	Warwick, RI	02887
Schaumburg, IL	60194	Tampa, FL	33630	Washington, DC	20013
Schenectady, NY	12301	Taunton, MA	02780	Waterbury, CT	06701
Scottsdale, AZ	85251	Taylor, MI	48180	Waterloo, IA	50701
Scranton, PA	18505	Tempe, AZ	85282	Watertown, NY	13601
Seal Beach, CA	90740	Temple, TX	76501	Waukegan, IL	60085
Seaside, CA	93955	Terre Haute, IN	47808	Waukesha, WI	53186
Seattle, WA	98109	Texarkana, TX	75501	Wausau, WI	54401
Selma, AL	36701	Texas City, TX	75501	Wauwatosa, WI	53213
Shaker Heights, OH	44120	Thornton, CO	80229	Weirton, WV	26062
Shawnee, KS	66202	Thousand Oaks, CA	91360	West Allis, WI	53213
Shawnee, OK	74801	Tinley Park, IL	60477	West Covina, CA	91793
Sheboygan, WI	53081	Titusville, FL	32780	Westfield, MA	01085
Shelton, CT	06484	Toledo, OH	43601	Westfield, NJ	07090
Sherman, TX	75090	Topeka, KS	66603	West Haven, CT	06516
Shreveport, LA	71102	Torrance, CA	90510	West Jordan, UT	84084
Simi Valley, CA	93065	Torrington, CT	06790	Westland, MI	48185
Sioux City, IA	51101	Trenton, NJ	08650	West Memphis, AR	72301
Sioux Falls, SD	57101	Troy, MI	48099	West Mifflin, PA	15122
Skokie, IL	60076	Troy, NY	12180	Westminster, CA	92683
Slidell, LA	70458	Tucson, AZ	85726	Westminster, CO	80030
Somerville, MA	02143	Tulsa, OK	74101	West New York, NJ	07093
Somerville, NJ	08876	Turlock, CA	95380	West Orange, NJ	07052
South Bend, IN	46624	Tuscaloosa, AL	35403	West Palm Beach, FL	33401
South Euclid, OH	44121	Tustin, CA	92680	Wheaton, IL	60187
Southfield, MI	48037	Twin Falls, ID	83301	Wheat Ridge, CO	80033
South Gate, CA	90280	Tyler, TX	75712	Wheeling, WV	26003
Southgate, MI	48195	Union City, CA	94587	White Plains, NY	10602
South San Francisco, CA	94080	Union City, NJ	07087	Whittier, CA	90605
Sparks, NV	89431	University City, MO	68130	Wichita, KS	67276
Spartanburg, SC	29301	Upland, CA	91786	Wichita Falls, TX	76307
Spokane, WA	99210	Upper Arlington, OH	43221	Wilkes-Barre, PA	18701
Springfield, IL	62703	Urbana, IL	61801	Williamsport, PA	17701
Springfield, MA	01101	Utica, NY	13504	Wilmette, IL	60091
Springfield, MO	65801	Vacaville, CA	95688	Wilmington, DE	19850
Springfield, OH	45501	Valdosta, GA	31601	Wilmington, NC	28402
Springfield, OR	97477	Vallejo, CA	94590	Wilson, NC	27893
Stamford, CT	06904	Valley Stream, NY	11580	Winona, MN	55987
State College, PA	16801	Vancouver, WA	98661	Winston-Salem, NC	27102
Sterling Heights, MI	48077	Vicksburg, MS	39180	Woburn, MA	01801
Steubenville, OH	43952	Victoria, TX	77901	Woodland, CA	95695
Stillwater, OK	74074	Vineland, NJ	08360	Woonsocket, RI	02895
Stockton, CA	95208	Virginia Beach, VA	23450	Worcester, MA	01613
Stow, OH	44224	Visalia, CA	93277	Wyandotte, MI	48192
Strongsville, OH	44136	Vista, CA	92083	Wyoming, MI	49509
Suffolk, VA	23434	Waco, TX	76701	Yakima, WA	98903
Sunnyvale, CA	94086	Walla Walla, WA	99362	Yonkers, NY	10701
Sunrise, FL	33338	Walnut Creek, CA	94596	Yorba Linda, CA	92686
Superior, WI	54880	Waltham, MA	02154	York, PA	17405
Syracuse, NY	13220	Warner Robins, GA	31093	Youngstown, OH	44501
Tacoma, WA	98413	Warren, MI	48089	Yuma, AZ	85364
Tallahassee, FL	32301	Warren, OH	44481	Zanesville, OH	43701

Magazines and Newspapers

Magazines

Consumerism

Accent on Living
P.O. Box 700
Gillum Road and High Drive
Bloomington, IL 61701

Backpacker
1515 Broadway
11th Floor
New York, NY 10036

Bicycling Magazine
Rodale Press
33 East Minor Street
Emmaus, PA 18049

Boating
Ziff-Davis Publishing Company
1 Park Avenue
New York, NY 10016

Camera 35
150 East 58th Street
New York, NY 10022

Camping Magazine
5000 State Road
Martinsville, IN 46151

Car and Driver
2002 Hogback Road
Ann Arbor, MI 48104

Changing Times
The Kiplinger Magazine
1729 H Street, NW
Washington, DC 20006

Concern
Consumer Education Resource Network
1500 Wilson Boulevard
Suite 800
Rosslyn, VA 22209

Consumer Reports
256 Washington Street
Mount Vernon, NY 10553

Consumers Digest
5705 North Lincoln Avenue
Chicago, IL 60659

Forbes
60 Fifth Avenue
New York, NY 10011

Gray Panther Network
311 South Juniper Street
Suite 601
Philadelphia, PA 19107

High Fidelity
ABC Leisure Magazines
825 Seventh Avenue
New York, NY 10019

Modern Maturity
American Association of Retired Persons
3200 East Carson Street
Lakewood, CA 90712

Modern Photography
ABC Leisure Magazines
825 Seventh Avenue
New York, NY 10019

Money
Time, Inc.
Time and Life Building
New York, NY 10020
Subscriptions:
    Time, Inc.
    591 North Fairbanks Court
    Chicago, IL 60611

Cooking and Dining

Better Homes and Gardens Holiday
    Cooking and Entertaining
Locust and 17th
Des Moines, IA 50336

Bon Appetit
5900 Wilshire Boulevard
Los Angeles, CA 90036

Gourmet
560 Lexington Avenue
New York, NY 10022

Entertainment

Back Stage
330 West 42nd Street
New York, NY 10036

National Enquirer
600 SE Coast Avenue
Lake Worth, FL 33464

Star Magazine
660 White Plains Road
Tarrytown, NY 10591

TV Guide Magazine
4 Radnor Corporate Center
Radnor, PA 19088

General Interest

Ebony
820 South Michigan Avenue
Chicago, IL 60605

LIFE
Time & Life Building
New York, NY 10020

National Geographic
17th and M Streets, NW
Washington, DC 20036

People
Time & Life Building
Rockefeller Center
New York, NY 10020

Psychology Today
One Park Avenue
New York, NY 10016

Reader's Digest
Pleasantville, NY 10570

The Saturday Evening Post
1100 Waterway Boulevard
Indianapolis, IN 46202

Smithsonian
900 Jefferson Drive, SW
Washington, DC 20560

Health and Nutrition

East West Journal
17 Station Street
Brookline, MA 02146

Prevention
33 East Minor Street
Emmaus, PA 18049

Weight Watchers Magazine
360 Lexington Avenue
New York, NY 10017

Home and Gardening

Better Homes and Gardens
1716 Locust Street
Des Moines, IA 50336

The Family Handyman
1999 Shepard Road
St. Paul, MN 55116

Horticulture
755 Boylston Street
Boston, MA 02116

House and Garden
The Condé Nast Building
350 Madison Avenue
New York, NY 10017

House Beautiful
1700 Broadway
New York, NY 10019

Metropolitan Home
Locust at 17th
Des Moines, IA 50336

Literary

The Atlantic
8 Arlington Street
Boston, MA 02116

Harper's Magazine
666 Broadway
New York, NY 10012

The New Yorker
25 West 43rd Street
New York, NY 10036

Saturday Review Magazine
214 Massachusetts Avenue, NE
Suite 460
Washington, DC 20002

Men's Interests

Esquire
Two Park Avenue
New York, NY 10016

Gentlemen's Quarterly (GQ)
350 Madison Avenue
New York, NY 10017

Penthouse
909 Third Avenue
New York, NY 10022

Playboy
919 North Michigan Avenue
Chicago, IL 60611

News

Newsweek
444 Madison Avenue
New York, NY 10022

Time
Time & Life Building
New York, NY 10022

U.S. News & World Report
2400 N Street, NW
Washington, DC 20037

Parenting

American Baby
575 Lexington Avenue
New York, NY 10022

Expecting
685 Third Avenue
New York, NY 10017

Parents Magazine
685 Third Avenue
New York, NY 10017

Public, Social, and Political Affairs

Note: *See also* News section.

Entrepreneur
1541 NW 15th Street
Ft. Lauderdale, FL 33311

Mother Jones
1663 Mission Street
San Francisco, CA 94103

The Nation
72 Fifth Avenue
New York, NY 10011

The New Republic
1220 19th Street, NW
Washington, DC 20036

Science and Mechanics

Home Mechanix
1515 Broadway
New York, NY 10036

Popular Mechanics Magazine
224 West 57th Street
New York, NY 10019

Science Digest
1775 Broadway
New York, NY 10019

Scientific American
415 Madison Avenue
New York, NY 10017

Sports

Field and Stream
1515 Broadway
12th Floor
New York, NY 10036

Travel

Travel & Leisure
1120 Avenue of the Americas
New York, NY 10036

Women's Interests

Bride's
The Condé Nast Building
350 Madison Avenue
New York, NY 10017

Cosmopolitan
224 West 57th Street
New York, NY 10019

Essence
1500 Broadway
New York, NY 10036

Family Circle
110 Fifth Avenue
New York, NY 10011

Glamour
350 Madison Avenue
New York, NY 10017

Good Housekeeping
959 8th Avenue
New York, NY 10019

Ladies' Home Journal
100 Park Avenue
New York, NY 10017

Mademoiselle
350 Madison Avenue
New York, NY 10017

McCall's
230 Park Avenue
New York, NY 10169

Modern Bride
One Park Avenue
New York, NY 10016

Ms.
119 West 40th Street
New York, NY 10018

New Woman
215 Lexington Avenue
New York, NY 10016

Playgirl
801 2nd Avenue
New York, NY 10017

Redbook
224 West 57th Street
New York, NY 10019

Vogue
350 Madison Avenue
New York, NY 10017

Woman's Day
1515 Broadway
New York, NY 10036

Women's Circle
23 Herrick Road
Peabody, MA 01960

Working Woman
342 Madison Avenue
New York, NY 10173

Newspapers

National

USA Today
1000 Wilson Boulevard
Arlington, VA 22209

Wall Street Journal
200 Liberty Street
New York, NY 10281

Major Daily by State

Alabama

Birmingham News
2200 4th Avenue, N
Birmingham, AL 35202

Birmingham Post-Herald
2200 4th Avenue, N
Birmingham, AL 35202

Huntsville News
2117 West Clinton Avenue
Huntsville, AL 35801

Alabama Journal
200 Washington Avenue
Montgomery, AL 36102

Montgomery Advertiser
200 Washington Avenue
Montgomery, AL 36102

Alaska

Anchorage Daily News
1001 Northway Drive
Anchorage, AK 99508

Anchorage Times
820 West 4th Avenue
Anchorage, AK 99501

Arizona

Arizona Republic
120 East Van Buren Street
Phoenix, AZ 85004

Phoenix Gazette
120 East Van Buren Street
Phoenix, AZ 85004

Arizona Daily Star
4850 South Park Avenue
Tucson, AZ 85726

Tucson Citizen
4850 South Park Avenue
Tucson, AZ 85726

Arkansas

Arkansas Gazette
112 West Third
Little Rock, AR 72201

Little Rock Arkansas Democrat
Capitol Avenue and Scott Street
Little Rock, AR 72201

California

Press-Telegram
604 Pine Avenue
Long Beach, CA 90844

Los Angeles Daily Journal
210 South Spring Street
Los Angeles, CA 90012

Los Angeles Herald Examiner
1111 South Broadway
Los Angeles, CA 90015

Los Angeles Times
Times Mirror Square
Los Angeles, CA 90053

The Tribune
409 13th Street
Oakland, CA 94623

Sacramento Bee
21st and Q Streets
Sacramento, CA 95813

San Diego Transcript
2131 Third Avenue
San Diego, CA 92101

San Diego Union
350 Camino de la Reina
San Diego, CA 92108

San Francisco Chronicle
901 Mission Street
San Francisco, CA 94103

San Francisco Examiner
110 5th Street
San Francisco, CA 94103

Colorado

Boulder Daily Camera
1048 Pearl Street
Boulder, CO 80302

Daily Journal
101 University Boulevard
Denver, CO 80206

Denver Post
650 15th Street
Denver, CO 80202

Connecticut

Hartford Courant
285 Broad Street
Hartford, CT 06115

New Haven Register
40 Sargent Drive
New Haven, CT 06511

The Advocate
75 Tresser Boulevard
Stamford, CT 06901

Delaware

Evening Journal
831 Orange Street
Wilmington, DE 19801

District of Columbia

Washington Post
1150 15th Street, NW
Washington, DC 20071

Florida

Fort Lauderdale News
101 North New River Drive, E
Ft. Lauderdale, FL 33302

Miami Herald
No. 1 Herald Plaza
Miami, FL 33132

Orlando Sentinel
633 North Orange Avenue
Orlando, FL 32801

Georgia

Atlanta Daily World
145 Auburn Avenue, NE
Atlanta, GA 30335

Atlanta Journal
72 Marietta Street
Atlanta, GA 30303

Hawaii

Hawaii Hochi
917 Kokea Street
Honolulu, HI 96817

Honolulu Advertiser
605 Kapiolana Boulevard
Honolulu, HI 96813

Idaho

Idaho Statesman
1200 North Curtis Road
Boise, ID 83706

Illinois

Chicago Defender
2400 South Michigan Avenue
Chicago, IL 60616

Chicago Sun Times
401 North Wabash Avenue
Chicago, IL 60611

Chicago Tribune
435 North Michigan Avenue
Chicago, IL 60611

Indiana

Herald-Telephone
1900 South Walnut
Bloomington, IN 47401

Indianapolis News
307 North Pennsylvania Street
Indianapolis, IN 46204

Indianapolis Star
307 North Pennsylvania Street
Indianapolis, IN 46204

Iowa

Des Moines Register
715 Locust Street
Des Moines, IA 50304

Des Moines Tribune
715 Locust Street
Des Moines, IA 50304

Kansas

Kansas City Kansan
901 North 8th Street
Kansas City, KS 66101

Lawrence Journal World
6th and North H Streets
Lawrence, KS 66044

Capital-Journal
616 Jefferson
Topeka, KS 66607

Wichita Eagle-Beacon
825 East Douglas
Wichita, KS 67202

Kentucky

Courier-Journal
525 West Broadway
Louisville, KY 40202

Louisiana

Baton Rouge Advocate
525 Lafayette Street
Baton Rouge, LA 70802

Daily Record
931 Canal Street
518 Audubon Building
New Orleans, LA 70112

Times-Picayune
3800 Howard Avenue
New Orleans, LA 70140

Maine

Evening Express
390 Congress Street
Portland, ME 04104

Portland Press Herald
390 Congress Street
Portland, ME 04104

Maryland

The Baltimore Sun
Calvert and Center Streets
Baltimore, MD 21278

Massachusetts

Boston Globe
135 Morrissey Boulevard
Boston, MA 02107

Boston Herald
One Herald Square
Boston, MA 02106

Michigan

Detroit Free Press
321 Lafayette
Detroit, MI 48231

Detroit News
615 Lafayette Boulevard
Detroit, MI 48231

Minnesota

Minneapolis Star and Tribune
425 Portland Avenue
Minneapolis, MN 55488

St. Paul Pioneer Press and Dispatch
345 Cedar Street
St. Paul, MN 55101

Mississippi

Jackson Clarion-Ledger
311 East Pearl Street
Jackson, MS 39205

Missouri

Kansas City Star
1729 Grand Avenue
Kansas City, MO 64108

Kansas City Times
1729 Grand Avenue
Kansas City, MO 64108

St. Louis Post-Dispatch
900 North Tucker Boulevard
St. Louis, MO 63101

Montana

Billings Gazette
401 North Broadway
Billings, MT 59101

Great Falls Tribune
205 River Drive, S
Great Falls, MT 59403

Nebraska

Lincoln Star-Journal
P.O. Box 81609
926 P Street
Lincoln, NE 68501

Daily Record
2511 Leavenworth
Omaha, NE 68105

Omaha World-Herald
World-Herald Square
Omaha, NE 68102

Nevada

Las Vegas Review-Journal
1111 West Bonanza
Las Vegas, NV 89125

Las Vegas Sun
121 South Highland
Las Vegas, NV 89127

Reno Gazette Journal
955 Kuenzli Street
Reno, NV 89520

New Hampshire

Nashua Telegraph
60 Main Street
Nashua, NH 03061

New Jersey

Press and Sunday Press
1900 Atlantic Avenue
Atlantic City, NJ 08404

Star-Ledger
Star-Ledger Plaza
Newark, NJ 07101

The Times
500 Perry Street
Trenton, NJ 08605

New Mexico

Albuquerque Journal
7777 Jefferson, NE
Albuquerque, NM 87109

Albuquerque Tribune
7777 Jefferson, NE
Albuquerque, NM 87109

New York

New York Daily News
220 East 42nd Street
New York, NY 10017

New York Newsday
780 Third Avenue
New York, NY 10017

New York Post
210 South Street
New York, NY 10002

New York Times
229 West 43rd Street
New York, NY 10036

North Carolina

Charlotte Observer
600 South Tryon Street
Charlotte, NC 28202

Durham Sun
115 Market Street
Durham, NC 27702

News and Observer
215 South McDowell Street
Raleigh, NC 27602

Raleigh Times
215 South McDowell Street
Raleigh, NC 27602

North Dakota

Bismarck Tribune
707 East Front Avenue
Bismarck, ND 58501

Ohio

Cincinnati Enquirer
617 Vine Street
Cincinnati, OH 45201

Cincinnati Post
125 East Court Street
Cincinnati, OH 45202

Cleveland Plain Dealer
1801 Superior Avenue
Cleveland, OH 44114

Columbus Dispatch
34 South Third Street
Columbus, OH 43215

Oklahoma

Daily Oklahoman
500 North Broadway
Oklahoma City, OK 73125

Tulsa Daily Business Journal
8545 East 41st Street
Tulsa, OK 74145

Tulsa Tribune
315 South Boulder Avenue
Tulsa, OK 74102

Oregon

Daily Journal of Commerce
2014 NW 24th Avenue
Portland, OR 97210

The Oregonian
1320 SW Broadway
Portland, OR 97201

Pennsylvania

Philadelphia Daily News
400 North Broad Street
Philadelphia, PA 19101

Philadelphia Enquirer
400 North Broad Street
Philadelphia, PA 19101

Pittsburgh Post-Gazette
50 Boulevard of Allies
Pittsburgh, PA 15222

Pittsburgh Press
34 Boulevard of Allies
Pittsburgh, PA 15230

Rhode Island

Evening Bulletin
75 Fountain Street
Providence, RI 02902

Providence Journal
75 Fountain Street
Providence, RI 02902

South Carolina

Charleston News and Courier
134 Columbus Street
Charleston, SC 29402

Columbia Record
Stadium Road
Columbia, SC 29202

South Dakota

Argus Leader
200 South Minnesota Avenue
Sioux Falls, SD 57117

Tennessee

Commercial Appeal
495 Union Avenue
Memphis, TN 38101

Knoxville Journal
210 West Church Avenue
Knoxville, TN 37901

Nashville Banner
1100 Broadway
Nashville, TN 37202

The Tennessean
1100 Broadway
Nashville, TN 37202

Texas

Austin American-Statesman
166 East River Drive
Austin, TX 78704

Dallas Morning News
Communications Center
Dallas, TX 75265

Dallas Times Herald
1101 Pacific
Dallas, TX 75202

El Paso Herald-Post
401 Mills Avenue
El Paso, TX 79901

Fort Worth Star-Telegram
400 West 7th Street
Ft. Worth, TX 76102

The Citizen
17511 El Camino Real
Houston, TX 77058

Houston Chronicle
801 Texas Avenue
Houston, TX 77002

Utah

Salt Lake City Deseret News
30 East First, South
Salt Lake City, UT 84110

Salt Lake Tribune
143 South Main
Salt Lake City, UT 84111

Vermont

Brattleboro Reformer
Black Mountain Road
Brattleboro, VT 05301

Burlington Free Press
191 College Street
Burlington, VT 05401

Virginia

Alexandria Gazette
717 North St. Asaph Street
Alexandria, VA 22314

Ledger-Star
150 West Brambleton Avenue
Norfolk, VA 23510

Richmond News Leader
333 East Grace Street
Richmond, VA 23219

Washington

Seattle Post-Intelligencer
101 Elliott Avenue, W
Seattle, WA 98119

Seattle Times
Fairview Avenue North and John Street
Seattle, WA 98111

West Virginia

Charleston Daily Mail
1001 Virginia Street
Charleston, WV 25301

The Intelligencer
1500 Main Street
Wheeling, WV 26003

Wisconsin

Madison Capital Times
1901 Fish Hatchery Road
Madison, WI 53713

Wisconsin State Journal
1901 Fish Hatchery Road
Madison, WI 53713

Milwaukee Journal
333 West State Street
Milwaukee, WI 53203

Milwaukee Sentinel
918 North 4th Street
Milwaukee, WI 53201

Wyoming

Wyoming Eagle
110 East 17th Street
Cheyenne, WY 82001

Wyoming State Tribune
110 East 17th Street
Cheyenne, WY 82001

Parenting

Adoption

Adoptee/Natural Parent Locators-International
P.O. Box 1283
Canyon Country, CA 91351
805-251-3536

Adoptive Parents Committee
210 Fifth Avenue
New York, NY 10010
212-683-9221

Committee for Single Adoptive Parents
P.O. Box 15084
Chevy Chase, MD 20852

Yesterday's Children
5945 Fiddletown Place
San Jose, CA 95120
408-268-5654

Single-Parent Families

America's Society of Separated and Divorced Men
575 Keep Street
Elgin, IL 60120
312-695-2200

Big Brothers/Big Sisters of America
230 North 13th Street
Philadelphia, PA 19107
215-567-2748

League for Human Rights in Divorce
P.O. Box 985
Southampton, NY 11968
516-283-5010

National Committee for Adoption
2025 M Street, NW
Suite 512
Washington, DC 20036
202-463-7559

National Council on Family Relations
1910 West County Road B
Suite 147
St. Paul, MN 55113
612-633-6933

Orphan Voyage
2141 Road 2300
Cedaredge, CO 81413
303-856-3937

Shared Parenting Association
P.O. Box 430306
6510 SW 93rd Avenue
Miami, FL 33143

Radio and Television Networks

American Broadcasting Companies (ABC)
1330 Avenue of Americas
New York, NY 10019
  ABC Communications
  ABC Entertainment
  ABC News and Sports
  ABC Radio Networks
  ABC Television Network
  Broadcast Group
  Broadcast Operations and Engineering
  Television Stations
  Video Enterprises
  Radio

American Business Network (BIZ NET)
1615 H Street, NW
Washington, DC 20062

Arts & Entertainment Cable Network (A&E)
555 Fifth Avenue
New York, NY 10017

Associated Press Radio Network
1825 K Street, NW
Suite 615
Washington, DC 20006

Black Entertainment Television
1232 31st Street, NW
Washington, DC 20077

Cable Network News (CNN)
P.O. Box 105264
1050 Techwood Drive, NW
Atlanta, GA 30318

Cable Satellite Public Affairs Network (C-SPAN)
400 North Capitol Street, NW
Suite 412
Washington, DC 20001

CBS, Inc.
51 West 52nd Street
New York, NY 10019

  CBS/Broadcast Group
  51 West 52nd Street
  New York, NY 10019

    CBS Magazines Division
    CBS/Publishing Group
    CBS/Records Group
    CBS Technology Center

  CBS Entertainment Division
  CBS Television City
  7800 Beverly Boulevard
  Los Angeles, CA 90036

  CBS News Division
  524 West 57th Street
  New York, NY 10019

  CBS Operations and Engineering Division
  524 West 57th Street
  New York, NY 10019

  CBS Radio Division
  51 West 52nd Street
  New York, NY 10019

  CBS Television Network (CTN)
  51 West 52nd Street
  New York, NY 10019

    CBS Sports Division (CSD)
    CBS Television Stations Division (CTS)

  CBS Theatrical Films Division
  4024 Radford Avenue
  Studio City, CA 91604

Entertainment and Sports Programming Network (ESPN)
ESPN Plaza
Bristol, CT 06010

Hughes Television Network
4 Penn Plaza
New York, NY 10001

The Learning Channel
1414 22nd Street, NW
Washington, DC 20037

Madison Square Garden Network
Two Pennsylvania Plaza
New York, NY 10001

MTV Networks, Inc.
1775 Broadway
New York, NY 10019

Mutual Broadcasting System
1755 South Jefferson Davis Highway
Arlington, VA 22202

National Broadcasting Company, Inc. (NBC)
30 Rockefeller Plaza
New York, NY 10020

  NBC Corporate Communications
  NBC Corporate Planning
  NBC Entertainment
  NBC Legal and Standards
  NBC News
  NBC Operations and Technical Services
  NBC Personnel and Labor Relations
  NBC Sports
  NBC Television Network
  NBC Television Stations

National Broadcasting Network
11906 Madison Avenue
Lakewood, OH 44107

National Christian Network
1150 West King Street
Cocoa, FL 32922

National Public Radio (NPR)
2025 M Street, NW
Washington, DC 20036

Public Broadcasting Service (PBS)
Headquarters
1320 Braddock Place
Alexandria, VA 22314

  National Press Relations/CA
  4401 Sunset Boulevard
  Suite 335
  Los Angeles, CA 90027

  National Press Relations/NY
  609 Fifth Avenue
  New York, NY 10017

Reuters Information Services
1700 Broadway
New York, NY 10019

Sheridan Broadcast Network
1500 Chamber of Commerce Building
Pittsburgh, PA 15219

Sportsvision
820 West Madison
Oak Park, IL 60302

United Press International Radio
1400 I Street
Washington, DC 20005

United Stations Radio Networks
1440 Broadway
New York, NY 10018

UPI Cable News
220 East 42nd Street
New York, NY 10017

USA Network
1230 Avenue of the Americas
New York, NY 10020

Time & Life Building
Chicago, IL 60611

2500 Fisher Building
Detroit, MI 48202

1900 Avenue of the Stars
Los Angeles, CA 90067

The Weather Channel
2840 Mt. Wilkinson Parkway
Atlanta, GA 30339

Owner:
Landmark Communications, Inc.
150 West Brambleton Avenue
Norfolk, VA 23501

Washington News Bureau:
1776 G Street, NW
Washington, DC 20006

London News Bureau:
11 Grape Street
London WC2H89R
England

Sports Organizations and Halls of Fame

American and National Basketball Associations
645 Fifth Avenue
New York, NY 10022

American and National Leagues of Professional Baseball Clubs
350 Park Avenue
New York, NY 10022

American Hockey League
218 Memorial Avenue
West Springfield, MA 01089

Association of Sports Museums and Halls of Fame
101 West Sutton Place
Wilmington, DE 19810

Baseball and Sports Hall of SHAME
P.O. Box 6218
West Palm Beach, FL 33405

International Boxing Hall of Fame
P.O. Box 425
Canastota, NY 13032

Naismith Memorial Basketball Hall of Fame
P.O. Box 179
1150 West Columbus Avenue
Springfield, MA 01101

National Association of Professional Baseball Leagues
(minor league clubs)
P.O. Box A
201 Bayshore Drive, SE
St. Petersburg, FL 33731

National Baseball Hall of Fame
P.O. Box 590
Cooperstown, NY 13326

National Bowling Association
377 Park Avenue South
7th Floor
New York, NY 10016

National Football Foundation and Hall of Fame
Bell Tower Building
1865 Palmer Avenue
Larchmont, NY 10538

National Football League
410 Park Avenue
New York, NY 10022

National Hockey League
960 Sun Life Building
1155 Metcalfe Street
Montreal, PQ, Canada H3B 2W2

National Sports Association
518 Barneson Avenue
San Mateo, CA 94402

National Tennis Foundation and Hall of Fame
100 Park Avenue
New York, NY 10017

Professional Bowler's Association of America
1720 Merriman Road
Akron, OH 44313

Professional Golfer's Association of America
Box 109601
Palm Beach Gardens, FL 33410

Where to Write Your Senators and Representatives

Senators' and representatives' offices are housed in the Capitol Building as well as in six other buildings listed below. However, constituents can write to their senators and representatives as follows.

Senator's name
United States Senate
Washington, DC 20510

Representative's name
United States House of Representatives
Washington, DC 20515

Most government departments and agencies have their own ZIP Codes; the correct one should be used. The Senate ZIP Code differs from that of the House. All Senate office buildings have the 20510 ZIP Code, and all House office buildings have the 20515 ZIP Code.

Listings of specific addresses of members of Congress are in the more current edition of *The Congressional Staff Directory* or *Congressional Quarterly's Washington Directory*, both of which are available in local libraries. These books also list the home offices of members of Congress. Local telephone directories may also be consulted.

Both the Senate and House have offices in the Capitol Building, but additional offices are housed at the following buildings:

Senate Offices

Dirksen Senate Office Building
Constitution Avenue between 1st and 2nd Streets, NE

Hart Senate Office Building
2nd Street and Constitution Avenue, NE

Russell Senate Office Building
Constitution Avenue between Delaware Avenue and
  1st Street, NE

House Offices

Cannon House Office Building
Independence Avenue between C and 1st Streets, SE

Longworth House Office Building
Independence Avenue between C and South Capitol
  Streets, SE

Rayburn House Office Building
Independence Avenue, between South Capitol and 1st
  Streets, SE

Additional Sources of Information

Brobeck, Stephen. *The Product Safety Book*. Dutton, 1983.

Congressional Staff Directory. Congressional Staff Directory, 1987.

Eiler, Andrew. *The Consumer Protection Manual*. Facts on File, 1984.

Everton, George B., ed. *The Handy Book for Genealogists*. Everton, 1986.

Gill, Kay, and Wilson, Robert. *Consumer Sourcebook,* 4th ed. Gale Research, 1987.

Post-Purchase Remedies. United States Federal Trade Commission, Office of Policy Planning and
  Evaluation, 1980.

Shilling, Dana. *Fighting Back: A Consumer's Guide for Getting Satisfaction*. Quill, 1982.

19

Travel

Traveler's Checklist

Things to Do

Arrange for the post office to hold your mail, or have someone collect it daily.
Stop all deliveries to your home.
Arrange for the care of animals, plants, and lawn.
Put valuables in a safe deposit box.
Notify neighbors and police of absence and let them know how you can be reached.
Leave a key with a neighbor.
Arrange for travelers' insurance coverage, if needed.
Notify travel agent of any special needs you might have, such as the use of an airport wheelchair.
Reconfirm your airline ticket and other reservations.
Tag your luggage with brightly colored stickers or ribbons for easy identification.
Set timers or leave a light on.
Empty refrigerator and turn it on low.
Turn off hot water.
Lock all doors and windows.

Things to Bring

Airline or other tickets and travel documents.
Auto registration, if driving.
Passport, visas, and health certificates.
Medical information and doctor's name and telephone number.
Special prescriptions or prescription medications.
Insurance papers.
Credit cards.
Travelers checks and personal checks.
Cash, including some in the currency of the country to which you are traveling.
Names and addresses of people to contact in an emergency.
Names, addresses, phone numbers, reservation numbers, and dates for places where you will be staying.
Lightweight fold-up tote bag for purchases.
Addresses of friends and family to whom to send mail.

Toll-Free Numbers for Rental Cars and Hotels/Motels

Note: In some areas dialing "1" before the number may be necessary.

Car Rental Agencies

Avis 800-331-1212
Budget 800-527-0700
Hertz 800-654-3131
National 800-227-7368

Rent-a-Wreck 800-423-2158
Thrifty 800-367-2277
Ugly Duckling 800-528-1584
Value 800-327-2501

International Car Rental Agencies

Auto Europe 800-223-5555
Avis 800-331-2112
Europcar 800-CarRent
Hertz 800-654-3001

Hotels/Motels

Best Western 800-528-1234
Hilton 800-445-8667
Holiday Inn 800-HOLIDAY
Hotels of the World 800-223-6800
     Atlantic City, Reno, Las Vegas, and Tahoe Hotels 800-255-5722
        Condo Reservations 800-321-2525
Howard Johnson 800-654-2000
Hyatt 800-228-9000
Marriott 800-228-9290
Ramada Inn 800-2RAMADA
Red Lion 800-547-8010

Airline Codes and Toll-Free Airline Numbers

Note: In some areas, dialing "1" before the number may be necessary.

EI	AerLingus 800-223-6537	NW	Northwest Airlines, domestic 800-225-2525
AM	Aeromexico 800-237-6639		Northwest Airlines, international 800-447-4747
AC	Air Canada 800-422-6232		
AF	Air France 800-237-2747	PA	Pan Am 800-442-5896
AS	Alaska Airlines 800-426-0333	PI	Piedmont Airlines 800-251-5720
AZ	Alitalia 800-223-5730	QF	Qantas 800-227-4500
AA	American Airlines 800-433-7300	RC	Republic Airlines 800-441-1414
BA	British Airways 800-247-9297	SA	Scandinavian Air 800-221-2350
BR	British Caledonian 800-231-0270	SR	Swissair 800-221-4750
CO	Continental Airlines 800-525-0280	TW	TWA, domestic 800-221-2000
DL	Delta Airlines 800-221-1212	TW	TWA, international 800-892-4141
EA	Eastern Airlines 800-Eastern	UA	United Airlines 800-241-6522
IB	Iberia Airlines 800-221-9741	AL	US Air 800-428-4322
JL	Japan Airlines 800-525-3663	WO	World Airways 800-772-2600
LH	Lufthansa 800-645-3880		

National Weather Service Average Temperatures (Fahrenheit)—North America

Location	*December–March* *(high/low)*	*June–August* *(high/low)*
Acapulco	87/70	89/75
Albuquerque	72/40	91/62
Austin	63/42	93/72
Bermuda	68/58	84/73
Boston	40/22	80/58
Cancún	87/70	89/75
Chicago	34/18	82/64
Dallas	58/37	92/72
Denver	43/17	85/57
Dominican Republic	85/69	88/72
Honolulu	76/68	84/72
Jackson Hole, WY	36/11	80/52
Lake Tahoe	50/16	89/40
Las Vegas	65/34	103/71
Los Angeles	66/47	76/58
Mexico City	72/43	75/53
Miami	76/59	88/75
Montreal	24/10	72/54
Nassau	77/67	88/76
New Orleans	65/48	90/76
New York City	41/27	80/65
Palm Beach	79/43	95/73
Philadelphia	42/29	83/64
Port au Prince	86/68	70/73
St. Thomas	85/72	89/76
San Juan	82/71	87/76
Tucson	65/39	97/71
Vancouver	44/36	67/53
Washington, DC	45/29	85/64
Yellowstone National Park	32/6	75/46

National Weather Service Average Temperatures (Fahrenheit)—Outside North America

Location	December–March (high/low)	June–August (high/low)
Amsterdam	40/32	69/53
Athens	58/44	90/72
Bali	90/74	94/76
Bangkok	89/70	90/75
Bogotá	67/48	64/50
Buenos Aires	87/62	57/40
Cairo	67/48	94/69
Caracas	77/57	78/63
Dublin	47/36	67/51
Guam	90/72	86/69
Hong Kong	68/57	87/59
Israel	57/41	90/65
Istanbul	48/38	80/64
Kathmandu	65/36	84/70
Lima	75/53	77/61
Lisbon	55/44	84/63
London	44/35	70/52
Manila	87/70	90/75
Montevideo	84/72	77/70
Munich	36/23	73/53
Nairobi	77/54	69/51
New Delhi	71/43	96/80
Panama City	88/71	86/70
Paris	44/36	76/58
Quito	77/57	78/65
Rio de Janeiro	82/71	76/70
Rome	55/42	85/66
Santiago	86/70	78/69
Seoul	30/20	81/69
Singapore	88/74	87/73
Taiwan	70/61	90/72
Tokyo	47/32	81/69

Air Mileage from New York City— Domestic

Albuquerque	1,810	Boston	188
Atlanta	747	Chicago	711
Baltimore	170	Denver	1,628

Detroit	483	Philadelphia	83
Kansas City, MO	1,097	Phoenix	2,142
Los Angeles	2,446	Portland	2,455
Memphis	953	St. Louis	873
Miami	1,095	Salt Lake City	1,972
Nashville	758	San Francisco	2,568
New Orleans	1,173	Seattle	2,419
Omaha	1,144	Washington, DC	204

Air Mileage from New York City— Foreign

Acapulco	2,260	Lima	3,651
Amsterdam	3,639	Lisbon	3,366
Antigua	1,783	London	3,456
Aruba	1,963	Madrid	3,588
Athens	4,927	Manchester	3,336
Barbados	2,100	Mexico City	2,086
Bermuda	771	Milan	4,004
Bogotá	2,487	Nassau	1,101
Brussels	3,662	Oslo	3,671
Buenos Aires	5,302	Paris	3,628
Caracas	2,123	Reykjavík	2,600
Copenhagen	3,849	Rio de Janeiro	4,816
Curaçao	1,993	Rome	4,280
Frankfurt	3,851	St. Croix	1,680
Geneva	3,859	San Juan	1,609
Glasgow	3,211	Santo Domingo	1,560
Hamburg	3,806	Tel Aviv	5,672
Kingston	1,583	Zurich	3,926

Foreign Currencies

This chart lists the official names for selected currencies around the world. Colonial legacies have made certain names—dollar, peso, franc, and pound, for example—widespread. The traveler should not assume equivalency in value, or transferability, among units sharing a name; that is, one cannot spend Central African *francs* in France or Turkish *lira* in Rome.

Afghanistan	afghani	Antigua	East Caribbean dollar
Albania	lek	Argentina	austral
Algeria	dinar	Australia	dollar
Andorra	French franc	Austria	schilling
	Spanish peseta	Bahamas	dollar
Angola	kwanza	Bahrain	dinar

Bangladesh	taka	Guinea Bissau	peso
Barbados	dollar	Guyana	dollar
Belau	dollar	Haiti	gourde
Belgium	franc	Honduras	lempira
Belize	dollar	Hungary	forint
Benin	franc CFA*	Iceland	krona
Bhutan	ngultrum	India	rupee
Bolivia	peso	Indonesia	rupiah
Bophuthatswana	South African rand	Iran	rial
Botswana	pula	Iraq	dinar
Brazil	cruzado	Ireland	pound
Brunei	dollar	Israel	shekel
Bulgaria	lev	Italy	lira
Burkina Faso	franc CFA	Ivory Coast	franc CFA
Burma	kyat	Jamaica	dollar
Burundi	franc	Japan	yen
Cambodia	riel	Jordan	dinar
Cameroon	franc CFA	Kenya	shilling
Canada	dollar	Kiribati	Australian dollar
Cape Verde	escudo	Korea, North	won
Central Africa	franc CFA	Korea, South	won
Chad	franc CFA	Kuwait	dinar
Chile	peso	Laos	kip
China	yuan	Lebanon	pound
Ciske	South African rand	Lesotho	loti
Colombia	peso	Liberia	dollar
Comoros	franc CFA	Libya	dinar
Congo	franc CFA	Liechtenstein	Swiss franc
Costa Rica	colon	Luxembourg	franc
Cuba	peso	Madagascar	franc
Cyprus	pound	Malawi	kwacha
Czechoslovakia	koruna	Malaysia	ringgit
Denmark	krone	Maldives	rupee
Djibouti	franc	Mali	franc CFA
Dominica	East Caribbean dollar	Malta	pound
Dominican Republic	peso	Marshalls	dollar
Ecuador	sucre	Mauritania	ouguiya
Egypt	pound	Mauritius	rupee
El Salvador	colon	Mexico	peso
Equatorial Guinea	ekuele	Micronesia	dollar
Ethiopia	birr	Monaco	French franc
Fiji	dollar	Mongolia	tugrik
Finland	markka	Morocco	dirham
France	franc	Mozambique	metical
Gabon	franc CFA	Namibia	South African rand
Gambia	dalasi	Nauru	Australian dollar
Germany, East	mark	Nepal	rupee
Germany, West	mark	Netherlands	guilder
Ghana	cedi	New Zealand	dollar
Greece	drachma	Nicaragua	cordoba
Grenada	East Caribbean dollar	Niger	franc CFA
Guatemala	quetzal	Nigeria	naira
Guinea	syli	Norway	krone

Oman	rial	Sweden	krona
Pakistan	rupee	Switzerland	franc
Panama	balboa	Syria	pound
Papua New Guinea	kina	Taiwan	New Taiwan dollar
Paraguay	guarani	Tanzania	shilling
Peru	inti	Thailand	baht
Philippines	peso	Togo	franc CFA
Poland	zloty	Tonga	dollar
Portugal	escudo	Transkei	South African rand
Qatar	riyal	Trinidad and Tobago	dollar
Rumania	lei	Tunisia	dinar
Rwanda	franc	Turkey	lira
St. Kitts	East Caribbean dollar	Tuvalu	Australian dollar
St. Lucia	East Caribbean dollar	Uganda	shilling
St. Vincent	East Caribbean dollar	United Arab Emirates	dirham
San Marino	Italian lira	United Kingdom	pound sterling
São Tomé and Principe	dobra	United States	dollar
Saudi Arabia	riyal	Uruguay	peso
Senegal	franc CFA	Vanuatu	vatu
Seychelles	rupee	Vatican City	lira
Sierra Leone	leone	Venda	South African rand
Singapore	dollar	Venezuela	bolivar
Solomons	dollar	Vietnam	dong
Somalia	shilling	Western Samoa	tala
South Africa	rand	Yemen, North	rial
Soviet Union	ruble	Yemen, South	dinar
Spain	peseta	Yugoslavia	dinar
Sri Lanka	rupee	Zaire	zaire
Sudan	pound	Zambia	kwacha
Suriname	guilder	Zimbabwe	dollar
Swaziland	lilangeni		

* Colonies Françoise d'Afrique

Foreign Visa Requirements

This listing is prepared solely for the information of U.S. citizens traveling as tourists and does not apply to persons planning to immigrate to foreign countries. A visa is generally an endorsement or stamp placed by officials of a foreign country on a U.S. passport that allows the bearer to visit that country.

   IMPORTANT: TRAVELERS SHOULD CHECK PASSPORT AND VISA REQUIREMENTS WITH THE CONSULAR OFFICIALS OF THE COUNTRIES TO BE VISITED WELL IN ADVANCE OF THEIR DEPARTURE DATES, SINCE SUCH INFORMATION IS SUBJECT TO CHANGE.

Passports

While a U.S. passport is not required by U.S. laws for travel to or in most countries in North, South, or Central America or adjacent islands, except Cuba, a passport is required under the laws or regulations of some of those countries and a valid U.S. passport is the best travel documentation available.

Persons who travel to a country where a U.S. passport is not required should be in possession of documentary evidence of their U.S. citizenship and identity to facilitate reentry into the United States. Those countries that do not require a passport to enter or depart frequently require the traveler to have documentary evidence of U.S. citizenship and identity. Documentary evidence of U.S. citizenship may be a previously issued U.S. passport, birth certificate, certificate of naturalization, certificate of citizenship, or report of birth abroad of a citizen of the United States. Documentary evidence of identity may be a previous U.S. passport, certificate of naturalization, certificate of citizenship, valid driver's license, or government (federal, state, or municipal) identification card or pass. Persons traveling in countries having requirements for evidence of citizenship and identity are cautioned that they may experience serious difficulties or delays if they do not have the necessary documents. Inquire before departure at the Embassy in Washington, D.C. or the local consulate of the country to be visited for specific requirements.

Visas

NECESSARY VISAS SHOULD BE OBTAINED BEFORE PROCEEDING ABROAD. Most foreign consular representatives are located in principal cities, particularly Chicago, New Orleans, New York, San Francisco, and Washington, D.C. In many instances, a traveler may be required to obtain visas from the consular office in the area of his/her residence. **IT IS THE RESPONSIBILITY OF THE TRAVELER TO OBTAIN VISAS, WHERE REQUIRED, FROM THE APPROPRIATE EMBASSY OR NEAREST CONSULAR OFFICE.** The addresses of foreign consular offices in the United States may be obained by consulting the **CONGRESSIONAL DIRECTORY,** which is available in most libraries, or city telephone directories. Tourists may be required to present other documentation at the port of entry of countries to be visited. Further assistance may be obtained from travel agents and from visa information services such as World Wide Visas (800-527-1861) and International Visa Service (800-843-0050).

Immunizations

Under the international health regulations adopted by the World Health Organization, a country may require international certificates of vaccination against yellow fever and cholera. Because smallpox has been eradicated, such vaccinations should NOT be given. Check with health care providers or your records to ensure measles, mumps, rubella, polio, diphtheria, tetanus, and pertussis immunizations are up to date. Prophylactic medication for malaria and certain other preventive measures are advisable for some travelers. NO immunizations are required to return to the United States. Pertinent information is included in "Health Information for International Travel," available from the U.S. Government Printing Office, Washington, D.C. 20402 for $4.75, or it may be obtained from your local health department or physician.

An increasing number of countries are establishing regulations regarding AIDS testing, particularly for long-term residents and students. Check with the embassy or consulate of the country you plan to visit for the latest information.

Afghanistan Valid passport and visa required. Tourist visa, valid 3 months from date of issue, allows stay up to 30 days and can be extended; $10 if obtained in person and $14 if obtained by mail; 3 photos. For specific requirements, check Embassy, Washington, DC 20008 (202-234-3770).

Albania Passport and visa required. Apply Albanian Mission, 131 rue de la Pompe, Paris 16e France, or Via Asmara 9, Rome, Italy, or any other country that maintains diplomatic relations with Albania. Currently visas are issued only to business representatives and groups of at least 10 persons.

Algeria Passport and visa required. Tourist visa, valid 3 months, 4 photos, $11.25. No personal checks. Obtain visa prior to airport arrival. Proof of onward/return ticket and sufficient funds for travel required. Apply Embassy, Washington, DC 20008 (202-328-5300), and check specific requirements.

Andorra *See* France.

Angola Passport and visa required. American citizens should be aware that there is no U.S. representation in Angola at this time. For travel to Angola, contact the Angolan Permanent Representative to the UN, 747 3rd Avenue, 18th Floor, New York, NY 10017.

Anguilla *See* United Kingdom.

Antigua and Barbuda Passport and visa not required for tourist stay up to 6 months. Proof of citizenship required. Return/onward ticket and/or proof of funds necessary. Check Embassy of Antigua and Barbuda, Intelsat Building, 3400 International Drive NW, Washington, DC 20008 (202-362-5122/5166/5211/5225) for specific requirements.

Argentina Passport and visa required. Tourist visa valid up to 4 years from date of issue; multiple entries, no charge. Each entry valid for stay of up to 3 months and may be extended for succeeding periods of 3 months. Children under 14 not accompanied by both parents require notarized authorization. Visas are issued by consulates in Baltimore, Chicago, Houston, Los Angeles, Miami, New Orleans, New York, San Francisco, and Puerto Rico. Check Embassy, Washington, DC (202-939-6400) or consulate for specific requirements.

Aruba Valid passport or proof of U.S. citizenship required. Visa not required for stay up to 14 days. Tourists may be asked to show onward/return ticket, necessary documents, or sufficient funds for stay. Permission of local authorities required for a maximum stay up to 90 days. Check Netherlands Embassy or nearest consulate for specific requirements.

Australia Valid passport and visa required. Transit visa not required for stay up to 72 hours. Visitor visa valid up to 5 years; multiple entries, stay of 6 months, no charge, 1 photo. Upon arrival, onward/return transportation required.

Apply Consulate General, San Francisco, CA 94108-4979; New York, NY 10111; Chicago, IL 60601-4675; Honolulu, HI 96813-4299; Los Angeles, CA 90046; Houston, TX 77056-9998; or the Embassy, Washington, DC 20036-2273 (202-797-3000). Check Consulate General/Embassy for regulations for entry other than visitor. **Norfolk Island**—Passport and visa not required for stay up to 30 days. Visitors must possess confirmed accommodations and onward/return transportation. Check Embassy of Australia for specific requirements.

Austria Passport required. Visa not required for stay up to 3 months. Visa required for stay over 3 months, no charge. Check Embassy, Washington, DC 20008 (202-232-2674) or consulate for specific requirements.

Azores *See* Portugal.

Bahamas Passport and visa not required of tourist with onward/return ticket and sufficient identification of citizenship (birth certificate or voter registration card) for stay up to 8 months. Passport and residence/work permit required for residence, business, or missionary work. Business representatives should inquire about work permit and traveling salesman's license. Apply Embassy, Washington, DC 20037 (202-338-3940) or Consulates General, New York, NY 10017 or Miami, FL 33131, and check specific requirements. Permit required to import pets.

Bahrain Passport required. No tourist visas issued at ths time. Transit visa available at Bahrain International Airport for temporary stay up to 72 hours; must have return/onward ticket. Bussiness, work, or resident visas valid for 3 months and require letter from company or No Objection Certificate from the Immigration Department in Bahrain. Apply Embassy of the State of Bahrain, 3502 International Drive NW, Washington, DC 20008 (202-342-0741/2) or the Permanent Mission of the State of Bahrain to the UN, 2 UN Plaza, East 44th Street, New York, NY 10017, and check specific requirements.

Bangladesh Passport required. Visa not required for tourist stay up to 14 days. Visitors must possess onward/return ticket. Check specific requirements with the Embassy of the People's Republic of Bangladesh, Washington, DC 20007 (202-342-8372) or Consulate General, New York, NY 10016.

Barbados Every visitor is required to be in possession of a valid passport or travel document. U.S. citizens traveling directly from the U.S. to Barbados may be admitted without a passport for a period not exceeding 3 months provided identity and national status are established to the satisfaction of immigration authorities. Such evidence includes a certified copy of a birth certificate, naturalization certificates, or similar legal proof of U.S. citizenship and a document that gives positive identification (photo I.D. such as driver's license or job identification card). Visas not required for U.S. citizen tourists for a stay of up to 6 months. Business visas, $25 single entry and $30 multiple entry. (A work permit may be required.) Visitors must possess valid return tickets to U.S. or a third country. Check Embassy, Washington, DC 20008 (202-939-9200) or Consulate General, New York, NY (212-867-8435) for specific requirements.

Belgium Passport required. Visa not required for business or tourist stay up to 90 days. Temporary residence permit required for stays over 90 days. For residence authorization, consult Embassy, Washington, DC 20008 (202-333-6900) or consulate for specific requirements.

Belize (formerly British Honduras) Passport required. Visa not required for tourists up to 6 months if in possession of return/round-trip ticket beginning in and returning to the U.S. Check Embassy of Belize, 1575 I. Street NW, Suite 695, Washington, DC 20005 (202-289-1416/7) for specific requirements.

Benin Passport and visa required. Entry/transit visa, 7 days, $8. Extensions may be obained for tourism, business, and short- or long-stay visa from the Immigration Office in Benin. Three photos and proof of return/onward ticket required. No personal checks. Apply Embassy, Washington, DC 20008 (202-232-6656) and check specific requirements.

Bermuda *See* United Kingdom.

Bhutan Passport and visa required. Visas issued by Department of Tourism in Bhutan. Unrestricted tourism is not permitted; visitors must be part of a group. The Bhutan travel service in New York has information on group tours (212-838-6382); check mission in New York (212-826-1919) for specific requirements.

Bolivia Passport required. Visa not required for tourist stay up to 90 days. Visa required for students, missionaries, diplomats, and officials issued at no charge. Business and/or work purposes visa required, $50. Include self-addressed, stamped envelope. Check Embassy, Washington, DC 20008 (202-483-4410) or consulate for specific requirements and entry of pets.

Bonaire *See* Netherlands Antilles

Botswana, Republic of Passport required. Visa not required for stay up to 30 days. Visitors staying over 30 days should apply for permission from Immigration and Passport Control Office in Gaborone. Check Embassy, Washington, DC 20008 (202-244-4990) or consulate for specific requirements.

Brazil Passport and visa required. Tourists must have onward/return ticket or bank introduction letter attesting to financial capability. One photo. Children 3 months to 6 years must have polio vaccination. Children not accompanied by both parents require notarized permission to travel in Brazil. Bearers of work visas and business travelers, excluded, must register with local immigration authorities. Check Embassy, Washington, DC 20008 (202-745-

2828) or consulate for specific requirements and entry of pets.

Brunei Passport and visa required. Apply Embassy, 2600 Virginia Avenue NW, Suite 300, Washington, DC 20037 (202-342-0159) and check specific requirements.

Bulgaria Passport and visa required. Tourist visa valid for stay over 30 hours and up to 30 days, $14. Business visa, for stay up to 60 days, $14, requires invitation from Bulgarian organization or its representative in the United States. Visitors visa requires letter of invitation for stay up to 90 days, issued to relatives, friends, etc. and may be extended, $14. Transit visa requires visa for next country of travel, valid up to 30 hours, $9. No personal checks. Include fee of $3, 1 photo, and self-addressed envelope. Apply Embassy, Washington, DC 20008 (202-387-7969) and check specific requirements.

Burkina Faso (formerly Upper Volta) Passport and visa required. Tourist/transit visa, valid up to 3 months from date of issue, $20; 2 photos. Include $1.50 for return of passport by registered mail. Apply Embassy, Washington, DC 20008 (202-332-5577) or the honorary consuls in Los Angeles or New Orleans, and check specific requirements.

Burma Passport and visa required. Tourist visa $5, valid up to 7 days, 1 entry, 3 photos; visa for next destination or onward/return ticket required. Overland travel into and out of Burma not permitted. Enclose stamped, self-addressed envelope (registered/certified) for return of passport. A minimum of 100 U.S. dollars must be changed for local currency on arrival. Apply Embassy, Washington, DC 20008 (202-332-9044) or Permanent Mission of Burma to the UN, New York, NY 10021 (212-535-1311) and check specific requirements.

Burundi, Republic of Valid passport required. Transit visa, up to 48 hours, $11. Entry visa, 1 month, $11, 3 photos. Include return postage of $1.20. Obtain before arrival, because airport visas cause delays. Apply Embassy, Washington, DC 20007 (202-342-2574) or Permanent Mission of Burundi to the UN, New York, NY 10017 and check specific requirements.

Cambodia *See* Kampuchea.

Cameroon Passport, visa, and return/onward ticket required. Tourist visa, valid 20 days, may be extended 10 days, 1 entry, $29.23, 2 photos. Tourists require a bank statement. Apply Embassy, Washington, DC 20008 (202-265-8790); include certified or special delivery return envelope for return of passport, and check specific requirements. Obtain visas before arrival because airport visas are difficult to obtain.

Canada Passport or visa not required for tourists entering from the U.S. for a stay of up to 90 days, but tourists should carry personal identification; birth certificate, naturalization certificate, alien registration card, and valid or expired passports are excellent for identification purposes. U.S. citizens entering Canada from a third country are required to have a valid passport or official U.S. travel document. Passport and visa are required for immigration, i.e., landed immigrant status. Employment authorization is required for persons seeking to enter Canada to take previously secured temporary work. Student authorization is required for persons seeking to enter Canada to attend an educational institution. Temporary workers and students can check with Canadian Embassy, Washington, DC 20036 (202-785-1400) or nearest consulate for specific details.

Canal Zone *See* Panama.

Cape Verde Passport and visa required. Tourist visa, valid up to 30 days, can be extended, $13.50, 1 photo. Include stamped envelope for return of passport. Allow 3 to 4 weeks. Apply Embassy, Washington, DC 20007 (202-965-6820) and check specific requirements.

Cayman Islands *See* United Kingdom.

Central African Republic Passport and visa required. Visa $20, 3 photos. If applying by mail, include stamped return envelope. A letter from company/organization guaranteeing onward return ticket also is required. Yellow fever and cholera immunizations required. Visa must be obtained before arrival and also is required for transiting the country. Apply Embassy, Washington, DC 20008 (202-483-7800) and check specific requirements.

Chad Passport and visa required. Transit visa without stay/stay up to 1 week, $12.25, onward ticket required. Tourist or business visa valid up to 2 months for stays up to 30 days extendable, $12.25, 1 entry. Round-trip ticket, 3 photos, and proof of yellow fever vaccination required. Those applying by mail should include a registered or certified return envelope. Business visas require letter from company describing purpose of trip. Apply Embassy, Washington, DC 20009 (202-462-4009) and check specific requirements.

Chile Passport required. Visa not required for stay up to 3 months; may apply for an additional 3 months. Check Embassy, Washington, DC 20036 (202-785-3159) or consulate for specific requirements.

China, People's Republic of Passport and visa required. Visa applications may be submitted to the Chinese Embassy, 2300 Connecticut Avenue NW, Washington, DC 20008 (202-328-2500) or the Chinese Consulates General in Houston, New York, or San Francisco. To qualify for a visa, the traveler must show a ''letter of confirmation'' from the China International Travel Service (CITS) or an invitation from an individual or institution in China. CITS is the agency with exclusive responsibility for all foreign tourism in China (not including ''Overseas Chinese''). CITS tours

may be booked through several different travel agencies and airlines in the United States and abroad. Such tours are often advertised in newspapers and magazines. Visas for tour group members are usually obtained by the travel agent as part of the tour package. All persons planning travel to China should allow at least 3 weeks' processing time. The current visa fee of $7 and 2 photographs must accompany each visa application form. Tourists must present evidence of hotel reservation and/or tourist card. Persons transiting China, regardless of whether they are required to pass through customs and immigration, must have transit visas, or they will be fined $1,000. *See also* Taiwan.

Colombia Passport, visa/tourist card, and proof of onward/return ticket required for stay up to 90 days; extensions must be requested from Colombian immigration authorities. Tourists arriving by ship should get tourist card before departing the U.S. All persons with tourist cards assessed $15 departure tax. U.S. citizens under age 18 departing Colombia with one parent or alone must present authenticated written authorization from absent parent(s) or legal guardian. Apply Embassy, Washington, DC 20008 (202-387-8338) and check specific requirements.

Comoros Islands Passport and visa required. Visa issued at airport by immigration officer on arrival.

Congo, People's Republic of (Brazzaville) Passport and visa required. Tourists must have confirmed hotel reservations. Apply Representative of People's Republic of Congo to the United Nations, New York, NY 10021.

Cook Islands Passport required. Visa or entry permit not required for stays less than 31 days. Must have advance hotel reservations and onward/return transportation.

Costa Rica Valid passport required. (U.S. travelers are sometimes admitted with only proof of U.S. citizenship rather than a valid passport.) Either a visa or tourist card is required. Visas may be obtained before arrival from Embassy, Washington, DC 20008 (202-234-2945) or Consulate (202-328-6628) or nearest Costa Rican consulate. Tourist cards valid for stays up to 30 days may be purchased in lieu of a visa at the airport upon arrival and may be extended up to 90 days by permission of Costa Rican Immigration authorities. For stays over 30 days, a passport and exit visa are required. Check Embassy, Washington, DC 20008 (202-234-2945) or Consulate (202-328-6628) or nearest consulate for specific requirements.

Côte d'Ivoire (Ivory Coast) Passport and visa required. Visa valid 1 to 90 days, no charge, 4 photos. Proof of yellow fever vaccination required. Onward/return ticket and financial guarantee while in country are required. Visa must be obtained prior to arrival. Include postage for return of passport by registered mail. For further details, contact

Embassy, 2424 Massachusetts Avenue NW, Washington, DC 20008 (202-483-2400) or honorary consulates.

Cuba Passport and visa required. Tourist visa $24. Apply Embassy of the Czechoslovak Socialist Republic, Cuban Interests Section, 2639 16th Street NW, Washington, DC 20009 (202-797-8518), or authorized agencies located in Los Angeles, Miami, New York, Puerto Rico, and Washington, DC; check specific requirements.

Curacao *See* Netherlands Antilles.

Cyprus Passport required. Visa not required. Check Embassy, Washington, DC 20008 (202-462-5772) for specific requirements.

Czechoslovakia Passport and visa required. Tourist-transit visa valid 1 entry, $14; 2 entries, $28; 2 photos. Personal checks and machine stamps not accepted. Tourist/transit visas valid for 5 months. Check Embassy, Washington, DC 20008 (202-363-6315) for business, multiple-entry, and group visas.

Dahomey *See* Benin.

Denmark (including Greenland) Passport required. Tourist/business visa not required for stay up to 3 months. (Period begins when entering Scandinavian area: Finland, Iceland, Norway, Sweden.) Special rules apply for entry into the U.S.-operated defense area in Greenland. Check Embassy, Washington, DC 20008 (202-234-4300) or consulate for specific requirements and residence work permits.

Djibouti, Republic of Passport and visa required. Must have advance tickets for onward or return air travel. Check French Consulate, Washington, DC 20007 (202-944-6200) or other French Consulates in the United States for specific requirements.

Dominica Passport and visa not required for tourist stay up to 6 months. Document establishing nationality and identity and return/onward ticket necessary. Check British Embassy or nearest consulate for longer stay and specific requirements.

Dominican Republic Passport/tourist card required. Tourist card valid 60 days, $5; proof of citizenship required. Visa, no charge. Check Embassy, Washington, DC 20008 (202-332-6280) or consulate for longer stay and specific requirements.

East Germany *See* German Democratic Republic.

Egypt, Arab Republic of Passport and visa required. Tourist visa, valid 3 months, $10 (cash or money order), 1 photo. Maximum Egyptian currency allowed into and out of Egypt is LE20. Individuals must register within 7 days of arrival with either local authorities or at hotel where they are staying. No limit to amount of foreign currency brought into Egypt provided currency is declared on Form "D" on arrival. Individuals must present Form "D" and bank receipts upon departure. A minimum of U.S. $150 must be exchanged on arrival. Check Consulate, Washington, DC 20008 (202-234-3903) or consulates in Chicago, Houston, San Francisco, or New York for specific requirements.

El Salvador Passport and visa required. U.S. citizens must be in possession of at least U.S. $300 upon arrival as evidence of financial solvency. Check Embassy, Washington, DC 20008 (202-265-3480) or nearest consulate for specific requirements.

Equador Valid passport, Migratory Control Card (no charge), and return/onward ticket required for stays up to 3 months. Check Embassy, Washington, DC 20009 (202-234-7166) or consulate for specific requirements.

Equatorial Guinea Passport and visa required. Check specific requirements with Embassy, 801 Second Avenue, Suite 1403, New York, NY 10017 (212-599-1523).

Estonia Passport required. Visas for entry or transit are issued by Soviet diplomatic and consular representatives. Check Mission to the UN, 1 UN Plaza, New York, NY 10017 for specific requirements. (This information does not imply U.S. government recognition of country's forcible annexation by the Soviet Union.)

Ethiopia Passport and visa required. Tourist visa for stay up to 30 days, 1 photo, $4.85 plus $1.55 cash or money order to cover mail service. Visa fee for business visa up to 30 days, $7.25 plus $1.55 for mail service. Certificate of Immunization against yellow fever required. Apply at Embassy, Washington, DC 20008 (202-234-2281) or Mission, New York, NY 10017, and check specific requirements.

Fiji Passport and onward/return ticket required. For holders of U.S. passports, visa issued on arrival for stay up to 30 days; can be extended to maximum of 6 months. Check Embassy, 2233 Wisconsin Avenue NW, #240, Washington, DC 20007 (202-337-8320) or Mission to the UN, New York, NY 10017 (212-355-7316) for specific requirements.

Finland Passport required. Visa not required for stay up to 3 months. (Period begins when entering Scandinavian area: Sweden, Norway, Denmark, Iceland.) Check Embassy, Washington, DC 20016 (202-363-2430) or consulate for specific requirements.

France and Overseas Territories, Andorra, and Monaco Passport and visa required to visit France, Andorra, Monaco Martinique, Guadeloupe, Saint-Barthelemy, Guiana, Reunion, Saint Pierre et Miquelon, French Austral Antarctic Lands, Wallis et Futuna Islands, New Caledonia, Tahiti, and dependencies. (Visas for French Overseas Departments [French West Indies] and Territories [Polynesia], excluding New Caledonia, valid 1 entry, up to 3 months, may be obtained at port of entry.) Visas must be obtained before arrival. Transit visa for a stay of 1 to 3 days is $3. Multiple entry visa valid for 3 months is $9. A multiple entry visa valid for 1 to 3 years (for stays not to exceed 90 days) is also available for $15. Photo, along with completed application, required. Passport must be valid for 2 months beyond length of visa. Visas may also be obtained by mail—send completed application, valid passport, and money order or certified check for category of visa requested, photo (optional), and return postage sufficient for certified mail to French Consulate, Washington, DC 20007 (202-944-6200) or apply at French consulates in Boston, Chicago, Detroit, Houston, Los Angeles, Miami, New York, New Orleans, Puerto Rico, or San Francisco, and check requirements. Applicants applying by mail should allow sufficient time for processing. (The requirement that U.S. citizens obtain French visas is a temporary measure effective until further notice.) Visas for travel to France can also be obtained from a French consulate in a third country.

Gabon Passport and visa required. Visa applicants must obtain visa before arrival. Submit valid passport, 2 photos, a smallpox (if available) and yellow fever vaccination certificate, 2 completed application forms, and a fee of $20 for a single-entry visa valid up to 1 month and $50 for a multiple-entry visa valid for 3 to 4 months. Include $20 processing fee. Details on travel arrangements, including flight numbers and departure dates, are required of tourists and business applicants. For a business visa, a letter from the applicant's company is also required. Apply Embassy, Washington, DC 20009 (202-797-1000), and check specific requirements.

Gambia, Republic of The Passport and visa required. Entry/transit visa, $8, 2 photos. Apply Embassy of the Republic of The Gambia, 1785 Massachusetts Avenue NW, Washington, DC 20036 (202-265-3252) or Permanent Mission of The Gambia to the UN, 19 East 47th Street, New York, NY 10017 for specific requirements.

German Democratic Republic (East Germany) (GDR) Passport and visa required. Visas are issued by the Embassy of the GDR in Washington, DC or at a border crossing point upon presentation of travel vouchers or visa entitlement certificates. These may be obtained from the GDR Reisebuero or through a local travel agent. Travel vouchers are based on confirmed hotel accommodations and also may be issued at border crossing points to tourists arriving by motor vehicle or air. Visa entitlement certificates, which require about 6 weeks to obtain, are for persons making private arrangements when staying with relatives or friends. The fee for a single-entry visa is the convertible currency equivalent of 15 GDR marks and of 40 GDR marks for a multiple-entry visa. Transit visas for travel through the GDR to West Berlin or another country are issued at the border. Permission for 1-day visits to East Berlin from West Berlin may be obtained without advance application at the sector crossing line in Berlin. The United States does not recognize East Berlin as part of the GDR; therefore, official

(nontourist) travelers should consult the Department of State before traveling to East Berlin or applying for GDR visas. For further information on tourist visits, contact the Embassy of the GDR, 1717 Massachusetts Avenue NW, Washington, DC 20036 (202-232-3134).

Germany, Federal Republic of (West Germany) Passport required. Tourist/business visa not required for stay up to 3 months in the Federal Republic of Germany including West Berlin if stay is temporary. For longer stays, obtain temporary residence permit from local alien office. Check Embassy, Washington, DC 20007 (202-298-4000) or consulate for specific requirements.

Ghana Passport and visa required. Tourist visa, valid up to 14 days, $20, 4 photos. Onward/return ticket and financial guarantee while in the country required. Visas take at least 3 working days to process and travelers must have valid certificate of immunization against yellow fewer and cholera. For stays over 14 days, apply well in advance of departure to Embassy, Washington, DC 20009 (202-462-0761) or Ghana Consulate General, 19 East 47th Street, New York, NY 10017. If applying by mail, include self-addressed, stamped, certified envelope for return of passport.

Gibraltar Passport required. Visa not required for tourists. Check British Embassy or nearest consulate for specific requirements, including employment regulations.

Great Britain and Northern Ireland *See* United Kingdom.

Greece Passport required. Visa not required for stay up to 3 months for business/pleasure. Check Embassy, Washington, DC 20008 (202-667-3168) or consulate for specific requirements.

Greenland *See* Denmark.

Grenada Passport and visa not required for tourist stay up to 3 months extendable to maximum of 6 months. Tourists need proof of U.S. citizenship (i.e., passport, birth certificate). Check Embassy, Washington, DC 20009 (202-265-2561) for specific requirements.

Guadeloupe *See* France.

Guatemala Proof of U.S. citizenship (passport, birth certificate, etc.) and tourist card or visa requied. Tourist card issued from consulate or airline serving Guatemala upon presentation of proof of U.S. citizenship and picture identification, $1. Tourist card must be used within 30 days from the date of issuance for stay up to 6 months at the discretion of Guatemalan immigration authorities upon arrival. Visas (issued for tourist and business stays) valid for duration of U.S. passport, multiple entries, no charge, no forms. Length of stay determined at the discretion of Guatemalan immigration authorities upon arrival. Holder must present U.S. passport personally to Immigration Department for stays over 30 days. Visas are issued only by Guatemalan consulates upon presentation of U.S. passport either personally or by mail. Check Embassy, Washington, DC 20008 (202-745-4952) or consulate for specific requirements.

Guiana, French *See* France.

Guinea Passport and visa required. Visa $20, 2 completed applications, 2 photos required. Proof of yellow fever and cholera vaccinations required. As malaria is prevalent, suppressants are recommended. Upon arrival, travelers are sometimes required to surrender their passport to airport authorities and may retrieve it the next day at police headquarters. Sometimes visitors are summoned to police headquarters to explain purpose of their visit. $12 departure tax, $7 if traveling to another African country. Guinean currency may not be taken out of the country. Apply for visa at Embassy, Washington, DC 20009 (202-797-1000) and check specific requirements.

Guinea-Bissau Passport and visa required. Travelers must declare all currency upon entering and leaving the country. Visitors are advised to carry U.S. dollars for paying hotel bills and other expenses. Apply for visa at Permanent Mission of Guinea-Bissau to the UN, 211 East 43rd Street, Suite 604, New York, NY 10017 and check specific requirements.

Guyana Passport and visa required. To qualify for a visa, applicant must have proof of sufficient funds for stay and 3 photos. Apply Embassy, Washington, DC 20008 (202-265-6900) and check specific requirements.

Haiti Passport and visa not required of tourists for stay up to 3 months. Proof of U.S. citizenship required, i.e., valid U.S. passport or birth certificate. Tourist card, valid 90 days, $5; obtain on arrival. Check Embassy, Washington, DC 20008 (202-332-4090) or consulate for specific requirements.

Holy See, Apostolic Nunciature of the Valid passport required. Visa not required for tourist stay up to 3 months. For longer stays, consult Apostolic Nunciature of the Holy See, Washington, DC 20008–3687 and check specific requirements.

Honduras Passport valid for at least 6 months, visa, and onward/return ticket required. Visa issued for stay up to 30 days, no charge. Apply Embassy, Washington, DC 20008 (202-966-7700) and check specific requirements.

Honduras, British *See* Belize.

Hong Kong Passport required. Tourist visa not required for stay up to 1 month with onward/return transportation by sea/air. Visa may be extended 1 month at a time up to 3 months by application at Hong Kong immigration. $15 departure tax for air travelers leaving Hong Kong. Confirmed hotel and flight reservations recommended during peak travel months of April/May and October/November.

Visa required for work or study. Apply British Embassy or consulate and check specific requirements.

Hungary Passport and visa required. Passport must be valid at least 1 month beyond expiration date of visa. Transit visa allows for stay up to 48 hours or entry visa for stay up to 30 days, 1 entry; $10, 2 photos, 1 application required. Double transit visa allows for stay up to 48 hours or double entry visa for stay up to 30 days, 2 entries; $20, 4 photos, 3 application forms required. Transit and entry visas are valid for 6 months from date of issuance. Multiple-entry visa valid up to 1 year for stays up to 30 days; $40, 2 photos, 1 application form. Apply Embassy, Consulate General, Budapest's Ferihegy Airport, or frontier crossing points (except if traveling by train or boat). For business visa and specific requirements, check Embassy, 3910 Shoemaker Street NW, Washington, DC 20008 (202-362-6730) or Consulate General, 8 East 75th Street, New York, NY 10021 (212-879-4127).

Iceland Passport required. Visa not required for stay up to 3 months. (Period begins when entering Scandinavian area: Denmark, Finland, Norway, Sweden.) Check Embassy, Washington, DC 20008 (202-265-6653) or Consulate General, New York, NY 10017 for specific requirements.

India Passport and visa required. Visa valid for stay up to 3 months, $15, 1 photo, and application form required. Onward/return ticket and financial guarantee while in country required. Visa must be obtained before arrival. Include postage, $4.15, or stamped, certified return envelope for return of passport. Check Embassy, Washington, DC 20008 (202-939-9839) or consulates in New York, Chicago, or San Francisco for specific requirements.

Indonesia Passport valid beyond 6 months of arrival and onward/return ticket required. Visa not required for tourist or business stay up to 2 months (non-extendable). Check Embassy, Washington, DC 20036 (202-293-1745) for specific requirements and for travel other than tourist.

Iran Passport and visa required. Apply Embassy of Algeria, Iranian Interests Section, Washington, DC 20007, and check specific requirements.

Iraq Passport required. No tourist visas issued at this time. Inquire Embassy of India, Iraqi Interests Section, 1801 P Street NW, Washington, DC 20036 (202-483-7500).

Ireland Valid passport required. Visa not required for tourist stay up to 90 days. Tourists may be asked to show onward/return ticket, necessary travel documents, or sufficient funds for stay. For residence authorization and work permits, consult Embassy, Washington, DC 20008 (202-462-3939) or Consulate for specific requirements.

Israel Passport valid beyond 9 months of arrival and onward/return ticket required. Visa not required for tourist stay up to 3 months. Apply at Israeli Ministry of Interior for extension. Holders of official/diplomatic passports must obtain visas prior to entry. Check Embassy, Washington, DC 20008 (202-364-5557) or Consulate for specific requirements and sensitive area warning.

Italy Valid passport required. Visa not required for tourist stay up to 3 months. For stays over 3 months, residence, or employment and for all students, obtain visa before departure. Apply Embassy, Washington, DC 20009 (202-328-5500) or Consulates General in New York, Chicago, Boston, Houston, Los Angeles, New Orleans, Philadelphia, San Francisco, Detroit, or Newark; and check specific requirements.

Ivory Coast *See* Côte d'Ivoire.

Jamaica Passport and visa not required of tourists for visit up to 6 months in direct travel from U.S., Puerto Rico, or U.S. Virgin Islands. Tourists must have return ticket, proof of citizenship, photo identification, and sufficient funds. Tourist card issued on arrival, returned to immigration authorities on departure. Passport but no visa required if not arriving in direct travel from U.S. territory. Visa required for business or study, no charge. Business visas usually valid up to 14 days; inquire about work permit before arrival. Apply Embassy, Washington, DC 20006 (202-452-0660); Consulates General, New York, NY 10017, Miami, FL 33131; or consulates, Atlanta, GA 30032-0386, Chicago, IL 60601, or Los Angeles, CA 90018; or Honorary Consul, San Francisco, CA 94542; check specific requirements.

Japan Passport and visa required. Transit visas available for stay up to 15 days. Short-stay visas (for tourism, business, news reporting, meetings, etc.) for up to 90 days are also available. Posting visa (for business, religious mission, news reporting); working visa (for professors, entertainers, technicians, etc.); and specified visa (for students, trainees, persons joining their families, etc.) for stays up to 3 years (but for some purposes, up to 6 months or 1 year) are available; 2 photos, and documents required. Multiple-entry visas must be used within 60 months of issue (some purposes of entry are single entry and are valid for 3 months from date of issue). No charge. Check Embassy, Washington, DC 20008 (202-939-6700) or consulates general of Japan for specific requirements and information regarding visas.

Jordan Passport and visa required. Visa valid up to 4 years, multiple entries, no charge. Apply Embassy, Washington, DC 20008 (202-966-2664) or consulates; check specific requirements.

Kampuchea, People's Republic of Passport and visa required. The U.S. does not maintain diplomatic or consular relations with Kampuchea and has no third country representing U.S. interests there. Travel is therefore not recommended by U.S. citizens. Application for a visa must

be directed to the Embassy of Kampuchea. Such embassies are located in Laos, the U.S.S.R., and Vietnam.

Kenya Passport and visa required. Visa valid up to 6 months and up to 12 months in special cases: 1 entry, $10; multiple entries within 1 year in special cases, $60. Transit visa $6, valid up to 7 days. Obtain visa before arrival. Apply Embassy, Washington, DC 20008 (202-387-6101); Kenya Tourist Office, 60 East 56th Street, New York, NY 10022 or Beverly Hills, CA 90212; check specific requirements.

Kiribati (formerly Gilbert Islands) Passport and visa required. Apply at British Embassy or consulates and check specific requirements.

Korea, North Passport and visa required. The U.S. does not maintain diplomatic or consular relations with North Korea and has no third country representing U.S. interests there. Travel is therefore not recommended by U.S. citizens. Application for a visa must be directed to the Embassy of North Korea. Such embassies are located in Czechoslovakia, Denmark, Egypt, Malaysia, Norway, Pakistan, and Singapore.

Korea, South Passport and visa required. No charge. All visas valid for multiple entries within 60 months. Transit visa valid up to 15 days. Tourist visa valid up to 90 days. Entry visa valid up to 90 days. One photo and 1 affidavit of support required. Fine imposed for overstaying visa and for entry visa holder not registering within 60 days after entry. Check Embassy, Washington, DC 20037 (202-939-5600) or consulate for specific requirements.

Kuwait Passport and visa required. Passport must be valid for 6 months beyond expiration date. Visa must be obtained before arrival. Transit visa valid 72 hours, 2 photos, requires proof of onward/return transportation; no charge. Entry visa for business visitors, for visits to friends or relatives, or for employment, valid within 6 months from date of issue for stay up to 1 month, requires 2 application forms and permit/letter and/or no-objection certificate, 2 photos; no charge. Apply Embassy, Washington, DC 20008 (202-966-1897) or Consulate of the State of Kuwait, 321 East 44th Street, New York, NY 10017 (212-973-4318). Include stamped, self-addressed, certified or registered envelope if applying by mail and check specific requirements.

Laos Passport and visa required. Check Embassy, Washington, DC 20008 (202-332-6416) for specific requirements.

Latvia Passport required. Visas for entry or transit are issued by Soviet diplomatic and consular representatives. (This information does not imply U.S. government recognition of country's forcible annexation by Soviet Union.)

Lebanon Passport and visa required. Effective January, 1987, U.S. passports are not valid for travel in, to, or through Lebanon without express authorization from the Department of State. Application for exemptions to this passport restriction should be submitted in writing to Passport Services, U.S. Department of State, 1425 K Street NW, Washington, DC 20524, Attention: CA/PPT/C, Room 300. Entry visa valid 3 or 6 months, multiple entries, $40. Group visa (over 10) available on request. When applying by mail, include self-addressed, stamped envelope or $2 for mailing costs. Apply Embassy, 2560 28th Street NW, Washington, DC 20008 (202-939-6300); check specific requirements.

Leeward Islands *See* United Kingdom.

Lesotho Passport required. Visa not required for tourist stay up to 3 months. For longer stays and for stays other than tourist, check Embassy, 1430 K Street NW, Washington, DC 20005 (202-628-4833).

Liberia Passport and visa required. Transit visitor with onward ticket can remain at airport up to 48 hours. Entry visa valid 3 months, 1 entry, no fee, 2 photos; obtain before arrival. Yellow fever vaccination and medical certificate attesting to traveler's good health required. Exit permit required, 1 photo; obtain on arrival. Apply Embassy, Washington, DC 20011 (202-723-0437). Check Embassy or nearest consulate for specific requirements.

Libya Passport and visa required. Effective December 10, 1981, U.S. passports are not valid for travel in, to, or through Libya without express authorization from the Department of State. Application for exemptions to this passport restriction should be submitted in writing to Passport Services, U.S. Department of State, 1425 K Street NW, Washington, DC 20524, Attention: CA/PPT/C, Room 300.

Liechtenstein Passport required. Visa not required for tourist/business stay up to 3 months. Check Swiss Embassy or consulate for specific requirements.

Lithuania Passport required. Visas for entry or transit are issued by Soviet diplomatic and consular representatives. (This information does not imply U.S. government recognition of country's forcible annexation by Soviet Union.)

Luxembourg Valid passport required. Visa required for stays over 3 months, $18, plus return postage for registry, 4 photos. All travelers must be in possession of sufficient funds and onward/return ticket. For student/employment entry and other specific requirements, check Embassy, Washington, DC 20008 (202-265-4171) or consulate.

Macau Passport and visa required. Apply Portuguese Consulate in Hong Kong. Check Portuguese Embassy or consulate for specific requirements.

Madagascar, Democratic Republic of Passport and visa required. One month, 1 entry: $22.50; multiple entries: $44.15; cash, certified check, or money order only, 4 photos. If applying by mail, include a stamped return envelope for registered return mail. Verification of round-trip airline

ticket or sufficient funds required. Applications for longer-term visas over 30 days generally take at least 2 months for approval, so allow sufficient time for such requests. Check Embassy, Washington, DC 20008 (202-265-5525); Permanent Mission to the UN, New York, NY 10017 (212-968-9491); or honorary consulates in Philadelphia, PA or Palo Alto, CA for specific requirements or longer stays.

Madeira *See* Portugal.

Malawi Passport required. Visa not required for stay up to 1 year. Entry visa, no charge, for stay over 1 year; 2 photos required. Check specific regulations regarding women's dress and men's hair length with the Embassy, 2408 Massachusetts Avenue NW, Washington, DC 20008 (202-797-1007) or Malawi Mission to the UN, 600 3rd Avenue, New York, NY 10016 (212-949-0180).

Malaysia Passport valid at least 1 month beyond stay required. Visa not required for purposes of tourism, transit, social visits, or business for stays up to 3 months. Visa required for employment, research, educational purposes, and other professional visits, $3. Apply Embassy, Washington, DC 20008 (202-328-2700) or Consulate General, New York, NY 10017 or Los Angeles, CA 90071; check specific requirements.

Maldives (Maldive Islands) Passport required. Tourist visa issued upon arrival at airport; no costs or photos involved. Visitors must possess proof of onward/return transportation and a minimum of $10 or its equivalent in acceptable foreign currency per person per day of stay. Check Embassy, 25 Melbourne Avenue, Colombo 4, Sri Lanka for specific requirements.

Mali Passport and visa required. Visa valid 1 week, $17; must be obtained before arrival; 2 photos required. Apply Embassy, Washington, DC 20008 (202-332-2249). If applying by mail, include stamped, self-addressed envelope. Apply for extensions in Mali. If in a country without Malian mission, cable visa request to "Le Directeur National des Services de Police, Bamako, Mali." Check Embassy for specific requirements.

Malta Passport required. Visa not required for stay up to 3 months. Check Embassy, Washington, DC 20008 (202-462-3611) or consulate for specific requirements.

Marshall Islands, Republic of the Entry permit not required of tourist/visitor up to 30 days. Entry permit for all other travelers and for stays over 30 days may be required. Obtain necessary forms from airline or shipping agent serving Marshall Islands. Must have proof of U.S. citizenship (passport or birth certificate), sufficient funds for stay, onward/return ticket, and valid visa for next destination if appropriate; 30-day extensions may be granted. Apply Chief of Immigration, Government of the Marshall Islands, Majuro, Marshall Islands 96960. Check Representative Office,

1901 Pennsylvania Avenue NW, Washington, DC 20006 (202-223-4952) or office in Honolulu (808-942-4422) for specific requirements.

Martinique *See* France.

Mauritania Passport and visa required. Obtain visa before arrival. Visa valid 3 months; $10, 4 photos. Apply Embassy, Washington, DC 20008 (202-232-5700) or Mission of Mauritania to the UN, New York, NY 10018; check specific requirements.

Mauritius Passport required. Visa not required for stay up to 3 months if in possession of return/onward ticket. Check Embassy, Washington, DC 20008 (202-244-1491) for specific requirements.

Mayotte Island *See* France.

Mexico Passport and visa not required of U.S. citizens for tourism up to 90 days or transit. A tourist card is required and is issued upon proof of U.S. citizenship through (a) presentation of a valid U.S. passport, (b) a U.S. birth certificate, or (c) a certified copy of a U.S. birth certificate. With (b) and (c), photo identification is also required. Tourist cards are free and may be obtained from Mexican consulates, Mexican tourism offices, Mexican immigration offices at ports of entry, and most airlines serving Mexico. Tourist card valid 3 months, 1 entry, no charge; stays of up to 180 days are authorized upon proof of adequate funds. Tourist cards may be revalidated up to the 180-day maximum at any local office of the Mexican Department of the Interior. If children are included with parents, all must leave Mexico together unless prior arrangements are made with the Mexican Department of Immigration. Children traveling with one parent (or with a relative or friend) must have the written, notarized consent from the other parent(s) to travel and it must be authenticated at a Mexican consulate. If the child is traveling alone and bears an American passport, no authorization is needed. If the child is traveling alone but bears only his/her birth certificate, authorization is needed from both parents. Such authorization must be notarized and legalized by a Mexican consulate. For entry for other than tourism or transit, check with the consular section of the Embassy of Mexico, Washington, DC 20036 (202-293-1711) or the nearest Mexican consulate about required documentation and specific requirements.

Micronesia, Federated States of (Kosrae, Yap, Ponape, and Truk) Entry permit not required of tourist/visitor up to 30 days. Entry permit for all other travelers and for stays over 30 days may be required. Obtain necessary forms from airline or shipping agent serving Micronesia. Must have proof of U.S. citizenship (passport or birth certificate), sufficient funds for stay, onward/return ticket, a valid visa for next destination if appropriate; 30-day extensions may be granted. Apply Chief of Immigration, Government of Micronesia, Kolonia, Ponape, 96941. Check Representative

Office, 706 G Street SE, Washington, DC 20003 (202-544-2640) or offices in Honolulu, Guam, and Tokyo for specific requirements.

Miquelon *See* France.

Monaco *See* France.

Mongolia Passport and visa required. Visa must be obtained at a Mongolian mission overseas, such as in the United Kingdom or France. Check entry requirements with Mongolian Mission to the UN, New York, NY 10021 (212-861-9460).

Montserrat *See* United Kingdom.

Morocco Passport required. Visa not required for stay up to 3 months. Apply with local authorities for longer stay. Check Embassy, Washington, DC 20009 (202-462-7979) or consulate for specific requirements.

Mozambique, People's Republic of Passport and visa required. Visa must be obtained before arrival. Visa valid 30 days from date of issue; $9, and 2 photos required. Yellow fever inoculation may be required. Currency must be declared upon arrival. Apply for visa at Embassy, Washington, DC 20036 (202-293-7146) and check specific requirements.

Nauru, Republic of Passport and visa required. Passengers must have tickets for onward/return transportation. Apply consulates in Honolulu 96813 or Guam 96910 and check requirements.

Nepal Passport and visa required. Visa valid 3 months for stay up to 30 days, $10 per person, 1 photo. Apply Embassy, Washington, DC 20008 (202-667-4550); Nepal Mission, 820 Second Avenue, Suite 1200, New York, NY 10017; or any Nepalese mission abroad. Visa valid 7 days issued at Kathmandu Airport upon arrival.

Netherlands Passport required. Visa not required for pleasure/business up to 90 days. Tourist may be asked to show onward/return ticket, necessary travel documents, or sufficient funds for stay. For residence authorization and work permit, consult Embassy, Washington, DC 20008 (202-244-5300) or nearest consulate for specific requirements.

Netherlands Antilles (Bonaire, Curacao, Saba, Statia [formerly St. Eustatius], St. Martin [St. Maarten]) Valid passport or proof of U.S. citizenship required. Visa not required for stay up to 14 days. Tourist may be asked to show onward/return ticket, necessary travel documents, or sufficient funds for stay. Permission of local authorities required for a maximum stay up to 90 days. Check Netherlands Embassy or nearest consulate for specific requirements.

New Caledonia *See* France.

New Guinea, Papua *See* Papua New Guinea.

New Zealand Passport required. Passport must be valid at least 3 months beyond the intended date of departure from New Zealand. Visa not required for stay up to 3 months. Onward/return tickets required. Longer stays may also require evidence of funds. Contact Embassy, Washington, DC 20008 (202-328-4800); or Consulate General, New York, NY 10111; Los Angeles, CA 90024; check specific requirements.

Nicaragua Passport and visa required. Tourist may be asked to show onward/return ticket and sufficient funds ($200) for stay. Check Embassy, Washington, DC 20009 (202-387-4371) for specific requirements.

Niger Passport and visa required. Transit/tourist visa for stay up to 1 week, $2.10; 1 week to 30 days, $4.20; 30 to 90 days, $8.30; 3 photos. Visa must be used within 3 months from date of issuance. Stays over 3 months require prior arrangements with immigration officials in Niamey. Tourist visa requires letter from travel agent regarding round-trip ticket (2 copies). If applying by mail, stamped return envelope either registered or certified must be included. Yellow fever vaccination required for all travelers. If traveling by road, cholera vaccination and letter from the bank certifying visitor has at least $500 in savings account (2 copies) required. Prior authorization from the Minister of Interior in Niamey or from the Prefecture in Agadez must be obtained before taking any photographs or filming. Check Embassy, Washington, DC 20008 (202-483-4224) for specific requirements.

Nigeria Passport and visa required. Transit visa, $2.55, valid 1 entry within 3 months, 1 photo. No personal checks. All persons must carry passport/onward ticket at all times. Apply Embassy, Washington, DC 20037 (202-822-1500); or Nigeria Consulate General, New York, NY 10022; San Francisco, CA 94108; or Atlanta, GA 30303; check specific requirements.

Niue Passport required. Visa not required for stay up to 30 days. Visitors must possess confirmed accommodations and onward/return transportation. Check Embassy of New Zealand for specific requirements.

Norfolk Island *See* Australia.

Northern Mariana Islands *See* Trust Territory of the Pacific Islands.

Norway Passport required. Visa not required for stay up to 3 months. (Period begins when entering Scandinavian area: Finland, Sweden, Denmark, Iceland.) Check Embassy, Washington, DC 20008 (202-333-6000) or consulate for specific requirements.

Okinawa *See* Japan.

Oman Passport required. Tourist visa not issued. Business visitors require either a business visa (2 photos, 1 entry, valid 3 months) or a nonobjection certificate, plus a letter from individual's company and letter of invitation from sponsor in Oman. For specific requirements, check Embassy of the Sultanate of Oman, Washington, DC 20008 (202-387-1980).

Pakistan Passport and visa required. Visa must be obtained before arrival. No charge, 1 photo. Visa valid up to 3 months, multiple entries. If applying by mail, submit passport, visa application, 1 photo, and self-addressed, stamped envelope. Apply Embassy, Washington, DC 20008 (202-939-6200) or Consulate, New York, NY 10021; check specific requirements.

Palau, Republic of The U.S. continues to exercise trusteeship of the Republic of Palau. Entry permit not required of tourist/visitor up to 30 days. Entry permit for all other travelers and for stays over 30 days may be required. Obtain necessary forms from airline or shipping agent serving Palau. Must have proof of U.S. citizenship (passport or birth certificate), sufficient funds for stay, onward/return ticket, and valid visa for next destination if appropriate; 30-day extensions may be granted. Apply Chief of Immigration, Government of the Republic of Palau, Koror, Western Caroline Islands 96940.

Panama Valid passport and visa or tourist card, evidence of citizenship and round-trip/onward ticket required. Tourist visa, valid 30 days, no charge. Tourist card, valid 30 days, fee charged; obtain from airline serving Panama. Travelers on international flights staying overnight in Panama must have visa or tourist card. Check Embassy, Washington, DC 20008 (202-483-1407) or consulate (202-265-0330) for specific requirements.

Papua New Guinea Passport required. Visa not required if arriving via Jackson Airport, Port Moresby, for stay up to 30 days; no extensions. Must have onward/return ticket. Visa required for visits over 30 days. Check Embassy, Washington, DC 20036 (202-659-0856) for specific requirements.

Paraguay Passport required; visa not required for stay up to 90 days. Check Embassy, Washington, DC 20008 (202-483-6960) or consulate for specific requirements.

Peru Valid passport required. Visa not required for tourist stay up to 90 days. Tourists must have onward/return ticket. For specific information regarding business travelers and artists, check Embassy, Washington, DC 20036 (202-833-9860) or consulate.

Philippines, Republic of the For entry at Manila International Airport, visa not required for transit/tourist stay up to 21 days; must have passport valid for at least 6 months; onward/return tickets. Visa required for stays over 21 days and up to maximum stay of 59 days; 1 photo, onward/return tickets, no charge. If applying by mail, include stamped, self-addressed envelope. For entry at military bases of military personnel and dependents and for other types of visas, check Embassy (202-483-1414) or consulates general for specific requirements.

Poland Passport and visa required. Regular visa issued for tourism, business, and visits to relatives for stay up to 90 days, single entry, $18. Transit visa, valid 24 hours, single entry, $12, 2 photos. Currency exchange required is $15 per day, except for students and persons visiting relatives: $7 per day. Apply Embassy, Washington, DC 20008 (202-234-3800) or Consulate General, Chicago, IL 60610, or New York, NY 10016; check specific requirements.

Portugal Valid passport required. Visa not required for visit up to 60 days. Visa must be used within 120 days. Check Embassy, Washington, DC 20008 (202-332-3007) or Consulate General, New York, NY 10020; San Francisco, CA 94115; or Consulate, Boston, MA 02115; Newark, NJ 07102; Providence RI 02903; New Bedford, MA 02740; Chicago, IL 60635; or Miami, FL 33132 for fees, entry of pets, departure tax, and specific requirements.

Qatar Passport and visa required. No tourist visas issued at this time. Visa for travel other than tourism valid 6 months; 2 photos, no charge. Check specific requirements with Embassy of State of Qatar, Washington, DC 20037 (202-338-0111).

Reunion *See* France.

Romania Passport and visa required. Transit visa valid 72 hours; single entry, $12; double entry, $14. Tourist visa valid 6 months from date of issue, 1 entry, $12. Apply Embassy or any border point of entry open to tourist traffic. No application or photos required. Entry–exit visa for business, educator, etc; one entry, $18; multiple entries, $46. Application accepted only at Embassy. Bearers of reentry permits must apply at Embassy as well. Currency exchange of $10 per day is required of all visitors. Check Embassy for exceptions. Include self-addressed, stamped envelope for return of passport by mail. For specific requirements, check Embassy, 1607 23rd Street NW, Washington, DC 20008 (202-232-4748/49).

Rwanda Passport and visa required. Visa must be obtained in advance for stay up to 30 days, $15, 2 photos. Include fee of $1.50 or stamped, self-addressed envelope for return of passport by mail. Yellow fever and cholera vaccinations required. Apply Embassy, Washington, DC 20009 (202-232-2882); check specific requirements.

Saba *See* Netherlands Antilles.

Sabah *See* Malaysia.

St. Barthelemy *See* France.

Saint Kitts and Nevis Passport and visa not required for stay up to 6 months. Return ticket to U.S., proof of U.S.

citizenship (passport or birth certificate), and document establishing identity necessary. Apply Embassy, Washington, DC 20036 (202-833-3550) for specific requirements.

Saint Lucia Passport and visa not required for tourist stay up to 6 months. Proof of U.S. citizenship, return/onward ticket, and/or proof of funds necessary. Check Embassy of Saint Lucia, 2100 M Street NW, Suite 309, Washington, DC 20037 (202-463-7378/9) or Saint Lucia's Permanent Mission to UN, 41 East 42nd Street, Suite 315, New York, NY 10017 for specific requirements.

St. Martin (St. Maarten) *See* Netherlands Antilles.

St. Pierre *See* France.

Saint Vincent and the Grenadines Passport and visa not required for tourist stay up to 6 months. Proof of citizenship, return/onward ticket, and/or proof of funds necessary. Check Consulate of Saint Vincent and the Grenadines, 801 Second Avenue, 21st Floor, New York, NY 10017 (212-687-4490) for specific requirements.

Salvador *See* El Salvador.

Samoa, Western Valid passport and onward/return tickets required. Visa not required for stay up to 30 days. For longer stays contact Embassy of New Zealand, Washington, DC, or nearest New Zealand consulate general and check specific requirements.

San Marino, Republic of Same requirements as Italy. For specific information, check with Consulate General, 1155 21st Street NW, 4th Floor, Lafayette Center, Washington, DC 20036 (202-233-3517) or consulates in New York or Detroit.

São Tomé and Principe Passport and visa required. Check Embassy, 801 Second Avenue, Suite 1504, New York, NY 10017 (212-697-4211) for specific requirements.

Sarawak *See* Malaysia.

Saudi Arabia Passport and visa required. No tourist visa issued at this time. Travelers transiting Saudi Arabia must be in possession of a valid visa. All persons going to Saudi Arabia for purposes of long-term employment require certification that they are free of the AIDS virus. For specific information regarding business, visitor, or work visa, check Embassy, Washington, DC 20037 (202-342-3800) or Consulate General, Houston, TX 77057; Los Angeles, CA 90024; or New York, NY 10017.

Scotland *See* United Kingdom.

Senegal Passport and visa required. Transit visa, valid up to 5 days, $5.10. Entry visa (tourist or business), valid 3 days to 3 months, $5.10, 3 photos. No personal checks. Include fee for return of passport by registered mail. Apply Embassy, Washington, DC 20008 (202-234-0540) or UN Mission, New York, NY 10017; check specific requirements.

Seychelles Valid passport required. Visitors' visa issued upon arrival, no charge, for stay up to 1 month, extendable up to 1 year. Tourists must have onward/return tickets and sufficient funds for stay. Check specific requirements with the Permanent Mission of Seychelles to the UN, 820 Second Avenue, Suite 203, New York, NY 10017 (212-687-9766).

Sierra Leone Valid passport and visa required. Transit visa may be obtained upon arrival. Ordinary visa, valid up to 1 month for 1 entry within 3 months, $20.50, 3 photos. Return/onward ticket and proof of financial support from bank or employer are required. Include $1 postage fee for return registered mail. Visitors must declare the amount of foreign currency they are carrying (and exchanging) on an exchange control form (M) which is certified and stamped at port of entry. A minimum of 100 U.S. dollars must be exchanged by all travelers over the age of 16 upon entry. Apply Embassy, Washington, DC 20009 (202-939-9261) or Permanent Mission, New York, NY 10022 (212-570-0030); check specific requirements.

Singapore Valid passport required. Visa not required for tourist or social visit for stay up to 90 days. Visa required for other purposes, $7.20, 3 photos. Apply Embassy, Washington, DC 20009 (202-667-7555); check specific requirements.

Solomon Islands Passport and visitors' permit required. Obtain permit on arrival that is valid for stay up to 2 months in any 1 year. Must have onward/return ticket and sufficient funds for stay.

Somali Democratic Republic Passport and visa required. Visa valid 3 months; 4 photos, $13. Traveler must have onward ticket. Check Embassy, Washington, DC 20037 (202-342-1575) for specific requirements. Where consulate of Somalia not available, contact Consulate of Italy.

South Africa, Republic of Valid passport and visa required. Visa valid 1 year; multiple entries if passport remains valid; no charge; obtain before arrival. Must have onward/return transportation. Apply in jurisdiction closest to residence: Embassy, Washington, DC 20008 (202-232-4400) or Consultate General, New York, NY 10022; Beverly Hills, CA 90210; Houston, TX 77056; or Chicago, IL 60611; check specific requirements. Allow 1 month to process visa.

Soviet Union *See* Union of Soviet Socialist Republics.

Spain Valid passport required. Visa not required for tourists for stay up to 6 months. For longer stays, check Embassy, Washington, DC 20009 (202-265-0190) or consulate for specific requirements. All Americans using diplomatic or official passports must possess a visa to enter Spain.

Sri Lanka (formerly Ceylon) Passport required. Tourist visa not required for stay up to 1 month with valid passport; visa (if necessary) for next destination, sufficient funds for stay, and onward/return ticket are required. For tourist stays over 30 days, a visa is required. Visa also required for travel for purposes other than tourism, valid 1 month, 2 photos, $2.52. Include return postage of $2. Apply Embassy, Washington, DC 20008 (202-483-4025) or consulates in Chicago, Los Angeles, or New Orleans; check specific requirements.

Statia (formerly St. Eustatius) *See* Netherlands Antilles.

Sudan Passport valid at least 6 months from date of entry and visa required. Transit visa for stay from 1 to 7 days, valid 3 months, 1 photo, $6. Valid visa is required for next destination. Single-entry tourist or business visa for stays from 8 days to 3 months also available, 1 photo, $9. Visitors must possess proof of onward/return transportation or letter from their bank attesting to sufficient funds for travel in the Sudan. Business travelers also require letter from sponsoring company. Yellow fever and cholera vaccinations recommended. Applicants applying by mail should send a stamped return envelope with their application. Check Embassy Washington, DC 20008 (202-338-8565) or consulate for specific requirements.

Suriname Passport and visa required, $17 for multiple entry visa valid 12 months, 2 photos; $5 for registered return mail. Application must be completed in duplicate. Visitors to Suriname are required to exchange the equivalent of 500 Surinamese guilders (U.S. $283) and children under the age of 12 are required to exchange the equivalent of U.S. $140 at port of entry. Travelers must have sufficient currency for this transaction. Apply Embassy, Washington, DC 20037 (202-338-6980) or Consulate in Miami (305-871-2790); check requirements.

Swaziland Passport required. Visitors entering from South Africa report to Immigration Department or police station within 48 hours except when lodging in a hotel on night of arrival. Visitors entering from Mozambique exempt. Temporary residence permit required for stay over 60 days. Apply Immigration Department, Mbabane. Visa required for Republic of South Africa if entering from Swaziland. Check Embassy, Washington, DC 20008 (202-362-6683) for specific requirements.

Sweden Valid passport required. Visa not required for stay up to 3 months. (Period begins when entering Scandinavian area: Finland, Norway, Denmark, Iceland.) Check Embassy, Washington, DC 20037 (202-944-5600) or consulate for specific requirements.

Switzerland Passport required. Tourist/business visa not required for stay up to 3 months. Check Embassy, Washington, DC 20008 (202-745-7900) or consulate for specific requirements.

Syrian Arab Republic Passport and visa required. Visitors must possess valid visa before arrival. Transit visa is available for stays up to 3 days; visitors must enter and leave via Damascus International Airport, $5. Entry visa valid 6 months, 1 entry, or valid 3 months, 2 entries; $18, 1 photo. Include self-addressed, stamped envelope for return of passport by mail. Check Embassy, Washington, DC 20008 (202-232-6313) for specific requirements.

Tahiti, Society Islands *See* France.

Taiwan Passport and visa required. Transit visas are for a maximum stay of 2 weeks and cannot be extended. Visitor visas limit stay to 2 months, renewable twice for total stay of 6 months; multiple entries, 2 photos, no charge. Passport must be valid at least 6 months beyond visa issuance date. For stays over 6 months, apply for resident visa 1 month in advance. Check with unofficial Coordination Council for North American Affairs (CCNAA) for business travel and specific requirements. The CCNAA Headquarters is at 4201 Wisconsin Avenue NW, Washington, DC 20016. Additional offices are in Atlanta, Boston, Chicago, Honolulu, Houston, Kansas City, Los Angeles, New York, San Francisco, and Seattle.

Tanzania Passport and visa required. Passport must be valid 6 months beyond entry. Single-entry tourist visa valid for 6 months from date of issue for stay up to 30 days, $10.50; 1 photo, 2 application forms required. No personal checks. Proof of sufficient funds and onward/return transportation required. Visitors wishing to stay beyond 30 days should extend their visas at Tanzanian Immigration Office. Apply Embassy, Washington, DC 20008 (202-939-6125); check specific requirements. **Zanzibar:** Visas for Mainland Tanzania are also valid for Zanzibar.

Thailand Passport required. Visa not required for stay up to 15 days if in possession of onward/return ticket and arrive and depart from Don Muang Airport in Bangkok. Transit visa, $10, for stay up to 30 days; tourist visa, $15, for stay up to 60 days. Nonimmigrant or business visa, $20, for stay up to 90 days; 3 photos. Include postage for return of passport. Apply Embassy, Washington, DC 20008 (202-483-7200) or Royal Thai Consulate General in New York, Los Angeles, or Chicago; check specific requirements.

Togo Passport required. Visa not required for stay up to 3 months. Americans traveling in remote areas in Togo occasionally require visas. Yellow fever vaccinations are required. Check with Embassy, Washington, DC 20008 (202-234-4212) for specific requirements.

Tonga Passport required. Visa not required for stay up to 30 days. Visitors must possess onward/return transportation. Check with Consulate General in San Francisco, 2900 Vallejo Street, 94123 (415-567-4331) for specific requirements.

Trieste *See* Italy for City of Trieste and Yugoslavia for other areas included in former free territory.

Trinidad and Tobago Passport required. Visa not required for tourist/business stay up to 2 months; must have onward/return ticket. Persons entering for employment, residence, etc., or staying longer than 2 months, check visa requirements with Embassy (202-467-6490) or consulate well in advance of departure.

Trust Territory of the Pacific Islands *See* Palau, Republic of.

Tunisia Passport required. Visa not required of tourists for stay up to 4 months. Check Embassy, Washington, DC 20005 (202-862-1850) or consulate for specific requirements.

Turkey Passport required. Visa not required for stay up to 3 months. Travelers to Turkey other than tourists are required by Turkish law to obtain a visa in advance. Visa also required for tourist stays over 3 months: 1 entry, $3; multiple entries, $10. Apply Embassy, Washington, DC 20008 (202-387-3200); check specific requirements.

Turks and Caicos *See* United Kingdom.

Tuvalu Passport and visa required. Visitors' permit issued on arrival. Travelers must possess onward/return transportation and sufficient funds for stay. Check British Embassy or consulates or immigration officer, Office of Chief of Police, Funa, Futi, Tuvalu for specific requirements.

Uganda Passport and visa required. Transit visa, valid for entry within 3 months, $10.50. Ordinary or continuous tourist visa, valid for entry within 3 months, $10.50. Single-entry visa for business representatives/educators, valid for entry within 3 months, $10.50. Nontourists must present a letter of intent. Obtain visa before arrival; 2 photos required. Yellow fever and cholera vaccinations are required, and it is suggested that you carry malaria pills. Apply Embassy, Washington, DC 20011; Uganda Mission to the UN, New York, NY 10017; or Uganda high commissions/embassies abroad; or write Principal Immigration Officer, P.O. Box 7165, Kampala, Uganda. Check Embassy (202-726-7100) or consulate for specific requirements and clothing requirements.

Union of Soviet Socialist Republics Passport and visa required. Visa valid for 1 entry, no charge; 3 photos and passport or photocopy of passport required. For more information, check with a travel agency or the consular office of the U.S.S.R Embassy, Washington, DC 20008 (202-332-1513, 332-1482, or 332-1483) or the Consulate General in San Francisco (415-922-6642).

United Arab Emirates (UAE) Passport and visa required. Tourist/business visa, valid 2 months, for stay up to 30 days; 1 entry, $18. Multiple-entry visa (issued only to business travelers), valid up to 6 months from date of issue for maximum stay of 30 days per entry, $225; 3 photos, 3 completed application forms required. Business travelers require letter from company; sponsor in UAE must send letter or Telex to UAE Embassy confirming trip. Applications by mail should include self-addressed, stamped, certified, or registered return envelope. Apply Embassy, Washington, DC 20037 (202-338-6500); check specific requirements.

United Arab Republic *See* Egypt, Arab Republic of.

United Kingdom (England, Northern Ireland, Scotland, Wales) Passport required. Visa not required for stay up to 6 months. Check British Embassy, Washington, DC 20008 (202-462-1340) or consulate for specific requirements and laws/regulations for travelers other than tourists. **Bermuda** Passport and visa not required for tourist stay up to 6 months. Onward/return documents and proof of identity and citizenship required (passport, birth certificate, or voter registration card). Apply Board of Immigration for work permit. **British West Indies (Anguilla, Montseratt, Cayman Islands, Turks and Caicos)** Passport and visa not required for tourist stay up to 6 months. Travelers must possess proof of citizenship (passport, birth certificate, or voter registration card) and proof of identity, onward/return transportation, and sufficient funds for stay. **British Virgin Islands (Anegarda, Jost van Dyke, Tortola, Virgin Gorda)** Passport and visa not required for tourist stay up to 3 months. Must have proof of identity and citizenship (passport or birth certificate) and onward/return transportation and sufficient funds for stay. Check British Embassy or consulate for specific requirements regarding dependencies.

Upper Volta *See* Burkina Faso.

Uruguay Passport required. Visa not required for stay up to 3 months. Check Embassy, Washington, DC 20006 (202-331-1313) or consulate for specific requirements.

Vanuatu (formerly New Hebrides) Passport required. Visa not required for stay up to 30 days. Inquire at the British Embassy or nearest consulate for specific requirements.

Vatican *See* Holy See.

Venezuela Passport and visa/tourist card required. Tourist card can be obtained from carriers, no charge, valid 60 days; cannot be extended. Tourist visa valid 60 days, no charge; requires personal appearance before consulate; may be extended in the country. Business visa, valid 30 days, issued at consulate. All travelers except tourists required to pay $18 exit tax. Check Embassy, Washington, DC 20008 (202-797-3800) or consulate for specific requirements.

Vietnam, Socialist Republic of Passport and visa required. The U.S. does not maintain diplomatic or consular relations with Vietnam and has no third country representing U.S. interests there. Travel is therefore not recommended for U.S. citizens. Application for a visa must be directed to a representative of Vietnam. Such representatives are located in Canada, France, and the United Kingdom.

Virgin Islands (British) *See* United Kingdom.

Wales *See* United Kingdom.

West Germany *See* Germany, Federal Republic of.

West Indies (British) *See* United Kingdom.

West Indies (French) *See* France.

Yemen Arab Republic (Northern Yemen) Passport and visa required. Single-entry visa, valid 30 days. Tourist visa, $10; business visa, $20; valid 30 days; 4 photos. Transit visa, no charge. If applying by mail, include return postage fee. All visitors must exchange $150 (U.S.) or the equivalent at an airport bank on arrival before being admitted. Apply for visa at Embassy, Washington, DC 20037 (202-965-4760) or Yemen Mission to the UN, 747 Third Avenue, New York, NY 10017; check specific requirements.

Yemen, People's Democratic Republic of (Southern Yemen) Passport and visa required. The U.S. does not maintain diplomatic or consular relations with the People's Republic of Yemen. Because there is no direct U.S. representation in that country, travel by U.S. citizens is not recommended. Application for a visa must be directed to a representative of Southern Yemen. Such representatives are located in the United Kingdom, France, Egypt, and Indonesia.

Yugoslavia Passport and visa required. Visa valid up to 1 year, no charge. Check Embassy, Washington, DC 20008 (202-462-6566) or consulate for specific requirements.

Zaire (formerly Congo, Democratic Republic of the [Kinshasa]) Passport and visa required. Transit visa, valid up to 8 days; 1 way, $8; round trip, $16. Tourist visa, valid 1 to 3 months; 1 entry, $20; multiple entries, $24. Tourist visa, valid 6 months; 1 entry, $28; multiple entries, $48; 3 photos required. Must have proof of onward/return ticket. Include self-addressed, stamped envelope for return of passport. No personal checks. Apply Embassy, Washington, DC 20009 (202-234-7690), or Permanent Mission to the UN of the Republic of Zaire, New York, NY 10017. Check Embassy/Mission for specific requirements.

Zambia Passport and visa required. Tourist visa valid up to 6 months, $3.51. Business visa valid up to 6 months, $3.51. Visitors must obtain visa before arrival. Apply Permanent Mission of Zambia to the UN, New York, NY 10022 or Embassy, Washington, DC 20008 (202-265-9717); check specific requirements.

Zanzibar *See* Tanzania.

Zimbabwe Passport, onward/return ticket, and sufficient funds for stay required. Apply Embassy, Washington, DC 20008 (202-332-7100) and check specific requirements.

Passport Applications

Passports are valid for ten years when issued to travelers 18 years of age or older; younger travelers must renew their passports every five years. Application guidelines follow.

1. Secure proof of citizenship, such as a birth certificate or an expired passport. Citizens not born in the United States must submit proof of their parents' citizenship and their marriage certificate, as well as proof of their own legal entry into the United States.
2. An application requires submission of two identical $2'' \times 2''$ photographs taken within the previous six months: these may be in color or black and white.
3. Proof of identity, with a physical description of the applicant and his or her signature, also is required; a driver's license may be used.
4. The fee is $42 for adults and $27 for children, payable in check or money order to Passport Services.
5. The initial passport application must be made in person at a federal or state court of record, a designated post office, a passport agency, or a U.S. embassy. Renewal applications need not be made in person, provided that the previously issued passport was granted within the last 12 years to an applicant older than 16.
6. Name changes, address changes, and other changes in passport information should be reported to one of the above-mentioned offices and accompanied by appropriate documents.

U.S. Passport Agencies

In Guam, Puerto Rico, and the U.S. Virgin Islands, passports are issued by the chief executive officer of the local government. In foreign countries, apply to a U.S. consular office. In the United States, passports are issued not only through the agencies listed below but also at many post offices.

Boston
John F. Kennedy Building
Government Center
Room E123
Boston, MA 02203
617-565-3940

Chicago
Kluczynski Federal Office Building
230 South Dearborn
Suite 380
Chicago, IL 60604
312-353-5426

Honolulu
New Federal Building
300 Ala Moana Boulevard
Room C 1-06
Honolulu, HI 96850
808-546-2130

Houston
One Allen Center
500 Dallas Street
Houston, TX 77002
713-229-3607

Los Angeles
Federal Building
11000 Wilshire Boulevard
Room 13100
West Los Angeles, CA 90024
213-209-7070

Miami
Federal Office Building
51 SW 1st Avenue
16th Floor
Miami, FL 33130
305-536-5395

New Orleans
Postal Service Building
701 Loyola Avenue
Room T-12005
New Orleans, LA 70113
504-589-6728

New York City
630 5th Avenue
Room 270
New York, NY 10111
212-541-7700

Philadelphia
Federal Office Building
600 Arch Street
Room 4426
Philadelphia, PA 19106
215-597-7480

San Francisco
525 Market Street
Suite 200
San Francisco, CA 94105
415-974-7972

Seattle
Federal Office Building
915 2nd Avenue
Room 992
Seattle, WA 98174
206-442-7941

Stamford
One Landmark Square
Broad and Atlantic Streets
Stamford, CT 06901
203-325-3538

Washington
1425 K Street, NW
Washington, DC 20524
202-523-1355

Customs Information

At reentry into the United States, you must declare all articles in your possession that you have acquired abroad, stating their actual purchase price or, if they were not purchased, their market value in the country where you acquired them. You will fill out a declaration form before reaching customs to show to the federal inspectors.

If you were out of the country for 48 hours or more, you will be exempt from paying duty and federal tax on the first $400 worth of goods. Generally, values above that amount are subject to duty at a straight 10 percent. For example, if you bring in $600 worth of goods, you will pay about $20 in duty. If you are traveling with your family, remember that each family member is allowed the same $400 exemption.

The items brought into the United States must be for your own use or for personal gifts. You may not resell them for profit.

If you leave the United States with foreign-made goods already in your possession, be sure to register them, using their serial numbers, with the customs office *before* leaving or bring proof (sales slips, for example) with you that you bought them in the United States. If you lack proof of domestic purchase or registration, you may be charged duty upon reentry.

There are customs restrictions on bringing in certain plants, animals, medications, and foods, and children may not bring in alcohol. You can get a list of restricted items from the U.S. Department of Agriculture, Washington, DC 20205.

Further information may be obtained from your local office of the Treasury Department and from the U.S. Customs Service, P.O. Box 7407, Washington, DC 20004. The telephone number is 202-566-8195.

State Tourism Offices

Alabama Bureau of Tourism
532 South Perry Street
Montgomery, AL 36130
205-261-4169

Alaska Division of Tourism
Box E
Juneau, AK 99811
907-465-2010

Arizona Office of Tourism
1480 East Bethany Home Road
Phoenix, AZ 85014
602-255-3618

Arkansas Department of Parks and Tourism
One Capitol Mall
Little Rock, AR 72201
501-682-7777

California Tourism Office
1121 L Street
Sacramento, CA 95814
916-322-1396

Colorado Tourism Board
1625 Broadway
Suite 1700
Box 38700
Denver, CO 80202
303-592-5410

Connecticut Department of Economic Development
210 Washington Street
Hartford, CT 06106
203-566-3977

D.C. Convention and Visitors Association
1575 I Street, NW
Suite 250
Washington, DC 20005
202-789-7000

Delaware Tourism Office
99 King Highway
Box 1401
Dover, DE 19903
302-736-4271

Florida Division of Tourism
126 Van Buren Street
Tallahassee, FL 32301
904-487-1462

Georgia Department of Industry and Trade
Box 1776
Atlanta, GA 30301
404-656-3590

Hawaii Visitors Bureau
2270 Kala Kaua Avenue
Honolulu, HI 96800
808-923-1811

Idaho Travel Council
State Capitol Building
Boise, ID 83720
208-334-2470

Illinois Travel Information Center
c/o Department of Commerce and Community Affairs
310 South Michigan Avenue
Chicago, IL 60604
312-793-2094

Indiana Department of Commerce, Tourist Development Division
1 North Capital Street
Suite 700
Indianapolis, IN 46204
317-232-8860

Iowa Development Commission, Tourist Travel Division
600 East Court Avenue
Des Moines, IA 50309
515-281-3100

Kansas Department of Travel and Tourism
400 West 8th Street
5th Floor
Topeka, KS 66603
913-296-2009

Kentucky Department of Travel Development
Capitol Plaza Tower
Frankfort, KY 40601
502-564-4930

Louisiana Office of Tourism
Box 94291
Baton Rouge, LA 70804
504-925-3860

Maine Publicity Bureau
97 Winthrop Streep
Hallowell, ME 04347
207-289-2423

Maryland Office of Tourist Development
45 Calvert Street
Annapolis, MD 21401
301-269-3517

Massachusetts Department of Commerce and Development, Division of Tourism
100 Cambridge Street
Boston, MA 02202
617-727-3201

Michigan Department of Commerce, Travel Bureau
Box 30226
Lansing, MI 48909
517-373-0670

Minnesota Office of Tourism
375 Jackson Street
250 Skyway Level
St. Paul, MN 55101
612-348-4313

Mississippi Department of Economic Development, Division of Tourism
1301 Walter Sillers Building
Box 849
Jackson, MS 39205
601-359-3414

Missouri Division of Tourism
Truman State Office Building
Box 1055
Jefferson City, MO 65102
314-751-4133

Montana Travel Promotion Division
1424 9th Avenue
Helena, MT 59620
406-444-2654

Nebraska Department of Economic Development, Division of Travel and Tourism
301 Centennial Mall South
Box 94666
Lincoln, NE 68509
402-471-3796

Nevada Commission on Tourism
Capitol Complex
Carson City, NV 89710
702-733-2323

New Hampshire Office of Vacation Travel
Box 856
Concord, NH 03301
603-271-2343

New Jersey Office of Travel and Tourism
CN-826
Trenton, NJ 08625
609-292-2470

New Mexico Tourism and Travel
Joseph Montoya Building
1100 St. Francis Drive
Santa Fe, NM 87503
505-827-0291

New York Division of Tourism
One Commerce Plaza
Albany, NY 12245
518-474-4116

North Carolina Travel and Tourism Division
430 Salisbury Street
Box 25249
Raleigh, NC 27611
919-733-4171

North Dakota Tourism Division
Liberty Memorial Building
Capitol Grounds
Bismarck, ND 58505
701-224-2525

Ohio Department of Development, Division of Travel and Tourism
Box 1001
Columbus, OH 43266
614-466-8844

Oklahoma Tourism and Recreation Department
505 Will Rogers Building
Oklahoma City, OK 73105
405-521-2406

Oregon Economic Development, Division of Tourism
595 Cottage Street, NE
Salem, OR 97310
503-378-3451

Pennsylvania Bureau of Travel Development
416 Forum Building
Harrisburg, PA 17120
717-787-5453

Rhode Island Tourism Division
7 Jackson Walkway
Providence, RI 02903
401-277-2601

South Carolina Department of Parks, Recreation, and Tourism
Box 71
Columbia, SC 29202
803-734-0127

South Dakota Division of Tourism
Capitol Lake Plaza
711 Wells Avenue
Pierre, SD 57501
605-773-3301

Tennessee Department of Tourism
Box 23170
Nashville, TN 37202
615-741-2158

Texas Travel and Information Division
Box 5064
Austin, TX 78763
512-463-8971

Utah Travel Council
Council Hall
Capitol Hill
Salt Lake City, UT 84114
801-533-5681

Vermont Travel Division
134 State Street
Montpelier, VT 05602
802-828-3236

Virginia Division of Tourism
202 West 9th Street
Suite 500
Richmond, VA 23219
804-786-4484

Washington Tourism Development
101 General Administration Building
Olympia, WA 98504
206-753-5600

West Virginia Tourism Information Office
State Capitol Complex
Charleston, WV 25305
304-348-2286

Wisconsin Division of Tourism
123 West Washington Avenue
Box 7606
Madison, WI 53707
608-266-2161

Wyoming Travel Commission
Frank Norris Jr. Travel Center
Cheyenne, WY 82002
307-777-7777

Government Tourist Information Centers

Aruba Tourism Authority
1270 Avenue of the Americas
New York, NY 10020
212-246-3030

Australian Tourist Commission
489 Fifth Avenue
New York, NY 10017
800-445-4400

Austrian National Tourist Office
11601 Wilshire Boulevard
Los Angeles, CA 90025
213-477-3332

Bahamas Tourist Office
150 East 52nd Street
New York, NY 10022
212-758-2777

Barbados Board of Tourism
800 2nd Avenue
New York, NY 10017
212-986-6516

Belgian Tourist Office
745 5th Avenue
New York, NY 10151
212-758-8130

Bermuda Department of Tourism
310 Madison Avenue
New York, NY 10017
800-223-6106

Brazilian Consulate General
3810 Wilshire Boulevard
Los Angeles, CA 90010
213-382-3133

British Tourist Office
40 West 57th Street
New York, NY 10019
212-581-4700

Bulgarian Balkan Holidays
161 East 86th Street
New York, NY 10028
212-722-1110

Canadian Consulate
300 South Grand Avenue
Los Angeles, CA 90071
213-687-7432
See also Quebec.

Chilean National Tourist Board
510 West 6th Street
Los Angeles, CA 90014
213-627-4293

Chinese Tourist Board
60 East 42nd Street
New York, NY 10165
212-867-0271

Colombian Government Tourist Office
140 East 57th Street
New York, NY 10022
212-688-0151

Costa Rican Tourist Board
3540 Wilshire Boulevard
Los Angeles, CA 90010
213-382-8080

Cyprus Consulate General
13 East 40th Street
New York, NY 10016
212-686-6016

Czechoslovakia CEDOK
10 East 40th Street
New York, NY 10016
212-689-9720

Denmark Tourist Board
655 3rd Avenue
New York, NY 10017
212-949-2333

Dominican Republic Tourist Center
485 Madison Avenue
New York, NY 10022
212-826-0750

Egyptian Tourist Authority
323 Geray Street
San Francisco, CA 94102
415-781-7676

French Government Tourist Office
610 5th Avenue
New York, NY 10020
212-757-1125

German National Tourist Office
747 3rd Avenue
New York, NY 10017
212-308-3300

Greek National Tourist Organization
645 5th Avenue
New York, NY 10022
212-421-5777

Grenada Department of Tourism
141 East 44th Street
New York, NY 10017
212-687-9554

Haitian National Office of Tourism
630 5th Avenue
New York, NY 10020
212-757-3517

Honduran Tourist Bureau
1138 Fremont Avenue
South Pasadena, CA 91030
213-682-3377

Hong Kong Tourist Association
548 5th Avenue
New York, NY 10036
212-869-5008

Hungarian IBUSZ Travel Bureau
630 5th Avenue
New York, NY 10111
212-582-7412

India Tourist Office
30 Rockefeller Plaza North
New York, NY 10112
212-586-4901

Indonesian Tourist Office
3457 Wilshire Boulevard
Los Angeles, CA 90010
213-387-2078

Ireland Tourist Board
757 3rd Avenue
New York, NY 10017
212-418-0800

Israeli Government Tourist Office
350 5th Avenue
New York, NY 10018
212-560-0621

Italian Tourist Office
630 5th Avenue
New York, NY 10020
212-245-4961

Jamaican Tourist Board
866 2nd Avenue
New York, NY 10017
212-688-7650

Japan National Tourist Office
360 Post Street
San Francisco, CA 94108
415-989-7140

Kenyan Tourist Office
424 Madison Avenue
New York, NY 10017
212-486-1300

Korean National Tourist Office
510 West 6th Street
Los Angeles, CA 90014
213-623-1226

Luxembourg National Tourist Office
801 2nd Avenue
New York, NY 10017
212-370-9850

Macau Tourist Office
P.O. Box 1860
3133 Lake Hollywood Drive
Los Angeles, CA 90078
213-851-3402

Malaysian Tourist Centre
818 West 7th Street
Los Angeles, CA 90017
213-689-9702

Mexican Tourist Office
10100 Santa Monica Boulevard
Los Angeles, CA 90067
213-203-8151

Monaco Government Tourist Office
845 3rd Avenue
New York, NY 10022
212-759-5227

Morocco National Tourist Office
20 East 46th Street
New York, NY 10017
212-557-2520

Netherlands Board of Tourism
355 Lexington Avenue
New York, NY 10017
212-370-7367

New Zealand Tourist Office
630 5th Avenue
New York, NY 10111
212-698-4680

Norway Scandinavia Tourist Offices
655 3rd Avenue
New York, NY 10017
212-949-2333

Panama Tourist Bureau
2355 Salzedo Street
Coral Gables, FL 33134
305-442-1892

Philippine Department of Tourism
3460 Wilshire Boulevard
Los Angeles, CA 90010
213-487-4525

Polish ORBIS Travel Bureau
500 5th Avenue
New York, NY 10110
212-391-0844

Portuguese Tourism Office
548 5th Avenue
New York, NY 10036
212-354-4403

Puerto Rican Tourism Office
1290 Avenue of the Americas
New York, NY 10104
212-541-6630

Quebec Tourism
17 West 50th Street
New York, NY 10020
212-397-0220

Rumanian National Tourist Office
573 3rd Avenue
New York, NY 10016
212-697-6971

Singapore Tourist Board
342 Madison Avenue
New York, NY 10173
212-687-0385

South African Tourism Board
747 3rd Avenue
New York, NY 10017
212-838-8841

Soviet INTOURIST Travel Office
630 5th Avenue
New York, NY 10111
212-757-3884

Spanish National Tourism Office
665 5th Avenue
New York, NY 10022
212-759-8822

Sri Lankan Tourist Board
2148 Wyoming Avenue
Washington, DC 20008
202-483-4025

Swedish Tourist Board
655 3rd Avenue
New York, NY 10017
212-949-2333

Swiss National Tourist Office
608 5th Avenue
New York, NY 10020
212-757-5944

Tahitian Tourist Board
12233 Olympic Boulevard
Los Angeles, CA 90064
212-207-1919

Taiwan Visitors Association
1 World Trade Center
New York, NY 10048
212-466-0691

Thailand Tourism Authority
3440 Wilshire Boulevard
Los Angeles, CA 90010
213-382-2353

Trinidad Tourist Board
400 Madison Avenue
New York, NY 10017
212-838-7750

Tunisian Tourist Office
1515 Massachusetts Avenue, NW
Washington, DC 20005
202-862-1850

Turkish Tourism Office
821 United Nations Plaza
New York, NY 10017
212-687-2194

Venezuelan Tourist Bureau
7 East 51st Street
New York, NY 10022
212-355-1101

Virgin Islands Tourism Office
1270 Avenue of the Americas
New York, NY 10021
212-582-4520

Yugoslavian Tourist Office
630 5th Avenue
New York, NY 10111
212-757-2801

BEST VACATION BETS

Sylvia McNair's book *Vacation Places Rated* assesses over 100 U.S. vacation areas, rating them on such features as urban activities, climate, access to recreational areas, population density, and "special attractions" like amusement parks and professional sports events. These are McNair's top ten choices:

1. Seattle area, including Mount Rainier and the North Cascades, Washington
2. Los Angeles
3. Hawaii
4. Miami, the Gold Coast, and the Keys, Florida
5. San Francisco
6. Boston
7. Chicago
8. Denver and Rocky Mountain National Park, Colorado
9. New York City
10. Tampa Bay area and the southwest coast, Florida

Theme Parks

Although the traditional American tourist attractions—from Mount Rushmore to the Grand Canyon to the Statue of Liberty to the Golden Gate—are still high on many travelers' itineraries, since the 1950s the greatest volume of visitors has been seen at "theme" amusement parks modeled on the pioneering, enormously successful Disneyland. U.S. amusement parks entertain over 170 million visitors a year. These are the top ten according to the U.S. Travel Data Center.

1. Walt Disney World, Buena Vista, Florida
2. Disneyland, Anaheim, California
3. Universal City Studios Tour, Universal City, California
4. Knott's Berry Farm, Buena Park, California
5. Six Flags/Great Adventure, Jackson, New Jersey
6. Busch Gardens, Tampa, Florida
7. Six Flags/Great America, Gurnee, Illinois
8. Sea World, Orlando, Florida
9. Cedar Point, Sandusky, Ohio
10. Kings Island, Cincinnati, Ohio

Traveling Tips for the Disabled

Determination and good planning are the keys to enjoyable travel for the disabled. If you are disabled, check with your health insurance agent about vacation coverage. In addition, engage a travel agent who specializes in travel for the disabled. Here are some further tips.

Air Travel

Telephone the airline ahead of time about accommodations and possible extra charges. Virtually all major airports have some barrier-free facilities, and special arrangements can be made for disabled passengers.

Buses

Because of space limitations, bus lines generally are less accommodating than other carriers. However, many do have special seating and reduced rates.

Railroads

Trains normally have seating arrangements and toilet facilities for the handicapped. Call ahead to arrange for seating and assistance.

Sea Travel

Travel by ship is possible, but it can be difficult, since ocean-going vessels are not designed for the handicapped. Generally they are not barrier-free.

Parks/Camping

Many domestic and international campsites provide accommodations for the disabled, and some European sites are even designated as "Handi-Camps." A directory of U.S. camps for the handicapped is available from the Easter Seal Society, and a national park guide is available for the handicapped from the National Park Service, U.S. Department of the Interior, Washington, DC 20240.

Hotels/Motels

Many hotel and motel chains have special facilities, as do some nonchain hotels and motels. Check with your travel agent.

Further Information

- Society for the Advancement of Travel for the Handicapped (SATH) (1-718-858-5483).
- Mobility International, for information about travel in the United Kingdom.
- National Park Service, for information on U.S. highway rest areas for disabled travelers.

TRAVELING WITH PETS

Although most travelers leave home without them, vacationing with pets is possible; if you plan carefully, taking your pet along can save on guilt, worry, and even money. It's easier to leave the goldfish in the care of friends, but the family dog can go with you almost anywhere. Information and suggestions to make this easier appear below.

Travel checklist

Proper identification (name and address tag)
Certificate of good health signed by your veterinarian
Proof of up-to-date immunizations
Pet carrier
Pet toys
Blanket
First aid kit, including bandages, antiseptic, and medications (including tranquilizers) prescribed by your
    veterinarian
Food (and can opener, if needed)
Thermos of water
Plastic bowls
Leash and muzzle
Flea powder or flea collar
Grooming tools

Pretravel suggestions

Introduce your pet to car travel with trial runs.
Allow your pet to become familiar with the pet carrier before your trip.
Do not feed your pet for several hours before the trip.
Exercise your pet right before leaving.

Travel restrictions

Automobile: No restrictions.
Bus: Except for seeing-eye dogs, pets are prohibited on buses in interstate travel.
Train: Pets may be taken only in private compartments or in the baggage car.
Airplane: Pets can come on board in pet carriers or can remain in the baggage compartment. Restrictions
    vary, so inquire of individual airlines in advance.
National park: Pets are allowed on leashes except in bathing areas.
State and private park: Restrictions vary; check with the individual facility.
Hotel, motel, and campground: Most do accept pets; notify the owner ahead of time.

International travel (including Hawaii)

Most countries require a recent certificate of good health and proof of immunizations. In addition, the following places may require a quarantine (at the owner's expense) for the number of days indicated.

Hawaii	180	Norway	120
Hong Kong	180	Panama	180
Jamaica	180	Singapore	30
Jordan	42	Sweden	120
Korea	21	Trinidad and Tobago	180
Malta	180	United Kingdom	180
Mauritius	180		

Returning home

Upon your return, a quarantine officer at customs will check documents and inspect your animal. The official may require confinement of any animal that you have purchased abroad; typically confinement is in your own home rather than in official quarantine. Pets purchased abroad also will require proof of immunization, certificates of good health, and payment of an import duty.

TRAVELERS' FIRST-AID KIT

Antiseptic lotion or ointment
Aspirin or acetaminophen
Cold and cough remedies
Gauze bandages and adhesive tape, elastic bandages
Heating pad
Ice pack
Identification bracelet
Insect repellent and insect bite medication
Medical information regarding condition, allergies, medications, blood type, and special needs
Milk of magnesia and diarrhea medication
Moleskin for blisters and calluses
Physician's name, address, and telephone number
Prescription medications and refills
Sunscreen and sunburn relief lotion
Telephone numbers of emergency contacts
Thermometer
Throat lozenges
Vitamins

International Auto Registration Marks

Country	Mark	Country	Mark
Afghanistan	AFG	Central African Republic	RCA
Albania	AL	Chile	RCH
Alderney (Channel Islands)	GBA	Colombia	CO
Algeria	DZ	Congo	RCR
Andorra	AND	Costa Rica	CR
Argentina	RA	Cuba	C
Australia	AUS	Cyprus	CY
Austria	A	Czechoslovakia	CS
Bahamas	BS	Denmark	DK
Bahrain	BRN	East Germany	DDR
Bangladesh	BD	Ecuador	EC
Barbados	BDS	Egypt	ET
Belgium	B	El Salvador	ES
Belize	BH	Faroe Islands	FR
Benin	DY	Fiji	FJI
Botswana	RB	Finland	SF
Brazil	BR	France	F
Brunei	BRU	Gambia	WAG
Bulgaria	BG	Gibraltar	GBZ
Burma	BRU	Great Britain	GB
Burundi	RU	Greece	GR
Cambodia	K	Grenada	WG
Canada	CDN	Guatemala	GCA

Guernsey	GBG	Papua New Guinea	PNG
Guyana	GUY	Paraguay	PY
Hong Kong	HK	Peru	PE
Hungary	H	Philippines	RP
Iceland	IS	Poland	PL
India	IND	Portugal	P
Indonesia	RI	Ruanda	RWA
Iran	IR	Rumania	RO
Iraq	IRQ	St. Lucia	WL
Ireland	IRL	St. Vincent	WV
Isle of Man	GBM	San Marco	RSM
Israel	IL	Senegal	SN
Italy	I	Seychelles	SY
Ivory Coast	CI	Sierre Leone	WAL
Jamaica	JA	Singapore	SGP
Japan	J	South Africa	ZA
Jersey	GBJ	South Korea	ROK
Jordan	HKJ	South Yemen	ADN
Kampuchea	K	Soviet Union	SU
Kenya	EAK	Spain	E
Laos	LAO	Sri Lanka	CL
Lebanon	RL	Suriname	SME
Lesotho	LS	Swaziland	SD
Liberia	LB	Sweden	S
Libya	LAR	Switzerland	CH
Luxembourg	L	Tanzania	EAT
Madagascar	RM	Thailand	T
Malawi	MW	Trinidad and Tobago	TT
Mali	RMM	Tunisia	TN
Malta	M	Turkey	TR
Mauritania	RIM	Uganda	EAU
Mauritius	MS	United States	USA
Mexico	MEX	Uruguay	ROU
Morocco	MA	Vatican City	V
Netherlands	NL	Venezuela	YV
New Zealand	NZ	Vietnam	VN
Niger	RN	West Germany	D
Nigeria	WAN	Yugoslavia	YU
Norway	N	Zaire	ZRE
Pakistan	PAK	Zimbabwe	ZW
Panama	PA		

Additional Sources of Information

AYH Handbook and Hostelers Manual: Europe. American Youth Hostels, 1987.
AYH Handbook and Hostelers Manual: United States. American Youth Hostels, 1987.
The Stephen Birnbaum Travel Guides. Houghton-Mifflin, 1976.
The Business Traveler's Handbook, Prentice-Hall, 1983.

Fodor's Guides. Fodor's Travel Publications, 1980—.

Frommer's Guides. Prentice-Hall, 1977—.

Grimes, Paul, *The New York Times Practical Traveler*. Times Books, 1985.

Hadley, Linda. *Fielding's Guide to Traveling with Children in Europe*. William Morrow, 1972.

Kirk, Robert William. *You Can Travel Free*. Pelican, 1985.

Mobil Travel Guides. 6 vols. Prentice-Hall, 1987.

The Official Airline Guides. Dun and Bradstreet, 1988.

Rand McNally European Atlas. Rand McNally, 1988.

Rand McNally Road Atlas of Britain. William Collins, 1985.

Rand McNally Road Atlas: United States, Canada and Mexico. Rand McNally, 1988.

Simony, Maggy. *The Traveler's Reading Guide*. Facts on File, 1987.

for the Homemaker

Washing Fabrics

Washer Loads

Cottons and Linens

Fabrics must be of fast color and sturdy construction. Wash in very hot water with all-purpose detergent for a full washer cycle. Results are better if white fabrics are washed by themselves. Two large sheets or tablecloths and a variety of smaller articles wash more effectively than a load made up of all large articles.

A load may include:

cotton dresses	shirts	sheets	T-shirts
cotton nightwear	cotton slips	socks	towels
pillowcases	table linen		

Load size: For good washability, load washer about 3 pounds lighter than manufacturer's recommendation (6 pounds in a 9-pound washer).

Lightweight or Sheer Cottons

Wash in warm water, or cool water for dark colors, with an all-purpose detergent and a shortened washing cycle.

A load may include:

blouses	petticoats	negligees and robes
dresses	slips	

Load size: About 3 pounds lighter than manufacturer's recommendation.

Similarly Soiled Articles of Synthetic Fibers

Use warm or cool water, an all-purpose detergent, and a shortened cycle. Include white nylons in an all-white load only; they easily pick up color from other fabrics. If articles are badly soiled, a hot-water wash may be needed.

Load size: A 3- or 4-pound load of easy-care fabrics washes and dries with fewer wrinkles than a capacity load.

Heavy Work Clothes and Other Badly Soiled Laundry

Divide into loads according to color. Use hot water unless running colors or shrinkage is a problem. Use plenty of all-purpose detergent. Pretreat, soak, and use full washer cycle.

A load may include:

children's sturdy play clothes	heavy socks
coveralls, overalls, work pants	shirts, skirts, slacks, shorts
shop or laboratory coats	

Load size: Light. Allow plenty of room for washer action.

Articles That May Run

Some dark-colored cottons, denims, socks, and jeans may be washed together if you do not mind some mixing of colors. Otherwise, sort out the fabrics that are likely to bleed color and wash them separately. Use cool wash water at full washer cycle or shorter if clothes are only lightly soiled.

Miscellaneous Items

These include bulky pieces, blankets, bedspreads, and throw rugs, which need to be washed separately because they fill the washer. Woolens, electric blankets, sweaters, and other items also may require special handling.

Soaking

Generally it pays to soak heavily soiled work and play clothes, dusty curtains and draperies, heavily soiled slipcovers, and certain stained articles to help loosen stains.

The most satisfactory way of soaking clothes is to agitate them in the washer for a few minutes in warm water with detergent. The addition of detergent helps hold the dirt suspended in the water. Use about half the amount of detergent needed for washing. Extract water and follow with a complete washing cycle.

If you have only a few items to soak, use a small container rather than the washer. Submerge clothes in a warm detergent solution and let them soak for 15 minutes. Soaking to remove stains may take longer. Stir the clothes around a bit, extract water, and add the garments to a normally soiled load of similar fabrics for the complete washing cycle. If soaked clothes are extremely dirty, wash them by themselves.

Water Temperature

Medium-hot water (approximately 120° F) is a good temperature for washing some bright or dark colors that do not actually run in the wash but that may fade in time from washing in hot water. This temperature also works well for washing lingerie that you do not want to put in very hot water.

The "warm" setting of an automatic washer usually controls the temperature at about 100° F. Most washers rinse with water at this temperature. In some cycles, and at the "cold" setting, cold water may be used.

Cold water (80° F or less) is recommended for lightly soiled items and fabrics and fibers that lose color, wrinkle, or shrink in hot water.

For more information on the right temperature for various washing jobs, consult the Wash-Water Temperatures guide on page 494.

Rinsing

If you are not getting good rinsing in your washer, you may be overloading or adding too much detergent, or the extraction of the wash water may not be as effective as it should be. See that the spinning mechanism of the washer is in perfect working order.

Fabric Softeners

Fabric softeners, which generally are added to rinse water, make textiles soft and fluffy. They also reduce the static electricity that builds up on some fabrics when they rub against each other and minimize wrinkles and deep creases.

Softener is added to the final rinse water in proportion to the weight of clothes rather than the amount of rinse water. Use softener each time you want fabrics softened; the effect is lost in the next washing. An overdose of softener may decrease the absorbency of fabrics. Some fabric softeners come in disposable sheets that are added to the dryer.

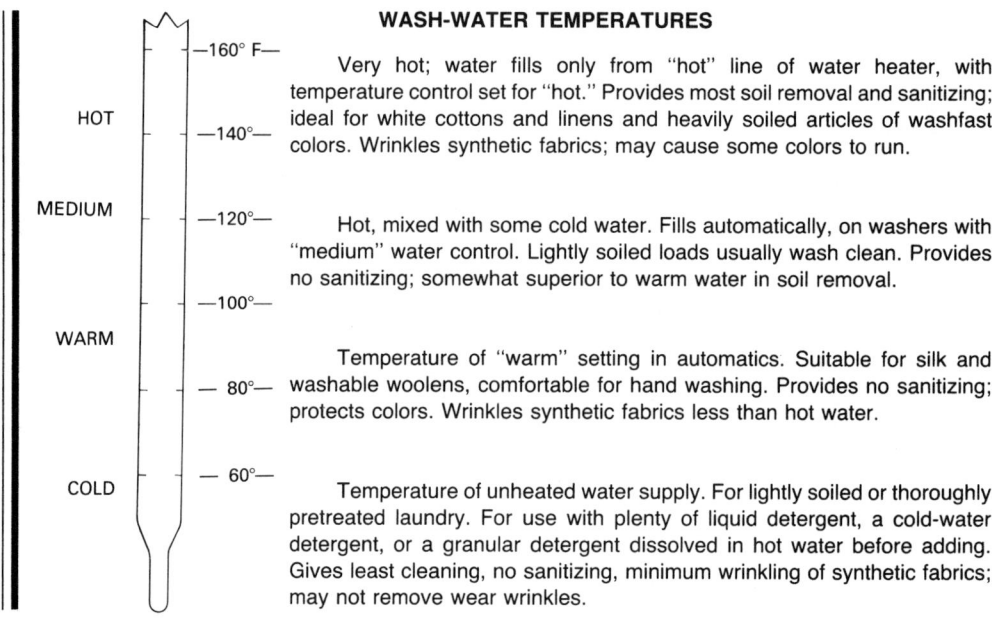

WASH-WATER TEMPERATURES

Very hot; water fills only from "hot" line of water heater, with temperature control set for "hot." Provides most soil removal and sanitizing; ideal for white cottons and linens and heavily soiled articles of washfast colors. Wrinkles synthetic fabrics; may cause some colors to run.

Hot, mixed with some cold water. Fills automatically, on washers with "medium" water control. Lightly soiled loads usually wash clean. Provides no sanitizing; somewhat superior to warm water in soil removal.

Temperature of "warm" setting in automatics. Suitable for silk and washable woolens, comfortable for hand washing. Provides no sanitizing; protects colors. Wrinkles synthetic fabrics less than hot water.

Temperature of unheated water supply. For lightly soiled or thoroughly pretreated laundry. For use with plenty of liquid detergent, a cold-water detergent, or a granular detergent dissolved in hot water before adding. Gives least cleaning, no sanitizing, minimum wrinkling of synthetic fabrics; may not remove wear wrinkles.

Stain Removal

Many common stains fall into one of three categories—greasy, nongreasy, and combination. These stains can be removed by following the appropriate method for each given below. When necessary, separate directions are given for washable and nonwashable articles. Directions for nonwashables are for articles made of fabrics that are not damaged by the application of small amounts of water.

Greasy Stains

Washable Articles

Regular washing, either by hand or by machine, removes some greasy stains. Some stains can be removed by rubbing soap or detergent into the stain and then rinsing with warm water. On some wash-and-wear or permanent-press fabrics, it may be necessary to rub soap or detergent thoroughly into the stain and allow it to stand for several hours, or overnight, before rinsing. Often, however, a grease solvent is necessary; this is effective even after an article has been washed. Sponge the stain thoroughly with the grease solvent and dry. Repeat if necessary. It often takes extra time to remove greasy stains from a fabric with a special finish.

A yellow stain may remain after a solvent treatment if the stain has been set by age or heat. To remove a yellow stain, use a chlorine or peroxygen bleach. If it is safe for the fabric, the strong sodium perborate treatment is usually the most effective.

Nonwashable Articles

Sponge stains well with grease solvent and dry. Repeat if necessary. It may take extra time to remove greasy stains from fabrics with a special finish.

A yellow stain may remain after a solvent treatment if the stain has been set by age or heat. To remove a yellow stain, use a chlorine or peroxygen bleach. If safe for the fabric, the strong sodium perborate treatment is usually the most effective.

Nongreasy Stains

Many fresh stains can be removed by simple treatments. Stains set by heat or age may be difficult or impossible to remove.

Washable Articles

Sometimes, regular laundry methods will remove nongreasy stains; in other cases, laundering will actually set the stains. Sponge the stain with cool water or soak it in cool water for 30 minutes or longer; some stains require an overnight soak. If the stain persists after sponging or soaking, work a soap or detergent into it, then rinse. If the stain remains after detergent treatment, use a chlorine or peroxygen bleach.

Nonwashable Articles

Sponge the stain with cool water. If it remains, rub soap or detergent on the stain and work it into the fabric. Rinse. A final sponging with alcohol helps to remove the soap or detergent and to dry the fabric more quickly. Test alcohol on the fabric first to be sure it does not affect the dye. Dilute the alcohol with two parts of water before using it on acetate. If the stain remains after rinsing, use a chlorine or peroxygen bleach.

Combination Stains

Combination stains are caused by materials that contain both greasy and nongreasy substances.

Washable Articles

Sponge the stain with cool water or soak in cool water for 30 minutes or longer. If the stain persists, work soap or detergent into it, then rinse thoroughly. Allow the article to dry. If a greasy stain remains, sponge with a grease solvent. Allow the article to dry. Repeat if necessary. If a colored stain remains after the fabric dries, use a chlorine or peroxygen bleach.

Nonwashable Articles

Sponge the stain with cool water. If it remains, rub soap or detergent on the stain and work it into the fabric. Rinse the spot well with water. Allow the article to dry. If a greasy stain remains, sponge with a grease solvent. Allow to dry. Repeat if necessary. If a colored stain remains after fabric dries, use a chlorine or peroxygen bleach.

Specific Stains

Acids

If an acid is spilled on a fabric, rinse the area with water immediately. Then apply ammonia to the stain. Rinse again with water. Strong acids, such as sulfuric (used in batteries) and hydrochloric (used for cleaning brick), may damage or destroy some fibers before the acid can be rinsed out. The amount of damage depends on the kind of fiber and acid and on the concentration and temperature of the acid solution. Often, however, thorough rinsing before the acid dries on the fabric will prevent serious damage. Diluted solutions of weak acids, such as acetic (vinegar), will not damage fibers.

Both weak and strong acids may change the color of some dyes. The use of ammonia after rinsing with water neutralizes any acid left in the fabric and sometimes restores colors that have changed.

Adhesive Tape

Scrape gummy matter from stains carefully with a dull table knife; avoid damaging fabric. Sponge with a grease solvent.

Alcoholic Beverages

Follow directions for nongreasy stains. An alternate method, if alcohol does not affect the color of the fabric, is to sponge the stain with rubbing alcohol. Dilute alcohol with two parts of water before using on acetate. If a stain remains, use a chlorine or peroxygen bleach.

The alcohol in alcoholic beverages will cause bleeding of some dyes, which results in loss of color or formation of a dye ring around the edge of the stain. When either change occurs, the original appearance of the fabric cannot be restored.

Alkalis

If an alkali is spilled on a fabric, rinse the area with water immediately. Then apply vinegar to the stain. Rinse again with water. Strong alkalis, such as lye, may damage or destroy some fibers before they can be rinsed out. The amount of damage depends on the kind of fiber and alkali and on the concentration and temperature of the alkali solution. In many cases, however, prompt rinsing will prevent serious damage. Silk and wool are the fibers most easily damaged by alkalis. Diluted solutions of such weak alkalis as ammonia will not damage fibers. Both strong and weak alkalis may change the color of some dyes. The use of vinegar after rinsing with water neutralizes any alkali left in the fabric and sometimes restores colors that have changed.

Antiperspirants and Deodorants

Wash or sponge the stain thoroughly with soap or detergent and warm water. Rinse. If the stain is not removed, use a chlorine or peroxygen bleach. Antiperspirants that contain such substances as aluminum chloride are acid; they may cause fabric damage and change the color of some dyes. Fabric color may be restored by sponging with ammonia. Dilute ammonia with an equal volume of water for use on wool or silk. Rinse.

Blood

Follow directions for nongreasy stains, with one variation. If the stain is not removed by soap or detergent, put a few drops of ammonia on it and repeat the treatment with detergent. Rinse. Follow with a bleach treatment if necessary. Blood stains that have been set by heat will be difficult to remove.

Bluing

Follow directions for nongreasy stains.

Butter and Margarine

Follow directions for greasy stains.

Candy and Syrup

For chocolate candy and syrup, follow directions for combination stains. For other candy and syrup, follow directions for nongreasy stains.

Carbon Paper

Work soap or detergent into the stain; rinse well. If the stain is not removed, put a few drops of ammonia on it and repeat the treatment; rinse well. Repeat again if necessary.

Catsup and Chili

Follow directions for nongreasy stains.

Chewing Gum

Scrape gum off without damaging fabric. The gum can be scraped off more easily if it is first hardened by rubbing it with ice. If a stain remains, sponge thoroughly with a grease solvent.

Chlorine

Use one of the following treatments to remove yellow chlorine bleach stains from fabrics with resin finishes, or to prevent such stains from appearing. Always treat the fabric before ironing it. On some fabrics, the yellow stains form before ironing; on others, after ironing. In either case, ironing before the chlorine is removed weakens the fibers.

Yellow stains caused by the use of chlorine bleach on wool and silk cannot be removed. White or faded spots caused by use of chlorine bleach on colored fabrics cannot be restored to the original color.

Treatment for any fabric. Rinse fabric thoroughly with water. Then soak for 30 minutes or longer in a solution containing one teaspoon of sodium thiosulfate to each quart of warm water. Rinse thoroughly. To strengthen the treatment, make the sodium thiosulfate solution as hot as is safe for the fabric.

Treatment for white or colorfast fabrics. Rinse the fabric thoroughly with water. Then use a color remover, following the directions given on the package for removing stains.

Chocolate

Follow directions for combination stains.

Cocoa

Follow directions for nongreasy stains.

Coffee and Tea

With cream. Follow directions for combination stains.

Without cream. Follow directions for nongreasy stains. Alternatively, for both types of stains, and if safe for the fabric, pour boiling water through the spot from a height of 1 to 3 feet.

Correction Fluid

Sponge the stain with acetone or amyl acetate. Use amyl acetate on acetate, Arnel, Dynel, and Verel; use acetone on other fabrics.

Cosmetics

(eye shadow, lipstick, liquid makeup, mascara, pancake makeup, powder, blush)

Washable articles. Apply undiluted liquid detergent to the stain, or dampen the stain and rub in soap or detergent until thick suds are formed. Work in until the outline of the stain is gone; then rinse well. Repeat if necessary. It may help to dry the fabric between treatments.

Nonwashable articles. Sponge with a grease solvent until no more color is removed. If the stain is not removed, use the method given for washable articles.

Crayon

Follow directions for cosmetics.

Cream

Follow directions for combination stains.

Dyes

Follow directions for nongreasy stains; if bleach is needed, use chlorine bleach or color remover. A long soak in sudsy water often is effective on fresh dye stains.

Egg

Follow directions for nongreasy stains.

Fish Slime, Mucus, Vomit

Follow directions for nongreasy stains or treat the stain with a lukewarm solution of salt and water—¼ cup salt to each quart of water. Sponge the stain with solution or soak the stain in it. Rinse well.

Flowers

See Grass, Flowers, and Foliage.

Food Coloring

Follow directions for nongreasy stains.

Fruit, Fruit Juices

Follow directions for nongreasy stains or, if it is safe for the fabric, pour boiling water through the spot from a height of 1 to 3 feet. When any fruit juice is spilled on a fabric, it is a good idea to sponge the spot immediately with cool water. Some fruit juices, citrus among them, are invisible on the fabric after they dry but turn yellow on aging or heating. This yellow stain may be difficult to remove.

Furniture Polish

Follow directions for greasy stains or, if the polish contains wood stain, follow directions given for paint.

Glue and Mucilage

Airplane glue, household cement. Follow directions for correction fluid.
Casein glue. Follow directions for nongreasy stains.
Plastic glue. Wash the stain with soap or detergent and water before the glue hardens; some types of glues cannot be removed after they have hardened.

To remove some dried plastic glue stains, immerse the stain in a hot 10-percent acetic acid solution or hot vinegar. Keep acid or vinegar at or near the boiling point until the stain is removed. This may take 15 minutes or longer. Rinse with water.

Other types of glues and mucilage. Follow directions for nongreasy stains, but soak the stain in hot water instead of cool.

Grass, Flowers, and Foliage

Washable articles. Work soap or detergent into the stain, then rinse. If it is safe for the dye, sponge the stain with alcohol. Dilute the alcohol with two parts of water for use on acetate. If the stain remains, use a chlorine or peroxygen bleach.

Nonwashable articles. Use the methods for washable articles, but try alcohol first if it is safe for the dye.

Gravy, Meat Juice

Follow directions for combination stains.

Grease (car grease, lard)

Follow directions for greasy stains.

Gum

See Chewing Gum.

Ice Cream

Follow directions for combination stains.

Ink, Ballpoint

Sponge the stain repeatedly with acetone or amyl acetate, or spray it with hair spray. This will remove fresh stains. Old stains may also require bleaching. Washing removes some types of ballpoint ink stains but sets other types. To see if the stain will wash out, mark a scrap of similar material with the ink and wash it.

Ink, Black (India ink)

Treat the stain as soon as possible. These stains are very hard to remove if dry.

Washable articles. Force water through the stain until all loose pigment is removed; otherwise, the stain will spread when treated. Wash with soap or detergent, several times if necessary. Then soak the stain in warm suds containing 1 to 4 tablespoons of ammonia to a quart of water. Dried stains may need to be soaked overnight. An alternative method is to force water through the stain until all loose pigment is removed, wet the spot with ammonia, and then work soap or detergent into it. Rinse. Repeat if necessary.

Nonwashable articles. Force water through stain until all loose pigment is removed; otherwise, the stain will spread when you treat it. Sponge stain with a solution of water and ammonia (1 tablespoon of ammonia per 1 cup of water). Rinse with water. If stain remains, moisten it with ammonia, then work soap or detergent into it. Rinse. Repeat if necessary. If ammonia changes the color of the fabric, sponge first with water, then moisten with vinegar. Rinse well.

Ink, Drawing (colors other than black)

Follow directions for nongreasy stains. If bleach is needed, use a color remover if it is safe for the dye. If a color remover is not safe, try other bleaches.

Ink, Writing

Washable articles. Follow directions for nongreasy stains. Because writing inks vary greatly in composition, it may be necessary to try more than one kind of bleach. Try a chlorine bleach on all fabrics for which it is safe. For other fabrics, try peroxygen bleach. A few types of inks require treatment with color removers. A strong bleach treatment may be needed. However, a strong bleach may leave a faded spot on some colored fabrics. If a yellow stain remains after bleaching, treat it as a rust stain.

Nonwashable articles. If possible, use a blotter (for small stains) or absorbent powder to remove excess ink before it soaks into the fabric. Then follow directions for washable articles.

Iodine

Washable articles. Three methods for removing iodine stains are given below. If the method you try first does not remove the stain, try another.

Water—Soak in cool water until the stain is removed; some stains require soaking overnight. If the stain remains, rub it with soap or detergent and wash it in warm suds. If the stain is not removed, soak the fabric in a solution containing 1 tablespoon of sodium thiosulfate to each pint of warm water, or sprinkle the crystals on the dampened stain. Rinse well as soon as the stain is removed.

Steam—Moisten the stain with water; then hold it in the steam from a boiling tea kettle.

Alcohol—If alcohol is safe for the dye, cover the stain with a pad of cotton soaked in it. If necessary, keep the pad wet for several hours. Dilute with two parts of water for use on acetate.

Nonwashable articles. Try the steam or alcohol methods given above.

Lacquer

Follow directions for correction fluid.

Margarine

See Butter and Margarine.

Mayonnaise and Salad Dressing

Follow directions for combination stains.

Medicines

Gummy, tarry, and with an oily base. Follow directions for grease stains.

In sugar syrup or in water. Wash the stain out with water.

Dissolved in alcohol (tinctures). Sponge the stain with alcohol. Dilute with two parts of water for use on acetate.

With iron. Follow directions for rust.

With dyes. Follow directions for dyes.

Mercurochrome and Merthiolate

Washable articles. Soak overnight in a warm soap or detergent solution that contains 4 tablespoons of ammonia to each quart of water.

Nonwashable articles. If safe for the dye, sponge with alcohol as long as any of the stain is removed. Dilute the alcohol with two parts of water for use on acetate. If the stain remains, place a pad of cotton saturated with alcohol on it. Keep the pad wet until the stain is removed; this may take an hour or more. If alcohol is not safe for the dye, wet the stain with liquid detergent. Add a drop of ammonia with a medicine dropper. Rinse with water, and repeat if necessary.

Metals

To remove stains caused by tarnished brass, copper, tin, and other metals, use vinegar, lemon juice, acetic acid, or oxalic acid. The two acids, because they are stronger, will remove stains that cannot be removed by vinegar or lemon juice. As soon as the stain is removed, rinse well with water. Do not use chlorine or peroxygen bleaches. These bleaches may cause damage because the metal in the stain hastens their action.

Mildew

Washable articles. Treat mildew spots while they are fresh, before the mold growth has a chance to weaken the fabric. Wash the mildewed article thoroughly, and dry it in the sun. If the stain remains, treat it with a chlorine or peroxygen bleach.

Nonwashable articles. Send the article to a dry cleaner promptly.

Milk

Follow directions for nongreasy stains.

Mud

Let the stain dry, then brush well. If the stain remains, follow directions for nongreasy stains. Stains from iron-rich clays not removed by this method should be treated as rust stains.

Mustard

Washable articles. Rub soap or detergent into the dampened stain; rinse. If the stain is not removed, soak the article in a hot detergent solution for several hours, or overnight if necessary. If the stain remains, use a bleach.

Nonwashable articles. If alcohol is safe for the dye, sponge the stain with it. Dilute the alcohol with two parts of water for use on acetate. If alcohol cannot be used, or if it does not remove the stain completely, follow the treatment for washable articles but omit the soaking.

Nail Polish

Follow directions for correction fluid. Nail polish removers also can be used to remove stains. Before using nail polish remover on acetate, Arnel, Dynel, or Verel, test it on a scrap of material to make sure it will not damage the fabric.

Oil (fish-liver oil, linseed oil, machine oil, mineral oil, vegetable oil)

Follow directions for greasy stains.

Paint, Varnish

Treat stains promptly, as they are always harder—and sometimes impossible—to remove after they have dried on fabric. Because there are so many different kinds of paints and varnishes, no one method will remove all stains. Read the label on the container; if a certain solvent is recommended as a thinner, it may be more effective in removing stains than the solvents recommended.

Washable articles. To remove fresh stains, rub soap or detergent into the stain and wash. If the stain has dried or is only partially removed by washing, sponge it with turpentine until no more paint or varnish is removed (for aluminum paint stains, dry-cleaning may be more effective than turpentine). While the stain is still wet with the solvent, work soap or detergent into it, put the article in hot water, and soak it overnight. Thorough washing will remove most types of paint stains. If the stain remains, repeat the treatment.

Nonwashable articles. Sponge fresh stains with turpentine until no more paint is removed (for aluminum paint stains, dry-cleaning may be more effective than turpentine). If the stain remains, put a drop of liquid detergent on it and work it into the fabric with the edge of the bowl of a spoon. Alternately, sponge the stain with turpentine and treat with detergent as many times as necessary. If alcohol is safe for the dye, sponge the stain with it to remove turpentine and detergent. Dilute the alcohol with two parts of water for use on acetate. If alcohol is not safe for the dye, sponge the stain first with warm soap or detergent solution, then with water.

Pencil

A soft eraser will remove pencil marks from some fabrics. If the marks cannot be erased, follow directions for carbon paper.

Perfume

Follow directions for alcoholic beverages.

Perspiration

Wash or sponge the stain thoroughly with soap or detergent and warm water. Work carefully, because some fabrics are weakened by perspiration; silk is the fiber most easily damaged. If perspiration has changed the color of the fabric, try to restore it by treating it with ammonia or vinegar. Apply ammonia to fresh stains and vinegar to old stains; rinse with water.

If an oily stain remains, follow directions for greasy stains. Remove any yellow discoloration with a chlorine or peroxygen bleach. If it is safe for fabric, the strong sodium perborate treatment recommended for greasy-stain removal is often the most effective for these stains.

Plastic

To remove stains caused by plastic hangers or buttons that have softened and adhered to the fabric, dry-cleaning is the safest and most effective method.

Rust

Oxalic-acid method. Moisten the stain with oxalic acid solution (1 tablespoon of oxalic acid crystals in 1 cup warm water). If the stain is not removed by a single treatment, heat the solution and repeat. If the stain is stubborn, place oxalic acid crystals directly on it. Moisten the stain with water as hot as is safe for the fabric and allow it to stand a few minutes, or dip it in hot water. Repeat if necessary. Do not use this method on nylon. Rinse the article thoroughly. If it is allowed to dry in the fabric, oxalic acid will cause damage. PRECAUTION: OXALIC ACID IS POISONOUS IF SWALLOWED.

Cream-of-tartar method. If the treatment is safe for the fabric, boil the stained article in a solution containing 4 teaspoons of cream of tartar to each pint of water. Boil until the stain is removed. Rinse thoroughly.

Lemon-juice method. Spread the stained portion over a pan of boiling water and squeeze lemon juice on it; or sprinkle salt on the stain, squeeze lemon juice on it, and spread the fabric in the sun to dry. Rinse thoroughly. Repeat if necessary.

Color removers can be used to remove rust stains from white fabrics.

Sauces, Soups

Follow directions for combination stains.

Scorch Stains

If the article is washable, follow the directions for nongreasy stains. To remove light scorch stains from an article that is nonwashable, apply hydrogen peroxide. The strong treatment may be needed to remove the stains. Repeat if necessary. Severe scorch stains cannot be removed, however, because the fabric already has been damaged.

Shellac

Using alcohol, sponge or soak the stain. Dilute the alcohol with two parts water for use on acetate. If alcohol bleeds the dye, try turpentine.

Shoe Polish

Because there are many different kinds of shoe polish, no one method will remove all stains. It may be necessary to try more than one of the methods given below.

1. Follow directions for cosmetics.
2. Sponge the stain with alcohol if it is safe for the dye in the fabric. Dilute the alcohol with two parts water for use on acetate.
3. Sponge the stain with grease solvent or turpentine. If turpentine is used, remove it by sponging with a warm soap or detergent solution or with alcohol.

If the stain is not removed by any of these methods, use a chlorine or peroxygen bleach. If safe for the fabric, the strong sodium perborate treatment recommended for greasy-stain removal is often the most effective.

Silver Nitrate

Dampen the stain with water. Then put a few drops of tincture of iodine on the stain. Let it stand for a few minutes. Then treat it as an iodine stain. Unless a stain on silk or wool is treated when fresh, a yellow or brown discoloration will remain.

Soft Drinks

Follow directions for nongreasy stains. When any soft drink is spilled on a fabric, sponge the spot immediately with cool water. Some soft drinks are invisible after they dry but turn yellow on aging or heating. The yellow stain may be difficult to remove.

Soot, Smoke

Follow directions for cosmetics.

Syrup

See Candy and Syrup.

Tar

Follow directions for greasy stains. If the stain is not removed by this method, sponge it with turpentine.

Tea

See Coffee and Tea.

Tobacco

Follow directions for grass.

Typewriter Ribbon

Follow directions for carbon paper.

Unknown Origin

If the stain appears greasy, treat it as a greasy stain; otherwise, treat it as a nongreasy stain.

Urine

To remove stains caused by normal urine, follow directions for nongreasy stains. If the color of the fabric has been changed, sponge the stain with ammonia. If this treatment does not restore the color, sponging with acetic acid or vinegar may help. If the stain is not removed by one or both of these methods, see directions for medicines and yellowing.

Vegetables

Follow directions for nongreasy stains.

Walnuts, Black

These stains are very difficult to remove.

Washable articles. If the treatment is safe for fabric, boil washable articles in soap or detergent solution. This will remove fresh stains. If the stain is not removed, use a strong chlorine or sodium perborate bleach treatment. If the stain remains, treat it as a rust stain.

Nonwashable articles. These stains cannot be removed at home. Send the article to a dry cleaner.

Wax (floor, furniture, car)

Follow directions for greasy stains.

Yellowing; Brown Stains

To remove storage stains—or unknown yellow or yellow-brown stains—from fabrics, use as many of the following treatments as necessary, if safe for the fabric, in the order given.

1. Wash.
2. Use a mild treatment of a chlorine or peroxygen bleach.
3. Use the oxalic-acid method for treating rust stains.
4. Use a strong treatment of a chlorine or peroxygen bleach.

Cooking Equivalents and Substitutions

Common Kitchen Measures

pinch (a few grains) = less than $\frac{1}{8}$ teaspoon	2 cups = 1 pint
3 teaspoons = 1 tablespoon	2 pints = 1 quart
2 tablespoons = 1 fluid ounce	4 quarts = 1 gallon
4 tablespoons = $\frac{1}{4}$ cup	2 dry pints = 1 dry quart
5 tablespoons + 1 teaspoon = $\frac{1}{3}$ cup	8 dry quarts = 1 peck
16 tablespoons = 1 cup	4 pecks = 1 bushel
1 cup = $\frac{1}{2}$ pint or 8 fluid ounces	

Cooking Measurement Abbreviations

Measure	Abbreviation	Measure	Abbreviation
teaspoon	tsp.	gram	g
tablespoon	tbsp.	milligram	mg
ounce	oz.	kilogram	kg
fluid ounce	fl. oz.	liter	l
pint	pt.	milliliter	ml
pound	lb.	degrees Fahrenheit	°F
quart	qt.	degrees Celsius	°C

Metric Cooking Measure Equivalents

Customary	Metric
1 teaspoon	4.9 milliliters
1 tablespoon	14.8 milliliters
1 ounce (dry)	28.35 grams
1 fluid ounce	29.57 milliliters
1 cup	236.6 milliliters
1 pint	437.2 milliliters
1 quart	946.4 milliliters
0.9 quart (dry)	1 liter
1.06 quarts (liquid)	1 liter
1 pound	454 grams
2.2 pounds	1 kilogram
32° Fahrenheit (freezing point)	0° Celsius
212° Fahrenheit (boiling point)	100° Celsius

Food Weights and Measures

Bread

1-pound loaf	12 to 16 slices
1 slice	½ cup soft or ¼ cup dry bread crumbs

Dairy

1 pound cheese	4 to 5 cups, shredded
1 pound cottage cheese	2 cups
3 ounces cream cheese	6 tablespoons
8 ounces cream cheese	1 cup
1 pound butter	2 cups (4 sticks)
1 quart milk	4 cups
1 pound instant nonfat dry milk	5 quarts liquid skim milk
13-ounce can evaporated milk	1⅔ cups
½ pint cream	1 cup
1 cup heavy cream	2 cups, whipped

Eggs

3 to 4	1 cup
8 to 10 whites	1 cup
12 to 14 yolks	1 cup
1 yolk	2 tablespoons

Flour

1 pound all-purpose flour	4 cups, sifted
1 pound cake flour	4¾ to 5 cups, sifted
1 pound whole-wheat flour	3½ to 3¾ cups, unsifted
1 pound cornmeal	3 cups

Fruit

juice of 1 medium lemon	2 to 3 tablespoons
juice of 1 medium orange	⅓ to ½ cup
grated rind of medium orange	1 tablespoon
1 apple	1 cup, sliced
1 pound apples	3 cups, pared and sliced
3 to 4 bananas (1 pound)	1¾ cups, mashed
1 pound cherries	2 cups, pitted
1 pound cranberries	2 cups, pitted
1 pound grapes	2½ cups, seeded
1 pound raisins	2½ cups
1 pound cut candied fruit	3 cups
1 pound finely cut dates	1½ cups

Meat and poultry

1 pound ground cooked meat	5 cups
1 pound diced cooked meat	5 cups
3½-pound chicken	3 cups diced, cooked

Nuts

1 pound almonds in shell	1¼ cups, shelled
1 pound pecans in shell	2 cups, chopped
1 pound walnuts in shell	1½ to 1¾ cups, chopped
¼ pound chopped nuts	about 1 cup

Sweeteners and flavorings

1 pound confectioners' sugar	3½ cups
1 pound brown sugar	2¼ to 2½ cups, firmly packed
1 pound granulated sugar	2 cups
1 pound honey, molasses, or syrup	1⅓ cups
1 pound cocoa	4 cups
1 ounce unsweetened chocolate	1 square
6-ounce package chocolate chips	1 cup

Vegetables

1 whole bay leaf	¼ teaspoon, crushed
1 pound split peas	2½ cups
1 large green pepper	1 cup, diced
¼ pound sliced mushrooms (1¼ cups)	¼ to ½ cup, cooked
1 medium onion	½ cup, chopped
1 pound potatoes (3 medium)	2½ cups, sliced
1 pound green beans (3 cups)	2½ cups, cooked
1 pound cabbage	2½ cups, cooked
1 pound carrots	2½ cups, diced, or 2 cups, cooked
1 medium bunch celery	4½ cups, chopped
1 pound tomatoes (3 medium)	1½ cups, cooked

Food Substitutions

Ingredient	Substitution
Baking powder (1 teaspoon)	¼ teaspoon baking soda + ½ teaspoon cream of tartar
Baking powder (1¼ teaspoons)	½ teaspoon baking soda + 2 tablespoons vinegar
Black pepper	White pepper or paprika
Bouillon (1 cup)	1 bouillon cube dissolved in 1 cup hot water
Bread crumbs (1 cup)	¾ cup cracker crumbs
Butter (1 cup)	1 cup margarine *or*
	1 cup vegetable shortening *or*
	⅞ cup lard
Buttermilk or sour milk (1 cup)	1 cup yogurt *or*
	1 cup whole milk + 1 tablespoon lemon juice *or*
	1 tablespoon vinegar *or*
	1¾ teaspoons cream of tartar
Carrots	Parsnips or baby white turnips
Chocolate:	
semisweet (1⅔ ounces)	1 ounce unsweetened chocolate + 4 teaspoons sugar
unsweetened (1 ounce— 1 square)	3 tablespoons cocoa powder + 1 tablespoon shortening
Cream, heavy (1 cup)	⅞ cup buttermilk or yogurt + 3 tablespoons butter
Croutons	Cubes of crustless white bread sautéed in butter
Curry powder	Turmeric plus cardamom, ginger powder, and cumin
Dry mustard	Prepared mustard
Egg, for thickening or baking	2 egg yolks
Flour:	
all-purpose, for thickening	1½ teaspoons cornstarch *or*
	1½ teaspoons arrowroot *or*
	1 tablespoon quick-cooking tapioca
all-purpose, for bread baking	Up to ½ cup bran, whole-wheat flour, or cornmeal + enough all-purpose flour to fill cup
cake (1 cup sifted)	1 cup minus 2 tablespoons all-purpose flour
Fresh herbs (1 tablespoon)	⅓ to ½ teaspoon dried herbs
Honey (1 cup)	1¼ cups sugar + ¼ cup liquid
Lemon juice	Vinegar *or* lime juice *or* white wine
Mayonnaise, homemade (½ cup)	½ cup commercial mayonnaise + ½ teaspoon lemon juice and ½ teaspoon prepared mustard
Olive oil	Vegetable oil

Ingredient	*Substitution*
Onion, chopped (1 cup)	1 tablespoon instant minced onion, reconstituted
Parsley	Chervil
Scallions	Green or white onions, or onion powder to taste
Shallots	2 parts onion + 1 part garlic
Sugar, granulated (1 tablespoon)	1 tablespoon maple sugar
(1 cup)	1¾ cups confectioners' sugar *or*
	1 cup molasses + ½ teaspoon baking soda
Tomato sauce (2 cups)	¾ cup tomato paste + 1 cup water
Wine vinegar	Cider vinegar with a little red wine *or* white distilled vinegar with a little white wine
Yeast, active dry (1 tablespoon— 1 package)	1⅗-ounce cake yeast

Kosher Substitutions

According to Jewish dietary laws, certain food items, such as pork products, shellfish, and some cuts of beef, are not allowed to be eaten. Also, meat and dairy products are not to be eaten at the same time. Below is a list of ingredients that may be problematic in preparing a kosher dish. On the right are acceptable replacements for these items.

Ingredient	*Substitution*
Butter	In pastry: margarine or vegetable shortening
	To sauté vegetables: margarine
	To fry meat or poultry: equal parts rendered chicken fat and oil; oil; equal parts oil and margarine
Ham or bacon	Used as flavoring: an equal quantity of anchovies, mushrooms, or pungent vegetables
Milk or cream	In chicken stew, soup, or sauce: for each ½ cup, ½ cup chicken stock mixed with 1 egg yolk and 1 teaspoon cornstarch
	In pancakes: an equal quantity of water, 1 tablespoon oil for each cup of flour, and twice as many eggs
Shellfish	An equal amount of firm fish

Cooking Times and Servings Sizes

Oven Temperatures

175° to 225° F	Warm
250° to 275° F	Very slow
300° to 325° F	Slow
350° to 375° F	Moderate
400° to 425° F	Hot
450° to 475° F	Very hot

Cooking Times for Meat, Poultry, Fish

To Roast Beef (325° F)

Cut	Weight in pounds	Minutes per pound	Internal temperature (F)
Standing rib	4 to 8		
rare		20 to 25	140°
medium		25 to 30	160°
well-done		30 to 35	170°
Rolled rib	5 to 7		
rare		30 to 35	140°
medium		35 to 40	160°
well-done		40 to 45	170°
Rib eye	4 to 6		
rare		20	140°
medium		22	160°
well-done		24	170°
Sirloin tip	3½ to 4	35 to 40	160°
Tenderloin (roast at 425°)			
whole	4 to 6	10	140°
half	2 to 3	20	140°

To Broil Steak (2 inches from preheated oven broiler)

1-inch-thick sirloin, porterhouse, T-bone, or rib
rare	5 minutes each side
medium	7 minutes each side
well-done	10 minutes each side

1½-inch-thick sirloin, porterhouse, T-bone, or rib
rare	6 minutes each side
medium	8 minutes each side
well-done	12 minutes each side

For filet mignon, decrease the cooking time by 1 minute on each side. When grilling steak over hot charcoals, have the grill 3 inches from the fire and cook the meat 1 minute less on each side.

To Roast Veal (325° F)

Cut	Weight in pounds	Minutes per pound	Internal temperature (F)
Leg	5 to 8	25 to 30	170°
Loin	4 to 6	30 to 35	170°
Rib (rack)	3 to 5	35 to 40	170°
Rolled rump	3 to 5	40 to 45	170°
Rolled shoulder	4 to 6	40 to 45	170°

To Roast Lamb (325° F)

Cut	Weight in pounds	Minutes per pound	Internal temperature (F)
Leg	5 to 8	30 to 35	175° to 180°
Shoulder	4 to 6	30 to 35	175° to 180°
Cushion shoulder	3 to 5	30 to 35	175° to 180°
Rib (rack)	4 to 5	40 to 45	175° to 180°
Rolled shoulder	3 to 5	40 to 45	175° to 180°
Crown roast	4 to 6	40 to 45	175° to 180°

To Broil Lamb

Broil 1-inch chops or patties about 6 minutes on each side, 1½-inch chops 9 minutes on each side, and 2-inch chops 11 minutes on each side.

To Roast Pork (350° F)

Cut	Weight in pounds	Minutes per pound	Internal temperature (F)
Loin, center	3 to 5	40	185°
Loin, half	5 to 7	45	185°
Loin, rolled	3 to 5	50	185°
Sirloin	3 to 4	50	185°
Crown	4 to 6	45	185°
Picnic shoulder	5 to 8	40	185°
Rolled shoulder	3 to 5	45	185°
Fresh ham (leg)			
whole	10 to 14	30	185°
half	5 to 7	40	185°
Spareribs	3	40	185°

To Broil Pork

Chops (¾ to 1 inch thick), shoulder steaks (½- to ¾-inch thick), and patties (1 inch thick) should be broiled about 11 minutes on each side.

To Roast Ham and Other Cured Pork (325° F)

Cut	Weight in pounds	Minutes per pound	Internal temperature (F)
Whole ham	10 to 14		
uncooked		20	160°
fully cooked		10	130°
Half ham	5 to 7		
uncooked		25	160°
fully cooked		15	130°
Picnic shoulder	5 to 8	30	170°
Rolled shoulder	2 to 4	40	170°

For all boneless meat, allow ⅓ to ½ pound per serving; if the meat contains bone, estimate ½ to ¾ pound per serving.

To Roast Chicken (375° F)

Chickens weighing between 2 and 4 pounds can be roasted for 30 minutes per pound. Add 15 minutes to the total roasting time if the chicken is stuffed. When the chicken is done, a meat thermometer inserted in the thickest part of the thigh will read 190° F; a thermometer inserted in the stuffing will read 165° F. Estimate ½ pound per serving.

To Roast Turkey (325° F)

Ready-to-cook weight in pounds	*Total number of hours*
4 to 8	3 to 4
8 to 12	4 to 4½
12 to 16	4½ to 5
16 to 20	6 to 7½
20 to 24	7½ to 9

Turkey is done when a meat thermometer inserted in the thickest part of the thigh reads 185° F, or when a thermometer inserted in the stuffing reads 165° F. Plan on ½ pound per serving.

To Roast Duck or Goose (325° F)

Roast duck or goose about 30 minutes per pound. Estimate 1 pound per serving.

To Cook Fish

Fish can be cooked at either a very high temperature for a short time or a low temperature for a longer period. Following are general guidelines:
  Baked: 10 minutes at 500° F
  Broiled: 15 minutes
  Deep-fried: 2 minutes at 370° F
  Pan-fried: 10 minutes
  Poached or steamed: 10 minutes per pound
Allow ¾ to 1 pound of whole fish per serving, ½ pound per serving of dressed fish, fillets, and steaks.

To Cook Shellfish

There are many ways to cook shellfish. Here are just a few.
  Starting with boiling water, drop in seafood and let it simmer as follows: shrimp, 5 minutes; crab, 20 minutes; lobster, 20 to 40 minutes.
  Clams can be steamed until their shells just open.
  Shrimp, scallops, clams, and oysters can be deep-fried at 370° F for about 3 minutes.
Allow the following quantities per serving:
  1 quart unshelled soft-shell clams
  1 to 2 crabs
  1 small lobster or 1 pound unshelled lobster
  6 to 8 oysters
  ⅔ cup or ⅓ pound shelled scallops
  ¼ pound unshelled shrimp

Cooking Times for Fresh Vegetables

Vegetable	Amount per Serving	Cooking Time (in minutes)*
Artichoke	1 whole	30 to 40
Asparagus	5 to 7 stalks	10 to 15
Beans (green and wax)	⅓ pound	5 to 10
Beans (lima)	¾ pound	20 to 25
Beets	⅓ pound	35 to 45, whole
Broccoli	½ pound	10 to 15
Brussels sprouts	⅓ pound	5 to 10
Cabbage	⅓ pound	5
Carrots	⅓ pound	10 to 15
Cauliflower	⅓ pound	20 to 25, whole; 10 to 15, flowerets
Corn	1 to 2 ears	5
Eggplant	¼ medium, sliced, broiled or sautéed	5 to 10
Mushrooms	¼ pound, caps or sliced, sautéed	5
Onions	⅓ pound	20 to 30, whole
Peas	½ pound	5 to 10
Peppers (green)	1 medium, sliced, sautéed	3 to 5
Potatoes	1 medium	20 to 25, sliced; 1½ hours, baked, 350° F
	3 small new	20 to 25, whole
Potatoes (sweet) or yams	1 medium, sliced	30 to 35
Spinach	½ pound	5
Squash (summer) or zucchini	½ pound, sliced, boiled or sautéed	5 to 10
Tomatoes	½ pound, sliced	5 to 10 (without water)
Turnips	⅓ pound, cubed	25 to 30

* Boiled or steamed unless otherwise noted.

Cooking Time for Fresh Fruit

To cook any of the fruits below, prepare the fruit according to the directions and add to the proper amount of boiling water. Add sugar and cook for the appropriate time.

Fruit	Amount[1]	How to Prepare	Amount of Boiling Water (cups)	Amount of Sugar (cups)	Cooking Time After Adding Fruit (in minutes)
Apples	8 medium	Pare and slice	½	¼	8 to 10 (slices); 12 to 15 (sauce)
Apricots	15	Halve; pit and peel if desired	½	¾	5
Cherries	1 quart	Remove pits	1	⅔	5
Cranberries	1 pound	Sort	1 or 2, as desired[2]	2	5
Peaches	6 medium	Pare, pit, and halve or slice	¾	¾	5
Pears	6 medium	Pare, core, and halve or slice	⅔	⅓	10 (soft varieties); 20 to 25 (firm varieties)
Plums	8 large	Halve, pit	½	⅔	5
Rhubarb	1½ pounds	Slice	¾	⅔	2 to 5

[1] Makes 6 servings, about ½ cup each.
[2] Cranberries make 6 servings with 1 cup water; 8 servings with 2 cups water.

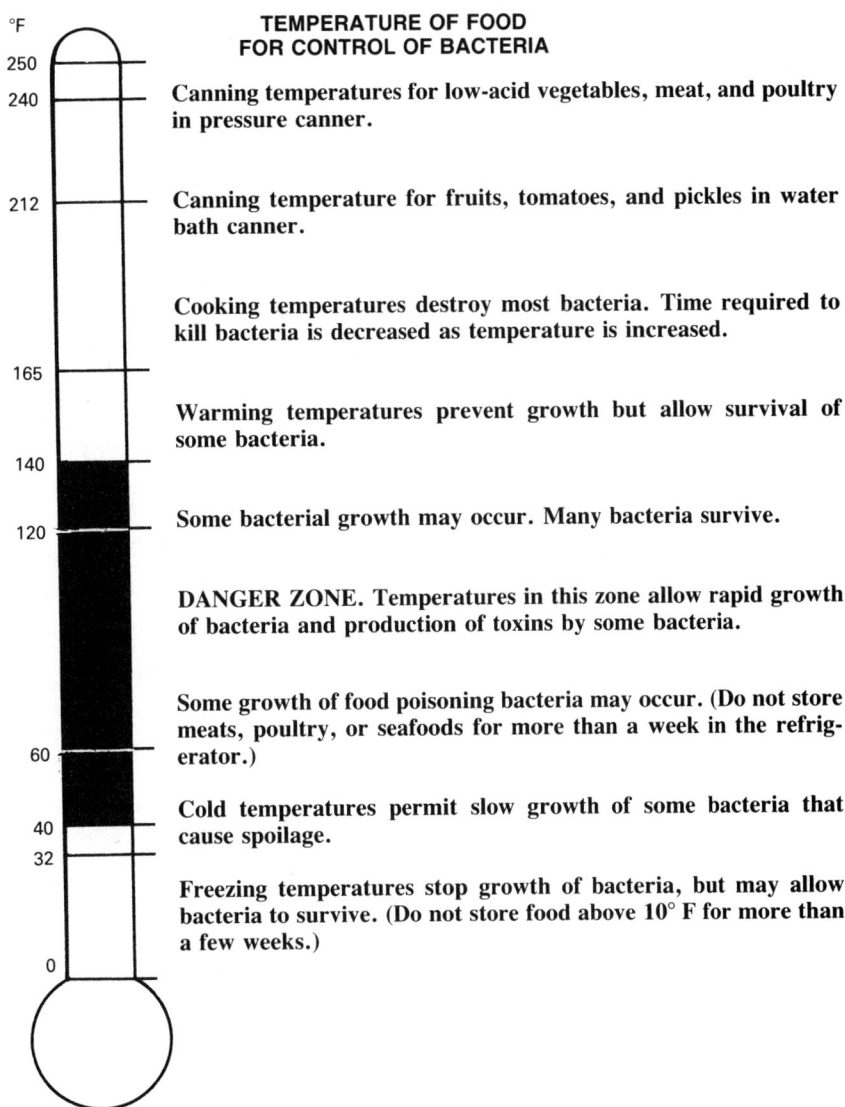

**TEMPERATURE OF FOOD
FOR CONTROL OF BACTERIA**

°F

250

240 — Canning temperatures for low-acid vegetables, meat, and poultry in pressure canner.

212 — Canning temperature for fruits, tomatoes, and pickles in water bath canner.

Cooking temperatures destroy most bacteria. Time required to kill bacteria is decreased as temperature is increased.

165

Warming temperatures prevent growth but allow survival of some bacteria.

140

Some bacterial growth may occur. Many bacteria survive.

120

DANGER ZONE. Temperatures in this zone allow rapid growth of bacteria and production of toxins by some bacteria.

Some growth of food poisoning bacteria may occur. (Do not store meats, poultry, or seafoods for more than a week in the refrigerator.)

60

Cold temperatures permit slow growth of some bacteria that cause spoilage.

40

32

Freezing temperatures stop growth of bacteria, but may allow bacteria to survive. (Do not store food above 10° F for more than a few weeks.)

0

HOW TO STORE COFFEE

Bean form:	
room temperature	4 to 5 weeks
freeze	5 to 6 months
	(grind amount needed only)
refrigerator	avoid
Ground:	
room temperature	7 to 10 days
freezer	5 to 6 weeks
refrigerator	up to 3 weeks

Herbs and Spices

Herbs can provide creative, flavorful alternatives to salt for seasoning foods. Through the skillful use of herbs and spices, you can create imaginative flavors and turn simple foods into gourmet delights.

Herbs and spices differ only in that herbs grow in temperate areas while spices grow in tropical regions. Many people like to grow their own herbs in order to have a fresh supply throughout the growing season. Professional cooks also prefer fresh herbs. But fresh herbs are less concentrated, and two to three times as much of them should be used if a recipe calls for dried herbs.

Here are some tips for cooking with herbs and spices.

- In general, the weaker the flavor of the main staple item, the lower the level of added seasoning required to achieve a satisfactory balance of flavor in the end product.

- Dried herbs are stronger than fresh, and powdered herbs are stronger than crumbled. A useful formula is ¼ teaspoon powdered herb = ¾ to 1 teaspoon crumbled = 2 teaspoons fresh.

- Leaves should be finely chopped because the more cut surface exposed, the more flavor will be absorbed.

- A mortar and pestle can be kept in the kitchen to powder-dry herbs when necessary.

- Scissors are often the best utensil for cutting fresh herbs.

- Be conservative with amounts until you are familiar with the strength of an herb. The aromatic oils can be too strong if a great deal is used.

- The flavoring of herbs is lost by extended cooking. Add herbs to soups or stews about 45 minutes before completing the cooking. For cold foods such as dips, cheeses, vegetables, and dressings, herbs should be added several hours, or even overnight, before using.

- For casseroles and hot sauces, add finely chopped fresh or dried herbs directly to the mixture.

- To become familiar with the specific flavor of an herb, try mixing it with butter and/or cream cheese, letting it set for at least an hour, and then spreading it on a plain cracker.

- Dried herbs should be stored in plastic bags, boxes, or tins rather than cardboard containers; they should be out of direct sunlight and away from the stove.

HERBAL SALT SUBSTITUTES

These can be placed in shakers and used instead of salt.

Basic salt substitute	Use 2 teaspoons garlic powder and 1 teaspoon each of basil, oregano, and powdered lemon rind (or dehydrated lemon juice). Put ingredients into a blender and mix well. Store in a glass container and add rice to prevent caking.
Tangy salt substitute	Mix well 3 teaspoons basil, 2 teaspoons each of savory (summer is best), celery seed, ground cumin seed, sage, and marjoram, and 1 teaspoon lemon thyme. Powder with a mortar and pestle.
Spicy seasoning	Mix in a blender 1 teaspoon each of cloves, pepper, and coriander seed (crushed), 2 teaspoons paprika, and 1 tablespoon rosemary. Store in an airtight container.

Selecting Herbs and Spices to Go with Foods

What Goes with What

Beef:	bay leaf, chives, cloves, cumin, garlic, hot pepper, marjoram, rosemary, savory
Bread:	allspice, caraway, cardamom, curry powder, marjoram, oregano, poppy seed, rosemary, thyme
Cakes:	allspice, cardamom, ginger
Cheese:	anise, basil, chervil, chives, curry, dill, fennel, garlic, chives, marjoram, oregano, parsley, sage, thyme
Fish:	sweet basil, chervil, dill, fennel, French tarragon, garlic, parsley, thyme
Fruit:	anise, cinnamon, coriander, cloves, ginger, lemon verbena, mint, rose geranium, sweet cicely
Lamb:	garlic, marjoram, oregano, rosemary, thyme
Pork:	coriander, cumin, garlic, ginger, hot pepper, pepper sage, savory, thyme
Poultry:	garlic, oregano, rosemary, sage, savory
Salads:	anise, basil, chives, dill, French tarragon, garlic chives, marjoram, mint, oregano, parsley, savory, sorrel, tarragon (many are best used fresh or added to salad dressing; otherwise, use herb vinegars for extra flavor)
Sauces:	allspice, basil, cardamom, chili powder, chives, cumin, curry, fennel, ginger, marjoram, oregano, parsley, rosemary
Soups:	bay, chervil, French tarragon, marjoram, parsley, savory, rosemary
Stews:	allspice, basil, cardamom, chili powder, curry, dill, ginger, parsley, sage
Vegetables:	basil, chervil, chives, dill, French tarragon, marjoram, mint, parsley, pepper, thyme

Chemical Additives

The information on the following pages comes from the Center for Science in the Public Interest and is available from the organization as a color chart entitled "Chemical Cuisine." The address is 1501 16th Street, NW, Washington, DC 20036.

Following each entry is a letter that corresponds to one of the three categories below.

(A) Avoid. The additive is unsafe in the amounts normally consumed or is poorly tested.

(C) Caution. The additive may be unsafe, is poorly tested, or is used in foods that people tend to eat too much of.

(S) Safe. The additive appears to be safe.

Definitions of additive terms

Antioxidants retard the oxidation of unsaturated fats and oils, colorings, and flavorings. Oxidation leads to rancidity, flavor changes, and loss of color. Most of these effects are caused by the reaction of oxygen in the air with fats.

Chelating agents trap trace amounts of metal atoms that would otherwise cause food to discolor or go rancid.

Emulsifiers keep oil and water mixed together.

Flavor enhancers contribute little or no flavor of their own, but accentuate the natural flavor of foods. They are most often used when very little of a natural ingredient is present.

Thickening agents are natural or chemically modified carbohydrates that absorb some of the water that is present in food, thereby making the food thicker. Thickening agents "stabilize" factory-made foods by keeping the complex mixtures of oils, water, acids, and solids well mixed.

ALGINATE; PROPYLENE GLYCOL ALGINATE
Thickening agent, foam stabilizer
Ice cream, cheese, candy, yogurt

Alginate, an apparently safe derivative of seaweed (kelp), maintains the desired texture in dairy products, canned frosting, and other factory-made foods. Propylene glycol alginate, a chemically modified algin, thickens acidic foods (soda pop, salad dressing) and stabilizes the foam in beer. (S)

ALPHA TOCOPHEROL (vitamin E)
Antioxidant, nutrient
Vegetable oil

Vitamin E is abundant in whole wheat, rice germ, and vegetable oils. It is destroyed by the refining and bleaching of flour. Vitamin E prevents oils from turning rancid. (S)

ARTIFICIAL COLORINGS

Most artificial colorings are synthetic chemicals that do not occur in nature. Though some are safer than others, colorings are not listed by name on labels. Colorings are used almost solely in foods of low nutritional value (candy, soda pop, gelatin desserts, etc.). In addition to the problems mentioned below, there is evidence that colorings may cause hyperactivity in some sensitive children. The use of coloring usually indicates that fruit or other natural ingredients have not been used.

BLUE NO. 1
Beverages, candy, baked goods

This dye has been inadequately tested; there are suggestions of a small cancer risk. (A)

BLUE NO. 2
Pet food, beverages, candy

The largest, most recent study suggested, but did not prove, that this dye causes brain tumors in male mice. The Food and Drug

CITRUS RED NO. 2
Skin of some Florida oranges only

Studies indicate that this additive causes cancer. The dye does not seep through the orange skin into the pulp. (A)

GREEN NO. 3
Candy, beverages

A 1981 industry-sponsored study gave hints of bladder cancer, but the FDA reanalyzed the data using other statistical tests and concluded that the dye is safe. This possibly carcinogenic dye is rarely used. (A)

RED NO. 3
Cherries in fruit cocktail, candy, baked goods

The evidence that this dye causes thyroid tumors in rats is "convincing," according to a 1983 committee report requested by the FDA. (A)

RED NO. 40
Soft drinks, candy, gelatin desserts, pastry, pet food, sausage

This is the most widely used food dye. While it is one of the most tested food dyes, the key tests with mice were flawed and inconclusive. An FDA review committee acknowledged problems but said that evidence of harm was not "consistent" or "substantial." (C)

YELLOW NO. 5
Gelatin dessert, candy, pet food, baked goods

This second most widely used coloring causes allergic reactions, primarily in aspirin-sensitive persons. This dye is the only one that must be labeled by name on food labels. (C).

YELLOW NO. 6
·Beverages, sausage, baked goods, candy, gelatin

Recent industry-sponsored animal tests indicate that this dye causes tumors of the adrenal gland and kidney. It may also cause occasional allergic reactions. This dye is contaminated with cancer-causing impurities. (A)

ARTIFICIAL FLAVORINGS
Soft drinks, candy, breakfast cereals, gelatin desserts, other food items

Hundreds of chemicals are used to mimic natural flavors; many may be used in a single flavoring, as in cherry soda pop. Most flavoring chemicals also occur in nature and are probably safe, but they may cause hyperactivity in some children. (A)

ASCORBIC ACID (VITAMIN C); ERYTHOBIC ACID
Antioxidant, nutrient, color stabilizer
Oily foods, cereals, soft drinks, cured meats

Ascorbic acid helps maintain the red color of cured meat and prevents the formation of nitrosamines (*see also* SODIUM NITRITE). It helps prevent loss of color and flavor by reacting with unwanted oxygen. It is used as a nutrient additive in drinks and breakfast cereals. Sodium ascorbate is a more soluble form of ascorbic acid. Erythorbic acid (sodium erythorbate) serves the same functions as ascorbic acid but has no value as a vitamin. (S)

ASPARTAME
Artificial sweetener
Drink mixes, gelatin desserts, other foods

Aspartame, made up of two amino acids, was thought to be the perfect artificial sweetener, but questions have arisen about the quality of the cancer tests done on it. In addition, some individuals have reported severe adverse behaviorial effects after drinking diet soda. People with PKU (phenylketonuria) should avoid it. (C)

BETA CAROTENE
Coloring; nutrient
Margarine, shortening, non-dairy whiteners, butter

Beta carotene is used as an artificial coloring and a nutrient supplement. The body converts it to vitamin A, which is part of the light-detection mechanism of the eye. (S)

BROMINATED VEGETABLE OIL (BVO)
Emulsifier, clouding agent
Soft drinks

BVO keeps flavor oils in suspension and gives a cloudy appearance to citrus-flavored soft drinks.The residues of BVO found in body fat are cause for concern. Safer substitutes are available. (A)

BUTYLATED HYDROXY-ANISOLE (BHA)
Antioxidant
Cereals, chewing gum, potato chips, oils, other edibles

BHA retards rancidity in fats, oils, and oil-containing foods. While most studies indicate it is safe, a 1982 Japanese study demonstrated that it causes cancer in rats. This synthetic chemical often can be replaced by safer chemicals. (A)

BUTYLATED HYDROXY-TOLUENE (BHT)
Antioxidant
Cereals, chewing gum, potato chips, oils, other edibles

BHT retards rancidity in oils. It both increased and decreased the risk of cancer in various animal studies. Residues of BHT occur in human fat. BHT is unnecessary or is easily replaced by safe substitutes. (A)

CAFFEINE
Stimulant
Coffee, tea, cocoa (natural), soft drinks (additive)

Caffeine may cause miscarriages or birth defects and should be avoided by pregnant women. It also keeps many people from sleeping. New evidence indicates that caffeine may cause fibrocystic breast disease in some women. (A)

CALCIUM (OR SODIUM) PROPIONATE
Preservative
Bread, rolls, pies, cakes

Calcium propionate prevents mold growth on bread and rolls. The calcium is a beneficial mineral; the propionate is safe. Sodium propionate is used in pies and cakes, because calcium alters the action of chemical leavening agents. (S)

CALCIUM (OR SODIUM) STEAROYL LACTYLATE
Dough conditioner, whipping agent
Bread dough, cake fillings, artificial whipped cream, processed egg whites

This additive strengthens bread dough so it can be used in bread-making machinery for more uniform grain and greater volume. It acts as a whipping agent in dried, liquid, or frozen egg whites and artificial whipped cream. Sodium stearoyl fumarate serves the same purpose. (S)

CARRAGEENAN
Thickening and stabilizing
agent
*Ice cream, jelly, chocolate
milk, infant formula*

Carrageenan is obtained from seaweed. Large amounts of carrageenan have harmed test animals' colons; the small amounts in food are probably safe. Better tests are needed. (C)

CASEIN; SODIUM CASEIN-
ATE
Thickening and whitening agent
*Ice cream, ice milk, sherbet,
coffee creamers*

Casein, the principal protein in milk, is a nutritious protein that contains adequate amounts of all the essential amino acids. (S)

CITRIC ACID; SODIUM CI-
TRATE
Acid flavoring, chelating agent
*Ice cream, sherbet, fruit
drinks, candy, carbonated
beverages, instant potatoes*

Citric acid is versatile, widely used, cheap, and safe. It is an important metabolite in virtually all living organisms and is especially abundant in citrus fruits and berries. It is used as a strong acid, a tart flavoring, and an antioxidant. Sodium citrate, also safe, is a buffer that controls the acidity of gelatin desserts, jam, ice cream, candy, and other foods. (S)

CORN SYRUP
Sweetener, thickener
*Candy, toppings, syrups, snack
foods, imitation dairy foods*

Corn syrup is a sweet, thick liquid made by treating cornstarch with acids or enzymes. It may be dried and used as corn syrup solids in coffee whiteners and other dry products. Corn syrup contains no nutritional value other than calories, promotes tooth decay, and is used mainly in low-nutrition foods. (C)

DEXTROSE (GLUCOSE,
CORN SUGAR)
Sweetener, coloring agent
*Bread, caramel, soda pop,
cookies, other foods*

Dextrose is an important chemical in every living organism. A sugar, it is a source of sweetness in fruits and honey. Added to foods as a sweetener, it represents empty calories and contributes to tooth decay. Dextrose turns brown when heated and contributes to the color of bread crust and toast. (C)

DIGLYCERIDES *See* MON-
OGLYCERIDES AND DI-
GLYCERIDES.

ETHYLENEDIAMINE TE-
TRAACETIC ACID (EDTA)
Chelating agent
*Salad dressing, margarine,
sandwich spreads, mayon-
naise, processed fruits and
vegetables, canned shellfish,
soft drinks*

Modern food-manufacturing technology, which involves metal rollers, blenders, and containers, results in trace amounts of metal contamination in food. EDTA traps metal impurities, which would otherwise promote rancidity and the breakdown of artificial colors. (S)

FERROUS GLUCONATE
Coloring, nutrient
Black olives, vitamin pills

Used by the olive industry to generate a uniform jet-black color and in pills as a source of iron, this substance is safe. (S)

FUMARIC ACID
Tartness agent
*Powdered drinks, pudding, pie
fillings, gelatin desserts*

A solid at room temperature, inexpensive, and highly acidic, fumaric acid is the ideal source of tartness and acidity in dry food products. However, it dissolves slowly in cold water, a drawback cured by adding dioctyl sodium sulfosuccinate (DSS), a poorly tested, detergentlike additive. (S)

GELATIN
Thickening and gelling agent
*Powdered dessert mix, yogurt,
ice cream, cheese spreads,
beverages*

Gelatin is a protein obtained from animal bones, hooves, and other parts. It has little nutritional value, because it contains little or none of several essential amino acids. (S)

GLYCERIN (GLYCEROL)
Maintainer of water content
Marshmallows, candy, fudge, baked goods

Glycerin forms the backbone of fat and oil molecules and is quite safe. The body uses it as a source of energy or as a starting material in making more complex molecules. (S)

GUMS (ARABIC, FURCELLERAN, GHATTI, GUAR, KARAYA, LOCUST, BEAN, TRAGACANTH)
Beverages, ice cream, frozen puddings, salad dressings, dough, cottage cheese, candy, drink mixes

Gums derive from natural sources (bushes, trees, or seaweed) and are poorly tested. They are used to thicken foods, prevent sugar crystals from forming in candy, stabilize beer foam (arabic), form gel in pudding (furcelleran), encapsulate flavor oils in powdered drink mixes, and keep oil and water mixed in salad dressings. Tragacanth sometimes causes severe allergic reactions. (C)

HEPTYL PARABEN
Preservative
Beer, noncarbonated soft drinks

Heptyl paraben—short for the heptyl ester of parahydroxybenzoic acid—is a preservative. Studies suggest that this chemical is safe, but, like other additives in alcoholic beverages, it has never been tested in the presence of alcohol. (C)

HYDROGENATED VEGETABLE OIL
Source of oil or fat
Margarine, processed foods

Vegetable oil, usually a liquid, can be made into a semisolid by treating it with hydrogen. Unfortunately, hydrogenation converts some of the polyunsaturated oil to saturated fat. High-fat diets promote obesity, heart disease, and possibly cancer. (C)

HYDROLYZED VEGETABLE PROTEIN (HVP)
Flavor enhancer
Instant soups, frankfurters, sauce mixes, beef stew

HVP consists of vegetable (usually soybean) protein that has been chemically broken down into the amino acids of which it is composed. HVP is used to bring out the natural flavor of food. (S)

INVERT SUGAR
Sweetener
Candy, soft drinks, many other foods

Invert sugar, an even mixture of dextrose and fructose, two sugars, is sweeter and more soluble than sucrose (table sugar). Invert sugar forms when sucrose is split in two by an enzyme or acid. It contributes to tooth decay. (C)

LACTIC ACID
Acidity regulator
Spanish olives, cheese, frozen desserts, carbonated beverages

This safe acid occurs in almost all living organisms. It inhibits spoilage in Spanish-type olives, balances the acidity in cheese-making, and adds tartness to frozen desserts, carbonated fruit-flavored drinks, and other goods. (S)

LACTOSE
Sweetener
Whipped topping mix, breakfast pastry

Lactose is a carbohydrate found only in milk. One-sixth as sweet as table sugar, it is added to food as a slightly sweet source of carbohydrate. Milk turns sour when bacteria convert lactose to lactic acid. Many non-Caucasians have trouble digesting lactose. (S)

LECITHIN
Emulsifier, antioxidant
Baked goods, margarine, chocolate, ice cream

A common constituent of animal and plant tissues, lecithin is a source of the nutrient choline. It keeps soil and water from separating, retards rancidity, reduces spattering in a frying pan, and leads to fluffier cakes. Major sources are egg yolks and soybeans. (S)

MANNITOL
Sweetener, antiabsorbent
Chewing gum, low-calorie foods

Not quite as sweet as sugar and poorly absorbed by the body, mannitol contributes only half as many calories as sugar. Used as the "dust" on chewing gum, it prevents gum from absorbing moisture and becoming sticky. (S)

MONOGLYCERIDES and DIGLY-CERIDES
Emulsifiers
Baked goods, margarine, candy, peanut butter

These substances make bread softer, improve the stability of margarine, and make caramel less sticky. They prevent staleness and keep the oil in peanut butter from separating. Monoglycerides and diglycerides are safe, though most foods they are used in are high in refined flour, sugar, or fat. (S)

MONOSODIUM GLUTAMATE (MSG)
Flavor enhancer
Soup, seafood, poultry, cheese, sauces, stews, other foods

This amino acid brings out the flavor of protein-containing foods. Large amounts of MSG fed to infant mice destroyed nerve cells in the brain. Public pressure forced baby food companies to stop using MSG. MSG causes ''Chinese restaurant syndrome,'' a burning sensation in the back of the neck and forearms, tightness of the chest, and headache, in some people. (C)

PHOSPHORIC ACID; PHOS-PHATES
Acidulant, chelating agent, buffer, emulsifier, nutrient, discoloration inhibitor
Baked goods, cheese, powered foods, cured meats, soft drinks, breakfast cereals, dehydrated potatoes

Phosphoric acid acidifies and flavors cola beverages. Phosphate salts are used in hundreds of processed foods for many purposes. Calcium and iron phosphates act as mineral supplements. Sodium aluminum phosphate is a leavening agent. Calcium and ammonium phosphates serve as food for yeast in bread. Sodium and pyrophosphate prevents discoloration in potatoes and sugar syrups. Phosphates are not toxic, but their widespread use has led to dietary imbalances that may be contributed to osteoporosis. (C)

POLYSORBATE 60
Emulsifier
Baked goods, frozen desserts, imitation dairy products

Polysorbate 60 is short for polyoxyethylene-(20)-sorbitan monostearate. Along with its close relatives, polysorbate 65 and 80, it works the same way that monoglycerides and diglycerides do, but smaller amounts are needed. They keep baked goods from going stale, keep dill oil dissolved in bottled dill pickles, help coffee whiteners dissolve in coffee, and prevent oil from separating out of artificial whipped cream. (S)

PROPYL GALLATE
Antioxidant
Vegetable oils, meat products, potato sticks, chicken soup base, chewing gum

This substance retards the spoilage of fats and oils and is often used with BHA and BHT because of the synergistic effect these additives have. The best long-term feeding study on this additive, in 1981, was peppered with suggestions but not proof of cancer. (A)

QUININE
Flavoring
Tonic water, quinine water, bitter lemon

This drug can cure malaria and is used as a bitter flavoring in a few soft drinks. There is a slight chance that quinine may cause birth defects, so pregnant women should avoid quinine-containing beverages and drugs. Quinine has been very poorly tested. (C)

SACCHARIN
Synthetic sweetener
Diet products

Saccharin is 350 times sweeter than sugar. Studies have not shown that saccharin helps people lose weight. In 1977 the FDA proposed that saccharin be banned because of repeated evidence that it causes cancer. It is gradually being replaced by aspartame. (A)

SALT (SODIUM CHLORIDE)
Flavoring
Most processed foods

Salt is used liberally in many processed foods. Other additives contribute additional sodium. A diet high in sodium may cause high blood pressure, which increases the risk of heart attack and stroke. (C)

SODIUM BENZOATE
Preservative
Fruit juices, carbonated drinks, pickles, preserves

Manufacturers have used sodium benzoate for over 70 years to prevent the growth of microorganisms in acidic foods. (S)

SODIUM CARBOXYMETHYL-
CELLULOSE (CMC)
Thickening and stabilizing agent
*Ice cream, beer, pie fillings, icings,
diet foods, candy*

CMC is made by reacting cellulose with a derivative of acetic acid. Studies indicate that it is safe. (S)

SODIUM NITRITE; SODIUM NI-
TRATE
Preservative, coloring, flavoring
*Bacon, ham, frankfurters, luncheon
meats, smoked fish, corned beef*

Nitrite can lead to the formation of small amounts of potent cancer-causing chemicals (nitrosamines), particularly in fried bacon. Nitrite is tolerated in foods because it can prevent the growth of bacteria that cause botulism poisoning. Nitrite also stabilizes the red color in cured meats and gives a characteristic flavor. Companies should find safer methods of preventing botulism. Sodium nitrate is used in dry-cured meats because it slowly breaks down into nitrite. (A)

SORBIC ACID; POTASSIUM
SORBATE
Prevents growth of mold
*Cheese, syrup, jelly, cakes, wines,
dry fruits*

These additives occur naturally in many plants and are safe under normal circumstances. (S)

SORBITAN MONOSTEARATE
Emulsifier
*Cakes, candy, frozen puddings, ic-
ings*

Like monoglycerides, diglycerides, and polysorbates, this additive keeps oil and water mixed. In chocolate candy, it prevents the discoloration that normally occurs when the candy is warmed up and then cooled down. (S)

SORBITOL
Sweetener, thickening agent, maintainer of moisture
*Dietetic drinks and foods, candy,
shredded coconut, chewing gum*

Sorbitol occurs naturally in fruits and berries and is a close relative of the sugars; however, it is half as sweet as sugar. It is used in noncariogenic chewing gum because oral bacteria do not metabolize it well. Large amounts of sorbitol (2 ounces for adults) have a laxative effect, but otherwise it is safe. Diabetics use sorbitol because it is absorbed slowly and does not cause blood sugar to increase rapidly. (S)

STARCH; MODIFIED STARCH
Thickening agent
Soups, gravies, baby foods

Starch, the major component of flour, potatoes, and corn, is used as a thickening agent. However, it does not dissolve in cold water. Chemists have solved this problem by reacting starch with various chemicals. These modified starches are added to some foods to improve their consistencies and to keep the solids suspended. Starch and modified starches make foods look thicker and richer than they really are. (S)

SUGAR (SUCROSE)
Sweetener
Table sugar, sweetened foods

Surcrose, ordinary table sugar, occurs naturally in fruit, sugar cane, and sugar beets. Americans consume about 65 pounds of refined sugar per year. Sugar, corn syrup, and other refined sweeteners make up about one-eighth of the average diet, but they contain no vitamins, minerals, or protein. (C)

SULFUR DIOXIDE; SODIUM
BISULFITE
Preservative, bleach
*Dried fruits, wines, processed pota-
toes*

Sulfiting agents prevent discoloration (in dried fruits, some "fresh" shrimp, and some dried, fried, and frozen potatoes) and bacterial growth (in wines). They also destroy vitamin B_1 and can cause severe reactions in asthmatics. This additive has caused at least seven deaths. (A)

VANILLIN; ETHYL VANILLIN
Substitute for vanilla
*Ice cream, baked goods, beverages,
chocolate, candy, gelatin desserts*

Vanilla flavoring is derived from a bean, but vanillin, the major flavor component of vanilla, is cheaper to produce in a factory. A derivative, ethyl vanillin, comes closer to matching the taste of real vanilla. Both chemicals are safe. (S)

Outlawed Additives

Name	Year Outlawed	Use
Cobalt sulfate	1966	Beer foam stabilizer
Cyclamate	1970	Artificial sweetener
Dulcin	1950	Artificial sweetener
Green No. 1	1966	Coloring agent
Orange B	1978	Coloring agent
Red No. 2	1976	Coloring agent
Safrole	1960	Root beer flavoring
Violet No. 1	1973	Coloring agent

Alcoholic Drink Recipes

Except where otherwise indicated, *shake* means to shake with cracked ice and then strain into a glass; *stir* means to stir over ice in the glass; and *straight up* means served without ice.

Alexander

Shake 1 oz. brandy, 1 oz. crème de cacao, and 1 oz. cream.

Bacardi Cocktail

Shake 1½ oz. Bacardi rum, the juice of ½ lime, and ½ teaspoon grenadine.

B & B

Stir ½ oz. benedictine and ½ oz. brandy (or cognac); B & B may also be served straight up.

Black Russian

Stir 1½ oz. vodka and ¾ oz. Kahlua.

Black Velvet

Pour equal parts Guinness stout and champagne over ice in a tall glass.

Bloody Mary

Shake or stir 1½ oz. vodka, 3 oz. tomato juice, the juice of ½ lemon, a dash each of Worcestershire and Tabasco sauce, and a pinch each of salt, pepper, and celery salt.

Bronx Cocktail

Shake 1 oz. gin, ½ oz. dry vermouth, ½ oz. sweet vermouth, and ½ oz. orange juice.

Bullshot

Substitute consommé for tomato juice and follow the directions for Bloody Mary.

Champagne Cocktail

Mix 1 lump sugar, 2 dashes angostura bitters, and 1 oz. brandy; top with chilled champagne.

Cuba Libre (Rum and Coke)

Over ice in a tall glass, pour 1 oz. light rum and the juice of ½ lime; top with cola.

Daiquiri

Shake 1½ oz. light rum, the juice of 1 lime, and 1 teaspoon powdered sugar (often served with the addition of crushed fruit or fruit juice as strawberry daiquiri, peach daiquiri, etc.; blended with crushed ice, it becomes a frozen daiquiri).

Gibson

A martini with the addition of a pearl onion instead of the traditional olive.

Gimlet

Shake 1 oz. gin and 1 oz. Rose's lime juice or the juice of 1 lime.

Gin and Tonic

Pour 2 oz. gin over ice in a tall glass; top with tonic water.

Gin Fizz

Shake 2 oz. gin, the juice of ½ lemon, and 1 teaspoon powdered sugar; top with soda water in a tall glass.

Grasshopper

Shake ½ oz. crème de menthe, ½ oz. white crème de cacao, and ½ oz. cream.

Harvey Wallbanger

Add 1 oz. Galliano to a Screwdriver.

Jack Rose

Shake 1½ oz. apple brandy, the juice of ½ lime, and 1 teaspoon grenadine.

Kir

To a glass of chilled white wine, add 1 teaspoon crème de cassis.

Mai Tai

Shake 2 oz. rum, 1 oz. curaçao, the juice of ½ lime, ½ oz. grenadine, ½ oz. almond-flavored syrup, and ½ teaspoon powdered sugar; serve over crushed ice.

Manhattan

Stir with cracked ice 1½ oz. whiskey, ¾ oz. sweet vermouth, and a dash of angostura bitters; serve over ice or straight up with a maraschino cherry.

Margarita

Shake 1½ oz. tequila, ½ oz. Cointreau or triple sec, and the juice of ½ lime; serve in a chilled, salt-rimmed glass.

Martini

Stir gin and dry vermouth; strain into a chilled glass. The original ratio of gin to vermouth was 2:1, but contemporary tastes tend toward "drier" ratios of 3:1, 5:1, and even 7:1. Serve straight up with an olive or, less traditionally, over ice or with a lemon twist. Made with a pearl onion, it is called a Gibson; with vodka, a vodka martini or Vodkatini.

Mint Julep

Mix in a tall glass 1 lump sugar, 1 tablespoon water, and 4 sprigs of mint; fill the glass with crushed ice; add 2 oz. bourbon, and serve with straws, without stirring.

Old-Fashioned

Mix in a short glass ½ lump sugar, 2 dashes angostura bitters, and 1 dash water; stir in ice cubes and 2 oz. whiskey.

Orange Blossom

Shake 1 oz. gin and 1 oz. orange juice.

Pimm's Cup

Over ice in a tall glass, pour 1 oz. Pimm's No. 1 Cup; top with lemonade, 7-Up, or ginger ale.

Piña Colada

Over crushed ice in a tall glass, pour ½ oz. light rum, ½ oz. dark rum, 1 oz. each of orange, lime, and pineapple juice, and 1 dash of grenadine; top with coconut milk.

Pink Gin

Add 1 dash angostura bitters to 2 oz. gin. Pink Gin may be served straight up or with water or soda and ice.

Planter's Punch

Over crushed ice in a tall glass, pour 2 oz. soda water, the juice of 2 limes, and 2 teaspoons powdered sugar; stir to frost glass; add 2 dashes angostura bitters and 2 oz. rum.

Rickey

Over cracked ice, pour 2 oz. gin and the juice of ½ lime; top with soda water. This traditional gin rickey is often modified by substituting other spirits: hence, Scotch rickey, Irish rickey, etc.

Rob Roy

Using Scotch whiskey, follow the directions for a Manhattan.

Rusty Nail

Stir 2 oz. Scotch whiskey with 1 oz. Drambuie.

Salty Dog

Stir 2 oz. gin, 2 oz. grapefruit juice, and ¼ teaspoon salt.

Sangre

A Bloody Mary made with tequila instead of vodka.

Screwdriver

Over ice in a tall glass, pour 2 oz. vodka; top with orange juice.

7 & 7

Over ice, pour 1½ oz. Seagram's whiskey; top with 7-Up.

Sidecar

Shake 1 oz. brandy, ½ oz. Cointreau or Triple Sec, and the juice of ½ lemon.

Singapore Sling

Shake 2 oz. gin, ½ oz. cherry brandy, the juice of ½ lemon, and 1 teaspoon powdered sugar; pour over ice cubes in a tall glass and top with soda water.

Stinger

Shake or stir 1 oz. brandy and 1 oz. white crème de menthe.

Tequila Sunrise

Shake or stir in a tall glass 1½ oz. tequila and 3 oz. orange juice; add 1 oz. grenadine; do not stir.

Toddy

Dissolve 1 lump sugar in a little water in a short glass; add 2 oz. spirits (brandy, gin, rum, or whiskey) and top with water (with boiling water, the drink is a hot toddy).

Tom Collins

Shake 2 oz. gin, the juice of ½ lemon, and 1 teaspoon powdered sugar; pour over ice cubes in a tall glass and top with soda water (made with vodka in place of gin, this is a Vodka Collins).

Whiskey Sour

Shake 2 oz. whiskey, the juice of 1 lemon, and ½ teaspoon powdered sugar.

White Lady

Shake 1½ oz. gin, 1 teaspoon powdered sugar, 1 teaspoon cream, and 1 egg white.

Zombie

Blend with cracked ice 3 oz. rum, ½ oz. apricot brandy, 1 oz. pineapple juice, the juice of 1 lime and 1 orange, and 1 teaspoon powdered sugar. Strain into a tall frosted glass; float ½ oz. rum (151 proof) on top before serving with straws.

Mixing Drinks

Always be sure of your ingredients and measure them accurately. A jigger is 1½ ounces, a pony ¾ ounce, a bar spoon ½ teaspoon, and a dash 7 to 10 drops.

Ice should always be the first ingredient that goes into the glass. Use new ice for every drink and do not let drinks stand too long before serving. The best bartenders chill cocktail glasses in the refrigerator before serving.

Drinks containing fruit juices, eggs, or other dissimilar ingredients should always be shaken fast and vigorously. The ingredients will mix more readily and completely in a shaker or an electric blender. Never shake drinks mixed with carbonated water or ginger ale. Stir them smoothly and not too vigorously for about half a minute. This will keep the drink sparkling and prevent a flat taste. It also will chill the drink properly and thoroughly.

When a drink calls for fruit juice, use fresh juice if possible. The juice is put into the mixing glass with the proper amount of sugar or other sweetener before the liquor.

Fine granulated sugar can be used for sweetening in most cases. Many people prefer simple syrup, which can easily be made by dissolving ½ pound of fine granulated sugar in ¾ cup of boiling water. One teaspoon of simple syrup is equivalent to one of sugar.

For drinks requiring a twist of lemon, orange, or lime, use a piece of peel about 1½ inches long and ¼ inch wide. Twist this over the drink to extract a bit of oil, and then drop in the peel.

Liquor Needed for Drinks Served

Liquor is commonly sold in fifths. One fifth is equivalent to 25 ounces. Liquor is also available in liter measures. One liter holds 33.9 ounces.

Number of People	Number of Drinks (for cocktails)	Amount Needed
4	10 to 16	1 fifth
6	15 to 22	2 fifths
8	18 to 24	2 fifths
12	20 to 40	3 fifths
20	40 to 65	4 fifths
	(for buffet or dinner)	
4	8 cocktails	1 fifth
	8 glasses of wine	2 one-liter bottles
	4 liqueurs	1 fifth
	10 highballs	1 fifth
6	12 cocktails	1 fifth
	12 glasses of wine	3 one-liter bottles
	8 liqueurs	1 fifth
	16 highballs	2 fifths
8	16 cocktails	1 fifth
	16 glasses of wine	3 one-liter bottles
	16 liqueurs	1 fifth
	18 highballs	2 fifths
20	40 cocktails	3 fifths
	40 glasses of wine	7 one-liter bottles
	25 liqueurs	2 fifths
	50 highballs	4 fifths
	(for after-dinner party)	
4	12 to 16	1 fifth
6	18 to 26	2 fifths
8	20 to 34	2 fifths
12	25 to 45	3 fifths
20	45 to 75	5 fifths

Wines and Their Service

Red table wines should be served cool or at room temperature. Room temperature means about 65 to 68° F, so some cooling may be necessary. Red wines go well with all foods with the possible exception of fish and seafood. White table wines, rosé wines, and all sparkling wines, both red and white, should be served well chilled. Dry wines should not be served with sweet dishes.

So that corks stay moist and tight, store wines on their side. If the cork is removed an hour or two before serving, red wines will expand a bit and give off a delightful scent. Smell the cork to see if it is sour-smelling; if so, the wine has started to turn to vinegar and should not be served; it can, however, be kept for cooking.

Many good wines will contain a small amount of sediment. This is harmless and will settle on the bottom of the bottle if it is stood upright for about two hours before serving. When serving champagne, hold the bottle at a slight angle for a few seconds after the cork is removed. This will reduce the amount of frothing and will maintain a maximum amount of sparkle.

Wineglasses should be placed to the right of the water goblet; they are arranged according to their use, the first wineglass being closest to the water goblet. If more than one wine is served, the glasses used first are removed when the course is through.

The person serving should fill his or her own glass one-quarter full and then taste the wine to check the quality and flavor. Then the other glasses should be filled half to three-quarters full, but never to the very top. Wine is poured as soon as a course is served. The person pouring should not lift the glasses from the table.

When more than one wine is served, remember that light wine comes before heavy or full wine, dry white wine precedes sweet red wine, and dry red wine is served before white sweet wine. The "correct" wine is always the one you like best; however, certain wines complement certain foods. The following wine and food list is a guide to what people generally like. One's own taste should be the final judge.

Canapes, crackers, olives, cheese dips, other hors d'oeuvres: sherry, vermouth, or champagne.

Soups: sherry or Madeira.

Seafood: Chablis, Rhine wine, Moselle, dry sauterne, white Burgundy.

Fowl: Rhine wine, dry sauterne, champagne, Bordeaux, white or red Burgundy (with game).

Meats: claret, red Burgundy, rosé (with cold cuts).

Cheese or nuts: port, sherry, red Burgundy, muscatel, zinfandel, Barbera.

Desserts: sweet sauterne, champagne, port, muscatel, Tokay.

After dinner: brandy, Cointreau, benedictine, crème de menthe.

Clothing Size Conversion Tables

Women

Blouses and Sweaters

U.S.	32	34	36	38	40	42	44
British	34	36	38	40	42	44	46
Continental	40	42	44	46	48	50	52

Coats and Dresses

U.S.	8	10	12	14	16	18	20
British	30	32	34	36	38	40	42
Continental	36	38	40	42	44	46	48

Shoes

U.S.	5–5½	6–6½	7–7½	8–8½	9
British	3½–4	4½–5	5½–6	6½–7	7½
Continental	36	37	38	39	40

Stockings

U.S. and British	8	8½	9	9½	10	10½
Continental	0	1	2	3	4	5

Men

Hats

U.S.	6⅝	6¾	6⅞	7	7⅛	7¼	7⅝	7½
British	6½	6⅝	6¾	6⅞	7	7⅛	7¼	7⅜
Continental	53	54	55	56	57	58	59	60

Shirts

U.S. and British	14	14½	15	15½	16	16½	17
Continental	36	37	38	39	41	42	43

Shoes

U.S.	7	7½	8	8½	9	9½	10	10½	11
British	6½	7	7½	8	8½	9	9½	10	10½
Continental	39	40	41	42	43	43	44	44	45

Socks

U.S. and British	9½	10	10½	11	11½	12	12½
Continental	39	40	41	42	43	44	45

Suits and Coats

U.S. and British	34	36	38	40	42	44	46
Continental	44	46	48	50	52	54	56

Standard Sizes Chart

Interior materials

Walls	Thicknesses (in inches)	Lengths (in feet unless otherwise indicated)	Widths (in feet unless otherwise indicated)
Decorative hardboard (embossed surface)	¼	4 to 16	4
Fiberboard (burlap or cork-surfaced)	¹⁵⁄₃₂	8, 10, 12, 14	4
Gypsum board (plain or vinyl-surfaced)	¼, ⅜, ½	6 to 16	2, 4
Hardboard (tempered or untempered)	⅜, ³⁄₁₆, ¼, ⁵⁄₁₆	6 to 16	4
Hardwood plywood (prefinished)	⁵⁄₃₂, ³⁄₁₆, ¼, ⁷⁄₁₆	7, 8	4
Hardwood plywood (veneered paneling)	⅛ to ¾	7, 8, 9, 10	4
Particle-core plywood	¾, ⁷⁄₁₆	7, 8, 9, 10	4
Plastic-surfaced hardboard	⅛, ³⁄₁₆, ¼	6, 7, 8, 10	16", 4
Prefinished hardboard	⅛, ³⁄₁₆, ¼	6 to 16	16", 4
Textured plywood (rough-sawn, brushed, grooved)	⅜, ⅝	8, 9, 10	4
Unfinished plywood	¾ to 1⅞	8, 9, 10	4
Vinyl-surfaced plywood	³⁄₁₆, ¼, ⁵⁄₁₆	7, 8	4
Wood-grained hardboard	³⁄₁₆, ¼	7, 8, 9, 10	4

Ceilings	Thicknesses (in inches)	Lengths	Widths
Acoustical panels	½, ¾, 1	2, 8, 10, 12, 14	2, 4
Acoustical tile	½	12"	12"
Decorative acoustical tile (embossed, textured, etc.)	½	12", 2, 4	12", 2
Fiberglass acoustical panels	2	8, 10½, 12½, 14, 16	4
Plastic-surfaced hardboard blocks	¼	16"	16"
Wood-grained planks	½	4	5³⁄₁₆", 6⅜", 8³⁄₁₆"

Floors	Thicknesses (in inches)	Lengths	Widths
Asphalt (or asphalt-asbestos) tile	⅛, ³⁄₁₆	9"	9"
Ceramic-tile sheets	⅛, ¼	12"	12"
Indoor–outdoor carpet		as desired	3, 6, 9, 12, 15
Indoor–outdoor carpet tile		9", 12"	9", 12"
Sheet vinyl		as desired	6, 9, 12
Vinyl and vinyl-asbestos tile	.050 to ⅛	9", 12", 18", 36"	4", 9", 12", 18", 36"
Wood parquet blocks	⁵⁄₁₆, ⁷⁄₁₆	9", 10"	9", 10"
Wood strips	⅜	2"	1 to 8

Bathroom fixtures	*Lengths*	*Depths*	*Heights*
Bathtubs	4'6", 5', 5'6"	2', 2'6", 2'7", 2'8"	1'2", 1'3", 1'4"
Compact corner tubs	3'2", 3'6", 4'	3'3", 3'10", 4'1½"	12"
One-piece fiberglass recessed shower units	3', 4', 5'	3'	6'1½"
One-piece fiberglass tub/shower units	5'	2'8⅞"	6'1½"
Shower stalls	2'6" to 3'6"	2'6" to 3'6"	6'3" to 6'5"
Sinks	19" to 30"	16" to 20"	2'7" (counter height)
Toilets (tank size)	18" to 23½"	25" to 30"	18½" to 40"

Kitchen equipment	*Widths (in inches)*	*Depths (in inches)*	*Heights (in inches unless otherwise indicated)*
Built-in ovens (set in cabinet)	23¾ to 36	23½	29¾
Built-in ranges (set in countertop)	12 to 42	19 to 22	34 to 36
Dishwashers	24	24¼ to 30	34 to 36
Double sinks (set in counters)	32	20	2'7"
Drop-in ranges and ovens (recessed into base cabinets)	30	24 to 27¼	34 to 36
Free-standing ranges and ovens	20 to 42	24¾ to 26⅝	35 to 36
Freezers (chest)	46½ to 72	29, 32	36, 37
Freezers (upright)	24 to 32	26 to 32	57 to 71
Ranges and eye-level ovens	30	27⅛ to 28¾	59⅛, 64⅛
Refrigerators	28 to 35	25 to 30	61 to 36
Single sinks (set in counters)	24, 30	21	2'7"
Slide-in ranges and ovens (set between base cabinets)	20 to 36	24 to 26⅞	34 to 36
Triple sinks (set in counters)	42, 45	21, 22	2'7"

Exterior materials

Siding	*Thicknesses (in inches)*	*Lengths (in feet unless otherwise indicated)*	*Widths*
Aluminum (horizontal)		9'4½", 10, 12½, 16	8", 10"
Hardboard lap (horizontal)	⅜, ⁷⁄₁₆	12, 16	6", 8", 9", 10", 12"
Hardboard panels (vertical)	¼, ⁵⁄₁₆, ⅜, ⁷⁄₁₆	6, 7, 8, 9, 10, 16	4'
Plywood panels (vertical—rough-sawn, brushed, grooved)	⅜, ½, ⅝	8, 9, 10, 12	4'
Prefinished steel (horizontal)		12'6"	8", 9½"
Vinyl lap (horizontal)		12½"	8", 12"
Vinyl V-grooved (vertical)		10	10"
Wood lap (horizontal)	½, ⅝, ¾	3 to 20	6", 8", 10", 12"

Doors and windows	Thicknesses (in inches)	Heights	Widths
Bifold, 2-door units	1⅛, 1⅜	6'8"	2', 2'8", 3'
Bifold, 4-door units	1⅛, 1⅜	6'8"	3', 4', 5', 6'
Flush (hollow, solid)	1⅜, 1¾, 2¼	6'8", 7'	6"
Louvered	1⅛, 1⅜	6'6", 6'8", 7'	1'3" to 3'
Panel	1⅜, 1¾	6'8", 7'	1'2" to 3'4"
Sash (with one or more glass panels)	1⅜, 1¾	6'8", 7'	2' to 3'6"
Sliding glass, 2-panel units		6'8"	5', 6', 6'2¼", 8', 8'¼"
Sliding glass, 3-panel units		6'8"	9', 9¾", 12', 12'¾"
Steel entry (single, double, sidelight)	1¾	6'8"	2'8", 3'

Additional Sources of Information

Organizations and Services

Energy Conservation Center
Public Service Electric and Gas Company
P.O. Box 1258
Newark, NJ 07101
800-854-4444

Specialists can provide information on specific energy needs such as weatherization, appliance efficiency and rebates, and home energy audit publications. The center receives calls weekdays between 9 A.M. and 5 P.M., EST.

Genova Plumbers Hotline
7034 East Court Street
Davison, MI
800-521-7488
800-572-5398 (in Michigan)

The staff can suggest solutions to plumbing problems involving gutters and plastic fittings as well as more technical problems. The hotline operates weekdays between 8 A.M. and 5 P.M., EST.

Major Appliance Consumer Action Panel (MACAP)
20 North Wacker Drive
Chicago, IL 60606
800-621-0477
312-984-5858 (in Illinois, Alaska, and Hawaii)

MACAP answers questions about problems with major appliances. It is open weekdays from 8:30 A.M. to 5 P.M., CST.

Shopsmith, Inc.
6640 Poe Avenue
Dayton, OH 45414
800-543-7586

Shopsmith will answer questions related to woodworking. If they cannot answer your question, they will research the information and call back. Call weekdays between 9 A.M. and 6 P.M. and Saturdays between 9 A.M. and 1 P.M., EST.

Soap and Detergent Association
475 Park Avenue South
New York, NY 10016
212-725-1262

This association will answer questions on all aspects of soaps and detergents. They also have free publications. Call Monday through Friday from 9 A.M. to 4:45 P.M., EST.

Books

Alth, Max. *The Do-It-Yourself Encyclopedia of Materials.* Crown, 1982.

Brody, Jane. *Jane Brody's Good Food Book.* Bantam, 1987.

Canning, Freezing and Drying. Lane, 1981.

Claiborne, Craig. *The (Original) New York Times Cookbook.* Harper & Row, 1961.

Cunningham, Marion, ed. *Fannie Farmer Cookbook.* Knopf, 1979.

Heinerman, John. *The Complete Book of Spices.* Keats, 1983.

Lichine, Alexis. *Alexis Lichine's New Encyclopedia of Wines & Spirits,* 5th ed. Knopf, 1987.

McGowan, John, and DuBern, Roger. *Good Housekeeping Book of Home Maintenance.* Hearst, 1985.

Mr. Boston Official Bartender's Guide. Warner, 1987.

Netzer, Corinne T. *The Brand-Name Calorie Counter.* Dell, 1986.

Pinkham, Mary Ellen. *Mary Ellen's Best of Helpful Kitchen Hints.* Warner, 1980.

Reader's Digest Complete Do-it-Yourself Manual. Reader's Digest, 1987.

Reader's Digest How to Do Just About Anything: A Money-Saving A to Z Guide to Over 1200 Practical Problems. Reader's Digest, 1986.

Rombauer, Irma S., and Becker, Marion R. *Joy of Cooking.* Bobbs-Merrill, 1978.

Root, Waverley. *Food: An Authoritative Visual History and Dictionary of the Foods of the World.* Simon & Schuster, 1980.

Root, Waverley, ed. *Herbs and Spices: A Guide to Culinary Seasoning.* McGraw-Hill, 1985.

Simon, André L. *A Concise Encyclopedia of Gastronomy.* Overlook, 1983.

Time/Life Complete Home Repair Manual. Prentice-Hall, 1987.

21

The Outdoors

Poisonous Cultivated and Wild Plants

The following chart lists 50 poisonous plants. It tells which portions, or areas, of the plant are toxic, describes symptoms of the illnesses they cause, and indicates which plants are or may be fatal.

Plants	*Toxic Portions*	*Symptoms of Illness; Degree of Toxicity*
Autumn crocus	Bulbs	Nausea, vomiting, diarrhea; may be fatal.
Azalea	All parts	Nausea, vomiting, depression, breathing difficulty, prostration, coma; fatal.
Belladonna	Young plants, seeds	Nausea, twitching muscles, paralysis; fatal.
Bittersweet	Leaves, seeds, roots	Vomiting, diarrhea, chills, convulsions, coma.
Bleeding heart (Dutchman's-breeches)	Foliage, roots	Nervous symptoms, convulsions.
Buttercups	All parts	Digestive system injury.
Caladium	All parts	Intense burning and irritation of the tongue and mouth; can be fatal if the base of the tongue swells, blocking air passage of the throat.
Castorbean	Seeds, foliage	Burning in mouth, convulsions; fatal.
Cherry	Twigs, foliage	Gasping, excitement, prostration.
Daffodil	Bulbs	Nausea, vomiting, diarrhea; may be fatal.
Daphne	Berries (red or yellow)	Severe burns to mouth and digestive tract followed by coma; fatal.
Delphinium	Young plants, seeds	Nausea, twitching muscles, paralysis; fatal
Dumbcane (Dieffenbachia)	All parts	Intense burning and irritation of the tongue and mouth; fatal if the base of the tongue swells, blocking air passage of the throat.
Elderberry	Roots	Nausea and digestive upset.
Elephant ear	All parts	Intense burning and irritation of the tongue and mouth; fatal if the base of the tongue swells, blocking air passage of the throat.
English holly	Berries	Severe gastroenteritis.
English ivy	Leaves, berries	Stomach pains, labored breathing, possible coma.
Foxglove	Leaves, seeds, flowers	Irregular heartbeat and pulse, usually accompanied by digestive upset and mental confusion; may be fatal.
Goldenchain	All parts, especially seeds	Excitement, staggering convulsions, coma; may be fatal.
Horse chestnut	All parts	Nausea, twitching muscles, sometimes paralysis.
Hyacinth	Bulbs	Nausea, vomiting, diarrhea; may be fatal.
Hydrangea	Buds, leaves, branches	Severe digestive upset, gasping, convulsions; may be fatal.
Iris	Freshly underground portions	Severe but not usually serious digestive upset.
Jack-in-the-pulpit	All parts, especially roots	Intense irritation and burning of the tongue and mouth.
Jimson weed (thorn apple; datura)	All parts	Abnormal thirst, distortion of vision, delirium, incoherence, coma; may be fatal.
Larkspur	Young plants, seeds	Nausea, twitching muscles, paralysis; fatal.

Plants	*Toxic Portions*	*Symptoms of Illness; Degree of Toxicity*
Laurel	All parts	Nausea, vomiting, depression, breathing difficulty, prostration, coma; fatal.
Lily of the valley	Leaves, flowers	Irregular heartbeat and pulse usually accompanied by digestive upset and mental confusion; may be fatal.
Mayapple	Unripe apples, leaves and roots	Diarrhea, severe digestive upset.
Mistletoe	All parts, especially berries	Fatal.
Monkshood	All parts, especially roots	Digestive upset and nervous excitement; juice in plant parts is fatal.
Morning glory	Seeds	Large amounts cause severe mental disturbances; fatal.
Mushrooms, wild	All parts of many varieties	Fatal.
Narcissus	Bulbs	Nausea, vomiting, diarrhea; may be fatal.
Nightshade	All parts, especially unripe berries	Intense digestive disturbances and nervous symptoms; often fatal.
Oak	Foliage, acorns	Gradual kidney failure.
Oleander	All parts	Severe digestive upset, heart trouble, contact dermatitis; fatal.
Philodendron	All parts	Intense burning and irritation of the tongue and mouth; fatal if the base of the tongue swells, blocking air passage of the throat.
Poinsettia	All parts	Severe digestive upset; fatal.
Poison hemlock	All parts	Stomach pains, vomiting, paralysis of the central nervous system; may be fatal.
Poison ivy and oak	All parts	Intense itching, watery blisters, red rash.
Poppy	Foliage, roots	Nervous symptoms, convulsions.
Potato	Foliage, green parts of vegetable	Intense digestive disturbances, nervous symptoms.
Privet	Berries, leaves	Mild to severe digestive disturbances; may be fatal.
Rhododendron	All parts	Nausea, vomiting, depression, breathing difficulty, prostration, coma; fatal.
Rhubarb	Leaf blade	Kidney disorder, convulsions, coma; fatal.
Rosary pea	Seeds, foliage	Burning in mouth, convulsions; fatal.
Snowdrop	Bulbs	Vomiting, nervous excitement.
Tomato	Vines	Digestive upset, nervous disorders.
Wisteria	Seeds, pods	Mild to severe digestive disturbances.

frost Dates for Spring

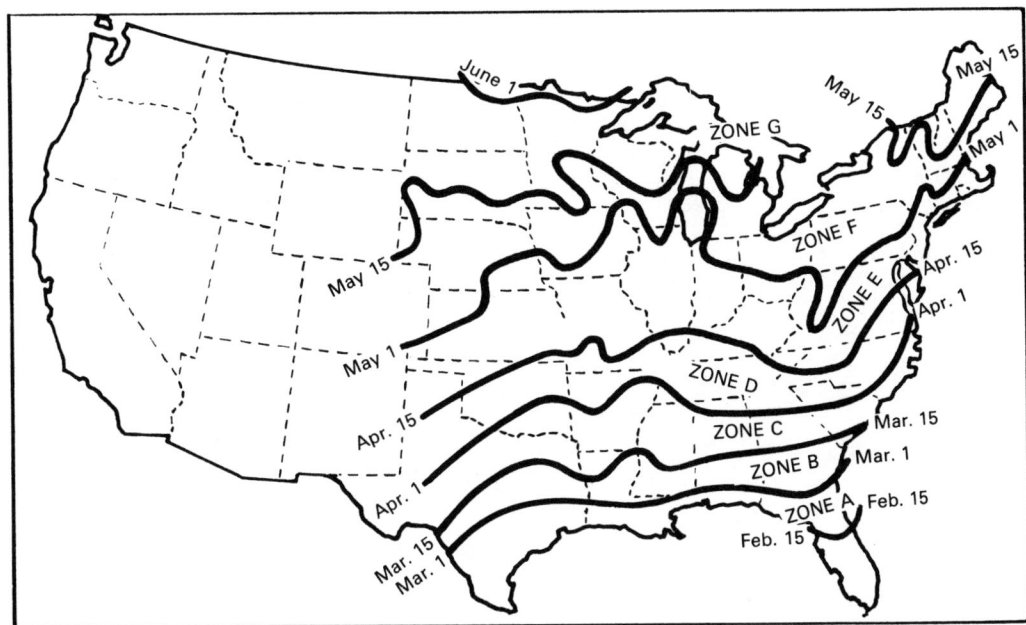

A zone map of the United States based on the average dates of the latest killing frost in spring east of the Rocky Mountains. **Source: United States Department of Agriculture.**

frost Dates for Autumn

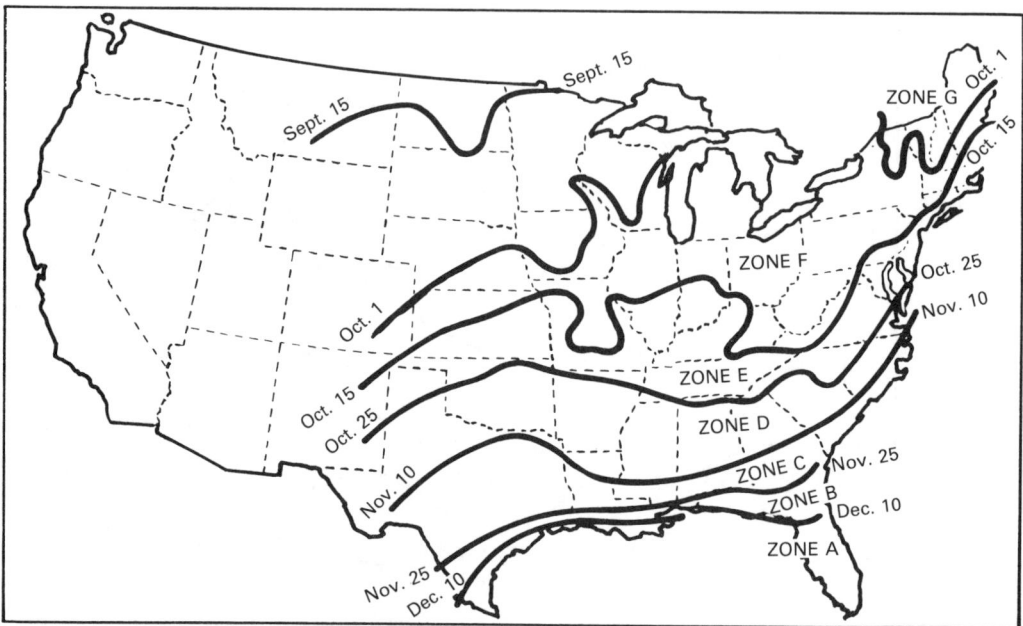

A zone map of the central and eastern part of the United States based on the average dates of the first killing frost in autumn. **Source: United States Department of Agriculture.**

Germination Tables

Annual Flowers

	Approximate number of days until germination		Approximate number of days until germination
Acrolinium	8–10	Four-o'clock	12–15
Ageratum	7–11	Gaillardia	12–15
Alyssum, sweet	10–13	Gomphrena	20–25
Browallia	18–20	Helichrysum	5–10
Cacalia	8–12	Larkspur	15–20
Calendula	10–12	Lupine	25–30
California poppy	5–10	Marigold	5–8
Candytuft	6–9	Nicotiana	20–25
Canterburybell	12–15	Petunia	18–20
Celosia (coxcomb)	20–25	Phlox Drummondi	20–25
		Pinks	5–8
Centaurea (ragged robin)	5–20	Portulaca	18–20
		Scabiosa	18–20
Chrysanthemum	6–8	Snapdragon	20–25
Cosmos	5–15	Sweetpea	15–20
Cynoglossum	11–15	Verbena	8–10
Flax	13–16	Zinnia	5–8

Vegetable Garden Plants

	Approximate number of days until germination		Approximate number of days until germination
Asparagus	21–28	Kohlrabi	6–8
Beans, bush	6–10	Lettuce	6–10
Beans, bush lima	6–10	Muskmelon	6–10
Beans, pole	6–10	Mustard	4–5
Beans, pole lima	7–12	Okra	15–20
Beets	7–10	Onion	8–12
Broccoli	6–10	Parsley	18–24
Brussels sprouts	6–10	Parsnip	12–18
Cabbage	6–10	Peas	6–10
Cabbage, Chinese	6–10	Pepper	10–14
Carrots	10–15	Pumpkin	6–10
Cauliflower	6–10	Radish	4–6
Celery	12–20	Rhubarb	12–14
Chard, Swiss	7–10	Rutabaga	4–7
Collards	6–10	Spinach	6–12
Corn, sweet	7–12	Squash, bush	6–10
Cress, garden	4–5	Squash, vine	6–10
Cucumber	6–8	Tomato	6–10
Eggplant	10–15	Turnip	4–7
Endive	8–12	Watermelon	8–12

Ground Covers

Botanical Name	Common Name
Sun	
Antennaria neodioica (1, 6)	Pussytoes
Arctostaphylas uva-ursi (1, 2, 3, 6)	Bearberry
Cotoneaster apiculata (1)	Cranberry cotoneaster
Cotoneaster dammeri and *cultivars* (1)	Bearberry cotoneaster
Euonymus colorata (3, 4, 6)	Purpleleaf wintercreeper
Juniperus horizontalis and *cultivars* (6)	Creeping juniper
Juniperus procumbens nana (4, 6)	Japanese juniper
Lonicera japonica halliana (3, 4, 6)	Hall's honeysuckle
Pachistima canbyi (1, 2, 6)	Pachistima
Potentilla tridentata (1, 2, 6)	Wineleaf cinquefoil
Potentilla verna nana (1, 5)	Cinquefoil
Sedum species (5, 6)	Stonecrop
Waldsteinia ternata (1, 3, 6)	Barren strawberry
Shade	
Ajuga reptans and *cultivars* (3, 4)	Carpet bugle
Convallaria majalis (4, 5)	Lily of the valley
Euonymus fortunei varieties (3, 4, 6)	Wintercreeper
Hedera helix and *cultivars* (4, 6)	English ivy
Hosta species (5)	Plantain lily
Liriope spicata (6)	Lily turf
Pachysandra terminalis (2, 6)	Japanese spurge
Vinca minor and *cultivars* (3, 6)	Periwinkle or myrtle

1. Requires well-drained soil
2. Requires acid soil
3. Good in sun or shade
4. Confine; may grow out of bounds
5. Herbaceous
6. Foliage retention in winter

VINES FOR SPECIAL USES

Botanical name	Common name
Akebia quinata (1, 2, 3, 4)	Five-leaf akebia
Clematis species and *hybrids* (1, 2, 3, 4)	Virgin's-bower
Euonymus fortunei (2, 3)	Wintercreeper
Hedera helix and *cultivars* (2)	English ivy
Hydrangea petiolaris (1, 2)	Climbing hydrangea
Parthenocissus tricuspidata (2)	Boston ivy
Wisteria floribunda (1, 2, 3, 4)	Japanese wisteria

1. Flowering
2. Wall cover
3. Screening
4. Trellis

Botanical Names of Plants

Common name	Botanical name	Common name	Botanical name
Acacia, giraffe	*Acacia giraffae*	Cabbage	*Brassica oleracea*
Adder's-tongue	*Erythronium sibiricum*		*B. oleracea capitata*
	Ophioglossum vulgatum islandicum	Kerguelen	*Pringlea antiscorbutica*
		Cacao	*Theobroma cacao*
Alder, European	*Alnus glutinosa*	Calotrope, fantan	*Calotropis procera*
hazel	*A. rugosa*	Capeberry, South African	*Myrica cordifolia*
red	*A. rubra*	Carpotroche	*Carpotroche brasiliensis*
Alfalfa	*Medicago sativa*	Carrot	*Daucus carota*
Almond	*Prunus amygdalus*	Cashew	*Anacardium occidentale*
Aloe	*Aloe* sp.	Castor bean	*Ricinus communis*
Amaryllis	*Amaryllis* sp.	Catalpa, Chinese	*Catalpa ovata*
Angelica	*Angelica polyclada*	northern	*C. speciosa*
garden	*A. archangelica*	Cedar	*Cedrus* sp.
Apple	*Malus pumila*	California incense	*Libocedrus decurrens*
	M. sylvestris	Celery, garden	*Apium graveolens dulce*
Apricot	*Prunus armeniaca*	wild	*A. graveolens*
Arborvitae, eastern	*Thuja occidentalis*	Chaulmoogra tree	*Gynocardia odorata*
giant	*T. plicata*	common	*Hydnocarpus anthelmintica*
Arum, East Asian	*Pinellia ternata*		
Ash, European	*Franxinus excelsior*	wight	*H. wightiana*
green	*F. pennsylvanica*	Cherry, black	*Prunus serotina*
white	*F. americana*	mazzard	*P. avium*
Asparagus, garden	*Asparagus officinalis*	pin	*P. pennsylvanica*
Aspen, European	*Populus tremula*	Chestnut, Chinese	*Castanea mollissima*
quaking	*P. tremuloides*	common horse-	*Aesculus hippocastanum*
Aster	*Aster* sp.	Chickpea, gram	*Cicer arietinum*
Attalea	*Attalea funifera*	Chinaberry	*Melia azedarach*
Avocado, American	*Persea americana*	Chrysanthemum, corn	*Chrysanthemum segetum*
		Pyrenees	*C. maximum*
		Cinchona, ledgerbark	*Cinchona ledgeriana*
Balloon vine	*Cardiospermum halicacabum*	Clarkia, rose	*Clarkia elegans*
		Clover, alsike	*Trifolium hybridum*
Balsam, garden	*Impatiens balsamina*	burdock	*T. lappaceum*
Barley	*Hordeum vulgare*	crimson	*T. incarnatum*
Bean, broad	*Vicia faba*	Egyptian	*T. alexandrinum*
kidney	*Phaseolus vulgaris*	Persian	*T. resupinatum*
sieva	*P. lunatus*	red	*T. pratense*
Beech, American	*Fagus grandifolia*	strawberry	*T. fragiferum*
European	*F. sylvatica*	subterranean	*T. subterraneum*
Beet, common	*Beta vulgaris*	suckling	*T. dubium*
Birch, European white	*Betula pendula*	yellow sweet	*Melilotus officinalis*
paper	*B. papyrifera*	white	*Trifolium repens*
sweet	*B. lenta*	white sweet	*Melilotus alba*
white	*B. populifolia*	Clubmoss, common	*Lycopodium clavatum*
yellow	*B. lutea*	Cocklebur, oriental	*Xanthium orientale*
Blackberry	*Rubus* sp.	Coconut	*Cocos nucifera*
Bladderpod	*Lesquerella densipila*	Coffee, Arabian	*Coffea arabica*
Blood-lily, Katharine	*Haemanthus katharinae*	Coneflower, pinewoods	*Rudbeckia bicolor*
Blueberry, highbush	*Vaccinium corymbosum*	Coreopsis, goldenwave	*Coreopsis drummondii*
Brake, sword	*Pteris ensiformis*	lance	*C. lanceolata*
Bryony, white	*Bryonia alba*	plains	*C. tinctoria*
Buckwheat	*Fagopyrum sagittatum*	Corn	*Zea mays*
Buttercup, creeping	*Ranunculus repens*	Cornflower	*Centaurea cyanus*

Common name	Botanical name	Common name	Botanical name
Coronilla, crownvetch	*Coronilla varia*	Fig	*Ficus carica*
Cosmos	*Cosmos* sp.	Filbert	*Corylus* sp.
Cotton, Levant	*Gossypium herbaceum*	Fir, cascades	*Abies amabilis*
Sea Island	*G. barbadense*	grand	*A. grandis*
upland	*G. hirsutum*	noble	*A. procera*
Coventry bells	*Campanula trachelium*	red	*A. magnifica*
Cowpea	*Vigna glabra*	white	*A. concolor*
common	*V. sinensis*	Flax, common	*Linum usitatissimum*
yard-long	*V. sesquipedalis*	Forget-me-not	*Myosotis* sp.
Crotalaria	*Crotalaria vitellina*	Foxglove, common	*Digitalis purpurea*
Croton, purging	*Croton tiglium*	Grecian	*D. lanata*
Cucumber	*Cucumis sativus*	Frenchweed	*Thlaspi arvense*
Currant, European black	*Ribes nigrum*		
red	*R. sativum*	Ginkgo	*Ginkgo biloba*
Cypress, Arizona	*Cupressus arizonica*	Gladiolus, common horti-	*Gladiolus hortulanus*
bald	*Taxodium distichum*	cultural	
		Gooseberry, Chinese	*Actinidia chinensis*
Dahlia	*Dahlia* sp.	Gourd, snake	*Trichosanthes* sp.
Dandelion	*Taraxacum officinale*	Grape, European	*Vitis vinifera*
Daphne	*Daphne* sp.	fox	*V. labrusca*
Date	*Phoenix dactylifera*	roundleaf	*Ribes rotundifolium*
Davallia, Fiji	*Davallia fejeensis*	Grass, Bermuda	*Cynodon dactylon*
Desert willow	*Chilopsis linearis*	buffalo	*Buchloe dactyloides*
Dock, curly	*Rumex crispus*	Canada blue-	*Pao compressa*
Dogbane	*Apocynum* sp.	canary	*Phalaris canariensis*
Dogwood, cornelian cherry	*Cornus mas*	cocksfoot orchard	*Dactylis glomerata*
flowering	*C. florida*	colonial bent-	*Agrostis tenuis*
Dollar plant	*Lunaria annua*	common carpet-	*Axonopus affinis*
Douglas fir	*Pseudotsuga menziesii*	crested wheat-	*Asgropyron cristatum*
common	*P. taxifolia*	dallis	*Paspalum dilatatum*
		desert wheat-	*Agropyron desertorum*
Eggplant	*Solanum melongena*	Italian rye-	*Lolium multiflorum*
garden	*S. melongena esculentum*	Johnson	*Sorghum halepense*
Elm, American	*Ulmus americana*	Kentucky blue-	*Poa pratensis*
Endive	*Cichorium endivia*	perennial rye-	*Lolium perenne*
Erysimum, plains	*Erysimum asperum*	quack	*Agropyron repens*
Eucalyptus	*Eucalyptus* sp.	reed canary	*Phalaris arundinacea*
Euphorbia, snow-on-the-	*Euphorbia marginata*	Sudan	*Sorghum vulgare suda-*
mountain			*nense*
False-cypress, Lawson's	*Chamaecyparis lawsoniana*	Hackberry, common	*Celtis occidentalis*
nootka	*C. nootkatensis*	Hart's-tongue	*Phyllitis scolopendrium*
Fern, common staghorn	*Platycerium bifurcatum*	Hemlock, eastern	*Tsuga canadensis*
common sword	*Nephrolepis exaltata*	western	*T. heterophylla*
filmy	*Hymenophyllum atrovirens*	Hemp	*Cannabis sativa*
grape	*Botrychium virginianum*	Hibiscus, kenaf	*Hibiscus cannabinus*
holly	*Cyrtomium falcatum*	Hickory, shagbark	*Carya ovata*
lady	*Athyrium filix-femina*	Holly, American	*Ilex opaca*
maidenhair	*Adiantum pedatum*	English	*I. aquifolium*
pine	*Anemia adiantifolia*	Hollyhock	*Althaea rosea*
royal	*Osmunda regalis*	Horsetail, common	*Equisetum arvense*
tropical	*Gleichenia flabellata*	Hyssop, hedge	*Gratiola* sp.
water	*Azolla pinnata*		
wood	*Thelypteris normalis*	Indigo	*Indigofera* sp.
Fescue, alta	*Festuca elatior arundina-*	Iris, blue flag	*Iris versicolor*
	cea	German	*I. germanica*
meadow	*F. elatior*	grass	*I. graminea*
red	*F. rubra*	Ironweed, kinka oil	*Vernonia anthelmintica*

Common name	Botanical name	Common name	Botanical name
Jacaranda	*Jacaranda* sp.	Okra	*Hibiscus esculentus*
Jimsonweed	*Datura stramonium*	Olive	*Olea europaea sativa*
Juniper, Savin	*Juniperus sabina*	common	*O. europaea*
		Oncoba, gorli	*Oncoba echinata*
Kale	*Brassica oleracea acephala*	Onion, garden	*Allium cepa*
Kamala tree	*Mallotus philippinensis*	Orange, sweet	*Citrus sinensis*
Knotweed, prostrate	*Polygonum aviculare*	trifoliate	*Poncirus trifoliata*
Lamb's quarter	*Chenopodium album*	Palm, African oil	*Elaeis guineensis*
Larch, western	*Larix occidentalis*	Pansy, wild	*Viola tricolor*
Larkspur, rocket	*Delphinium ajacis*	Parinarium	*Parinarium* sp.
Lemon	*Citrus limon*	Parsley	*Petroselinum crispum*
Lentil	*Lens culinaris*	common curly	*P. latifolium*
Lespedeza, common	*Lespedeza striata*	Parsnip	*Pastinaca sativa*
Korean	*L. stipulacea*	Pea, field	*Pisum sativum arvense*
wand	*L. intermedia*	garden	*P. sativum*
Lettuce	*Lactuca sativa*	sweet	*Lathyrus odoratus*
Licania	*Licania rigida*	Peach	*Prunus persica*
Lilac, common	*Syringa vulgaris*	Peanut	*Arachis hypogaea*
Lily, regal	*Lilium regale*	Pear	*Pyrus communis*
Linden, American	*Tilia americana*	Peavine, flat	*Lathyrus sylvestris*
Litsea	*Litsea* sp.	Pecan	*Carya illinoensis*
Locust, black	*Robinia pseudoacacia*	Peony, fernleaf	*Paeonia tenuifolia*
Lotus, East Indian	*Nelumbo nucifea*	Pepper, bush red	*Capsicum frutescens*
Lupine	*Lupinus arcticus*	Pepperwort	*Marsilea minuta*
tree	*L. angustifolius*	Perilla, common	*Pefrilla frutescens*
		Persimmon, common	*Diospyros virginiana*
Macadamia, Queenslandnut	*Macadamia ternifolia*	Petunia	*Petunia* sp.
Magnolia, great-leaved	*Magnolia macrophylla*	Phlox, Drummond	*Phlox drummondii*
southern	*M. grandiflora*	Pine, Austrian	*Pinus nigra*
Malope	*Malope trifida*	eastern white	*P. strobus*
Mango, common	*Mangifera indica*	jack	*P. banksiana*
Maple, red	*Acer rubrum*	loblolly	*P. taeda*
silver	*A. saccharinum*	longleaf	*P. palustris*
sugar	*A. saccharum*	ponderosa	*P. ponderosa*
Marattia	*Marattia salicina*	shore	*P. contorta*
Marbleseed, western	*Onosmodium occidentale*	shortleaf	*P. echinata*
Marigold	*Tagetes* sp.	slash	*P. caribea*
winter cape	*Dimorphotheca aurantiaca*	sugar	*P. lambertiana*
Meadowrue, Sierra	*Thalictrum polycarpum*	western white	*P. monticola*
Milkweed, common	*Asclepias syriaca*	Pineapple	*Ananas comosus*
Millet, pearl	*Pennisetum glaucum*	Pink, clove	*Dianthus caryophyllus*
Morning glory, common	*Ipomoea purpurea*	Pistachio	*Pistacia* sp.
orizaba	*I. orizabensis*	Plum, garden	*Prunus domestica*
Muskmelon	*Cucumis melo*	Japanese	*P. salicina*
Mustard, black	*Brassica nigra*	Podocarpus	*Podocarpus* sp.
white	*B. hirta*	Polypody, rock	*Polypodium virginianum*
		Pomegranate, common	*Punica granatum*
Nasturtium	*Tropaeolum* sp.	Poplar, eastern	*Populus deltoides*
Niger seed	*Guizotia abyssinica*	Mongolian	*P. suaveolens*
		yellow, or tulip	*Liriodendron tulipifera*
Oak, black	*Quercus velutina*	tree	
English	*Q. robur*	Poppy, corn	*Papaver rhoeas*
scarlet	*Q. coccinea*	opium	*P. somniferum*
southern red	*Q. falcata*	oriental	*P. orientale*
white	*Q. alba*	Portulaca, common	*Portulaca grandiflora*
Oat, common	*Avena sativa*	Potato	*Solanum tuberosum*

Common name	Botanical name	Common name	Botanical name
Primrose, evening	*Oenothera biennis*	Strawberry, chiloe	*Fragaria chiloensis*
Lemarck	*O. lamarckiana*	pine	*F. ananassa*
Pumpkin	*Cucurbita pepo*	Strophanthus	*Strophanthus glaber*
Purslane, common	*Portulaca oleracea*	arrow poison	*S. sarmentosus*
Pycnanthus, akomu	*Pycnanthus kombo*	Sugarcane	*Saccharum officinarum*
		Sumac	*Rhus*, sp.
Quillwort	*Isoetes braunii*	Sunflower, common	*Helianthus annuus*
		Sweetcane	*Saccharum spontaneum*
Radish, garden	*Raphanus sativus*	Sweetgum, American	*Liquidambar styraciflua*
Rape, bird	*Brassica campestris*	Sweet potato	*Ipomoea batatas*
winter	*B. napus*	Sweet william	*Dianthus barbatus*
Red cedar, eastern	*Juniperus virginiana*		
Redtop	*Agrostis alba*	Tallow wood	*Ximenia americana*
Redwood	*Sequoia sempervirens*		*X. caffra*
Rhododendron, catawba	*Rhododendron cataw-*	Tara vine	*Taraktogenos kurzii*
	biense	Tetradenia, Asian	*Tetradenia glauca*
Rhubarb, garden	*Rheum rhaponticum*	Timothy	*Phleum pratense*
medicinal	*R. officinale*	Tobacco	*Nicotiana glutinosa*
sorrel	*R. palmatum*	common	*N. tabacum*
Rice	*Oryza sativa*	Tomato, common	*Lycopersicon esculentum*
Rose, cabbage	*Rosa centifolia*	Trefoil, bird's foot	*Lotus corniculatus*
Rubber, para	*Havea brasiliensis*	Tulip	*Tulipa* sp.
Rutabaga	*Brassica napobrassica*	Tung oil tree	*Aleurites fordii*
Rye	*Secale cereale*	Tupelo, water	*Nyssa aquatica*
		Turnip	*Brassica rapa*
Safflower	*Carthamus tinctorius*		
Sage, garden	*Salvia officinalis*	Vetch, common	*Vicia sativa*
scarlet	*S. splendens*	hairy	*V. villosa*
Salsify, vegetable-oyster	*Tragopogon porrifolius*	Hungarian	*V. pannonica*
Scammony, glorybind	*Convolvulus scammonia*	narrow leaf	*V. angustifolia*
Scarlet runner	*Phaseolus coccineus*	one-flower	*V. articulata*
Sequoia, giant	*Sequoiadendron giganteum*	purple	*V. benghalensis*
	Sequoia gigantea	tiny	*V. hirsuta*
Sesame, oriental	*Sesamum indicum*	wooly pod	*V. dasycarpa*
Snapdragon, common	*Antirrhinum majus*	Violet, field	*Viola arvensis*
Sorghum	*Sorghum bicolor*		
	S. vulgare	Walnut, eastern black	*Juglans nigra*
Soybean	*Glycine max*	Waterlily	*Nymphaea alba*
Spicebush, Japanese	*Lindera obtusiloba*	Watermelon	*Citrullus vulgaris*
Spiderwort	*Tradescantia paludosa*	Waterweed, Canadian	*Elodea canadensis*
Virginia	*T. virginiana*	Wheat	*Triticum aestivum*
Spikemoss	*Selaginella selaginoides*	Willow, basket	*Salix viminalis*
Spinach	*Spinacia oleracea*	big catkin	*S. gracilistyla*
Spruce, Norway	*Picea abies*	black	*S. nigra*
red	*P. rubens*	pussy	*S. discolor*
Sitka	*P. sitchensis*	white	*S. alba*
white	*P. glauca*		
Spurge, South American	*Sebastiania fruticosa*	Yellow trumpet, Florida	*Stenolobium stans*
Spurry, corn	*Spergula avensis*	Yew, English	*Taxus baccata*
Sterculia, hazel	*Sterculia foetida*	Pacific	*T. brevifolia*
Stillingia	*Stillingia* sp.	Yucca	*Yucca* sp.
Stock, common	*Matthiola incana*		
		Zinnia, oblong leaf	*Zinnia angustifolia*

National Park Directory

Acadia National Park
Bar Harbor, Maine
Area: 41,634 acres
Season: May through November

Major attractions: Mountains (highest point on Atlantic Coast) showing marine erosion and glaciation; lakes; forests; marine life.

Activities: Camping, fishing, hiking, horseback riding, nature walks, picnicking, swimming, sea cruises.

Arches National Park
Moab, Utah
Area: 73,379 acres
Season: Year-round

Major attractions: Huge rock formations caused by erosion; mountains; Colorado River gorge.

Activities: Camping, fishing, canoeing, white-water boating.

Badlands National Park
Wall, South Dakota
Area: 243,303 acres
Season: Year-round

Major attractions: Multicolored peaks and spires caused by erosion; fossil sites; Pine Ridge Indian Reservation near site of Wounded Knee battleground.

Activities: Camping, fishing, hiking, picnicking.

Big Bend National Park
Maverick or Persimmon Gap, Texas
Area: 708,221 acres
Season: Year-round

Major attractions: Mountains; canyons; desert; U.S. and Mexican flowers; trees; wildlife.

Activities: Camping, boating, fishing, hiking, horseback riding, picnicking, pack trips.

Biscayne National Park
Key Biscayne, Florida
Area: 173,040 acres
Season: Year-round

Major attractions: Underwater coral reefs; marine life.

Activities: Boating, diving.

Bryce Canyon National Park
Bryce Canyon, Utah
Area: 35,836 acres
Season: Year-round

Major attractions: Multicolored rock erosions.

Activities: Camping, fishing, hiking, boating, picnicking, museum tours.

Canyonlands National Park
Moab, Utah
Area: 337,258 acres
Season: Year-round

Major attractions: Rock formations; ancient cliff dwellings; Green River and Colorado River canyons.

Activities: Boating, white-water trips, hiking, camping, fishing, horseback riding, picnicking.

Capitol Reef National Park
Torrey, Utah
Area: 241,905 acres
Season: Year-round

Major attractions: Colorful rock formations; desert plants and wildlife; pioneer exhibits.

Activities: Camping, hiking, fishing, four-wheel-drive trails.

Carlsbad Caverns National Park
Carlsbad, New Mexico
Area: 46,753 acres
Season: Year-round

Major attractions: Possibly world's largest cavern with spectacular underground formations; above-ground desert plants and rock formations.

Activities: Cavern tours, nature walks, picnicking, camping, nearby fishing.

Channel Islands National Park
Santa Barbara, California
Area: 249,355 acres
Season: Year-round

Major attractions: Marine life and sea birds.

Activities: Hiking, nature walks, boating, fishing, picnicking.

Crater Lake National Park
Medford, Oregon
Area: 160,290 acres
Season: July to October

Major attractions: Deepest lake in the United States (2,000 feet) in crater of extinct volcano; multicolored rocks; forests; mountain flowers and wildlife.

Activities: Camping, hiking, fishing, boating, horseback riding.

Denali National Park
Anderson, Alaska
Area: 4,726,909 acres
Season: June to September

Major attractions: Peaks of Alaska Range, including Mount McKinley (20,320 feet); rare wildlife and subarctic plant life; huge Denali fault; break in earth's crust.

Activities: Camping, hiking, fishing, big-game hunting.

Everglades National Park
Homestead, Florida
Area: 1,410,533 acres
Season: Year-round

Major attractions: Immense subtropical wilderness; mangrove swamps; wild animals and rare birds.

Activities: Boating, camping, fishing, guided tours, hiking, nature walks, picnicking.

Gates of the Arctic National Park
Wiseman, Alaska
Area: 8,300,000 acres
Season: June to September

Major attractions: Snow-covered peaks of Endicott Mountains north of Arctic Circle; tundra and taiga in valleys; wildlife.

Activities: Big-game hunting, fishing, camping.

Glacier Bay National Park
Yakutat, Alaska
Area: 3,226,000 acres
Season: May to October

Major attractions: Great Mendenhall Glacier; iceberg formations from glaciers; dense coastal rain forests; wildlife; nearby, Mount Logan, highest point in Canada (19,850 feet).

Activities: Camping, hiking, hunting, fishing.

Glacier National Park
West Glacier, Montana
Area: 1,056,000 acres
Season: June through September

Major attractions: Rugged mountain peaks of Continental Divide; glaciers; numerous alpine lakes and streams; rare wildflowers; wildlife; ancient Blackfoot hunting grounds.

Activities: Hiking on old hunting and exploration trails, nature walks, horseback riding, camping, fishing.

Grand Canyon National Park
Grand Canyon, Arizona
Area: 1,218,376 acres
Season: Year-round

Major attractions: Mile-deep, 1.5-billion-years-old canyon of Colorado River, showing geologic features with fossil plants and animals; multicolored rocks; wide range of wild plants and animals; Havasupai Indian reservation.

Activities: Camping, hiking, horseback riding, boating, white-water trips, nature walks, picnicking.

Grand Teton National Park
Moose, Wyoming
Area: 301,291 acres
Season: June to September

Major attractions: Mountains; trails of famous early explorers; perennial snow fields; wild plants, animals, and birds.

Activities: Camping, hiking, fishing, boating, horseback riding.

Great Smoky Mountains National Park
Gatlinburg, Tennessee/Asheville, North Carolina
Area: 512,673 acres
Season: Year-round

Major attractions: Highest mountains in the eastern United States (6,500 feet); geologic formations; wildlife.

Activities: Camping, fishing, hiking, nature walks, museums, horseback riding, picnicking.

Guadalupe Mountains National Park
Pine Springs, Texas
Area: 77,518 acres
Season: Year-round

Major attractions: Desert wilderness; ancient Apache hunting grounds; wildlife; highest point in Texas (8,749 feet).

Activities: Camping, hiking.

Haleakala National Park
Kahului, Maui, Hawaii
Area: 28,655 acres
Season: Year-round

Major attractions: Dormant Haleakala volcano (10,023 feet) with overlook; semitropical vegetation.

Activities: Hiking, nature walks, picnicking.

Hawaii Volcanoes National Park
Island of Hawaii
Area: 229,178 acres
Season: Year-round

Major attractions: Volcano activity; semitropical plants; birds.

Activities: Hiking, nature walks.

Hot Springs National Park
Hot Springs, Arkansas
Area: 1,032 acres
Season: Year-round

Major attractions: Ancient hot springs for bathing with reputed therapeutic benefits.

Activities: Bathing, museum tours, hiking, nature trails, picnicking, camping, fishing, and boating nearby.

Isle Royale National Park
Houghton, Michigan
Area: 539,339 acres
Season: May to September

Major attractions: Geologic phenomena; hardwood and evergreen forests; prehistoric iron mines; wildlife.

Activities: Camping, hiking (160 miles of foot trails), fishing, boating (no cars permitted on island).

Katmai National Park
King Salmon, Alaska
Area: 3,700,000 acres
Season: May to September

Major attractions: Aleutian Mountains; Brooks River; Valley of 10,000 Smokes; wildlife.

Activities: Fishing, wildlife photography.

Kenai Fjords National Park
Kenai, Alaska
Area: 670,000 acres
Season: May to September

Major attractions: Wrangell Mountains; wildlife; whale watching; ancient Indian copper mines.

Activities: Fishing, hunting, camping, wildlife photography, hiking, bird watching (150 species).

Kings Canyon National Park
Fresno, California
Area: 460,331 acres
Season: May to October

Major attractions: High Sierra peaks; giant sequoia trees; mile-deep canyon; alpine lakes; glaciers and snowfields; wildlife.

Activities: Camping, hiking, horseback riding, fishing, photography, winter skiing.

Kobuk Valley National Park
Kotzebue, Alaska
Area: 1,750,000 acres
Season: June to September

Major attractions: Baird Mountain peaks; forests; tundra; great sand dunes; prehistorical archeological sites; wildlife.

Activities: Camping, trophy fishing, photography, hunting.

Lake Clark National Park
Anchorage, Alaska
Area: 2,874,000 acres
Season: May to September

Major attractions: Aleutian Range peaks; Cook Inlet; Eskimo and Athabascan Indian archeological sites; fossils; forests; wildlife.

Activities: Camping, fishing, boating, canoeing, hiking, bird-watching, hunting.

Lassen Volcanic National Park
Susanville, California
Area: 105,922 acres
Season: May to October

Major attractions: Cascade Mountains; dense evergreen forests; volcanic lakes (intermittent eruptions since 1914); hot springs; ancient Indian rock carvings.

Activities: Fishing, camping, hiking (150 miles of trails), boating, winter ski tours.

Mammoth Cave National Park
Mammoth Cave, Kentucky
Area: 51,354 acres
Season: Year-round

Major attractions: Large cavern (150 miles of passageways), underground river, blind fish, unusual geologic formations.

Activities: Boating, camping, fishing, hiking, nature walks, picnicking.

Mesa Verde National Park
Mesa Verde, Colorado
Area: 51,333 acres
Season: May to October

Major attractions: Prehistoric cliff dwellings; semiarid landscape; lookout showing six mountain ranges in four states; 2-million-acre San Juan National Forest nearby.

Activities: Fishing, hunting, hiking, horseback riding; dude ranches nearby.

Mount Rainier National Park
Longmire, Washington
Area: 241,571 acres
Season: May to November

Major attractions: Mountain terrain featuring glaciers, alpine lakes, streams, wildlife, marshes, and swamps.

Activities: Hiking, horseback riding, fishing, camping, guided climbs to summit (14,410 feet) for experienced mountaineers.

North Cascades National Park
Marblemount, Washington
Area: 504,781 acres
Season: June through September

Major attractions: Alpine wilderness area featuring mountains, lakes, forests, glaciers, wildlife, and gold rush and logging campsites.

Activities: Camping, fishing, hiking, boating, winter ski tours.

Olympic National Park
Port Angeles, Washington
Area: 896,600 acres
Season: Year-round

Major attractions: Rain forests of giant evergreens; mountains; glaciers; alpine lakes; meadows; wildlife; rocky beaches on peninsula between Pacific Ocean and Puget Sound.

Activities: Camping, fishing, hiking, hunting, horseback riding, boating.

Petrified Forest National Park
Holbrook, Arizona
Area: 93,530 acres
Season: Year-round

Major attractions: World's largest display of petrified coniferous trees in six groups of logs now in the form of jasper and agate; prehistoric Indian rock carvings; painted desert of eroded layers of red and yellow sediment; Mogollon Plateau cliffs (Tonto Rim) nearby.

Activities: Hiking, nature walks, picnicking; fishing, camping, horseback riding, hunting nearby.

Platt National Park
Sulphur, Oklahoma
Area: 912 acres
Season: Year-round

Major attractions: Mineral springs; wild animals; birds and plants.

Activities: Camping, fishing, hiking, nature walks, picnicking.

Redwood National Park
Orick, California
Area: 110,180 acres
Season: Year-round

Major attractions: Redwood forests, including trees topping 300 feet; Pacific Ocean coastline; coast ranges; wildlife.
Activities: Camping, hiking, fishing; hunting, white-water trips nearby.

Rocky Mountain National Park
Estes Park, Colorado
Area: 255,794 acres
Season: June to October

Major attractions: Mountains; lakes; streams; forests; wildflower meadows; wild animals.
Activities: Camping, hiking, fishing, boating, hunting, horseback riding, mountaineering classes, winter skiing; dude ranches nearby.

Sequoia National Park
Three Rivers, California
Area: 386,683 acres
Season: June to October

Major attractions: High Sierra peaks, including Mount Whitney (14,494 feet); lakes, streams, and glaciers; redwood forests; wildlife.
Activities: Camping, hiking, fishing, horseback riding, photographic trips.

Shenandoah National Park
Luray, Virginia
Area: 212,303 acres
Season: Year-round

Major attractions: Blue Ridge Mountains; hardwood forests; wildflowers.
Activities: Camping, fishing, hiking, horseback riding, nature walks, picnicking.

Theodore Roosevelt Memorial National Park
Medora, North Dakota
Area: 70,436 acres
Season: May to October

Major attractions: Missouri River Badlands; petrified forest; deep canyons; virgin prairies; site of former President Theodore Roosevelt's ranch; wildlife.
Activities: Hiking, camping, picnicking, winter snowmobiling.

Virgin Islands National Park
St. John, U.S. Virgin Islands
Area: 15,150 acres
Season: Year-round

Major attractions: Tropical plant and animal life; marine life; coral reefs; sandy beaches; colonial plantations; prehistoric rock carvings.
Activities: Camping, fishing, hiking, nature walks, picnicking, swimming, diving.

Voyageurs National Park
Kabetogama, Minnesota
Area: 219,400 acres
Season: May to September

Major attractions: Evergreen forests; ancient rock outcroppings; bogs; glacial lakes; sandy beaches; wildlife.
Activities: Boating (access to interior is mainly by boat), camping, fishing, hiking, canoeing.

Wind Cave National Park
Hot Springs, South Dakota
Area: 28,060 acres
Season: Year-round

Major attractions: Limestone caverns; bison herds; wildlife.
Activities: Camping, hiking, nature walks, picnicking.

Wrangell–St. Elias National Park
Cordova, Alaska
Area: 8,945,000 acres
Season: May to October

Major attractions: Largest U.S. national park; greatest concentration of peaks over 14,500 feet in North America; rugged coastline; boreal forests; alpine tundra; wildlife.
Activities: Big-game hunting, fishing, camping, boating.

Yellowstone National Park
Idaho–Montana–Wyoming border area
Area: 2,221,773 acres
Season: June to September

Major attractions: Oldest national park; spectacular wilderness; Old Faithful geyser; hot springs; lakes, streams, and waterfalls; "glass mountain" of obsidian; wildlife; alpine meadows.
Activities: Camping, hiking, fishing, photography, horseback riding, boating, canoeing, picnicking, winter ski touring; dude ranches nearby.

Yosemite National Park
Yosemite Village, California
Area: 758,020 acres
Season: June to October

Major attractions: Mountain peaks over 10,000 feet; spectacular granite domes and monoliths; waterfalls; glaciers; hardwood and evergreen forests; wildlife.
Activities: Camping, hiking (Pacific Crest and John Muir trails), fishing, overnight saddle trips, downhill and cross-country skiing in winter.

Zion National Park
Springdale, Utah
Area: 143,254 acres
Season: Year-round

Major attractions: Huge canyons and gorges carved by mountain rivers; colorful rock cliffs; wildlife.
Activities: Camping, hiking, horseback riding, boating.

National Wildlife Refuges Locations and Facilities

This is not a listing of the entire Refuge System, but only those refuges that offer visitor opportunities. The address given is that of the office that administers the refuge; it does not necessarily reflect the location of the refuge.

Refuge conditions and activities are varied and subject to change. Please check with the refuge manager regarding conditions, regulations, and handicapped facilities before taking a trip to a refuge.

	Recommended best wildlife viewing season(s)				Visitor center, contact station	Foot trails	Auto tour	Bicycling	Boating—nonmotorized	Boating—motorized	Environmental study area	Backcountry use	Hunting	Fishing	Camping	Picnicking	Swimming	Refuge leaflet	Species list	Food/lodging nearby
	Spring	Summer	Fall	Winter																
ALABAMA																				
Bon Secour, P.O. Box 1650, Gulf Shores, AL 36542	■		■	■		■														■
Choctaw, Box 808, Jackson, AL 36545		■	■	■																■
Eufaula, Route 2, Box 97-B, Eufaula, AL 36027 (Alabama and Georgia)	■		■	■	■	■	■		■	■			■	■				■	■	■
Wheeler, Box 1643, Decatur, AL 35602	■		■	■	■	■	■		■	■			■	■				■	■	■
Blowing Wind Cave		■																		
ALASKA																				
Alaska Maritime (Headquarters), 202 West Pioneer Avenue, Homer, AK 99603	■		■		■				■	■					■	■		■		■
Alaska Peninsula Unit																				
Aleutian Islands Unit, Box 5251, FPO Seattle, WA 98791	■								■	■		■	■	■	■	■		■	■	
Bering Sea Unit		■																		
Chukchi Sea Unit		■																		
Gulf of Alaska Unit		■																		
Alaska Peninsula, P.O. Box 277, King Salmon, AK 99613	■		■		■				■	■		■	■	■	■			■		
Artic, 101 12th Avenue, Box 20, Fairbanks, AK 99701	■		■						■	■		■	■	■	■	■		■		
Becharof, P.O. Box 277, King Salmon, AK 99613	■		■		■				■	■		■	■	■	■			■		
Innoko, General Delivery, McGrath, AK 99627	■								■	■		■	■	■	■	■		■		
Izembek, Pouch #2, Cold Bay, AK 99571	■				■				■	■	■	■	■	■	■	■		■		
Kanuti, 101 12th Avenue, Box 20, Fairbanks, AK 99701	■								■	■		■	■	■	■	■		■		
Kenai, P.O. Box 2139, Soldotna, AK 99669	■		■		■	■			■	■		■	■	■	■	■		■		
Kodiak, P.O. Box 825, Kodiak, AK 99615	■		■		■	■			■	■		■	■	■	■	■		■	■	
Koyukuk, Box 287, Galena, AK 99741	■								■	■		■	■	■	■	■		■		
Nowitna, Box 287, Galena, AK 99741	■								■	■		■	■	■	■	■		■		
Selawik, Box 270, Kotzebue, AK 99752	■								■	■		■	■	■	■			■		
Tetlin, Box 155, Tok, AK 99780	■		■		■	■			■	■		■	■	■	■	■		■		
Togiak, P.O. Box 10201, Dillingham, AK 99576	■		■						■	■		■	■	■	■	■		■		
Yukon Delta, P.O. Box 346, Bethel, AK 99559	■		■						■	■		■	■	■	■	■		■		
Yukon Flats, 101 12th Avenue, Box 20, Fairbanks, AK 99701	■		■						■	■		■	■	■	■	■		■		

National Wildlife Refuges Locations and Facilities (Continued)

Refuge conditions and activities are varied and subject to change. Please check with the refuge manager regarding conditions, regulations, and handicapped facilities before taking a trip to a refuge.

Location	Spring	Summer	Fall	Winter	Visitor center, contact station	Foot trails	Auto tour	Bicycling	Boating—nonmotorized	Boating—motorized	Environmental study area	Backcountry use	Hunting	Fishing	Camping	Picnicking	Swimming	Refuge leaflet	Species list	Food/lodging nearby
ARIZONA																				
Cabeza Prieta, Box 418, Ajo, AZ 85321	■			■	■						■	■	■					■	■	
Cibola, Box AP, Blythe, CA 92225 (Arizona and California)			■	■	■			■	■	■			■	■				■	■	■
Havasu, Box A, Needles, CA 92363 (Arizona and California)			■	■				■	■	■			■	■	■	■	■	■	■	■
Imperial, Box 72217, Martinez Lake, AZ 85364 (Arizona and California)			■	■	■	■	■		■	■			■	■	■	■		■	■	■
Kofa, Box 6290, Yuma, AZ 85364			■	■	■	■							■			■		■	■	■
ARKANSAS																				
Big Lake, Box 67, Manila, AR 72442	■	■	■	■			■		■	■			■	■				■	■	■
Felsenthal, P.O. Box 1157, Crossett, AR 71635	■	■	■	■			■		■	■			■	■				■	■	■
Holla Bend, Box 1043, Russellville, AR 72801	■	■	■			■	■		■				■	■				■	■	■
Wapanocca, Box 279, Turrell, AR 72384	■	■	■		■	■	■		■				■	■				■	■	
White River, Box 308, 321 West 7th Street, De Witt, AR 72042	■	■	■		■	■			■				■	■				■	■	■
CALIFORNIA																				
Cibola (See Arizona)																				
Havasu (See Arizona)																				
Imperial (See Arizona)																				
Kern, Box 219, Delano, CA 93216			■	■	■	■	■				■		■					■	■	■
Klamath Basin Refuges, Route 1, Box 74, Tulelake, CA 96134			■	■														■	■	
Bear Valley (See Oregon)																				
Clear Lake	■	■	■										■							
Klamath Forest (See Oregon)																				
Lower Klamath (Oregon and California)	■		■	■			■		■				■					■	■	■
Tule Lake	■		■	■			■		■				■					■	■	■
Upper Klamath (See Oregon)																				
Modoc, Box 1610, Alturas, CA 96101	■		■	■		■	■		■				■					■	■	■
Sacramento Valley Refuges, Route 1, Box 311, Willows, CA 95988																				
Colusa	■		■	■			■						■	■				■	■	■
Delevan	■		■	■			■						■	■				■	■	■
Sacramento	■		■	■		■	■						■	■				■	■	■

Sutter

Salton Sea, P.O. Box 120, Calipatria, CA 92223

Tijuana Slough

San Francisco Bay, Box 524, Newark, CA 94560-0524

Antioch Dunes

Humboldt Bay

Salinas River

San Pablo Bay

San Luis, Box 2176, Los Banos, CA 93635

Kesterson

Merced

COLORADO

Arapaho, Box 457, Walden, CO 80480

Browns Park, 1318 Highway 318, Maybell, CO 81640

Alamosa/Monte Vista, Box 1148, Alamosa, CO 81101

CONNECTICUT

Salt Meadow, Box 307, Charlestown, RI 02813

DELAWARE

Bombay Hook, Route 1, Box 147, Smyrna, DE 19977

Prime Hook, Route 1, Box 195, Milton, DE 19968

FLORIDA

Chassahowitzka, Route 2, Box 44, Homosassa, FL 32646

Cedar Keys

Crystal River

Egmont Key

Lower Suwannee

Passage Key

Pinellas

Hobe Sound, P.O. Box 645, Hobe Sound, FL 33455

J. N. "Ding" Darling, 1 Wildlife Drive, Sanibel, FL 33957

Caloosahatchee

Island Bay

Matlacha Pass

Pine Island

Lake Woodruff, Box 488, DeLeon Springs, FL 32028

Loxahatchee, Route 1, Box 278, Boynton Beach, FL 33437

Merritt Island, Box 6504, Titusville, FL 32780

Pelican Island

National Key Deer, Box 510, Big Pine Key, FL 33043

Crocodile Lake

Great White Heron

Key West

St. Marks, Box 68, St. Marks, FL 32355

St. Vincent, Box 447, Apalachicola, FL 32320

553

Refuge conditions and activities are varied and subject to change. Please check with the refuge manager regarding conditions, regulations, and handicapped facilities before taking a trip to a refuge.

Location	Spring	Summer	Fall	Winter	Visitor center, contact station	Foot trails	Auto tour	Bicycling	Boating—nonmotorized	Boating—motorized	Environmental study area	Backcountry use	Hunting	Fishing	Camping	Picnicking	Swimming	Refuge leaflet	Species list	Food/lodging nearby
GEORGIA																				
Eufaula (See Alabama)																				
Okefenokee, Rt. 2, Box 338, Folkston, GA 31537	■	■	■	■	■	■	■		■	■		■	■	■				■	■	■
Piedmont, Round Oak, GA 31038	■	■	■	■	■	■	■						■	■				■	■	■
Savannah Coastal Refuges, Box 8487, Savannah, GA 31402																				
Blackbeard Island (Georgia)	■		■	■		■							■	■						■
Harris Neck (Georgia)	■	■	■	■		■	■						■	■				■	■	■
Pinckney Island (South Carolina)	■	■	■	■		■		■					■	■					■	■
Savannah (Georgia and South Carolina)	■	■	■	■	■	■	■	■	■				■	■				■	■	■
Tybee (South Carolina)	■		■	■														■	■	■
Wassaw (Georgia)	■	■	■	■									■	■				■		
Wolf Island (Georgia)	■		■	■			■						■	■				■		
HAWAII																				
Hawaiian and Pacific Islands Refuges, P.O. Box 50167, 300 Ala Moana Boulevard, Honolulu, HI 96850																				
Hawaiian Islands				■							■							■	■	
James C. Campbell			■	■							■							■	■	
Kakahaia																				
Kilauea Point, Box 87, Kilauea, Kauai, HI 96754	■	■	■	■	■	■													■	■
Hanalei	■	■	■	■					■		■							■	■	■
IDAHO																				
Deer Flat, Box 448, Nampa, ID 83653-0448	■	■	■	■	■	■	■	■	■	■			■	■		■		■	■	■
Snake River Islands	■	■	■	■									■	■					■	■
Kootenai, Star Route 1, Box 160, Bonners Ferry, ID 83805	■	■	■		■	■	■		■	■			■	■				■	■	■
Southeast Idaho Refuges, 250 S. Fourth Avenue, Pocatello, ID 83201																				
Bear Lake, 370 Webster, P.O. Box 9, Montpelier, ID 83254	■	■	■			■	■			■			■	■					■	■
Camas, HC 69, Box 1700, Hamer, ID 83425	■	■	■				■						■	■					■	
Grays Lake, HC 70, Box 4090, Wayan, ID 83285	■	■											■						■	
Minidoka, Route 4, P.O. Box 290, Rupert, ID 83350	■		■						■	■			■	■				■	■	■

ILLINOIS

Chautauqua, Route 2, Havana, IL 62644

Crab Orchard, Box J, Carterville, IL 62918

Mark Twain, 311 North 5th Street, Suite 100, Great River Plaza, Quincy, IL 62301

    Batchtown Division, Box 142, Brussels, IL 62013

    Calhoun Division, Box 142, Brussels, IL 62013

    Gardner Division, P.O. Box 88, Annada, MO 63330

    Gilbert Lake Division, Box 142, Brussels, IL 62013

    Keithsburg Division, Route 1, Wapello, IA 52653

Upper Mississippi River Wild Life and Fish Refuge (*See* Minnesota)

    Savanna District, Box 250, Savanna, IL 61074

INDIANA

Muscatatuck, Box 189 A, Route 7, Seymour, IN 47274

IOWA

Des Soto, Box 114, Missouri Valley, IA 51555 (Iowa and Nebraska)

Mark Twain (*See* Illinois)

    Big Timber Division, Route 1, Wapello, IA 52653

    Louisa Division, Route 1, Wapello, IA 52653

    Union Slough, Route 1, Box 52, Titonka, IA 50480

Upper Mississippi River Wild Life and Fish Refuge (*See* Minnesota)

    McGregor District, P.O. Box 460, McGregor, IA 52157

KANSAS

Flint Hills, Box 128, Hartford, KS 66854

Kirwin, Kirwin, KS 67644

Quivira, Box G, Stafford, KS 67578

LOUISIANA

Bogue Chitto, 1010 Gause Boulevard, Building 936, Slidell, LA 70458

Catahoula, P.O. Drawer LL, Jena, LA 71342

D'Arbonne, Box 3065, Monroe, LA 71201

    Upper Quachita

Delta-Breton, Venice, LA 70091

Lacassine, Route 1, Box 186, Lake Arthur, LA 70549

Sabine, MRH 107, Hackberry, LA 70645

Tensas River, Merchant's National Bank Building, 820 South Street,
    Vicksburg, MS 39180

MAINE

Moosehorn, Box X, Calais, ME 04619

    Cross Island

    Franklin Island

    Petit Manan

Rachel Carson, Route 2, Box 751, Wells, ME 04090

MARYLAND

Blackwater, Route 1, Box 121, Cambridge, MD 21613

Eastern Neck, Route 2, Box 225, Rock Hall, MD 21661

555

National Wildlife Refuges
Locations and Facilities (Continued)

Refuge conditions and activities are varied and subject to change. Please check with the refuge manager regarding conditions, regulations, and handicapped facilities before taking a trip to a refuge.

Location	Spring	Summer	Fall	Winter	Visitor center, contact station	Foot trails	Auto tour	Bicycling	Boating—nonmotorized	Boating—motorized	Environmental study area	Backcountry use	Hunting	Fishing	Camping	Picnicking	Swimming	Refuge leaflet	Species list	Food/lodging nearby
MASSACHUSETTS																				
Great Meadows, Weir Hill Rd., Sudbury, MA 01776	■		■		■	■		■	■	■	■							■	■	■
Oxbow	■	■	■										■	■					■	
Parker River, Northern Boulevard, Plum Island, Newburyport, MA 01950	■		■			■		■				■	■	■				■	■	■
Monomoy	■		■															■	■	■
Nantucket	■		■											■						■
MICHIGAN																				
Seney, Seney, MI 49883	■		■		■	■			■		■		■	■				■	■	■
Shiawassee, 6975 Mower Road, Route 1, Saginaw, MI 48601	■		■		■	■		■	■				■			■		■	■	■
MINNESOTA																				
Agassiz, Middle River, MN 56737	■		■	■		■	■												■	■
Big Stone, 25 NW 2nd Street, Ortonville, MN 56278	■		■	■		■	■												■	■
Minnesota Valley, 4101 E. 78th Street, Bloomington, MN 55420	■		■	■	■	■			■	■	■			■				■	■	■
Minnesota Wetlands Complex, Route 1, Box 76, Fergus Falls, MN 56537																				
Detroit Lakes Wetland Management District, Route 3, Box 47D, Detroit Lakes, MN 56501	■		■																	
Fergus Falls, Wetland Management District, Route 1, Box 76, Fergus Falls, MN 56537	■		■																	
Litchfield Wetland Management District, 305 North Sibley, Litchfield, MN 55353	■		■																	
Morris Wetland Management District, Route 1, Box 208, Mill Dam Road, Morris, MN 56267	■		■	■	■															
Rice Lake, Route 2, McGregor, MN 55760	■		■		■	■	■												■	■
Sherburne, Route 2, Zimmerman, MN 55398	■		■	■	■	■	■		■										■	■
Tamarac, Rural Route, Rochert, MN 56578	■		■	■	■	■	■		■										■	■
Upper Mississippi River Wild Life and Fish Refuge (Headquarters), 51 East 4th Street, Winona, MN 55987 (Illinois, Iowa, Minnesota, and Wisconsin)																				
Winona District	■		■	■		■			■	■	■		■	■	■	■	■	■	■	■
MISSISSIPPI																				
Mississippi Sandhill Crane Complex, Box 699, Gautler, MS 39553	■		■	■	■	■					■								■	■
Noxubee, Route 1, Box 142, Brooksville, MS 39739	■		■	■	■	■	■			■				■		■		■	■	■
Yazoo, Route 1, Box 286, Hollandale, MS 38748	■		■	■	■	■	■		■	■				■				■	■	■
Hillside	■		■	■					■	■				■					■	■

Morgan Brake

Panther Swamp

MISSOURI

Mark Twain (See Illinois)

Clarence Cannon, Box 88, Annada, MO 63330

Mingo, Route 1, Box 103, Puxico, MO 63960

Squaw Creek, Box 101, Mound City, MO 64470

Swan Lake, Box 68, Sumner, MO 64681

MONTANA

Benton Lake, Box 450, Black Eagle, MT 59414

Bowdoin, Box J, Malta, MT 59538

Charles M. Russell, Box 110, Lewistown, MT 59457

Lee Metcalf, Box 257, Stevensville, MT 59870

Medicine Lake, Medicine Lake, MT 59247

National Bison Range, Moiese, MT 59824

Red Rock Lakes, Monida Star Route, Box 15, Lima, MT 59739

NEBRASKA

Crescent Lake, HC 68, Box 21, Ellsworth, NE 69340

DeSoto (See Iowa)

Fort Niobrara, Hidden Timber Route, HC 14, Box 67, Valentine, NE 69201

Valentine

Rainwater Basin Wetland Management District, Box 1786, Kearney, NE 68847

NEVADA

Desert National Wildlife Range, 1500 North Decatur Boulevard, Las Vegas, NV 89108

Ash Meadows

Pahranagat

Ruby Lake, Ruby Valley, NV 89833

Sheldon, P.O. Box 111, Room 308, U.S. Post Office Building, Lakeview, OR 97630

Stillwater, Box 1236, 1510 Rio Vista Road, Fallon, NV 89408

Fallon

NEW HAMPSHIRE

Wapack, Weir Hill Road, Sudbury, MA 01776

NEW JERSEY

Edwin B. Forsythe, Box 72, Oceanville, NJ 08231

Brigantine

Barnegat, Box 544, Barnegat, NJ 08005

Great Swamp, Pleasant Plains Road, RD 1, Box 152, Basking Ridge, NJ 07920

NEW MEXICO

Bitter Lake, Box 7, Roswell, NM 88201

Bosque del Apache, Box 1246, Socorro, NM 87801

Sevilleta, San Acacia, NM 87831

Grulla, Box 549, Muleshoe, TX 79347

Las Vegas, Route 1, Box 399, Las Vegas, NM 87701

Maxwell, Box 276, Maxwell, NM 87728

557

National Wildlife Refuges
Locations and Facilities (Continued)

Refuge conditions and activities are varied and subject to change. Please check with the refuge manager regarding conditions, regulations, and handicapped facilities before taking a trip to a refuge.

	Spring	Summer	Fall	Winter	Visitor center, contact station	Foot trails	Auto tour	Bicycling	Boating—nonmotorized	Boating—motorized	Environmental study area	Backcountry use	Hunting	Fishing	Camping	Picnicking	Swimming	Refuge leaflet	Species list	Food/lodging nearby
NEW YORK																				
Iroquois, P.O. Box 517, Alabama, NY 14003	■		■	■	■	■			■				■	■				■	■	■
Montezuma, RD 1, Box 1411, Seneca Falls, NY 13148	■		■	■	■		■						■	■				■	■	■
Wertheim, P.O. Box 21, Shirley, NY 11967	■		■	■		■			■									■	■	■
Morton	■	■	■	■																■
Oyster Bay	■			■						■				■						■
Target Rock	■	■	■	■		■												■	■	■
NORTH CAROLINA																				
Great Dismal Swamp (See Virginia)																				
Mackay Island, Knotts Island, NC 27950 (North Carolina and Virginia)	■		■	■		■	■						■	■				■	■	
Mattamuskeet, Route 1, Box N-2, Swanquarter, NC 27885	■		■	■	■		■		■				■	■				■	■	
Cedar Island	■	■	■	■																
Pungo	■			■			■													
Swanquarter	■	■	■	■									■	■						
Pea Island, Box 150, Rodanthe, NC 27968	■	■	■	■	■	■				■				■				■	■	■
Pee Dee, Box 780, Wadesboro, NC 28170	■	■	■	■		■				■			■	■				■	■	■
NORTH DAKOTA																				
Arrowwood, Rural Route 1, Pingree, ND 58476	■		■		■	■	■						■	■				■	■	■
Long Lake, Moffit, ND 58560	■		■		■	■	■						■					■	■	
Valley City Wetland Management District, Rural Route 1, Valley City, ND 58072	■	■																		
Audubon, Rural Route 1, Coleharbor, ND 58531	■		■		■	■	■			■			■	■				■	■	■
Des Lacs, Box 578, Kenmare, ND 58746	■		■		■								■					■	■	■
Crosby Wetland Management District, Box 148, Crosby, ND 58730	■		■							■										
Lake Ilo, Dunn Center, ND 58626	■									■				■					■	■
Lostwood, Rural Route 2, Kenmare, ND 58746	■		■			■	■						■					■	■	
Devils Lake Wetland Management District, Box 908, Devils Lake, ND 58301	■		■									■						■	■	■
Sullys Hill National Game Preserve, Ft. Totten, ND 58335	■		■			■	■									■		■	■	■
J. Clark Salyer, Upham, ND 58789	■		■			■	■						■	■				■	■	
Kulm Wetland Management District, Box E, Kulm, ND 58456	■		■															■	■	■
Tewaukon, Rural Route 1, Cayuga, ND 58013	■					■							■	■				■	■	■

Ottawa, 14000 W. State, Route 2, Oak Harbor, OH 43449

OKLAHOMA

Optima, Box 628, Guymon, OK 73942

Salt Plains, Route 1, Box 76, Jet, OK 73749

Sequoyah, Route 1, Box 18A, Vian, OK 74962

Tishomingo, Route 1, Box 151, Tishomingo, OK 73460

Washita, Route 1, Box 68, Butler, OK 73625

Wichita Mountains Wildlife Refuge, Route 1, Box 448, Indiahoma, OK 73552

OREGON

Hart Mountain National Antelope Refuge, Box 111, Room 308, U.S. Post Office Building, Lakeview, OR 97630

Klamath Basin Refuges, Route 1, Box 74, Tulelake, CA 96134

Bear Valley

Clear Lake (*See* California)

Klamath Forest

Lower Klamath (Oregon and California)

Tule Lake (*See* California)

Upper Klamath

Lower Columbia River Refuges, 1309 NE 134th Street, Vancouver, WA 98665

Columbian White-tailed Deer (Oregon and Washington)

Lewis and Clark

Ridgefield (*See* Washington)

Willapa (*See* Washington)

Malheur, P.O. Box 113, Burns, OR 97720

Umatilla, P.O. Box 239, Umatilla, OR 97882 (Oregon and Washington)

Cold Springs

McKay Creek

Western Oregon Refuges, Route 2, Box 208, Corvallis, OR 97333

Ankeny

Baskett Slough

Brandon Marsh

Cape Meares

William L. Finley

PENNSYLVANIA

Erie, RD 1, Wood Duck Lane, Guy Mills, PA 16327

Tinicum National Environmental Center, Suite 104, Scott Plaza 2, Philadelphia, PA 19113

PUERTO RICO

Caribbean Islands, Box 510, Carr. 301, KM 5.4, Boqueron, PR 00622

Buck Island (Virgin Islands)

Cabo Rojo (Puerto Rico)

Culebra (Puerto Rico)

Desecheo (Puerto Rico)

Green Cay (Virgin Islands)

Sandy Point (Virgin Islands)

National Wildlife Refuges
Locations and Facilities (Continued)

Refuge conditions and activities are varied and subject to change. Please check with the refuge manager regarding conditions, regulations, and handicapped facilities before taking a trip to a refuge.

	Spring	Summer	Fall	Winter	Visitor center, contact station	Foot trails	Auto tour	Bicycling	Boating—nonmotorized	Boating—motorized	Environmental study area	Backcountry use	Hunting	Fishing	Camping	Picnicking	Swimming	Refuge leaflet	Species list	Food/lodging nearby
RHODE ISLAND																				
Ninigret, Box 307, Charlestown, RI 02813	■	■	■	■										■						■
Block Island		■	■											■						■
Sachuest Point	■	■		■		■								■					■	■
Trustom Pond	■	■		■		■					■								■	■
SOUTH CAROLINA																				
Cape Romain, Route 1, Box 191, Awendaw, SC 29429	■	■	■	■	■	■	■		■	■			■	■						■
Carolina Sandhills, Route 2, Box 130, McBee, SC 29101	■	■	■	■	■	■	■		■	■			■	■	■			■	■	■
Pinckney Island (*See Georgia*)																				
Santee, Route 2, Box 66, Summerton, SC 29148	■	■			■	■	■	■	■	■			■	■				■	■	■
Savannah (*See Georgia*)																				
SOUTH DAKOTA																				
Lacreek, HWC 3, Box 14, Martin, SD 57551	■	■	■		■		■		■				■	■		■			■	■
Lake Andes, Route 1, Box 77, Lake Andes, SD 57356	■	■	■		■		■		■	■			■	■		■			■	■
Karl E. Mundt	■	■	■	■														■		
Madison Wetland Management District, Box 48, Madison, SD 57042	■	■	■		■								■	■					■	
Sand Lake, Rural Route 1, Columbia, SD 57433	■	■	■	■	■		■		■				■	■			■		■	■
Waubay, Rural Route 1, Box 79, Waubay, SD 57273	■	■	■	■	■	■	■						■	■		■			■	■
TENNESSEE																				
Cross Creeks, Route 1, Box 229, Dover, TN 37058	■	■	■	■	■		■		■	■			■	■				■	■	■
Hatchie, Box 187, Brownsville, TN 38012	■	■	■	■		■			■	■			■	■				■	■	■
Lower Hatchie	■	■		■									■	■						■
Reelfoot, Route 2, Highway 157, Union City, TN 38261	■	■	■	■	■		■		■	■			■	■					■	■
Lake Isom	■	■		■									■	■						■
Tennessee, Box 849, Paris, TN 38242	■	■	■	■	■		■				■		■	■					■	■

TEXAS

Anahuac, Box 278, Anahuac, TX 77514

McFaddin

Texas Point

Aransas, Box 100, Austwell, TX 77950

Attwater Prairie Chicken, Box 518, Eagle Lake, TX 77434

Brazoria, Box 1088, Angleton, TX 77515

Big Boggy

San Bernard

Hagerman, Route 3, Box 123, Sherman, TX 75090

Laguna Atascosa, Box 450, Rio Hondo, TX 78583

Muleshoe, Box 549, Muleshoe, TX 79347

Buffalo Lake, Box 228, Umbarger, TX 79091

Grulla (See New Mexico)

Santa Ana, Route 1, Box 202A, Alamo, TX 78516

Rio Grande Valley

UTAH

Bear River Migratory Bird Refuge, Box 459, Brigham City, UT 84302

Fish Springs, Dugway, UT 84022

Ouray, 447 E. Main Street, Suite 4, Vernal, UT 84078

VERMONT

Missisquoi, Route 2, Swanton, VT 05488

VIRGINIA

Back Bay, Pembroke Office Park, Suite 218, Virginia Beach, VA 23462

Chincoteague, Box 62, Chincoteague, VA 23336

Great Dismal Swamp, P.O. Box 349, Suffolk, VA 23434 (North Carolina and Virginia)

Mackay Island (See North Carolina)

Mason Neck, 14416 Jefferson Davis Highway, Suite 20-A, Lorton, VA 22191

Presquile, Box 620, Hopewell, VA 23860

WASHINGTON

Columbia, 44 South 8th Avenue, P.O. Drawer F, Othello, WA 99344

Lower Columbia River Refuges, 1309 NE 134th Street, Vancouver, WA 98685

Columbian White-tailed Deer (Oregon and Washington)

Conboy Lake

Lewis and Clark (See Oregon)

Ridgefield

Willapa

Nisqually, 100 Brown Farm Road, Olympia, WA 98506

Dungeness

San Juan Islands

Turnbull, Route 3, Box 385, Cheney, WA 99004

Umatilla, P.O. Box 239, Umatilla, OR 97882 (Oregon and Washington)

McNary

Toppenish

561

National Wildlife Refuges
Locations and Facilities (Continued)

Refuge conditions and activities are varied and subject to change. Please check with the refuge manager regarding conditions, regulations, and handicapped facilities before taking a trip to a refuge.

	Spring	Summer	Fall	Winter	Visitor center, contact station	Foot trails	Auto tour	Bicycling	Boating—nonmotorized	Boating—motorized	Environmental study area	Backcountry use	Hunting	Fishing	Camping	Picnicking	Swimming	Refuge leaflet	Species list	Food/lodging nearby
WISCONSIN																				
Horicon, Route 2, Mayville, WI 53050	■	■	■		■	■					■		■	■				■	■	■
Necedah, Star Route West, Box 386, Necedah, WI 54646	■	■	■	■	■	■	■				■		■	■				■	■	■
Trempealeau, Route 1, Trempealeau, WI 54661	■		■			■	■	■	■				■	■				■	■	■
Upper Mississippi River Wild Life and Fish Refuge (See Minnesota)																				
La Crosse District, Room 208, P.O. Building, Box 415, La Crosse, WI 54601	■		■						■	■		■		■	■	■	■	■	■	■
McGregor District (See Iowa)																				
WYOMING																				
National Elk Refuge, Box C, Jackson, WY 83001	■		■	■	■				■				■	■				■	■	■
Seedskadee, P.O. Box 67, Green River, WY 82935	■		■										■	■				■		

Cloud Nomenclature

For illustrations of cloud types, see page 565.

altocumulus (Ac) Similar to cirrocumulus, with patches of small clouds occasionally separated by thin breaks. Although altocumulus clouds also may be identified by a "mackerel sky" pattern, they are lower, at around 10,000 feet, and the clumps of white or gray water droplets or ice crystals are larger. The clouds may develop directly overhead, depending on the temperature of the atmosphere, and may produce a shower.

altostratus (As) Dull, drab gray or blue middle-level clouds that usually contain moisture in the form of water droplets. Altostratus clouds are often opaque, giving a "ground glass" view of the sun or moon behind them. They may be a source of virga, filaments of ice crystals or water droplets that fall toward Earth but evaporate before touching the ground.

cirrocumulus (Cc) Loosely packed sheets of small white cloud segments at altitudes of around 18,000 to 20,000 feet, forming a "mackerel sky" resembling scales on a fish. The clouds may consist of ice crystals or water droplets or both. The patchy appearance is caused by vertical air currents at the cloud level, indicating a lack of stability and a possible approaching storm.

cirrostratus (Cs) Translucent veils of white fibrous cloud that tend to occur at altitudes of around 20,000 feet or more. Cirrostratus clouds often cover the entire sky and may cause the appearance of halos or reflected images of the sun or moon. They may signal an approaching storm.

cirrus (Ci) Generally, the highest clouds, forming "mares' tails" at altitudes between 20,000 and 40,000 feet. The clouds may appear as delicate white filaments, featherlike tufts, or fibrous bands of ice crystals.

cumulonimbus (Cb) Thunderstorm clouds that may vary considerably in altitude from ominously dark lower portions below 5,000 feet to white anvil-shaped tops that may reach upward to 50,000 feet. They contain large amounts of moisture, some of which may be in the form of hail. The cumulonimbus cloud may appear alone or as part of a wall of advancing storm clouds.

cumulus (Cu) Low-level billowy clouds that are usually dark on the bottom while the top resembles a giant white cotton ball. A cumulus cloud may be relatively tall, extending from a base around 2,000 feet to a top near 10,000 feet above ground. It casts a dark shadow and may be a source of moisture but generally produces no more than a summer shower.

nimbostratus (Ns) Low, dark rain clouds with ragged tops that have bottoms only a few hundred feet above ground and may range upward to an altitude of 3,000 feet. They obscure the sun and are associated with continuous rain, sleet, or snow but are rarely accompanied by thunder or lightning.

stratocumulus (Sc) Dark, gray rolls of clouds that usually cover the entire sky at an altitude from 1,500 to 6,500 feet. The rounded segments may appear checkered or wavelike and there may or may not be breaks of blue sky between segments. Stratocumulus clouds contain moisture but are usually not rain producers.

stratus (St) Wispy foglike clouds that hover a few hundred feet above ground, sometimes obscuring hills or tall buildings. They may begin as ground fog and can be a source of drizzle.

Beaufort Scale of Wind Force

Beaufort no.	Knots (mph)	Description	Effect at sea	Effect ashore
0	Less than 1	Calm	Sea is like a mirror.	Smoke rises vertically.
1	1–3 (1–3)	Light air	Ripples with the appearance of a scale are formed but without foam crests.	Wind vanes are not moved, but wind direction is shown by smoke drift.
2	4–6 (4–7)	Light breeze	Small wavelets, still short but more pronounced, appear; crests have a glassy appearance but do not break.	Wind is felt on face; leaves rustle; ordinary vane is moved by wind.
3	7–10 (8–12)	Gentle breeze	Large wavelets appear. Crests begin to break. Foam is of glassy appearance, perhaps with scattered white horses.	Leaves and small twigs are in constant motion; wind extends light flag.

Beaufort Scale of Wind Force *(Continued)*

Beaufort no.	Knots (mph)	Description	Effect at sea	Effect ashore
4	11–16 (13–18)	Moderate breeze	Small waves appear, becoming longer; there are fairly frequent white horses.	Dust and loose paper are raised; small branches are moved.
5	17–21 (18–24)	Fresh breeze	Moderate waves arise, taking a more pronounced long form; many white horses are formed (with chance of some spray).	Small trees in leaf begin to sway; crested wavelets form on inland waters.
6	22–27 (25–31)	Strong breeze	Large waves begin to form; the white foam crests are more extensive everywhere (probably with some spray).	Large branches are in motion; whistling is heard in telegraph wires; umbrellas are used with difficulty.
7	28–33 (32–38)	Moderate gale (high wind)	Sea heaps up and white foam from breaking waves begins to be blown in streaks along the direction of the wind. Spindrift begins.	Whole trees are in motion; inconvenience is felt in walking against the wind.
8	34–40 (39–46)	Fresh gale	Moderately high waves of greater length appear; edges of crests break into spindrift. The foam is blown in well-marked streaks along the direction of the wind.	Twigs are broken off trees, and the wind generally impedes progress.
9	41–47 (47–54)	Strong gale	High waves appear. Dense streaks of foam arise along the direction of the wind. Sea begins to roll. Spray may affect visibility.	Slight structural damage occurs (chimney pots and slate removed).
10	48–55 (55–63)	Storm	Very high waves with long overhanging crests appear. The resulting foam in great patches is blown in dense white streaks along the direction of the wind. On the whole, the surface of the sea takes on a white appearance. The rolling of the sea becomes heavy and shocklike. Visibility is affected.	It is seldom experienced inland. Trees are uprooted; considerable structural damage occurs.
11	55–63 (64–73)	Violent storm	Exceptionally high waves appear. (Small and medium-sized ships might for a long time be lost to view behind the waves.) The sea is completely covered with long white patches of foam lying along the direction of the wind. Everywhere the edges of the wave crests are blown into froth. Visibility is affected.	It is very rarely experienced and is accompanied by widespread damage.
12	Above 63 (73)	Hurricane	The air is filled with foam and spray. The sea is completely white with a driving spray; visibility is very seriously affected.	

CIRRUS

CIRRO-STRATUS

CIRRO-CUMULUS

ALTO-CUMULUS

ALTO-STRATUS

CUMULO-NIMBUS

CUMULUS

STRATO-CUMULUS

NIMBO-STRATUS

STRATUS

Lunar and Solar Eclipses

An eclipse occurs when a celestial body, such as the sun or moon, produces a shadow so that another celestial body seems to disappear. An eclipse of the moon (lunar eclipse) occurs when the sun, Earth, and moon are in a straight line so that the moon is in the shadow of Earth. An eclipse of the sun occurs when the sun, moon, and Earth are in a straight line so that the moon casts a shadow on Earth. As each of the celestial bodies is in constant motion with respect to the others, and the alignment of the bodies is not always perfect, an eclipse seldom lasts more than a few minutes. The eclipse may be total or partial.

Because a lunar eclipse results in the total surface of the moon being in the shadow of Earth, the eclipse is visible from any point on Earth. But the shadow of a solar eclipse is visible only along an arc-shaped path on a portion of Earth, and it moves at a speed of between 1,060 and 2,100 miles per hour, depending on the latitude of the shadow, the rotation of Earth, and the speed of the moon through its own orbit. An annual eclipse is one in which the moon's shadow allows the corona, or outer fringe, of the sun to reach Earth.

Because the sun, Earth, and moon travel in relatively predictable orbits, astronomers since the days of ancient Babylonia (700 B.C.) have been able to calculate the future dates on which the sun, Earth, and moon will once again be in alignment. Therefore, they can forecast the time and place of eclipses many years in advance. For example, at regular intervals of 18 years, 9 to 11 days (depending on leap years), and 8 hours (a period of one saros), the sun and moon will return to the same orbital node relative to Earth. During one saros, there are usually 41 total or partial solar eclipses and 29 lunar eclipses, or an average of about four eclipses a year. But each successive solar eclipse is observed about 120 degrees to the west of the previous phenomenon and can be expected to recur at the same longitude on Earth after a period equivalent to three times the length of one saros. Each solar eclipse may affect an area only about 100 miles wide and any given place on Earth can expect a total eclipse about once every 400 years.

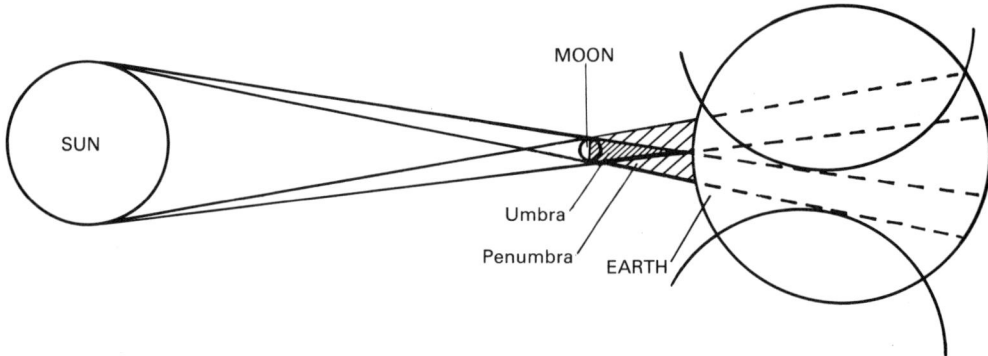

A total eclipse of the sun takes place when Earth, the moon, and the sun are in alignment in such a way that the umbra of the shadow of the moon reaches Earth (the umbra is the dark central part of the cone-shaped shadow projecting from the moon to Earth during this phenomenon). All the light of the sun is blocked or eclipsed because of the moon's position. The penumbra (the lighter shadow) shows a partial solar eclipse. The two arcs indicate positions of Earth where a total eclipse would not be possible.

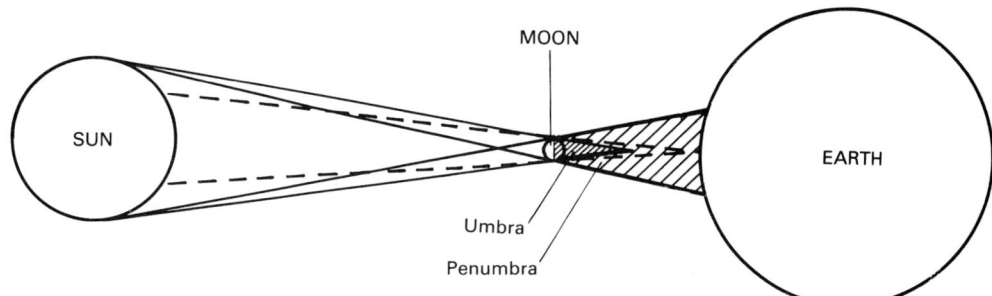

In an annular solar eclipse, the alignment is just the same as in a total solar eclipse, but the moon is too far away from Earth at the time for the umbra of the shadow to reach Earth. The circle of the moon is not large enough to block our seeing the sun, so a ring of light can be seen surrounding the moon's circle.

Total Eclipses of the Sun During the Twentieth Century

Date	Approximate duration (min:sec)	Maximum width (miles)	Course of central line
1900 May 28	2:10	58	Mexico, United States, Spain, North Africa
1901 May 18	6:71	149	Indian Ocean, Sumatra, Borneo, New Guinea
1903 September 21	2:02	157	Antarctica
1904 September 9	6:19	146	Pacific Ocean
1905 August 30	3:46	123	Canada, Spain, North Africa, Arabia
1907 January 14	2:24	119	Soviet Union, China
1908 January 3	4:20	93	Pacific Ocean
1908 December 23	0:12	6	South America, Atlantic Ocean, Indian Ocean
1909 June 17	0:24	32	Greenland, Soviet Union
1910 May 9	4:14	. . .	Antarctica
1911 April 28	4:58	120	Pacific Ocean
1912 April 17	0:02	1	Atlantic Ocean, Europe, Soviet Union
1912 October 10	2:20	54	Brazil, South Atlantic Ocean
1914 August 21	2:15	113	Greenland, Europe, Middle East
1916 February 3	2:36	69	Pacific Ocean, South America, Atlantic Ocean
1918 June 8	2:23	70	Pacific Ocean, United States
1919 May 29	6:50	153	South America, Atlantic Ocean, Africa
1921 October 1	1:52	189	Antarctica
1922 September 21	6:39	142	Indian Ocean, Australia
1923 September 10	3:37	106	Pacific Ocean, Central America
1925 January 24	2:32	130	Northeast United States, Atlantic Ocean
1926 January 14	4:11	92	Africa, Indian Ocean, Borneo
1927 June 29	0:50	48	England, Scandinavia, Arctic Ocean, Soviet Union
1928 May 19	. . .	. . .	(Umbra barely touched Antarctica)
1929 May 9	5:07	122	Indian Ocean, Malaya, Philippines
1930 April 28	0:01	1	Pacific Ocean, United States, Canada
1930 October 21	1:55	54	South Pacific Ocean
1932 August 31	1:45	104	Arctic Ocean, East Canada
1934 February 14	2:53	79	Borneo, Pacific Ocean
1936 June 19	2:31	83	Greece, Turkey, Soviet Union, Pacific Ocean
1937 June 8	7:04	156	Pacific Ocean, Peru
1938 May 29	4:04	. . .	South Atlantic Ocean
1939 October 12	1:32	276	Antarctica

Total Eclipses of the Sun During the Twentieth Century *(Continued)*

Date	Approximate duration (min:sec)	Maximum width (miles)	Course of central line
1940 October 1	5:35	137	South America, Atlantic Ocean, Africa
1941 September 21	3:22	91	Soviet Union, China, Pacific Ocean
1943 February 4	2:39	146	Japan, Pacific Ocean, Alaska
1944 January 25	4:09	91	South America, Atlantic Ocean, Africa
1945 July 9	1:35	57	Canada, Greenland, Scandinavia, Soviet Union
1947 May 20	5:14	124	Argentina, Brazil, Central Africa
1948 November 1	1:56	53	Africa, Indian Ocean
1950 September 12	1:13	90	Arctic Ocean, Soviet Union, Pacific Ocean
1952 February 25	3:50	89	Africa, Arabia, Iran, Soviet Union
1954 June 30	2:35	96	United States, Canada, Scandinavia, Soviet Union
1955 June 20	7:08	159	Indian Ocean, Thailand, Pacific Ocean
1956 June 8	4:44	269	South Pacific Ocean
1957 October 23	. . .	. . .	(Umbra touched Antarctica)
1958 October 12	5:11	131	Pacific Ocean, Argentina
1959 October 2	3:01	76	Atlantic Ocean, Africa
1961 February 15	2:44	164	Europe, Soviet Union
1962 February 5	4:08	92	Borneo, New Guinea, Pacific Ocean
1963 July 20	1:40	63	Pacific Ocean, Alaska, Canada
1965 May 30	5:61	124	New Zealand, Pacific Ocean
1966 November 12	1:57	53	South America, Atlantic Ocean
1967 November 2	. . .	. . .	(Umbra touched Antarctica)
1968 September 22	0:40	68	Soviet Union
1970 March 7	3:28	99	Pacific Ocean, Mexico, Eastern United States
1972 July 10	2:36	111	Soviet Union, North Canada
1973 June 30	7:04	160	Atlantic Ocean, Central Africa, Indian Ocean
1974 June 20	5:08	216	Indian Ocean, Australia
1976 October 23	4:46	125	Africa, Indian Ocean, Australia
1977 October 12	2:37	63	Pacific Ocean, Colombia, Venezuela
1979 February 26	2:52	195	Northwest United States, Canada, Greenland
1980 February 16	4:08	93	Africa, Indian Ocean, India, China
1981 July 31	2:03	68	Soviet Union, Pacific Ocean
1983 June 11	5:11	125	Indian Ocean, New Guinea
1984 November 22	1:59	53	New Guinea, South Pacific Ocean
1985 November 12	1:59	. . .	Antarctica
1986 October 3	0:01	1	North Atlantic Ocean
1987 March 29	0:08	3	South Atlantic Ocean, Central Africa
1988 March 18	3:46	109	Sumatra, Borneo, Philippines
1990 July 22	2:33	130	Soviet Union, Pacific Ocean
1991 July 11	6:54	161	Hawaii, Mexico, South America
1992 June 30	5:20	186	South Atlantic Ocean
1994 November 3	4:51	119	Bolivia, Brazil, South Atlantic Ocean
1995 October 24	2:10	49	India, Southeast Asia, Indonesia
1997 March 9	2:50	231	Soviet Union, Arctic Ocean
1998 February 26	4:08	95	Pacific Ocean, Venezuela, Atlantic Ocean
1999 August 11	2:23	70	Central Europe, Middle East, India

Constellations

Twelve Zodiacal Consellations

Aquarius, the Water-Bearer
Ares, the Ram
Cancer, the Crab
Capricorn, the Goat
Gemini, the Twins
Leo, the Lion

Libra, the Balance or Scales
Pisces, the Fishes
Sagittarius, the Archer
Scorpio, the Scorpion
Taurus, the Bull
Virgo, the Virgin

Twenty-nine North of the Zodiac

Andromeda, the Chained Lady
Aquila, the Eagle
Auriga, the Charioteer
Bootes, the Wagoner
Camelopardalis, the Camelopard
Canes Venatici, the Hunting Dog
Cassiopeia, the Lady in the Chair
Cepheus, the King
Coma Bereniceses, Berenice's Hair
Corona Borealis, the Northern Crown
Cygnus, the Swan
Delphinus, the Dolphin
Draco, the Dragon
Equuleus, the Colt
Hercules (Kneeling)

Lacerta, the Lizard
Leo Minor, the Lesser Lion
Lynx, the Lynx
Lyra, the Lyre or Harp
Ophiuchus, the Serpent Holder (sometimes
    called Serpentarius)
Pegasus, the Winged Horse
Perseus, the Hero (with Medusa's head)
Sagitta, the Arrow
Scutum, the Shield
Sepens, the Serpent
Triangulum, the Triangle
Ursa Major, the Greater Bear
Ursa Minor, the Lesser Bear
Vulpecula, the Fox (and the Goose)

Forty-nine South of the Zodiac

Antila (Pneumatica), the Air Pump
Apus (Avis Indica), Bird of Paradise (or of India)
Ara, the Altar
Argo Navis, the Ship (may include Carina, the Keel;
    Malus, the Mast; Puppis, the Stern; Vela, the Sails)
Caelum (Sculptorium), the (Engraver's) Tool
Canis Major, the Greater Dog
Canis Minor, the Lesser Dog
Carina, the Keel (Argo Navis)
Centaurus, the Centaur
Cetus, the Whale
Chamaeleon, the Chameleon
Circinus, the Pair of Compasses
Columba (Noachi), (Noah's) Dove
Corona Australis, the Southern Crown
Corvus, the Crow
Crater, the Bowl
Crux Australis, the Southern Cross
Darado (Xiphias), the Gilthead or Swordfish
Eridanus, the River Po

Fornax (Chemicae), the (Chemist's) Furnace or Retort
Grus, the Crane
Horologium, the Clock
Hydra, the Water-Serpent or Hydra (fem.)
Hydrus, the Water-Snake or Sea-Serpent (masc.)
Indus, the Indian
Lepus, the Hare
Lupus, the Wolf
Malus, the Mast (Argo Navis)
Mensa (Mons Mensae), the Table Mountain
Microscorpium, the Microscope
Monoceros, the Unicorn
Musca (Apis), the Fly or Bee
Norma, the Square or Rule
Octans, the Octant
Orion, the Hunter
Pavo, the Peacock
Phoenix, the Fabulous Bird
Pictor (Equuleus Pictorius), the Painter's Easel or Little Horse
Piscis Austrinus, the Southern Fish
Puppis, the Stern (Argo Navis)
Pyxis (nautica), the (Ship's) Compass
Reticulum, the Reticule or Net
Sculptor (Apparatus Sculptorius), the Sculptor's Tools
Sextans, the Sextant
Telescopium, the Telescope
Triangulum Australe, the Southern Triangle
Tucana, the Toucan
Vela, the Sails (Argo Navis)
Volcans (Piscius Volans), the Flying Fish

Additional Sources of Information

Organizations and Services

American Astronomical Society
211 FitzRandolph Road
Princeton, NJ 08540

American Horticultural Society
Mount Vernon, VA 22121

American Institute of Biological Scientists
1401 Wilson Boulevard
Arlington, VA 22209

American Meteorological Society
45 Beacon Street
Boston, MA 02108

American Museum of Natural History
Central Park West and 79th Street
New York, NY 10024

Appalachian Mountain Club
5 Joy Street
Boston, MA 02108

Bureau of Outdoor Recreation
Interior Building
18th and C Streets
Washington, DC 20240

Garden Club of America
598 Madison Avenue
New York, NY 10022

Men's Garden Clubs of America
5560 Merle Hay Road
Des Moines, IA 50323

National Oceanic and Atmospheric Administration
6010 Executive Boulevard
Rockville, MD 20852

National Parks and Conservation Association
1701 18th Street, NW
Washington, DC 20009

National Park Service
Interior Building
18th and C Streets
Washington, DC 20240

National Recreation and Park Association
1601 North Kent Street
Arlington, VA 22209

National Weather Service Public Affairs
8060 13th Street
Silver Springs, MD 20910

National Wildlife Federation
1412 16th Street, NW
Washington, DC 20036

Sierra Club
530 Bush Street
San Francisco, CA 94108

U.S. Department of Interior
Interior Building
18th and C Streets
Washington, DC 20240

U.S. Fish and Wildlife Service
Interior Building
18th and C Streets
Washington, DC 20240

The Wilderness Society
1901 Pennsylvania Avenue, NW
Washington, DC 20006

Books

Alden, Peter. *Peterson's First Guide to Mammals*. Houghton-Mifflin, 1987.

Asimov, Isaac. *The Universe: From Flat Earth to Quasars*. Avon, 1976.

Audubon Society and Little, Elbert L., Jr. *Audubon Field Guide to North American Trees*. Knopf, 1980.

Berry, Richard. *Discover the Stars: Star Watching Using the Naked Eye, Binoculars or a Telescope*. Crown, 1987.

Encyclopedia of Astronomy. McGraw-Hill, 1983.

Faust, Joan Lee, ed. *The New York Times Garden Book*. Ballantine, 1977.

Hardy, Ralph, et al. *The Weather Book*. Little, Brown, 1982.

Muirden, James. *The Amateur Astronomer's Handbook*, 3rd ed. Harper & Row, 1982.

Peterson, Roger T. *Peterson's First Guide to Birds*. Houghton-Mifflin, 1986.

Peterson, Roger T. *Peterson's First Guide to Wildflowers*. Houghton-Mifflin, 1986.

Rand McNally Cosmopolitan World Atlas, rev. ed. Rand McNally, 1987.

Rand McNally Road Atlas and Vacation Guide. Rand McNally, 1987.

Weather and Forecasting. Macmillan Field Guide Series, 1987.

Woodall's North American Campground Directory. Woodall, 1988.

Wyman, Donald. *The Gardening Encyclopedia*. Macmillan, 1987.

22

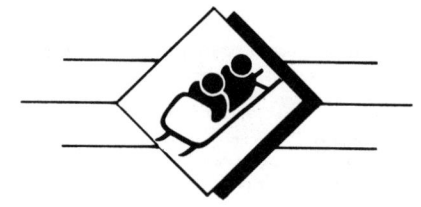

Sports and Games

Baseball

Baseball, named for the three bases and home plate that are parts of the playing field, has nine players on each side. The offensive team sends to home plate one batter at a time, who with a wooden or metal bat attempts to hit a small cowhide-covered ball thrown from the pitcher to the catcher, two members of the defensive team. The defensive team also consists of four infielders and three outfielders. If the batter hits the ball on the ground, he must run toward first base; he is out if a defensive player throws the ball to a teammate standing on first base before the runner reaches the base. The batter is also out if the ball he hits is caught by a defensive player before it hits the ground, of if the batter fails in three attempts to strike the pitched ball or fails to hit three pitches determined by the umpire to be strikes. This last situation is called a strikeout. Outs may also be made by tagging a baserunner with the ball when the runner is between bases, or by stepping on second base, third base, or homeplate while holding the ball if the runner is forced to move to that base because the batter or another baserunner is moving to occupy the preceding base. The offensive team attempts to score runs by causing offensive baserunners to go around all four bases and cross home plate safely. This can be done by accumulating hits, balls hit between the two foul lines that go uncaught, allowing a batter to safely reach first base (a single), second base (a double), or third base (a triple), thus driving runners ahead of him to circle the bases. Batters can also reach base and move the runners ahead up a base by obtaining a walk, four pitches determined by the umpire not to be strikes that the batter does not swing at. Runs also can be scored with a home run, whereby a batter hits the ball over the outfield fence or far enough that he can circle the bases. The game is divided into nine innings, with three outs for each team in each inning. The batting, or offensive, team takes the field (defensive positions) after making three outs, when the opponents become batters. At the end of nine innings, the team that has accumulated the most runs is the winner.

BASEBALL FIELD
(1) Pitcher; (2) catcher; (3) first baseman; (4) second baseman; (5) third baseman; (6) shortstop; (7) left fielder; (8) center fielder; (9) right fielder.

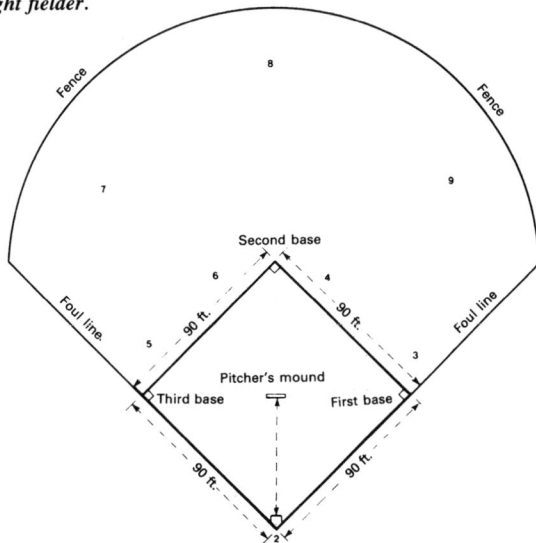

U.S. and Canadian Major League Teams

American League

Eastern Division	Western Division
Baltimore Orioles	California Angels
Boston Red Sox	Chicago White Sox
Cleveland Indians	Kansas City Royals
Detroit Tigers	Minnesota Twins
Milwaukee Brewers	Oakland Athletics
New York Yankees	Seattle Mariners
Toronto Blue Jays	Texas Rangers

National League

Eastern Division	Western Division
Chicago Cubs	Atlanta Braves
Montreal Expos	Cincinnati Reds
New York Mets	Houston Astros
Philadelphia Phillies	Los Angeles Dodgers
Pittsburgh Pirates	San Diego Padres
St. Louis Cardinals	San Francisco Giants

World Series

Every year since 1903 (with the exception of 1904), the winners of major league baseball's American League pennant have played the winners of the National League pennant in the World Series. This has been a best-of-seven-game series since 1905; the first team to win four games becomes champion. The results since 1903 follow.

	Winner	League	Loser	League	Games
1903	Boston Red Sox	AL	Pittsburgh Pirates	NL	5–3
1904	No series				
1905	New York Giants	NL	Philadelphia Athletics	AL	4–1
1906	Chicago White Sox	AL	Chicago Cubs	NL	4–2
1907	Chicago Cubs	NL	Detroit Tigers	AL	4–0
1908	Chicago Cubs	NL	Detroit Tigers	AL	4–1
1909	Pittsburgh Pirates	NL	Detroit Tigers	AL	4–3
1910	Philadelphia Athletics	AL	Chicago Cubs	NL	4–1
1911	Philadelphia Athletics	AL	New York Giants	NL	4–2
1912	Boston Red Sox	AL	New York Giants	NL	4–3
1913	Philadelphia Athletics	AL	New York Giants	NL	4–1
1914	Boston Braves	NL	Philadelphia Athletics	AL	4–0
1915	Boston Red Sox	AL	Philadelphia Phillies	NL	4–1
1916	Boston Red Sox	AL	Brooklyn Dodgers	NL	4–1
1917	Chicago White Sox	AL	New York Giants	NL	4–2
1918	Boston Red Sox	AL	Chicago Cubs	NL	4–2
1919	Cincinnati Reds	NL	Chicago White Sox	AL	5–3
1920	Cleveland Indians	AL	Brooklyn Dodgers	NL	5–2
1921	New York Giants	NL	New York Yankees	AL	5–3

	Winner	League	Loser	League	Games
1922	New York Giants	NL	New York Yankees	AL	4–0
1923	New York Yankees	AL	New York Giants	NL	4–2
1924	Washington Senators	AL	New York Giants	NL	4–3
1925	Pittsburgh Pirates	NL	Washington Senators	AL	4–3
1926	St. Louis Cardinals	NL	New York Yankees	AL	4–3
1927	New York Yankees	AL	Pittsburgh Pirates	NL	4–0
1928	New York Yankees	AL	St Louis Cardinals	NL	4–0
1929	Philadelphia Athletics	AL	Chicago Cubs	NL	4–1
1930	Philadelphia Athletics	AL	St. Louis Cardinals	NL	4–2
1931	St. Louis Cardinals	NL	Philadelphia Athletics	AL	4–3
1932	New York Yankees	AL	Chicago Cubs	NL	4–0
1933	New York Giants	NL	Washington Senators	AL	4–1
1934	St. Louis Cardinals	NL	Detroit Tigers	AL	4–3
1935	Detroit Tigers	AL	Chicago Cubs	NL	4–2
1936	New York Yankees	AL	New York Giants	NL	4–2
1937	New York Yankees	AL	New York Giants	NL	4–1
1938	New York Yankees	AL	Chicago Cubs	NL	4–0
1939	New York Yankees	AL	Cincinnati Reds	NL	4–0
1940	Cincinnati Reds	NL	Detroit Tigers	AL	4–3
1941	New York Yankees	AL	Brooklyn Dodgers	NL	4–1
1942	St. Louis Cardinals	NL	New York Yankees	AL	4–1
1943	New York Yankees	AL	St. Louis Cardinals	NL	4–1
1944	St. Louis Cardinals	NL	St. Louis Browns	AL	4–2
1945	Detroit Tigers	AL	Chicago Cubs	NL	4–3
1946	St. Louis Cardinals	NL	Boston Red Sox	AL	4–3
1947	New York Yankees	AL	Brooklyn Dodgers	NL	4–3
1948	Cleveland Indians	AL	Boston Braves	NL	4–2
1949	New York Yankees	AL	Brooklyn Dodgers	NL	4–1
1950	New York Yankees	AL	Philadelphia Phillies	NL	4–0
1951	New York Yankees	AL	New York Giants	NL	4–2
1952	New York Yankees	AL	Brooklyn Dodgers	NL	4–3
1953	New York Yankees	AL	Brooklyn Dodgers	NL	4–2
1954	New York Giants	NL	Cleveland Indians	AL	4–0
1955	Brooklyn Dodgers	NL	New York Yankees	AL	4–3
1956	New York Yankees	AL	Brooklyn Dodgers	NL	4–3
1957	Milwaukee Braves	NL	New York Yankees	AL	4–3
1958	New York Yankees	AL	Milwaukee Braves	NL	4–3
1959	Los Angeles Dodgers	NL	Chicago White Sox	AL	4–2
1960	Pittsburgh Pirates	NL	New York Yankees	AL	4–3
1961	New York Yankees	AL	Cincinnati Reds	NL	4–1
1962	New York Yankees	AL	San Francisco Giants	NL	4–3
1963	Los Angeles Dodgers	NL	New York Yankees	AL	4–0
1964	St. Louis Cardinals	NL	New York Yankees	AL	4–3
1965	Los Angeles Dodgers	NL	Minnesota Twins	AL	4–3
1966	Baltimore Orioles	AL	Los Angeles Dodgers	NL	4–0
1967	St. Louis Cardinals	NL	Boston Red Sox	AL	4–3
1968	Detroit Tigers	AL	St. Louis Cardinals	NL	4–3
1969	New York Mets	NL	Baltimore Orioles	AL	4–1
1970	Baltimore Orioles	AL	Cincinnati Reds	NL	4–1
1971	Pittsburgh Pirates	NL	Baltimore Orioles	AL	4–3
1972	Oakland Athletics	AL	Cincinnati Reds	NL	4–3
1973	Oakland Athletics	AL	New York Mets	NL	4–3
1974	Oakland Athletics	AL	Los Angeles Dodgers	NL	4–1

	Winner	*League*	Loser	*League*	*Games*
1975	Cincinnati Reds	NL	Boston Red Sox	AL	4–3
1976	Cincinnati Reds	NL	New York Yankees	AL	4–0
1977	New York Yankees	AL	Los Angeles Dodgers	NL	4–2
1978	New York Yankees	AL	Los Angeles Dodgers	NL	4–2
1979	Pittsburgh Pirates	NL	Baltimore Orioles	AL	4–3
1980	Philadelphia Phillies	NL	Kansas City Royals	AL	4–2
1981	Los Angeles Dodgers	NL	New York Yankees	AL	4–2
1982	St. Louis Cardinals	NL	Milwaukee Brewers	AL	4–3
1983	Baltimore Orioles	AL	Philadelphia Phillies	NL	4–1
1984	Detroit Tigers	AL	San Diego Padres	NL	4–1
1985	Kansas City Royals	AL	St. Louis Cardinals	NL	4–3
1986	New York Mets	NL	Boston Red Sox	AL	4–3
1987	Minnesota Twins	AL	St. Louis Cardinals	NL	4–3
1988	Los Angeles Dodgers	NL	Oakland Athletics	AL	4–1

Basketball

Basketball usually is played indoors on a rectangular wooden court by two teams, each with five players. At both ends of the court are suspended two goals, or baskets, consisting of a circular metal rim 10 feet above the floor attached to a square backboard made of wood, plastic, or fiberglass. A cord net is hung below the rim. The object is to shoot the ball so that it goes through the basket from above and to prevent your opponents from doing the same. Basketball uses a large rubber ball covered with leather.

Play begins with a jump ball. The official throws the ball upward at the center circle between two opposing players. The two players try to tip or slap the ball to a teammate and thus gain possession of the ball. Each team defends one goal. There is an offensive and defensive half of the court for each team, divided by the mid-court line. The ball can be advanced down the court by passing to a teammate, dribbling (bouncing the ball while walking or running), or shooting the ball at the basket. Running or walking while holding the ball is not permitted. If a shot goes in the basket, two points are awarded to the shooting team. If a shot is missed (usually hitting the rim or backboard), a defensive player may rebound the ball (catch it as it bounces away from the basket). He then may begin to advance the ball to the other end of the court in preparation for a shot by his team. An offensive player may also rebound a missed shot and shoot again. A shot made from beyond the three-point line (23 feet 9 inches from the rim) scores three points instead of the usual two.

Holding, pushing, grabbing, and similar types of body contact are not permitted; these are called fouls. They may result in a foul shot or free throw, an unimpeded shot taken by the offended player from a line on the court 15 feet from the basket. A successful free throw scores one point.

Professional basketball games are divided into four 12-minute quarters; the team with more points at the end of that time wins the game.

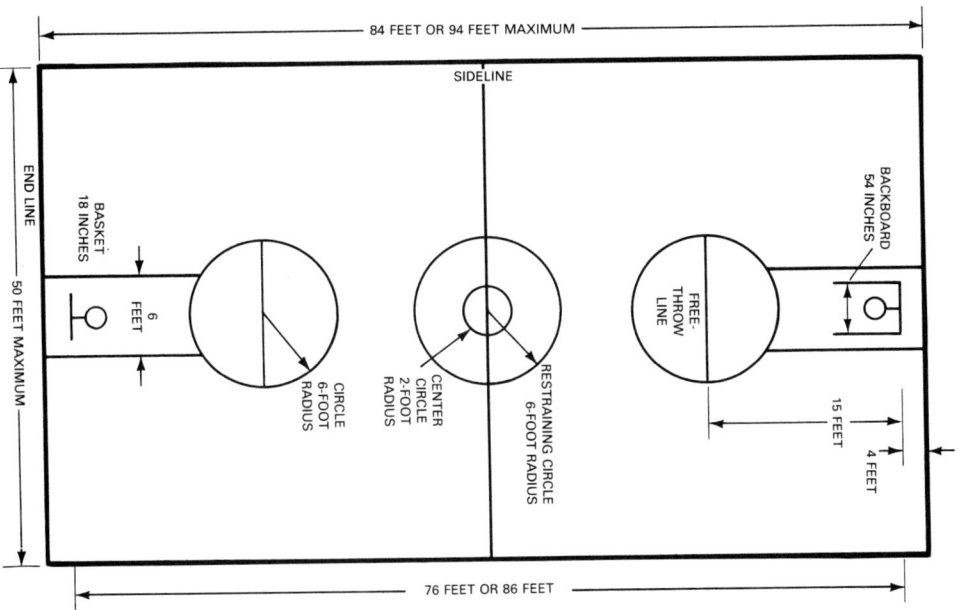

National Basketball Association (NBA)

Eastern Conference

Atlantic Division

Boston Celtics
Charlotte Hornets
New Jersey Nets
New York Knickerbockers
Philadelphia 76ers
Washington Bullets

Central Division

Atlanta Hawks
Chicago Bulls
Cleveland Cavaliers
Detroit Pistons
Indiana Pacers
Milwaukee Bucks

Western Conference

Midwest Division

Dallas Mavericks
Denver Nuggets
Houston Rockets
Miami Heat
San Antonio Spurs
Utah Jazz

Pacific Division

Golden State Warriors
Los Angeles Clippers
Los Angeles Lakers
Phoenix Suns
Portland Trailblazers
Sacramento Kings
Seattle Supersonics

National Basketball Association Champions

Each year the Eastern conference champions meet the Western Conference champions in a seven-game series for the NBA championship. The playoffs and the championship series, played in the spring, mark the end of the basketball season that started the previous winter.

Year	Winners	Conference	Losers	Conference
1947	Philadelphia Warriors	E	Chicago Stags	W
1948	Baltimore Bullets	W	Philadelphia Warriors	E
1949	Minneapolis Lakers	W	Washington Capitols	E
1950	Minneapolis Lakers	W	Syracuse Nationals	E
1951	Rochester Royals	W	New York Knickerbockers	E
1952	Minneapolis Lakers	W	New York Knickerbockers	E
1953	Minneapolis Lakers	W	New York Knickerbockers	E
1954	Mineapolis Lakers	W	Syracuse Nationals	E
1955	Syracuse Nationals	E	Fort Wayne Pistons	W
1956	Philadelphia Warriors	E	Fort Wayne Pistons	W
1957	Boston Celtics	E	St. Louis Hawks	W
1958	St. Louis Hawks	W	Boston Celtics	E
1959	Boston Celtics	E	Minneapolis Lakers	W
1960	Boston Celtics	E	St. Louis Hawks	W
1961	Boston Celtics	E	St. Louis Hawks	W
1962	Boston Celtics	E	Los Angeles Lakers	W
1963	Boston Celtics	E	Los Angeles Lakers	W
1964	Boston Celtics	E	San Francisco Warriors	W
1965	Boston Celtics	E	Los Angeles Lakers	W
1966	Boston Celtics	E	Los Angeles Lakers	W
1967	Philadelphia 76ers	E	San Francisco Warriors	W
1968	Boston Celtics	E	Los Angeles Lakers	W
1969	Boston Celtics	E	Los Angeles Lakers	W
1970	New York Knickerbockers	E	Los Angeles Lakers	W
1971	Milwaukee Bucks	W	Baltimore Bullets	E
1972	Los Angeles Lakers	W	New York Knickerbockers	E
1973	New York Knickerbockers	E	Los Angeles Lakers	W
1974	Boston Celtics	E	Milwaukee Bucks	W
1975	Golden State Warriors	W	Washington Bullets	E
1976	Boston Celtics	E	Phoenix Suns	W
1977	Portland Trail Blazers	W	Philadelphia 76ers	E
1978	Washington Bullets	E	Seattle Supersonics	W
1979	Seattle Supersonics	W	Washington Bullets	E
1980	Los Angeles Lakers	W	Philadelphia 76ers	E
1981	Boston Celtics	E	Houston Rockets	W
1982	Los Angeles Lakers	W	Philadelphia 76ers	E
1983	Philadelphia 76ers	E	Los Angeles Lakers	W
1984	Boston Celtics	E	Los Angeles Lakers	W
1985	Los Angeles Lakers	W	Boston Celtics	E
1986	Boston Celtics	E	Houston Rockets	W
1987	Los Angeles Lakers	W	Boston Celtics	E
1988	Los Angeles Lakers	W	Detroit Pistons	E
1989	Detroit Pistons	E	Los Angeles Lakers	W

Bowling

Bowling, or tenpins, is an indoor sport in which a player attempts to knock down ten wooden pins that are arranged in a triangular formation. This is accomplished by rolling a ball down a wooden lane, or alley. The ball, which usually weighs about 16 pounds, is fitted with three holes for thumb and finger grips. Each game is divided into ten frames, and the bowler is allowed a maximum of two rolls per frame, except for the last frame, where he is allowed three. If a player knocks down all ten pins with one roll, it is called a strike; the second roll of the frame is not used, except for the tenth frame, where three strikes are possible. If a player knocks down all ten pins using both rolls of the frame, it is called a spare. The number of pins knocked down by the end of the game determines the score, with spares scoring 10 plus the number of pins knocked down on the next roll and strikes scoring 10 plus the number of pins knocked down on the next two rolls. A perfect game of 12 consecutive strikes scores 300.

BOWLING ALLEY

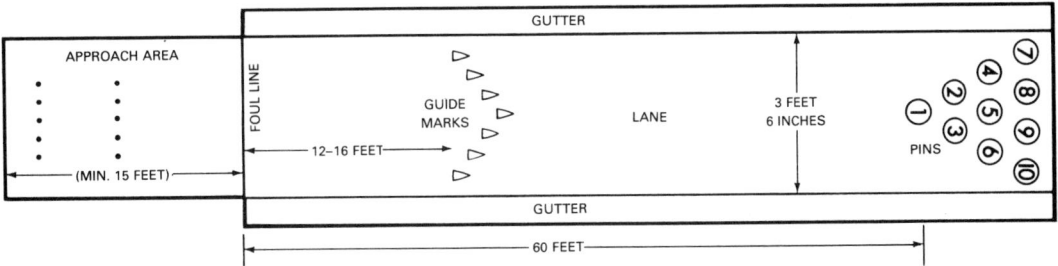

Football

American football has 11 players on each team and is played on a large rectangular field. At each end of the field is an end zone, where the H-shaped goal posts are placed. The object is to gain possession of an inflated leather or pigskin ball and move it across the opponents' goal line by running or passing, thus scoring a touchdown, which is worth six points. Passing the ball is usually done by the quarterback. Points also are scored by kicking the ball through the goalposts. This opportunity is given automatically after a touchdown; the point is called a point after touchdown, or extra point. A field goal scores three points. The defensive team can score by downing an offensive player in his own end zone. This is called a safety and scores two points.

The offensive team must gain 10 yards in four tries, called downs, or give up possession of the ball. If 10 or more yards are gained, the offense has four more downs to advance the ball. If on the fourth down (or, rarely, before) it seems unlikely that the 10-yard minimum will be reached, the offense has the option of kicking the ball to the opponents. This is called a punt, and the defensive team, after catching the ball, goes on offense. The defensive team may also gain possession of the ball, and thus become the offense, by catching a ball passed by the quarterback and intended for a teammate (interception), or by recovering the ball after it has been dropped by an offensive player (fumble). The defense hinders the attempts of the offense to gain yardage by tackling the ball carrier and pulling him to the ground. Because blocking and tackling can be very rough, football players wear protective helmets and substantial padding.

The game is divided into four 15-minute periods; the team with the most points after the end of that time is the winner.

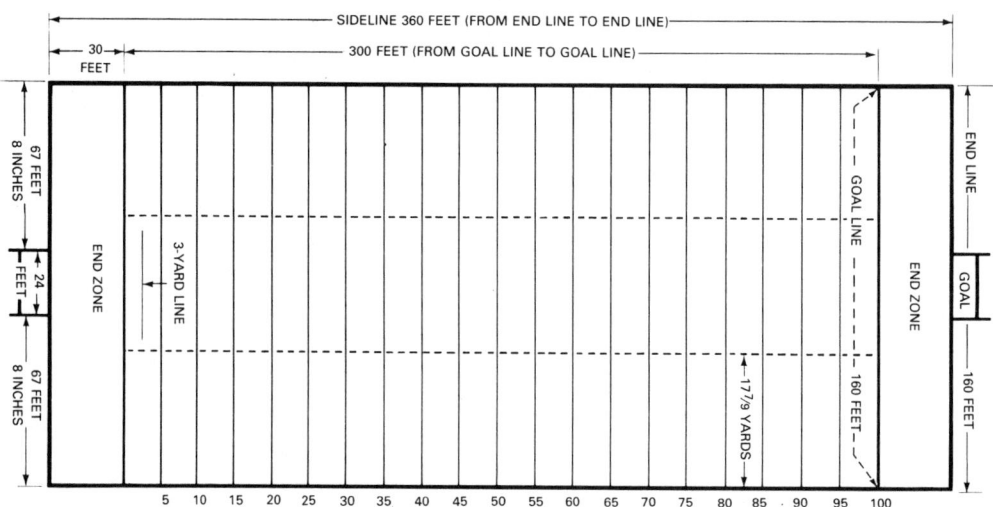

National Football League (NFL)

National Conference

Eastern Division

Dallas Cowboys
New York Giants
Philadelphia Eagles
Phoenix Cardinals
Washington Redskins

Central Division

Chicago Bears
Detroit Lions
Green Bay Packers
Minnesota Vikings
Tampa Bay Buccaneers

Western Division

Atlanta Falcons
New Orleans Saints
Los Angeles Rams
San Francisco 49ers

American Conference

Eastern Division

Buffalo Bills
Indianapolis Colts
Miami Dolphins
New England Patriots
New York Jets

Central Division

Cincinnati Bengals
Cleveland Browns
Houston Oilers
Pittsburgh Steelers

Western Division

Denver Broncos
Kansas City Chiefs
Los Angeles Raiders
San Diego Chargers
Seattle Seahawks

The Super Bowl

The Super Bowl, played in January, marks the end of the professional football season that began the previous fall. The first four Super Bowls were played between the champions of the National Football League and those of the American Football League. The two leagues then merged; the game has since been played between the National Football Conference champions and the American Football Conference champions. The winners and losers follow.

	Year	Winners	League	Losers	League	Score
I	1967	Green Bay Packers	NFL	Kansas City Chiefs	AFL	35–10
II	1968	Green Bay Packers	NFL	Oakland Raiders	AFL	33–14
III	1969	New York Jets	AFL	Baltimore Colts	NFL	16–7
IV	1970	Kansas City Chiefs	AFL	Minnesota Vikings	NFL	23–7
V	1971	Baltimore Colts	AFC	Dallas Cowboys	NFC	16–13
VI	1972	Dallas Cowboys	NFC	Miami Dolphins	AFC	24–3
VII	1973	Miami Dolphins	AFC	Washington Redskins	NFC	14–7
VIII	1974	Miami Dolphins	AFC	Minnesota Vikings	NFC	24–7
IX	1975	Pittsburgh Steelers	AFC	Minnesota Vikings	NFC	16–6
X	1976	Pittsburgh Steelers	AFC	Dallas Cowboys	NFC	21–17
XI	1977	Oakland Raiders	AFC	Minnesota Vikings	NFC	32–14
XII	1978	Dallas Cowboys	NFC	Denver Broncos	AFC	27–10
XIII	1979	Pittsburgh Steelers	AFC	Dallas Cowboys	NFC	35–31
XIV	1980	Pittsburgh Steelers	AFC	Los Angeles Rams	NFC	31–19
XV	1981	Oakland Raiders	AFC	Philadelphia Eagles	NFC	27–10
XVI	1982	San Francisco 49ers	NFC	Cincinnati Bengals	AFC	26–21
XVII	1983	Washington Redskins	NFC	Miami Dolphins	AFC	27–17
XVIII	1984	Los Angeles Raiders	AFC	Washington Redskins	NFC	38–9
XIX	1985	San Francisco 49ers	NFC	Miami Dolphins	AFC	38–16
XX	1986	Chicago Bears	NFC	New England Patriots	AFC	46–10
XXI	1987	New York Giants	NFC	Denver Broncos	AFC	39–20
XXII	1988	Washington Redskins	NFC	Denver Broncos	AFC	42–10
XXIII	1989	San Francisco 49ers	NFC	Cincinnati Bengals	AFC	20–16

Golf

Golf is an outdoor game in which players hit a small hard ball with specially designed clubs that consist of a metal shaft and a wooden or metal club head. The object is to strike the ball with the club so that the ball goes into a cup that is sunk in the ground and marked with a flag. A standard golf course is divided into 18 holes, each with a tee, where the initial stroke is made; a grass fairway; and a green, a smooth grass surface where the cup is located. Each player attempts to reach the green and hit the ball into the cup using as few strokes as possible. Obstacles—such as water, tall grass called rough, or traps filled with sand—may be found near the green or fairway. As many as 14 different types of clubs may be used depending on the length of shot required or the terrain. The distance from tee to cup varies greatly, but generally it is from 100 to 600 yards. The length and difficulty of the hole determine the par, the number of strokes that a good golfer would need to put the ball into the cup. After 18 holes, the player with the lowest number of strokes is the winner of that round. Golf tournaments are typically won by the player with the best (lowest) cumulative score after four rounds.

The Masters

Four major golf tournaments carry the most important titles in professional golf. They are the Masters, the Professional Golfer's Association Tournament (PGA), the U.S. Open, and the British Open. The Masters, played at the Augusta National Golf Club in Augusta, Georgia, is the most sought-after title in professional golf. The winners of the Masters Tournament follow.

Year	Winner	Score	Year	Winner	Score
1934	Horton Smith	284	1962	Arnold Palmer*	280
1935	Gene Sarazen*	282	1963	Jack Nicklaus	286
1936	Horton Smith	285	1964	Arnold Palmer	276
1937	Byron Nelson	283	1965	Jack Nicklaus	271
1938	Henry Picard	285	1966	Jack Nicklaus*	288
1939	Ralph Guldahl	279	1967	Gay Brewer	280
1940	Jimmy Demaret	280	1968	Bob Goalby	277
1941	Craig Wood	280	1969	George Archer	281
1942	Byron Nelson*	280	1970	Billy Casper*	279
1943	No tournament held		1971	Charles Coody	279
1944	No tournament held		1972	Jack Nicklaus	286
1945	No tournament held		1973	Tommy Aaron	283
1946	Herman Keiser	282	1974	Gary Player	278
1947	Jimmy Demaret	281	1975	Jack Nicklaus	276
1948	Claude Harmon	279	1976	Ray Floyd	271
1949	Sam Snead	282	1977	Tom Watson	276
1950	Jimmy Demaret	283	1978	Gary Player	277
1951	Ben Hogan	280	1979	Fuzzy Zoeller*	280
1952	Sam Snead	286	1980	Severiano Ballesteros	275
1953	Ben Hogan	274	1981	Tom Watson	280
1954	Sam Snead*	289	1982	Craig Stadler*	284
1955	Cary Middlecoff	279	1983	Severiano Ballesteros	280
1956	Jack Burke	289	1984	Ben Crenshaw	277
1957	Doug Ford	283	1985	Bernhard Langer	282
1958	Arnold Palmer	284	1986	Jack Nicklaus	279
1959	Art Wall, Jr.	284	1987	Larry Mize*	285
1960	Arnold Palmer	282	1988	Sandy Lyle	281
1961	Gary Player	280	1989	Nick Faldo	283

* Won in a playoff.

Ice Hockey

Ice hockey is played on a rectangular rink that is surrounded by a wooden wall. At each end of the ice is placed a netted goal. Six skaters make up each team, including the goalie, whose job it is to protect the goal. By using wooden sticks, the players attempt to propel a rubber disc, called the puck, across the ice and into the opponents' goal. This scores a point.

The game begins with a faceoff in the center of the ice. The official drops the puck between two players, one from each team. Both teams try to gain control of the puck and to advance it toward the opponent's goal by skating with the puck, passing it to a teammate, or shooting it directly toward the goal. The defense tries to hinder this advance by deflecting or intercepting a pass or shot or by bodychecking an opposing player. This is physically blocking an opponent with a hip or shoulder.

There is a wide range of penalties for which the offending player may be removed from the ice for a stated number of minutes. During this time, the penalized team plays with one fewer player than its opponents, giving a power play to the fully manned team. Penalty times range from two minutes for minor violations to ejection from the game for the most serious fouls. Holding on to the puck or to an opponent, checking from behind, tripping, using the stick illegally, and fighting all normally result in penalties. The offensive player in control of the puck must cross his own blue line before any of his teammates. In moving down the ice and attacking the opponent's end, if an attacking player without the puck crosses that line first, he is offside. This is a violation, leading to a resetting of the puck and a new faceoff.

Hockey is a rough sport and players wear hip pads, shoulder pads, padded gloves, and helmets. The game consists of three 20-minute periods with rest periods in between. The team with more goals at the end of that time wins the game.

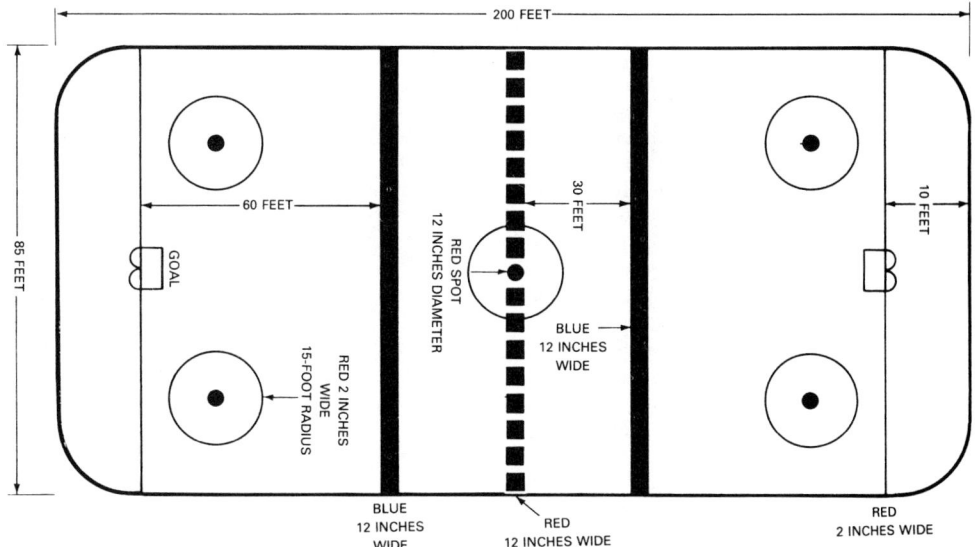

National Hockey League

Wales Conference

Adams Division

Boston Bruins
Buffalo Sabres
Hartford Whalers
Montreal Canadiens
Quebec Nordiques

Patrick Division

New Jersey Devils
New York Islanders
New York Rangers
Philadelphia Flyers
Pittsburgh Penguins
Washington Capitals

Campbell Conference

Norris Division

Chicago Black Hawks
Detroit Red Wings
Minnesota North Stars
St. Louis Blues
Toronto Maple Leafs

Smythe Division

Calgary Flames
Edmonton Oilers
Los Angeles Kings
Vancouver Canucks
Winnipeg Jets

The Stanley Cup

The Stanley Cup is awarded to the championship team following a best-of-seven-games series between professional ice hockey conference champions. Until 1910, amateurs and professionals were permitted to play on the same teams, but since 1910, the cup has been presented to entirely professional teams and since 1917 to the champions of the National Hockey League (NHL). Stanley Cup winners follow.

1894	Montreal A.A.A.	1925	Victoria Cougars	1957	Montreal Canadiens
1895	Montreal Victorias	1926	Montreal Maroons	1958	Montreal Canadiens
1896	Winnipeg Victorias	1927	Ottawa Senators	1959	Montreal Canadiens
1897	Montreal Victorias	1928	New York Rangers	1960	Montreal Canadiens
1898	Montreal Victorias	1929	Boston Bruins	1961	Chicago Black Hawks
1899	Montreal Victorias	1930	Montreal Canadiens	1962	Toronto Maple Leafs
1900	Montreal Shamrocks	1931	Montreal Canadiens	1963	Toronto Maple Leafs
1901	Winnipeg Victorias	1932	Toronto Maple Leafs	1964	Toronto Maple Leafs
1902	Montreal A.A.A.	1933	New York Rangers	1965	Montreal Canadiens
1903	Ottawa Silver Seven	1934	Chicago Black Hawks	1966	Montreal Canadiens
1904	Ottawa Silver Seven	1935	Montreal Maroons	1967	Toronto Maple Leafs
1905	Ottawa Silver Seven	1936	Detroit Red Wings	1968	Montreal Canadiens
1906	Montreal Wanderers	1937	Detroit Red Wings	1969	Montreal Canadiens
1907	Kenora Thistles (Jan.)	1938	Chicago Black Hawks	1970	Boston Bruins
	Montreal Wanderers (March)	1939	Boston Bruins	1971	Montreal Canadiens
1908	Montreal Wanderers	1940	New York Rangers	1972	Boston Bruins
1909	Ottawa Senators	1941	Boston Bruins	1973	Montreal Canadiens
1910	Montreal Wanderers	1942	Toronto Maple Leafs	1974	Philadelphia Flyers
1911	Ottawa Senators	1943	Detroit Red Wings	1975	Philadelphia Flyers
1912	Quebec Bulldogs	1944	Montreal Canadiens	1976	Montreal Canadiens
1913	Quebec Bulldogs	1945	Toronto Maple Leafs	1977	Montreal Canadiens
1914	Toronto Ontarios	1946	Montreal Canadiens	1978	Montreal Canadiens
1915	Vancouver Millionaires	1947	Toronto Maple Leafs	1979	Montreal Canadiens
1916	Montreal Canadiens	1948	Toronto Maple Leafs	1980	New York Islanders
1917	Seattle Metropolitans	1949	Toronto Maple Leafs	1981	New York Islanders
1918	Toronto Arenas	1950	Detroit Red Wings	1982	New York Islanders
1919	Championship series unfinished	1951	Toronto Maple Leafs	1983	New York Islanders
1920	Ottawa Senators	1952	Detroit Red Wings	1984	Edmonton Oilers
1921	Ottawa Senators	1953	Montreal Canadiens	1985	Edmonton Oilers
1922	Toronto St. Patricks	1954	Detroit Red Wings	1986	Montreal Canadiens
1923	Ottawa Senators	1955	Detroit Red Wings	1987	Edmonton Oilers
1924	Montreal Canadiens	1956	Montreal Canadiens	1988	Edmonton Oilers

Tennis

Tennis is played either indoors or outdoors on a rectangular court, which may be grass, clay, or synthetic. A small felt-covered rubber ball is hit back and forth over a net with the use of wooden or metal rackets, which are fitted with strings made of lamb's gut, nylon, or synthetic material. The net, which is 3 feet above the court's surface at its midpoint, is stretched across the court. Tennis may be played either as singles, with one player on each side, or as doubles, with two players on each side. In doubles, the court is 9 feet wider than in singles, because of the addition of two doubles alleys.

To initiate play, the server stands behind the baseline and to the right of the center mark and hits the ball with the racket so that the ball lands in the diagonally opposite service court of the opponent. If this first serve does not land in this service area because it is hit too long or too wide, or hits the net, the server may try again with a second serve. If this second serve is not a legal serve, the receiver scores a point. At each point the serve alternates left to right, with the server always serving from behind the baseline to the diagonally opposite service court. The receiver attempts to return a legal serve by hitting the ball anywhere into the opponent's court, which includes the alleys in doubles. Play continues until one player (or one team, in doubles) fails to make a legal return. A point is then scored by the opponent.

Four points constitute a game, designated as 15, 30, 40, and game; a player must win each game by at least two points. Thus, if after six points in any game each player has scored three, the score is 40–40 (this is called deuce). One player must then score two consecutive points to win the game; this player has the advantage after winning the first of these two points. Having the advantage, if the player wins the second consecutive point, he or she wins the game; but if the opponent wins that point, the score goes back to 40–40, or deuce. Play then continues until one player wins the game by scoring two consecutive points.

Each player (or team, in doubles) alternates by serving one game and receiving the next. The first to win six games wins a set, provided the margin of victory is two games or more. Thus, if the score reaches six games to four, the set is over, but at six to five, play continues. If the score reaches six to six, a tiebreaker is usually employed. A match consists of the best two out of three sets in women's play and usually the best three out of five in men's play.

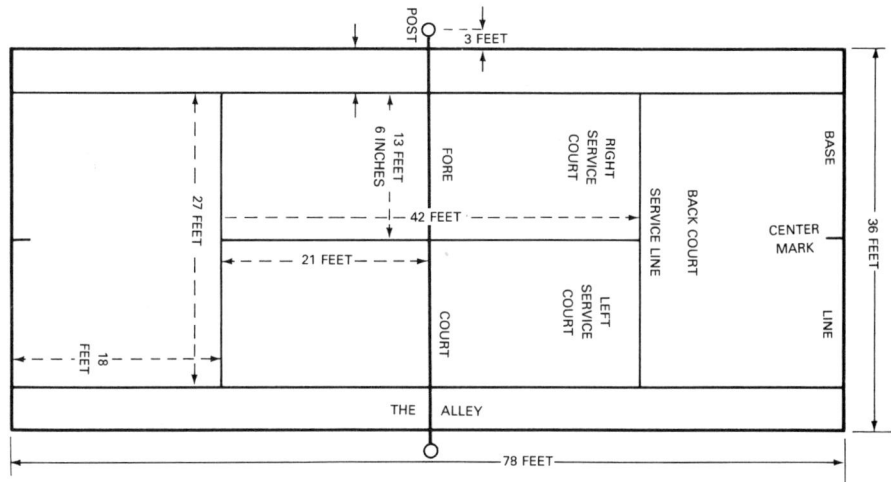

Wimbledon

There are four major championships in professional tennis that make up the Grand Slam: the French Open, the Australian Open, the U.S. Open, and the All-England Lawn Tennis Championships, better known as Wimbledon. Wimbledon is the oldest and most prestigious tournament of the four. The winners since 1877 follow.

Men's Singles Champions

1877	Spencer W. Gore	1915	No tournament held	1953	Vic Seixas
1878	P. F. Hadow	1916	No tournament held	1954	Jaroslav Drobny
1879	J. T. Hartley	1917	No tournament held	1955	Tony Trabert
1880	J. T. Hartley	1918	No tournament held	1956	Lew Hoad
1881	William Renshaw	1919	Gerald Patterson	1957	Lew Hoad
1882	William Renshaw	1920	Bill Tilden	1958	Ashley Cooper
1883	William Renshaw	1921	Bill Tilden	1959	Alex Olmedo
1884	William Renshaw	1922	Gerald Patterson	1960	Neale Fraser
1885	William Renshaw	1923	William Johnston	1961	Rod Laver
1886	William Renshaw	1924	Jean Borotra	1962	Rod Laver
1887	Herbert Lawford	1925	Jean Rene Lacoste	1963	Chuck McKinley
1888	Ernest Renshaw	1926	Jean Borotra	1964	Roy Emerson
1889	William Renshaw	1927	Henri Cochet	1965	Roy Emerson
1890	Willoughby Hamilton	1928	Jean Rene Lacoste	1966	Manuel Santana
1891	Wilfred Baddeley	1929	Henri Cochet	1967	John Newcombe
1892	Wilfred Baddeley	1930	Bill Tilden	1968	Rod Laver
1893	Joshua Pim	1931	Sidney Wood	1969	Rod Laver
1894	Joshua Pim	1932	Ellsworth Vines	1970	John Newcombe
1895	Wilfred Baddeley	1933	Jack Crawford	1971	John Newcombe
1896	Harold Mahoney	1934	Fred Perry	1972	Stan Smith
1897	Reginald Doherty	1935	Fred Perry	1973	Jan Kodes
1898	Reginald Doherty	1936	Fred Perry	1974	Jimmy Connors
1899	Reginald Doherty	1937	Donald Budge	1975	Arthur Ashe
1900	Reginald Doherty	1938	Donald Budge	1976	Bjorn Borg
1901	Arthur Gore	1939	Bobby Riggs	1977	Bjorn Borg
1902	H. Laurence Doherty	1940	No tournament held	1978	Bjorn Borg
1903	H. Laurence Doherty	1941	No tournament held	1979	Bjorn Borg
1904	H. Laurence Doherty	1942	No tournament held	1980	Bjorn Borg
1905	H. Laurence Doherty	1943	No tournament held	1981	John McEnroe
1906	H. Laurence Doherty	1944	No tournament held	1982	Jimmy Connors
1907	Norman Brookes	1945	No tournament held	1983	John McEnroe
1908	Arthur Gore	1946	Yvon Petra	1984	John McEnroe
1909	Arthur Gore	1947	Jack Kramer	1985	Boris Becker
1910	Anthony F. Wilding	1948	Bob Falkenburg	1986	Boris Becker
1911	Anthony F. Wilding	1949	Ted Schroeder	1987	Pat Cash
1912	Anthony F. Wilding	1950	Budge Patty	1988	Stefan Edberg
1913	Anthony F. Wilding	1951	Dick Savitt		
1914	Norman Brookes	1952	Frank Sedgman		

Women's Singles Champions

1884	Maud Watson	1888	Lottie Dod	1892	Lottie Dod
1885	Maud Watson	1889	Blanche Bingley Hillyard	1893	Lottie Dod
1886	Blanche Bingley	1890	L. Rice	1894	Blanche Bingley Hillyard
1887	Lottie Dod	1891	Lottie Dod	1895	Charlotte Cooper

1896	Charlotte Cooper	1927	Helen Wills	1958	Althea Gibson
1897	Blanche Bingley Hillyard	1928	Helen Wills	1959	Maria Bueno
1898	Charlotte Cooper	1929	Helen Wills	1960	Maria Bueno
1899	Blanche Bingley Hillyard	1930	Helen Wills Moody	1961	Angela Mortimer
1900	Blanche Bingley Hillyard	1931	Cilly Aussem	1962	Karen Susman
1901	Charlotte Cooper Sterry	1932	Helen Wills Moody	1963	Margaret Smith
1902	Muriel Robb	1933	Helen Wills Moody	1964	Maria Bueno
1903	Dorothea Douglass	1934	Dorothy Round	1965	Margaret Smith
1904	Dorothea Douglass	1935	Helen Wills Moody	1966	Billie Jean King
1905	May Sutton	1936	Helen Jacobs	1967	Billie Jean King
1906	Dorothea Douglass	1937	Dorothy Round	1968	Billie Jean King
1907	May Sutton	1938	Helen Wills Moody	1969	Ann Jones
1908	Charlotte Cooper Sterry	1939	Alice Marble	1970	Margaret Smith Court
1909	Dora Boothby	1940	No tournament held	1971	Evonne Goolagong
1910	Dorothea Douglass Chambers	1941	No tournament held	1972	Billie Jean King
1911	Dorothea Douglass Chambers	1942	No tournament held	1973	Billie Jean King
1912	Ethel Larcombe	1943	No tournament held	1974	Chris Evert
1913	Dorothea Douglass Chambers	1944	No tournament held	1975	Billie Jean King
1914	Dorothea Douglass Chambers	1945	No tournament held	1976	Chris Evert
1915	No tournament held	1946	Pauline Betz	1977	Virginia Wade
1916	No tournament held	1947	Margaret Osborne	1978	Martina Navratilova
1917	No tournament held	1948	A. Louise Brough	1979	Martina Navratilova
1918	No tournament held	1949	A. Louise Brough	1980	Evonne Goolagong
1919	Suzanne Lenglen	1950	A. Louise Brough	1981	Chris Evert Lloyd
1920	Suzanne Lenglen	1951	Doris Hart	1982	Martina Navratilova
1921	Suzanne Lenglen	1952	Maureen Connolly	1983	Martina Navratilova
1922	Suzanne Lenglen	1953	Maureen Connolly	1984	Martina Navratilova
1923	Suzanne Lenglen	1954	Maureen Connolly	1985	Martina Navratilova
1924	Kitty McKane	1955	A. Louise Brough	1986	Martina Navratilova
1925	Suzanne Lenglen	1956	Shirley Fry	1987	Martina Navratilova
1926	Kitty McKane Godfree	1957	Althea Gibson	1988	Steffi Graf

Volleyball

Volleyball is played either outdoors or indoors on a rectangular court, with six players to a side. An inflated ball is hit back and forth over a net; the players try to prevent the ball from hitting the court on their own side. The net's top is 8 feet above the floor (slightly lower in women's play). To initiate play the ball is served by hitting it with the hand or fist and thereby sending it over the net toward the opponent's court. After the serve, the ball may be hit with any part of the body. The ball may be hit a maximum of three times by each team, the third hit sending the ball over the net. Catching or holding the ball is not permitted.

If the receiving team allows the ball to hit the floor on its side, or hits the ball out of bounds, the serving team scores a point and serves again. If the serving team allows the ball to hit the floor, hits it out of bounds, or fails to make a legal serve, the serve is transferred to the opponents, but no point is scored. The first team to reach 15 points wins the game, provided the margin of victory is at least two points. In championship play, a match is won by winning three out of five games. (*See illustration of court on page 588.*)

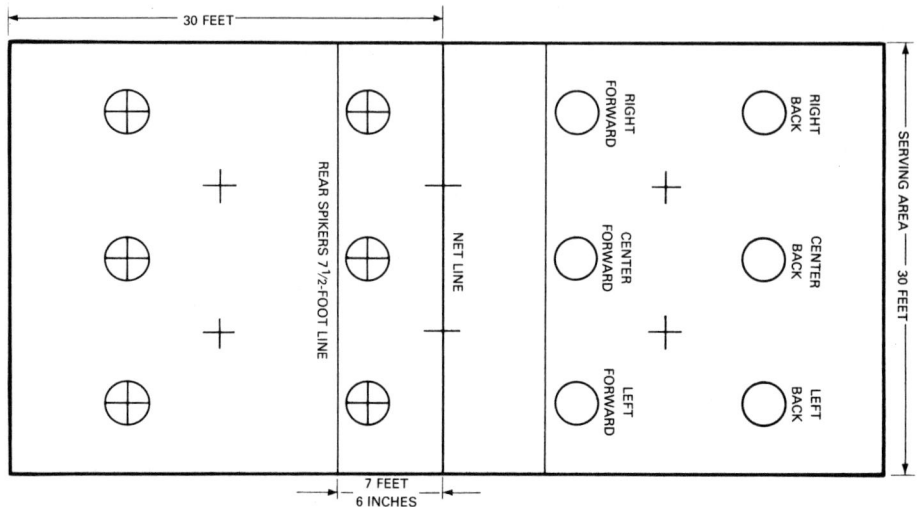

HORSE RACING

The Triple Crown

The best-known horse races in America are the Kentucky Derby, the Preakness, and the Belmont Stakes. These three races for three-year-olds make up horse racing's Triple Crown. Eleven horses have won all three events.

Year	Horse	Year	Horse
1919	Sir Barton	1946	Assault
1930	Gallant Fox	1948	Citation
1935	Omaha	1973	Secretariat
1937	War Admiral	1977	Seattle Slew
1941	Whirlaway	1978	Affirmed
1943	Count Fleet		

Winning Horses in the Kentucky Derby

(Held at Churchill Downs; 1¼ miles)

1875	Aristides	1887	Montrose	1899	Manuel
1876	Vagrant	1888	Macbeth II	1900	Lieutenant Gibson
1877	Baden Baden	1889	Spokane	1901	His Eminence
1878	Day Star	1890	Riley	1902	Alan-a-Dale
1879	Lord Murphy	1891	Kingman	1903	Judge Himes
1880	Fonso	1892	Azra	1904	Elwood
1881	Hindoo	1893	Lookout	1905	Agile
1882	Apollo	1894	Chant	1906	Sir Huon
1883	Leonatus	1895	Halma	1907	Pink Star
1884	Buchanan	1896	Ben Brush	1908	Stone Street
1885	Joe Cotton	1897	Typhoon H	1909	Wintergreen
1886	Ben Ali	1898	Plaudit	1910	Donau

1911	Meridian	1938	Lawrin	1965	Lucky Debonair
1912	Worth	1939	Johnstown	1966	Kauai King
1913	Donerail	1940	Gallahadion	1967	Proud Clarion
1914	Old Rosebud	1941	Whirlaway	1968	Forward Pass*
1915	Regret	1942	Shut Out	1969	Majestic Prince
1916	George Smith	1943	Count Fleet	1970	Dust Commander
1917	Omar Khayyam	1944	Pensive	1971	Canonero II
1918	Exterminator	1945	Hoop Jr.	1972	Riva Ridge
1919	Sir Barton	1946	Assault	1973	Secretariat
1920	Paul Jones	1947	Jet Pilot	1974	Cannonade
1921	Behave Yourself	1948	Citation	1975	Foolish Pleasure
1922	Morvich	1949	Ponder	1976	Bold Forges
1923	Zev	1950	Middleground	1977	Seattle Slew
1924	Black Gold	1951	Count Turf	1978	Affirmed
1925	Flying Ebony	1952	Hill Gail	1979	Spectacular Bid
1926	Bubbling Over	1953	Dark Star	1980	Genuine Risk
1927	Whiskery	1954	Determine	1981	Pleasant Colony
1928	Reigh Count	1955	Swaps	1982	Gato del Sol
1929	Clyde Van Dusen	1956	Needles	1983	Sunny's Halo
1930	Gallant Fox	1957	Iron Liege	1984	Swale
1931	Twenty Grand	1958	Tim Tam	1985	Spend a Buck
1932	Burgoo King	1959	Tomy Lee	1986	Ferdinand
1933	Brokers Tip	1960	Venetian Way	1987	Alysheba
1934	Cavalcade	1961	Carry Back	1988	Winning Colors
1935	Omaha	1962	Decidedly	1989	Sunday Silence
1936	Bold Venture	1963	Chateauguay		
1937	War Admiral	1964	Northern Dancer		

* In 1968, Dancer's Image finished first but was disqualified.

AUTO RACING

Indianapolis 500 Winners

1911	Ray Harroun	1938	Floyd Roberts	1965	Jim Clark
1912	Joe Dawson	1939	Wilbur Shaw	1966	Graham Hill
1913	Jules Goux	1940	Wilbur Shaw	1967	A. J. Foyt
1914	Rene Thomas	1941	Floyd Davis–Mauri Rose	1968	Bobby Unser
1915	Ralph DePalma	1942	No race held	1969	Mario Andretti
1916	Dario Resta	1943	No race held	1970	Al Unser
1917	No race held	1944	No race held	1971	Al Unser
1918	No race held	1945	No race held	1972	Mark Donohue
1919	Howard Wilcox	1946	George Robson	1973	Gordon Johncock
1920	Gaston Chevrolet	1947	Mauri Rose	1974	Johnny Rutherford
1921	Tommy Milton	1948	Mauri Rose	1975	Bobby Unser
1922	Jimmy Murphy	1949	Bill Holland	1976	Johnny Rutherford
1923	Tommy Milton	1950	Johnnie Parsons	1977	A. J. Foyt
1924	L. L. Corum-Joe Boyer	1951	Lee Wallard	1978	Al Unser
1925	Peter DePaolo	1952	Troy Ruttman	1979	Rick Mears
1926	Frank Lockhart	1953	Bill Vukovich	1980	Johnny Rutherford
1927	George Souders	1954	Bill Vukovich	1981	Bobby Unser
1928	Louis Meyer	1955	Bob Sweikert	1982	Gordon Johncock
1929	Ray Keech	1956	Pat Flaherty	1983	Tom Sneva
1930	Billy Arnold	1957	Sam Hanks	1984	Rick Mears
1931	Louis Schneider	1958	Jimmy Bryan	1985	Danny Sullivan
1932	Fred Frame	1959	Rodger Ward	1986	Bobby Rahal
1933	Louis Meyer	1960	Jim Rathmann	1987	Al Unser
1934	Bill Cummings	1961	A. J. Foyt	1988	Rick Mears
1935	Kelly Petillo	1962	Rodger Ward	1989	Emerson Fittipaldi
1936	Louis Meyer	1963	Parnelli Jones		
1937	Wilbur Shaw	1964	A. J. Foyt		

Olympic Games

Summer Games			*Winter Games*	
Year	*Location*		*Year*	*Location*
1896	Athens, Greece		1924	Chamonix, France
1900	Paris, France		1928	St. Moritz, Switzerland
1904	St. Louis, Missouri		1932	Lake Placid, New York
1908	London, England		1936	Garmisch-Partenkirchen, Germany
1912	Stockholm, Sweden		1948	St. Moritz, Switzerland
1920	Antwerp, Belgium		1952	Oslo, Norway
1924	Paris, France		1956	Cortina, Italy
1928	Amsterdam, The Netherlands		1960	Squaw Valley, California
1932	Los Angeles, California		1964	Innsbruck, Austria
1936	Berlin, Germany		1968	Grenoble, France
1948	London, England		1972	Sapporo, Japan
1952	Helsinki, Finland		1976	Innsbruck, Austria
1956	Melbourne, Australia		1980	Lake Placid, New York
1960	Rome, Italy		1984	Sarajevo, Yugoslavia
1964	Tokyo, Japan		1988	Calgary, Canada
1968	Mexico City, Mexico			
1972	Munich, West Germany			
1976	Montreal, Canada			
1980	Moscow, USSR			
1984	Los Angeles, California			
1988	Seoul, South Korea			

1988 Olympic Events

Summer Games

Men

Boxing
Canoeing
Judo
Soccer (team)
Water polo (team)
Weightlifting
Wrestling
    Freestyle
    Greco-Roman

Men's swimming

50 m, 100 m, 200 m, 400 m, 1500 m freestyle
100 m, 200 m backstroke
100 m, 200 m breast stroke
100 m, 200 m butterfly
200 m, 400 m individual medley
400 m, 800 m freestyle medley
400 m medley relay
Springboard dive
Platform dive

Men's track and field

100 m, 200 m, 400 m dash
800 m, 1500 m, 5000 m, 10,000 m run
Marathon
110 m, 400 m hurdles
3000 m steeplechase
20 km, 50 km walk
400 m relay (4 × 100)
1600 m relay (4 × 400)
High jump
Long jump
Triple jump
Pole vault
Shot put
Discus throw
Javelin throw
Hammer throw
Decathlon

Men and women

Archery
Basketball (team)
Cycling
Equestrian*
Fencing
Field hockey
Gymnastics
Handball (team)
Kayaking
Rowing
Shooting
Table tennis
Tennis
Volleyball (team)
Yachting

Women's swimming

50 m, 100 m, 200 m, 400 m, 800 m freestyle
100 m, 200 m backstroke
100 m, 200 m breast stroke
100 m, 200 m butterfly
200 m, 400 m individual medley
400 m freestyle relay
400 m medley relay
Springboard dive
Platform dive
Synchronized swimming

Women's track and field

100 m, 200 m, 400 m dash
800 m, 1500 m, 3000 m run
100 m, 400 m hurdles
400 m relay (4 × 100)
1600 m relay (4 × 400)
Marathon
High jump
Long jump
Shot put
Discus throw
Javelin throw
Heptathlon
Modern pentathlon

* In equestrian sports, men and women compete against one another.

Winter Games

Except for biathlon, bobsledding, and ice hockey, all winter sports at the 1984 and 1988 games were divided into two classes, one for men and the other for women. Biathlon, bobsledding, and ice hockey were played by men only. In paired figure skating and ice dancing, men and women performed together.

10 K biathlon
20 K biathlon
30 K biathlon relay
4-man bobsledding
2-man bobsledding
Figure skating
Ice dancing
Ice hockey
Luge
Alpine skiing
  Downhill
  Slalom
  Giant slalom
  Super giant slalom

Nordic skiing
  Men's cross country
    15 K, 30 K, 50 K
    40 K relay
    combined cross country and jumping
    ski jumping: 90 m, 70 m
  Women's cross country
    5 K, 10 K, 20 K
    20 K relay
Speed skating
  Men: 500 m, 100 m, 1500 m, 5 K, 10 K
  Women: 500 m, 100 m, 1500 m, 3 K, 5 K

Board Games

Backgammon

Backgammon is a board game played by two players, each with 15 markers, or stones, which at the beginning of the game are placed in a standard initial configuration (see diagram) on the board. The board is divided into two tables, each with 12 triangular spaces, or points. Each player rolls two dice to determine the number of points moved by the stones, with black moving around the board in one direction and white moving in the opposite direction. The numbers on each die can be combined to move one stone the total amount indicated, or each die's value can be applied separately to single stones. If "doubles" are thrown (i.e., two 6s), the player can move twice as many points as are shown on the dice—in this case, four stones can move six spaces each, one can move six spaces and one eighteen spaces, two can move 12 spaces each, or one stone can move 24 spaces. The object of the game is to be the first person to move his or her stones around the board and then off, called bearing off.

Any number of stones of the same color may stay on one point, but stones of the opposite color may not occupy the same point. A point occupied by two or more stones of the same color is said to be closed; it prevents the opponent from landing there. A point occupied by one marker (or none) is open. A single stone on any point is called a blot, and the opponent may land there with a hit. This sends the blot back to the beginning by placing it on the bar. It must enter the game again by rolling a number on one of the dice corresponding to an open point or to one occupied by stones of the same color before the owner may make another move.

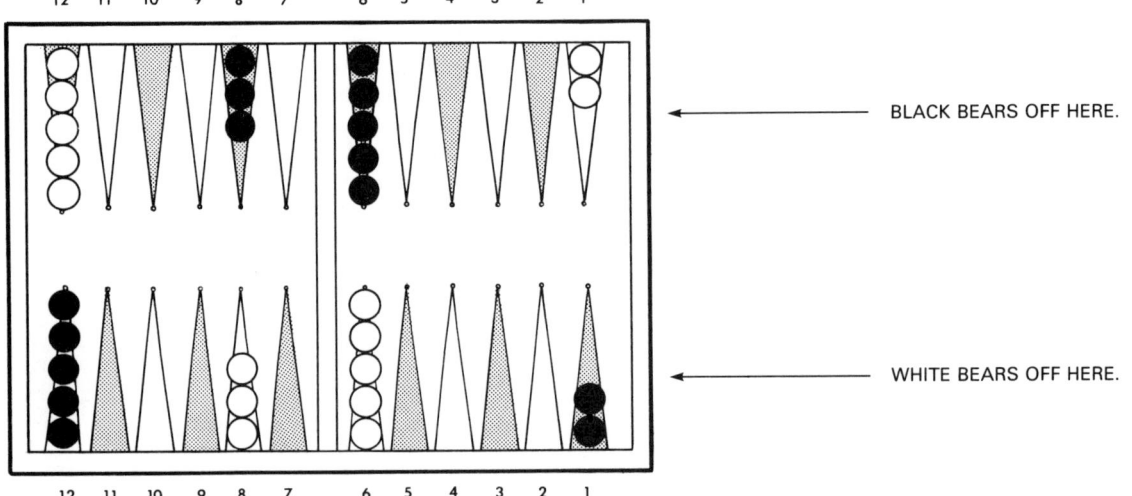

White moves counterclockwise from top to bottom.
Black moves clockwise from bottom to top.

Backgammon depends on the roll of the dice and is therefore partially a game of chance, but it can also involve complex strategy and tactics. The game may make use of the doubling cube, which is a die with a number on each face (2, 4, 8, 16, 32, 64). Using this cube, either player can at any point in the game double the stakes, whether they be points, as in tournament play, or money, as in the gambling version.

Checkers

Checkers is played by two players on a board with 64 squares alternating light and dark. Only the dark squares of the board are used. The board is eight squares wide and eight squares long. Each player uses 12 wooden discs called checkers, usually red for one player and black for the other. The pieces are set up on the dark squares of the first three ranks, four in each rank. The players alternate turns by moving one checker forward diagonally toward the opposing player's checkers. The object is to jump over the opponent's pieces, which are then removed from play. A player wins when all the opponent's pieces have been removed. If a player manages to advance a piece to the last rank on the opposite end of the board, that piece becomes a king and thereby acquires the capability of moving backward as well as forward.

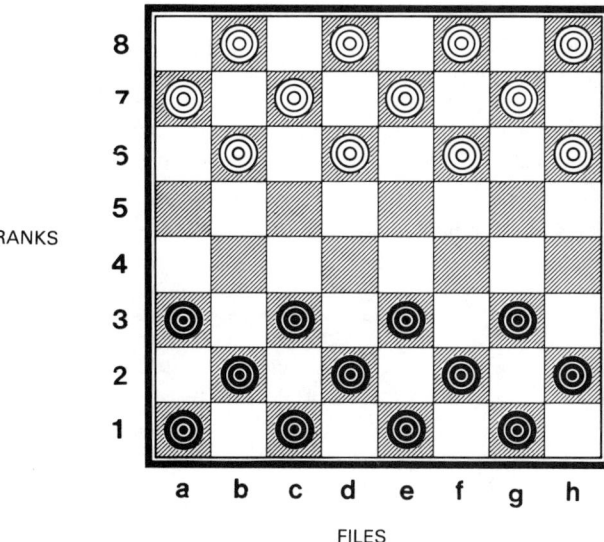

Chess

Chess is a game for two players, one of them directing the white pieces and one of them the black pieces. It is played on a board with 64 squares of alternating colors, black and white. The board is eight squares wide and eight long. Squares on the board are normally referred to by coordinates, using numbered ranks and lettered files. Each player has 16 pieces: eight pawns, two rooks, two knights, two bishops, a queen, and a king. To start the game, the pieces are set up using the 32 spaces of ranks 1 and 2 (for one color) and 7 and 8 (for the other color). Rooks occupy the outermost files (a and h), with knights placed next to them (b and g); next to them are the bishops (c and f). Toward the center of the board (d and e) the king and queen are placed, with the white queen on a white square and the black queen on a black square. The pawns are placed in front of these pieces, using ranks 2 and 7.

The object of the game is to capture the opponent's king by placing him in checkmate. In this position, the king is under attack by an opposing piece (check), and wherever the king moves, it remains under attack by that or another opposing piece. The attacking side thus wins the game. If a player feels that checkmate is unavoidable, he or she may give up, or resign. If neither white nor black is able to checkmate the opponent or force resignation, a tie may be agreed upon. This is called a stalemate.

Any piece may capture, or take, an opponent's piece by landing on the square occupied by that piece. However, the king can not be captured and is instead put into check when attacked. If a piece is captured, it is removed from the board and, with one rare exception, it may not be used again. The exception is called queening, whereby a captured queen may return to the game to replace a pawn that has safely reached the last rank (1 or 8).

Each type of piece moves in a prescribed way. A rook moves forward or back, left or right as many squares in one direction as is desired. Knights move two squares in one direction (forward, back, left, or right) and one square at right angles to the first direction— or one square in one direction and two squares at right angles to the first move—resulting in an L-shaped move. The knight is the only piece that may jump over another piece. Bishops move diagonally any number of spaces in one direction. The queen moves forward, back, left, right, or diagonally any number of spaces in one direction. The king moves as the queen does, but one space at a time. Pawns move forward only, one space at a time, except for the first move, which may be two spaces. Pawns capture pieces by moving diagonally. There are only two instances in which pieces may move in other than these prescribed ways:

1. *Castling* is a two-part move involving the king and a rook. If neither of these pieces has moved previously, and if there are no pieces placed between them, the king may

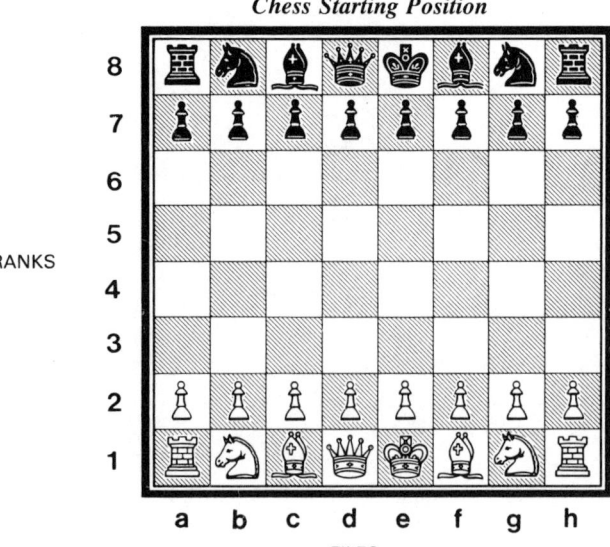

Chess Starting Position

RANKS

FILES

move two spaces toward the rook, and the rook may move to the far side next to the king.

2. If, by moving ahead two squares on an opening move, a black pawn becomes placed next to an opposing white pawn on the same rank, the white pawn may take the black pawn by moving diagonally to the square immediately behind it. This is called taking *en passant*, or capturing in passing. Of course, a black pawn may capture a white pawn in the same way.

Monopoly

Monopoly uses a board with 40 spaces around the perimeter. Players, starting with a fixed amount of money, roll two dice and, in turn, advance their tokens around the board the number spaces indicated by the dice. If a player lands on any of 22 properties, that player may buy it at a stated price. This money goes into the bank. The player then receives a deed for that property, which states the rent that an opposing player must pay the owner if he or she lands on it. The object of the game is to accumulate the properties and, by charging rent when an opponent lands there, to drive opposing players into bankruptcy. Properties are grouped by colors, with two or three to a group. If a player acquires all the properties within a single color, that player may develop those properties by purchasing houses and hotels. These dramatically increase the rent.

In addition to the color-coded properties, which are given street names, there are also four railroads and two utility companies that may be purchased. These also carry rents, but they may not be developed. If a player lands on any of six spaces, three called ''Chance'' and three ''Community Chest,'' that player must pick up a card from two piles placed in the center of the board and follow its instructions. These involve monetary transactions either beneficial or harmful to the player. There is a neutral space called ''Free Parking,'' a ''Jail'' space, two tax spaces, and a space called ''Go.'' Play begins on the Go space and the players collect $200 each time they circle the board and pass it.

In informal play, Monopoly may involve considerable negotiation and trading among players. The game ends when all but one player has gone bankrupt; the remaining player is the winner.

THE MOST LANDED-ON SPACES ON THE MONOPOLY GAME BOARD

According to Irvin R. Hertzel of Iowa State University, there are 10 spaces on the Monopoly game board you can count on landing on more than the others. Using a computer, Hertzel, a mathematician, was able to figure out the overall probability of landing on each square. The following are the 10 most landed-on spaces.

1. Illinois Avenue
2. Go
3. B.&O. Railroad
4. Free Parking
5. Tennessee Avenue
6. New York Avenue
7. Reading Railroad
8. St. James Place
9. Water Works
10. Pennsylvania Railroad

Scrabble

Scrabble® is a word game for two, three, or four players. The game uses a Scrabble® board with 225 spaces, 100 lettered tiles, and a tile rack. Each player, starting with seven letters, attempts to form words on the board using letters from his or her own hand and from words on the board. Words may read from left to right or from top to bottom. Usually a new word uses one letter from a word already on the board, with which it interlocks at right angles, as in a crossword. Letters may be added to an existing word to form a new one.

Each player, after using some or all his or her tiles to form a word on the board, replenishes the playing hand from the pool of remaining tiles, which are face down. Thus each player always has seven tiles with which to form words, except toward the end of the game, when the pool runs out.

Each letter has a numerical value associated with it; this number is marked on the tile. Players score for each word formed, based on the value of each letter in the word. These are recorded using pencil and paper. Scores may be augmented by using certain premium spaces on the board. These special spaces result in doubling or tripling the values of single letters or complete words. When no player is able to form additional words, each player's score is tallied. Values of unplayed letters for each player are subtracted. The highest score wins the game.

Card Games

Blackjack

Blackjack is a gambling game using a standard 52-card deck. A counts as 1 or 11; K, Q, J, and 10 count as 10 each; all other cards count their face number. The object is to hold two or more cards totaling 21 or as close to 21 as possible without going over. Cards are dealt one at a time, clockwise, starting with the player at the dealer's left. Each player receives one down card and one face-up card. After this initial deal, each player may stand and refuse more cards or take additional cards face-up. For example, having been dealt a king down and a six up (totaling 16), if the player chooses to take an additional card and receives another six, that player is out with 22. An ace and a picture card or a 10 is called blackjack; it totals 21 and beats all other hands.

Various betting methods are used, but usually bets are made before and after the initial deal and after each subsequent deal. All players play against the dealer, and bets are settled depending on which hands are closest to but not over 21; if the dealer has the same count as a given player, the hand is considered a stand-off.

Bridge

Contract bridge uses a standard 52-card deck and is a game for four players, in partnerships of two. The teams are designated North–South and East–West. Cards in each suit rank A (high), K, Q, J, 10, 9, . . . 2 (low), and suits rank spades (high), hearts, diamonds, and clubs (low). Each player receives cards, dealt one at a time clockwise starting at the dealer's left.

Each player in turn gets a chance to make a bid, which is a statement of the intention to win more than six tricks. At the same time the player either declares a high-ranking suit (trump) or declares no trump. If a player chooses not to bid, he or she may pass. Bids go around the table in clockwise rotation, with each bid being higher than any preceding bid. A bid may be doubled by an opponent or redoubled by a partner. These double the scoring value of a bid if it is played. This bidding segment of the game is called the auction, and the highest bid becomes the contract. One member of the contracting team declares the trump and becomes the declarer. That person's partner spreads his or her hand face up on the table and becomes the dummy.

The object of the game is to win tricks in order to fulfill the contract or to defeat the opponent's attempt to fulfill it. The player to the dealer's left leads, and all players must follow suit if possible. A trick is won by the highest card of the suit led if no trump is played, or by the highest trump player.

When all 13 tricks have been taken, the result is scored. There is a complicated scoring system depending primarily on whether or not the contract was made and by how much. The two members of a partnership score their combined tricks as a single unit. Extra points may be scored in several ways. A bonus is scored if a doubled or redoubled bid is made. One of two types of slams is scored if the contracting team wins 12 tricks or all 13. Honors points are scored when a player receives certain cards in the deal (A, K, Q, J, 10 of trump, or the four aces if no trump has been declared).

When a side accumulates 100 or more points in trick scores, the game is over. The side that first wins two out of three games wins a rubber. After each rubber, partnerships may change and play may begin again.

Pinochle

Pinochle is played by two to four players and uses a 48-card deck, which includes two of each rank from 9 to A in all four suits. The rank of cards in each suit is A (high), 10, K, Q, J, 9. Cards are dealt three at a time, clockwise, starting to the dealer's left. In two-hand pinochle, both players receive 12 cards; in three-hand (auction pinochle), each receives 15; and in four-hand (partnership pinochle), each receives 12 cards. The remaining cards, if any, form the stock. After an ad hoc high-ranking suit, called trump, has been determined, the player to the left of the dealer leads by placing a card in the middle, followed by each player in rotation. Tricks are won by the high trump or by the higher card of the suit led if no trump is played. The winner of the trick leads for the next trick. Except in two-hand pinochle, a player must always follow the suit that is led, if possible.

Scoring is done by examining cards taken in tricks, with each ace counting 11, each ten 10, each king 4, each queen 3, and each jack 2. Nines do not score. Points can also be scored by winning the last trick. In addition, certain combinations of cards, called melds, have scoring value. These include the flush (A, 10, K, Q, J in the same suit), the marriage (K and Q in the same suit), groups of cards of the same rank (four aces, four kings, etc.), and two special melds, the nine of trump and the pinochle (queen of spades and jack of diamonds).

Points taken in tricks are added to those accumulated by melding. Usually the player or team that first reaches 1,000 points wins the game.

Poker

Poker is a popular card game using a standard 52-card deck, with cards ranking A (high), K, Q, J, 10, 9, . . . 2 (low). The ace can also rank low if used as part of A-2-3-4-5. Jokers are sometimes used as wild cards, which can stand for any card the holder chooses. There are hundreds of forms of poker, but invariably the cards are dealt clockwise, one at a time, starting with the player to the dealer's left. Usually each player receives five cards face down, but depending on the type of poker, more cards may be dealt, or some may be face up.

Poker is a gambling game using chips of different monetary value. Bets by players go into a pile of chips called the pot. The object is to win the pot, either by showing the best hand or by making a bet that no one is willing to match. The rank of poker hands without wild cards is as follows:

1. *Straight flush:* five cards in sequence in the same suit
2. *Four of a kind:* any four cards of the same rank
3. *Full house:* three of a kind and a pair
4. *Flush:* five cards of the same suit
5. *Straight:* five cards in sequence, regardless of suit
6. *Three of a kind:* three cards of the same rank
7. *Two pair:* two cards of the same rank and two others of a different rank
8. *One pair:* two cards of the same rank
9. *High card:* five unmatched cards, one with the highest rank of the five.

Rummy

Rummy uses a regular deck of 52 cards. The cards rank K (high), Q, J, 10, . . . 2, A (low). Cards are dealt one at a time, clockwise, starting at the dealer's left. The number of cards dealt to each player depends on the number of players in the game: with two players, 10 cards each; with three or four players, seven cards each; with five or six players, six cards each. The undealt remainder of the deck is placed face down, forming the stock. Its top card is turned up next to the stock, forming the discard file. The object is to form groups (three or more cards of the same rank) or sequences (three or more cards of the same suit in sequence of rank). This is called melding.

One at a time and proceeding clockwise, players draw one card from the top of the stack or the top of the discard pile. If melding is possible, groups or sequences are placed face up in front of the player. A player may also lay off, or add to his or her own or an opponent's melds. A player's turn ends by placing one card face up on the discard pile. When one player melds all the cards remaining in a hand, that player goes out, thus ending that deal, which is then scored. The player going out scores his or her own melds plus the points left in the opponents' hands. The other players score just their own melds. Aces count as one; all picture cards count as 10; and the rest of the cards count as their face number. High score wins.

Except when going out, a player must discard one card after each play, whether or not that player has melded or laid off.

Solitaire

Solitaire, or Patience, refers to a group of card games played by one person. The most popular and best known of these games is Klondike. Using a standard 52-card deck, a tableau or layout is dealt in front of the player, consisting of seven piles of cards. The first pile on the far left has one card, the second pile two, and so on to the far right pile, which has seven cards. These cards are face down except for the top card in each pile. On these piles, descending sequences are built in alternating colors. For example, a red nine may be placed on a black ten. Entire sequences or individual cards may be moved from pile to pile, provided correct colors and sequences are maintained. If a down card in a pile is revealed, it is turned face up and may then become part of a sequence. When a pile is exhausted, a king may replace it.

When they become available, aces are placed above the original layout. The object is to build sequences in suit from the four aces (the foundations) up to the four kings, thus using all cards of the original layout as well as the remaining cards, which form the stock. From the stock, the player turns up one card at a time, forming a waste pile. The top card of the waste pile is available for play on the layout or foundations. The player goes through the stock only once and wins the game if he or she successfully places the entire deck on the foundations. Many players employ alternative, more liberal methods of dealing the stock.

Additional Sources of Information

Organizations and Services
General

Amateur Athletic Union of the U.S.
3400 West 86th Street
P.O. Box 68207
Indianapolis, IN 46268
317-872-2900

National Collegiate Athletic Association (NCAA)
Nall Avenue at 63rd Street
P.O. Box 1906
Mission, KS 66201
913-384-3220

U.S. Olympic Committee
1750 East Boulder Street
Colorado Springs, CO 80909
303-632-5551

Baseball

American League
350 Park Avenue
New York, NY 10022
212-371-7600

Baseball Hall of Fame
Box 590
Cooperstown, NY 13326
607-547-9988

Major League Baseball Commissioner's Office
350 Park Avenue
New York, NY 10022
212-371-7800

National League
350 Park Avenue
New York, NY 10022
212-371-7300

Basketball

Naismith Memorial Basketball Hall of Fame
P.O. Box 179, Highland Station
1150 West Columbus Avenue
Springfield, MA 01101
413-781-6500

National Baseball Association
645 Fifth Avenue
New York, NY 10022
212-826-7000

Football

National Football League
410 Park Avenue
New York, NY 10022
212-758-1500

Pro Football Hall of Fame
2121 George Halas Drive, NW
Canton, OH 44708
216-456-8207

Golf

Ladies Professional Golf Association (LPGA)
4675 Sweetwater Boulevard
Sugar Land, TX 77479
713-980-5742

U.S. Golf Association
Liberty Corner Road
Far Hills, NJ 07931
201-234-2300

Professional Golfer's Association of America
100 Avenue of the Champions
Palm Beach Gardens, FL 33410
305-626-3600

U.S. Golf Association Hall of Fame
Golf House
Far Hills, NJ 07931
201-234-2300

Hockey

Hockey Hall of Fame
Exhibition Place
Toronto, Ontario, Canada M6K 3C3
416-595-1345

National Hockey League
500 Fifth Avenue
34th Floor
New York, NY 10110
212-398-1100

Horse Racing

National Museum of Racing
Union Avenue
Saratoga Springs, NY 12866
518-584-0400

U.S. Trotting Association
750 Michigan Avenue
Columbus, OH 43215
614-224-2291

Thoroughbred Racing Association of North America
3000 Marcus Avenue
Lake Success, NY 11042
516-328-2660

Tennis

International Tennis Hall of Fame and Museum
194 Bellevue Avenue
Newport, RI 02840
401-849-3990

U.S. Tennis Association
1212 Avenue of the Americas
New York, NY 10036
212-302-3322

Track and Field

Intercollegiate Association of Amateur Athletes of America (IC4A)
P.O. Box 3
Centerville, MA 02632
617-771-5060

International Amateur Athletics Federation
3 Hans Crescent
Knightsbridge
London SWIX OLN, England
+44 +1 /581-8771

U.S. Track and Field Hall of Fame
P.O. Box 297
Angola, IN 46703
219-495-7735

Books

Ainslie, Tom. *Ainslie's Complete Guide to Thoroughbred Racing.* Simon & Schuster, 1988.

Collins, Bud, and Hollander, Zander. *Bud Collins' Modern Encyclopedia of Tennis.* Doubleday, 1980.

Fischler, Shirley, and Fischler, Stan. *The Complete Record of Professional Ice Hockey.* Macmillan, 1983.

Fisher, David, and Bragonier, Reginald, Jr. *What's What in Sports: The Visual Glossary of the Sports World.* Hammond, 1984.

Frommer, Harvey. *Sports Lingo: A Dictionary of the Language of Sports.* Atheneum, 1983.

Hollander, Zander. *The Complete Handbook of Pro Basketball.* New American Library, annual.

Menke, Frank G. *The Encyclopedia of Sports,* 5th rev. ed. A.S. Barnes, 1975.

Morrison, Ian. *The Hamlyn Encyclopedia of Golf.* Salem House, 1986.

Neft, David S., and Cohen, Richard M. *Sports Encyclopedia: Baseball,* 7th ed. St. Martin's, 1987.

Neft, David S., et al. *Sports Encyclopedia: Pro-Football, the Modern Era. 1960–The Present.* St. Martin's, 1987.

Odd, Gilbert. *Encyclopedia of Boxing.* Crescent, 1983.

The Oxford Companion to Sports and Games. Oxford University Press, 1974.

Reichler, Joseph L. *The Baseball Encyclopedia: The Complete and Official Record of Major League Baseball,* 7th ed. Macmillan, 1989.

Treat, Roger. *The Encyclopedia of Football,* 16th rev. ed. Doubleday, 1979.

Webster's Sports Dictionary. G & C Merriam, 1976.

23

Health

Anatomical Drawings with Parts of the Body Labeled

The Skeletal System

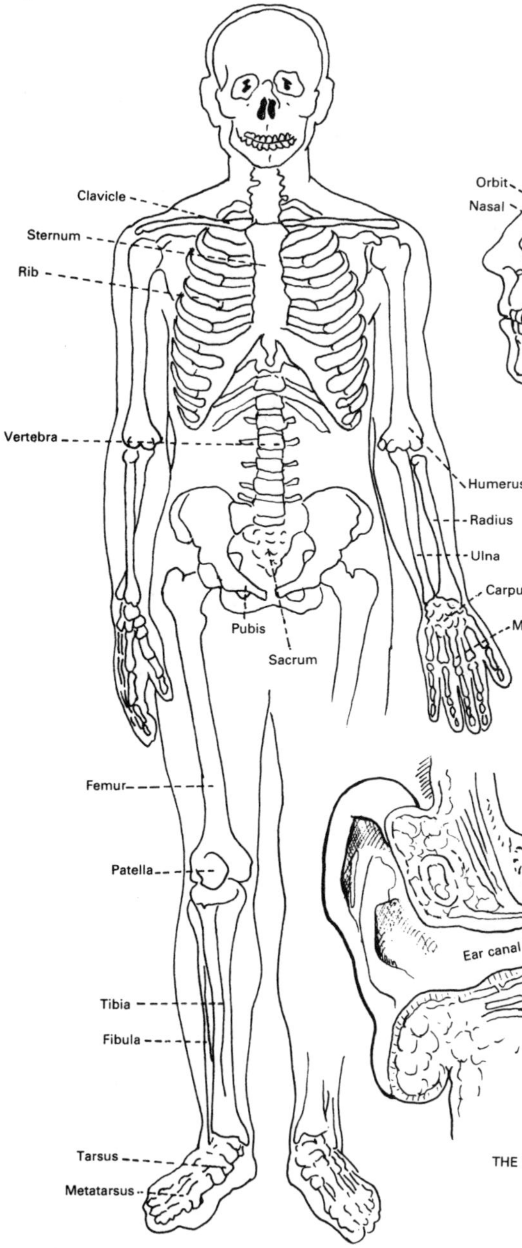

THE SKULL

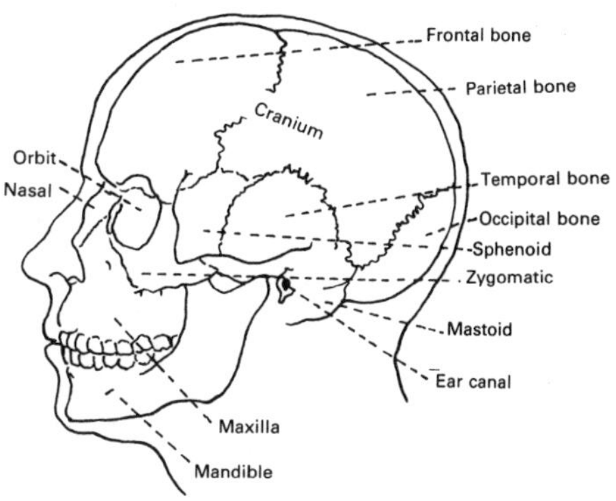

Frontal bone

Parietal bone

Orbit

Nasal

Cranium

Temporal bone

Occipital bone

Sphenoid

Zygomatic

Mastoid

Ear canal

Maxilla

Mandible

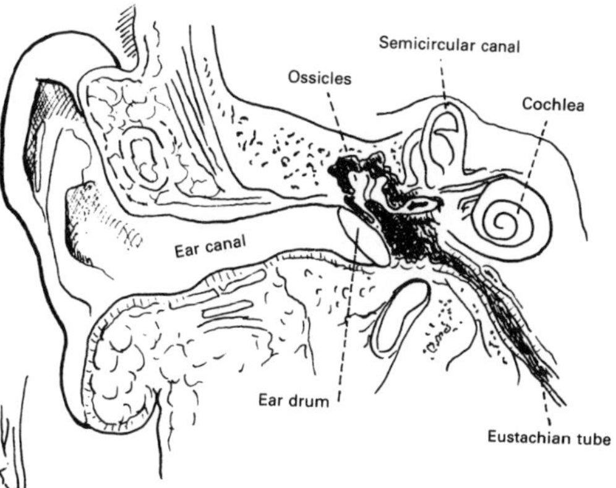

Clavicle

Sternum

Rib

Vertebra

Humerus

Radius

Ulna

Carpus

Metacarpus

Pubis

Sacrum

Femur

Patella

Tibia

Fibula

Tarsus

Metatarsus

Semicircular canal

Ossicles

Cochlea

Ear canal

Ear drum

Eustachian tube

THE EAR

The Muscles

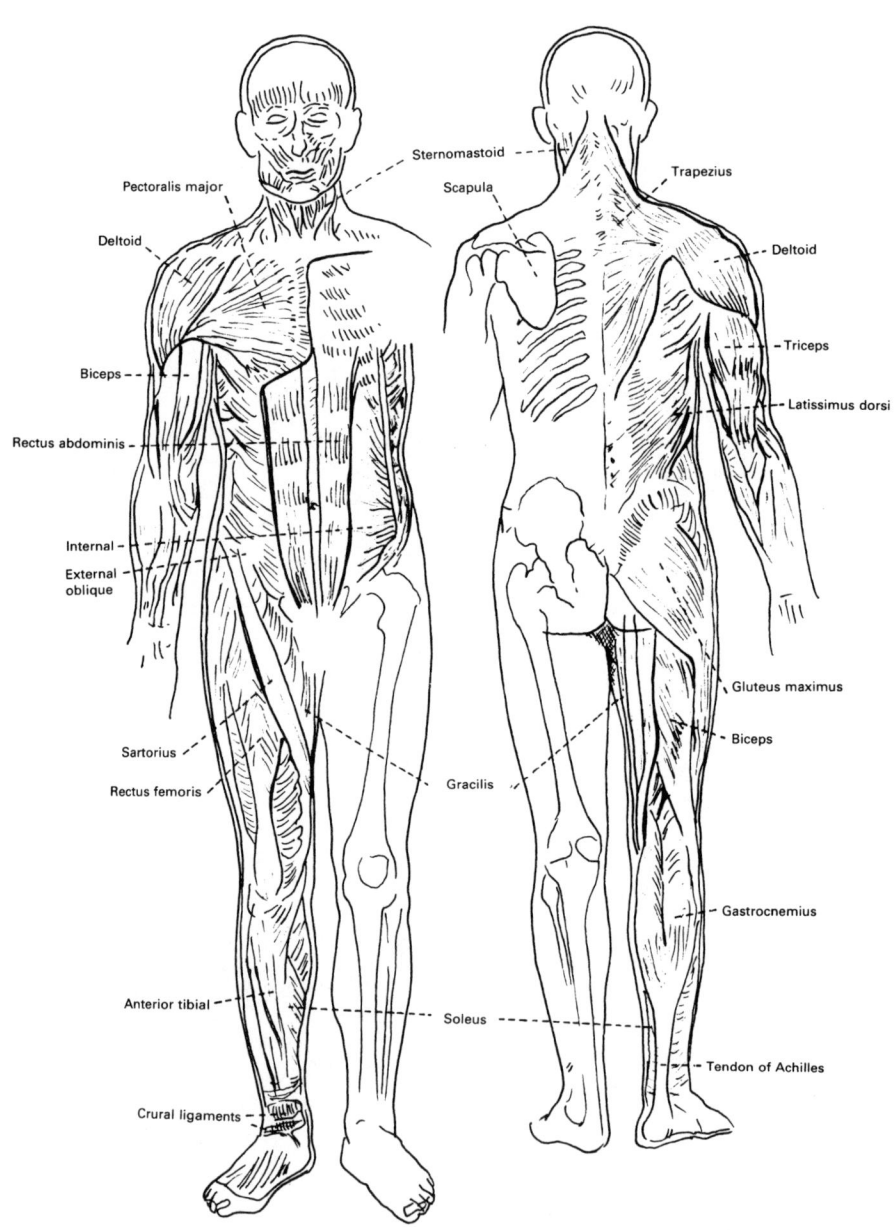

Pectoralis major

Deltoid

Biceps

Rectus abdominis

Internal

External oblique

Sartorius

Rectus femoris

Anterior tibial

Crural ligaments

Sternomastoid

Scapula

Gracilis

Soleus

Trapezius

Deltoid

Triceps

Latissimus dorsi

Gluteus maximus

Biceps

Gastrocnemius

Tendon of Achilles

The Alimentary System

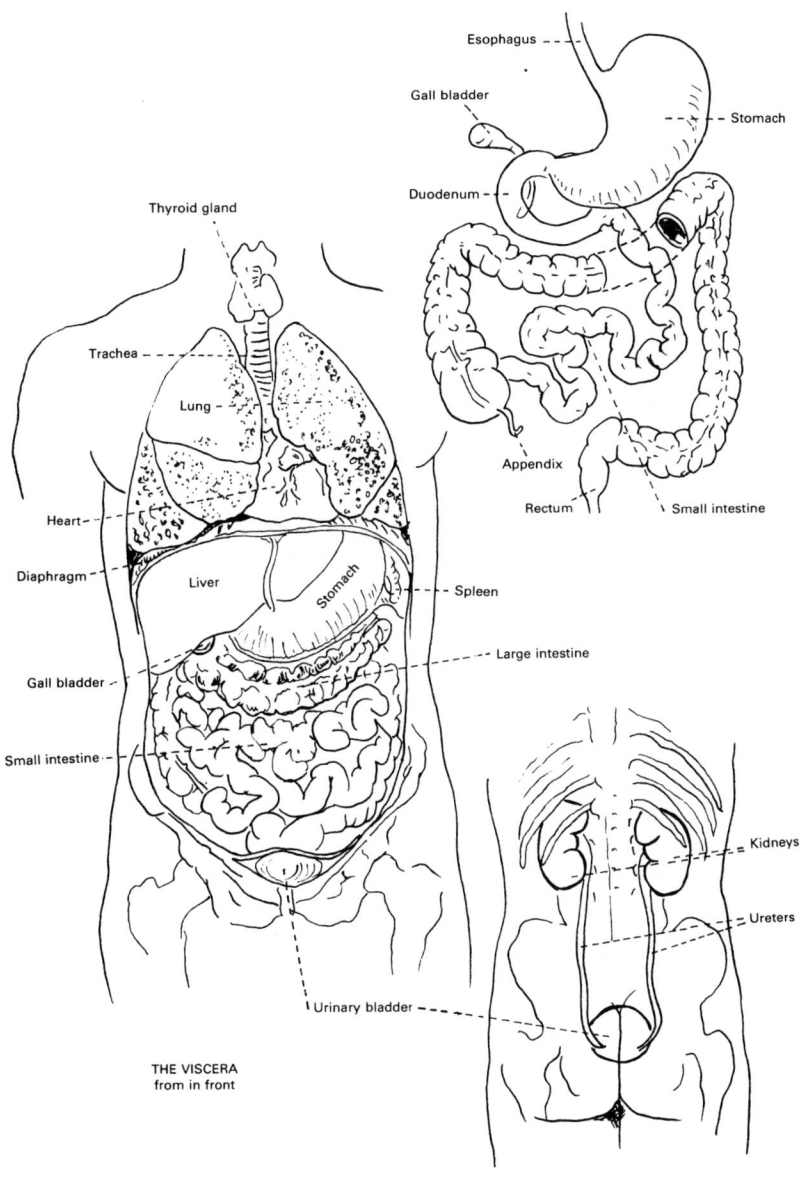

Esophagus

Gall bladder

Duodenum

Stomach

Thyroid gland

Trachea

Lung

Heart

Diaphragm

Liver

Stomach

Spleen

Gall bladder

Large intestine

Small intestine

Appendix

Rectum

Small intestine

THE VISCERA
from in front

Urinary bladder

Kidneys

Ureters

THE URINARY TRACT

The Brain and Spinal Cord

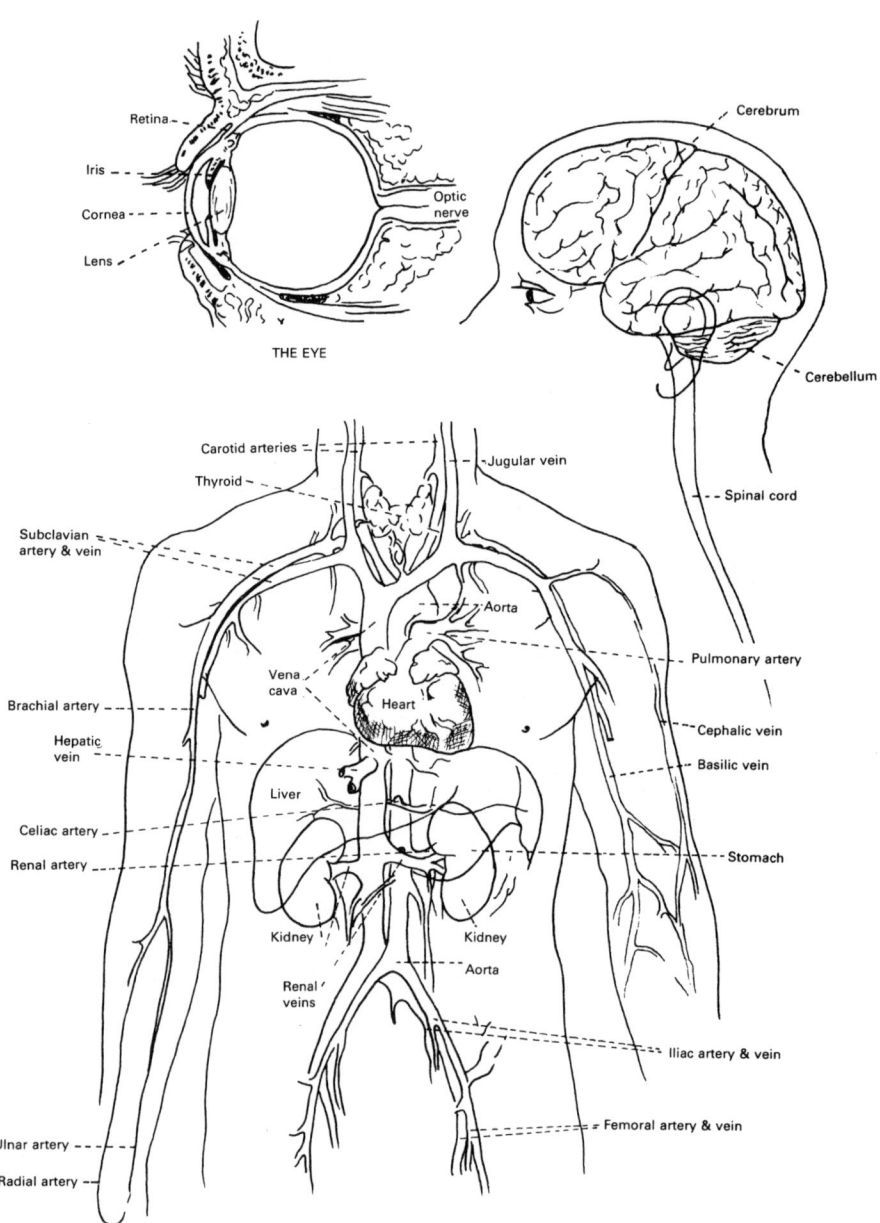

THE EYE

The Heart and Great Vessels

Height and Weight Charts for Adults and Children

Height and Weight Charts for Adults

Desirable Weights in Pounds for Persons 25 to 29 Years Old

Men

Height (in shoes)	Small frame	Medium frame	Large frame
5 ft. 2 in.	128–134	131–141	138–150
5 ft. 3 in.	130–136	133–143	140–153
5 ft. 4 in.	132–138	135–145	142–156
5 ft. 5 in.	134–140	137–148	144–160
5 ft. 6 in.	136–142	139–151	146–164
5 ft. 7 in.	138–145	142–154	149–168
5 ft. 8 in.	140–148	145–157	152–172
5 ft. 9 in.	142–151	148–160	155–176
5 ft. 10 in.	144–154	151–163	158–180
5 ft. 11 in.	146–157	154–166	161–184
6 ft.	149–160	157–170	164–188
6 ft. 1 in.	152–164	160–174	168–192
6 ft. 2 in.	155–168	164–178	172–197
6 ft. 3 in.	158–172	167–182	176–202
6 ft. 4 in.	162–176	171–187	181–207

Women

Height (in shoes)	Small frame	Medium frame	Large frame
4 ft. 10 in.	102–111	109–121	118–131
4 ft. 11 in.	103–113	111–123	120–134
5 ft.	104–115	113–126	122–137
5 ft. 1 in.	106–118	115–129	125–140
5 ft. 2 in.	108–121	118–132	128–143
5 ft. 3 in.	111–124	121–135	131–147
5 ft. 4 in.	114–127	124–138	134–151
5 ft. 5 in.	117–130	127–141	137–155
5 ft. 6 in.	120–133	130–144	140–159
5 ft. 7 in.	123–136	133–147	143–163
5 ft. 8 in.	126–139	136–150	146–167
5 ft. 9 in.	129–142	139–153	149–170
5 ft. 10 in.	132–145	142–156	152–173
5 ft. 11 in.	135–148	145–159	155–176
6 ft.	138–151	148–162	158–179

Height and Weight Charts for Children

Desirable Weights in Pounds for Boys and Girls 5 to 18 Years Old

Boys

Height (in inches)	5	6	7	8	9	10	11	12	13	14	15	16	17	18
38	34	34												
39	35	35												
40	36	36												
41	38	38	38											
42	39	39	39	39										
43	41	41	41	41										
44	44	44	44	44										
45	46	46	46	46	46									
46	47	48	48	48										
47	49	50	50	50	50	50								
48		52	53	53	53	53								
49		55	55	55	55	55	55							
50		57	58	58	58	58	58	58						
51			61	61	61	61	61	61	61					
52			63	64	64	64	64	64	64					
53			66	67	67	67	68	68						
54				70	70	70	70	71	71	72				
55				72	72	73	73	74	74	74				
56				75	76	77	77	77	78	78	80			
57					79	80	81	81	82	83	83			
58					83	84	84	85	85	86	87			
59						87	88	89	89	90	90	90		
60						91	92	92	93	94	95	96		
61							95	96	97	99	100	103	106	
62							100	101	102	103	104	107	111	116
63							105	106	107	108	110	113	118	123
64								109	111	113	115	117	121	126
65								114	117	118	120	122	127	131
66									119	122	125	128	132	136
67									124	128	130	134	136	139
68										134	134	137	141	143
69										137	139	143	146	149
70										143	144	145	148	151
71										148	150	151	152	154
72											153	155	156	158
73											157	160	162	164
74											160	164	168	170

Girls

Height (in inches)	5	6	7	8	9	10	11	12	13	14	15	16	17	18
38	33	33												
39	34	34												
40	36	36	36											
41	37	37	37											
42	39	39	39											
43	41	41	41	41										
44	42	42	42	42										
45	45	45	45	45	45									
46	47	47	47	48	48									
47	49	50	50	50	50	50								
48		52	52	52	52	53	53							
49			54	55	55	56	56							
50			56	57	58	59	61	62						
51			59	60	61	61	63	65						
52			63	64	64	64	65	67						
53			66	67	67	68	68	69	71					
54				69	70	70	71	71	73					
55				72	74	74	74	75	77	78				
56					76	78	78	79	81	83				
57					80	82	82	82	84	88	92			
58						84	86	86	88	93	96	101		
59						87	90	90	92	96	100	103	104	
60						91	95	95	97	101	105	108	109	111
61							99	100	101	105	108	112	113	116
62							104	105	106	109	113	115	117	118
63								110	110	112	116	117	119	120
64								114	115	117	119	120	122	123
65								118	120	121	122	123	125	126
66									124	124	125	128	129	130
67									128	130	131	133	133	135
68									131	133	135	136	138	138
69										135	137	138	140	142
70										136	138	140	142	144
71										138	140	142	144	145

Table of Approximate Dates of Childbirth

Find the date of the last menstrual period in the top line (light-face type) of the pair of lines. The dark number (boldface type) in the line below will be the expected day of delivery.

January	1 2 3 4 5 6 7 8 9 10 11 12 13 14 15 16 17 18 19 20 21 22 23 24 25 26 27 28 29 30 31	
October	**8 9 10 11 12 13 14 15 16 17 18 19 20 21 22 23 24 25 26 27 28 29 30 31 (1 2 3 4 5 6 7**	**November**
February	1 2 3 4 5 6 7 8 9 10 11 12 13 14 15 16 17 18 19 20 21 22 23 24 25 26 27 28	
November	**8 9 10 11 12 13 14 15 16 17 18 19 20 21 22 23 24 25 26 27 28 29 30 (1 2 3 4 5**	**December**
March	1 2 3 4 5 6 7 8 9 10 11 12 13 14 15 16 17 18 19 20 21 22 23 24 25 26 27 28 29 30 31	
December	**6 7 8 9 10 11 12 13 14 15 16 17 18 19 20 21 22 23 24 25 26 27 28 29 30 31 (1 2 3 4 5**	**January**
April	1 2 3 4 5 6 7 8 9 10 11 12 13 14 15 16 17 18 19 20 21 22 23 24 25 26 27 28 29 30	
January	**6 7 8 9 10 11 12 13 14 15 16 17 18 19 20 21 22 23 24 25 26 27 28 29 30 31 (1 2 3 4**	**February**
May	1 2 3 4 5 6 7 8 9 10 11 12 13 14 15 16 17 18 19 20 21 22 23 24 25 26 27 28 29 30 31	
February	**5 6 7 8 9 10 11 12 13 14 15 16 17 18 19 20 21 22 23 24 25 26 27 28 (1 2 3 4 5 6 7**	**March**
June	1 2 3 4 5 6 7 8 9 10 11 12 13 14 15 16 17 18 19 20 21 22 23 24 25 26 27 28 29 30	
March	**8 9 10 11 12 13 14 15 16 17 18 19 20 21 22 23 24 25 26 27 28 29 30 31 (1 2 3 4 5 6**	**April**
July	1 2 3 4 5 6 7 8 9 10 11 12 13 14 15 16 17 18 19 20 21 22 23 24 25 26 27 28 29 30 31	
April	**7 8 9 10 11 12 13 14 15 16 17 18 19 20 21 22 23 24 25 26 27 28 29 30 (1 2 3 4 5 6 7**	**May**
August	1 2 3 4 5 6 7 8 9 10 11 12 13 14 15 16 17 18 19 20 21 22 23 24 25 26 27 28 29 30 31	
May	**8 9 10 11 12 13 14 15 16 17 18 19 20 21 22 23 24 25 26 27 28 29 30 31 (1 2 3 4 5 6 7**	**June**
September	1 2 3 4 5 6 7 8 9 10 11 12 13 14 15 16 17 18 19 20 21 22 23 24 25 26 27 28 29 30	
June	**8 9 10 11 12 13 14 15 16 17 18 19 20 21 22 23 24 25 26 27 28 29 30 (1 2 3 4 5 6 7**	**July**
October	1 2 3 4 5 6 7 8 9 10 11 12 13 14 15 16 17 18 19 20 21 22 23 24 25 26 27 28 29 30 31	
July	**8 9 10 11 12 13 14 15 16 17 18 19 20 21 22 23 24 25 26 27 28 29 30 31 (1 2 3 4 5 6 7**	**August**
November	1 2 3 4 5 6 7 8 9 10 11 12 13 14 15 16 17 18 19 20 21 22 23 24 25 26 27 28 29 30	
August	**8 9 10 11 12 13 14 15 16 17 18 19 20 21 22 23 24 25 26 27 28 29 30 31 (1 2 3 4 5 6**	**September**
December	1 2 3 4 5 6 7 8 9 10 11 12 13 14 15 16 17 18 19 20 21 22 23 24 25 26 27 28 29 30 31	
September	**7 8 9 10 11 12 13 14 15 16 17 18 19 20 21 22 23 24 25 26 27 28 29 30 (1 2 3 4 5 6 7**	**October**

Life Expectancy Tables

by Race, Sex, and Age

| Age (years) | Expectation of life in years | | | | | Expected deaths per 1,000 alive at specified age | | | | |
| | Total | White | | Black | | Total | White | | Black | |
		Male	Female	Male	Female		Male	Female	Male	Female
At birth	74.6	71.7	78.7	65.4	73.6	11.15	10.79	8.60	21.05	17.23
1	74.5	71.5	78.4	65.9	73.9	0.75	0.80	0.59	1.22	0.92
2	73.5	70.5	77.4	64.9	72.9	0.59	0.60	0.47	1.00	0.76
3	72.6	69.6	76.4	64.0	72.0	0.47	0.47	0.37	0.81	0.62
4	71.6	68.6	75.5	63.0	71.0	0.39	0.39	0.31	0.66	0.51
5	70.8	67.6	74.5	62.1	70.1	0.33	0.35	0.26	0.54	0.42
6	69.7	66.6	73.5	61.1	69.1	0.30	0.33	0.23	0.45	0.34
7	68.7	65.7	72.5	60.1	68.1	0.26	0.30	0.20	0.38	0.29
8	67.7	64.7	71.5	59.2	67.2	0.23	0.27	0.18	0.33	0.25
9	66.7	63.7	70.6	58.2	66.2	0.20	0.22	0.16	0.30	0.23
10	65.7	62.7	69.6	57.2	65.2	0.18	0.19	0.14	0.30	0.22
11	64.7	61.7	68.6	56.2	64.2	0.18	0.18	0.14	0.32	0.23
12	63.7	60.7	67.6	55.2	63.2	0.22	0.25	0.17	0.38	0.25
13	62.8	59.8	66.6	54.3	62.2	0.31	0.39	0.21	0.48	0.27
14	61.8	58.8	65.8	53.3	61.2	0.44	0.60	0.28	0.61	0.31
15	60.8	57.8	64.6	52.3	60.3	0.59	0.83	0.36	0.75	0.36
16	59.8	56.9	63.7	51.4	59.3	0.73	1.04	0.43	0.91	0.41
17	58.9	55.9	62.7	50.4	58.3	0.84	1.22	0.49	1.10	0.47
18	57.9	55.0	61.7	49.5	57.3	0.92	1.34	0.51	1.32	0.54
19	57.0	54.1	60.7	48.5	56.4	0.97	1.41	0.51	1.55	0.61
20	56.0	53.1	59.8	47.6	55.4	1.02	1.47	0.50	1.81	0.69
21	55.1	52.2	58.8	46.7	54.4	1.07	1.53	0.50	2.06	0.77
22	54.2	51.3	57.8	45.8	53.5	1.10	1.57	0.50	2.27	0.84
23	53.2	50.4	56.9	44.9	52.5	1.12	1.58	0.51	2.42	0.90
24	52.3	49.4	55.9	44.0	51.6	1.13	1.57	0.52	2.53	0.94
25	51.3	48.5	54.9	43.1	50.6	1.13	1.55	0.53	2.62	0.98
26	50.4	47.6	54.0	42.2	49.7	1.14	1.52	0.54	2.74	1.04
27	49.4	46.7	53.0	41.3	48.7	1.14	1.51	0.55	2.88	1.09
28	48.5	45.7	52.0	40.4	47.8	1.16	1.50	0.56	3.05	1.16
29	47.6	44.8	51.0	39.6	46.6	1.18	1.51	0.57	3.26	1.24
30	46.6	43.9	50.1	38.7	45.9	1.21	1.52	0.59	3.49	1.33
31	45.7	42.9	49.1	37.8	45.0	1.24	1.54	0.61	3.72	1.43
32	44.7	42.0	48.1	37.0	44.0	1.28	1.57	0.65	3.93	1.53
33	43.8	41.1	47.2	36.1	43.1	1.33	1.61	0.69	4.12	1.65
34	42.8	40.1	46.2	35.3	42.2	1.38	1.66	0.74	4.30	1.77
35	41.9	39.2	45.2	34.4	41.2	1.46	1.73	0.81	4.50	1.91
36	41.0	38.3	44.3	33.6	40.3	1.54	1.82	0.80	4.73	2.07
37	40.0	37.3	43.3	32.7	39.4	1.64	1.92	0.96	4.99	2.24
38	39.1	36.4	42.3	31.9	38.5	1.76	2.04	1.05	5.26	2.42
39	38.2	35.5	41.4	31.0	37.6	1.89	2.18	1.15	5.57	2.61

Life Expectancy Table by Race, Sex, and Age (Continued)

| Age (years) | | Expectation of life in years | | | | | Expected deaths per 1,000 alive at specified age | | | | |
| | | White | | Black | | | White | | Black | |
	Total	Male	Female	Male	Female	Total	Male	Female	Male	Female
40	37.2	34.6	40.4	30.2	36.7	2.05	2.35	1.27	5.89	2.81
41	36.3	33.6	39.5	29.4	35.8	2.23	2.55	1.40	6.26	3.05
42	35.4	32.7	38.5	28.6	34.9	2.44	2.78	1.55	6.75	3.33
43	34.5	31.8	37.6	27.8	34.0	2.69	3.06	1.71	7.40	3.67
44	33.6	30.9	36.7	27.0	33.1	2.97	3.39	1.90	8.16	4.05
45	32.7	30.0	35.7	26.2	32.2	3.29	3.76	2.10	9.02	4.47
46	31.8	29.1	34.8	25.4	31.4	3.64	4.17	2.33	9.90	4.92
47	30.9	28.2	33.9	24.7	30.5	4.02	4.64	2.58	10.74	5.39
48	30.0	27.4	33.0	23.9	29.7	4.45	5.17	2.88	11.51	5.89
49	29.1	26.5	32.1	23.2	28.9	4.91	5.77	3.20	12.23	6.41
50	28.3	25.7	31.2	22.5	28.1	5.42	6.42	3.56	12.97	6.98
51	27.4	24.8	30.3	21.8	27.3	5.97	7.12	3.94	13.81	7.58
52	26.6	24.0	29.4	21.1	26.5	6.56	7.90	4.34	14.81	8.24
53	25.8	23.2	28.5	20.4	25.7	7.20	8.76	4.76	16.02	8.97
54	24.9	22.4	27.7	19.7	24.9	7.89	9.70	5.19	17.40	9.75
55	24.1	21.6	26.0	19.1	24.1	8.63	10.72	5.64	18.85	10.56
56	23.3	20.8	25.9	18.4	23.4	9.42	11.80	6.15	20.35	11.41
57	22.6	20.1	25.1	17.8	22.7	10.28	12.95	6.72	22.03	12.36
58	21.8	19.3	24.3	17.2	21.9	11.22	14.14	7.37	23.94	13.46
59	21.0	18.6	23.4	16.6	21.2	12.23	15.41	8.10	26.02	14.66
60	20.3	17.9	22.6	16.0	20.5	13.33	16.76	8.89	28.35	16.01
61	19.6	17.2	21.8	15.5	19.9	14.49	18.22	9.74	30.74	17.37
62	18.8	16.5	21.0	14.9	19.2	15.71	19.83	10.61	32.81	18.55
63	18.1	15.8	20.3	14.4	18.6	16.98	21.63	11.51	34.37	19.44
64	17.4	15.2	19.5	13.9	17.9	18.31	23.62	12.45	35.54	20.13
65	16.7	14.5	18.7	13.4	17.3	19.72	25.74	13.45	36.43	20.69
70	13.5	11.5	15.1	10.9	14.1	29.70	39.52	20.78	51.45	30.79
75	10.7	9.0	11.8	9.0	11.5	44.31	60.15	32.76	68.22	42.55
80	8.1	6.9	8.8	7.1	9.0	66.98	90.04	53.49	93.33	62.99
85 and over	6.1	5.2	6.5	6.0	7.4	1,000.00	1,000.00	1,000.00	1,000.00	1,000.00

The above figures are based on statistics published in the early 1980s.

Deaths and Death Rates

Death Rates, 1960 to 1985, and Deaths, 1970 to 1985, from Selected Causes

Beginning in 1970, the table on the following pages excludes death of nonresidents of the United States. The standard population for this table is the total population of the United States enumerated in 1940. Beginning in 1979, deaths are classified according to the ninth revision of *International Classification of Diseases;* for earlier years, they are classified according to the revision in use at that time.

Cause of death	Crude death rate per 100,000 population[1]					Age-adjusted death rates per 100,000 population[1]			Deaths (1,000)		
	1960	1970	1980	1984	1985	1970	1980	1985	1970	1980	1985
All causes	945.7	945.3	878.3	862.3	873.9	714.3	585.8	546.1	1,921.0	1,989.8	2,086.4
Major cardiovascular diseases	515.1	496.0	436.4	411.6	409.6	340.1	256.0	224.0	1,008.0	988.5	977.9
Diseases of heart	369.0	362.0	336.0	323.0	323.5	253.6	202.0	180.5	735.5	761.1	771.2
Percent of total	38.7	38.3	38.3	37.5	37.0	35.5	34.5	33.1	38.3	38.2	37.0
Rheumatic fever and rheumatic heart disease	10.3	7.3	3.5	2.9	2.8	6.3	2.6	1.9	14.9	7.8	6.6
Hypertensive heart disease[2]	37.0	7.4	10.9	10.0	9.9	4.9	6.8	5.9	15.0	24.8	23.7
Ischemic heart disease	296.9	328.1	249.7	228.9	224.8	228.1	149.8	125.5	666.7	565.8	536.8
Other diseases of endocardium	24.9	3.3	3.2	3.7	4.0	2.3	2.0	2.2	6.7	7.2	9.5
All other forms of heart disease		15.9	68.7	78.1	81.5	12.0	40.8	45.1	32.3	155.5	194.6
Hypertension[2]	7.1	4.1	3.5	3.3	3.2	2.9	2.0	1.8	8.3	7.8	7.8
Cerebrovascular diseases	108.0	101.9	75.1	65.3	64.1	66.3	40.8	32.3	207.2	170.2	153.1
Atherosclerosis	20.0	15.6	13.0	10.3	10.0	8.4	5.7	4.0	31.7	29.4	23.9
Other	11.0	12.5	8.8	9.2	9.2	8.8	5.5	5.4	25.3	20.0	22.0
Malignancies[3]	149.2	162.8	183.9	191.8	193.3	129.9	132.8	133.6	330.7	416.5	461.6
Percent of total	15.6	17.2	20.9	22.2	22.1	18.2	22.7	24.5	17.2	20.9	22.1
Of respiratory and intrathoracic organs	22.2	34.2	47.9	52.3	53.3	28.4	36.4	38.8	69.5	108.5	127.3
Of digestive organs and peritoneum	50.8	46.6	48.8	49.3	48.8	35.2	33.0	31.6	94.7	110.6	116.6
Of genital organs	21.6	20.3	20.5	20.7	20.8	15.6	13.6	13.0	41.2	46.4	49.7
Of breast	13.4	14.7	15.8	16.8	16.9	12.6	12.5	12.7	29.9	35.9	40.4
Of urinary organs	7.1	7.6	7.9	7.9	7.9	5.7	5.2	5.0	15.5	17.8	18.9
Leukemia	7.1	7.1	7.3	7.2	7.3	5.8	5.4	5.0	14.5	16.5	17.3
Accidents and adverse effects	52.3	56.4	46.7	39.3	39.1	53.7	42.3	34.7	114.6	105.7	93.5
Motor vehicle	21.3	26.9	23.5	19.6	19.2	27.4	22.9	18.8	54.6	53.2	45.9
All other	31.0	29.5	23.3	19.7	19.9	26.3	19.5	16.0	60.0	52.5	47.6
Chronic obstructive pulmonary diseases and allied conditions[4]	9.9	15.2	24.7	29.2	31.3	11.6	15.9	18.7	30.9	56.1	74.7
Bronchitis, chronic and unspecified	1.8	2.9	1.6	1.5	1.5	2.1	1.0	0.8	5.8	3.7	3.6
Emphysema	5.2	11.2	6.1	5.6	5.9	8.4	4.0	3.7	22.7	13.9	14.2
Asthma	3.0	1.1	1.3	1.5	1.6	1.0	1.0	1.2	2.3	2.9	3.9
Other	(5)	(5)	15.7	20.6	22.2	(5)	9.9	12.9	(5)	35.6	53.0
Pneumonia and influenza	[6]37.3	30.9	24.1	24.9	28.3	22.1	12.9	13.4	62.7	54.6	67.6
Pneumonia	[6]32.9	29.0	22.9	24.4	27.5	20.8	12.4	13.0	59.0	51.9	65.6
Influenza	4.4	1.8	1.2	0.5	0.9	1.3	0.5	0.3	3.7	2.7	2.1

Cause of death	Crude death rate per 100,000 population[1]					Age-adjusted death rates per 100,000 population[1]			Deaths (1,000)		
	1960	1970	1980	1984	1985	1970	1980	1985	1970	1980	1985
Diabetes melitus	16.7	18.9	15.4	15.1	15.5	14.1	10.1	9.6	38.3	34.9	37.0
Suicide	10.6	11.6	11.9	12.4	12.3	11.8	11.4	11.5	23.5	26.9	29.5
Chronic liver disease and cirrhosis	11.3	15.5	13.5	11.6	11.2	14.7	12.2	9.6	31.4	30.6	26.8
Nephritis, nephrotic syndrome, and nephrosis	7.6	4.4	7.4	8.5	8.9	3.5	4.5	4.9	8.9	16.8	21.3
Homicide and legal intervention	4.7	8.3	10.7	8.4	8.3	9.1	10.8	8.3	16.8	24.3	19.9
Certain conditions originating in the perinatal period	37.4	21.3	10.1	8.0	8.1	(x)	(x)	(x)	43.2	22.9	19.2
Septicemia	1.1	1.7	4.2	6.4	7.2	1.4	2.6	4.1	3.5	9.4	17.2
Congenital anomalies	12.2	8.3	6.2	5.5	5.4	(x)	(x)	(x)	16.8	13.9	12.8
Other infective and parasitic diseases	4.3	3.4	2.2	2.9	3.4	2.8	1.8	2.8	6.9	5.1	8.1
Benign neoplasms[7]	2.7	2.4	2.7	2.7	2.8	2.0	2.0	1.9	4.8	6.2	6.7
Ulcer of stomach and duodenum	6.3	4.2	2.7	2.8	2.8	3.2	1.7	1.5	8.6	6.1	6.6
Hernia of abdominal cavity and intestinal obstruction[8]	5.1	3.6	2.4	2.2	2.2	2.6	1.4	1.1	7.2	5.4	5.4
Anemias	1.9	1.7	1.4	1.5	1.5	1.3	0.9	0.9	3.4	3.2	3.7
Cholelithiasis and other disorders of gallbladder	2.6	2.0	1.5	1.3	1.2	1.3	0.8	0.6	4.0	3.3	3.0
Nutritional deficiencies	(5)	1.2	1.0	1.1	1.2	0.8	0.5	0.5	2.5	2.4	2.9
Infections of kidney	4.3	4.0	1.2	0.9	0.8	2.8	0.7	0.4	8.2	2.7	2.0
Tuberculosis	6.1	2.6	0.9	0.7	0.7	2.2	0.6	0.5	5.2	2.0	1.8
Meningitis	1.3	0.8	0.6	0.5	0.5	0.8	0.6	0.4	1.7	1.4	1.2
Viral hepatitis	0.5	0.5	0.4	0.4	0.4	0.5	0.3	0.3	1.0	0.8	0.9
Hyperplasia of prostate	2.5	1.1	0.3	0.2	0.2	0.6	0.2	0.1	2.2	0.8	0.5
Acute bronchitis and bronchiolitis	0.7	0.6	0.3	0.2	0.3	0.5	0.2	0.1	1.3	0.6	0.6
Symptoms, signs, and ill-defined conditions	11.4	12.7	12.7	12.6	13.0	10.4	9.8	9.3	25.8	28.8	31.0
All other causes	39.7	53.5	53.0	59.6	64.4	44.0	36.8	40.2	108.8	120.0	153.0

x Not applicable.
[1] Based on resident population enumerated as of April 1 for 1960, 1970, and 1980 and estimated as of July 1 for other years.
[2] With or without renal disease.   [3] Includes other types of malignancies not shown separately.   [4] Prior to 1980, data are shown for bronchitis, emphysema, and asthma.
[5] Included in "all other causes."   Comparable data not available separately.   [6] Excludes pneumonia of newborn.   [7] Includes neoplasm of unspecified nature; beginning in 1980, also includes carcinoma in situ.   [8] Without mention of hernia.
Source: U.S. National Center for Health Statistics, *Vital Statistics of the United States*, annual; and unpublished data.

Home Remedies

The following should not be considered medical advice and is presented for informational purposes only. Always consult a doctor for medical problems.

acetaminophen A painkiller and fever reducer for persons allergic to aspirin.

alcohol A mild antiseptic or germ killer used topically.

ammonia For fainting, used as "smelling salts" by holding an open container under the victim's nose so vapor can be inhaled. Ammonia can also be used as a counterirritant and to neutralize insect bites.

aspirin A relatively safe, effective, and inexpensive painkiller and inflammation and fever reducer.

baking soda Used to neutralize acid burns.

benzalkonium chloride A detergent-type cleanser and disinfectant for treating wounds.

boric acid A weak germ and fungus killer, used as dusting powder.

burned toast Used as a substitute for activated charcoal (*see* universal antidote).

calamine lotion Used for sunburn and minor thermal (heat) burns that do not result in blisters.

chloride of lime (bleaching powder) A disinfectant. Avoid direct contact with the wound.

coffee Used as a stimulant in shock cases if the victim is conscious and bleeding internally.

egg white Used as a demulcent to soothe the stomach and retard absorption of a poison.

epsom salts Dissolved in warm water, can be used in treating wounds and to make wet dressings for them.

flour Made into a thin paste, can be used as a demulcent to soothe the stomach and retard absorption of a poison.

hydrogen peroxide A germ killer when in direct contact with bacteria.

milk Used as a demulcent to soothe the stomach and retard absorption of a poison.

milk of magnesia Used as a substitute for magnesium oxide (*see* universal antidote). Milk of magnesia is also used in small doses as an antacid for stomach upset.

mineral oil Used as drops to treat thermal (heat) burns of the eye.

oil of cloves Used for temporary relief of a toothache.

olive oil Used as drops to treat thermal (heat) burns of the eye. Olive oil is also used as an emollient to soften skin.

petrolatum (vaseline) A skin softener and protective ointment used on wound dressings.

powdered mustard (dry mustard) Used as an emetic. Dissolve one to three teaspoonfuls in a glass of warm water.

salt *See* table salt.

soap suds (not detergents) Used as an emetic and as an antidote for poisoning by certain metal compounds, such as mercuric chloride. Soap and clean water can also be used to cleanse wounds.

starch, cooked Made into a thin paste as a demulcent to soothe the stomach and retard absorption of a poison.

table salt Used as an emetic. Dissolve two teaspoonfuls in a glass of warm water. (Clean sea water can be used if an emetic or a wound cleanser is needed for an accident near an ocean beach.)

tea Made strong, used as a substitute for tannic acid. Tea is also used as a stimulant in shock cases when appropriate.

universal antidote Recommended as an antidote for poisoning when the poison cannot be identified. The universal antidote is made by mixing ½ ounce activated charcoal, ¼ ounce magnesium oxide, and ¼ ounce tannic acid in a glass of water.

vaseline *See* petrolatum.

vinegar (acetic acid) Used to neutralize alkali burns.

SHELF LIFE OF MEDICINE

Pharmacists generally do not mark containers with expiration dates, though the containers usually show the dates of the original prescriptions. If a prescription drug is more than one year old but is not in its original container clearly showing the expiration date, it should be replaced. First-aid creams in tubes usually have expiration dates marked on the tube, but the dates are generally hard to see. After the components separate, the creams should not be used. Vitamins and minerals will keep for a long time if protected from heat, moisture, and light. A good rule of thumb about the shelf life of drugs is "When in doubt, throw it out." Below is a list of the shelf life of some common drugs.

Cold tablets	1–2 years
Laxatives	2–3 years
Minerals	6 years or more
Nonprescription painkiller tablets	1–4 years
Prescription antibiotics	2–3 years
Prescription antihypertension tablets	2–4 years
Travel sickness tablets	2 years
Vitamins	6 years or more

Infectious Diseases and How They Are Spread

Disease	Agent	Transmission
AIDS (acquired immune deficiency syndrome)	Virus	Contact of body fluid (semen, blood, vaginal secretions) with that of an infected person. Sexual contact and sharing of unclean paraphernalia for intravenous drugs are the most common means of transmission.
Blastomycosis	Fungus	Inhaling contaminated dust
Botulism	Bacteria	Consuming contaminated food
Chicken pox	Virus	Direct or indirect contact with infected person
Common cold	Virus	Direct or indirect contact with infected person
Diphtheria	Bacteria	Direct contact with infected person
Encephalitis	Virus	Mosquito bite
Gonorrhea	Bacteria	Sexual contact
Hepatitis	Virus	Direct or indirect contact with infected person
Herpes simplex	Virus	Direct contact with infected person
Histoplasmosis	Fungus	Inhaling contaminated dust
Hookworm	Nematode	Contact with contaminated soil
Infectious mononucleosis	Virus	Direct or indirect contact with infected person
Influenza	Virus	Direct or indirect contact with infected person
Lyme disease	Bacteria	Deer tick bite
Malaria	Protozoa	Mosquito bite
Measles	Virus	Direct or indirect contact with infected person
Mumps	Virus	Direct or indirect contact with infected person
Pertussis (whooping cough)	Bacteria	Direct or indirect contact with infected person
Poliomyelitis	Virus	Direct contact with infected person
Rubella (German measles)	Virus	Direct or indirect contact with infected person

Scarlet fever	Bacteria	Direct or indirect contact with infected person
Spotted fever	Rickettsia	Tick bite
Syphilis	Bacteria	Sexual contact
Tapeworm	Nematode	Consuming infected meat or fish
Toxoplasmosis	Protozoa	Consuming raw meat; contact with contaminated soil
Trichomoniasis	Protozoa	Sexual contact
Typhus	Rickettsia	Lice, flea, tick bite
Yellow fever	Virus	Mosquito bite

Combining Forms of Medical Terms

Prefix	Meaning of prefix	Example
a-, ab-, an-	away, lack of, without	astigmatism
acro-	extremity, end	acroparesthesia
adeno-	gland	adenous
adreno-	adrenal gland	adrenocortex
aero-	gas, air	aerophagia
allo-	different, another	allorhythmia
ambi-	both, both sides	ambidextrous
antero-	before, in front of	anterograde
anti-	against	antiseptic
arterio-	artery	arteriospasm
arthro-, arthr-	joint	arthritis
bacterio-	bacteria	bacteriological
blephari-	eyelash, eyelid	blepharitis
brady-	slow	bradycardia
broncho-	windpipe	bronchospasm
cardio-	heart, heart region	cardiovascular
cephalo-	head	cephalometry
cerebro-	brain	cerebrovascular
cervico-	neck	cervicobrachial
chole-	bile	cholecystis
chondro-	cartilage	chondroblastoma
chromo-	color	chromogen
chylo-	lymph	chylomicron
contra-	against, opposite	contraindication
costo-	rib	costochondral
cyst-	bladder, sac	cystitis
dacryo-	tears	dacryocystitis
derma-	skin	dermatitis
dextro-	right side	dextromanual
dys-	abnormal, bad, painful	dysentery
encephalo-, encephal-	brain	encephalitis
endo-	inside	endocardium
entero-	intestines	enterospasm
ep-, epi-	at, over, upon	epiglottis
ex-, exo-	out, outside	excrement
fibrino-	threadlike	fibrinogen
fibro-	fiber, fibrous	fibrocystic
galact-	milk	galactose

Prefix	*Meaning of prefix*	*Example*
gastro-	stomach	gastroenteric
gloss-	tongue	glossitis
hemi-	half	hemiplegic
hepato-	liver	hepatocolic
hydro-	water	hydrocephalic
hyper-	above, beyond	hyperacidity
hypo-	below, less	hypoglycemia
ileo-	end of small intestine	ileocolic
ilio-	flank, upper hip bone	iliopelvic
infra-	below, inferior	infraorbital
inter-	between	interdigital
intra-	within	intrauterine
kerat-	cornea, hard tissue	keratoid
laryngo-, larying-	voice box	laryngitis
leuko-, leuk-	white	leukocyte
mega-	abnormally large	megacolon
mela-	black	melanin
myelo-, myel-	marrow, nerve sheath	myelination
myo-	muscle	myospasm
neo-	new	neoplasm
nephro-, nephr-	kidney	nephritis
neuro-, neuri-, neur-	nerve	neuritis
osteo-	bone	osteoarthritis
peri-, pneumo-	around or about the lungs or air	pericardial pneumonia
sacro-	sacrum (triangular bone above tailbone)	sacroiliac
sero-	serum, blood	serofibrous
tachy-	rapid	tachycardia
thrombo-	blood clot	thrombosis
tracheo-	windpipe	tracheotomy
utero-	uterus, womb	uterotomy
vaso-	blood vessel	vasodilator
ventro-	belly, abdominal	ventroptosia
zymo-	enzyme, fermentation	zymocide

Breast Self-Examination (BSE)

It is important for you to know the signs of breast cancer, because most breast cancers are discovered by women themselves, not their doctors. If you discover any of the signs of breast cancer, see your doctor immediately. It is a frightening experience to find a lump or another possible cancer sign, but you should know that 8 of 10 lumps are *not* cancerous. Many women have naturally lumpy breasts. But your doctor should determine whether a lump or other sign is actually cancer or a harmless condition.

Ask for a Breast Exam

Don't be embarrassed. Asking your doctor or nurse for a breast examination as part of an office visit is one good way to learn what is normal for your breasts. But examination by a doctor is not enough—you, too, should examine your breasts monthly. Ask your doctor or nurse to teach you breast self-examination (BSE) to be sure you are practicing it correctly.

Practice Breast Self-Examination

Breast self-examination is an important key to early diagnosis. Along with regular examination by your physician, monthly BSE can give you peace of mind because it helps you know how your breasts normally feel.

Knowing the normal feel of your breasts makes it easier to notice any changes early, when treatment is most effective. To examine your breasts correctly, you should follow the six steps described.

1. Stand before a mirror. Inspect both breasts for anything unusual, such as any discharge from the nipples or puckering, dimpling, or scaling of the skin.

   The next two steps are designed to emphasize any changes in the shape or contour of your breasts. As you do them, you should be able to feel your chest muscles tighten.

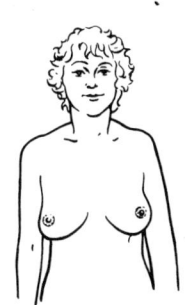

2. Watching closely in the mirror, clasp hands behind your head and press hands forward.

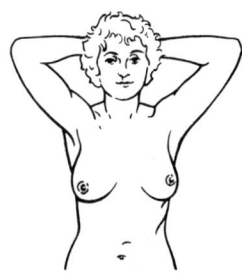

3. Next, press hands firmly on hips and bow slightly toward the mirror as you pull your shoulders and elbows forward.

   Some women do the next part of the exam in the shower: Fingers glide over soapy skin, making it easy to concentrate on the texture underneath.

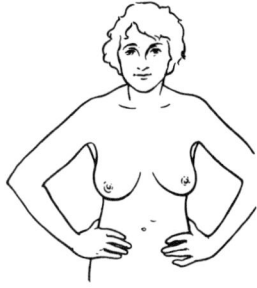

4. Raise your left arm. Use three or four fingers of your right hand to explore your left breast firmly, carefully, and thoroughly. Beginning at the outer edge, press the flat part of your fingers in small circles, moving the circles slowly around the breast. Gradually work toward the nipple. Be sure to cover the entire breast. Pay special attention to the area between the breast and the armpit, including the armpit itself. Feel for any unusual lump or mass under the skin.

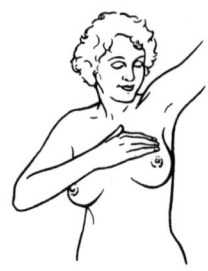

5. Gently squeeze the nipple and look for a discharge. Repeat the exam on your right breast.

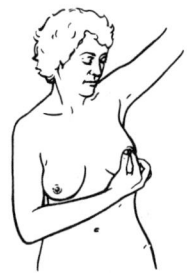

6. Repeat steps 4 and 5 lying down. Lie flat on your back with your left arm over your head and a pillow or folded towel under your left shoulder. This position flattens the breast and makes it easier to examine. Use the same circular motion described earlier. Repeat on your right breast.

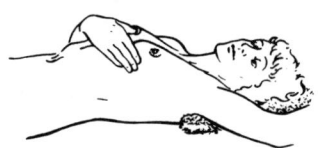

When to Examine Your Breasts

Every month! If you menstruate, the best time to practice BSE is two or three days after the end of your period, when your breasts are least likely to be tender or swollen. If you no longer menstruate, choose a day such as your birthdate to practice BSE. That way, you will remember to do it every month.

Recommended Daily Dietary Allowances (RDAs)

Recommended Daily Dietary Allowances (RDAs) of Calories and Proteins

	Age	Pounds	Height (in inches)	Calories needed	Grams of protein needed
Males	11–14	97	63	2,800	44
	15–18	134	69	3,000	54
	19–22	147	69	3,000	54
	23–50	154	69	2,700	56
	51 +	154	69	2,400	58
Females	11–14	97	62	2,400	44
	15–18	119	65	2,100	48
	19–22	128	65	2,100	46
	23–50	128	65	2,000	46
	51 +	128	65	1,800	46
Pregnant				+ 300	+ 30
Nursing				+ 500	+ 20

Recommended Daily Dietary Allowances (RDAs) of Fat-Soluble Vitamins (in International Units)

	Age	Pounds	Height (in inches)	Vitamin A	Vitamin D	Vitamin E
Males	11–14	97	63	5,000	400	12
	15–18	134	69	5,000	400	15
	19–22	147	69	5,000	400	15
	23–50	154	69	5,000		15
	51 +	154	69	5,000		15
Females	11–14	97	62	4,000	400	12
	15–18	119	65	4,000	400	12
	15–22	128	65	4,000	400	12
	23–50	128	65	4,000		12
	51 +	128	65	4,000		12
Pregnant				5,000	400	15
Nursing				6,000	400	15

**Recommended Daily Dietary Allowances (RDAs)
of Water-Soluble Vitamins (in Milligrams)**

	Age	Pounds	Height (in inches)	Vitamin C	Folic acid	Niacin	Riboflavin	Thiamine	Vitamin B-6	Vitamin B-12
Males	11–14	97	63	45	400	18	1.5	1.4	1.6	3.0
	15–18	134	69	45	400	20	1.8	1.5	2.0	3.0
	19–22	147	69	45	400	20	1.8	1.5	2.0	3.0
	23–50	154	69	45	400	18	1.6	1.4	2.0	3.0
	51+	154	69	45	400	16	1.5	1.2	2.0	3.0
Females	11–14	97	62	45	400	16	1.3	1.2	1.6	3.0
	15–18	119	65	45	400	14	1.4	1.1	2.0	3.0
	19–22	128	65	45	400	14	1.4	1.1	2.0	3.0
	23–50	128	65	45	400	13	1.2	1.0	2.0	3.0
	51+	128	65	45	400	12	1.1	1.0	2.0	3.0
Pregnant				60	800	+2	0.3	+0.3	2.5	4.0
Nursing				80	600	+4	+0.5	+0.3	2.5	4.0

Nutritive Values of foods

Composition of Foods (100 grams, Edible Portion)

Food and description	Water (percent)	Food energy (calories)	Protein (grams)	Fat (grams)	Carbohydrate Total (grams)	Carbohydrate Fiber (grams)	Ash (grams)
Ale, *See* Beverages, alcoholic: Beer							
Almonds, roasted and salted	.7	627	18.6	57.7	19.5	2.6	3.5
Apple butter	51.6	58	.4	.8	46.8	1.1	.4
Apple juice, canned or bottled	87.8	47	.1	Trace	11.9	.1	.2
Apples, raw, fresh, not pared	84.4	58	.2	.6	14.5	1	.3
Apricots, raw	85.3	51	1.0	.2	12.8	.6	.7
Asparagus, cooked spears, boiled, drained	93.6	20	2.2	.2	3.6	.7	.4
Avocados, raw	74	167	2.1	16.4	6.3	1.6	1.2
Baby foods:							
Cereals:							
Barley, added nutrients	6.6	348	13.4	1.2	73.6	1.2	5.2
Oatmeal, added nutrients	7	375	16.5	5.5	66	1.5	5
Desserts, canned:							
Custard pudding	76.5	100	2.3	1.8	18.6	.2	.8
Fruit pudding	75.7	96	1.2	.9	21.6	.3	.6
Dinners, canned:							
Beef noodle	88.2	48	2.8	1.1	6.8	.3	1.1
Cereal, egg yolk, bacon	84.7	82	2.9	4.9	6.6	.1	.9
Beef with vegetables	81.6	87	7.4	3.7	6	.2	1.3
Chicken with vegetables	79.6	100	7.4	4.6	7.2	.2	1.2
Turkey with vegetables	81.3	86	6.7	3.2	7.6	.5	1.2
Veal with vegetables	85	63	7.1	1.6	5.1	.2	1.2

Recommended Daily Dietary Allowances (RDAs) of Minerals (in Milligrams)

	Age	Pounds	Height (in inches)	Calcium	Phosphorus	Iodine	Iron	Magnesium	Zinc
Males	11–14	97	63	1,200	1,200	130	18	350	15
	15–18	134	69	1,200	1,200	150	18	400	15
	19–22	147	69	800	800	140	10	350	15
	23–50	154	69	800	800	130	10	350	15
	51+	154	69	800	800	110	10	350	15
Females	11–14	97	62	1,200	1,200	115	18	300	15
	15–18	119	65	1,200	1,200	115	18	300	15
	19–22	128	65	800	800	100	18	300	15
	23–50	128	65	800	800	100	18	300	15
	51+	128	65	800	800	80	10	300	15
Pregnant				1,200	1,200	125	*18+	450	20
Nursing		1,200	1,200	150	18	450	25		

* A pregnant woman usually requires iron supplement tablets because of the difficulty in providing an adequate iron intake in an otherwise balanced diet.

Calcium (milligrams)	Phosphorus (milligrams)	Iron (milligrams)	Sodium (milligrams)	Potassium (milligrams)	Vitamin A value (international units)	Thiamine (milligrams)	Riboflavin (milligrams)	Niacin (milligrams)	Ascorbic Acid (milligrams)
235	504	4.7	198	773	0	.05	.92	3.5	0
14	36	.7	2	252	0	.01	02	.2	2
0	9	.6	1	101	—	.01	.02	.1	1
7	10	.3	1	110	90	.03	.02	.1	4
17	23	.5	1	281	2,700	.03	.04	.6	10
21	50	.6	1	183	900	.16	.18	1.4	26
10	42	.6	4	604	290	.11	.20	1.6	14
736	821	53.2	452	413	(0)	3.71	1.20	32.2	(0)
757	734	48.2	437	374	(0)	2.58	1.05	21.3	(0)
64	62	.3	150	94	100	.02	.12	.1	1
27	34	.3	128	75	100	.03	.05	.1	3
12	29	.5	269	159	620	.02	.05	.5	2
29	60	.8	301	36	520	.05	.06	.4	—
13	84	1.2	304	113	1,100	.07	.17	1.6	2
22	85	.9	265	71	1,000	.09	.15	1.6	2
38	63	.6	348	122	1,000	.13	.13	1.8	2
11	71	.8	323	95	800	.08	.15	2	2

Composition of Foods (100 grams, Edible Portion) *(Continued)*

Food and description	Water (percent)	Food energy (calories)	Protein (grams)	Fat (grams)	Carbohydrate Total (grams)	Fiber (grams)	Ash (grams)
Fruits, canned:							
Applesauce	80.8	72	.2	.2	18.6	.5	.2
Bananas	77.5	84	.4	.2	21.6	.1	.3
Peaches	78.1	81	.6	.2	20.7	.5	.4
Pears	82.2	66	.3	.1	17.1	1	.3
Plums with tapioca	74.8	94	.4	.2	24.3	.3	.3
Prunes with tapioca	76.7	86	.3	.2	22.4	.3	.4
Meats, poultry, and eggs, canned:							
Beef, strained	80.3	99	14.7	4	(0)	(0)	1
Beef heart	81.1	93	13.5	3.8	.4	(0)	1.2
Chicken	77.2	127	13.7	7.6	(0)	(0)	1.5
Lamb, strained	79.3	107	14.6	4.9	(0)	(0)	1.2
Liver, strained	79.7	97	14.1	3.4	1.5	(0)	1.3
Pork, strained	77.7	118	15.4	5.8	(0)	(0)	1.1
Veal, strained	80.7	91	15.5	2.7	(0)	(0)	1.1
Vegetables, canned:							
Beans, green	92.5	22	1.4	.1	5.1	.8	.9
Beets, strained	89.2	37	1.4	.1	8.3	.6	1
Carrots	91.5	29	.7	.1	6.8	.6	.9
Peas, strained	85.5	54	4.2	.2	9.3	.8	.8
Spinach, creamed	88.1	43	2.3	.7	7.5	.4	1.4
Squash	92.1	25	.7	.1	6.2	.8	.9
Sweet potatoes	82.3	67	1.0	.2	15.5	.5	1
Tomato soup, strained	83.4	54	1.9	.1	13.5	.2	1.1
Bacon, Canadian, broiled or fried, drained	49.9	277	27.6	17.5	.3	0	4.7
Bacon, cured:							
Canned	16.7	685	8.5	71.5	1.0	0	2.3
Broiled or fried, drained	8.1	611	30.4	52	3.2	0	6.3
Baking powders:							
Cream of tartar, with tartaric acid	1.0	78	.1	Trace	18.9	Trace	—
Sodium aluminum sulfate with monocalcium phosphate mono-hydrate	1.6	129	.1	Trace	31.2	Trace	—
Bamboo shoots, raw	91.0	27	2.6	.3	5.2	.7	.9
Bananas, raw, common	75.7	85	1.1	.2	22.2	.5	.8
Barley, pearled, light	11.1	349	8.2	1.0	78.8	.5	.9
Bass, striped, oven-fried	60.8	196	21.5	8.5	6.7	—	2.5
Beans, common:							
White, cooked	69	118	7.8	.6	21.2	1.5	1.4
Canned, solids and liquids, with pork and tomato sauce	70.7	122	6.1	2.6	19	1.4	1.6
Beans, lima, boiled, drained	71.1	111	7.6	.5	19.8	1.8	1
Beans, snap, green, boiled, drained	92.4	25	1.6	.2	5.4	1	.4
Bean sprouts, mung, boiled, drained	91	28	3.2	.2	5.2	.7	.4
Beef:							
Chuck, choice, braised or pot-roasted (81% lean, 19% fat)	49.4	327	26	23.9	0	0	.7
Corned, cooked, medium fat	43.9	372	22.9	30.4	0	0	2.9
Hamburger:							
Lean, cooked	60.0	219	27.4	11.3	0	0	1.3
Regular, cooked	54.2	286	24.2	0	0	0	1.3

Calcium (milli-grams)	Phospho-rus (milli-grams)	Iron (milli-grams)	Sodium (milli-grams)	Potassium (milli-grams)	Vitamin A value (interna-tional units)	Thiamine (milli-grams)	Riboflavin (milli-grams)	Niacin (milli-grams)	Ascorbic Acid (milli-grams)
4	7	.4	6	64	40	.01	.02	.1	Trace
13	10	.2	29	118	70	.02	.02	.7	35
6	14	.3		80	500	.01	.02	.7	3
7	8	.2	4	62	30	.02	.02	.2	2
5	12	.4	38	44	250	.01	.02	.2	2
7	21	.9	33	120	400	.02	.06	.4	4
8	127	2	228	183	—	.01	.16	3.5	0
5	155	3.7	208	—	—	.6	.62	3.6	0
—	129	1.9	263	96	—	.02	.16	3.5	0
9	124	2.1	241	181	—	.02	.17	3.3	—
6	182	5.6	253	202	24,000	.05	2.00	7.6	10
8	130	1.5	223	178	—	.19	.20	2.7	—
10	145	1.7	226	214	—	.03	.20	4.3	—
33	25	1.1	213	93	400	.02	.06	.3	3
18	27	.7	212	228	20	.02	.03	.1	3
23	21	.5	169	181	13,000	.02	.03	.4	3
11	63	1.2	194	100	500	.08	.09	1.2	10
64	63	.6	272	142	5,000	.02	.13	.3	6
24	17	.4	292	138	2,400	.02	.04	.3	8
16	34	.4	187	180	4,900	.04	.03	.4	8
24	52	.4	294	200	1,000	.05	.12	.7	3
19	218	4.1	2,555	432	(0)	.92	.17	5	—
15	92	1.4	—	—	(0)	.23	.10	1.5	—
14	224	3.3	1,021	236	(0)	.51	.34	5.2	—
0	0	0	7,300	3,800	(0)	(0)	(0)	(0)	(0)
1,932	2,904	—	10,953	150	(0)	(0)	(0)	(0)	(0)
13	59	.5	—	533	20	.15	.07	.6	4
8	26	.7	1	370	190	.05	.06	.7	10
16	189	2	3	160	(0)	.12	.05	3.1	(0)
—	—	—	—	—	—	—	—	—	—
50	148	2.7	7	416	0	.14	.07	.7	0
54	92	1.8	463	210	130	.08	.03	.6	2
47	121	2.5	1	422	280	.18	.10	1.3	17
50	37	.6	4	151	540	.07	.09	.5	12
17	48	.9	4	156	20	.09	.10	.7	6
11	140	3.3	60	370	40	.05	.20	4	—
9	93	2.9	1,740	150	—	.02	.18	1.5	0
12	230	3.5	48	558	20	.09	.23	6	—
11	194	3.2	47	450	40	.09	.21	5.4	—

Composition of Foods (100 grams, Edible Portion) *(Continued)*

Food and description	Water (percent)	Food energy (calories)	Protein (grams)	Fat (grams)	Carbohydrate Total (grams)	Fiber (grams)	Ash (grams)
Ribs, roasted (55% lean, 45% fat)	36.3	481	18.3	44.7	0	0	.7
T-bone steak, choice, broiled (56% lean, 44% fat)	36.4	473	19.5	43.2	0	0	.9
Beef greens, common, boiled, drained	93.6	18	1.7	.2	3.3	1.1	1.2
Beets, boiled, drained	90.1	32	1.1	.1	7.2	.8	.7
Beverages, alcoholic:							
Beer, alcohol 4.5% by volume (3.6% by weight)	92.1	42	.3	0	3.8	—	.2
Gin, rum, vodka, whiskey:							
80-proof (33.4% alcohol by weight)	66.6	231	—	—	Trace	—	—
86-proof (36.0% alcohol by weight)	64	249	—	—	Trace	—	—
90-proof (37.9% alcohol by weight)	62.1	262	—	—	Trace	—	—
94-proof (39.7% alcohol by weight)	60.3	275	—	—	Trace	—	—
100-proof (42.5% alcohol by weight)	57.5	295	—	—	Trace	—	—
Wines:							
Dessert, alcohol 18.8% by volume (15.3% by weight)	76.7	137	.1	0	7.7	—	.2
Table, alcohol 12.2% by volume (9.9% by weight)	85.6	85	.1	0	4.2	—	.2
Beverages, carbonated, nonalcoholic:							
Cola	90	39	(0)	(0)	10	0)	—
Ginger ale	92	31	(0)	(0)	8	(0)	—
Root beer	89.5	41	(0)	(0)	10.5	(0)	—
Biscuits, baking powder, baked with enriched flour	27.4	369	7.4	17	45.8	.2	2.4
Blackberries, canned, solids and liquid, juice pack	85.8	54	.8	.8	12.1	2.7	.5
Blueberries, canned, solids and liquid, water pack	89.3	39	.5	.2	9.8	1	.2
Bouillon cubes or powder	4	120	20	3	5	—	68
Bran flakes (40% bran), added thiamine	3	303	10.2	1.8	80.6	3.6	4.4
Brazil nuts	4.6	654	14.3	66.9	10.9	3.1	3.3
Breads:							
White:							
Enriched, with 1% to 2% nonfat dry milk	35.8	269	8.7	3.2	50.4	.2	1.9
Toasted	25.3	314	10.1	3.7	58.7	.2	2.2
Whole-wheat, with 2% nonfat dry milk	36.4	243	10.5	3.0	47.7	1.6	2.4
Toasted	24.3	289	12.5	3.6	56.7	1.9	2.9
Broccoli spears, boiled, drained	91.3	26	3.1	.3	4.5	1.5	.8
Bulgur, dry, from hard red winter wheat	10	354	11.2	1.5	75.7	1.7	1.6
Buns. *See* Rolls and buns							

Calcium (milligrams)	Phosphorus (milligrams)	Iron (milligrams)	Sodium (milligrams)	Potassium (milligrams)	Vitamin A value (international units)	Thiamine (milligrams)	Riboflavin (milligrams)	Niacin (milligrams)	Ascorbic Acid (milligrams)
8	153	2.4	60	370	90	.05	.14	3.4	—
8	166	2.6	60	370	80	.06	.16	4.1	—
99	25	1.9	76	332	5,100	.07	.15	.3	15
14	23	.5	43	208	20	.03	.04	.3	6
5	30	Trace	7	25	—	Trace	.03	.6	—
—	—	—	1	2	—	—	—	—	—
—	—	—	1	2	—	—	—	—	—
—	—	—	1	2	—	—	—	—	—
—	—	—	1	2	—	—	—	—	—
—	—	—	1	2	—	—	—	—	—
8	—	—	4	75	—	.01	.02	.2	—
9	10	.4	5	92	—	Trace	.01	.1	—
—	—	—	—	—	(0)	(0)	(0)	(0)	(0)
—	—	—	—	—	(0)	(0)	(0)	(0)	(0)
—	—	—	—	—	(0)	(0)	(0)	(0)	(0)
121	175	1.6	626	117	Trace	.21	.21	1.8	Trace
25	17	.9	1	170	150	.02	.03	.3	10
10	9	.7	1	60	40	.01	.01	.2	7
—	—	—	24,000	100	—	—	—	—	—
71	495	4.4	925	—	(0)	.40	.17	6.2	(0)
186	693	3.4	1	715	Trace	.96	.12	1.6	—
70	87	2.4	507	85	Trace	.25	.17	2.3	Trace
81	101	2.8	590	99	Trace	.23	.20	2.7	Trace
99	228	2.3	527	273	Trace	.26	.12	2.8	Trace
118	271	2.7	627	325	Trace	.25	.15	3.4	Trace
88	62	.8	10	267	2,500	.09	.20	.8	90
29	338	3.7	—	229	(0)	.28	.14	4.5	(0)

Composition of Foods (100 grams, Edible Portion) *(Continued)*

Food and description	Water (percent)	Food energy (calories)	Protein (grams)	Fat (grams)	Carbohydrate		Ash (grams)
					Total (grams)	Fiber (grams)	
Butter	15.5	716	.6	81	.4	0	2.5
Buttermilk, fluid, cultured (from skim milk)	90.5	36	3.6	.1	5.1	0	.7
Cabbage, common:							
Raw	92.4	24	1.3	.2	5.4	.8	.7
Shredded, boiled, drained	93.9	20	1.1	.2	4.3	.8	.5
Cakes:							
Baked from home recipes:							
Angelfood	31.5	269	7.1	.2	60.2	0	1
Boston cream pie	34.5	302	5	9.4	49.9	0	1.2
Chocolate with chocolate icing	22	369	4.5	16.4	55.8	.3	1.3
Fruitcake, dark, with enriched flour	18.1	379	4.8	15.3	59.7	.6	2.1
White, without icing	24.2	375	4.6	16	54	.1	1.2
Candy:							
Chocolate:							
Bittersweet	1.8	477	7.9	39.7	46.8	1.8	2.3
Fudge	8.2	400	2.7	12.2	75	.2	1.8
Semisweet	1.1	507	4.2	35.7	57	1	1.2
Sweet	.9	528	4.4	35.1	57.9	.5	1.2
Hard	1.4	386	0	1.1	97.2	0	.3
Jelly beans	6.3	367	Trace	.5	93.1	Trace	.1
Marshmallows	17.3	319	2.0	Trace	80.4	0	.3
Peanut brittle	2	421	5.7	10.4	81	.5	.9
Carrots:							
Raw	88.2	42	1.1	.2	9.7	1	.8
Boiled, drained	91.2	31	.9	.2	7.1	1	.6
Cauliflower:							
Raw	91	27	2.7	.2	5.2	1	.9
Boiled, drained	92.8	22	2.3	.2	4.1	1	.6
Celery, raw	94.1	17	.9	.1	3.9	.6	1
Cheeses:							
Cheddar	37	398	25	32.2	2.1	0	3.7
Cottage, creamed	78.3	106	13.6	4.2	2.9	0	1
Cream	51	374	8	37.7	2.1	0	1.2
Parmesan	30	393	36	26	2.9	0	5.1
Pasteurized process, American	40	370	23.2	30	1.9	0	4.9
Cherries:							
Canned, sour, red, solids and liquid, water pack	88	43	.8	.2	10.7	.1	.3
Raw, sweet	80.4	70	1.3	.3	17.4	.4	.6
Chestnuts, fresh	52.8	194	2.9	1.5	42.1	1.1	1
Chewing gum	3.5	317	—	—	95.2	—	1.3
Chicken:							
Roasted light meat without skin	63.8	166	31.6	3.4	0	0	1.2
Roasted dark meat without skin	64.4	176	28	6.3	0	0	1.2
Chili con carne, canned:							
With beans	72.4	133	7.5	6.1	12.2	.6	1.8
Without beans	66.9	200	10.3	14.8	5.8	.2	2.2
Chocolate syrup, fudge type	25.4	330	5.1	13.7	54	.4	1.4
Clams, raw, soft, meat only	80.8	82	14	1.9	1.3	—	2
Cocoa, dry powder, high-fat, plain	3	299	16.8	23.7	48.3	4.3	5

Calcium (milligrams)	Phosphorus (milligrams)	Iron (milligrams)	Sodium (milligrams)	Potassium (milligrams)	Vitamin A value (international units)	Thiamine (milligrams)	Riboflavin (milligrams)	Niacin (milligrams)	Ascorbic Acid (milligrams)
20	16	0	987	23	3,300	—	—	—	0
121	95	Trace	130	140	Trace	.04	.18	.1	1
49	29	.4	20	233	130	.05	.05	.3	47
44	20	.3	14	163	130	.04	.04	.3	33
9	22	.2	283	88	0	.01	.14	.2	0
	101	.5	186	89	210	.03	.11	.2	Trace
70	131	1	235	154	160	.02	.10	.2	Trace
72	113	2.6	158	496	120	.13	.14	.8	Trace
63	91	.2	323	76	30	.01	.08	.2	Trace
58	284	5	3	615	40	.03	.17	1	0
77	84	1	190	147	Trace	.02	.09	.2	Trace
30	150	2.6	2	325	20	.01	.08	.5	0
90	142	1.4	33	269	19	.02	.14	.3	Trace
21	7	1.9	32	4	0	0	0	0	0
12	4	1.1	12	1	0	0	Trace	Trace	0
18	6	1.6	39	6	0	0	Trace	Trace	0
35	95	2.3	31	151	0	.16	.03	3.4	0
37	36	.7	47	341	11,000	.06	.05	.6	8
33	31	.6	33	222	10,500	.05	.05	.5	6
25	56	1.1	13	295	60	.11	.10	.7	78
21	42	.7	9	206	60	.09	.08	.6	55
39	28	.3	126	341	240	.03	.03	.3	9
750	478	1.0	700	82	(1,130)	.03	.46	.1	(0)
94	152	.3	229	85	(170)	.03	.25	.1	(0)
62	95	.2	250	74	(1,540)	(.02)	.24	.1	(0)
1,140	781	.4	734	149	(1,060)	.02	.73	.2	(0)
697	771	.9	1,136	80	(1,220)	.02	.41	Trace	(0)
15	13	.3	2	130	680	.03	.02	.2	5
22	19	.4	2	191	110	.05	.06	.4	10
27	88	1.7	6	454	—	.22	.22	6	—
—	—	—	—	—	(0)	(0)	(0)	(0)	(0)
11	265	1.3	64	411	60	.04	.10	11.6	—
13	229	1.7	86	321	150	.07	.23	5.6	—
32	126	1.7	531	233	60	.03	.07	1.3	—
38	152	1.4	—	—	150	.02	.12	2.2	—
127	159	1.3	89	284	150	.04	.22	.4	Trace
—	183	3.4	36	235	—	—	—	—	—
133	648	10.7	6	1,522	30	.11	.46	2.4	0

Composition of Foods (100 grams, Edible Portion) *(Continued)*

Food and description	Water (percent)	Food energy (calories)	Protein (grams)	Fat (grams)	Carbohydrate Total (grams)	Fiber (grams)	Ash (grams)
Coconut meat:							
Dried, unsweetened	3.5	662	7.2	64.9	23	3.9	1.4
Fresh	50.9	346	3.5	35.3	9.4	4	.9
Cod, broiled	64.6	170	28.5	5.3	0	0	—
Coffee, instant, water-soluble solids:							
Beverage	98.1	1	Trace	Trace	Trace	Trace	.1
Dry powder	2.6	129	Trace	Trace	(35.)	Trace	9.7
Coleslaw, with mayonnaise	79	144	1.3	14	4.8	.7	.9
Cookies:							
Assorted, packaged, commercial	2.6	480	5.1	20.2	71	.1	1.1
Chocolate chip, home recipe, with enriched flour	3	516	5.4	30.1	60.1	.4	1.4
Oatmeal with raisins	2.8	451	6.2	15.4	73.5	.4	2.1
Corn, sweet, boiled, drained, white and yellow, kernels, cut off cob before cooking	76.5	83	3.2	1	18.8	.7	.5
Cornbread, southern style, with whole-ground cornmeal	53.9	207	7.4	7.2	29.1	.5	2.4
Cornflour	12	368	7.8	2.6	76.8	.7	.8
Corn grits, degermed, enriched, cooked	87.1	51	1.2	.1	11	.1	.6
Cornstarch	12	362	.3	Trace	87.6	.1	.1
Crackers, saltines	4.3	433	9	12	71.5	.4	3.2
Cranberry sauce, sweetened, canned, strained	62.1	146	.1	.2	37.5	.2	.1
Cream:							
Half-and-half	79.7	134	3.2	11.7	4.6	0	.6
Heavy whipping	56.6	352	2.2	37.6	3.1	0	.4
Cress, garden, raw	89.4	32	2.6	.7	5.5	1.1	1.8
Cucumbers, raw, not pared	95.1	15	.9	.1	3.4	.6	.5
Dates, domestic, natural and dry	22.5	274	2.2	.5	72.9	2.3	1.9
Doughnuts:							
Cake-type, enriched flour	23.7	391	4.6	18.6	51.4	.1	1.7
Yeast-leavened, enriched flour	28.3	414	6.3	26.7	37.7	.2	1
Eggs, chicken:							
Fried	67.7	216	13.8	17.2	.3	0	1
Poached	73.3	163	12.7	11.6	.8	0	1.4
Scrambled	72.1	173	11.2	12.9	2.4	0	1.4
Endive, raw	93.1	20	1.7	.1	4.1	.9	1
Fats, cooking (vegetable fat)	0	884	0	100	0	0	0
Figs, dried, uncooked	23	274	4.3	1.3	69.1	5.6	2.3
Frankfurters. *See* Sausage							
Fruit cocktail, canned, solids and liquid, light syrup pack	83.6	60	.4	.1	15.7	.4	.2
Gelatin dessert, with water, plain	84.2	59	1.5	0	14.1	0	.2
Goose, domesticated, roasted	39.1	426	23.7	36.0	0	0	1.2
Grapefruit, raw, pulp, all varieties	88.4	41	.5	.1	10.6	.2	.4
Grape juice, canned or bottled	82.9	66	.2	Trace	16.6	Trace	.3
Haddock, dipped in egg, milk, and breadcrumbs, fried	66.3	165	19.6	6.4	5.8	—	1.9
Halibut, Atlantic and Pacific, broiled	66.6	171	25.2	7	0	0	1.7

Calcium (milli-grams)	Phospho-rus (milli-grams)	Iron (milli-grams)	Sodium (milli-grams)	Potassium (milli-grams)	Vitamin A value (interna-tional units)	Thiamine (milli-grams)	Riboflavin (milli-grams)	Niacin (milli-grams)	Ascorbic Acid (milli-grams)
26	187	3.3	—	585	0	.06	.04	.6	0
13	95	1.7	23	256	0	.05	.02	.5	3
31	274	1	110	407	180	.08	.11	3	—
2	4	.1	1	36	0	0	Trace	.3	0
179	383	5.6	72	3,256	0	0	.21	30.6	0
44	29	.4	120	199	160	.05	.05	.3	29
37	163	.7	365	67	80	.03	.05	.4	Trace
34	99	2.1	348	117	110	.11	.11	.9	Trace
21	102	2.9	162	370	50	.11	.08	.5	Trace
3	89	.6	Trace	165	400	.11	.10	1.3	7
120	211	1.1	628	157	150	.13	.19	.6	1
6	(164)	1.8	(1)	—	340	.20	.06	1.4	(0)
1	10	.3	—	11	60	.04	.03	.4	(0)
(0)	(0)	(0)	Trace	Trace	(0)	(0)	(0)	(0)	(0)
20	90	1.2	(1,100)	(120)	(0)	.01	.04	1	(0)
6	4	.2	1	30	20	.01	.01	Trace	2
108	85	Trace	46	129	480	.03	.16	.1	1
75	59	Trace	32	89	1,540	.02	.11	Trace	1
81	76	1.3	14	606	9,300	.08	.26	1	69
25	27	1.1	6	160	250	.03	.04	.2	11
59	63	3	1	648	50	.09	.10	2.2	0
40	190	1.4	501	90	80	.16	.16	1.2	Trace
38	76	1.5	234	80	60	.16	.17	1.3	0
60	222	2.4	338	140	1,420	.10	.30	.1	0
55	203	2.2	271	128	1,170	.08	.25	.1	0
80	189	1.7	257	146	1,080	.08	.28	.1	0
81	54	1.7	14	294	3,300	.07	.14	.5	10
0	0	0	0	0	—		0	0	0
126	77	3	34	640	80	.10	.10	.7	(0)
9	12	.4	5	164	140	.02	.01	.5	2
—	—	—	51	—	—	—	—	—	—
(11)	(240)	(2.1)	—	—	—	(.08)	(.24)	(8.1)	—
16	16	.4	1	135	80	.04	.02	.2	38
11	12	.3	2	116	—	.04	.02	.2	Trace
40	247	1.2	177	348	—	.04	.07	3.2	2
16	248	.8	134	525	680	.05	.07	8.3	—

Composition of Foods (100 grams, Edible Portion) *(Continued)*

Food and description	Water (percent)	Food energy (calories)	Protein (grams)	Fat (grams)	Carbohydrate Total (grams)	Carbohydrate Fiber (grams)	Ash (grams)
Ham. *See* Pork							
Herring, pickled, Bismarck type	59.4	223	20.4	15.1	0	0	4
Hickory nuts	3.3	673	13.2	68.7	12.8	1.9	2
Horseradish, prepared	87.1	38	1.3	.2	9.6	.9	1.8
Ice cream and frozen custard:							
Regular, about 10% fat	63.2	193	4.5	10.6	20.8	0	.9
Rich, about 16% fat	62.8	222	2.6	16.1	18.0	0	.5
Ice cream cones	8.9	377	10	2.4	77.9	.2	.8
Jams and preserves	29	272	.6	.1	70	1.0	.3
Kale, boiled, drained, leaves and stems	91.2	28	3.2	.7	4	1.1	.9
Kidneys, beef, braised	53	252	33	12	.8	0	1.2
Leg of lamb, lean, roasted	61.6	192	28.6	7.7	0	0	2.1
Lemonade concentrate, frozen, diluted with 4⅓ parts water, by volume	88.5	44	.1	Trace	11.4	Trace	Trace
Lemon juice, raw	91	25	.5	.2	8	Trace	.3
Lemon peel, candied	17.4	316	.4	.3	80.6	2.3	—
Lentils, whole, cooked	72	106	7.8	Trace	19.3	1.2	.9
Lettuce, raw, Boston, Bibb	95.1	14	1.2	.2	2.5	.5	1
Liver, beef, fried	56	229	26.4	10.6	5.3	0	1.7
Lobster, northern, canned or cooked	76.8	95	18.7	1.5	.3	—	2.7
Macadamia nuts	3	691	7.8	71.6	15.9	2.5	1.7
Macaroni, enriched, cooked (tender stage)	72	111	3.4	.4	23	.1	1.2
Mackerel, Atlantic, canned, solids and liquid	66	183	19.3	11.1	0	0	3.2
Mackerel, Pacific, canned, solids and liquid	66.4	180	21.1	10	0	0	2.5
Mangoes, raw	81.7	66	.7	.4	16.8	.9	.4
Margarine	15.5	720	.6	81	.4	0	2.5
Marmalade, citrus	29	257	.5	.1	70.1	.4	.3
Milk, cow's:							
Canned:							
Condensed (sweetened)	27.1	321	8.1	8.7	54.3	0	1.8
Evaporated (unsweetened)	73.8	137	7	7.9	9.7	0	1.6
Dry, skim, instant	4	359	35.8	.7	51.6	0	7.9
Fluid:							
Skim	90.5	36	3.6	.1	5.1	0	.7
Whole, 3.7% fat	87.4	65	3.5	3.5	4.9	0	.7
Milk, human, U.S. samples	85.2	77	1.1	4	9.5	0	.2
Molasses, cane, light	24	252	—	—	65	—	6.3
Mushrooms, canned, solids and liquid	93.1	17	1.9	.1	2.4	.6	1.6
Muskmelons:							
Cantaloupes	91.2	30	.7	.1	7.5	.3	.5
Honeydews	90.6	33	.8	.3	7.7	.6	.6
Mussels, Atlantic and Pacific, raw, meat and liquid	83.8	66	9.6	1.4	3.1	—	2.1
Mustard, prepared, yellow	80.2	75	4.7	4.4	6.4	1	4.3
Mustard greens, boiled, drained	92.6	23	2.2	.4	4	.9	.8

Calcium (milli-grams)	Phos-phorus (milli-grams)	Iron (milli-grams)	Sodium (milli-grams)	Potassium (milli-grams)	Vitamin A value (interna-tional units)	Thiamine (milli-grams)	Riboflavin (milli-grams)	Niacin (milli-grams)	Ascorbic Acid (milli-grams)
—	—	—	—	—	—	—	—	—	—
Trace	360	2.4	—	—	—	—	—	—	—
61	32	.9	96	290	—	—	—	—	—
146	115	.1	63	181	440	.04	.21	.1	1
78	61	Trace	33	95	660	.02	.11	.1	1
156	198	.4	232	244	Trace	.05	.21	.5	Trace
20	9	1	12	88	10	.01	.03	.2	2
134	46	1.2	43	221	7,400	—	—	—	62
18	244	13.1	253	324	1,150	.51	4.82	10.7	—
12	237	2.2	290	290	—	.16	.30	6.1	—
1	1	Trace	Trace	16	Trace	Trace	.01	.1	7
7	10	.2	1	141	20	.03	.01	.1	46
—	—	—	—	—	—	—	—	—	—
25	119	2.1	—	249	20	.07	.06	.6	0
35	26	2	9	264	970	.06	.06	.3	8
11	476	8.8	184	380	53,400	.26	4.19	16.5	27
65	192	.8	210	180	—	.10	.07	—	—
48	161	2.0	—	264	0	.34	.11	1.3	0
8	50	.9	1	61	(0)	.14	.08	1.1	(0)
185	274	2.1	—	—	430	.06	.21	5.8	—
260	288	2.2	—	—	30	.03	8.8	—	
10	13	.4	7	189	4,800	.05	.05	1.1	35
20	16	0	987	23	3,300	—	—	—	0
35	9	.6	14	33	—	.02	.02	.1	6
262	206	.1	112	314	360	.08	.38	.2	1
252	205	.1	118	303	320	.04	.34	.2	1
1,293	1,005	.6	526	1,725	30	.35	1.78	.9	7
121	95	Trace	52	145	Trace	.04	.18	.1	1
118	93	Trace	50	144	140	.03	.17	.1	1
33	14	.1	16	51	240	.01	.04	.2	5
165	45	4.3	15	917	—	.07	.06	.2	
6	68	.5	400	197	Trace	.02	.25	2.0	2
14	16	.4	12	251	3,400	.04	.03	.6	33
14	16	.4	12	251	40	.04	.03	.6	23
—	—	—	—	—	—	—	—	—	—
84	73	2	1,252	130	—	—	—	—	—
138	32	1.8	18	220	5,800	.08	.14	.6	48

Composition of Foods (100 grams, Edible Portion) *(Continued)*

Food and description	Water (percent)	Food energy (calories)	Protein (grams)	Fat (grams)	Carbohydrate Total (grams)	Carbohydrate Fiber (grams)	Ash (grams)
Nectarines, raw	81.8	64	.6	Trace	17.1	.4	.5
Noodles, egg, enriched, cooked	70.4	125	4.1	1.5	23.3	.1	.7
Oatmeal, cooked	86.5	55	2	1	9.7	.2	.8
Ocean perch, Atlantic (redfish), dipped in egg, milk, and bread-crumbs, fried	59	227	19	13.3	6.8	0	1.9
Okra, boiled, drained	91.1	29	2	.3	6	1	.6
Oleomargine. *See* Margarine							
Olives:							
Green	78.2	116	1.4	12.7	1.3	1.3	6.4
Ripe, salt-cured, oil-coated, Greek-style	43.8	338	2.2	35.8	8.7	3.8	(9.5)
Onions, mature (dry):							
Boiled, drained	91.8	29	1.2	.1	6.5	.6	.4
Raw	89.1	38	1.5	.1	8.7	.6	.6
Onions, young green, raw, bulb and entire top	89.4	36	1.5	.2	8.2	(1.2)	.7
Opossum, roasted	57.3	221	30.2	10.2	0	0	2.3
Orange juice:							
Frozen concentrate, unsweetened:							
Diluted with 3 parts water, by volume	88.1	45	.7	.1	10.7	Trace	.4
Undiluted	58.2	158	2.3	.2	38	.2	1.3
Raw, all commercial varieties	88.3	45	.7	.2	10.4	.1	.4
Orange peel, candied	17.4	316	.4	.3	80.6	—	1.3
Oranges, all commercial varieties, peeled	86	49	1	.2	12.2	.5	.6
Oysters:							
Raw, meat only:							
Dipped in egg, milk, and bread-crumbs, fried	54.7	239	8.6	13.9	18.6	Trace	1.5
Eastern	84.6	66	8.4	1.8	3.4	—	1.8
Pacific and Western (Olympia)	79.1	91	10.6	2.2	6.4	—	1.7
Pancakes, home recipe, enriched flour	50.1	231	7.1	7	34.1	.1	1.7
Papayas, raw	58.7	39	.6	.1	10	.9	.6
Parsley, raw	85.1	44	3.6	.6	8.5	1.5	2.2
Parsnips, boiled, drained	82.2	66	1.5	.5	14.9	2	.9
Peaches:							
Canned, solids and liquid, heavy syrup pack	79.1	78	.4	.1	20.1	.4	.3
Raw	89.1	38	.6	.1	9.7	.6	.5
Peanut butter, with small amounts of added fat, salt	1.8	581	27.8	49.4	17.2	1.9	3.8
Peanuts:							
Raw, without skins	5.4	568	26.3	48.4	17.6	1.9	2.3
Roasted, salted	1.6	585	26.0	49.8	18.8	2.4	3.8
Pears:							
Canned, solids and liquid, heavy syrup pack	79.8	76	.2	.2	19.6	.6	.2
Raw, including skin	83.2	61	.7	.4	15.3	1.4	.4

Calcium (milligrams)	Phosphorus (milligrams)	Iron (milligrams)	Sodium (milligrams)	Potassium (milligrams)	Vitamin A value (international units)	Thiamine (milligrams)	Riboflavin (milligrams)	Niacin (milligrams)	Ascorbic Acid (milligrams)
4	24	.5	6	294	1,650	—	—	—	13
10	59	.9	2	44	70	.14	.08	1.2	(0)
9	57	.6	218	61	(0)	.08	.02	.1	(0)
33	226	1.3	153	284	—	.10	.11	1.8	—
92	41	.5	2	174	490	(.13)	(.18)	(.9)	20
61	17	1.6	2,400	55	300	—	—	—	—
—	29	—	3,288	—	—	—	—	—	—
24	29	.4	7	110	40	.03	.03	.2	7
27	36	.5	10	157	40	.03	.04	.2	10
51	39	1	5	231	(2,000)	.05	.05	.4	32
—	—	—	—	—	—	.12	.38	—	—
9	16	.1	1	186	200	.09	.01	.3	45
33	55	.4	2	657	710	.30	.05	1.2	158
11	17	.2	1	200	200	.09	.03	.4	50
—	—	—	—	—	—	—	—	—	—
41	20	.4	1	200	200	.10	.04	.4	(50)
152	241	8.1	206	203	440	.17	.29	3.2	—
94	143	5.5	73	121	310	.14	.18	2.5	—
85	153	7.2	—	—	—	.12	—	1.3	30
101	139	1.3	425	123	120	.17	.22	1.3	Trace
20	16	.3	3	234	1,750	.04	.04	.3	56
203	63	6.2	45	727	8,500	.12	.26	1.2	172
45	62	.6	8	379	30	.07	.08	.1	10
4	12	.3	2	130	430	.01	.02	.6	3
9	19	.5	1	202	1,330	.02	.05	1	7
63	407	2	607	670	—	.13	.13	15.7	0
59	409	2	5	674	0	.99	.13	15.8	0
74	401	2.1	418	674	—	.32	.13	17.2	0
5	7	.2	1	84	trace	.01	.02	.1	1
8	11	.3	2	130	20	.02	.04	.1	4

Composition of Foods (100 grams, Edible Portion) *(Continued)*

Food and description	Water (percent)	Food energy (calories)	Protein (grams)	Fat (grams)	Carbohydrate		Ash (grams)
					Total (grams)	Fiber (grams)	
Peas, green, immature:							
Boiled, drained	81.5	71	5.4	.4	12.1	2	.6
Canned:							
Alaska, regular pack, solids and liquids	82.6	66	3.5	.3	12.5	1.5	1.1
Low-sodium pack, solids and liquids	85.9	55	3.6	.3	9.8	1.3	.4
Peppers, sweet, immature, green, raw	93.4	22	1.2	.2	4.8	1.4	.4
Persimmons, native, raw	64.4	127	.8	.4	33.5	1.5	.9
Pickles:							
Cucumber:							
Dill	93.3	11	.7	.2	2.2	.5	3.6
Fresh (as bread-and-butter pickles)	78.7	73	.9	.2	17.9	.5	2.3
Sour	94.8	10	.5	.2	2	.5	2.5
Pies:							
Baked, piecrust with unenriched flour:							
Apple	47.6	256	2.2	11.1	38.1	.4	1
Chocolate meringue	48.4	252	4.8	12	33.5	.2	1.2
Pecan	19.5	418	5.1	22.9	51.3	.5	1.2
Raisin	42.5	270	2.6	10.7	43	.3	1.2
Rhubarb	47.4	253	2.5	10.7	38.2	.6	1.2
Pimientos, canned, solids and liquid	92.4	27	.9	.5	5.8	.6	.4
Pineapple:							
Candied	18	316	.8	.4	80	.8	.8
Raw	85.3	52	.4	.2	13.7	.4	.4
Pineapple juice, canned, unsweetened	85.6	55	.4	.1	13.5	.1	.4
Pizza, with cheese, home recipe, sausage topping	50.6	234	7.8	9.3	29.6	.3	2.7
Plantain, raw	66.4	119	1.1	.4	31.2	.4	.9
Plums, raw, Damson	81.1	66	.5	Trace	17.8	.4	.6
Pollock, cooked, creamed (with flour, butter, milk)	74.7	128	13.9	5.9	4	—	1.5
Popcorn, popped, oil and salt added	3.1	456	9.8	21.8	59.1	1.7	6.2
Pork, fresh:							
Bacon:							
Fat class (25% lean, 75% fat)	26.4	631	7.1	66.6	0	0	.3
Thin class (40% lean, 60% fat)	34.3	545	9.4	56	0	0	.5
Composite of trimmed lean cuts (ham, loin, shoulder, spareribs):							
Medium-fat class (77% lean, 23% fat), roasted	45.2	373	22.6	30.6	0	0	1.6
Ham, roasted (72% lean, 28% fat)	43.7	394	21.9	33.3	0	0	1
Potato chips	1.8	568	5.3	39.8	50	(1.6)	3.1
Potatoes:							
Baked in skin	75.1	93	2.6	.1	21.1	.6	1.1
Boiled in skin	79.8	76	2.1	.1	17.1	.5	.9
French-fried	44.7	274	4.3	13.2	36	1	1.8

Calcium (milligrams)	Phosphorus (milligrams)	Iron (milligrams)	Sodium (milligrams)	Potassium (milligrams)	Vitamin A value (international units)	Thiamine (milligrams)	Riboflavin (milligrams)	Niacin (milligrams)	Ascorbic Acid (milligrams)
23	99	1.8	1	196	540	.28	.11	2.3	20
20	66	1.7	236	96	450	.09	.05	.9	
20	66	1.7	3	96	450	.09	.05	.9	9
9	22	.7	13	213	420	.08	.08	.5	128
27	26	2.5	1	310	—	—	—	—	66
26	21	1	1,428	200	100	Trace	.02	Trace	6
32	27	1.8	673	—	140	Trace	.03	Trace	9
17	15	3.2	1,353	—	100	Trace	.02	Trace	7
8	22	.3	301	80	30	.02	.02	.4	1
69	98	.7	256	139	190	.03	.12	.2	Trace
47	103	2.8	221	123	160	.16	.07	.3	Trace
18	40	.9	285	192	Trace	.03	.03	.3	1
64	26	.7	270	159	50	.02	.04	.3	3
7	17	1.5	—	—	2,300	.02	.06	.4	95
—	—	—	—	—	—	—	—	—	—
17	8	.5	1	146	70	.09	.03	.2	17
15	9	.3	1	149	50	.05	.02	.2	9
17	92	1.2	729	168	560	.09	.12	1.5	9
7	30	.7	5	385	—	.06	.04	.6	14
18	17	.5	2	299	(300)	.08	.03	.5	—
—	—	—	111	238	—	.03	.13	.7	Trace
8	216	2.1	1,940	—	—	—	.09	1.7	0
4	62	1.1	*	—	(0)	.35	.08	1.8	—
5	92	1.4	*	—	(0)	.46	.11	2.4	—
10	232	2.9	*	—	(0)	.50	.23	4.9	—
10	225	2.9	*	—	(0)	.49	.22	4.4	—
40	139	1.8	—	1,130	Trace	.21	.07	4.8	16
9	65	.7	—	503	Trace	.10	.04	1.7	20
7	53	.6	—	407	Trace	.90	.04	1.5	16
15	111	1.3	—	853	Trace	.13	.08	3.1	21

Composition of Foods (100 grams, Edible Portion) *(Continued)*

Food and description	Water (percent)	Food energy (calories)	Protein (grams)	Fat (grams)	Carbohydrate Total (grams)	Fiber (grams)	Ash (grams)
Potato salad, home recipe, with mayonnaise and French dressing, hard-cooked eggs, seasonings	72.4	145	3	9.2	13.4	.4	2
Pretzels	4.5	390	9.8	4.5	75.9	.3	5.3
Prunes, cooked, fruit and liquid, added sugar	50.7	180	1.2	.2	47.1	(.8)	.8
Puddings, starch base, home recipe							
Chocolate	65.8	148	3.1	4.7	25.7	.2	.7
Vanilla (blancmange)	76	111	3.5	3.9	15.9	Trace	.7
Pumpkin, canned	90.2	33	1	.3	7.9	1.3	.6
Raccoon, roasted	54.8	255	29.2	14.5	0	0	1.5
Radishes, raw, common	94.5	17	1	.1	3.6	.7	.8
Raisins, natural, uncooked	18	289	2.5	.2	77.4	.9	1.9
Raspberries, raw, black	80.8	73	1.5	1.4	15.7	5.1	.6
Rhubarb, cooked, added sugar	62.8	141	.5	.1	36	.6	.6
Rice, white, enriched, commercial, cooked	72.6	109	2	.1	24.2	.1	1.1
Rice products, breakfast:							
Flakes, added nutrients	3.2	390	5.9	.3	87.7	.6	2.9
Puffed or oven-popped, presweetened, honey, added nutrients	1.8	388	4.2	.7	90.6	.2	2.7
Rolls and buns, commercial, ready-to-serve							
Danish pastry	22	422	7.4	23.5	45.6	.1	1.5
Plain pan rolls, enriched	31.4	298	8.2	5.6	53	.2	1.8
Salad dressings, commercial:							
Blue and Roquefort cheese	32.2	504	4.8	52.3	7.4	.1	3.2
French, low fat	77.3	96	.4	4.3	15.6	.3	2.4
Italian	27.5	552	.2	60	6.9	Trace	5.4
Mayonnaise	15.1	718	1.1	79.9	2.2	Trace	1.7
Mayonnaise-type	40.6	435	1	42.3	14.4	—	1.7
Thousand Island	32	502	.8	50.2	15.4	.3	1.6
Salami. *See* Sausage							
Salmon, broiled or baked	63.4	182	27	7.4	0	0	1.6
Sauerkraut, canned, solids and liquid	92.8	18	1.0	.2	4.0	.7	2
Sausage, cold cuts, and luncheon meats:							
Brown-and-serve sausage, browned	39.9	422	16.5	37.8	2.8	0	3
Frankfurters, cooked	57.3	304	12.4	27.2	1.6	—	1.5
Liverwurst, smoked	52.6	319	14.8	27.4	2.3	0	2.9
Meatloaf	64.1	200	15.9	13.2	3.3	0	3.5
Polish-style sausage	53.7	304	15.7	25.8	1.2	0	3.6
Pork sausage, links or bulk, cooked	34.8	476	18.1	44.2	Trace	0	2.9
Salami, dry	29.8	450	23.8	38.1	1.2	0	7.1
Scrapple	61.3	215	8.8	13.6	14.6	.1	1.7
Vienna sausage, canned	63	240	14	19.8	.3	0	2.9
Scallops, bay and sea:							
Raw	79.8	81	15.3	.2	3.3	—	1.4
Steamed	73.1	112	23.2	1.4	—	—	—

Calcium (milligrams)	Phosphorus (milligrams)	Iron (milligrams)	Sodium (milligrams)	Potassium (milligrams)	Vitamin A value (international units)	Thiamine (milligrams)	Riboflavin (milligrams)	Niacin (milligrams)	Ascorbic Acid (milligrams)
19	63	.8	480	296	180	.07	.06	.9	11
22	131	1.5	1,680	130	(0)	.02	.03	.7	(0)
31	37	1.5	4	329	760	.03	.07	.7	1
96	98	.5	56	171	150	.02	.14	.1	Trace
117	91	Trace	65	138	160	.03	.16	.1	1
25	26	.4	2	240	6,400	.03	.05	.6	5
—	—	—	—	—	—	.59	.52	—	—
30	31	1	18	322	10	.03	.03	.3	26
62	101	3.5	27	763	20	.11	.08	.5	1
30	22	.9	1	199	Trace	(.03)	(.09)	(.9)	18
78	15	.6	2	203	80	(.02)	(.05)	(.3)	6
10	28	.9	374	28	(0)	.11	—	1	(0)
29	132	1.6	987	180	(0)	.35	.05	4.4	(0)
46	74	.9	706	—	(0)	.33	—	4.6	(0)
50	109	.9	366	112	310	.07	.15	.8	Trace
74	85	1.9	506	95	Trace	.28	.18	2.2	Trace
81	74	.2	1,094	37	210	.01	.10	.1	2
11	14	.4	787	79	—	—	—	—	—
10	4	.2	2,092	15	Trace	Trace	Trace	Trace	—
18	28	.5	597	34	280	.02	.04	Trace	—
14	26	.2	586	9	220	.01	.03	Trace	—
11	17	.6	700	113	320	.02	.03	.2	3
—	414	1.2	116	443	160	.16	.06	9.8	—
36	18	.5	747	140	50	.03	.04	.2	14
—	—	—	—	—	—	—	—	—	—
5	102	1.5	—	—	—	.15	.20	2.5	—
10	245	5.9	—	—	6,530	.17	1.44	8.2	—
9	178	1.8	—	—	—	.13	.22	2.5	—
9	176	2.4	—	—	(0)	.34	.19	3.1	—
7	162	2.4	958	269	(0)	.79	.34	3.7	—
14	283	3.6	—	—	—	.37	.25	5.3	—
5	64	1.2	—	—	—	.19	.09	1.8	—
8	153	2.1	—	—	—	.08	.13	2.6	—
26	208	1.8	255	396	—	—	.06	1.3	—
115	338	3	265	476	—	—	—	—	—

Composition of Foods (100 grams, Edible Portion) *(Continued)*

Food and description	Water (percent)	Food energy (calories)	Protein (grams)	Fat (grams)	Carbohydrate Total (grams)	Fiber (grams)	Ash (grams)
Sesame seeds, dry, whole	5.4	563	18.6	49.1	21.6	6.3	5.3
Shad, baked with butter or margarine and bacon slices	64	201	23.2	11.3	0	0	1.4
Sherbet, orange	67	134	.9	1.2	30.8	0	.4
Shrimp:							
French-fried, dipped in egg, breadcrumbs, and flour, or butter	56.9	225	20.3	10.8	10	—	2
Raw	78.2	91	18.1	.8	1.5	—	1.4
Syrups:							
Cane	26	263	0	0	68	0	1.5
Maple	33	252	—	—	65	—	.7
Sorghum	23	257	—	—	68	—	2.4
Table blends, chiefly light and dark corn syrup	24	290	0	0	75	0	.7
Soups, commercial, canned, prepared with equal volume of water:							
Bean with pork	84.4	67	3.2	2.3	8.7	.6	1.4
Beef noodle	93.2	28	1.6	1.1	2.9	Trace	1.2
Celery, cream of	92.3	36	.7	2.1	3.7	.2	1.2
Chicken, cream of	91.9	39	1.2	2.4	3.3	.1	1.2
Clam chowder, Manhattan type	91.9	33	1	5	.2	1.2	
Minestrone	89.5	43	2	1.4	5.8	.3	1.3
Mushroom, cream of	89.6	56	1	4	4.2	.1	1.2
Pea, split	85.4	59	3.5	1.3	8.4	.2	1.4
Tomato	90.5	36	.8	1	6.4	2	1.3
Vegetable beef	91.9	32	2.1	.9	3.9	.2	1.2
Vegetable with beef broth	91.7	32	1.1	.7	5.5	.3	1
Soybean flour, full-fat	8	421	36.7	20.2	30.4	2.4	4.6
Soybean milk, fluid	92.4	33	3.4	1.5	2.2	0	.5
Soybeans, cooked, dry mature seeds	71	130	11	5.7	10.8	1.6	1.5
Spaghetti, enriched:							
Cooked, firm (8–10 min.)	63.6	148	5	.5	30.1	.1	1.3
Cooked, tender (14–20 min.)	72	111	3.4	.4	23	.1	1.2
In tomato sauce with cheese, home recipe	77	104	3.5	3.5	14.8	.2	1.2
With meatballs, in tomato sauce, home recipe	70	134	7.5	4.7	15.6	.3	2.2
Spinach, boiled, drained	92	23	3	.3	3.6	.6	1.1
Squash:							
Summer:							
All varieties, boiled, drained	95.5	14	.9	.1	3.1	.6	.4
Winter: Butternut, baked	79.6	68	1.8	.1	17.5	1.8	1
Zucchini and Cocozelle, green	96	12	1.0	.1	2.5	.6	.4
Starch. *See* Cornstarch							
Strawberries, raw	89.9	37	.7	.5	8.4	1.3	.5
Sugar, beet or cane:							
Brown	2.1	373	0	0	96.4	0	1.5
Granulated	.5	385	0	0	99.5	0	Trace
Powdered	.5	385	0	0	99.5	0	Trace
Sunflower seed kernels, dry	4.8	580	24	47.3	19.9	3.8	4

Calcium (milligrams)	Phosphorus (milligrams)	Iron (milligrams)	Sodium (milligrams)	Potassium (milligrams)	Vitamin A value (international units)	Thiamine (milligrams)	Riboflavin (milligrams)	Niacin (milligrams)	Ascorbic Acid (milligrams)
1,160	616	10.5	60	725	30	.98	.24	5.4	0
24	313	.6	79	377	30	.13	.26	8.6	—
16	13	Trace	10	22	60	.01	.03	Trace	2
72	191	2	186	229	—	.04	.08	2.7	—
63	166	1.6	140	220	—	.02	.03	3.2	—
60	29	3.6	—	425	0	.13	.06	.1	0
104	8	1.2	10	176	—	—	—	—	0
172	25	12.5	—	—	—	—	.10	.1	—
46	16	4.1	68	4	0	0	0	0	0
25	51	.9	403	158	260	.05	.03	.4	1
3	20	.4	382	32	20	.02	.03	.4	Trace
20	15	.2	398	45	80	.01	.02	Trace	Trace
10	14	.2	404	33	170	.01	.02	.2	Trace
14	19	.4	383	75	360	.01	.01	.4	—
15	24	.4	406	128	960	.03	.02	.4	—
17	21	.2	398	41	30	.01	.05	.3	Trace
12	16	.6	384	110	180	.10	.06	.6	Trace
6	14	.3	396	94	410	.02	.02	.5	5
5	20	.3	427	66	1,100	.02	.02	.4	—
8	16	.3	345	98	1,300	.02	.01	.5	—
199	558	8.4	1	1,660	110	.85	.31	2.1	0
21	48	.8	—	—	40	.08	.03	.2	0
73	179	2.7	2	540	30	.21	.09	.6	0
11	65	1.1	1	79	(0)	.18	.10	1.4	(0)
8	50	.9	1	61	(0)	.14	.08	1.1	(0)
32	54	.9	(382)	163	430	.10	.07	.9	5
50	95	1.5	407	268	640	.10	.12	1.6	9
93	38	2.2	50	324	8,100	.07	.14	.5	28
25	25	.4	1	141	390	.05	.08	.8	10
40	72	1	1	609	6,400	.05	.13	.7	8
25	25	.4	1	141	300	.05	.08	.8	9
21	21	1	1	164	60	.03	.07	.6	59
85	19	3.4	30	344	0	.01	.03	.2	0
0	0	.1	1	3	0	0	0	0	0
0	0	.1	1	3	0	0	0	0	0
120	837	7.1	30	920	50	1.96	.23	5.4	—

Composition of Foods (100 grams, Edible Portion) *(Continued)*

Food and description	Water (percent)	Food energy (calories)	Protein (grams)	Fat (grams)	Carbohydrate		Ash (grams)
					Total (grams)	Fiber (grams)	
Sweetbreads, beef, braised	49.6	320	25.9	23.2	0	0	1.3
Sweet potatoes, baked in skin	63.7	141	2.1	.5	32.5	.9	1.2
Swordfish, broiled, with butter or							
margarine	64.6	174	28	6	0	0	1.7
Tapioca cream pudding	71.8	134	5	5.1	17.1	0	1
Tea, instant, beverage	99.4	2	—	Trace	.4	Trace	Trace
Tomatoes, ripe:							
Canned, solids and liquid	93.7	21	1	.2	4.3	.4	.8
Raw	93.5	22	1.1	.2	4.7	.5	.5
Tomato juice, canned or bottled	93.6	19	.9	.1	4.3	.2	1.1
Tongue, beef, medium-fat, braised	60.8	244	21.5	16.7	.4	0	.6
Tuna, canned:							
In oil, drained solids	60.6	197	28.8	8.2	0	0	2
In water, solids and liquid	70	127	28	.8	0	0	1.2
Turkey, all classes, total edible,							
roasted	55.4	263	27	16.4	0	0	1.2
Turnip greens, boiled, drained	93.2	20	2.2	.2	3.6	.7	.8
Turnips, boiled, drained	93.6	23	.8	.2	4.9	.9	.5
Walnuts, black	3.1	628	20.5	59.3	14.8	1.7	2.3
Watercress	93.3	19	2.2	.2	3	.7	1.2
Whale meat, raw	70.9	156	20.6	7.5	0	0	1
Wheat flour, whole (from hard							
wheats)	12	333	13.3	2	71	2.3	1.7
Whisky. *See* Beverages, alcoholic							
Wine. *See* Beverages, alcoholic							
Yogurt:							
Made from partially skimmed							
milk	89	50	3.4	1.7	5.2	0	.7
Made from whole milk	88	62	3	3.4	4.9	0	.7
Zucchini. *See* Squash							
Zwieback	5	423	10.7	8.8	74.3	.3	1.2

* Average value per 100 g of pork of all cuts is 70 mg for raw meat and 65 mg for cooked meat.

Calcium (milli-grams)	Phos-phorus (milli-grams)	Iron (milli-grams)	Sodium (milli-grams)	Potassium (milli-grams)	Vitamin A value (interna-tional units)	Thiamine (milli-grams)	Riboflavin (milli-grams)	Niacin (milli-grams)	Ascorbic Acid (milli-grams)
—	364	—	116	433	—	—	—	—	—
40	58	.9	12	300	8,100	.09	.07	.7	22
27	275	1.3	—	—	2,050	.04	.05	10.9	—
105	109	.4	156	135	290	.04	.18	.1	1
Trace	—	Trace	—	25	—	—	.01	Trace	—
6	19	.5	130	217	900	.05	.03	.7	17
13	27	.5	3	244	900	.06	.04	.7	23
7	18	.9	200	227	800	.05	.03	.8	16
7	117	2.2	61	164	—	.05	.29	3.5	—
(8)	234	1.9	—	—	80	.05	.12	11.9	—
16	190	1.6	41	279	—	—	.10	13.3	—
—	—	—	—	—	—	—	—	—	—
184	37	1.1	—	—	6,300	.15	.24	.6	69
35	24	.4	34	188	Trace	.04	.05	.3	22
Trace	570	6.0	3	460	300	.22	.11	.7	—
151	54	1.7	52	282	4,900	.08	.16	.9	79
12	144	—	78	22	1,860	.09	.08	—	6
41	372	3.3	3	370	(0)	.55	.12	4.3	(0)
120	94	Trace	51	143	70	.04	.18	.1	1
111	87	Trace	47	132	140	.03	.16	.1	1
13	69	.6	250	150	40	.05	.07	.9	(0)

Vitamin/Food Chart
(best food sources for each vitamin)

Vitamin	Chief functions	Results of deficiency	Characteristics	Good sources	Daily allowances recommended
VITAMIN A Provitamin, carotene	Essential for maintaining the integrity of epithelial membranes; helps maintain resistance to infections; necessary for the formation of rhodopsin and prevention of night blindness	*Mild:* Retarded growth; increased susceptibility to infection; abnormal function of gastrointestinal, genitourinary, and respiratory tracts due to altered epithelial membranes; dry, shriveled, thickened skin, sometimes pustule formation; night blindness *Severe:* Xerophthalmia, a characteristic eye disease, and other local infections	Fat-soluble; not destroyed by ordinary cooking temperatures; destroyed by high temperatures when oxygen is present; marked capacity for storage in liver NOTE: Excessive intake of carotene, from which vitamin A is formed, may produce yellow discoloration of the skin (carotenemia).	Animal fats (butter, cheese, cream, egg yolk, whole milk); fish liver oil; liver; vegetables (green leafy, especially escarole, kale, and parsley, and yellow, especially carrots) *Artificial:* Concentrates in several forms; irradiated fish oils	*Males* (11–51+ yrs.): 1,000 mg retinol equivalents *Females* (11–51+ yrs.): 800 mg retinol equivalents *In pregnancy:* 1000 mg retinol equivalents *In lactation:* 1200 mg retinol equivalents *Children:* 400–700 mg retinol equivalents *Infants:* 400 mg retinol equivalents
THIAMINE Vitamin B₁	Important role in carbohydrate metabolism; essential for maintenance of normal digestion and appetite; essential for normal functioning of nervous tissue	*Mild:* Loss of appetite; impaired digestion of starches and sugars; colitis, constipation, or diarrhea; emaciation *Severe:* Nervous disorders of various types; loss of coordinating power of muscles; beriberi; paralysis	Water-soluble; not readily destroyed by ordinary cooking temperature; destroyed by exposure to heat, alkali, or sulfites; not stored in body	Widely distributed in plant and animal tissues but seldom occurs in high concentration, except in brewer's yeast; other good sources are whole-grain cereals, peas, beans, peanuts, oranges, heart, liver, kidney, many vegetables and fruits, and nuts *Artificial:* Concentrates from yeast; rice polishings; wheat germ	*Males* (11–51+ yrs.): 1.2–1.5 mg *Females* (11–51+ yrs.): 1.0–1.1 mg *In pregnancy:* 1.4–1.6 mg *In lactation:* 1.5–1.7 mg *Children:* 0.7–1.2 mg *Infants:* 0.3–0.5 mg

	Functions	Deficiency Symptoms	Properties	Sources	Daily Requirements
RIBOFLAVIN Vitamin B$_2$	Important in formation of certain enzymes and in cellular oxidation; normal growth; prevention of cheilosis and glossitis	Impaired growth; lassitude and weakness; cheilosis; glossitis, atrophy of skin; anemia; photophobia; cataracts	Water-soluble; alcohol-soluble; not destroyed by heat in cooking unless with alkali; unstable in light, especially in presence of alkali	Eggs, green vegetables, liver, kidney, lean meat, milk, wheat germ, dried yeast, enriched foods	*Males (11–51⁺ yrs.):* 1.4–1.7 mg *Females (11–51⁺ yrs.):* 1.2–1.3 mg *In pregnancy:* 1.6 mg
NIACIN Nicotinic acid Nicotinamide Antipellagra vitamin	As the component of two important enzymes, it is important in glycolysis, tissue respiration, and fat synthesis; nicotinic acid but not nicotinamide causes vasodilation and flushing; prevents pellagra	Pellagra; gastrointestinal disturbances; mental disturbances	Soluble in hot water and alcohol; not destroyed by heat, light, air, or alkali; not destroyed in ordinary cooking	Yeast, lean meat, fish, legumes, whole-grain cereals and peanuts, enriched foods	*Males (11–51⁺ yrs.):* 16–19 mg *Females (11–51⁺ yrs.):* 13–15 mg *In pregnancy:* 17 mg *In lactation:* 20 mg *Children:* 9–16 mg *Infants:* 6–8 mg
VITAMIN B$_{12}$ Cyanocobalamin	Produces remission in pernicious anemia; essential for normal development of red blood cells	Pernicious anemia	Soluble in water or alcohol; unstable in hot alkaline or acid solutions	Liver, kidney, dairy products; most of vitamin required by humans is synthesized by intestinal bacteria	*Males and females (11–51⁺ yrs.):* 3 mcg *In pregnancy:* 4 mcg *In lactation:* 5 mcg *Children:* 2–5 mcg *Infants:* 1–2 mcg

Vitamin/Food Chart (Continued)

Vitamin	Chief functions	Results of deficiency	Characteristics	Good sources	Daily allowances recommended
VITAMIN C Ascorbic acid	Essential to formation of intracellular cement substances in a variety of tissues including skin, dentin, cartilage, and bone matrix; important in healing of wounds and fractures of bones; prevents scurvy; facilitates absorption of iron	*Mild:* Lowered resistance to infections; joint tenderness; susceptibility to dental caries, pyorrhea, and bleeding gums *Severe:* Hemorrhage; anemia; scurvy	Soluble in water; easily destroyed by oxidation and heat hastens the process; lost in cooking, particularly if water in which food was cooked is discarded; loss is greater if cooked in iron or copper utensils; quick-frozen foods lose little; stored in the body to a limited extent	Abundant in most fresh fruits and vegetables, especially citrus fruit and juices, tomatoes and oranges *Artificial:* Ascorbic acid; cevitamic acid	*Males (11–51⁺ yrs.):* 50–60 mg *Females (11–51⁺ yrs.):* 50–60 mg *In pregnancy:* 80 mg *In lactation:* 100 mg *Children:* 45 mg *Infants:* 35 mg The infant diet is likely to be deficient in vitamin C unless orange or tomato juice or another form is added.
VITAMIN D	Regulates absorption of calcium and phosphorus from the intestinal tract; antirachitic	*Mild:* Interferes with utilization of calcium and phosphorus in bone and teeth formation; irritability; weakness *Severe:* Rickets may be common in young children; osteomalacia in adults	Soluble in fats and organic solvents; relatively stable under refrigeration; stored in liver; often associated with vitamin A	Butter, egg yolks, fish liver oils, fish having fat distributed through the flesh, such as salmon, tuna fish, herring, and sardines, liver, oysters, yeast, and foods irradiated with ultraviolet light; formed in the skin by exposure to sunlight; artificially prepared forms exist	*Males and Females (11–51⁺ yrs.):* 200–400 IU;* after age 22, none except during pregnancy or lactation *In pregnancy:* 400–600 IU *In lactation:* 400–600 IU *Children:* 400 IU *Infants:* 400 IU

VITAMIN E Alpha tocopherol	Normal reproduction in rats; prevention of muscular dystrophy in rats	Red blood cell resistance to rupture is decreased	Fat soluble Stable to heat in absence of oxygen	Lettuce and other green, leafy vegetables, wheat germ oil, margarine, rice	*Males* *(11–51 + yrs.):* 8–10 mg α-tocopherol *Females* *(11–51 + yrs.):* 8 mg α-tocopherol *In pregnancy:* 10 mg α-tocopherol *In lactation:* 11 mg α-tocopherol *Children:* 10–15 IU *Infants:* 5 IU
VITAMIN B₆ Pyridoxine	Essential for metabolism of tryptophan; needed for utilization of certain other amino acids	Dermatitis around eyes and mouth; neuritis; anorexia; nausea and vomiting	Soluble in water and alcohol; rapidly inactivated in presence of heat, sunlight, or air	Blackstrap molasses, meat, cereal grains, wheat germ	*Males and Females* *(11–51 + yrs.):* 1.8–2.2 mg *In pregnancy:* 2.6 mg *In lactation:* 2.5 mg *Children:* 0.9–1.6 mg *Infants:* 0.3–0.6 mg
FOLACIN	Essential for normal functioning of hematopoietic system	Anemia	Slightly soluble in water; easily destroyed by heat in presence of acid; decreases when food is stored at room temperature NOTE: A large dose may prevent the appearance of anemia in a case of pernicious anemia but still permits neurological symptoms to develop.	Glandular meats, yeast, green, leafy vegetables	*Males and Females* *(11–51 + yrs.):* 400 mg *In pregnancy:* 800 mg *In lactation:* 500 mg *Children:* 100–300 mg *Infants:* 30–45 mg

* International Units

VACCINES

Vaccines are disease-specific immunizations. The period of effectiveness for common vaccines is shown below:

Vaccine	Immunization Period
Combination (diphtheria, tetanus toxoids, and whooping cough)	5–10 years
Diphtheria (antitoxin)	2–3 months
Diphtheria (toxoid)	5–10 years
Measles (attenuated virus)	Over 10 years
Measles (immune blood serum, gamma globulin, or placental extract)	A few weeks
Mumps (attenuated virus)	Probably life
Poliomyelitis (dead or attenuated virus)	Unknown
Rabies (attenuated virus)	Unknown
Rubella (attenuated virus)	Unknown
Tetanus (antitoxin)	A few weeks
Tetanus (toxoid)	5–10 years
Typhoid (dead germs)	2–3 years
Whooping cough (dead germs)	2–5 years

Activities and the Calories They Consume

(for a person weighing approximately 150 pounds)

Activity	Calories expended per hour
Rest and light activity	*50–200*
Lying down or sleeping	80
Sitting	100
Typing	110
Driving	120
Standing	140
Housework	180
Shining shoes	185
Moderate activity	*200–350*
Bicycling (5½ mph)	210
Walking (2½ mph)	210
Gardening	220
Canoeing (2½ mph)	230
Golf (foursome)	250
Lawn-mowing (power mower)	250
Fencing	300
Rowing a boat (2½ mph)	300
Swimming (¼ mph)	300
Calisthenics	300
Walking (3¼ mph)	300
Badminton	350
Horseback riding (trotting)	350

Square dancing	350
Volleyball	350
Roller-skating	350
Stacking heavy objects (boxes, logs)	350
Vigorous activity	*over 350*
Baseball pitching	360
Ditch-digging (hand shovel)	400
Ice-skating (10 mph)	400
Chopping or sawing wood	400
Bowling (continuous)	400
Tennis	420
Water-skiing	480
Hill-climbing (100 feet per hour)	490
Basketball	500
Football	500
Skiing (10 mph)	600
Squash and handball	600
Bicycling (13 mph)	660
Rowing (machine)	720
Scull-rowing (race)	840
Running (10 mph)	900

Safe Alcohol Consumption

The effects of drinking alcoholic beverages depend in part on the amount of actual ethyl alcohol consumed and one's body weight. The level of alcohol in the blood is calculated in terms of milligrams (1 milligram = $\frac{1}{30,000}$ of an ounce) of pure alcohol per deciliter (1 deciliter = 3.5 fluid ounces) of blood. This is usually expressed as mg/dl. Twelve ounces of beer, 4 ounces of wine, or a 1.5-ounce shot of 80-proof whiskey, gin, or vodka contain approximately the same amount of ethyl alcohol, 8 grams, or 8,000 mg.

Blood alcohol concentrations often are expressed as a percentage of blood, as .05 percent for 50 milligrams of alcohol per deciliters (dl) of blood. It is recommended that drinkers keep their blood alcohol concentration (BAC) below 0.4 percent.

Depending on body weight and other factors, it takes the average adult nearly one hour for his or her liver to metabolize (break down) 8 grams of alcohol. Alcohol tends to accumulate in the blood because it is absorbed faster than it is metabolized.

Alcohol is absorbed through the membranes of the mouth and esophagus, from the stomach, and from the intestines. The rate of absorption is affected by proteins, fats, and carbohydrates in the digestive tract, which can slow absorption; by carbonation in drink mixers, which increases absorption; by the amount of water added to dilute the alcoholic beverage or the water or soft drinks consumed between alcoholic beverages; and by the presence of congeners (chemicals such as methyl alcohol, tannins, and histamines) present in the type of alcoholic beverage being consumed. The health of the drinker is also important, as a healthy liver metabolizes alcohol more efficiently.

A blood level of 20 to 30 mg/dl (the equivalent of .02 to .03 percent, or one or two drinks for an average adult) causes central nervous system changes in behavior, coordination, and ability to think clearly. Because alcohol is an anesthetic, the drinker may not notice the changes in his or her own behavior.

At a blood level of 50 mg/dl (.05 percent), the drinker may experience sedation or a tranquilized feeling. Between 50 and 150 mg/dl (.05 to .15 percent), there is a definite loss of coordination.

A concentration of 80 to 100 mg/dl (.08 to .10 percent) is considered evidence of "legal intoxication" in many states, even though the alcohol level may be estimated by a breath test rather than actual blood analysis.

At blood levels between 150 and 200 mg/dl (.15 and .20 percent), a person is obviously intoxicated and may show signs of delirium.

At levels between 300 and 400 mg/dl (.30 and .40 percent), the drinker usually loses consciousness.

At an alcohol blood level above 500 mg/dl (.50 percent), the heart and respiration become so depressed that they cease to function, and death follows.

Drinking and Driving

It is unsafe to drink and drive; in addition, many states have very strict driving while intoxicated (DWI) laws. The following chart is intended as a general guideline of how long to wait after imbibing before driving a motor vehicle. The time varies, however, from person to person, and the best rule is "Don't drink and drive." In the following chart, one drink equals 1½ ounces of liquor (86 proof) or 4 ounces of wine or champagne or 12 ounces of beer.

Body Weight (pounds)	1 drink	2 drinks	3 drinks	4 drinks	5 drinks	6 drinks
100–119	0 hours	3 hours	6 hours	10 hours	13 hours	16 hours
120–139	0 hours	2 hours	5 hours	8 hours	10 hours	12 hours
140–159	0 hours	2 hours	4 hours	6 hours	8 hours	10 hours
160–179	0 hours	1 hour	3 hours	5 hours	7 hours	9 hours
180–199	0 hours	0 hours	2 hours	4 hours	6 hours	7 hours
200–219	0 hours	0 hours	2 hours	3 hours	5 hours	6 hours
Over 220	0 hours	0 hours	1 hour	3 hours	4 hours	6 hours

Additional Sources of Information

Organizations and Services

Alcoholics Anonymous World Services Office
468 Park Avenue South
New York, NY 10016

The American Academy of Allergy and Immunology
611 East Wells Street
Milwaukee, WI 53202

American Diabetes Association
2 Park Avenue
New York, NY 10016

American Heart Association
New York City Affiliate
205 East 42nd Street
New York, NY 10017

American Medical Association
535 North Dearborn Street
Chicago, IL 60610

Cancer Information Clearinghouse
National Cancer Institute
9000 Rockville Pike
Building 31, Room 10A18
Bethesda, MD 20205

Cancer Information Service
National Cancer Institute
9000 Rockville Pike
Bethesda, MD 20205

Center for Science in the Public Interest
1501 16th Street, NW
Washington, DC 20036

Centers for Disease Control
1600 Clifton Road, NW
Atlanta, GA 30333

Health and Human Services Department
200 Independence Avenue, SW
Washington, DC 20201

National Institute of Child Health and Human
  Development
9000 Rockville Pike
Bethesda, MD 20892

National Institute on Drug Abuse Prevention
5600 Fishers Lane
Rockville, MD 20857

National Institutes of Health
9000 Rockville Pike
Bethesda, MD 20892

National Library of Medicine
8600 Wisconsin Avenue
Bethesda, MD 20894

National Women's Health Network
224 7th Street, SE
Washington, DC 20003

The Nutrition Information Center
The New York Hospital–Cornell Medical Center
Memorial Sloan-Kettering Cancer Center
515 East 71st Street
Room 904
New York, NY 10021

The President's Council on Physical Fitness and Sports
450 Fifth Street, NW
Suite 7103
Washington, DC 20001

Smokenders
P.O. Box 3146
Glen Ellyn, IL 60138

U.S. Public Health Service
5600 Fishers Lane
Rockville, MD 20857

Books

American Medical Directory, 1988. 31st ed. American Medical Association, 1906–.

Anderson, Kenneth. *Orphan Drugs*. Linden Press, 1983.

Anderson, Kenneth. *Symptoms After 40*. Arbor House, 1987.

Blake, John Ballard, and Roos, Charles. *Medical Reference Works*. Medical Library Association, 1967–75.

Boston Women's Health Book Collective. *The New Our Bodies, Ourselves*. Simon & Schuster, 1985.

Brace, Edward R., and Anderson, Kenneth N. *The New Pediatric Guide to Drugs & Vitamins*. Price Stern, 1987.

Brace, Edward R., and Pacanowski, John P. *Childhood Symptoms*. Harper & Row, 1985.

Brody, Jane. *Jane Brody's Nutrition Book*. Norton, 1981.

Brody, Jane. *Jane Brody's The New York Times Guide to Personal Health*. Avon, 1983.

Directory of Medical Specialists, 22nd ed. 3 vols. Marquis Who's Who, 1985.

Friedman, Jo-Ann. *Home Health Care: A Guide for Patients and Their Families*. Norton, 1986.

Kutsky, Roman J. *Handbook of Vitamins and Hormones*, 2nd ed. Van Nostrand Reinhold, 1981.

Medical Books for the Lay Person. Boston Public Library, 1976.

Merck Manual of Diagnosis and Therapy, 15th ed. Merck, Sharp & Dohme, 1987.

Miller, Benjamin F., and Keane, Claire B. *Encyclopedia and Dictionary of Medicine, Nursing, and Allied Health*. Saunders, 1987.

Physician's Desk Reference, 1988. Medical Economics, 1947–.

Urdang Dictionary of Current Medical Terms. Wiley, 1981.

Wilson, Doris B., and Wilson, Wilfred. *Human Anatomy*, 2nd ed. Oxford University Press, 1982.

Wolman, Benjamin B., ed. *International Encyclopedia of Psychiatry, Psychology, Psychoanalysis, and Neurology*. 12 vols. Van Nostrand Reinhold, 1977.

24

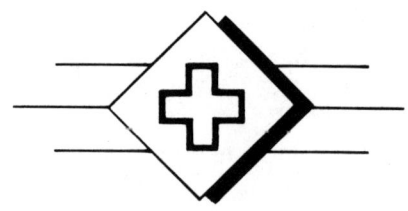

First Aid

Life-Saving Procedures

The American Medical Association recommends that, when a person is injured or becomes suddenly ill, priority be given to these objectives:

1. Maintain breathing
2. Maintain circulation
3. Prevent loss of blood

4. Prevent further injury
5. Prevent shock
6. Summon professional medical services

Maintaining Breathing and Circulation

When breathing stops, the victim has enough oxygen in the blood and other tissues to sustain life for only a very few minutes. Any delay in restoring the flow of oxygen to the brain and other body organs can result in death or permanent damage. Start artificial respiration and manual external cardiac massage immediately if the person is not breathing. Basic cardiopulmonary resuscitation (CPR)—mouth-to-mouth breathing and external cardiac massage—does not require equipment. It can be done by only one or two rescuers, but having more rescuers increases the chances for success.

If you are not directly involved in the rescue effort, you can help by calling a doctor, emergency medical services (EMS), or the police or fire department. But rescuers should not wait for professional support to arrive. Seconds count. Rescue may involve three related actions: opening an airway to the lungs, restoring breathing, and restoring circulation.

First, place the victim on his or her back on a hard, flat surface, such as the floor. If breathing has stopped because of poisonous gas or lack of oxygen, move the victim quickly to fresh air before beginning CPR.

Second, examine the victim closely for possible injuries or other obstacles that would interfere with CPR action. Check for a pulse in the carotid artery, on either side of the neck beneath the chin. Try to get the attention of the victim by talking, pinching, or tapping. If there is no response, assume that the person is unconscious. Look, listen, and feel for any signs of air moving in or out of the victim's lungs.

Mouth-to-Mouth Breathing

If there are no signs of breathing or there is no significant pulse, take the first step in artificial respiration by placing one hand under the victim's neck and the other on the forehead in order to tilt the head back. This extends the neck and helps prevent the tongue from dropping back into the throat, blocking the airway. If available, a plastic "stoma," or oropharyngeal airway device, should be inserted now. If none is available, turn the hand on the victim's forehead so that the thumb and index finger can pinch closed his or her nostrils. Your mouth should be placed over the victim's mouth so as to make an airtight seal.

Next, blow into the victim's mouth four times in succession, making each puff of increasing strength and volume. The victim's chest should expand. After the first set of puffs, remove your mouth and allow the victim's chest to fall. The mouth-to-mouth cycle of puffs should be repeated every five seconds (see sidebar "Mouth-to-Mouth Breathing," page 654).

If the victim's chest fails to expand, the problem may be an airway obstruction. Mouth-to-mouth respiration should be interrupted briefly to apply first aid for choking (see section on choking, pages 664–65).

MOUTH-TO-MOUTH BREATHING

If there are no signs of breathing, place one hand under the victim's neck and gently lift. At the same time, push with the other hand on the victim's forehead. This will move the tongue away from the back of the throat to open the airway.

While maintaining the backward head tilt position, place your cheek and ear close to the victim's mouth and nose. Look for the chest to rise and fall while you listen and feel for breathing. Check for about 5 seconds.

Next, while maintaining the backward head tilt, pinch the victim's nose with the hand that is on the victim's forehead to prevent leakage of air, open your mouth wide, take a deep breath, seal your mouth around the victim's mouth, and blow into the victim's mouth with four quick but full breaths. For an infant, give gentle puffs and blow through the mouth *and* nose and do not tilt the head back as far as for an adult.

If you do not get an air exchange when you blow, it may help to reposition the head and try again.

If there is still no breathing, give one breath every 5 seconds for an adult and one gentle puff every 3 seconds for an infant until breathing resumes.

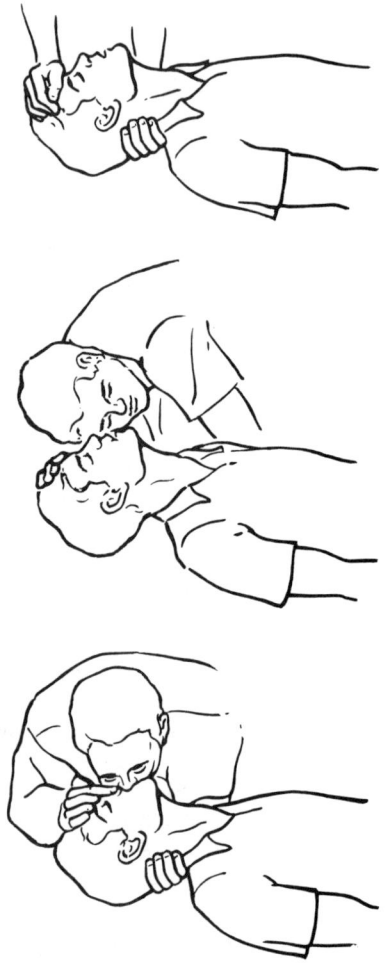

Cardiac Massage

Check the carotid artery pulse again. If there is no pulse, begin external cardiac massage by squeezing the heart between the sternum (breastbone) and the spinal column. To begin external cardiac massage, take a position facing the victim and uncover his or her chest. Find the bottom (xiphoid process) of the breastbone and place your index and middle fingers next to it to mark the location. Next, place the heel of your other hand on the sternum, just above the xiphoid process. Remove your first hand and place it on the second, interlocking the fingers. Holding your arms straight, rock back and forth from the hips and press downward so the sternum is depressed between one and two inches. Do not press on the xiphoid process and do not exert enough pressure to cause internal injuries to the liver or other organs in the area.

If possible, mouth-to-mouth breathing and external cardiac massage should be combined at a rate of 12 breath cycles and 60 chest compressions per minute. If at least two rescuers are available, one should perform mouth-to-mouth breathing while the other does chest compressions.

Check frequently for signs of a carotid artery pulse, a return of normal skin coloring, or signs of spontaneous breathing. Even if normal breathing returns, remain ready to resume CPR if necessary and until a doctor or other professional medical help arrives.

Mouth-to-Nose Breathing

When mouth-to-mouth breathing is not feasible, mouth-to-nose breathing can be performed in a similar manner by placing your mouth over the victim's nose and holding his or her lips closed between the thumb and forefinger.

For Small Children

If the victim is a small child, your mouth can be placed over both the nose and mouth. Be careful about extending the neck of an infant, because soft tissues in the neck may obstruct the upper airway if the head is tilted too far.

External cardiac massage for a small child should be done with the pressure of two thumbs or two fingers and compression should be limited to a depth of only one-half to one inch, depending on the size of the child.

For Drowning Victims

If drowning is the cause, do not wait until the victim can be transported to shore or placed on a flat surface to begin CPR. Mouth-to-mouth artificial respiration can be started while the victim is in a boat or is floating in the water. (See also section on drowning, page 667.)

Preventing Loss of Blood

Heavy bleeding, or hemorrhaging, is a life-threatening emergency. Bleeding from a large artery can result in death in less than five minutes. As with maintaining breathing and circulation, immediate action is needed. Notify a doctor, emergency medical service (EMS), the police, or the fire department. If the victim can be moved safely and quickly, take him or her to a nearby hospital emergency room.

Covering the Wound

Unless there are injuries or other conditions that might interfere, keep the victim lying down with the bleeding part of the body raised higher than the rest of the body. If the bleeding is external, as from an open wound, place a clean cloth, handkerchief, pad, or similar object directly over the wound and press firmly, with both hands if necessary.

If blood soaks through the cloth, add more cloth and keep pressing, but do not take off the original pad or cloth until the bleeding is under control. Ice placed directly over the wound may help reduce the blood flow by causing constriction of the blood vessel that is the source of blood loss.

Apply firm pressure to the pressure point (see sidebar and section on pressure points, below) that can control blood flow to the wound. If possible, apply pressure to the pressure point with one hand while your other hand presses a pad over the wound. Do not apply a tourniquet unless there is no other way to stop the loss of blood. A tourniquet can result in the death of tissues to an arm, leg, hand, or foot and may lead to amputation.

General Care of the Victim

Heavy bleeding leads to symptoms of shock: thirst, cold and clammy skin, dizziness, and falling blood pressure. Keep the victim flat and covered with a blanket or coat. Also, maintain body temperature by making sure the victim is not lying on a cold or damp surface.

Unless the victim is unconscious or suffering from an abdominal wound, allow him or her to drink water or other beverages as needed; blood loss requires replacement of fluids. Do not give a wounded person alcoholic beverages, which would have the effect of increasing fluid depletion.

If the victim has suffered an open abdominal or chest wound and professional medical help is not immediately available, cover any protruding organs with a clean damp cloth held in place with a bandage or by hand pressure.

An open chest wound may result in a lung collapse unless the wound can be covered quickly with a gauze or cloth pad held in place by a firm bandage to prevent air from moving in or out of the lung. If a gauze pad is not available, make a pad from plastic sheeting, aluminum foil, or other clean material to form an airtight seal. If a bandage is not available, use a belt to hold the pad in place. Do not touch an open wound except as necessary to apply pressure or a pad or other dressing. Never try to explore a wound to locate fragments of metal, glass, or other debris that may have caused the injury.

Pressure Points

Fingers usually can be applied without worsening a victim's condition to control bleeding at a pressure point. There are a half-dozen pressure points where bleeding from an artery can be stopped or reduced by pressing the artery against a bone located next to it.

One of the main pressure points is in the area of the groin, where the femoral artery, supplying blood from the thigh to the foot, passes over one of the bones of the pelvis.

Bleeding in the upper arm may be controlled by pressing on an artery that passes over the top rib of the chest. Loss of blood for most of the rest of the arm can usually be stopped by compressing an artery that passes close to the upper arm bone at a point about halfway between the shoulder and elbow. A pressure point for bleeding from the neck, mouth, or

---

PRESSURE POINTS

PRESSURE POINT FOR NECK, MOUTH, OR THROAT

To stop bleeding from the neck, mouth, or throat area, apply pressure at a point on the neck where an artery passes alongside the trachea, or windpipe. Place the thumb of the hand against the back of the victim's neck and the fingers on the neck just below the larynx, or Adam's apple. Then push the fingers against the artery.

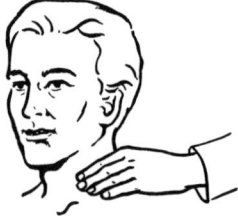

STOP BLEEDING FROM
TWO-THIRDS OF ARM

An artery supplying the lower arm passes close to the bone of the upper arm about halfway along the length of the upper arm. By applying pressure at that point, pressing the artery against the arm bone, bleeding from nearly any point beyond can be stopped.

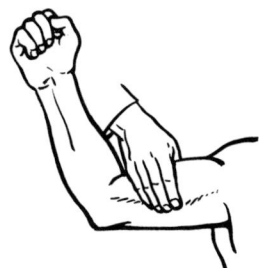

PRESSURE POINT IN UPPER ARM

A pressure point for controlling the loss of blood in the area of the upper arm, shoulder, or armpit should be found where an artery passes over the outer surface of the top rib. Place the thumb in the position shown (the top rib is indicated in the drawing) and the fingers over the shoulder so they press against the area behind the collarbone. Apply pressure to the artery crossing the top rib.

BLEEDING BELOW EYE
AND ABOVE JAWBONE

Bleeding from an artery supplying the area of the face below the level of the eye usually can be controlled by finding the pressure point that is located along the edge of the jawbone.

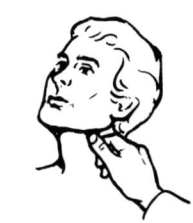

BLEEDING FROM HEAD ABOVE EYE LEVEL

For bleeding above the level of the eye, the rescuer should be able to find a pressure point where an artery passes over one of the skull bones in front of the upper portion of the ear, as shown in the drawing.

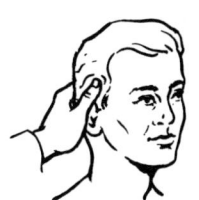

PRESSURE POINT FOR LEG

To stop bleeding from a leg or foot, apply pressure at a point in the area of the groin where the femoral artery passes over one of the bones of the pelvis, as shown in the drawing. If the blood flow slackens or stops, you can assume you have found the pressure point.

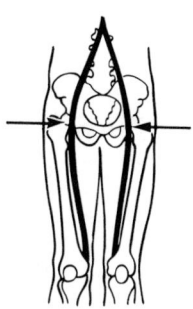

throat area is near the base of the neck, where an artery passes alongside the trachea, or windpipe, just below the Adam's apple. Bleeding from the head between the level of the eye and the jawbone usually can be stopped by pressing on an artery that crosses the edge of the jawbone. For bleeding above the eye level, there is a pressure point in front of the upper portion of the ear.

If at first you do not find the exact pressure point location, try again. The locations may vary somewhat with different body builds. You will know when you find the correct place, because bleeding will diminish or stop. As when a tourniquet is used, remember to release pressure at intervals to allow some blood to flow to deprived tissues. Do not continue compressing an artery if bleeding stops. If a tourniquet is applied, as when it may be necessary to stop the loss of blood from an arm or leg so seriously damaged it may have to be amputated, be sure to advise the doctor or EMS personnel who will eventually take charge. Better yet, attach a note or write a message with lipstick on the victim's forehead that a tourniquet has been used. Do not assume that a hospital emergency-room doctor or intern many miles away will be aware that a tourniquet, or any other special first-aid measures, may have been applied at the scene of the accident.

Preventing Further Injury

First aid in an emergency should be limited to no more than is necessary to save a life or prevent further injury. In most cases, do not move an injured person from an accident site before a doctor, emergency personnel, or police or fire personnel arrive. An exception is a situation, such as a building fire or potential explosion, in which the lives of the rescuers as well as the victims could be in danger. If there is an injury to the neck or spine, a victim should not be moved until a stretcher or other carrying device that provides firm support is available. Improper movement of the victim could cause a broken or dislocated bone that may damage an internal organ or pinch or sever a vital nerve trunk and result in death or permanent disability.

If the victim appears to have a head injury, movement should be delayed until a doctor has examined the person. Even then, any movement should be supervised by a physician. Do not move the head, or other body parts, if there is bleeding from the nose, mouth, or ears. If the victim is unconscious, you must assume that he or she has a head injury.

Never assume that an unconscious, disoriented, or apparently incoherent person is drunk. The victim may have suffered a head injury in a fall, a physical assault, or an accident. There are numerous causes of impaired consciousness, including brain hemorrhage, concussion, carbon monoxide poisoning, epilepsy, encephalitis, diabetic coma, hypoglycemia, heart trouble, psychiatric disorders, and barbiturates or other medications. Never give alcoholic beverages to an accident victim, and never offer fluids of any kind to a person who is unconscious or semiconscious or who has internal injuries.

Preventing Shock

Shock can be expected at any accident scene. It is a common, natural reaction to any severe physical or psychological injury. Generally, shock results from an automatic change in a person's blood circulation, as nature suddenly diverts blood to the vital organs in an effort to ensure the victim's survival. However, the natural reaction can also lead to death through circulatory collapse.

Shock prevention is next in priority to maintaining respiration and control of bleeding. Watch for—but do not wait for—the common shock signs: (1) a weak, rapid pulse, (2) skin that is cold and moist with "cold sweat," (3) dilated pupils or eyes that appear "vacant," (4) restless or abnormally anxious behavior, (5) nausea or thirst, (6) faintness and weakness. If the person becomes quiet and slips into unconsciousness, shock has already progressed beyond the first stages.

A usual first-aid measure for shock is to position the victim so the head is lower than the rest of the body, thus allowing gravity to pull blood toward the brain. An exception may be necessary if the victim has a head injury and cannot be moved.

Keep the victim warm and protected from the weather. However, do not provide too much warmth, which could lead to sweating with loss of vital body fluids and redirection of the blood flow from the vital organs to the surface of the body. Fluids may be given to a shock victim under certain circumstances—if the person is conscious, does not have internal injuries, and can swallow. Fluids can be vital for the survival of a victim who has suffered burns. It is better to give fluids in the early stages of shock, because fluids may not be absorbed from the digestive system later. If the accident site is some distance from the nearest hospital or doctor's office, small amounts of warm water or tea may be offered. But do not offer fluids if emergency service personnel or other professional help are nearby and the victim is likely to be anesthetized for surgery. If a physician is available, by telephone or otherwise, let the doctor make the final decision about fluids for accident victims.

Some persons at an accident scene may suffer only minor cuts and bruises but experience psychological shock. The signs and symptoms are the same as for victims with serious physical injuries. Time and personnel permitting, emotional shock cases should receive the same care for their shock symptoms as the severely injured. If those with psychological shock are allowed to slip into unconsciousness with possible circulatory failure, their condition will obviously complicate the overall rescue effort.

Treatment for Health Emergencies

Burns

Burns can be caused by contact with heat, chemicals, electricity, or radiation. One of the effects is "burn shock," in which body fluid is diverted from normal blood flow to the brain, heart, and other vital organs to the burned area of the body. Burn shock is the same as physical or psychological shock and can even follow severe sunburn. Small thermal burns, as may occur from fire, steam, or touching a hot object, usually result in pain, a reddened skin area, and blisters. In many cases, the burn can be treated with ice or cold water. Do not try to open a blister. It can be protected by a pad held in place with a loose bandage.

Never apply ointments or grease, including butter or margarine, baking soda, or other household substances, to a burned skin area.

A severe or extensive thermal burn requires professional care in a hospital. A doctor and/or emergency personnel should be summoned. While waiting for professional medical care, the victim should be made to lie down with the head and chest lower than the legs (shock position). Cover the burn area with a clean cloth to exclude air. Infection is a common complication if the skin is broken. If the victim is conscious and can swallow, provide adequate nonalcoholic liquids to drink. Because of burn shock, body tissues require fluid replacement.

First- and Second-Degree Burns

First-degree burns are marked by redness or other skin discoloration, pain, and swelling. An ordinary sunburn is typical of a first-degree burn. These burns generally are treated as small thermal burns and usually will heal with the application of cold water followed by a dry dressing.

Second-degree burns are often the result of exposure to flame, scalding liquids, or a very severe sunburn. The skin is usually reddish, mottled, and damaged, with signs of body fluid loss. These burns are treated as extensive thermal burns, requiring professional medical care.

Third-Degree Burns

Third-degree burns are marked by damage to tissues beneath the skin. The area may resemble a second-degree burn at first, but it quickly progresses to a whitish or charred coloration. Third-degree burns often result from contact with high-voltage electricity, steam, or boiling water, or from an accident in which the person is trapped in burning clothing. A third-degree burn is a true medical emergency. While ice or cold water may be used as a first-aid measure for first- or second-degree burns, nothing should be applied to a third-degree burn. Do not even remove clothing from burn areas. However, burn areas can be covered temporarily with sterile dressings, clean sheets, or even plastic garment bags. Do not put plastic materials over facial burns.

If the third-degree burn victim is conscious and not vomiting, small amounts of fluid should be offered. The recommended beverage is lukewarm water containing a teaspoon of salt and one-half teaspoon of baking soda per quart of liquid, to be sipped at a rate of one ounce every four or five minutes while waiting for professional medical help.

Chemical Burns

Chemical burns, either acid or alkali, are generally corrosive reactions that tend to affect the skin, eyes, and digestive tract. They usually result from spills, leaks, and splashes. A strong acid or alkali can cause permanent tissue damage. An alkali burn may be more serious than an acid burn because an acid usually is neutralized by contact with body tissues, whereas an alkali can continue causing damage until it is neutralized by another substance or washed away with copious amounts of water.

As a result, all chemical burns should be flooded—not merely rinsed—with water. It is usually important to remove contaminated clothing, which tends to absorb the chemical and hold it next to the skin, exacerbating the damage. Water flooding should continue while clothing is being removed. If possible, insert a hose under the clothing to inject water between the skin and the contaminated fabric.

Poisoning

A poison is anything that may be injurious to health or dangerous to life if it is swallowed, inhaled, or touched by the skin. Common sources of poisons include contaminated foods, carbon monoxide gas, cleaning products and solvents, certain household plants, pesticides, and medicines.

Food Poisoning

Food poisoning may be caused by enterotoxins, or poisons produced by bacteria that may or may not still be in the food. Symptoms usually include nausea and vomiting, cramps, diarrhea, fever, and headache, which may begin minutes to hours after the food has been eaten.

First aid in most cases includes bed rest, preferably close to a bathroom, and avoidance of any food or beverage until vomiting has stopped. When vomiting has ended, the victim should be offered sweetened tea or soft drinks and strained broth or bouillon with a little salt added. It is important to replace the body fluids and electrolytes (minerals) lost in vomiting or diarrhea.

In addition to vomiting, cramps, or diarrhea, symptoms of poisoning may include loss of consciousness, confusion or disorientation, an unusual odor on the breath, pain or a burning sensation in the mouth or throat, and stains or discoloration in or about the mouth from the leaves or berries of poisonous plants.

If the symptoms are severe, with signs of shock or the presence of blood or mucus in the diarrhea, a doctor should be notified.

A potentially fatal form of food poisoning that does not always cause vomiting or diarrhea is botulism. It is caused by a bacteria-produced poison, usually found in home-canned or processed foods. Botulism attacks the nervous system. The victim may feel no symptoms for a day or two, then experience visual problems, dry mouth and swallowing difficulty, and constipation as the poison gradually paralyzes various organ systems. Immediate hospitalization is needed to prevent the spread of the paralyzing effects to the respiratory system.

In any case of a swallowed poison, the container of food or other substance should be saved, with the label and any remaining contents, so that doctors or Poison Control Center personnel can recommend the most rapid and effective treatment.

First aid for most cases of swallowed poisons depends on the type of substance involved and the condition of the victim. Do not try to induce vomiting in any poisoning victim if he or she is unconscious or having convulsions.

Corrosive Poisons

Do not induce vomiting if the victim may have swallowed a corrosive substance, such as an acid or alkali, or has a burning pain in the mouth or throat. Examples of corrosive substances are toilet bowl cleaners, drain cleaners, lye, washing soda, and chlorine bleach.

- Do not attempt to ''neutralize'' swallowed acids or alkalis.
- Do not use activated charcoal for swallowed corrosive poisons.
- Do give the victim adequate amounts of milk or water.
- Do begin CPR if breathing stops.

Petroleum Distillates

For swallowed petroleum distillates, such as gasoline, kerosene, lighter fluid, paint thinner, or furniture polish, call the nearest Poison Control Center or hospital emergency room immediately for specific instructions. The exact type and amount of the poison may determine the treatment. Some products contain more than one kind of poison.

Symptoms may include coughing, choking, cyanosis (blue skin), breath-holding, a burning sensation in the stomach, lethargy, coma, convulsions, and spontaneous vomiting.

- Do not induce vomiting. There is a great risk that some of the vomited poison may enter the lungs; some hydrocarbon products are more than a hundred times as poisonous in the lungs as in the digestive tract.
- Do, if recommended by a doctor, give the person a glass of milk to dilute the poison and reduce stomach irritation.

Noncorrosive Poisons

Most medicines, such as aspirin, may be noncorrosive poisons. Generally, the doctor may recommend that you try to induce vomiting if the person has swallowed a noncorrosive poison that is not a petroleum distillate product. If you do not know whether the swallowed substance is corrosive or noncorrosive—or even if it is actually poisonous—call a Poison Control Center.

To induce vomiting, use syrup of ipecac (1 tablespoon for a child; 2 tablespoons for an adult) when it is available. The syrup of ipecac should be followed with one or more 8-ounce glasses of water.

If the person does not vomit within 15 minutes after one dose of syrup of ipecac, repeat the dose.

If syrup of ipecac is not available, use soapy water or a handwashing liquid detergent dissolved in water, or place the handle of a spoon or your finger at the back of the victim's throat. If the victim is a child, hold the child with the head lower than the hips while you induce vomiting. This position will reduce the chance of vomit entering the lungs.

Save a sample of the vomit so it can be analyzed in a medical laboratory.

Inhaled Poisons

A common type of inhaled poison is carbon monoxide gas, as produced by a car or truck engine in a confined area or by a faulty furnace or fireplace. The first symptoms are usually headache, yawning, breathing difficulty, dilated pupils, dizziness, faintness, ringing in the ears (tinnitus), nausea, and heart palpitations, followed by loss of consciousness. A distinctive sign is a cherry-red coloring of the mucous membranes. Persons with a light complexion may show a similar bright red coloring of the skin.

First aid requires fresh air and oxygen. Give mouth-to-mouth resuscitation until an emergency medical unit can arrive to provide 100-percent oxygen by mask. Do not give any stimulants, but keep the victim warm and as quiet as possible.

In rescuing a person from an inhaled poison, such as smoke or carbon monoxide, protect yourself against becoming a victim of the same dangerous situation. Be sure that oxygen is available by opening doors or windows of an enclosed space. If possible, carry an independent air supply if you must enter a confined or overheated area to rescue a victim of inhaled poisons. When a second rescuer is present, tie a rope around your waist and give the other end to the second rescuer, who can pull you to safety if you also are overcome by poisonous fumes.

Plant Poisons

The major contact poison plants in North America are poison ivy, poison oak, and poison sumac. They are usually identified by their clusters of three shiny leaflets. Signs and symptoms of contact with these plants include itching skin and blisters. These are effects of a poisonous resin in the leaves. Some first-aid relief can be had by diluting and washing away the resin with a strong laundry soap and water. Follow-up treatments can include mild wet dressings or starch or oatmeal baths to relieve the itching. Do not break the blisters. If there is oozing and crusting of the blisters, exposing them to dry air may give some relief. More serious adverse effects can result from chewing the leaves of poison ivy or inhaling the smoke of plants being burned. Swallowing or inhaling the resin causes painful swelling of the lining of the throat, accompanied by fever and weakness. The symptoms may require professional medical treatment.

Insect Bites

Bites or stings of ants, bees, hornets, wasps, yellow jackets, mosquitoes, and other insects usually result in the injection of substances under the skin of the person attacked. The body's reaction may vary from mild itching to a severe form of shock, depending on the venom or other foreign protein injected and the sensitivity of the person to the substance. Some hypersensitive persons can experience an extreme allergic reaction, known as *anaphylactic shock,* marked by breathing difficulty or circulatory failure within a few minutes after a bite or sting. Such individuals require special prescription drugs that should be carried when they expect to be near stinging or biting insects.

For most people who experience insect bites and stings, first aid may require only the application of ice or a cold compress to slow the rate of venom absorption. If the insect leaves its stinger in the skin, remove it with care, as the venom sac usually is still attached and should not be squeezed.

Ticks and other insects that may cling to the skin may require application of a petroleum product or similar irritant in order to remove them. In addition to local pain, swelling, and irritation, bites of ticks and other insects can result in serious infections requiring hospitalization.

Snake Bites

Most snake bites should be treated like those of any wild animal. If the bite is from a poisonous snake, the symptoms may vary according to the type of snake and its venom. But most poisonous snake bites will be followed immediately by an intense pain and a feeling of numbness in the bite area. The bite of a pit viper, such as a rattlesnake, cottonmouth, or copperhead, is often identified by fang punctures about one-half inch apart. It may also produce swelling. Other snake bites may or may not leave fang marks. A coral snake-bite wound may show a chewing action of the snake's jaws.

In general, a snake-bite victim should remain still. Any body movement will tend to increase the spread of venom. If the bite is in an arm or leg, the limb should be immobilized and kept lower than the level of the heart. If a hospital or other medical facility is less than 30 to 40 minutes away, the victim should be delivered there for professional care as quickly as possible. Other first-aid measures are suggested only for cases in which a doctor or hospital is not easily available.

A constriction band should be tied around the arm or leg a few inches above the bite and between the bite and the heart. The bite may be washed with soap and water and covered with a sterile dressing. Ice or a cold compress can be applied, but not directly over the bite. As in any other serious injury, the victim should be monitored closely for signs of shock. In some cases, an incision can be made in the bite area for removal of some of the venom by suction. However, incision and suction should be performed only if a doctor is not available and immediately after the bite has been inflicted. The person making the incision should be aware that when cutting into an arm or leg, there is a high risk of causing permanent damage to nerves, blood vessels, muscles, or other tissue.

Animal Bites

Animal bites, whether by a pet or a wild animal, can cause a puncture wound, laceration, or an avulsion, in which part of the flesh is torn away. First aid should be directed toward control of bleeding and protecting the wound from infection until it can be examined by a doctor. Unless the wound is extremely painful or bleeding profusely, clean it with soap and water and cover it with a sterile dressing before taking the victim to a doctor's office or hospital emergency room.

Many animal bites require a tetanus shot and, if the animal is identified as being rabid, additional protection against rabies. In most communities, local health authorities require notification of any serious animal bite.

Electric Shock

Severe electric shock can be caused by contact with ordinary electric lines in a home, office, or factory, as well as by high-voltage lines or a lightning bolt. An electric charge can have a number of effects on the body, including muscular contractions or seizures, paralysis of the lungs, abnormal heart function, bone fractures, thermal burns, and changes in blood chemistry.

Saving a person from further injury or death by electrocution should be done carefully so that the rescuer does not also become a victim. The electric shock victim first must be safely separated from contact with the electricity by turning the electricity off or by removing a wire or electric appliance with an insulated tool, such as a dry stick. In some cases, it may be easier to throw a loop of rope or cloth about the victim's arm or leg and drag him or her away from the source of electricity. If the victim is alive but unconscious, summon a doctor or emergency medical personnel. If breathing has stopped or there is no pulse, begin CPR immediately while awaiting the arrival of medical professionals.

Choking

Obstruction of the airways leading to the lungs can be caused by food, candy, chewing gum, or other objects accidentally inhaled. If air is unable to reach the lungs, the body's oxygen supply can become exhausted in a few minutes, resulting in death.

NOTE: A person whose windpipe (trachea) is blocked cannot talk but must make those around aware that he or she is choking, using sign language or any other means so that first aid can be given immediately.

There are two accepted ways of giving first aid to a choking person.

1. The Heimlich maneuver, which consists of a series of thrusts to the upper abdomen. Stand behind the victim and put your arms around his or her upper abdomen so that your hands can be clasped in a fist at the bottom of the victim's breastbone. Then quickly push your fist upward into the victim's chest, putting pressure on the lungs so that any air in them will be squeezed backward up into the windpipe, pushing the obstruction into the mouth. The Heimlich maneuver may have to be repeated six or more times to dislodge a foreign body in the throat. If the victim is pregnant, or very obese, the rescue pressure should be directed through the chest rather than the abdomen.

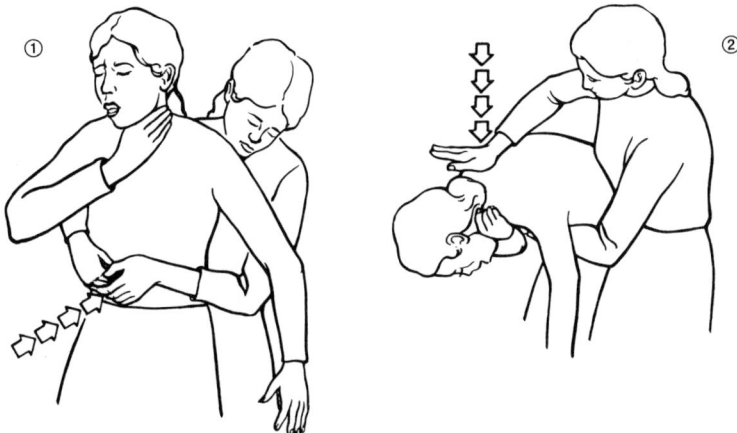

2. Firm blows over the spinal column between the shoulder blades. Stand behind the choking person and help him or her lean over, using one hand on the victim's chest to lend support. Then hit high on the back with the heel of your hand. Four or more back blows may ne needed to dislodge the object in the windpipe.

Frostbite

The most common cold-weather injury is frostbite. Severe cold can constrict the blood vessels, thereby reducing the normal flow of warm blood to the exposed tissues. The symptoms usually include a very cold feeling in the exposed skin area followed by a loss of feeling. The skin may appear flushed or red at first, but later it becomes white or a grayish yellow. Because of the loss of feeling, the victim is often unaware of the danger of frostbite.

The victim should be taken into a warm environment and all tight or wet clothing in the affected body area should be removed. The frostbitten area should be immersed in warm—but not extremely hot—water (experts recommend a water temperature of around 105°).

You can offer the victim hot coffee, tea, cocoa, or soup, but smoking should be avoided because it has an effect similar to that of cold, causing constriction of blood vessels. Do not rub the frostbitten tissues. If bleeding, swelling from fluid accumulation, or other complications develop after the exposed areas have thawed, notify a doctor immediately.

Abrasions

A minor break in the skin, such as may be caused by scraping or rubbing against a rough surface, should be washed with soap and water and treated with mild antiseptic, such as hydrogen peroxide. Then cover the abrasion with a sterile gauze dressing held in place with a bandage. If signs of infection appear, consult a doctor.

Black Eyes and Bruises

Black eyes and bruises are actually a type of closed wound in which blood from a damaged vessel in the soft tissues has leaked into a space beneath the skin. Apply ice or a cold compress to reduce the swelling and control the further loss of blood under the skin. In most cases, the pool of blood will be reabsorbed and the skin color will return to normal.

Boils and Blisters

A *boil* is a tender, often painful, pus-filled swelling of the skin. A boil is also known as a *furuncle,* and a group of furuncles is a *carbuncle.* Boils should be treated quickly and carefully to prevent the spread of a more serious infection and the formation of a scar. A boil around the nose or face can be particularly serious and should be treated with antibiotics by a doctor. Most other boils should be treated with moist heat to cause spontaneous rupture and drainage. The pus contains staphylococcus bacteria and should not be allowed to spread the infection.

Blisters are fluid-filled skin eruptions that may be caused by allergy, injury, sunburn, insect bites, infection, or drug reaction. Correcting the cause is important if the cause is an infection, allergy, or drug reaction. Most ordinary blisters can be treated with a mild antiseptic and a protective dressing. Do not puncture a blister. If the blister is accidentally broken, treat it as a wound.

Concussions

A concussion can result from a head injury and may be accompanied by a brief or longer period of unconsciousness. The victim may experience headache, blurred vision, or other signs of nervous system damage and may lapse into a coma. The victim, even if conscious, should be treated as an unconscious person. Keep the person quiet and warm, watch for signs of shock, and help maintain breathing if necessary while awaiting arrival of a doctor or emergency medical personnel.

Convulsions

A convulsion, or seizure, involves a disturbance of the nervous system that affects the muscles of movement. The person experiencing a convulsion may have uncontrollable twitching of the muscles, or the muscles may become rigidly contracted. There are many possible causes and types of such seizures. In general, however, first aid should be aimed at protecting the victim from self-injury. Place a firm but soft object, such as a folded handkerchief, in the mouth to protect the tongue. Do not try to protect the tongue with a hard object that may damage the teeth and do not insert your fingers between the jaws of the victim. Clothing about the neck should be loosened. Place pillows, cushions, or rolled blankets about the head and body. Meanwhile, summon a doctor or EMS.

Drowning

Drowning is a form of asphyxiation due to an inability of the victim to get oxygen into the lungs. It may also be complicated by inhalation of fluid into the lungs. First aid for a drowning victim requires CPR procedures (described on page 654) to maintain breathing and circulation. Do not waste time trying to squeeze water out of the lungs, particularly if the accident occurred in fresh water. If the victim has been in sea water, try to keep the body positioned with the head and chest lower than the abdomen and legs to assist fluid drainage from the lungs.

Heat Cramps, Heat Exhaustion, Heat Stroke

Prolonged exposure to high temperatures can lead to several life-threatening health problems. The most serious effects are heat exhaustion and heat stroke. *Heat cramps* are usually in the form of painful muscle spasms caused by excessive sweating and loss of body salt. The skin may be hot and dry or cool and clammy. In most cases, heat cramps can be treated with food and liquid containing sodium chloride (ordinary table salt).

Heat exhaustion, or heat prostration, is due to loss of body fluid. It is marked by nausea, weakness, excessive sweating, and faintness. The skin is pale and clammy, the pulse is weak, and the victim may show signs of shock. The loss of body fluid results in loss of blood volume and, in turn, a deficiency of oxygenated blood reaching the brain. Have the victim lie flat with the head down and give him or her small sips of cool, slightly salted liquids every few minutes. Do not give the victim too much fluid too rapidly.

Heat stroke, or sunstroke, is the most serious type of heat injury. It may begin suddenly with headache, dizziness, and fatigue. The skin is hot, dry, and flushed and the pulse is extremely rapid. The victim can develop a very high fever of around 105° F, experience convulsions, or become unconscious. Unless first aid is given immediately, the person may suffer circulatory collapse and die. Cool the body by wrapping the victim in wet clothing or bedding. Use snow or ice, if available, or immerse the person in cool water while awaiting the arrival of an emergency medical crew or a physician. Check the victim's temperature every 10 minutes to make sure the body temperature does not fall too rapidly. Hypothermia, or excessively cold body temperature, could complicate the condition.

Nosebleeds

Nosebleeds are usually caused by rupture of the numerous capillaries in the soft tissues near the tip of the nose. A nosebleed may be started by an injury, high blood pressure, physical activity, or sudden change in atmospheric pressure, as may occur in traveling from sea level to a mountaintop. First aid requires keeping the victim quiet and in a seated position with the head leaning forward. Apply pressure to the outside of the bleeding nostril, or insert gauze pads in one or both nostrils and squeeze the outside of the nose toward the midline. Also, apply ice or a cold compress to the nose and surrounding areas of the face. If the nose continues to bleed, notify a doctor.

FIRST-AID KITS

Many people are confused about the meanings of terms, such as bandages and dressings, used by health professionals. A *bandage* is a strip or muslin, gauze, or other material used to hold a compress or dressing in place. A *roller bandage* is a long strip of cloth that can be used as a dressing or compress as well as a bandage. A *triangular bandage* is one cut from a square of cloth along a diagonal line.

A *compress* is a square of fabric, generally of flannel or wool, used to apply heat, cold, or medications to the skin. A *dressing* can be anything placed over an open wound to control bleeding, absorb blood or secretions, and prevent infectious agents from entering the body through the wound. The best kind of dressing is a piece of sterile gauze, but in an emergency, any clean material may become a dressing—even sheet plastic or a newspaper. However, fluffy materials, such as cotton wool, should not be used because the loose fibers will stick to body tissues. Dressings are held in place by bandages.

An ideal family first aid kit should contain the following:

12	4-by-4-inch sterile dressings in sealed envelopes
12	2-by-2-inch sterile dressings in sealed envelopes
2	15-foot roller bandages, 1 inch wide
2	15-foot roller bandages, 2 inches wide
1	roll of adhesive tape
4	triangular bandages with safety pins
1	clean bedsheet
2	small bath towels
2	large bath towels
1	pair of blunt-nose scissors
1	pair of tweezers
1	pair of needle-nose pliers
1	eyedropper
1	set of measuring spoons
12	wooden tongue blades (for finger splints)
12	wood splints, 12–18 inches long
1	bar of antiseptic soap
1	package of salt
1	package of baking soda
1	package of aspirin tablets
1	package of antihistamine tablets
1	package of anti-motion sickness tablets
1	large package of adhesive bandages, assorted sizes
1	package of paper cups

Directory of Poison Control Centers

Following is a list of state coordinators' offices.

Alabama

Department of Public Health
Montgomery, AL 36117
205-832-3194

Alaska

Department of Health and Social Services
Juneau, AK 99811
907-465-3100

Arizona

College of Pharmacy
University of Arizona
Tucson, AZ 85724
602-626-6016
800-362-0101

Arkansas

University of Arkansas
Medical Science Campus
Little Rock, AR 72201
501-661-6161

California

Department of Health Services
Sacramento, CA 95814
916-322-4336

Colorado

Department of Health
EMS Division
Denver, CO 80220
303-320-8476

Connecticut

University of Connecticut
Health Center
Farmington, CT 06032
203-674-3456

Delaware

Wilmington Medical Center
Delaware Division
Wilmington, DE 19801
302-655-3389

District of Columbia

Department of Human Services
Washington, DC 20009
202-673-6741
202-673-6736

Florida

Department of Health and Emergency Medical Services
Tallahassee, FL 32301
904-487-1566

Georgia

Department of Human Resources
Atlanta, GA 30308
404-894-5170

Hawaii

Department of Health
Honolulu, HI 96801
808-531-7776

Idaho

Department of Health and Welfare
Boise, ID 83701
208-334-2241

Illinois

Division of Emergency Medical Services and Highway
  Safety
Springfield, IL 62761
217-785-2080

Indiana

State Board of Health
Indianapolis, IN 46206
317-633-0332

Iowa

Department of Health
Des Moines, IA 50319
515-281-4964

Kansas

Department of Health and Environment
Topeka, KS 66620
913-862-9360
Ext. 451

Kentucky

Department for Human Resources
Frankfort, KY 40601
502-564-3970

Louisiana

Emergency Medical Services of Louisiana
Baton Rouge, LA 70801
504-342-2600

Maine

Maine Poison Control Center
Portland, ME 04102
207-871-2950

Maryland

Maryland Poison Information Center
University of Maryland
School of Pharmacy
Baltimore, MD 21201
301-528-7604

Massachusetts

Department of Public Health
Boston, MA 02111
617-727-2700

Michigan

Department of Public Health
Lansing, MI 48909
517-373-1406

Minnesota

State Department of Health
Minneapolis, MN 55404
612-296-5281

Mississippi

State Board of Health
Jackson, MS 39205
601-354-6660

Missouri

Missouri Division of Health
Jefferson City, MO 65102
314-751-2713

Montana

Department of Health and Environmental Sciences
Montana Poison Control System
Cogswell Building
Helena, MT 59620
406-449-3895
800-525-5042

Nebraska

Department of Health
Lincoln, NE 68502
402-471-2122

Nevada

Department of Human Resources
Carson City, NV 86710
702-885-4750

New Hampshire

New Hampshire Poison Center
May Hitchcock Hospital
2 Maynard Street
Hanover, NH 03755
603-643-4000

New Jersey

Department of Health, Accident Prevention and Poison
   Control Program
Trenton, NJ 08625
609-292-5666

New Mexico

New Mexico Poison, Drug Information and Medical
   Crisis Center
University of New Mexico
Albuquerque, NM 87131
505-843-2551
800-432-6866

New York

Department of Health
Albany, NY 12237
518-474-3785

North Carolina

Duke University Medical Center
Durham, NC 27710
919-684-8111

North Dakota

Department of Health
Bismarck, ND 58505
701-224-2388

Ohio

Department of Health
Columbus, OH 43216
614-466-5190

Oklahoma

Oklahoma Poison Control Center
Oklahoma Children's Memorial Hospital
P.O. Box 26307
Oklahoma City, OK 73126
405-271-5454
800-522-4611

Oregon

Oregon Poison Control and Drug Information Center
University of Oregon
Health Sciences Center
Portland, OR 97201
503-225-8968
800-452-7165

Pennsylvania

Director, Division of Epidemiology
Department of Health
P.O. Box 90
Harrisburg, PA 17108
717-787-2307

Rhode Island

Rhode Island Poison Control Center
Rhode Island Hospital
593 Eddy Street
Providence, RI 02902
401-277-5727

South Carolina

Department of Health and Environmental Control
Columbia, SC 29201
803-758-5654

South Dakota

Department of Health
Pierre, SD 57501
605-773-3361

Tennessee

Department of Public Health
Division of Emergency Services
Nashville, TN 37216
615-741-2407

Texas

Department of Health
Division of Occupational Health
Austin, TX 78756
512-458-7254

Utah

Utah Department of Health
Division of Family Health Services
Salt Lake City, UT 84113
801-533-6161

Vermont

Department of Health
Burlington, VT 05401
802-862-5701

Virginia

Bureau of Emergency Medical Services
Richmond, VA 23219
804-786-5188

Washington

Department of Social and Health Services
Seattle, WA 98115
206-522-7478

West Virginia

Department of Health
Charleston, WV 25305
304-348-2971

Wisconsin

Department of Health and Social Services
Division of Health
Madison, WI 53701
608-267-7174

Wyoming

Office of Emergency Medical Services
Department of Health and Social Services
Cheyenne, WY 82001
307-777-7955

THE SIGNS AND SIGNALS OF HEART ATTACKS AND STROKES

Heart Attack Warning Signs

- Uncomfortable pressure, fullness, squeezing, or pain in the center of the chest lasting 2 minutes or more
- Spreading of pain to shoulders, neck, or arms
- Severe pain, dizziness, fainting, sweating, nausea, or shortness of breath

Not all of these signals are always present. Don't wait! Get help immediately.

Stroke Warning Signs

- Sudden, temporary weakness or numbness of the face, arm, and leg on one side of the body
- Temporary loss of speech, or trouble speaking or understanding speech
- Temporary dimness or loss of vision, particularly in one eye
- Unexplained dizziness, unsteadiness, or sudden falls

Many major strokes are preceded by "little strokes," warning signals like the above experienced days, weeks, or months before the more severe event.

In Case of Emergency

- If you are having chest discomfort that lasts for 2 minutes or more, call the emergency medical services (EMS) in your area.
- If you can get to a hospital faster by car, have someone drive you.

Before an Emergency

- Find out which hospitals in your area offer 24-hour emergency cardiac care.
- Select in advance the facility nearest your home and office, and tell your family and friends so that they will know what to do.
- Keep a list of emergency rescue service numbers next to your telephone and in a prominent place in your pocket, wallet, or purse.

Additional Sources of Information

Organizations and Services

American College of Emergency Physicians
P.O. Box 61991
Dallas, TX 75261

American Medical Association
535 North Dearborn Street
Chicago, IL 60610

American National Red Cross
17th and D Streets
Washington, DC 20006
202-737-8300

National Association of Emergency Medical Technicians
P.O. Box 334
Newton Highlands, MA 02161

Books

American National Red Cross Standard First Aid and Personal Safety. Doubleday, 1989.

Bevar, James. *The Pocket Medical Encyclopedia and First Aid Guide.* Simon & Schuster, 1979.

Consumer Guide editors and Charles Mosher. *Emergency First Aid.* Fawcett, 1980.

Emergency Family First Aid Guide. Simon & Schuster, 1978.

Henderson, John. *Emergency Medical Guide.* McGraw-Hill, 1978.

Nourse, Alan E. *The Outdoorsman's Medical Guide: Common Sense Advice and Essential Health Care for Campers, Hikers and Backpackers.* Harper & Row, 1974.

Rothenberg, Robert. *First Aid: What to Do in an Emergency.* Crown, 1976.

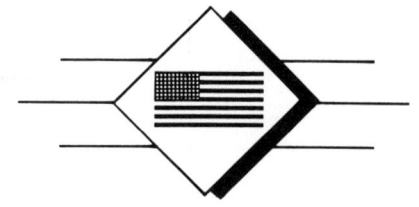

The United States

United States Map

ATLANTIC OCEAN

PACIFIC OCEAN

ME
NH
VT
MA
RI
CT
NJ
DE
MD
NY
PA
WV
VA
NC
SC
OH
KY
GA
MI
IN
TN
AL
IL
MS
LA
WI
MO
AR
MN
IA
OK
TX
ND
SD
NE
KS
FL
MT
WY
CO
NM
ID
UT
AZ
WA
NV
OR
CA
AK
HI
PR

Population

The United States boasts a heterogenous population, which, since the last census was taken in 1980, has risen 6.9 percent, from 226.5 million to 242.2 million. The tables in this section were drawn primarily from the Department of Commerce, Bureau of the Census, and reflect the most accurate profiles available of the population by race, sex, age, and region.

Total U.S. Population by Age, Sex, and Race

	Birth to 14	*15 to 29*	*30 to 44*	*45 to 59*	*60 to 79*	*80 and over*	*All ages*
	(numbers in thousands)						
WHITE							
Male	21,548	25,638	23,018	14,406	13,403	1,795	99,808
Female	20,444	25,012	23,000	15,198	16,949	3,890	104,493
BLACK							
Male	4,048	4,084	2,756	1,596	1,254	173	13,892
Female	3,937	4,278	3,234	1,950	1,685	299	15,414
SPANISH ORIGIN							
Male	2,843	2,909	1,978	965	468*	NA	9,294
Female	2,733	1,950	1,951	1,052	578*	NA	9,208
OTHER RACES							
Male	1,017	1,018	878	434	280	34	3,661
Female	990	977	957	498	344	49	3,811
ALL PERSONS							
Male	26,612	30,741	26,653	16,436	14,939	1,981	117,360
Female	25,371	30,297	27,190	17,646	18,978	4,237	123,718

* Indicates that some figures are not available within this age group.

NA = Not available.

State Populations

State	Population	Rank	Percent of U.S. total
Alabama	3,893,888	22	1.7
Alaska	401,851	51	0.2
Arizona	2,718,425	29	1.2
Arkansas	2,365,000	33	1.0
California	23,667,565	1	10.5
Colorado	2,889,735	28	1.3
Connecticut	3,107,576	25	1.4
Delaware	594,317	48	0.3
District of Columbia	638,432	47	0.3
Florida	9,746,324	7	4.3
Georgia	5,463,105	13	2.4
Hawaii	964,691	39	0.4
Idaho	944,038	41	0.4
Illinois	11,426,518	5	5.0
Indiana	5,490,260	12	2.4
Iowa	2,913,808	27	1.3
Kansas	2,364,236	32	1.0
Kentucky	3,660,257	23	1.6
Louisiana	4,206,312	19	1.9
Maine	1,125,027	38	0.5
Maryland	4,216,975	18	1.9
Massachusetts	5,737,037	11	2.5
Michigan	9,262,078	8	4.1
Minnesota	4,075,970	21	1.8
Mississippi	2,520,638	31	1.1
Missouri	4,916,759	15	2.2
Montana	786,690	44	0.4
Nebraska	1,569,825	35	0.7
Nevada	800,493	43	0.4
New Hampshire	920,610	42	0.4
New Jersey	7,364,823	9	3.3
New Mexico	1,302,981	37	0.6
New York	17,558,072	2	7.8
North Carolina	5,881,813	10	2.6
North Dakota	652,717	46	0.3
Ohio	10,797,624	6	4.8
Oklahoma	3,025,290	26	1.3
Oregon	2,633,149	30	1.2
Pennsylvania	11,863,895	4	5.2
Rhode Island	947,154	40	0.4
South Carolina	3,121,833	24	1.4
South Dakota	690,768	45	0.3
Tennessee	4,591,120	17	2.0
Texas	14,229,288	3	6.3
Utah	1,461,037	36	0.6
Vermont	511,456	49	0.2
Virginia	5,346,818	14	2.4
Washington	4,132,180	20	1.8
West Virginia	1,950,279	34	0.9
Wisconsin	4,705,521	16	2.1
Wyoming	469,557	50	0.2

Immigration Statistics

Immigration, 1820–1986

(in thousands, except rate, for fiscal years ending in year shown, except as noted)

Period	Total Number	Rate[1]	Period or year	Total Number	Rate[1]	Year	Total Number	Rate[1]
1820–1986	**53,122**	**3.4**	1931–40.	528	.4	1972	385	1.8
			1941–50.	1,035	.7	1973	400	1.9
1820–30[2]	152	1.2	1951–60.	2,515	1.5	1974	395	1.9
1831–40[3]	599	3.9	1961–70.	3,322	1.7	1975	386	1.8
1841–50[4]	1,713	8.4	1971–80[6]	4,493	2.1	1976	399	1.9
1851–60[4]	2,598	9.3	1981–86.	3,466	2.4	1977	462	2.1
1861–70[5]	2,315	6.4	1965	297	1.5	1978	601	2.8
1871–80.	2,812	6.2	1966	323	1.6	1979	460	2.1
1881–90.	5,247	9.2	1967	362	1.8	1980	531	2.3
1891–1900	3,688	5.3	1968	454	2.3	1981	597	2.6
1901–10.	8,795	10.4	1969	359	1.8	1982	594	2.6
1911–20.	5,736	5.7	1970	373	1.8	1983	560	2.4
1921–30.	4,107	3.5	1971	370	1.8	1984	544	2.3
						1985	570	2.4
						1986	602	2.5

[1] Annual rate per 1,000 U.S. population. Rate computed by dividing sum of annual immigration totals by sum of annual U.S. population totals for same number of years.   [2] October 1, 1819–September 30, 1830.   [3] October 1, 1830–December 31, 1840.   [4] Calendar years.   [5] January 1, 1861–June 30, 1870.   [6] Includes transition quarter, July 1 to September 30, 1976.

Immigrants, by Country of Birth, 1961–86

(in thousands)

Country of birth	1961–1970, total	1971–1980, total	1981–1985, total	1986	Country of birth	1961–1970, total	1971–1980, total	1981–1985, total	1986
All countries	**3,321.7**	**4,493.3**	**2,864.4**	**601.7**	Asia—cont'd.				
					Lebanon	7.5	33.8	17.0	4.0
Europe[1]	**1,238.6**	**801.3**	**321.8**	**62.5**	Pakistan	4.9	31.2	25.8	6.0
Austria	13.7	4.7	1.9	.5	Philippines	101.5	360.2	221.2	52.6
Belgium	8.5	4.0	2.6	.6	Thailand	5.0	44.1	26.3	6.2
Czechoslovakia	21.4	10.2	5.1	1.1	Turkey	6.8	18.6	11.4	1.8
Denmark	11.8	4.5	2.5	.6	Vietnam	4.6	179.7	234.8	30.0
Finland	5.8	3.4	1.6	.3					
France	34.3	17.8	10.1	2.5	**North America[1]**	**1,351.1**	**1,645.0**	**885.7**	**207.7**
Germany	200.0	66.0	34.5	7.1	Canada	286.7	114.8	55.6	11.0
Greece	90.2	93.7	16.3	2.5	Mexico	443.3	637.2	335.2	66.5
Hungary	17.3	11.6	3.7	1.0	Caribbean[1]	519.5	759.8	371.6	101.6
Ireland	42.4	14.1	5.6	1.8	Barbados	9.4	20.9	9.4	1.6
Italy	206.7	130.1	17.8	3.1	Cuba	256.8	276.8	58.9	33.1
Netherlands	27.8	10.7	5.6	1.3	Dominican Republic	94.1	148.0	104.6	26.2
Norway	16.4	4.0	1.9	.4	Haiti	37.5	58.7	43.9	12.7
Poland	73.3	43.6	36.3	8.5	Jamaica	71.0	142.0	100.5	19.6
Portugal	79.3	104.5	21.4	3.8	Trinidad and Tobago	24.6	61.8	17.0	2.9
Rumania	14.9	17.5	16.8	5.2					
Soviet Union[2]	15.7	43.2	39.5	2.6	**Central America[1]**	**97.7**	**132.4**	**123.1**	**28.4**
Spain	30.5	30.0	7.6	1.6	El Salvador	15.0	34.4	42.9	10.9
Sweden	16.7	6.3	4.7	1.1	Guatemala	15.4	25.6	19.9	5.2
Switzerland	16.3	6.6	3.2	.7	Nicaragua	10.1	13.0	14.3	2.8
United Kingdom	230.5	123.5	71.7	13.7	Panama	18.4	22.7	15.4	2.2
Yugoslavia	46.2	42.1	8.1	2.0					
					South America[1]	**228.3**	**284.4**	**184.0**	**41.9**
Asia[1]	**445.3**	**1,633.8**	**1,376.3**	**268.2**	Argentina	42.1	25.1	10.2	2.2
Cambodia	1.2	8.4	70.1	13.5	Brazil	20.5	13.7	8.7	2.3
China: Mainland	96.7	202.5	180.9	25.1	Colombia	70.3	77.6	51.6	11.4
Taiwan				13.4	Ecuador	37.0	50.2	22.2	4.5
Hong Kong	25.6	47.5	25.7	5.0	Guyana	7.1	47.5	42.7	10.4
India	31.2	176.8	119.7	26.2	Peru	18.6	29.1	21.8	4.9
Iran	10.4	46.2	62.5	16.5					
Iraq	6.4	23.4	12.9	1.3	**Africa[1]**	**39.3**	**91.5**	**77.0**	**17.5**
Israel	12.9	26.6	16.3	3.8	Egypt	17.2	25.5	14.2	3.0
Japan	38.5	47.9	20.0	4.0					
Jordan	14.0	29.6	14.9	3.1	**Australia**	**9.9**	**14.3**	**6.6**	**1.4**
Korea	35.8	272.0	166.0	35.8	**New Zealand**	**3.7**	**5.3**	**3.2**	**.6**
Laos	.1	22.6	97.4	7.8	**Other countries**	**5.5**	**17.7**	**9.8**	**1.9**

[1] Includes countries not shown separately.   [2] Europe and Asia.

Immigrants Admitted, by Class of Admission, 1970–86

Class of admission	1970	1975	1980	1983	1984	1985	1986
Immigrants, total	373,326	386,194	530,639	559,763	543,903	570,009	601,708
Subject to limitations[1]	287,283	281,561	289,479	269,213	262,016	264,208	266,968
Relative preferences.	92,432	95,945	216,856	213,488	212,324	213,257	212,939
Unmarried sons and daughters of U.S. citizens and their children (1st preference) . . .	1,089	871	5,668	6,892	7,569	9,319	10,910
Spouses, unmarried sons and daughters of resident aliens, and their children (2d preference)	30,714	43,077	110,269	116,623	112,309	114,997	110,926
Married sons and daughters of U.S. citizens (4th preference)[2]	8,350	3,623	10,752	20,948	14,681	18,460	20,702
Brothers and sisters of U.S. citizens (5th preference)[2]	52,279	48,374	90,167	69,025	77,765	70,481	70,401
Occupational preferences	34,016	29,334	44,369	55,468	49,521	50,895	53,625
Immigrants in professions (3d preference) . . .	10,142	8,363	8,238	12,338	10,691	10,947	11,763
Other workers (6th preference)	8,786	6,724	12,599	12,708	11,393	11,425	11,399
Their spouses and children	15,088	14,247	23,532	30,422	27,437	28,523	30,463
Conditional entrants[3]	9,863	9,129	12,222	(X)	(X)	(X)	(X)
Nonpreference (includes private bill cases)[4] . . .	36,057	25,961	—	—	—	7	—
Natives of Western Hemisphere, their spouses and children[5]	102,529	96,547	15,913	49	(X)	(X)	(X)
Cuban Refugee Act (Act of November 1966)[6]	12,208	24,554	(X)	(X)	(X)	(X)	(X)
Other[7].	178	91	119	208	171	49	404
Exempt from numerical limitations	86,043	104,633	241,160	290,550	281,887	305,801	334,740
Immediate relatives	79,213	91,504	151,131	172,006	177,783	198,143	216,821
Wives of U.S. citizens	36,276	33,719 ⎱	90,887	107,349	111,653	124,093	131,545
Husbands of U.S. citizens.	15,619	21,901 ⎰					
Children of U.S. citizens.	18,095	22,315	26,562	29,960	31,559	35,064	40,044
Orphans	(NA)	5,633	5,139	7,127	8,327	9,286	9,945
Parents of U.S. citizens.	9,223	13,569	33,682	34,697	34,571	38,986	45,232
Refugees.	144	879	75,835	102,685	92,127	95,040	104,383
Cuban Refugee Act, November 1966[6].	124	879	6,021	3,274	3,460	14,288	30,152
Indochinese Refugee Act, October 1977	(X)	(X)	22,497	3,122	875	166	136
Refugee-Parolee Act, October 1978	(X)	(X)	46,058	13,409	7,657	3,766	1,720
Asylees, Refugee Act of 1980	(X)	(X)	1,250	2,914	5,607	5,000	5,000
Refugees, Refugee Act of 1980.	(X)	(X)	(X)	79,965	74,528	71,820	67,375
Other refugees	20	—	9	1	—	—	—
Special immigrants.	1,844	2,854	3,142	3,175	2,338	2,551	2,992
Ministers of religion[2].	1,497	1,231	1,529	1,734	1,540	1,853	2,060
Employees of U.S. government abroad[2]	290	1,622	1,354	529	535	479	773
Foreign medical graduates, I&NA Amendments of 1981[2].	(X)	(X)	(X)	790	174	87	48
Other special immigrants.	57	1	259	122	89	132	111
Children born abroad to resident aliens or subsequent to issuance of visa	3,012	3,636	4,059	3,501	3,759	3,508	3,554
Aliens adjusted[8].	1,543	591	254	144	132	105	95
Spouses of U.S. citizens and their children, Act of April 1970	9	5,057	6,612	5,786	5,464	6,225	6,647
Investors, I&NA Amendments of 1981[2]	(X)	(X)	(X)	616	128	52	40
Virgin Islands Nonimmigrants Act of September 1982[2]	(X)	(X)	(X)	2,517	15	(X)	(X)
Others not subject to numerical limitation	278	112	127	120	141	177	208

— Represents zero.   (NA) Not available.   (X) Not applicable.

[1] From 1970 to December 1976, preference classifications were applied only to Eastern Hemisphere immigrants.   [2] Includes spouses and children.   [3] Prior to 1981, conditional entrants were a 7th preference class.   [4] Through 1975, includes private bill cases. No nonpreference visas issued since 1978. 1985 data represent prior contested cases.   [5] No visas issued after 1982.   [6] As of January 1977, Act of November 1966 not subject to numerical limitations.   [7] Beginning in 1980, includes private bill cases.   [8] Under sections 244 and 249, Immigration and Naturalization Act.

Estimated Refugee Arrivals by Selected Country of Citizenship, 1982–86

Country of citizenship	1982	1983	1984	1985	1986	Country of citizenship	1982	1983	1984	1985	1986
Total.........	97,300	60,700	70,600	67,800	62,250	Hungary.........	450	650	550	500	650
						Iran............	—	900	2,850	3,450	3,200
Afghanistan	4,250	2,900	2,000	2,200	2,400	Iraq............	2,000	1,600	150	250	300
Angola..........	100	—	100	50	—	Laos	9,600	2,950	7,200	5,250	12,900
Bulgaria.........	100	150	150	150	150	Poland	6,500	5,550	3,950	2,850	3,600
Cambodia........	20,850	13,200	19,850	19,250	10,050	Rumania.........	2,900	3,750	4,250	4,500	2,600
Cuba	500	650	50	150	150	Soviet Union	2,750	1,400	750	650	800
Czechoslovakia....	700	1,250	800	950	1,400	Vietnam.........	41,700	23,050	24,950	25,400	22,450
Ethiopia.........	3,150	2,550	2,500	1,750	1,250	Others[1].........	1,750	150	500	450	350

— Represents zero. [1] Includes those from countries other than those listed, those whose country of citizenship is unknown, and those with no country of citizenship.

Immigrants Admitted as Permanent Residents Under Refugee Acts, by Country of Birth, 1961–86

(for fiscal years ending in year shown, covers immigrants who were allowed to enter the United States under the 1953 Refugee Relief Act and later acts)

Country of birth	1961–1970, total	1971–1980, total	1981–1985, total	1986	Country of birth	1961–1970, total	1971–1980, total	1981–1985, total	1986
Total	212,843	539,447	554,026	104,383	Asia[1]	19,895	210,683	436,183	58,685
Europe[1]	55,235	71,858	71,083	11,868	Cambodia.......	—	7,739	68,936	13,300
Austria........	233	185	182	53	China: Mainland .. }	5,308	13,760	5,317	{ 618
Bulgaria	1,799	1,238	513	134	Taiwan ... }				{ 1
Czechoslovakia...	5,709	3,646	3,601	841	Indonesia	7,658	222	913	148
Germany	665	143	287	104	Japan..........	554	56	91	5
Greece........	586	478	800	27	Korea..........	1,316	65	99	6
Hungary........	4,044	4,358	1,616	543	Laos	—	21,690	96,643	7,556
Italy..........	1,198	346	177	24	Vietnam	7	150,266	216,079	23,930
Netherlands	3,134	8	7	—	Others	5,052	16,885	48,105	13.121
Poland	3,197	5,882	14,596	3,949					
Portugal	1,361	21	18	—	North America	132,068	252,633	34,515	31,086
Rumania........	7,158	6,812	12,979	4,308	Cuba	131,557	251,514	32,458	30,333
Soviet Union	871	31,309	35,318	1,654	Others	511	1,119	2,057	753
Spain	4,114	5,317	378	114					
Yugoslavia	18,299	11,297	186	32	South America	123	1,244	927	195
Others	2,867	818	425	85	Africa	5,486	2,991	11,281	2,547
					Others..........	36	38	37	2

— Represents zero. [1] Through 1970, Turkey is included in Europe; thereafter, it is included in Asia.

Refugee Arrivals by Selected Area of Citizenship and State, 1980–86

(for fiscal years ending in years shown)

State	Southeast Asia[1]			Eastern Europe[2]/ Soviet Union, 1986	Other,[3] 1986	State	Southeast Asia[1]			Eastern Europe[2]/ Soviet Union, 1986	Other,[3] 1986
	1980	1985	1986	1986	1986		1980	1985	1986	1986	1986
U.S.	[4]166,727	[4]49,853	[4]45,391	9,077	7,204	Mississippi. . . .	436	128	137	4	1
						Missouri	1,713	629	713	189	86
Alabama	853	206	276	14	4	Montana	540	31	33	3	2
Alaska.	111	24	39	14	12	Nebraska.	741	74	126	41	28
Arizona.	1,254	871	657	150	133	Nevada	719	163	131	27	100
Arkansas	1,112	114	137	18	2	New Hampshire	130	143	46	15	4
California.	48,540	16,107	15,168	1,811	3,066	New Jersey	1,613	507	436	399	126
Colorado	2,792	539	515	74	128	New Mexico . . .	1,274	271	126	9	20
Connecticut	1,770	608	521	237	38	New York	5,938	2,185	1,946	1,602	729
Delaware	72	7	30	3	6	North Carolina	1,734	540	473	71	31
District of						North Dakota. . .	331	92	51	62	7
Columbia	3,191	200	107	64	125	Ohio	2,465	778	594	156	81
Florida	2,926	1,104	883	217	121	Oklahoma	2,204	506	393	21	38
Georgia	2,427	1,043	823	85	120	Oregon	6,213	767	713	107	38
Hawaii	2,385	302	251	10	—	Pennsylvania . . .	6,689	1,744	1,380	370	79
Idaho	335	211	201	117	5	Rhode Island . . .	1,132	492	371	57	2
Illinois.	7,012	1,776	1,548	847	239	South Carolina	573	61	71	3	10
Indiana	1,585	242	191	67	36	South Dakota. . .	389	36	40	53	27
Iowa	2,837	563	751	35	6	Tennessee	2,032	591	811	77	38
Kansas	1,924	803	517	7	14	Texas	12,251	4,219	3,493	376	477
Kentucky.	790	354	387	3	18	Utah	3,568	815	620	79	18
Louisiana.	2,116	725	599	5	16	Vermont	151	39	25	94	4
Maine	278	214	150	83	36	Virginia	3,153	1,211	1,177	39	341
Maryland.	1,257	546	502	170	317	Washington	7,972	2,443	2,100	285	141
Massachusetts . .	3,748	2,520	1,941	293	87	West Virginia. . .	213	22	13	6	5
Michigan	3,142	362	491	495	142	Wisconsin	2,492	420	737	41	17
Minnesota	7,425	1,480	1,936	69	82	Wyoming.	113	6	9	3	1

— Represents zero. [1] Vietnam, Laos, and Cambodia. [2] Czechoslovakia, Hungary, Poland, and Rumania.
[3] Afghanistan, Iran, Iraq, and Ethiopia. [4] Includes those in Guam and whose destination is unknown.

Economic Statistics

Federal Government Receipts by Source

	1987	1988	Percent change
Tax Sources			
Income			
Individual	364.0	392.8*	+1.1
Corporate	104.8	117.2	+1.1
Social insurance taxes and contributions:			
Employment	273.2	307.4	+1.1
Unemployment	23.8	22.2	
Other retirement contributions	4.4	3.5	−0.8
Excise	32.6	33.4	+1.0
Estate and gift	6.0	5.8	−0.1
Other Sources			
Customs duties	14.4	15.3	+1.1
Miscellaneous	19.1	18.9	−0.1
Total Receipts	824.4	916.6	+1.1

* Dollars in billions

Federal Government Expenditures

	1987	1988	Percent change
Agriculture	31.1	26.3	−0.8
Commerce and housing credit	9.3	2.5	−0.3
Community and regional development	6.2	5.5	−0.9
Defense	282.2	297.6	+1.1
Education, training, employment, and social services	29.8	28.4	−1.0
Energy	3.8	3.3	−0.9
General government	6.8	7.5	+1.1
General-purpose fiscal assistance	1.9	1.5	−0.8
Health	39.7	38.9	−1.0
Income security	124.9	124.8	−0.1
International affairs	14.6	15.2	+1.0
Justice administration	8.3	9.2	+1.1
Natural resources and environment	13.9	14.2	+1.0
Science, space, and technology	9.5	11.4	+1.2
Social Security and Medicare	270.4	280.9	+1.0
Transportation	27.0	25.5	+1.0
Veterans benefits and services	26.7	27.2	+1.0
Net interest	137.5	139.0	+1.0
Allowances	—	−0.8	—
Undistributed offsetting receipts	−37.1	−45.4	+8.2
Total Expenditures	1,015.6	1,024.3	+1.0

Per Capita Personal Income by States

State	1980	1984	1985	1986[1]	State	1980	1984	1985	1986[1]
Alabama	$ 7,465	$ 9,987	$10,670	$11,115	Montana	$ 8,342	$10,607	$10,984	$11,904
Alaska	13,007	17,550	18,140	17,744	Nebraska	8,895	12,572	13,286	13,777
Arizona	8,854	11,822	12,771	13,220	Nevada	10,848	13,298	14,479	15,074
Arkansas	7,113	9,734	10,471	10,773	New Hampshire	9,150	13,386	14,947	15,922
California	11,021	14,471	16,070	16,778	New Jersey	10,966	15,389	17,214	18,284
Colorado	10,143	13,848	14,797	15,113	New Mexico	7,940	10,256	10,909	11,037
Connecticut	11,532	16,547	18,101	19,208	New York	10,179	14,341	16,083	17,118
Delaware	10,059	13,692	14,269	15,010	North Carolina	7,780	10,852	11,605	12,245
District of Columbia	12,251	16,870	18,239	18,980	North Dakota	8,642	12,290	12,052	12,284
Florida	9,246	12,773	13,744	14,281	Ohio	9,399	12,326	13,223	13,743
Georgia	8,021	11,548	12,546	13,224	Oklahoma	9,018	11,629	12,215	12,368
Hawaii	10,129	13,028	13,845	14,691	Oregon	9,309	11,613	12,630	13,217
Idaho	8,105	10,146	11,130	11,432	Pennsylvania	9,353	12,292	13,426	13,944
Illinois	10,454	13,705	14,736	15,420	Rhode Island	9,227	12,860	13,926	14,670
Indiana	8,914	11,725	12,443	12,944	South Carolina	7,392	10,111	10,626	11,096
Iowa	9,226	12,123	12,603	13,222	South Dakota	7,800	10,904	11,159	11,850
Kansas	9,880	13,311	13,782	14,379	Tennessee	7,711	10,400	11,230	11,831
Kentucky	7,679	10,232	10,815	11,129	Texas	9,439	12,575	13,467	13,523
Louisiana	8,412	10,741	11,261	11,227	Utah	7,671	9,715	10,491	10,743
Maine	7,760	10,849	11,873	12,709	Vermont	7,957	10,828	12,111	12,845
Maryland	10,394	14,443	15,862	16,588	Virginia	9,413	13,291	14,553	15,374
Massachusetts	10,103	14,755	16,387	17,516	Washington	10,256	12,755	13,882	14,498
Michigan	9,801	12,621	13,608	14,064	West Virginia	7,764	9,708	10,190	10,530
Minnesota	9,673	13,212	14,092	14,737	Wisconsin	9,364	12,378	13,152	13,796
Mississippi	6,573	8,684	9,182	9,552	Wyoming	11,018	12,238	13,212	13,230
Missouri	8,812	12,075	13,228	13,657	*United States*	9,494	12,772	13,867	14,461

[1] Preliminary.

Household Type, by Median Income and Income Level, 1985

		Family households				Nonfamily households				
				Male house-holder, wife absent	Female house-holder, husband absent		Single-person household			Multiple-person house-hold
Item	All house-holds	Total	Married couple			Total	Total	Male house-holder	Female house-holder	
Median income (in dollars):										
All households	**23,618**	**28,022**	**31,161**	**24,354**	**14,316**	**13,798**	**11,884**	**16,312**	**9,774**	**28,773**
White	24,908	29,404	31,660	25,799	16,544	14,391	12,327	17,267	10,138	30,053
Black	14,819	17,053	24,685	16,901	9,574	9,571	8,360	11,114	6,691	19,573
Hispanic[1]	17,465	19,478	22,366	22,430	8,993	10,914	8,984	11,507	6,581	21,000
Number (1,000):										
All households	**88,458**	**63,558**	**50,933**	**2,414**	**10,211**	**24,900**	**21,178**	**8,285**	**12,893**	**3,722**
Under $5,000	6,784	2,947	1,103	152	1,693	3,837	3,748	1,064	2,684	88
$5,000–$9,999	10,997	5,307	2,984	251	2,072	5,690	5,401	1,506	3,895	288
$10,000–$14,999	10,149	6,436	4,665	246	1,525	3,713	3,364	1,264	2,099	350
$15,000–$19,999	9,674	6,629	5,042	277	1,311	3,046	2,599	1,107	1,492	447
$20,000–$24,999	8,838	6,528	5,189	317	1,021	2,310	1,899	865	1,034	412
$25,000–$34,999	15,007	11,894	10,147	457	1,290	3,114	2,390	1,334	1,056	724
$35,000–$49,999	13,947	12,052	10,794	401	857	1,897	1,132	691	440	764
$50,000 and over	13,061	11,767	11,010	314	442	1,294	645	453	192	649

[1] Hispanic persons may be of any race.

Income of Households—Aggregate and Mean—by Race and Hispanic Origin of Householder, 1985

Characteristic	All races[1] Aggregate money income (in billions)	All races[1] Mean income (in dollars)	White Aggregate money income (in billions)	White Mean income (in dollars)	Black Aggregate money income (in billions)	Black Mean income (in dollars)	Hispanic[2] Aggregate money income (in billions)	Hispanic[2] Mean income (in dollars)
Total	2,571.1	29,066	2,317.1	30,259	189.4	19,335	113.8	21,823
Age of householder:								
15–24	97.5	17,708	87.8	18,567	7.6	11,223	8.4	15,419
25–34	569.5	27,904	506.6	29,257	48.0	19,163	33.1	20,893
35–44	640.8	35,606	573.4	37,184	48.2	23,696	28.7	24,408
45–54	501.9	38,316	444.6	40,438	41.6	24,728	22.2	28,091
55–64	411.8	32,045	379.3	33,342	24.7	19,721	13.3	23,253
65 and over	349.6	18,800	325.5	19,440	19.3	11,747	8.1	14,804
Region:								
Northeast	578.1	31,146	530.2	32,259	37.7	20,620	19.7	19,220
Midwest	615.0	28,149	568.1	28,916	39.0	20,204	8.6	24,012
South	819.7	27,044	717.8	28,945	92.0	17,826	36.5	21,801
West	558.3	31,475	501.0	31,920	20.7	23,618	49.0	22,713
Size of household:								
One person	338.8	15,997	303.5	16,550	30.0	11,995	9.7	12,135
Two persons	818.8	29,525	763.3	30,632	43.3	18,312	23.9	21,261
Three persons	551.8	34,300	497.8	36,001	40.1	21,347	23.1	22,428
Four persons	511.9	37,161	459.6	38,711	36.9	24,817	27.5	25,278
Five persons	229.0	36,495	196.5	38,395	22.9	25,607	15.3	24,879
Six persons	77.5	36,257	64.5	38,750	8.5	24,658	7.6	26,174
Seven persons or more	43.3	34,053	32.0	38,102	7.7	23,565	6.6	25,202
Educational attainment of householder:								
Elementary school:								
Less than 8 years	92.2	13,938	73.1	14,470	16.0	11,612	22.2	15,247
8 years	99.1	17,329	89.4	17,721	7.8	13,293	7.3	17,615
High school:								
1–3 years	214.9	19,419	184.0	20,379	28.0	14,750	15.2	17,786
4 years	827.5	26,462	747.5	27,343	64.7	19,429	32.6	23,709
College:								
1–3 years	480.7	31,416	433.8	32,414	37.0	23,347	19.0	29,043
4 years or more	856.8	46,349	789.3	47,175	36.0	35,141	17.4	38,278
Occupation of longest job of householder:								
Total[3]	2,164.0	34,121	1,952.8	35,244	155.1	24,116	99.2	25,459
Managerial and professional specialty	803.3	47,042	744.6	47,731	34.9	36,191	19.8	37,917
Technical, sales, and administrative support	518.1	33,437	470.9	34,467	35.2	23,570	19.6	27,118
Service workers	149.7	22,169	120.2	23,651	25.0	17,324	12.2	20,247
Farming, forestry, and fishing	45.6	19,756	41.9	20,183	2.1	12,001	3.4	16,350
Precision production, crafts, and repair	349.2	32,110	320.6	32,338	20.8	27,996	18.7	25,384
Operators, fabricators, and laborers	296.7	27,314	253.3	28,015	37.1	23,037	25.3	23,080

[1] Includes other races not shown separately.   [2] Hispanic persons may be of any race.
[3] Includes persons in armed forces not shown separately.

Federal Receipts by Source and Outlays by Function, 1970–87

(in billions of dollars)

Source or function	1970	1975	1980	1981	1982	1983	1984	1985	1986	1987, est.	Percent distribution 1980	Percent distribution 1987
Surplus or deficit (−) . .	−2.8	−53.2	−73.8	−78.9	−127.9	−207.8	−185.3	−212.3	−220.7	−173.2	(X)	(X)
BY SOURCE												
Total receipts¹	**192.8**	**279.1**	**517.1**	**599.3**	**617.8**	**600.6**	**666.5**	**734.1**	**769.1**	**842.4**	**100.00**	**100.00**
Individual income taxes	90.4	122.4	244.1	285.9	297.7	288.9	298.4	334.5	349.0	364.0	47.20	43.21
Corporation income taxes	32.8	40.6	64.6	61.1	49.2	37.0	56.9	61.3	63.1	104.8	12.49	12.44
Social insurance taxes and contributions . . .	44.4	84.5	157.8	182.7	201.5	209.0	239.4	265.2	283.9	301.5	30.52	35.79
Employment taxes and contributions	39.1	75.2	138.7	163.0	180.7	185.8	209.7	234.6	255.1	273.2	26.83	32.44
Unemployment insurance	3.5	6.8	15.3	15.8	16.6	18.8	25.1	25.8	24.1	23.8	2.97	2.82
Contributions for other insurance and retirement	1.8	2.6	3.7	4.0	4.2	4.4	4.6	4.8	4.7	4.4	.72	.53
Excise taxes	15.7	16.6	24.3	40.8	36.3	35.3	37.4	36.0	32.9	32.6	4.70	3.87
Estate and gift taxes . . .	3.6	4.6	6.4	6.8	8.0	6.1	6.0	6.4	7.0	6.0	1.24	.71
Customs duties	2.4	3.7	7.2	8.1	8.9	8.7	11.4	12.1	13.3	14.4	1.39	1.71
Miscellaneous receipts	3.4	6.7	12.7	13.8	16.2	15.6	17.0	18.5	19.9	19.1	2.47	2.27
Federal Reserve earning deposits	**3.3**	**5.8**	**11.8**	**12.8**	**15.2**	**14.5**	**15.7**	**17.1**	**18.4**	**15.8**	**2.28**	**1.88**
BY FUNCTION												
Total outlays¹	**195.6**	**332.3**	**590.9**	**678.2**	**745.7**	**808.3**	**851.8**	**946.3**	**989.8**	**1,015.6**	**100.00**	**100.00**
National defense¹	**81.7**	**86.5**	**134.0**	**157.5**	**185.3**	**209.9**	**227.4**	**252.7**	**273.4**	**282.2**	**22.68**	**27.79**
Department of Defense, military	80.2	85.9	131.0	153.8	180.7	204.4	220.8	245.4	265.6	274.2	22.16	27.00
Atomic energy defense activities . . .	1.4	1.5	2.9	3.4	4.3	5.2	6.1	7.1	7.4	7.4	.49	.73
Defense-related activities	.1	−.9	.1	.3	.3	.3	.5	.3	.3	.6	.02	.06
International affairs¹ . . .	**4.3**	**7.1**	**12.7**	**13.1**	**12.3**	**11.8**	**15.9**	**16.2**	**14.2**	**14.6**	**2.15**	**1.44**
International development and humanitarian assistance	2.3	3.1	3.6	4.1	3.8	4.0	4.5	5.4	5.0	4.4	.61	.43
Conduct of foreign affairs	.4	.7	1.4	1.3	1.6	1.8	1.9	2.1	2.3	2.7	.23	.27
Foreign information and exchange	.2	.3	.5	.5	.6	.6	.7	.8	.9	1.0	.09	.10
International financial program activities	.3	.4	2.4	2.0	.9	−1.1	.9	−1.5	−4.5	−2.1	.41	−.21
International security assistance	1.1	2.5	4.8	5.1	5.4	6.6	7.9	9.4	10.5	8.6	.81	.84

Source or function	1970	1975	1980	1981	1982	1983	1984	1985	1986	1987, est.	Percent distribution 1980	Percent distribution 1987
Income security	**15.6**	**50.2**	**86.5**	**99.7**	**107.7**	**122.6**	**112.7**	**128.2**	**119.8**	**124.9**	**14.64**	**12.30**
General retirement and disability insurance	1.0	4.7	5.1	5.4	5.6	5.6	5.4	5.6	5.3	5.5	.86	.55
Federal employee retirement and disability	5.5	13.2	26.6	31.3	34.3	36.5	38.1	38.6	41.4	43.6	4.50	4.29
Housing assistance	.5	2.1	5.6	7.8	8.7	10.0	11.3	25.3	12.4	12.9	.95	1.27
Food and nutrition assistance	1.0	6.6	14.0	16.2	15.6	18.0	18.1	18.5	18.6	19.4	2.37	1.91
Other income security	4.3	10.1	17.2	19.4	19.8	21.1	21.4	22.7	24.4	25.5	2.91	2.51
Unemployment insurance	3.4	13.5	18.0	19.7	23.7	31.5	18.4	17.5	17.8	18.0	3.05	1.77
Health	**5.9**	**12.9**	**23.2**	**26.9**	**27.4**	**28.6**	**30.4**	**33.5**	**35.9**	**39.7**	**3.92**	**3.91**
Health-care services	4.0	9.5	18.0	21.2	21.8	23.0	24.5	27.0	28.9	32.0	3.05	3.15
Health research	1.1	1.9	3.4	3.8	3.9	4.0	4.4	4.9	5.4	5.9	.58	.58
Education and training of health-care work force	.6	.9	.7	.8	.7	.6	.4	.5	.5	.5	.12	.04
Consumer and occupational health and safety	.2	.6	1.0	1.0	1.0	1.1	1.1	1.2	1.2	1.2	.17	.12
Social Security and Medicare	**36.5**	**77.5**	**150.6**	**178.7**	**202.5**	**223.3**	**235.8**	**254.4**	**268.9**	**279.5**	**25.49**	**27.52**
Social Security	30.3	64.7	118.5	139.6	156.0	170.7	178.2	188.6	198.8	207.9	20.06	20.47
Medicare	6.2	12.9	32.1	39.1	46.6	52.6	57.5	65.8	70.2	71.6	5.43	7.05
Veterans' benefits and services[1]	**8.7**	**16.6**	**21.2**	**23.0**	**24.0**	**24.8**	**25.6**	**26.3**	**26.4**	**26.7**	**3.59**	**2.63**
Income security	5.5	7.9	11.7	12.9	13.7	14.3	14.4	14.7	15.0	15.1	1.98	1.48
Education, training, and rehabilitation	1.0	4.6	2.3	2.3	1.9	1.6	1.4	1.1	.5	.4	.40	.04
Hospital and medical care	1.8	3.7	6.5	7.0	7.5	8.3	8.9	9.5	9.9	10.3	1.10	1.01
Housing	.1	(Z)	(−Z)	.2	.1	(Z)	.2	.2	.1	.1	(X)	.01
Education, training, employment, and social services[1]	**8.6**	**16.0**	**31.8**	**33.7**	**27.0**	**26.6**	**27.6**	**29.3**	**30.6**	**29.8**	**5.39**	**2.94**
Elementary, secondary, and vocational education	2.9	4.4	6.9	7.2	6.8	6.3	6.5	7.6	7.8	7.6	1.17	.75
Higher education	1.4	2.2	6.7	8.9	7.2	7.2	7.4	8.2	8.4	7.5	1.14	.74
Research and general education aids	.4	.8	1.2	1.0	1.0	1.1	1.2	1.1	1.2	1.4	.20	.14
Training and employment	1.6	4.1	10.3	9.2	5.5	5.3	4.6	5.0	5.3	5.0	1.75	.49
Social services	2.3	4.4	6.1	6.9	6.0	6.1	7.2	6.7	7.2	7.5	1.03	.74

Federal Receipts by Source and Outlays by Function, 1970–87 *(Continued)*

(in billions of dollars)

Source or function	1970	1975	1980	1981	1982	1983	1984	1985	1986	1987, est.	Percent distribution 1980	Percent distribution 1987
Commerce and housing credit	2.1	9.9	9.4	8.2	6.3	6.7	6.9	4.2	4.4	9.3	1.59	.92
Mortgage credit and thrift insurance . . .	.1	6.0	5.6	4.7	4.0	3.9	3.8	.9	1.9	5.5	.95	.54
Payment to Postal Service	1.5	3.0	1.2	1.4	.2	1.1	1.2	1.4	.8	1.8	.21	.18
Other commerce	.5	1.0	2.5	2.1	2.1	1.7	1.9	2.0	1.8	2.0	.43	.20
Transportation[1]	7.0	10.9	21.3	23.4	20.6	21.3	23.7	25.8	28.1	27.0	3.61	2.66
Ground transportation	4.7	7.0	15.3	17.1	14.3	14.3	16.2	17.6	18.7	17.9	2.58	1.76
Air transportation . . .	1.4	2.4	3.7	3.8	3.5	4.0	4.4	4.9	5.3	5.3	.63	.52
Water transportation	.9	1.4	2.2	2.4	2.7	3.0	3.0	3.2	4.0	3.7	.38	.37
Natural resources and environment[1]	3.1	7.3	13.9	13.6	13.0	12.7	12.6	13.4	13.6	13.9	2.35	1.36
Water resources	1.5	2.6	4.2	4.1	3.9	3.9	4.1	4.1	4.0	4.2	.71	.41
Conservation and land management	.4	.7	1.0	1.2	1.1	1.5	1.3	1.5	1.4	1.6	.18	.16
Recreational resources	.4	.8	1.7	1.6	1.4	1.5	1.6	1.6	1.5	1.6	.28	.16
Pollution control and abatement	.4	2.5	5.5	5.2	5.0	4.3	4.0	4.5	4.8	4.5	.93	.45
Other natural resources	.4	.8	1.4	1.5	1.5	1.5	1.6	1.7	1.9	1.9	.24	.19
Energy[1]	1.0	2.9	10.2	15.2	13.5	9.4	7.1	5.7	4.7	3.8	1.72	.37
Supply	.9	2.4	8.4	10.2	8.3	6.1	3.3	2.6	2.8	1.9	1.42	.19
Conservation	—	(Z)	.6	.7	.5	.5	.5	.5	.5	.4	.10	.04
Emergency preparedness	—	(Z)	.3	3.3	3.9	1.9	2.5	1.8	.6	.7	.06	.07
Information, policy, and regulation	.1	.4	.9	1.0	.9	.9	.3	.7	.8	.7	.15	.07
Community and regional development	2.4	4.3	11.3	10.6	8.3	7.6	7.7	7.7	7.2	6.2	1.90	.61
Community development	1.4	2.3	4.9	5.1	4.6	4.4	4.5	4.6	4.1	4.3	.83	.42
Area and regional development	.7	1.6	4.3	3.8	3.8	3.2	3.0	3.1	2.7	1.9	.73	.19
Disaster relief and insurance	.3	.4	2.0	1.7	−.1	(−Z)	.1	(−Z)	.4	(−Z)	.35	(−Z)
Agriculture[1]	5.2	3.0	8.8	11.3	15.9	22.9	13.6	25.6	31.4	31.1	1.50	3.06
Farm income stabilization	4.6	2.2	7.4	9.8	14.3	21.3	11.9	23.8	29.6	29.2	1.26	2.87
Research and services	.6	.9	1.4	1.5	1.6	1.6	1.7	1.8	1.8	1.9	.24	.19
Net interest	14.4	23.2	52.5	68.7	85.0	89.8	111.1	129.4	136.0	137.5	8.89	13.54
General purpose fiscal assistance	.4	7.2	8.5	6.9	6.4	6.5	6.8	6.4	6.4	1.9	1.45	.19
Revenue sharing	—	6.1	6.8	5.1	4.6	4.6	4.6	4.6	5.1	.1	1.16	.01

Source or function	1970	1975	1980	1981	1982	1983	1984	1985	1986	1987, est.	Percent distribution 1980	Percent distribution 1987
General science, space, and technology[2] . . .	**4.5**	**4.0**	**5.8**	**6.5**	**7.2**	**7.9**	**8.3**	**8.6**	**9.0**	**9.5**	**.99**	**.94**
General science and basic research	.9	1.0	1.4	1.5	1.6	1.6	1.8	2.0	2.2	2.3	.23	.22
Space flight	2.3	1.7	2.6	3.1	3.5	4.1	4.0	4.0	3.8	4.3	.44	.42
Space science, applications and technology	1.2	1.3	1.9	1.9	2.1	2.2	2.4	2.6	3.0	2.9	.31	.29
General government[1] . . .	**1.8**	**3.2**	**4.4**	**4.6**	**4.5**	**4.8**	**5.1**	**5.2**	**6.1**	**6.8**	**.75**	**.67**
Legislative functions	.3	.6	1.0	1.0	1.2	1.2	1.3	1.4	1.4	1.7	.18	.16
Management, direction (Exec. Branch)	(Z)	.1	.1	.1	.1	.1	.1	.1	.1	.1	.02	.01
Central fiscal operations.	.9	1.9	2.6	2.6	2.6	3.1	3.3	3.5	3.6	4.5	.44	.44
General property and records management	.6	.4	.3	.1	.2	.2	.2	.1	.5	(Z)	.06	(Z)
Justice administration . .	**1.0**	**3.0**	**4.6**	**4.8**	**4.7**	**5.1**	**5.7**	**6.3**	**6.6**	**8.3**	**.78**	**.82**
Federal law enforcement	.6	1.3	2.2	2.4	2.5	2.9	3.2	3.5	3.6	4.6	.38	.46
Federal judicial activities[3]	.2	.6	1.3	1.5	1.5	1.6	1.8	2.1	2.2	2.6	.23	.25
Federal correctional activities.	.1	.2	.3	.4	.4	.4	.5	.5	.6	.8	.06	.07
Criminal justice assistance	.1	.9	.7	.5	.3	.2	.1	.2	.2	.3	.11	.03
Undistributed offsetting receipts	**−8.6**	**−13.6**	**−19.9**	**−28.0**	**−26.1**	**−34.0**	**−32.0**	**−32.7**	**−33.0**	**−37.1**	**−3.37**	**−3.65**
Employer share, employee retirement	−8.4	−11.2	−15.8	−17.9	−19.8	−23.5	−25.3	−27.2	−28.3	−31.3	−2.68	−3.08
Rents and royalties[5]	−.2	−2.4	−4.1	−10.1	−6.3	−10.5	−6.7	−5.5	−4.7	−3.9	−.69	−.38

— Represents zero.   (X) Not applicable.   (Z) Less than $50 million.   [1] Totals reflect interfund and intragovernmental transactions and/or other functions not shown separately.   [2] Includes supporting space activities.   [3] Includes litigative activities.   [4] Includes sale of major assets (−1.9) not shown separately.   [5] On Outer Continental Shelf.

Federal Budget—Summary, 1945–87[1]

(in billions of dollars, except percent)

Year	Receipts			Outlays					Surplus or deficit (−)		
	Total[1]	Federal funds	Trust funds	Total[1]	Federal funds	Trust funds	Human resources	National defense	Total[1]	Federal funds	Trust funds
1945.	45.2	41.9	3.6	92.7	94.8	− .6	1.9	83.0	− 47.6	− 53.0	4.3
1950.	39.4	35.3	3.5	42.6	38.4	5.1	14.2	13.7	− 3.1	− 3.1	− 1.6
1955.	65.5	58.2	3.1	68.4	62.3	3.0	14.9	42.7	− 3.0	− 4.2	.1
1960.	92.5	75.6	7.8	92.2	74.9	8.1	26.2	48.1	.3	.8	− .3
1961.	94.4	75.2	9.4	97.7	79.4	9.0	29.8	49.6	− 3.3	− 4.2	.4
1962.	99.7	79.7	9.9	106.8	86.5	8.9	31.6	52.3	− 7.1	− 6.8	1.0
1963.	106.6	84.0	10.8	111.3	90.6	8.1	33.5	53.4	− 4.8	− 6.6	2.7
1964.	112.6	87.5	11.2	118.5	96.1	9.2	35.3	54.8	− 5.9	− 8.6	2.0
1965.	116.8	90.9	11.5	118.2	94.9	9.2	36.6	50.6	− 1.4	− 3.9	2.3
1966.	130.8	101.4	12.9	134.5	106.6	10.8	43.3	58.1	− 3.7	− 5.2	2.1
1967.	148.8	111.8	16.5	157.5	127.5	13.4	51.3	71.4	− 8.6	− 15.7	3.1
1968.	153.0	114.7	17.6	178.1	143.1	16.9	59.4	81.9	− 25.2	− 28.4	.6
1969.	186.9	143.3	20.1	183.6	148.2	15.7	66.4	82.5	3.2	− 4.9	4.4
1970.	192.8	143.2	22.3	195.6	156.3	17.8	75.3	81.7	− 2.8	− 13.2	4.5
1971.	187.1	133.8	26.0	210.2	163.7	22.2	91.9	78.9	− 23.0	− 29.9	3.8
1972.	207.3	148.8	28.4	230.7	178.1	25.5	107.2	79.2	− 23.4	− 29.3	2.9
1973.	230.8	161.4	41.2	245.7	187.0	30.9	119.5	76.7	− 14.9	− 25.7	10.3
1974.	263.2	181.2	46.1	269.4	201.4	33.9	135.8	79.3	− 6.1	− 20.1	12.2
1975.	279.1	187.5	51.0	332.3	248.2	45.6	173.2	86.5	− 53.2	− 60.7	5.4
1976.	298.1	201.1	61.8	371.8	277.2	56.2	203.6	89.6	− 73.7	− 76.1	5.6
1976[5].	81.2	54.1	13.3	96.0	66.9	13.8	52.1	22.3	− 14.7	− 12.8	− .5
1977.	355.6	241.3	70.3	409.2	304.5	56.9	221.9	97.2	− 53.6	− 63.1	13.4
1978.	399.6	270.5	76.9	458.7	342.4	59.9	242.3	104.5	− 59.2	− 71.9	17.0
1979.	463.3	316.4	86.0	503.5	374.9	65.7	267.6	116.3	− 40.2	− 58.5	20.3
1980.	517.1	350.9	94.7	590.9	433.5	84.8	313.4	134.0	− 73.8	− 82.6	9.9
1981.	599.3	410.4	106.0	678.2	496.2	94.2	362.0	157.5	− 78.9	− 85.8	11.8
1982.	617.8	409.3	122.1	745.7	543.4	107.9	388.7	185.3	− 127.9	− 134.2	14.2
1983.	600.6	382.3	147.3	808.3	613.2	124.4	426.0	209.9	− 207.8	− 230.8	22.9
1984.	666.5	419.6	158.1	851.8	637.8	125.4	432.0	227.4	− 185.3	− 218.2	32.6
1985.	734.1	459.5	197.5	946.3	725.9	152.7	471.8	252.7	− 212.3	− 266.4	44.8
1986.	769.1	473.5	206.9	989.8	756.5	161.4	481.6	273.4	− 220.7	− 283.0	45.5
1987, est.	842.4	526.1	215.1	1,015.6	769.1	164.8	500.5	282.2	− 173.2	− 243.0	50.3

(NA) Not applicable.   [1] Includes off-budget receipts, outlays, and interfund transactions.   [2] End of fiscal year.   [3] Gross national product as of fiscal year.   [4] Change from 1944; from previous year shown for all other years.   [5] Represents transition quarter, July–September.

Out-standing gross debt[2]	Average annual percent change				Outstand-ing gross debt	Percent of GNP[3]				Outstand-ing gross debt	Outlays, off-budget
		Outlays					Outlays				
	Receipts	Total	Federal funds	Trust funds		Total	Human resources	National defense		
260.1	3.2	1.5	2.8	(NA)	[4]27.5	43.6	.9	39.1	122.5	.1
256.9	−2.7	−14.4	−16.6	(NA)	−.3	16.0	5.3	5.1	96.3	.5
274.4	10.7	10.0	10.2	−10.0	1.3	17.7	3.9	11.1	71.0	4.0
290.9	7.2	6.1	3.7	21.9	1.2	18.2	5.2	9.5	57.4	10.9
292.9	2.0	6.0	6.0	10.7	.7	18.9	5.8	9.6	56.5	11.7
303.3	5.6	9.3	9.0	−.8	3.5	19.2	5.7	9.4	54.4	13.5
310.8	6.9	4.2	4.7	−8.8	2.5	18.9	5.7	9.1	52.9	15.0
316.8	5.7	6.5	6.0	12.8	1.9	18.8	5.6	8.7	50.3	15.7
323.2	3.7	−.3	−1.3	.8	2.0	17.6	5.4	7.5	48.0	16.5
329.5	12.0	13.8	12.4	16.8	2.0	18.2	5.9	7.9	44.6	19.7
341.3	13.7	17.0	19.7	24.3	3.6	19.8	6.5	9.0	43.0	20.4
369.8	2.8	13.1	12.2	26.2	8.3	21.0	7.0	9.6	43.5	22.3
367.1	22.2	3.1	3.6	−7.4	−.7	19.8	7.1	8.9	39.5	25.2
382.6	3.2	6.5	5.5	13.6	4.2	19.8	7.6	8.3	38.6	27.6
409.5	−2.9	7.4	4.7	24.5	7.0	19.9	8.7	7.5	38.8	32.8
437.3	10.8	9.8	8.8	15.0	6.8	20.0	9.3	6.9	37.9	36.9
468.4	11.3	6.5	5.0	21.0	7.1	19.2	9.3	6.0	36.6	45.6
486.2	14.0	9.6	7.7	9.7	3.8	19.0	9.6	5.6	34.3	52.1
544.1	6.0	23.4	23.2	34.4	11.9	21.8	11.4	5.7	35.7	60.4
631.9	6.8	11.9	11.7	23.3	16.1	21.9	12.0	5.3	37.2	69.6
646.4	(NA)	(NA)	(NA)	(NA)	(NA)	21.4	11.6	5.0	36.0	19.4
709.1	19.3	10.1	9.8	1.3	12.2	21.2	11.5	5.0	36.7	80.7
780.4	12.4	12.1	12.4	5.2	10.1	21.1	11.2	4.8	35.9	89.7
833.8	16.0	19.8	9.5	9.6	6.8	20.6	10.9	4.8	34.1	100.0
914.3	11.6	17.4	15.6	29.1	9.7	22.1	11.7	5.0	34.2	114.3
1,003.9	15.9	14.8	14.5	11.1	9.8	22.7	12.1	5.3	33.6	135.2
1,147.0	3.1	10.0	9.5	14.6	14.2	23.8	12.4	5.9	36.5	151.4
1,381.9	−2.8	8.5	12.8	15.3	20.5	24.3	12.8	6.3	41.6	147.1
1,576.7	11.0	5.2	4.0	.4	14.1	23.1	11.7	6.2	42.8	165.8
1,827.2	10.1	11.1	13.8	22.3	15.9	24.0	12.0	6.4	46.4	176.8
2,132.9	4.8	4.6	4.3	5.7	16.7	23.8	11.6	6.6	51.2	183.5
2,372.4	9.5	2.6	1.7	2.1	11.2	23.0	11.3	6.4	53.7	194.5

Federal Budget Surplus or Deficit, 1935–87

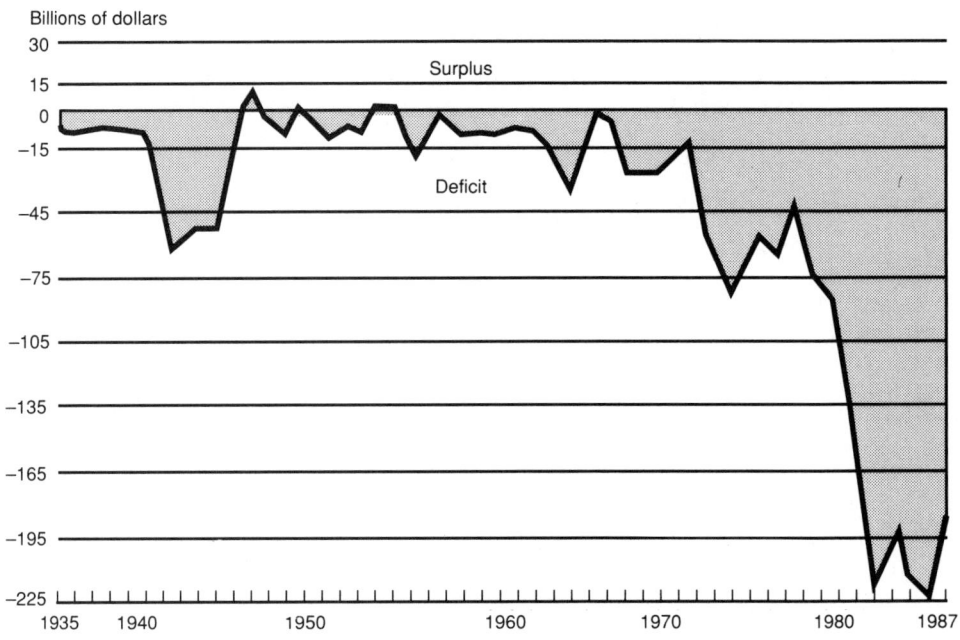

State Government

All states (except Nebraska) have a lawmaking body, in most cases called a *legislature* or *general assembly,* that is divided into two houses. (Nebraska's state government is unicameral, or single-chambered, and all its officials are called senators.) In most states, the upper house is called the Senate and the lower house is called the House of Representatives. State senators usually are elected every four years, while representatives or assembly members are elected every two years. State legislatures generally meet biennially, though a few meet annually.

The table on page 693 shows the name of each of the 50 states along with the year it became a state, the official abbreviation used by the United States Postal Service, the capital, and the name of the lawmaking body.

State Facts

State	Date Entered Union	Postal Abbreviation	Capital	Name of Lawmaking Body
Alabama	1819	AL	Montgomery	Legislature
Alaska	1959	AK	Juneau	Legislature
Arizona	1912	AZ	Phoenix	Legislature
Arkansas	1836	AR	Little Rock	General Assembly
California	1850	CA	Sacramento	Legislature[1]
Colorado	1876	CO	Denver	General Assembly
Connecticut	1788	CT	Hartford	General Assembly
Delaware	1787	DE	Dover	General Assembly
Florida	1845	FL	Tallahassee	Legislature
Georgia	1788	GA	Atlanta	General Assembly
Hawaii	1959	HI	Honolulu	Legislature
Idaho	1890	ID	Boise	Legislature
Illinois	1818	IL	Springfield	General Assembly
Indiana	1816	IN	Indianapolis	General Assembly
Iowa	1846	IA	Des Moines	General Assembly
Kansas	1861	KS	Topeka	Legislature
Kentucky	1792	KY	Frankfort	General Assembly
Louisiana	1812	LA	Baton Rouge	Legislature
Maine	1820	ME	Augusta	Legislature
Maryland	1788	MD	Annapolis	General Assembly[2]
Massachusetts	1788	MA	Boston	General Court
Michigan	1837	MI	Lansing	Legislature
Minnesota	1858	MN	St. Paul	Legislature
Mississippi	1817	MS	Jackson	Legislature
Missouri	1821	MO	Jefferson City	General Assembly
Montana	1889	MT	Helena	Legislative Assembly
Nebraska	1867	NE	Lincoln	Legislature
Nevada	1864	NV	Carson City	Legislature[1]
New Hampshire	1788	NH	Concord	General Court
New Jersey	1787	NJ	Trenton	Legislature[3]
New Mexico	1912	NM	Santa Fe	Legislature
New York	1788	NY	Albany	Legislature[1]
North Carolina	1789	NC	Raleigh	General Assembly
North Dakota	1889	ND	Bismarck	Legislative Assembly
Ohio	1803	OH	Columbus	General Assembly
Oklahoma	1907	OK	Oklahoma City	Legislature
Oregon	1859	OR	Salem	Legislative Assembly
Pennsylvania	1787	PA	Harrisburg	General Assembly
Rhode Island	1790	RI	Providence	General Assembly
South Carolina	1788	SC	Columbia	General Assembly
South Dakota	1889	SD	Pierre	Legislature
Tennessee	1796	TN	Nashville	General Assembly
Texas	1845	TX	Austin	Legislature
Utah	1896	UT	Salt Lake City	Legislature
Vermont	1791	VT	Montpelier	General Assembly
Virginia	1788	VA	Richmond	General Assembly[2]
Washington	1889	WA	Olympia	Legislature
West Virginia	1863	WV	Charleston	Legislature[2]
Wisconsin	1848	WI	Madison	Legislature[1]
Wyoming	1890	WY	Cheyenne	Legislature

[1] The lower house is called the Assembly.

[2] The lower house is called the House of Delegates.

[3] The lower house is called the General Assembly.

TERRITORIES AND COMMONWEALTHS

Name	Date Acquired	Abbreviation	Capital	Legislature
American Samoa	1899	—	Pago Pago	Legislature
Canal Zone		CZ	Balboa Heights	Canal Zone Government
Guam	1950	—	Agana	Legislature*
Midway Islands	1867	—		Administered by U.S. Navy
Northern Mariana Islands	1947	—	Saipan	Legislature
Puerto Rico	1898	PR	San Juan	Legislative Assembly
Virgin Islands	1927	VI	Charlotte Amalie	Legislature*
Wake Islands	1899	—		Administered by U.S. Air Force

* Legislatures are unicameral.

State Flowers, Birds, Mottos, and Nicknames

State	Flower	Bird	Motto	Nickname
Alabama	Camellia	Yellowhammer	We dare defend our rights	Heart of Dixie; Camellia State
Alaska	Forget-me-not	Willow ptarmigan	North to the future	The Last Frontier
Arizona	Saguaro	Cactus wren	Diat Deus (God enriches)	Grand Canyon State
Arkansas	Apple blossom	Mockingbird	Regnat populus (The people rule)	Land of Opportunity
California	Golden poppy	California valley quail	Eureka (I have found it)	Golden State
Colorado	Blue columbine	Lark bunting	Nil sine numine (Nothing without providence)	Centennial State
Connecticut	Mountain laurel	American robin	Qui transtulit sustinet (He who transplanted still sustains)	Constitution State; Nutmeg State
Delaware	Peach blossom	Blue hen chicken	Liberty and independence	First State; Diamond State
District of Columbia	American Beauty rose	Wood thrush	Justitia Omnibus (Justice for all)	Capital City
Florida	Orange blossom	Mockingbird	In God we trust	Sunshine State
Georgia	Cherokee rose	Brown thrasher	Wisdom, justice, and moderation	Empire State of the South; Peace State
Hawaii	Hibiscus	Nene goose	The life of the land is perpetuated in righteousness	Aloha State
Idaho	Syringa	Mountain bluebird	Esto perpetua (It is perpetual)	Gem State
Illinois	Native violet	Cardinal	State sovereignty—national union	Prairie State

State	Flower	Bird	Motto	Nickname
Indiana	Peony	Cardinal	Crossroads of America	Hoosier State
Iowa	Wild rose	Goldfinch	Our liberties we prize and our rights we will maintain	Hawkeye State
Kansas	Sunflower	Western meadowlark	Ad astra per aspera (To the stars through difficulties)	Sunflower State
Kentucky	Goldenrod	Kentucky cardinal	United we stand, divided we fall	Bluegrass State
Louisiana	Magnolia	Eastern brown pelican	Union, justice and confidence	Pelican State
Maine	Pine cone and tassel	Chickadee	Dirigo (I direct)	Pine Tree State
Maryland	Black-eyed Susan	Baltimore oriole	Fatti maschii, parole femine (Manly deeds, womanly words)	Old Line State; Free State
Massachusetts	Mayflower	Chickadee	Ense petit placidam sub libertate (By the sword we seek peace, but peace only under liberty)	Bay State; Colony State
Michigan	Apple	Robin	Si quaeris peninsulam amoenam (If you seek a pleasant peninsula, look about you)	Great Lake State; Wolverine State
Minnesota	Showy lady slipper	Common loon	L'Etoile du nord (Star of the north)	North Star State; Gopher State
Mississippi	Magnolia	Mockingbird	Virtute et armis (By valor and arms)	Magnolia State
Missouri	Hawthorn	Bluebird	Salus populi suprema lex esto (The welfare of the people shall be the supreme law)	Show-Me State
Montana	Bitterroot	Western meadowlark	Oro y plata (Gold and silver)	Treasure State
Nebraska	Goldenrod	Meadowlark	Equality before the law	Cornhusker State
Nevada	Sagebrush	Mountain bluebird	All for our country	Sagebrush State; Battle-Born State
New Hampshire	Purple lilac	Purple finch	Live free or die	Granite State
New Jersey	Purple violet	Eastern goldfinch	Liberty and prosperity	Garden State
New Mexico	Yucca	Roadrunner	Crescit eundo (It grows as it goes)	Land of Enchantment
New York	Rose (any color)	Bluebird	Excelsior (Ever upward)	Empire State
North Carolina	Dogwood	Cardinal	Esse quam videri (To be rather than to seem)	Tar Heel State; Old North State
North Dakota	Wild prairie rose	Western meadowlark	Liberty and union, now and forever, one and inseparable	Peace Garden State

State	Flower	Bird	Motto	Nickname
Ohio	Scarlet carnation	Cardinal	With God, all things are possible	Buckeye State
Oklahoma	Mistletoe	Scissor-tailed flycatcher	Labor omnia vincit (Labor conquers all things)	Sooner State
Oregon	Oregon grape	Western meadowlark	The union	Beaver State
Pennsylvania	Mountain laurel	Ruffed grouse	Virtue, liberty and independence	Keystone State
Rhode Island	Violet	Rhode Island hen	Hope	Little Rhody; Ocean State
South Carolina	Carolina jessamine	Carolina wren	Dum spiro spero (While I breathe, I hope)	Palmetto State
South Dakota	Pasqueflower	Pheasant	Under God, the people rule	Coyote State; Sunshine State
Tennessee	Iris	Mockingbird	Agriculture and commerce	Volunteer State
Texas	Bluebonnet	Mockingbird	Friendship	Lone Star State
Utah	Sego Lily	Seagull	Industry	Beehive State
Vermont	Red clover	Thrush	Freedom and unity	Green Mountain State
Virginia	Flowering dogwood	Cardinal	Sic semper tyrannis (Thus always to tyrants)	Old Dominion
Washington	Rhododendron	Willow goldfinch	Alki (By and by)	Evergreen State
West Virginia	Big rhododendron	Cardinal	Montani semper liberi (Mountaineers are always free)	Mountain State
Wisconsin	Wood violet	Robin	Forward	Badger State
Wyoming	Indian paintbrush	Meadowlark	Equal rights	Equality State

United States Territories and Commonwealths

	Flower	Bird	Motto
American Samoa	Paogo (Ula-fala)		Samoa Muamua le Atua (In Samoa, God is first)
Guam	Puti tai nobio (bougainvillea)	Toto (fruit dove)	Where America's day begins
Puerto Rico	Maga	Reinita	Joannes est nomen eius (John is his name)
Virgin Islands	Yellow elder or yellow trumpet	Yellow breast	

State Name Origins

Alabama Originally the name for "tribal town," the territory of Alabama was later the home of the Alabama, or Alibamon, Indians of the Creek confederacy.

Alaska The Russians adopted the word meaning "great lands" or "land that is not an island" from the Aleutian word *alakshak*.

Arizona The Spanish coined the name either from the Pima Indian word meaning "little spring place" or from the Aztec *arizuma*, meaning "silver-bearing."

Arkansas Once the territory of the Siouan Quapaw (downstream people), *Arkansas* is the French derivative of this Indian name.

California The name of a fictitious earthly paradise in *Las Serged de Esplandian,* a sixteenth-century Spanish romance. It is believed that Spanish conquistadors named this state.

Colorado A Spanish word for "red." The name *Colorado* first referred to the Colorado River.

Connecticut The Algonquin and Mohican Indian word for "long river place."

Delaware This version of the name of Lord De La Warr, a governor of Virginia, was first used to name the Delaware River and later adopted by the Europeans to rename the local Indians, originally called the Lenni-Lenape.

District of Columbia Named for Christopher Columbus in 1791.

Florida In his search for the "Fountain of Youth," Ponce de Leon named this region "flowery Easter" or "feast of flowers" on Easter Sunday, 1513.

Georgia Named for King George II of England, who granted James Oglethorpe a charter to found the colony of Georgia in 1732.

Hawaii Commonly believed to be an English adaptation of the native word for "homeland," *hawaiki* or *owhyhee*.

Idaho A name coined by the state meaning "gem of the mountains" or "light on the mountains." Originally the name *Idaho* was to be used for the Pike's Peak mining territory in Colorado, and later for the mining territory of the Pacific Northwest. Others believe the name derives from the Kiowa Apache word for the Comanche.

Illinois From the French version of the Algonquin word meaning "men" or "soldiers," *Illini*.

Indiana English-speaking settlers named the territory to mean "land of the Indians."

Iowa The Sioux word for "one who puts to sleep" or "beautiful land."

Kansas Derived from the Sioux word for those who lived south (the "south wind people") of their territory, which was mainly Wisconsin, Iowa, Minnesota, and North and South Dakota.

Kentucky Originally the term for the Kentucky Plains in Clark County, *Kentucky* is believed to derive from the Indian word meaning "dark and bloody ground," "meadow land," or "land of tomorrow."

Louisiana Present-day Louisiana is just a fraction of the territory that was named for the French king Louis XIV by Sieur de La Salle.

Maine Originally a French territory, *Maine* was the ancient French word for "province." It is also believed that it refers to the mainland, as distinct from the many islands off the state's coast.

Maryland Named for Queen Henrietta Maria, wife of Charles I of England.

Massachusetts The name of the Indian tribe that lived near Milton, Massachusetts, meaning "large hill place."

Michigan Believed to be from the Chippewa word *micigama*, meaning "great water," after Lake Michigan, although Alouet defined it in 1672 as designating a clearing.

Minnesota Named from the Sioux description of the Minnesota River, "sky-tinted water" or "muddy water."

Mississippi Most likely derived from the Chippewa words *mici* (great) and *zibi* (river), it was first written by La Salle's lieutenant Henri de Tonti as "Michi Sepe."

Missouri Meaning "muddy water," this state is named after an Algonquin Indian tribe.

Montana Derived from the Latin word meaning "mountainous."

Nebraska Descriptive of the Platte River, *Nebraska* is from the Omaha or Otos Indian word for "broad water" or "flat river."

Nevada Spanish word meaning "snow-clad."

New Hampshire Captain John Mason named this colony for his home county in England in 1629.

New Jersey Named after the Isle of Jersey in England by John Berkeley and Sir George Carteret.

New Mexico Named by the Spanish for the territory north and west of the Rio Grande.

New York Originally named New Netherland, New York was later named after the Duke of York and Albany, who received a patent to the region from his brother Charles II of England and captured it from the Dutch in 1644.

North Carolina From the Latin name *Carolus*, meaning "Charles." The colony was originally given to Sir Robert Heath by Charles I and was to be called Province of Carolana. Carolana was divided into North and South Carolina in 1710.

North Dakota From the Sioux word meaning "friend" or "ally."

Ohio From an Iroquois Indian word variously meaning "great," "fine," or "good river."

Oklahoma The Choctaw Indian word meaning "red man," which was coined by the Reverend Allen Wright, a Choctaw-speaking Indian.

Oregon Though its exact origin is unclear, one theory maintains that it may have been a variation on the name of the Wisconsin River, which was called *Ouaricon-sint* on a French map dated 1715. Later, the English explorer Major Robert Rogers named a river "called by the Indians Ouragon" in his request to seek a Northwest Passage from the Great Lakes. Another theory derives the word from the Algonquin *wauregan*, meaning "beautiful water."

Pennsylvania Named after the colony's founder, the Quaker William Penn. The literal translation is "Penn's woods."

Rhode Island Possibly named by Giovanni de Verrazano, who charted an island about the size of an island of the same name in the Mediterranean. Another theory suggests Rhode Island was named Roode Eylandt by Dutch explorer Adrian Block because of its red clay.

South Carolina *See* North Carolina.

South Dakota *See* North Dakota.

Tennessee The state of Franklin, or Frankland, from 1784 to 1788, it was finally named after the Cherokee villages called *tanasi* on the Little Tennessee River.

Texas Also written *texias, tejas,* and *teysas, Texas* is a variation on the Caddo Indian word for "friend" or "ally."

Utah Meaning "upper" or "higher," *Utah* is derived from a name used by the Navajos (Utes) to designate a Shoshone tribe.

Vermont It is believed Samuel de Champlain coined the name from the French words *vert* (green) and *mont* (mountain). Later, Dr. Thomas Young proposed this name when the state was formed in 1777.

Virginia Named for the Virgin Queen of England, Queen Elizabeth I, by Sir Walter Raleigh, who first visited its shores in 1584.

Washington Originally named the Territory of Columbia, it was changed to *Washington* in honor of the first U.S. President because of the already existing District of Columbia.

West Virginia Named when this area refused to secede from the Union in 1863.

Wisconsin A Chippewa word that was spelled *Ouisconsin* and *Mesconsing* by early explorers. Wisconsin was formally named by Congress when it became a state.

Wyoming The Algonquin word meaning "large prairie place," the name was adopted from Wyoming Valley, Pennsylvania, the site of an Indian massacre. It was widely known from Thomas Campbell's poem "Gertrude of Wyoming."

ADMISSION OF THE 13 ORIGINAL STATES

State	Date of Admission
1. Delaware	December 7, 1787
2. Pennsylvania	December 12, 1787
3. New Jersey	December 18, 1787
4. Georgia	January 2, 1788
5. Connecticut	January 9, 1788
6. Massachusetts	February 6, 1788
7. Maryland	April 28, 1788
8. South Carolina	May 23, 1788
9. New Hampshire	June 21, 1788
10. Virginia	June 25, 1788
11. New York	July 26, 1788
12. North Carolina	November 21, 1789
13. Rhode Island	May 29, 1790

SECESSION OF AMERICAN STATES

State	Secession Date
1. South Carolina	December 20, 1860
2. Mississippi	January 9, 1861
3. Florida	January 10, 1861
4. Alabama	January 11, 1861
5. Georgia	January 19, 1861
6. Louisiana	January 26, 1861
7. Texas	February 1, 1861
8. Virginia	April 17, 1861
9. Arkansas	May 6, 1861
10. North Carolina	May 20, 1861
11. Tennessee	June 8, 1861

READMISSION OF AMERICAN STATES

State	Date of Readmission
1. Tennessee	July 24, 1866
2. Arkansas	June 22, 1868
3. Alabama	June 25, 1868
4. Florida	June 25, 1868
5. Georgia	June 25, 1868*
6. Louisiana	June 25, 1868
7. North Carolina	June 25, 1868
8. South Carolina	June 25, 1868
9. Virginia	January 26, 1870
10. Mississippi	February 23, 1870
11. Texas	March 30, 1870

* readmitted a second time July 15, 1870

The Declaration of Independence

IN CONGRESS, JULY 4, 1776

The Unanimous Declaration of the Thirteen United States of America

When in the course of human events, it becomes necessary for one people to dissolve the political bands which have connected them with another, and to assume among the powers of the earth, the separate and equal station to which the laws of Nature and of Nature's God entitle them, a decent respect to the opinions of mankind requires that they should declare the causes which impel them to the separation.

We hold these truths to be self-evident, that all men are created equal, that they are endowed by their Creator with certain unalienable rights, that among these are life, liberty and the pursuit of happiness. That to secure these rights, governments are instituted among men, deriving their just powers from the consent of the governed,—That whenever any form of government becomes destructive of these ends, it is the right of the people to alter or to abolish it, and to institute new government, laying its foundation on such principles and organizing its powers in such form, as to them shall seem most likely to effect their safety and happiness. Prudence, indeed, will dictate that governments long established should not be changed for light and transient causes; and accordingly all experience hath shown, that mankind are more disposed to suffer, while evils are sufferable, than to right themselves by abolishing the forms to which they are accustomed. But when a long train of abuses and usurpations, pursuing invariably the same object evinces a design to reduce them under absolute despotism, it is their right, it is their duty, to throw off such government, and to provide new guards for their future security.—Such has been the patient sufferance of these Colonies; and such is now the necessity which constrains them to alter their former systems of government. The history of the present King of Great Britain is a history of repeated injuries and usurpations, all having in direct object the establishment of an absolute tyranny over these States. To prove this, let facts be submitted to a candid world.

He has refused his assent to laws, the most wholesome and necessary for the public good.

He has forbidden his Governors to pass laws of immediate and pressing importance, unless suspended in their operation till his assent should be obtained; and when so suspended, he has utterly neglected to attend to them.

He has refused to pass other laws for the accommodation of large districts of people, unless those people would relinquish the right of representation in the legislature, a right inestimable to them and formidable to tyrants only.

He has called together legislative bodies at places unusual, uncomfortable, and distant from the depository of their public records, for the sole purpose of fatiguing them into compliance with his measures.

He has dissolved Representative Houses repeatedly, for opposing with manly firmness his invasions on the rights of the people.

He has refused for a long time, after such dissolutions, to cause others to be elected; whereby the legislative powers, incapable of annihilation, have returned to the people at large for their exercise; the State remaining in the mean time exposed to all the dangers of invasion from without, and convulsions within.

He has endeavoured to prevent the population of these States; for that purpose obstructing the laws for naturalization of foreigners; refusing to pass others to encourage their migrations hither, and raising the conditions of new appropriations of lands.

He has obstructed the administration of justice, by refusing his assent to laws for establishing judiciary powers.

He has made judges dependent on his will alone, for the tenure of their offices, and the amount and payment of their salaries.

He has erected a multitude of new offices, and sent hither swarms of officers to harass our people, and eat out their substance.

He has kept among us, in times of peace, standing armies without the consent of our legislatures.

He has affected to render the military independent of and superior to the civil power.

He has combined with others to subject us to a jurisdiction foreign to our constitution, and unacknowledged by our laws; giving his assent to their acts of pretended legislation:

For quartering large bodies of armed troops among us:

For protecting them, by a mock trial, from punishment for any murders which they should commit on the inhabitants of these States:

For cutting off our trade with all parts of the world:

For imposing taxes on us without our consent:

For depriving us in many cases, of the benefits of trial by jury:

For transporting us beyond seas to be tried for pretended offenses:

For abolishing the free system of English laws in a neighbouring province, establishing therein an arbitrary government, and enlarging its boundaries so as to render it at once an example and fit instrument for introducing the same absolute rule into these colonies:

For taking away our charters, abolishing our most valuable laws, and altering fundamentally the forms of our governments:

For suspending our own legislatures, and declaring themselves invested with power to legislate for us in all cases whatsoever.

He has abdicated government here, by declaring us out of his protection and waging war against us.

He has plundered our seas, ravaged our coasts, burnt our towns, and destroyed the lives of our people.

He is at this time transporting large armies of foreign mercenaries to complete the works of death, desolation and tyranny, already begun with circumstances of cruelty and perfidy scarcely paralleled in the most barbarous ages, and totally unworthy of the head of a civilized nation.

He has constrained our fellow citizens taken captive on the high seas to bear arms against their country, to become the executioners of their friends and brethren, or to fall themselves by their hands.

He has excited domestic insurrections amongst us, and has endeavoured to bring on the inhabitants of our frontiers, the merciless Indian savages, whose known rule of warfare is an undistinguished destruction of all ages, sexes and conditions.

In every stage of these oppressions we have petitioned for redress in the most humble terms: Our repeated petitions have been answered only by repeated injury. A prince, whose character is thus marked by every act which may define a tyrant, is unfit to be the ruler of a free people.

Nor have we been wanting in attentions to our British brethren. We have warned them from time to time of attempts by their legislature to extend an unwarrantable jurisdiction over us. We have reminded them of the circumstances of our emigration and settlement here. We have appealed to their native justice and magnanimity, and we have conjured them by the ties of our common kindred to disavow these usurpations, which, would inevitably interrupt our connections and correspondence. They too have been deaf to the voice of justice and of consanguinity. We must, therefore, acquiesce in the necessity which denounces our separation, and hold them, as we hold the rest of mankind, enemies in war, in peace friends.

WE, THEREFORE, the Representatives of the United States of America, in General Congress, Assembled, appealing to the Supreme Judge of the world for the rectitude of out intentions, do, in the name, and by authority of the good people of these Colonies, solemnly publish and declare, That these United Colonies are, and of right ought to be FREE AND INDEPENDENT STATES; that they are absolved from all allegiance to the British Crown, and that all political connection between them and the State of Great Britain, is and ought to be totally dissolved; and that as free and independent States, they have full power to levy war, conclude peace, contract alliances, establish commerce, and to do all other acts and things which independent States may of right do. And for the support of this Declaration, with a firm reliance on the protection of Divine Providence, we mutually pledge to each other our lives, our fortunes and our sacred honor.

JOHN HANCOCK.

New Hampshire

JOSIAH BARTLETT	MATTHEW THORNTON
WM. WHIPPLE	

Massachusetts Bay

SAML ADAMS	ROBT TREAT PAINE
JOHN ADAMS	ELBRIDGE GERRY

Rhode Island

STEP. HOPKINS	WILLIAM ELLERY

Connecticut

ROGER SHERMAN   WM. WILLIAMS
SAML HUNTINGTON   OLIVER WOLCOTT

New York

WM. FLOYD   FRANS. LEWIS
PHIL. LIVINGSTON   LEWIS MORRIS

New Jersey

RICHD. STOCKTON   JOHN HART
JNO WITHERSPOON   ABRA CLARK
FRAS. HOPKINSON

Pennsylvania

ROBT MORRIS   JAS. SMITH
BENJAMIN RUSH   GEO. TAYLOR
BENJA. FRANKLIN   JAMES WILSON
JOHN MORTON   GEO. ROSS
GEO. CLYMER

Delaware

CAESAR RODNEY   THO M'KEAN
GEO READ

Maryland

SAMUEL CHASE   CHARLES CARROLL
WM. PACA   of Carrollton
THOS. STONE

Virginia

GEORGE WYTHE   THOS. NELSON JR.
RICHARD HENRY LEE   FRANCIS LIGHTFOOT LEE
TH JEFFERSON   CARTER BRAXTON
BENJA. HARRISON

North Carolina

WM HOOPER   JOHN PENN
JOSEPH HEWES

South Carolina

EDWARD RUTLEDGE   THOMAS LYNCH JUNR.
THOS. HEYWARD JUNR.   ARTHUR MIDDLETON

Georgia

BUTTON GWINNETT   GEO WALTON.
LYMAN HALL

The Constitution of the
United States of America

PREAMBLE

WE THE PEOPLE of the United States, in order to form a more perfect Union, establish justice, insure domestic tranquility, provide for the common defense, promote the general welfare, and secure the blessings of liberty to ourselves and our posterity, do ordain and establish this Constitution for the United States of America.

ARTICLE I

SECTION 1. All legislative powers herein granted shall be vested in a Congress of the United States, which shall consist of a Senate and House of Representatives.

SECTION 2. The House of Representatives shall be composed of members chosen every second year by the people of the several States, and the electors in each State shall have the qualifications requisite for electors of the most numerous branch of the State Legislature.

No person shall be a Representative who shall not have attained to the age of twenty-five years, and been seven years a citizen of the United States, and who shall not, when elected, be an inhabitant of that State in which he shall be chosen.

Representatives and direct taxes shall be apportioned among the several States which may be included within this Union, according to their respective numbers, which shall be determined by adding to the whole number of free persons, including those bound to service for a term of years, and excluding Indians not taxed, three-fifths of all other persons. The actual enumeration shall be made within three years after the first meeting of the Congress of the United States, and within every subsequent term of ten years, in such manner as they shall by law direct. The number of representatives shall not exceed one for every thirty thousand, but each State shall have at least one Representative; and until such enumeration shall be made, the State of New Hampshire shall be entitled to choose three, Massachusetts eight, Rhode Island and Providence Plantations one, Connecticut five, New York six, New Jersey four, Pennsylvania eight, Delaware one, Maryland six, Virginia ten, North Carolina five, South Carolina five, and Georgia three.

When vacancies happen in the representation from any State, the executive authority thereof shall issue writs of election to fill such vacancies.

The House of Representatives shall choose their Speaker and other officers; and shall have the sole power of impeachment.

SECTION 3. The Senate of the United States shall be composed of two Senators from each State, chosen by the legislature thereof, for six years and each Senator shall have one vote.

Immediately after they shall be assembled in consequence of the first election, they shall be divided as equally as may be into three classes. The seats of the Senators of the first class shall be vacated at the expiration of the second year, of the second class at the expiration of the fourth year, and of the third class at the expiration of the sixth year, so that one-third may be chosen every second year; and if vacancies happen by resignation, or otherwise, during the recess of the legislature of any State, the executive thereof may make temporary appointments until the next meeting of the legislature, which shall then fill such vacancies.

No person shall be a Senator who shall not have attained to the age of thirty years, and been nine years a citizen of the United States, and who shall not, when elected, be an inhabitant of that State for which he shall be chosen.

The Vice President of the United States shall be President of the Senate, but shall have no vote, unless they be equally divided.

The Senate shall choose their other officers, and also a President pro tempore, in the absence of the Vice President, or when he shall exercise the office of President of the United States.

The Senate shall have the sole power to try all impeachments. When sitting for that purpose, they shall be on oath or affirmation. When the President of the United States is tried, the Chief Justice shall preside: and no person shall be convicted without the concurrence of two thirds of the members present.

Judgment in cases of impeachment shall not extend further than to removal from office, and disqualification to hold and enjoy any office of honor, trust or profit under the United States: but the party convicted shall nevertheless be liable and subject to indictment, trial, judgment and punishment, according to law.

SECTION 4. The times, places and manner of holding elections for Senators and Representatives, shall be prescribed in each State by the legislature thereof; but the Congress may at any time by law make or alter such regulations, except as to the places of choosing Senators.

The Congress shall assemble at least once in every year, and such meeting shall be on the first Monday in December, unless they shall by law appoint a different day.

SECTION 5. Each House shall be the judge of the elections, returns and qualifications of its own members, and a majority of each shall constitute a quorum to do business; but a smaller number may adjourn from day to day, and may be authorized to compel the attendance of absent members, in such manner, and under such penalties as each House may provide.

Each House may determine the rules of its proceedings, punish its members for disorderly behaviour, and, with the concurrence of two-thirds, expel a member.

Each House shall keep a journal of its proceedings, and from time to time publish the same, excepting such parts as may in their judgment require secrecy; and the yeas and the nays of the members of either house on any question shall, at the desire of one-fifth of those present, be entered on the journal.

Neither House, during the session of Congress, shall, without the consent of the other, adjourn for more than three days, nor to any other place than that in which the two Houses shall be sitting.

SECTION 6. The Senators and Representatives shall receive a compensation for their services, to be ascertained by law, and paid out of the Treasury of the United States. They shall in all cases, except treason, felony and breach of the peace, be privileged from arrest during their attendance at the session of their respective Houses, and in going to and returning from the same; and for any speech or debate in either House, they shall not be questioned in any other place.

No Senator or Representative shall, during the time for which he was elected, be appointed to any civil office under the authority of the United States, which shall have been created, or the emoluments whereof shall have been increased during such time; and no person holding any office under the United States, shall be a member of either House during his continuance in office.

SECTION 7. All bills for raising revenue shall originate in the House of Representatives; but the Senate may propose or concur with amendments as on other bills.

Every bill which shall have passed the House of Representatives and the Senate, shall, before it becomes a law, be presented to the President of the United States; if he approves he shall sign it, but if not he shall return it, with his objections to that House in which it shall have originated, who shall enter the objections at large on their journal, and proceed to reconsider it. If after such reconsideration two thirds of that House shall agree to pass the bill, it shall be sent, together with the objections, to the other House, by which it shall likewise be reconsidered, and if approved by two thirds of that House, it shall become a law. But in all such cases the votes of both Houses shall be determined by yeas and nays, and the names of the persons voting for and against the bill shall be entered on the journal of each House respectively. If any bill shall not be returned by the President within ten days (Sundays excepted) after it shall have been presented to him, the same shall be a law, in like manner as if he had signed it, unless the Congress by their adjournment prevent its return, in which case it shall not be a law.

Every order, resolution, or vote to which the concurrence of the Senate and House of Representatives may be necessary (except on a question of adjournment) shall be presented to the President of the United States; and before the same shall take effect, shall be approved by him, or being disapproved by him, shall be repassed by two thirds of the Senate and House of Representatives, according to the rules and limitations prescribed in the case of a bill.

SECTION 8. The Congress shall have power to lay and collect taxes, duties, imposts and excises, to pay the debts and provide for the common defense and general welfare of the United States; but all duties, imposts and excises shall be uniform throughout the United States;

To borrow money on the credit of the United States;

To regulate commerce with foreign nations, and among the several States, and with the Indian tribes;

To establish a uniform rule of naturalization, and uniform laws on the subject of bankruptcies throughout the United States;

To coin money, regulate the value thereof, and of foreign coin, and fix the standard of weights and measures;

To provide for the punishment of counterfeiting the securities and current coin of the United States;

To establish post offices and post roads;

To promote the progress of science and useful arts, by securing for limited times to authors and inventors the exclusive right to their respective writings and discoveries;

To constitute tribunals inferior to the Supreme Court;

To define and punish piracies and felonies committed on the high seas, and offenses against the law of nations;

To declare war, grant letters of marque and reprisal, and make rules concerning captures on land and water;

To raise and support armies, but no appropriation of money to that use shall be for a longer term than two years;

To provide and maintain a navy;

To make rules for the government and regulation of the land and naval forces;

To provide for calling forth the militia to execute the laws of the Union, suppress insurrections and repel invasions;

To provide for organizing, arming, and disciplining the militia, and for governing such part of them as may be employed in the service of the United States, reserving to the States respectively, the appointment of the officers, and the authority of training the militia according to the discipline prescribed by Congress;

To exercise exclusive legislation in all cases whatsoever, over such district (not exceeding ten miles square) as may, by cession of particular States, and the acceptance of Congress, become the seat of the Government of the United States, and to exercise like authority over all places purchased by the consent of the legislature of the State in which the same shall be, for the erection of forts, magazines, arsenals, dock-yards, and other needful buildings;—And

To make all laws which shall be necessary and proper for carrying into execution the foregoing powers, and all other powers vested by this Constitution in the Government of the United States, or in any department or officer thereof.

SECTION 9. The migration or importation of such persons as any of the States now existing shall think proper to admit, shall not be prohibited by the Congress prior to the year one thousand eight hundred and eight, but a tax or duty may be imposed on such importation, not exceeding ten dollars for each person.

The privilege of the writ of habeas corpus shall not be suspended, unless when in cases of rebellion or invasion the public safety may require it.

No bill of attainder or ex post facto law shall be passed.

No capitation, or other direct, tax shall be laid, unless in proportion to the census or enumeration herein before directed to be taken.

No tax or duty shall be laid on articles exported from any State.

No preference shall be given by any regulation of commerce or revenue to the ports of one State over those of another: nor shall vessels bound to, or from, one State, be obliged to enter, clear, or pay duties in another.

No money shall be drawn from the Treasury, but in consequence of appropriations made by law; and a regular statement and account of the receipts and expenditures of all public money shall be published from time to time.

No title of nobility shall be granted by the United States: And no person holding any office of profit or trust under them, shall, without the consent of the Congress, accept of any present, emolument, office, or title, of any kind whatever, from any King, Prince, or foreign State.

SECTION 10. No State shall enter into any treaty, alliance, or confederation; grant letters of marque and reprisal; coin money; emit bills of credit; make any thing but gold and silver coin a tender in payment of debts; pass any bill of attainder, ex post facto law, or law impairing the obligation of contracts, or grant any title of nobility.

No State shall, without the consent of the Congress, lay any imposts or duties on imports or exports, except what may be absolutely necessary for executing its inspection laws: and the net produce of all duties and imposts, laid by any state on imports or exports, shall be for the use of the Treasury of the United States; and all such laws shall be subject to the revision and control of the Congress.

No State shall, without the consent of Congress, lay any duty of tonnage, keep troops, or ships of war in time of peace, enter into any agreement or compact with another State, or with a foreign power, or engage in war, unless actually invaded, or in such imminent danger as will not admit of delay.

ARTICLE II

SECTION 1. The executive power shall be vested in a President of the United States of America. He shall hold his office during the term of four years, and together with the Vice President, chosen for the same term, be elected, as follows:

Each State, shall appoint, in such manner as the legislature thereof may direct, a number of electors, equal to the whole number of Senators and Representatives to which the State may be entitled in the Congress; but no Senator or Representative, or person holding an office of trust or profit under the United States, shall be appointed an elector.

The electors shall meet in their respective States, and vote by ballot for two persons, of whom one at least shall not be an inhabitant of the same State with themselves. And they shall make a list of all the persons voted for, and of the number of votes for each; which list they shall sign and certify, and transmit sealed to the seat of the Government of the United States, directed to the President of the Senate. The President of the Senate shall, in the presence of the Senate and House of Representatives, open all the certificates, and the votes shall then be counted. The person having the greatest number of votes shall be the President, if such number be a majority of the whole number of electors appointed; and if there be more than one who have such majority, and have an equal number of votes, then the House of Representatives shall immediately choose by ballot one of them for President; and if no person have a majority, then from the five highest on the list the said House shall in like manner choose the President. But in choosing the President, the votes shall be taken by States, the representation from each State having one vote; a quorum for this purpose shall consist of a member or members from two thirds of the States, and a majority of all the States shall be necessary to a choice. In every case, after the choice of the President, the person having the greatest number of votes of the electors shall be the Vice President. But if there should remain two or more who have equal votes, the Senate shall choose from them by ballot the Vice President.

The Congress may determine the time of choosing the electors, and the day on which they shall give their votes; which day shall be the same throughout the United States.

No person except a natural born citizen, or a citizen of the United States, at the time of the adoption of this Constitution, shall be eligible to the office of President; neither shall any person be eligible to that office who shall not have attained to the age of thirty-five years, and been fourteen years a resident within the United States.

In case of the removal of the President from office, or of his death, resignation, or inability to discharge the powers and duties of the said office, the same shall devolve on the Vice President, and the Congress may by law provide for the case of removal, death, resignation, or inability, both of the President and Vice President, declaring what officer shall then act as President, and such officer shall act accordingly, until the disability be removed, or a President be elected.

The President shall, at stated times, receive for his services, a compensation, which shall neither be increased nor diminished during the period for which he shall have been elected, and he shall not receive within that period any other emolument from the United States, or any of them.

Before he enter on the execution of his office, he shall take the following oath or affirmation:—''I do solemnly swear (or affirm) that I will faithfully execute the office of President of the United States, and will to the best of my ability, preserve, protect and defend the Constitution of the United States.''

Section 2. The President shall be Commander in Chief of the Army and Navy of the United States, and of the militia of the several States, when called into the actual service of the United States; he may require the opinion, in writing, of the principal officer in each of the executive departments, upon any subject relating to the duties of their respective offices, and he shall have power to grant reprieves and pardons for offenses against the United States, except in cases of impeachment.

He shall have power, by and with the advice and consent of the Senate, to make treaties, provided two thirds of the Senators present concur; and he shall nominate, and by and with the advice and consent of the Senate, shall appoint ambassadors, other public ministers and consuls, Judges of the Supreme Court, and all other officers of the United States, whose appointments are not herein otherwise provided for, and which shall be established by law: but the Congress may by law vest the appointment of such inferior officers, as they think proper, in the President alone, in the courts of law, or in the heads of departments.

The President shall have power to fill up all vacancies that may happen during the recess of the Senate, by granting commissions which shall expire at the end of their next session.

SECTION 3. He shall from time to time give to the Congress information of the State of the Union, and recommend to their consideration such measures as he shall judge necessary and expedient; he may, on extraordinary occasions, convene both Houses, or either of them, and in case of disagreement between them, with respect to the time of adjournment, he may adjourn them to such time as he shall think proper; he shall receive ambassadors and other public ministers; he shall take care that the laws be faithfully executed, and shall commission all the officers of the United States.

SECTION 4. The President, Vice President and all civil officers of the United States, shall be removed from office on impeachment for, and conviction of, treason, bribery, or other high crimes and misdemeanors.

ARTICLE III

SECTION 1. The judicial power of the United States, shall be vested in one Supreme Court, and in such inferior courts as the Congress may from time to time ordain and establish. The judges, both of the Supreme and inferior Courts, shall hold their offices during good behaviour, and shall, at stated times, receive for their services, a compensation, which shall not be diminished during their continuance in office.

SECTION 2. The judicial power shall extend to all cases, in law and equity, arising under this Constitution, the laws of the United States, and treaties made, or which shall be made, under their authority;—to all cases affecting ambassadors, other public ministers and consuls;—to all cases of admiralty and maritime jurisdiction;—to controversies to which the United States shall be a party;—to controversies between two or more States;—between a State and citizens of another State;—between citizens of different States,—between citizens of the same State claiming lands under grants of different States, and between a State, or the citizens thereof, and foreign States, citizens or subjects.

In all cases affecting ambassadors, other public ministers and consuls, and those in which a State shall be a party, the Supreme Court shall have original jurisdiction. In all the other cases before mentioned, the Supreme Court shall have appellate jurisdiction, both as to law and fact, with such exceptions, and under such regulations as the Congress shall make.

The trial of all crimes, except in cases of impeachment, shall be by jury; and such trial shall be held in the State where the said crimes shall have been committed; but when not committed within any State, the trial shall be at such place or places as the Congress may by law have directed.

SECTION 3. Treason against the United States, shall consist only in levying war against them, or in adhering to their enemies, giving them aid and comfort. No person shall be convicted of treason unless on the testimony of two witnesses to the same overt act, or on confession in open court.

The Congress shall have power to declare the punishment of treason, but no attainder of treason shall work corruption of blood, or forfeiture except during the life of the person attainted.

ARTICLE IV

SECTION 1. Full faith and credit shall be given in each State to the public acts, records, and judicial proceedings of every other State. And the Congress may by general laws prescribe the manner in which such acts, records, and proceedings shall be proved, and the effect thereof.

SECTION 2. The citizens of each State shall be entitled to all privileges and immunities of citizens in the several States.

A person charged in any State with treason, felony, or other crime, who shall flee from justice, and be found in another State, shall on demand of the executive authority of the State from which he fled, be delivered up, to be removed to the State having jurisdiction of the crime.

No person held to service or labour in one State, under the laws thereof, escaping into another, shall, in consequence of any law or regulation therein, be discharged from such service or labour, but shall be delivered up on claim of the party to whom such service or labour may be due.

SECTION 3. New States may be admitted by the Congress into this Union; but no new State shall be formed or erected within the jurisdiction of any other State; nor any State be formed by the junction of two or more States, or parts of States, without the consent of the legislatures of the States concerned as well as of the Congress.

The Congress shall have power to dispose of and make all needful rules and regulations respecting the Territory or other property belonging to the United States; and nothing in this Constitution shall be so construed as to prejudice any claims of the United States, or of any particular State.

SECTION 4. The United States shall guarantee to every State in this Union a republican form of Government, and shall protect each of them against invasion; and on application of the legislature, or of the executive (when the legislature cannot be convened) against domestic violence.

ARTICLE V

The Congress, whenever two thirds of both Houses shall deem it necessary, shall propose amendments to this Constitution, or on the application of the legislatures of two thirds of the several States, shall call a convention for proposing amendments, which, in either case, shall be valid to all intents and purposes, as part of this Constitution, when ratified by the legislatures of three fourths of the several States, or by conventions in three fourths thereof, as the one or the other mode of ratification may be proposed by the Congress; provided that no amendment which may be made prior to the year one thousand eight hundred and eight shall in any manner affect the first and fourth clauses in the Ninth Section of the First Article; and that no State, without its consent, shall be deprived of its equal suffrage in the Senate.

ARTICLE VI

All debts contracted and engagements entered into, before the adoption of this Constitution, shall be as valid against the United States under this Constitution, as under the Confederation.

This Constitution, and the laws of the United States which shall be made in pursuance thereof; and all treaties made, or which shall be made, under the authority of the United States, shall be the supreme law of the land; and the judges in every State shall be bound thereby, any thing in the Constitution or laws of any State to the contrary notwithstanding.

The Senators and Representatives before mentioned, and the members of the several State legislatures, and all executive and judicial officers, both of the United States and of the several States, shall be bound by oath or affirmation, to support this Constitution; but no religious test shall ever be required as a qualification to any office or public trust under the United States.

ARTICLE VII

The ratification of the conventions of nine States shall be sufficient for the establishment of this Constitution between the States so ratifying the same.

Done in convention by the unanimous consent of the States present the seventeenth day of September in the year of our Lord one thousand seven hundred and eighty seven and of the independence of the United States of America the twelfth. In witness whereof we have hereunto subscribed our names,

GO. WASHINGTON—*Presid't.*
and deputy from Virginia

Attest WILLIAM JACKSON *Secretary*

New Hampshire

JOHN LANGDON   NICHOLAS GILMAN

Massachusetts

NATHANIEL GORHAM   RUFUS KING

Connecticut

WM. SAML. JOHNSON   ROGER SHERMAN

New York

ALEXANDER HAMILTON

New Jersey

WIL: LIVINGSTON   WM. PATERSON
DAVID BREARLEY   JONA: DAYTON

Pennsylvania

B. FRANKLIN   THOS. FITZSIMONS
THOMAS MIFFLIN   JARED INGERSOLL
ROBT MORRIS   JAMES WILSON
GEO. CLYMER   GOUV MORRIS

Delaware

GEO: READ   RICHARD BASSETT
GUNNING BEDFORD JUN   JACO: BROOM
JOHN DICKINSON

Maryland

JAMES MCHENRY   DANL CARROLL
DAN OF ST. THOS. JENIFER

Virginia

John Blair—   James Madison jr.

North Carolina

Wm. Blount   Hu Williamson
Richd. Dobbs Spaight

South Carolina

J. Rutledge   Charles Pinckney
Charles Cotesworth   Pierce Butler
  Pinckney

Georgia

William Few   Abr Baldwin

Amendments

ARTICLE I

Congress shall make no law respecting an establishment of religion, or prohibiting the free exercise thereof; or abridging the freedom of speech, or of the press; or the right of the people peaceably to assemble, and to petition the Government for a redress of grievances.

ARTICLE II

A well regulated militia, being necessary to the security of a free State, the right of the people to keep and bear arms, shall not be infringed.

ARTICLE III

No soldier shall, in time of peace be quartered in any house, without the consent of the owner, nor in time of war, but in a manner to be prescribed by law.

ARTICLE IV

The right of the people to be secure in their persons, houses, papers, and effects, against unreasonable searches and seizures, shall not be violated, and no warrants shall issue, but upon probable cause, supported by oath or affirmation, and particularly describing the place to be searched, and the persons or things to be seized.

ARTICLE V

No person shall be held to answer for a capital, or otherwise infamous crime, unless on a presentment or indictment of a Grand Jury, except in cases arising in the land or naval forces, or in the militia, when in actual service in time of war or public danger; nor shall any person be subject for the same offense to be twice put in jeopardy of life or limb; nor shall be compelled in any criminal case to be a witness against himself, nor be deprived of life, liberty, or property, without due process of law; nor shall private property be taken for public use, without just compensation.

ARTICLE VI

In all criminal prosecutions, the accused shall enjoy the right to a speedy and public trial, by an impartial jury of the State and district wherein the crime shall have been committed, which district shall have been previously ascertained by law, and to be informed of the nature and cause of the accusation; to be confronted with the witnesses against him; to have compulsory process for obtaining witnesses in his favor, and to have the assistance of counsel for his defense.

ARTICLE VII

In suits at common law, where the value in controversy shall exceed twenty dollars, the right of trial by jury shall be preserved, and no fact tried by a jury, shall be otherwise reexamined in any Court of the United States, than according to the rules of the common law.

ARTICLE VIII

Excessive bail shall not be required, nor excessive fines imposed, nor cruel and unusual punishments inflicted.

ARTICLE IX

The enumeration in the Constitution, of certain rights, shall not be construed to deny or disparage others retained by the people.

ARTICLE X

The powers not delegated to the United States by the Constitution, nor prohibited by it to the States, are reserved to the States respectively, or to the people.

ARTICLE XI

The judical power of the United States shall not be construed to extend to any suit in law or equity, commenced or prosecuted against one of the United States by citizens of another State, or by citizens or subjects of any foreign State.

ARTICLE XII

The electors shall meet in their respective States, and vote by ballot for President and Vice President, one of whom, at least, shall not be an inhabitant of the same State with themselves; they shall name in their ballots the person voted for as President, and in distinct ballots the person voted for as Vice President, and they shall make distinct lists of all persons voted for as President, and of all persons voted for as Vice President, and of the number of votes for each, which lists they shall sign and certify, and transmit sealed to the seat of the government of the United States, directed to the President of the Senate;—The President of the Senate shall, in the presence of the Senate and House of Representatives, open all the certificates and the votes shall then be counted;—The person having the greatest number of votes for President, shall be the President, if such number be a majority of the whole number of electors appointed; and if no person have such majority, then from the persons having the highest numbers not exceeding three on the list of those voted for as President, the House of Representatives shall choose immediately, by ballot, the President. But in choosing the President, the votes shall be taken by States, the representation from each State having one vote; a quorum for this purpose shall consist of a member or members from two-thirds of the States, and a majority of all the States shall be necessary to a choice. And if the House of Representatives shall not choose a President whenever the right of choice shall devolve upon them, before the fourth day of March next following, then the Vice President shall act as President, as in the case of the death or other constitutional disability of the President.— The person having the greatest number of votes as Vice President, shall be the Vice President, if such number be a majority of the whole number of electors appointed, and if no person have a majority, then from the two highest numbers on the list, the Senate shall choose the Vice President; a quorum for the purpose shall consist of two-thirds of the whole number of Senators, and a majority of the whole number shall be necessary to a choice. But no person constitutionally ineligible to the office of President shall be eligible to that of Vice President of the United States.

ARTICLE XIII

SECTION 1. Neither slavery nor involuntary servitude, except as a punishment for crime whereof the party shall have been duly convicted, shall exist within the United States, or any place subject to their jurisdiction.

SECTION 2. Congress shall have power to enforce this article by appropriate legislation.

ARTICLE XIV

SECTION 1. All persons born or naturalized in the United States, and subject to the jurisdiction thereof, are citizens of the United States and of the State wherein they reside. No State shall make or enforce any law which shall abridge the privileges or immunities of citizens of the United States; nor shall any State deprive any person of life, liberty, or property, without due process of law; nor deny to any person within its jurisdiction the equal protection of the laws.

SECTION 2. Representatives shall be apportioned among the several States according to their respective numbers, counting the whole number of persons in each State, excluding Indians not taxed. But when the right to vote at any election for the choice of electors for President and Vice President of the United States, Representatives in Congress, the executive and judicial officers of a State, or the members of the legislature thereof, is denied to any of the male inhabitants of such State, being twenty-one years of age, and citizens of the United States, or in any way abridged, except for participation in rebellion, or other crime, the basis of representation therein shall be reduced in the proportion which the number of such male citizens shall bear to the whole number of male citizens twenty-one years of age in such State.

SECTION 3. No person shall be a Senator or Representative in Congress, or elector of President and Vice President, or hold any office, civil or military, under the United States, or under any State, who, having previously taken an oath, as a member of Congress, or as an officer of the United States, or as a member of any State legislature, or as an executive or judicial officer of any State, to support the Constitution of the United States, shall have engaged in insurrection or rebellion against the same, or given aid or comfort to the enemies thereof. But Congress may by a vote of two-thirds of each house, remove such disability.

SECTION 4. The validity of the public debt of the United States, authorized by law, including debts incurred for payment of pensions and bounties for services in suppressing insurrection or rebellion, shall not be questioned. But neither the United States nor any State shall assume or pay any debt or obligation incurred in aid of insurrection or rebellion against the United States, or any claim for the loss or emancipation of any slave; but all such debts, obligations and claims shall be held illegal and void.

SECTION 5. The Congress shall have power to enforce, by appropriate legislation, the provisions of this article.

ARTICLE XV

SECTION 1. The right of citizens of the United States to vote shall not be denied or abridged by the United States or by any State on account of race, color, or previous condition of servitude.

SECTION 2. The Congress shall have power to enforce this article by appropriate legislation.

ARTICLE XVI

The Congress shall have power to lay and collect taxes on incomes, from whatever source derived, without apportionment among the several States, and without regard to any census or enumeration.

ARTICLE XVII

SECTION 1. The Senate of the United States shall be composed of two Senators from each State, elected by the people thereof, for six years; and each Senator shall have one vote. The electors in each State shall have the qualifications requisite for electors of the most numerous branch of the State legislatures.

SECTION 2. When vacancies happen in the representation of any State in the Senate, the executive authority of such State shall issue writs of election to fill such vacancies: *Provided,* That the legislature of any State may empower the executive thereof to make temporary appointments until the people fill the vacancies by election as the legislature may direct.

SECTION 3. This amendment shall not be so construed as to affect the election or term of any Senator chosen before it becomes valid as part of the Constitution.

ARTICLE XVIII

SECTION 1. After one year from the ratification of this article the manufacture, sale, or transportation of intoxicating liquors within, the importation thereof into, or the exportation thereof from the United States and all territory subject to the jurisdiction thereof for beverage purposes is hereby prohibited.

SECTION 2. The Congress and the several States shall have concurrent power to enforce this article by appropriate legislation.

SECTION 3. This article shall be inoperative unless it shall have been ratified as an amendment to the Constitution by the legislatures of the several States, as provided in the Constitution, within seven years from the date of the submission hereof to the States by the Congress.

ARTICLE XIX

SECTION 1. The right of citizens of the United States to vote shall not be denied or abridged by the United States or by any State on account of sex.

SECTION 2. Congress shall have power to enforce this article by appropriate legislation.

ARTICLE XX

SECTION 1. The terms of the President and Vice President shall end at noon on the 20th day of January, and the terms of Senators and Representatives at noon on the 3d day of January, of the years in which such terms would have ended if this article had not been ratified; and the terms of their successors shall then begin.

SECTION 2. The Congress shall assemble at least once in every year, and such meeting shall begin at noon on the 3d day of January, unless they shall by law appoint a different day.

SECTION 3. If, at the time fixed for the beginning of the term of the President, the President elect shall have died, the Vice President elect shall become President. If a President shall not have been chosen before the time fixed for the beginning of his term, or if the President elect shall have failed to qualify, then the Vice President elect shall act as President until a President shall have qualified; and the Congress may by law provide for the case wherein neither a President elect nor a Vice President elect shall have qualified, declaring who shall then act as President, or the manner in which one who is to act shall be selected, and such person shall act accordingly until a President or Vice President shall have qualified.

SECTION 4. The Congress may by law provide for the case of the death of any of the persons from whom the House of Representatives may choose a President whenever the right of choice shall have devolved upon them, and for the case of the death of any of the persons from whom the Senate may choose a Vice President whenever the right of choice shall have devolved upon them.

SECTION 5. Sections 1 and 2 shall take effect on the 15th day of October following the ratification of this article.

SECTION 6. This article shall be inoperative unless it shall have been ratified as an amendment to the Constitution by the legislatures of three-fourths of the several States within seven years from the date of its submission.

ARTICLE XXI

SECTION 1. The eighteenth article of amendment to the Constitution of the United States is hereby repealed.

SECTION 2. The transportation or importation into any State, Territory, or possession of the United States for delivery or use therein of intoxicating liquors, in violation of the laws thereof, is hereby prohibited.

SECTION 3. This article shall be inoperative unless it shall have been ratified as an amendment to the Constitution by conventions in the several States, as provided in the Constitution, within seven years from the date of the submission hereof to the States by the Congress.

ARTICLE XXII

SECTION 1. No person shall be elected to the office of the President more than twice, and no person who has held the office of President, or acted as President, for more than two years of a term to which some other person was elected President shall be elected to the office of the President more than once. But this article shall not apply to any person holding the office of President when this article was proposed by the Congress, and shall not prevent any person who may be holding the office of President, or acting as President, during the term within which this article becomes operative from holding the office of President or acting as President during the remainder of such term.

SECTION 2. This article shall be inoperative unless it shall have been ratified as an amendment to the Constitution by the legislatures of three-fourths of the several States within seven years from the date of its submission to the States by the Congress.

ARTICLE XXIII

SECTION 1. The District constituting the seat of Government of the United States shall appoint in such manner as the Congress may direct:

A number of electors of President and Vice President equal to the whole number of Senators and Representatives in Congress to which the District would be entitled if it were a State, but in no event more than the least populous State; they shall be in addition to those appointed by the States, but they shall be considered, for the purposes of the election of President and Vice President, to be electors appointed by a State; and they shall meet in the District and perform such duties as provided by the twelfth article of amendment.

SECTION 2. The Congress shall have power to enforce this article by appropriate legislation.

ARTICLE XXIV

SECTION 1. The right of citizens of the United States to vote in any primary or other election for President or Vice President, for electors for President or Vice President, or for Senator or Representative in Congress, shall not be denied or abridged by the United States or any State by reason of failure to pay any poll tax or other tax.

SECTION 2. The Congress shall have power to enforce this article by appropriate legislation.

ARTICLE XXV

SECTION 1. In case of the removal of the President from office or of his death or resignation, the Vice President shall become President.

SECTION 2. Whenever there is a vacancy in the office of the Vice President, the President shall nominate a Vice President who shall take office upon confirmation by a majority vote of both Houses of Congress.

SECTION 3. Whenever the President transmits to the President pro tempore of the Senate and the Speaker of the House of Representatives his written declaration that he is unable to discharge the powers and duties of his office, and until he transmits to them a written declaration to the contrary, such powers and duties shall be discharged by the Vice President as Acting President.

SECTION 4. Whenever the Vice President and a majority of either the principal officers of the executive departments or of such other body as Congress may by law provide, transmit to the President pro tempore of the Senate and the Speaker of the House of Representatives their written declaration that the President is unable to discharge the powers and duties of his office, the Vice President shall immediately assume the powers and duties of the office as Acting President.

Thereafter, when the President transmits to the President pro tempore of the Senate and the Speaker of the House of Representatives his written declaration that no inability exists, he shall resume the powers and duties of his office unless the Vice President and a majority of either the principal officers of the executive department or of such other body as Congress may by law provide, transmit within four days to the President pro tempore of the Senate and the Speaker of the House of Representatives their written declaration that the President is unable to discharge the powers and duties of his office. Thereupon Congress shall decide the issue, assembling within forty-eight hours for that purpose if not in session. If the Congress, within twenty-one days after receipt of the latter written declaration, or, if Congress is not in session, within twenty-one days after Congress is required to assemble, determines by two-thirds vote of both Houses that the President is unable to discharge the powers and duties of his office, the Vice President shall continue to discharge the same as Acting President; otherwise, the President shall resume the powers and duties of his office.

ARTICLE XXVI

SECTION 1. The right of citizens of the United States who are 18 years of age or older, to vote shall not be denied or abridged by the United States or by any State on account of age.

SECTION 2. The Congress shall have power to enforce this article by appropriate legislation.

The Emancipation Proclamation

President Lincoln first issued the Emancipation Proclamation, freeing the slaves, on September 22, 1862. The final proclamation was issued on January 1, 1863, as follows:

By the President of the United
States of America:

A Proclamation.

Whereas on the 22d day of September, A.D. 1862, a proclamation was issued by the President of the United States, containing, among other things, the following, to wit:

"That on the 1st day of January, A.D. 1863, all persons held as slaves within any State or designated part of a State the people whereof shall then be in rebellion against the United

States shall be then, thenceforward, and forever free; and the executive government of the United States, including the military and naval authority thereof, will recognize and maintain the freedom of such persons and will do no act or acts to repress such persons, or any of them, in any efforts they may make for their actual freedom.

"That the executive will on the 1st day of January aforesaid, by proclamation, designate the States and parts of States, if any, in which the people thereof, respectively, shall then be in rebellion against the United States; and the fact that any State or the people thereof shall on that day be in good faith represented in the Congress of the United States by members chosen thereto at elections wherein a majority of the qualified voters of such States shall have participated shall, in the absence of strong countervailing testimony, be deemed conclusive evidence that such State and the people thereof are not then in rebellion against the United States."

Now, therefore, I, Abraham Lincoln, President of the United States, by virtue of the power in me vested as Commander-in-Chief of the Army and Navy of the United States in time of actual armed rebellion against the authority and government of the United States, and as a fit and necessary war measure for suppressing said rebellion, do, on this 1st day of January, A.D. 1863, and in accordance with my purpose so to do, publicly proclaimed for the full period of one hundred days from the first day above mentioned, order and designate as the States and parts of States wherein the people thereof, respectively, are this day in rebellion against the United States the following, to wit:

Arkansas, Texas, Louisiana (except the parishes of St. Bernard, Plaquemines, Jefferson, St. John, St. Charles, St. James, Ascension, Assumption, Terrebonne, Lafourche, St. Mary, St. Martin, and Orleans, including the city of New Orleans), Mississippi, Alabama, Florida, Georgia, South Carolina, North Carolina, and Virginia (except the forty-eight counties designated as West Virginia, and also the counties of Berkeley, Accomac, Northampton, Elizabeth City, York, Princess Anne, and Norfolk, including the cities of Norfolk and Portsmouth), and which excepted parts are for the present left precisely as if this proclamation were not issued.

And by virtue of the power and for the purpose aforesaid, I do order and declare that all persons held as slaves within said designated States and parts of States are, and henceforward shall be, free; and that the Executive Government of the United States, including the military and naval authorities thereof, will recognize and maintain the freedom of said persons.

And I hereby enjoin upon the people so declared to be free to abstain from all violence, unless in necessary self-defense; and I recommend to them that, in all cases when allowed, they labor faithfully for reasonable wages.

And I further declare and make known that such persons of suitable condition will be received into the armed service of the United States to garrison forts, positions, stations, and other places, and to man vessels of all sorts in said service.

And upon this act, sincerely believe to be an act of justice, warranted by the Constitution upon military necessity, I invoke the considerate judgment of mankind and the gracious favor of Almighty God.

The Monroe Doctrine

In his message to Congress on December 2, 1823, President James Monroe established what has come to be known as the Monroe Doctrine, a statement of U.S. foreign policy that expresses opposition to the extension of European control or influence in the Western Hemisphere. Following is part of Monroe's message:

In the discussions to which this interest has given rise, and in the arrangements by which they may terminate, the occasion has been deemed proper for asserting as a principle in which rights and interest of the United States are involved, that the American continents, by the free and independent condition which they have assumed and maintain, are henceforth not to be considered as subjects for future colonization by any European power. . . . We owe it, therefore, to candor and to the amicable relations existing between the United States and those powers to declare that we should consider any attempt on their part to extend their system to any portion of this hemisphere as dangerous to our peace and safety. With the existing colonies or dependencies of any European power we have not interfered and shall not interfere. But with the governments who have declared their independence and maintain it, and whose independence we have, on great consideration and on just principles, acknowledged, we could not view any interposition for the purpose of oppressing them or controlling in any other manner their destiny by any European power in any other light than as the manifestation of an unfriendly disposition toward the United States.

The Pledge of Allegiance

I pledge allegiance to the flag of the United States of America, and to the Republic for which it stands, one nation under God, indivisible, with liberty and justice for all.

The phrase "under God" was added to the pledge by an Act of Congress in 1954. The original pledge, written in 1892 by Francis Bellamy, contained the phrase "my flag."

The U.S. Flag

History

The "Stars and Stripes" as we know it today, with its blue field of 50 white stars and 13 red and white stripes representing the original 13 colonies, underwent several transformations.

The first flag raised in the United States was hoisted by John Cabot in 1497; it flew the banners of England and St. Mark. As settlers populated the colonies, each territory adopted its own flag. By 1707, each colony had its own state flag, the forerunners of the individual state flags today. The first colonial flag representing all the colonies, however, was believed to have been raised on Prospect Hill in Boston at the Battle of Bunker Hill. The "Continental Colors" bore the cross of the British flag in the upper left corner with 13 alternating red and white stripes extending horizontally. In 1777 the first Continental Congress "Resolved, that the Flag of the United States be thirteen stripes alternate red and white, that the Union be thirteen stars white on a blue field, representing a constellation."

As the new Union grew, Congress voted in 1794 to add two stripes and two stars to represent the two new states of Vermont and Kentucky. This flag is believed to be the one nicknamed the "Star-Spangled Banner." By 1818 five more states had joined, and on April 4 Congress voted to keep the number of stripes at 13 and to add a star to the field for every new state, the stars for the new states being added the July 4th after each state's admission to the Union.

The table below shows the order in which states joined the Union and the number of revisions the flag went through before arriving at its current design.

The U.S. Flag: 1777–1960

Date Used	Number of Stars	Designs	States Represented
June 14, 1777	13	1	Original 13 colonies
May 1, 1795	15	2	Vermont, Kentucky
July 4, 1818	20	3	Tennessee, Ohio, Louisiana, Indiana, Mississippi
July 4, 1819	21	4	Illinois
July 4, 1820	23	5	Alabama, Maine
July 4, 1822	24	6	Missouri
July 4, 1836	25	7	Arkansas
July 4, 1837	26	8	Michigan
July 4, 1845	27	9	Florida
July 4, 1846	28	10	Texas
July 4, 1847	29	11	Iowa
July 4, 1848	30	12	Wisconsin
July 4, 1851	31	13	California
July 4, 1858	32	14	Minnesota
July 4, 1859	33	15	Oregon
July 4, 1861	34	16	Kansas
July 4, 1863	35	17	West Virginia
July 4, 1865	36	18	Nevada
July 4, 1867	37	19	Nebraska
July 4, 1877	38	20	Colorado

Date Used	Number of Stars	Designs	States Represented
July 4, 1890	*43*	*21*	*North Dakota, South Dakota, Montana, Washington, Idaho*
July 4, 1891	*44*	*22*	*Wyoming*
July 4, 1896	*45*	*23*	*Utah*
July 4, 1908	*46*	*24*	*Oklahoma*
July 4, 1912	*48*	*25*	*New Mexico, Arizona*
July 4, 1959	*49*	*26*	*Alaska*
July 4, 1960	*50*	*27*	*Hawaii*

Care and Use of the Flag

Wherever and whenever it is displayed, the first requirement for flying the flag is that it be flown with respect. To show respect and honor to the symbol of the United States, fly it only in good weather, on all holidays and special occasions, and on official buildings such as schools when they are in session, post offices, courthouses, and the like. The flag generally is flown only from sunrise to sunset and at full staff. If it is displayed at night, it should be lit. Fly the flag at half staff to commemorate the death of an official and until noon on Memorial Day.

The White House flag is flown only when the President is in residence and only from sunrise to sunset. At the Capitol building, the flag flies over the appropriate wing when the House or Senate is in session. The flag is flown all night long and is lit by lights from the Capitol dome. Other special national monuments also fly the flag at night, notably Fort McHenry National Monument in Baltimore, Maryland, where Francis Scott Key was inspired to write "The Star-Spangled Banner."

When handling the flag, never let it touch the ground. When it flies with other flags, it should appear prominently above them. The flag should be to its own right (to the left, viewed face-on) with its staff in front of the staff of the other flag when placed against a wall with another flag. In a group of flags, the U.S. flag should be at the center. (The flag of the United Nations and a Navy Chaplain's church pennant may be flown above the U.S. flag.)

Hoist the flag quickly and lower it ceremoniously to the tempo of "Taps." If the flag is hung from a rope attached to a building, the field of stars should face away from the building; when hung over a street, the Union side should face north or east.

On a platform, the flag may be hung flat against the wall behind and above the speaker with the field of stars to the audience's left. In a church, the flag on its staff should be to the right of the speaker's platform and other flags to the left of the platform. If the flag is flown anywhere else in the chancel or on a platform, it should be to the right of the audience as they face the platform.

Salute when the flag passes in a parade or review, is being raised or lowered, is present at the playing of the national anthem, or is present at the saying of the Pledge of Allegiance.

Civilians should salute the flag by standing at attention and placing their right hands over their hearts. Men should remove their hats and hold them over their left shoulders with their right hand. Military personnel in uniform should give the military salute. Noncitizens should stand at attention.

Presidents of the United States

President	Term	Years of Birth and Death	Party	Vice President	Congresses
1. George Washington	4/30/1789– 3/3/1797	1732–1799	F	John Adams	1, 2, 3, 4
2. John Adams	3/4/1797– 3/3/1801	1735–1826	F	Thomas Jefferson	5, 6
3. Thomas Jefferson	3/4/1801– 3/3/1805	1743–1826	D-R	Aaron Burr	7, 8
	3/4/1805– 3/3/1809			George Clinton	9, 10
4. James Madison	3/4/1809– 3/3/1813	1751–1836	D-R	George Clinton	11, 12
	3/4/1813– 3/3/1817			Elbridge Gerry	13, 14
5. James Monroe	3/4/1817– 3/3/1821	1758–1831	D-R	Daniel D. Tompkins	15, 16, 17, 18
	3/4/1821– 3/3/1825				
6. John Quincy Adams	3/4/1825– 3/3/1829	1767–1848	D-R	John C. Calhoun	19, 20
7. Andrew Jackson	3/4/1829– 3/3/1833	1767–1845	D-R	John C. Calhoun	21, 22
	3/4/1833– 3/3/1837			Martin Van Buren	23, 24
8. Martin Van Buren	3/4/1837– 3/3/1841	1782–1862	D	Richard M. Johnson	25, 26
9. William Henry Harrison	3/4/1841– 4/4/1841	1773–1841	W	John Tyler	27
10. John Tyler	4/6/1841– 3/3/1845	1790–1862	W	—	27, 28
11. James K. Polk	3/4/1845– 3/3/1849	1795–1849	D	George M. Dallas	29, 30
12. Zachary Taylor	3/4/1850– 7/9/1850	1784–1850	W	Millard Fillmore	31
13. Millard Fillmore	7/10/1850– 3/3/1853	1800–1874	W	—	31, 32
14. Franklin Pierce	3/4/1853– 3/3/1857	1804–1869	D	William R. King	33, 34
15. James Buchanan	3/4/1857– 3/3/1861	1791–1868	D	John C. Breckinridge	35, 36
16. Abraham Lincoln	3/4/1861– 3/3/1865	1809–1865	R	Hannibal Hamlin	37, 38
	3/4/1865– 4/15/1865			Andrew Johnson	39
17. Andrew Johnson	4/15/1865– 3/3/1869	1808–1875	NU	—	39, 40
18. Ulysses S. Grant	3/4/1869– 3/3/1873	1822–1885	R	Schuyler Colfax	41, 42
	3/4/1873– 3/3/1877			Henry Wilson	43, 44

President	Term	Years of Birth and Death	Party	Vice President	Congresses
19. Rutherford B. Hayes	3/4/1877– 3/3/1881	1822–1893	R	William A. Wheeler	45, 46
20. James Garfield	3/4/1881– 9/19/1881	1831–1881	R	Chester A. Arthur	47
21. Chester A. Arthur	9/20/1881– 3/3/1885	1829–1886	R	—	47, 48
22. Grover Cleveland	3/4/1885– 3/3/1889	1837–1908	D	Thomas A. Hendricks	49, 50
23. Benjamin Harrison	3/4/1889– 3/3/1893	1833–1901	R	Levi P. Morton	51, 52
24. Grover Cleveland	3/4/1893– 3/3/1897	1837–1908	D	Adlai E. Stevenson	53, 54
25. William McKinley	3/4/1897– 3/3/1901	1843–1901	R	Garret A. Hobart	55, 56
	3/4/1901– 9/14/1901			Theodore Roosevelt	57
26. Theodore Roosevelt	9/14/1901– 3/3/1905	1858–1919	R	—	57, 58
	3/4/1905– 3/3/1909			Charles W. Fairbanks	59, 60
27. William H. Taft	3/4/1909– 3/3/1913	1857–1930	R	James S. Sherman	61, 62
28. Woodrow Wilson	3/4/1913– 3/3/1917 3/14/1917– 3/3/1921	1856–1924	D	Thomas R. Marshall	63, 64, 65, 66
29. Warren G. Harding	3/4/1921– 8/2/1923	1865–1923	R	Calvin Coolidge	67
30. Calvin Coolidge	8/3/1923– 3/3/1925	1872–1933	R	—	68
	3/4/1925– 3/3/1929			Charles G. Dawes	69, 70
31. Herbert C. Hoover	3/4/1929– 3/3/1933	1874–1964	R	Charles Curtis	71, 72
32. Franklin D. Roosevelt	3/4/1933– 1/20/1941	1882–1945	D	John N. Garner	73, 74, 75, 76
	1/20/1941– 1/20/1945			Henry A. Wallace	77, 78
	1/20/1945– 4/12/1945			Harry S Truman	79
33. Harry S Truman	4/12/1945– 1/20/1949	1844–1972	D	—	79, 80
	1/20/1949– 1/20/1953			Alben W. Barkley	81, 82
34. Dwight D. Eisenhower	1/20/1953– 1/20/1961	1890–1969	R	Richard M. Nixon	83, 84, 85, 86
35. John F. Kennedy	1/20/1961– 11/22/1963	1917–1963	D	Lyndon B. Johnson	87, 88
36. Lyndon B. Johnson	11/22/1963– 1/20/1965	1908–1973	D	—	88
	1/20/1965– 1/20/1969			Hubert H. Humphrey	89, 90

President	Term	Years of Birth and Death	Party	Vice President	Congresses
37. Richard M. Nixon	1/20/1969–1/20/1973	1913–	R	Spiro T. Agnew	91, 92, 93
	1/20/1973–8/9/1974			Gerald R. Ford	93
38. Gerald R. Ford	8/9/1974–1/20/1977	1913–	R	Nelson A. Rockefeller	93, 94
39. James (Jimmy) Carter	1/20/1977–1/20/1981	1924–	D	Walter F. Mondale	95, 96
40. Ronald Reagan	1/20/1981–1/20/1985	1911–	R	George Bush	97, 98
	1/20/1985–1/20/1989				99, 100
41. George Bush	1/20/1989	1924–	R	J. Danforth Quayle	101

F = Federalist; D-R = Democratic-Republican; D = Democrat; W = Whig; R = Republican; NU = National Union Party, a coalition of Republicans and War Democrats (Andrew Johnson was a Democrat).

THE SEQUENCE OF PRESIDENTIAL SUCCESSION

1. Vice President
2. Speaker of the House
3. President Pro Tempore of the Senate
4. Secretary of State
5. Secretary of the Treasury
6. Secretary of Defense
7. Attorney General
8. Secretary of the Interior
9. Secretary of Agriculture
10. Secretary of Commerce
11. Secretary of Labor
12. Secretary of Health and Human Services
13. Secretary of Housing and Urban Development
14. Secretary of Transportation
15. Secretary of Energy
16. Secretary of Education

Any successor to the presidency must meet the requirements for the office as established in the Constitution.

Vice Presidents of the United States

Vice President	Years of Birth and Death	President	Party
1. John Adams	1735–1826	George Washington	F
2. Thomas Jefferson	1743–1826	John Adams	F
3. Aaron Burr	1756–1836	Thomas Jefferson	D-R
4. George Clinton	1739–1812	Thomas Jefferson	D-R
		James Madison	D-R
5. Elbridge Gerry	1744–1814	James Madison	D-R
6. Daniel D. Tompkins	1774–1825	James Madison	D-R
7. John C. Calhoun	1782–1850	John Quincy Adams	D-R
		Andrew Jackson	
8. Martin Van Buren	1782–1862	Andrew Jackson	D-R
9. Richard M. Johnson	1780–1850	Martin Van Buren	D
10. John Tyler	1790–1862	William Henry Harrison	W
11. George M. Dallas	1792–1864	James K. Polk	D
12. Millard Fillmore	1800–1874	Zachary Taylor	W
13. William R. King	1786–1853	Franklin Pierce	D
14. John C. Breckinridge	1821–1875	James Buchanan	D
15. Hannibal Hamlin	1809–1891	Abraham Lincoln	R
16. Andrew Johnson	1808–1875	Abraham Lincoln	R
17. Schuyler Colfax	1823–1885	Ulysses S. Grant	R
18. Henry Wilson	1812–1875	Ulysses S. Grant	R
19. William A. Wheeler	1819–1887	Rutherford B. Hayes	R
20. Chester A. Arthur	1829–1886	James Garfield	R
21. Thomas A. Hendricks	1819–1885	Grover Cleveland	D
22. Levi P. Morton	1824–1920	Benjamin Harrison	R
23. Adlai E. Stevenson	1835–1914	Grover Cleveland	D
24. Garret A. Hobart	1844–1899	William McKinley	R
25. Theodore Roosevelt	1858–1919	William McKinley	R
26. Charles W. Fairbanks	1852–1918	Theodore Roosevelt	R
27. James S. Sherman	1855–1912	William H. Taft	R
28. Thomas R. Marshall	1854–1925	Woodrow Wilson	D
29. Calvin Coolidge	1872–1933	Warren G. Harding	R
30. Charles G. Dawes	1865–1951	Calvin Coolidge	R
31. Charles Curtis	1860–1936	Herbert C. Hoover	R
32. John N. Garner	1868–1967	Franklin D. Roosevelt	D
33. Henry A. Wallace	1888–1965	Franklin D. Roosevelt	D
34. Harry S Truman	1884–1972	Franklin D. Roosevelt	D
35. Alben W. Barkley	1877–1956	Harry S Truman	D
36. Richard M. Nixon	1913–	Dwight D. Eisenhower	R
37. Lyndon B. Johnson	1908–1973	John F. Kennedy	D
38. Hubert H. Humphrey	1911–1978	Lyndon B. Johnson	D
39. Spiro T. Agnew	1918–	Richard M. Nixon	R
40. Gerald R. Ford	1913–	Richard M. Nixon	R
41. Nelson A. Rockefeller	1908–1979	Gerald R. Ford	R
42. Walter F. Mondale	1928–	James (Jimmy) Carter	D
43. George Bush	1924–	Ronald Reagan	R
44. J. Danforth Quayle	1947–	George Bush	R

Weather Charts

Average Precipitation for Selected States and Cities
(in inches)

State	*City*	*Jan/Feb*	*Mar/Apr*	*May/Jun*	*Jul/Aug*	*Sep/Oct*	*Nov/Dec*
Alabama	Mobile	4.8	6	5.3	7.3	4.6	4.6
Alaska	Juneau	3.7	3.1	3.2	4.6	7.0	5.0
Arizona	Phoenix	0.7	0.6	0.2	0.4	0.6	0.7
California	Los Angeles	3.4	1.8	0.1	0.03	0.3	2.0
	San Francisco	4.0	2.1	0.2	0.08	0.7	3.0
Colorado	Denver	0.6	1.5	2.1	1.7	1.1	0.7
Connecticut	Hartford	3.4	4.1	3.4	3.6	3.7	4.2
Delaware	Wilmington	3.1	3.7	3.4	4.0	3.3	3.4
District of Columbia		2.7	3.3	3.9	4.0	3.2	3.2
Florida	Jacksonville	3.3	3.5	5.2	6.9	5.4	2.3
	Miami	2.1	2.5	7.9	6.5	7.6	2.3
Georgia	Atlanta	4.7	5.2	3.7	4.1	2.9	3.8
Hawaii	Honolulu	3.3	2.5	0.9	0.6	1.3	3.3
Idaho	Boise	1.4	1.1	1.1	0.4	0.7	1.3
Illinois	Chicago	1.5	3.2	3.7	3.6	2.9	2.1
Indiana	Indianapolis	2.6	3.7	3.9	3.9	2.6	3.0
Iowa	Des Moines	1.1	2.7	4.1	3.7	2.7	1.5
Kansas	Dodge City	0.5	1.7	3.2	2.8	1.6	0.7
Kentucky	Louisville	3.3	4.4	3.9	3.7	3.1	3.5
Louisiana	New Orleans	5.1	4.6	4.9	6.4	4.3	4.7
Maine	Portland	3.7	4.0	3.2	2.8	3.6	4.6
Massachusetts	Boston	3.9	3.9	3.2	3.2	3.4	4.6
Michigan	Detroit	1.8	2.9	3.1	3.2	2.2	2.4
Minnesota	Duluth	1.1	2.0	3.6	4.1	2.8	1.5
	Minneapolis	0.9	1.9	3.7	3.6	2.2	1.1
Mississippi	Jackson	5.0	5.9	3.9	4.1	3.1	4.8
Missouri	Kansas City	1.0	2.4	3.8	3.4	2.9	1.2
	St. Louis	1.9	3.5	3.6	3.1	2.5	2.4
Montana	Helena	0.6	0.9	1.9	1.1	0.8	0.6
Nebraska	Omaha	0.9	2.4	4.2	3.9	2.3	1.1
Nevada	Reno	1.1	0.6	0.4	0.3	0.3	0.9
New Jersey	Atlantic City	3.3	3.4	2.9	4.2	2.8	3.5
New Mexico	Albuquerque	0.4	0.5	0.5	1.4	0.9	0.5
New York	Albany	2.4	3.0	3.3	3.2	3.1	3.0
	Buffalo	2.7	3.0	2.8	3.6	3.2	3.5
	New York	3.2	3.9	3.5	3.9	3.6	4.0
North Carolina	Raleigh	3.5	3.3	3.7	4.4	3.0	3.0
North Dakota	Bismarck	0.5	1.1	2.6	1.9	1.1	0.5
Ohio	Cleveland	2.4	3.2	3.4	3.4	2.6	2.8
	Columbus	2.5	3.3	3.9	3.9	2.4	2.6
Oklahoma	Oklahoma City	1.2	2.5	4.7	2.7	2.9	1.4
Oregon	Portland	5.1	3.0	1.8	0.8	2.4	5.8
Pennsylvania	Philadelphia	3.0	3.7	3.6	4.0	3.1	3.4
	Pittsburgh	2.7	3.5	3.4	3.6	2.7	2.5
Rhode Island	Providence	3.9	4.2	3.2	3.5	3.7	4.4
South Carolina	Charleston	3.4	3.5	5.5	6.9	3.9	2.7
South Dakota	Huron	0.6	1.6	3.0	2.2	1.4	0.6
Tennessee	Memphis	4.5	5.6	4.4	3.9	3.0	4.6
	Nashville	4.4	5.2	4.2	3.6	3.2	4.1
Texas	Dallas-Ft. Worth	1.8	3.0	3.5	1.9	2.9	1.8
	Houston	3.3	3.5	4.4	3.5	4.3	3.6

State	*City*	*Jan/Feb*	*Mar/Apr*	*May/Jun*	*Jul/Aug*	*Sep/Oct*	*Nov/Dec*
Utah	Salt Lake City	1.4	2.0	1.3	1.3	0.8	1.0
Vermont	Burlington	1.8	2.6	3.3	3.7	3.0	2.6
Virginia	Norfolk	3.5	3.4	3.7	5.3	3.9	3.1
	Richmond	3.2	3.3	3.6	5.1	3.6	3.4
Washington	Seattle	5.1	3.0	1.5	1.0	2.7	5.6
Wisconsin	Milwaukee	1.5	3.0	3.4	3.3	2.6	2.0
Wyoming	Lander	0.6	1.4	2.1	0.6	1.1	0.7

Average Temperatures and Wind Speeds for Selected States and Cities

Numbers in parentheses indicate number of years that city has recorded wind speed. All wind speeds are expressed in miles per hour; temperature is expressed in degrees Fahrenheit. T = temperature; W = wind speed.

State	*City*	*Jan/Feb*		*Mar/Apr*		*May/Jun*		*Jul/Aug*		*Sep/Oct*		*Nov/Dec*	
		T	*W*	*T*	*W*	*T*	*W*	*T*	*W*	*T*	*W*	*T*	*W*
Alabama	Mobile (33)	53	10.6	66	10.7	78	8.3	82	6.8	74	8.1	56	19.2
Alaska	Juneau (38)	25	8.6	35	8.8	50	8.1	56	7.6	46	8.9	30	9.0
Arizona	Phoenix (36)	54	5.6	65	6.9	82	7.0	91	6.9	79	6.1	57	5.2
California	Los Angeles (33)	58	7.0	61	8.3	67	8.1	75	7.7	72	7.0	61	6.5
	San Francisco (54)	51	7.8	54	11.2	59	13.6	63	13.1	63	10.2	52	7.0
Colorado	Denver (33)	33	9.1	43	10.1	62	9.3	72	8.4	58	8.1	36	8.7
Connecticut	Hartford (27)	27	9.5	43	10.1	62	9.3	72	8.4	58	8.1	36	8.7
Delaware	Wilmington (33)	32	10.4	47	10.9	67	9.0	76	7.6	62	8.1	41	9.4
District of Columbia (33)		33	10.3	48	10.8	67	9.0	75	8.2	61	8.5	40	9.5
Florida	Jacksonville (32)	54	8.9	64	9.1	77	8.3	81	7.3	74	8.2	58	8.1
	Miami (32)	68	9.8	74	10.6	80	9.0	83	7.9	80	8.8	71	9.4
Georgia	Atlanta (43)	43	10.8	58	10.5	73	8.3	79	7.3	68	8.2	49	9.5
Hawaii	Honolulu (32)	73	10.3	75	10.2	79	9.4	81	8.4	81	8.4	76	8.5
Illinois	Chicago (23)	24	11.6	43	12	64	9.9	73	9.3	60	8.1	34	10.9
Indiana	Indianapolis (33)	28	11.0	46	11.6	68	9.1	74	7.3	61	8.4	37	10.5
Iowa	Des Moines (32)	22	11.8	43	13.1	67	10.9	75	8.9	60	10.0	33	11.5
Kentucky	Louisville (34)	35	9.7	51	10.2	70	7.8	77	6.6	64	7.0	42	9.1
Louisiana	New Orleans (33)	54	9.6	65	9.7	78	7.5	82	6.1	74	7.4	58	8.8
Maine	Portland (41)	23	9.4	38	10.0	58	8.6	68	7.5	54	8.0	32	8.9
Massachusetts	Boston (24)	31	14.2	44	13.6	64	11.8	73	10.8	60	11.7	40	13.3
Michigan	Detroit (47)	25	11.6	41	11.3	63	9.5	72	8.2	58	9.2	35	11.3
Minnesota	Duluth (32)	9	11.7	31	12.4	55	1.4	64	9.7	49	11.0	21	11.6
	Minneapolis (43)	15	10.4	38	11.7	64	10.8	72	9.2	56	10.1	26	10.6
Mississippi	Jackson (18)	48	8.6	61	8.8	76	6.6	82	5.7	71	6.4	52	7.8
Missouri	Kansas City (9)	29	11.3	49	12.4	71	10.1	78	8.8	63	9.5	38	11.1
	St. Louis (32)	32	10.7	50	11.7	71	9.1	78	7.8	64	8.3	40	10.1
Nebraska	Omaha (45)	22	11.2	43	11.8	67	10.7	75	9.0	59	9.7	32	10.8
Nevada	Reno (39)	35	5.9	44	7.8	34	7.6	69	6.5	55	5.4	37	5.2
New Jersey	Atlantic City (23)	35	11.8	47	12.2	64	10.0	74	8.6	63	8.7	43	10.9
New Mexico	Albuquerque (42)	37	8.4	30	10.6	70	10.4	78	8.7	63	8.5	40	7.8
New York	Albany (43)	22	9.7	41	10.7	63	8.7	70	7.3	56	7.8	33	9.2
	Buffalo (42)	25	14.2	39	13.2	61	11.4	70	10.2	57	10.9	35	13.1
	New York (57)	33	10.8	47	10.8	67	8.5	76	7.7	63	8.5	42	9.7
North Carolina	Raleigh (32)	41	8.8	54	9.3	71	7.4	78	6.5	66	7.0	46	8.0
North Dakota	Bismarck (42)	11	10.1	35	11.7	60	11.3	70	9.4	52	10.1	22	9.8
Ohio	Cleveland (40)	27	12.3	43	12.1	63	9.9	71	8.6	59	9.6	37	12.2
	Columbus (32)	29	10.3	46	10.5	66	8.1	73	6.7	60	7.3	37	9.7

Average Temperatures and Wind Speeds for Selected States and Cities *(Continued)*

State	City	Jan/Feb T	W	Mar/Apr T	W	May/Jun T	W	Jul/Aug T	W	Sep/Oct T	W	Nov/Dec T	W
Oklahoma	Oklahoma City (33)	39	13.3	55	14.9	73	12.7	82	10.9	68	11.6	45	12.6
Oregon	Portland (33)	41	9.6	48	7.8	60	7.1	68	7.4	59	6.5	44	9.0
Pennsylvania	Philadelphia (41)	32	10.8	48	11.3	68	9.3	76	8.0	63	8.6	41	9.9
	Pittsburgh (29)	28	10.7	45	10.7	64	8.6	72	7.4	59	8.0	37	10.2
Rhode Island	Providence (28)	29	11.6	43	12.2	63	10.7	72	9.4	59	9.6	38	10.8
Tennessee	Memphis (33)	42	10.4	58	10.9	75	8.5	82	7.3	69	7.7	47	9.6
	Nashville (40)	39	9.3	55	9.8	72	7.4	79	6.3	66	6.5	45	8.7
Texas	Dallas-Fort Worth (28)	47	11.5	61	12.8	78	10.9	86	9.3	74	9.4	52	10.7
	Houston (12)	53	8.5	65	9.3	78	7.9	83	6.4	74	6.7	57	7.7
Utah	Salt Lake City (52)	32	7.9	45	9.4	37	9.4	77	9.6	59	8.8	35	7.7
Vermont	Burlington (38)	18	9.4	36	9.3	60	8.6	69	7.6	54	8.4	30	9.6
Virginia	Norfolk (33)	41	11.7	54	12.0	72	9.9	78	8.8	67	10.0	48	10.8
	Richmond (33)	38	8.2	53	8.9	70	7.5	78	6.5	65	6.7	45	7.5
Wisconsin	Milwaukee (41)	21	12.8	39	13.1	60	11.2	70	9.6	57	11.0	31	12.5

Average Percentage of Possible Sunshine for Selected Cities

State	City	Length of record (yr.)	Jan.	Feb.	Mar.	Apr.	May	June	July	Aug.	Sept.	Oct.	Nov.	Dec.	Annual
Alabama.........	Montgomery	34	48	54	59	65	65	65	62	64	62	66	56	50	60
Alaska	Juneau[2].........	33	32	32	37	39	39	34	31	32	26	19	23	20	22
Arizona	Phoenix..........	89	78	80	83	88	93	94	85	85	89	88	83	77	85
Arkansas	Little Rock	36	48	55	59	63	69	74	73	73	69	70	57	49	63
California ....:..	Los Angeles[3]......	32	69	72	73	70	66	65	82	83	79	73	74	71	73
	Sacramento	36	45	61	72	81	88	93	97	96	93	85	63	46	77
	San Francisco[4].....	38	56	62	69	73	72	73	66	65	72	70	62	53	66
Colorado	Denver	35	71	71	70	68	64	71	72	72	75	72	65	67	70
Connecticut	Hartford	30	57	58	56	57	58	61	64	63	60	57	47	49	57
Delaware	Wilmington[2].......	39	50	54	56	57	56	62	62	62	59	69	52	49	57
District of Columbia	Washington	36	48	52	55	58	59	65	64	64	62	59	52	47	57
Florida..........	Jacksonville.......	33	58	61	67	71	69	63	61	60	55	58	60	56	62
	Miami...........	8	67	65	77	79	70	75	79	75	72	72	66	67	72
Georgia ....'.	Atlanta	49	49	54	58	65	68	67	63	65	64	68	60	51	61
Hawaii..........	Honolulu.........	32	62	64	68	66	68	70	73	75	75	68	61	58	67
Idaho...........	Boise	42	39	50	62	67	71	75	87	84	81	68	44	38	64
Illinois	Chicago[1]	39	45	51	56	63	65	72	74	76	69	68	52	45	63
	Peoria...........	41	46	50	51	54	59	66	68	67	65	61	45	40	56
Indiana..........	Indianapolis.......	40	41	50	50	54	60	66	67	70	66	62	43	39	56
Iowa	Des Moines	34	51	54	54	55	60	68	72	70	66	62	50	45	59
Kansas	Wichita	31	59	60	60	63	65	70	75	75	68	66	58	58	65
Kentucky	Louisville	37	42	48	49	54	61	66	66	67	65	61	47	41	56
Louisiana	New Orleans	11	48	53	57	63	61	67	62	60	63	67	55	53	59
Maine	Portland	44	56	59	56	55	55	59	64	64	62	58	48	53	57
Maryland	Baltimore	34	51	55	55	56	56	62	65	62	60	58	51	48	57
Massachusetts.....	Boston	49	53	56	57	57	59	64	67	66	64	60	51	52	59
Michigan	Detroit[1]..........	32	32	43	49	52	59	65	70	65	61	56	35	32	54
	Sault Ste. Marie....	43	36	46	54	55	57	58	63	58	45	40	24	27	47

State	City	Length of record (yr.)	Jan.	Feb.	Mar.	Apr.	May	June	July	Aug.	Sept.	Oct.	Nov.	Dec.	Annual
Minnesota	Duluth	34	49	52	55	55	56	58	65	61	52	46	35	39	52
	Minneapolis-St. Paul	46	52	58	55	56	60	64	71	68	61	55	39	40	57
Mississippi	Jackson.	20	47	56	59	63	63	70	65	64	61	66	55	49	60
Missouri.	Kansas City.	12	59	56	58	64	64	69	74	68	65	60	50	50	61
	St. Louis.	25	52	53	54	56	61	67	71	65	64	60	47	42	58
Montana.	Great Falls	40	49	55	65	61	62	64	79	76	68	60	46	44	61
Nebraska	Omaha	48	54	53	54	57	60	67	74	71	67	65	51	47	60
Nevada	Reno[5]	38	65	68	76	81	82	85	92	93	92	83	71	64	79
New Hampshire . . .	Concord	43	52	55	52	53	54	58	63	60	56	54	42	47	54
New Jersey	Atlantic City	24	49	51	53	55	54	58	60	63	60	56	49	44	54
New Mexico.	Albuquerque	45	72	73	73	77	80	83	76	76	79	79	77	72	76
New York	Albany	46	45	51	52	53	55	59	63	60	57	51	36	38	52
	Buffalo	41	32	38	45	52	58	65	68	64	59	51	29	27	49
	New York[3,6]	100	50	55	56	59	61	64	65	64	63	61	52	49	58
North Carolina	Charlotte.	34	55	60	63	69	69	70	68	69	67	68	61	58	65
	Raleigh	30	54	59	62	63	59	61	61	61	59	61	60	55	60
North Dakota	Bismarck.	45	54	54	59	59	62	64	75	73	66	58	45	47	60
Ohio	Cincinnati[1].	66	41	44	50	55	60	66	68	66	66	58	44	38	56
	Cleveland	41	31	37	44	52	58	65	67	63	60	53	32	26	49
	Columbus	33	36	42	43	52	56	60	60	60	61	56	38	31	49
Oklahoma.	Oklahoma City . . .	30	59	61	64	66	66	74	78	79	72	69	61	58	67
Oregon.	Portland	35	27	37	46	52	58	55	70	65	61	42	29	21	47
Pennsylvania.	Philadelphia.	42	50	53	55	56	56	62	62	62	60	59	52	49	56
	Pittsburgh	32	33	38	44	48	52	57	59	57	58	52	38	29	47
Rhode Island	Providence	31	56	57	56	56	57	60	63	60	61	60	50	52	57
South Carolina	Columbia	31	57	61	64	69	68	67	67	68	65	67	65	60	65
South Dakota	Rapid City.	42	55	59	61	59	58	62	72	73	69	65	55	53	62
Tennessee	Memphis.	34	50	54	56	64	69	74	74	75	70	70	58	50	64
	Nashville.	42	41	48	51	58	61	66	64	65	63	63	50	42	56
Texas.	Dallas-Ft. Worth . . .	6	53	58	59	64	64	71	81	77	74	61	62	56	65
	El Paso.	42	77	82	85	87	89	89	80	81	82	84	82	78	83
	Houston	15	43	51	47	51	57	64	66	64	62	61	53	55	56
Utah	Salt Lake City	46	46	55	63	67	72	79	83	82	83	72	54	43	67
Vermont.	Burlington.	41	41	48	50	49	55	59	64	60	54	48	30	32	49
Virginia	Norfolk[1]	21	56	59	60	65	65	68	64	65	64	58	58	55	61
	Richmond	34	53	58	60	65	65	68	66	66	64	60	58	53	61
Washington	Seattle	18	24	37	49	53	56	54	65	64	59	44	29	20	46
	Spokane	36	27	38	53	60	63	65	80	77	70	53	28	21	53
West Virginia	Parkersburg[1]	83	32	37	44	50	56	59	62	59	59	54	37	30	49
Wisconsin.	Milwaukee	44	44	47	50	53	59	64	70	66	59	55	40	37	54
Wyoming	Cheyenne . . , ...	45	62	65	65	61	59	65	68	67	68	68	60	59	64
Puerto Rico	San Juan.	29	66	69	74	68	60	61	67	66	60	61	58	58	64

[1] For period of record through 1981.   [2] For period of record through 1978.   [3] For period of record through 1976.   [4] For period of record through 1973.   [5] For period of record through 1980.   [6] City office data.

Important Dates in American History

Date	Event
1492	Columbus sails to Caribbean Islands.
1497	John Cabot explores North America from Canada to Delaware.
1513	Juan Ponce de Leon explores Florida.
1524	Giovanni da Verrazano leads French expedition along the coast from Carolina to Nova Scotia, entering New York harbor.
1565	St. Augustine, Florida, is founded.
1579	Francis Drake claims California for Britain.
1586	St. Augustine is destroyed by Francis Drake.
1587	Virginia Dare is the first baby born in America to English parents.
1607	The first European settlement in America is established at Jamestown, Virginia.
1609	Henry Hudson explores New York harbor and the Hudson River to Albany; Samuel de Champlain explores Lake Champlain in upstate New York; Spaniards settle Santa Fe, New Mexico.
1619	The first black slaves land at Jamestown, Virginia; the House of Burgesses, the first representative assembly in America, is established in Virginia.
1620	Pilgrims land in Plymouth, Massachusetts; the Mayflower Compact is drafted and signed.
1623	The Dutch found New Netherland (later New York).
1626	Peter Minuit buys Manhattan Island from Native Americans.
1630	The Massachusetts Bay Colony is founded.
1631	Roger Williams, pioneer of religious tolerance, arrives in America.
1634	Maryland is founded as a Catholic colony.
1635	New Hampshire is founded by Captain John Mason; the first public school, the Boston Latin School, is established.
1636	Harvard, the first college in America, is founded; Roger Williams founds Providence, Rhode Island.
1639	The first constitution in America is written, the Fundamental Orders of Connecticut.
1647	Margaret Brent is the first woman to claim the right to vote.
1648	The first labor organization in the United States is authorized in the Massachusetts Bay Colony.

Date	Event
1654	The first Jews arrive in New Amsterdam.
1663	The Colony of New Jersey is founded by Sir William Berkeley and Sir George Carteret; the Carolinas are founded.
1664	The English capture New Netherland.
1682	William Penn founds Pennsylvania.
1688	The first formal protest against slavery is made, by Pennsylvania Quakers.
1692	Nineteen persons (mostly women) are executed for "witchcraft" in Salem, Massachusetts.
1712	A slave revolt in New York leads to the execution of 21 blacks; six commit suicide.
1731	The first circulating library is founded, in Philadelphia.
1732	Georgia is founded by James Oglethorpe and others; Benjamin Franklin publishes the first *Poor Richard's Almanac*.
1741	The second slave uprising takes place in New York; 13 are hanged, 13 burned, and 71 deported.
1749	Black slavery is legalized in Georgia.
1754	The French and Indian War begins (called the Seven Years' War in Europe).
1758	The first Indian reservation is established.
1763	The French and Indian War ends.
1764	The Sugar Act places duties on lumber, foodstuffs, molasses, and rum in the colonies.
1765	Passage of the Stamp Act by Britain leads to the Declaration of Rights, signed by nine colonies opposed to taxation without representation.
1766	Britain repeals the Stamp Act.
1767	The Townshend Acts levy taxes on glass, painter's lead, paper, and tea.
1770	Five colonists are killed in the Boston Massacre.
1773	The Boston Tea Party takes place.
1774	The Intolerable Acts passed by Parliament curtail Massachusetts' self-rule and bar the use of Boston Harbor until tea is paid for.
1775	The American Revolution begins with the battles of Lexington and Concord.

Date Event

1776 France and Spain each donate 1 million livres in arms to Americans; the Declaration of Independence is drafted and signed; Nathan Hale is executed by the British as a spy; the first fraternity, Phi Beta Kappa, is founded at the College of William and Mary; the Journeymen Printers' Strike is the first in the United States.

1777 The Continental Congress adopts a flag with stars and stripes; Washington defeats Lord Cornwallis at the battle of Princeton; Major General John Burgoyne captures Fort Ticonderoga, but Americans defeat him at Saratoga.

1778 France agrees to assist the United States and sends a fleet; the British evacuate Philadelphia.

1779 George Washington orders a military campaign against the Iroquois.

1780 Benedict Arnold is discovered to be a traitor and escapes to the British.

1781 Colonial and French armies defeat the British at Yorktown, the last major battle of the Revolutionary War.

1783 The Revolutionary War ends with a treaty.

1784 The first daily newspaper, *Pennsylvania Packet and General Advertiser*, is published in Philadelphia.

1787 The Constitutional Convention begins in Philadelphia.

1788 New Hampshire ratifies the Constitution, putting it into effect.

1789 George Washington is chosen the first President; John Adams, Vice President; Thomas Jefferson, secretary of state; and Alexander Hamilton, secretary of the treasury.

1790 Congress meets in Philadelphia, the temporary capital, and votes to found a new capital on the Potomac River; the United States signs the first treaty with the Iroquois.

1791 The Bill of Rights goes into effect; Vermont is the first state to enter the Union after the original 13 colonies.

1793 The invention of the cotton gin by Eli Whitney revives slavery in the South.

1794 Suppression by the U.S. militia of the Whiskey Rebellion, in which farmers protest the liquor tax of 1791, established the authority of the new federal government.

1800 John Brown, abolitionist, is born.

Date Event

1801 Tripoli declares war on the United States.

1803 The Supreme Court declares an act of Congress unconstitutional in *Marbury v. Madison*; the United States buys the Louisiana Territory from Napoleon, doubling its land holdings.

1804 President Jefferson orders the Lewis and Clark expedition to explore the northwest; Vice President Aaron Burr and Alexander Hamilton duel; Hamilton dies the next day.

1805 Conflict with Tripoli ends.

1808 The importation of slaves is outlawed (about 250,000 slaves are illegally imported between 1808 and 1860).

1810 Margaret Fuller, feminist and transcendentalist, is born.

1811 Harriet Beecher Stowe is born.

1812 The War of 1812 begins.

1814 The war of 1812 ends with the Treaty of Ghent.

1815 Florida is ceded to the United States by Spain; Elizabeth Cady Stanton, suffragist, is born.

1816 The first savings bank is established, the Provident Institute for Savings, in Boston.

1817 Black abolitionist Frederick Douglass is born.

1818 Lucy Stone, feminist theorist, is born.

1820 Susan B. Anthony, suffragist and abolitionist, is born.

1821 Elizabeth Blackwell, the first U.S. woman physician, is born; Missouri is admitted to the Union as a slave state; Troy Female Seminary, the first women's college in the United States, is founded by Emma Willard.

1825 The Erie Canal is opened, cutting travel time from New York City to Buffalo and the Great Lakes by one-third.

1827 *Freedom's Journal*, the first black U.S. newspaper, is published.

1828 The first Native American newspaper, *Cherokee Phoenix*, begins publication.

1829 The first school for the blind is incorporated in the United States.

1830 Mary Harris (Mother) Jones is born; President Jackson signs the Indian Removal Act.

1831 Nat Turner leads a slave rebellion in Virginia.

1832 The first meeting of the New England Anti-Slavery Society is held; Oberlin College, Ohio, becomes the first college to establish coeducation.

Date *Event*

1836 Texans are besieged at the Alamo in San Antonio; Texas declares independence from Mexico.

1837 The panic of 1837 begins a seven-year depression.

1838 Cherokees begin the Trail of Tears, their 1,200-mile forced march to Oklahoma.

1841 Oberlin College, Ohio, becomes the first college to confer degrees on women; the first wagon train leaves from Independence, Missouri, for California.

1843 Sojourner Truth, former slave, begins an abolitionist lecture tour.

1844 The first telegraph message is sent from Washington to Baltimore by Samuel F. B. Morse.

1846 The United States declares war on Mexico; as a result, the United States obtains Texas, California, Arizona, New Mexico, Nevada, Utah, and part of Colorado; a treaty with Great Britain gives the United States the Oregon Territory to the 49th parallel; Henry David Thoreau is jailed for tax resistance.

1847 The first postage stamp is issued; Michigan becomes the first state to abolish capital punishment.

1848 The United States signs the Treaty of Guadalupe Hidalgo with Mexico, ending the Mexican War and increasing U.S. territory; the first women's rights convention is held in Seneca Falls, New York; gold is discovered in California.

1849 Eighty thousand gold prospectors flood California.

1850 Senator Henry Clay's Compromise of 1850 admits California to the Union as a nonslave state, while Utah and New Mexico enter with no decision on slavery.

1852 *Uncle Tom's Cabin*, by Harriet Beecher Stowe, is published.

1853 The American Labor Union is founded.

1854 The Republican party is formed in opposition to the Kansas–Nebraska Act, which left the issue of slavery to a vote by settlers.

1857 The Dred Scott decision by the Supreme Court upholds slavery.

1858 The Lincoln–Douglas debates are held in Illinois.

1859 John Brown, abolitionist, captures the U.S. arsenal at Harper's Ferry, West Virginia; Brown is hanged for treason.

1860 A nationwide shoemakers' strike wins workers higher wages; Charlotte Perkins Gilman, feminist theorist, is born; the National Labor Union is founded; social reformer Jane Addams is born.

Date *Event*

1861 The American Miners Association, the first national coal miners' union, is founded; the Civil War begins when Confederates fire on Fort Sumter, South Carolina.

1862 Slavery is abolished in Washington, D.C.; the Homestead Act grants land to settlers.

1863 Harriet Tubman frees 750 slaves in a raid; President Lincoln delivers the Gettysburg Address and issues the Emancipation Proclamation; draft riots in New York City kill approximately a thousand, including blacks who are hanged by a mob.

1864 Black prisoners of war are massacred by Confederate soldiers at Fort Pillow, Tennessee; General Sherman marches through Georgia, capturing Atlanta; the *New Orleans Tribune*, a black-run daily newspaper, begins publication; 133 Cheyenne and Arapahoe are killed by Colorado cavalry volunteers at Sand Creek.

1865 The Confederacy surrenders at Appomattox, Virginia, ending the Civil War; the first state civil rights law is passed, in Massachusetts; the Thirteenth Amendment abolishes slavery; the Ku Klux Klan is formed in Pulaski, Tennessee; President Lincoln is assassinated.

1868 Impeachment proceedings begin against President Andrew Johnson; the Fourteenth Amendment is ratified, guaranteeing due process to all but Native Americans; a U.S.–Sioux treaty is signed at Fort Laramie, Wyoming.

1869 Emma Goldman, anarchist, is born; the first national black labor group, the Colored National Labor Convention, meets in Washington, D.C.; the Central Pacific and Union Pacific railroads are linked at Promontory, Utah, forming the first transcontinental railroad; Wyoming territory is the first to grant suffrage to women.

1870 The first woman candidate for U.S. President, Victoria Claflin Woodhull, announces she will run; the Great Chicago Fire takes place; the first sorority, Kappa Alpha Theta, is established at De Pauw University; Ada H. Kepley, the first American woman graduate of a law school, receives degree from Union College of Law, Chicago.

1872 Susan B. Anthony is arrested for voting; the Amnesty Act restores rights to Southern citizens except for 500 Confederate leaders; Yellowstone, the first U.S. national park, opens in Wyoming.

1873 The first illustrated daily newspaper, *New York Daily Graphic*, is established.

Date *Event*

1875 Mary McLeod Bethune, black educator and activist, is born; the Civil Rights Act gives equal rights to blacks in public accommodations and jury duty.

1876 General Custer is defeated at the battle of the Little Bighorn.

1877 The United States violates its treaty with the Dakota Sioux by seizing the Black Hills; Chief Joseph surrenders with a starving remnant of Nez-Percé people.

1881 Sitting Bull surrenders; President Garfield is shot and killed; Booker T. Washington founds Tuskegee Institute for blacks.

1883 Margaret Sanger, birth control advocate, is born; the Supreme Court rules that Native Americans are aliens; Sojourner Truth dies; the Civil Rights Act of 1875 is invalidated by the Supreme Court.

1884 Eleanor Roosevelt is born.

1885 The first skyscraper is built in Chicago.

1886 The Haymarket Square massacre takes place in Chicago as a bomb explodes and protestors demanding an eight-hour day are arrested; Geronimo surrenders to Arizona Territory leaders; the American Federation of Labor (AFL) is founded.

1887 Crazy Horse is assassinated while in custody.

1890 The United Mine Workers is formed; Sitting Bull is killed by police at Standing Rock Reservation, South Dakota; 200 Sioux are massacred by troops at Wounded Knee, South Dakota; William Kemmler is the first criminal to be executed by electrocution, at Auburn Prison, New York; Ellis Island becomes a port of entry for immigrants.

1893 NAACP leader Walter White is born; financial panic lasting for four years begins.

1896 The Supreme Court's *Plessy v. Ferguson* decision upholds the "separate but equal" doctrine.

1898 The United States declares war on Spain; U.S. troops invade Puerto Rico to liberate it from Spain; Admiral Dewey captures Manila.

1899 Philippine insurrection against U.S. rule begins; *The Awakening,* an early feminist novel by Kate Chopin, is published; the Open Door Policy makes China an international market and preserves its integrity as a nation.

1900 The International Ladies Garment Workers Union is founded; prohibitionist Cary Nation leads the first bottle-smashing raid, in Wichita, Kansas.

1901 President McKinley is assassinated.

Date *Event*

1902 The last Philippine resistance to U.S. intervention ends.

1903 Panama declares its independence from Colombia, with U.S. support, and signs the Panama Canal Treaty; Orville and Wilbur Wright make the first flights in a mechanically propelled plane.

1905 The Niagara Movement, later to become the NAACP, is founded.

1906 The San Francisco earthquake and fire occurs.

1907 Charles Curtis of Kansas becomes the first Native American U.S. senator.

1908 The United States bars Japanese immigration; women demonstrate in New York City, demanding an end to sweatshops and child labor; the Federal Bureau of Investigation (FBI) is established.

1909 The National Association for the Advancement of Colored People (NAACP) is founded; Native American leader Geronimo dies.

1911 The Triangle Shirt Waist Company fire in New York City kills 146 sweatshop workers, mostly women, and leads to demands for better working conditions.

1912 The "Bread and Roses" strike by 10,000 textile workers begins in Lawrence, Massachusetts; folk singer Woody Guthrie is born.

1913 Ratification of the Sixteenth Amendment authorizes income tax; the Federal Reserve System is adopted; the first important U.S. exhibition of modern art is held at the New York City Armory; Harriet Tubman, leader of the Underground Railroad, dies.

1914 The Colorado National Guard burns a striking miner's camp and kills 13 children and seven adults in the Ludlow Massacre.

1915 The Women's International League for Peace and Freedom is founded; 25,000 women march in New York City demanding suffrage; Haiti becomes a U.S. protectorate after U.S. troops land there.

1916 The National Women's Party is founded; the first public birth control clinic opens, in Brooklyn, New York; Jeannette Rankin of Montana becomes the first woman elected to the House of Representatives; Margaret Sanger is arrested for operating a birth control clinic; the United States buys the Virgin Islands from Denmark; a military government is established in the Dominican Republic as the country is occupied by U.S. Marines.

1917 Women picket the White House for the right to vote; Puerto Rico becomes a U.S. territory; the United

Date	Event

States declares war on Germany, entering World War I; a wartime draft is enacted; Emma Goldman is sentenced to two years for aiding draft resisters.

1918 The Sedition Act becomes law; World War I ends.

1919 The Supreme Court holds that freedom of speech does not apply to draft resistance; a women's suffrage bill passes the House of Representatives; the Communist Party of America is founded; Congress overrides President Wilson's veto of Prohibition legislation.

1920 Five thousand alleged subversives are arrested nationwide in "Palmer raids"; the sale of alcoholic beverages is banned under the Eighteenth Amendment; women win the right to vote with ratification of the Nineteenth Amendment; the League of Women Voters is founded; the first transcontinental airmail route is established between New York City and San Francisco.

1921 Immigration is curtailed by quotas set by Congress; the Ku Klux Klan begins a revival of violence against blacks in the North, South, and Midwest; major powers meet at the Limitation of Armaments Conference to reduce naval construction, outlaw poison gas, restrict submarine attacks on merchantmen, and discuss the integrity of China.

1922 Rebecca L. Felton, from Georgia, is appointed the first woman U.S. senator.

1923 The War Resisters League is founded.

1924 The Supreme Court upholds the involuntary sterilization of mentally retarded persons; Native Americans are declared citizens by Congress; the first U.S. gay rights organization, the Society for Human Rights, is founded in Chicago.

1925 Nellie Taylor Ross, the first woman governor in the United States, is sworn in, in Wyoming; Malcolm X (Malcolm Little), black leader, is born; John T. Scopes is convicted of teaching the theory of evolution; Tennessee bans the teaching of evolution.

1927 Charles Lindbergh makes the first intercontinental flight.

1929 The stock market crashes, beginning the Great Depression.

1931 The Scottsboro Boys trial begins in Alabama; the Empire State Building opens in New York City.

1932 Hattie Caraway, of Tennessee, is the first woman elected to the U.S. Senate.

Date	Event

1933 President Franklin Roosevelt closes all U.S. banks; during the "100 days," a special session of Congress, important New Deal legislation is passed, including the establishment of the National Recovery Administration and the Tennessee Valley Authority (TVA); Frances Perkins, Secretary of Labor, becomes the first woman Cabinet member; the Twenty-first Amendment, ending Prohibition, is passed.

1935 The Works Projects Administration (WPA) is established; the National Labor Relations Act, recognizing workers' right to organize and bargain collectively, passes; President Roosevelt signs the Social Security Act.

1937 Amelia Earhart and her co-pilot disappear over the Pacific.

1938 The national minimum wage is enacted; the "War of the Worlds" broadcast by Orson Welles causes nationwide fear that Martians have invaded Earth.

1939 Sit-down strikes are outlawed by the Supreme Court; World War II begins with the German invasion of Poland.

1940 The Alien Registration Act (Smith Act) is passed; Congress approves the first peacetime draft.

1941 The Ford Motor Company signs its first contract with the United Auto Workers; the Japanese attack Pearl Harbor, bringing the United States into World War II.

1942 President Roosevelt issues an executive order to intern 120,000 Japanese-Americans on the West Coast; the Manhattan Project begins developing the atomic bomb.

1943 President Roosevelt bars all war contractors from racial discrimination.

1944 Allies stage the D-Day invasion of Normandy; Congress passes the G.I. Bill of Rights, providing veterans' benefits.

1945 The Yalta conference, attended by Roosevelt, Churchill, and Stalin, brings Russia into World War II against Japan; Roosevelt dies; Truman becomes President; Nazi Germany and Japan are defeated, ending World War II in Europe and the Pacific; U.S. troops liberate the concentration camp at Dachau; the first atomic bomb is exploded, at Alamogordo, New Mexico; the United States drops atomic bombs on Hiroshima and Nagasaki; Congress passes the Communist Control Act; the United Nations Charter is adopted.

Date *Event*

1946 The Atomic Energy Commission is formed; the Philippines is given independence.

1947 The first draft-card burning takes place; the cold war begins; aid is given to Greece and Turkey under the Truman Doctrine; Jackie Robinson, the first black major league baseball player, appears in his first game with the Brooklyn Dodgers; the Marshall Plan for European recovery is announced; the Department of Defense is created; the Central Intelligence Agency (CIA) and the National Security Council are established under the National Security Act; the House of Representatives cites the Hollywood Ten, accused of subversion, for contempt of Congress.

1948 Twelve Communist party leaders are indicted by the United States on grounds that they advocated the overthrow of the government.

1949 The North Atlantic Treaty Organization (NATO) is formed by the United States, Canada, and 10 European nations.

1950 The United States recalls all consular personnel from the People's Republic of China; Truman orders the development of the hydrogen bomb; Senator Joseph McCarthy accuses State Department employees of Communist party affiliation; two of the Hollywood Ten are imprisoned for refusing to cooperate with the House Un-American Activities Committee; the Korean conflict begins; the United States sends 35 military advisers and agrees to give military and economic aid to South Vietnam.

1951 Julius and Ethel Rosenberg and Morton Sobel are convicted of espionage conspiracy; the Mattachine Society, an early gay rights organization, is formed in California; atomic energy is first used to generate electricity in the United States; Korean cease-fire talks begin.

1952 The United States explodes the world's first hydrogen bomb; the Immigration and Naturalization Act is passed, lifting the last racial and ethnic barriers to naturalization.

1953 President Truman announces development of the hydrogen bomb; Julius and Ethel Rosenberg are executed; Vice President Richard Nixon gives his "Checkers" speech; the Korean conflict ends.

1954 Seven thousand square miles of the Pacific are irradiated by a Bikini Island hydrogen bomb test, which contaminates Japanese fishermen; the U.S. Air Force begins flying French reinforcements to Indochina; the *Brown v. Board of Education* ruling by the Supreme Court outlaws segregation in public

Date *Event*

schools; the Senate censures Joseph McCarthy; the Southeast Asia Treaty Organization (SEATO) is formed, comprising the United States, Great Britain, France, Australia, New Zealand, the Philippines, Pakistan, and Thailand.

1955 Rosa Parks refuses to give up her bus seat to a white person and begins the Montgomery, Alabama, bus boycott; the AFL and CIO merge, electing George Meany the first president; the United States agrees to help train the South Vietnamese army.

1956 Passage of the Federal Aid Highway Act inaugurates the first interstate highway system.

1957 Elizabeth Eckford is blocked from becoming the first black student at Little Rock Central High School; nine black students enroll at Little Rock High School with the help of federal troops; Congress approves the first bill protecting blacks' right to vote since the Reconstruction era.

1958 The United States launches its first satellite into orbit.

1959 Alaska and Hawaii become the forty-ninth and fiftieth states, respectively.

1960 More than 70,000 black and white students participate in sit-ins to protest a Greensboro, North Carolina, incident in which four blacks were denied service at a lunch counter.

1961 The United States breaks diplomatic ties with Cuba; the Bay of Pigs invasion of Cuba is thwarted; "freedom riders" test segregation laws in the Deep South; the Student Non-Violent Coordinating Committee (SNCC) voter registration drive begins in the South; the FBI launches its Socialist Worker Disruption Program; Alan B. Shepard, Jr. travels on the first U.S. manned space flight.

1962 The United States announces resumption of atmospheric nuclear testing after test-ban negotiations fail; James Meredith becomes the first black to enroll at the University of Mississippi; President Kennedy orders a blockade of Cuba, which begins the Cuban Missile Crisis; John H. Glenn, Jr. becomes the first American to orbit in space; *Silent Spring,* by Rachel Carson, is published, launching the environmental movement.

1963 The Supreme Court rules that states must provide free legal counsel for indigents; blacks in Birmingham, Alabama, begin mass demonstrations for civil rights; the Supreme Court bars mandatory Bible readings in public schools; Martin Luther King, Jr. leads a civil rights march on Washington, D.C.; a

Date *Event*

White House–Kremlin "hot line" is installed; the War Resisters League organizes its first demonstration against U.S. involvement in Vietnam; President Kennedy is assassinated; Congress passes the first Clean Air Act.

1964 The Twenty-fourth Amendment eliminates the poll tax in federal elections; a Civil Rights Act is passed by Congress; Congress passes the Gulf of Tonkin Resolution, giving President Lyndon Johnson power to wage war in Indochina; Martin Luther King, Jr. receives the Nobel Peace Prize; Panama suspends relations with the United States, which offers to negotiate a new Canal treaty.

1965 Malcolm X, black leader, is assassinated; 49 people are arrested during protests at Chase Manhattan Bank against loans to South Africa; Martin Luther King, Jr. leads a march on Selma, Alabama; a massive electric power failure blacks out most of the Northeast for the night of November 9–10; the Supreme Court holds that the "right of privacy" covers the use of contraceptives.

1966 Federal courts outlaw the last poll tax; the National Organization for Women (NOW) is founded; Medicare begins to pay the health-care expenses of U.S. citizens age 65 and older.

1967 Two hundred thousand people march against the Vietnam War in New York City; Thurgood Marshall becomes the first black Supreme Court justice; six days of racial rioting in Newark, New Jersey, leave 23 dead; week-long racial rioting in Detroit leaves 43 dead; J. Edgar Hoover, director of the FBI, authorizes activities against black nationalist groups.

1968 Four black student demonstrators are killed by police in Orangeburg, South Carolina; 500 unarmed Vietnamese are killed by U.S. troops in the My Lai massacre; Martin Luther King, Jr. is assassinated; Robert F. Kennedy is assassinated hours after his California primary victory; the American Indian Movement is founded; a coalition of women's groups interrupts the Miss America Pageant in the first mass demonstration of the modern women's movement; the United States ends the bombing of North Vietnam; Representative Shirley Chisholm, from New York, becomes the first black woman elected to Congress.

1969 The Stonewall rebellion, at a bar in New York City, starts the modern gay rights movement; the Woodstock festival in upstate New York draws 300,000 for "three days of peace and music"; the Chicago Seven conspiracy trial begins, in which seven de-

Date *Event*

fendants are accused of inciting a riot at the 1968 Democratic National Convention; 2 million people nationwide demonstrate against U.S. involvement in Vietnam; 78 Native Americans seize Alcatraz Island, demanding it be made into a cultural center; Black Panthers Fred Hampton and Mark Clark are murdered by Chicago police; the United States begins peace talks with Vietnam, as troop withdrawal starts; Neil Armstrong becomes the first man to walk on the moon.

1970 Chicano activists gather in Crystal City, Texas, to found La Raza Unida Party; U.S. postal workers hold their first strike; the Ohio National Guard kills four students in a Vietnam War protest at Kent State University; Mississippi police kill two black students at Jackson State University; President Nixon signs a law giving 18-year-olds the right to vote; the United Farm Workers begins a lettuce boycott; the Environmental Protection Agency (EPA) is established; Congress passes the Occupational Safety and Health Act; the Chicago Seven are found not guilty, though five are convicted of crossing state lines with intent to incite riots; the first two U.S. women generals are named by President Nixon.

1971 Five hundred thousand people demonstrate in Washington, D.C., against the Vietnam War and 14,000 are arrested; Native Americans leave Alcatraz Island after holding it for 19 months.

1972 The Watergate break-in, which leads to the resignation of President Nixon, takes place; Nixon makes an unprecedented visit to China; the Senate approves a constitutional amendment barring discrimination against women because of their sex and sends the measure to the states to ratify.

1973 A peace treaty is signed with Vietnam in Paris; President Nixon signs the Endangered Species Act; Oglala Sioux occupy Wounded Knee, South Dakota, and declare an independent Oglala Sioux nation; Spiro T. Agnew resigns as Vice President, and Gerald Ford becomes the first appointed Vice President; Nixon fires Archibald Cox, special prosecutor in the Watergate case, and William Ruckelshaus in the "Saturday Night Massacre"; Attorney General Elliot Richardson resigns; five of seven defendants in the Watergate trial plead guilty, and two are convicted; the Supreme Court rules that a state may not prevent a woman from having an abortion during the first six months of pregnancy; Congress overrides Nixon's veto of the War Powers Act, which curbs a President's power to commit armed forces to hostilities abroad without congressional approval.

Date Event

1974 The Organization of Petroleum Exporting Countries (OPEC) lifts the oil embargo; the Coalition of Labor Union Women is founded; the House Judiciary Committee votes Articles of Impeachment against President Nixon, and Nixon resigns; President Ford pardons former President Nixon.

1975 North Vietnamese troops enter Saigon; the Mohawk tribe reclaims part of its homeland in New York State; former Attorney General John N. Mitchell and ex-presidential advisers H. R. Haldeman and John D. Ehrlichman are found guilty in the Watergate trial; Congress votes $405 million in aid for South Vietnamese refugees; Vice President Rockefeller's blue-ribbon panel uncovers illegal CIA operations, including records on 300,000 persons and groups and infiltration by agents into black, antiwar, and political movements.

1976 The death penalty is ruled by the Supreme Court to be a constitutionally acceptable form of punishment. The nation celebrates its Bicentennial.

1977 President Carter pardons 10,000 Vietnam draft resisters; the Department of Energy is established; the National Women's Conference convenes in Houston.

1978 The "longest walk," by 300 Native Americans, begins, to protect treaty rights; gay activist and City Council member Harvey Milk and Mayor George Moscone are assassinated in San Francisco; the Senate votes to give the Panama Canal to Panama. The Middle East "Framework for Peace" is signed by Egypt and Israel after a Camp David conference led by President Carter.

1979 The Three Mile Island nuclear power plant has a near meltdown; 110,000 demonstrate in Washington, D.C., against nuclear power; Iranian students seize the U.S. embassy in Teheran.

1980 Thirty thousand people march on Washington against draft registration; 50,000 march in Chicago for passage of the Equal Rights Amendment (ERA); President Carter announces an embargo on the sale of grain and high technology to the Soviet Union because of its invasion of Afghanistan; the U.S. Olympic Committee votes not to participate in the Olympic Games in Moscow.

1981 Iran releases 52 American hostages held 444 days; 100,000 protest U.S. intervention in El Salvador; Sandra Day O'Connor is appointed the first woman Supreme Court justice; 11,500 air traffic controllers strike and are fired by President Reagan; the first reusable spacecraft, the shuttle *Columbia,* completes its two-day mission.

Date Event

1982 The ERA lapses without ratification; the Vietnam War Memorial is dedicated in Washington; Anne M. Gorsuch becomes the first Cabinet-level administrator to be cited for contempt of Congress, for refusing to turn over documents from the Environmental Protection Agency.

1983 The Puget Sound Women's Peace Camp is founded; the Seneca Falls, New York, women's peace encampment begins; 5,000 U.S. Marines and Army Rangers invade the island of Grenada; Congress applies the War Powers Act, demanding that troops leave Grenada; Federal District Judge Jack Tanner orders Washington State to pay female employees according to "comparable worth"; Dr. Sally K. Ride becomes the first American woman astronaut to travel in space; the Supreme Court holds that the Internal Revenue Service can deny tax exemptions to private schools that practice racial discrimination.

1984 Dr. Kathryn D. Sullivan becomes the first woman astronaut to walk in space; Geraldine A. Ferraro is the first woman candidate on a major party ticket to run for Vice President; the CIA acknowledges that it mined Nicaraguan harbors, touching off a controversy in Congress; veterans of the Vietnam War reach an out-of-court settlement with seven chemical companies in their class-action suit relating to the use of Agent Orange; a Salt Lake City federal judge rules that the United States had been negligent in its above-ground testing of nuclear weapons in Nevada from 1951 to 1962; the Senate votes to impose economic sanctions on South Africa in protest against apartheid; Palestinian Liberation Organization (PLO) hijackers seize an Italian cruise ship with Americans abroad, killing one; the United States and the Soviet Union meet at their first summit conference in six years; Congress passes the Gramm-Rudman Act in an attempt to curb the federal deficit.

1985 The United States and the Soviet Union agree to resume negotiations on reducing nuclear arms and the space weapons race. Soviet leader Chernenko dies and is succeeded by Mikhail Gorbachev. The Supreme Court bars public school teachers from positions in parochial schools. A summit meeting agreement is reached by Reagan and Gorbachev on stepping up arms control talks and cultural ties.

1986 The first official observance of the birthday of Martin Luther King, Jr. takes place; the space shuttle *Challenger* explodes moments after liftoff, killing all crew members, including a civilian, Christa McAuliffe; the United States bombs Tripoli and Benghazi, Libya, in retaliation against terrorist at-

Date *Event*

tacks; the antiviral drug azidothymidine (AZT) is found to improve the health of some AIDS patients; U.S. officials announce that AIDS cases and deaths will increase tenfold in the next five years; Congress passes antidrug legislation; the United States imposes more economic sanctions against South Africa; President Reagan walks out on arms talks with Soviet leader Mikhail Gorbachev in Iceland because of a disagreement over the development of the U.S. "Star Wars" program.

1987   The Iran–contra affair dominates public attention when it is revealed that arms were traded for hostages and money was funneled to Swiss bank accounts and used to finance the contras in Nicaragua; insider trading is revealed on Wall Street during the bull market; the United States violates the SALT II treaty with the Soviet Union; President Reagan appoints a commission to study the AIDS crisis and backs AIDS education; a clean-water act is passed over a presidential veto; the United States imposes duties on Japanese imports to curb the trade deficit; in a

Date *Event*

landmark case, surrogate mother Mary Beth Whitehead is denied custody of "Baby M"; the drug AZT is approved for fighting AIDS; animal forms are granted patent rights; U.S. ships are involved in a conflict in the Persian Gulf; Robert Bork is nominated by President Reagan to the Supreme Court but withdraws in the face of strong opposition; the Federal Communications Commission (FCC) drops the Fairness Doctrine, which allowed equal time on radio and television for controversial issues; "Black Monday" marks the end of the bull market, when Wall Street experiences its three biggest one-day point losses ever.

1988   Panamanian General Noriega is indicted on drug bribery charges, disrupting U.S.–Panama relations. Supreme Court Justice Anthony Kennedy is confirmed. The U.S.–Canada Trade Agreement approves lower barriers to trade. The space shuttle *Discovery* is launched successfully after delays caused by the 1986 tragedy. The U.S. agrees after a 13-year hiatus to meet with the Palestine Liberation Organization.

Government Benefits

The federal government provides financial assistance to U.S. citizens through a number of its agencies. You will find most government offices listed in the phone book under "U.S. Government." (See also the "Toll Free Numbers" section of this book for a listing of Federal Information Centers.) To name just a few of the agencies that offer aid to U.S. citizens, the Department of Education oversees student financial assistance, the Department of Health and Human Services provides for Medicare/Medicaid, the Department of Housing and Urban Development offers federal funds for low-income housing, and the Small Business Administration offers loans to small businesses. In this section, the benefits most Americans can receive from Social Security and Medicare hospital and medical insurance are outlined.

Social Security Benefits

Every working American is entitled to retirement benefits by the age of 62 under the Social Security program. To become eligible, a worker pays into the Social Security fund based on his or her primary insurance amount (PIA), which is adjusted annually according to the average indexed monthly earnings (AIME), which are standardized by law. Social Security benefits increase based on the Consumer Price Index (CPI). The worker's full PIA becomes available when he or she retires at 62 or 65, becomes disabled, or dies. In May of 1987, for example, the average monthly benefits payable to retirees was $491, while the average amount for disabled workers was $488. Spouses and families are also eligible for benefits under certain circumstances (see below).

To become fully insured and earn *retirement benefits,* a worker must have earned one quarter of coverage for every year since the age of 21 (or since 1950), up to but not including the time when he or she reaches age 62, becomes disabled, or dies. (Some very old persons who do not qualify by these standards can still receive benefits.) For every $460 of annual earnings, a worker in 1987 earns one quarter of coverage, with a maximum of four quarters per year. *Disability benefits* are paid to those who are fully insured plus have 20 quarters of coverage out of the potential 40 calendar quarters. However, blind persons qualify simply by being fully insured, while those people disabled before 31 years of age can qualify for benefits with a briefer period of coverage. *Survivor benefits* are available to the survivors of those who had at least 6 quarters of coverage in the 13 quarters preceding death.

Retirement Benefits

At the age of 62, workers can retire and begin collecting Social Security. Coverage for retirement at this age, however, is only 80 percent of PIA, the full amount allowable. Those who retire at age 65 or later receive the full amount of their PIA. A delayed retirement credit applies to those workers who reach 65 after 1981. Their benefits increase 3 percent for each year between ages 65 and 70 that they did not receive benefits. This credit is 1 percent a year for workers reaching 65 before 1982, although the credit will rise from 3 percent to 8 percent per year from 1990 to 2008.

Spouses of workers who receive Social Security retirement or disability benefits may get a spouse's insurance benefit of half of the worker's PIA when the spouse reaches 65. As with the worker's benefits, spouses may begin getting reduced payments at age 62. Payments are also available for divorced spouses provided they were married to the worker for at least 10 years.

Disability Benefits

If a worker is unable to work because he or she is severely disabled, Social Security offers a monthly disability payment. The worker receives the payments until he or she is able to work again. If the worker is still disabled by age 65, the payments become those for a retired worker.

If a fully insured worker retires or is disabled, his or her spouse and children under 18 are entitled to half of the unreduced benefit. Benefits usually stop after children reach 18, though payments can continue until the nineteenth year provided the child is enrolled in an elementary or secondary school full time. The benefits are limited to a maximum amount, and individual benefits are adjusted after the family receives the maximum allowed.

Survivor Benefits

Benefits to survivors of fully insured workers are available under one or more of the five conditions listed:

1. If the spouse is 65 or older, he or she will receive the full amount of the deceased's PIA and may begin collecting at a reduced rate at age 60. If the worker had begun collecting Social Security before the age of 65, spouses 62 and over may collect benefits at the same reduced amount the worker would have received if alive, but not less than 82½ percent of the worker's PIA.

If the widow or widower of a deceased worker becomes disabled before or within seven years after the spouse's death, the last month he or she received mother's or father's insurance benefits, or the last month he or she received the surviving spouse's benefits, that person may receive 71½ percent of the worker's PIA.

2. As with children of disabled or retired workers, surviving children receive benefits until they are 18 or 19 if they are enrolled in school full time. Benefits for such children are three-quarters of the amount the worker would have received had he or she lived to collect full benefits.

3. The spouse of a deceased worker receives an additional 75 percent of the PIA provided he or she cares for a child 16 years of age or younger; payments also are made to divorcees of a deceased worker if the marriage lasted at least 10 years. Payments to the spouse stop when the child reaches age 16, even if payments to the child continue. Payments will start again when the spouse is 60 (50 if disabled), unless the spouse remarries before the age of 60 (50 if disabled). If the child in care is disabled, benefits continue after he or she reaches 16 years of age.

4. Parents who were dependent on a child for at least half of their support and who have reached the age of 62 may receive payments of 75 percent of the worker's PIA. A sole surviving parent receives 82½ percent of the PIA.

5. A cash payment of $255 is made to a spouse who lived with the deceased worker or to a spouse or child eligible for immediate monthly survivor benefits.

Self-Employed and Household Workers

Self-employed persons may receive the same benefits as other workers, but they must contribute to Social Security by filing taxes on a quarterly basis. As with other workers, self-employed workers earn a quarter of coverage for every $460 (as of 1987), with a limit of four quarters per year.

Household workers—maids, cooks, laundry workers, nursemaids, baby-sitters, chauffeurs, etc.—also are covered provided they are paid $50 or more in cash per quarter by at least one employer. Carfare can be applied if it is paid in cash, but room and board cannot be claimed. Whether the job is regular, full time, or part time, household workers can receive this benefit by showing their Social Security cards to their employers. The employer will then deduct the Social Security tax from payment and send it to the government.

Farm Owners and Workers

Self-employed farmers pay contributions to Social Security at the same rate as other self-employed persons. They can report two-thirds of their gross earnings if their earnings are $2,400 or less. Those whose gross income is $2,400 or more, and whose net income is $1,600 or less, can report $1,600. Cash or crop shares from a tenant or share farmer can be counted only if the farmer participated materially in the production or management.

Farm employees may claim Social Security only if they earn $150 or more in cash during the year or if they worked on 20 or more days for cash figured on a time basis.

Medicare

Medicare provides hospital and medical insurance for Social Security and Railroad Retirement beneficiaries 65 and over. It also provides for those persons who are entitled to receive Social Security disability benefits for two years and to those with end-stage renal disease. Persons aged 65 and over not otherwise eligible for hospital benefits may receive them by paying a special monthly premium on a voluntary basis. (The hospital insurance program paid almost $55 billion in 1987 while about $25 billion was paid for medical insurance.) Those eligible for hospital benefits may apply for medical benefits by paying a monthly premium.

Hospital Insurance

Those eligible for hospital insurance are covered for the following:

1. Limit of 90 days of hospital care during an illness beginning with the first day of the stay at a hospital or a skilled-nursing facility. The coverage ends when the patient has not been a bed patient in the hospital for 60 consecutive days.

Medicare pays all but $520 for the first 60 days and all but $130 for the remaining days up to 90. A 60-day lifetime reserve can be used after the initial 90 days. All but $260 a day of expenses are paid during the reserve days. Mental hospital pay is limited to 190 days.

2. A stay up to 100 days in a skilled-nursing facility. Medicare pays for the first 20 days; for 80 days after that, insurance pays all but $65. However, a three-day hospital stay must precede the stay in the skilled-nursing facility for a patient to qualify.

3. All visits by nurses and health workers except doctors for one year after release from a hospital or extended-care facility.

Medical Insurance

Medical insurance is available to those who enroll in the Medicare program and pay a monthly premium ($17.90 in 1987, with the government covering the rest). The monthly premium is deducted from the payments persons receive from Social Security, Railroad Retirement, or Civil Service retirement benefits. Persons may enroll ten months before age 65 or in a three-month period after their sixty-fifth birthday. For coverage to begin in the month a person turns 65, that person must enroll three months before his or her birthday. Those who do not enroll during these periods may still apply, but their premium will be 10 percent higher for each year they did not enroll.

Except for doctors' charges for X-ray or clinical laboratory services for hospital-bed patients, which are paid in full by individuals, members of this program pay 20 percent (after the first $75) of the total amount required for the following services:

1. Hospital, office, or home physicians' and surgeons' fees.
2. Diagnostic tests, surgical dressings, and splints; rental or purchase of medical equipment; the services of a physical therapist at home or in the office; outpatient physical therapy received from a hospital or an extended-care facility for those who have used up their hospital insurance coverage.
3. Physical therapy furnished under the supervision of a practicing hospital, clinic, skilled-nursing facility, or agency.
4. Certain services by podiatrists.
5. All outpatient services of a participating hospital (including diagnostic tests).
6. Services of licensed chiropractors who meet government standards, but only for manual manipulation treatment of the spine and treatment of subluxation of the spine proven by X-ray.
7. Supplies related to colostomies.

Monthly Payments for Selected Families

Beneficiary Family	Career Earnings Level/Average ($18,456)*	Low Earnings ($6,968)*	Maximum Earnings ($43,800)*
Retiring at 65 (PIA)	$ 593.80	$391.10	$ 789.20
Retiring at 65 (maximum family benefit)	1,079.90	612.80	1,380.60
Disabled at 55 (maximum family benefit)	943.00	625.80	1,253.70
Disabled at 65			
Worker	628.00	417.00	835.00
Worker, spouse, 1 child	943.00	625.80	1,253.70
Retiring at 62			
Worker[2]	502.00	333.00	662.00
With spouse claiming benefits at 62[2]	737.00	489.00	972.00
65 or over	816.00	541.00	1,075.00
Widow or widower claiming benefits at 60	424.00	279.00	564.00
65 or over[3]	593.00	391.00	789.00
Disabled widow or widower claiming benefits at age 50–59[4]	424.00	279.00	564.00
1 surviving child	445.00	293.00	591.00
Widow or widower 65 and over and 1 child	1,038.00	612.80	1,380.00
Widowed parent and 1 child	890.00	586.00	1,182.00
Widowed parent and 2 children	1,079.00	612.80	1,380.60

* Figures for 1987.   [1] Estimate.   [2] Assumes maximum reduction.   [3] A widow or widower's benefit amount is limited to the amount the spouse would have received if still living.   [4] Effective January 1984, disabled widows or widowers claiming benefits at age 50–59 will receive benefits equal to 71½ percent of PIA.

Crime Rates

Crimes and Crime Rates, by Type: 1977–86

Data refer to offenses known to the police.

Item and year	Total	Violent crime						Property crime			
		Total	*Murder*[1]	*Forcible rape*	*Robbery*	*Aggravated assault*		*Total*	*Burglary*	*Larceny—theft*	*Motor vehicle theft*
Number of offenses (1,000):											
1977	10,985	1,030	19.1	63.5	413	534		9,955	3,072	5,906	978
1978	11,209	1,086	19.6	67.6	427	571		10,123	3,128	5,991	1,004
1979	12,250	1,208	21.5	76.4	481	629		11,042	3,328	6,601	1,113
1980	13,408	1,345	23.0	83.0	566	673		12,064	3,795	7,137	1,132
1981	13,424	1,362	22.5	82.5	593	664		12,062	3,780	7,194	1,088
1982	12,974	1,322	21.0	78.8	553	669		11,652	3,447	7,143	1,062
1983	12,109	1,258	19.3	78.9	507	653		10,851	3,130	6,713	1,008
1984	11,882	1,273	18.7	84.2	485	685		10,609	2,984	6,592	1,032
1985	12,430	1,328	19.0	87.7	498	723		11,103	3,073	6,926	1,103
1986	13,211	1,488	20.6	90.4	543	834		11,723	3,241	7,257	1,224
Percent change, number of offenses:											
1977–86	20.3	44.5	7.8	42.4	31.5	56.1		17.8	5.5	22.9	25.2
1982–86	1.8	12.5	−1.9	14.8	−1.9	24.6		.6	−6.0	1.6	15.2
1985–86	6.3	12.1	8.6	3.2	9.0	15.4		5.6	5.5	4.8	11.0
Rate per 100,000 inhabitants:											
1977	5,078	476	8.8	29.4	191	247		4,602	1,420	2,730	452
1978	5,140	498	9.0	31.0	196	262		4,643	1,435	2,747	461
1979	5,566	549	9.7	34.7	218	286		5,017	1,512	2,999	506
1980	5,950	597	10.2	36.8	251	299		5,353	1,684	3,167	502
1981	5,858	594	9.8	36.0	259	290		5,264	1,650	3,140	475
1982	5,604	571	9.1	34.0	239	289		5,033	1,489	3,085	459
1983	5,175	538	8.3	33.7	217	279		4,637	1,338	2,869	431
1984	5,031	539	7.9	35.7	205	290		4,492	1,264	2,791	437
1985	5,207	556	7.9	36.7	209	303		4,651	1,287	2,901	462
1986	5,480	617	8.6	37.5	225	346		4,863	1,345	3,010	508
Percent change, rate per 100,000 inhabitants:											
1977–86	7.9	29.7	−2.3	27.6	18.0	40.1		5.7	−5.3	10.3	12.4
1982–86	−2.2	8.1	−5.5	10.3	−5.8	19.7		−3.4	−9.7	−2.4	10.7
1985–86	5.2	11.0	8.9	2.2	8.0	14.3		4.6	4.5	3.8	9.9

[1] Includes nonnegligent manslaughter.

Crimes and Crime Rates, by Type and Area: 1985 and 1986

In thousands, except rate. Rate per 100,000 population. Estimated totals based on reports from city and rural law enforcement agencies representing 96 percent of the national population.

Type of crime	1985 MSA's[1] Total	1985 MSA's[1] Rate	1985 Other cities Total	1985 Other cities Rate	1985 Rural areas Total	1985 Rural areas Rate	1986 MSA's[1] Total	1986 MSA's[1] Rate	1986 Other cities Total	1986 Other cities Rate	1986 Rural areas Total	1986 Rural areas Rate
Total	10,767	5,921	1,051	4,580	612	1,803	11,482	6,236	1,097	4,793	631	1,854
Violent crime	1,197	658	73	319	56	168	1,348	732	80	350	60	175
Murder and nonnegligent manslaughter	16	9	1	5	2	6	18	10	1	5	2	5
Forcible rape.	76	42	5	21	6	18	79	43	5	22	6	18
Robbery	483	266	10	44	5	15	527	286	11	49	5	15
Aggravated assault.	622	342	57	249	44	129	725	394	63	274	47	137
Property crime	9,569	5,262	978	4,262	555	1,635	10,134	5,504	1,017	4,443	572	1,678
Burglary	2,632	1,447	229	999	212	625	2,781	1,510	239	1,046	221	649
Larceny—theft	5,915	3,253	704	3,067	307	906	6,213	3,374	731	3,191	314	921
Motor vehicle theft	1,023	562	45	195	35	104	1,140	819	47	206	37	108

[1]Metropolitan Statistical Areas.

Crime Rates by State, 1980 to 1986, and by Type, 1986

Offenses known to the police per 100,000 population. Based on Bureau of Census estimated resident population as of July 1, except April 1, 1980 census counts.

Region, division, and state	1980, total	1984, total	1985, total	1986 Total	1986 Violent crime Murder[1]	1986 Violent crime Forcible rape	1986 Violent crime Robbery	1986 Violent crime Aggravated assault	1986 Property crime Burglary	1986 Property crime Larceny—theft	1986 Property crime Motor vehicle theft
U.S..	5,950	5,031	5,207	5,480	8.6	37.5	225	346	1,345	3,010	508
Region:											
Northeast.	5,767	4,562	4,627	4,732	6.8	28.3	298	296	1,043	2,473	587
Midwest	5,529	4,675	4,658	4,832	6.6	[2]35.4	179	290	1,082	2,792	448
South	5,573	4,899	5,256	5,709	10.6	40.6	199	371	1,523	3,107	458
West	7,388	6,210	6,405	6,644	9.2	44.3	251	423	1,671	3,662	584
New England	5,713	4,376	4,487	4,503	3.5	25.2	151	239	1,064	2,398	622
Maine.	4,368	3,527	3,672	3,461	2.0	14.8	28	102	803	2,347	164
New Hampshire	4,680	3,138	3,252	3,330	2.2	21.5	24	92	755	2,208	228
Vermont	4,988	3,968	3,888	3,977	2.1	21.8	22	103	949	2,697	181
Massachusetts	6,079	4,588	4,758	4,723	3.6	29.7	193	331	1,071	2,189	906
Rhode Island	5,933	4,774	4,723	4,902	3.5	21.4	119	192	1,294	2,568	705
Connecticut	5,882	4,629	4,705	4,829	4.6	23.8	192	205	1,198	2,758	447
Mid-Atlantic	5,786	4,625	4,675	4,810	8.0	29.3	348	316	1,035	2,498	575
New York	6,912	5,577	5,589	5,768	10.7	30.5	514	431	1,221	2,924	637
New Jersey	6,401	4,856	5,094	5,241	5.2	33.2	269	265	1,071	2,822	776
Pennsylvania	3,736	3,060	3,037	3,102	5.5	25.1	152	176	735	1,654	354

Region, division, and state	1980, total	1984, total	1985, total	1986							
					Violent crime				Property crime		
				Total	Mur-der[1]	Forci-ble rape	Rob-bery	Aggra-vated assault	Bur-glary	Lar-ceny–theft	Motor vehi-cle theft
East North Central	**5,800**	**5,000**	**4,916**	**5,058**	**7.5**	**[2]39.4**	**213**	**316**	**1,118**	**2,845**	**518**
Ohio	5,431	4,273	4,187	4,359	5.5	38.6	142	235	988	2,574	376
Indiana	4,930	3,929	3,914	3,855	6.0	25.9	90	186	887	2,333	328
Illinois	6,269	5,304	5,303	5,546	8.9	[2]32.4	325	434	1,180	2,938	628
Michigan	6,675	6,556	6,366	6,491	11.3	67.4	301	424	1,509	3,378	800
Wisconsin	4,799	4,172	4,017	4,097	3.1	20.1	73	162	783	2,802	254
West North Central	**4,874**	**3,904**	**4,046**	**4,296**	**4.6**	**26.1**	**97**	**228**	**995**	**2,665**	**281**
Minnesota	4,799	3,842	4,134	4,362	2.5	31.8	102	148	1,004	2,785	288
Iowa	4,747	3,800	3,943	4,151	1.8	12.5	42	179	956	2,801	158
Missouri	5,433	4,297	4,366	4,654	9.2	29.2	170	370	1,136	2,500	439
North Dakota	2,964	2,583	2,679	2,605	1.0	11.6	7	32	385	2,049	120
South Dakota	3,243	2,613	2,641	2,716	4.0	17.7	16	87	554	1,939	99
Nebraska	4,305	3,497	3,695	3,856	3.1	24.6	51	184	748	2,677	168
Kansas	5,379	4,339	4,375	4,823	4.4	32.9	80	252	1,188	3,008	258
South Atlantic	**6,081**	**5,033**	**5,375**	**5,724**	**9.8**	**40.1**	**222**	**412**	**1,473**	**3,159**	**407**
Delaware	6,777	5,007	4,961	4,832	4.9	56.9	124	241	1,042	3,090	272
Maryland	6,630	5,215	5,373	5,602	9.0	43.6	304	476	1,246	2,978	545
District of Columbia[3]	10,236	8,799	8,007	8,339	31.0	52.4	754	668	1,728	4,131	975
Virginia	4,620	3,784	3,779	3,860	7.1	26.5	106	167	813	2,522	219
West Virginia	2,552	2,336	2,253	2,317	5.9	18.9	41	99	625	1,358	169
North Carolina	4,640	4,044	4,121	4,332	8.1	26.4	88	354	1,225	2,423	208
South Carolina	5,439	4,663	4,841	5,137	8.6	41.3	99	525	1,340	2,846	277
Georgia	5,604	4,498	5,110	5,455	11.2	43.9	214	319	1,453	2,984	430
Florida	8,402	6,821	7,574	8,228	11.7	52.7	367	605	2,221	4,373	598
East South Central	**4,161**	**3,519**	**3,651**	**3,910**	**9.6**	**32.5**	**127**	**280**	**1,115**	**2,030**	**316**
Kentucky	3,434	2,959	2,947	3,092	6.7	23.1	83	222	824	1,740	193
Tennessee	4,498	3,890	4,167	4,534	10.4	47.0	208	274	1,325	2,126	544
Alabama	4,934	3,902	3,942	4,288	10.1	28.4	112	408	1,159	2,304	267
Mississippi	3,417	3,060	3,266	3,345	11.2	25.8	65	172	1,076	1,845	150
West South Central	**5,657**	**5,489**	**5,991**	**6,706**	**12.3**	**45.8**	**207**	**360**	**1,828**	**3,639**	**615**
Arkansas	3,811	3,368	3,585	3,925	8.1	28.9	80	278	1,030	2,305	195
Louisiana	5,454	5,111	5,564	6,078	12.8	40.1	224	482	1,461	3,417	442
Oklahoma	5,053	4,893	5,425	6,014	8.1	36.4	107	285	1,787	3,142	649
Texas	6,143	6,030	6,569	7,408	13.5	51.6	240	354	2,049	3,987	714
Mountain	**6,831**	**5,779**	**6,183**	**6,323**	**7.4**	**38.4**	**127**	**335**	**1,540**	**3,911**	**366**
Montana	5,024	4,653	4,549	4,479	2.9	17.3	20	118	793	3,314	215
Idaho	4,782	3,672	3,908	4,207	3.2	20.0	21	178	1,003	2,800	181
Wyoming	4,896	3,683	4,015	4,357	5.3	21.9	22	243	817	3,078	169
Colorado	7,333	6,471	6,919	7,032	7.0	42.3	145	329	1,792	4,231	486
New Mexico	5,979	6,243	6,486	6,626	11.5	46.9	130	538	1,845	3,712	343
Arizona	8,171	6,499	7,116	7,321	9.3	43.0	169	437	1,908	4,337	419
Utah	5,881	4,766	5,317	5,478	3.2	25.3	59	180	915	4,074	223
Nevada	8,854	6,561	6,575	6,290	12.6	64.9	287	354	1,604	3,489	478

Crime Rates by State, 1980 to 1986, and by Type, 1986 *(Continued)*

					1986						
					Violent crime				Property crime		
Region, division, and state	1980, total	1984, total	1985, total	Total	Murder[1]	Forcible rape	Robbery	Aggravated assault	Burglary	Larceny—theft	Motor vehicle theft
Pacific....................	7,588	6,369	6,486	6,761	9.9	46.4	296	455	1,719	3,572	664
Washington	6,915	6,102	6,529	6,880	5.0	53.4	135	244	1,861	4,267	315
Oregon	6,687	6,244	6,730	7,081	6.6	51.1	206	286	1,967	4,163	402
California.................	7,833	6,468	6,518	6,763	11.3	44.9	343	521	1,696	3,384	762
Alaska....................	6,210	6,115	5,877	6,246	8.6	72.7	88	401	1,162	3,910	604
Hawaii...................	7,482	5,484	5,201	5,671	4.8	31.0	106	103	1,339	3,759	328

[1]Includes nonnegligent manslaughter.   [2]Forcible rape figures furnished by the state-level Uniform Crime Reporting (UCR) Program administered by the Illinois Department of State Police were not in accordance with national UCR guidelines. The 1986 forcible rape totals for most agencies in Illinois were, therefore, estimated using the national rate of forcible rapes when grouped by like agencies.   [3]Includes offenses reported by the police at the National Zoo.

Crime Rates, by Type—Selected Cities: 1986

Offenses known to the police per 100,000 population, as of July 1.

City	Crime index, total	Violent crime					Property crime			
		Total	Murder	Forcible rape	Robbery	Aggravated assault	Total	Burglary	Larceny—theft	Motor vehicle theft
Total, 12,297 agencies	6,031	687	9.0	40	242	362	5,065	1,402	3,128	535
Total, 8,298 cities	7,363	864	10.5	46	326	431	6,102	1,603	3,825	674
Selected cities:										
Baltimore, MD	8,458	1,944	30.6	84	1,020	808	6,515	1,828	3,810	877
Chicago, IL	(1)	(1)	24.8	(1)	1,030	1,116	7,543	1,874	4,054	1,615
Dallas, TX	15,143	1,896	34.1	123	914	825	13,247	3,709	7,942	1,595
Detroit, MI.............	12,801	2,487	59.1	123	1,497	807	10,314	3,553	3,852	2,909
Houston, TX............	9,448	1,156	22.9	86	614	434	8,292	2,502	3,869	1,921
Indianapolis, IN	6,317	915	13.4	93	334	475	5,402	1,752	2,936	713
Los Angeles, CA.........	9,550	2,036	25.6	71	918	1,021	7,515	1,969	3,819	1,727
Memphis, TN	9,823	1,587	24.4	139	881	542	8,236	2,776	3,498	1,962
New York, NY	8,847	1,995	22.0	49	1,126	798	6,852	1,732	3,924	1,196
Philadelphia, PA	5,233	1,046	20.8	66	586	373	4,187	1,165	2,226	796
Phoenix, AZ............	9,641	996	13.2	61	321	602	8,644	2,760	5,274	610
San Antonio, TX.........	11,396	709	18.4	92	371	228	10,687	3,320	6,442	925
San Diego, CA	7,885	843	10.1	39	394	400	7,042	1,734	4,000	1,308
San Francisco, CA	7,546	1,267	15.2	66	678	508	6,280	1,342	4,027	910
Washington, DC	8,332	1,505	31.0	52	754	668	6,827	1,727	4,124	975

[1] The rates for 1986 for forcible rape, violent crime, and crime index total are not shown because the forcible rape figures were not in accordance with national Uniform Crime Reporting guidelines.

Victimization Rates for Crimes Against Persons: 1973–85

Rates per 1,000 persons, 12 years old and over. Includes attempted crimes. Data based on National Crime Survey. Totals exclude personal larceny.

Year and Crime	Total[1]	White	Black	His-panic[2]	Male White	Male Black	Male His-panic[2]	Female White	Female Black	Female His-panic[2]	Victim–offender relationship Stranger	Victim–offender relationship Non-stranger
1973	33	32	42	36	43	53	53	21	32	22	22	11
1974	33	32	41	34	44	54	49	21	29	20	22	11
1975	33	32	43	40	42	53	50	21	34	30	21	11
1976	33	31	44	35	42	55	55	21	36	23	21	12
1977	34	33	42	40	45	57	50	22	29	32	21	13
1978	34	33	41	37	45	54	54	22	30	23	21	12
1979	35	34	42	41	44	53	55	24	32	29	22	12
1980	33	32	41	40	43	53	54	22	31	27	21	12
1981	35	33	50	39	44	61	53	23	40	26	23	12
1982	34	33	44	40	42	57	49	25	33	32	22	12
1983	31	30	41	38	39	50	48	21	33	29	18	13
1984	31	30	41	35	38	51	45	22	33	26	17	14
1985	30	29	38	30	38	47	33	21	31	27	18	12

[1] Includes races not shown separately. [2] Hispanic persons may be of any race.

Victimization Rates for Crimes Against Households: 1973–85

Rates per 1,000 households. Includes attempted offenses. Data based on National Crime Survey.

Year and Household Characteristic	Total	Burglary Total[1]	Burglary White	Burglary Black	Larceny Total[1]	Larceny White	Larceny Black	Motor vehicle theft Total[1]	Motor vehicle theft White	Motor vehicle theft Black
1973	218	92	87	133	107	108	104	19	18	24
1974	236	93	88	135	124	125	112	19	18	26
1975	237	92	87	129	125	127	115	19	19	27
1976	229	89	84	131	124	126	112	17	16	21
1977	229	89	84	122	123	124	116	17	16	21
1978	223	86	83	115	120	120	121	18	17	21
1979	235	84	80	114	134	133	133	18	17	22
1980	227	84	81	115	127	125	134	17	16	25
1981	226	88	83	134	121	119	142	17	16	24
1982	208	78	73	117	114	111	132	16	15	25
1983	190	70	67	98	105	103	119	15	13	25
1984	179	64	61	92	99	97	115	15	14	26
1985: All households.	**174**	**63**	**60**	**83**	**97**	**95**	**120**	**14**	**13**	**22**
Homeowner	145	50	48	71	83	80	115	11	10	25
Renter	226	84	84	93	123	124	124	19	19	20
Households with income of										
Under $7,500	195	86	83	100	98	98	102	11	11	10
$ 7,500–$9,999	177	60	63	46	101	98	125	15	17	(B)
$10,000–$14,999	182	67	66	78	101	97	135	14	12	29
$15,000–$24,999	176	59	57	80	104	100	136	14	11	35
$25,000–$29,999	162	54	51	96	95	92	149	13	10	48
$30,000–$49,999	173	58	56	90	99	95	154	16	15	32
$50,000 and over	180	56	55	94	104	102	156	21	20	(B)

(B) Estimated number of victimizations too small to be statistically reliable. [1] Includes other races not shown separately.

GOVERNMENT STRUCTURE AND HOW A BILL BECOMES LAW

The chart below shows the structure of the U.S. Government and its departments and agencies as of July 1, 1985. As the chart shows, the Constitution set forth the organization of the government, which operates on a system of checks and balances. The three branches of government, the legislative, executive, and judicial, each have the power to check the other. The legislative branch, the Congress, has the power to propose and make laws; the executive branch contains the office of the President, who has the ultimate power to enforce the law and oversee the government; and the judicial branch explains the law by ruling on the constitutionality of laws and trying cases.

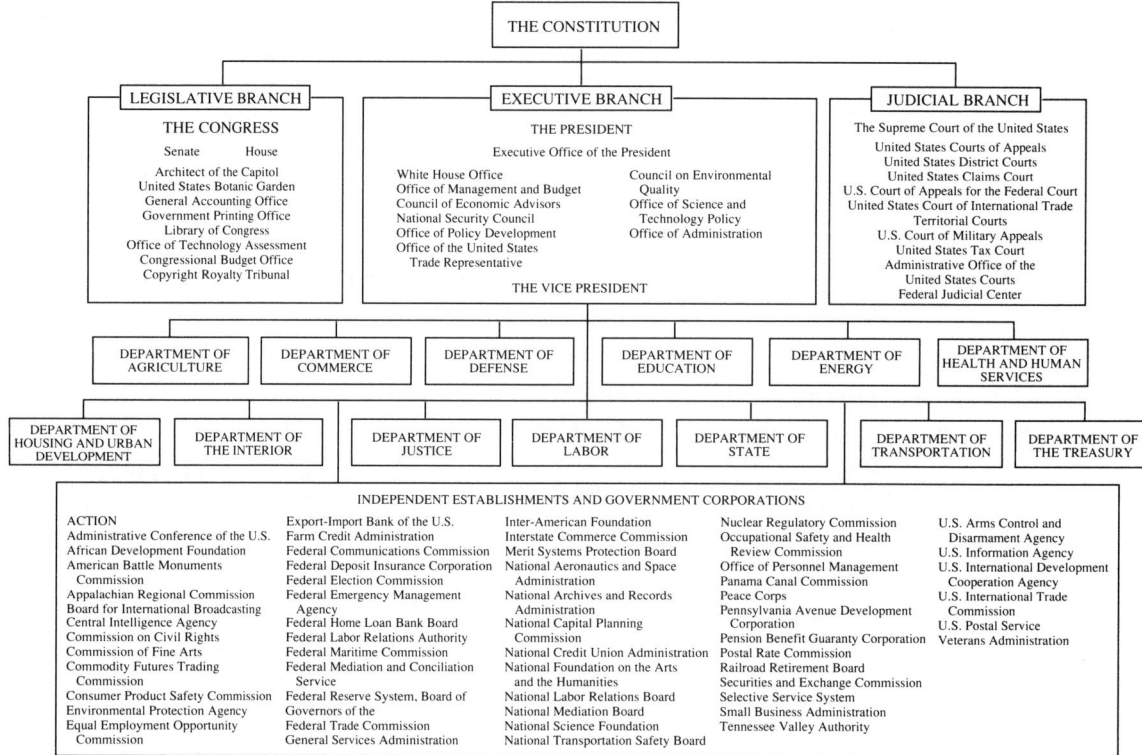

How a Bill Becomes Law

First Reading

To become law, a bill is introduced by a senator or representative in the Senate or Congress and is assigned a number or title by the clerk of the House. The bill is then assigned to the committee of the Senate or House that is responsible for the particular area the bill relates to (for example, a bill providing aid to farmers would go to the Committee on Agriculture). The committee debates the bill, listens to the opinions of interested people and members of the Congress, and sometimes offers amendments to the bill. The bill is then voted on by the committee and, if passed, is sent back to the clerk of the House. If the bill is unacceptable to the committee when they receive it, they may table it, killing consideration of the bill. This process is called the first reading of the bill.

Second and Third Readings

In the second reading, the clerk of the House reads the bill to the House, which then debates it and suggests amendments. At the third reading, after the bill is debated, a vote is called for and the title of the bill is read before the vote.

Passage

If the bill passes, it is sent to the other house, where it is again debated, amendments are added, and a vote is taken. If it passes with amendments, a joint congressional committee (composed of members of both the House and Senate) tries to reach a compromise between the two versions of the bill. If the bill is not passed by the second house, it dies.

Veto Power

When the bill is passed, it is sent to the President, who has the power to veto it. He may send the bill back to the house that originally produced it, offering his suggestions for revision. If the President signs the bill, it becomes a law.

Once back in the house, the bill is debated again in light of the President's comments and a roll-call vote is taken. To remain an active bill, it must receive at least a two-thirds vote from that house. If it does not, it is defeated. If the bill does get the support of two-thirds of that house, it is sent to the other house, where it again must receive a vote of two-thirds to override a presidential veto.

The bill is returned to the President. If the President holds on to the bill for 10 days (not including Sunday), it automatically becomes law without his signature. The President may still kill the bill through a *pocket veto* if Congress has adjourned within those 10 days.

Additional Sources of Information

Andriot, Donna; Andriot, Jay; and Andriot, Laurie. *Guide to U.S. Government Statistics*. Documents Index, 1987.

Barone, Michael, and Ujifusa, Grant, eds. *The Almanac of American Politics*. National Journal, 1987.

Barraclough, E. M. C., and Crampton, W. G., eds. *Flags of the World*. Frederick Warne, 1978.

Baydo, Gerald. *A Synoptic History of America's Past*. Random House, 1981.

Campbell, Gordon. *The Book of Flags*. Oxford University Press, 1965.

Congress and the Nation: 1981–1984. Congressional Quarterly, published every four years.

Congressional Quarterly Almanac. Congressional Quarterly, annual.

Congressional Quarterly Weekly. Congressional Quarterly, weekly.

Consumer's Resource Handbook. U.S. Office of Consumer Affairs, January 1986.

Cordasco, Francesco. *Immigrant Children in American Schools.* A. M. Kelly, 1976.

The Flag Book of the United States. National Flag Foundation, 1977.

Garwood, Alfred N. *Almanac of the Fifty States.* Information Publications, 1987.

Gebhart, John R. *Your State Flag.* Franklin, 1975.

Gervasi, Tom. *Arsenal of Democracy III.* Grove Press, 1984.

Golab, Caroline. *Immigrant Destinations.* Temple University Press, 1977.

Hatch, Jane M. *The American Book of Days,* 3rd ed. H. W. Wilson, 1978.

Lesko, Matthew. *Information U.S.A.* Viking, 1986.

Manchee, Fred B. *Our Heritage of Flowers: The Official Flowers of the United States and Canada.* Holt, Rinehart and Winston, 1970.

McClellan, Grant S. *Immigrants, Refugees, and U.S. Policy.* H. W. Wilson, 1981.

Ornstein, Norman, ed. *Vital Statistics on Congress.* American Enterprise Institute for Public Policy Research, 1988.

Smith, Whitney. *The Flag Book of the United States.* William Morrow, 1970.

26

The World

Countries of the World

Afghanistan
Area: 647,500 km² (250,000 sq. mi.)
Capital: Kabul
Government: Communist
Population: 14,183,671
Languages: Pashtu, Afghan Persian, Turkic
Religions: Sunni Muslim, Shi'a Muslim

Albania
Area: 28,750 km² (11,100 sq. mi.)
Capital: Tirana
Government: Communist
Population: 3,085,985
Languages: Albanian Tosk, Greek
Religions: Muslim, Eastern Orthodox, Roman Catholic
(before atheism campaign of 1967)

Algeria
Area: 2,381,740 km² (919,592 sq. mi.)
Capital: Algiers
Government: Republic
Population: 23,460,614
Languages: Arabic, French, Berber
Religions: Sunni Muslim, Christian, Jewish

Andorra
Area: 450 km² (188 sq. mi.)
Capital: Andorra la Vella
Government: Co-principality
Population: 47,973
Languages: Catalan, French, Castilian
Religion: Roman Catholic

Angola
Area: 1,246,700 km² (481,352 sq. mi.)
Capital: Luanda
Government: Marxist
Population: 7,950,244
Languages: Portuguese, Bantu
Religions: Roman Catholic, Protestant, indigenous
  beliefs

Anguilla
Area: 91 km² (37 sq. mi.)
Capital: The Valley
Government: British dependent territory
Population: 6,828
Language: English
Religions: Anglican, Methodist, Roman Catholic

Antigua and Barbuda
Area: 440 km² (171 sq. mi.)
Capital: St. John's
Government: British independent territory
Population: 69,280
Languages: English, local dialects
Religions: Anglican, other Protestant faiths, Roman
  Catholic

Argentina
Area: 2,766,890 km² (1,072,163 sq. mi.)
Capital: Buenos Aires
Government: Republic
Population: 31,144,775
Languages: Spanish, English, Italian, German, French
Religions: Roman Catholic, Protestant, Jewish

Aruba
Area: 193 km² (75 sq. mi.)
Capital: Oranjestad
Government: Netherlands independent territory
Population: 62,125
Languages: Dutch, Papiamento, Spanish
Religions: Roman Catholic, Protestant, Jewish, Hindu,
  Muslim

Australia
Area: 7,686,850 km² (2,985,184 sq. mi.)
Capital: Canberra
Government: Federal parliamentary state affiliated
  with Great Britain
Population: 16,072,986
Languages: English, native languages
Religions: Anglican, other Protestant faiths, Roman
  Catholic

Austria
Area: 83,850 km² (32,563 sq. mi.)
Capital: Vienna
Government: Federal republic
Population: 7,569,283
Language: German
Religions: Roman Catholic, Protestant

Bahamas
Area: 13,940 km² (5,414 sq. mi.)
Capital: Nassau
Government: Independent commonwealth affiliated
  with Great Britain
Population: 238,817
Languages: English, Creole
Religions: Anglican, other Protestant faiths, Roman
  Catholic

Bahrain
Area: 620 km² (240 sq. mi.)
Capital: Manama
Government: Traditional monarchy
Population: 464,102
Languages: Arabic, English, Farsi, Urdu
Religions: Shi'a Muslim, Sunni Muslim

Bangladesh
Area: 144,000 km² (55,598 sq. mi.)
Capital: Dhaka
Government: Republic
Population: 107,087,586
Languages: Bangla, English
Religions: Muslim, Hindu, Buddhist, Christian

Barbados
Area: 430 km² (166 sq. mi.)
Capital: Bridgetown
Government: Independent sovereign state within
  British Commonwealth
Population: 323,839
Language: English
Religions: Anglican, Methodist, Roman Catholic,
  Moravian

Barbuda
See Antigua and Barbuda.

Belgium
Area: 30,510 km² (11,783 sq. mi.)
Capital: Brussels
Government: Constitutional monarchy
Population: 9,873,066
Languages: Flemish, French, German
Religions: Roman Catholic, Protestant

Belize
Area: 22,960 km² (8,867 sq. mi.)
Capital: Belmopan
Government: Parliamentary independent state of
  British Commonwealth
Population: 168,204
Languages: English, Spanish Maya, Carib
Religions: Roman Catholic, Anglican, Seventh-Day
  Adventist

Benin
Area: 112,620 km² (43,484 sq. mi.)
Capital: Porto-Novo
Government: Soviet-type civilian government
Population: 4,339,096
Languages: French, Fon, Yoruba, tribal dialects
Religions: Indigenous beliefs, Muslim, Christian

Bermuda
Area: 50 km² (19 sq. mi.)
Capital: Hamilton
Government: British dependent territory
Population: 58,033
Language: English
Religions: Anglican, other Protestant faiths, Roman
  Catholic

Bhutan
Area: 47,000 km² (1,815 sq. mi.)
Capital: Thimphu
Government: Monarchy
Population: 1,472,911
Languages: Dzongkha, other Tibetan dialects, Nepalese
Religions: Lamaistic Buddhism, Hindu

Bolivia
Area: 1,098,580 km² (424,164 sq. mi.)
Capital: La Paz
Government: Republic
Population: 6,309,642
Languages: Spanish, Quechua, Aymara
Religions: Roman Catholic, Protestant

Botswana
Area: 600,370 km² (231,805 sq. mi.)
Capital: Gaborone
Government: Parliamentary republic affiliated with
  British Commonwealth
Population: 1,149,141
Languages: English, Setswana
Religions: Indigenous beliefs, Christian

Brazil
Area: 8,511,970 km² (3,286,488 sq. mi.)
Capital: Brasilia
Government: Federal republic
Population: 147,094,739
Languages: Portuguese, English
Religion: Roman Catholic

British Indian Ocean Territory
Area: 80 km² (31 sq. mi.)
Capital: None
Government: British colony
Population: No permanent civilian population.
  Consists mainly of Diego Garcia and 2,300 other
  islands strategically located in the central
  Indian Ocean.

British Virgin Islands
Area: 150 km² (58 sq. mi.)
Capital: Road Town
Government: British dependent territory
Population: 12,374
Language: English
Religions: Anglican, other Protestant faiths, Roman
  Catholic

Brunei
Area: 5,770 km² (2,226 sq. mi.)
Capital: Bandar Seri Begawan
Government: Constitutional sultanate
Population: 249,961
Languages: Malay, English, Chinese
Religions: Muslim, Christian, Buddhist

Bulgaria
Area: 110,910 km² (42,823 sq. mi.)
Capital: Sofia
Government: Communist
Population: 8,960,749
Language: Bulgarian
Religions: Bulgarian Orthodox, Muslim, Jewish,
  Roman Catholic, Protestant, Gregorian-Armenian

Burkina Faso
Area: 274,200 km² (105,869 sq. mi.)
Capital: Ouagadougou
Government: Military
Population: 8,276,272
Languages: French, Sudanic tribal dialects
Religions: Indigenous beliefs, Muslim, Christian

Burma
Area: 676,550 km² (261,218 sq. mi.)
Capital: Rangoon
Government: Republic
Population: 38,822,484
Languages: Burmese, ethnic dialects
Religions: Buddhist, indigenous beliefs, Muslim, Christian

Burundi
Area: 27,830 km² (10,747 sq. mi.)
Capital: Bujumbura
Government: Republic
Population: 5,005,504
Languages: Kirundi, French, Swahili
Religions: Roman Catholic, Protestant, indigenous
  beliefs, Muslim

Cambodia
Area: 181,040 km² (69,900 sq. mi.)
Capital: Phnom Penh
Government: Communist
Population: 6,536,079
Languages: Khmer, French
Religion: Theravada Buddhist

Cameroon
Area: 475,440 km² (183,569 sq. mi.)
Capital: Yaounde
Government: Unitary republic
Population: 10,255,332
Languages: English, French, African languages
Religions: Indigenous beliefs, Christian, Muslim

Canada
Area: 9,976,140 km² (3,851,809 sq. mi.)
Capital: Ottawa
Government: Federal state affiliated with Great Britain
Population: 25,857,943
Languages: English, French
Religions: Roman Catholic, United Church, Anglican

Cape Verde
Area: 4,030 km² (1,557 sq. mi.)
Capital: Praia
Government: Republic
Population: 344,282
Languages: Portuguese, Crioulo
Religions: Roman Catholic, indigenous beliefs

Cayman Islands
Area: 260 km² (100 sq. mi.)
Capital: George Town
Government: British dependent territory
Population: 23,192
Language: English
Religions: United Church, Anglican, Roman Catholic

Central African Republic
Area: 622,980 km² (240,535 sq. mi.)
Capital: Bangui
Government: Republic (with military rule since 1981)
Population: 2,669,293
Languages: French, Sangho, Arabic, Hunsa, Swahili
Religions: Indigenous beliefs, Protestant, Roman
  Catholic, Muslim, animist

Chad
Area: 1,284,000 km² (495,750 sq. mi.)
Capital: N'Djamena
Government: Republic
Population: 4,646,054
Languages: French, Arabic, Sara, Sango, African dialects
Religions: Muslim, indigenous beliefs, Christian

Chile
Area: 756,950 km² (292,258 sq. mi.)
Capital: Santiago
Government: Republic with military rule
Population: 12,448,008
Language: Spanish
Religions: Roman Catholic, Protestant, Jewish

China
Area: 9,596,960 km² (3,691,500 sq. mi.)
Capital: Beijing
Government: Communist
Population: 1,064,147,038
Languages: Mandarin, Yue, Wu, Fuzhou, Minan,
  Xiang, Gan, Hakka, local dialects
Religions: Confucianist, Taoist, Buddhist, Muslim,
  Christian

Christmas Island
Area: 130 km² (50 sq. mi.)
Capital: The Settlement
Government: Australian territory
Population: 2,243
Languages: English, Chinese, Malayan

Colombia
Area: 1,138,910 km² (439,737 sq. mi.)
Capital: Bogotá
Government: Republic
Population: 30,660,504
Language: Spanish
Religion: Roman Catholic

Comoros
Area: 2,170 km² (838 sq. mi.)
Capital: Moroni
Government: Independent republic
Population: 415,220
Languages: Shaafi Islam, Malagasy, French
Religions: Sunni Muslim, Roman Catholic

Congo
Area: 342,000 km² (126,360 sq. mi.)
Capital: Brazzaville
Government: People's republic
Population: 2,082,154
Languages: French, Lingala, Kikongo
Religions: Animist, Christian, Muslim

Cook Islands
Area: 230 km² (89 sq. mi.)
Capital: Avarua
Government: Self-governing in association with New
 Zealand
Population: 17,898
Language: English
Religion: Cook Islands Christian Church

Costa Rica
Area: 50,700 km² (19,600 sq. mi.)
Capital: San Jose
Government: Democratic republic
Population: 2,811,652
Language: Spanish
Religion: Roman Catholic

Cuba
Area: 110,860 km² (42,827 sq. mi.)
Capital: Havana
Government: Communist
Population: 10,259,473
Language: Spanish
Religion: Roman Catholic

Cyprus
Area: 9,250 km² (3,572 sq. mi.)
Capital: Nicosia
Government: Republic
Population: 683,651
Languages: Greek, Turkish, English
Religions: Greek Orthodox, Muslim, Armenian,
 Maronite

Czechoslovakia
Area: 127,870 km² (49,375 sq. mi.)
Capital: Prague
Government: Communist
Population: 15,581,993
Languages: Czech, Slovak, Hungarian
Religions: Roman Catholic, Protestant, Eastern
 Orthodox

Denmark
Area: 43,070 km² (16,632 sq. mi.)
Capital: Copenhagen
Government: Constitutional monarchy
Population: 5,121,766
Languages: Danish, Faroese, Greenlandic, German
Religions: Protestant, Roman Catholic

Djibouti
Area: 22,000 km² (8,880 sq. mi.)
Capital: Djibouti
Government: Republic
Population: 312,405
Languages: French, Arabic, Somali, Afar
Religions: Muslim, Christian

Dominica
Area: 750 km² (299 sq. mi.)
Capital: Roseau
Government: Independent state within British
 Commonwealth
Population: 94,191
Languages: English, French patois
Religions: Roman Catholic, Anglican, other Protestant
 faiths

Dominican Republic
Area: 48,730 km² (18,703 sq. mi.)
Capital: Santo Domingo
Government: Republic
Population: 6,960,743
Language: Spanish
Religion: Roman Catholic

East Germany *See* German Democratic Republic.

Ecuador
Area: 283,560 km² (109,484 sq. mi.)
Capital: Quito
Government: Republic
Population: 9,954,609
Languages: Spanish, Quechua
Religion: Roman Catholic

Egypt
Area: 1,001,450 km² (386,663 sq. mi.)
Capital: Cairo
Government: Republic
Population: 51,929,962
Languages: Arabic, English, French
Religions: Muslim, Coptic Christian

El Salvador
Area: 21,040 km² (8,124 sq. mi.)
Capital: San Salvador
Government: Republic
Population: 5,260,478
Language: Spanish
Religion: Roman Catholic

Equatorial Guinea
Area: 28,050 km² (10,831 sq. mi.)
Capital: Malabo
Government: Republic
Languages: Spanish, pidgin English, Fang
Religions: Christian, pagan

Ethiopia
Area: 1,221,900 km² (471,800 sq. mi.)
Capital: Addis Ababa
Government: Unitary single-party People's Republic
Population: 46,706,229
Languages: Amharic, Tigrinya, Orominga, Arabic,
 English
Religions: Muslim, Ethiopan Orthodox, animist

Falkland Islands
Area: 12,170 km² (4,699 sq. mi.)
Capital: Stanley
Government: British dependent territory
Population: 1,821
Language: English
Religion: Anglican

Faroe Islands
Area: 1,400 km² (541 sq. mi.)
Capital: Torshavn
Government: Self-governing province of Denmark
Population: 46,429
Languages: Faroese, Danish
Religion: Evangelical Lutheran

Fiji
Area: 18,270 km² (7,056 sq. mi.)
Capital: Suva
Government: Independent parliamentary state within
    British Commonwealth
Population: 727,902
Languages: English, Fijian, Hindustani
Religions: Christian, Hindu, Muslim

Finland
Area: 337,030 km² (130,557 sq. mi.)
Capital: Helsinki
Government: Republic
Population: 4,939,880
Languages: Finnish, Swedish, Lapp, Russian
Religions: Evangelical Lutheran, Greek Orthodox

France
Area: 547,030 km² (211,208 sq. mi.)
Capital: Paris
Government: Republic
Population: 55,596,030
Languages: French, regional dialects
Religions: Roman Catholic, Protestant, Jewish, Muslim

French Guiana
Area: 91,000 km² (35,135 sq. mi.)
Capital: Cayenne
Government: French department
Population: 92,038
Language: French
Religion: Roman Catholic

French Polynesia
Area: 4,000 km² (1,544 sq. mi.)
Capital: Papeete
Government: French territory
Languages: Polynesian, Chinese, French
Religions: Protestant, Roman Catholic

Gabon
Area: 267,670 km² (103,347 sq. mi.)
Capital: Libreville
Government: Republic
Population: 1,039,006
Languages: Fang, Myene, Bateke, Bapounou/Eschira,
    Bandjabi
Religions: Christian, Muslim, animist

Gambia
Area: 11,300 km² (4,361 sq. mi.)
Capital: Banjul
Government: Independent republic affiliated with
    Senegal
Population: 760,362
Languages: English, Mandinka, Wolof, Fula, local
    dialects
Religions: Muslim, Christian, indigenous beliefs

German Democratic Republic (East Germany)
Area: 108,330 km² (41,767 sq. mi.)
Capital: East Berlin
Government: Communist
Population: 16,610,265
Language: German
Religions: Protestant, Roman Catholic

Germany, Federal Republic of (West Germany)
Area: 248,580 km² (96,025 sq. mi.)
Capital: Bonn
Government: Federal republic
Population: 60,989,419
Language: German
Religions: Roman Catholic, Protestant

Ghana
Area: 238,540 km² (92,100 sq. mi.)
Capital: Accra
Government: Military
Population: 13,948,925
Languages: English, Akan, Mole-Dagbani, Ewe,
    Ga-Adangbe
Religions: Indigenous beliefs, Muslim, Christian

Gibraltar
Area: 6.5 km² (2.5 sq. mi.)
Capital: Gibraltar
Government: British dependent territory
Population: 29,048
Languages: English, Spanish, Italian, Portuguese,
    Russian
Religions: Roman Catholic, Anglican, Jewish

Greece
Area: 131,940 km² (50,944 sq. mi.)
Capital: Athens
Government: Parliamentary
Population: 9,987,785
Languages: Greek, English, French
Religions: Greek Orthodox, Muslim

Greenland
Area: 2,175,600 km² (840,000 sq. mi.)
Capital: Godthab
Government: Self-governing province of Denmark
Population: 54,205
Languages: Danish, Eskimo dialects
Religions: Evangelical Lutheran

Grenada
Area: 340 km² (133 sq. mi.)
Capital: St. George's
Government: Independent state affiliated with Great
   Britain
Population: 84,748
Languages: English, French
Religions: Roman Catholic, Anglican, other Protestant
   faiths

Guadeloupe
Area: 1,780 km² (687 sq. mi.)
Capital: Basse-Terre
Government: French department
Population: 336,354
Languages: French, Creole
Religions: Roman Catholic, Hindu, pagan African

Guatemala
Area: 108,890 km² (42,042 sq. mi.)
Capital: Guatemala
Government: Republic
Population: 8,622,387
Languages: Spanish, Quiche, Cakchiquel, Kekchi,
   Amerindian dialects
Religions: Roman Catholic, Protestant, traditional
   Mayan

Guernsey
Area: 194 km² (75 sq. mi.)
Capital: St. Peter Port
Government: British dependency
Population: 52,947
Languages: English, French, Norman-French
Religions: Anglican, other Protestant faiths, Roman
   Catholic

Guinea
Area: 245,860 km² (94,926 sq. mi.)
Capital: Conakry
Government: Republic
Population: 6,737,760
Languages: French, tribal languages
Religions: Muslim, indigenous beliefs, Christian

Guinea-Bissau
Area: 36,120 km² (13,948 sq. mi.)
Capital: Bissau
Government: Republic
Population: 928,425
Languages: Portuguese, Criolo, tribal languages
Religions: Indigenous beliefs, Muslim, Christian

Guyana
Area: 214,970 km² (83,000 sq. mi.)
Capital: Georgetown
Government: Cooperative republic
Population: 765,844
Languages: English, Amerindian dialects
Religions: Christian, Hindu, Muslim

Haiti
Area: 27,750 km² (10,714 sq. mi.)
Capital: Port-au-Prince
Government: Provisional military
Population: 6,187,115
Languages: French, Creole
Religions: Roman Catholic, voodoo, Protestant

Honduras
Area: 112,090 km² (43,277 sq. mi.)
Capital: Tegucigalpa
Government: Republic
Population: 4,823,818
Languages: Spanish, Amerindian dialects
Religions: Roman Catholic, Protestant

Hong Kong
Area: 1,040 km²
Capital: Victoria
Government: British colony (until 1997)
Population: 5,608,610
Languages: Cantonese, English
Religions: Local religions, Christian

Hungary
Area: 93,030 km² (35,921 sq. mi.)
Capital: Budapest
Government: Communist
Population: 10,609,447
Language: Hungarian (Magyar)
Religions: Roman Catholic, Protestant

Iceland
Area: 103,000 km² (39,769 sq. mi.)
Capital: Reykjavik
Government: Republic
Population: 244,676
Language: Icelandic
Religions: Evangelical Lutheran, other Protestant
   faiths, Roman Catholic

India
Area: 3,287,590 km² (1,269,213 sq. mi.)
Capital: New Delhi
Government: Federal republic
Population: 800,325,817
Languages: Hindi, English, official and local
   languages, including 24 used by over 1 million
   people
Religions: Hindu, Muslim, Christian, Sikh, Buddhist

Indonesia
Area: 1,904,570 km² (735,272 sq. mi.)
Capital: Jakarta
Government: Republic
Population: 180,425,534
Languages: Indonesian, Javanese, English, Dutch
Religions: Muslim, Protestant, Roman Catholic, Hindu

Iran
Area: 1,648,000 km² (636,296 sq. mi.)
Capital: Teheran
Government: Theocratic republic
Population: 50,407,763
Languages: Farsi, Turki, Kurdish, Arabic, English, French
Religions: Shi'a Muslim, Sunni Muslim, Zoroastrian, Jewish, Christian, Baha'i

Iraq
Area: 434,920 km² (167,925 sq. mi.)
Capital: Baghdad
Government: Republic
Population: 16,970,948
Languages: Arabic, Kurdish, Assyrian, Armenian
Religions: Shi'a Muslim, Sunni Muslim, Christian

Ireland
Area: 70,280 km² (27,136 sq. mi.)
Capital: Dublin
Government: Republic
Population: 3,534,553
Languages: Irish Gaelic, English
Religions: Roman Catholic, Anglican

Israel
Area: (excluding occupied territories) 20,770 km² (8,019 sq. mi.)
Capital: Jerusalem
Government: Republic
Population: 4,222,118 (excluding occupied territories)
Languages: Hebrew, Arabic, English
Religions: Jewish, Muslim, Christian, Druze
See also West Bank and Gaza Strip.

Italy
Area: 301,230 km² (116,318 sq. mi.)
Capital: Rome
Government: Republic
Population: 57,350,850
Languages: Italian, German, French, Slovene
Religion: Roman Catholic

Ivory Coast
Area: 322,460 km² (124,504 sq. mi.)
Capital: Abidjan (also Yamoussoukro)
Government: Republic
Population: 10,766,632
Languages: French, Dioula, tribal languages
Religions: Indigenous beliefs, Muslim, Christian

Jamaica
Area: 10,990 km² (4,409 sq. mi.)
Capital: Kingston
Government: Independent state within British Commonwealth
Population: 2,455,536
Languages: English, Creole
Religions: Anglican, other Protestant faiths, Roman Catholic, spiritualist cults

Japan
Area: 372,310 km² (143,751 sq. mi.)
Capital: Tokyo
Government: Constitutional monarchy
Population: 122,124,293
Language: Japanese
Religions: Shinto, Buddhist, Christian

Jersey
Area: 117 km² (45 sq. mi.)
Capital: Saint Helier
Government: British dependency
Population: 80,511
Languages: English, French, Norman-French
Religions: Anglican, other Protestant faiths, Roman Catholic

Jordan
Area: 97,740 km² (37,738 sq. mi.)
Capital: Amman
Government: Constitutional monarchy
Population: 2,761,695 (excluding West Bank)
Languages: Arabic, English
Religions: Sunni Muslim, Christian
See also West Bank and Gaza Strip.

Kampuchea
See Cambodia.

Kenya
Area: 582,650 km² (224,961 sq. mi.)
Capital: Nairobi
Government: Republic within British Commonwealth
Population: 22,377,802
Languages: English, Swahili, local languages
Religions: Protestant, Roman Catholic, indigenous beliefs, Muslim

Kiribati
Area: 710 km² (277 sq. mi.)
Capital: Tarawa
Government: Republic
Population: 66,441
Languages: English, Gilbertese
Religions: Roman Catholic, Protestant, Seventh-Day Adventist, Baha'i

Korea, North
Area: 120,540 km² (46,540 sq. mi.)
Capital: P'yongyang
Government: Communist
Population: 21,447,977
Language: Korean
Religions: Buddhist, Confucianist

Korea, South
Area: 98,480 km² (38,221 sq. mi.)
Capital: Seoul
Government: Republic
Population: 41,986,669
Languages: Korean, English
Religions: Confucianist, Christian, Buddhist, Shamanist, Chondokyo

Kuwait
Area: 17,820 km² (6,880 sq. mi.)
Capital: Kuwait
Government: Constitutional monarchy
Population: 1,863,615
Languages: Arabic, English
Religions: Sunni Muslim, Shi'a Muslim, Christian, Hindu, Parsi

Laos
Area: 236,800 km² (91,400 sq. mi.)
Capital: Vientiane
Government: Communist
Population: 3,765,887
Languages: Lao, French, English
Religions: Buddhist, animist

Lebanon
Area: 10,400 km² (3,950 sq. mi.)
Capital: Beirut
Government: Republic
Population: 3,320,522
Languages: Arabic, French, Armenian, English
Religions: Muslim, Druze, Christian

Lesotho
Area: 30,350 km² (11,720 sq. mi.)
Capital: Maseru
Government: Constitutional monarchy affiliated with British Commonwealth
Population: 1,621,932
Languages: Sethoso, English, Zulu, Xhosa
Religions: Christian, indigenous beliefs

Liberia
Area: 111,370 km² (43,000 sq. mi.)
Capital: Monrovia
Government: Republic, with military rule
Population: 2,384,189
Languages: English, Niger-Congo
Religions: Christian, Muslim, indigenous beliefs

Libya
Area: 1,759,540 km² (679,363 sq. mi.)
Capital: Tripoli
Government: Republic, with military rule
Population: 3,306,825
Languages: Arabic, Italian, English
Religion: Sunni Muslim

Liechtenstein
Area: 160 km² (62 sq. mi.)
Capital: Vaduz
Government: Constitutional monarchy
Population: 27,074
Languages: German, Alemannic
Religions: Roman Catholic, Protestant

Luxembourg
Area: 2,586 km² (999 sq. mi.)
Capital: Luxembourg
Government: Constitutional monarchy
Population: 366,127
Languages: Luxembourgian, German, French, English
Religions: Roman Catholic, Protestant, Jewish

Macau
Area: 20 km² (8 sq. mi.)
Capital: Macau
Government: Chinese territory under Portuguese administration
Population: 437,822
Languages: Chinese, Portuguese
Religions: Buddhist, Roman Catholic

Madagascar
Area: 587,040 km² (226,658 sq. mi.)
Capital: Antananarivo
Government: Presidential with Supreme Revolutionary Council
Population: 10,730,754
Languages: French, Malagasy
Religions: Indigenous beliefs, Christian, Muslim

Malawi
Area: 118,480 km² (45,747 sq. mi.)
Capital: Lilongwe
Government: Republic
Population: 7,437,911
Languages: English, Chichewa, Tombuka
Religions: Protestant, Roman Catholic, Muslim, indigenous beliefs

Malaysia
Area: 329,750 km² (127,581 sq. mi.)
Capital: Kuala Lumpur
Government: Constitutional monarchy with hereditary rulers in peninsular states
Population: 16,068,516
Languages: Malay, English, Tamil, Mandarin, Hakka, tribal dialects
Religions: Muslim, Buddhist, Hindu, Christian, Confucianist

Maldives
Area: 300 km² (115 sq. mi.)
Capital: Male
Government: Republic
Population: 195,837
Languages: Dihevi, English
Religion: Sunni Muslim

Mali
Area: 1,240,000 km² (478,767 sq. mi.)
Capital: Bamako
Government: Republic
Population: 8,422,810
Languages: French, Bambara
Religions: Muslim, indigenous beliefs, Christian

Malta
Area: 320 km² (122 sq. mi.)
Capital: Valletta
Government: Independent republic affiliated with British Commonwealth
Population: 361,704
Languages: Maltese, English
Religion: Roman Catholic

Man, Isle of
Area: 588 km² (227 sq. mi.)
Capital: Douglas
Government: Self-governing British dependent
    territory
Population: 64,934
Languages: English, Manx Gaelic
Religions: Anglican, other Protestant faiths, Roman
    Catholic

Martinique
Area: 1,100 km² (425 sq. mi.)
Capital: Fort-de-France
Government: French department
Population: 344,922
Languages: French, Creole patois
Religions: Roman Catholic, Hindu, pagan African

Mauritania
Area: 1,030,700 km² (1,781,000 sq. mi.)
Capital: Nouakchott
Government: Republic
Population: 1,863,208
Languages: Hasaniya, Arabic, French, Toucouleur,
    Fula, Sarakole, Wolof
Religion: Muslim

Mauritius
Area: 1,860 km² (790 sq. mi.)
Capital: Port Louis
Government: Independent state affiliated with Great
    Britain
Population: 1,079,627
Languages: English, Creole, French, Hindi, Urdu,
    Hakka, Bojpoori
Religions: Hindu, Roman Catholic, Anglican, Muslim

Mayotte
Area: 375 km² (145 sq. mi.)
Capital: Dzaoudzi
Government: French territory
Population: 64,481
Languages: Mahorian, French
Religions: Muslim, Christian

Mexico
Area: 1,972,550 km² (756,062 sq. mi.)
Capital: Mexico City
Government: Federal republic
Population: 81,860,566
Language: Spanish
Religions: Roman Catholic, Protestant

Monaco
Area: 1.9 km² (.7 sq. mi.)
Capital: Monaco
Government: Constitutional monarchy
Population: 28,641
Languages: French, English, Italian, Monegarque
Religion: Roman Catholic

Mongolia
Area: 1,565,000 km² (604,250 sq. mi.)
Capital: Ulaanbaatar
Government: Communist
Population: 2,011,066
Languages: Khalkha Mongol, Turkic, Russian,
    Chinese
Religions: Tibetan Buddhist, Muslim

Montserrat
Area: 100 km² (38.6 sq. mi.)
Capital: Plymouth
Government: British indepenent territory
Population: 12,076
Language: English
Religions: Anglican, other Protestant faiths, Roman
    Catholic

Morocco
Area: 446,550 km² (177,115 sq. mi.)
Capital: Rabat
Government: Constitutional monarchy
Population: 23,361,495
Languages: Arabic, French, Berber dialects
Religions: Muslim, Christian, Jewish

Mozambique
Area: 801,950 km² (309,496 sq. mi.)
Capital: Maputo
Government: People's republic
Population: 14,535,805
Languages: Portuguese, indigenous languages
Religions: Indigenous beliefs, Christian, Muslim

Namibia
Area: 824,290 km² (318,259 sq. mi.)
Capital: Windhoek
Government: South African administrative
    protectorate
Population: 1,273,263
Languages: Afrikaans, German, English, indigenous
    languages
Religions: Christian, indigenous beliefs

Nauru
Area: 20 km² (8 sq. mi.)
Capital: None (government agencies in Yaren District)
Government: Republic
Population: 8,748
Languages: Nauruan, English
Religions: Protestant, Roman Catholic

Nepal
Area: 140,800 km² (54,362 sq. mi.)
Capital: Kathmandu
Government: Constitutional monarchy
Population: 17,814,294
Languages: Nepali, local languages
Religions: Hindu, Buddhist, Muslim, Christian

Netherlands
Area: 37,310 km² (15,770 sq. mi.)
Capitals: Amsterdam and The Hague
Government: Constitutional monarchy
Population: 14,641,554
Language: Dutch
Religions: Roman Catholic, Protestant

Netherlands Antilles
Area: 960 km² (371 sq. mi.)
Capital: Willemstad (on Curacao)
Government: Autonomous Netherlands territory
Population: 182,218
Languages: Dutch, Papiamento, English, Spanish
Religions: Roman Catholic, Protestant, Jewish,
  Seventh-Day Adventist

New Caledonia
Area: 19,060 km² (7,359 sq. mi.)
Capital: Noumea
Government: French territory
Population: 149,795
Languages: French, Melanesian-Polynesian dialects
Religions: Roman Catholic, Protestant

New Zealand
Area: 268,680 km² (103,736 sq. mi.)
Capital: Wellington
Government: Independent state within
British   Commonwealth
Population: 3,307,239
Languages: English, Maori
Religions: Christian, Hindu, Confucian

Nicaragua
Area: 130,000 km² (50,193 sq. mi.)
Capital: Managua
Government: Republic
Population: 3,319,059
Languages: Spanish, English, Amerindian dialects
Religion: Roman Catholic

Niger
Area: 1,267,000 km² (489,191 sq. mi.)
Capital: Niamey
Government: Republic (under military control)
Population: 6,988,540
Languages: French, Hausa, Djerma
Religions: Muslim, indigenous beliefs, Christian

Nigeria
Area: 923,770 km² (356,669 sq. mi.)
Capital: Lagos
Government: Military
Population: 108,579,764
Languages: English, Hausa, Yoruba, Ibo, Fulani
Religions: Muslim, Christian, indigenous beliefs

Niue
Area: 260 km² (100 sq. mi.)
Capital: Alofi
Government: Self-governing territory affiliated with
  New Zealand
Population: 2,602
Languages: Polynesian/Tongan-Samoan, English
Religions: Niuean, Mormon, Roman Catholic,
  Jehovah's Witness, Seventh-Day Adventist

Norfolk Island
Area: 40 km² (15.4 sq. mi.)
Capital: Kingston
Government: Australian territory
Population: 2,537
Languages: English, Norfolk
Religions: Anglican, other Protestant faiths, Roman
  Catholic, Seventh-Day Adventist

Norway
Area: 324,220 km² (149,411 sq. mi.)
Capital: Oslo
Government: Constitutional monarchy
Population: 4,178,545
Languages: Norwegian, Lapp, Finnish
Religions: Evangelical Lutheran, other Protestant
  faiths, Roman Catholic

Oman
Area: 212,460 km² (82,030 sq. mi.)
Capital: Muscat
Government: Absolute monarchy
Population: 1,226,923
Languages: Arabic, English, Baluchi, Zanzibari
Religions: Ibadhi Muslim, Sunni Musim, Shi'a Muslim,
  Hindu

Pakistan
Area: 803,940 km² (310,404 sq. mi.)
Capital: Islamabad
Government: Federal republic
Population: 104,600,799
Languages: Urdu, English, Punjabi, Sindhi, Pushtu,
  Baluchi
Religions: Muslim, Christian, Hindu

Panama
Area: 77,080 km² (29,762 sq. mi.)
Capital: Panama
Government: Centralized republic
Population: 2,274,833
Languages: Spanish, English
Religions: Roman Catholic, Protestant

Papua New Guinea
Area: 461,690 km² (178,704 sq. mi.)
Capital: Port Moresby
Government: Independent parliamentary state within
  British Commonwealth
Population: 3,395,000
Languages: English, pidgin English, Motu, local
  dialects
Religions: Roman Catholic, Protestant

Paraguay
Area: 406,750 km² (157,048 sq. mi.)
Capital: Asuncion
Government: Republic
Population: 4,251,924
Languages: Spanish, Guarani
Religions: Roman Catholic, Mennonite, other
    Protestant faiths

Peru
Area: 1,285,220 km² (496,225 sq. mi.)
Capital: Lima
Government: Republic
Population: 20,738,218
Languages: Spanish, Quechua, Aymara
Religion: Roman Catholic

Philippines
Area: 300,000 km² (115,831 sq. mi.)
Capital: Manila
Government: Republic
Population: 61,524,761
Languages: Pilipino (Tagalog), English
Religions: Roman Catholic, Protestant, Muslim,
    Buddhist

Pitcairn Islands
Area: 47 km² (18 sq. mi.)
Capital: Adamstown
Government: British dependent territory
Population: 62
Languages: English, English/Tahitian dialect
Religion: Seventh-Day Adventist

Poland
Area: 312,680 km² (120,727 sq. mi.)
Capital: Warsaw
Government: Communist
Population: 37,726,699
Language: Polish
Religions: Roman Catholic, Uniate, Greek Orthodox,
    Protestant

Portugal
Area: 92,080 km² (35,553 sq. mi.)
Capital: Lisbon
Government: Republic
Population: 10,314,727
Language: Portuguese
Religions: Roman Catholic, Protestant

Qatar
Area: 11,000 km² (4,416 sq. mi.)
Capital: Doha
Government: Traditional monarchy
Population: 315,741
Languages: Arabic, English
Religion: Muslim

Reunion
Area: 2,510 km² (969 sq. mi.)
Capital: Saint-Denis
Government: French department
Population: 549,697
Languages: French, Creole
Religion: Roman Catholic

Rumania
Area: 237,500 km² (91,699 sq. mi.)
Capital: Bucharest
Government: Communist
Population: 22,936,503
Languages: Rumanian, Hungarian, German
Religions: Rumanian Orthodox, Roman Catholic,
    Protestant, Jewish

Russia
See Soviet Union.

Rwanda
Area: 26,340 km² (10,169 sq. mi.)
Capital: Kigali
Government: Republic (under military control)
Population: 6,811,336
Languages: Kingyarwanda, French, Kiswahili
Religions: Roman Catholic, Protestant, Muslim,
    indigenous beliefs

St. Christopher and Nevis
Area: 360 km² (139 sq. mi.)
Capitals: Basseterre; Charlestown
Government: Independent state within British
    Commonwealth
Population: 54,775
Language: English
Religions: Anglican, other Protestant faiths, Roman
    Catholic

St. Helena
Area: 310 km² (120 sq. mi.)
Capital: Jamestown
Population: 8,524
Language: English
Religions: Anglican, other Protestant faiths, Roman
    Catholic

St. Lucia
Area: 620 km² (238 sq. mi.)
Capital: Castries
Government: Independent state within British
    Commonwealth
Population: 152,305
Languages: English, French patois
Religions: Roman Catholic, Protestant, Anglican

St. Vincent and the Grenadines
Area: 340 km² (150 sq. mi.)
Capital: Kingstown
Government: Independent state within British
    Commonwealth
Population: 131,215
Languages: English, French patois
Religions: Anglican, other Protestant faiths, Roman
    Catholic, Seventh-Day Adventist

San Marino
Area: 60 km² (23 sq. mi.)
Capital: San Marino
Government: Republic
Population: 22,791
Language: Italian
Religion: Roman Catholic

São Tomé and Principe
Area: 960 km² (372 sq. mi.)
Capital: São Tomé
Government: Republic
Population: 114,025
Language: Portuguese
Religions: Roman Catholic, Protestant, Seventh-Day
   Adventist

Saudi Arabia
Area: 2,149,690 km² (830,000 sq. mi.)
Capital: Riyadh
Government: Monarchy
Population: 14,904,794
Language: Arabic
Religion: Muslim

Senegal
Area: 196,190 km² (75,954 sq. mi.)
Capital: Dakar
Government: Republic affiliated with Gambia
Population: 7,064,025
Languages: French, Wolof, Pulaar, Dialo, Mandingo
Religions: Muslim, indigenous beliefs, Christian

Seychelles
Area: 280 km² (119 sq. mi.)
Capital: Victoria
Government: Republic within British Commonwealth
Population: 67,552
Languages: English, French, Creole
Religions: Roman Catholic, Anglican

Sierra Leone
Area: 71,740 km² (27,699 sq. mi.)
Capital: Freetown
Government: Republic
Population: 3,754,088
Languages: English, Mende, Krio, Temne

Singapore
Area: 580 km² (239 sq. mi.)
Capital: Singapore
Government: Republic within British Commonwealth
Population: 2,616,236
Languages: Chinese, Tamil, Malay, English
Religions: Buddhist, Muslim, Christian, Hindu, Sikh,
   Taoist, Confucianist

Solomon Islands
Area: 28,450 km² (10,983 sq. mi.)
Capital: Honiara
Government: Independent parliamentary state within
   British Commonwealth
Population: 301,180
Languages: Melanesian, pidgin English, local dialects
Religions: Anglican, other Protestant faiths, Roman
   Catholic, Seventh-Day Adventist

Somalia
Area: 637,660 km² (246,201 sq. mi.)
Capital: Mogadishu
Government: Republic
Population: 7,741,859
Languages: Somali, Arabic, Italian, English
Religion: Sunni Muslim

South Africa
Area: 1,221,040 km² (471,445 sq. mi.)
Capital: Pretoria, Cape Town
Government: Republic
Population: 34,313,356
Languages: Afrikaans, English, Zulu, Xhosa, Tswana
Religions: Christian, Hindu, Muslim

Soviet Union (Union of Soviet Socialist Republics)
Area: 22,402,200 km² (8,649,498 sq. mi.)
Capital: Moscow
Government: Communist
Population: 284,008,160
Languages: Russian, local languages and dialects
Religions: Russian Orthodox, Muslim, Jewish,
   Protestant, Georgian Orthodox, Roman Catholic

Spain
Area: 504,750 km² (194,897 sq. mi.)
Capital: Madrid
Government: Parliamentary monarchy
Population: 39,000,084
Languages: Castilian Spanish, Catalan, Galician,
   Basque
Religion: Roman Catholic

Sri Lanka
Area: 65,610 km² (25,332 sq. mi.)
Capital: Colombo
Government: Republic
Population: 16,406,576
Languages: Sinhala, Tamil, English
Religions: Buddhist, Hindu, Christian, Muslim

Sudan
Area: 2,505,810 km² (967,500 sq. mi.)
Capital: Khartoum
Government: Republic
Population: 23,524,622
Languages: Arabic, Nubian, Ta Bedawie, Nilotic,
   Nilo-Hamitic, Sudanic, English
Religions: Sunni Muslim, indigenous beliefs, Christian

Suriname
Area: 163,270 km² (63,037 sq. mi.)
Capital: Paramaribo
Government: Military-civilian rule
Population: 388,636
Languages: Dutch, English, Sranan Tongo, Javanese
Religions: Hindu, Muslim, Roman Catholic, Protestant

Swaziland
Area: 17,360 km² (6,704 sq. mi.)
Capital: Mbabane
Government: Independent monarchy within British
   Commonwealth
Population: 715,160
Languages: English, siSwati
Religions: Christian, indigenous beliefs

Sweden
Area: 449,960 km² (173,654 sq. mi.)
Capital: Stockholm
Government: Constitutional monarchy
Population: 8,383,026
Languages: Swedish, Lapp, Finnish
Religions: Evangelical Lutheran, Roman Catholic

Switzerland
Area: 41,290 km² (15,943 sq. mi.)
Capital: Bern
Government: Federal republic
Population: 6,572,739
Languages: German, French, Italian, Romansch
Religions: Roman Catholic, Protestant, Jewish

Syria
Area: 185,180 km² (71,498 sq. mi.)
Capital: Damascus
Government: Republic
Population: 11,147,763
Languages: Arabic, Kurdish, Armenian, Aramaic,
   Circassian, French, English
Religions: Sunni Muslim, Alawite Druze, other Muslim
   sects, Christian

Taiwan
Area: 35,980 km² (13,892 sq. mi.)
Capital: Taipei
Government: Republic
Population: 19,768,035
Languages: Mandarin, Taiwanese, Hakka
Religions: Buddhist, Confucianist, Taoist, Christian

Tanzania
Area: 945,090 km² (364,900 sq. mi.)
Capital: Dar es Salaam
Government: Republic
Population: 23,502,472
Languages: Swahili, English
Religions: Christian, Muslim, indigenous beliefs

Thailand
Area: 514,000 km² (198,457 sq. mi.)
Capital: Bangkok
Government: Constitutional monarchy
Population: 53,645,823
Languages: Thai, English, local dialects
Religions: Buddhist, Muslim

Togo
Area: 56,790 km² (21,162 sq. mi.)
Capital: Lomé
Government: Republic
Population: 3,228,635
Languages: French, Ewe, Mina, Dagoma, Kabye
Religions: Indigenous beliefs, Christian, Muslim

Tokelau
Area: 10 km² (4 sq. mi.)
Capital: None (various local government agencies)
Government: New Zealand territory
Population: 1,713
Languages: Polynesian Tokelauan, English
Religions: Protestant, Roman Catholic

Tonga
Area: 700 km² (270 sq. mi.)
Capital: Nuku'alofa
Government: Constitutional monarchy within British
   Commonwealth
Population: 98,689
Languages: Tongan, English
Religion: Christian

Trinidad and Tobago
Area: 5,130 km² (1,981 sq. mi.)
Capital: Port-of-Spain
Government: Parliamentary democracy
Population: 1,250,839
Languages: English, Hindi, French, Spanish
Religions: Roman Catholic, Hindu, Protestant, Muslim

Tunisia
Area: 163,610 km² (63,170 sq. mi.)
Capital: Tunis
Government: Republic
Population: 7,561,641
Languages: Arabic, French
Religions: Muslim, Christian, Jewish

Turkey
Area: 780,580 km² (301,382 sq. mi.)
Capital: Ankara
Government: Republican parliamentary democracy
Population: 52,987,778
Languages: Turkish, Kurdish, Arabic
Religions: Sunni Muslim, Christian, Jewish

Turks and Calicos Islands
Area: 430 km² (166 sq. mi.)
Capital: Grand Turk (Cockburn Town)
Government: British dependent territory
Population: 9,052
Language: English
Religions: Anglican, other Protestant faiths, Roman
   Catholic, Seventh-Day Adventist

Tuvalu
Area: 26 km² (9.5 sq. mi.)
Capital: Funafuti
Government: Independent state within British
  Commonwealth
Population: 8,329
Languages: Tuvaluan, English
Religion: Protestant

Uganda
Area: 236,040 km² (91,134 sq. mi.)
Capital: Kampala
Government: Republic
Population: 15,908,896
Languages: English, Lugandan, Swahili, Bantu,
  Nilotic
Religions: Roman Catholic, Protestant, Muslim,
  indigenous beliefs

United Arab Emirates
Area: 83,600 km² (32,278 sq. mi.)
Capital: Abu Dhabi
Government: Federation of six Arab states
Population: 1,846,373
Languages: Arabic, Farsi, English, Hindi, Urdu
Religions: Muslim, Christian, Hindu

United Kingdom
Area: 244,820 km² (94,525 sq. mi.)
Capital: London
Government: Constitutional monarchy
Population: 56,845,195
Languages: English, Welsh, Scottish Gaelic
Religions: Anglican, other Protestant faiths, Roman
  Catholic, Jewish

United States
Area: 9,372,610 km² (3,615,122 sq. mi.)
Capital: Washington, DC
Government: Federal republic
Population: 243,084,000
Language: English
Religions: Protestant, Roman Catholic, Jewish

Uruguay
Area: 176,220 km² (68,037 sq. mi.)
Capital: Montevideo
Government: Republic
Population: 2,964,952
Language: Spanish
Religions: Roman Catholic, Protestant, Jewish

USSR *See* Soviet Union.

Vanuatu
Area: 14,760 km² (5,700 sq. mi.)
Capital: Port-Vila
Government: Republic
Population: 149,652
Languages: English, French, Bislama
Religion: Christian

Vatican City
Area: 0.438 km² (108.7 acres)
Capital: Vatican City
Government: Independent papal state
Population: 738
Languages: Italian, Latin
Religion: Roman Catholic

Venezuela
Area: 912,050 km² (352,144 sq. mi.)
Capital: Caracas
Government: Republic
Population: 18,291,134
Languages: Spanish, local Amerindian dialects
Religion: Roman Catholic

Vietnam
Area: 329,560 km² (128,402 sq. mi.)
Capital: Hanoi
Government: Communist
Population: 63,585,121
Languages: Vietnamese, French, Chinese, English,
  Khmer, tribal dialects
Religions: Buddhist, Confucianist, Taoist, Roman
  Catholic, indigenous beliefs, Muslim, Protestant

Wallis and Futuna Islands
Area: 200 km² (77 sq. mi.)
Capital: Mata-Utu
Government: French territory
Population: 14,593
Languages: French, Polynesian dialects
Religion: Roman Catholic

West Bank and Gaza Strip
Area: 5,860 km² (2,263 sq. mi.)
Capital: None
Government: Israeli military rule
Population: 1,529,235
Languages: Arabic, Hebrew, English
Religions: Muslim, Jewish, Christian

Western Sahara
Area: 266,000 km² (102,703 sq. mi.)
Capital: None
Government: Moroccan administrative protectorate
Population: 250,000
Languages: Hassaniya Arabic, Moroccan Arabic
Religion: Muslim

Western Samoa
Area: 2,860 km² (1,097 sq. mi.)
Capital: Apia
Government: Constitutional monarchy under native
  chief
Population: 175,084
Languages: Samoan, English
Religions: Roman Catholic, Protestant, Seventh-Day
  Adventist, Mormon

West Germany *See* Germany, Federal Republic of.

Yemen Arab Republic (North Yemen)
Area: 195,000 km² (75,290 sq. mi.)
Capital: Sanaa
Government: Republic
Population: 6,533,265
Languages: Arabic
Religion: Muslim

Yemen People's Democratic Republic (South Yemen)
Area: 332,970 km² (128,560 sq. mi.)
Capital: Yemen
Government: Republic
Population: 2,451,131
Language: Arabic
Religions: Sunni Muslim, Christian, Hindu

Yugoslavia
Area: 255,800 km² (98,766 sq. mi.)
Capital: Belgrade
Government: Communist
Population: 23,430,830
Languages: Serbo-Croatian, Slovene, Macedonian, Albanian, Hungarian
Religions: Eastern Orthodox, Roman Catholic, Muslim, Protestant

Zaire
Area: 2,345,410 km² (905,365 sq. mi.)
Capital: Kinshasa
Government: Republic
Population: 32,342,947
Languages: French, English, Lingala, Swahili, Kingwana, Kikongo, Tshiluba
Religions: Roman Catholic, Protestant, Kimbanguist, Muslim, indigenous beliefs

Zambia
Area: 752,610 km² (290,586 sq. mi.)
Capital: Lusaka
Government: One-party state
Population: 7,281,738
Languages: English, local languages and dialects
Religions: Christian, Muslim, Hindu, indigenous beliefs

Zimbabwe
Area: 390,580 km² (150,804 sq. mi.)
Capital: Harare
Government: Independent parliamentary democracy
Population: 9,371,972
Languages: English, Shona, Si Ndebele
Religions: Christian, indigenous beliefs, Muslim

Great Events in World History

1,600,000 B.C. Earliest humanlike ancestors.

250,000 B.C. Earliest Homo sapiens.

70,000 B.C. Neanderthals use stone tools and fire.

40,000 B.C. Ice Age ends: Cro-Magnons migrate into Europe.

30,000 B.C. Neanderthals disappear.

28,000 B.C. Asians cross land bridge between Asia and America.

20,000 B.C. European cave art exists.

8000 B.C. Agriculture develops in Near East.

7000 B.C. First walled cities, pottery, and use of metals appear.

4236 B.C. Earliest date on Egyptian calendar.

3760 B.C. Earliest date on Jewish calendar.

3100 B.C. Egypt united under first dynasty.

3000 B.C. Phoenicians migrate to eastern Mediterranean.

2780 B.C. First Egyptian pyramid built.

2697 B.C. Huang-ti becomes "Yellow Emperor" of China.

2150 B.C. Aryans invade Indus Valley.

2000 B.C. Bronze age begins in Europe.

1760 B.C. Shang dynasty is founded in China.

1400 B.C. Iron Age begins in Asia.

1250 B.C. Exodus of Israelites from Egypt.

1193 B.C. Greeks destroy city of Troy.

1050 B.C. Dorian tribes invade Peloponnesus.

1000 B.C. Hebrews establish Jerusalem as capital of Israel.

994 B.C. Teutons migrate to Rhine River area.

815 B.C. Carthage is founded by Phoenicians.

776 B.C. First Olympic Games are held in Greece.

753 B.C. Rome is founded.

580 B.C. King Nebuchadnezzar builds Hanging Gardens of Babylon.

563 B.C. Buddha is born.

551 B.C. Confucius is born.

336 B.C. Alexander III, king of Macedonia, begins world conquest.

321 B.C. Chandragupta founds first empire of India.

215 B.C. Great Wall of China is built.

55 B.C. Julius Caesar conquers Gaul, invades Britain.

5 B.C. Jesus Christ is born.

30 A.D. Jesus is executed.

64 A.D. Rome under Nero is partly destroyed by fire.

79 A.D. Eruption of Vesuvius destroys Pompeii.

268 A.D. Goths invade Greece.

370 A.D. Asian Huns invade Europe.

406 A.D. Vandals invade Gaul; Romans leave Britain.

410 A.D. Goths sack Rome.

425 A.D. Angles, Saxons, and Jutes invade Britain.

433 A.D. Attila the Hun begins reign.

476 A.D. Goths depose Western Roman emperor, Romulas Augustus; Middle Ages begin.

570 A.D. Muhammad is born at Mecca.

620 A.D. Vikings invade Ireland.

632 A.D. Muhammad dies.

634 A.D. Muslims begin conquest of Near East and Africa.

711 A.D. Moors invade Spain.

768 A.D. Reign of Charlemagne begins.

800 A.D. Charlemagne is crowned Holy Roman emperor.

814 A.D. Arabic numerals are established.

862 A.D. Viking Russ tribe seizes control of northern Russia.

874 A.D. Vikings settle Iceland.

900 A.D. Spain begins to drive out Moors.

932 A.D. Printed books from woodblocks are developed in China.

981 A.D. Eric the Red begins settlement of Greenland.

1000 A.D. Vikings begin exploration of North America.

1021 Muslim Druse sect is found by Caliph al-Hakim.

1054 Byzantine Empire breaks with Holy Roman Church.

1066 Normans conquer Britain.

1096 First Crusade is launched to oust Muslims from Holy Land.

1148 Second Crusade begins.

1156 Civil wars are fought in Japan.

1161 Chinese use explosives in warfare.

1189 Last recorded Viking voyage to North America.

1190 Genghis Khan begins conquest of Asia.

1204 Crusaders capture and sack Constantinople.

1210 Mongols invade China.

1215 England's Magna Carta is signed by King John.

1228 Sixth Crusade results in capture of Jerusalem.

1240 Mongols capture Moscow, destroy Kiev.

1260 Kublai Khan founds Yuan dynasty in China.

1271 Marco Polo leaves for China to visit Kublai Khan.

1274 Mongols attempt invasion of Japan but fail.

1291 Crusades end as Muslims rout Christians in Palestine.

1336 Civil war lasting until 1392 begins in Japan.

1337 Hundred Years' War between England and France begins.

1347 Bubonic plague spreads from China to Cyprus.

1348 Black Death (plague) spreads to England.

1351 Plague reaches Russia; Europe's toll tops 25 million.

1363 Tamerlane begins conquest of Asia.

1368 Mongol dynasty ends in China; Ming dynasty begins.

1390 Turks conquer Asia Minor.

1402 Tamerlane conquers Ottoman Empire.

1431 Jeanne d'Arc is burned as a witch at Rouen.

1453 Hundred Years' War ends; fall of Constantinople ends Byzantine Empire; Middle Ages end; Renaissance begins.

1454 Movable-type printing press is introduced.

1455 England's War of the Roses is fought.

1478 Spanish Inquisition is begun by Ferdinand and Isabella; period of exploration by Europeans begins.

1482 Portuguese colonize African Gold Coast.

1488 Bartholomew Diaz sails around Cape of Good Hope.

1492 Christopher Columbus discovers West Indies.

1497 John Cabot discovers Newfoundland.

1500 Pedro Cabral discovers Brazil.

1502 Columbus discovers Nicaragua.

1505 Portuguese colonize Mozambique.

1507 First world map showing "America" is produced.

1513 Balboa discovers the Pacific Ocean.

1517 Martin Luther's Reformation begins.

1522 Magellan circumnavigates the world.

1534 Henry VIII is excommunicated and founds Church of England.

1541 Hernando de Soto discovers Mississippi River.

1557 Portuguese establish colony at Macao.

1558 Elizabeth I becomes queen of England.

1582 Gregorian calendar is introduced.

1588 Spanish Armada is defeated by English fleet.

1595 Dutch colonize Guinea Coast.

1600 English East India Company is chartered.

1602 Dutch East India Company is formed.

1604 Russia begins settlement in Siberia.

1606 Willem Jansz discovers Australia.

1607 English found North American colony of Virginia.

1610 Hudson Bay is discovered.

1618 Thirty Years' War begins.

1619 First black slaves arrive in Virginia.

1620 English Pilgrims reach Cape Cod, found Plymouth Colony.

1626 Dutch found New Amsterdam (New York).

1633 Colony of Connecticut is established.

1637 Russian explorers reach Pacific coast of Siberia.

1642 French found Montreal in Canada; King Charles I battles Parliament in English Civil War.

1652 English and Dutch begin series of wars.

1654 Portuguese take Brazil from Dutch.

1655 England takes Jamaica from Spain.

1661 English take control of Bombay in India.

1664 England takes New Amsterdam (New York) from Dutch; Manchu dynasty is founded in China.

1683 Turkish army overruns Vienna.

1686 English establish Dominion of New England.

1704 English seize Gibraltar from Spain.

1759 England captures Quebec in war with France.

1763 Peace of Paris gives Canada to England.

1767 Townshend Acts tax American colony imports; Mason-Dixon line is established.

1770 Boston Massacre occurs; Townshend Acts are repealed except for tea tax.

1773 Boston Tea Party occurs.

1774 First Continental Congress of American colonies is held.

1775 War of Independence begins in Massachusetts.

1776 Declaration of Independence is signed.

1781 English General Cornwallis surrenders at Yorktown.

1783 Treaty of Paris ends American War of Independence; India Act allows English control of India.

1787 United States Constitution takes effect.

1788 First English convicts are transported to Australia.

1789 George Washington becomes first U.S. President; French Revolution begins.

1791 U.S. Bill of Rights takes effect.

1792 France is declared a republic; Denmark becomes first country to ban slave trade.

1793 First free settlers migrate to Australia; French Reign of Terror exists.

1798 Napoleon Bonaparte invades Egypt, capturing Cairo.

1803 Louisiana Purchase is completed.

1804 Lewis and Clark begin exploration of American Northwest; Bonaparte crowns himself Napoleon I, emperor of France.

1806 Napoleon dissolves Holy Roman Empire.

1807 England abolishes slave trade.

1812 War is fought between England and United States; Napoleon invades Russia, occupies Moscow.

1814 Napoleon is exiled to Elba.

1815 Napoleon is defeated at Battle of Waterloo and exiled again.

1819 Florida is ceded by Spain to United States.

1820 Missouri Compromise on U.S. slave states becomes effective.

1823 Monroe Doctrine against foreign activity in Americas is adopted.

1833 England bans slavery and child labor in factories.

1836 Texas secedes from Mexico; battle of the Alamo is fought.

1846 War is fought between Mexico and United States; Irish potato famine is suffered, with deaths reaching 1 million.

1848 Revolutions erupt throughout Europe; Marx and Engels produce *The Communist Manifesto;* United States takes California and New Mexico from Mexico.

1854 Crimean War is fought; Japan ends isolation, signs U.S. commercial treaty.

1860 South Carolina secedes from United States.

1861 U.S. Civil War begins.

1863 President Abraham Lincoln abolishes slavery in United States.

1865 U.S. Civil War ends; President Lincoln is assassinated.

1867 United States acquires Alaska from Russia; Dominion of Canada is established.

1868 Japan ends 700-year shogun rule, begins modernization.

1869 Suez Canal is completed.

1870 Franco-Prussian War is fought.

1883 Germany introduces health insurance.

1898 War between Spain and United States is fought over Cuba; United States acquires Hawaiian Islands.

1900 Boxer Rebellion erupts in China, hundreds of Europeans are killed; England and Germany begin arms race.

1902 Boer War ends; England acquires South African states.

1903 Panama, aided by U.S., secedes from Colombia.

1904 Russo-Japanese War is fought; Japan acquires Korea and Manchuria.

1906 Earthquake destroys much of San Francisco.

1909 England introduces old-age pensions; assembly line production is introduced in Detroit.

1912 Chinese revolution ends Manchu dynasty, republic is formed; passenger ship *Titanic* sinks, with 1,513 lives lost; Balkan wars begin.

1914 World War I follows assassination of Austrian archduke; trench warfare begins; airplanes are used as weapons; Panama Canal opens.

1915 Poison gas is first used by Germans in warfare.

1916 Tanks are first used by England in warfare.

1917 United States joins Allies in European fighting; Bolsheviks led by Lenin seize power in Russia; Balfour Declaration urges Jewish state in Palestine.

1918 Russia withdraws from World War I fighting; Kaiser of Germany abdicates; Germany forms republic after revolt; armistice ends World War I.

1919 Treaty of Versailles causes heavy German economic losses; League of Nations is founded; Sinn Fein rebellion erupts in Ireland; Benito Mussolini introduces fascism in Italy; Gandhi begins passive resistance movement in India.

1920 Civil war is fought in Ireland; England establishes a Palestinian Jewish state; United States prohibits use of alcoholic beverages.

1921 Irish Free State is established.

1922 Union of Soviet Socialist Republics is established; fascists march on Rome; Mussolini is named prime minister of Italy.

1923 Adolf Hitler forms National Socialist Party in Germany; Turkey becomes a republic after revolt ends sultanate.

1924 Joseph Stalin succeeds Lenin as leader of Soviet Union; new Chinese government is formed with communist members.

1927 Purge of communists leads to civil war in China.

1929 U.S. stock market crash triggers worldwide depression; fighting begins between Jews and Arabs in Palestine.

1931 Japanese organize puppet state in Manchuria; Spain becomes a republic, King Alfonso is deposed; British Empire status is changed to British Commonwealth.

1933 Adolf Hitler is named chancellor of Germany, and National Socialists (Nazis) purge opposition; Stalin purges opposition in Russia; United States ends prohibition experiment.

1934 Hitler assumes title of ''Fuhrer''; Mao Tse-tung starts ''Long March'' of Chinese communists.

1935 Italy invades Ethiopia; Hitler renounces Versailles Treaty and begins open rearmament.

1936 Germany reoccupies Rhineland and forms ''Axis'' with Italy; General Franco begins Spanish Civil War; King Edward of England abdicates to marry an American.

1937 Japanese invade China, capturing Peking and Shanghai; German aircraft bomb Spain in support of Franco.

1938 Germany annexes Austria and gains Czechoslovakia's Sudetenland in Munich Pact.

1939 Germany annexes Czechoslovakia; Franco captures Madrid, and Spanish Civil War ends; Italy invades Albania; Germany invades Poland, triggering World War II; Russo-Finnish War ends in defeat of Finland.

1940 Germany invades France, Belgium, Denmark, and Norway; Battle of Britain prevents German invasion of England; Japan joins Berlin–Rome Axis; Italy invades Greece and joins war against England and France.

1941 Germany invades Russia; Italy and Germany invade Egypt; Japanese attack U.S. bases in Hawaii; U.S. joins Allies in war against Axis powers.

1942 Japanese capture Philippines and much of Southeast Asia; Battle of Midway alters naval balance in Pacific; Germans begin retreat in North Africa.

1943 United States begins recapture of Japanese Pacific bases; Allies invade Sicily; Italians surrender; Germans surrender to Russians at Stalingrad.

1944 Allies invade Normandy; German retreat begins; Allies liberate Rome, Paris, and Brussels; U.S. forces defeat Japanese navy in Leyte Gulf.

1945 Yalta Conference is attended by United States, Great Britain, and Soviet Union; Germany surrenders; Mussolini is assassinated; Hitler commits suicide; atom bombs are dropped at Hiroshima and Nagasaki; Japan surrenders, ending World War II; Potsdam Conference discusses postwar settlements.

1946 League of Nations is replaced by United Nations; Ho Chi Minh begins war against French in Indochina; German war crimes trials are held in Nuremberg.

1947 Marshall Plan aids European war recovery; Arabs reject plan for separate Jewish and Arab states; independent states of India and Pakistan are formed.

1948 Nation of Israel is established; war begins between Israel and Arab League; Gandhi is assassinated by a Hindu extremist; communists gain control of Czechoslovakia; Korea is divided into North Korea and South Korea; Berlin is blockaded by Soviet Union.

1949 Mao Tse-tung's communists gain control of China; Nationalist Chinese move government to Taiwan; South Africa establishes apartheid policy; Germany is divided into East Germany and West Germany; North American Treaty Organization (NATO) is formed.

1950 North Korean troops invade South Korea.

1951 Chinese communists occupy Tibet.

1952 Jawaharlal Nehru is elected first prime minister of India.

1953 Stalin dies and is replaced by Malenkov; USSR announces development of hydrogen bomb; Vietnamese Viet Minh forces invade Laos.

1954 Viet Minh troops defeat French at Dien Bien Phu; Vietnam is divided into North Vietnam and South Vietnam; South-East Asia Treaty Organization (SEATO) is formed.

1955 European communist states sign Warsaw Pact; Argentine President Juan Peron is exiled.

1956 Soviets crush anti-Russian uprising in Hungary; Egypt nationalizes Suez Canal, British withdraw; Israel invades Egypt.

1957 Russia launches first artificial satellite, Sputnik I; Fidel Castro begins revolution in Cuba; European Common Market is formed.

1958 Egypt, Syria, and Yemen form United Arab States; Charles de Gaulle is elected president of France; United States launches an artificial satellite, Explorer I.

1959 Fidel Castro overthrows Fulgencio Batista and becomes Cuban premier.

1960 Many European colonies in Africa gain independence.

1961 Bay of Pigs invasion of Cuba fails; Russian Yuri Gargarin is first man in space; communists build Berlin Wall; United States sends thousands of military advisers to Vietnam.

1962 Soviet missile crisis threatens in Cuba; Algeria gains independence from France.

1963 Russian Valentina Kareshkova is first woman in space; President Kennedy is assassinated; United States, Great Britain, and Soviet Union sign nuclear test ban treaty; North Vietnamese boats attack U.S. Navy in Gulf of Tonkin; President Lyndon Johnson orders attack on North Vietnam.

1965 U.S. Marines are sent to Vietnam; U.S. aircraft begin air strikes against North Vietnam.

1966 China undergoes "Cultural Revolution."

1967 Six-Day War between Israel and Arabs is fought; Israel occupies Jerusalem and West Bank of Jordan River.

1968 Martin Luther King, Jr. is assassinated; U.S. senator Robert Kennedy is assassinated; Soviets invade Czechoslovakia to crush uprising; Vietcong stage Tet offensive in South Vietnam; U.S. troop deployment in Vietnam passes 500,000; North Korea seizes U.S. Navy ship *Pueblo*.

1969 U.S. military begins withdrawal from Vietnam; U.S. astronauts land on the moon.

1970 U.S. troops invade Cambodia.

1971 Communist China replaces Taiwan in United Nations.

1972 President Nixon travels to China to renew relations; Great Britain takes over direct rule of Northern Ireland.

1973 Military coup in Chile overthrows Marxist government; Arabs attack Israel in October War; participants in Vietnam War sign peace agreements.

1974 Watergate scandal ends Nixon term in White House.

1975 Vietnam War ends with communist seizure of Saigon; communists take control of government of Cambodia; U.S. and Soviet spacecraft link up in space.

1978 United States votes to return Canal Zone to Panama in year 2000.

1979 Ayatollah Khomeini gains control of Iran; Shah of Iran leaves; Iranians seize U.S. Embassy in Teheran, holding hostages; Soviet Union invades Afghanistan; Israel and Egypt sign peace treaty.

1980 War begins between Iran and Iraq; Solidarity trade union confronts communists in Poland.

1981 United States begins series of space shuttle flights; assassination attempt is made on President Ronald Reagan; assassination attempt is made on Pope John Paul II; Sandra Day O'Connor becomes first woman on U.S. Supreme Court.

1982 Falklands War between Argentina and England is fought; Israel withdraws troops from Egypt's Sinai.

1983 Soviets shoot down South Korean airliner, and 269 are killed; Sally Ride is first U.S. woman in space; bomb kills 237 U.S. Marines in Beirut, Lebanon; U.S. forces invade island of Grenada.

1984 Marines withdraw from Beirut; Geraldine Ferraro is nominated as U.S. vice president.

1985 Mikhail Gorbachev becomes leader of Soviet Union.

1986 U.S. space shuttle explodes in flight, killing crew; Corazon Aquino is elected president of Philippines; U.S. aircraft raid Libya in retaliation for terrorism; nuclear accident occurs at Soviet Chernobyl power station.

1987 U.S. stock market crashes with 508-point loss; Iran-contra aid scandal involves U.S. officials; United States and Soviet Union agree to reduce nuclear arms; U.S. Navy ship *Stark* is attacked in Persian Gulf.

1988 Panamanian General Noriega is indicted in U.S. Courts, disrupting Panamanian economy; cease-fire agreement is signed between Nicaraguan government and contra leaders; Iran accepts peace plan offer by Iraq; King Hussein abandons claim to West Bank territory and cedes authority to Palestine Liberation Organization; George Bush is elected President; U.S. space shuttle program makes first two successful trips since 1986 disaster; Palestine Liberation Organization recognizes Israel as a state and renounces terrorism; Soviet leader Gorbachev agrees to reduce European forces in U.N. address; devastating earthquake in Armenia kills tens of thousands.

Significant Figures in World History

3500 B.C. Menes unites kingdoms of Egypt, introduces irrigation.

2780 B.C. Imhotep designs first step pyramid at Saqqara, Egypt.

2700 B.C. Cheops builds Great Pyramid at Giza.

2697 B.C. Huang-ti becomes legendary "Yellow Emperor" of China.

2640 B.C. Si Ling-chi introduces silk production in China.

2340 B.C. Sargon establishes Semitic and Sumerian civilizations.

1750 B.C. Hammurabi, Babylonian king, issues code of laws.

1270 B.C. Abulfaraj, Syrian historian, compiles first encyclopedia.

1250 B.C. Moses, Hebrew lawgiver, leads Israelites from Egypt to Canaan.

1100 B.C. Pa-out-She, Chinese scholar, compiles first dictionary.

1000 B.C. David, first king of Judah, establishes Jerusalem as capital.

760 B.C. Homer, poet, writes *Iliad* and *Odyssey*.

730 B.C. Ahaz, prince of Judah, invents sundial.

700 B.C. Sennacherib, Syrian king, builds first aqueduct.

673 B.C. Terpander, Greek musician, develops stringed instruments.

600 B.C. Lao-tze develops philosophy of Taoism.

563 B.C. Siddhartha Gautama develops Buddhist philosophy.

559 B.C. Cyrus establishes Persian Empire.

551 B.C. K'ung Fu-tzu develops philosophy of Confucianism.

550 B.C. Anaximander invents star charts and model of spherical Earth.

540 B.C. Pythagoras, mathematician, studies musical harmonics.

508 B.C. Cleisthenes introduces democratic government in Athens.

485 B.C. Aeschylus writes first early Greek tragedies.

480 B.C. Sophocles writes early Greek tragic poems.

460 B.C. Pericles establishes democracy in Athens.

450 B.C. Euripides writes Greek tragedies; Herodotus becomes known as father of history.

440 B.C. Democritus introduces concept of atomic structure of matter; Hippocrates becomes known as father of medicine; Socrates teaches that virtue and knowledge are identical.

400 B.C. Aristophanes introduces political satire in Greek comedies; Plato writes dialogues that help shape Western thought.

340 B.C. Aristotle contributes to development of logical thought.

334 B.C. Alexander the Great begins conquest of known world.

321 B.C. Chandagupta forms first great empire in India.

300 B.C. Euclid develops deductive system of mathematics; Meng-tse spreads philosophy of Confucius in Orient.

250 B.C. Aristrarchus develops modern concept of universe.

236 B.C. Asoka, emperor of India, becomes Buddhist missionary.

221 B.C. Shih Hwang-ti, first emperor of China, begins Great Wall.

220 B.C. Archimedes, Greek mathematician, develops physics and mechanics.

218 B.C. Hannibal leads army from Spain over Alps to Italy.

160 B.C. Hipparchus develops trigonometry.

78 B.C. Julius Caesar begins his climb as ruler of Roman Empire.

63 B.C. Cicero, orator, compiles record of Roman life.

38 B.C. Horace, Roman poet, writes classic satires.

30 B.C. Virgil, Roman poet, writes *Aeneid*.

27 B.C. Caesar Augustus becomes first Roman emperor.

5 B.C. Jesus of Nazareth, Christian leader, is born.

32 A.D. Saul of Tarsus begins early Christian missionary work.

105 A.D. T'sai Lun invents paper manufacture.

132 A.D. Bar-Kokhba leads Roman revolt and makes Israel independent.

250 A.D. Mani founds Manichaeism, religion popular in Middle Ages.

312 A.D. Constantine becomes first Christian emperor of Rome.

391 A.D. Augustine begins work as founder of Christian theology.

451 A.D. Attila, leader of Huns, invades Europe.

520 A.D. Aryabhata is among first to use algebra.

550 A.D. Justinian codifies Roman law in Corpus Juris Civilis.

570 A.D. Muhammad, founder of Islam, is born.

768 A.D. Charlemagne becomes king of the Franks.

786 A.D. Harun al-Rashid makes Baghdad center of Islamic culture.

886 A.D. Alfred the Great introduces 24-hour-day measurement system.

936 A.D. Otto I establishes Holy Roman Empire.

995 A.D. Fugiware Michinaga founds Japanese Golden Age.

1002 Leif Ericsson establishes North American colony.

1054 Abdallah ben Yassim spreads Islamic culture in Africa.

1066 William the Conqueror establishes Norman culture in Britain.

1096 Pope Urban II begins series of Crusades to free Holy Land.

1162 Thomas à Becket becomes archbishop of Canterbury.

1190 Temujin (Genghis Khan) begins conquest of Asia and Near East.

1210 Francis of Assisi founds Franciscan religious order.

1215 King John signs Magna Carta, foundation of modern democracy.

1250 Roger Bacon, English philosopher, invents magnifying lens.

1259 Thomas Aquinas develops official Roman Catholic philosophy.

1264 Simon de Montfort founds House of Commons in Parliament.

1269 Petrus Peregrinus invents 360-degree compass.

1271 Marco Polo begins 24-year journey to court of Kublai Khan.

1295 King Edward I summons first representative Parliament.

1326 Rinaldo di Villamagna invents firing cannon.

1368 Chu Yuan-chang overthrows Mongols, founds Ming dynasty.

1369 Tamerlane becomes ruler of land from India to Egypt.

1387 Geoffrey Chaucer writes *Canterbury Tales*.

1419 Henry the Navigator begins period of African explorations.

1429 Jeanne d'Arc, peasant girl, leads French army against English.

1454 Johannes Gutenberg perfects movable-type printing press.

1474 Regiomontanus develops lunar nautical navigation.

1478 Ferdinand and Isabella establish Spanish Inquisition.

1482 Leonardo da Vinci, painter, creates many modern devices.

1489 Johann Widman introduces (+) and (−) signs in mathematics.

1492 Christopher Columbus discovers West Indies and South America.

1497 John Cabot discovers Newfoundland.

1498 Vasco da Gama sails around Cape of Good Hope to India.

1510 Michelangelo paints ceiling of Sistine Chapel.

1513 Italo Balboa discovers Pacific Ocean at Panama.

1517 Martin Luther posts 95 theses protesting church indulgences.

1519 Ferdinand Magellan begins first trip to circumnavigate world.

1521 Hernan Cortes conquers Aztec and claims Mexico for Spain.

1531 Francisco Pizarro begins conquest of Peru.

1532 Niccolò Machiavelli outlines principles of power politics.

1534 John Calvin begins Reformation program in Switzerland; Henry VIII is excommunicated and creates Church of England; Ignatius Loyola founds Society of Jesus (Jesuits).

1540 Nicolaus Copernicus revises heliocentric planet system theory.

1547 Ivan IV becomes first czar of united Russia.

1558 Elizabeth I rules England at start of colonization period.

1582 Pope Gregory XIII introduces calendar still in use.

1585 Galileo Galilei develops understanding of many laws of nature.

1588 Francis Drake leads English destruction of Spanish fleet.

1589 John Harington invents flush toilet.

1590 Hans Janssen makes compound telescope and microscope lenses.

1592 William Shakespeare emerges as successful British dramatist.

1605 Francis Bacon, essayist, teaches inductive reasoning.

1607 John Smith founds English colony at Jamestown, Virginia.

1610 William Harvey discovers blood circulation.

1611 Johannes Kepler explains movements of the planets.

1614 John Napier develops logarithmic calculator.

1628 René Descartes, mathematician and philosopher, founds analytical geometry.

1631 William Oughtred introduces multiplication ($\times$) sign; Rembrandt becomes famous as prodigious portrait painter.

1642 Blaise Pascal invents calculating machine.

1644 Oliver Cromwell leads revolt against English King Charles I.

1656 Isaac Newton develops principles of integral calculus.

1683 Anton van Leeuwenhoek discovers bacteria with microscope.

1688 John Locke outlines political revolutionary theory.

1696 Peter the Great leads Russian modernization program.

1703 Gottfied Leibnitz invents binary system of arithmetic.

1730 Voltaire leads struggle for French justice and enlightenment.

1733 John Kay starts Industrial Revolution with flying shuttle.

1747 Johann S. Bach creates library of vocal and instrumental music.

1750 Jean-Jacques Rousseau, philosopher, writes on political economy.

1766 Leonhard Euler founds science of pure mathematics.

1769 Wolfgang Mozart begins career as musical composer. James Watt advances Industrial Revolution with steam engine.

1770 Immanuel Kant, philosopher, supports American colonies.

1776 Thomas Jefferson prepares Declaration of Independence; Adam Smith writes *Wealth of Nations;* George Washington leads revolution of English colonies.

1781 Benjamin Franklin begins peace negotiations with British.

1783 Montgolfier brothers introduce hot-air balloon travel.

1785 Charles Coulomb discovers rule of electrical forces.

1789 Georges Danton leads French Revolution; Antoine Lavoisier founds modern scientific chemistry.

1791 Thomas Paine publishes *Rights of Man.*

1793 Maximilien Robespierre leads French Reign of Terror; Touissaint-Breda leads revolt ending French slavery.

1795 Ludwig van Beethoven begins career as musical composer.

1796 Edward Jenner introduces vaccination against smallpox; Napoleon Bonaparte begins conquest of Europe and Mediterranean.

1798 Thomas Malthus publishes essay on population explosion; Eli Whitney, cotton-gin inventor, introduces mass production.

1800 Alessandro Volta invents method for storing electricity.

1803 John Dalton explains atomic nature of matter.

1804 Meriwether Lewis and William Clark begin exploration of Louisiana Purchase.

1807 Robert Fulton develops steam-powered water travel.

1809 David Ricardo develops modern concepts of finance.

1811 Simón Bolívar frees part of South America from Spanish rule.

1812 Bryan Donkin develops canned-food process.

1815 Duke of Wellington crushes Napoleon in battle of Waterloo.

1819 Hans Christian Oersted discovers electromagnetism.

1821 Michael Faraday develops electric motor principle; José San Martín frees Chile and Argentina from Spanish control.

1823 James Monroe issues doctrine against foreign interference.

1825 George Stephenson develops steam-locomotive land travel.

1833 Charles Babbage invents differential calculating machine.

1836 Sam Houston gains independence of Texas from Mexico.

1837 Louis Daguerre invents photography.

1840 Samuel Morse patents electric telegraph system.

1846 William Morton introduces use of anesthetic gases.

1848 Karl Marx and Friedrich Engels produce *Communist Manifesto.*

1854 Matthew Perry ends Japanese isolation with U.S. trade treaty.

1855 Florence Nightingale introduces battlefield nursing care.

1857 Gregor Mendel begins experiments on hereditary factors.

1859 Charles Darwin publishes *Origin of Species;* Edwin Drake develops technique for drilling oil wells; Etienne Lenoir invents internal combustion engine.

1860 Giuseppe Garibaldi begins nationalist movements in Europe.

1862 Richard Gatling invents machine gun.

1863 Abraham Lincoln proclaims abolition of slavery in United States.

1864 James Maxwell begins studies of electromagnetic radiation; Alfred Nobel invents nitroglycerine and dynamite explosives; Louis Pasteur disproves doctrine of spontaneous generation.

1867 Joseph Lister introduces antiseptic practices in hospitals.

1869 Ferdinand de Lesseps completes Suez Canal construction.

1871 Otto von Bismarck defeats France and forms new German Reich.

1874 Paul Cézanne leads Impressionist movement in painting.

1875 Leo Tolstoy becomes established as great Russian author.

1876 Alexander Graham Bell patents the telephone.

1877 Nikolaus Otto invents four-stroke internal combustion engine.

1879 Thomas Edison develops carbon-filament electric light.

1882 William Jenny designs first "skyscraper" office building. Robert Koch discovers cause of tuberculosis and cholera.

1885 Gottlieb Daimler builds first gasoline-powered automobile.

1889 Herman Hollerith develops data-processing computer.

1892 Rudolph Diesel invents compression-ignition (diesel) engine; Dmitri Ivanovsky discovers viruses.

1894 Sun Yat-sen begins move to end Manchu dynasty in China; Guglielmo Marconi invents wireless telegraphy.

1895 Sigmund Freud develops method of psychoanalysis; Louis and Auguste Lumière introduce motion pictures; Wilhelm Roentgen discovers X-rays; Joseph Thomson discovers the electron.

1896 Henri Becquerel develops science of radioactivity.

1897 Ferdinand Braun invents the cathode-ray tube; Ivan Pavlov conducts conditioned-reflex experiments; Ronald Ross discovers cause of malaria, the mosquito.

1898 Christiaan Eijkman discovers vitamin-deficiency diseases.

1900 Max Planck introduces general quantum theory.

1901 Karl Landstiner develops human blood-group system.

1902 William Bayliss and Ernest Starling discover hormones; William Carrier invents air conditioning for workplace; Pierre and Marie Curie discover radium.

1903 Orville and Wilbur Wright fly first practical airplane.

1904 John Fleming invents ratio vacuum tube.

1905 Albert Einstein develops special theory of relativity.

1907 Pablo Picasso and Georges Braque found Cubist movement in art.

1908 William d'Arcy discovers oil in Persian Gulf region.

1909 Fritz Haber develops synthetic ammonia process.

1910 Thomas Morgan introduces gene theory of heredity.

1913 Niels Bohr applies quantum theory to subatomic physics; Henry Ford develops moving assembly line for mass production.

1914 George Goethals completes Panama Canal.

1915 Walter Wilson and William Tritton develop British army tank.

1917 Paul Langevin and Robert Boyle develop SONAR detection system; Vladimir Lenin leads Bolshevik revolution in Russia.

1919 Mahatma Gandhi begins passive-resistance campaign in India; Benito Mussolini founds Italian fascist movement.

1920 Woodrow Wilson helps form League of Nations.

1921 Karel Capek introduces concept of robots.

1924 Josef Stalin succeeds Lenin as leader of Soviet Union; Louis de Broglie develops particle-wave dualism theory.

1925 Erwin Schrodinger develops science of wave mechanics.

1927 Niels Bohr proposes fission of uranium with neutrons; Werner Heisenberg discovers uncertainty principle in physics; Chiang Kai-shek succeeds Sun Yat-sen in China.

1928 Andre Bocage develops tomography technique for CAT scans; Alexander Fleming discovers penicillin; Chandrasekhara Raman discovers particles in visible light.

1929 Hans Berger develops ''brain-wave'' electroencephalograph; Max Knoll and Ernst Ruska invent electron microscope; Joseph Stalin succeeds Lenin as leader of Soviet Union.

1930 Vannevar Bush develops mechanical differential analyzer; Ernest Lawrence and N. E. Edlefsen invent nuclear cyclotron.

1931 Karl Jansky develops radio astronomy; Wolfgang Pauli discovers neutrino; Vladimir Zworykin invents television camera.

1932 Wallace Carothers and Arnold Collins invent nylon and neoprene; John Cockcroft and Ernest Walton bombard lithium with protons; William Kouwenhaven invents heart defibrillator; Harold Urey discovers deuterium (heavy hydrogen).

1933 Edwin Armstrong develops frequency modulation (FM) radio; Adolf Hitler becomes dictator of Nazi Germany; Franklin D. Roosevelt becomes thirty-second president of United States.

1934 Mao Tse-tung leads China's communist army on ''Long March.''

1935 Heinrich Focke develops first practical helicopter; John Keynes authors concept of government role in economy; Hans von Ohain and Frank Whittle invent jet aircraft engines.

1936 Francisco Franco begins Spanish Civil War.

1938 Edward Kendall and Philip Hench develop corticosteroid drugs.

1940 Winston Churchill becomes prime minister of Great Britain. John Randall invents cavity magnetron (radar tube).

1941 Peter Goldmark develops color television system.

1942 Enrico Fermi builds first nuclear reactor.

1943 Max Newman and T. H. Flowers build electronic computer; Selman Waksman develops streptomycin.

1944 Howard Aiken builds sequence-controlled calculator.

1945 William Kolff develops artificial kidney; J. R. Oppenheimer develops first atomic bomb.

1946 John Mauchly and J. P. Eckert build ENIAC electronic computer; Ho Chi Minh begins war against France and United States in Vietnam.

1947 Dennis Gabor develops 3-D holography; Willard Libby develops radiocarbon dating technique; Charles Yeager is first to fly at supersonic speed.

1948 William Shockley develops transistor.

1950 Paul Charpentier develops chlorpromazine tranquilizer; Harry Truman sends U.S. troops to fight communists in Korea.

1951 Gregory Pincus develops oral contraceptive.

1952 Edward Teller develops hydrogen bomb.

1953 Francis Crick and James Watson map DNA molecule; John Gibbon develops heart-lung machine; Nathan Kline develops antihypertensive drug reserpine.

1955 Severo Ochoa synthesizes ribonucleic acid (RNA); Jonas Salk announces existence of killed-virus polio vaccine.

1956 Arthur Kornberg synthesizes DNA with enzymes, nucleotides; Choh Hao Li isolates human growth hormone.

1957 Fidel Castro begins communist revolution in Cuba; Alick Isaacs and Jean Lindemann discover interferon; Clarence Lillehie develops artificial-heart pacemaker; Sergei Pavlovich produces Sputnik I, Soviet satellite; Bruce Sabin develops live-virus polio vaccine.

1958 Charles de Gaulle becomes president of French Fifth Republic; Charles Townes and Arthur Leonard develop optical laser.

1959 Leo Esaki develops commercial tunnel diode.

1960 D. R. Herriott develops argon ion laser; John F. Kennedy becomes youngest U.S. president.

1961   Yuri Gagarin becomes first human to orbit Earth.

1963   Murray Gell-Mann discovers quarks (subatomic particles); Marten Schmidt finds quasars (quasistellar radio sources).

1967   Jocelyn Bell discovers pulsars.

1969   Neil Armstrong and Edwin Aldrin walk on surface of the moon.

1972   John Charnley develops artificial hip; John Hughes discovers brain chemical enkephalin.

1973   Paul Berg develops recombinant DNA.

1975   Cesar Milstein develops monoclonal antibodies.

1978   Tony Allison develops organ transplant drug cyclosporin A; Patrick Steptoe develops method for test-tube baby.

1979   Ayatollah Khomeini leads revolution against Shah of Iran; Margaret Thatcher becomes prime minister of Great Britain.

1980   Ronald Reagan is elected President of United States.

1985   Michael Phelps develops positron emission tomography; Mikhail Gorbachev becomes leader of Soviet Union.

1988   George Bush is elected President of United States.

World Exploration and Discovery

40,000 B.C.   Cro-Magnons migrate to Europe from Near East.

28,000 B.C.   Humans migrate from Asia to Americas over land bridge.

5000 B.C.   Sumerians migrate to Mesopotamia.

2300 B.C.   Semites migrate from Arabia to Mesopotamia.

2000 B.C.   Israelites migrate from Euphrates Valley to Canaan.

1000 B.C.   Phoenician sailors explore Britain and western Africa.

700 B.C.   Central Asian tribes migrate to Persia.

640 B.C.   Greek explorer Colaeus reaches Gibraltar and Spain.

600 B.C.   Egyptian pharaoh Necho circumnavigates Africa; Greek explorer Midacritus finds tin in England or Brittany.

510 B.C.   Greek traveler Scylax explores Indus River, Red Sea, and Arabia.

500 B.C.   Bantu tribes migrate through eastern Africa; Greek explorer Hekataios travels to Spain and North Africa; Carthaginian explorer Himlico visits French Atlantic Coast.

480 B.C.   Carthaginian admiral Hanno explores west coast of Africa.

424 B.C.   Greek traveler Herodotus visits North Africa, Italy, and Arabia.

400 B.C.   Greek explorer Ctesias travels to Ganges River in India.

345 B.C.   Greek explorer Pythias explores northwest European coastline.

327 B.C.   Alexander the Great leads army to Indus Valley of India.

325 B.C.   Greek admiral Nearchus attempts to circumnavigate Arabia.

302 B.C.   Greek traveler Megasthenes visits India, Tibet, and Ceylon.

218 B.C.   Hannibal leads army with elephants from Spain to Italy.

138 B.C.   Decimus Brutus becomes first Roman to reach west coast of Spain.

128 B.C.   Chinese explorer of central Asia has contact with Greeks.

112 B.C.   Greek explorer Eudoxus sails to India and western Africa.

100 B.C.   Greek explorer Hippalus finds direct ocean route to India.

55 B.C.   Julius Caesar leads Roman army to Britain.

20 A.D.   King Juba of Morocco explores Canary Islands.

80 A.D.   Gnaeus Agricola explores Atlantic coast of Britain.

100 A.D.   Roman explorer Julius Maternus crosses Sahara to Sudan; Alexander, Greek trader, sails to Vietnam and Cambodia; Chinese explorer Kan Ying reaches Black Sea and turns back.

370 A.D.   Huns, nomadic Mongols, invade Europe and reach Gaul.

400 A.D.   Chinese monk Fa Hsien visits India, Ceylon, and Java.

407 A.D.   Northern European Goths and Vandals spread to Mediterranean.

431 A.D. Gunavarman, prince of Kashmir, travels to Java and China.

570 A.D. Brendan, Irish monk, reportedly discovers America.

620 A.D. Vikings explore Ireland.

645 A.D. Chinese monk Yuan Chuang travels overland to India and returns.

861 A.D. Vikings discover Iceland.

872 A.D. Iraqi traveler Ibn Wahab visits China.

900 A.D. Mayans migrate from Central America to Yucatan Peninsula; Arab traveler Ibn Rosteh explores Malay Peninsula and Java.

921 A.D. Arabian diplomat Ahmad Ibn Fodhlan explores Russia and Poland.

950 A.D. Maori sailors discover New Zealand.

980 A.D. Arabs migrate to east coast of Africa.

981 A.D. Eric the Red discovers Greenland.

986 A.D. Viking sailor Bjarne Herjulfsson sights North America.

1000 A.D. Leif Ericsson explores Atlantic coast of North America.

1002 Thorwald Ericsson explores American coast below New England.

1007 Viking Thorfinn Karlsefni establishes North American colony.

1150 Polynesian Toi Kai Rakan opens settlement of New Zealand.

1165 Spanish rabbi Benjamin visits synagogues of Asia and Near East.

1245 Franciscan monk Giovanni Carpini travels to Mongol capital.

1271 Marco Polo begins 24-year journey to Orient and Near East.

1291 Vivaldi brothers try sailing Atlantic from Genoa to India; Italian explorer Malocello discovers Canary Islands.

1337 Josef Faquin circumnavigates known world of fourteenth century.

1350 Polynesian chief Marutuahu established colony in New Zealand.

1419 Portuguese king Henry begins African exploration.

1431 Portuguese explorer discovers Azores.

1440 Italian explorer Niccolò Conti travels in Indonesia and Malaya.

1446 Portuguese explorer Nuno Tristao is lost on second trip to Africa.

1455 Venetian sailor Cadamosto discovers Cape Verde Islands.

1482 Portuguese navigator Diego Cao explores Congo River; Portugal establishes African Gold Coast settlements.

1488 Portuguese explorer Bartholomeu Dias sails around Cape of Good Hope.

1492 Christopher Columbus discovers the West Indies; German navigator Martin Behaim shows Earth is spherical.

1493 Pope Alexander VI divides New World between Spain and Portugal.

1494 Bartolome Colon, brother of Columbus, explores Haiti.

1495 Francisco de Almeida establishes Portuguese naval bases in eastern Africa.

1497 Italian John Cabot discovers Newfoundland for England.

1498 Columbus discovers South America and Trinidad; Portuguese navigator Vasco da Gama finds sea route to India.

1499 Spanish explorer Vincent Yañez Pinzon discovers mouth of Amazon River.

1500 Portuguese explorer Pedro Cabral discovers Brazil.

1501 Amerigo Vespucci explores coast of Brazil; Spanish explorer Rodrigo Bastidas discovers Colombia.

1502 Columbus discovers Nicaragua; Spaniard Alonso de Ojeda explores Haiti, Guiana, and Venezuela.

1504 Portuguese explorer Pacheco Pereira visits India.

1505 Portuguese establish settlements in Mozambique; Portuguese nobleman Tristão da Cunha leads expedition to India.

1507 German maps by Martin Waldseemuller identify New World as ''America.''

1510 Afonso de Albuquerque establishes Portuguese base in India at Goa.

1512 Spanish priest Bartolomé Las Casas is missionary to Cuban Indians.

1513 Balboa, in Panama, discovers Pacific Ocean; Ponce de Leon explores Florida and West Indies; Portuguese reach Canton, China.

1514 Spanish explorer Francisco de Montejo travels to West Indies.

1516 Spanish explorer Juan Diaz de Solís discovers Rio de la Plata, Uruguay.

1517 Spanish explorer Fernandez de Cordoba discovers Mayan ruins.

1518 Pedro Alvarado explores Southeast Mexico for Spain; Spanish conquistador Juan de Grijalva discovers Aztec Empire.

1519 Hernan Cortes conquers Mexico for Spain.

1521 Ferdinand Magellan dies in an attempt to circumnavigate Earth.

1522 Spanish navigator Juan Sebastián Elcano is first to circumnavigate Earth.

1524 Italian explorer Giovanni da Verrazano discovers New York harbor; Francisco Pizarro explores the west coasts of Panama and Peru.

1526 Italian Sebastian Cabot explores Rio de la Plata, Uruguay.

1527 Cabeza de Vaca begins trek from Florida to Mexican west coast.

1528 Spanish explorer Panfilo de Narvaez dies near mouth of Mississippi.

1530 German adventurer Nikolaus Federmann explores Venezuela, Colombia, and the Andes.

1533 Spanish conquistador Francisco Pizarro conquers Peru; Spanish conquistador Sebastián de Benalcázar conquers Ecuador.

1535 Jacques Cartier explores Saint Lawrence River; Spanish explore Chile; Spanish explorer Antonio de Mendoza establishes city of Buenos Aires.

1536 Spaniard Jiménez de Quesada explores Colombia and Orinoco River; Spanish conquistador Domingo de Irala explores Parana and Paraguay rivers.

1540 Vásquez de Coronado explores Arizona and New Mexico; Spanish monk Andres Urdaneta explores Philippine Islands.

1541 Hernando de Soto discovers Mississippi River; Francisco de Orellana travels Amazon River from source in Peru to mouth; Gonzalo Pizarro crosses the Andes from Ecuador to the Amazon River.

1542 Portuguese explorer Mendes Pinto is first European in Japan.

1544 Spanish conquistadors explore coast of Oregon.

1553 English explorer Richard Chancellor establishes Russian trade route.

1554 English explorer Sir Hugh Willoughby dies seeking Northeast Passage.

1557 Portuguese establish Chinese base at Macao.

1562 French explorer Jan Ribault establishes colony in South Carolina.

1564 Miguel López de Legazpe claims Marianas and Philippines for Spain and founds Manila.

1569 Spanish explorer Alvaro Bazan crosses Chaco of South America.

1576 English explorer Sir Martin Frobisher searches for Northwest Passage.

1581 Cossack Timofeevich extends Russian territory into Siberia.

1582 Cossack Koltso aids Timofeevich in exploration of Siberia; Spanish explorer Berrio navigates Orinoco River.

1584 Sir Walter Raleigh explores Virginia and North Carolina.

1592 Explorer Cornelis de Houtman discovers Dutch route to East Indies.

1594 Dutch explorer Willem Barents searches for Northeast Passage.

1595 Dutch establish settlements on Guinea Coast.

1598 Van Neck leads second Dutch expedition to East Indies; English explorer Will Adams travels to Japan.

1602 Englishman Bartholomew Gosnold explores New England coast.

1603 Samuel de Champlain explores Saint Lawrence River as "route to China."

1607 Englishman John Smith helps establish Jamestown, Virginia.

1608 Champlain founds city of Quebec; John Smith explores Cape Cod and Chesapeake Bay.

1610 Henry Hudson discovers Hudson Bay and River; Dutch navigator Willem Schouten sails around Cape Horn.

1613 Dutch colonist Jan Coen establishes factories in Indonesia; English explorer William Baffin discovers Baffin Bay and Island.

1614 Dutch captain Christianssen establishes fort at Albany, New York.

1615 Champlain explores lakes Huron and Ontario.

1617 Dutch explorers Jakob LeMaire and Willem Schouten start trip around world.

1618 French explorer Imbert finds Timbuktu in Africa.

1620 English Pilgrims reach Cape Cod.

1626 French establish settlements in Madagascar; Dutch settle New Amsterdam in North America; French missionary Jean de Brébeuf explores Lake Huron region.

1631 English captain Thomas James explores James Bay in Canada.

1637 Russian explorers reach Pacific coast of Siberia.

1642 French explorer Sieur de Maisonneuve founds city of Montreal; Dutch explorer Abel Tasman discovers Van Dieman's Land (Tasmania).

1645 Capuchin monks explore Congo River.

1646 French missionary Isaac Jogues discovers Lake George.

1649 Cossack Dezhnev explores Siberia and Alaska for Russia; Cossack Stadukhin explores the Lena and Kolyma rivers in Siberia.

1652 Dutch colonist Jan van Riebeek founds Cape of Good Hope settlement.

1659 French fur trader Pierre Radisson explores Minnesota.

1670 French fur trader Perrot explores upper Mississippi region.

1673 French explorers Louis Joliet and Jacques Marquette navigate the length of the Mississippi.

1675 Belgian explorer Louis Hennepin discovers Niagara Falls and Mississippi source.

1679 Frenchman Daniel Duluth explores Minnesota and Great Lakes.

1681 Sieur de La Salle explores Mississippi and names delta area Louisiana; English buccaneer William Dampier explores South Pacific islands.

1682 Buero da Silva explores Central Mountains region of Brazil; Pieres de Campos explores rivers of South America.

1683 Dutch explorer Aerssen establishes colony of Surinam; German naturalist Kaempfer visits Java, Thailand, and Japan.

1685 French missionary Claude Allouez explores western Lake Superior.

1697 Cossack Atlasov explores Kamchatka Peninsula for Russia.

1699 William Dampier explores northwest cost of Australia.

1721 Norwegian missionary Hans Egede is first European in Greenland in 200 years.

1723 Russian adventurer Fedorov explores northwest cost of America.

1732 Gvozdev explores Bering Sea and Alaska coastline for Russia.

1741 Russian explorer Chrikov discovers some Aleutian Islands.

1744 Frenchman Charles La Condamine measures arc of meridian in Andes.

1745 Basov explores Aleutian Islands for Russia.

1767 English navigator James Cook explores east coast of Australia.

1772 English explorer Samuel Hearne is first European to reach Arctic Ocean; Frenchman Yves Kerguélen-Trémarec discovers Antarctic islands; James Cook searches for possible continent of Antarctica.

1776 Cook searches for possible Atlantic–Pacific maritime passage.

1784 Daniel Boone explores Appalachian and Ozark areas.

1789 Scottish fur trader Sir Alexander Mackenzie explores western Canada.

1790 Russian fur trader Aleksandr Baranov explores Alaska; American explorer Robert Gray discovers Columbia River.

1797 German adventurer Hornemann explores caravan routes of Sahara Desert.

1798 British explorer George Bass circumnavigates Tasmania.

1799 German explorer Alexander von Humboldt tours North and South America.

1802 English explorer Matthew Flinders circumnavigates Australia; Portuguese explorers cross Africa.

1804 Lewis and Clark begin exploration of Louisiana Purchase; Russian Lisyanskii explores Pacific from Hawaii to Alaska.

1805 Canadian Fraser explores Canada west of Rocky Mountains; Russian navigator Adam Krusenstern maps Sakhalin, discovers Amur's mouth.

1815 Russian navigator Otto Kotzebue discovers many Pacific islands.

1818 French explorer René Caillé crosses Sahara, reaching Timbuktu.

1819 English explorer Sir William Parry finds Northwest Passage in Arctic.

1820 American Nathaniel Palmer discovers Palmer Peninsula of Antarctica.

1821 Russian Fabian Bellinghausen leads South Pole expedition.

1825 British explorer Sir John Franklin surveys Canadian Arctic region.

1828 German physicist Georg Erman circumnavigates Earth, studying magnetic fields.

1829 English explorer Freemantle founds West Australia colony.

1830 British Lander brothers explore Niger River and delta.

1831 American Benjamin Bonneville explores Rocky Mountains and California; British explorer James Ross finds North Magnetic Pole.

1835 British colonist Bourke explores new areas of Australia; American pioneer Jim Bowie explores U.S. Southwest.

1837 American trapper Joseph Walker explores Sierra Mountains.

1840 Frenchman Dumont d'Urville discovers Antarctic islands.

1842 John Fremont begins exploration west of Rockies.

1843 British colonist Edward Eyre explores South and West Australia; Scottish explorer Sir James Ross proves Antarctica has ice barrier.

1846 German explorer Friedrich Leichhardt disappears crossing Australia.

1847 French naturalist Comte de Castelnau crosses South America west to east.

1848 American explorer Elisha Kane surveys Gulf of Mexico.

1850 English naval officer Sir Robert McClure discovers Northwest Passage.

1851 German explorer Heinrich Barth crosses Sahara Desert twice; American explorer Savage rediscovers Yosemite Valley.

1853 Englishman Sir Richard Burton is first non-Muslim to visit Mecca and Medina; American explorer Elisha Kane leads Arctic expedition.

1854 U.S. Commodore Matthew Perry ends isolation of Japan; German Schlagintweit brothers explore Central Asia; Portuguese explorer Silva Porto crosses South Africa, west to east.

1855 Russian adventurer Nevelskoi explores Amur and proves Sakhalin is an island.

1856 Scottish missionary David Livingstone explores Africa; English explorers Richard Burton and John Speke discover Lake Tanganyika; English explorer Gregory crosses Australia east to west.

1857 British explorer John Speke discovers Lake Victoria.

1860 Irish explorer Robert Burke is first to cross Australia south to north; German explorer Karl Decken leads Kilimanjaro Mountain expedition; John Speke and James Grant prove Lake Victoria is source of Nile; American Isaac Hayes searches for "open sea" above Arctic Circle.

1863 Frenchman Louis Faidherbe explores Senegal and Niger River in Africa.

1864 Hermann Schlagintweit is first European to cross Kuenlun range.

1866 Doudart explores Mekong River route to source for France.

1871 Russian naturalist Aleksi Fedchenko explores Asian mountain ranges; British journalist Henry Stanley finds missing Livingstone; American Charles Hall is first to explore above 82 degrees north latitude.

1872 French colonist Francis Garnier searches for China–Tibet river route.

1874 John and Alexander Forrest survey western Australia.

1878 German Eduard Schnitzer (Emin Pasha) explores African lake country; English explorer Sir George Nares surveys Magellan Strait; Russian Grigori Potanin explores Gobi Desert of Mongolia.

1879 Swedish explorer Nils Nordenskjöld discovers Northeast Passage; Russian Nikolai Przhevalski is first to cross Tibet's Humboldt Mountains; Joseph Thompson explores Great Rift Valley of Africa.

1880 French colonist Pierre Brazza explores African river routes to sea.

1882 French explorer Pierre Bonvalot discovers ancient cities of Asia.

1883 French officer Foucauld explores Algerian oases and Morocco.

1885 Portuguese explorer Capelo crosses South Africa.

1888 Norwegian Fridtjof Nansen explores Greenland ice cap; French explorer Louis Binger leads African scientific expedition.

1889 German explorer Hans Meyer is first to scale Kilimanjaro peak; Austrian Oskar Baumann explores African rivers and lakes.

1891 German Erich von Drygalski explores West Greenland.

1892 Scottish oceanographer William Bruce explores Antarctic coastline; Englishman William Conway is first to scale 23,000-foot Himalayan peaks; American Robert Peary explores Greenland and proves it is an island.

1893 Swedish engineer Andre explores Arctic by balloon; German explorer Goetzen crosses Africa east to west.

1894 Englishwoman Mary Kingsley explores Ogowe River in Africa.

1895 French explorer Charles Bonin crosses Tibet and Mongolia; Englishman Frederick Jackson explores Franz Josef Land in Arctic.

1897 Gerlache de Gomery leads Belgian Antarctic expedition.

1899 Sweden's Sven Hedin finds sources of Bramaputra and Indus rivers.

1900 Norwegian Carsten Borchgrevink is early Antarctic explorer.

1906 Norwegian Roald Amundsen is first to navigate Northwest Passage.

1908 British explorer Sir Ernest Shackleton nearly reaches South Pole.

1909 American explorer Robert Peary is first to reach North Pole.

1910 Bavarian officer Wilhelm Filchner leads German Antarctic expedition.

1911 Norwegian explorer Roald Amundsen reaches South Pole; American explorer Bingham discovers Machu Picchu in Peru; British explorer Sir Douglas Mawson leads Antarctic expedition.

1912 British explorer Robert Scott reaches South Pole.

1913 Theodore Roosevelt explores central Brazilian rivers.

1926 Americans Floyd Bennett and Richard Byrd fly over North Pole; American Lincoln Ellsworth flies over North Pole; Italian engineer Umberto Nobile flies over North Pole, from Norway to Alaska.

1927 American Charles Lindbergh is first to fly solo across Atlantic Ocean.

1929 American explorer Richard Byrd is first to fly over South Pole; German Hugo Eckener makes round-the-world flight.

1931 Eckener flies over North Pole.

1932 British explorer St. John Philby crosses Arabia's Rub-al-Kali Desert; Jean Piccard explores stratosphere in balloon gondola.

1935 Lincoln Ellsworth flies over South Pole.

1937 Russian aviator Valeri Chkalov is first to fly from USSR to America over North Pole.

1947 Norwegian Thor Heyerdahl sails balsa raft from Peru to Polynesia.

1953 British mountaineer Sir Edmund Hillary and Tenzing Norgay of Nepal scale Mount Everest.

1956 Heyerdahl explores Easter Island and eastern Pacific.

1958 American explorer Anderson crosses North Pole in submarine.

1961 Russian cosmonaut Yuri Gagarin is first man to orbit Earth.

1962 John Glenn is first American to orbit Earth.

1969 American astronauts Neil Armstrong and ''Buzz'' Aldrin land on moon.

1976 Mars space probes, Viking 1 and 2, are launched by NASA.

1981 Space shuttle Columbia, the world's first reusable spacecraft, orbits Earth 36 times, carrying two astronauts, marking the beginning of the U.S. space shuttle program.

1986 Experimental airplane Voyager, using a single load of fuel, completes a flight around the world, setting a record for distance flown without refueling.

Major World Cities

City	Population (est.)
Addis Ababa, Ethiopia	1,423,000
Capital since 1896	
Ahmedabad, India	2,548,000
Founded in 1411	
Alexandria, Egypt	2,705,000
Founded by Alexander the Great, 332 B.C.	
Algiers, Algeria	2,500,000
Founded in tenth century on Roman site	
Amman, Jordan	800,000
Site of biblical city of Ammonites	
Amsterdam, The Netherlands	679,000
Founded in 1300	
Ankara, Turkey	2,252,000
Capital of Galacia around 300 B.C.	

City	*Population (est.)*
Athens, Greece	3,000,000
Ancient Greek city-state in 700 B.C.	
Auckland, New Zealand	895,000
Founded 1840, original capital	
Baghdad, Iraq	3,500,000
Center of Islamic culture since 813	
Baku, USSR	1,700,000
Founded in ninth century	
Bandung, Indonesia	1,600,000
Founded in 1810	
Bangalore, India	2,900,000
Founded in sixteenth century	
Bangkok, Thailand	5,180,000
Capital since 1782	
Barcelona, Spain	1,800,000
Founded by Carthaginians around 300 B.C.	
Barranquilla, Colombia	900,000
Inland seaport since 1935	
Beirut, Lebanon	750,000
Site of ancient Phoenician settlement	
Belgrade, Yugoslavia	1,250,000
Site of Singidunum, ancient Roman camp	
Belo Horizonte, Brazil	2,500,000
Cattle and cotton-trading center	
Birmingham, England	1,020,000
Market town since before thirteenth century	
Bogotá, Colombia	4,000,000
Founded by conquistadors in 1538	
Bombay, India	8,300,000
Established in early Christian era	
Brisbane, Australia	1,160,000
Founded in 1824 as a penal colony	
Brussels, Belgium	1,000,000
Capital since 1530	
Bucharest, Rumania	1,975,000
Capital since 1861	
Budapest, Hungary	2,200,000
Site of Aquincum, second-century Roman camp	
Buenos Aires, Argentina	3,100,000
Settled by conquistadors in 1536	
Cairo, Egypt	12,680,000
Site of seventh-century Arab military camp	
Calcutta, India	9,840,000
Developed from 1690 English factory site	
Calgary, Alberta, Canada	600,000
Originally (1875) Northwest Mounted Police post	
Cali, Colombia	1,325,000
Founded by conquistadors in 1536	
Canton, China	7,060,000
Inland seaport since third century B.C.	
Cape Town, South Africa	1,100,000
Founded in 1652 as Dutch naval base	
Caracas, Venezuela	3,000,000
Founded by conquistadors in 1567	

City	*Population (est.)*
Casablanca, Morocco	2,200,000
Site of ancient City of Anfa	
Chicago, Illinois	3,000,000
Originally portage site for fur traders	
Chittagong, Bangladesh	1,450,000
Portuguese trading post in 1600s	
Chungking, China	4,080,000
Former capital of Nationalist China	
Cologne, West Germany	929,000
Site of Roman (50 A.D.) Colonia Agrippina	
Copenhagen, Denmark	1,400,000
Capital since 1443	
Córdoba, Argentina	1,095,000
Founded in 1573; university founded 1613	
Damascus, Syria	1,210,000
City of Egyptians and Hittites before 1000 B.C.	
Delhi, India	6,000,000
Thirteenth-century capital of northern India	
Dhaka, Bangladesh	4,000,000
Capital since 1971 secession from Pakistan	
Dnepropetrovsk, USSR	1,100,000
Founded in 1787 at Cossack village site	
Donetsk, USSR	1,050,000
Founded in 1870; called Stalino until 1961	
Dresden, East Germany	528,000
Originally (922 A.D.) a Slavonic settlement	
Dublin, Ireland	547,000
Originally a ninth-century Viking base	
Düsseldorf, West Germany	568,000
Rhine River port since eleventh century	
East Berlin, East Germany	1,150,000
Part of divided city since 1945	
Edmonton, Alberta, Canada	670,000
Originally (1795) Hudson Bay trading post	
Essen, West Germany	649,000
Ruhr Valley city founded in ninth century	
Frankfurt, West Germany	600,000
Site of ancient Roman military camp	
Fukuoka, Japan	1,300,000
Thirteenth-century seaport on Hakata Bay	
Genoa, Italy	750,000
Roman settlement in third century B.C.	
Glasgow, Scotland	780,000
Founded by sixth-century missionaries	
Gorky, USSR	1,405,000
Founded in 1221; renamed for Maxim Gorky	
Guadalajara, Mexico	2,960,000
Originally founded in 1530	
Guatemala City, Guatemala	1,190,000
Founded as capital in 1776	
Guayaquil, Ecuador	1,598,000
Founded by conquistadors in 1535	
Hamburg, West Germany	1,700,000
Founded in ninth century by Charlemagne	

City	*Population (est.)*
Harbin, China	3,500,000
Village until linked by railroad in 1898	
Havana, Cuba	2,000,000
Founded in 1519 as Spanish navy base	
Ho Chi Minh City, Vietnam	3,500,000
Formerly Saigon, ancient Khmer village	
Hyderabad, India	2,600,000
Founded as Golconda; capital in 1589	
Hyderabad, Pakistan	830,000
Founded in 1768 as capital of Sind	
Ibadan, Nigeria	1,000,000
Founded around 1830 as military camp	
Istanbul, Turkey	5,650,000
Until 300 A.D., Byzantium; until 1930, Constantinople	
Jakarta, Indonesia	7,650,000
Founded in 1619 as Batavia; renamed 1971	
Johannesburg, South Africa	1,695,000
Founded as gold-mining camp in 1886	
Kanpur, India	1,597,000
Village until ceded to British in 1801	
Karachi, Pakistan	5,260,000
Founded in 1725 as Hindu trading center	
Kharkov, USSR	1,560,000
Founded in 1654 as outpost of Moscow	
Kiev, USSR	2,500,000
Russian "Mother of Cities," founded 882	
Kinshasa, Zaire	3,325,000
Founded in 1881 as Leopoldville; renamed 1966	
Kobe, Japan	1,500,000
Ancient fishing village until 1868	
Kuala Lumpur, Malaysia	1,200,000
Founded as tin-mining settlement in 1857	
Kuibyshev, USSR	1,250,000
Founded in 1586; temporary Russian capital in World War II	
Lagos, Nigeria	1,100,000
Former slave trading center; now the capital	
Lahore, Pakistan	3,000,000
Capital of Mogul sultans in eleventh century	
La Paz, Bolivia	1,000,000
Founded in 1548; capital since 1898	
Leipzig, East Germany	550,000
Founded in eleventh century; Bach was organist here	
Leningrad, USSR	5,000,000
Founded in 1703 as St. Petersburg; renamed 1924	
Lima, Peru	4,980,000
Site of oldest university of Americas (1551)	
Lisbon, Portugal	935,000
Ancient Phoenician, Carthaginian trading center	
Liverpool, England	509,000
Chartered in 1207 by King John	
Lodz, Poland	850,500
Founded in 1423; belonged to Russia until 1919	
London, England	6,750,000
Established in 43 A.D. as Roman town of Londinium	

City	*Population (est.)*
Los Angeles, California	3,200,000
Founded in 1781 as capital of Spanish colony	
Madras, India	4,400,000
Founded in 1640 as British outpost	
Madrid, Spain	3,250,000
A Moorish fortress until 932	
Managua, Nicaragua	700,000
Established as capital in 1855 to end feud	
Manila, Philippines	1,800,000
Founded by Spanish in 1571	
Marseilles, France	849,000
Originally Massilia, Ionian Greek Colony, in 600 B.C.	
Mecca, Saudi Arabia	550,000
Birthplace of Muhammad in 570	
Medellín, Colombia	1,390,000
Coffee, drugs, mining center founded 1675	
Melbourne, Australia	3,000,000
Founded 1835 by Tasmanian settlers	
Mexico City, Mexico	12,650,000
Aztec capital until captured by Cortes in 1521	
Milan, Italy	1,700,000
Ancient Celtic town captured by Romans in 222 B.C.	
Minsk, USSR	1,500,000
Eleventh-century city on Moscow–Warsaw rail link	
Monterrey, Mexico	2,240,000
Founded in 1579; invaded by U.S. troops in 1846	
Montevideo, Uruguay	1,350,000
Settled by Spanish in 1726; capital since 1828	
Montreal, Quebec, Canada	2,900,000
Site of Indian encampment; founded by French in 1642	
Moscow, USSR	8,500,000
Founded in 1147; became capital around 1340	
Munich, West Germany	1,250,000
Founded in 1158; birthplace of Nazi movement, 1923	
Nagoya, Japan	2,200,000
Buddhist temple site in second century; now an industrial city	
Nanking, China	4,700,000
Founded in 1368; twice capital in twentieth century	
Naples, Italy	1,250,000
Named Neapolis (New City) by Greek settlers around 600 B.C.	
New York City, New York	7,000,000
Founded in 1609 as New Amsterdam by Dutch; renamed 1664	
Novosibirsk, USSR	1,400,000
"Chicago of Siberia," founded 1893 on Trans-Siberian Railway	
Odessa, USSR	1,295,000
Founded by Tartars in fourteenth century	
Osaka, Japan	2,575,000
Founded in sixteenth century as capital city	
Ottawa, Ontario, Canada	800,000
Selected as capital in 1858 by Queen Victoria	
Palermo, Sicily	822,000
Founded by Phoenicians in eighth century B.C.	
Paris, France	2,195,000
Grew from pre-Roman settlement named Lutetia Parisiorum	

City	*Population (est.)*
Peking, China	10,000,000
Founded around 1122 B.C.; renamed Beijing in 1949	
Port-au-Prince, Haiti	750,000
Founded by sugar planters in 1749; capital since 1804	
Porto Alegre, Brazil	1,300,000
Founded in 1742 by settlers from Azores	
Prague, Czechoslovakia	1,200,000
Grew from tenth-century trading center	
Pusan, South Korea	3,500,000
Originally a fishing village; opened to trade in 1443	
Pyongyang, North Korea	1,500,000
Existed as Heijo, Korean cultural center, in 1100 B.C.	
Quebec City, Quebec, Canada	580,000
Site of Indian settlement visited by Cartier in 1535	
Quezon City, Philippines	1,400,000
Founded in 1940 as site of future capital	
Quito, Ecuador	1,200,000
Originally Quito Indian camp; captured by Incas in 1470	
Rangoon, Burma	2,300,000
Existed as fishing village in sixth century	
Recife, Brazil	1,300,000
Settled by Portuguese in 1535	
Rio de Janeiro	5,750,000
Founded by Portuguese in 1502; capital since 1889	
Riyadh, Saudi Arabia	1,250,000
One-time center of classic Arabic architecture	
Rome, Italy	3,000,000
According to legend, founded in 753 B.C. by Romulus	
Rosario, Argentina	1,000,000
City in La Pampa region; founded in 1730	
Rotterdam, The Netherlands	560,000
North Sea port chartered in 1328	
Salvador, Brazil	2,000,000
Founded in 1549 as Bahia	
Santiago, Chile	4,300,000
Founded in 1541 by Spanish conquistadors	
Santo Domingo, Dominican Republic	1,500,000
Oldest continuous European settlement in Americas, founded in 1496	
São Paulo, Brazil	12,500,000
Founded in 1554 by Jesuit missionaries on Indian campsite	
Sapporo, Japan	1,500,000
Founded in 1869 in government plan to develop Hokkaido Island	
Seoul, South Korea	10,000,000
Originally named Keijo, a Korean capital since 1392	
Seville, Spain	770,000
Originally Hispalis, a Phoenician trading center	
Shanghai, China	12,000,000
Existed as Hu-tsen in Sung dynasty, eleventh century	
Shenyang, China	5,250,000
Formerly Mukden, capital city of twelfth-century Tartars	
Singapore, Singapore	2,650,000
Original Singhapura, destroyed in 1365; refounded in 1819	

City	*Population (est.)*
Sofia, Bulgaria	1,100,000
Founded as Sardica by second-century Romans; capital since 1879	
Stockholm, Sweden	1,440,000
Originally a fishing village, founded in thirteenth century	
Surabaja, Indonesia	2,300,000
Grew from seventeenth-century Javanese trading post	
Sverdlovsk, USSR	1,290,000
Founded in 1721 as Ekaterinburg (Catherine); renamed in 1924	
Sydney, Australia	3,400,000
First British settlement in Australia, 1788	
Taipei, Taiwan	2,500,000
Settled in eighteenth century by Chinese mainland immigrants	
Tashkent, USSR	1,950,000
Ancient central Asian city; existed in first century B.C.	
Tbilisi, USSR	1,050,000
Also called Tiflis; settled in fourth century B.C.	
Teheran, Iran	6,100,000
Settled in thirteenth century by refugees from Mongol invasion	
Tianjin, China	7,910,000
Also called Tientsin, ancient trading center	
Tokyo, Japan	8,535,000
Founded in twelfth century as fortress for warlord	
Toronto, Ontario, Canada	3,000,000
Originally Fort Rouille, 1749; York, 1793; renamed 1834	
Tripoli, Libya	598,000
Founded as Oea by Phoenicians in seventh century B.C.	
Tunis, Tunisia	602,000
Pre-Carthaginian city with access to Mediterranean	
Turin, Italy	1,180,000
Ancient Roman city of Augusta Taurinorum	
Valencia, Spain	760,000
Former city of Romans, Visgoths, Moors	
Vancouver, British Columbia, Canada	1,360,000
Originally settled in 1875 as Granville; renamed 1886	
Vienna, Austria	1,550,000
Capital of the Austro-Hungarian Empire 1278–1918; now capital of the Austrian republic	
Volgograd, USSR	968,000
Founded in 1589 as Tsaritsyn; later Stalingrad; renamed 1961	
Warsaw, Poland	1,780,000
Settled in eleventh century; capital since 1596	
Washington, DC	765,000
Founded in 1790 on site selected by George Washington	
Wellington, New Zealand	600,000
Founded in 1840; replaced Auckland as capital in 1865	
Yokohama, Japan	3,280,000
Feudal fishing village until opened to foreign trade in 1859	

The United Nations

The United Nations organization was established during World War II as an outgrowth of an agreement among 26 countries fighting the Germany–Italy–Japan Axis. It replaced the League of Nations as an instrument for the promotion of international peace and security.

The name was suggested by U.S. President Franklin D. Roosevelt in 1941 and was officially adopted the following year. The United Nations was formally organized on June 26, 1945, following an initial San Francisco conference to draft a charter.

The basic charter contains 19 chapters, divided into 111 articles, and provides for the support of a number of international organs and agencies. These include the General Assembly, Security Council, Secretariat, International Court of Justice, Trusteeship Council, Economic and Social Council, World Health Organization, Food and Agricultural Organization, International Bank for Reconstruction and Development, International Labor Organization, International Monetary Fund, International Civil Aviation Organization, International Telecommunications Union, Universal Postal Union, World Meteorological Organization, and Educational, Scientific, and Cultural Organization (UNESCO).

The United Nations System

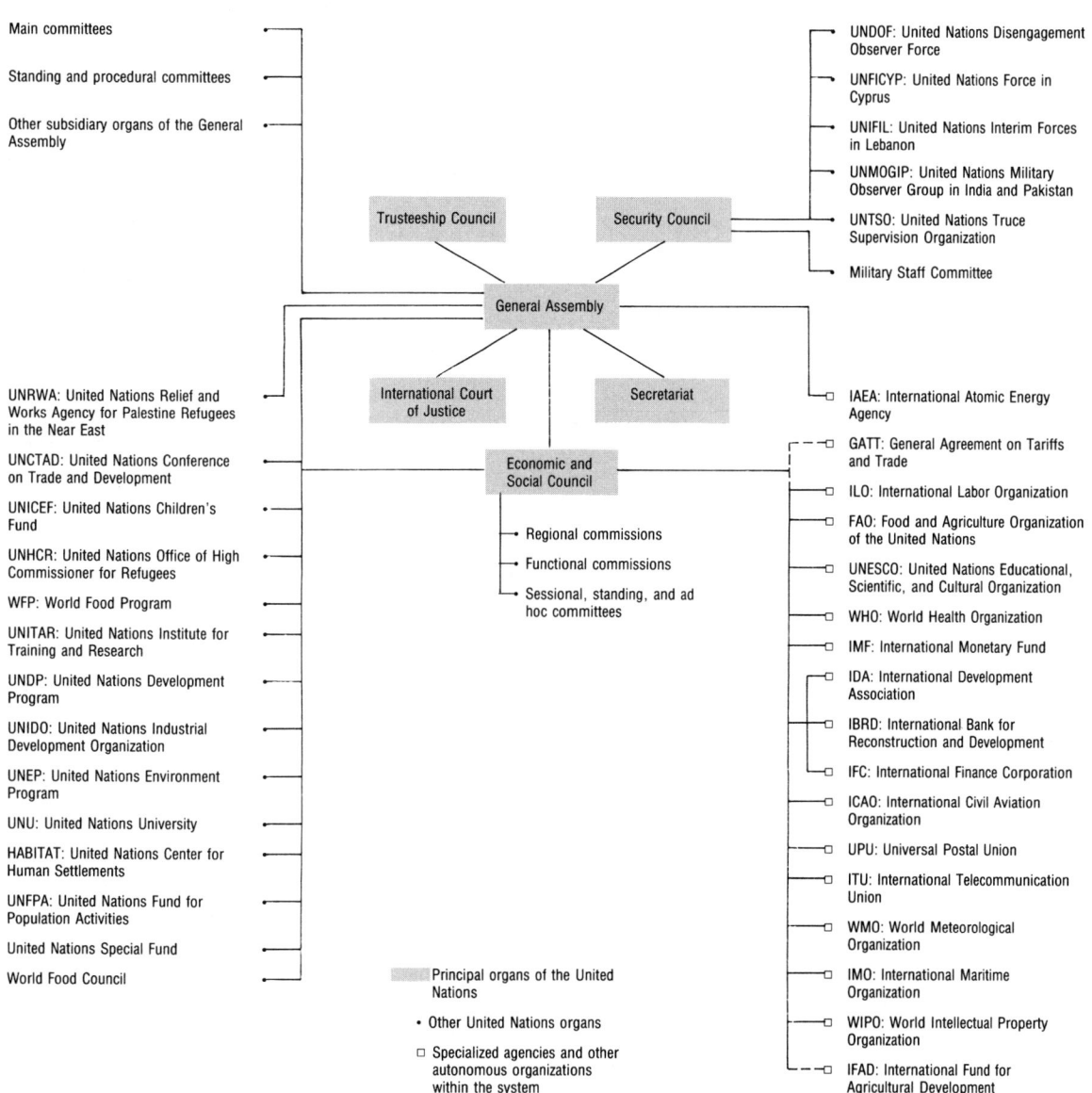

Main committees

Standing and procedural committees

Other subsidiary organs of the General Assembly

Trusteeship Council

Security Council

General Assembly

International Court of Justice

Secretariat

Economic and Social Council

- Regional commissions
- Functional commissions
- Sessional, standing, and ad hoc committees

UNDOF: United Nations Disengagement Observer Force

UNFICYP: United Nations Force in Cyprus

UNIFIL: United Nations Interim Forces in Lebanon

UNMOGIP: United Nations Military Observer Group in India and Pakistan

UNTSO: United Nations Truce Supervision Organization

Military Staff Committee

UNRWA: United Nations Relief and Works Agency for Palestine Refugees in the Near East

UNCTAD: United Nations Conference on Trade and Development

UNICEF: United Nations Children's Fund

UNHCR: United Nations Office of High Commissioner for Refugees

WFP: World Food Program

UNITAR: United Nations Institute for Training and Research

UNDP: United Nations Development Program

UNIDO: United Nations Industrial Development Organization

UNEP: United Nations Environment Program

UNU: United Nations University

HABITAT: United Nations Center for Human Settlements

UNFPA: United Nations Fund for Population Activities

United Nations Special Fund

World Food Council

IAEA: International Atomic Energy Agency

GATT: General Agreement on Tariffs and Trade

ILO: International Labor Organization

FAO: Food and Agriculture Organization of the United Nations

UNESCO: United Nations Educational, Scientific, and Cultural Organization

WHO: World Health Organization

IMF: International Monetary Fund

IDA: International Development Association

IBRD: International Bank for Reconstruction and Development

IFC: International Finance Corporation

ICAO: International Civil Aviation Organization

UPU: Universal Postal Union

ITU: International Telecommunication Union

WMO: World Meteorological Organization

IMO: International Maritime Organization

WIPO: World Intellectual Property Organization

IFAD: International Fund for Agricultural Development

Principal organs of the United Nations

- Other United Nations organs

□ Specialized agencies and other autonomous organizations within the system

International Organizations

A	AAPSO	Afro-Asian People's Solidarity Organization
	ADB	Asian Development Bank
	AfDB	African Development Bank
	AIOEC	Association of Iron Ore Exporting Countries
	ANRPC	Association of Natural Rubber Producing Countries
	ANZUS	ANZUS Council; treaty signed by Australia, New Zealand, and the United States
	APC	African Peanut (Groundnut) Council
	. . .	Arab League (League of Arab States)
	ASEAN	Association of Southeast Asian Nations
	ASPAC	Asian and Pacific Council
	ASSIMER	International Mercury Producers Association
B	BENELUX	Belgium, Netherlands, Luxembourg Economic Union
	BLEU	Belgium-Luxembourg Economic Union
C	CACM	Central American Common Market
	CARICOM	Caribbean Common Market
	CARIFTA	Caribbean Free Trade Association
	CCC	Customs Cooperation Council
	CDB	Caribbean Development Bank
	CEAO	West African Economic Community
	CEMA	Council for Mutual Economic Assistance
	CENTO	Central Treaty Organization
	CIPEC	Intergovernmental Council of Copper Exporting Countries
	. . .	Colombo Plan
	. . .	Council of Europe
D	DAC	Development Assistance Committee (OECD)
E	EAMA	African States associated with the EEC
	EC	European Communities
	ECA	Economic Commission for Africa (UN)
	ECE	Economic Commission for Europe (UN)
	ECLA	Economic Commission for Latin America (UN)
	ECOSOC	Economic and Social Council (UN)
	ECOWAS	Economic Community of West African States
	ECWA	Economic Commission for Western Asia (UN)
	EEC	European Economic Market
	EFTA	European Free Trade Association

	EIB	European Investment Bank
	ELDO	European Space Vehicle Launcher Development Organization
	EMS	European Monetary System
	ENTENTE	Political-Economic Association of Ivory Coast, Benin, Niger, Burkina Faso, and Togo
	ESCAP	Economic and Social Commission for Asia and the Pacific (UN)
	ESRO	European Space Research Organization
F	FAO	Food and Agriculture Organization (UN)
G	G-77	Group of 77
	GA	General Assembly (UN)
	GATT	General Agreement of Tariffs and Trade (UN)
	GCC	Gulf Cooperation Council
I	IADB	Inter-American Defense Board
	IAEA	International Atomic Energy Agency (UN)
	IATP	International Association of Tungsten Producers
	IBA	International Bauxite Association
	IBEC	International Bank for Economic Cooperation
	IBRD	International Bank for Reconstruction and Development (''World Bank,'' UN)
	ICAC	International Cotton Advisory Committee
	ICAO	International Civil Aviation Organization (UN)
	ICCAT	International Commission for the Conservation of Atlantic Tunas
	ICCO	International Cocoa Organization
	ICEM	Intergovernmental Committee for European Migration
	ICES	International Commission for the Exploration of the Seas
	ICJ	International Court of Justice (UN)
	ICO	International Coffee Organization
	IDA	International Development Association (IBRD affiliate, UN)
	IDB	Inter-American Development Bank
	IDB	Islamic Development Bank
	IEA	International Energy Agency (associated with OECD)
	IFAD	International Fund for Agricultural Development (UN)
	IFC	International Finance Corporation (IBRD affiliate, UN)
	IHO	International Hydrographic Organization
	IIB	International Investment Bank
	ILO	International Labor Organization (UN)
	. . .	International Lead and Zinc Study Group
	IMF	International Monetary Fund (UN)
	IMO	International Maritime Organization (UN)

	INRO	International Natural Rubber Organization
	INTELSAT	International Telecommunications Satellite Organization
	IOOC	International Olive Oil Council
	IPU	Inter-Parliamentary Union
	IRC	International Rice Council
	ISO	International Sugar Organization
	ITC	International Tin Council
	ITU	International Telecommunication Union (UN)
	IWC	International Whaling Commission
	IWC	International Wheat Council
L	LAIA	Latin American Integration Association
N	NAM	Nonaligned Movement
	NATO	North Atlantic Treaty Organization
O	OAPEC	Organization of Arab Petroleum Exporting Countries
	OAS	Organization of American States
	OAU	Organization of African Unity
	OCAM	Afro-Malagasy and Mauritian Common Organization
	ODECA	Organization of Central American States
	OECD	Organization for Economic Cooperation and Development
	OIC	Organization of the Islamic Conference
	OPEC	Organization of Petroleum Exporting Countries
P	PAHO	Pan American Health Organization
S	SAARC	South Asian Association for Regional Cooperation
	SADCC	Southern African Development Coordination Committee

Country Membership in International Organizations

	International Organizations																	
Country	ADB	**ARAB** LEAGUE	ASEAN	CACM	CARICOM	CEMA	EC	G-77	GCC	IDB[a]	IDB[b]	INTELSAT	LAIA	NAM	NATO	OAPEC	OAS
Afghanistan	●							●			●	●		●			
Albania						●d											
Algeria		●						●			●	●		●		●	
Andorrac																	
Angola								●				●		●			
Antigua and Barbuda					●			●									●

	SC	Security Council (UN)
	SELA	Latin American Economic System
	SPC	South Pacific Commission
	SPEC	South Pacific Bureau for Economic Cooperation
	SPF	South Pacific Forum
T	TC	Trusteeship Council (UN)
	TDB	Trade and Development Board (UN)
U	UDEAC	Economic and Customs Union of Central Africa
	UEAC	Union of Central African States
	UNCTAD	UN Conference on Trade and Development
	UNDP	UN Development Program
	UNESCO	UN Educational, Scientific, and Cultural Organization
	UNICEF	UN Children's Fund
	UNIDO	UN Industrial Development Organization
	UPEB	Union of Banana Exporting Countries
	UPU	Universal Postal Union (UN)
W	WEU	Western European Union
	WFC	World Food Council (UN)
	WFTU	World Federation of Trade Unions
	WHO	World Health Organization (UN)
	WIPO	World Intellectual Property Organization (UN)
	WMO	World Meteorological Organization (UN)
	WPC	World Peace Council
	WSG	International Wool Study Group
	WTO	World Tourism Organization

						United Nations Organizations																
OAU	OECD	OIC	OPEC	SELA	WFTU	FAO	GATT	IAEA	IBRD	ICAO	ICJ	IDA	IFAD	IFC	ILO	IMF	IMO	ITU	UNESCO	UPU	WHO	WMO
		●c			●	●		●	●	●	●	●	●	●	●	●		●	●	●	●	●
					●	●		●			●							●	●	●	●	●
●		●	●			●	●	●	●	●	●	●	●		●	●	●	●	●	●	●	●
																			●			
●					●	●	●			●	●		●		●			●	●	●	●	●
						●		●	●	●					●	●				●	●	●

International Organizations

Country	ADB	ARAB LEAGUE	ASEAN	CACM	CARICOM	CEMA	EC	G-77	GCC	IDBᵃ	IDBᵇ	INTELSAT	LAIA	NAM	NATO	OAPEC	OAS
Argentina								•		•		•	•	•			•
Australia	•											•					
Austria	•									•		•					
Bahamas					•			•		•				•			•
Bahrain		•						•	•		•			•		•	
Bangladesh	•							•			•	•		•			
Barbados					•			•		•		•		•			•
Belgium	•						•			•		•			•		
Belize					•			•									
Benin								•						•			
Bhutan	•							•						•			
Bolivia								•		•		•	•	•			•
Botswana								•						•			
Brazil			•					•		•		•	•				•
Brunei			•														
Bulgaria						•								•			
Burkina Faso								•			•	•		•			
Burma	•							•									
Burundi								•						•			
Cambodia	•							•						•			
Cameroon								•			•	•		•			
Canada	•									•		•			•		
Cape Verde								•						•			
Central African Republic								•			•			•			
Chad								•			•			•			
Chile								•		•		•	•				•
China, People's Republic of												•					
Colombia								•		•		•	•	•			•
Comoros								•			•			•			
Congo								•				•		•			
Cook Islands[c]	•																
Costa Rica				•				•		•		•					•
Cuba						•		•						•			•
Cyprus								•				•		•			
Czechoslovakia						•											
Denmark	•						•			•		•			•		
Djibouti		•						•			•			•			
Dominica					•			•									•
Dominican Republic								•		•		•					•
Ecuador								•		•		•	•	•			•
Egypt		•[e]						•			•	•		•		•[c]	
El Salvador				•				•		•		•					•
Equatorial Guinea								•						•			
Ethiopia								•				•		•			
Fiji	•							•				•					
Finland	•									•		•					
France	•						•			•		•			•		
French Guiana[c]																	
Gabon								•			•	•		•			
Gambia, The								•			•			•			

						United Nations Organizations																
OAU	OECD	OIC	OPEC	SELA	WFTU	FAO	GATT	IAEA	IBRD	ICAO	ICJ	IDA	IFAD	IFC	ILO	IMF	IMO	ITU	UNESCO	UPU	WHO	WMO
				●	●	●	●	●	●	●	●	●	●	●	●	●	●	●	●	●	●	●
	●					●	●	●	●	●	●	●	●	●	●	●	●	●	●	●	●	●
	●				●	●	●	●	●	●	●	●	●	●	●	●	●	●	●	●	●	●
						●	●	●	●	●	●				●	●	●	●	●	●	●	●
		●				●	●	●	●	●	●				●	●	●	●	●	●	●	●
		●			●	●	●	●	●	●	●	●	●	●	●	●	●	●	●	●	●	●
			●			●	●					●	●	●	●	●	●	●	●	●	●	●
	●					●	●	●	●	●	●	●	●	●	●	●	●	●	●	●	●	●
						●	●		●	●	●	●	●	●	●	●		●	●	●	●	●
●		●			●	●	●		●	●	●		●	●	●	●		●	●	●	●	●
						●			●		●	●	●		●			●	●	●	●	●
			●			●		●	●	●	●	●	●	●	●	●		●	●	●	●	●
●						●	●		●	●	●	●	●	●	●	●		●	●	●	●	●
		●				●	●	●	●	●	●	●	●	●	●	●	●	●	●	●	●	●
	●																●					
					●	●		●		●	●				●		●	●	●	●	●	●
●	●				●	●	●		●	●	●	●	●	●	●	●		●	●	●	●	●
						●	●	●	●	●	●	●	●		●	●	●	●	●	●	●	●
●						●	●		●	●	●	●	●	●	●	●		●	●	●	●	●
		●			●	●	●	●	●	●	●	●	●	●	●	●	●	●	●	●	●	●
●		●				●	●		●	●	●	●	●	●	●	●		●	●	●	●	●
	●					●	●	●	●	●	●	●	●	●	●	●	●	●	●	●	●	●
●						●	●		●	●	●	●	●	●	●	●		●	●	●	●	●
●						●	●		●	●	●	●	●		●	●		●	●	●	●	●
●		●				●	●		●	●	●	●	●	●	●	●		●	●	●	●	●
			●			●	●	●	●	●	●	●	●	●	●	●	●	●	●	●	●	●
					●	●	●		●	●	●	●	●	●	●	●	●	●	●	●	●	●
			●	●	●	●	●	●	●	●	●	●	●	●	●	●	●	●	●	●	●	●
●	●					●			●	●	●	●	●		●	●		●	●	●	●	●
●					●	●	●		●	●	●	●	●	●	●	●		●	●	●	●	●
											●			●			●					
		●				●		●	●	●	●	●	●	●	●	●	●	●	●	●	●	●
		●		●		●	●	●		●	●			●	●		●	●	●	●	●	●
					●	●	●	●	●		●	●	●	●	●	●	●	●	●	●	●	●
					●	●	●	●		●	●				●		●	●	●	●	●	●
	●					●	●	●	●	●	●	●	●	●	●	●	●	●	●	●	●	●
●		●			●	●		●	●	●	●	●	●	●	●	●	●		●	●	●	●
						●	●		●	●	●	●	●	●	●	●		●	●	●	●	●
			●	●	●	●	●		●	●	●	●	●	●	●	●	●	●	●	●	●	●
		●	●	●	●	●	●	●	●	●	●	●	●	●	●	●	●	●	●	●	●	●
●		●				●	●	●	●	●	●	●	●	●	●	●	●	●	●	●	●	●
		●			●	●	●	●	●	●	●	●	●	●	●	●	●	●	●	●	●	●
●						●	●		●	●	●	●	●	●		●	●	●	●	●	●	
●					●	●	●		●	●	●	●	●	●	●	●	●	●	●	●	●	●
	●					●	●	●	●	●	●	●	●	●	●	●	●	●	●	●	●	●
	●				●	●	●	●	●	●	●	●	●	●	●	●	●	●	●	●	●	●
					●																	
●		●	●			●	●	●	●	●	●	●	●	●	●	●	●	●	●	●	●	●
●		●			●	●	●		●	●	●	●	●	●		●	●	●	●	●	●	●

Country	ADB	ARAB LEAGUE	ASEAN	CACM	CARICOM	CEMA	EC	G-77	GCC	IDB[a]	IDB[b]	INTELSAT	LAIA	NAM	NATO	OAPEC	OAS
German Democratic Republic						•											
Germany, Federal Republic of	•						•			•		•			•		
Ghana								•				•		•			
Greece							•					•			•		
Grenada					•			•						•			•
Guadeloupe[c]																	
Guatemala				•				•		•		•					•
Guinea								•			•	•		•			
Guinea-Bissau								•			•			•			
Guyana					•			•		•				•			
Haiti								•		•		•					•
Honduras				•				•		•		•					•
Hong Kong[c]	•																
Hungary						•											
Iceland												•					
India	•							•				•		•			
Indonesia	•		•					•			•	•		•			
Iran								•				•		•			
Iraq		•						•			•	•		•		•	
Ireland							•					•					
Israel										•		•					
Italy	•						•			•		•			•		
Ivory Coast								•				•		•			
Jamaica					•			•		•		•		•			•
Japan	•									•		•					
Jordan		•						•			•	•		•			
Kenya								•				•		•			
Kiribati[c]	•																
Korea, North[c]								•						•			
Korea, South[c]	•							•				•					
Kuwait		•						•	•		•	•		•		•	
Laos	•							•						•			
Lebanon		•						•			•	•		•			
Lesotho								•						•			
Liberia								•						•			
Libya		•						•			•	•		•		•	
Liechtenstein[c]												•					
Luxembourg							•					•			•		
Madagascar								•				•		•			
Malawi								•				•		•			
Malaysia	•		•					•			•	•		•			
Maldives	•							•			•			•			
Mali								•			•	•		•			
Malta								•						•			
Martinique[c]																	
Mauritania		•						•			•	•		•			
Mauritius								•						•			
Mexico								•		•		•	•				•
Monaco[c]												•					
Mongolia						•											

						United Nations Organizations																
OAU	OECD	OIC	OPEC	SELA	WFTU	FAO	GATT	IAEA	IBRD	ICAO	ICJ	IDA	IFAD	IFC	ILO	IMF	IMO	ITU	UNESCO	UPU	WHO	WMO
					•			•			•				•		•	•	•	•	•	•
	•					•	•	•	•	•	•	•	•	•	•	•	•	•	•	•	•	•
•						•	•	•	•	•	•	•	•	•	•	•	•	•	•	•	•	•
	•					•	•	•	•	•	•	•	•	•	•	•	•	•	•	•	•	•
		•				•	•		•	•	•	•	•	•	•	•		•	•	•	•	
					•																	
		•			•	•	•	•	•	•	•	•	•	•	•	•	•	•	•	•	•	•
•			•			•			•	•	•	•	•	•	•	•	•	•	•	•	•	•
•			•			•	•		•	•	•	•	•	•	•	•	•	•	•	•	•	•
				•	•	•	•		•	•	•	•	•	•	•	•	•	•	•	•	•	•
				•		•	•	•	•	•	•	•	•	•	•	•	•	•	•	•	•	•
				•	•	•			•	•	•	•	•	•	•	•	•	•	•	•	•	•
																	•					•
					•	•	•	•	•	•	•				•	•	•	•	•	•	•	•
	•					•	•	•	•	•	•	•			•	•	•	•	•	•	•	•
		•	•		•	•	•	•	•	•	•	•	•	•	•	•	•	•	•	•	•	•
		•	•		•	•		•	•	•	•	•	•	•	•	•	•	•	•	•	•	•
		•	•		•	•		•	•	•	•	•	•	•	•	•	•	•	•	•	•	•
	•		•		•	•		•	•	•	•	•	•	•	•	•	•	•	•	•	•	•
						•	•	•	•	•	•	•	•	•	•	•	•	•	•	•	•	•
	•					•	•	•	•	•	•	•	•	•	•	•	•	•	•	•	•	•
•						•	•	•	•	•	•	•	•	•	•	•	•	•	•	•	•	•
	•					•	•	•	•	•	•		•	•	•	•	•	•	•	•	•	•
	•					•	•	•	•	•	•	•	•	•	•	•	•	•	•	•	•	•
			•		•	•	•	•	•	•	•	•	•	•	•	•	•	•	•	•	•	•
•						•					•											
					•						•							•	•	•	•	•
		•	•		•	•	•	•	•	•	•	•	•	•	•	•	•	•	•	•	•	•
					•	•		•	•	•	•	•	•		•	•		•	•	•	•	•
	•		•	•	•		•	•	•	•	•	•	•	•	•	•	•	•	•	•	•	•
•						•	•		•	•	•	•	•	•	•	•		•	•	•	•	•
•							•	•	•	•	•	•	•	•	•	•		•	•	•	•	•
•		•	•			•		•	•	•	•	•	•	•	•	•		•	•	•	•	•
								•				•						•	•		•	
	•					•	•	•	•	•	•	•	•	•	•		•	•	•	•	•	•
•					•	•	•	•	•	•	•	•	•	•	•	•	•	•	•	•	•	
•						•	•		•	•	•	•	•	•	•	•		•	•	•	•	•
	•					•	•		•	•	•	•	•		•	•	•	•	•	•	•	•
	•					•	•		•	•	•	•	•	•	•	•	•	•	•	•	•	•
•	•					•	•	•	•	•	•	•	•	•	•	•	•	•	•	•	•	•
						•	•		•	•	•		•		•	•		•	•	•	•	•
					•																	
•	•					•	•		•	•	•	•	•	•	•	•	•	•	•	•	•	•
•					•	•	•		•	•	•	•	•	•	•	•	•	•	•	•	•	•
		•				•			•	•	•	•	•	•	•	•	•	•	•	•	•	•
							•		•									•	•	•	•	
					•	•					•					•		•	•	•	•	•
	•					•	•	•	•	•	•	•	•	•	•	•	•	•	•	•	•	•

International Organizations

Country	ADB	ARAB LEAGUE	ASEAN	CACM	CARICOM	CEMA	EC	G-77	GCC	IDBa	IDBb	INTELSAT	LAIA	NAM	NATO	OAPEC	OAS
Morocco		●						●		●		●		●			
Montserrat					●												
Mozambique								●						●			
Namibia[c]																	
Nauru[c]																	
Nepal	●							●						●			
Netherlands	●						●			●		●			●		
Netherlands Antilles[c]																	
New Caledonia[c]																	
New Zealand	●											●					
Nicaragua				●				●		●		●		●			
Niger								●				●		●			
Nigeria								●				●		●			
Norway	●											●			●		
Oman		●						●	●	●		●	●	●			
Pakistan	●							●		●		●		●			
Panama								●	●			●		●			●
Papua New Guinea	●							●				●					
Paraguay								●	●			●	●				●
Peru								●	●			●	●	●			●
Philippines	●							●				●					
Poland						●											
Portugal							●			●	●				●		
Qatar		●						●	●	●		●		●		●	
Reunion[c]																	
Rumania						●		●									
Rwanda								●						●			
St. Christopher and Nevis					●												●
St. Lucia					●			●						●			●
St. Vincent and the Grenadines					●			●						●			●
San Marino[c]																	
São Tomé and Principe								●						●			
Saudi Arabia		●						●	●	●		●		●		●	
Senegal								●		●		●		●			
Seychelles								●						●			
Sierra Leone								●		●				●			
Singapore	●		●					●				●		●			
Solomon Islands	●							●									
Somalia		●						●		●		●		●			
South Africa												●					
Spain							●		●			●			●		
Sri Lanka	●							●				●		●			
Sudan		●						●			●	●		●			
Suriname								●	●			●		●			●
Swaziland								●						●			
Sweden	●									●		●					
Switzerland[c]	●									●		●					
Syria		●						●		●		●		●		●	
Taiwan[c]	●																
Tanzania								●				●		●			

						United Nations Organizations																
OAU	OECD	OIC	OPEC	SELA	WFTU	FAO	GATT	IAEA	IBRD	ICAO	ICJ	IDA	IFAD	IFC	ILC	IMF	IMO	ITU	UNESCO	UPU	WHO	WMO
																				•		
•						•	•		•	•	•	•				•		•	•	•	•	•	•
		•				•										•			•		•	
										•								•		•		
						•		•	•	•	•	•	•	•	•	•	•	•	•	•	•	•
	•					•	•	•	•	•	•	•	•	•	•	•	•	•	•	•	•	•
																					•	•
					•																	•
	•				•	•	•	•	•	•	•	•	•	•	•	•	•	•	•	•	•	•
				•	•	•	•	•	•	•	•	•	•	•	•	•	•	•	•	•	•	•
•		•				•	•	•	•	•	•	•	•	•	•	•	•	•	•	•	•	•
•			•			•	•	•	•	•	•	•	•	•	•	•	•	•	•	•	•	•
	•					•	•	•	•	•	•	•	•	•	•	•	•	•	•	•	•	•
		•			•	•				•	•	•			•	•	•	•	•	•	•	•
		•			•	•	•	•	•	•	•	•	•	•	•	•	•	•	•	•	•	•
			•		•	•		•	•	•	•	•	•	•	•	•	•	•	•	•	•	•
						•	•	•	•	•	•	•	•	•	•	•	•	•	•	•	•	•
		•			•	•		•	•	•	•	•	•	•	•	•	•	•	•	•	•	•
			•		•	•	•	•	•	•	•	•	•	•	•	•	•	•	•	•	•	•
					•	•	•	•	•	•	•				•	•	•	•	•	•	•	•
					•	•	•	•		•	•				•	•	•	•	•	•	•	•
	•					•	•	•	•	•	•		•	•	•	•	•	•	•	•	•	•
		•	•			•	•	•	•	•	•		•		•	•	•	•	•	•	•	•
					•																	
					•	•	•	•	•	•	•		•		•	•	•	•	•	•	•	•
•						•	•	•	•	•	•	•	•	•	•	•	•	•	•	•	•	•
						•			•	•	•					•		•	•			
					•	•	•		•	•	•	•	•	•	•	•	•		•	•	•	•
					•	•	•		•	•	•	•	•				•	•	•	•	•	•
											•							•	•	•	•	•
•						•	•		•	•	•	•	•	•	•	•	•	•	•	•	•	•
	•	•	•			•		•		•	•	•	•	•	•	•	•	•	•	•	•	•
•		•			•	•	•	•	•	•	•	•	•	•	•	•	•	•	•	•	•	•
•		•				•	•		•	•	•	•		•	•	•	•		•	•	•	•
•		•				•	•	•	•	•	•	•	•	•	•	•	•	•	•	•	•	•
						•	•	•	•	•	•		•	•	•	•	•		•	•	•	•
						•			•		•	•	•	•	•	•			•	•		
•		•			•	•			•	•	•	•	•	•		•	•	•	•	•	•	•
					•		•	•	•	•	•	•	•		•		•		•		•	•
	•					•	•	•	•	•	•	•	•	•	•	•	•	•	•	•	•	•
•		•			•	•	•		•	•	•	•	•	•		•	•	•	•	•	•	•
				•		•	•		•	•	•	•		•		•	•	•	•	•	•	•
•						•	•		•	•	•	•	•		•	•	•	•	•	•	•	•
	•					•	•	•		•	•		•		•	•	•	•	•	•	•	•
	•					•	•	•		•	•	•	•		•	•	•	•	•	•	•	•
		•			•	•			•	•	•	•	•	•		•	•	•	•	•	•	•
•						•	•	•	•	•	•	•	•	•	•	•	•	•	•	•	•	•

Country	ADB	ARAB LEAGUE	ASEAN	CACM	CARICOM	CEMA	EC	G-77	GCC	IDBa	IDBb	INTELSAT	LAIA	NAM	NATO	OAPEC	OAS
					International Organizations												
Thailand	•		•									•					
Togo								•						•			
Tongac	•																
Trinidad and Tobago					•			•		•		•		•			•
Tunisia		•						•			•	•		•		•	
Turkey											•	•			•		
Tuvaluc																	
Uganda								•			•	•		•			
Union of Soviet Socialist Republics						•											
United Arab Emirates		•						•	•			•		•		•	
United Kingdom	•						•			•		•			•		
United States	•									•		•			•		•
Uruguay								•		•		•	•				•
Vanuatu	•						•	•						•			
Vatican Cityc												•					
Venezuela								•		•		•					•
Vietnam	•					•		•				•		•			
Western Samoa	•							•									
Yemen, People's Democratic Republic of		•						•						•			
Yemen Arab Republic		•						•			•	•		•			
Yugoslavia								•		•		•		•			
Zaire								•				•		•			
Zambia								•				•		•			
Zimbabwe								•									

a Inter-American Development Bank b Islamic Development Bank c Not a member of U.N. d Ceased to participate in 1961 e Suspended

INTERNATIONAL CONVERSIONS

To convert from	To	Multiply by	To convert from	To	Multiply by
Acres	Hectares	0.4046856	Gallons, US liquid	Liters	3.785412
Acres	Kilometers, square	0.004046856	Gallons, US liquid	Meters, cubic	0.003785412
Acres	Meters, square	4046.856	Grams	Ounces, troy	0.032151
Centimeters	Meters	0.01	Grams	Pounds, troy	0.002679
Centimeters, square	Meters, square	0.0001	Hectares	Kilometers, square	0.01
Degrees, Fahrenheit	Degrees, Celsius	subtract 32 and multiply by 5/9	Hectares	Meters, squares	10.000
			Inches	Centimeters	2.54
Feet	Centimeters	30.48	Inches	Meters	0.0254
Feet	Meters	0.3048	Inches, cubic	Milliliters	16.387064
Feet	Kilometers	0.0003048	Inches, cubic	Liters	0.016387064
Feet, cubic	Liters	28.316847	Inches, cubic	Meters, cubic	0.000016387064
Feet, cubic	Meters, cubic	0.28316847	Inches, square	Centimeters, square	6.4516
Feet, square	Centimeters, square	929.0304	Inches, square	Meters, square	0.00064516
Feet, square	Meters, square	0.09290304	Kilograms	Ounces, troy	32.15075

United Nations Organizations

OAU	OECD	OIC	OPEC	SELA	WFTU	FAO	GATT	IAEA	IBRD	ICAO	ICJ	IDA	IFAD	IFC	ILO	IMF	IMO	ITU	UNESCO	UPU	WHO	WMO
						•	•	•	•	•	•	•	•	•	•	•	•	•	•	•	•	•
•						•	•		•	•	•	•	•	•	•	•	•	•	•	•	•	•
						•	•					•						•	•	•	•	
		•	•			•	•		•	•	•	•	•	•	•	•	•	•	•	•	•	•
•		•				•	•	•	•	•	•	•	•	•	•	•	•	•	•	•	•	•
	•	•				•	•	•	•	•	•	•	•	•	•	•	•	•	•	•	•	•
						•													•			
•		•				•	•	•	•	•	•	•	•	•	•	•	•	•	•	•	•	•
					•			•		•	•				•		•	•	•	•	•	•
		•	•			•	•	•	•	•	•	•	•	•	•	•	•	•	•	•	•	
	•					•	•	•	•	•	•	•	•	•	•	•	•		•		•	•
	•					•	•	•	•	•	•	•	•	•	•	•	•	•	•		•	•
		•				•	•	•	•	•	•	•	•	•	•	•	•	•	•	•	•	•
						•		•	•	•	•		•		•		•			•	•	•
						•											•		•			
	•	•	•		•	•		•	•	•	•		•	•	•	•	•	•	•	•	•	•
					•	•		•	•	•	•	•	•	•	•	•	•		•	•	•	•
	•				•	•	•		•	•	•	•	•		•	•	•	•	•	•	•	•
						•		•	•	•	•	•	•	•		•		•	•			
	•				•	•		•	•	•	•	•	•	•	•	•	•	•	•	•	•	•
						•		•	•	•	•	•	•	•	•	•	•	•	•	•	•	•
•						•		•	•	•	•	•	•	•	•	•	•	•	•	•	•	•
•						•		•	•	•	•	•	•	•				•	•	•	•	•
•				•		•	•		•	•	•	•	•	•	•		•		•	•	•	•

d Ceased to participate in 1961   e Suspended

INTERNATIONAL CONVERSIONS

To convert from	To	Multiply by	To convert from	To	Multiply by
Kilograms	Pounds, troy	2.679229	Miles, statute	Meters	1609.344
Kilograms	Tons, metric	0.001	Miles, statute	Kilometers	1.609344
Kilometers, square	Hectares	100	Ounces, avoirdupois	Grams	28.349523
Liters	Milliliters	1000	Ounces, avoirdupois	Kilograms	0.028349523
Liters	Meters, cubic	0.001	Ounces, troy	Pounds, troy	0.083333
Meters	Millimeters	1000	Ounces, troy	Grams	31.10348
Meters	Centimeters	100	Pints, liquid	Milliliters	473.176473
Meters	Kilometers	0.001	Pints, liquid	Liters	0.473176473
Meters, cubic	Liters	1000	Pounds, avoirdupois	Grams	453.59237
Meters, cubic	Tons, register	0.353147	Pounds, avoirdupois	Kilograms	0.45359237
Miles, nautical	Kilometers	1.852	Pounds, avoirdupois	Quintals	0.00453592
Miles, square	Hectares	258.9998	Pounds, avoirdupois	Tons, metric	0.000453592
Miles, square	Kilometers, square	2.589998	Pounds, troy	Ounces, troy	12
Miles, statute	Centimeters	160934.4	Pounds, troy	Grams	373.241722

MATHEMATICAL CONVERSIONS

To convert from	To	Multiply by	To convert from	To	Multiply by
Quarts, dry	Liters	1.101221	Tons, metric	Quintals	10
Quarts, dry	Dekaliters	0.1101221	Tons, register	Meters, cubic	2.831685
Quarts, liquid	Milliliters	946.352946	Tons, short	Kilograms	907.185
Quarts, liquid	Liters	0.946352946	Tons, short	Tons, metric	0.907185
Quintals	Tons, metric	0.1	Yards	Centimeters	91.44
Ton-miles, long	Ton-kilometers, metric	1.635169	Yards	Meters	0.9144
Ton-miles, short	Ton-kilometric, metric	1.459972	Yards, cubic	Liters	764.5549
Tons, long	Kilograms	1016.047	Yards, cubic	Meters, cubic	0.7645549
Tons, long	Tons, metric	1.016047	Yards, square	Meters, square	0.836127

Foreign Dialing Codes

Note: For international telephone calls automatically routed through AT&T, dial "011," then dial the code for that country, the city code if one is indicated, and the subscriber telephone number to be reached. Other long-distance telephone services may have other procedures and should be consulted for their specific instructions.

Algeria	213	Denmark	45	Greece	30
American Samoa	684	(Aalborg 8)		(Athens 1)	
Andorra	33	(Copenhagen 1 or 2)		(Rhodes 241)	
(all points 628)		Ecuador	593	Guam	671
Argentina	54	(Cuneca 7)		Guantanamo Bay U.S. naval	53
(Buenos Aires 1)		(Quito 2)		base	
Australia	61	Egypt	20	(all points 99)	
(Melbourne 3)		(Alexandria 3)		Guyana	592
(Sydney 2)		(Port Said 66)		(Georgetown 2)	
Austria	43	El Salvador	503	Haiti	509
(Vienna 222)		England *See* United Kingdom.		(Port-au-Prince 1)	
Bahrain	973	Ethiopia	251	Honduras	504
Belgium	32	(Addis Ababa 1)		Hong Kong	852
(Brussels 2)		Fiji	679	(Hong Kong 5)	
(Ghent 91)		Finland	358	(Kowloon 3)	
Belize	501	(Helsinki 0)		Hungary	36
Bolivia	591	France	33	(Budapest 1)	
(Santa Cruz 33)		(Marseille 91)		Iceland	354
Brazil	55	(Nice 93)		(Akureyri 6)	
(Brasilia 61)		(Paris 13, 14, or 16)		(Hahnarfjorour 1)	
(Rio de Janeiro 21)		French Antilles	596	India	91
Cameroon	237	French Polynesia	689	(Bombay 22)	
Chile	56	Gabon	241	(New Delhi 11)	
(Santiago 2)		German Democratic Republic	37	Indonesia	62
Colombia	57	(East Berlin 2)		(Jakarta 21)	
(Bogotá 1)		Germany, Federal Republic of	49	Iran	98
Costa Rica	506	(Frankfurt 69)		(Teheran 21)	
Cyprus	357	(Munich 89)		Iraq	964
Czechoslovakia	42	(West Berlin 30)		(Baghdad 1)	
(Prague 2)					

Ireland	353	New Caledonia	687	Sri Lanka	94
(Dublin 1)		New Zealand	64	(Kandy 8)	
(Galway 91)		(Auckland 9)		Suriname	597
Israel	972	(Wellington 4)		Sweden	46
(Haifa 4)		Nicaragua	505	(Göteborg 31)	
(Jerusalem 2)		(Managua 2)		(Stockholm 8)	
(Tel Aviv 3)		Nigeria	234	Switzerland	41
Italy	39	(Lagos 1)		(Geneva 22)	
(Florence 55)		Norway	47	(Lucerne 41)	
(Rome 6)		(Bergen 5)		(Zurich 1)	
(Venice 41)		(Oslo 2)		Taiwan	886
Ivory Coast	225	Oman	968	(Tainan 6)	
Japan	81	Pakistan	92	(Taipei 3)	
(Tokyo 3)		(Islamabad 51)		Thailand	66
(Yokohama 45)		Panama	507	(Bangkok 2)	
Jordan	962	Papua New Guinea	675	Tunisia	216
(Amman 6)		Paraguay	595	(Tunis 1)	
Kenya	254	(Asuncion 21)		Turkey	90
Korea, South	82	Peru	51	(Istanbul 1)	
(Pusan 51)		(Arequipa 54)		(Izmir 51)	
(Seoul 2)		(Lima 14)		United Arab Emirates	971
Kuwait	965	Philippines	63	(Abu Dhabi 2)	
Liberia	231	(Manila 2)		(Al Ain 3)	
Libya	218	Poland	48	(Dubai 4)	
(Tripoli 21)		(Warsaw 22)		(Ras Al Khainah 77)	
Liechtenstein	41	Portugal	351	(Sharjah 6)	
(all points 75)		(Lisbon 1)		(Umm Al Quwain 6)	
Luxembourg	352	Qatar	974	United Kingdom	44
Malawi	265	Rumania	40	(Belfast 232)	
(Domasi 531)		(Bucharest 0)		(Cardiff 222)	
Malaysia	60	Saipan	670	(Glasgow 41)	
(Kuala Lumpur 3)		San Marino	39	(London 1)	
Mexico	52	(all points 541)		Uruguay	598
(Mexico City 5)		Saudia Arabia	966	(Mercedes 532)	
(Tijuana 66)		(Riyadh 1)		(Montevideo 2)	
Monaco	33	Senegal	221	Vatican City	39
(all points 93)		Singapore	65	(all points 6)	
Morocco	212	South Africa	27	Venezuela	58
(Agadir 8)		(Cape Town 21)		(Caracas 2)	
Namibia	264	(Pretoria 12)		(Maracaibo 61)	
(Olympia 61)		Spain	34	Yemen Arab Republic	967
Netherlands	31	(Barcelona 3)		(Amran 2)	
(Amsterdam 20)		(Las Palmas,		Yugoslavia	38
(The Hague 70)		Canary Islands 28)		(Belgrade 11)	
Netherlands Antilles	599	(Madrid 1)			
(Aruba 2978)		(Seville 54)			

Seven Wonders of the Ancient World

Artemision at Ephesus, the temple of the Greek goddess Artemis (also the Roman goddess Diana), was begun in 541 B.C. at Ephesus (now a site in Turkey) and completed 220 years later. The temple was 425 feet long and 220 feet wide with 127 marble columns, each 60 feet tall. The gates were made of cypress and the ceiling of cedar. The temple was destroyed by the Goths in 262 A.D.

The Colossus of Rhodes, a 100-foot-tall bronze statue of the sun god Helios, was erected between 292 and 280 B.C. in the harbor at Rhodes. According to legend, it appeared to stand astride the harbor but was actually on a promontory overlooking it. The statue was toppled by an earthquake around 224 B.C. and lay in ruins until 653 A.D., when the remains were sold as scrap metal.

The Hanging Gardens of Babylon, a series of five terraces of glazed brick, each 50 feet above the next, was erected by King Nebuchadnezzar for his wife, Amytis, in 562 B.C. The terraces, featuring rare and exotic plants, were connected by a winding stairway. A pumping device supplied water so the gardens could be irrigated by fountains.

The Mausoleum at Halicarnassus, a 140-foot-high white marble structure, was built in 352 B.C. at Halicarnassus (now a site in Turkey) in memory of King Mausolus of Caria. Its massive base contained a sarcophagus and supported 36 columns crowned with a stepped pyramid on which was constructed a marble chariot. It was destroyed for the use of stone to build a castle for the Knights of Saint John in 1402.

Olympian Zeus, a statue of the supreme god in Greek mythology, was executed in gold and ivory for the temple at Olympia. The figure of the seated Zeus was 40 feet tall and rested on a base that was 12 feet high. The portions of the statue representing the flesh of the god were covered with marble and his cloak was made of gold. Golden lions rested near his feet.

The Pyramids of Egypt were started by Khufu (Cheops) around 2700 B.C. as tombs for the ancient kings. The three largest and finest were erected during the Fourth dynasty at Gizeh, near Cairo. The largest of the group is the Khufu Pyramid, built of limestone blocks from a base 756 feet wide on each side and covering an area of 13 acres. It is 482 feet high. Smaller pyramids were built for wives and other members of the royal families.

The Tower of Pharos was a great lighthouse built on the island of Pharos, at Alexandria, Egypt, during the reign of Ptolemy Philadelphus, 285 B.C. Also called The Pharos, it was 500 feet tall with a ramp leading to the top. Light was produced with a fire and reflectors and could be seen from a distance of 42 miles.

Royal Rulers of Europe and Asia

Europe and Russia

Great Britain

William I the Conqueror	1066–1087	Edward III	1327–1377
William II	1087–1100	Richard II	1377–1399
Henry I	1100–1135	Henry IV	1399–1413
Stephen	1135–1154	Henry V	1413–1422
Henry II	1154–1189	Henry VI	1422–1461
Richard I	1189–1199	Edward IV	1461–1483
John	1199–1216	Edward V	1483
Henry III	1216–1272	Richard III	1483–1485
Edward I	1272–1307	Henry VII	1485–1509
Edward II	1307–1327	Henry VIII	1509–1547

Edward VI	1547–1553
Mary I	1553–1558
Elizabeth I	1558–1603
James I	1603–1625
Charles I	1625–1649
(Commonwealth period)	1649–1660
Charles II	1660–1685
James II	1685–1688
William III and Mary II	1689–1694
William III (alone)	1694–1702
Anne	1702–1714
George I	1714–1727
George II	1727–1760
George III	1760–1820
George IV	1820–1830
William IV	1830–1837
Victoria	1837–1901
Edward VII	1901–1910
George V	1910–1936
Edward VIII	1936
George VI	1936–1952
Elizabeth II	1952–

France

Henri I	1031–1060
Philip I	1060–1108
Louis VI	1108–1137
Louis VII	1137–1180
Philip II	1180–1223
Louis VIII	1223–1226
Louis IX	1226–1270
Philip III	1270–1285
Philip IV	1285–1314
Louis X	1314–1316
John I	1316
Philip V	1316–1322
Charles IV	1322–1328
Philip VI	1328–1350
John II	1350–1364
Charles V	1364–1380
Charles VI	1380–1422
Charles VII	1422–1461
Louis XI	1461–1483
Charles VIII	1483–1498
Louis XII	1498–1515
François I	1515–1547
Henri II	1547–1559
François II	1559–1560
Charles IX	1560–1574
Henri III	1574–1589
Henri IV	1589–1610
Louis XIII	1610–1643

Louis XIV	1643–1715
Louis XV	1715–1774
Louis XVI	1774–1792
(First Republic)	1792–1804
Napoleon I	1804–1814
Louis XVIII	1814–1824
Charles X	1824–1830
Louis Philippe	1830–1848
(Second Republic)	1848–1852
Napoleon III	1852–1870
(Third Republic)	1870–1914

Germany

Frederick I	1710–1713
Frederick William I	1713–1740
Frederick II	1740–1786
Frederick William II	1786–1797
Frederick William III	1797–1840
Frederick William IV	1840–1861
William I	1861–1888
Frederick III	1888
William II	1888–1918

Russia

Ivan III	1462–1505
Vasilly III	1505–1533
Ivan IV	1533–1584
Theodore I	1584–1598
Boris Godunov	1598–1605
Theodore II	1605
Demetrius I	1605–1606
Basil IV	1606–1610
Wladyslaw (Polish Prince)	1610–1613
Mikhail Romanov	1613–1645
Alexis I	1645–1676
Theodore III	1676–1682
Ivan V and Peter I	1682–1689
Peter I (alone)	1689–1725
Catherine I	1725–1727
Peter II	1727–1730
Anna	1730–1740
Ivan VI	1740–1741
Elizabeth	1741–1762
Peter III	1762
Catherine II	1762–1796
Paul I	1796–1801
Alexander I	1801–1825
Nicholas I	1825–1855
Alexander II	1855–1881
Alexander III	1881–1894
Nicholas II	1894–1917

Asia

China

Yuan (Kublai Khan) dynasty	1260–1368
Ming dynasty	1368–1644
Manchu (Ch'ing) dynasty	1644–1912
Shun Chih	1644–1661
K'ang Hsi	1661–1722
Yung Cheng	1722–1735
Ch'ien Lung	1735–1796
Chia Ch'ing	1796–1820
Tao Kuang	1820–1851
Hsien Feng	1851–1861

T'ung Chi	1861–1875
Kuang Hsu	1875–1898
Tzu Hsi	1898–1908
P'u Yi	1908–1912

Japan

Tokugawa Shogun rule	1603–1867
Mutsuhito (Meiji)	1867–1912
Taisha	1912–1926
Hirohito	1926–1989

Additional Sources of Information

Books

Central Intelligence Agency. *The World Factbook*. U.S. Government Printing Office, published annually.

Grun, Bernard. *The Timetables of History*. Touchstone, 1987.

The Harper Atlas of World History. Harper and Row, 1987.

Hellemans, Alexander, and Bunch, Bryan. *The Timetables of Science*. Simon & Schuster, 1988.

Hoffman, Mark S. *The World Almanac and Book of Facts*. Pharos Books, published annually.

Kurian, George T. *World Data*. World Almanac Publications, 1983.

Maps on File. Facts on File, 1987.

The New International World Atlas. Rand McNally, 1989.

Simony, Maggy. *The Travelers Reading Guide*. Revised Edition. Facts on File, 1987.

Urdang, Laurence. *The World Almanac Dictionary of Dates*. World Almanac Publications, 1982.

Wetterau, Bruce. *Macmillan Concise Dictionary of World History*. Macmillan, 1986.

Organizations and Services

The Asia Foundation
550 Kearney Street
San Francisco, CA 94108

Bureau of Public Affairs
U.S. Department of State
2201 C Street, NW
Washington, DC 20520

Carnegie Endowment for International Peace
11 Dupont Circle
Washington, DC 20036

Central Intelligence Agency
Public Affairs Director
Washington, DC 20505

European Community Information Service
2100 M Street, NW
Washington, DC 20037

Middle East Institute
1761 N Street, NW
Washington, DC 20036

Organization of American States
Pan-American Union Building
17th Street and Constitution Avenue
Washington, DC 20006

United Nations Headquarters
United Nations Plaza
New York, NY 10017

United Nations Information Centre
2101 L Street, NW
Washington, DC 20037

United States Mission to the United Nations
799 United Nations Plaza
New York, NY 10017

World Institute
777 United Nations Plaza
New York, NY 10017

INDEX

807